THE ROMANTIC REVOLUTION
IN AMERICA

FOREWORD

In justification of the choice of writers and allotment of space in the following pages, let it be said frankly that I have been guided by what I conceived to be the historical significance of the several documents. With aesthetic judgments I have not been greatly concerned. I have not wished to evaluate reputations or weigh literary merits, but rather to understand what our fathers thought, and why they wrote as they did. This will serve to explain the considerable number of pages devoted to southern letters, as well as to certain well-nigh forgotten figures. For the purpose I had in view such a method was inevitable. Lost causes have a way of shrinking in importance in the memory of later generations, and the historian must go back to the days before their overthrow, and view them in the light of their hopes. Time is not always a just winnower; it is partial to success and its verdict too often inclines to the side of the biggest cannon or the noisiest *claque*. The exhuming of buried reputations and the revivifying of dead causes is the familiar business of the historian, in whose eyes forgotten men may assume as great significance as others with whom posterity has dealt more generously. Communing with ghosts is not unprofitable to one who listens to their tales. To our fathers John Taylor and Beverley Tucker and Fisher Ames were living figures; they spoke for their generation, and they may have something still to say to a later generation. For dealing at length with such men as Hugh Legaré and Gilmore Simms and John P. Kennedy and Herman Melville, no apologies need be offered. They have too long been slighted. Walt Whitman I have chosen to regard as the forerunner of a later school, and have reserved the consideration of his work for another study. Certain other men I have omitted regretfully out of regard to space—diverse figures such as Orestes Brownson, Albert Brisbane, and John Esten Cooke, together with a group of poets and essayists, who though they have long been reckoned ghosts are nevertheless well worth knowing. Even echoes imply substance somewhere.

V. L. P.

Seattle, February 22, 1926.

INTRODUCTION

INTRODUCTION

THE present volume is the second in a proposed study of the main tendencies of American thought as expressed in our literature. In the preceding volume I have considered the incoming into America of certain old-world ideals and institutions, and the subjection of those ideals and institutions to the pressure of a new environment, from which resulted the overthrow of the principles of monarchy and aristocracy, and the setting up of the principle of republicanism. In the present study I purpose considering certain new growths that sprang up in the land thus cleared—what particular forms they assumed and why they assumed such forms. The delimitations of the period to be treated of are fixed by two wars that disturbed the normal unfolding of national experience: the War of 1812 that hastened the development of nineteenth-century ideals, and the Civil War that uprooted certain of the crasser growths of those vigorous years. The half century that lay between these dramatic episodes was a period of extravagant youth, given over to a cult of romanticism that wrought as many marvels as Aaron's rod. In the South, in New England, and on the western frontier, it laid hold of men's minds, consuming the stubble of eighteenth-century harvests, sweeping away the drab realisms of a cautious past, and offering in their stead more alluring ideals. Revolutions, greater and lesser, trod on each other's heels; the common adventure led into unexplored paths; and the final outcome for which it was all preparing was the emergence of a new middle class that in the succeeding half century was to subdue America to middle-class ends.

Such drastic overturnings of the customary and familiar, such swift ruptures with the past, quite evidently do not come from trivial causes. Men do not put off the old before the new is ready; and if in those credulous years they turned romantic and refused to heed the counsels of experience, it was because the soil had been new-plowed for the growing of such crops as their fathers had not known. The grapes from which the wine of romance is vinted, it must not be forgotten, are rooted in the common earth. The loveliest romantic dreams spring from a parentage that is humbly prosaic. There is no more fruitful source of romantic hope than a fluid economics that overflows all narrow preëmptions and sweeps away the restrictions that hamper free endeavor. With fresh economic realms to conquer, the dullest plodder discovers a stimulus in anticipation that sets him upon creating a Utopia. The breaking up of the static, the bold adventuring upon new worlds, is the fertile soil in which romance springs most luxuriantly. It needs no uncommon eyes, surely, to discover in the swift changes that came to America in the wake of the second English war, the seed-bed of those ebullient romanticisms which in politics and economics, in theology and literature, turned away so contemptuously from the homespun past. Of a sudden America was becoming a new world with potentialities before undreamed of; and this new America was no longer content with the narrow ways of a more cautious generation. The older America of colonial days had been static, rationalistic, inclined to pessimism, fearful of innovation, tenacious of the customary. It conceived of human nature as evil, and accounting men incurably wicked, it opened no doors to Utopian dreams of a golden future. The round of daily life was confined within a narrow domestic economy, with few and rare changes in social status. Growth in population came mainly from natural increase. Exploitation was laborious, and such wealth as was laid by was gained in shop and field, in fisheries and shipping. With its expectations cramped by a drab agrarianism, it was content to remain primitively self-sufficient, not given to seeking riches by speculative short-cuts, clinging to the habitual, distrustful of change.

During the thirty-odd years between the Peace of Paris and the end of the War of 1812 that older America was dying. The America that succeeded was a shifting, restless world, youthfully optimistic, eager to better itself, bent on finding easier roads to wealth than the plodding path of natural increase. It conceived of human nature as acquisitive, and accounting acquisitiveness a cardinal virtue, it set out to inquire what opportunities awaited it in the unexploited resources of the continent. The cautious ways of earlier generations were become as much out of date as last year's almanac. New commonwealths were rising in the wilderness; immigration from war-torn Europe was pouring in; wild lands were daily coming on the market. Money was to be made by the enterprising, and the multitude of the enterprising was augmenting with the expansion of the settlements. The ideal of a static society having been put away, progress was assumed to be the first law of nature, and innovation was accepted as the sign and seal of progress. It was our first great period of exploitation, and from it emerged, as naturally as the cock from the mother egg, the spirit of romance, gross and tawdry in vulgar minds, dainty and refined in the more cultivated. But always romance. The days of realism were past, and it was quietly laid away with the wig and smallclothes of an outgrown generation.

Unfortunately economic romance is more imperious in its demands than literary romance. Its dreams follow objective desires, and in America of those days of new beginnings the desires of diverse economic groups conducted straight to antagonistic imperialisms. The major interests of the three great sections of the country differentiated more and more sharply. The East was discovering its Utopia in an industrial capitalistic order. With the flocking of immigrants to the factories began the extraordinary expansion of the cities and the movement of centralization that was eventually to transform America from a rural to an urban society, supplanting the farmer by the business man and disintegrating the traditional psychology. The new manufacturing and the new finance were subjecting an agrarian people to the dislocations and readjustments implied in the industrial revolution, the outcome of which no man could foresee. The reaction of this new industrialism upon the South was immediate. With the improvements in textile manufacturing came greater demands upon the new southern staple, and an agriculture that had long been static with its traditional crops of indigo, rice, and tobacco, began to look forward confidently to a Utopia founded on cotton, and conceived an imperialistic dream of expanding fields of white bolls and black slaves, reaching into Mexico and embracing the West Indies. The new South left off apologizing for slavery and hoping for its ultimate extinction. Slavery had become enormously profitable and it proposed to exploit the negro as frankly as New England was exploiting the Irish immigrant, but more humanely if possible, in something of the patriarchal spirit.

Meanwhile in the Inland Empire was arising an economics that looked with little favor on the imperialisms of eastern capitalism or southern slavery; an economics equalitarian in temper, decentralizing in impulse; nourished on the idealism of the Declaration of Independence, but interpreting it to mean the natural right of every free citizen to satisfy his acquisitive instinct by exploiting the national resources in the measure of his shrewdness. Democratic in professions, it was middle-class in spirit and purpose. Discovering the inflowing tide of immigration to be favorable to speculation, it sought its Utopia in county-seat towns where land holdings mounted in value with every new wave. No narrow horizons bounded a realm that stretched to the Pacific and into the remote Northwest, and no stodgy ways of money-getting could satisfy men whose imaginations ranged through such spaces. This country was theirs to do with as they chose, and if eastern capitalism or southern slavery interfered with their inalienable rights, their Sharp's rifles were at hand for defense. In the vast territory drained by the Mississippi—the "Valley of Democracy," a recent writer has chosen to call it—was conceived what may be accounted the most romantic dream that ever visited the native mind of America. It impressed de Tocqueville, who discovered the poetry of America in this romance of a moving frontier, in the vision that led the pioneer on his conquering way westward, hewing at an interminable wilderness that was matched only by his ambitions.

Such swift expansions, such mounting romanticisms of temper, must inevitably provide themselves with correspondent philosophies to phrase the new aspirations. The nineteenth century was not content to think in the narrower terms of the eighteenth, but must refashion its thought to suit the romantic style. The modes which it came to accept were for the most part of European origin, adapted to new-world needs. From France and England, and later from Germany, came variant schools of romantic theory that at bottom were a common glorification of the ideal of individualism; and this very diversity of interpretation made possible in America an appeal to different classes and diverse interests, the sum total of which was a many-sided contribution to social theory, but a contribution which carried within it the seeds of later conflict.

The first stage in the romanticization of American thought resulted from the naturalization of French revolutionary theory. Its devious progress through the country can be traced fairly accurately. Landing first in Virginia in the early seventeen-seventies, it met with a hospitable reception from the generous planter society and spread widely there the fashion of Physiocratic agrarianism. Traveling thence westward into the Inland Empire it domesticated itself in frontier log cabins under the guise of an assertive individualism, to issue later as the coon-skin democracy of the Jacksonian revolution. Eventually reaching New England, the last haven and refuge of eighteenth-century realism, it disarmed Yankee antagonism by assuming the dress of Unitarianism and preached the doctrine of human perfectibility with such conviction as to arouse the conscience of New England to an extraordinary enthusiasm for reforming man and society. And coming finally to New York it inoculated the mind of the emerging proletariat with its doctrine of the rights of man, with Fourieristic and other Utopias, and turmoiled contemporary politics with equalitarian Locofoco programs. No other philosophy assumed so many and such attractive disguises, or wrought such changes in American ideals, as this French romanticism with its generous humanitarian impulses. The ground was ready for the seed it was to sow, and if in the judgment of a hostile philosophy the crop turned out to be tares, increasing thousands believed it to be excellent wheat, to the growing of which America was to be dedicated henceforth.

The rival philosophy, which came to view with increasing dislike the doctrines of French romanticism, was of English middle class origin and sprang from the long struggle of that class to loose the hands of the landed gentry from control of the state. Phrased persuasively by Adam Smith, it embodied the principle of liberalism as that principle was understood by men of affairs. It conceived of a social Utopia that must result if economic forces were given free play; if governmental restrictions on trade were done away with and individual enterprise were free to buy and sell in the open market. Springing from the same root of individualism that brought forth French romanticism, it flowered in an economics that denied the aspirations of the French school. Assuming as its determining principle the common instinct of acquisitiveness, it set up the economic man as the criterion of conduct and proposed to reorder society to the single end of trade. Thus sanctioned and given free rein, the principle of acquisitiveness set forth on its triumphant march through western civilization. Accepted by the English middle class as the ultimate social philosophy sufficient to all needs, it presented to willing eyes the ideal of exploitation as the goal of social progress.

But transported to America, the new philosophy soon discovered unforeseen obstacles in its path. The acquisitive instinct was here enormously strengthened by the vast unpreëmpted resources lying all about, but unfortunately those resources were too great or too speculative to be exploited by individual effort. Capital was wanting, and unless collective funds were available, exploitation must be slow and inadequate. There was need of the state to further the opening up of western lands and to throw its guardianship about an infant industrialism. Roads and canals could not wait on individual enterprise; tariffs and subsidies could flow only from the government. Hence arose a modification of *laissez faire*, from which resulted the theory that a democratic state stands *in loco parentis* to the economic interests of its citizens, and should guarantee the progressive well-being of strategic groups on whose prosperity depended the common well-being. It was this modification of the English philosophy that the Whig party came to embody in its platform, and which by pooling the interests of western speculators, eastern financiers and New England industrialists, sponsored the "American Plan," a curiously ingenious scheme to milk the cow and divide the milk among those who superintended the milking.

Meanwhile in the imperialistic South was arising a distinctive philosophy, native to the special conditions imposed by slavery, that was to set it apart from both eastern and western economics and draw it inevitably into a narrowing isolation. Frankly defensive in purpose, rejecting alike French equalitarianism and English individualism, it sought to justify the institution of slavery by an appeal to realism and square it to the theory of democracy by analogy with northern industrialism. The conception of a Greek democracy, which was the last citadel of the southern mind, was a skillful compromise between the antagonistic principles of aristocracy and democracy, the most romantic ideal brought forth by our golden age of romance. Assuming the middle-class principle of exploitation as the creative source of every civilization, it proposed to erect a free state on the basis of a slave proletariat after the model of ancient Athens. A democracy, it argued, is possible only among equals. In every society hitherto the inevitable inequality between economic classes has nullified every democratic program. Master and man, exploiter and exploited, are necessarily opposed in vital economic interests; and this potential clash, this fundamental antagonism of classes, has been intensified by the rise of industrialism. Exploitation has been brutalized by the impersonal wage-system, and the proletariat has been reduced to sodden and embittered beasts. If now as honest realists we recognize frankly that equality cannot exist between inferior and superior races, if we accept the inevitable proletarian status of the negro, if finally we concede the truism that the lifelong relations between master and slave are more humane than the temporary relations between wage-giver and wage-earner, we shall concern ourselves less with a romantic equalitarianism and more with a rational conception of a democracy of equals that may conceivably erect a civilization worthy of the name.

It was an ingenious theory, but unfortunately it left out of account the ambitions of the middle class, and it was this class that in the end destroyed it. Whether they will it or not, imperialisms have a way of clashing with rival imperialisms. Reality persists though romance may deny it, and in their several programs the three diverse sections of America were driving blindly to a collision. In that bitter collision the dream of the South was destroyed. With the overthrow of the aristocratic principle in its final refuge the ground was cleared of the last vestiges of the eighteenth century. Thenceforth America was to become wholly middle class, and such romance as it might bring forth was to be of another sort.

The literature of this extraordinarily vigorous period we are now to deal with, not in the narrow field of *belles lettres* alone but in the outlying fields of social and political philosophies. The difficulties in the way are many. To endeavor to penetrate critically to the intellectual core of a period, to weigh this romance in realistic scales, to take off the outer wrappings and lay bare the inner truth, is no May-day undertaking. The critic finds himself at every turn confronted by reputations distorted by contemporary praise or censure. In the formal biographies written in that golden age of myth-making, criticism too often gave way to eulogy. Our fathers wrote like gentlemen, but unfortunately too often they believed that in preparing a biography a gentleman was under obligation to speak well of the dead. No blemishes were to be recognized, no disagreeable truths to find a place in their immaculate pages. In consequence scarcely a single commentary of the times is to be trusted, and the critic is reduced to patching together his account out of scanty odds and ends, or else settling down to do a series of full-length portraits, in which work, quite evidently, he will not get far. The inadequacies of the present study I am painfully conscious of: its omissions, its doubtful interpretations, its hasty generalizations, its downright guesses; but in the present lack of exact knowledge of the history of American letters, I do not see how such inadequacies can be avoided.

CONTENTS

xi

Part III

The Romance of the West

BOOK III: THE MIND OF NEW ENGLAND

PART I

The Twilight of Federalism

PART II

The Rise of Liberalism

BOOK ONE: THE MIND OF THE SOUTH

BOOK ONE

THE MIND OF THE SOUTH

To those who follow the main-traveled road of American experience, as we know it today, the mind of the old South seems curiously remote. It is so archaic, so wholly apart from all present-day ambitions, as to appear singular. Yet the continental highways we now travel so familiarly, it must be remembered, were not the highways of an earlier America. It is the North that has changed, and not the South, and the nationality that sits so easily upon us would have seemed ominous to the simpler world that determined the ideals of the Old Dominion. The southern mind has grown old-fashioned, but it is native and of long and honorable descent. It derived its singularity from the eighteenth century in which it took shape; and it retained the clear impress of its origins long after the eighteenth century had become an anachronism in America. It was primarily political, of the French rather than the English school; but it was economic also, out of Quesnay and Du Pont de Nemours rather than Adam Smith, with a frank bias towards the Physiocratic agrarianism that was so congenial to the needs and temper of a plantation society; and this political agrarianism, parochial in its outlook rather than national, suffices to explain the singularity of the southern mind in the eyes of a later industrialized America.

Simple and homogeneous in the early years of the nineteenth century, it nevertheless carried the seeds of disruption within it. Beneath the surface of this common political agrarianism disintegrating forces were at work, that were to produce broad cleavages of thought and lead to sharp differences of outlook and polity. An old South and a new South dwelt side by side, and to the West lay a frontier that took particular form as it came under the determining influence of one or the other. Virginia and South Carolina were the germinal centers of southern culture, from which issued the creative ideas that gave special forms to the brood of frontier states. Kentucky and Tennessee were the intellectual heirs of Virginia; Alabama and Mississippi were the intellectual heirs of South Carolina. Of these two schools of thought that looked in different directions and sought different ends, Jefferson and Calhoun were the intellectual leaders; and the contrasts in their philosophies—the rejection by the latter of equalitarian idealism, and the substitution of economic realism—mark the diverse tendencies which in the end disrupted the South. Jackson and Lincoln were followers of the Jeffersonian school; Jefferson Davis finally went with Calhoun; and Henry Clay, lacking an adequate philosophy, wavered between them. The differences between these men were open and patent, and any analysis of the mind of the South, any attempt to understand the conflict of tendencies that marked the development of southern thought between 1800 and 1860, must give due weight to such differences. The problem, therefore, instead of being single is threefold, and involves an examination of the mind of Virginia, the mind of South Carolina, and the mind of the new West from the Ohio River to the Gulf.

PART ONE: THE VIRGINIA RENAISSANCE

CHAPTER I

THE OLD DOMINION

THE history of the Old Dominion is an easy chapter in the text-book of economic determinism. It is a modern instance that exemplifies the law of land distribution and political control as laid down by James Harrington; it is another Oceana seated by the James River, that would not suffer a king to rule because gentlemen held the land and acknowledged no feudal dues or royal prerogatives. On the surface its history seems little more than a bundle of paradoxes. From the raw materials of English middle-class stock it created a distinguished and capable aristocracy, that was restrained from feudal tyranny by a vigorous yeomanry that held its land in fee simple and stoutly maintained its rights. Established on a slave economy, it adopted an agrarian economy, espoused a republic, and accepted the doctrine of democratic equalitarianism. It was generous, humanitarian, independent; parochial in its jealousies, yet farsighted in outlook; tenacious of its authority and quick to defend it, yet never mean or grasping. During the noonday of its power its influence was always on the side of local democratic freedom and the common well-being. It opposed the encroachments of the centralizing state and the spirit of capitalistic exploitation; yet its domestic economy rested on the most primitive of all exploitation.

But these paradoxes disappear when the history of Virginia is interpreted in the light of its land economy. By force of circumstances the Old Dominion became broadly American in its social philosophy, the interpreter of America to herself. Native conditions created there a native psychology, and this native psychology spread widely through the frontier states where a like economics provided suitable breeding places. Virginia was the mother of the agrarian West, as New York, Philadelphia, and Boston were the progenitors of the mercantile and industrial

East; and in the frequent clashes between country and town, between agrarianism and capitalism, the ideas of Virginia have commonly opposed the ideas of the northern cities. Between the older colonial America and later industrial America, stand the ideals of the Old Dominion, more humane and generous than either, disseminating the principles of French romantic philosophy, and instilling into the provincial American mind, static and stagnant in the grip of English colonialism, the ideal of democratic equalitarianism and the hope of humane progress. The nineteenth century first entered America by way of the James River.

The renaissance in Virginia began with the transition from middle-class to plantation ideals that marked the last half of the eighteenth century; and it was given intellectual stimulus by the libertarian natural-rights philosophy that in England and France was undermining the old order. There were no cities either mercantile or social, in the Old Dominion, and no industrialism. Life everywhere centered in the plantation. The navigable rivers of the tide-water region were favorable to the development of a decentralized economics, and in spite of royal commands to create adequate seaports, and heavy taxes by the commonwealth, trading towns did not prosper. For two hundred years Virginia refused to create a native middleman group to handle its staples, but preferred to deal through British factors and ship directly, preferably in Dutch bottoms. Each planter insisted on putting his hogsheads of tobacco aboard ship at his own wharf, and receiving his merchandise direct from London. The system was wasteful, and Madison was active in an attempt to limit by law the ports of entry to two, in order to build up a middleman machinery; but the plan broke on the fixed prejudices of plantation masters who had come to share the old English dislike of tradesmen. Virginia stubbornly refused to adopt middle-class methods, even though refusal cost her dear. She preferred to be exploited by British factors rather than create a domestic class to devour her resources.

The system had grown up in earlier times when the merchant spirit was strong in Virginia. It is often assumed that the Virginia aristocracy was descended from emigrant Cavaliers who fled from England during the commonwealth period; but the facts of history do not bear out such a theory. It was descended largely from vigorous middle-class stock—from men who had been merchants in England and in turning planters brought to the business qualities that had been developed in mercantile pursuits. In the seventeenth century Virginia society exhibited few of the usual characteristics of the Cavalier. It was frankly *bourgeois*, pushing, avaricious, keen in driving hard bargains, with no high sense of honor, canny rather than impulsive, preferring the law to the duel, hating war and only half-hearted in defense against the Indians—a little world of London burgesses new seated on the banks of the James and the Rappahannock. "Beyond doubt," concludes a recent student, "the most numerous section of the Virginia aristocracy was derived from the English merchant class" (Thomas J. Wertenbaker, *Patrician and Plebeian in Virginia*, p. 28), pretty much the same class that settled Boston and Philadelphia. For a hundred and fifty years these merchant ideals characterized Virginia society. Speculation in land was universal; exploitation was open and shameless; the highest officials took advantage of their positions to loot the public domain, resorting to divers sharp practices from tax dodging to outright theft. One gentleman added a cipher to a grant for two thousand acres, and although the fraud was commonly known, so great was his influence that no one disputed his title to twenty thousand acres. While governor, Alexander Spotswood issued patents for sixty thousand acres to dummy holders, who deeded the land to him after he had retired from office.[1]

In the third quarter of the eighteenth century such practices came to an end. The merchant spirit died out among the Virginia planters, and the Cavalier spirit took its place. A high sense of personal and civic honor became the hall-mark of the landed aristocracy, and for upwards of a hundred years this common code gave to Virginia an enviable distinction. Both in national and commonwealth politics her representatives were clean-handed and jealous to deserve the public faith reposed in them. Among the planters were good business men, of course, notably Washington, who under his stately manners concealed a capable mind for speculative affairs. He engaged in various enterprises; speculated heavily in western lands; was president of the Potomac Company, organized to improve navigation and connect his holdings with salt water; and at his death was one of the wealthiest men in America. But such a career was very unusual in Virginia after

[1] For these and other facts, see Wertenbaker's book (mentioned above), pp. 95-99.

the Revolutionary War. Washington, indeed, may properly be regarded as the last of the eighteenth-century gentlemen, who like Colonel William Byrd was interested in accumulating vast holdings as well as cultivating his plantation. Even more characteristic of an earlier day was John Marshall, the last of the great Virginia Federalists, who was nearer akin to Robert Morris, with whom he had business dealings, than with Jefferson or John Randolph of Roanoke.

The opportunity for such careers in Virginia was passing. Population was draining off into the West and few immigrants came to settle. With no rapidly growing cities the incentive to speculate in unearned increment was lacking and liquid capital was inadequate. The economics of plantation life developed agrarian rather than capitalistic interests. In the midst of a rapidly changing America, a world given over to exploitation, increasingly middle class and contemptuous of the older aristocratic order, the Old Dominion remained static and unchanging. The plantation aristocracy was marooned by the rising tide. It repudiated the ways of trade and industry and sharply criticised the North for its plebeian spirit. "Commerce is certainly beneficial to society in a secondary degree," said Governor Tyler in 1810, addressing the Virginia legislature, "but it produces also what is called citizens of the world—the worst citizens in the world" (quoted in Wertenbaker, *Patrician and Plebeian in Virginia*, p. 102). Enterprising young men who a generation before would have been strong Federalists and supported the new capitalism, found such an atmosphere stifling and migrated to the new South—to Kentucky, Tennessee, Mississippi, or farther West still, where greater opportunity awaited them. Virginia produced no more Washingtons or Marshalls, but turned whole-heartedly to the school of Jefferson, providing the leaders of states-rights agrarianism. She broke off all intellectual alliances with the mercantile and industrial North, and withdrew within her own plantation world.

Purged thus of its Federalist remnant Virginia became increasingly libertarian in its social and political philosophy. Its mind had taken form at the time when French humanitarianism was in the air, and it discovered much in the new philosophy that appealed to its romantic spirit. A quick and jealous concern for personal liberty and the rights of man was a common passion. The gentlemen of the Old Dominion were bound together by caste solidarity, but they remained strikingly individual, never amenable to group coercion, expressing their convictions freely and ready to uphold their views by the code of the duel. "No people ever lived," said Alexander H. Stephens in 1867, "more devoted to the principles of liberty, secured by free democratic institutions, than the people of the South" (*Constitutional View*, etc., Vol. I, p. 539). The right of dissent from majority opinion was the imprescriptible right of every gentleman. In no other part of America could the career of John Randolph be paralleled—a free-lance critic of politicians and political measures, who turned his caustic wit against whom he would, an arch individualist in opinions as other Americans were in acquisitiveness. Politics was an absorbing game in Virginia. Debarred from commercial pursuits, ambitious young Virginians went in for law and politics, with an eye upon a congenial career at Washington. This serves to explain the long predominance of southern leadership in the national government. For two generations the South provided a surprising number of first-class men whose influence was commanding. Until the problem of slavery became acute, and leadership passed from moderate Virginians to Fire Eaters from further south, the influence of Virginia at Washington was thrown on the side of republican simplicity, low taxes and the decentralization of power. The armed clash over slavery very probably might have been averted if the spirit of the Old Dominion had prevailed.

CHAPTER II

THE HERITAGE OF JEFFERSONIANISM

I

To the young Virginia Republicans of the year 1800, Jeffersonianism seemed to be a comprehensive social philosophy peculiarly adapted to their needs. It offered a practical and humane program of national development in harmony with existing fact and native genius. It had not yet been distorted by the caprice of circumstance into a somewhat nebulous idealism, nor confined within the narrower limits of political equalitarianism and states-rights theory. By later generations Jefferson has been interpreted too exclusively in terms of the Declaration of Independence, the glowing idealism of which has proved curiously elastic and has been stretched by later libertarian movements to meet their special and particular ends: by the Jacksonian democracy in their struggle for manhood suffrage; by the Abolitionists in their attack upon a slave-sanctioning Constitution; by other idealists in their various crusades. The great name of Jefferson, in consequence, has come to be commonly associated with the conception of democracy and the ideal of social justice. But to his young Virginia followers in the morning of the Republican movement, the perennial suggestiveness of their leader lay in the fact that he embodied for them the many-sided liberalism of French revolutionary thought, its economic and social idealisms equally with political. They interpreted him more adequately, for they understood, as later interpreters frequently have not, how deeply the roots of his natural-rights philosophy went down into current economics. Of the different French writers who gave shape and substance to his thinking, the strongest creative influence on the mature Jefferson came from the Physiocratic group, from Quesnay, Condorcet, Mirabeau, Du Pont de Nemours, the brilliant founders of an economy that was primarily social rather than narrowly industrial or financial. Historically the Physiocratic school is as sharply aligned with idealistic agrarianism as the Manchester school is aligned with capitalistic industrialism. The conception that agriculture is the single productive form of labor, that from it alone comes the *produit net* or ultimate net labor increment, and that bankers, manufacturers and middlemen belong to the class of sterile workers, profoundly impressed the Virginia mind, bred up in a plantation economy and concerned for the welfare and dignity of agriculture.

Franklin had first given currency to the Physiocratic theory in America a generation earlier, but it was Jefferson who spread it widely among the Virginia planters. He did more; he provided the new agrarianism with a politics and a sociology. From the wealth of French writers he formulated a complete libertarian philosophy. His receptive mind was saturated with romantic idealism which assumed native, congenial form in precipitation. From Rousseau, Godwin and Paine, as well as from Quesnay and Condorcet, came the idea of political justice and the conception of a minimized political state, assuming slightly different forms from filtering through different minds. The early doctrine of *laissez faire, laissez passer*—a phrase given currency by Gournay, the godfather of the Physiocratic school—proved to be curiously fruitful in the field of political speculation, as in economic. From it issued a sanction for natural rights, the theory of progress, the law of justice, and the principle of freedom. The right of coercion was restricted by it to the narrowest limits, and the political state was shorn of all arbitrary power. "Authority," the Physiocratic thinkers concluded, "should only employ the force of the community to compel madmen and depraved men to make their conduct conform to the principles of justice."

So far Jefferson went gladly with the Physiocrats, but in their acceptance of a benevolent despotism he discovered a denial of their first principles, and turned to the more congenial democratic group. With the political principles of Godwin and Paine he was in hearty accord. With them he accepted as an historical fact the principle that government is everywhere and always at war with natural freedom, and from this he deduced the characteristic doctrine that the lover of freedom will be jealous of delegated power, and will seek to hold the political state to strict account. From this same principle, following Paine, he deduced the doctrine of the terminable nature of compact, which he set over against the legal doctrine of inviolability. In this matter French liberalism and English legalism were at opposite poles. Replying to Burke's doctrine of irrevocable compact, Paine had written *The Rights of Man*, which Jefferson did much to popularize in America, and with the broad principles of which he was in complete accord. "The earth belongs in usufruct to the living," Paine had argued, and the dead possess no rights over it. Government from the grave is a negation of the inalienable rights of the new-born; hence social justice demands that a time limit should automatically revoke all compacts. Since no generation can rightly deed away the heritage of the unborn, the natural limit of every compact is the lifetime of the generation ratifying it. "No society," Jefferson said, "can make a perpetual Constitution, or even a perpetual law."

In this suggestive theory of the terminable nature of compact is to be found the philosophical origin of the later doctrine of states rights. However deeply it might be covered over by constitutional lawyers and historians who defended the right of secession, the doctrine was there implicitly, and the southern cause would have been more effectively served if legal refinements had been subordinated to philosophical justification of this fundamental doctrine. With a frank contempt for all legalists Jefferson believed that social well-being was not to be bounded by constitutional limitations or statutory enactments; that political action should be governed by reason rather than by historical precedent. He had discovered that the political state does not remain static, but gathers power by the law of physical attraction; with increasing power it becomes increasingly dangerous to natural freedom; hence a long-established and venerable constitution may become, by reason of its hold upon the popular affection, the most useful of agencies to cloak aggressions on the rights of the people. The love of profits is always seeking to overthrow the rule of justice. Human selfishness persistently distorts civic conduct, warping it from ideal ends. But the shortcomings of existing political states cannot abrogate the law of justice or destroy the love of freedom. To safeguard freedom from encroachment by the political state, and to establish the rule of justice, were always the great and difficult ends that Jefferson aimed at, and as a follower of the Physiocratic school and a Virginia planter he turned naturally to a *laissez faire* agrarianism in opposition to a centralizing capitalism.

But he was much too sound a political thinker and too sagacious a party leader to rest his case upon abstract theory. In all his later writings and counsels he kept his mind close to economic fact, and the Jeffersonian movement was a long and effective training school in the economic basis of politics. It habituated the motley rank and file of the electorate to think in economic terms and to regard political parties as the instruments of economic groups. This was in keeping with the soundest eighteenth-century tradition, before romantic dogma had divorced politics and realism; and in so far Jefferson agreed with his Federalist opponents, Hamilton and John Adams. A decade of acrimonious debate had made it plain to the common voter that the real struggle in America lay between the rival capitalist and agrarian interests, of which the Federalist and Republican parties were the political instruments. The Congressional enactments of the first twelve years had further clarified the issue. The funding plan had visibly increased the number and wealth of the rising capitalist group. The first banks were being erected and the complex machinery of modern credit— the hated "paper system" that had driven out the traditional me- tallic currency—was being rapidly built up. A small financial group in the northern cities was growing powerful from discount- ing and money-brokerage. The truth was slowly coming home to the farmers and small men that war is profitable to the few at the cost of the many; that from the egg of war-financing was hatched a brood of middlemen who exploited the post-war hardships and grew rich from the debts that impoverished the producing farmers. This ambitious class, hitherto negligible in America, was provided with the means to make a vigorous fight; it invoked the political state as an ally, and under Hamilton's leadership used the admin- istration to serve its financial interests. It looked with open hos- tility upon every agrarian program, was cynical towards French romantic theories, and was restrained by no scruples. To loose the hands of this capable class from the helm of government, to keep America agricultural, and the Federal state secondary in all but necessary police powers to the several commonwealths, was the avowed and logical purpose of the Jeffersonian Republicans.[1]

The leaders of the movement were men who in capacity and training were worthy opponents of the capable Federalists. In surprising number they were from the Old Dominion, gentlemen of the best Virginia stock, who in the last decades of the eighteenth

[1] See Charles A. Beard, *The Economic Origins of Jeffersonian Democracy*, Chap- ter XIII.

century engrafted upon a generous plantation tradition the Physiocratic doctrines of France. A finer race of gentlemen America
has never produced, and it was fortunate for the Jacksonian movement, which produced no notable thinkers and contributed little
to political and economic theory, that the preceding generation had
given adequate form to the philosophy of agrarianism. That theory
took definite shape between 1800 and 1820. In the days of Hamilton's control of the Treasury Department, the agrarian opposition was weakened by the lack of such a theory; but the necessities of the situation were a prod to the young Republicans, and
the philosophy of agrarianism rapidly crystallized. In its final form
it was an extraordinarily interesting and native expression of two
hundred years' experience of a society founded on agriculture—
a reasoned defense of an older America against the ambitions of
a younger and more vigorous.

II

JOHN TAYLOR

An Agrarian Economist

The intellectual leader of the young Republicans in the great
attack on the economics of Federalism was a thinker too little
recognized by later Americans. His just fame has been obscured
with the cause for which he labored, and his reputation lies
buried with the old agrarian *régime*. Nevertheless John Taylor of
Caroline County, Virginia, "the philosopher and statesman of
agrarianism," was the most penetrating critic of Hamiltonian
finance and the most original economist of his generation. Unambitious, simple, honest, calm and dignified in bearing, he embodied the heroic virtues of the great age of Virginia.   In his
Thirty Years' View, Thomas H. Benton describes him thus:

> I can hardly figure to myself the ideal of a republican statesman more
> perfect and complete than he was in reality:—plain and solid, a wise
> counsellor, a ready and vigorous debater, acute and comprehensive, ripe
> in all historical and political knowledge, innately republican—modest,
> courteous, benevolent, hospitable,—a skilful, practical farmer, giving
> his time to his farm and his books, when not called by an emergency to
> the public service—and returning to his books and his farm when the
> emergency was over. . . . He belonged to that constellation of great men
> which shone so brightly in Virginia in his day, and the light of which was
> not limited to Virginia, or our America, but spread through the bounds
> of the civilized world. (Chapter XVIII.)

Taylor was a member of Congress at the time of the funding operations and contributed two notable pamphlets to the public discussion: the first, issued in 1793, entitled *An Examination of the Late Proceedings in Congress Respecting the Official Conduct of the Secretary of the Treasury;* the second, issued the following year, entitled *An Inquiry into the Principles and Tendencies of Certain Public Measures.* Twenty years later, in 1814, he embodied his matured convictions in a stout volume, printed at Fredericksburg, entitled *An Inquiry into the Principles and Policy of the Government of the United States.* The work is tediously prolix—dressed, according to Benton, "in a quaint Sir Edward Coke style"—even more tediously moralistic; but in spite of very evident stylistic shortcomings, it deserves, in the opinion of Professor Beard, "to rank among the two or three really historic contributions to political science which have been produced in the United States" (*Economic Origins of Jeffersonian Democracy*, p. 323). It was the last of the eighteenth-century works, solidly reasoned, keeping a main eye upon economics and refusing to wander off into the bog of constitutionalism, concerned rather with the springs and sources of political action and the objectives of political parties. It summed up adequately the agrarian argument against capitalism, analyzed the current tendencies, and provided a convenient handbook for the Jacksonian movement, from which the latter drew freely in the dispute over the Bank.

Like Jefferson's, the agrarianism of Taylor was founded in the Physiocratic economy. He was convinced that the tiller of the soil was the only true economist, and that if republican America were to retain its republican virtues it must guard against every system of exploitation, for in exploitation lay the origin of social caste. America had rid itself of the feudal principle of a landed aristocracy, which in the past had provided the machinery of exploitation, by the abolition of the law of primogeniture and entail, only to be confronted by a graver danger, the new aristocracy of liquid wealth. His main purpose, therefore, was an examination of the sources of power of the capitalistic order, and the successive steps by which it had risen to power. His analysis is acute and reveals a mind concerned with the realities that lie beneath outward appearances. It is the economics of history that concern him most, for as fully as John Adams he was convinced that economics determine the form of the political state. In his analysis of the origins of government, he discovers in every society a master class that becomes the beneficiary of sovereign power: the political state is first erected and thereafter used to safeguard the past acquisitions and to further the present ambitions of a dominant economic group which calls itself an aristocracy; and such an aristocracy imposes its will upon the exploited mass, crudely by the sword and purse, and subtly by the skillful use of psychology. Once in control of the political state it intrenches itself behind certain fictions which profess to carry moral sanction. This political jugglery plays many tricks to catch the gullible; arrayed in the garb of patriotism, loyalty, obedience to authority, law and order, divine right, it carries a weighty appeal. When these moral fictions fail, the fictions of the law step in, and such doctrines as the sacredness of contract translate the stealings of the master class into vested interests which the state is bound to protect. There is a fine irony in Taylor's implied references to Burke's doctrine of a changeless constitution based on a non-revocable compact, and Hamilton's doctrine of the public faith, which, he argues, were clearly designed to sacrifice the common good to the interests of a class:

> Law enacted for the benefit of a nation, is repealable; but law enacted for the benefit of individuals, though oppressive to a nation, is a charter, and irrepealable. . . . Posterity, being bound by the contracts of its ancestry, in every case which diminishes its rights, man is daily growing less free by a doctrine which never increases them. A government intrusted with the administration of publick affairs for the good of a nation, has a right to deed away that nation for the good of itself or its partisans, by law charters for monopolies or sinecures; and posterity is bound by these deeds. But although an existing generation can never reassume the liberty or property held by its ancestors, it may recompense itself by abridging, or abolishing the right of its descendants. (Page 61.)

The two theories to which he devotes chief attention are the natural aristocracy theory of John Adams, and the capitalistic aristocracy theory of Hamilton. The first of these takes its bias from stressing the inequality inherent in the nature of men; individuals are biologically unequal; and from this fact Adams deduces that the thrifty rise to opulence and the thriftless sink into poverty by reason of individual qualities. Society can neither keep a strong man down nor thrust a weak man up. Between the rich and the poor, the capable and incapable, a state of war exists,

held in check by the strong hand in feudal and monarchical societies, but necessarily open and bitter in a democracy. Hence the
inevitable failure of democracy wherever it is tried, and the necessity of nicely calculated checks in a republic to prevent the equal
tyranny of an aristocracy and a mob. The second theory, the
Hamiltonian, justifies itself by the same theory of human nature.
It accepts the fact of social inequality as inherent in men, but it
sees no reason to pursue Utopian dreams. Recognizing the universal fact of economic control, it erects the state upon exploitation
as preferable to anarchy. This capitalistic state it defends before
a gullible public by eloquent appeals to the national faith, the
security of property, the fear of lawlessness.

Having thus analyzed the two theories Taylor seeks to cut the
ground from under both by arguing that social classes cannot be
historically explained by the fact of biological inequality amongst
individuals, but rather by accidental opportunity, unscrupulous-
ness, and brute force. All aristocracies, whether feudal, natural,
or capitalistic, take their origin and uphold their dominion, not
from superior excellence or capacity, but from exploitation, that
beginning in a small way grows by what it feeds on till it assumes
the proportions of a colossus. Exploitation breeds a continually
augmenting exploitation that conducts inevitably to caste regimentation. All aristocracies are founded in social theft. They
are not established in the morality of nature, but exist as parasites
on the social wealth; they levy upon the producer; and the only
preventive is to destroy the foundations on which they rest by
taking from them the means of exploitation.

In conjuring up phantom dangers of feudal aristocracies, Taylor
pointed out, John Adams was fighting dead issues. No feudal
aristocracy could arise in America; land was too plentiful and the
quick jealousy of the people would strike it down. The danger to
republican institutions was closer at hand; it was the poison of the
new capitalism that was spreading its virus through all the veins
of the national life. And in order that the American people might
know something of the history of this innovating force which they
must reckon with, John Taylor proceeded to open to them a page
in the economics of capitalism. The aristocracy of credit, founded
on "monopoly and incorporation," he pointed out, had arisen
first in England with the growing power of the middle class; it
had gone forward swiftly in consequence of the Napoleonic wars,

and through the agencies of the Bank of England and the Consolidated Debt, it had secured control of the public credit. It had
arisen first in America in consequence of the financial disturbance
resulting from the Revolutionary War, and had further strengthened its position by the War of 1812. Ambitious men had taken
advantage of the national necessities to create an artificial paper
system identical with that of England. They had profited immensely from the funding operations and the National Bank;
they were setting up their private banks in every city and town,
and through the manipulation of credit were taking heavy toll
of the national production. A money monopoly was the most
dangerous of all monopolies, and the master of all.

Taylor had grown up under the traditional domestic economy.
He was habituated to think of production in terms of consumption,
and of money as a stable measure of exchange. He could not
adjust his mind to the theory of production for profit, of middleman speculation, as socially legitimate; and when that speculation
extended to the national currency, and exacted its profits from
the medium of exchange, he took alarm. Gold and silver are
fairly stable commodities that allow of no sudden increase or
diminution, and in consequence a specie currency does not readily
lend itself to speculative juggling. But a paper system has no
natural limitations. Expanded and contracted at the will of
speculators, it subjects the business of the country to the exploitation of money brokers. Vast sums had thus been taken from the
people by the funding operations. Gold and silver had been driven
out of circulation, and with their disappearance a riot of speculation had begun by which only the brokers had profited. Such
was the origin of the new money aristocracy that had already
taken possession of the state and was using it for the sole end of
exploitation. America must make choice between agrarianism
and capitalism; the two were incompatible, John Taylor was convinced, and unless the ambitions of the paper-money aristocracy
were held in check, the American producer would come under the
heel of middle-class exploitation.

So suggestive was the reasoning of Taylor, so interesting for
the light it throws on the agrarian mind of the Virginia Republicans, that it will be well to set down his theses in compact form.
As summarized admirably by Professor Beard, his argument runs
thus:

1. The masses have always been exploited by ruling classes, royal, ecclesiastical, or feudal, which have been genuine economic castes sustaining their power by psychological devices such as "loyalty to the throne and altar."

2. Within recent times a new class, capitalistic in character, has sprung up, based on exploitation through inflated public paper, bank stock, and a protective tariff, likewise with its psychological devices, "public faith, national integrity, and sacred credit."

3. In the United States, this class was built up by Hamilton's fiscal system, the bank, and protective tariff, all of which are schemes designed to filch wealth from productive labor, particularly labor upon the land.

4. Thus was created a fundamental conflict between the capitalistic and agrarian interests which was the origin of parties in the United States.

5. Having no political principles, capitalism could fraternize with any party that promised protection, and in fact after the victory of the Republicans successfully entrenched itself in power under the new cover.

6. The only remedy is to follow the confiscatory examples of other classes and destroy special privilege without compensation. (*Economic Origins of Jeffersonian Democracy*, p. 351.)

In the great battle of ideas that followed the conflict of interests, the Virginia agrarians armed themselves with trenchant weapons. In intellectual equipment they were a match for the ablest of the Federalists; in social idealism, in generous concern for the *res publica*, or common public business, in sober and practical humanitarianism, they were far superior. Between John Taylor of Virginia, spokesman of planter agrarianism, and Fisher Ames of Massachusetts, spokesman of Boston Federalism, the contrast could scarcely be greater. It is a contrast in social culture, in humane ideals, in interpretations of the native genius of America; and in the comparison it is not the Virginia Republican who suffers.

CHAPTER III

JOHN MARSHALL

Last of the Virginia Federalists

UNLIKE John Taylor of Caroline, whose fame lies buried with his cause, the reputation of John Marshall has taken on immense proportions with the later triumph of his principles. There is abundant reason for the veneration in which he has come to be held by present-day disciples of Hamilton. More than any other man he saved the future for Federalism. During the critical years of the Jeffersonian and Jacksonian assaults upon the outworks of nationalism, he held the inner keep of the law, and prepared for the larger victories that came long after he was in his grave. His strategic judicial decisions served as a causeway over which passed the eighteenth-century doctrine of the sovereignty of the law, to unite with the new philosophy of capitalistic exploitation. The turbid waters of frontier leveling and states-rights democracy washed fiercely about him, but he went on quietly with his self-appointed work. He was one man who would not bow his neck to the majority yoke, would not worship the democratic Baal. He profoundly distrusted the principle of confederation. Convinced that the "continental belt" must be buckled tightly, he gave unstinted service to the cause of consolidation. The imperative need of a sovereign political state to curb the disintegrating forces of America was axiomatic in his thinking. Looking upon all democratic aspirations as calculated to destroy federal sovereignty, and convinced that the principle of equalitarianism was a bow strung to wield against society, he stoutly upheld the principle of minority rule as the only practical agency of stable and orderly government. Holding such views it was a matter of high and patriotic duty with Marshall to use his official position to prevent the majority will from endangering interests which were far more sacred in his eyes than any natural rights propagated in the hothouse of French philosophy. He was the last of the old school of Federalists and the first of the new.

That John Marshall should have come out of Virginia is perhaps

the most ironical fact in the political history of the Old Dominion.
Quite unrepresentative of the dominant planter group that had
gone over to Jefferson, bitterly hostile to the agrarian interests
that spoke through John Taylor, he was the leader of a small
remnant of Virginians who followed Washington through the
fierce extremes of party conflict.   He was the last and ablest representative of that older middle-class Virginia, given to speculation and intent on money-making, that was being superseded by a
cavalier Virginia concerned about quite other things than financial
interests.   He belonged rather to Boston than to Richmond.   His
intense prejudices were primarily property prejudices.   He was
the Fisher Ames of the South, embodying every principle of the
dogmatic tie-wig school of New England Federalists.   Profoundly
influenced by Hamilton and Robert Morris, he seems to have
found the Boston group more congenial in temper and outlook.
The explanation of his strong property-consciousness is to be
discovered both in his material ambitions and his professional interests.   He was a business man rather than a planter.   He was
heavily involved in land speculation and held stock in numerous
corporations launched to exploit the resources of the state.   Robert
Morris, whose daughter married Marshall's younger brother, was
his financial adviser and advanced money with which to purchase
the Fairfax estate, an investment that cost the buyers the very
considerable sum of fourteen thousand pounds and numerous
lawsuits.   He was a director in banks and a legal adviser in
important cases involving property rights.   His financial interests
overran state boundaries and his political principles followed
easily in their train, washing away all local and sectional loyalties.

Like his kinsman Jefferson, Marshall was bred on the Virginia
frontier, and to the end of his life he retained the easy and careless
democracy of dress and manners that marked his early environment.   In his deportment he was far removed from the prim
respectability of the Boston Federalists. A friendly, likable man,
fond of pitching horseshoes and sitting in a game of cards, he
was outwardly a genial member of the crude little Richmond
world where politics and law and speculation engrossed the common
attention. An easy-going nature, he was wholly wanting in intellectual interests. Strangely ill-read in the law, he was even more
ignorant of history and economics and political theory. His
mind took an early set, and hardened into rigidity during the

reactionary years that lay between Shays's Rebellion and the rise of Napoleon. Of social and humanitarian interests he was utterly devoid. One might as well look for the sap of idealism in a last year's stump as in John Marshall. French romantic philosophy he regarded as the mother of all vicious leveling. There is no indication that he had ever heard of the Physiocratic school of economics, or had looked into the writings of Rousseau or Godwin or Paine. The blind sides of his mind were many; his intellectual contacts were few; yet what he saw and understood he grasped firmly. The narrowness of his outlook intensified the rigidity with which he held to his fixed opinions; and his extraordinary courage coupled with a dominant personality clothed his strategic position as Chief Justice with fateful influence on the later institutional development of America.

Although Marshall's later fame is the fame of a lawyer, he was in reality a politician whom fate in the person of John Adams placed on the Supreme Court bench at a critical moment, where his political opinions translated themselves into the organic law of the land, and shaped the constitution to special and particular ends. Masterful, tenacious, manipulating his fellow judges like putty, he was a judicial sovereign who for thirty-five years molded the plastic constitution to such form as pleased him, and when he died the work was so thoroughly done that later generations have not been able to undo it. His political opinions, therefore, become a matter of very great importance to the historian, for they help to explain the peculiar direction taken by our constitutional development. Materials for a just estimate of his remarkable career were long wanting, but with the appearance of Beveridge's able and explicit *Life of John Marshall* it is now possible to view him in exact historical perspective. Carefully documented, the work is a genial and readable interpretation that will go far to revivify the fame of the great Federalist. And yet in spite of its abundant documentation—drawn perhaps somewhat overmuch from Federalist sources—it is essentially a *biographie à thèse* that is careful to magnify the nationalism of its hero and to minify the property consciousness. It provides a picturesque setting, but it is a bit careless in its evaluation of the rival philosophies then struggling for supremacy. Concerning the economics of the great contest between Federalism and Republicanism it offers very inadequate information, with the result that Jefferson is reduced to the status of a master politician set over against the constructive statesman. The intellectual limitations of the lawyer have reacted in these pages upon his political enemy. Certain of the old Federalist prejudices have come to life again in these entertaining pages.

The two fixed conceptions which dominated Marshall throughout his long career on the bench were the sovereignty of the federal state and the sanctity of private property; and these found their justification in the virulence of his hatred of democracy. No man in America was less democratic in his political convictions. Underneath the free and easy exterior of the Chief Justice was as stalwart a reactionary as ever sat on the Supreme Court bench. He was utterly indifferent to popular views, and he calmly overturned the electoral verdicts of his fellow Americans with the deliberateness of a born autocrat. Not only were his important decisions political opinions, but they were Federalist opinions. America had made definite choice between the Federalist and Republican theories of government. It had repudiated the rule of "gentlemen of principle and property" and set up a very different rule. But to this mandate of the supposedly sovereign people Marshall declined to yield. Defeated at the polls, no longer in control of the executive and legislative branches of the government, Federalism found itself reintrenched in the prejudices of John Marshall. He boldly threw down the gage to the majority will, and when the long fierce struggle was over, he had effectively written into the fundamental law of the land the major tenets of the repudiated philosophy. "Judicial statesmanship," Mr. Beveridge calls these political decisions, and bids us admire statesmanship on the bench; yet the phrase runs so far as to merge the judge in the politician—an honest but somewhat indiscreet admission that the law may be twisted to partisan ends. The frankly political nature of Marshall's decisions was universally recognized at the time, and this explains the intense partisanship they evoked, the fury of the Republicans and the extravagant praise of the Federalists. The so-called Jeffersonian assault on the judiciary, of which so much has been made by the orthodox historians, and which came near to wrecking the system, was not primarily an attack upon the courts but upon political judges who used their places to serve party ends. It is a dangerous thing for the bench to twist the law to partisan or class purposes, yet to this very thing John Marshall was notoriously given.

As a judicial statesman, then, rather than a lawyer, Marshall is to be judged, and to such a business the political historian is more competent than the legalist. His important decisions fall into two main groups: those like Marbury *vs.* Madison that assert the supremacy of the judiciary over the legislature—that is, the power of the Supreme Court to nullify an act of Congress; and those like the Yazoo Fraud case and the Dartmouth College case, that assert the irrevocable nature of contracts. The first was an official pronouncement of the principle that Hamilton had elaborated in *The Federalist*, namely, that the constitution is a law and as such lies within the field of judicial interpretation. This was sound Federalist doctrine, and Marshall welcomed the opportunity to engraft it upon the fundamental law of the land, going far out of his way to bring it within the judicial purview.[1] It was a bold and skillful move, and as Beveridge remarks, it announced a principle that "is wholly and exclusively American. It is America's contribution to the science of the law" (Beveridge, *Life of John Marshall*, p. 142). A contribution, it should be added, which with the multiplying of republican constitutions in the later nineteenth century was pretty generally rejected.

Even more partisanly Federalist were the decisions touching the nature of contract. These reached to the heart of the bitter opposition of the commercial and financial interests to the legislative acts of populistic majorities. Suffering heavily from the postwar confusions, those majorities had struck blindly at the profiteers whose well-feathered nests were securely protected by the law. The revolt was natural and human; a rough sense of social justice lay behind it; but because it struck at the most prosperous and capable members of society, who held the professional classes in retainer and dominated the agencies of publicity, it aroused an extraordinarily vindictive opposition. Dip into the literature of the seventeen-eighties and nineties anywhere, in the *Anarchiad* and the *Echo* of the Hartford Wits, or the private letters of indignant gentlemen, and the animus of the respectable classes is clamorously revealed. At bottom it was no other than this, that the law of business must be made the law of the land, and that any populistic tampering with such law was wicked and anarchistic. How determining was this spirit in the matter of the Constitutional

---

[1] For an excellent discussion see Beveridge, *Life of John Marshall*, Vol. III, Chap. III.

Convention is sufficiently well known. In the new constitution certain practices of populistic majorities were estopped—the emission of bills of credit and paper money, and laws impairing the obligation of contracts; but such provisions, strictly interpreted, did not reach to all cases. There were still gaps in the law of business through which populistic majorities might force their bills. To stop those gaps and complete the great work of rendering business secure was the problem to which Marshall addressed himself; and in the Yazoo Fraud case and the Dartmouth College case, he brought the long Federalistic struggle to a triumphant issue.

An examination of the first of these two celebrated cases will suffice to reveal the spirit of his judicial statesmanship. The state of Georgia, through its Legislature, had contracted to sell thirty-five million acres of land—the great part of the territory now comprising the states of Alabama and Mississippi—to certain speculative companies "at less than one and one-half cents an acre." The passage of the bill was marked by more than the usual jobbery, so common with a generation fond of looting the public domain. The fraud was so gross that the state of Georgia was thrown into a fury that visited itself upon the corrupt legislators. A new legislature repealed the law and rescinded the contract; but some of the land had already been resold to investors in Boston and Philadelphia, who brought their claims before the Supreme Court. The state of mind in which the chief justice heard the argument is thus suggested by Beveridge: "Marshall was profoundly interested in the stability of contractual obligations. The repudiation of these by the legislature of Virginia had powerfully and permanently influenced his views upon this subject. Also Marshall's own title to part of the Fairfax estate had more than once been in jeopardy. At that very moment a suit affecting the title of his brother's to certain Fairfax lands was pending in Virginia courts" (Vol. III, p. 584). To suggest that a nicer judicial honor would have inhibited Marshall from sitting in the case is perhaps going too far if one accepts the principle of judicial statesmanship. Certainly Marshall discovered none of the scruples that must have troubled George Wythe. In awarding claims for compensation to the investors he held that the act of the Georgia legislature was a contract and as such was inviolable. The crux of the decision, however, lay in the pronouncement that the courts cannot examine the motives that induce legislators to enact a law, that the people are bound by their agents and must suffer the penalties of choosing unwise or corrupt agents. The upshot of the verdict, in plain language, was that a legislative contract is sacred no matter how corruptly got. A curious decision, surely, for one who professed to venerate the common law. A Virginian of the type of John Randolph would never have reasoned thus to a conclusion that laid open the public domain to the deals of clever lobbyists and encouraged the betrayal of official stewardship. He would scarcely have sacrificed the public interests to the law of business.

The bitter hostility which Marshall's decisions aroused in his native commonwealth reveals how far the Virginia of Jefferson had traveled from the Federalism of the commercial North. The states-rights philosophy and the philosophy of consolidation were at swords' points; the agrarian and capitalistic economies were engaged in a mortal duel; that it should have been a Virginian who saved the day for the Hamiltonians, erecting the old Federalism into the law of the land, and conducting by his decisions straight to an augmented, consolidated state, under the shadow of whose power the development of corporate finance might go forward without agrarian let or hindrance, was a bitter brew for the Jeffersonian planters to drink. As Marshall grew old he drew farther away from his fellow Virginians. In his last years he was perhaps the most reactionary man in America. "Should Jackson be elected," he wrote in 1828, "I shall look upon the government as virtually dissolved" (Beveridge, Vol. IV, p. 463). His last hatreds he divided between Old Hickory and the rising democratic movement. He bitterly resisted the spread of manhood suffrage; he would make no change even in the antiquated judicial system of Virginia; he would have no overturning of anything established. A stubborn autocrat he remained to the end, and there was a certain ironic fitness in his last encounter with the executive power. The autocratic lawyer met his match in the autocratic soldier who grimly remarked, "John Marshall has made his decision, now let him enforce it."

Nearly a century has passed since these happenings [concludes Beveridge] and Marshall's attitude now appears to have been that of cold reaction; but he was as honest as he was outspoken in his resistance to democratic reforms. He wanted good government, safe government.

He was not in the least concerned in the rule of the people as such. Indeed, he believed that the more they directly controlled public affairs the worse the business of government would be conducted. He feared that sheer majorities would be unjust, intolerant, tyrannical, and he was certain that they would be untrustworthy and freakishly changeable. (Vol. IV, p. 507.)

A strong, resourceful, honest, capable man was John Marshall. In so far there is pretty common agreement. Beyond this, comes in the sundering blade of political theory. Concerning the wisdom of his judicial statesmanship it is idle to expect Federalist and Democrat to agree.

CHAPTER IV

THE OLDER PLANTATION MIND

I

PLANTATION BACKGROUNDS

THE literary renaissance of Virginia began in the late twenties when the English romantic movement reached the quiet plantations. Till then the Virginia mind had lingered pleasantly in the twilight of the liberal eighteenth century, following ways of thought it had learned of revolutionary France, and writing with a leisurely finish it had learned of Augustan England. In that older Virginia dignified sentiment was accepted as the hall-mark of breeding— a sentiment somewhat ornate and consciously elegant, that recognized its obligations to a strict morality, and laid its nosegay at the feet of the pure and beautiful and good. When the Virginian essayed somewhat infrequently to commit his thoughts to paper, he wrote as an old-fashioned gentleman, conscious of his social responsibility, consulting classic standards of taste, and embellishing his sentences with bits of choice Latin. But after the year 1830 sentiment gave place to romance, and dignity to exuberance of fancy. A new generation, trained in the school of Sir Walter Scott, fell to the pleasant task of portraying the familiar plantation life in glowing colors and investing it with romantic charm.

The plantation tradition, it will be remembered, first took shape in the Old Dominion and assumed its salient features at the hands of Virginia romantics. Its development was contemporary with the New England transcendental movement, and in origin and spirit it was as native to Virginia as the philosophy of idealism was native to Massachusetts. Inspired by an over-seas romanticism, it accepted the materials it found at hand and transmuted the easy-going plantation life into enduring romance. The work was begun by Kennedy in his idyllic *Swallow Barn*. The picture thus slightly sketched was given stronger colors by Caruthers, and received completer form from John Esten Cooke. From their hands Thomas Nelson Page took his materials to refashion to suit the taste of a later day. No realism added its sobering touches to the romantic picture thus early drawn, and none has since been added. A golden light still lingers upon the old plantation. Memories are still too dear to the Virginian to suffer any lessening of the reputed splendors of *ante bellum* days. The tragedy of a lost cause has woven itself into the older romance and endowed the tradition with an added sanction. It has long since spread beyond the confines of Virginia and become a national possession. North as well as South is so firmly convinced of its authenticity that realism has never had the temerity to meddle with it.[1]

It was a romanticizing age, and in Virginia congenial materials were ready to hand. The distinction of a plantation aristocracy set in the midst of a bucolic republican society, with its genial hospitality, its individuality, its sharp contrasts of whites and blacks, its clutter of cabins for background to the pillared mansion, its wide neighborhood interests, its outdoor life, its patriarchal spirit, was a distinction that no romantic could overlook, the most individual and native picturesque in all America. Life on the plantation was uncramped by the drab routine and skimpy meanness of the New England farm; it was unsoiled by the coarseness and vulgarity of the frontier; it had none of the sordidness of the middle-class town. It might be wasteful, but it was good material for literature; and hence the Virginia romantic had no need to seek the picturesque in England and Spain, as Irving had done. He had only to pick and choose from the familiar stuff lying all about him, emphasizing the agreeable, overlooking the unpleasant, fashioning his figures and action to suit the ideal of a golden age of plantation society. Yet the result, it must be confessed, is not wholly adequate. Virginia has suffered gravely from the want of a sober realism. It is not so much that the worst did not get into the romantic tradition—shortcomings in Virginia life which even Wirt hints at—as that the best did not get in. The plantation master of the romantics falls grossly short of the reality that Virginia provided. The simple dignity of John Taylor, the ingrained Puritanism of Lee and Jackson, the catholic culture and fine integrity of George Wythe, have been left out of the tradition. The Virginian created by the romantics is absurdly inferior to such men, who by any standard were as admirable a group of

[1] For an excellent study, see Francis Pendleton Gaines, *The Southern Plantation*, 1925.

gentlemen as America has ever bred. A little honest realism would have corrected the picture, to the advantage of the Old Dominion.

At the time when the romantics were beginning their work of constructing the plantation tradition the intellectual renaissance of Virginia was passing. With the fading of the French influence after 1820 came increasing isolation and a conscious sectionalism. Intellectual discipline and catholic tastes became rarer. Virginia had no share in the revolutionary enthusiasms of the Utopian thirties and forties, when New England expected the Promised Land to appear at the next turn in the road; it received no stimulus from the expansive systems of thought that were setting all Europe in ferment. The new Germany seems to have made no impression on the Virginia mind, neither its philosophical idealism nor its provocative higher criticism. The new interest in social speculation and experiment that arose in Massachusetts with the beginnings of industrialism awakened no response in Virginia. Plantation society was static, and social speculation was unwelcome. The theories of Comte, of Fourier, of Owen were unknown; Utopian experiments were untried. If Virginia escaped the curse of industrialism it lacked the intellectual stimulus that came to New England with the rise of the textile mills. Social unrest bred no protests against the plantation order. The revolutionary mood was gone, and after 1820 the stimulus to intellectual life grew weaker. English romanticism as exemplified in the work of Scott and Tom Moore was the single foreign influence that spread amongst the plantations, and the new literature accepted the cult of the picturesque romantic. With the passing of the great age of Virginia the tradition of her greatness remained to be gathered up and preserved.

II

WILLIAM WIRT

To Virginia gentlemen of the old school it must have seemed a bit ironical that William Wirt should have come to be accepted as the literary representative of the Old Dominion in the days of John Randolph of Roanoke. Born in Maryland in 1772 of Swiss parentage, Wirt belonged to Virginia only by adoption, and although on terms of intimacy with the plantation gentry he embodied few of the traits that went to the making of the plantation tradition. In temperament he was far removed from the easy-going planter. A certain canny thrift marked him, a pronounced desire to rise in the world and cut a distinguished figure. He was careful to make a good investment of his talents, attentive to profitable undertakings, whether in law or eloquence or speculation. His mature life ran a singularly prosperous and dignified course. He gathered property and reputation and office, and in every position he acquitted himself honorably. To do less than well in any undertaking he would have accounted a stain upon his reputation. In every company he made himself liked. There was none of the aggressive individualism of John Randolph, in wait for an opportunity to send home a shaft of rankling wit, but always a studious concern to please. He was troubled that anyone should think his criticism severe in *The British Spy*, and he hesitated long before publishing his *Patrick Henry* for fear offense would be taken at the few blemishes he discovered in his hero. An honest man and a capable, sterling after his kind but not notably intellectual, not creative, he owed his advancement to very practical qualities: an engaging personality and genial wit, a knack at formal oratory, a graceful pen, a persevering pursuit of his profession, the cultivation of desirable friendships. An excellent lawyer, he never turned aside from the law to meddle with politics; yet he was on good terms with the politicians, and he reached the top of his ambition by appointment to the Attorney-Generalship of the United States, a post which he held for upwards of twelve years.

In training and culture Wirt was of the sound eighteenth-century tradition. He was bred in the classics, English literature, and the common law. When he set up in his profession his library consisted of Blackstone, *Don Quixote*, and *Tristram Shandy*. His literary taste was formed by the later writers of the eighteenth century, by Gray, Hervey, Young, Ossian, Burke, Sterne, rather than by Pope and Dryden. In *The British Spy* he praises Bacon highly and lavishes commendation upon Addison, regretting that the *Spectator* "should be thrown by, and almost entirely forgotten, while the gilded blasphemies of infidels, and the 'noontide trances' of pernicious theorists, are hailed with rapture, and echoed around the world" (*Letter X*). Yet the determining influence in his own writings, it is clear, came from the sentimentalists and from Burke. From the former he caught the note of polite emotion. and from the latter the strain of sonorous eloquence. His well-bred sensibilities were constantly in the service of his pen or tongue, to lend pathos to an affecting bit of description or to transport his hearers by a melting appeal. A look, a gesture, a pose, was nicely calculated to bring sympathetic tears to the eyes of his auditors. To touch the emotions he considered the triumph of art, and to conduct through the emotions to a sound morality, its sole justification.

As a member of the Virginia bar Wirt took pride in the tradition of sober culture that had grown up amongst its distinguished practitioners. The members of that bar were gentlemen as well as lawyers, who would rather go wrong in their legal authorities than in their classical embellishments; they were orators as well, careful of their diction and meticulous in rounding a period. In these excellent qualities Wirt early distinguished himself. He had read more than most, and apposite quotations from the classics came easily to his pen to grace the pellucid flow of his English. One of the signal triumphs of his life was when in an elaborate legal argument before the Supreme Court at Washington, he retorted a passage of the *Aeneid* upon his opponent, to provide a text for a burst of the exuberant rhetoric that so delighted his generation (*The British Spy*, 1855, pp. 88–90). His love of ornate speech seems to us curiously old-fashioned, yet it was the manner of the times, and he gave himself to it with enthusiasm—*vivo gurgite exundans*, as he would have chosen to say. The chief interest of his life was oratory, and how skillful a practitioner he was adjudged by his own generation is revealed in the comment of a contemporary who often admired "the blaze of his reasoning and declamation":

The march of his mind is direct to its object, the evolutions by which he attains it, are so new and beautiful, and apparently necessary to the occasion, that your admiration is kept alive, your fancy delighted, and your judgment convinced, through every stage of the process. . . . There is no weak point in his array, no chink in the whole line of his extended works. Then the sweet melody of voice, the beautiful decorations of fancy, the easy play of a powerful reason, by which all this is accomplished, amaze and delight. His pathos is natural and impressive; there is a pastoral simplicity and tenderness in his pictures of distress, when he describes female innocence, helplessness, and beauty, which the husband on whom she smiled should have guarded from even the winds of heaven which might visit it too roughly, "shivering at midnight on the winter banks of the Ohio, and mingling her tears with the torrent, which froze as they fell;" it is not a theatrical trick, to move a fleeting pity, but a deep and impressive appeal to the dignified charities of our nature. (*Ibid.*, pp. 84–85.)

Wirt's literary reputation rests chiefly upon *The British Spy* and *Sketches of the Life and Character of Patrick Henry*, both of which may be characterized in the admirable phrase above quoted, as studies in "the dignified charities of our nature." The former was done hastily at the age of thirty, the latter was toiled over for years and appeared when he was forty-five. They were received with vast approval and set him quite in the front rank of American literary fame. Yet the contemporary popularity of *The British Spy* is inexplicable to us today. It is astonishing that so slight a thing should have achieved so great a reputation, and it suggests the depths of literary poverty in which the Virginia of 1803 was sunk. The work is a miscellany—hodgepodge perhaps is a juster term— of character sketches, geology, description, rhapsody, moralizing, with the faintest suggestion of criticism. The sketch which achieved the greatest celebrity, the description of the blind preacher (*Letter VII*, pp. 195–202), is elaborately artificial and sentimental, done from Sterne. The sketches of contemporary politicians, and in particular that of Jefferson, contributed much to current appeal, and the casual criticism aroused a mild remonstrance. There is a certain grace of style after the late eighteenth-century manner, abundant sentiment and little wit. Perhaps the happiest touch is the title; only a British spy could discover material for criticism in the excellent life and ideal institutions of Virginia, or insinuate that the commonwealth was lacking in public spirit— that its roads were as bad as its schools, and that the "one object throughout the state" was "to grow rich." But it was a very moral spy who was troubled that "the noxious weed of infidelity had struck a deep, a fatal root, and spread its pestilential branches far around"; and who lamented that "our eccentric and fanciful countryman, Godwin, had contributed not a little to water and cherish this pernicious exotic" (*Letter VII*, p. 203).

The demands made upon the dignified charities of our nature Wirt found more insistent when he came to write the life of Patrick Henry. He was troubled by his materials, as well as by the want of them. He complains repeatedly in his letters of the difficulties of the task. There were blemishes in the character of his god, spots that marred his divinity; yet how to clean them away and not spoil the natural appearance was a problem. He could not tell Virginians that Patrick Henry in his old age was grasping and vain, that he changed his politics as he grew rich. The idea was too repugnant to his own good nature, and to the taste of the times. The age was sentimental and romantic even in its eulogy. It took seriously the motto, *de mortuis nil nisi bonum;* it was patriotically engaged in making a myth out of the figures and events of the Revolution; and sober truth is not to be expected from the stately biographies that emerged from this period of excessive patriotism. The writers were too much in awe of their subjects, too much concerned to present them in full dress with wig and cloak and sword, and see to it that they acted a proper part. It was in this attitude that Wirt first approached his theme, but failing to achieve the desired result, he turned the work into eulogy of Henry's oratory. This was the most congenial of tasks to one so deeply interested in the art of the orator. The fragmentary records that had come down were a challenge to his inventiveness, and he set himself to recreate the lost speeches, from scanty notes. How admirably he succeeded is shown in the celebrated "give me liberty, or give me death" speech, that became at once an American classic. One could forgive him much for such a masterpiece.

The leaders of that older Virginia society were lawyers rather than planters, and Wirt's excursions into the field of *belles lettres* were only pleasant outings from the court-room. His intellectual interests were narrow. Though bred in an atmosphere of politics, he cared nothing for political theory, was wholly unread in the political classics, and untouched by the flood of social speculation that came with the French Revolution. He drifted politically with the stream of his generation, taking color from the changing waters. Brought up a Jeffersonian Republican, he remained curiously ignorant of the economic and political philosophy of agrarianism. He was little given to abstract speculation on the rights of man, and was never partisan to a cause. He was a genial embodiment of those colorless times when the enthusiasms of eighteenth-century liberalism were dead and the romanticisms of nineteenth-century exploitation were not yet risen, known in the history books as the era of good feeling. Fundamentally conservative and somewhat conventional, he would not look with approval upon the new men and new ways that came in with the western democracy. Upon the accession of Jackson he went over to the Whig party. He supported Clay, yet for some reason, perhaps a harmless vanity, he accepted a nomination for the presidency by the Anti-Masons in 1832 and went down before the hosts of the Jacksonians. Two years later his blameless life was brought to a close. A kindly and honorable gentleman of old-fashioned tastes, with a culture founded in Blackstone, embellished by Addison and Sterne, and given a classic dignity by Livy, he filled the measure of the excellencies as they were understood in the Old Dominion in the days before romance had created the plantation tradition.

III

NATHANIEL BEVERLEY TUCKER
A Virginia Fire Eater

In striking contrast to the amiable Attorney-General was another Virginia lawyer and judge who ventured into literature and whose one important novel created a mighty stir in its day. Beverley Tucker was twelve years younger than Wirt. Half brother of John Randolph of Roanoke, for some years on the bench in Missouri, and long professor of law at William and Mary College, he was a well-known figure in the Old Dominion, and his vigorous speech was much applauded at conventions where southern gentlemen met to talk over their grievances. In him were richly embodied all the picturesque parochialisms that plantation life encouraged. He was so completely and exclusively Virginian as to deserve the epithet "Virginianissimus." He never traveled, never compared diverse civilizations, never questioned the excellence of that in which he had been bred. His loyalty to his native commonwealth was a consuming jealousy for its honor, and he tucked the horizons of Virginia about him like a Hudson's Bay blanket and defied the cold winds of the North. Beyond Mason and Dixon's line lay a foreign country, and he judged all foreign countries by their size and color on his wall map. He was the arch-romantic of his generation and his *Partisan Leader* is the repository of the curious political and economic romanticisms of the ardent southern mind.

Over his after-dinner bottle of Madeira, Beverley Tucker may well have been the raciest and most delightful of companions. Like Samuel Johnson, he found his pleasure in a mind well stocked with robust prejudices and a wit to phrase them tellingly. He never spared his epithets nor hesitated to damn an opponent.

Like Fisher Ames, he coddled an aggravated case of political spleen and luxuriated in a picturesque pessimism. The clouds hung low over his mind, and the future of Virginia appeared as black to him as the future of Massachusetts appeared desperate to the Boston Federalist. His pessimism no doubt was a solace to his old age and provided a sauce for his dinner. Temperamently he was curiously like the New England Jeremiah. He followed Calhoun with the unreasoning and passionate conviction with which Fisher Ames followed Hamilton. He foresaw a future laid waste by the ravenings of democracy, and like Ames he took pleasure in sketching the dark picture. It would be no fault of his if the easygoing planters remained indifferent to the political monster that in the guise of Jacksonian democracy had made his den at Washington and was preparing to devour the liberties of sovereign commonwealths. He would make haste, while the shadows of those liberties remained, to arouse Virginia to its peril before the jaws closed upon it.

It was to this end that he wrote *The Partisan Leader*, an obvious attempt to dramatize the political philosophy of Calhoun and breathe into it a war psychology. Its single purpose was to popularize the doctrine of secession and encourage Virginia to act upon it. The book was printed at Washington by the notorious Duff Green, who had quitted Jackson and gone over to Calhoun, and appeared under the pen name of Edward William Sidney. Written in the last years of Jackson's second term, it prophesied Van Buren's succession and his setting up a dictatorship. The beginning of the action is projected thirteen years into the future. Van Buren is assumed to be in his third term and is seeking election a fourth time. He is in secure and insolent possession of "the presidential throne." He has surrounded himself with a horde of democratic sycophants; his political machine is well oiled and the army and navy are at his bidding. Virginia has been split asunder by factions. Mercenaries in Van Buren's pay occupy the public stations, and supported by Federal bayonets they carry things with a high hand. The lower South, under the leadership of South Carolina, has already seceded, and freed from the exploitation of northern tariffs is economically rejuvenated. The Virginia patriots are biding their time, working under cover and making detailed plans to carry the commonwealth over to the new Confederacy when the hour shall strike. The hand of fate is no other than economic pressure. The free South has provided an eloquent object lesson to Virginia planters. By reason of a trade treaty with England, by the terms of which each country exports to the other its natural wares unvexed by artificial restrictions—an industrial economy and an agricultural mutually benefiting by the exchange —the cotton and tobacco growers to the south of Virginia are enjoying a prosperity unshared by the exploited planters of the Old Dominion. When economic depression shall have finally opened the eyes of Virginians to the folly of a federal union that sacrifices southern interests to fatten northern manufacturers, the commonwealth must drop into the lap of the Confederacy like a ripe persimmon. In the meantime a mysterious Mr. B.—presumably Calhoun—moves adroitly behind the scenes, shaping matters for the great event—a super-statesman, a man of godlike sagacity and divine benevolence, a heroic embodiment of all the magnanimous southern virtues, compared with whom Webster and Clay are common political mercenaries and Jackson a paltry charlatan.

It is a romantically extravagant book, quite the absurdest in the library of the old South. It possesses no savor of humor or pleasantry of satire. Tucker was too deadly in earnest to play with his theme. He had so long and bitterly brooded over the supposed wrongs of Virginia that he had lost all sense of proportion. He lacks a cool skill in dissection; he has not learned the gentlemanly art of flaying his victim; he defends Virginia with a matchlock instead of a rapier. Gilmore Simms credited him with one of the most finished prose styles of the day, and a very recent critic remarks that "no other American of the time wrote with such classical restraint and pride as Tucker" (*Cambridge History of American Literature*, Vol. I, p. 312). But there is little evidence of such mastery in *The Partisan Leader*. It is the work of an unpracticed writer, with a command of rhetoric to furnish forth a southern stump-speaker, but quite inadequate to the needs of a competent novelist. Compared with Simms or Kennedy he is a mere bungler. His characters are as wooden as Cooper's females, and his plot is grossly distorted by his polemics. The drama sags under the weight of the sacred cause. There is inadvertent comedy in the picture of Van Buren as the man on horseback—the sleek, well-groomed politician of history rises somewhat inadequately to the rôle. In comparison with Kennedy's *Quodlibet* his attack upon Jackson is only caricature. Beverley Tucker was a patriotic

Virginian whose craftsmanship proved inadequate to the serious business in hand.

The backgrounds of his thought are clearly Jeffersonian. His prejudices run strongly for eighteenth-century *laissez faire*. He is a confirmed agrarian and his hatred of industrialism amounts to an obsession. He will have nothing to do with protective tariffs that lay a tax upon the planter to aid the manufacturer. In his advocacy of political decentralization he is a disciple of Calhoun, but more pessimistic than his master. Southern interests can be adequately protected, he is convinced, only by a jealous insistence on the sovereign powers of Virginia, and so long as Virginia remains within the centralizing federal Union those sovereign powers will suffer a subtle diminution. The simple-minded and magnanimous southern planter was no match in the political game with unscrupulous and ambitious Northerners. But in certain significant aspects of his political philosophy, Beverley Tucker broke with the Jeffersonian tradition. Two current developments had quite destroyed his faith in the democracy of Jefferson. The rise of Jacksonianism had seated the rabble in power, and the spread of Abolitionism was threatening to infect that triumphant rabble with its poison. The very life of Virginia was at the mercy of a hostile democracy, and to protect themselves and their slaves from the encroachments of a democratized federal government seemed to him the urgent business of the southern planters. Unless a move were made speedily it would be too late, for the power of the northern democracy was fast outstripping the confederate power of the South.

Tucker's intense prejudices color every judgment, and in consequence his misunderstanding of the North was colossal. He imagined a profit-mongering clown whom he dubbed Yankee, and solemnly assured himself that it was an authentic likeness. The Abolitionist was a Yankee with an added Puritan malignancy. In his defense of slavery Tucker has corrected the sentimental mistake of Jefferson in assuming the extinction of slavery to be desirable, but he professes an equally humanitarian spirit. His benevolence toward the negro is so warmly generous that one is ready to weep at the sad fate of the faithful slave who is in danger of being turned out into the cold world by the wicked Abolitionists. The loyal attachment between master and servant, he argues, is too finely generous to be understood by the mercenary North. The Yankees "have not the qualities which would enable them to comprehend the negro character. Their calculating selfishness can never understand his disinterested devotion. Their artificial benevolence is no interpreter of the unsophisticated heart. . . . They know no more of the feelings of our slaves, than their fathers could comprehend of the loyalty of the gallant cavaliers from whom we spring; and for the same reason. The generous and self-renouncing must ever be a riddle to the selfish" (p. 205, edition of 1861). Hence it is the clear duty of the magnanimous planter to keep his generous and self-renouncing slaves out of the clutches of the selfish Abolitionists.

Something of the ardency of Beverley Tucker's convictions is revealed in certain fragments of his letters to Gilmore Simms, to whom he poured out his heart in uncensored words, and whose magazine, *The Southern Quarterly Review*, he made use of to further the cause. In those letters he writes himself down a frank and whole-hearted Tory. There is an inveterate and ingrained aristocracy of temperament that will not mince words when it comes to dealing with democracy. In his comment on the growing democratic spirit he is virulent. He has lost all hope for Virginia in the year of grace 1851. "She is sunk in the slough of democracy, which has no sense of honor, no foresight, and is never valiant but against its own instruments" (W. P. Trent, *William Gilmore Simms*, p. 186). Georgia is in an even worse way. His spleen at the commonwealth of Stephens and Toombs—"filled as that State is with Yankee traders"—spits out venom: "She has been bought, and her price is in the pockets of those she trusted." He quotes sardonically the comment of a Georgia senator: "The State of Georgia is a damned rascal. I bought and sold her, and will buy her and sell her again when I please" (*ibid.*, p. 182). His only hope is in South Carolina, and he pleads with Simms for decisive action. Calhoun's kingdom is singularly blessed, for no base democracy there sullies the purity of manly councils. As early as 1820 Tucker had come to realize that the Union was a curse to the South. "I vowed then, and I have repeated the vow, *de die in diem*, that I will never give rest to my eyes nor slumber to my eyelids until it is shattered into fragments. . . . Time was when I might have been less desperate, because I could have sought refuge under some emperor or king. But all such refuges are broken up, and there is now no escape from the many-headed despotism of numbers, but by a strong and bold stand on the banks of the Potomac. . . . If we will not *have* slaves, we must *be* slaves." He then makes his great appeal:

And what are our democracies but mobs? South Carolina alone can act, because she is the only State in which the gentleman retains his place and influence, and in which the statesman has not been degraded from his post. You are fast coming to that hopeless and irreclaimable condition; and then all hope of action is gone. Work now. . . . The twilight is already upon you, and hence I fear you will not act even *now*. And if not now—never, never, never! (*Ibid.*, p. 187.)

It was not granted to Beverley Tucker to know what harvests were to be gathered from his sowings. He did not live to see the fields of his beloved commonwealth drenched in the blood that he had done more than his share to let. In that bitter struggle it is certain that he would have borne his part valiantly. He had sown to the wind, and he would have welcomed the whirlwind. But the outcome must have broken his proud heart, and it is well that he was not spared to see his hopes turn to ashes in his mouth.

CHAPTER V

ADVENTURES IN ROMANCE

I

WILLIAM ALEXANDER CARUTHERS

A Virginia Liberal

IN the early thirties came the transition in Virginia from the essay-sketch that had prevailed since the appearance of *The British Spy*, to the full blown romance of love and adventure. The older type had been a blend of nature description, social observation, character sketches, with somewhat injudicious portions of sentiment and moralizing, and with frequent resort to the old letter-form of fiction that lingered out a surprising old age. Not only is the transition revealed in the work of John P. Kennedy, whose *Swallow Barn*, written in 1832, was followed in 1835 by *Horseshoe Robinson*, but quite as strikingly in the work of Dr. William Alexander Caruthers, whose *Kentuckian in New York, or, the Adventures of Three Southerns*, published in 1834, was followed at once by *The Cavaliers of Virginia*, 1834–35.

Dr. Caruthers was a genial and cultivated Virginian from the Piedmont region, with a ready wit and a clever pen, who had pretty well rid himself of the intense and narrow parochialisms that restricted the sympathies of Beverley Tucker. He was a Virginia liberal of the older school, before the renaissance of the slave cause transferred southern leadership to the South Carolina group, and he shared none of Tucker's partisanship for Calhoun. He had traveled widely both south and north, and had discovered that human nature was much the same on both sides of Mason and Dixon's line. This experience qualified him to become a shrewd and kindly interpreter of both sections of the country, and his *Kentuckian in New York* was an excellent contribution to the cause of intersectional good-will. He sends two young South Carolinians just out of college on a trip north, who fall in with a Kentuckian on the way, and together they enjoy life in New York City, lose their hearts and meet with divers romantic and amusing adventures. A fourth character, a young Virginian, he sends to South Carolina, likewise to lose his heart and encounter adventures; and the copious letters that travel between them are filled with intelligent comment on unfamiliar ways. The writers are generous-minded young liberals with keen eyes, and their observations still make excellent reading after nearly a hundred years.

The South Carolinian who falls romantically in love with a New York girl is far from a Calhoun Fire Eater. He can see good even in the Yankee, whom he defends against the common southern prejudice by arguing that Yankee chicanery has resulted from a niggardly environment and the competition that comes with over-population, a competition that Virginia has been spared by the draining off of her population west; and as for the Yankee "canting and sniveling," "tell me," he remarks, "if you have not, in the very bosom of your great valley, as genuine Presbyterians and Round-heads as ever graced the Rump Parliament, or sung a psalm on horseback? And to give the devil his due, these same Presbyterians are no bad citizens of a popular government" (Vol. I, p. 72). Virginia has judged the North out of her prejudices rather than knowledge, and the advice Caruthers gives his Virginia neighbors, as an antidote to the suspicions of Beverley Tucker, is to travel beyond the boundaries of the Old Dominion.

Every southern should visit New-York. It would allay provincial prejudices, and calm his excitement against his northern countrymen. The people here are warm-hearted, generous, and enthusiastic, in a degree scarcely inferior to our own southerns. . . . Many of these Yorkers are above local prejudices, and truly consider this as the commercial metropolis of the Union, and all the people of the land as their customers, friends, patrons, and countrymen. Nor is trade the only thing that flourishes. The arts of polished and refined life, refined literature, and the profounder studies of the schoolmen, all have here their distinguished votaries,—I say distinguished, with reference to the standard of science in our country. (Vol. I, p. 181.)

The material prosperity of the North contrasts painfully in his mind with the condition of his native Carolina, and there is a note of apprehension in his comment:

The more I see of these northern states, the more I am convinced that some great revolution awaits our own cherished communities. Revolutions, whether sudden or gradual, are fearful things; we learn to feel attachments to those things which they tear up, as a poor cripple feels attached to the mortified limb, that must be amputated to save his life. A line of demarkation in such a case is distinctly drawn between the diseased and the healthy flesh. Such a line is now drawing between the

slave and free states, I fear. God send that the disease may be cured
without amputation, and before mortification takes place. I know that
this latter is your own belief. What think you now, since you have seen
the greater extent of the disease? (Vol. I, p. 165.)

The question is addressed to another young man on his travels,
a young Virginian who has gone south, and who is even more
troubled at what he finds. He cannot bring himself to think well
of the sacred institution as he sees it in South Carolina. There it
is laid bare in all its naked exploitation. The humaner relations
between the races that he has known in Virginia have been destroyed by the absentee system with its drivers and overseers—
"to these animals," he says, "I have always had an utter aversion."
The evils of the large-scale system have carried farther; slavery in
the Carolinas has destroyed the middle class of yeomen, unduly
exalted the aristocracy and utterly debased the poor white. The
single spot he heartily approves in the two commonwealths is
Salem, a Moravian settlement where no slavery exists, where all
work, and where education is thought so well of that the daughters
of the first southern families go there for their schooling. In Salem
he found an answer to the southern problem far more competent
than Nullification.

Here, then, is a triumphant answer—an answer in deeds, instead of
words—in the happiness, and the substantial wealth of these simple and
primitive Moravians. Here . . . is an industrious, intelligent, and
healthy community, in the very heart of all the misery I have described.
Let us then improve by the lesson, seek out the sources of their prosperity,
find the point where their plans diverge from ours, and, my word for it
. . . we become a great, a flourishing, and a happy people. (Vol. I, p. 80.)

To the problem of slavery he returns constantly, and his views
may perhaps be sufficiently understood from the following passages:

The poor of a slave-country are the most miserable and the most
wretched of all the human family. The grades of society in this state are
even farther apart than in Virginia. Here, there is one immense chasm
from the rich to the abject poor. In the valley of Virginia, or in the
country where you are, there are regular gradations. The very happiest,
most useful, and most industrious class of a well-regulated community, is
here wanting. Their place is filled up by negroes; in consequence of which,
your aristocrats are more aristocratic, and your poor still poorer. The
slaves create an immeasurable distance between these two classes, which
can never be brought together until this separating cause be removed.
You know I am no *abolitionist*, in the incendiary meaning of the term;

yet I cannot deny from you and myself, that they are an incubus upon our prosperity. This we would boldly deny, if a Yankee uttered it in our hearing; but to ourselves, we must e'en confess it. If I am, therefore, an abolitionist, it is not for conscience-sake, but from policy and patriotism. (Vol. I, pp. 76–77.)

With us [in Virginia] slavery is tolerable, and has something soothing about it to the heart of the philanthropist; the slaves are more in the condition of tenants to their landlords—they are viewed as rational creatures, and with more kindly feelings. . . . *Here* slavery is intolerable; a single individual owning a hundred or more, and often not knowing them when he sees them. . . . The slaves here are plantation live-stock; not domestic and attached family servants, who have served around the person of the master from the childhood of both. . . . Here, besides your white overseers, you have your black *drivers;*—an odious animal, almost peculiar to the far south. It is horrible to see one slave following another at his work, with a cow-skin dangling at his arm, and occasionally tying him up and flogging him when he does not get through his two tasks a day. . . . I do not observe much difference between the North and South Carolinians, except in the case of those who inhabit the most southern portions of the latter state. There your rich are more princely and aristocratic, and your poor more wretched and degraded; but to tell you the plain truth, many of your little slaveholders are miserably poor and ignorant; and what must be the condition of that negro who is a slave to one of these miserable wretches? (Vol. II, pp. 115–119.)

To the solution of the difficult problem Caruthers offers no easy plan. He cannot go with the northern "enthusiasts" who propose immediate emancipation. They do not comprehend the complexity of the problem. "We cannot set slaves free among us. Such a course would dissolve the social compact. It would set at defiance all laws for the protection of life, liberty, and property, either among them or the whites." He foresaw clearly what happened during the unhappy days of reconstruction. "Would it be any reparation of an hereditary wrong, to plunge the subjects of that wrong, with ourselves, into irretrievable ruin, to attain nominal justice?" The free negroes would constitute a menace more serious than the northern city mobs, which latter Caruthers had no liking for. "These city mobocracies, composed as they are, principally of wild Irish, are terrible things"; how much worse would be a negro mobocracy? A confirmed agrarian, he finds his chief hope in a vigorous yeomanry, and until the South shall develop that, matters must go ill with it. In the midst of the Carolina system his thoughts return fondly to his native state. He is under no illusion in regard to the tide-water region of Virginia. It has

lived a generous life, but spendthrift and wasteful, and has come to evil days. But in the West, beyond the mountains, a newer and more vigorous age is rising that "will sweep away the melancholy vestiges of a former and more chivalrous and generous age."

Poor, exhausted eastern Virginia! she is in her dotage. Her impassable roads protect her alike from the pity and contempt of foreign travellers; but with all her weakness, with all the imbecilities of premature age upon her, I love her still. (Vol. II, p. 194.)

Of this more vigorous age the prototype is the title-hero of the volume, the stalwart Kentuckian whose native intelligence and racy speech delight the Carolinian. This free son of the untamed West is portrayed with bold strokes, and if his talk leans somewhat heavily on the current convention of frontier humor, if Montgomery Damon in his picturesque exaggerations suggests Davy Crockett, the result is none the less salty. Caruthers does not descend to caricature, but writes with gusto, and the Kentuckian's single letter is a little masterpiece in the vein of the free frontier humor that was competing with the cavalier romantic for popular approval. His whimsicalities, Caruthers tells us, he hopes will encourage "a smile of good-humor" so that this maiden product of the author's pen may find its way into the good graces of the reader—a course reckoned "the more necessary by a southern aspirant, as there is evidently a current in American literature, the fountainhead of which lies north of the Potomac, and in which a southern is compelled to navigate up the stream if he jumps in too far south" (Vol. II, p. 218.)

The Cavaliers of Virginia, or the Recluse of Jamestown, announced in the postscript to the *Kentuckian in New York*, and published soon afterwards, is a full-fledged historical romance, with Bacon's Rebellion for a background and a somewhat melodramatic figure of a recluse warrior for its romantic hero. There is brisk action, dramatic Indian fights, much ruffling of young cavaliers, and a fine aristocratic swagger, but Caruthers' sympathies seem to incline to the more democratic elements and in the end his rebellious hero proves himself a match for the brisk young blades. There is excellent reading in it, as there is in his last work, *The Knights of the Horse-Shoe; a Traditionary Tale of the Cocked Hat Gentry in the Old Dominion*, published in 1845, and reissued as late as 1909; a genial story of Governor Spotswood's time. Caruthers deserved a better fate than fell to his lot. In spite of his excellent work surprisingly little is known about him; even the spelling of his name and the date of his death are matters about which there is disagreement. From a slight sketch contributed to *The Knicker-bocker Magazine* for July, 1838, *Climbing the Natural Bridge*, it is known that he was a student at Washington College, now Washington and Lee, at Lexington, Virginia, in the year 1818, and the signature affixed carries only one "r." He seems to have removed later to Savannah, Georgia, an enthusiastic description of which he gives in the *Kentuckian in New York*. No doubt he there practiced medicine and died in his prime, perhaps in the year 1846. Virginia historians have inconsiderately neglected a cultivated and open-minded writer who embodied the finer spirit of the Old Dominion and whose stories have contributed their portion to the plantation tradition.

II

JOHN PENDLETON KENNEDY
A Southern Whig

A far more prosperous course was run by John P. Kennedy, whose sympathies drew him north rather than south, and who early learned that it is better to serve a rising than a decaying order. Very like Caruthers in temperament and gifts, a liberal in all his sympathies, he found the ties that bound him to the Old Dominion more fragile, and the drift of circumstance carrying him with the stronger current. It was a kindly fate that took him in charge, bringing him abundant prosperity and contemporary fame.

One of the most attractive figures of his generation was this son of a Maryland father and a Virginia mother. A gentleman of much personal distinction, high-minded and of wide culture, endowed with a pleasant wit, easy manners and generous nature, he is an agreeable representative of the *ante bellum* Southerns, an American Victorian of the Cobden-Bright school, standing midway between the northern radical and the southern Fire Eater. Like Henry Clay, he was a Whig engrafted on a Jeffersonian root. Born and educated in Baltimore, he was a son of the borderland, with strong ties of kinship and love that drew him to the Old Dominion, and even stronger ties of intellectual, social and financial interests that drew him towards Philadelphia and New York,

Saratoga and Newport. As a young man he found his inspiration in the life of William Wirt, whose biography he afterwards wrote. Like Wirt, he dreamed of combining law and letters and adopting the life of a southern gentleman; but he discovered little that was congenial in the exactions of the law, and in spite of considerable success as attorney for certain Baltimore interests, he largely abandoned the profession. He loved his Chaucer and Shakespeare more than his Coke and Blackstone: he was more interested in Dickens and Thackeray and Carlyle and Irving and Scott than in John Marshall's decisions, and he followed the more congenial path. He tried his hand likewise at politics. He was a member of Congress for six years, was Secretary of the Navy during the last months of President Fillmore's administration, and was of service to the Whig party as spokesman on dignified occasions. But he was never a practical politician, and the rough and tumble of political life he found utterly distasteful. As he grew older he unconsciously drew further away from his southern antecedents. In his later years there was little to distinguish him from Irving and Robert C. Winthrop and other northern friends. He had left the world of Beverley Tucker far behind him. He had severed all ties with Virginia and South Carolina, and during the Civil War he was a militant Unionist, though it cost him much grief and the loss of old friendships.

Kennedy's life ran an usually placid and prosperous course, greatly unlike that of Gilmore Simms. His father was a Scotch-Irish merchant of Baltimore who married Nancy Pendleton, daughter of an excellent Virginia family with many honorable connections. His early years were not unlike Irving's—a little Latin and Greek and much outdoor life, with a desultory education got from vagrant books. The course of study at the local college afforded far less intellectual stimulus than *Tristram Shandy*, over which he pored of evenings, dissecting the prose style to discover the secret of its charm, and filling his notebooks with elaborately colloquial sentences, highly seasoned with dashes and exclamation points. Graduating at eighteen, he enlisted in a Baltimore regiment to fight the British, who were preparing their raid on Washington. He went through the campaign as a summer lark, emerging unscathed from the single skirmish. The field was lost, but whether the honor of the crack Fifth was left on the battle ground may be judged from Kennedy's humorous comment. "Soon we had the famous 'trial of souls'—the battle of Bladensburg. The drafted militia ran away at the first fire, and the Fifth Regiment was driven off the field with the bayonet. We made a fine scamper of it. I lost my musket in the mêlée while bearing off a comrade" (Tuckerman, *Life of Kennedy*, p. 79).

Throughout his twenties Kennedy was a studious dilettante in letters and politics and law. He married but lost his wife and son within the year; with his friend Peter Hoffman Cruse he published a series of Baltimore sketches in two volumes entitled *The Red Book;* and at the age of thirty-four married again. His second wife was the daughter of Edward Gray, a wealthy Baltimore cotton-spinner who at the age of eighteen had emigrated from northern Ireland to Philadelphia, became a bank clerk and a Federalist simultaneously, adopted Washington and Hamilton— whom he occasionally met in a professional way—as his particular heroes, prospered greatly, purchased the Ellicott Mills a few miles out of Baltimore, and set up a half feudal estate vastly attractive to discriminating visitors like Irving.

Kennedy's marriage to Elizabeth Gray in 1829 seems to have been the turning-point of his life. Before this he had been a disinterested liberal in his views, concerning himself in a political way with such humanitarian issues as the repeal of the brutal debtor laws. He had never been an avowed Jeffersonian like William Wirt and many of his Virginia connections, but the Jeffersonian idealism must have appealed to the generous sympathies of the young man. Immediately upon being taken into the Gray family he adopted its ample scale of living, its genial hospitality, its social and political philosophy. The influence of the masterful Edward Gray was thenceforth a dominant creative factor in Kennedy's life, and he followed faithfully in the footsteps of his father-in-law. The profits of the Ellicott Mills had been greatly increased by the tariff act of 1824. Naturally Edward Gray was an ardent protectionist, and Kennedy frankly espoused the same policy. He accepted Henry Clay as his political leader, was sent to Congress on a protectionist platform, lectured before Workingmen's Institutes on the advantages of industrial development, and gained a very considerable reputation as an expounder of the American Plan. After the war he became a Republican, voted for Grant, and adopted extreme nationalist views. That the family income was dependent on tariff favors is a detail which only a more realistic generation would suggest in explanation of his political course; the fact remains, nevertheless, that the youthful disciple of William Wirt adopted the new philosophy of prosperity, became president of the board of directors of the Baltimore and Ohio Railway, invested in West Virginia coal lands, and was by way of becoming a captain of industry. The break with his southern antecedents was complete and final; he went with his native city in preferring the industrial to the plantation economy.

Baltimore in Kennedy's day was a thriving port with a growing trade to the West Indies and Europe. It had long been a convenient market for the tobacco of Virginia, and with the development of the clipper service its over-sea commerce expanded greatly. Unlike Charleston, the mercantile interests predominated over the planter. Middle-class ideals, to be sure, were still tempered by the dignified decorum that lingered on from the eighteenth century. Merchants still emulated the gentry and strove for personal distinction. They professed benevolent ideals and their talk was much of public spirit and the progress of the town. They adopted the romantic faith of their class in the beneficent processes of trade and industry in furthering social well-being, and they endowed Mechanics Institutes and founded public libraries and museums with all the ardor of converts. In this agreeable work of expounding the gospel of progress, Kennedy joined heartily. It satisfied the latent idealism of his nature and recompensed him for the loss of his Virginia heritage. Intellectually he was too honest to pervert the gospel of progress to selfish class interest and seek to hide the perversion behind sonorous platitudes, as his friend Robert C. Winthrop of Boston was guilty of doing. He had too much love for the English language to misuse it even in defense of the family income. He could not contract his mind to the compass of a Whig politician's. His defense of industrialism, in consequence, embodies the spirit of the best English liberalism as that liberalism was interpreted by Victorian Englishmen. He seems to have been honestly convinced that the future well-being of America was dependent upon the development of an industrialism to provide an economic balance between manufactures and agriculture.

Like his friend Irving, Kennedy was a devout romantic, with a love of the old-time picturesque; but as a consistent Whig he would spin and weave his romance out of domestic materials, refusing to import. He was a child of the effervescent days following 1812, when the static eighteenth century was breaking up and an ebullient romanticism was permeating the land. Of this youthful period his thought reveals the clear impress. Washington Irving from long pottering over the old-world picturesque had become English romantic, with an inveterate dislike of all innovation. The vulgar nineteenth century was destroying for him the charm of the eighteenth; he would have had the world remain as it was before the American and French revolutions had despoiled life of picturesque feudal ways. Whereas Kennedy, sharing in a romanticism that was economic and social—that was creating a wonderful America of the future out of the raw materials of life—was content to remain native, at home in the land of his birth. He might turn to the past for the figures and scenes of his stories, but he discovered in the activities of the present materials for romance quite as fascinating. He was wholly Victorian in his genial optimism. He was receptive to new ideas and promising ventures. He listened sympathetically to inventors and scientists and promoters. He was instrumental in securing Congressional aid to erect Morse's telegraph line between Washington and his native city. As Secretary of the Navy he provided for Commodore Perry's expedition to Japan, and the expedition to search for Dr. Kane in the Arctic regions. But unfortunately his economic romanticism gradually undermined his literary romanticism; he outgrew his earlier literary ambitions, and the romances of his later life never got written. In the end the gospel of progress was his undoing.

That the generous comfort in which he lived afforded him leisure, means of travel, contact with distinguished people, goes without saying; but that it was favorable to letters is far from clear. Divided interests consumed his energies and kept him an amateur to the last. His literary development was an evolution from a sketchy and humorous Addisonian, with its echoes of the eighteenth century, to the full Victorian romantic. The foreign elements from an earlier time slowly settled to the bottom of the vat and left the pure wine of romance. But it took time. Like other amateurs he was influenced by current literary successes, and was much given to following the changing fashions. His three best-known books, written between the ages of thirty-six and forty-five, are unlike enough to have been written by different men. *Swallow Barn,* like the youthful sketches of *The Red Book*, is Irvingesque, and the Irving influence crops out again in a late book *Quodlibet;* but *Horseshoe Robinson* is substantial Revolutionary romance, done in sober narrative with touches of realism; and *Rob of the Bowl* is light and whimsical cavalier romance, all atmosphere and small talk, utterly unlike Irving. It is in this latter book, perhaps, written in 1838 at the age of forty-two, that Kennedy really found himself; he seems to move through the scenes more easily and with greater delight than in any other of his pages.

That the leisurely sketches of *Swallow Barn* belong to the school of Irving is a fact as obvious as Kennedy's love for the idling plantation life. Quite too much, however, has been made of this imitativeness—it is an imitativeness rather of method than of theme or style. If it was not quite a pioneer work in the field of local description, it was amongst the earliest. Paulding had dealt with Dutch colonial life, and Timothy Flint and James Hall had begun the descriptive literature of the West; but little else had been done at the time *Swallow Barn* appeared. Longstreet's *Georgia Scenes* came out two years later. Intrinsically as well as historically the work is curiously suggestive. Nowhere else does the plantation life of the Old Dominion in the days before its decline appear so vividly as in these discursive pages: "the mellow, bland, and sunny luxuriance of her old-time society—its good fellowship, its hearty and constitutional *companionableness*, the thriftless gaiety of the people, their dogged but amiable invincibility of opinion, and that overflowing hospitality which knows no ebb."

Like Irving, Kennedy went back to the old home, but that old home was Virginia and not England; and there he found still lingering on the great plantations charmingly romantic anachronisms that had disappeared elsewhere—a spontaneous romanticism of temperament that gave color and zest to the daily routine. The aloofness of plantation life had bred in the Virginia gentry a piquant individuality, a distinction as of old morocco or calfskin. Philly Wart, the shrewdly humorous fox-hunting lawyer; old Mr. Tracy of The Brakes, "turning a little sour with age" and resembling "that waterish, gravelly soil that you see sometimes around a spring, where nothing grows but sheep-sorrel," who cherishes a hereditary boundary dispute, pursuing his hypothetical rights through all the law courts and discovering, when the matter has been amicably settled by arbitration, that much of the zest has

gone out of his life; the heroine Bel Tracy, a frank wholesome girl
with a dash of Di Vernon in her romantic affectations that lead
her to play at hawking: such figures fit as naturally into the background as the pampered house servants, the horseback riding, the
constant visiting, the abundant dinners. Especially the dinners,
when the neighborhood is invited in. The table spread with
opulent hospitality and careless profusion—the baked ham at
one end and the saddle of roast mutton at the other, with fried
chicken, oysters, crabs, sweet potatoes, jellies, custards—a prodigal feast that only outdoor stomachs could manage, and all by
way of preliminary to the dusty wine-bottles and easy stories
that hold the men long after the ladies have withdrawn. Surely
the romance of Old Virginia, preserved in these light-hearted
discursive pages, is worth remembering by later generations who
have forgotten how to live so genially.

In 1832 when *Swallow Barn* was written, the southern mind was
just at the turn in its attitude towards slavery, and Frank Meriwether, a Virginian Sir Roger de Coverley, bred in the humanitarianism of the older liberals, accepts the institution as a present
evil that is in a way of natural extinction. Slavery in *Swallow
Barn* is kept in the background. There are slaves, of course, on
the plantation, many of them; but they are in the tobacco fields
or the quarters, far from the mansion; and not till near the end of
the book does Kennedy's curiosity induce him to visit the cabins
and draw out Frank Meriwether in talk on slavery. The result is
what one could have foreseen. The plantation master was the
victim of a benevolent romanticism that vaguely looks for a solution to colonization schemes that will return the negro to Africa;
but like other southern gentlemen he is somewhat testy at the suggestion of outside interference. Slavery he regards as an exclusive
southern problem, to be solved by those who understand its complex domestic implications. It would be better for everybody if
Abolition busybodies would mind their own affairs and cease
stirring up feelings where no good can come of it. To prove that
Virginia gentlemen are aware of their responsibility, Meriwether
offers a half humorous suggestion that negro emancipation might
well follow the example of English villeinage, with a slow break-up
of the system, the emancipated negro to remain in a protective
feudal relation to his master. It was an amiable notion to play
with, and it fitted the feudal psychology of the plantation.

In these early sketches Kennedy revealed an easy knack at writing that gave promise of excellent work later. He has lightness, grace, refinement, an eye sensitive to picturesque effects, delight in line and texture and color, an agreeable wit and playful sentiment, a relish for English idiom and the literary colloquial. In *Horseshoe Robinson*, written three years later, he abandoned the essay-sketch and turned to the school of historical romance then in full swing. The story is done in the orthodox manner of the thirties; it is compounded of equal parts gentry and commoners, the former providing respectability and the latter dramatic interest, the whole garnished with a few historical figures. There is quite obvious concern for authentic reality. The title-hero, a shrewd homespun scout, is carefully drawn from life; the background of bushwhackings and forays and onsets, and the numerous company of blackguards and honest folk, are painted in skillfully; and the whole conducts to a dramatic finale in the battle of King's Mountain. It is an excellent tale, quite worth reading today, but scarcely comparable in vividness and brisk action—in picaresque realism which any true war story must embody—with *The Partisan* of Gilmore Simms, written in the same year of 1835. Realism was not Kennedy's forte and after *Horseshoe Robinson* he abandoned the field of the Revolution which offered so rich an opportunity for the robuster genius of the Charleston romancer.

In *Rob of the Bowl* Kennedy opened a promising vein that he never adequately explored—the vein of the cavalier romantic. Temperamentally he was ill fitted to deal with rollicking action or picaresque adventure; he preferred the leisurely, discursive romantic, subdued to gentle raillery or humorous tenderness. One trembles to think what Simms would have made of the materials that Kennedy brought together in this tale of old St. Mary's in the days of Charles II. Here is the raw stuff of a true bloody-bones thriller: a gentlemanly blackguard with the stumps of his legs bound in a huge rocking trencher and moving about with the help of crutches, who is deep in the contraband trade; a swaggering young pirate, a Brother of the Bloody Coast, who falls in love with the daughter of the Collector of the Port and kidnaps her from her father's house; a romantic lover, slender and clerkly, but skillful with the rapier, who turns out to be the son of Rob; a haunted house that covers the smuggling operations of Rob and Captain Cocklescraft; and all this set against a background of partisan struggle between Roundhead and Cavalier, Protestant and Catholic, in the early days of the Maryland settlement.

But in the handling the story is far removed from a bloody-bones tale. The action is deliberately subdued to the humoresque; atmosphere is studiously created; adventure is held in strict subjection to the whimsical; and a mellow old-time flavor is imprisoned in the leisurely pages. Kennedy had an appreciative eye for picturesque characters, and in *Rob of the Bowl* he has gathered a choice group, limned—as he would choose to say—with a partial hand. Garret Weasel, the garrulous pot-valiant innkeeper, and Dorothy his termagant spouse; Captain Jasper Dauntless, the cogging, wheedling swordsman who twists Dame Dorothy about his fingers and inveigles his host into undue commerce with his cups—these to be sure are stock characters, but they are done with excellent vivacity. Their abundant talk is well seasoned, and if the action sometimes drags, the company is good and the drinking is a sufficient end in itself. All the while he is writing Kennedy keeps half an eye on Elizabethan literature to assure himself of the exact turn of phrase. His vocabulary is saturated with the homely old speech, and his characters talk as if they had culled all the simples of English cottage gardens to garnish the staple of their wit. He has a keener delight than Simms in the picturesque archaic. He far surpasses Irving in easy mastery of the old-fashioned colloquial, as indeed he surpasses all our early novelists. He delights in the courtly wit of the Cavalier equally with the humors of Dogberry and Falstaff and Captain Bobadil, and he quite evidently is seeking to cross the sparkle of Congreve with the robustness of the Elizabethans. The result may sometimes appear a bit self-conscious; his phrases too often seem to be on dress parade; but he can plead his precedents in justification. In its fondness for the literary colloquial his prose style almost suggests Thackeray, and it is this suggestion, perhaps, that gave rise to the tradition that Kennedy wrote for the former a certain chapter of *The Virginians*. That he supplied Thackeray with materials for his Virginia backgrounds may be accepted as true, but the indebtedness probably went no further.

Rob of the Bowl is certainly Kennedy's best work, as it is one of the most finished and delightful of our earlier romances. Although it ran to six editions, the latest in 1907, it has scarcely received the recognition its lightness of touch deserves. But instead of opening the vein further he turned away to venture in new fields. *Quodlibet,* written in 1840,[1] is a surprising successor to *Rob*—a satire on Jacksonian democracy, done with a light touch and great good humor. In those acrimonious days when Old Hickory's attack on the Bank so embittered its Whig partisans, Kennedy kept his temper, tipped his shafts with laughter and sent them neatly between the joints of the Democratic armor. Against such amusing satire fustian is helpless. The book is keen, vivacious, sparkling. The supposed follies of Jacksonianism—its deification of the majority vote, its cant of the sovereign people, its hatred of all aristocrats, its demagoguery and bluster and sheer buncombe—are hit off with exuberant raillery. The story professes to be an account of the rise to prosperity of the Borough of Quodlibet, under the beneficent smile of Democratic finance. Mean and insignificant before the coming of Jackson, with the removal of the "Deposites," "like Jeshurun, it waxed fat," with its rows of brick shops built on speculation and its Patriotic Copper-Plate Bank that issued an unlimited supply of beautifully engraved notes as a stimulus to enterprise. To be sure the bank broke and the cashier absconded with his family to Europe, but its untoward end was attributed by all Jacksonian New Lights to the vile machinations of the Whigs. It was certainly Nick Biddle and the Barings, with their hatred of Old Bullion Benton's democratic gold coinage, that were the devil in the pot to spill the people's porridge.

Yet even in its laughter Kennedy's political bias is sharply and narrowly partisan. The satire is a capitalistic counter to the agrarian attack on the rising money power, and it is colored by the chagrin of gentlemen who find themselves displaced by plebeians. Something of the old aristocratic contempt for the plain man functioning as a political animal lingers in its pages, which the bubbling humor does not wholly conceal. In Jackson's onslaught on the Bank, Kennedy discovers only an impudent demagoguery; it is selfish and stupid, turmoiling the country for partisan ends and seeking to cover its petty spite with the mantle of patriotism. The Old Hero cuts a sorry figure in these brisk pages, and Van Buren a

[1] The characteristic title is *Quodlibet: Containing some Annals thereof, with an Authentic Account of the Origin and Growth of the Borough and the Sayings and Doings of Sundry Townspeople: Interspersed with Sketches of the Most Remarkable and Distinguished Characters of that Place and its Vicinity. Edited by Solomon Secondthoughts, Schoolmaster, from original MSS. Indited by him, and now made Public at the Request and under the Patronage of the Great New Light Democratic Central Committee of Quodlibet.*

still sorrier one. The satire sparkles amusingly, but it is drawn from the old Federalist vintage and it preserves the flavor of a time when gentlemen frankly resented the rule of the unwashed majority. For that very reason *Quodlibet* is an unusually interesting document. It is the most vivacious criticism of Jacksonianism in our political library, one of our few distinguished political satires, and it deserves a better fate than to gather dust on old shelves.

After *Quodlibet* Kennedy did little else. The last twenty years of his life were largely wasted. His dignified life of William Wirt, published in 1849, seems to have met with approval, for it ran to six editions. Our grandfathers liked stately narrative that portrayed their subjects in full dress; and Kennedy gave them an impeccably respectable work in which all the rugosities of character were ironed out neatly and a fine starchy effect achieved. It is hard to understand how a writer so keen to detect the whimsical should have drawn so lifeless a picture of the genial Attorney-General. Perhaps the memory of Wirt's reputed greatness rested too heavily upon him; or it may have been that a lawyer in old Virginia lived as colorless a life as the narrative suggests; at any rate the novelist who never had failed to breathe life into the characters of his fiction, somehow failed in depicting this excellent gentleman of the old school. During the Civil War Kennedy contributed to the northern cause his *Letters of Mr. Paul Ambrose on the Great Rebellion in the United States*, in which he again showed that he could keep his temper and argue calmly. It was a difficult theme for which he was inadequately equipped. His constitutional argument is not impressive and it makes an ill showing when set over against Alexander H. Stephens' *Constitutional View of the War between the States*. He was a man of letters rather than a lawyer, and if he had eschewed politics and law and stuck to his pen our literature would have been greatly in his debt. Few Americans of his day were so generously gifted; none possessed a lighter touch. He has been somewhat carelessly forgotten even by our literary historians who can plead no excuse for so grave a blunder.

EDGAR ALLAN POE
Romantic

It is from this slovenly background of aristocratic Virginia, with its liberalisms and conservatisms running at cross purposes, that the enigmatical figure of Poe emerged to vex the northern critics. In so far as any particular environment determined his highly individual and creative nature, it was the indolent life of the planter gentry, shot through with a pugnacious pride of locality, with a strong dislike of alien ways, with haughtiness, dissipation, wastefulness, chivalry. In his proud, irascible individualism that went out of its way to pick a quarrel, there is something of the spirit of John Randolph of Roanoke, but pied and streaked with unfortunate qualities that to many observers seemed the marks of the mere charlatan. As a southern gentleman he imbibed the common dislike of New England, and this dislike was aggravated by its diverse conception of the functions of art, and by the misfortunes that attended his literary career. An aesthete and a craftsman, the first American writer to be concerned with beauty alone, his ideals ran counter to every major interest of the New England renaissance: the mystical, optimistic element in transcendentalism; the social conscience that would make the world over in accordance with French idealism, and that meddled with its neighbor's affairs in applying its equalitarianism to the negro; the pervasive moralism that would accept no other criteria by which to judge life and letters—these things could not fail to irritate a nature too easily ruffled. The Yankee parochialisms rubbed across his Virginia parochialisms; and when to these was added a Yankee preëmption of the field of literary criticism, when a little clique engaged in the business of mutual admiration puffed New England mediocrities at his expense, the provocation was enough to arouse in a sensitive southern mind an antagonism that rivaled Beverley Tucker's. In his unhappy pilgrimage through life Poe was his own worst enemy, but he took comfort in charging his ill fortune upon the malignancy of others.

Southern though he was in the deep prejudices of a suspicious nature, his aloofness from his own Virginia world was complete. Aside from his art he had no philosophy and no programs and no causes. He got from Virginia what was bad rather than good, and his alienation from the more generous southern ideals did him harm. It was perhaps harder to be an artist in that slack southern society than in New England—harder to be a romantic concerned only with twilight melancholy. It would have been hard enough anywhere in Jacksonian America. His romanticisms were of quite another kind than those his countrymen were pursuing; and the planter sympathized with them no more than did the New York literati, or the western men of letters. In a world given over to bumptious middle-class enthusiasms, there would be scant sympathy for the craftsman and dreamer. There was no unearned increment to be got from investments in "the misty mid-region of Weir," which Poe threw on the market. The technician concerned with the values of long and short syllables would find few congenial spirits in a world of more substantial things; and the purveyors of shoddy tales would not take it kindly if their shortcomings were pointed out and a more competent craftsmanship insisted upon. And so, like Herman Melville, Poe came to shipwreck on the reef of American materialisms. The day of the artist had not dawned in America.

So much only need be said. The problem of Poe, fascinating as it is, lies quite outside the main current of American thought, and it may be left with the psychologist and the belletrist with whom it belongs. It is for abnormal psychology to explain his "neural instability amounting almost to a dissociated or split personality," his irritable pride, his quarrelsomeness, his unhappy persecution complex, his absurd pretentions to a learning he did not possess, his deliberate fabrications about his life and methods of work, his oscillations between abstinence and dissipation, between the morbidly grotesque and the lucidly rational, his haunting fear of insanity that drove him to demonstrate his sanity by pursuing complex problems of ratiocination. Such problems are personal to Poe and do not concern us here. And it is for the belletrist to evaluate his theory and practice of art: his debt to Coleridge and Schlegel; the influence of the contemporary magazine on his conception of the length of a work of the imagination; the value of his theory of the tyrannizing unity of mood in the poem and short story; the provocation to the craftsman of the pretentiousness of contemporary American literature, joined to a flabby and crude technique; the grossness of the popular taste and the validity of his critical judgments. Whatever may be the final verdict it is clear that as an aesthete and a craftsman he made a stir in the world that has not lessened in the years since his death, but has steadily widened. Others of greater repute in his day have fared less prosperously in later reputation. He was the first of our artists and the first of our critics; and the surprising thing is that such a man should have made his appearance in an America given over to hostile ideals. He suffered much from his aloofness, but he gained much also. In the midst of gross and tawdry romanticisms he refused to be swallowed up, but went his own way, a rebel in the cause of beauty, discovering in consequence a finer romanticism than was before known in America.

PART TWO: THE RENAISSANCE OF SLAVERY

CHAPTER I
SOUTHERN IMPERIALISM

I

By the year 1824 a change was becoming evident in the South that was to affect profoundly the course of southern thought in regard to her peculiar institution. The passing of the long Virginia hegemony was a sign that southern opinion was undergoing a revolutionary overturn, and that leadership henceforth would rest with men of a different philosophy. The humanitarian spirit that marked the thought of the preceding generation was dying out, to be replaced by a frank recognition of local economic interests. Expectation that slavery was on the way to natural extinction was yielding to the conviction that the system was too profitable to the South to permit its extinction, and this in turn bred an imperious desire to spread it westward to the Pacific. With this significant shift from apology to imperialism, it became clear to ardent pro-slavery men that lukewarm Virginians of the old tradition were not the spokesmen to entrust with the fortunes of the South, and leadership passed to the South Carolina school. In that momentous shift much was implied. It was more than a shift from Jefferson to Calhoun, from humanitarian idealism to economic realism. It marked the complete ascendancy of a small minority of gentleman planters over the inarticulate mass of southern yeomanry, and the assertion of the aristocratic ideal as the goal of southern society. It denied the principle of democracy as that principle was understood in the North and West, and it rejected the new humanitarian spirit of western civilization. It abandoned the Jeffersonian equalitarianism that was so deeply rooted in the southern mind from Kentucky to Georgia; it cast aside the agrarianism of John Taylor and the older Virginians; and it set up in place of these congenial conceptions the alien ideal of a Greek democracy. More momentous still, it threw down the

61

gauntlet to the ideals of the middle class, then in the first flush of a triumphant career, and in the armed clash that eventually resulted, it was destroyed by that class.

The intellectual capital of southern imperialism was Charleston, but its numerical strength lay in the Black Belt, with South Carolina to the east and Texas to the west, a compact territory the heart of which was Georgia, Alabama, Mississippi and Louisiana. In this new South that was rapidly passing through its frontier development, the patriarchal system of Virginia gave way to a system of negro exploitation, more naked as it passed further westward. It was here that the proportion of slaves to whites was greatest; it was here that slave labor was most profitable; and it was here in consequence that the slave economy was most militant. The Black Belt became the native habitat of the southern Fire Eater. In the late twenties and early thirties South Carolina provided the outstanding leaders of the new school; but the philosophy of imperialism spread rapidly and western men came more and more to the front. George McDuffie and Bob Toombs, perhaps the boldest of the loquacious tribe of Fire Eaters, came from Georgia; Alexander H. Stephens was bred in the same turbulent state; L. Q. C. Lamar and Jefferson Davis were from Mississippi. For the most part self-made, products of a frontier environment, these western extremists had got from Jefferson little more than an assertive individualism that easily espoused the states-rights philosophy and prompted them to defend their immediate interests. It was this vigorous group that largely created the new southern psychology and prodded the southern mind along the path marked out for it to travel. Democratic in their attitude towards the white voter, middle class in their love of exploitation, they retained little of the spirit of the Virginia school.

The expansion of the South to the Gulf region came a generation later than the settlement of the Ohio valley. The Creek Indians who clung tenaciously to the rich lands of Mississippi were long an obstacle to the white advance, and the settlers filtered in slowly. Moreover the slave economy was ill fitted to the business of pioneering. It was difficult to transport negroes and establish great plantations in a wilderness; there was too little security in a region that offered every temptation to the slave to run away. The plantation system could prosper only after a considerable degree of development had been effected and sufficient negroes

provided. On the other hand, the rich soil, virgin and productive, offered every inducement for large-scale production of cotton, tobacco and sugar. Here the economics of slavery could be fairly tested, and if the system were found to be profitable it would spread of its own impulse beyond the Mississippi, becoming more imperialistic with every extension, ambitious to seize Texas with its filibusters, looking as far as California and the Oregon territory for future expansion. But while planning for such expansion it must secure its strategic front at Washington, making certain that no rival economy should control the central government to its disadvantage. It was an ambitious program, but it was all implicit in the evident fact that slavery in the Black Belt proved to be profitable.

The explanation of this sudden prosperity of the Black Belt is a matter of familiar knowledge. Coincident with the first westward expansion of slavery came a revolution in the technique of the English cotton industry that brought about corresponding changes in southern agriculture. The production of cotton textiles in England had long been held back by the difficulty of spinning a fine and even thread. When this problem was solved at the beginning of the century by the invention of new machines, the cotton industry at once developed amazingly, making heavy demands upon the supply of American raw materials. This supply in turn was greatly increased by the invention of the cotton gin, and the combined result of these inventions was an upheaval in southern agriculture. In the eighteenth century the southern staples were tobacco, rice and indigo; by 1825 the staples had become cotton, tobacco and sugar. Almost in a decade cotton had become king. In 1791, three years after Andrew Jackson settled in Nashville, the total export of cotton was only 200,000 pounds. In 1803 it had risen to 40,000,000 pounds, and by 1860 the export for the year was of the value of nearly two hundred millions of dollars. Such figures provide a sufficient explanation of the militant spirit of the slave economy after 1820. Here was an enormous vested interest, the economic life of the South, that could not suffer its present or future profits to be put in jeopardy by any political party on any pretext. Its well-being and its prestige were both at stake. The peculiar institution, which a generation before was commonly believed to be in the way of natural extinction, had the South by the throat.

It was the strategic weakness of the South that the spirit of exploitation, which following the peace of 1783 had spread through America like the itch, should there have assumed its most hateful form, far more revolting to the humanitarian sense and far less justifiable to uneasy consciences than wage slavery. With every extension the system became necessarily more brutal in exploitation. As new plantations were opened the natural increase of negroes was inadequate to meet the pressing demands for slaves. Since the abolition of the traffic with Africa the occasional smuggling by venturesome runners—many of whom were respectable New England church members—had provided a totally inadequate supply of raw material; the price of slaves rose steadily, and this in turn led to increasing speculation in negroes. Buying and selling by middlemen went on briskly, to the horror of northern humanitarians and the concern of southern. So brutal and open was the exploitation that Alexander H. Stephens—the kindest-hearted of men—went so far as to advocate the reopening of the slave trade with Africa, as the lesser of the two evils. The better South hated what it could not help. Although the slave trader remained a social pariah with whom no gentleman would associate, his business was a necessary evil of the system and could not be eradicated.

The reaction of the slave system upon the southern people, both plantation masters and poor whites, was wholly evil. The generous culture of Virginia failed to take root in the Black Belt. The development of the plantation system under hired overseers infected the masters, few in numbers and absolute in power, with an exaggerated sense of their own greatness. The aristocratic spirit of the Old Dominion had been tempered by a feeling of patriarchal responsibility that humanized the relations between master and slave, and more generous social contacts had created an admirable republican squirearchy. But in the frontier Gulf states the rapid expansion of the plantation system created an aristocracy given to swaggering, *bourgeois* in spirit, arrogant in manners. Republican simplicity was losing vogue and there was much loose talk about the superiority of the classes. It is said that when Alexander H. Stephens was appointed a delegate to the Confederate Convention at Montgomery, he refused to attend till he was assured that the jingoes would make no attempt to set up a monarchy. Gideon Welles is authority for the story that when news came to Washington of the secession of South Carolina, Mrs. Jefferson Davis was all aflutter: "She said she wanted to get rid of the old government; that they would have a monarchy South, and gentlemen to fill official positions" (*Diary*, Vol. II, p. 256). Such stories were probably the result of war hysteria; nevertheless they suggest a bias in the southern temper that reveals how far the new South had drifted from its Jeffersonian moorings.

Of this new South with its grandiose dreams of slave imperialism, fate selected Jefferson Davis to be the political leader and spokesman. The choice may have proved unfortunate, but it was logical. Much calumny has been heaped upon his name, but that is the common fate of partisans of lost causes. The real Jefferson Davis is to be sought in some mean between the extravagant adulation of his friends and the slanders of his enemies. Not a great man certainly; in no sense comparable to Lee or Stonewall Jackson or Alexander H. Stephens; he was very far from a petty or time-serving nature. As time softens the old animosities it reveals the features of a high-minded southern gentleman who possessed the virtues and the weaknesses of his race. Simple and austere in tastes, he was the product of a crossing of the southern Puritan with the aristocratic tradition of the Old Dominion. If he was not of the old cavalier stock he was a gentleman by instinct and training. His father was half Welsh, half English; his mother Scotch-Irish. He came of Revolutionary stock. After the war his father settled in Georgia and later removed to Kentucky, where the son was born in Todd County in 1808. While still a small child he was taken to Wilkinson County, Mississippi, where he was brought up on a plantation. Educated at Lexington, Kentucky, and at West Point, he proved a serious, capable student, who loved reading but possessed little intellectual curiosity. His ideas were few, but those he embraced he clung to with the tenacity of a strong nature. Resigning from the army after a few years of honorable service, he settled down as a plantation master. He was summoned from his isolation by the call for troops to serve in the Mexican campaign, went through several battles with unusual distinction, and proved himself an extremely able officer. With his military fame the path to political preferment was open and he demonstrated his ability in Congress. At the outbreak of the secession movement he was eager to receive the appointment as commander of the southern armies, but fate called him to the presidency of the Confederacy and he devoted his best strength unselfishly to the cause, only to find the accumulated bitterness of the North heaped upon his single head. It was an unhappy lot, but there was iron in him, and he bore it like a man.

Jefferson Davis was cut out of the same tough oak that fashioned John C. Calhoun. Hard and unyielding, tenacious of opinion, dictatorial, somewhat inclined to arrogance, he might break, but he would not bend. The Scotch-Irish stock was rarely genial or tolerant, and Davis possessed none of the seeming pliability of Lincoln that yielded the non-essentials to secure the essentials. Utterly lacking in humor and easy-going good nature, he offended by his very virtues. Profoundly Puritan, he was narrow and rigid, a legalist in temperament, proud and jealous of authority. Meticulously honest, he could not get on well with men; he quarreled with his generals and wore himself out trying to do everything himself. Politically he was a strict constructionist of the most rigid views. He refused to follow Calhoun into the camp of Nullification. His patriotism was extreme, and only a greater loyalty to his state made him an advocate of secession. At bottom he was a Jeffersonian and to the end of his life he was faithful to the principles of his party. Kindly and humane, he treated his dependents with singular consideration. He set up a curious little democracy amongst the slaves of his plantation, and his negroes were devoted to him with rare loyalty. There was in his nature not the slightest trace of the exploiter; he was a patriarchal master after the old Virginia ideal, with no hint of the speculator or middleman. The background of his thought was agrarian and he shared with Jefferson a dislike for capitalistic industrialism. The President of the Confederacy may have been an unfortunate civil leader, but the slanders that so long clung to his name are only worthy of the gutter. The sin that he was led into was not counted a sin in his southern decalogue; it was the sin, not of secession, but of imperialism—a sin common to all America in those drunken times when the great West invited exploitation.

CHAPTER II

WINDS OF POLITICAL DOCTRINE

I

AN economic revolution so widespread and profound could not fail to impress its ideals on current political thought. In the year 1825 three streams of tendency were flowing through the southern mind, rising from different sources, incompatible in spirit and purpose, strong in their diverse appeals; and in the end the major current was certain to engulf the lesser. The humanitarianism of Virginia, the individualism of the new West, and the imperialism of the Black Belt might seem to mingle their waters for a time, but there would be confusions of thought and diversity of counsels until one or another had worn a deeper channel through which the dominant opinion might run. There could be no more fascinating study in the economics of political theory than the changing mind of the South during the critical decades from 1820 to 1850, as it followed the course determined by its peculiar institution. Political thought passed under the jurisdiction of slavery, and every southern writer took his daily bearings from that polar fact. It is unintelligent to charge upon southern politicians a lack of consistency—to point out that after 1820 Calhoun reversed himself on every major political principle. It was true of Calhoun, as it was true of Webster and true of Clay. In a rapidly changing America, with economics in a state of flux, men were no longer free political agents, guiding themselves by the fixed stars of accepted theory; they were borne like corks on the current of the times, and their inconsistency is the surest evidence that they spoke for their constituents. The North and the South were at the parting of the ways, and if southern imperialism created for its needs a philosophy of particularism, it was met by a counter philosophy of nationalism created for its needs by northern capitalism, which likewise was following the path of its manifest destiny. The charge of innovation, indeed, lies more justly against northern theory than southern; it was Webster rather than Calhoun who ignored the teachings of the fathers.

Of these three streams of tendency it was the new imperialism of the Black Belt that wore the deepest channel, gathering its tributaries till it was swollen to an overwhelming flood that drew in every lesser current. Every other interest was eventually sacrificed to slavery, every ambition was laid upon that consuming altar. Southern political thought, in consequence, came to be an ingenious study in the strategy of defense. From the somewhat vague doctrine of states rights as struck off by the Virginia school was elaborated a complete philosophy of particularism with its principle of a protective state veto. Tremendous as was the stir created by the doctrine of Nullification, that doctrine was little more than a warning gesture, a militant expression of the southern temper. The time was not ripe for the critical issue, the philosophy of the new South was not yet clarified; the objective was clearly seen, but the defenses were incomplete, the line of campaign not yet laid down. That great work was in the skillful hands of Calhoun, and much was yet to be done. The deeper purpose that lay behind the gesture of Nullification was the purpose of erecting in the slave states a civilization founded on a landed aristocracy that should serve as a sufficient counterweight to the mercantile and industrial civilization of the North; and in the event that the institution of slavery were not assured of peaceful extension through the new West, to secede and establish a southern Confederacy wherein a generous civilization might develop, modeled after the Greek democracy. Such at least was the dream of the noblest minds of the South.

Thrown early upon the defensive, southern political thought found too little time to examine fundamental principles. The necessities of the situation entailed a meticulous constitutional debate, in which the terms of the Constitution were examined with microscopic care, and interpreted in the light of their historical origin. Something of the sterility of the lawyer's mind marked the long debate; and little of the suggestiveness of the philosopher's. Acute as was Calhoun's reasoning, it reveals the weakness of contemporary political thought, northern as well as southern. It concerned itself too exclusively with government under the Constitution—its origin, the just interpretation of the terms of the fundamental law, the potentialities of consolidation inherent in the principle of loose construction. To the broader problems of the nature and functions of the political state—questions that had so deeply interested the speculative minds of the French school—quite inadequate consideration was given. The drift of circumstance was in the way of creating a leviathan state. Southern orators railed at consolidation in abundant and florid language, but they concerned themselves little with the deeper problem of the relation of the political state to the well-being of the citizen. This common weakness is strikingly evident in the work of Calhoun's successor, Alexander H. Stephens, whose interest was so exclusively historical and constitutional as almost to exclude him from a place among political philosophers.

II

JOHN C. CALHOUN
Realist

The greatest figure in that long controversy was certainly John C. Calhoun, a man who set his face like flint against every northern middle-class ambition, and with his dream of a Greek democracy steered his beloved South upon the rocks. A truly notable figure was this ascetic Carolinian. In the passionate debates over slavery he daily matched powers with Webster and Clay and proved himself intellectually the greatest of the three. He is the one outstanding political thinker in a period singularly barren and uncreative. His influence was commanding. Tall, lean, eager, with no humor, no playfulness, lacking the magnetic personality of Clay and the ornate rhetoric of Webster, speaking plainly and following his logic tenaciously, this gaunt Scotch-Irishman became by virtue of intellect and character, driven by an apostolic zeal, the master political mind of the South, an uncrowned king who carried his native Carolina in his pocket like a rotten borough. Long before his death he had expanded a political philosophy into a school of thought. What he planned a hundred disciples hastened to execute. Like Jefferson he was a pervasive influence in shaping men's opinions. It was impossible to ignore him or to escape the admonitory finger that pointed at every weak and shuffling compromiser.

Whatever road one travels one comes at last upon the austere figure of Calhoun, commanding every highway of the southern mind. He subjected the philosophy of the fathers to critical analysis; pointed out wherein he conceived it to be faulty; cast aside some of its most sacred doctrines; provided another foundation for the democratic faith which he professed. And when he had finished the great work of reconstruction, the old Jeffersonianism that had satisfied the mind of Virginia was reduced to a thing of shreds and patches, acknowledged by his followers to have been a mistaken philosophy, blinded by romantic idealism and led astray by French humanitarianism. To substitute realism for idealism, to set class economics above abstract humanitarianism, was the mission to which Calhoun devoted himself. He undid for the plantation South the work of his old master. Speaking in the name of democracy, he attacked the foundations on which the democratic movement in America had rested, substituting for its libertarian and equalitarian doctrines conceptions wholly alien and antagonistic to western democracy, wholly Greek in their underlying spirit.

Calhoun's career was linked indissolubly with slavery. He was the advocate and philosopher of southern imperialism, and in defense of that imperialism he elaborated those particularist theories which prepared the way for the movement of secession. Born and bred in South Carolina, he was enveloped from infancy in the mesh of southern provincialisms. Except for two years at Yale, where he graduated in the class of 1804, and eighteen months reading law in Connecticut, his life was spent between Washington and his plantation. He was in temperament a Puritan, of that Scotch-Irish strain which, scattered along the wide American frontier, greatly modified the American character and gave to the South such different leaders as Stonewall Jackson and Jefferson Davis. It was a hard, stern race—that Scotch-Irish—little responsive to humanitarian appeal; and Calhoun was harder and sterner than most. He held his emotions in strict subjection to his reason. Intent on thinking every problem through from premise to conclusion, concerned always with fundamental principles, he would have become, in an environment congenial to humanistic thought, a distinguished intellectual. His mind would have lost its rigidity and become pliable from contact with diverse streams of theory, and his speculations would have found new horizons from more generous intellectual acquisitions. But unhappily there was nothing either at Washington or in South Carolina that tended to liberalize his thinking. He had not gone to school, as Jefferson had done, to the great thinkers of Europe; he had not found an intellectual stimulus in revolutionary systems of philosophy. He dwelt all his life in the arid world of politicians. His two years at Yale may even be accounted a calamity. Timothy Dwight and Calhoun were cut out of the same cloth. The South Carolina Puritan would only be confirmed in his dogmatisms by the most dogmatic of Yankee Puritans; and in consequence his career, like Jonathan Edwards', suffered from a narrow, ingrowing intellectualism. He was a potential intellectual whose mind was unfertilized by contact with a generous social culture.

Calhoun's public life covered the forty years from 1810 to 1850, from the first administration of Madison to that of Zachary Taylor. For nearly half of the total period, up to the year 1828, he was a politician of ability but without distinction. He entered Congress at a time when the young men from the South and West were becoming impatient with the cautious policy of the old Republicans led by Jefferson and Madison. The war psychology was mounting under British pin-pricks, and the young nationalists, forgetful that bayonets and cannon and ships are not easily defeated by rhetoric, were eager to teach the Mistress of the Seas some much-needed international manners. In those early years Calhoun joined with Clay in driving through Congress a war policy. In this he seems to have represented his constituents, whose patriotism was always somewhat bellicose. During the shameful war experience, the cool analytical Calhoun came near to exhibiting the tawdry marks of the jingo; and thereafter for years there was little to distinguish him from a Hamiltonian Federalist. He was a throughgoing nationalist of the school of loose construction. He advocated a protective tariff on the ground that "it would form a new and most powerful cement, far outweighing any political objections that might be urged against the system" (Gaillard Hunt, *John C. Calhoun*, p. 29). As yet he had discovered no constitutional scruples against the exercise of this or other implied powers. He was, he said, "no advocate for refined arguments on the Constitution. The instrument is not intended as a thesis for the logician to exercise his ingenuity on. It ought to be construed with plain, good sense; and what can be more express than the Constitution on this point?" (*ibid.*, p. 30). As Secretary for War in Monroe's cabinet he was an advocate of internal improvements, and he submitted to Congress an elaborate report on a proposed system of roads and canals. Until the critical year 1828 there was little in Calhoun's career to distinguish him from Clay. The tide of national expansion was running strong; the growth of exploitation was creating a middle-class psychology; and Calhoun in these earlier years was as unconsciously middle class as afterwards he became consciously aristocratic. He sprang from an acquisitive race, and to the end of his life some remnants of the old instincts clung to him despite his repudiation of the middle-class political philosophy.

The year 1828, marked by a fierce discussion in South Carolina of the Tariff of Abominations, proved the turning-point of his career. As Vice President he had been little more than a spectator of the growing discontent in his native state at the contrast between the industrial prosperity of New England and the agricultural depression of the South. But he could no longer remain an idle spectator. Pamphlets and newspaper articles were appearing that sharply challenged his position. Capitalistic Federalism and democratic equalitarianism were equally under fire. The celebrated Dr. Cooper, an Englishman long resident in South Carolina, who had suffered under the Alien and Sedition law, had vigorously attacked the natural-rights dogma, and was active in arousing the public mind against Calhoun's consolidationist tendencies.[1] The publication in 1821 of Yates's *Minutes of Debates of the Constitutional Convention* had awakened widespread interest in an historical interpretation of the Constitution, and the time was ripe for a new period of constitutional debate. The tariff act of 1828 provided the immediate occasion. It opened the flood gates, and the waters of states-rights doctrine that had long been gathering rushed forth in a torrent. Calhoun hesitated no longer. The problem and the solution had both clarified themselves in his mind, and he at once took the lead in directing the unrest to achieve a definite end.

Calhoun's contribution to political theory—a contribution that elevates him to a distinguished place among American political thinkers—was the child of necessity, and received its particularist bias from the exigencies of sectional partisanship. With the rapid expansion of the nation westward, and the consequent augmenting of a potentially hostile free-soil power, the South was doomed to become increasingly a minority voice in the councils of government; and if it were to preserve its peculiar institution it must find more adequate means of self-protection than it had enjoyed hitherto.

---

[1] See Merriam, *American Political Theories*, p. 231; Gaillard Hunt, *John C. Calhoun*, p. 64.

The tendencies most to be feared, in his judgment, were the spontaneous drift towards consolidation, and an uncritical faith in numerical majorities. He was convinced that America had too thoughtlessly accepted the principle of political democracy as a sufficient safeguard against the danger of arbitrary government. Soon or late it must discover, what the South already was discovering, that numerical democracy, unrestrained by constitutional limitations on its will, is no friend to political justice. The critical test of every government is the measure of protection afforded its weakest citizen; and judged by this test a democratic state, when power has come to be centralized in few hands, may prove to be no other than a tyrant. Irresponsible in its unrestraint, the majority vote may easily outdo an Oriental despot in arbitrary rule, and the more power it wields the more ruthless will be its disregard of minority opinion. The political philosopher who proposes to formulate an ideal democratic system of government, therefore, must deal critically with this fundamental problem of political justice, for upon the solution will turn the excellence and permanence of every democracy. It was to this baffling problem that Calhoun addressed himself.

In seeking a constitutional defense for the threatened southern interests, he drew from the two great reservoirs of American constitutional theory. From the Jeffersonian Republicans he derived his familiar doctrine of states rights in opposition to the consolidating principle; from the Federalists of the Montesquieu school he drew his theory of static government, resulting from exactly balanced powers; and from the amalgamation of these diverse theories he formulated a new principle. Both schools of earlier thought, he had come to believe, had been sound in their major premises, but both had gone astray in certain important deductions. The experience of forty years, with the democracy constantly augmenting its powers, had demonstrated to Calhoun's satisfaction both the grave danger that lay in the principle of consolidation, and the insufficiency of existing checks on the Federal government. The prime mistake of the Jeffersonians, he conceived, was their belief that the democratic majority will necessarily serve the cause of political justice; and the miscalculation of the Federalists resulted from the belief that the division of powers provided in the Constitution was adequate to prevent arbitrary government. He now proposed to correct these two mistakes by providing an additional check through the simple expedient—as logical as it was efficacious, granted his premises—of recognizing the veto power of the individual commonwealth upon an act of the Federal government. Stripped of its states-rights limitation, this was in germ the principle of the referendum, modified, however, by certain suggestive provisions.

The veto-power as a protective principle Calhoun regarded as the hallmark of constitutional government. Granted that sovereignty under the Constitution inheres in the people, and that all authority is delegated, it follows that government is no more than an agent with strictly defined fiduciary powers, all the acts of which are subject to review by the principal. Whether such review shall be immediate and plenary, or at more or less remove and limited, becomes therefore a fundamental question of constitutional polity. Unfortunately much confusion has resulted from an intentional vagueness, contributed by interested groups to further particular ends, in the common understanding of the terms, the people and government. The former is rarely, as is usually assumed, a homogeneous body with common interests, but a congeries of individuals and groups and classes with diverse and often antagonistic interests; and the latter—in a republic— is never a sacred entity, the residuary legatee of sovereignty, to criticize which is to commit the crime of *lèse-majesté*, but a group of officials invested with temporary authority and actuated by motives common to all men. A necessary preliminary, therefore, to an intelligent understanding of the principle of veto is a critical analysis of these much misunderstood terms.

Calhoun was far too honest a realist to be under any hallucinations in regard to political government. He estimated at its full significance "the never-ending audacity of elected persons." Power he knew to be the most insidious of poisons; every government is liable to the disease of auto-intoxication. Seated securely in office the agent assumes all the prerogatives of the principal and clothes his acts with the sanctity of sovereignty. Armed with the taxing power, he distributes penalties and benefits with partial hand, and unless an adequate defense protects the weaker interests they will suffer a legal exploitation. Every government justly rests under suspicion, and only the most critical scrutiny of its conduct can keep it decently honest. Popular government, from which the Republicans hoped too much, changes only the outward form of the selfish struggle for power by substituting party rule for class rule. With its disciplined party machine the lure of political spoil encourages the most shameless exploitation of the weaker groups, who have no recourse.[2] Hence, the more popular the government, the more ruthless becomes the majority rule; and any system of checks and balances that does not adequately restrain this inherent tendency of party rule must prove a failure. However carefully the political philosopher may provide for a division of powers among executive, legislature and judiciary, he must fail of his object, for a regnant majority will control all three branches of government, and thus intrenched will defy the protests of the minority. The Montesquieu theory had proved a failure in practice.

An even greater danger, in Calhoun's judgment, lay in the current misinterpretation of the term "the people," the result of which was the obscuring of the economic basis of society and the befuddling of the whole problem of government. To this disastrous result, he believed, both schools of political thought had contributed. The early Republicans had oversimplified the political problem by assuming a clear division between ruler and subject. The conception was a heritage from European experience, where it had taken form as a strategic move to align the unthinking mass against a despotic monarchy. The Jeffersonians had used it to like purpose in their struggle against consolidation, appealing to a common democracy against the aristocracy. The early Federalists were even more blameworthy, for, understanding clearly the economic origins of political power and the economic ends served by the political state, they made their knowledge serve their interests and concealed their designs by deceptive appeals to patriotism. Every realist knows that "the people" is a political fiction. Society is made up of individuals, each with his particular interest. The total interests of the subject-citizens are necessarily complex. Group and classify them as he may, the political philosopher can never merge the parts in a coalescing whole, but must recognize that the problem remains one of adjustments and compromises. It follows therefore that any facile assumption that government represents the people or rests on the will of the people is a disastrous fallacy. Popular government rests on the will of the majority; aristocratic government rests on the will of the aristocracy; and

[2] See "A Disquisition on Government" in Calhoun's *Works*, Vol. I, pp. 41-42.

despotic government rests on the will of the despot. It is an axiom that the political state is partisan to those who administer it. The stakes of rulership are high; the game of politics never lacks its devotees; the business of deceiving the people in order to pluck the goose has long been one of the respectable professions.

The perennial problem of constitutional government, then, in Calhoun's philosophy, remains what it was seen to be by the Federalist followers of Montesquieu—the problem of restraining government by constitutional checks to the end that it be kept just. Existing machinery having demonstrated its inadequacy, it remained to provide more effective. Freedom Calhoun regarded as the crown jewel of civilization, hardly won, easily lost. But freedom was not to be measured by *habeas corpus* acts and similar legal restraints on tyranny; it was freedom from legal exploitation and statutory dictatorship. "The abuse of delegated power, and the tyranny of the stronger over the weaker interests, are the two dangers, and the only two to be guarded against; and if this be done effectually, liberty must be eternal. Of the two, the latter is the greater and most difficult to resist" (*Works*, Vol. VI, p. 32). In more definite terms the problem is thus stated:

Two powers are necessary to the existence and preservation of free States: a power on the part of the ruled to prevent rulers from abusing their authority, by compelling them to be faithful to their constituents, and which is effected through the right of suffrage; and a power to compel the parts of society to be just to one another, by compelling them to consult the interest of each other—which can only be effected . . . by requiring the concurring assent of all the great and distinct interests of the community to the measures of the Government. This result is the sum-total of all the contrivances adopted by free States to preserve their liberty, by preventing the conflicts between the several classes or parts of the community. (*Ibid.*, Vol. VI, pp. 189-190.)

In elaboration of the second phase of the problem Calhoun contributed the principle on which his reputation as a political thinker must rest—the doctrine of a concurrent majority. He found his solution in an expansion of the principle of democracy—recovering the true principle, he was fond of insisting—by superimposing upon the consolidated, indiscriminate numerical majority the will of a geographical majority; or in other words, by a special form of sectional referendum.

It results, from what has been said, that there are two different modes in which the sense of the community may be taken: one, simply, by the right of suffrage, unaided; the other, by the right through a proper organism. Each collects the sense of the majority. But one regards numbers only, and considers the whole community one unit, having but one common interest throughout; and collects the sense of the greater number of the whole, as that of the community. The other, on the contrary, regards interests as well as numbers;—considering the community as made up of different and conflicting interests as far as the action of the government is concerned; and takes the sense of each, through its majority or appropriate organ, and the united sense of all, as the sense of the entire community. The former of these I call the numerical, or absolute majority; and the latter, the concurrent, or constitutional majority. ("A Disquisition on Government," in *Works*, Vol. I, p. 28.)

In such speculation on the possibility of achieving political justice by the machinery of representation, Calhoun was face to face with a revolutionary conception—the conception of proportional economic representation. The idea was implicit in his assumption of an existing economic sectionalism that must find adequate expression through political agencies. He had come to understand the futility of a miscellaneous numerical majority; he had only to go back to eighteenth-century philosophy and substitute economic classes for economic sectionalism, finding his social cleavages in economic groups instead of geographical divisions, to have recast the whole theory of representation. Clearly, he had made enormous strides in his thinking. He had long since put behind him the philosophy of Jefferson. He had subjected the principle of democracy to critical scrutiny. But instead of rejecting it as an unworkable hypothesis, as the Hamiltonian Federalists had done, he proposed to establish it on a sound and permanent basis. The ideal of democracy he conceived to be the noblest in the whole field of political thought, but misunderstood and misapplied as it had been in America, it had become the mother of every mischief. This betrayal of democracy he laid at the door of the Jeffersonians. They had accepted too carelessly the romantic dogmas of the French school, and had come to believe that democracy was synonymous with political equalitarianism.

It was this false notion that had debased the noble ideal, and delivered it over to the hands of the mob. To assert that men are created free and equal is to fly in the face of every biological and social fact. The first business of the true democrat, therefore, was to reëxamine the nature of democracy and strip away the false assumptions and vicious conclusions that had done it incalculable injury. The Greeks, he pointed out, understood its essential nature better than the moderns. Democracy assumes a co-partnership among equals. Its only rational foundation is good will, and it can function only through compromise. From this it follows that in a society composed of high and low, capable and weak, worthy and unworthy—as every historical society has been composed—a universal democracy is impractical. The numerous body of social incompetents will suffer one of two fates: they will be exploited by the capable minority under the guise of free labor, or they will be accepted as the wards of society and protected by the free citizens—they must inevitably become either wage slaves or bond slaves, in either case incapable of maintaining the rights of free members of the commonwealth. Democracy is possible only in a society that recognizes inequality as a law of nature, but in which the virtuous and capable enter into a voluntary co-part-nership for the common good, accepting wardship of the incompe-tent in the interests of society. This was the Greek ideal and this ideal had created Greek civilization.

Calhoun was thus brought face to face with the natural-rights theory, which the glowing rhetoric of the Declaration of Independ-ence had disseminated throughout America, and which lay as a virus at the heart of Jacksonianism. To destroy that theory, he believed, was a necessary preliminary to any rational theory of democracy, and he turned to the business with characteristic frankness. Upon the venerable dogmas he threw the light of his realism, subjecting them to critical analysis. The origin of govern-ment in compact was only a myth. The amiable being known as man in a state of nature, whose portrait had been drawn by the French romantics, he discovered in neither social nor biological history. The true origin of government, he asserted in common with John Adams, is to be found in practical necessity; government arises, as Hobbes had pointed out, from the universal fact of human selfishness. It has always been found necessary to lodge coercive powers in certain hands as a social protection against individual aggression; and since all men are impelled by self-interest, political systems are determined in form and scope by this universal in-stinct. Without government there is anarchy; with government there is potential tyranny. The crucial problem to be solved by the political philosopher, hence, is to determine the just delimitation between sovereign power and individual liberty; the one protecting the rights of the whole, the other keeping open fresh opportunity to advance.

Having thus established government on the firm basis of social necessity, he proceeded to examine the romantic dogmas of liberty and equality.

It follows, from what has been stated, that it is a great and dangerous error to suppose that all people are equally entitled to liberty. It is a reward to be earned, not a blessing to be gratuitously lavished on all alike;—a reward reserved for the intelligent, the patriotic, the virtuous and deserving;—and not a boon to be bestowed on a people too ignorant, degraded and vicious, to be capable either of appreciating or of enjoying it. Nor is it any disparagement to liberty, that such is, and ought to be the case. On the contrary its greatest praise,—its proudest distinction is, that an all-wise Providence has reserved it, as the noblest and highest reward for the development of our faculties, moral and intellectual. A reward more appropriate than liberty could not be conferred on the deserving;—nor a punishment inflicted on the undeserving more just, than to be subject to lawless and despotic rule. This dispensation seems to be the result of some fixed law;—and every effort to disturb or defeat it, by attempting to elevate a people in the scale of liberty, above the point to which they are entitled to rise, must ever prove abortive, and end in disappointment. . . . There is another error, not less great and dangerous, usually associated with the one which has just been considered. I refer to the opinion, that liberty and equality are so intimately united, that liberty cannot be perfect without perfect equality. That they are united to a certain extent,— and that equality of citizens, in the eyes of the law, is essential to liberty in a popular government, is conceded. But to go further, and make equality of *condition* essential to liberty, would be to destroy both liberty and progress. The reason is, that inequality of condition, while it is a necessary consequence of liberty, is, at the same time, indispensable to progress. . . . It is, indeed, this inequality of condition between the front and rear ranks, in the march of progress, which gives so strong an impulse to the former to maintain their position, and to the latter to press forward into their files. This gives to progress its greatest impulse. To force the front rank back to the rear, or attempt to push forward the rear into line with the front, by the interposition of the government, would put an end to the impulse, and effectually arrest the march of progress. ("A Disquisition on Government," in *Works*, Vol. I, pp. 55–56.)

It was the persuasive ideal of a Greek democracy in the plantation states that lay back of Calhoun's defense of slavery—a defense that thrusts into sharp relief the change of southern attitude in the decade of the thirties. The earlier Jeffersonian attitude had been fairly expressed by a Georgia representative in the debate on the Missouri question:

Believe me, sir, I am not a panegyrist of slavery. It is an unnatural state; a dark cloud which obscures half the lustre of our free institutions! . . . Would it be fair; would it be manly; would it be generous; would it be just, to offer contumely and contempt to the unfortunate man who wears a cancer in his bosom, because he will not submit to cautery at the hazard of his existence? (Quoted in Hunt, *John C. Calhoun*, p. 53.)

But with slavery put upon its defense, the southern spokesmen passed from apology to praise. From the first, Calhoun accepted the system implicitly, but now he subjected it to critical analysis in the light of his theory of a Greek democracy. Over against it he set the northern system of wage labor, and he came to the conclusion that the latter was more brutal and inhumane than the former. He was convinced that heretofore the South had made a serious mistake in apologizing for its peculiar institution, and in expecting its eventual extinction. In this matter the fathers had been wrong. No serious-minded Southerner any longer believed that slavery was on the way to natural extinction. It was spreading daily and must be permitted to spread. The hopes of southern civilization were bound up with it. The North must be brought to recognize it as a beneficent institution, necessary to a free, cultivated democracy, the only alternative to those fierce conflicts between wage labor and capital which already in the manufacturing states were threatening the permanence of American institutions. In a speech delivered in 1838, Calhoun thus sketched the new southern conception:

Many in the South once believed that it [slavery] was a moral and political evil. That folly and delusion are gone. We see it now in its true light, and regard it as the most safe and stable basis for free institutions in the world. It is impossible with us that the conflict can take place between labor and capital, which makes it so difficult to establish and maintain free institutions in all wealthy and highly civilized nations where such institutions as ours do not exist. The Southern States are an aggregate, in fact, of communities, not of individuals. Every plantation is a little community, with the master at its head, who concentrates in himself the united interests of capital and labor, of which he is the common representative. These small communities aggregated make the State in all, whose action, labor, and capital is equally represented and perfectly harmonized. Hence the harmony, the union, the stability of that section which is rarely disturbed, except through the action of this Government. The blessing of this state of things extends beyond the limits of the South. It makes that section the balance of the system; the great conservative power, which prevents other portions, less fortunately constituted, from rushing into conflict. . . . Such are the institutions which these deluded madmen are stirring heaven and earth to destroy, and which we are called on to defend by the highest and most solemn obligations that can be imposed on us as men and patriots. ("Remarks on the State Rights Resolutions in Regard to Abolition. January 12, 1838," in *Works*, Vol. III, p. 180.)

Thus in the end the political philosopher turns partisan to a cause. His fruitful speculations on the theory of representation, his inquiry into the economic basis of politics, remained incomplete, the larger reaches only half explored. Espousing the ideal of democracy, he yielded to the seductions of a Greek republic. Beginning as a Jeffersonian, he ended as the philosopher of a slave aristocracy, from whose principles men like Governor McDuffie of South Carolina deduced the dictum that "the laboring population of no nation on earth are entitled to liberty, or capable of enjoying it." It was a curious dream, yet no more curious than his faith in an obsolete article in the Constitution to withstand the advance of a hostile economy. There is something almost tragic in the self-deception of this clear-minded realist in his appeal to a paper defense against economic forces. "The Constitution—no interference—no discrimination," he cried passionately in repudiating the right of Abolition petition. "These are the grounds on which the battle may be safely fought. . . . You must tell these deluded fanatics, you have no right to intermeddle in any form or shape. . . . Expediency, justice, plighted faith, and the Constitution: these, and these only, can be relied on to avert conflict" (*Works*, Vol. III, p. 190).

Lost faiths and repudiated prophets go down to a common grave. The living have little inclination to learn from the dead. The political principles of Calhoun have had scant justice done them by later generations who incline to accept the easy opinion that the cause which triumphs is altogether the better cause. What Calhoun so greatly feared has since come about. He erected a last barrier against the progress of middle-class ideals—consolidation in politics and standardization in society; against a universal cash-register evaluation of life: and the barrier was blown to pieces by the guns of the Civil War. Historically he was the last spokesman of the

great school of the eighteenth century, the intellectual descendant
of John Adams. The two men were much alike in the broad
principles of their political philosophy, and identical necessities
brought them to identical conclusions. They agreed in the fundamental principle that property will rule by reason of its inherent
power, and that political justice is attainable only by a nicely
calculated system of checks and balances, which provides each
important group with a defensive veto. But in the social experience
on which Adams founded his doctrine, political antagonism was
potential in rival classes, and justified a division of powers on the
model of the British constitution. In the intervening years, however, the economic alignment had become sectional, the rise of
party government had created a new problem, and the earlier
division of powers seemed to demand a supplementary veto if the
nice balance contemplated in the Constitution were to be maintained. This was the kernel of the states-rights doctrine which
Calhoun elaborated with such skill. That he should have associated
the principle with a cause that was doomed was disastrous to the
just fame of Calhoun. More, it was disastrous to the vital democratic principle of decentralized powers. In championing a
Greek democracy Calhoun affronted the latent idealism of America,
and the harm he did to agrarian democracy was incalculable.

III

ALEXANDER H. STEPHENS

Constitutionalist

Southern scholars are pretty well agreed that the ablest defender
of the doctrine of secession was Alexander H. Stephens, the Georgia
commoner. He was sprung from the plain people. Brought up
in severe poverty, self-taught, the friend of the poor, he was no
child of an exclusive planter aristocracy, and was never quite
trusted by them. The victim of a slight, ramshackly physique,
never weighing a hundred pounds, never knowing a well day, fear-
fully handicapped in the everyday matter of living, it is amazing
that soul and body held together for seventy-one years and more
amazing that he accomplished what he did. "Throughout life,"
says one of his biographers, "he was practically a brain without a
body." Temperamentally despondent, he was driven into restless

activity to forget self. His will was fine-tempered steel and ill
health never broke his courage even when it laid him on his back.
He feared nothing, but took a position and argued a cause without
regard to personal consequences. He never flinched from the
personal encounters which the lawless code of Georgia politics
invited. A morbid consciousness of his feeble physique sometimes
drove him into truculence, and on one occasion he was stabbed
eighteen times by a certain ornament of the Georgia bench, and
saved his life only by grasping the blade that was driven at his
throat. But such encounters can be explained on the ground of
overcorrection; the real Stephens was gentle, peace-loving, hating
all swaggerers military or civilian, "a man of generous sympathies,
of broad humanity, a democrat of democrats, a friend of all the
world" (Pendleton, *Alexander H. Stephens*, p. 253). The words
Non sibi sed aliis, cut in his tombstone at Crawfordville, come
nearer the truth than epitaphs usually do. He was never selfishly
ambitious and he could justly say after the fall of the Confederacy,
"I am old and weak in bodily infirmity, but I have done my duty
to God and my country, and I am ready for whatever fate may be
assigned me" (*ibid.*, p. 393).

Stephens was a lifelong student of politics, regarding it as "one
of the most intricate, as well as interesting subjects that can engage
the attention of reflecting minds." He was not a political philosopher like Calhoun, concerned with principle and theory, but a
constitutional historian concerned to trace the genesis and development of the fundamental law of the land. He was probably more
widely read in the early literature of the Constitution than any
other man of his generation. He had thumbed and dog-eared
Elliot's *Debates*, and could cite dates and explain circumstances
for the elucidation of doubtful points or the correcting of an unhistorical interpretation. He knew the genesis of every article, of
almost every word in the Constitution, and the reasons which
determined the special form which each assumed; and this exact
knowledge equipped him for the task of critical commentator on
earlier commentators. Unfortunate was the theorizer who fell
into his hands. Federalist expositors like Story and Motley, given
to rash generalization from inadequate data, suffered disaster
under his critical inspection. With his fund of historical knowledge
he was amply prepared for the labor of love to which he turned
after the war, and in his *Constitutional View of the War between the*

States he produced one of the most notable studies in the origin of the Constitution that we have.

Certain deep personal needs, taking form in passionate conviction, determined the bias of Stephens' political philosophy, which was quite simple, consistent and inflexible, from his first entry into public life until his death. There was no subtlety in his intellectual processes, no balancing uncertainly between diverse appeals, but a clear faith which he expounded to the common voter in confident expectation that it would awaken sympathetic response. His extensive reading was not so much a disinterested search for light on the ideal relations of men in society, as for confirmation of certain prepossessions. That those prepossessions were shared by his fellow Georgians, that they were the natural product of existing social conditions, gave to them an added sanction. The creative source of his philosophy was a passionate love of freedom; and his meditations convinced him that the only freedom worth a tuppence is civil liberty under civil law—that the test of any civilization is the concern it manifests for the safeguarding of such liberty by exact and adequate constitutional provisions. His reverence for law was a religion with him, and his love of the Constitution as the fostering mother of the law was only this side idolatry. "No stronger or more ardent Union man ever lived than I was," he asserted late in life. Intense loyalty was almost commonplace amongst the people from whom he sprang. Love of the Union, and of the Constitution as a guarantee of that Union, was far stronger in the South before the Civil War than in the North. But it was the Constitution of the fathers, not a newfangled consolidating instrument that drew all power to Washington, that they loved. Pride of locality—naïve though it might be and provincial—the spontaneous pride of a simple untraveled people—was rooted in the southern heart. It was nourished by a deep love of homestead and neighborhood, natural to an agrarian society; and it came to political expression in the doctrine that the commonwealth must be free to manage its own affairs in its own way. The theory of states rights, amongst such a people, was not an abstract principle but an expression of the psychology of localism created by everyday habit. This explains the intensity of conviction which colors the thought of Stephens. The principle of local sovereignty was inbred. He rarely deigns to argue the question. He never concerned himself with abstract argument—as Jefferson had done

—to prove the superior excellence of local home rule. This failure, indeed, may perhaps be accounted his greatest weakness as a political thinker. Rather he was concerned to prove that state sovereignty existed prior to the Union, that it was jealously guarded at the making of the Constitution, that it had never been surrendered, and hence was the constitutional order until destroyed by the Civil War. But if he refrained from abstract argument touching the desirability of localizing political power, he exhibited a Jeffersonian fear of unregulated power which consolidation makes possible.

This passionate love of freedom he exemplified in his own career. He followed his convictions and spoke his own mind, regardless of occasion or circumstance. He was no man's tool. He hated a demagogue and never curried favor with his constituents or calculated popular response. In his public life he considered himself a representative of the people of Georgia, and the one object of his labors was the preservation of that constitutional liberty in which they had grown up. In furtherance of this policy he found himself not infrequently at odds with other southern leaders. He vigorously opposed his party in its Mexican war policy, looking upon it as no other than imperialistic vandalism aimed at a weaker neighbor for the purpose of extending slave territory. There was no glamor for him in military victories; he would not concede that a republic might plead manifest destiny in extenuation of armed aggression, or that the ends of civilization may be furthered by war. In a speech opposing the policy of his fellow Whigs, he thus expressed his conception of national progress:

I am no enemy to the extension of our domain, or the enlargement of the boundaries of the republic. I trust the day is coming, and not far distant, when the whole continent will be ours; when our institutions shall be diffused and cherished, and republican government enjoyed, throughout the length and breadth of this land. . . . That this is our ultimate destiny, if wise counsels prevail, I confidently believe. But it is not to be accomplished by the sword. . . . Republics never spread by arms. We can properly enlarge only by voluntary accessions. . . .

There is much said in this country of the party of progress. I profess to be of that party; but I am far from advocating that kind of progress which many of those who seem anxious to appropriate the term exclusively to themselves are using their exertions to push forward. Theirs, in my opinion, is a downward progress. It is a progress of party, of excitement, of lust of power; a spirit of war, aggression, violence and licentiousness. It is a progress which, if indulged in, would soon sweep over all law, all order, and the Constitution itself. . . . It is to progress in *these* essential attributes of national greatness that I would look: the improvement of mind, the "increase and diffusion of knowledge among men," the erection of schools, colleges and temples of learning; the progress of intellect over matter; the triumph of mind over the animal propensities; the advancement of kind feeling and good will among the nations of the earth; the cultivation of virtue and the pursuits of industry; the bringing into subjection and subservience to the use of man of all the elements of nature around us; in a word, the progress of civilization, and everything that elevates and ennobles man. This . . . is not to be done by wars, whether foreign or domestic. Fields of blood and carnage may make men brave and heroic, but seldom tend to make nations either virtuous or great. (Quoted in Pendleton, *Alexander H. Stephens*, pp. 79–80.)

A man of peace, Stephens was greatly agitated over the movement of secession. He fought the Fire Eaters to the bitter end in his native state, but like other high-minded Southerners he went out with his commonwealth. Loyalty to Georgia was stronger than loyalty to the nation. But in the new order he preserved his old principles. The Jeffersonian democrat could not forget his teachings. When the Confederacy was discussing its proposed Constitution, he took alarm at some loose talk about the desirability of setting up a monarchy. His old friend Bob Toombs, one of the ablest of the southern leaders, quite frankly preferred the English system to the American. [3] There seems to have been considerable comment to like effect amongst the Tory hot-heads; but the wind was not blowing in that direction and such straws were only the stirrings of vagrant eddies. The Constitution as adopted was more democratic than the older instrument—an outcome to which Stephens contributed greatly.

As Vice President of the Confederacy he constituted himself the special guardian of constitutional liberty, and his jealous concern at what he regarded as administrative usurpations of power brought on grave differences with President Davis. Even in the urgent crises of war he would not sanction the use of extra-constitutional powers. He knew better than most that power grows by what it feeds on, that too often war destroys the liberty it professes to be serving. To win the war and lose the peace, to secede in defense of constitutional rights and then tamely yield them up, seemed to him a pitiful ending, and when President Davis suspended the right of *habeas corpus* and his generals

[3] See Pendleton, *Alexander H. Stephens*, p. 231, note.

proclaimed martial law, he took alarm. "All such orders," he said, "are palpable and dangerous usurpations, and if permitted to continue will end in military despotism. . . . Better in my judgment that Richmond should fall, and that the enemy's armies should sweep our whole country from the Potomac to the Gulf than that our people should submissively yield obedience to one of these edicts of our own generals" (Pendleton, *Alexander H. Stephens*, p. 292). Freedom of speech he would not have interfered with under any excuse. The suspension of civil law he considered a threat aimed at every citizen of the South. He had heard, he said, that one purpose of the act was "to control certain elections and certain expected assemblages in North Carolina"—where there was a good deal of disaffection—"to put a muzzle upon certain presses, and a bit in the mouth of certain speakers of that State. If this be so, I regard it as the more dangerous to public liberty" (*ibid.*, p. 313). To the question, "Can you not trust the President?" he replied in words that deserve to be remembered:

To the question of whether I would not or cannot trust him with these high powers not conferred by the Constitution, my answer is: I am utterly opposed to everything looking to or tending toward dictatorship in this country. There is no man living and not one of the illustrious dead, whom, if now living, I would so trust. . . . I would not turn on my heel to choose between masters. I was not born to acknowledge a master from either the North or the South. I shall never choose between candidates for that office. I have no wish or desire to live after the degradation of my country, and have no intention to survive its liberties, if life be the necessary sacrifice of their maintenance to the utmost of my abilities. (*Ibid.*, pp. 313–314.)

No argument of expediency, no appeal to military necessity ever moved him from the belief that the sole justification of government is the maintenance of liberty, and that the sole guarantee of such liberty is the orderly process of civil law. He was harassed by the encroachment upon individual freedom demanded by war, north as well as south. "The North to-day," he said, "presents the spectacle of a free people having gone to war to make freemen of slaves, while all they have as yet attained is to make slaves of themselves" (*ibid.*, p. 293). Perhaps no other public man in America kept his head amidst the passions of the time so completely as Stephens. He was utterly beyond reach of jingo appeal, and he suffered what the individual must expect to suffer who pits his single conscience against the mass will. He was branded as a traitor, and only his extraordinary hold on the affections of the plain people of Georgia saved him from the bitterest experience.

During the black period following the southern collapse, when he was disfranchised, broken in health past mending, and hated by the followers of President Davis, Stephens sought distraction in writing American history. Three and a half years, from 1867 to 1870, he devoted to his *Constitutional View of the Late War between the States*. The case for states rights has never been more convincingly put than in this monumental study. The first volume in particular, which deals with the history of the Constitution, is an acute and able work. The thesis on which it rests is the doctrine which Paine and Jefferson derived from the French school, namely, that a constitutional compact is terminable. Elaborated by Stephens and applied to the case in question, the doctrine becomes this: that the right of secession is a civil as well as a revolutionary right; that it is implied in the compact originally entered into by the several states; that any state may rightfully take back what it had peacefully granted, when such action shall seem to it desirable. The sovereign commonwealth has never abrogated its sovereignty; the Constitution is a Federal compact amongst equals; the United States is a federated Union, not an organic nation. To conceive of the organic law as a consolidating instrument binding the individual citizen immediately to the central government, as Webster and Judge Story had done, was not only unhistorical but contrary to every fact and every tradition. To arrive at the principle of consolidation, and hold that the right of secession is only a revolutionary right, one must deliberately shut one's eyes to the early history of the Constitution.

Not content to prove the original compact nature of the Constitution—an argument that runs through fourteen hundred pages, buttressed by a mass of citations from all sources and wholly convincing in its evidence—Stephens undertakes to prove the wisdom of the fathers in establishing the federal union in compact. In respecting existing loyalties to the several commonwealths, they not only preserved the local democracies—which, as a Jeffersonian, Stephens believed were the foundation of good government—but they established the federal state on a strong and enduring foundation. The Hamiltonian consolidationists had asserted that a strong state must rest on the principle of coercive sovereignty, that it can he held together only through the exercise of

authority. Stephens replied by laying down the counter principle
that the secret of a strong and enduring state is to be discovered
in the spontaneous loyalty of its citizens, and that in consequence
a democracy which rests on the good will of the people as a whole
is the most enduring of all forms.

A Government, to be worth anything, . . . must be strong. Its parts
and members must be held together by force of some sort. This I cordially
admit. We do not differ as to the force or its extent; we differ only as to
its nature and character. Should it be a physical or moral force? In my
judgment, the strongest force that can hold the parts or constituent
elements of any Government together is the affection of the people towards it. (*Constitutional View, etc.*, Vol. I, p. 526.)

Affection, he reasoned, cannot be coerced. It must spring
spontaneously from the recognition that government is useful,
that it is just, that it treats all its parts and members equally,
that it is an agency erected by a free people to serve the ends of
freedom. Allegiance is an individual compact between the citizen
and government. Destroy the principle of voluntary allegiance,
seek to coerce the citizen, impose upon minorities the ruthless will
of majorities, subjugate individual commonwealths, and the federal Union which Jefferson believed to be "the strongest Government on Earth," would indeed become what Hamilton in
his blindness to the secret of power believed that it was—"a
frail and worthless fabric." "But the indissoluble union between
the several states of this Confederated Nation is, after all, not in
the *right*, but in the *heart*" (*ibid.*, Vol. I, p. 527). So long as the
rights of all are respected, the common interest and common
loyalty will preserve the union. Injustice alone is to be feared, for
no political bonds can long resist the action of this most potent
of social dissolvents.

Modern as Stephens was in the assertion of the principle of good
will as the source of sovereignty in democratic government, he
belonged to his own generation in his blindness to economic
motives. He thought exclusively in legal and constitutional terms;
he remained wholly a lawyer. It is hard to understand how one
so profoundly read in our political history should have failed to
discover the workings of economic forces beneath the surface of
politics. Calhoun, bred in the same Jeffersonian school, had found
his way through the mist of equalitarianism to the solid realism
of an earlier day; but to the last of his fourteen hundred pages of

exposition Stephens retained the illusion that the political state is something apart from economics and superior to it. He conceived of government as an end in itself, and this lends an air of unreality to his thinking. An ardent Jeffersonian, he reduced the philosophy of his master to the compact theory of government. The economic basis of Jefferson's philosophy, his love of an agrarian order and hatred of capitalistic exploitation—motives which serve to explain and justify his theory of local self government—Stephens wholly ignores. The result is a grotesque perversion of a philosophy which John Taylor had elaborated clearly. Jefferson was a much greater political thinker than Stephens conceived, although he called him the "greatest philosophical statesman" America has produced. In his estimate of Andrew Jackson he falls into the same mistake. He attempts to reduce the confused career of Jackson—half middle-class in his earlier years and later returning to agrarian principles—to the same narrow compass of the compact theory. Even Webster, for whom he entertained "the highest esteem and admiration," and in praise of whose moral qualities he is almost fulsome,[4] he quite failed to understand. Webster's theory of the Constitution, he clearly demonstrated, was utterly unhistorical; but Webster's economic alliances he ignored. What havoc was wrought in current politics by suffering political theory to obscure economic reality is suggested by the fact that Stephens, a Jeffersonian in every instinct, turned Whig and voted for Webster in 1852—after the latter's death. Politics makes strange bedfellows, yet it must have been an ample bed that could sleep the spokesman of an agrarian economy and the spokesman of capitalism side by side.

In his attitude towards slavery Stephens was a product of his Georgia environment. His views were ready-made, out of the common southern storehouse. The economic determinism which he ignored in politics had its revenge, and the man who often differed with his constituents on political issues fell victim to the subtle power of economics. As the South Carolina philosophy took form, issuing finally in the romantic conception of a Greek democracy, it imposed itself imperiously on the southern mind, on the commoner equally with the aristocrat. It was impossible to escape, unless, like Moncure Conway, one were of an idealistic temper far different from the common run. For Stephens it

[4] See *A Constitutional View*, etc., Vol. I, pp. 406–408.

proved impossible. In this matter of slavery he had no individual opinion; his mind was molded by the common psychology and became a repository of the common prejudice. He followed his fire-eating friend Bob Toombs into the camp of Calhoun, and talked about a Greek democracy in true Charleston style. In a speech delivered on March 21, 1861, shortly after he was chosen Vice President of the Confederacy, he gave expression to the new philosophy in these words:

The prevailing ideas entertained by . . . most of the leading statesmen at the time of the formation of the old Constitution were that the enslavement of the African was in violation of the laws of nature; that it was wrong in principle, socially, morally, and politically. It was an evil they knew not well how to deal with, but the general opinion of the men of that day was that, somehow or other in the order of Providence, the institution would be evanescent and pass away. . . . Those ideas, however, were fundamentally wrong. They rested upon the assumption of the equality of races. This was an error. Our new government is founded upon exactly the opposite idea; its foundations are laid, its corner-stone rests upon the great truth that the negro is not equal to the white man; that slavery—subordination to the superior race—is his natural and normal condition . . . in conformity with the ordinance of the Creator. . . . Our Confederacy is founded upon principles in strict conformity with these [Divine] laws. This stone which was rejected by the first builders "is become the chief of the corner"—the real "corner-stone" in our new edifice. (Pendleton, *Alexander H. Stephens*, pp. 251–254.)

To the end of his life Stephens saw no reason to change his opinion on negro slavery. He regarded it as more humane than wage slavery because of the patriarchal responsibility devolving upon the master. The institution was not founded, he said, on "the erroneous dogma of the greatest good to the greatest number," but on the broader principle of securing "the greatest good possible, morally, intellectually, and politically, to all classes of persons . . . without necessary wrong or detriment to any" (*Constitutional View, etc.*, Vol. I, pp. 539–542). In his relations with his own slaves he followed the best traditions of the South. His kindness won their loyalty and affection. "Ef he ain't in heaven," said a house servant after his death, "'tain't no use for anybody else to try to git dere" (Pendleton, *Alexander H. Stephens*, p. 100). To the argument of Hinton Helper that the system was economically ruinous to the poor white, he seems to have given no consideration; but to the argument of the Abolitionist that it was immoral, he replied with deep conviction. On that point he would not yield an inch. After quoting a miscellany of Biblical texts from the earliest Hebraic times down to Paul, he comments naïvely:

> To maintain that Slavery is *in itself sinful*, in the face of all that is said and written in the Bible upon the subject, with so many sanctions of the relation by the Deity himself, does seem to me to be little short of blasphemous! It is a direct imputation upon the wisdom and justice, as well as the declared ordinances of God, as they are written in the inspired oracles, to say nothing of their manifestation in the universe around us. (*Ibid.*, Vol. II, p. 83.)

It is doubtful wisdom for the layman to meddle with Scripture. Stephens was a sounder interpreter of the writings of the constitutional fathers than of the will of God.

A careful historian devoted to a single idea rather than a creative political thinker; a thorough democrat of the Jeffersonian school, humanitarian, liberty-loving, courageous; a man who devoted his life to the preservation of constitutional liberty as it had taken shape before the industrial revolution unsettled the basis of modern life, Alexander H. Stephens was an honest gentleman who bravely defended the traditions of the South in the face of a new order. He was of an earlier generation, instinctively hostile to all consolidation, which, under the impulse of economic evolution, was obliterating state lines, gathering financial power in great reservoirs, and creating a new alignment between labor and capital. With such evolution it was axiomatic that political practice should follow economic fact; that a consolidating wealth should create a consolidated political state. Great enterprises with ramifications in every section would not long tolerate a multitude of state sovereignties; sovereignty must be centralized at Washington where it could be guided and controlled. The war only hastened what in the nature of things was inevitable. Stephens rightly insisted that slavery was only the immediate *casus belli*. The deeper cause was the antagonistic conceptions of the theory and functions of the political state that emerged from antagonistic economic systems. That the principle of local self-government should have been committed to the cause of slavery, that it was loaded with an incubus certain to alienate the liberalism of the North, may be accounted one of the tragedies of American history. It was disastrous to American democracy, for it removed the last brake on the movement of consolidation, submerging the democratic individualism of the South in an unwieldy mass will, and surrendering the country to the principle of capitalistic exploitation. Stephens never seems to have realized this grave mistake in strategy. He never realized that the principle of democracy, in the cause of which he believed that he was faithful to the end, received a staggering blow from the enlistment of northern liberalism under the banners of a consolidating nationalism. He remained to the last an unreconstructed Jeffersonian, convinced that the lost cause was the cause of liberal democracy.

IV

FRANCIS LIEBER

A New-Modeled Federalism

To turn from Calhoun and Stephens to Francis Lieber is to pass from the South to the North, from an obsolescent political theory to a prophetic conception, from the doctrine of states rights to the principle of an evolving state that draws all lesser sovereignties into its orbit by the law of attraction. Joseph Story had educed the legal conception of the organic nature of the federal union from the terms of the Constitution; Francis Lieber provided a philosophical background that justified the same conclusion; and under the combined legal and philosophical attack the compact theory found its philosophical breastworks leveled, its natural-rights theory undermined, and its commanding position effectively turned.

The figure of our first academic political philosopher appears oddly out of place in the midst of South Carolina politicians, yet fate set the studious German in the thick of the Fire Eaters, to cogitate a philosophy of freedom in the land of slavery, and to justify the spirit of nationalism amongst the advocates of particularism. For twenty-one years he lived quietly in his southern classroom and study, disregarding the passions that buzzed about him, elaborating ideas that in later years came to exercise a determining influence upon our academic political thinkers, and publishing ponderous volumes that marked the beginning of the swing away from the natural-rights philosophy and towards the conception of an engrossing political state. Applying German liberalism to American constitutionalism, he succeeded in new-modeling the Federalism of Hamilton and sending it forth to meet the needs of an imperializing generation. He agreed with Calhoun in the latter's attack on French romantic theories; he agreed with Webstei in the conception of the organic nature of the federal compact; but he went further and elaborated a theory of the state as an historical development that receives its form and spirit from the impress of social needs. Building on a foundation provided by Montesquieu and Burke, guided by Hamilton and Marshall, he set about erecting a structure that in the hands of Theodore Woolsey and John W. Burgess came to overtop all local and state sovereignties—an imperial authority that, in the words of Burgess, must become "the organ of interpretation in last instance of the order of life for its subjects" (Merriam, *American Political Theories*, p. 299).   In that subtle shift of vocabulary from citizen to subject appears the final result of the speculations begun by Lieber, which in rejecting the natural-rights philosophy overthrew the defenses erected by the eighteenth century against an engrossing political state, and set the individual citizen at the mercy of a new divine-right sovereignty.   "Really the state cannot be conceived," according to Burgess, "without sovereignty, *i. e.* without unlimited power over its subjects; that is its very essence" (Merriam, *American Political Ideas: 1865–1917*, p. 380).

Between the democratic Stephens and the imperializing Burgess stands the work of Francis Lieber. Born in Germany in the year 1800, son of a well-to-do Berlin family, Lieber's youth and young manhood fell in stirring times. When only fifteen he served in the Waterloo campaign under Blücher, was wounded, stricken with typhus, and nearly lost his life. From those perilous experiences he emerged a pronounced liberal. During the Metternich reaction he fell under suspicion, served a prison term for his political opinions, graduated from the University of Jena, and in 1822 went to Greece with a group of young German idealists to serve the cause of revolution. Disgusted with the Greek character he made his way to Italy, fell in with the historian Niebuhr, became tutor to the latter's son for a year, continued his university studies, was a second time imprisoned, and finally in 1826 quitted a hopelessly reactionary Germany, spent a year in England, and then emigrated to America, following the example of Prof. Charles Follen. In Boston he taught gymnastics for a time, edited the *Encyclopedia Americana*, and in 1835 was appointed to the professorship of history and political economy in South Carolina College. Here he remained till 1856, teaching, writing, and ac‹

quiring academic fame. In 1855 he aspired to the presidency of the college, a post then vacant, but his political theories were in disrepute with the legislature, and his views on slavery were under general suspicion. Becoming embroiled with the politicians, he lost the post, resigned his professorship, and went to New York City, and in 1857 he was called to the new chair of history and political science at Columbia, where he remained till his death in 1872.

The two books on which rests his reputation, *Political Ethics* (1838–1839) and *Civil Liberty and Self-Government* (1853), are substantial volumes quite lacking the genial note that marks his *Stranger in America* (1834), a series of sketchy letters that among other things contains an extraordinarily vivid account of his experiences at Waterloo (*Letters VI, VII*). To a casual reader these excursions into the philosophy of politics are as soberly respectable as a judge's wig, as studiously conventional as a professor's gown. He went about the business of blowing up the accepted Jeffersonian philosophy decently, in the name of the law and under the high sanction of liberty. There can be no doubt that this German liberal was a passionate lover of liberty, and no doubt of his conviction that freedom is possible only in a society under the reign of law. Like Hamilton, he had no local ties or state loyalties to circumscribe his political allegiance. It was natural for him to think in terms of nationality. His bitter experience in Germany had laid open to him the fatal weakness of petty states, and he was loath to see repeated in America the history of warring antagonisms that disrupted the German people. He was a profound admirer of the British constitution, more English than German in his conception of liberty.

The nationalism of Lieber was identical with that of John Adams. It was, in a phrase, government by law. But this government by law was both political and legal. The former, he believed, was admirably provided for by the federal Constitution; the latter was equally provided for by the body of the Common Law; with these twin safeguards, he was convinced, the liberty of the citizen was assured. In his interpretation of the Constitution Lieber added little that was new. He followed the older Federalists back to Montesquieu, and accepted the existing system of constitutional checks as the final word of political wisdom. In *Civil Liberty and Self-Government* he glorifies the federal system as the apotheosis of representative republicanism, quite unconcerned at its undemocratic features. The sufficiency of the Common Law to all social needs and the implicit sovereignty of the judiciary, he regards as equally axiomatic. "The law," he says, "must be the lord and our 'earthly god,' and not a man, a set of men, or the multitude" (*Civil Liberty and Self-Government*, p. 208). Yet with the common blindness of the legalist, he proceeds to erect a profession above society, and exalts a group of judges, appointive and not elective, preferably holding office for life, as the embodiment of impartial justice. That it is a presumption contrary to fact seems not to have entered his mind. That judicial interpretation implies judicial legislation, and that judicial legislation implies the sovereignty of lawyers, are logical deductions of which his philosophy made no account. Unfriendly to a democracy, he was content to yield authority into the hands of the judiciary.

But if in his exaltation of the Common Law he was as extreme a legalist as Hugh Legaré, in his doctrine of historical evolution he discovered the seeds of freedom in what he calls institutions. By these he means the organic expressions of daily life, or the customs of society which take spontaneous form from its needs. It is no other than the social fabric that Tom Paine was fond of contrasting, in its pervasive and beneficent coöperation, with the repressive tyrannies of the political state. Where liberty reposes thus in the social fabric, Lieber argues, the sovereign power is held in check; and where institutional freedom has not taken root, the political state will run into absolutism.

"Liberty," he argues, "is a thing that grows, and institutions are its very garden beds. There is no liberty which as a national blessing has leaped into existence in full armor like Minerva from the head of Jove. Liberty is crescive in its nature. It takes time, and is difficult, like all noble things. . . . It must be defended, developed, conquered, and bled for. It can never be added, like a mere capital on a column; it must pervade the whole body" (*Civil Liberty and Self-Government*, pp. 334–335, third edition). "Liberty stands in need of character," and this character is received from social institutions. He then proceeds:

. . . An institution is a system or body of usages, laws, or regulations of extensive and recurring operation, containing within itself an organism by which it effects its own independent action, continuance, and generally its own farther development. Its object is to generate, effect, regulate, or sanction a succession of acts, transactions, or productions of a peculiar class or kind. The idea of an institution implies a degree of self-government. Laws act through human agents, and these are, in the case of institutions, their officers or members. (*Ibid.*, p. 300.)

It was the deep-rooted *civisme anglais*, he believed, that had developed the orderly liberty of the English race; and it is this same institutional spirit that provides the surest check upon the augmenting power of the political state. There can be no tyranny where society is trained and disciplined in liberty.

The creative source and origin of this excellent *civisme anglais* Lieber discovered in the principle of local self-government; in the exercise of local control of local interests; the enjoyment of innumerable lesser sovereignties within the larger national organism. These lesser sovereignties are both civil and social, and the amount of liberty enjoyed in a given society is measured by the independent vigor with which they function. The exercise of definite rights by the several states is clearly one of the important institutional functions of self-government, but it is only one. The New England town-meeting, county and city governments, are even more important, while outside these civil organisms are innumerable social organisms, exercising their common right of establishing by-laws for their own governance, and spreading the spirit of liberty through all the practices of society.

According to the Anglican view, institutional self-government consists in the fact that all the elementary parts of the government, as well as the highest and most powerful branches, consist in real institutions . . . [but it] consists, farther, in the unstinted freedom and fair protection which are granted to institutions of all sorts, commercial, religious, cultural, scientific, charitable, and industrial, to germinate and to grow—provided they are moral and do not invade the equal rights of others. It receives its aliment from a pervading spirit of self-reliance and self-respect—the real afflatus of liberty. (*Ibid.*, p. 320.)

This, quite evidently, is the spirit of *laissez faire* applied to political philosophy. A people thus used to order their social affairs, as the English people have long done, will prove competent to manage their political affairs; and the widespread spirit of individual independence will prevent the drift towards unregulated centralism with its corollary of tyrannical power. The conception of institutional liberty embodies much of the spirit of Jeffersonianism, and it goes back in its origins as far as Roger Williams.

The states-rights advocates, Lieber implies, were mistaken in seeking the principle of liberty through particularism. In magnifying the individual commonwealth they overlooked the more vital units of self-government. To erect the state above the nation was no lasting solution of the most difficult problem in political philosophy, namely, the coördination of sovereign power with individual liberty; it was only to substitute one sovereignty for another, whereas to encourage the spread of self-governing bodies through society was to provide the necessary countercheck to centralizing power and coördinate liberty and sovereignty under the reign of law.

A stimulating thinker was this German liberal with his historical method and his conception of an evolutionary freedom rooted in the institutions of the English people. He gave a new turn to speculation on the origin and nature of the political state, the immediate consequence of which was the repudiation of the compact theory and natural-rights philosophy by our academic political scientists. The organic conception of the political state fell in with the centralizing movement that followed the Civil War, a movement which the forces of institutional self-government have been powerless to prevent. On the whole the influence of Lieber has been rather against than for that liberty which was so dear to him, and the explanation is to be found in the tragic divorce, in his thinking, of politics and economics. His inveterate legalism and his failure to investigate the economics of politics proved in the end the undoing of his liberalism.

CHAPTER III

THE DREAM OF A GREEK DEMOCRACY

I

THE pronounced drift of southern thought, in the years immediately preceding the Civil War, towards the ideal of the Greek democracy, has been too carelessly forgotten by later times. It was no vagrant eddy but a broadening current of tendency. In its blend of romanticism and realism it fitted exactly the temper of the plantation mind, imparting a fine idealism to shiftless realities and setting a generous goal to be achieved by somewhat inadequate agencies. A humane and cultivated democracy, set free from the narrow exactions of economics to engage in the higher work of civilization, was a conception worthy of the generous southern mind, a conception that does not suffer by contrast with the northern dream of an exploitative industrialism. That it was an impossible dream does not lessen its significance as an expression of the best southern aspiration in the days when slavery was on the defensive.

It is plain enough now that this drift of thought resulted from the need of clarifying the logic of the situation, by bringing into harmony two seemingly irreconcilable facts, the system of negro slavery and the rising spirit of white democracy. The feudal principle, which lurks in the background of all slave systems and which was peculiarly congenial to the plantation temper, was confronted on every side by the stubborn democracy of the yeomanry. A hundred miles beyond Charleston the feudal spirit encountered the leveling individualism of the frontier; and this passion for equality, that grew fiercer with every remove westward, was a stumbling-block in the way of the planter aristocracy. Caught thus between the two forces of a Jeffersonian democracy and a slave economy, southern thought found in the Greek ideal the most natural compromise. Since manual labor was black, a white skin was a guarantee against serfdom, and the common race prejudice was accounted sufficient to draw even the poor whites to the support of slavery. The sharp cleavage between the races provided the basis for the conception of a common white democracy of the

99

master class, every member of which shared in the supremacy of
the race and was free to enjoy the profits of negro exploitation.
The enterprising small farmer might rise to be a gentlemanly
planter, providing his children with leisure to fit themselves for
citizenship in the commonwealth and assist in the great work of
creating a southern civilization. The Greek ideal, in short, met
the double need of southern economics and southern prejudices,
and made its appeal even to the frontier spirit of equalitarianism.

A native growth and rooted deep in southern realities, the new
conception emerged in response to the changing times. It may be
considered the plantation counterpart of northern industrialism,
marking the reaction of the southern mind to the economic revolution in western civilization. With their diverse economics, North
and South were facing in different directions, and the Greek ideal
was as natural in Charleston as industrial feudalism was natural in
Lowell. Created in part as an ingenious measure of defense, it
provided an excellent counter offensive against alien critics by
turning the light of inquiry upon the bases of capitalism and
thrusting upon the attention of godly Puritans the dependence of
culture upon exploitation. The new industrialism was creating
a new philosophy of labor, and this philosophy the southern
apologists seized upon and turned to their special ends. They
accepted certain of the capitalistic premises, but they interpreted
those premises in a spirit of drastic realism, deducing conclusions
disconcerting to the apologists of industrialism. In defending the
plantation system they attacked the factory system; in upholding
black slavery they attacked wage slavery; and in this game of the
pot and the kettle the exploitative root of both systems was
nakedly exposed.

The major premise of the new southern philosophy was identical
with that of northern capitalism, namely, that every civilization
rests on labor exploitation. However quaintly they might em-
broider this fact with romantic patterns, they saw it clearly and
deduced from it the conclusion that the North was indulging in a
vicious fallacy in confusing wage labor with free labor. In every
industrialized society, they pointed out, free labor is an anachronism; where it exists it is a hold-over from a simpler social order.
The development of industrialism tends to draw all labor into its
capacious maw, and the labor surplus that results from evicting
the peasant from the land creates a competitive labor market

that speedily reduces the laborer to the status of a wage-slave. Since slavery, then, in some form is the inevitable counterpart of modern civilization, the question that presses on the conscience of every enlightened and generous observer is the question of the relative well-being of the slave under the different systems. Upon this question the southern apologists turned their shrewdest analysis. They examined the condition of the proletariat in the English mill towns; they commented on the callous exploitation of the textile workers in Massachusetts; they assessed the waste in the labor turnover under the factory system; they considered the seeds of class war sown by industrialism and pointed out the insecurity of society under a system of capitalistic irresponsibility. In their estimate of the social evils of industrialism they concurred in the findings of Carlyle and antedated much of the criticism of Ruskin. The huge mass of unpalatable fact which they uncovered was the same mass that inspired George Ripley and Albert Brisbane and Horace Greeley to seek a way out by the path of coöperative commonwealths.

But in the hands of these apologists the argument was turned to the narrower end of proving that the southern field-hand fared better than the northern mill-hand. They recognized both systems as capitalistic, established in labor exploitation; but they proved to their own satisfaction that the southern was far humaner, more truly social. In the South, they pointed out, there was no waste in the labor turnover, no ugly labor scrap-heap, no ruthless efficiency in using up the human material. The master was responsible to society for the treatment and conduct of his slaves, and the southern conscience was far tenderer in the matter than the northern. The workers were never troubled by uncertain means of subsistence. The young were free from care, the old and infirm were adequately provided for. Living conditions were commonly pleasant, and the personal relations between master and slave kindly and loyal. When every argument against slavery had been urged it still remained true that the patriarchal tie that existed on the plantation was more humane than the cash-nexus of capitalism. In this fundamental matter Carlyle was right; and right also in his insistence on the need of capable masters. The South was fortunate in its system. On the self-sufficient plantations there was many an Abbot Sampson directing his little world wisely and humanely; collectively these Abbot Sampsons formed a capable and socially

responsible ruling class worthy of their trust. The economic returns of a wage-slave industrialism might be greater, but the returns in civilization were far less.[1]

Such, in brief, was the reaction of the southern mind in the early
fifties to the challenge of an industrializing generation. It was not
till the publication of *Uncle Tom's Cabin* in 1851 that southern
apologists were fully aroused to the need of counter propaganda.
They had been moving slowly towards the conception of a Greek
democracy under the leadership of Calhoun, but now under the
sharp prod of Abolitionism they turned militant. Facts were
collected and arguments clarified, and the war was carried home to
New England. In three years following *Uncle Tom*, according to a
recent student, fourteen pro-slavery novels appeared together with
other matter.[2] Much of the material made use of in these stories
was conveniently assembled in a work entitled *Pro-Slavery Argument*, published in 1852, a collaboration by Professor Dew of
William and Mary College, Chancellor Harper of the Supreme
Court of South Carolina, Governor Hammond of South Carolina, and Gilmore Simms. The first reviewed the Scriptural
authority for slavery; Chancellor Harper drew from Hobbes
the familiar argument that "a state of nature is a state of war";
Simms elaborated the patriarchal theory; but Governor Hammond developed the more significant argument of the degradation of the wage-slave, an argument elaborated at considerable
length in another work entitled *Letters on Slavery*, in which he
presented the results of his investigation of English factory conditions. The novels that Miss Tandy comments upon have been
pretty much forgotten, but the titles of some of them sufficiently
reveal the lines of attack. L. B. Chase's *English Serfdom and
American Slavery* (1854), J. W. Page's *Uncle Robin in His Cabin
in Virginia and Tom without One in Boston* (1855), and S. H.
Elliott's *New England Chattels* (1858) quite evidently reflect the

---

[1] The same argument was made use of by northern supporters of slavery.
Gordon Bennett's *New York Herald*, for example, "printed a description of slum
life in Liverpool, remarking that compared with the English laborer, 'the slave
lived like a prince.' He had his cabin, neat, clean, and weather-proof: he had his
own garden patch, over which he was lord paramount; he was well fed, well lodged,
well clothed, and rarely over-worked; sleek, happy, contented, enjoying his many
holidays with gusto, he lived to a great age" (quoted in Allan Nevins, *The Evening
Post: A Century of Journalism*, p. 271).

[2] See Jeannette Reid Tandy, "Pro-Slavery Propaganda in American Fiction in the
Fifties," *South Atlantic Quarterly*, January–March, 1922. See also Francis Pendleton Gaines, *The Southern Plantation*, Chapter III.

new southern philosophy. If the South were attacked, it was not without weapons to defend itself.

WILLIAM J. GRAYSON

Of this very considerable literature of defense, *The Hireling and the Slave* presents in convenient compass the most telling southern arguments, and reveals in its sharp contrast of realism and romanticism the common southern temper. Its author, William J. Grayson, was a cultivated South Carolinian who had served two terms in Congress and for years was collector of the Port of Charleston. He was widely read, was familiar with contemporary English writers on economics, and possessed a fluent pen. He had published "an elaborate heroic poem entitled *The Country*," in which he had sung "the praises of rural life and agricultural pursuits" (Introduction to Grayson's *Life of James L. Petigru*), and a volume entitled *Chicora and other Poems*, the title work of which was a romantic poem celebrating the primitive virtues of the Indian. Politically he was affiliated with the anti-Calhoun party of Unionists. His closest friend was James L. Petigru, a sketch of whose life he wrote as a last labor of love, during the unhappy days of the Charleston siege. He did not go so far as Petigru in refusing to have any part in a war that he opposed, but the tragedy of it cut him to the quick. He was no Fire Eater, but a southern moderate—a gentleman of old-fashioned tastes whose views may be taken as those of the cultivated Charleston group to which he belonged, of Petigru, of Legaré, of Alfred Huger.

The Hireling and the Slave, published in 1856 when Grayson was sixty-eight and dedicated to Petigru, is a poem in heroic couplets of approximately 1600 lines, divided into two parts. The first part draws a realistic picture of the life of the wage-slave, the second paints an idyllic picture of the life of the bond-slave. In this second part the spirit of romance holds high carnival; the descriptions are done with gusto and the rural pleasures that fall to the lot of the negro provide a striking contrast to the mean environment of the factory worker. About this contrast are grouped the lesser arguments: the hypocrisy of the Yankee Abolitionist, the sentimentalism of English humanitarians, the wisdom of providence in providing masters to protect the negro from destruction by a superior race and train him through apprenticeship in slavery to carry the blessings of civilization to Africa. The heroic couplet was deliberately adopted to offer "some variety to the poetic forms that are almost universally prevalent." "The poetry of the day is, for the most part," Grayson remarked, "subtile and transcendental in its character"; yet "the school of Dryden and Pope is not entirely forgotten," and "the most fastidious appetite may tolerate an occasional change of diet, and exchange dainties now and then for plainer fare" (*The Hireling and the Slave*, Preface, pp. xiv–xv). The poem seems to have been popular in the South, and a southern reviewer declared that "it ought to be on every man's mantel" (*Life of James L. Petigru*, p. vii).

In the preface Grayson discusses the subject of slavery with a candor somewhat unusual, acknowledging its evils, yet discovering compensations. As an expression of intelligent southern opinion on a question in which the passions of the country were becoming deeply engaged, his views deserve quotation. Slavery, he says,

. . . is that system of labor which exchanges subsistence for work, which secures a life-maintenance from the master to the slave, and gives a life-labor from the slave to the master. The slave is an apprentice for life, and owes his labor to his master; the master owes support, during life, to the slave. Slavery is the Negro system of work. He is lazy and improvident. Slavery makes all work, and it insures homes, food, and clothing for all. It permits no idleness, and it provides for sickness, infancy, and old age. It allows no tramping or skulking, and it knows no pauperism.

This is the whole system substantially. All cruelty is an abuse; does not belong to the institution; is now punished, and may be in time prevented. The abuses of slavery are as open to all reforming influences as those of any civil, social, or political condition. The improvement in the treatment of the slave is as marked as in that of any other laboring class in the world. . . . If slavery is subject to abuses, it has its advantages also. It establishes more permanent, and, therefore, kinder relations between capital and labor. It removes what Stuart Mill calls 'the widening and imbittering feud between the class of labor and the class of capital.' It draws the relation closer between master and servant. It is not an engagement for days or weeks, but for life. There is no such thing with slavery as a laborer for whom nobody cares or provides. The most wretched feature in hireling labor is the isolated, miserable creature who has no home, no food, and in whom no one is particularly interested. *This is seen among hirelings only.* (*Ibid.*, Preface, pp. vii–viii.)

The principle on which Grayson bases his argument is the principle that civilization rests on labor exploitation, but as a good churchman he attributes the evil to God and discovers the children of Adam to be suffering from the primeval curse—"Slave, hireling, help—the curse pursues him still." More specifically the thesis which he defends is this, "The state of the hireling and the slave [is] the same substantially—the condition hard labor, the reward subsistence;" and the conclusion which he draws is that the slave obtains a larger return for his labor than the factory hand. The picture he paints of the condition of the wage slave of England is Hogarthian in its details:

> There, unconcerned, the philanthropic eye
> Beholds each phase of human misery;
> Sees the worn child compelled in mines to slave
> Through narrow seams of coal, a living grave,
> Driven from the breezy hill, the sunny glade,
> By ruthless hearts, the drudge of labor made,
> Unknown the boyish sport, the hours of play,
> Stripped of the common boon, the light of day,
> Harnessed like brutes, like brutes to tug, and strain,
> And drag, on hands and knees, the loaded wain:
> There crammed in huts, in reeking masses thrown,
> All moral sense and decency unknown,
> With no restraint but what the felon knows,
> With the sole joy that beer or gin bestows,
> To gross excess and brutalizing strife,
> The drunken hireling dedicates his life:
> Starved else, by infamy's sad wages fed,
> There women prostitute themselves for bread,
> And mothers, rioting with savage glee,
> For murder'd infants spend the funeral fee;
> Childhood bestows no childish sports or toys,
> Age neither reverence nor repose enjoys,
> Labor with hunger wages ceaseless strife,
> And want and suffering only end with life;
> In crowded huts contagious ills prevail,
> Dull typhus lurks, and deadlier plagues assail,
> Gaunt Famine prowls around his pauper prey,
> And daily sweeps his ghastly hosts away;
> Unburied corses taint the summer air,
> And crime and outrage revel with despair. (*Ibid.*, pp. 24–25.)

Grayson does not stint his facts but traces the wretchedness of the wage-slave through all the phases of his misery to provide a background for the happier lot of the bond-slave. It is an unlovely picture, done with considerable vigor, from which one turns gladly to contemplate life on the southern plantation.

And yet the life, so unassailed by care,
So blessed with moderate work, with ample fare,
With all the good the starving pauper needs,
The happier slave on each plantation leads;
Safe from harassing doubts and annual fears,
He dreads no famine in unfruitful years;
If harvests fail from inauspicious skies,
The master's providence his food supplies;
No paupers perish here for want of bread,
Or lingering live, by foreign bounty fed;
No exiled trains of homeless peasants go,
In distant climes, to tell their tales of woe:
Far other fortune, free from care and strife,
For work, or bread, attends the Negro's life,
And Christian slaves may challenge as their own,
The blessings claimed in fabled states alone—
The cabin home, not comfortless, though rude,
Light daily labor, and abundant food,
The sturdy health that temperate habits yield,
The cheerful song that rings in every field,
The long, loud laugh, that freemen seldom share,
Heaven's boon to bosoms unapproached by care,
And boisterous jest and humor unrefined,
That leave, though rough, no painful sting behind;
While, nestling near, to bless their humble lot,
Warm social joys surround the Negro's cot,
The evening dance its merriment imparts,
Love, with its rapture, fills their youthful hearts,
And placid age, the task of labor done,
Enjoys the summer shade, the winter sun,
And, as through life no pauper want he knows,
Laments no poor-house penance at its close. (*Ibid.*, pp. 50–51.)

Convinced of the righteousness and humanity of slavery Grayson turns with scorn upon the Abolitionists and their meddlesome interference with the beneficent ways of Providence. With a few dexterous turns of the spit he browns each one nicely like a roasted goose. His descriptions strip off the gay plumage and reveal the naked fowl. He makes a good job of it, as witness these bits:

There supple Sumner, with the Negro cause,
Plays the sly game for office and applause;
What boots it if the Negro sink or swim?
He wins the Senate—'tis enough for him. . . .
He heeds nor court's decree nor Gospel light,
What Sumner thinks is right alone is right. . . .

There Greeley, grieving at a brother's woe,
Spits with impartial spite on friend and foe. . . .
To each fanatical delusion prone,
He damns all creeds and parties but his own,
Brawls, with hot zeal, for every fool and knave,
The foreign felon and the skulking slave; . . .
And faction's fiercest rabble always find
A kindred nature in the Tribune's mind;
Ready each furious impulse to obey,
He raves and ravens like a beast of prey. . . .

There Seward smiles the sweet perennial smile,
Skilled in the tricks of subtlety and guile;
The slyest schemer that the world e'er saw;
Peddler of sentiment and patent law;
Ready for fee or faction to display
His skill in either, if the practice pay. . . . (*Ibid.*, pp. 38–40.)

As he contemplates Mrs. Stowe his full wrath is stirred. He does not spare her sex. Southern chivalry serves the pure and good in lovely woman, not the malignant and selfish. An unsexed woman is hateful to it, and after extolling the true womanliness of Florence Nightingale, angel of mercy, Grayson pays his compliments to the Yankee propagandist thus:

Not such with Stowe, the wish or power to please,
She finds no joy in gentle deeds like these;
A moral scavenger, with greedy eye,
In social ills her coarser labors lie;
On fields where vice eludes the light of day,
She hunts up crimes as beagles hunt their prey;
Gleans every dirty nook—the felon's jail,
And hangman's mem'ry, for detraction's tale,
Snuffs up pollution with a pious air,
Collects a rumor here, a slander there;
With hatred's ardor gathers Newgate spoils,
And trades for gold the garbage of her toils.

In sink and sewer thus, with searching eye,
Through mud and slime unhappy wretches pry;
In fetid puddles dabble with delight,
Search every filthy gathering of the night;
Fish from its depths, and to the spacious bag
Convey with care the black, polluted rag;
With reeking waifs secure the nightly bed,
And turn their noisome stores to daily bread.

(*Ibid.*, pp. 42–43.)

The Hireling and the Slave, is vigorous propaganda, carefully documented and pointed with modern instances, the work of an intelligent and humane writer who might be blind to certain evils in slavery but whose eyes were open to the social ills that grew rankly in the muck of industrialism. Outside of the South few in America had as yet come to understand so much—a handful of New England idealists, Parker and William Henry Channing and Emerson and Wendell Phillips, and Orestes Brownson, and a handful of Utopians, Albert Brisbane and George Ripley and Horace Greeley. The inadequacy of southern thought was identical with that of northern: blinded by sectional economic interests, they saw only half the truth. They beheld the mote in a brother's eye, but considered not the beam that was in their own.

CHAPTER IV
ADVENTURES IN BELLES LETTRES

I

OLD CHARLESTON

IN the year 1825 the little city of Charleston, with its fourteen thousand whites and more than fourteen thousand blacks, was perhaps the most delightful spot in America. The Mecca of plantation fashion and the capital of plantation politics, it prided itself on its genial and distinguished society. It was the last stronghold in America of the older pride of aristocracy. The tone of society still remained pretty much what it had been before the schism of '76. Social lines were rigid and an old-fashioned conservatism of temper marked the upper class. Despite the large admixture of French Huguenot blood the manners and prejudices of the aristocracy retained the pronounced British cast that came down from pre-Revolutionary times, and if Dr. Johnson could have stepped from the Fleet Street of 1780 to the Charleston of 1825 he would have felt almost at home. "We are decidedly more English than any other city of the United States," said Hugh Legaré, whose love of the English character was second only to his love of Charleston. It was a gay world with its country squires and their horses and racing, its Madeira drinking, its promenades and dancing and assemblies; one to win the affection of all who liked lighthearted ways.

But underneath this gay life was a more serious Charleston, which in certain of its aspects was not unlike Boston. From both the Huguenot and Scotch-Irish strains came a sobering Puritanism that gave a serious cast to thoughtful natures and disciplined them in a strict morality. Calhoun was far more Puritan than Fisher Ames, and Hugh Legaré than Edward Everett. Life was likely to be a serious business to these southern Puritans, filled with weighty responsibilities, to be lived, like Milton's, as ever in the great Taskmaster's eye. Aristocrat though he was, young Hugh Legaré was no gay cavalier treading the primrose path, but as serious-minded as any Roundhead. Victorian in manners, he would have found the bluff speech of the old revolutionary, General Charles Cotesworth Pinckney—"more pregnant with meaning than prudish in dress"—somewhat too "salt" for refined ears. It was this note of Puritanism that marked the finest characters in Charleston and gave its tone to society; but it was a Puritanism of conduct rather than dogma. Charleston gentlemen were of the English church, and their Puritanism, unwarped by Calvinism, assumed a moral rather than a theological cast.

The lawyer came to assume the position of intellectual leadership taken by the minister in New England. A profound respect for law dominated the Charleston mind. Blackstone was the Charleston Bible, and the lawyer who was master of dignified oratory was looked upon with high regard. The aristocracy opened its doors to young James Louis Petigru, an Irish-Huguenot lawyer with his own way to make, but it closed them tightly against young Gilmore Simms, apprentice to an apothecary and unread in the classics. Ambitious youths therefore turned to the law as a congenial career, for there reputations lay, and political influence. A pronounced cult of the law, and regard for orderly procedure, went hand in hand with the old English respect for individual rights. Charleston gentlemen could not be coerced, even by their own politicians, and Legaré was bitter against the Nullifiers because the spirit of dictation was "alien to our old habitudes, to the gentle courage, the courteous hostility, the mild and merciful justice, the proud submission to *law* and respect for right, which once distinguished our low country society from and above all other American society" (*Writings*, Vol. I, p. 211).

Politically Charleston was of the old Federalist tradition, as that Federalism was embodied in the picturesque figure of General Pinckney. Outside the narrow circle of the aristocracy, Federalism had long since given way to a democratic faith with its background of states-rights Jeffersonianism; but it lingered amongst the gentry and provided the nucleus of the later Union party. Grayson tells a story of Petigru that suggests the bitterness of the back-country democracy towards the old Federalism. The latter one day was being abused by a swamp-sucker "who lavished on him all the foul epithets and appellations he could remember or invent, of which rogue and scoundrel were among the most moderate." At last he hit upon a term of reproach "which at that day comprised everything hateful—he called him a 'damned Federal,'" and was promptly knocked down for the insult (William J. Grayson, *James Louis Petigru*, pp. 83–84). But the Charleston vintage of Federalism was little more than a stout conservatism that idealized the Union and preached the sufficiency and sacredness of the law. It was social rather than political or economic—the assertion of the prescriptive right of gentlemen to govern the state. Jeffersonianism never took possession of the first circles of Charleston as it did in Virginia, and French revolutionary philosophy found there an uncongenial soil. The profound conservatism of the aristocracy is sufficiently expressed in a comment of Hugh Legaré—"The politics of the immortal Jefferson! Pish!" (*Writings*, Vol. I, p. 207.) Physiocratic agrarianism found few advocates amongst Carolina gentlemen. The Charleston mind was political and legal rather than economic in its interests, and as a commercial port Charleston was more sympathetic with capitalism than with agrarianism. Its politics, in which it found much diversion, it preferred highly seasoned, and when Nullification divided the state into hostile camps, the Nullifiers and Unionists brought Charleston to the verge of civil war. Respect for law and the amenities vanished before the hot demands of partisanship.

The culture of Charleston was as conservatively old-fashioned as its politics. Such a renaissance as it enjoyed before the Civil War wrought its destruction was delayed by its rejection of French romantic thought until the beginning of the thirties, and synchronized with the renaissance of New England. When the romantic spirit appeared about 1825, it was primarily English, of the school of Tom Moore. There had never been any literature in Charleston worthy of the name, except such as had come from London, bound in calfskin and tooled morocco. Those who affected a love of letters were still enamored of the heroic couplet and the Addisonian essay. Not until he went to Brussels in 1832 did Legaré, the most brilliant southern linguist, take up the study of German. The classics still dominated education, and literary taste inclined to a mingling of wit and sentiment. Young and Ossian and Mrs. Radcliffe held honored places on Charleston bookshelves. The young poets were deep in Byron, and Sir Walter was in high repute. But Wordsworth and Shelley and Keats were scarcely mentioned, and Carlyle could not hope to gain a hearing. Nevertheless by the year 1828 the example of the *North American Review* proved so stimulating an incentive that the scholarship of Charleston collaborated to establish the *Southern Review*, which ran a sober course for four years, providing a medium for learned articles on law, letters and politics. It was a serious venture that concerned itself little with *belles lettres*, but the intellectual resources were inadequate, and on Legaré's departure for Europe *The Review* came to an end. Later, Gilmore Simms labored to the same purpose, but even his enormous energy was insufficient to sustain a magazine esteemed worthy of southern genius, and the work languished. Facile writers were fewer in Charleston than in Boston.

But despite any shortcomings in the way of letters, to members of its polite circles Charleston was the most delightful of American cities, and its society the most distinguished. "I have never, since I could form an opinion on such matters," wrote Legaré from Brussels, where he mingled with the most cultivated society, "doubted of the immense superiority of Carolina society over all others on that continent, and now feel it more than ever" (*Writings*, Vol. I, p. 218). It was a common opinion of southern gentlemen, who, with their English notions of a landed aristocracy, believed that "fixed landed property is of the essence of civil society, properly so called." It embodied the planter ideal of a social capital, uncorrupted by a vulgar plutocracy. Its highways ran out to the plantations; the free citizen of the Greek democracy drew his wealth from the soil; the slave labored while the master rode to and fro from the city. Law and politics were regarded as respectable vocations for sons of gentlemen, but the ideal life was acknowledged to be that of the planter, with his three thousand acres, his three hundred negroes, his ricks of rice and bales of tobacco and cotton. The profits that came from the law were certain to be invested in land, and the young attorney dreamed of retiring in middle life to a well-stocked plantation. To become a member of the ruling squirarchy was an ambition that filled and satisfied the Charleston imagination.

II

WILLIAM CRAFTS
Charleston Wit

The slightness of literary achievement in the Charleston of 1825 is sufficiently attested by the considerable local fame that rewarded the efforts of the volatile William Crafts. Born in Charleston in

1789, the son of a well-to-do Yankee father and a southern mother, he was sent to Harvard to complete his education, distinguished himself in the classics and in declamation, achieved a gownsman's fame for the brisk informality of a Latin oration, and carried back to Charleston a great reputation as a wit and scholar. He went into the law but burnt too few candles at the shrine of Blackstone; was seized with political ambition and proposed to make a great name for himself as a statesman, but his politics were not agreeable to his constituents and his career failed to arrive. He was a graceful orator in the florid southern style, an agreeable fellow with a pleasant wit, who loved society, dabbled in prose and verse, but proved to be unstable. He spread too much canvas to the uncertain winds and his unballasted bark came to grief. He died at the age of thirty-seven, leaving his writings to be gathered up and published by his family—a miscellany that brought down upon it the severe judgment of Hugh Legaré.

William Crafts was a transplanted Bostonian who essayed to domesticate Harvard culture among the polite circles of Charleston. As an undergraduate he admired the graceful preaching of Buckminster and the acrid eloquence of Fisher Ames. The latter he seems to have adopted as his political godfather, and from him he accepted a decadent Federalism that got him into trouble when later he entered politics. But the chief model on whom he shaped his life seems to have been Robert Treat Paine, in the declining sun of whose fame the young Harvard undergraduate warmed himself. With a less pregnant wit, a less trenchant prose style, a less masculine oratory, he succeeded in becoming a smaller edition of a petty master. The parallelism in the lives of the two apostles of wit is striking. They were both dabblers, but Crafts possessed less skill and dabbled less felicitously. They both broke with the rigid decorum of their circles, but Paine achieved a more tragic shipwreck. They both marked the last ebbing of the eighteenth century before the wit ideal was submerged by the incoming tide of romanticism, and the reputations of both have been forgotten.

In Crafts' case, certainly, no injustice has been done. Such literary wealth as he displayed would seem notable only in an indigent society. His prose is vapid and feeble in the essay, and stilted and artificial in the oration. His verse is insignificant in quantity—two formal poems and a handful of occasional pieces—

and wanting in distinction of phrase or imagery. It is the work
of a graceful imitator of doubtful models. He wrote at the moment
when the long supremacy of Pope was yielding to the popularity
of Moore, and his verse wavered between the old loyalty and the
new love. *Sullivan's Island,* a carefully elaborated descriptive
poem, applies the structure and method of *Windsor Forest* to
a local theme, following the original so closely as to imitate the
detail. His skill in the grand manner may be judged by a single
passage that phrases feebly what Pope had done vigorously:

> When cooler gales foretell departing day,
> The plaintive curlew homeward wings his way—
> Now stoops, then soars, and fearing danger nigh,
> To guardian heaven pours forth its piteous cry.
> Alas! in vain. The fowler's fond reply,
> Still deemed its own, but tells it where to die.

The Raciad is less crudely imitative. It is a brisk and rather amusing account of the outpouring of Charleston society to the races,
the great event of the year in the gay southern capital. It is done
with some sprightliness, it is an amiable historical document,
but it is not important. When Crafts died in 1826 Charleston
had done little in the way of creative literature, but the stirring
of the waters was beginning. The following year a young apothecary just admitted to the bar published a volume entitled *Lyrical
and Other Poems,* first fruits of the colossal labors of Gilmore
Simms. In 1828 Hugh Legaré got *The Southern Review* on its
feet, a substantial magazine that aspired to be the mouthpiece of
southern culture. With the beginning of the thirties the Charleston
renaissance was under way.

III

HUGH SWINTON LEGARÉ

Charleston Intellectual

A far solider nature than the ebullient Crafts was Hugh Swinton
Legaré. Of distinguished social position, the most cultivated
mind in the South before the Civil War, and one of the most
cultivated in America, he was an embodiment of the serious
Charleston that served as counterweight to the gayer. In
Legaré the moral earnestness of the South came to its most
attractive expression. The repository of two streams of ethical

idealism, he was as Puritan as Calhoun. Natively aristocratic, with a high sense of personal integrity and civic responsibility, a profound student of law and letters, with the Charleston parochialism brushed away by wide travel and intimate acquaintance with old-world civilizations and classical cultures, he represented the excellent seriousness that came to flower on the Carolina plantation as well as in the New England meetinghouse. Southern Puritanism might be less ungainly than that of Massachusetts, but it was equally introspective, given to melancholy; and Hugh Legaré found his life as serious an affair, and as laborious, as any New England Calvinist discovered his to be. It is no holiday business to serve righteousness; wisdom does not flower in the primrose path of dalliance; and this Charleston gentleman emerged from a prolonged and arduous self-discipline as complete a Puritan as Theodore Parker.

Descended in the fifth generation from a Huguenot ancestor who settled in Charleston about 1695, he was French in name and by cherished family tradition, but in little else. Through successive intermarriages, the original French strain was pretty much diluted by the Scotch and English, and few Gallic traits came down to him. In temperament and sympathies he was the child of his mother, Mary Swinton, of Scotch Covenanter blood. The native seriousness that came to him by right of inheritance was intensified by fate. Inoculated for the smallpox in his fourth year, the poison lingered in his system, keeping him sickly for years and permanently stunting the lower half of his body. Thus set apart from active life, he turned to books and entered upon the career of a scholar. At the time of his death in 1842, at the age of forty-five, he was perhaps the best linguist and the most widely read man in America. A mature student of the classics, he was intimately acquainted with French, Spanish, Italian and German, and had added Romaic as a help to his Greek. This may seem a meager list in comparison with Theodore Parker's nineteen languages, but the substantial acquisitions he gathered from the several bodies of literature were far from meager.

Yet immense as were those acquisitions they were only supplementary to his professional studies. The Charleston Puritan gave to the study of law the same intensity that the Boston Puritan gave to theology. Not content with a three years' reading course in a law office, he went to Europe to pursue his studies more comprehensively. At the University of Edinburgh he plunged into an investigation of the Roman and Civil Law, which henceforth was to be his major intellectual interest. He found in the continental systems, he believed, a body of legal principles more comprehensive and philosophical than the English Common Law, and the ambition grew upon him to ingraft certain features of the Civil Law upon American practice. After two years' intense study he came home, engaged in active practice of his profession, and ten years later, at the age of thirty-five, was appointed *chargé d'affaires* at Brussels, where he spent four rich years. His diplomatic and social life was subordinated to his studies, into which he threw himself with the keenest zest, enlarging his knowledge of modern letters and adding to his encyclopedic knowledge of legal systems. In 1841 he was appointed Attorney-General of the United States in the cabinet of President Tyler, and upon Webster's retirement was given the additional portfolio of Secretary of State *ad interim*. While on a visit to Boston with President Tyler to assist in the Bunker Hill Monument celebration, he was taken suddenly ill and died at the home of his friend Professor Ticknor.

The man thus prematurely cut down was a nature of vast solidity. Profoundly serious, inclined to the blackest melancholy, as pessimistic as Fisher Ames, with no leaven of humor, no romance, no careless idling, he was a hard taskmaster to his days. He toiled prodigiously at his self-appointed tasks. His standards were severe, whether in letters or law or politics or morals. As a critic he dealt with substantial subjects: *The Constitutional History of Greece; The Origin, History and Influence of Roman Legislation; Early Spanish Ballads; Jeremy Bentham and the Utilitarians; Lord Byron's Character and Writings*—solid dissertations done with German thoroughness—reviews of huge compass that provided opportunity for independent treatises. As a lawyer he was rather a philosophical historian than a special pleader. He was far more given to exploring the labyrinths of ancient codes than to arguing cases. His legal erudition appalls the layman. He had sat at the feet of black-letter philosophers; he had been instructed by sages long since forgotten. His mind was an ample storehouse of archaic legal maxims. He delighted in the crabbed law Latin—its sententious phrases worn to the quick, the residuum and repository of the wisdom bequeathed by past generations. Richer in poetry than any verses of Byron were the

Latin words *habeas corpus* to one who, like this scholar, understood
how packed they were with English history, how rich in suggestion
to all who love English freedom.   From this immense erudition
came his love for old books and venerable authorities.   Blackstone
he looked upon as a modern—"a gentleman's law book, clear, but
not deep"; and the wisdom of my Lord Coke seemed to him not so
mellow as that drawn from the more capacious vats of earlier days.
He quoted Grotius and Vattel and Pufendorf and Bourlamaqui
more readily than the South Carolina Digest, and the names of
Papinian and Ulpian and Modestinus and Voet and Cujacius,
of the *Corpus Alaricianum*, of the Justinian, Gregorian, Hermoge-
nian, and Theodosian codes, slipped familiarly from his pen.   How
many outlandish authorities were contained in the huge inkwell
on his desk it is idle to conjecture.   Probably not three men in
America comprehended the significance of half the references that
he offered for the consideration of his fellow lawyers, or were
competent to question his deductions.   Even the learned Judge
Story and Chancellor Kent seem mere dabblers in comparison
with this philosophical historian.

Such learning must inevitably mold one's thinking in kindred
fields, and he came naturally to espouse what for want of an exacter
term may be called the Common Law theory of politics.   It is a
conception of law as an organic growth, the result of man's laborious search for a rational freedom in the social body, the single
and avowed end of which is justice.   It has taken form not by the
decrees of legislatures, but by decisions of the judiciary, tested
and reëxamined and reargued generation after generation; built
up code by code through slow evolution, the wisdom of the past
serving as counselor to the present; continuously expanding its
jurisdiction from the community to the nation, and from the
nation to a world society; the one guarantee of a sober and rational progress.   Theorists and philosophers come and go; revolutions succeed and fail; foolish statutes and temporary constitutions
have their day; but the organic body of the law survives all surface
change, building into the fabric of society what experience proves
to be good, sloughing off what experience has outgrown—the
tempered rule of social justice; the exact measure of every civilization compared with which the majority will is a crude and inadequate makeshift.

From such a conception it follows that government is little more than ancillary to the law, and political principles are sound in the measure that they are founded on legal principles. Thus by following the musty path of jurisprudence Legaré arrived at the same goal that John Cotton had reached two hundred years before— the apotheosis of magistracy. With the older Puritan he could assert, *Scripturae plenitudinem adoro*. The sufficiency of the law to social justice was axiomatic in his thinking. But the scriptures which he adored were the words of the judges, whose decisions were above the authority of legislator or governor and little concerned with a transient majority will. The old theocrat had set up his theocracy; the modern lexolater would set up his lexocracy; but the end was pretty much the same. Very likely Legaré, like the present-day lexolater, would deny the conclusion, yet it was implicit in his premises, and his scorn of political theory was sufficient proof. Practical politics he regarded as rather a trumpery business that achieves no solid results.[1] The political philosopher he was profoundly suspicious of. The flood of speculation let loose upon the world by the revolutions of the seventeenth and eighteenth centuries seemed to him to have invited disaster, and the political classics of those revolutions he cared little for. He distrusted the "era of illumination" that sacrificed use and wont to abstract theory. "We have not too much faith in the 'march of intellect,'" he remarked dryly, "and would not . . . pitch our anticipations in too high a key" (*ibid.*, Vol. II, p. 264). But his greatest contempt he reserved for the intellectual revolutionaries—"hair-brained metaphysicians and empirical demagogues" (*ibid.*, Vol. I, p. 216), who would upset the nice balance of the law. To this matter he returned again and again, with the scorn of the legal mind for ambitious political systems. "Innovators or Revolutionists, who go only for an imaginary abstract rectitude and symmetry of government," he said, "are always dangerous, and sometimes the greatest curse with which heaven in its wrath can visit an offending people"(*ibid.*, Vol. II, p. 286).

I have no faith at all in speculative politics. A theorist in government is as dangerous as a theorist in medicine, or in agriculture, and for precisely the same reasons—the subjects are too complicated and too obscure for simple and decisive experiments. I go for undisputed results in the long run. (*Ibid.*, Vol. I, p. 303.)

---

[1] See *Writings*, Vol. II, p. 104.

Man begins a revolution, but its issues are with God alone.   The voluntary revolutions of man have always been abrupt, violent and for the worse: so that the wisdom of antiquity laid it down, as a maxim, that every fundamental change in the State must needs be bloody and deadly. (*Ibid.*, Vol. II, p. 297.)

This inherent conservatism of the legal mind explains Legaré's intellectual sympathy with Federalism and his contempt for Jefferson.   The latter to him was the prince of demagogues, and his ink was vitriol when he wrote of him, as thus in one of his letters: "The immortal sayings and doings of the holy father in democracy—the servant of the servants of Demos (whose nose of wax he knew better than anybody how to shape to his own convenience,)—the infallible, though ever-changing, St. Thomas of *Canting*-bury.   And here, you may be sure, I *cross* myself devoutly and cry out, with an all-fervent benediction to that canonized worthy, *pax tecum* (pronounced, you know, *Scottice*, *pox tacum*)" (*Writings*, Vol. I, p. 208).   Modern political theories seemed to him mere upstart doctrines compared with the venerable principles of the law, and he came to look with suspicion on all political liberalism not sponsored by lawyers and supported by briefs.   A passionate lover of liberty, he was as distrustful of democracy as John Adams, and his condemnation was as frank— "that scene of wild impulse, and tyrannical misrule—a pure democracy" (*ibid.*, Vol. II, p. 271).   No state, Beverley Tucker pointed out, was so little democratic as South Carolina, and Legaré shared the common Charleston distrust of it.   As he watched England and France during the tumultuous thirties, and saw the struggle over Nullification at home, his concern for the future became acute and his pessimism as black as Fisher Ames'.   In a letter from Brussels, in the year 1833, shortly after the passage of the English Reform Bill, he wrote:

Mankind have too little sense to maintain, for any length of time, a well-tempered democracy, and a great deal too much to bear an unlimited one—the most dreadful form of " State sovereignty," beyond all doubt, in which the descendants of the father of the first murderer have ever given loose to their ruffian instinct of violence and oppression.   If they have a moderate policy of the kind, which happens (as all complicated machines will) to be occasionally a little out of order, their only idea of a remedy is to pull it down, and along with it every thing that makes a civil society worthy of its name.   Who could ever have dreamed that the law of brute

force which now crushes Europe . . . should be deliberately adopted in
America, instead of the really sublime institutions of a federal jurisdiction,
(fallible, of course, but generally right) and that this relapse into downright barbarism should be vaunted, by the most enlightened men in the
Southern States, as a *grand* improvement and the only thing wanting to
make our government as perfect as we have been swearing it was all along.
(*Ibid.*, Vol. I, p. 210.)

Back of this ingrained conservatism was a tender Puritan conscience that must twist his legal studies to ideal ends. After all it
was no other than a juridical romanticism that Hugh Legaré discovered in the bottom of his scholar's cup. As medieval as Sir
Walter, he sought his romance in old law-courts rather than in
feudal castles, in black-robed advocates rather than in knights and
ladies; and he persuaded himself that those old litigations, preserved in scraps of Latin and law French, were dramatic episodes in
the ceaseless battle for human rights, whereof the single objective
was justice. Slowly, stone upon stone, the lawyers were erecting
an impregnable citadel, within which justice kept her inviolable
court. It is a pleasant fiction still believed in by lawyers of the old
school, and to Legaré in his study it bore the very semblance of
truth. He had read too many law books; he had speculated too
little on politics; immersed in his codes, he had forgotten to inquire
into the hidden springs of sovereignty.   In his contempt for practical politics he had neglected to study even the primer of economic
determinism. To the economic historian, Legaré's boundless faith
in the sufficiency of legal processes is incomprehensible. A few
lessons from the wiser Jefferson would have taught him much that
he needed to know concerning the economic sources of power. In
his attitude towards the law Jefferson was a suspicious realist.
He had no faith in legal codes that had grown up under monarchical
and aristocratic systems, and he put no trust in government by
lawyers. He could not understand how the Common Law, interpreted by the Tory Blackstone, and applied by Federalist lawyers,
should serve the needs of a democracy. Democratic America, he
was convinced, must create a new democratic law, and hold its
judiciary in strict subjection to its will; to surrender sovereignty
to an aristocracy of the bench would mean the abdication of democracy. But Legaré refused to go to school to Jefferson. He
clung to his romantic conception of the law with the same passionate conviction that Calhoun clung to his romantic dream of a

Greek democracy; and with the ebbing of the romantic tide they were both left stranded.

But if Legaré was unsympathetic towards the new political theory that came from the French intellectuals, and frankly hostile to the new political practice that came in with the Jacksonians, he warmly approved the new economics that came with the Industrial Revolution. In his whole-hearted acceptance of Adam Smith he seems not a Carolinian at all, but an English liberal of the Cobden-Bright school. He adopted the principle of *laissez faire*, the gospel of progress, the attitude of optimism. He accepted the theory of the beneficence of commerce as a universal civilizing agency, and he looked forward confidently to an eventual parliament of man, a future federation of the world. Commerce in the end must outlaw war, and peace with freedom would spread the blessings of civilization to the ends of the earth.[2]

A convincing object-lesson in the sufficiency of the principle of *laissez faire*, he discovered in the amazing progress of America. The mainspring of that progress he found in economic freedom—freedom "from those undue restraints and that impertinent interference of government in the interests properly belonging to individuals." "I know," he said, "that the cardinal spring and source of our success is freedom—freedom of thought, freedom of speech, freedom of action, freedom of commerce" (*Writings*, Vol. I, p. 306). The greatest of these was free trade between the states. His travels in England and the contrast between English progress and continental backwardness confirmed him in this belief. "The doctrine of Free Trade," he asserted, "is a great fundamental doctrine of civilization. The world must come to it at last, if the visions of improvement in which we love to indulge are ever to be realized" (*ibid.*, Vol. I, p. 272). He went further and accepted the Industrial Revolution with its division of labor as a necessary agency of social amelioration. "It is evidently in the order of nature, and we must take it with all its good and all its evils together." In forecasting the effect of that revolution he was troubled by no fears.

Sir, it is a favorite phrase of those who boast of what is called "the march of intellect," that things are thus changed because the "schoolmaster is abroad." But I tell you that something far more effective than the schoolmaster, a mightier than Solomon, is abroad. It is the STEAM-ENGINE—in

2 See "The Arbitrament of National Disputes," in *Writings*, Vol. I, pp. 355-357.

its twofold capacity of a means of production and a means of transport—the most powerful instrument by far of pacification and commerce, and therefore of improvement and happiness that the world has ever seen; which, while it increases capital, and multiplies beyond all imagination the products of industry, brings the most distant people into contact with one another . . . effaces all peculiarities of national character, and promises, at no distant period, to make the whole Christian world, at least, one great family. . . .

A people well clad and well housed will be sure to provide themselves with all the other comforts of life; and it is the diffusion of these comforts, and the growing taste for them, among all classes of society in Europe—it is the desire of riches as it is commonly called, that is gradually putting an end to the destructive and bloody game of war, and reserving all the resources hitherto wasted by it, for enterprises of industry and commerce, prosecuted with the fiery spirit which once vented itself in scenes of peril and carnage. (*Ibid.*, Vol. I, pp. 285–286.)

Remembering how dependent were southern cotton interests on English industrialism and commerce, one can understand Legaré's acceptance of *laissez faire* economics. His idealism, his local pride, his romanticism, were all enlisted in its behalf, and he painted in glowing colors. But his frank advocacy of capitalism is harder to understand, except perhaps on the ground that Charleston was a considerable shipping port and his clients were engaged in commerce. In the bitter dispute with Jackson over the Bank, Legaré adopted northern views on national finance. Although nominally a Democrat, he had never been an agrarian, and he went with Webster and Clay against the subtreasury scheme and a metallic currency. His thoughtful speech on *The Spirit of the Sub-Treasury*, delivered in 1837, was thoroughgoing Whig doctrine, asserting the excellence of the modern banking system and extolling the economic fruitfulness of credit. He repudiated every principle of John Taylor; denied every dogma of agrarian economics; and eulogized the English financial system as the germinal source of English greatness. Applying the principle of credit to American conditions, he discovered the secret of American expansion in the principle of speculative borrowing, and expanded his doctrine of economic freedom by asserting that freedom to borrow was a necessary preliminary to freedom to work. "A people have been enriched by debt," he argued, overlooking the possible fallacy of a *post hoc ergo propter hoc*, "and 'by owing, owe not.'" As he contemplated the amazing progress of the nation, his lyric enthusiasm becomes prologue to a somewhat lame conclusion

that enthrones the banker as the fairy godmother of the hardy
pioneer.

There is a grandeur and a majesty in this irresistible onward march of
a race, created, as I believe, and elected to possess and people a continent.
. . . We may become so much accustomed to such things that they shall
make as little impression upon our minds as the glories of the Heavens
above us; but, looking on them, lately, as with the eyes of the stranger,
I felt, what a recent English traveller is said to have remarked, that far
from being without poetry, as some have vainly alleged, our whole country
is one great poem.   Sir, it is so; and if there be a man that can think of
what is doing, in all parts of this most blessed of all lands, to embellish
and advance it, who can contemplate that living mass of intelligence,
activity and improvement as it rolls on, in its sure and steady progress,
to the uttermost extremities of the west; who can see scenes of savage
desolation transformed, almost with the suddenness of enchantment, into
those of fruitfulness and beauty; crowned with flourishing cities, filled
with the noblest of all populations; if there be a man, I say, that can witness all this passing under his very eyes, without feeling his heart beat
high, and his imagination warmed and transported by it, be sure, sir, that
the raptures of song exist not for him. . . .

But of this rational, diffusive liberty, among a people so intelligent as
ours, the credit system is the natural fruit, the inseparable companion,
the necessary means and instrument.   It is part and parcel of our existence.   Who ever heard of CREDIT in a despotism, or an anarchy?   It
implies *confidence*—confidence in yourself, confidence in your neighbor,
confidence in your government, confidence in the administration of the
laws, confidence, in a word, in your destiny, and your fortune, in the des-
tinies and the fortunes of the country to which you belong; as, for instance,
in the case of a great national debt.   It is the fruit, I say, of all that is
most precious in civilized life, and to quarrel with it is to be ungrateful
to God for some of the greatest blessings he has vouchsafed to man.
(*Writings*, Vol. I, pp. 306–307.)

Such ebullient rhetoric fits the mouth of the politician rather than
the scholar, and such careless logic comes oddly from a southern
intellectual.   In his ignorance of the economics of John Taylor,
Legaré was unprovided with principles to reply to his own arguments, and unaware of the lameness of his confident conclusions.
But though he might glow with optimism as he contemplated the
westward expansion, for the future of the South and of his own
beloved state he was deep in pessimism.   From the first he had
dissented vigorously from the program of Nullification.   An ardent Union man, he believed with his friend James Petigru that
secession meant ruin for South Carolina.   Calhoun seemed to him
a monomaniac, consumed by a single idea.   He feared the hot

passion of the states-rights party and he was troubled over slavery.
His travels abroad had acquainted him with European views on
the subject; he watched the spread of English humanitarianism
and he had come to recognize the institution as an anachronism.
It seemed to him impossible for the South to withstand much longer
the augmenting pressure of civilized opinion. He could justify
slavery in his own eyes both by ancient law—*servitus est constitutio
juris gentium*—and by comparison of the condition of the negro
with that of the English wage worker. The ideal of a Greek democracy was vastly congenial to his aristocratic temperament, but
he knew that it was a romantic dream, and he was oppressed by the
shadow of impending ruin. Writing from Brussels on April 8,
1833, he concluded an anxious letter thus:

> It ends in my not knowing what to think, except that dangers are
> around and above and below and within our poor little State,—which
> may God preserve us from! I ask of heaven only that the little circle I
> am intimate with in Charleston should be kept together while I live,—
> in health, harmony and competence; and that, on my return, I may my-
> self be enabled to enjoy the same happiness, in my intercourse with it,
> with which I have been hitherto blessed. *We* are (I am quite sure) the
> *last* of the *race* of South-Carolina; I see nothing before us but decay and
> downfall,—but on that very account, I cherish its precious relics the
> more. . . . Yet my heart sinks within me often when I think of what
> may too soon be, and I say, in those touching words, "Why should not my
> countenance be sad, when the city, the place of my fathers' sepulchres,
> lieth waste, and her gates are burnt with fire." (*Writings*, Vol. I, p. 215.)

Thus like old John Winthrop two hundred years before, this
descendant of southern Pilgrims, this Charleston lawyer and
intellectual, found the words of the Hebrew Scriptures rising to his
lips in moments of deep emotion. In spite of travel and many
books and ripe culture and catholic sympathies, Hugh Legaré
remained Puritan at heart, sorely puzzled with life, the burden of
his days heavy upon him, walking soberly in the way of duty.
North or south, the Puritan was still Puritan, whether he were
Theodore Parker, the Boston radical, or Hugh Swinton Legaré,
the Charleston conservative.

IV

WILLIAM GILMORE SIMMS

Charleston Romancer

From the background of old Charleston emerged, about the year 1825, the figure of Gilmore Simms, lately a drug clerk but now come to the dignity of admission to the bar; a tall, vigorous young fellow, with little formal schooling, no Latin or Greek, without land or slaves, but heavily involved in Byronic odes and like unprofitable investments; a social nobody soon to be married at the age of twenty to a girl of no better station than his own, who offered himself as candidate for the poet laureateship of the South. A somewhat presumptuous proceeding on the part of a plebeian quite outside the cultivated circle of the Petigrus and Grimkés and Hugers and Legarés, who were the accepted custodians of Charleston culture and who did not take kindly to ambitious newcomers. They regarded literature as a polite art that could flourish only in polite circles, and they turned a cold shoulder upon a young man whose ways suggested the Carolina buckra.

After all these years one may well cherish a grudge against the amiable little city for its shabby treatment of Gilmore Simms. The most richly endowed of any son she ever gave birth to, he was snubbed for years by the social oligarchy and suffered keenly from the ostracism. His extreme parochialism made him the more sensitive to the slight. An ardent Southerner, loyal to all the Carolinian totems and taboos, he accepted the Charleston judgment in literature and politics as the very law and the prophets. He loved the soil of South Carolina, he loved the people and the way of life, and he was steeped as no other Carolinian in local history and tradition. He could perceive no shortcomings in a society he warmly admired, and he accepted the Charleston provincialisms as the lover accepts the mole on his mistress' cheek. The more Charleston snubbed him, the more admirable he professed to believe was an aristocracy that so jealously guarded its fine exclusiveness. His lifelong ambition was to receive recognition from his native city, and when after the death of his first wife and his marriage to the daughter of a prosperous planter, he gained admission into the ranks of the lesser gentry, he eagerly made common cause with them. He accepted the Carolinian standards and conventions; he advocated social caste: he honored the southern gentleman as God's best handiwork; he unconsciously reflected an aristocratic arrogance towards all social inferiors. He abandoned the Jeffersonian philosophy of his youth and adopted the revised gospel of Calhoun. He became, in short, a Carolina Fire Eater. He set up as a militant defender of slavery and collaborated with other eminent Carolinians to develop the pro-slavery argument.[3] He could have escaped the subtle compulsions of the southern system only by emptying his mind of his dearest prejudices, and this he had neither the will nor the wish to do. And so in spite of the fact that his every instinct was democratic, and every natural impulse generous and manly, he fought the battles of the peculiar institution as stoutly as if he had been born to his three hundred slaves; and he suffered in consequence the loss of pretty nearly everything, including his art. After his death, his friend Paul Hayne wrote of him: "Simms's genius *never had fair play!* Circumstances hampered him!" The judgment is just. Parochial Charleston brought about his literary undoing.

In taste and temperament Simms was a pronounced realist, but his career took shape from a generation given to every romantic excess. His genius, in consequence, was always at cross purposes with the popular taste. His realism turned naturally to low-life adventure; his upper-class romance became stilted and posturing, and his love of action degenerated into swashbuckling. That he survived such mishaps at all, suggests the enormous vitality of the man. If there had only been a little more of the intellectual in him, if he could have detached himself as an artist from the immediate and present, he might have risen superior to his unfortunate environment. But he was constitutionally incapable of aloofness, and hence incapable of criticism. To analyze, compare and judge was impossible to so ardent a nature. He must be partisan to a people and a cause, rather than to his art. The South that he loved was romantic, and he would appeal to the world as a Southerner. He wore his sectional prejudices as the southern politician wears his rumpled Prince Albert coat, broad-brimmed hat and black string tie. He never realized what a clutter of useless luggage he carried into his study. It is a pity that he constricted himself to the shell of an outworn order, instead of realizing that social orders and institutions are significant to the novelist

[3] See above, page 102.

only as he stands apart from them, observing their ways and considering their interplay in the lives of men and women. It was a major loss to American letters that he should not have striven to be an artist first, and a southern romantic only at a later and more convenient season. If he had served his art more jealously, if he had learned from Poe to refuse the demands of inconsequential things, he would have viewed his beloved Charleston with keener eyes and portrayed it more adequately.

But he would not serve his art alone. Unhappily he conceived that he owed an imperative duty to his native commonwealth, and in fulfillment of that duty he frittered away his enormous vitality in delivering patriotic orations and occasional addresses, serving in the Legislature, pottering over politics, lecturing upon literature, founding and editing magazines and essaying to bring culture to Charleston by fiery impetuosity of appeal. He struggled as few other Americans have done to further the cause of letters in a desperate environment; but creative literature could neither be cajoled nor coerced to take up an abode in the indolent little city, and Simms wore himself out in a fruitless undertaking. Our literature has suffered few greater losses than this wasting of the genius of Gilmore Simms in trumpery fields that belong to the literary dray horse. It was the inevitable outcome of the conflict between the creative artist and the citizen of South Carolina.

Little as he is known to later readers Simms is by far the most virile and interesting figure of the Old South. He was built on a generous plan. He was endowed with a rich and prodigal nature, vigorous, spontaneous, creative. There was in him much of Whitman's largeness and coarseness, much of his delight in the good things of earth. He wrote with extraordinary gusto, and his fine strong face suggests that he lived with equal gusto. As a professional man of letters he turned out an incredible amount of work, by ordinary two tales a year—solid works of five hundred pages each—together with poems and plays and pot-boiling stuff to tax the capacity of two or three hack writers. He poured out his material copiously, lavishly, with overrunning measure. His stories flow as generously as his Jamaica rum. He is a veritable geyser of invention, an abundant sea of salty speech. He has no sense of restraint; he does not stop to prune the tangle of his imagination; he refuses to strip the plot of extraneous incident to hasten its action. He is as episodic as Dickens at his worst, piling up action and multiplying threads till the story bogs down. The major plot is always struggling from hummock to hummock in the endless swamp where his characters slip in and out, rarely getting to firm ground, yet never quite submerged. Prodigal of adventure and loving action, clumsy as the natural man when confronted with sentiment, he is an American Fielding with a dash of Smollett. He is at ease only out of doors, in the fields and swamps and highways; there his speech becomes racy, and there the rich poetry of his nature, which somehow rarely got into his verse, comes to abundant and spontaneous expression. When he enters the drawing-room his stilted language betrays his lack of ease. He writes with his pen and not with his heart. The plantation tradition has him in its grip and his fine ladies and gentlemen are done up with much literary starch. But let him come upon a happy-go-lucky blackguard and he loves him as Fielding would have loved him. The amusing scene in which Lieutenant Porgy heaves a pot of hot hominy in the face of a Scotch dragoon is quite evidently reminiscent of Parson Adams' recourse to a dish of hog's blood in a certain tavern brawl.[4] Like Fielding also is his criterion of morality. A frank and generous nature is his infallible test of worth, and if his patriotism led him to bestow a large share of generosity on the patriots, and a correspondingly meager share on the Loyalists and British, he was but exercising an ancient prerogative of the romancer.

Contemporary romanticism engrafted on a nature fundamentally realistic developed a pronounced strain in his work which, for lack of an exacter word, we may call picaresque. This comes out at its worst in the crude border tales of *Richard Hurdis* and *Border Beagles*, stories marked by the coarseness of the eighteenth century, backwoods versions of *Jonathan Wild*. At its best it created a goodly company of blackguards that are an asset to American literature. Simms dearly loved a rogue, and the more picturesque the latter's knavery the more he loved him. A gentleman villain turns to a thing of wood in his hands, but a low-born rascal he creates out of living flesh and blood. A surprising number of low figures, both rogues and honest men, enliven his cluttered pages, individual, racy, often poetic. Realistic in speech and action, they are men of special gifts, nimble of wit and rich in imagination, sometimes fallen to base uses and sometimes ennobled

[4] See *Katherine Walton*, Chapter XLI.

by affection for their superiors. Thumbscrew, Supple Jack Bannister, and Joe Ballou, the partisan scouts; Isaac Muggs, mine host of the Black Riders; Goggle the half-breed; Hell Fire Dick of Tophet, the blackguard converted by *Pilgrim's Progress;* Sam Bostwick the Squatter—these are admirable figures, done with inimitable spirit, the choicest collection of homespun in American literature. They impart life and drama to Simms's tales. Remove them, and his romances are only a welter of stilted language and starchy situations. The scene, for example, between Jack Bannister and Isaac Muggs, in which the latter is converted to true republican principles by appeal to a backwoods ordeal by battle, is magnificent in its broad humor, and it is a pity that Simms did not give freer rein to his genius for such work. It is incomprehensible that a man who could put into the mouth of Thumbscrew such language as the following could have stooped to scribble the love scenes between Ernest Mellichampe and Janet Berkeley:

When it so happens that the things a man's got to love gits fewer and smaller, they gits more valuable, Airnest, in his sight; for he knows mighty well, if he loses them, that he's jist like an old bird that comes back to the tree when the blossoms and the flowers have all dropped off, and are rotting under it. It's mighty nigh to winter in his heart then, Airnest— mighty nigh—and the sooner he begins to look out a place to sleep in, the wiser man you may take him to be. (*Mellichampe*, Chapter IX.)

But Simms was too inveterately episodical to construct a pretty plot, and too careless in his generous southern hospitality to discriminate between guests at his board. He throws a huge miscellany on the table from which each may choose what pleases his taste.

Here again romanticism did him an evil turn. Southern taste was too aristocratic to like coarse fare. Gentlemen must dine like gentlemen even though black rascals served as waiters. Common fellows were well enough in the background, but they must not presume to crowd their betters from the table. In such matters Simms was constrained to follow the orthodox literary tradition. From Shakespeare to Scott the notion prevailed that legitimate romance must be conceived of as a flitch of bacon, the lean of vulgarity alternating with the fat of gentility. Hence Simms was forced to keep a weather eye on the popular taste lest it be offended by too free an offering of the low. His negroes, such as Scipio and Bram and Benny Bowlegs, are more worth while than their masters, and his swamp-suckers are done with more gusto than the officers; but when the plot demands the appearance of the gentry he sends his black-bottle rapscallions about their business. Except in occasional instances, as in the case of old Colonel Sinclair, the Carolinian baron—a testy old gentleman done in the best gouty manner—Simms does the "quality" badly and the canny reader soon learns to skip the genteel passages in order to visit with Lieutenant Porgy or follow the adventures of Hell Fire Dick or Supple Jack Bannister. There is ample fare at his generous board, but one must pick and choose.

The critics have made quite too much of the Gothic extravagancies that mar so many of his pages. It is true that Simms was a generous purveyor of "blood-pudding" romance with its gory exploitation of crime and mystery. Nothing can excuse or extenuate such folly in the abstract; but it is easily comprehensible. It was a part of the price which the professional man of letters had to pay as caterer to a provincial reading public. After the surprising success of *Guy Rivers*, Simms deliberately tested the taste of his readers by sending forth *Richard Hurdis* under a pen name; and the equal success of the latter convinced him that American readers liked such fare. He had a living to make; the market was limited, and he resolved to give the public what it wanted. This accounts for his major sins. An enormous number of chapters, together with whole volumes such as *Charlemont* and *Beauchampe*—preposterous accounts of a notorious murder case in Kentucky—deserve no better fate than the rubbish heap. They are in no sense literature; yet unfortunately the very great powers of Simms are too commonly measured by such trash, instead of by his Revolutionary tales.

Simms was a loving student of older English literature and drew much of his water from excellent wells. A happy instinct led him back to the robust time of Elizabeth and those masculine playwrights whose ample natures were so like his own. Shakespeare may be reckoned his particular master—especially the prose of Shakespeare with its Cheapside colloquialisms and racy idiomatic rhythms. No better training school could be desired, and his loving apprenticeship to the older vernacular serves to explain the source of Simms's greatest literary virtue. From long familiarity with the Elizabethans he derived his mastery of English idiom that sets him widely apart from most other contemporary Americans. In easy

outpouring of picturesque speech, of the lithe and muscular idiom
of the older literature, he was without a rival in his generation.
Many an old Elizabethan phrase lingered in the southern backwoods, and many an indigenous turn of speech had sprung from
homely new-world experience. All such Simms seized upon with
the relish of a gourmand, stirring them into the great pot from
which he ladled such generous spoonfuls. Later critics have been
singularly obtuse in their failure to do justice to his rich linguistic
equipment. Quite too much comment has been devoted to his
careless slips in rhetorical construction, and quite too little to his
command of masculine English prose. It is absurd to couple him
with Cooper in sinning against good writing. They are as unlike as
two men could well be. Simms is incomparably the greater master
of racy prose, as he is much the richer nature. The only contemporary indeed who approaches him is Melville in *Moby Dick*.
He is careless and slovenly enough in all conscience; when he goes
on a rampage he mouths his lines like any town crier. But though
he keeps a sharp eye on the groundlings, though he is often preposterous, he is rarely wooden, never feeble.

The Elizabethan influence comes out strikingly in the character of Lieutenant Porgy, the spoilt child of his imagination,
who runs through the Revolutionary romances as a sort of comic
chorus. Despite Professor Trent's opinion to the contrary, Porgy
is a South Carolinian Falstaff, quite evidently done with a close
eye to the original. He is a very mountain of a fellow, with huge
paunch and spindling shanks from too much sitting at the table
and in the saddle—the most amusing and substantial comic
character in our early fiction. As a South Carolina gentleman,
Porgy of course was no liar or coward or woman cheater. In battle
he is an avalanche of patriotic valor, and in his deference to the
weak and dependent, in his free-handed generosity that encum-
bers him with penniless hangers-on, he is model of southern chivalry. But in the far greater matters of the belly, he is strikingly
Falstaffian. He is not so much a valiant trencherman, as an artist in food and drink. He lived to eat and he ate to speculate on
the virtues of a good dinner. "He took philosophy with him to
the table, and grew wise over his wine" (*Woodcraft*, Chapter
XVIII). He is an epicure in words, a gourmand of wit. The
copious stream of his speech runs on in an endless flow, sometimes
roily but never stagnant. A pat aphorism or a picturesque phrase

is as succulent to him as Carolina terrapin. When philosophy
fails he stoops to horseplay, but his practical jokes are carried
off with theatrical splendor, with colossal assurance. Like Falstaff he is fond of practicing his wit on his followers. His
Bardolph is a certain Geordie Dennison, the swamp poet of
the troop; and Porgy honors him as one artist honors the craft
of another.

But the most satisfying comradeship lies between Porgy and
Black Tom, fellow practitioners of the gentle art of cookery,
sworn liegemen to roasts and soups and stews. Together they
make the swamp commissariat bloom like a Covent Garden
market. They are master foragers untroubled by an overnice
conscience. "Do as much stealing in an honest way as you can,"
the lieutenant remarks to Tom. "D—n the patriotism that can't
eat stolen fruit!" At a pinch the native resources of the swamp are
boldly commandeered The creative masterpiece of the valiant
Porgy was a notable banquet which he proffered General Greene
and his staff in their swamp quarters. His infinite resourcefulness
in this great affair, his huge inventiveness, elevate the dinner to
the rank of a culinary epic. The swamp frogs that he speared by
moonlight, and the young alligators that he took by subtle strata-
gem, were transmogrified into delectable dishes served to his guests
under the alluring names of *alerta* and *lagarta*.[5] The scene is done
with a gusto that only the worshiper of fleshpots could achieve.
Simms delighted in Porgy because he was himself something of a
Porgy. There is good fare for those who sit at table with the fat
humorist of *The Forayers;* the ready talk does not lack the salt of
wit. The later Porgy of *Woodcraft* scarcely comes up to the earlier.
His debts weigh too heavily on his spirits for the easy play of his
fancy; he is less redoubtable as a wooer than as a warrior;
nevertheless there is excellent humor to be enjoyed at Glen
Eberle, and some extraordinary pranks.

The two major themes with which his romances deal, as has been
often pointed out, are the frontier and the Revolution; but the intimate connection between them has not been so commonly remarked.
In much of his better work the two themes blend into one. The
conditions of civil war in the South thrust into sharp relief the
cultural and psychological frontier that clung to the outskirts
of the plantations—the ragged edges of a society that kept the

[5] See *The Forayers*, Chapters XLIII–XLVI.

poor whites submerged and bred a numerous progeny of coarse and primitive creatures, little better than social outcasts. Not the least of the curses of slavery—as Helper pointed out—was its blighting effect on the less prosperous whites who environed every plantation with its special frontier. With his strong bias towards realism Simms refused to romanticize what was inherently unlovely. Like Baldwin in his *Flush Times of Mississippi and Alabama*, he discovered an ample supply of blackguards and sharpers in the no man's land beyond the settlements. The log cabins of the swamp country harbored their motley crew in no wise different from their fellows of the farther frontier along the Mississippi; and these precious rascals he drags from their lurking-places to exhibit in the light of day. The frontier in consequence is rarely absent from his stories, and it is this picaresque interpretation that sets him so sharply off from Cooper. A recent student, in commenting on the contrast between the frontier of Cooper and Simms, suggests that "perhaps the earlier frontier had been intrinsically more dignified than that which Simms had observed; perhaps the difference is that Cooper's had lain deeper under the softening shadow of the past" (Van Doren, *The American Novel*, p. 65). But this is quite to miss the point, both of Cooper and Simms. The real explanation is to be sought in the different interpretations of the romantic and the realist. Cooper's frontier existed only in his imagination. When he came face to face with the reality, as in the case of old Aaron Thousandacres and his lawless brood, he hated it too frankly to portray it justly. The stern Puritan squatter and his fiercer wife are magnificent caricatures, drawn to serve a partisan purpose. They provide a romantic contrast to the honest Chainbearer, spokesman of the psychology of the settlements; but set beside Simon Suggs, master of the frontier technic of easy money, as depicted by Joseph Baldwin, they are as romantic as Cooper's Indians.

The picaresque note is frankly emphasized in Simms' Revolutionary tales. All the swamp-suckers and rapscallions found their heaven-sent opportunity in the disorders of civil war. No realist could write about the Revolution in South Carolina without noting the flocks of buzzards gathering to fall upon the carrion. War is not a heroic thing in these stirring pages. It invites debauchery and encourages brutality. Blackguards put a black stain on military glory. In the preface to *The Scout*, Simms remarks:

To burn and slay were not the simple performances of this reckless period and ravaged country. To burn in wantonness and to murder in cold blood, and by the cruellest tortures, were the familiar achievements of the time: . . . The face of the country was overrun by outlaws. Detached bands of ruffians, formed upon the frontiers of Georgia, and in the wilds of Florida—refugees from all the colonies—availed themselves of the absence of civil authority to effect a lodgment in the swamps, the forests, and the mountains. These, mounted on swift horses, traversed the state with the wind; now here, now there; one moment operating on the Savannah, the next on the Peedee; sometimes descending within sight of the smokes of the metropolis; and anon, building their own fires on the lofty summits of the Appalachian ridge.

Now and then in his pages war flashes out in romantic or heroic episodes, but for the most part it is mean and degrading, a thing to be hated. Simms loved action too keenly not to make the most of the countless onsets and forays, the ambushing of Hessians and the cutting off of wagon trains; he found in them material for many a brisk page and stirring adventure; but in the end it is the brutality of it all, the unhappy loosing of evil passions, that gives him most concern. It was a hard world, and the soft-hearted Jack Bannister, speaking with the tongue of Simms, could find comfort only in stoicism. "A man ought not to be too soft about the heart, in a world like this, so full of rascals that need the knockings of a hard and heavy hand."

It is this strong seasoning of the picaresque, perhaps, that accounts for the neglect that has befallen the work of Simms. Many blackguards and generous potations of Jamaica rum consorted ill with the genteel tradition in letters that grew up in the days following the Civil War; and romantic memories of a lost cause threw an idyllic haze over earlier times. The Revolutionary War lay too far in the past for a generation suffering from a great tragedy to concern itself with, and the vivid and vital work of Simms scarcely outlived its creator. The Revolutionary tales have been largely forgotten, and from his abundant work only *The Yemassee* has survived in popular affection, and this partly from the vogue of Cooper. The winnowing has been severe and scarcely just. The best of Simms is not in *The Yemassee*, but in those stirring tales of Marion's men who carried on a bushwhacking campaign under the hot sun of the dog days. *The Partisan* and *The Forayers* and *Woodcraft* deserve a better fate than has befallen them. The ghost of Cooper does not haunt their pages to challenge comparison, as it does *The Yemassee*, and bring into question their relative merits. There Simms is at home, in the swamps and fields and villages, with men whose ways he knew and loved, and his generous nature followed its own impulses.

But in dealing with the Indians he entered a domain preëmpted by the romantic, and his picaresque realism suffered a disastrous rivalry. Like Robert Montgomery Bird's *Nick of the Woods*, *The Yemassee* is heavily marked by the frontier psychology. It was unfortunate, perhaps, that Simms did not follow Cooper's example and plunge into the wilderness, leaving behind him the squatter and settler with their sordid prose. Instead, his Indians are encompassed by a dark background of civilization, and their tragic destiny is poignantly dramatized in the fate of young Occonestoga, besotted with the white man's rum, and doomed to a destruction far less poetic than befalls Uncas fighting his hereditary foes. Nevertheless a wealth of romantic material is crowded into the volume, enough to serve Cooper for half a dozen tales. In simplifying his plots to the uncomplicated problem of flight and pursuit, the latter gains in dramatic swiftness of movement, but he loses in abundance of accompanying action—the sense of cross purposes and many-sided activities, which *The Yemassee* so richly suggests. The latter is an elaborately carved and heavily freighted Spanish bark that is left far astern by the trim Yankee clipper ship; yet its cargo of the gold of the Indies is far richer. It is the familiar story of southern prodigality and wastefulness— an exuberant nature pouring out its wealth in spendthrift fashion, and failing to achieve the greater results attained by a simpler nature held in closer restraint. After all it is idle to compare Cooper and Simms, and even more futile to catalogue the latter as a disciple of the Cooper school. Simms was far too rich in his own right to live as a dependent on anyone, and certainly far too original to be an imitator. Nature was lavish in her gifts to him, and as if his fame as a story-teller is less than Cooper's, the debit must be charged against his unfortunate environment.

The later years of Simms were utterly devastated by the unhappy war, in which, as was to be expected, he was a stalwart and uncompromising partisan. His native commonwealth that had long treated him shabbily, sacrificed him in the end to her folly. It was his own fault of course, but how could one warped by the pervasive southern provincialism hope to escape? Scratch a Carolinian of the Calhoun school and you find a Fire Eater. In this respect Simms was not different from the McDuffies and Hamiltons from whom he took his cue—gentlemen whom, because they were politically prominent, he regarded as socially intelligent. That a man of such native powers as Simms should have taken seriously the Charleston politicians—blown up like a pig's bladder after butchering; that he should himself have aspired to become another such bladder—these are sobering facts to remind us that the man of letters is very likely to be a child outside his study walls. What was wrong with Simms that he read the signs of the times so badly? This, that he lived in a world of unreality, of social and economic romanticism, that was forever benumbing his strong instinct for reality. His father-in-law owned seventy slaves; his neighbors and acquaintances owned slaves; all South Carolina gentlemen owned slaves; and in judging this matter of slavery Gilmore Simms went unquestioningly with his little world. He who had drunk of the rich wine of Elizabethan culture came at last to drink himself under the table with his drafts of Charleston Jamaica. The dream of a Greek civilization based on black slavery was discovered in the bottom of the cup of southern romanticism. And Simms emptied his bottle with the rest. Charleston, no doubt, has paid a sufficiently heavy price for her too copious potations, but she can never atone for the undoing of her greatest son—for the foolish intoxication that befuddled the generous mind of Gilmore Simms. The loss is not Charleston's alone; it is a loss to our common American literature. There is food for thought in the words of the epitaph which he composed for himself: "Here lies one who, after a reasonably long life, distinguished chiefly by unceasing labors, has left all his better works undone." Juster words could not have been written, nor more tragic.

PART THREE: THE ROMANCE OF THE WEST

CHAPTER I

NEW WORLDS

I

WHILE Calhoun was instructing the South in the theory of a Greek democracy, other sons of the South were learning, in the new world to which they had removed, the ways of a very different democracy—a democracy native to the frontier and quite unconcerned with Greek ideals. In the Ohio valley was gathering a multitude of rough libertarians who had exchanged the restrictions of the old settlements for the freedom of the new. To these bumptious levelers rulership by established authorities made no appeal. They attached no respect to broadcloth, but preferred to manage their affairs in their own way by appeal to the majority. Taught by experience the worth of certain Jeffersonian principles, they took seriously the doctrine of equality and proposed to put it into practice. They were coonskin apostles of liberty and equality—if not of fraternity—backwoods democrats who by virtue of numbers established in common practice the principle of the sovereignty of the popular will. Springing up naturally on the frontier, the practice of democracy received from it a new validity and became the determining factor in the nationalism that America was creating in the early years of the nineteenth century. That it was a crude and often shoddy democracy, that it never justified its pretentions in the eyes of a critical realism, did not lessen the zeal with which men clung to it or weaken their loyalty. Democracy became the common faith of the West, and in becoming the common faith of the West it was put in the way of becoming the common faith of America.

If the romantic temper is a spontaneous by-product of social change, that temper found in the upheaval attending the western migration a plentiful aliment that had been wanting in the static eighteenth century. In that older world men had been held fast in the grip of the customary and familiar; but in the free West all

137

was new and strange. The crossing of the Appalachian barrier that had long held back the settlements was an adventurous undertaking that fired the imagination. Romantic in spirit and scope, it was meanly picaresque in a thousand unlovely details. Plain men engaged in it, provident and improvident, hard-working and shiftless; heroes had a share in it, but blackguards and outlaws and broken men—the lees and settlings thrown off from the older communities—had a share as well. The world that provided a stage for the courage of Daniel Boone and the fighting qualities of George Rogers Clark bred also the Davy Crocketts and Mike Finks and Col. William Suggses, who discovered there opportunities for the development of less admirable qualities; and it engulfed in its depths a host of nameless adventurers who drifted into the wilderness settlements, drank and quarreled and begot children, suffered from the chills and ague, spread a drab poverty along the frontier, and were put away under ground and forgotten by the more fortunate who salvaged prosperity from the abundant wreckage.

From this crude society emerged the new states with governments designed to serve simple ends. Jealousy for his sovereign right to do as he pleased was the chief concern of the free western voter; as a sovereign citizen he refused to be subject to the creature commonwealth. If governors and legislators and judges got uppish he would throw them out of office and put in others who better understood the rights of free Americans. It was this rude equalitarianism that marked the early stage of western commonwealth building. Naïve Jeffersonians, these frontier citizens had not learned from Hamilton how useful the political state may become to those who know how to control its policies to their particular ends; but that lesson they were soon to learn. The citizens of Georgia received excellent instruction from no less a man than Chief Justice Marshall in the matter of the Yazoo frauds; and as such lessons sank into their minds their political philosophy underwent a silent change. The coonskin individualism that created Jacksonian democracy was gradually undermined by a middle-class individualism that inclined to the Whiggery of Henry Clay. The former was a spontaneous expression of the frontier spirit, the latter a calculating expression of the maturing settlement. The one discovered its native habitat on the backwoods farm, the other in the county seat town. The one was agrarian *laissez faire*, the

other was exploitative paternalistic. The followers of Jackson
wanted the state kept simple and frugal, the followers of Clay
wanted it to engage in ambitious programs of internal improvement; and from these antagonistic principles emerged a bitter feud
between Democracy and Whiggery that in western townships
revived the old alignment of agrarian and Federalist of earlier
times.

In such a contest the principle of Whiggery must eventually
triumph. It was an expression of "the genius of the times."
Economics and psychology were daily arguing in its behalf. From
the first early settlements of the Ohio valley, it must be remembered, circumstances were creating a new middle class that was to
stamp itself indelibly on western life and institutions. The spirit
of speculation had entered the wilderness with the early surveyors.
With its vast resources the Inland Empire offered the first opportunity to exercise the newly won right to exploit the western hinterland, and it was seized upon greedily. Agriculture was still the
common business and land hunger the common passion. The
irruption of the land-hungry hordes upon the fertile Ohio valley, it
will be recalled, synchronized with the speculative debauch that
followed the conclusion of the peace of 1783, and this in turn was a
by-product of the sudden expansion of the new capitalistic finance.
Speculation had suddenly become every man's business, and wild
lands and wild-cat banks, joining fortunes for better or worse,
brought forth a characteristic progeny. The new gospel of progress
found more willing hearers than the old gospel of righteousness.
Every adventurer into the Ohio valley was a potential speculator,
and every settler was eager to sell out to a later comer at an advance. The real estate agent followed close on the footsteps of
Daniel Boone, quick to profit from the explorations. Land was
the staple commodity and such a turnover had never before been
known in America. Every clearing in the woods was speedily
capitalized, and every townsite was reckoned rich in potential
values. The new cities were founded in unearned increment and
prospered with its increase. With European peasants flocking
to the West from their poverty-stricken countries, and the exploited of the East seeking new openings there, it was an unlucky
speculator who could not exchange his paper values for substantial equivalents. Law, religion, education, culture, were pressed
into the service of speculation. How widely the spirit permeated

the West is suggested in the experience of Timothy Flint, frontier
missionary. Writing from Saint Charles, Missouri, in 1818, he
commented somewhat bitterly:

> Religion, when I came here was considered contemptible. The phalanx
> of opposition was in array from one end of the street to the other. Why
> did they invite me here? On speculation. A minister—a church—a
> school—are words to flourish in an advertisement to sell lots. (John
> Ervin Kirkpatrick, *Timothy Flint, etc.*, Appendix B, p. 293.)

From the determining factors, then, of abundant wild lands,
rapid increase in population, and an elastic credit, operating on a
vast scale, came the optimistic, speculative psychology of the new
West. It is the common disease of every period of unstable economics. It had traveled west with every extension of the frontier;
and it became acute in the Ohio valley in the romantic days following the War of 1812. In colonial times before the upheaval of the
Revolution, prices of land and commodities had been stable. The
basic silver currency varied little in quantity or value; coin was
scarce, but the occasional emission of paper money produced little
disturbance, for the reason that the farmer habitually reckoned his
income in the produce of his farm and fireside. But with the un-
settling of exchange values by the wide use of bank notes, prices
at once shifted to a speculative basis. The familiar commodities
ceased to have a fixed use value, and a cash psychology superseded
the traditional commodity value. The old stability was gone.
The familiar domestic economy that functioned primarily in terms
of consumption rather than profit disintegrated under the workings of a paper system and gave place to a speculative economy.

It was this revolution that set apart the new West from the older
traditional America and made it the special repository of the new
middle-class spirit of progress. The change had been long preparing. Writing from Boonesborough in January, 1776, the agent of
the Transylvania Land Company pointed out that the western
country "abounded with land mongers," and that his company had
already issued nine hundred patents.[1] These adventurous spirits
were only pioneers pointing the way for later hordes that after
1815 pushed eagerly onward. "Old America seems to be breaking up, and moving westward," commented a traveler in 1817 as he
watched the long line of Conestoga wagons moving towards Pitts-

[1] See James Hall, *Romance of American History*, Appendix.

burgh; and in the fall of the same year Timothy Flint said of Saint Charles, Missouri, that "there was an average of one hundred people every day coming to the town, or passing to near-by points. Nearly all were poor and not one family in fifty had a Bible" (Kirkpatrick, *Timothy Flint, etc.*, p. 102). "This western fever has seized old and young," remarks a character in Cooper's *Home as Found*, "and it has carried off many active families from our parts of the world. . . . Most of the counties adjoining our own have lost a considerable portion of their population." One reason for this vast exodus from the East is suggested by a recent student who remarks: "A considerable part of the significance of the frontier lies behind the frontier. In one sense, the westward expansion of the American people was a flight from the new industrialism" (Norman Ware, *The Industrial Worker*, p. xx). To these adventurers from the East was added an increasing immigration. During the period from the close of the Revolution to the War of 1812, the annual immigration averaged no more than four or five thousand. In the year 1817 it rose to 22,000, and thereafter an augmenting stream poured into America and filtered westward. They were natural prey to shrewd promoters, and in *Martin Chuzzlewit* Dickens has drawn a picture—not wholly caricature—of what befell some of them. But whatever might be their individual fate, they provided fuel to the fire that was consuming the old agrarianism and clearing the ground for the western middle class.

II

With land as its staple commodity the West naturally interpreted progress in terms of increasing land values; and these in turn were dependent on better markets, better roads, and a freely flowing tide of immigration. In a country of such vast distances internal improvements were an everyday necessity. With every mile that a turnpike was driven into the wilderness new opportunities were opened up. Monies paid for wild land went into the Federal treasury; it was only just, according to the western view, that such monies should return to the West in the form of public improvements, for with such improvements tax values were increased, prices of all commodities rose, and progress was furthered. The Federal government could not fairly leave its offspring to shift for themselves, but must consider itself *in loco parentis* to the rising commonwealths. It was a persuasive argument, appealing alike to farmer and speculator, to town and country, but it played havoc with the older Jeffersonianism. Jefferson thought always in terms of the agrarian producer functioning in a stable economic world; speculation was not in his philosophy; unearned increment was a crop he never calculated on; and in sympathy with an older liberalism he would reduce the state to the narrow rôle of policeman. But the new West, thinking in terms of its immediate needs, desired a broad and benevolent paternalism. It wanted the Federal government to butter its bread regardless of the ultimate cost of the butter.

The complete embodiment of this spirit of paternalistic progress was the master politician of the times, whose dramatic career, beginning as a Jeffersonian and ending as a Hamiltonian, suggests the confusions of a world in transition. Henry Clay was the hero of the new West, the spokesman of the new ambitions. A man of great personal charm, engaging manners, buoyant temperament, exuberant patriotism, and persuasive tongue, he migrated in 1797 at the age of twenty-one from Richmond, Virginia, to Lexington, Kentucky, then a booming county-seat town only twenty-two years removed from the building of its first blockhouse. The population of the state had more than doubled in seven years, and by 1797 it had risen above 180,000. Of this aggressive little world Clay soon became the accredited representative at Washington. He had been brought up under the old domestic economy and carefully tutored in the Jeffersonian philosophy. For four years he had been private secretary to George Wythe, a distinguished Virginian of the older generation, a profound lawyer and teacher, a scholarly political thinker, a humanitarian, and a confirmed agrarian. When Clay left Virginia he carried with him the Jeffersonianism of Wythe; but he was wanting in the trained intellect of his preceptor and his views were inadequately grounded. His subsequent career revealed him as an impressionable nature modifying his convictions with his environment. In Kentucky the spirit of speculative expansion seized him and inoculated his mind with the new gospel of progress. He early convinced himself that government was not doing its full duty unless it helped its citizens to make money, and he persistently pressed on Congress the need of federal aid to develop the West. In 1812 he fell victim to the war psychology, turned jingo, and substituted an ardent patriotism for sober reason. Thereafter he became increasingly nationalistic, demanding a strong army and navy, pleading for a loose construction of the constitution, arguing for paternalism. His Jeffersonianism was quietly put away like a garment out of style. Grossly ignorant of the schools of economic thought, he was an opportunist who shifted from the older domestic economy to the later capitalistic, without comprehending the significance of the change. Unread in history and political theory, he trusted his fluency to get him out of any inconsistencies he might blunder into. In the course of his long career he found himself at different times on both sides of every important question; yet gravitating to the middle-class position, the exponent of exploitation in the name of progress, spokesman of the commercial, financial and manufacturing interests, a new-model Federalist passionately defending the new money economy—a curious ending for one who began as a pupil of George Wythe.

And yet not curious when one considers the ambitions of the world that molded him. Clay was a born politician who rarely came to grips with reality. Devoted to the principles of republican liberty as he found them in the Constitution, he professed to believe that government could be trusted to distribute favors with impartial hand. Personally honest, he never realized how often he allowed himself to become the unconscious tool of powerful economic interests. With his desire to please everybody he was an easy prey for skillful lobbyists. He had been at one time attorney for the Bank, yet he denied vehemently that his defense of the institution had been influenced by such connection. He had become a Hamiltonian without gaining Hamilton's clear understanding of the economic basis of politics. A brilliant opportunist, he was guided by no fixed political principles but tacked with the shifting winds. A brilliant romantic, he was the persuasive prophet of an age that was dreaming of a prosperity that should gather in certain favored reservoirs through the agency of subsidies and taxes, and trickle thence through all the land to water the roots of industry. It was fitting that such a man should be the father of Whiggery, and fitting also that he should stand as the embodiment of the spirit of compromise. One great lesson, at least, he had learned, that greater men too often do not learn, the lesson that republican government rests on good will and that such good will demands a policy of give and take among rival interests. Compromise may be displeasing to earnest souls, but it is implied in any workable system of democratic rule.

Like Calhoun and Webster, Clay was a victim of changing times. If he had lived a generation later, when the middle-class revolution had been accomplished and the principle of capitalism was in undisputed control, he would have achieved a far greater personal success. But capitalism was not yet strong enough to uphold him against rival economies, and he failed of his lifelong ambition to be President. He was broken by the Jacksonian revolution, in spite of the fact that no other American politician has been so loved by a hero-worshiping electorate—and it should be added, has been so lovable.

CHAPTER II

TWO SPOKESMEN OF THE WEST

I

ANDREW JACKSON

Agrarian Liberal

CLAY's pleasant dream of a paternalistic prosperity for America got its first rude awakening from General Jackson and his motley following of western equalitarians and eastern proletarians. Gentlemen were suddenly reminded that the plain people had been overlooked in the distribution of benefits. The waters of prosperity, it would seem, had been trickling somewhat too scantily to them from the great reservoirs where they were impounded; and as they saw the wealth pouring into private ponds through governmental pipe lines, a natural human envy took possession of them. In theory the pipe lines belonged to them, and the impounded waters were to be used for common irrigation; but in practice the mains seemed to conduct only to Lowell industrialists and Philadelphia and New York capitalists, and the waters turned out to be privately owned. As the recognition of this fact came home to the producing mass it provided a rallying point for an anti-monopolist movement and determined the great objective of the Jacksonian attack, the assault on the Bank.

The driving force of the new Democracy was the same class-feeling that had done service a generation before, the will to destroy the aristocratic principle in government. This conscious class-feeling had been strengthened by the spread of the dogma of equalitarianism through the frontier, and this in turn had brought about an extension of manhood suffrage which enfranchised a numerous body of voters who turned against an aristocracy that had long resisted their demands for the vote. The spirit of 1798 was rising afresh, and the re-alignment assumed the form of a democratic-aristocratic struggle, which for the moment obscured the more significant fact of an emerging middle class. The battle seemed to lie between homespun and broadcloth for control of government, and this serves to explain the odium that quickly

145

attached to Jacksonian Democracy in polite circles. In drawing together mechanics and frontiersmen, the new party inevitably became a lower-class instrument, offensive to gentlemen of the old school of politics. The records of the times carry abundant evidence, often amusing, of this aristocratic contempt. In the early forties a girl of seventeen living on a Mississippi plantation, describing Jefferson Davis—whose wife she afterwards became—was surprised at the contrast between his politics and his manners. "Would you believe it," she wrote, "he is refined and cultivated, and yet he is a Democrat!" (*Jefferson Davis, A Memoir by his Wife*, Vol. I, p. 192.)

There were quite evident reasons for this aristocratic contempt. The new Democracy was heavily weighted with what gentlemen were pleased to call the rabble. Fresh Democratic recruits had been gathering since Jefferson molded the first party of protest. Industrialism was creating a city proletariat, and the frontier was producing the coonskin voter; neither as yet possessed any adequate political philosophy, but they needed no philosophy to enlist against the traditional privileges and perquisites of broadcloth. They had had their fill of such rule. The stake-in-society theory was worn threadbare, and other philosophies were preparing. Meanwhile in the person of Old Hickory they saw the visible embodiment of their vague aspirations, and they turned to him with an unquestioning loyalty that nothing could weaken. He was our first great popular leader, our first man of the people. If he aroused a wild enthusiasm in breasts covered by linsey-woolsey, it was because he believed that linsey-woolsey had its stake-in-society equally with broadcloth. He was one of our few Presidents whose heart and sympathy were with the plain people, and who clung to the simple faith that government must deal as justly with the poor as with the rich. Believing so, he could not be turned aside from his course by paid clamor, but with a courage rare in the White House he dared make a frontal attack on the citadel of exploitation in the face of an army of mercenaries.

The dramatic career of Andrew Jackson, so unlike that of Jefferson, which was determined by a speculative temperament and founded on a critical examination of diverse systems of society and politics, was shaped in large measure by prejudice and circumstance. A man of iron will and inflexible purpose, he was almost wholly lacking in political and social philosophy. His conclusions were the reactions of a simple nature of complete integrity, in contact with plain fact. Fundamentally realistic, he cherished few romanticisms. There was no subtlety in his mental processes and this lack kept him free from the temptation to follow devious paths beloved of politicians. He must take the shortest way to his objective, crashing through such obstacles as lay in his path. He was never a bookish man. He was surprisingly ill read, and his grammar and spelling were those of the plain people. He loved horse racing and was a master of profanity; yet in spite of characteristics that link him with Davy Crockett, he possessed an innate dignity and chivalry that set him far above the wag of the canebrakes. He was a born leader whose headlong onslaughts and rash mistakes might imperil the cause but could not shake the confidence of his followers. All who knew a man when they saw one respected Andrew Jackson. Imperious and dictatorial, he knew how to command but not to obey; he took orders from no one, not even his superiors, unless such orders fell in with his own plans. In short General Jackson represented the best which the new West could breed in the way of capable and self-reliant individualism, and the backwoodsmen loved him for the enemies he made, and backed him loudly in his fight against the aristocratic East.

When Jackson settled in Nashville in 1788, at the age of twenty-one, the Cumberland valley had somewhat under five thousand inhabitants scattered a distance of eighty-five miles along the river. The first settlements had been made only nine years before, and Nashville was a frontier post with frontier manners. Into this rough society the young Scotch-Irishman fitted easily. His smattering of the law sufficed to gain him clients and he soon became a local political leader. When he was only twenty-nine he was sent to Philadelphia as the first Congressman from the state of Tennessee, where he came in contact with the "aristocratic Neebobs" of the government and heartily disliked them. The next year he was sent to the Senate, but a single session satisfied him and he resigned to accept a judgeship in the state Supreme Court, which post he held for six years. During these early years he was unconsciously following the path that conducted straight to a middle-class philosophy. He threw himself into speculation, bought and sold land in great blocks, traded in horses and slaves, set up a general store, and was well on the road to wealth when the panic of 1795 caught him unprepared. He lost most of his extensive holdings, including his homestead and many of his slaves, and removed to a six hundred and forty acre tract eight miles from Nashville—the Hermitage—which was to become one of the famous places of America. With this removal his middle-class ambitions fell away and he became a planter with a simple agrarian point of view; and this old-fashioned agrarianism became in later years the determining force in all his political thinking.

He was fifty-eight when he emerged as a potential candidate for the Presidency in 1822, and for years his sole interests, other than those of his plantation, had been military. He was singularly wanting in any formulated political philosophy, and his reëlection to the Senate two years later did little to supply the lack. He had picked up some shreds of the protectionist theory and in a letter written in 1824 he went so far as to declare for a "judicious" protective tariff, basing his view on the grounds of the country's economic unpreparedness at the time of the War of 1812, on the lack of markets for the produce of western farms, and on the desirability of drawing labor from the farm to the factory. But he added a significant passage that reveals the agrarian bias of his mind. To the end of his life he insisted that he was an old Republican of 1798, and this comment of 1824 suffices to connect his later attack on the Bank with Jefferson's attack on Hamilton's fiscal policy.

> Beyond this, I look at the Tariff with an eye to the proper distribution of labor and revenue; and with a view to discharge our national debt. I am one of those who do not believe that a national debt is a national blessing, but rather a curse to a republic; inasmuch as it is calculated to raise around the administration a moneyed aristocracy dangerous to the liberties of the country. (Quoted in Bassett, *Life of Andrew Jackson*, Vol. I, p. 346.)

The tariff was the only question on which he was receptive to Whiggish arguments, and although he never openly repudiated a protectionist policy he soon grew lukewarm in its support. Such other fragments of Whiggery as found accidental lodgment in his mind were swept away in the fierce struggles that marked his years in the White House. During those eight years Jackson found himself, and the man who emerged from the struggle was an agrarian of the old Virginian school. As he came to understand the significance of the principle of exploitation he learned to interpret social

classes in terms of economics. He instinctively hated all aristocrats, extending his dislike to the circle that pretended to social
preëminence in Tennessee, speaking of them contemptuously as
the "aristocrats of Nashville." But in these later years a change in
his vocabulary appeared; his favorite phrases became "the monied
capitalists" and the "hydra of corruption." He had come to associate aristocracy with the control of the economics of society. He
was learning how aristocracies are built up through the instrumen-
tality of the state; and as that lesson sank into his mind his opposition to such class favoritism hardened into adamant. He would
put a stop to such practices, cost what it might. His attack on
the Bank was perhaps the most courageous act in our political
history; he knew how fiercely it would be defended; yet he was
amazed at the number of hornets that issued from the shaken
nest. "Such has been the scenes of corruption in our last congress," he wrote in 1833, "that I loath the corruption of human
nature and long for retirement, and repose on the Hermitage.
But until I can strangle this hydra of corruption, the Bank, I
will not shrink from my duty." And a little later, "I want re-
laxation from business and rest, but where can I get rest; I fear not
on this earth" (Bassett, *Life of Andrew Jackson*, Vol. II, pp. 635,
637).

As his policy unfolded it became clear that Jackson had not
changed with the changing times. He remained to the last the
product of an earlier domestic economy, with an old-fashioned
horror of debt. He was too generous to be frugal, too kind-hearted
to be thrifty, too honest to live above his means. He desired a
simple independence for himself and for his country. He believed
that the government should pay its debt, reduce its revenues, and
live simply. In his austere personal rectitude he exhibited a Puritan conviction of the sacredness of stewardship; he must return to
the common people, who had put their trust in him, an honest
reckoning of that trust. It was not in his nature to betray their
faith. He would have nothing to do with the new theory that
government is an agency to help business. To take profits from
an instrument erected supposedly for the common good was
abhorrent to his old-fashioned views; it was impossible for him to
lend the sanction of his office to particular or special interests;
and when circumstances made the Bank the central vexing problem of his administration, his position was predetermined by every

conviction of his mind. While he was President he would not allow the government to be used for business ends; he would not permit its funds or credit to be turned to private profits; he would not tolerate a money monopoly, no matter how conventionally correct its operations might be proved to be, that challenged the sovereignty of the national government. The twin powers of the purse and sword—to recall Clay's famous phrase that every Whig orator used on the stump—were in Jackson's opinion the ultimate tests of sovereignty; and to turn over the money of the government to private hands for private use, he believed, was as grave an abrogation of sovereign rights as would be the use of the army and navy by private interests for private ends.

In the judgment of many critics Jackson, in his ignorance of the intricacies of capitalistic finance, wantonly destroyed a necessary credit system, thereby bringing a devastating panic on the country. Whether or not that judgment is true is of little importance today. More interesting historically is the fact that in his attitude towards the Bank, as in his attitude towards internal improvements, Jackson returned to the agrarian position of Jefferson and John Taylor, nullifying for a time the victories gained by the middle class during the boom period of nationalism. The more he learned about the methods of capitalistic finance, the more he distrusted it. His prejudices were his strength. He disliked speculation and he could see nothing permanently wise or sound in a speculative economy that put American industry at the mercy of bankers to expand or contract credit. With an old-fashioned love of a stable currency he gave his warm support to the project to return the country to a specie basis. "The great desideratum, in modern times," he said in his message to the twenty-fourth Congress, "is an efficient check upon the power of banks, preventing that excessive issue of paper whence arise those fluctuations in the standard of value which render uncertain the rewards of labor." The establishment of additional mints to provide an adequate coinage of gold or silver became therefore a natural corollary of his attack upon bank currency. It was John Taylor's economics written into the law of the land.

In his attitude towards the state Jackson followed the nationalistic tendencies of the West. He was as patriotic as Clay, and in spite of strong states-rights sympathies he contemptuously rejected Calhoun's theory of nullification. But he had no love for an omnicompetent state. More and more he drifted back to the Jeffersonian position in his conception of the powers and duties of the federal government. Replying to the vote of censure of 1834, he stated his ideal of government in words that would have become Jefferson's first inaugural speech. He had been charged with being ambitious, to which he replied:

> The ambition which leads me on, is an anxious desire and a fixed determination, to return to the people, unimpaired, the sacred trust they have confided to my charge—to heal the wounds of the constitution and preserve it from further violation; to persuade my countrymen, so far as I may, that it is not in a splendid government, supported by powerful monopolies and aristocratical establishments, that they will find happiness, or their liberties protected, but in a plain system, void of pomp—protecting all, and granting favors to none—dispensing its blessings like the dews of heaven, unseen and unfelt, save in the freshness and beauty they contribute to produce. It is such a government that the genius of our people requires—such a one only under which our States may remain for ages to come, united, prosperous, and free. (Benton, *Thirty Years' View*, Vol. I, p. 427.)

The evils entailed on America by the Jacksonian revolution were many, but they cannot properly be charged against Andrew Jackson. They came in spite of him, and they came as a result of the great object lesson in the manipulation of the majority will that his popularity had laid bare. His instincts and the main outline of his policy were Jeffersonian; but neither he nor any other man was strong enough to stop the current of middle-class individualism then running. The American people were wanting in an adequate democratic program suited to the changing times, as they were wanting in desire for a social democracy. And when his capable hands fell from the machine he had created, it was seized by the politicians and used for narrow partisan ends. Yet one far-reaching result survived the movement, the popularization of the name of democracy and the naïve acceptance of the belief that the genius of America was democratic. In choosing a party name the Jacksonians were shrewder politicians and better prophets than the Whigs. For better or worse the American masses, and in particular the nationalistic West, had espoused the principle of democracy, and interpreted it in terms of political equalitarianism —a principle that had inspired a fanatical hatred in the breasts of old Federalists. To gentlemen of that earlier school democracy had meant the right of the propertyless majority to plunder the

minority in the name of the law. The later Whigs did not make
so blundering a mistake. Instead of proclaiming democracy the
mother of all mischiefs, they welcomed it as an effective aid
in vote-getting. Learning their lesson from Jackson, the Whig
politicians outdid him in democratic professions. They had discovered that business has little to fear from a skillfully guided
electorate; that quite the safest way, indeed, to reach into the public purse is to do it in the sacred name of the majority will. Perhaps the rarest bit of irony in American history is the later custodianship of democracy by the middle class, who while perfecting
their tariffs and subsidies, legislating from the bench, exploiting
the state and outlawing all political theories but their own, denounce all class consciousness as unpatriotic and all agrarian or
proletarian programs as undemocratic. But it was no fault of
Andrew Jackson if the final outcome of the great movement of
Jacksonian democracy was so untoward; it was rather the fault
of the times that were not ripe for democracy.

II

LINCOLN

Free-Soil Liberal

The equalitarian West that bred Andrew Jackson bred Lincoln
also, a man with the same homespun mind, the same sterling
integrity of nature, the same instinctive democracy, but shaped
by an environment in which the new philosophy of progress had
displaced the older agrarianism. The road of middle-class ideals
he traveled further than Jackson, but in the end he also turned
back to pick up once more the democratic faith then being repudiated by the proponents of slavery, north as well as south. Long an
ardent Whig of the Clay school, and thoroughly indoctrinated in a
paternalistic nationalism, he was brought, as every thoughtful
American of the times was brought, to weigh the program of
slave imperialism in the scales with the Declaration of Independence. The doctrines of that great document lay before every
man's feet in those uncertain days, to get over as one could. They
could not easily be evaded or got round; they must be dealt with.
Rufus Choate, representing Boston Toryism, had come upon them
and dismissed them as "glittering and sounding generalities."
Calhoun, representing southern imperialism, had come upon them

and essayed to destroy them by a critical realism. Lincoln, embodying the spontaneous liberalism of the West, came upon them and paused to take his bearings afresh. He could neither wave them aside nor destroy them. The deep-rooted equalitarianism of his simple social philosophy found in them an eloquent pronouncement of its democratic faith, that set him upon considering how such doctrine might be squared with the reality of slavery. The agrarianism of John Taylor and the Whiggery of Henry Clay could tell him nothing about that; he must seek elsewhere; and the solution he found in an amalgamation of equalitarianism and free-soilism, in an adaptation of western Whiggery to Jeffersonian principles.

Whatever party name he might call himself by, in his love of justice and his warm humanity Lincoln was essentially Jeffersonian. He respected property rights, but other rights he believed more sacred. And as he watched the emergence in the South of the ideal of a Greek democracy, as he considered how the party of Jackson had become the party of Calhoun and Douglas, bent solely on strengthening and spreading the institution of slavery, his equalitarianism took alarm. He could not sit quiet while the principles of the Declaration of Independence were being openly flouted; he must speak out; he must arouse the idealism of the people to deal with the iconoclasts. In an important pronouncement written in 1859, he set the problem before them thus:

Remembering . . . that the Jefferson party was formed upon its supposed superior devotion to the personal rights of men, holding the rights of property to be secondary only, and greatly inferior . . . it will be . . . interesting to note how completely the two [parties] have changed hands as to the principles upon which they were originally supposed to be divided. The Democracy of today hold the liberty of one man to be absolutely nothing, when in conflict with another's right of property; Republicans, on the contrary, are for both the man and the dollar, but in case of conflict the man before the dollar. . . . But, soberly, it is now no child's play to save the principles of Jefferson from total overthrow in this nation. . . . The principles of Jefferson are the principles and axioms of free society. And yet they are denied and evaded, with no small show of success. One dashingly calls them "glittering generalities." Another bluntly calls them "self-evident lies!" And others insidiously argue that they apply to "superior races." These expressions, differing in form, are identical in object and effect—the supplanting the principles of free government, and restoring those of classification, caste, and legitimacy. . . . They are the vanguard, the miners and sappers of returning despotism. We must repulse them, or they will subjugate us. (Letter to H. L. Prince and Others, April 6, 1859, in *Works*, Vol. V, pp. 125–126.)

Two conceptions were here competing in Lincoln's mind, the older equalitarianism that sprang from French humanitarianism and the newer economics that came from English *laissez faire;* and the attempt to reconcile them suggests how far he had traveled along the path of western Whiggery. With the spirit of enterprise he had no complaint; the ideal of progress was associated in his mind with a fluid economics that permitted the capable to rise through skillful exploitation. He had no love for the stable economics of the eighteenth century that Jackson preferred; the profit motive, functioning freely, he regarded as the legitimate driving force of society; but he was concerned that competition should be open to all on equal terms. As he watched the transition from an agrarian to an industrial order, he found himself more in sympathy with the new than the old. Accepting the principle of exploitation he came to the position of the little capitalist who believed that in America capitalism could be democratized by the simple method of keeping the opportunities for exploitation open to every citizen. It was common view of western Whiggery, and in so far Lincoln remained a Whig, content with a system which he accepted as peculiarly suited to the genius of the American people. In a late speech he summed it up thus:

What is the true condition of the laborer? I take it that it is best to leave each man free to acquire property as fast as he can. Some will get wealthy. I don't believe in a law to prevent a man from getting rich; it would do more harm than good. So while we don't propose any war upon capital, we do wish to allow the humblest man an equal chance to get rich with anybody else. When one starts poor, as most do in the race of life, free society is such that he knows he can better his condition; he knows that there is no fixed condition of labor for his whole life. . . . I want every man to have a chance—and I believe a black man is entitled to it—in which he can better his condition—when he may look forward and hope to be a hired laborer this year and the next, work for himself afterwards, and finally to hire men to work for him. That is the true system. (Speech at New Haven, March 6, 1860, in *Works*, Vol. V, pp. 360–361.)

But as a western man Lincoln was far more concerned over the application of *laissez faire* to the problem of western lands, and as he contemplated the practical workings of "squatter sovereignty" he learned how the free functioning of *laissez faire* may be interfered with by economic imperialisms. That lesson determined his final stand. The virgin prairies beyond the Mississippi were coveted equally by northern and southern exploiters; and who should finally possess them, whether the small freeholder or the slave-master, was a question that could not be put off forever. None knew this better than the small farmers who were already staking out homesteads there. If Congress yielded to the pro-slavery demands their economic future would be endangered. It was the free-soil West that sent the first anti-slavery men to Washington and provided the backbone of the new party. Not the respectable West, but the plain people, Whig as well as Democrat. "Much of the plain old Democracy is with us," said Lincoln in 1858, "while nearly all the old exclusive silk-stocking Whiggery is against us. I don't mean nearly all the old Whig party, but nearly all of the nice exclusive sort" (Letter to A. C. Henry, in *Works*, Vol. V, p. 95). It was no humanitarian regard for the rights of the negro that welded them into a militant party. Racially and economically the free-soiler was hostile to the black, whether slave or free. The Topeka constitution adopted by the Kansas free-soilers barred all negroes from the new state; Kansas was to be a white man's country. The free labor of the West wanted no competition with an alien race, and was prepared to fight both the white master and free black for exclusive possession of the national domain. There were few John Browns among these western homesteaders—uncompromising idealists who rebelled at the injustice done the negro. The free-soiler hated slavery because it threatened his immediate interests; nevertheless as the great struggle developed, the moral injustice of slavery was thrust to the fore and imparted a humanitarian motive to the free-soil argument. This humanitarian motive Lincoln seized upon, wedded it to the ideal of national union, and thus doubly armed went forth to the fight.

To amalgamate idealism and economics is no easy task. "Public opinion," he said in a speech at Hartford, "is founded, to a great extent, on a property basis." But it is not the sole basis. The ideal of justice comes in to upset all purely economic calculations. "The property basis will have its weight. The love of property and a consciousness of right and wrong have conflicting places in our organization, which often make a man's course seem crooked, his conduct a riddle" (*Works*, Vol. V, p. 330). Beyond question it was this recognition of the perennial conflict between economics and justice, between realism and idealism, that explains the hes-

itancies and harassing doubts that marked Lincoln's development.
To reconcile the principle of exploitation with the Declaration of
Independence it was necessary to stick like a flea to *laissez faire*—
to eliminate slave labor and accept only free labor. Lincoln was
a slow man and cautious, and he pulled himself forward to such a
position by main force. He was not a rare intellect like Thoreau,
to think swiftly to a conclusion and abide the consequences. He
was a political leader rather than an intellectual, and he could advance only a little ahead of the slow-moving mass he sought to
draw after him. A hundred invisible ties held him back—his
belief in the rights of local democracies, his respect for law and
order, his devotion to the Constitution, his recognition of property
interests in the slave, his understanding of the complexity of the
problem, with the entire economy of the South resting on a slave
basis. Here were difficulties enough to trouble an honest mind.
His practical sense, which is only another name for political realism,
restrained his idealism and made him of necessity an opportunist,
willing to yield much if he might save the Union. A simple, tolerant,
easy-going man, he was at bottom a realist who had come to understand what may be considered the greatest truth in political
science, namely, that an enduring state must rest on willing allegiance. Force cannot compel loyalty; authority may put down
revolt but it cannot destroy the seeds of discontent; for that only
the sovereignty of good will is competent, and in free states the
sovereignty of good will must rest upon compromise. Lincoln was a
better democrat than Jackson, for he would rather persuade than
drive. If Hamilton embodied the aristocratic principle of coercive
government, Lincoln embodied the democratic principle of give
and take, that prefers compromise to bayonets. With a cause resting on the common good will it might safely be trusted to muddle
through.

Slowly pushed forward by his cautious realism, Lincoln was
forty-nine before he reached the "divided house" position of the
Douglas debates, that was to entail such consequences. It was a
bold pronouncement to address to a generation desperately engaged
in erecting sham defenses against reality, in fleeing from the truth
that cried aloud to be heard. But he would not let men stop their
ears longer; the truth must be spoken to their understanding.

In my opinion [he said] agitation will not cease until a crisis shall have
been reached and passed. "A house divided against itself cannot stand."

I believe this government cannot endure permanently half slave and half free. I do not expect the Union to be dissolved—I do not expect the house to fall—but I do expect it will cease to be divided. It will become all one thing, or all the other. Either the opponents of slavery will arrest the further spread of it, and place it where the public mind shall rest in the belief that it is in the course of ultimate extinction; or its advocates will push it forward till it shall become alike lawful in all the States, old as well as new, North as well as South. (Speech at Springfield, June 16, 1858.)

The situation could not have been put more neatly. It was an appeal of honest realism to put away all shoddy romanticisms, all mean evasions, and to face the situation fairly; and it cut across the murky clouds like a flash of lightning. Thenceforth there could be no longer a conspiracy of silence; the problem of slavery had been brought home to the common mind and common conscience, the question of its relation to our national unity and national well-being had been brought out into the realm of homely discussion. It is the democratic way, and as an honest democrat, Lincoln stripped away all the protective coloring of lies that politicians use and appealed to the honesty of plain men. The same method he applied to the Dred Scott decision. He proposed to bring to the bar of the majority opinion the stale legal romanticisms of the Supreme Court. He refused to accept the divine right of the courts to rulership, he denied the sovereignty of the judiciary, and proposed to make a political issue of the matter. He would have it settled in town-meetings and at the polls, by the plain people, and not by lawyers and judges. It was a reversion to Jeffersonian principles, to the simple democratic creed that fundamentals of public policy must be determined by the people themselves.

Lincoln had thought his way slowly to the "divided house" position, but he could not pause there. Those were hurrying times, and the liberalism of yesterday was inadequate for the liberalism of today. A weak man or a time-server would have gone upon the rocks, and a man of unyielding policy must have broken; to be certain of one's conclusions was possible only to one who saw less than the whole. Patience and an open mind alone could be relied on, an intelligent opportunism alone would serve during the months the country was fiercely debating with itself; and the heart-breaking hesitation of Lincoln, the troublesome doubts and perplexed questionings, reveal as nothing else could the simple integrity of his nature. He must go forward, but he must carry the people with him, the North as a whole, the border states if possible, even the rebellious South if charity might suffice. Though in arms, they were Americans, and their hearts must be brought to willing allegiance; how otherwise could a democratic people emerge from the bitterness of civil war? He was not made for a dictator, and blood and iron he accounted poor cement to mend the sundered democracies. He trusted the better impulses of men to prevail in the end, because with Jefferson he believed in the essential justice of the plain people. In this faith he exemplified his democracy. Not a great political thinker, he was a great leader because he never forgot that he was one with those he led.

The slow unfolding of Lincoln's mind is sufficiently revealed in the changing quality of his speeches. He was rarely eloquent—never after the ornate fashion of the time; and the bits of Hebraic poetry that have come to be associated with his name are singularly few and belong to the last years of his life. His usual style was plain homespun, clear and convincing, but bare of imagery and lacking distinction of phrase. The thought seems to break into speech hesitatingly, in the way of a man visibly seeking to adapt his words to his meaning. Matter he judged to be of greater significance than manner. Few men who have risen to enduring eloquence have been so little indebted to rhetoric. Very likely his plainness of style was the result of deliberate restraint, in keeping with the simplicity of his nature. When he let himself go he discovered a well of poetry in his heart. When he chose he could even play the rhetorician. In those rare moments when he put caution behind him, his words fell into a stately rhythm that suggests the orator. Witness such a passage as this:

In those days our Declaration of Independence was held sacred by all, and thought to include all; but now, to aid in making the bondage of the negro universal and eternal, it is assailed and sneered at and construed, and hawked at and torn, till, if its framers could rise from their graves, they could not at all recognize it. All the powers of earth seem rapidly combining against him. Mammon is after him, ambition follows, philosophy follows, and the theology of the day is fast joining the cry. They have him in his prison-house; they have searched his person, and left no prying instrument with him. One after another they have closed the heavy iron doors upon him; and now they have him, as it were, bolted in with a lock of a hundred keys, which can never be unlocked without the concurrence of every key—the keys in the hands of a hundred different men, and they scattered to a hundred different and distant places; and they stand musing as to what invention, in all the dominions of mind and matter, can be produced to make the impossibility of his escape more complete than it is. (Speech at Springfield, June 27, 1857, in *Works*, Vol. II, pp. 327–328.)

But he did not often let himself go. As one reads his speeches one feels that an English diffidence held him back—this and the strong prose of his environment. Like a true Anglo-Saxon he was reluctant to speak out, afraid to let his emotions seize upon his speech. Only at the last did that diffidence yield to complete unconsciousness. The Gettysburg speech and the Second Inaugural are marked by the sincerity and self-effacement that ennobled the words of John Brown in the Virginia court-room—it is the eloquence which rises from the heart when life has been felt in its tragic reality, an eloquence that Webster could not rise to. Such words come only to those who have been purified by fire; they are the distillation of bitter experience. But the mass of his speeches are in quite another manner—that of the simple, everyday world that bred him. He had none of the itch of publicity that afflicts the second-rate mind. Webster was a magnificent poseur; Edward Everett repeated the same academic oration a hundred times; but Lincoln was too modest to pose and too honest to turn parrot and speak by rote. He was a man who loved to talk with his neighbors in homely metaphor, and it was then that his thought clothed itself in whimsical humor. He did not wear his heart on his sleeve, but like Mark Twain he let it slip out in a witticism.

Even more than Washington has Lincoln suffered at the hands of the myth makers. Of late years he has come to be looked upon too often as the invaluable asset of the political party that he honored in its founding, and too rarely as the embodiment of the kindly, liberal soul of our native democracy in the simpler days of a fluid economics and an unsophisticated equalitarianism. With his instinctive kindliness, his abiding faith in the good will of men, his dislike of coercion, his readiness to compromise, he may seem old-fashioned to a generation that has grown intolerant—but that is a reflection on our own times rather than on Lincoln. The real Lincoln can grow old-fashioned no more than Jefferson. As he went back in a day of sordid imperialisms to the earlier liberalism of the great Virginian, seeking to rescue the idealism of the Declaration of Independence from the desecration of the market place where it was openly flouted, so in a day of vaster imperialisms and greater complexity we may take counsel of his humanitarianism, his open-mindedness, his trust in tolerance and good will, his democratic faith that held firm in spite of disappointment. The market place is mighty now as it was then, and liberalism finds as few friends there; but when did its gods become immortal?

CHAPTER III

THE FRONTIER IN LETTERS

WHEN the West began to appear in literature in the late twenties and early thirties, it was the Ohio valley that became the beneficiary of the new interest, and over the vast region through which flowed the Beautiful River—as far as the Mississippi and beyond—was thrown the romance of the settlement. It was a beguiling theme with its background of dark forests and bloody Indian fights, with its venturesome flatboats that drifted with the current, its picturesque rivermen, "half horse, half alligator," who towed their heavy crafts upstream, its rude miscellany of settlers who intrusted their families and goods and cattle to great rafts and set forth hopefully on waters that were to bear them presumably to the Promised Land—a theme to appeal to imaginations easily stirred to romance. There was a darker side to be sure; wrecks in plenty littered the shores, wrecks of fortune and character and life; outlaws and blackguards thronged the river and preyed on the adventurers; but in spite of such misadventures the great movement was invested with dramatic interest, and the Ohio valley became the particular repository of the romance of the frontier, a monopoly which later times never despoiled it of and which only the Golden Coast of California ever remotely rivaled. It was fortunate in that its early history was recorded by a romanticizing generation that wove its myths about the wilderness scouts, that delighted in the picturesque talk of river boatmen and discovered themes for epics in the founding of new commonwealths.

From the first, therefore, the literature of the new West fell naturally into the romantic note. The early writers who essayed to deal with frontier materials were eastern men who proposed to exploit the romance of the Inland Empire as frankly as their fellow adventurers were exploiting the material resources. Gradually in their work two main conceptions crystallized, which came to overshadow all lesser themes: one localized itself in Kentucky and took form in the poetic conception of the Dark and Bloody ground; the other associated itself first with the rivermen but quickly diffused its spirit through the backwoods and took form in the conception of western humor. The first was a heritage from the early days when the Indian tribes fought for their ancient hunting grounds and fell upon the isolated stations with knife and tomahawk; the second grew up with a later generation that had penetrated far into the wilderness, where, stimulated by much whisky, its rough vigor found issue in exaggerated boasting. Each created its legendary hero about whom popular imagination wove its myths: the figure of Daniel Boone came to symbolize the heroic qualities of a race of scouts and backwoodsmen who matched their wits in woodcraft with the Indians and proved the quality of their Kentucky rifles in many a brush with the warriors; and the figure of Davy Crockett came to embody in the popular mind the loquacious eccentricities and exaggerated wit that were already passing into a literary tradition. Many hands contributed to the common work: writers as different as James Kirke Paulding with his *Westward Ho!*, Robert Montgomery Bird with his *Nick of the Woods*, Nathaniel Beverley Tucker with his *George Balcomb*, Albert Pike with his *Prose Sketches and Poems*, Augustus Longstreet with his *Georgia Scenes*, and Joseph G. Baldwin with his *Flush Times of Alabama and Mississippi*—to name only a few. From such diverse elements was created the new literature of the West that was contemporary with the rise of Jacksonian democracy and that gave wide currency to certain romantic conceptions.

I

THE ROMANTIC FRONTIER

Of this very considerable group of writers the two who earliest wrote from immediate first-hand knowledge of frontier life were Timothy Flint, Harvard graduate and missionary, and Judge James Hall, Pennsylvania lawyer, both of whom spent a considerable portion of their mature lives in the West. Of Timothy Flint's restless wanderings and periodic settlements, at Saint Charles, Missouri, at New Orleans, at Alexandria on the Red River in Louisiana, at Cincinnati, with frequent returns to his native Massachusetts and a short editorial experience in New York City, it is impossible to speak in detail; they suggest, however, the breadth and intimacy of his knowledge of the West got from twenty-five years' experience there from 1815 to his death in 1840. Few men traveled so widely through the frontier, or carried with them such keenly observant eyes. He wrote much, conducted for several years a literary magazine in Cincinnati, was for a short time editor of *The Knickerbocker Magazine* on the withdrawal of Charles Fenno Hoffman, and established a considerable reputation as a representative of western letters. Much of his work was frankly casual, but his *Recollections of the Last Ten Years, Passed in Occasional Residencies and Journeyings in the Valley of the Mississippi,* published in 1826, and his four novels published between 1826 and 1830, make up the first important contribution to the new literature of the West.

In temperament Timothy Flint seems to have been something of a realist. In his daily life he was frankly outspoken and critical, often to his own hurt, and some of the many troubles he met with in his honest preaching to frontier heathen, resulted from this plain speaking. He refused to measure life and conduct by the crude western standards, and the enmities resulting from such refusal brought about a rupture with the home society that had supported his missionary undertaking. It was this intellectual honesty that filled his *Recollections* with an invaluable body of observation and criticism, and constituted it an important source-book for later historians. Paulding early made use of it writing his *Westward Ho!*—published in 1832—and in his introduction, after paying tribute to Flint's "picturesque description," he went on to say that the work "has not met its deserts, and he should be highly gratified if this passing notice served in any way to call public attention to its interesting details." Unfortunately the occasional realism of the *Recollections* gave place in his novels to romance saturated with sentiment and heavily coated with moralizing. With a fund of exact information at his disposal he chose to turn away from reality and project his stories into regions he had visited only in imagination. *Francis Berrian, or the Mexican Patriot,* deals with a Southwest far beyond his extremest journeyings; *The Life and Adventures of Arthur Clenning* is a romanticized version of Robinson Crusoe; and *The Shoshonee Valley* is a romance conceived out of tales told him by far western travelers, woven into an extravagantly romantic plot. The only one of his tales that makes use of familiar settings is *George Mason, the Young Backwoodsman; or "Don't Give up the Ship,"* in which he put some of the materials gathered in his journeyings up and down the Mississippi, but sentimentalized and moralized out of all realism. It is a pity that Flint should have fallen in with the extremest mode of the times, for in many essential respects he was the best qualified man of the West to write an honest account of a world just taking form.

The literary reputation of Timothy Flint soon came to be overshadowed by that of Judge Hall. "Among writers of short narratives, the most characteristically Western fiction of the time," remarks a recent student, "James Hall was clearly preëminent; and he became the central figure in a kind of school of experimenters in the materials of frontier life" (Ralph Leslie Rusk, *The Literature of the Middle Western Frontier*, Vol. I, p. 274). In the early twenties he had ridden the circuit in Illinois as a very young lawyer, when the settlements were scattered thinly through the southern portion of the state. At Vandalia he started the *Illinois Monthly Magazine*, which survived for two years, when he removed to Cincinnati and established *The Western Monthly Magazine*, which in the four years from 1832 to 1836 became one of the "most important of the pioneer period." "The purpose," says the student above quoted, "was not so much to introduce the East to the West as to make the West conscious of itself" (Rusk, *ibid.*, Vol. I, p. 173). To this end Hall was writing and publishing short tales and descriptions, and he had already collected a miscellany of prose and verse by several hands which he issued as an annual, *The Western Souvenir, a Christmas and New Year's Gift for 1829*. Thus launched on a literary career, he wrote in the next twenty years a very considerable amount, including tales, sketches of manners, history and casual comment.

His best-known story is probably *Harpe's Head*, which he later incorporated with other tales in a volume entitled *Legends of the West: Sketches Illustrative of the Habits, Occupations, Privations, Adventures and Sports of the Pioneers of the West*, and published in 1832. The work proved popular and passed through half a dozen editions. Sketchy and loose in construction, it belongs to the school that hovered between the essay and the romance, delighting in the picturesque, exuding sentiment, and going out of its way to exploit the pleasantly horrible. It is a mingling of Virginia chivalry and frontier bravery, woven about a central plot of a daughter of a Virginia house who removes to Kentucky under tragic circumstances, is abducted by a roving band of Indians, and subsequently rescued. Additional romantic interest is sought in the melodramatic deeds of the title hero—a well-known border ruffian with an insatiable blood-lust who murders his unsuspecting victims wherever he comes upon them—and in the curious exploits in rattlesnake killing of Hark Short, a waif from the Carolina swamps who lives like a fox in his den. The interest of the story today lies in the pleasantly idealized descriptions of such scenes as the barbecue and the camp meeting, rather than in the portrayal of backwoods characters. Although Hall frequently professed his devotion to realism, there is little evidence of it; occasional figures like Pete Featherton, whose rifle had been bewitched, and occasional indulgence in a conventionalized backwoods dialect, serve only to heighten the somewhat gaudy romance of the whole. Yet even such timid ventures brought on his head criticism from a Cincinnati editor "for tiring the reader with vulgar backwoods expressions" (Rusk, *ibid.*, Vol. I, p. 282).

That Hall's interest in backwoods eccentricities of speech and manner suffered a heavy handicap from the romantic taste of his readers may easily be believed. Matter excluded from his tales he sometimes put into his introductions. Thus in the third edition of *Harpe's Head* he analyzed at some length certain characteristics of the crude pioneers who were creating the psychology of the West—their fondness for drinking, betting, horse-trading, stump-speaking, swearing. Particularly it is the exuberance of their picturesque language that he emphasized, an exuberance that was already becoming a literary tradition and that flowered in the cento of western folk ways that were gathered into the Davy Crockett myth. A single passage will suffice to suggest some of the elements from which Davy was created:

Though usually taciturn in the presence of strangers, [the frontiersman] is communicative to his friend or guest, has often strong colloquial powers, with quaint, singular, figurative, and even eloquent forms of expression. His language, which is commonly brief, sententious, and abrupt, becomes, when excited by the interest of the subject or by passion, highly expletive, and redundant with exaggerated forms and figures of comparison. When he swears—and he is probably not more given to this exceedingly vulgar vice than other men—but when he does swear in earnest, his philology becomes concentrated, and explodes with an appalling energy, which would have astonished even the celebrated army in Flanders. (*Ibid.*, Introduction, p. xii.)

In his last collection, *The Wilderness and the War Path*, published in 1846 and including some earlier tales, Hall contributed little that was new. There is the same heavy romance with touches of realism, and by way of reply to Bird's interpretation of the Indian character he exploits the romantic qualities of the red man; but his failures are commoner than his successes, and his work as a whole must be regarded as a sacrifice to the bad taste of his generation. From this judgment, perhaps, should be excepted his *Romance of American History*, which is still pleasantly readable.

II
THE REALISTIC FRONTIER

Far more vital than these literary tales with their heavy coating of romance are the few realistic sketches—only too rare in those exuberant days of the high-flown—that preserve the authentic ways of backwoods life in their rude vernacular. Of such sketches those that most faithfully reveal the impress of the frontier, preserving down to the present the note of verisimilitude, are *Georgia Scenes* by Augustus B. Longstreet, and the *Autobiography of Davy Crockett*, to which may be added, perhaps, Joseph G. Baldwin's *Flush Times of Alabama and Mississippi*.

1

AUGUSTUS LONGSTREET
The Georgia Frontier

For some reason no glamour has ever gathered about the Georgia frontier. It may be that fate conspired against it in bestowing no idealizing historian to throw a romantic haze over life in the pine woods. Or perhaps it was the Georgians themselves who did the commonwealth an evil turn. As a matter of sober fact what could even romance do with the raw materials that went to the making of this crude southern Yankee state? How could the most confirmed romantic discover rare graces in the indigenous Cracker, or weave poetry about the ubiquitous peddler with his pack of Yankee notions? Any honest historian could hardly avoid taking into account the ungainly throng that attended a gander pulling, or depict Ransy Sniffle as other than a pallid, pot-bellied, clay-eating grotesque. Crude, uncouth, drab, with primitive passions and unlovely manners, Georgia offered scanty materials for the most ardent eulogist. Frontier life there ran a petty round between fist fights and horse races, between politics and religion. These were the staples of everyday existence, as necessary to the natural man as whisky and salt pork; and the honest Georgian preferred his whisky straight and his politics and religion red-hot.   The Jeffersonian hated the Federalist vindictively; and Presbyterian, Baptist, and Methodist regarded each other malignantly, convinced that the devil was stoking his fires for the lost neighbor who persisted in sitting under the wrong preaching.   Denominationalism on the Georgia frontier was as harsh and unforgiving as political partisanship.   Alexander H. Stephens believed that the plain people of Georgia were the most democratic on the face of the earth, and the kindliest; yet the pugnacious little democrat was himself nearly butchered by a democratic neighbor.   In depicting such a society realism was the only honest method; but to make it palatable it must be well seasoned with humor.   If it were garnished with moralizing, so much the better.   There must be no subtleties in the treatment, no literary touches.   The humor must be in the backwoods vernacular, and the preaching open and aboveboard—frank pulpit-thumping lessons to awaken the surliest sinner.

For such business Gus Longstreet was ideally fitted.   A true child of the Georgia border, he never quite outgrew his early environment.   Born in Augusta in 1790 of New Jersey parents, Holland Dutch but with a large admixture of English blood,[1] he came of plain stock.   A driving, robust, energetic fellow, never squeamish, with a ready wit, he was at home amongst the plain people, the greatest wag in every gathering.   He could knock a man down or shoot out a squirrel's eye with any champion of them all; he could enter into a dance or a revival meeting with equal ardor, or take the stump against a seasoned campaigner.   A fellow must be simple-minded who would expect to get the best of him in swapping horses, or in the way of a practical joke.   It came hard for so vigorous a plebeian to settle down as a substantial citizen, and the dignified titles that he gathered in the course of a long and prosperous career—judge, doctor of laws, doctor of divinity— fitted him somewhat incongruously.   On the whole one prefers the plain Gus Longstreet to Judge Longstreet, but his neighbors, who thought they knew a man when they saw one, thrust his titles upon him.   Besides he had gone to college and was thereby lifted to a place of distinction which he could not avoid.   The process of

[1] The family name of Langestraet was given an English form by his grandfather.

scraping off the bark of the frontier followed orthodox southern lines. A few years' schooling at Dr. Moses Waddell's celebrated Academy, where at different times Calhoun, Crawford, McDuffie, Petigru and Legaré prepared for college, and two years at Yale, provided him with a stock of rusty Latin to suffice a college president; and a winter or two at the law school in Litchfield, Connecticut, following Calhoun's high example, furnished him with enough Blackstone to meet the demands of Georgia law courts. Thus provided intellectually, he went forth boldly to cope with the Georgia world as he found it.

It was a plebeian world that approved his plebeian qualities. There was nothing of the southern patrician in Gus Longstreet, nothing of the ascetic Puritan that marked so deeply men like Calhoun, Legaré, and the Grimkés. In his strong instinct of acquisitiveness, his canny thrift that never failed to seize advantage by the forelock, his desire to get on in the world while serving God, he was a Georgia Yankee, with an emotional religion that took comfort in discovering that God was always on his side of any controversy. Yankee also was his knack of doing many things well enough to impress his less capable neighbors. He was a frontier jack-of-all-trades, passing easily from one profession to another, lawyer, newspaper editor, writer, minister, politician, teacher, and between times busying himself with all sorts of odd jobs, doing everything readily and nothing thoroughly well. A good talker, his chief interests were politics, religion, and money-making. He wrote much in careless haste, apologizing always for the lack of finish; but except for the sketches which were gathered under the title of *Georgia Scenes*, he produced nothing that needs to be remembered. At the age of forty-eight he quitted the law for the Methodist ministry, proved to be a mediocre preacher, and was soon given the berth of president of Emory College, a denominational school then recently established at Oxford, for which his literary reputation and his reputed scholarship seemed to fit him. Later he was president for a few months of Centenary College, Louisiana, but found the place uncongenial, resigned, and was chosen president of the University of Mississippi, where he served seven years and made full use of the opportunity to speculate in real estate. At the age of sixty-six he was made president of the University of South Carolina, where he ruled patriarchally till the school was closed by the war.

How great a man he was judged to be by his fellow Georgians is hard for us to realize today. Throughout his later years he was regarded by his friends as the brightest ornament of Georgia society, a Christian gentleman who was a model to southern youth, a scholar who had brought honor to the commonwealth, an author who had silenced the reproach that the state had produced no literature. Yet it must be confessed that the Judge shrinks in compass when taken out of his native environment. Beside John P. Kennedy or Hugh Legaré, he lacks distinction either of mind or manner; compared with Gilmore Simms he is only an amateur in letters. His latest biographer [2] has sifted a mass of material to prove the solid and eminent worth of the man; yet no impression of intellectual vigor emerges from the analysis; one must take it on the authority of somewhat incompetent witnesses. The figure that emerges from the clutter of contemporary estimate is that of a capable, expansive, middle-class soul, disputatious in the lordly southern manner, genially domineering, magnificently superior to logic, given to erecting an imposing structure of convictions on the slightest of foundations, impatient of contradiction and inclined to lose his temper when the argument went against him— a witty, agreeable gentleman, at home amongst mediocre preachers, and an oracle to admiring friends. He was on terms of intimacy with not a single first-class mind. He had no intellectual curiosity and was incapable of rigorous intellectual processes. Yet good fortune had marked him for her own. A small investment in letters, made at odd moments between law cases and farming operations, returned him such dividends in the way of contemporary fame that for forty years thereafter he lived in the sunshine of a literary reputation. No other American, unless it were William Wirt, ever drew such ample revenues of popular praise from a casual investment, and certainly none ever expanded with greater self-satisfaction. To the end of his life he was the much-sought-after author of *Georgia Scenes*, and the most ambitious southern magazines were glad to publish his frequent effusions; in all of which the Judge delighted, for he was a simple soul and accounted himself an apostle of southern culture, a mentor of southern taste, and he loved to see his name in print.

As a man close to the people Longstreet reflected the current Georgia views on politics. He was an idolatrous admirer of

[2] John Donald Wade, *Augustus Baldwin Longstreet*.

Calhoun and George McDuffie. The former he rated "above William Pitt, or any other premier who ever lived before or since his day" (Wade, *Augustus Baldwin Longstreet*, p. 124) and the latter he regarded as "hardly inferior to him in anything." Calhoun's innate Hebraisms, so deeply imbued with a patriarchal spirit, fitted to a nicety his own Hebraized conception of a Jeffersonian order. Writing of Calhoun, in after years, Longstreet remarked with evident approval:

> I believe that he regarded the government of the children of Israel in the wilderness, the most perfect that ever existed on earth. Be that as it may, he called my attention to it more than once as exactly the government ours ought to be, or was intended to be. "There," said he, "each tribe had its place on the march and in the camp, each managed its own concerns in its own way, neither interfered in the slightest degree, with the private affairs of another, nor did their common head interfere with any of them in any matters, save such as were of equal interest to all, but unmanageable by them as separate and distinct communities." (*Ibid.*, p. 60.)

The background of his political thought was Jeffersonian agrarian. He was always a countryman at heart, and his dearest interests were agricultural. But he seems to have been quite unread in political theory, and probably had never heard of John Taylor's economic principles. Suffering from an incurable political itch, he was one of the earliest and most ardent of states-rights advocates. He went for Nullification before either Calhoun or McDuffie had espoused it; and he followed his premises through to the logical end of secession. But with the growth of northern Abolitionism his Jeffersonianism began to disintegrate. Garrison's appeal to equalitarianism and the rights of man aroused all his southern prejudices. A philosophy that could be turned against the sacred institution was no philosophy for a southern gentleman, and like Calhoun he repudiated the whole French liberal philosophy that he had imbibed in his youth. He even went so far as to play with Calhoun's doctrine of economic representation. Writing to President Lamar, of Texas, in the late thirties, he said, "A government should have a legislative assemblage to represent each of its large economic interests, one, say, agricultural, one manufacturing, one commercial. No bill not acceptable to all three of these assemblages should become a law" (*ibid.*, p. 138). But in defense of slavery he argued as a minister rather than an economist. He declined to consider it an economic question;

he would not discuss it as a social question; political theories, he believed, had nothing to do with it. The right to hold slaves he regarded as a moral question to be determined exclusively by the authority of the Bible, and on such a question he professed to speak with assurance. He was vastly annoyed at the Abolitionists' unchristian appeal to the old doctrine of equalitarianism, and in 1845 he wrote angrily, "Will not some of you accept my ideas and then argue through the question on that basis, without taking recourse to the Declaration of Independence or throwing up a breastwork out of the long-forsaken rubbish of the Social Contract, or bewildering your pursuers in the mazes of metaphysical subtlety?" (*ibid.*, p. 282). His religion was deeply involved in the institution of slavery, and it seemed to him uncharitable for an intellectual like Theodore Parker to question the sufficiency of a southern minister's texts, or to drag him beyond his intellectual depths. So exasperated did he grow that finally he would have no fellowship with northern Methodists, and was a prime mover in the great schism that rent the church into sectional branches. Abolitionism seemed to him hypocrisy and blasphemy and as a minister of Christ he could not hold fellowship with those who rejected the Master's word. After the war, in reviewing the long controversy, his Christian pugnacity flared up anew, and he flung at the northern churches the accusation that they had been "the most man-astounding, God-offending foes that we had" (*ibid.*, p. 367).

There could be no more telling commentary on the literary poverty of *ante-bellum* Georgia than the extraordinary popularity of Longstreet's sketches. Written for the most part between the years 1832 and 1836, while he was publishing the *State Rights Sentinel*, they profess to be authentic documents of frontier life in Georgia in the early years of the century, and the deliberate note of realism contributes to the impression of authenticity. The love of the romantic that spread like the plague among southern men of letters during the long reign of Sir Walter, fortunately did not infect the robust nature of Longstreet. The best of the sketches are spun out of the vernacular; they are as objective as Longstreet could make them—conscious studies in the local, done with obvious delight in butternut ways and frontier dialect. The quality of the work improves as he draws nearer the backwoods, and comes upon the unregenerate Cracker in his native habitat

There his humor has free play, exuding in practical jokes and ready repartee, in boyish pranks and homely idiom. And there he finds characters to his liking and bits of realistic drama. If one were to single out the sketch that is most indigenous to the Georgia frontier, the truest local document, the choice might well fall on *The Fight*, an account of a bloody meeting between back-woods gladiators brought on by skillful diplomacy of Ransy Sniffle, a grotesque clay-eater and Longstreet's favorite character. Other excellent sketches are *The Gander Pulling*, *The Shooting Match*, *Georgia Theatrics*, *The Horse Swap*, *The Militia Company Drill*—stories that throw an unromantic light on the ways of the Georgia Cracker. Longstreet was as uncritical as his readers and his frequent failures are glaring in their badness. Perhaps the worst of the sketches are the absurd *The "Charming Creature" as a Wife*, a crude sermon on the folly of marrying a lazy woman; *The Song*, an overdone burlesque, and the puerile *The Debating Society*, a heavy practical joke which for some inexplicable reason Poe thought the best of the whole.

Slight though the sketches in *Georgia Scenes* are, they embody solid merits; they are not literary and they are quite unaffected by Irving and the exploitation of the picturesque. Realism was only too rare in those days of high-flown romance, and how honestly realistic was Longstreet's work is revealed by a comparison with James Hall's contemporary stories of the West, such as *Harpe's Head*, or even with Kennedy's *Swallow Barn*. After all Gus Longstreet was an original, and he set the style that was followed in a long series of frontier sketches, and established the tradition of frontier humor that flowered at last in Mark Twain.

2

THE DAVY CROCKETT MYTH

The Narrative of the Life of David Crockett of the State of Tennessee was woven from the same stuff that Longstreet made use of, but the fabric is of far better texture. It is the great classic of the southern frontier, far more significant than *Georgia Scenes*, far more human and vital. Realistic in method, it is romantic in spirit. In its backwoods vernacular it purveys the authentic atmosphere of the cabin and the canebrake; it exhibits the honesty, the wit, the resourcefulness, the manly independence of a coon-

skin hero; it reveals, in short, under the rough exterior of a shiftless
squatter and bear-hunter, qualities that are sterling in every society
where manhood is held in repute. It is an extraordinary document,
done so skillfully from life that homespun becomes a noble fabric
and the crudest materials achieve the dignity of an epic.

The thing had long been waiting to be done. The literary
romantics had tried their hand at the frontier materials and had
failed, and then came a realist of the Georgia school who used the
stuff as he found it and created a lasting document. A practiced
writer collaborated with a picturesque talker, and the fame of
the Tennessee Congressman was made. Romantic America found
a new hero and Davy Crockett reaped a surprising reward. He
had the good fortune to preëmpt the romance of the backwoods, to
file on an unsurveyed tract of western life, and when the lines were
run it was found that his claim embraced all that was native and
picturesque along the Mississippi frontier. Popular imagination
seized upon him and endowed the mighty hunter of the canebrakes with the fugitive romance that had been gathering for
years. He was erected into a mythical figure that drew to itself
the unappropriated picturesque that sprang spontaneously from
the crude western life. How this astonishing result came about,
how good fortune came to single out Davy Crockett for her smiles,
offers a somewhat amusing commentary on the ways of an unsophisticated generation.

That in its later development, if not in the beginning, the Davy
Crockett myth was a deliberate fabrication scarcely admits of
doubt, nor that its immediate purpose was frankly partisan. It
did not spring from the soil of the Tennessee canebrakes; it
was created at Washington. It was not the spontaneous product
of popular imagination; it was the clever work of politicians.
The successive stages through which it passed in its triumphant
progress can be traced fairly accurately with the aid of a little
historical imagination. Roughly they were three; the exploitation
of Davy's canebrake waggery, the exploitation of his anti-Jack-
son spleen, and the exploitation of his dramatic death at the
Alamo. The first phase is embodied in the *Sketches and Eccentricities of Col. David Crockett, of West Tennessee* (1833); the second, in *An Account of Col. Crockett's Tour to the North and Down
East* (1835), and *The Life of Martin Van Buren* (1835); and the
last, in *Col. Crockett's Exploits and Adventures in Texas* (1836).

Midway between the first and second stages stands *A Narrative of the Life of David Crockett, of the State of Tennessee* (1834), which may be accepted in the main as authentic autobiography. None of the five was written by Crockett. He probably had a hand in the first in spite of his repudiation of the work, for most of the important facts of his life and the language of many of the picturesque episodes were taken from its pages to be reproduced in the *Narrative*. The *Tour* and *Martin Van Buren* were claimed by him and were certainly done under his eye and with his help, but the *Exploits* is quite as certainly sheer fabrication, done by a hack writer after Davy's death. It was the politicians who contributed most to the success of the myth. They exploited Davy as a convenient weapon against Jackson, saw their work prosper beyond all expectation, get out of their hands, enlarge itself to a cento of backwoods romance and pass into folklore. It was an unforeseen outcome that must have been vastly amusing to those who set the thing going.

The early thirties, it will be remembered, were robustious times when broadcloth in politics had suddenly gone out of style and homespun had come in. The new coonskin democracy had descended upon Washington, and picturesque figures provided with ample plugs of tobacco were making themselves free with Congressional perquisites. Nothing like it had been seen before in the city of dignified politicians, and the spectacle must have delighted the wags of the capital. But to the members of the overthrown dynasty the Jacksonian votes which these picturesque backwoodsmen represented were very far from amusing. The loss of desirable offices was a hard lesson that taught them the need of catering to this new element of the great American democracy. In their remunerative occupation as representatives of the prosperous and genteel constituencies of the East, the old-school politicians had too long overlooked the power of the plain voter which the progress of manhood suffrage was daily increasing. Hence began a desperate campaign to counteract the Jacksonian appeal. The coonskin vote could no longer be ignored and shrewd plans were laid to capture the backwoods for the new Whig party. The program of internal improvements was well enough in its way, and the old Revolutionary cry of the sword and the purse might prove useful; but the party needed a picturesque figure to draw the coonskin democracy to its standard. Men rather than principles appealed to the West, self-made men, speaking the western vernacular, imbibing western views with their whisky, uncorrupted by broadcloth. This explains the tremendous Whig hurrah over log cabins and hard cider that marked a later campaign; and this explains likewise the singular fate that overtook Davy Crockett, the bear-hunter from the canebrakes.

Davy had first come to Washington during Adams' administration, and in four years' loafing and boasting at the Congressional bar had achieved some distinction as a picturesque original with the tongue of a wag. He spoke rarely in the House and the few records in the *Congressional Debates* are sadly commonplace. Until after he broke with Jackson his political influence at Washington was negligible. But that fortunate break was the beginning of his fame. He had unwittingly made himself. He had become a valuable asset to the Whig party. To find a native Tennesseean, a real coonskin democrat, one who had served under Jackson and been sent to Congress as a Jacksonian, as authentic a Westerner as the General himself, at bitter personal odds with Old Hickory, ready to talk out in meeting and eager to repudiate the latter's attack upon the Bank, was a find indeed to the hard-pressed Whigs; and they would have been no politicians if they had not used what God sent. In consequence Davy soon found himself talked about. His picturesque eccentricities began to be exploited. His rugged western honesty was applauded; his shrewd backwoods intelligence was praised; his frontier humor was skillfully touched up; his characteristic motto, "go ahead," was seized upon as an expression of the progressive spirit of the lusty young Whig party. In short he was speedily turned into a myth by ways not unknown in our time, and sent forth as useful campaign material in the fight for political righteousness. Davy was vastly surprised at his sudden rise to fame. He had never realized how great a man he was; but he accepted it as an agreeable fact and went ahead.

The work had already begun with the publication of the *Sketches and Eccentricities of Col. David Crockett*, that came from the clever pen of some journalist with a liking for the new vein of backwoods humor. A Whig bias runs through the pages, but the book is more a character sketch than a political document. The first embroiderings laid upon the original homespun are seen in an extravagance of picturesque language—an extravagance quite lacking in the more realistic *Narrative*. A well-known passage professing to relate an occurrence on Davy's first trip to Washington will serve to reveal an early stage of the myth-making process—the fathering upon Davy of a type of humor then being exploited by clever young writers:

> I was *rooting* my way to the fire, not in a good humour, when some fellow staggered towards me, and cried out, "Hurrah for Adams!" Said I, "Stranger, you had better hurrah for hell, and praise your own country." Said he, "And who are you?"
>
> "I'm that same David Crockett, fresh from the backwoods, half-horse, half-alligator, a little touched with the snapping-turtle; can wade the Mississippi, leap the Ohio, ride upon a streak of lightning, and slip without a scratch down a honey locust; can whip my weight in wild-cats—and if any gentleman pleases, for a ten-dollar bill, he may throw in a panther—hug a bear too close for comfort, and eat any man opposed to Jackson." (*Ibid.*, Chapter XIII.)

The touching up of the picturesque in the *Sketches* seems to have been a little too much for Davy, who resented the note of clownishness; but he was not the man to permit undue modesty to blight so agreeable a myth in its tender stage. He loved to swagger in the public eye too much for that, and he joined heartily with his new political friends to clothe it in more dignified dress. His incredible egotism was aroused and he swallowed the Whig bait, hook, line and sinker. He began to take himself seriously and set about the business of propagating the myth. He conceived the plan of issuing in his own name books which he humorously claimed to have written in the same way that the President wrote his state papers. Some wag having suggested his name for the presidency to succeed Jackson, Davy was at great pains to advertise the fact to the world. To link himself with Jackson in the public eye and to contrast his own rugged honesty with the latter's reputed abandonment of democratic principles, was the single purpose of these Whig documents. The autobiography was quickly followed by the *Tour*, and this by the *Life of Martin Van Buren*, each more obvious propaganda than the last, and frankly designed to undermine the popularity of the President and his advisers with the coonskin democracy. Who the writer was that lent his pen to the work has never been determined. A recent student has adduced testimony to prove that it was Augustin S. Clayton, a Georgia Congressman, a ready talker and writer, a man of sound culture, a close friend of Longstreet and fond of the backwoods vernacular. The argument is plausible, but the case is not established.[3] In the *Life of Martin Van Buren* the mask is dropped and all the malicious gossip of the Congressional lobby is poured out on "little Van," the "heir-apparent to the 'government.'" The backwoods character is retained only in an occasional coarseness or deliberate lapse of grammar inserted in a text that is written with vigor and skill. The book is far less amusing than Kennedy's *Quodlibet*. Davy is pretty much lost out of its pages and its contribution to the myth was probably slight.

It is in the *Tour*, on the title page of which Davy formally accepts the brevet dignity of Colonel conferred upon him by the writer of the *Sketches*, that the myth expands more genially. A clever and amusing campaign document, it is a masterpiece of Whig strategy to gull the simple. The loquacious Davy joined heartily with his managers to cash in on his reputation. His egotism was played upon at every turn and he was quite unconscious that he had become a mere cat's-paw to pull Whig chestnuts out of the coals. He was paraded at meetings with Daniel Webster, given great dinners, applauded for his rustic wit and homespun honesty, presented with a fine rifle; and he seems never to have realized how grossly he was being exploited. His self-esteem was proof against dillusionment and he accepted the applause greedily. Wherever he went he was taken in charge by the young Whigs. Everything was carefully arranged beforehand. News was sent forward that he was coming; crowds were gathered to greet him; publicity was attended to; morning, noon, and night he was invited to speak, and the speeches were carefully reprinted—not the authentic speeches, probably, but good campaign material nevertheless. It was a gratifying experience and Davy swelled up like a turkey cock.

As a result of his tour he was immensely strengthened in his new political faith and became a staunch nationalist. When he first went to Congress he was anti-tariff and had won his seat on that issue; but he was invited to Lowell, shown an idyllic picture of contented and prosperous mill-hands, dined, given a prepared table of statistics proving how industrialism "is calculated not only to give individual happiness and prosperity, but to add to our national wealth and prosperity," and bidden Godspeed in the work of spreading the true gospel among the honest, simple-minded and patriotic frontiersmen. After having been presented

[3] See John Donald Wade, "The Authorship of David Crockett's *Autobiography*," *Georgia Historical Quarterly*, September, 1922.

by Mr. Lawrence with a fine suit of domestic broadcloth, Davy would have been an ingrate not to vote for a protective tariff. But alas! the opportunity never came. A backwoods constituency that had never been dined by Lowell capitalists and had little use for fine broadcloth, a constituency that persisted in throwing up coonskin caps for Old Hickory in spite of Lowell statistics, resented his apostasy from the Democratic faith and at the next election invited him to stay in the canebrakes. The gorgeous bubble was pricked. Davy had expanded under prosperity and could not now endure adversity. In a fit of anger he quitted his family and the state of Tennessee, went off on the mad chase to Texas and in March of the next year fell at the Alamo. Vain, ignorant Davy Crockett! A simple-minded frontiersman, he went down to Jericho and fell among thieves, and when they were done with him they left him despoiled politically but invested with a fame that has grown to this day. After his death other hands took up the work, wove around his name the humor and romance of the frontier, and made of him a legendary figure. It would have pleased Davy to know how the myth had prospered.[4]

Yet from this crude romanticism, this picturesque propaganda of coonskin days, one solid contribution remains—the autobiography. It is a striking bit of realism, done after the manner of the Longstreet school. There is politics in it, of course. Written just after Davy had gone through a bitter campaign from which he had emerged triumphant, it is a bold pronouncement that he wears no collar marked "My dog—Andrew Jackson." In the campaign of 1830 he had been defeated by the Jacksonians, but two years later he "made a mash" of his opponents, and the elation of that victory adds a certain cockiness to his habitual swagger. But it is much more than a political tract; it is a vital frontier document. The main facts of his biography, as set down there, may be accepted as true, and the general picture of backwoods existence in Tennessee; but the humor has been elaborated and the effect of the picturesque heightened by his collaborator. Such added touches were only natural. The real Davy was very far from romantic. An honest picture of the Tennessee democracy in its native habitat would reveal few idyllic features. It was a slovenly world and Davy was

---

[4] Among the miscellaneous material gathered together in the *Exploits and Adventures in Texas* and attributed to Davy is Longstreet's *Georgia Theatrics*, lifted verbatim from *Georgia Scenes*.

pretty much of a sloven. Crude and unlovely in its familiar details, with its primitive courtships and shiftless removals, its brutal Indian campaign and fierce hunting sprees, its rough equality, its unscrupulous politics, its elections carried by sheer impudence and whisky, the autobiography reveals the backwoods Anglo-Irishman as an uncivilized animal, responding to simple stimuli, yet with a certain rough vigor of character. Wastefulness was in the frontier blood, and Davy was a true frontier wastrel. In the course of successive removals he traversed the length of Tennessee, drinking, hunting, talking, speculating, begetting children, scratching a few acres of land to "make his crap," yet living for the most part off the country; and his last squatting place on the Obion River, seven miles from the nearest neighbor, was as primitive as the first. Willing to endure almost incredible hardships to obtain a keg of gunpowder to celebrate Christmas, risking his skin to kill a bear with a butcher knife, he was never much given to mending fences or enlarging his plow lands. He was a hunter rather than a farmer, and the lust of killing was in his blood. With his pack of hounds he slaughtered with amazing efficiency. A later generation would call him a game-hog. His family must have had Gargantuan appetites to have consumed one-tenth of the meat that fell before his beloved Betsy; the rest went to the dogs and hogs and buzzards. His hundred and five bears in a single season, his six deer shot in one day while pursuing other game—two of which were left hanging in the woods—serve to explain why the rich hunting grounds of the Indians were swept so quickly bare of game by the white invaders. Davy was but one of thousands who were wasting the resources of the Inland Empire, destroying forests, skinning the land, slaughtering the deer and bear, the swarms of pigeons and turkey, the vast buffalo herds. Davy the politician is a huge western joke, but Davy the wastrel was a hard, unlovely fact.

Strip away the shoddy romance that has covered up the real man and the figure that emerges is one familiar to every backwoods gathering, an assertive, opinionated, likable fellow, ready to fight, drink, dance, shoot or brag, the biggest frog in a very small puddle, first among the Smart Alecks of the canebrakes. Davy was a good deal of a wag, and the best joke he ever played he played upon posterity that has swallowed the myth whole and persists in setting a romantic halo on his coonskin cap. Yet in spite of the romantic machinery the play turns out to be broad farce.

BOOK TWO: THE MIND OF THE MIDDLE EAST

BOOK TWO

THE MIND OF THE MIDDLE EAST

THE literature of the Middle East during the years of the romantic revolution, unlike contemporary letters north and south, revealed no coalescing unity of spirit and purpose; it was rather the casual and somewhat fortuitous expression of two cities, both of which were divided by language and custom into fairly equal groups, and neither of which had developed a homogeneous native culture. There were no intellectual hinterlands to Philadelphia and New York, as there were to Boston and Charleston and Richmond; no common ideals spread over broad areas, no dominant schools of thought, no branching roots by which a common literature might be nourished. In consequence it may, perhaps, be reckoned a misuse of terms to speak of the mind of the Middle East, as one may speak of the mind of New England or of the Old Dominion, where in spite of pronounced variations of individual temperament a common culture had set its mark on the literature. There were few common ties and few intellectual sympathies to bind together the men of letters of New York or Philadelphia. Certainly Irving and Paulding and Cooper and Melville and Whitman reveal none of that strong community of taste and purpose that marks the Concord group, or the Boston-Cambridge group, or even the Charleston group. They expressed no common culture, they had been disciplined in no common faith, and they were held together by no common economic or political or intellectual interests; as a result their writing is a frank expression of individual temperament and taste, unfettered by schools, drawing its nourishment from no common soil. They stand on their own feet, and to understand them requires no critical examination of a complex cultural background. And yet this very diversity may prove to be symptomatic of the hurrying changes that the rise of the middle class was bringing to America—to the city perhaps even more dramatically than to the country. The confusions and

183

diversity of thought that mark the literature of Philadelphia and New York may, perhaps, most adequately suggest the mercurial temper of the revolutionary transition from the eighteenth century to the nineteenth, of which the romantic spirit was the natural expression.

CHAPTER I

THE OLD CAPITAL

I

In the year 1800 one might well have expected Philadelphia to retain indefinitely its proud ascendency as the cultural capital of America. For decades no other colonial city had come near to rivaling it as a pleasant center of wealth and refinement. Its society was accounted the politest and most agreeable in America, and during the Revolutionary War young British officers had found its hospitable drawing-rooms an agreeable substitute for London clubs. It had long prided itself on its culture and it was on chatty terms with the fine arts, with books and music and painting, with actors and plays and playhouses. It was the recognized center of the publishing business, and its busy presses turned out books and magazines and newspapers for remote colonial readers. Ambitious young men were drawn to it as by a magnet, and Matthew Carey from Ireland and William Cobbett from England were outstanding figures amongst the many who found Philadelphia as attractive as Franklin had earlier found it. Certainly it was the least provincial spot in America in 1800, managing to keep abreast of the latest English fashions in letters as well as smallclothes; and when the supercilious Tom Moore favored the city with his presence in the summer of 1804, he found there the companionship which in some measure compensated for the meanness of the rest of America, where he professed to see:

> One dull chaos, one unfertile strife,
> Betwixt half-polish'd and half-barbarous life,
> Where every ill the ancient world can brew
> Is mixed with every grossness of the new.[1]

The pronounced intellectual stir expressed itself not only in *belles lettres*, and in the scientific experiments of Franklin and Rittenhouse, but more adequately still in politics. Political disputation would seem, indeed, to have been the common Philadelphia passion. Party forces were more equally divided than in

[1] Quoted in Oberholtzer, *Literary History of Philadelphia*, p. 178.

Boston. From the beginnings of the Revolutionary disputes Philadelphia had produced notable disputants on both sides— pamphleteers like Joseph Galloway and John Dickinson, and satirists like Joseph Stansbury and Francis Hopkinson. In the succeeding decades partisan pens had augmented rather than abated their vigor. During Washington's administration the French Revolution shook Philadelphia as it shook no other American city, and the fierce battle between Federalist and Jacobin was waged with amazing fury and limitless invective. The deadly journalistic duel between Freneau and Fenno in their two *Gazettes* was reflected in the equally bitter duel of couplets between Matthew Carey and William Cobbett. If Philadelphia was not more catholic than Boston, it was at least better informed on party questions, for clever writers were daily flinging their arguments at its head. So long as the political capital of the nation remained in Philadelphia the city was clearly the place for the young American to sharpen his wits, inform his mind, and quicken his literary enthusiasm.

Economically the future of the city seemed equally bright. A younger generation of speculative merchants had taken the place of the older conservatives, and great fortunes were being made with a rapidity before unknown. When title to the western lands passed from the crown to the new republic, Philadelphia merchants took the lead in land speculation, and Robert Morris entered upon a spectacular career that profoundly impressed his generation. The city became the chief center of land speculation to which western and southern investors looked. Economic opportunities increased with the setting up of the new government, and the stir of national politics increased the general activity. With the establishment of the Bank, Philadelphia became the financial capital of the country, receiving and disbursing the monies of the government and attracting outside funds for investment. The decade of the nineties was its golden age. Then came the removal of the seat of the Federal government to Washington, and the gay little city underwent a swift eclipse. It was an unwilling victim to the topography of the North American continent. Between it and the Inland Empire, on which rested its future economic expansion, lay the Appalachian mountain range. To be sure, the opening of the Pittsburgh turnpike seemed to promise that Philadelphia should become the shipping port for the Ohio valley; but the law of gravity sent the produce of the back-country downstream to New Orleans, rather than upstream to the East. Mountains were a serious barrier then to cheap transportation, and in consequence the contributory hinterland to Philadelphia was narrowly restricted, and with the rise of the more fortunately situated New York her economic ascendency was lost past recovery.

A like unforeseen fate overtook the cultural aspirations of the ambitious little city. In the year 1799 Timothy Pickering, Secretary of State in Adams' cabinet, invited to Philadelphia as his secretary Joseph Dennie, a young Boston lawyer who had achieved a wide reputation as a writer of Addisonian essays; and with his coming the literary vigor of Philadelphia flared up in a last brilliant blaze. He established *The Port Folio*, gathered a club of congenial spirits, and gained an extraordinary reputation throughout the country at large. Dennie was a fierce Federalist who hated French Jacobinism with more than the ardor of his party, and he was encouraged by Tom Moore, who wrote,

> Long may you hate the Gallic dross that runs
> O'er your fair country and corrupts its sons.

But with the swift decay of Federalism Dennie's own fortunes fell into a like decay, and with the suspension of *The Port Folio* in 1809 the golden age of Philadelphia came to a definite end. Though it long retained its primacy as a publishing center, and though later *Godey's Lady's Book* became almost a national institution, its intellectual vigor lessened, and its literary leadership passed to other cities. It succumbed to the tastes of Victorianism and became the acknowledged home of "female genius" that for years fed the American reading public on cambric tea. It enjoyed no such renaissance as came to Boston and Charleston, and ambitious young writers abandoned it for more promising fields. While other cities were caught up in the swirl of romantic expansion that followed the War of 1812, Philadelphia remained content with the ways of the eighteenth century, immersed in an old-fashioned culture. With its geographical position disqualifying it to reap the harvest of the westward movement, and with no Merrimac falls to invite industrial development on a great scale, its fate was sealed. It had been a delightful capital for an older America, but it was too narrowly environed, too straitened in potential resources for exploitation, to become the capital of a more expansive and ambitious generation.

II

Yet it enjoyed a brief moment of literary creativeness before the hand of fate finally settled upon it. In the twilight of the eighteenth century the new liberalisms that were turmoiling Europe found their way to Philadelphia, and for the moment it seemed as if the city were to lead the thought of America in its venture into new fields. It was a convenient port for the unloading of foreign romanticisms, and under the stimulus of national politics the demand for such commodities was greatly increased. Certainly in no other American city did the French upheaval quicken so sympathetic a ferment, and with this ferment came a more romantic spirit in letters. The English pre-romantics found there responsive readers. In the verse of young Philadelphians began to appear a note of the vague, the mysterious, the melancholy, echoes of Gray and Cowper and Ossian, as a pleasant relief from vigorous satire as practiced by the Hartford Wits. But it was in the field of fiction that the new spirit most adequately revealed itself, and particularly in the work of a young Philadelphian who had broken wholly with the Federalism that immured the sympathies of young poets like William Cliffton, and welcomed the romantic philosophies then being formulated by radical thinkers in France and England.

Brockden Brown was fortunately spared the fate that might well have been his if circumstances had not determined otherwise. As a boy he had meditated epics on romantic historical figures, inspired perhaps by Dwight and Barlow; but from so profitless a career he was saved by an early introduction to overseas fashions. By William Godwin and Mary Wollstonecraft he was influenced as profoundly as was young William Ellery Channing a few years afterward, and with like results. Later generations have too carelessly forgotten how persuasive to young intellectuals, a century or more ago, was the philosophy of Godwin. To generous minds there was something vastly attractive in his confident appeal to reason and justice; and to a new world and a new venture in government it came with double appeal. How could the republican experiment better justify itself than by establishing justice in the new social order—justice for men and justice for women who had too long suffered under narrow handicaps? It was certainly an ideal worth serious consideration—particularly since the French school had suggested that the germinal source of social injustice must be sought in institutions rather than in the nature of man. It was natural enough for gentlemen who profited by social wrong to charge that injustice was inherent in human nature—that man's innate selfishness was to blame for the ills of society. But the new thinkers were of an inquiring turn of mind, and under their critical scrutiny the old conception was seen to rest on a perversion of fact. Gentlemen had got the cart before the horse. The crying evils of civilization, when analyzed, were traceable to vicious environment, to social and political maladjustments; not to human nature. The mind of the infant is plastic. Very well. If it is molded by social environment, why is it so often misshapen and perverted to base purposes, if institutions are not at fault? why may it not be molded to nobler ends under more beneficent institutions? Reason is a common possession; the ideal of justice is a common ideal. The evil genius that has hitherto thwarted their benevolent work is the overgrown political state, debased to selfish ends. Once let the beneficent sway of social instincts supersede the exploiting machinery of the political state, and reason must conduct to justice. The heart of man is sound. Let it be free to follow its natural promptings and war must give way to peace, the selfish struggle of classes disappear in a common brotherhood.

To an ardent young American like Brockden Brown, with the Hamiltonian struggle for power before his eyes, such a philosophy must have come with immense appeal. America confronted a future unmortgaged to the past; why should it repeat the old follies and mistakes that had reduced Europe to its present level? Here the pressure of vicious institutions was light as yet. Here the appeal to reason and justice was less hampered by selfish preëmptions. Let social commendation be bestowed on the uncorrupted heart, on generous impulses, on native integrity of character. Let education be a natural unfolding of humane instincts, not a sharpening of wits to overreach one's fellows. Let rewards go to frank, outspoken truth, rather than to chicanery and deceit. Inspired by such sentiments, Brockden Brown proposed to make fiction serve social ends. He would spread the gospel of Mary Wollstonecraft and Godwin by means of popular tales. The views of the former he elaborated in *Alcuin; A Dialogue*, which in the year 1798 presented for the consideration of the American people the Wollstonecraft feminism in such passages as this:

Marriage is an union founded on free and mutual consent. It cannot exist without friendship. It cannot exist without personal fidelity. As soon as the union ceases to be spontaneous, it ceases to be just. This is the sum. If I were to talk for months I could add nothing to the completeness of the definition.

But it is in *Arthur Mervyn* that he gives his fullest pronouncement of what he conceives must be done in America. He takes his hero fresh from the plowtail, one of nature's noblemen, and traces his triumphant course through the thick of sordid intrigue to a happy end. Generous in instincts, impulsive in sociability, responsive to suffering, hating injustice, loving the pure and disinterested, Arthur Mervyn is a Godwinian figure drawn to captivate the imagination with the social ideal. It is not so much the plot of the story that reveals the enormous influence of Godwin— patent as the likeness is to *Caleb Williams,* but rather the expansive nature of the title hero, whose instincts bid him espouse justice, and whose life is an implied criticism of all that is sordid and mean.

With the political romanticism of his work was joined a literary romanticism that likewise came from England, where it was muddying the stream of English fiction and turning it aside from the vigorous realism of the middle eighteenth century. The movement that Paulding dubbed the "blood-pudding school" was one of the by-products of the romantic development that ran a far more disastrous course in America than in England, distorting the growth of native fiction for half a century. It was perhaps unfortunate for the American novel that *Wieland* should have been Brockden Brown's most finished work, for it contributed in consequence more powerfully to the spread of the melodramatic. Lacking his strain of rationalism, other writers reveled increasingly in the luridly picaresque, till the popular taste was so debauched that Gilmore Simms found it well-nigh impossible to struggle against it. For this of course Brown was not to blame; yet his gross romanticisms of manner persisted long after his Godwinian romanticisms had faded out of the popular mind, if indeed they ever found lodgment there.

III

Brockden Brown's career was in a sense symbolic of the fate of his native city—a few brilliant years and then a swift decline. Death cut him down before he fulfilled his promise. Something of a like fate befell his most brilliant successor, Robert Montgomery Bird, probably the ablest man of letters that Philadelphia produced. Caught up by the romantic movement at the beginning of his precocious career, he plunged into dramatic writing and from 1830 to 1834, between the ages of twenty-four and twenty-eight, he wrote four plays for Edwin Forrest, one of which, *The Gladiator*, met with extraordinary success, both in this country and in England; and another, *The Broker of Bogota*, kept the stage for years. At the age of thirty he gave over the writing of plays and turned to other fields. The explanation of so unusual a course, according to a recent historian, is not far to seek. He had been overreached by Forrest, and after parting with his manuscripts to the actor, the playwright found himself in the condition of the farmer who after shipping his potatoes to market discovers himself to be in debt to the commission merchant.[2] That he determined to try a different crop was natural enough, but unfortunate for the American drama.

Of his subsequent ventures into the field of romantic fiction, one at least was an extraordinary success, rivaling if not surpassing *The Gladiator* in popular favor. *Nick of the Woods, or the Jibbenainosay* still remains one of the few outstanding tales of the Kentucky settlement. Published in Philadelphia in 1837, it has been reissued in successive editions, more than twenty in all down to the present. It was translated into German in 1838, into Dutch in 1877, and into Polish in 1905. There is abundant reason for its popularity. It is a story of calculating revenge, done with extraordinary vividness and set against a romantic background. A frontier Quaker, trusting in the spirit of good will, finds his non-resistance futile; he is set upon by Indians, his family murdered before his eyes, and himself scalped and left for dead beside his burnt cabin. Recovering, he sets forth on a fierce career. Under the mask of a non-resistant, so effectively worn as to awaken the contempt of the frontier Indian-haters, he became a hunter of men, and his secret passages through the wilderness leave no other trail than the marked bodies of slaughtered warriors. The Jibbenainosay is an uncanny figure who strikes with appalling suddenness, a Nemesis that fills the hearts of border Indians with terror and turns their dreams to nightmares—one of the most striking and fearful figures in our early fiction. The Indians whom

[2] See A. H. Quinn, *A History of the American Drama, etc.*, pp. 244–248.

he pursues so remorselessly are depicted as thorough savages. In describing them Bird has put all his romanticisms aside. There is no sentimentalizing of the noble red man in the brisk pages of *Nick of the Woods;* the warriors are dirty drunken louts, filled with an unquenchable blood-lust, whom the frontiersman kills with as little compunction as he would kill a rattlesnake. The ugly feud that so long soiled the Border is depicted with almost startling frankness, and through its worst phases moves the figure of Bloody Nathan, professing to be a man of peace whilst cutting an appalling lot of notches in his gun, an epileptic who perhaps deceives even himself.

If one likes stirring action that is certain to end in blood-letting, there is good foraging in *Nick of the Woods*, despite its excesses of conventional romance. And there is much else as well. Bird had evidently studied his western materials with some care, and he did his part to popularize certain conceptions that literature had come to associate with the Ohio valley. The character of Ralph Stackpole is clearly suggestive of the wild antics supposed to be common to the river boatmen. "The history of this wild scape-gallows," says Bird, "his prowess in the pin-fold and the battle-field, his adventure on the beech-tree, and his escape from the meshes of the law, with other characteristic events not included in our relation, are recollections still cherished in some parts of Kentucky, and made the theme of many a gleesome story." But what seems more suggestive today is Bird's conscious attempt to reproduce the new type of western humor that found its expression in the Davy Crockett myth. Perhaps the wild extravagance of Ralph Stackpole's vocabulary goes back to Mike Fink, perhaps it derives from Davy himself; at any rate the mode had spread so widely by 1837 that this Philadelphia man of letters had come to believe that such was the indigenous form of humor in the new West of the Ohio valley, and he took particular pains to draw the irrepressible Ralph with vigorous touches. A pronounced romantic, Bird unconsciously contributed his mite to the myth of western humor.

CHAPTER II

THE NEW CAPITAL

I

VERY different from the gay and cultivated Quaker City was the commercial port of Manhattan, with its Yankee energy ingrafted on the stolid Dutch stock, which fate seized upon and transformed into the greatest of our new cities, the favorite home of the genius of American enterprise. Never a cultural capital as Philadelphia had been, and as Charleston was becoming—a fact which Fenimore Cooper untactfully announced to the world—it was ambitious to acquire commercial and financial ascendency; and this ascendency of the economic over the cultural, this frank evaluation of progress in terms of exploitation, marks the definite transition from the eighteenth century to the nineteenth, the triumph of an aggressive middle class over the leisurely ways of an older landed aristocracy. The romance of expansion was creating there a new psychology, and this new psychology was preparing the city for leadership in the new age that was rising. Its strategic position brought to it the produce of the new settlements that were pushing west to the great lakes and beyond; its aggressive traders were reaching out for a share in the markets of the world; the plodding methods of money-getting that had satisfied an earlier generation no longer satisfied men who had discovered the richer possibilities of capitalistic manipulation. The potentialities that lay in the capitalistic system were shrewdly explored, and the necessary machinery of the new finance was devised. The acquisitive spirit of the city found itself in a position to profit from the rage of speculation that was running through the country, and it quickly outdistanced its rivals in the race for financial supremacy.

The changes that came to New York in the last years of the old century were enough to muddle a head stronger than Rip Van Winkle's. The quiet ways of colonial times were gone, and in their stead was a restless activity that had no leisure for its pipe and mug in the sleepy tavern. Business and politics could not wait on men who like Wouter Van Twiller pickled their dreams in tobacco smoke. The bewilderment of old Rip on his return from the hills was the bewilderment of the colonial mind in the presence of a new order. When Washington came to New York to assume the presidency, the town contained approximately 29,000 inhabitants, some two thousand of whom were slaves. Fifty years later the census of 1840 set down its population as 312,710. In 1789 Albany was a Dutch village of four or five thousand, and a few miles to the West lay an unbroken wilderness. Within the narrow zone of the quiet settlements old and new dwelt in close proximity. The most feudal of American aristocracies fringed the banks of the Hudson from Albany to Manhattan; and reaching out through the Mohawk valley that aristocracy was laying a network of speculative land-holdings through which a flood of Yankee pioneers was making its way from the long-settled lands of Connecticut and Massachusetts. The frontier was close at hand; the leveling spirit was near neighbor to the feudal; potential economic rivalries were becoming actual, and the days of a static, power-proud Dutch aristocracy were numbered. The spirit that had dominated the commonwealth from its founding was tenacious of life, but on January 26, 1839, died Stephen Van Rensselaer, last of the Patroons, courteous, dignified, a worthy embodiment of the old patriarchal virtues, who had outlived his age; and hard upon his death came the final break-up of the traditional order. The small men got the land they had long tilled and the influence of the Dutch gentry slowly disintegrated. A new order was rising that had discovered shorter roads to wealth than feudal rents. While the more energetic of the old order, men like Gouverneur Morris and Judge William Cooper, were deep in land speculation, in Manhattan a new aristocracy of capitalism was rising. Wall Street was losing the distinction of housing the most exclusive of the landed gentry, to gain a greater distinction as the home of the new aristocracy of credit. By 1825 the rise of industrialism, the development of banking, the completion of the Erie Canal, the influx of proletarian immigrants, and the drift of population to the towns had fixed the destiny of the city. In becoming the chief repository of the new capitalism New York had become the first and greatest of our middle-class capitals.

Of this new Manhattan the representative citizen was a man whose aggressive ambitions differentiated him sharply from Stephen Van Rensselaer, and whose dramatic career of exploitation seemed to Washington Irving to embody the romantic potentialities of America. John Jacob Astor was to the New York of 1825 what Robert Morris had been to Philadelphia a generation before—an evidence of the wealth that was to be got by those who would boldly exploit the vast resources of America. A German immigrant who landed in America with small funds, immediately following the Peace of Paris, Astor embarked in the fur trade, acquired a fortune which he invested in Manhattan land, and then laid his plans to engage in a great venture in imperialism. Stirred by the Lewis and Clarke expedition, he proposed to explore the virgin resources of the far Pacific Northwest. With the tacit approval of the government he undertook the hazardous project of the Astoria settlement, sent his agent to the Russian posts of Alaska, and by subsidizing an army of trappers proposed to gather the peltries of the entire Northwest for the rich Canton market. It was a grandiose conception worthy of a feudal baron of commerce. It was knit up with dreams of conquest; it necessarily entailed open warfare with the English companies whose ambitions were equally grandiose; it was certain to be attended by bitter hardships on the part of the venturesome agents to whom it was intrusted; and the outcome was uncertain as a gambler's chance. Irving has thrown over his narrative of the great venture a glamour of patriotism; to him it appeared as a plan of empire building; but whether patriotism or profit was the determining impulse in the mind of John Jacob Astor, the settlement of Astoria suggests the romantic aspirations that were making over the lethargic world of Dutch Manhattan, in the venturesome days of the new capitalism. Stephen Van Rensselaer and John Jacob Astor would have had difficulty in understanding each other.

II

In sharp contrast with Boston, New York was wanting in intellectual background and intellectual stimulus. It had never gone to school to dogmatic theology and neither clergy nor laity had been disciplined by a severe Puritan regimen. Gentlemen were little given to metaphysical speculation and the subtleties of creed never provided the staple of talk in the farmer's kitchen. The terrors of hell rarely troubled the sluggish imagination of the Dutch, and the extraordinary stimulus that came to the serious-minded New Englander from long contemplation of the ways of God, was lacking amongst a more prosaic people. No other stimulus supplied the want and in consequence ideas and books were held in low esteem and the things of the mind suffered. The English gentry commonly sent their sons to the English universities, but the Dutch by common report seem to have been indifferent to schooling and opportunities for education were sadly inadequate. The result was a low plane of intellectual life, which even in Cooper's time was remarked by him. There were brilliant and cultivated intellects, wits like Gouverneur Morris and statesmen like John Jay; yet even under the stimulus of Revolutionary and Constitutional controversy the contribution of New York to political theory was far slighter than that of New England or Virginia. *The Federalist* was its single notable production, and even in that the papers of Madison were no inconsiderable part. As a commercial port it attracted young men ambitious to rise in the world of affairs rather than in the world of letters. Unlike Philadelphia it had never been a cosmopolitan meeting ground for aspiring young intellectuals and purveyors of polite culture, nor an important center of printers, publishers and book dealers. Aside from Philip Freneau, who had long since established himself in New Jersey when he was not at sea, it had contributed little to pure literature, or even to the political satire that deluged Philadelphia. As a creative center it ranked far below Hartford, Connecticut, where in the seventeen-eighties and nineties wit had become a staple commodity for export. And yet despite its intellectual lethargy it was a pleasant little town, with a note of cosmopolitanism that rendered life amongst the upper classes genial and urbane. The spirit of aristocracy was as yet little weakened by alien newcomers from the more republican New England, and city and commonwealth were ruled by a little group of old-fashioned gentlemen who upheld the rigid Federalism of the tie-wig school.

In the year 1800 the political leaders of the state were men of long established reputations, Hamilton, Jay, Gouverneur Morris, Rufus King, with whom was closely associated the brilliant lawyer James Kent, afterward Chancellor. Only two of the five were of the older New York stock: Rufus King was from Maine, Hamilton from the West Indies, and Kent was of Yankee Presbyterian ancestry. Politics were already becoming turmoiled by faction, with bitter cleavages and vindictive struggles for the spoils of office that sadly confused the logic of the earlier alignment. The old Federalist party was led by the distinguished gentlemen named above; the Democratic party was led by the Livingstons and Clintons; and outside both was the ambitious Aaron Burr who played a lone hand against the field. After the death of Hamilton the disintegration of the old parties went forward rapidly. The Livingstons and Clintons broke, and a fierce political feud arose between them. The former were accounted the true Jeffersonians, but under the name of Lewisites they drifted towards the Federalist remnant; the Burrites went to pieces after the disgrace of their leader; and the Clintonians remained masters of the field, with a motley support drawn from Tammany Hall Irish, Wall Street bankers, and odds and ends of all factions. From this sordid situation, rendered conspicuous by the extension of suffrage under the new constitution, emerged two master politicians, adepts in all the arts of party manipulation, who exploited the prejudices of the voting masses in a way to justify the gloomy fear of demagoguery that haunted the minds of the old Federalists. Martin Van Buren and Thurlow Weed, Democrat and Whig, were finished products of the new school of practical politicians who held that office-holding was the great end of partisan struggle, and that principles must not stand in the way of success.

III

Through this fierce scramble of rival politicians moved a scholarly figure who preserved to the last the dignity and distinction of an earlier age. James Kent, whose long life and ripe legal learning were devoted to upholding what he conceived to be the ultimate principles of law and politics, was the chief political thinker of the transition days of New York. A disciple of Locke and Blackstone, remodeling seventeenth-century liberalism into eighteenth-century conservatism, he was concerned to erect the barriers of the Common Law about the unsurveyed frontiers of the American experiment, assigning exact metes and bounds beyond which it should not go. Like John Marshall and Joseph Story he was expert in devising legal springes to catch unwary democrats, and while the Jeffersonians were shouting over their victories at the polls, he was engaged in the strategic work of placing the Constitution under the narrow custodianship of the English law. An ardent Federalist and later an equally ardent Whig, he reveals in his precise thinking the intimate relations that every- where exist between economics, politics, and legal principles. With John Adams he accepted the dictum of Locke that "the great and chief end . . . of men's uniting into commonwealths, and putting themselves under government, is the preservation of their prop- erty"; and believing that the English Common Law was the se- curest of all agencies devised to safeguard the subject in the enjoy- ment of his property rights, he made no difficulty in imposing that law upon the Constitution, circumscribing the written document by Common Law fences. Government he conceived to be a pa- triarchal institution erected for the single purpose of coercing the vicious, and as such it must remain in the hands of the good, the wise and the wealthy. It did not need the authoritative pro- nouncement of his great master to convince him that the wealthy included the good and wise. Observation of the "barbarian Jackson" and his rude followers was enough to convince him of the truth of the fact. "All theories of government that suppose the mass of the people virtuous," he wrote to Webster, "and able and willing to act virtuously, are plainly utopian, and will remain so until the Saturnian age" (William Kent, *Memoirs and Letters of James Kent*, p. 207). Profoundly distrustful of democracy, he brought all his wide reading in the history of ancient and medie- val republics to demonstrate the favorite Federalist conviction— a conviction that Paulding in his *Letters from the South* paid his respects to [1]—that democracy is only a euphemism for mob-rule and that it must speedily conduct to anarchy and despotism. All leveling principles he repudiated without waiting to hear cause. Until necessity counseled otherwise he looked with sus- picion on the holders of liquid wealth, as likely to prove wanting in the wisdom and goodness that came naturally to the landed proprietor. He would have the many ruled by the few, but those few he would have owners of great estates.

After all, the learned Chancellor was only a transplanted Yankee of the Fisher Ames school, with something of the austerity and intellectual vigor of his two Puritan grandfathers. An ardent admirer of Hamilton, he early broke with the more liberal faith of his family and joined himself to the extreme Federalists. He was advanced rapidly by Governor Jay, enjoyed for years both office

[1] See *Letters*, etc., Vol. I, p. 207.

and distinction, and ably defended the party of his choice.   Fearful
of agrarian laws and the sequestration of property by the enfranchised poor, he fought stubbornly every proposal for an extension
of suffrage or a larger measure of self-government for the cities.
Defeated in the great constitutional convention of 1821 he soon
after lost his office and retired to write his *Commentaries on American Law*, a work that was to exercise a creative influence on the
later development of our jurisprudence.   That American law came
to be deeply colored by Federalist political theory, that it upheld
from the bench principles that had been repudiated at the polls,
was due in no little measure to the legal scholarship of this last of
the New York Federalists.   What a recent historian has borrowed
to describe another applies with equal felicity to Chancellor
Kent—"his pigmy hope that life would some day become somewhat
better, punily shivered by the side of his gigantic conviction that
it might be infinitely worse" (Fox, *Decline of Aristocracy in New
York Politics*, p. 243).   As he contemplated the ways of the triumphant Jacksonians, he found such consolation as he could in
turning back to an older century with its narrow outlook and sober
culture.   Writing to his brother in 1835, he said:

> There never was such misrule. Our Tory rich men are becoming startled
> and alarmed at our downhill course. My opinion is that the admission
> of universal suffrage and a licentious press are incompatible with govern-
> ment and security to property, and that the government and character
> of this country are going to ruin. This suffrage is too great an excitement
> for any political machine. It racks it to pieces, and morals go with it. It
> is probable England is going the same way. We are becoming selfish,
> profligate, crazy. . . . Give me the writings of Addison and Locke, and
> the Presbyterianism of Dr. Ripley, Dr. Stiles, and old Dr. Rogers. (Kent,
> *Memoirs and Letters of James Kent*, pp. 218-219.)

IV

With the extraordinary upheaval in economics and politics
New York unfortunately underwent no corresponding intellectual revolution.   The renaissance that a generation earlier had
created a new Virginia, and that was awakening in Massachusetts
a many-sided intellectual activity, touched the mind of New York
only lightly.   The ground was unprepared for the new philosophies.
To Virginia, French romantic theory had come with the appeal
of a new gospel for the reason that plantation economics fell in
with the major premises of Physiocratic liberalism, and the old-

world dogmas seemed to find new-world justification. To New England, German idealism had come likewise with the appeal of a new gospel, after Unitarianism had broken the fetters of Calvinism and set free its traditional idealism. But among the young men of New York in 1825 neither France nor Germany was a determining influence. With an inadequate cultural background and no responsive economics, they were attracted only casually to the current European liberalisms. They were wanting in idealism and in consequence the major intellectual and social movements of the times influenced the form and content of the new Knickerbocker literature far less profoundly than was the case in New England. New York was as insular as Charleston. That the growing economic unrest would ultimately find expression in a controversial or Utopian literature, was a matter of course; and that the cosmopolitanism of the city should make for vigorous discussion, was equally a matter of course. Nevertheless Albert Brisbane, William Leggett, Parke Godwin and Horace Greeley were far less representative of the dominant literary spirit than Irving and Halleck and Willis of the earlier group, or Stedman and Stoddard later.

The Knickerbocker movement was inaugurated by four young men whose clever sketches caught the provincial ear of polite society and set the new fashion in prose and verse. Irving and Paulding in *Salmagundi*, and Halleck and Drake in the *Croaker Papers*, were lucky adventurers whose slight crafts made the most prosperous of voyages. Bright young fellows with a charming literary swagger, they aspired to be wits and exploit the amusing foibles of Broadway. Twelve years separated the two ventures, and in the interval Byron and Scott had been supplanting Moore and Campbell in the esteem of the Town, and the literary mode of New York was changing. From their gay provincialism, happily Irving and Paulding later freed themselves; Drake died at the age of twenty-five; but Halleck retained to the end of a leisurely life the mannerisms of the Croaker period—a crochety wit who affected persiflage, a brisk young buck who gently slid into a *blasé* old buck, a free lance in verse who lived in state on the income of a small literary investment made in his twenties.

The very considerable reputation of Fitz-Greene Halleck resulted in part from the literary sterility of New York in his early days, and in part from the personal popularity of the man. A Connecticut Yankee, descended on his mother's side from old

John Eliot, he was drawn to the city as a promising field for an accountant, and eventually found his way into the office of John Jacob Astor by whom he was later pensioned. He accepted the views and shared the antipathies of his Wall Street associates, but with a certain affectation of individuality that took delight in shocking them by whimsical pronouncements in favor of the Catholic church and the monarchical system. There is perhaps a suggestion of seriousness in the remark that Bryant has preserved: "The ship of state," so he reports Halleck as saying, "must be governed and navigated like any other ship, without consulting the crew. What would become of the stanchest bark in a gale, if the captain were obliged to call all hands together and say: 'All you who are in favor of taking in sail, will please to say ay'" (*Orations and Addresses*, p. 186). His political affiliations were Federalist-Whig, and his satire exudes much of the old prejudice against the democratic mass. The pompous long-winded DeWitt Clinton was a fair mark for his shafts; [2] the demagoguery of office-seeking politicians was a fruitful theme for his wit; [3] and Halleck's satire plays upon them with good-natured raillery. But his gayety cannot hide a certain animus in dealing with the tousled-headed democracy. When the labor movement was painfully getting under way in New York Halleck contemplated the curious phenomenon with a tolerant contempt—in something of the spirit of a wit of pre-Revolutionary times who amused the Town with his couplet:

> Down at night a bricklayer or carpenter lies,
> Next sun a Lycurgus or Solon doth rise.

As an illustration of the attitude of polite society in New York a hundred years ago towards the aspirations of the proletariat, Halleck's forgotten *Epistle to Robert Hogbin, Esq., Chairman of the Committee of Working-Men*, etc., deserves quotation:

> Mr. Hogbin,—I work as a weaver—of rhyme—
>   And therefore presume with a working-man's grace,
> To address you as one I have liked for some time,
>   Though I know not (no doubt it's a fine one) your face.
>
> There is much in a name, and I'll lay you a wager
>   (Two ale-jugs from Reynolds), that Nature designed,
> When she formed you, that you should become the drum-major
>   In that choice piece of music, the Grand March of Mind.

---

[2] See *Governor Clinton's Speech*.   [3] See *The Recorder*.

A Hogbin! a Hogbin! how cheering the shout
   Of all that keep step to that beautiful air,
Which leads, like the treadmill, about and about,
   And leaves us exactly, at last, where we were!

Yes, there's much in a name, and a Hogbin's so fit is
   For that great moral purpose whose impulse divine
Bids men leave their own workshops to work in committees,
   And their own wedded wives to protect yours and mine! . . .

When the moment arrives that we've won the good fight,
   And broken the chains of laws, churches, and marriages,
When no infants are born under six feet in height,
   And our chimney-sweeps mount up a flue in their carriages—

That glorious time when our daughters and sons
   Enjoy a *blue Monday* each day of the week,
And a clean shirt is classed with the mastodon's bones,
   Or a mummy from Thebes, an undoubted antique—

Then, then, my dear Hogbin, your statue in straw,
   By some modern *Pig*malion delightfully wrought,
Shall embellish the Park, and our youths' only law
   Shall be to be Hogbins in feeling and thought.

In Halleck's better work there is sometimes evident a certain
critical detachment that permitted him to see both sides of his
theme. In the lines to his native Connecticut he has taken pretty
accurately the measure of the Puritan and the Yankee. He rests
under no awe in presence of the old worthies, and he throws overboard the pious fairy-tales of Cotton Mather—"that slanderer
of the memory of our fathers"—only to forgive the preacher who
scolded his friends "up from earth to heaven" because of the
"sour grapejuice in his disposition." Unfortunately little of his
work possesses the virility of *Connecticut*. His most ambitious
poem, *Fanny*, is a feeble and discursive satire on the social climber. It was a great favorite at the time and passed through several editions, but the sparkle is gone out of its affected jauntiness
and little has been lost in its being forgotten. Halleck's casual
literary activity continued only for the brief period between the
years 1819 and 1828; thereafter for close on forty years he was
content to turn out an occasional *jeu d'esprit*, enjoy the deepening
twilight of his reputation, and watch his fellow Yankee, Willis,
invest his talents in the ephemeral. The day of the wit was past
in New York.

CHAPTER III
TWO KNICKERBOCKER ROMANTICS

I

WASHINGTON IRVING

FORTUNATELY the stolid New York of earlier days was not to pass away without bequeathing to posterity some fragments of its chronicles. In the midst of a pleasant society of smallclothes and tie-wigs, of feudalism and Federalism, appeared young Washington Irving at the precise moment when Sansculottism was beginning to make a stir in the land, and gentlemen were putting away their knee-breeches to don a republican dress—a decline in taste to which he would not easily reconcile himself. A boyish wit from the eighteenth century, a genial loiterer in the twilight of the old, he found himself out of humor with the ambitions that were making over the little city he loved. The present seemed to him not so amusing as the past, nor so picturesque. That he had any business with the world of trade and speculation he could not believe. Its concerns were not his. Its new Wall Street counted for less in his eyes than the pipe of old Diedrich Knickerbocker. Its decadent Federalism that was clinging to the wreck of its hopes, and its roistering Democracy that wore greasy clothes, spoke with an Irish accent, and was marshaled to the polls by Tammany Hall, were of less consequence to him than the black bottle that brought such curious adventures to Rip Van Winkle. The wit and romance he took pleasure in were of another sort than the kind his generation was getting drunk on—more insubstantial, less heady, picturesque rather than profitable. So Irving gently detached himself from contemporary America, and detached he remained to the end of a loitering life, untroubled by material ambitions, enjoying the abundance of good things that fell in his way, mingling with prosperous folk and liking everybody—men as diverse as John Jacob Astor and Martin Van Buren and John P. Kennedy—and unconsciously taking the color of his environment, careful to turn into limpid prose such romantic tales as he came upon and achieving thereby both reputation and profit—a pleasant blame-

less way of living, certainly, yet curiously unrepresentative of the
America in which chance had set him and which was to claim him
as its first man of letters.

An incorrgible *flâneur*, Irving's business in life was to loaf and
invite the picturesque. A confirmed rambler in pleasant places,
in the many lands he visited he was a lover of the past rather than
the present, seeking to recreate the golden days of the Alhambra or
live over the adventurous mood of the fur trader. The immediate
and the actual was an unsatisfying diet for his dreams. There was
in him nothing of the calm aloofness of the intellectual that stands
apart to clarify its critical estimate, and none of the reforming
zeal of the Puritan that is at peace only in the thick of a moral crusade. The duty of saving the world was not laid on his untroubled
soul. No man of his generation was less of a rebel than Irving, and
he went his way unconcerned at things that quite upset Fenimore
Cooper's peace of mind. In his early days, to be sure, he broke
with the ambitious middle class—if gently drawing away can be
called breaking—because he could not bring himself to like its
ways and the devastation those ways were entailing on the leisurely
world he loved. Revolutions seemed to him somewhat vulgar
affairs. The French Revolution had brought destruction on too
many lovely things, and the industrial revolution was taking too
heavy a toll of the picturesque, to please him. He thought it
a pity that steam should drive the clipper ship from the seas and
put an end to snug posting in the tally-ho. Progress might be
bought at too dear a price. The bluff squire with his hounds, the
great hall with its ancient yuletide customs, the patriarchal relations between master and man, seemed to him more worth while
than the things progress was substituting for them; so he turned
away from the new and gently ingratiated himself into the past
in order to gather up such fragments of the picturesque as progress
had not yet destroyed.

But only for a time. His dislike of capitalism rested on no more
substantial basis than its substitution of vulgar trousers for gentlemanly smallclothes. It was too new to have achieved dignity
or the charm of assured position. When that time should come
and masters of finance should stand before the world as generous
dispensers of patronage, when the development of business should
have produced its new barons, Irving's dislike would lessen and
he would associate with the new capitalism on the same easy terms

that he associated with the old feudalism. In the meantime he stood apart, unconcerned with praise or blame. The industrial revolution might work itself out as it would. The seventeen years he spent abroad on his great pilgrimage were black years for England. Wretchedness and poverty were all about him if he chose to see. The "condition of England" question was rising out of the factory smoke to challenge the conscience of England. But he did not choose to see and his conscience was untroubled. As he idled about the countryside or visited the hospitable manor houses, his eye was caught by the grace of medieval spires rising from parish churches rather than by the condition of the proletariat. He saw no children working in the coalpits, for he did not choose to visit the collieries. He sympathized vaguely with the new social movements then getting under way, but it was not in his nature to be partisan to a cause. He may not have been a Tory but he had lived so long with Tories and enjoyed so frankly the charm of upper-class society, that his outlook was unconsciously determined by such intimate contacts. While Secretary to the Legation at London in the reform years from 1829 to 1831, he was aware of the tremendous stir all about him, but his infrequent references to the Reform Bill in his letters turned usually on its disastrous effects on the publishing business. Only once during his long residence abroad does he seem to have felt deeply the significance of the current revolutionary unrest, and the mood that swept him away from his habitual indifference bears the marks of a sudden awakening. Writing from London on March 1, 1831, he said:

We are in the beginning of an eventful week. . . . However, *the great cause of all the world* will go on. What a stirring moment it is to live in. I never took such intense interest in the newspapers. It seems to me as if life were breaking out anew with me, or that I were entering upon quite a new and almost unknown career of existence, and I rejoice to find my sensibilities, which were waning as to many objects of past interest, reviving with all their freshness and vivacity at the scenes and prospects opening around me. I trust, my dear Brevoort, we shall both be spared to see a great part of this grand though terrible drama that is about to be acted. There will doubtless be scenes of horror and suffering, but what splendid triumphs must take place over these vile systems of falsehood in every relation of human affairs, that have been woven over the human mind, and for so long a time have held it down in despicable thraldom. (Pierre M. Irving, *Life and Letters of Washington Irving*, Vol. II, p. 199.)

Irving lacked a month of being forty-nine when he wrote this confession of interest in matters political. It marks the first appearance of liberalism in his thinking, and the last—somewhat vague to be sure, unduly bottomed on romantic expectations, yet significant in so placid a life and explanatory of his course, when a year later he returned to America to knit up once more the raveled threads of his interests. It was as an incipient liberal that he came back to a land then in the first flush of the Jacksonian victory, eager to discover a romantic charm in the vast changes that had come during the seventeen years he had been abroad. He plunged into the business of re-discovery with enthusiasm. He was in want of new literary materials, and as he took his bearings, his creative interest was stirred to write on American themes. He went to Washington and for three months listened to the great debate on Nullification. He talked with business men and politicians, with those who were prosperous and prominent, and he drifted easily with the tide of liberalism. To be sure he could scarcely be called a Jacksonian. Parties and causes did not greatly interest him even then. An intelligent man, indeed, could hardly be less concerned about political principles. Thirty years before, as a clever young man about town, he had gone with the dominant Federalism of the times, and had amused himself with political ambitions. His brother Peter was editor of the Lewisite paper the *Chronicle*, but Josiah Ogden Hoffman, with whose firm Irving was connected during his desultory incursion into the law and to whose daughter Matilda he was betrothed, was an old Loyalist and ardent Hamiltonian. His wife, to whom Irving was warmly attached, was a daughter of John Fenno, Hamilton's editor. Under such tutelage it was natural for Irving to poke good-natured fun at President Jefferson's red velvet breeches in *Salmagundi;* but his venture into practical politics proving little to his taste, he quickly gave over such ambitions. In a letter to a clever young lady of Republican sympathies, he thus announced his abandonment of political hopes:

I am as deep in mud and politics as ever a modern gentleman would wish to be; and I drank beer with the multitude; and I talked hand-bill fashion with the demagogues; and I shook hands with the mob, whom my heart abhorreth. . . . Truly this saving one's country is a nauseous piece of business, and if patriotism is such a dirty virtue,—prythee, no more of it. (*Life and Letters*, Vol. I, Chap. XI.)

Years now separated him from that youthful experience. His long absence from his native land had completely alienated him from the fierce partisanship of contemporary America and he could view matters political with calm detachment. Inclined to make the best of any government *de facto*, he found it easy on his return to accept Jacksonianism, and he soon discovered a genuine liking for Old Hickory. "The more I see of this old cock of the woods," he wrote from Washington, "the more I relish his game qualities" (*ibid.*, Vol. II, p. 255). No doubt his early friend Paulding had much to do with his ready acceptance of the new order, although he had come in close contact with Martin Van Buren at the London legation and was drawn to him. "He is one of the gentlest and most amiable men I have ever met with," he wrote to his brother, "with an affectionate disposition that attaches itself to those around him, and wins their kindness in return" (*ibid.*, Vol. II, p. 220). Although distrustful of some of the "elbow counsellors" of the Democracy he found little cause for criticism and soon came to be regarded as one with them. The Jacksonians were eager to make political capital out of his literary reputation, and he was urged by Tammany Hall to stand for Congress and later to accept a mayoralty candidacy. In 1837, probably through the intervention of Paulding, he was offered a post in Van Buren's cabinet. These partisan offers he had the good sense to decline, but when in 1842 he was tendered the post of Minister to Spain he gladly seized the opportunity to revisit a land he loved. His nephew is explicit in his statement that the offer came wholly unsolicited, but Fenimore Cooper was of another opinion.[1] Very likely Cooper was misinformed, but whatever the truth the appointment was a godsend to Irving. His affairs were in a bad way. The popularity of his writings was on the wane, the panic had caught him with much of his capital invested in unprofitable land speculations, and the "Roost" at Tarrytown was a heavy drain, although he wrote whimsically, "I beat all the gentlemen farmers in my neighborhood, for I can manage to raise my vegetables and fruits at very little more than twice the market price" (*Life and Letters*,

---

[1] Writing to his wife a month afterwards, Cooper said: "By the way, Mrs. Willing has let out the secret of Irving's appointment. He wrote to Webster to remember him *if any good thing offered.* So that instead of not asking for the office, he asked for anything that was good. There has been more humbug practised concerning this man than concerning any other now living" (Cooper, *Correspondence of James Fenimore-Cooper*, Vol. II, p. 469).

Vol. II, p. 320). Only a severe nature like Cooper, sorely wounded by the angry reception of his own honest criticism, would cavil at an appointment so honorable to the government.

A friendly nature, Irving discovered friendliness wherever he went. His own generosity appealed to the generosity of others, and he found it easy in consequence to take a kindly view of men and parties. He was harassed by none of Cooper's quick suspicions and rigid principles, and it must be added he had none of Cooper's intuitive penetration into the secret springs of human action that made the latter so acute a critic of contemporary America. The sharp contrast in moods in which the two men returned to America from their travels, the one harshly critical of middle-class economics and frontier leveling, the other responding naïvely to the enthusiasm for speculative expansion and eager to exploit the romance of the westward movement, sufficiently reveals the difference between them. The one was a dogmatic Puritan with the dictatorial ways of the quarter-deck, the other was a play-boy of letters temperamentally incapable of critical analysis. There was not a grain of realism in Irving's nature. His cheerful optimism was little more than the optimism of the prosperous. Wholly ignorant of economics, he never comprehended the significance of the revolutions in process all about him, and this *naïveté* blinded him to the motive of John Jacob Astor in financing Astoria, as it blinded him to all the major forces of the times. He was easily brought to see the romance of the great struggle between rival companies for mastery of the fur trade, but he did not comprehend how the glamour he threw about the venture must inevitably strengthen his patron's investment in imperialism. Gullible as a child, he discovered nothing more significant in the great struggle between agrarianism and capitalism for control of government than the ungenerous suspicions and novel theories it bred. For the outstanding liberals of New York he had scant sympathy. William Leggett, Horace Greeley, Albert Brisbane, William Cullen Bryant, influenced his views far less than did the masters of Wall Street; and from the courageous movement of Locofocoism he drew back in distrust. The one letter in which he elaborated such political convictions as he had come to hold, is an interesting document that deserves quotation.

As far as I know my own mind, I am thoroughly a republican, and attached, from complete conviction, to the institutions of my country; but

I am a republican without gall, and have no bitterness in my creed. I have no relish for puritans either in religion or politics, who are for pushing principles to an extreme, and for overturning everything that stands in the way of their own zealous career. I have, therefore, felt a strong distaste for some of those locofoco luminaries who of late have been urging strong and sweeping measures, subversive of the interests of great classes of the community. Their doctrines may be excellent in theory, but, if enforced in violent and uncompromising opposition to all our habitudes, may produce the most distressing effects. The best of remedies must be cautiously applied, and suited to the taste and constitution of the patient. . . . Ours is a government of compromise. We have several great and distinct interests bound up together, which, if not separately consulted and severally accommodated, may harass and impair each other. . . . I always distrust the soundness of political councils that are accompanied by acrimonious and disparaging attacks upon any great class of our fellow-citizens. Such are those urged to the disadvantage of the great trading and financial classes of our country. You yourself know. . . how important these classes are to the prosperous conduct of the complicated affairs of this immense empire. You yourself know, in spite of all the common-place cant and obloquy that has been cast upon them by political spouters and scribblers, what general good faith and fair dealing prevails throughout these classes. Knaves and swindlers there are doubtless among them, as there are among all great classes of men; but I declare that I looked with admiration at the manner in which the great body of our commercial and financial men have struggled on through the tremendous trials which have of late overwhelmed them, and have endeavored, at every pecuniary sacrifice, to fulfill their engagements. (*Life and Letters*, Vol. II, pp. 312–313.)

This persuasive presentation of the philosophy of compromise, with its implicit defense of capitalism, marks Irving's drift back to the middle class with which he had long before broken. In the six years since his return he had watched the country react to the great panic, and he went with it in its veering towards the Whiggery of Henry Clay. The fragile bonds of his attachment to the Democracy were becoming tenuous; other attachments were insensibly drawing him towards the more congenial representatives of wealth. He had all his life associated with the Tory classes and it was easy for him to transfer his loyalty to the American Tories. Under such influences began a slow *rapprochement cordial* towards the new philosophy of progress. He was seized with the common mania of speculation and made some unfortunate investments in wild lands and railways that seriously hampered him later, and he commercialized his literary reputation by such money-making ventures as *Astoria* and the *Adventures of Captain Bonne-*

ville. He discovered a new romance in the great business of exploitation, and found the hand of God in the profits of unearned increment. In the letter above quoted from, he justified the ways of speculation thus:

> There are moral as well as physical phenomena incident to every state of things, which may at first appear evils, but which are devised by an all-seeing Providence for some beneficent purpose. Such is the spirit of speculative enterprise which now and then rises to an extravagant height, and sweeps throughout the land. . . . The late land speculations, so much deprecated, though ruinous to many engaged in them, have forced agriculture and civilization into the depths of the wilderness; have laid open the recesses of primeval forests; made us acquainted with the most available points of our immense interior; have cast the germs of future towns and cities and busy marts in the heart of savage solitudes, and studded our vast rivers and internal seas with ports that will soon give activity to a vast internal commerce. Millions of acres which might otherwise have remained idle and impracticable wastes, have been brought under the dominion of the plough, and hundreds of thousands of industrious yeomen have been carried into the rich but remote depths of our immense empire, to multiply and spread out in every direction, and give solidity and strength to our confederacy. All this has in a great measure been effected by the extravagant schemes of land speculators. I am, therefore, inclined to look upon them with a more indulgent eye than they are considered by those violent politicians who are prescribing violent checks and counter measures, and seem to have something vindictive in their policy. (*Life and Letters*, Vol. II, p. 314.)

Thus did Irving become completely domesticated in the new world that Rip Van Winkle had found so disconcerting when he came upon it out of the quiet colonial past. The rediscovery of America proved to be an agreeable business, and profitable in a professional way. His enthusiasms, which in 1831 he felt were "waning as to many objects of past interest," were stimulated by the vast stir of the country, and the spirit of romance once more ran briskly in his veins. The better part of a year he rambled widely about the country, in order, as he said, to get at home "upon American themes." He visited Boston and the White Mountains, then West to Ohio and St. Louis, then with an Indian commissioner he penetrated the southwest prairies as far as the wild Pawnee country beyond the South Canadian River, then to New Orleans and Charleston, finally settling down in Washington to immerse himself in politics. From there he passed over the Potomac for an extended trip through the Old Dominion, returning to New York

where he spent some time with Astor at Hell Gate, finally in 1835
settling at Tarrytown which was to be his home to the last. He
had definitely determined on his new field of work. His imagination had been stirred by his visit to the prairies; the romance of the
westward expansion was beginning to find expression in the works
of Timothy Flint and James Hall; the public interest was ripe and
John Jacob Astor was at hand to encourage him. Thus stimulated
Irving proposed to make the field of western romance his own, with
the result that he published in quick succession *A Tour of the
Prairies*, *Astoria*, and *The Adventures of Captain Bonneville*.

On the whole the new venture did not prosper. The spirit of the
West was not to be captured by one whose heart was in Spain.
In *A Tour of the Prairies* there is a certain homely simplicity and
straightforwardness that spring from a plain recital of undramatic
experience; and in *Astoria* there is an unembellished narrative of
appalling hardship and heroic endurance, with none of the tawdry
romantics that mar the work of Flint and Hall. Yet neither is
creatively imaginative, neither stirs one with a sense of high drama.
The atmosphere of Snake River could not be created in the quiet
study at the "Roost"; it needed the pen of a realist to capture the
romance of those bitter wanderings in mountain and sagebrush.
It is journeyman work, and on every page one is conscious of the
professional man of letters faithfully doing this day's allotment.
It is much the same with his *Life of Washington*. In this last great
undertaking Irving no longer writes with gusto. The golden days
of Diedrich Knickerbocker and Rip Van Winkle are long since
gone; the magic is departed from his pen; and a somewhat tired
old gentleman is struggling to fulfill his contract with his publisher.
It was a mistake to venture on the work, despite the fact that he
had long been planning it. His historical equipment was inadequate. He might make a pretty story out of Washington's early
life and his days with the army, but he was far too ignorant of
politics, too credulous in judging his materials, to interpret justly
the fierce party struggles that seethed about the President. Quite
unconsciously in this last work he returned to the political prejudices of his youth, and wrote an account of Washington's administrations deeply colored by his Federalist sources.

The most distinguished of our early romantics, Irving in the end
was immolated on the altar of romanticism. The pursuit of the
picturesque lured him away into sterile wastes, and when the will-

o'-the-wisp was gone he was left empty. A born humorist, the
gayety of whose spirits overflowed the brim, he was lacking in a
brooding intellectuality, and instead of coming upon irony at the
bottom of the cup—as the greater humorists have come upon it
after life has had its way with them—he found there only sentiment
and the dreamy poetic. As the purple haze on the horizon of his
mind was dissipated by a sobering experience, he tried to substitute an adventitious glamour; as romance faded, sentiment
supplied its place. So long as youth and high spirits endured, his
inkwell was a never-failing source of gayety, but as the sparkle
subsided he over-sweetened his wine. This suffices to account for
the fact that all his better work was done early; and this explains
why the Knickerbocker *History* remains the most genial and vital
of his volumes. The gayety of youth bubbles and effervesces in
those magic pages, defying time to do its worst. The critic may
charge the later Irving with many and heavy shortcomings, but
the romantic smoke-clouds that ascend from Wouter Van Twiller's
pipe cannot be dissipated by the winds of criticism.

II

JAMES KIRKE PAULDING

Far more native to the limitations and hardships of American
life and far more loyal to its homely aspirations was James Kirke
Paulding, whose literary reputation came to be so deeply overshadowed by that of his early friend. Sprung from plain stock—
whether English or Dutch his son remained in doubt, although
inclining to believe the former—and cradled in the fierce partisanship of the Revolutionary struggle, he never abandoned his inherited liberalism or found his love of country growing less. To
the end of his life he remained a primitive American of an earlier
generation, somewhat puzzled by the ways of another age that
speculated in prosperity by running in debt, and measured a man's
wealth by the amount he owed. His father had been an active
Whig in a Tory neighborhood who did not stint his service to the
Revolutionary cause. He was a member of the local Committee
of Safety, and acted as State Commissary to the Revolutionary
forces, a post which in the end brought him to ruin. In the dark
days of the struggle he pledged his private credit for supplies, and
was never reimbursed by a negligent commonwealth. The outcome was financial disaster. The father was imprisoned for debt

and his courage broken, and the family long suffered from want. "We were not only poor," the son wrote later, "but steeped in poverty." But there was excellent stuff in the awkward, dreamy country boy. He was "built of stubborn oak," he remarked whimsically, "seasoned in the school of poverty, like an old chimney-piece in a log cabin." When at the age of nineteen he was suddenly plunged into the world of New York City, he was shy, uncouth, self-educated, and felt himself an alien in Wall Street and Broadway. For the Federalist upper class he seems to have felt the instinctive hostility of the outsider; but through the agency of the Irvings—an elder sister having married William Irving—he was brought into the companionship of a group of clever young men, and under the stimulus of high talk and exuberant pranks, the latent idealism of his nature expanded freely. This was his university, and while it left something to be desired in the way of discipline, suffering too free a rein to his discursive fancy, it quickened his native wit, awakened his creative imagination, and put him to school to the pleasant craft of writing. The *Salmagundi Papers* were the first fruits of the literary apprenticeship of the group, and although Irving has come to receive the chief credit for them, the wit of Paulding seems quite as sprightly, and his gayety as fresh.

That his later career in letters was less notable resulted in part from the fact that he was an inveterate rambler by nature, and partly from the fact that writing with him was occasional, a pleasant relief from humdrum duties, and he did not choose to lay a curb on his vagrant ways. In letters as in life he was always discursive, forgetful of his objective in his delight at the beauty of the countryside, loading his pages down with nature descriptions and clogging the action of his tales with somewhat tedious homilies. After forty years of writing he remained still an amateur, incapable of pruning the wilful tangle of his fancy—an essayist of the leisurely school who ventured incautiously into the realms of verse and fiction without mastering the technic of the business. There was perhaps too much of the homespun in him to permit him to become an artist. The experience of his youth marked him too deeply, and all his life he remained as conscious a son of the people as Hamlin Garland was later, delighting to chronicle the ways of the obscure, somewhat militant in proclaiming the excellence of homely virtues. Formed in an environment that bred a spontaneous democracy, he was a confirmed equalitarian, untroubled by the itch to rise in the world or exploit his fellows. Alone among the Knicker-bocker group, he was a Jeffersonian in the fundamentals of his social creed; not in the lesser matters of Kentucky Resolutions and the like, but in his Physiocratic leanings, in his profound distrust of all middle-class programs and his preference for the simple country ways over the city economy; and it was this deep-rooted agrarianism that set him against capitalism and made him a later Jacksonian. In him there spoke out the authentic New York, not of Broadway merchants or Wall Street bankers, but of the plain rank and file of the people. Untouched by foreign travel but widely acquainted with his native America, he was fashioned out of the wool from the fireside loom and domestic dye-pot.

A writer so consciously and completely American would find abundant occasion to put his pen to the service of his country at a time when every English traveler turned critic and on his return home published a volume of truculent disparagement of ways and things American. For the most part those volumes were a defense of Toryism by the easy method of attacking democracy, and they annoyed Paulding beyond measure. He would not let them go un-answered, and from *The Diverting History of John Bull and Brother Jonathan* (1812) to *John Bull in America* (1825), he published five different replies, varying his attack from argument to burlesque. Something more than loyalty to his country seems to have spurred him on. His dislike of England was inveterate, partly because of the old Revolutionary feud, partly because of later antagonisms. Almost at the hour of his birth the Paulding family had been forced to quit their home for fear of the British and Tories who daily threatened them; and a deep hatred of the British Tory he drew in with his mother's milk. To him England was a Tory country, reeking with social injustice, the home of ancient abuses, and necessarily the implacable enemy of democratic America. He was convinced that want and tyranny and subserviency dogged the daily life of the English common people; and the English Reviews that attacked the ways of democracy with caustic British superior-ity, filled his honest republican heart with wrath, and he jabbed his quill into the tough skin of John Bull with patriotic vigor. The shame of the burning of the capitol rankled in the American heart, and Paulding discovered fresh grievances in remembering that from England had come the banking system and the "shin-

plaster dynasty" that would breed in the new country the evils of
the old if they were not looked to. He was convinced that the
mother country wished ill to her offspring, and he thanked God in
successive volumes that democratic America was not what Tory
England was.

For despite the English travelers—Weld, Parkinson, Ashe, Brad-
bury, Hall, Trollope, and all the rest of the loquacious tribe—
Paulding was persuaded that America constituted the hope of the
future. Here in this land he believed that men should eventually
achieve a measure of well-being undreamed of in the old world;
already the old tyrannies had been destroyed, the ancient poverty
abated. From this stubborn idealism nothing could turn him aside.
It finds expression in an early poem, and it provides the theme for
his last novel. *The Backwoodsman*, published in 1818, is a rambling
and somewhat plethoric idyll of the West, the hero of which is
an archetype of the oppressed and exploited, who finds a generous
asylum in the free land beyond the Alleghenies, and like Crèvecœur's Andrew the Hebridean, expands the horizons of his mind
under the beneficent touch of freedom. *The Puritan and His
Daughter*, written over thirty years later, deals with a different
phase of the same general theme. It is a vivid picture of the strife
engendered in America by immigrant families who bring hither
their old-world feuds and animosities, and the curative influence
of the free environment that, in discovering the good rather than
the bad in neighbors, draws together the younger generation despite
the jealous parental authority that would keep them apart. The
bigoted fathers make trouble enough—the fanatical Puritan who
fought with Cromwell and the headstrong Cavalier who defended
divine right—wilful men whom even the common frontier perils
cannot reconcile or make tolerant; but they are powerless to thwart
the ways of nature. The son of the Cavalier discovers an attractive
woman in the daughter of the Puritan, and when love walks in the
twilight what matters theology or politics. Youth has its own notions of divine right; in its creed the dogmas of John Calvin and
Robert Filmer have no place; and if the lovers are more tolerant
than the fathers it only proves that a freer environment will manage to soften the traditional animosities and beget a kindlier race
from the merging of classes. Such at least is the characteristic
thesis that Paulding elaborates through two volumes of discursive narrative interspersed with bits of vigorous action.

Of this kindly melting pot Paulding himself was a product. He had rid himself wholly of all ties that would bind him to Europe. He was partisan to no cause or party, literary or political, of the old world. He was content to be American and suffer his native land to bound his loyalties. In his own literary practice he refused to imitate the current English fashions and he spoke his mind freely to the American reading public for its greedy swallowing of cheap imported food. He did not take kindly to the English romantic writers, and went often out of his way to have a dig at his two pet aversions, Scott and Byron.[2] His amusing tale of *Koningsmarke, the Long Finne,* is a good-natured burlesque of certain romantic mannerisms of the Waverley novels, and a defense of Cooper's *Pioneers* for its homely realism. Paulding's dislike of the "blood-pudding" fiction that had come over from England, and that proved so disastrous to the genius of Gilmore Simms, was inveterate, and in his whimsical dedication of *The Puritan and His Daughter* to the sovereign people he comments on the public taste thus:

I am not ignorant of your preference for high-seasoned dishes of foreign cookery, most especially blood-puddings, plentifully spiced and sauced with adultery, seduction, poisoning, stabbing, suicide, and all other sublime excesses of genius. I am aware also that Your Majesty, being yourself able to perform impossibilities, believed nothing impossible. Possessing this clew to Your Majesty's royal approbation, I solemnly assure you I have gone as far as I could to secure it, with a safe conscience. I have laid about me pretty handsomely, and sprinkled a good number of pages with blood enough, I hope, to make a pudding. If I have any apology to make to Your Majesty, it is for permitting some of my people to die a natural death, a thing so unnatural that it has been banished from all works of fiction aiming at the least semblance to truth. . . . But, may it please Your Majesty, I am troubled with weak nerves, and my great grandfather was a Quaker. I am, therefore, naturally averse to bloodshed, and have more than once nearly fallen into convulsions over the pages of Monsieur Alexandre Dumas, whom I consider a perfect Guillotine among authors. In short, may it please Your Majesty, I abjure poisoning, or smothering with charcoal, and confess myself deplorably behind the spirit of this luminous age, which is as much in advance of all others, as the forewheel of a wagon is ahead of the hind ones.

In his politics—and as a good American of the times he took his politics seriously—Paulding found in the popular drift towards Jacksonian democracy an expression of his deepest convictions.

[2] See *Letters from the South,* Vol. I, *Letter XXII.*

It was moving in the direction he had long faced, and he went with it whole-heartedly, enjoyed some of the emoluments of office, and eventually served as Secretary to the Navy in the cabinet of Van Buren. With Jackson's attack on the Bank he must have been in deep sympathy, for his dislike of the new financial system was of long standing. His father had suffered heavily from a depreciated Continental currency, and he early came to distrust all banks and banking. His political views, indeed, were pretty much determined by the Physiocratic convictions that underlay his thinking. He had been a Jeffersonian long before the rise of Jacksonianism. Portions of his *Letters from the South*, published in 1817, seem like excerpts from the agrarian writings of John Taylor of Caroline. There is the same contemptuous analysis of the "shin-plaster dynasty," the same concern at the growth of trading towns, the same conviction that cities and poverty and low morals go hand in hand, the same trust in the perennial wholesomeness of country life. Such a passage as this will suffice to reveal his leanings towards a Physiocratic economy:

I was saying, that we have too many people living in cities, in proportion to our farmers, who, after all, are the backbone of every country, whence originates its riches and its solid strength. . . . Yet our people cling to the towns and cities, attracted by the hope of sudden wealth, and despising the slow, yet sure, rewards of agriculture, which, without leading a man to inordinate riches, secure him for ever from the chances of sinking into beggary or want. The race of paupers receives no recruits from them; for in all my sojournings, I may say with truth, that I never saw an industrious farmer forsaken, "or his seed begging bread." One great cause of the disproportion of numbers . . . between the agricultural and other classes of the community, is the great system of paper money, which has struck at the root of regular, persevering industry, whose rewards, though slow, are always certain. For some years back, hardly a tradesman in our cities, and of late in our little towns (each of which, however insignificant, has now its snug little bank) thinks of growing rich by his industry. No; he must get accommodations at some bank, and plunge into speculations: nor can you now go into a cobbler's stall without seeing a bank notice, or perhaps two or three, stuck up with an awl at the chimney-piece, to remind the honest gentleman that he owes a great deal more than he can pay. Thus is the axe laid to the very root of national morals, and consequently national prosperity, and the whole American people, farmers excepted, sunk into an abject subjection to banks and their directors. (*Letters from the South*, Vol. I, pp. 100–102.)

So confirmed an agrarian would easily arrive at agrarian conclusions in his meditations on the nature and functions of the political state. Unlike Irving, who, having no political convictions, was equally pleased with Whig or Democrat if he happened to be a gentleman, Paulding was something of a political philosopher with clear-cut doctrines. He was too shrewd an observer of ways political to be caught by party cries, or to ignore the class selfishness that would make government a party to its ends. As a Jeffersonian he retained an old-fashioned distrust of the political state. As an eighteenth-century liberal he would keep the state within narrow bounds. Jealous for a freedom worthy of free citizens, he wanted government to keep hands off what did not concern it. He would not have the state used as a cat's-paw to pull anybody's chestnuts out of the fire, whether in the form of Clay's American System, or what not. For protective tariffs and internal improvements—those grandiose schemes for hastening prosperity—he felt an old-fashioned repugnance that found issue in amusing caricature. In *Westward Ho!* he introduces a French publican of a Mississippi River village who does not care for Yankee improvements and describes them thus:

Diable! monsieur, another improvement; last year they assess me for one grand public improvement! one road to go somewhere, I don't know. Eh bien! I pay the money. Well, this year they assess me for one other grand public improvement—very grand—voilà, monsieur, one other road, right alongside the other, both going to the same place. Diable! I no want to travel on two turnpike roads. Ah! monsieur le colonel, I shall be very rich, O! very rich indeed, by these grand improvements. They take away all my land to make room for the grand improvement; they take away all my money to pay for him, and then they tell me my land worth four, six time so much as before. Peste! what that to me when my land all gone to the dem public improvement, hey? I shall be very rich then. Diable! I wish myself gone to some country where every thing was go backwards—what you call tail foremost, instead of forwards, for the dem march of improvement shall ruin me at last. (Vol. II, Chapter XVI.)

Satire aimed at the new gospel of progress is not infrequent in Paulding. In *Koningsmarke* he drew the picture of a politician that was perhaps intended for a burlesque of Henry Clay. The worthy Wolfgang Langfanger, member of the council of Elsingburgh, having "brought his private affairs into great confusion, by devoting too much time to the public good," began "to think it high time the public good should repay some part of its weighty obligations. He had accordingly invented, and persuaded the Heer Piper to put into practice, a system of internal improvement, which has been imitated, from time to time, in this country ever since with great success. The essence of his plan consisted in running in debt for the present, and living afterwards upon the anticipation of future wealth" (Book Second, Chapter VI). Big with his wonderful idea the busy councilor projected great docks and wharves for the commerce that was to be invited to come, a fine canal that would cut off a full six miles for barges that were not yet on the stocks, and a magnificent plan of new streets that led through houses that must be pulled down and fields that must forego their usual harvests. Such goodly improvements naturally cost money, and to maintain the public credit taxes were levied, and still more taxes, until, like the French tavern-keeper, the good people of Elsingburgh were brought to doubt the wisdom of investing in future prosperity at so high a present cost.

But the masterpiece of Langfanger's policy was that of pulling down an old market, and building a new one in another part of the village, in the management of which business he is supposed to have laid down the first principles of the great and thriving science of political economy, or picking people's pockets on a grand scale. He caused the people living near the old market to pay roundly for its removal as a nuisance; and then he caused the people that lived about where the new one was to be built, to pay roundly for the vast pleasure and advantage of its neighbourhood. Thus he pinched them through both ears, and got the reputation of a great financier. (Book Seventh, Chapter III.)

Koningsmarke is Paulding's most interesting work, and the utter neglect that has overtaken it is far from deserved. It is native and original, full of shrewd comment and sly satire, and it embodies most of Paulding's pet theories and aversions. Few books of the time are more amusing than this tale of the Long Finne who moves in a dark cloud of mystery woven by Bombie of the Frizzled Head, barks his sturdy shins on many a blood-curdling adventure, proves a true knight to his lady, and in the end turns out to be a very ordinary fellow who has been blown up to heroic size by the black art of romance. Paulding must have had great fun writing it, for his wit still preserves its freshness after a hundred years. It is a whimsical satire on the ways of the hour, literary and other, set against the background of an old Swedish settlement on the banks of the Delaware; but the chief purpose of its quizzical pages is the pouring of a broadside into the picturesque hull of contemporary fiction. It is an attack on the abundant extravagance of current romance that had been inflated by "Monk" Lewis and Sir Walter. Paulding cleverly hits off the high-flown and ghostly, the love of blood pudding, the snobbish contempt for the homely and native. Written in 1823, the year of Cooper's *Pioneers*, it defends the realism of characters and setting in that work against the charge of vulgarity and commonplace, but it takes pains to satirize Cooper's noble red man of the forest. Paulding's Indians are more like Bird's than Cooper's, material for burlesque rather than romance, but as he runs over the names of the warriors—"the Big Buffalo, the Little Duck-Legs, the Sharp-Faced Bear, the Walking Shadow, the Iron Cloud, the Jumping Sturgeon, the Belly Ache, and the Doctor, all legitimate sovereigns, with copper rings in their noses, blanket robes of state, and painted faces"—amusement at their childishness is tempered by the recognition that they have been overreached and dispossessed by the grasping white men.

In some of his later work the line between burlesque and serious is not so clearly marked, and one hesitates to pronounce whether *Westward Ho!* is a sober attempt at popular romance or a *reductio ad absurdum* of the current romantic flummery. Certainly it is a preposterous story with its melancholy hero driven mad by fear of madness and indulging in gibberish that comes straight out of Shakespeare, and with its ample crop of stock characters—Master Zeno Paddock and Mrs. Judith Paddock with their prying inquisitiveness, Colonel Dangerfield the easy-going Virginia gentleman who in staking his estate on a horse race embodies the plantation tradition, and Bushfield the backwoodsman who cannot live in a world that has left off its moccasins, and removes to a place where there are no laws and no lawyers and where constables do not visit a man who has thrashed his neighbor. *Westward Ho!* is not an amusing book; it is quite lacking in local color, and its casual bits of realism and occasional satire are too inconsequential to signify. *The Dutchman's Fireside*, written at about the same time, is far more successful. It purports to be an account of the Knickerbocker society in the days of the Old French war, and it contains some lovely pictures of old times that one reads with pleasure; but it indulges somewhat freely in adventure amongst the Indians and in the war, and its love story is needlessly romantic. Although Paulding still protests against a blood-pudding diet, he indulges occasionally in the high-flown, to the detriment of the idyllic note. Romance was all about him and he could not wholly escape its compulsions. Too casual in his work, too undisciplined in the craft of writing, he remained to the end an amusing amateur, a homespun man of letters who never took the trouble to master his technic. There was excellent stuff in him, solider perhaps than in Irving, but his failure suggests the difference between the journeyman and the artist.

CHAPTER IV

JAMES FENIMORE COOPER

Critic

FENIMORE COOPER is one of the puzzling figures of his generation. In his substantial character was embodied what may well appear no more than a bundle of contradictions. Romancer and social critic, feudal-minded yet espousing a republican faith, he pretty much baffled his own generation in its testy attempts to understand him, as he has pretty much baffled later times. No other major writer, unless it be Whitman, has been so misunderstood, and no other offers a knottier problem to the student of American letters. The stubborn clay of his nature was molded to a pattern unlike that of his fellows, and the difference was long accounted to him as a grave shortcoming. His outspoken individualism was a constant irritant to a sensitive majority, and his aloofness from the common enthusiasms was reckoned no better than treason to his native land. The right of the individual to question the herd pronouncements was a right not acknowledged by the herd, and the more it tried to silence Cooper's tongue the more caustic and loquacious it became. He refused to be silenced though it should come to open warfare. His later years in consequence were rendered unhappy by a thousand petty vexations, and his creative work was brought only this side of shipwreck.

How and why so great a misadventure befell him are questions of prime importance to which little attention has been given. That his tactlessness was at fault is commonly believed—his tactlessness and a certain pugnacious virtue that would inculcate righteousness by means of a broken head. But such an explanation, true enough so far as it goes, does not go far enough. The trouble lay deeper than that; it lay in the mind of Cooper himself, in the doubts and uncertainties that dwelt side by side with stubborn dogmatisms, troubling his speculations and perplexing his plainest counsels. And that trouble must be traced to an underlying conflict between the man and his age, between the ideal and the real, between high loyalties and petty fact. Fenimore Cooper

222

was the barometer of a gusty generation, sensitive to every storm on the far horizon. No other observer of that changing generation suffered so keenly in mind and conscience from the loosening of ancient ties, and none labored so hard to keep his countrymen to the strait path of an old-fashioned rectitude. His busy life covered the middle years of the great shift from an aristocratic order to a capitalistic order, and this revolutionary change provided him ample materials for brooding speculation. At every turn in the road fresh doubts assailed him. The perplexities and dogmatisms that clutter so many of his later pages, playing havoc with his romantic art, are a testimony to the confusions of a generation in the midst of epic changes. As honest a man as ever spoke his mind frankly, he endeavored to reconcile the irreconcilable, and establish sure standards amid the wreck of all standards. He could not drift. He must discover some working agreement between the old America and the new, between the reputed excellencies of the traditional aristocratic order, and the reputed justice of the democratic ideal. But unfortunately for this difficult business he was temperamentally ill-equipped. He was always at war with himself. His loyalties and his conscience ran at cross-purposes. His mind was packed with prejudices as an egg with meat. He was too partisan to compromise, and too honest to be content with the shoddy. His instinctive romanticisms were always being buffeted by fact, and his troubled mind in consequence was forever constructing laborious defense-mechanisms.

For those deep confusions that marred his later work and brought such bitter misunderstanding upon him, his heritage was much to blame. A romantic at heart, he was out of sympathy with the dominant romanticisms of his generation. Certain hold-overs from the past held him back from hearty participation in the present. He loved the world that was falling into decay too much to put away its virtues with its smallclothes; he would preserve what was excellent in the old to enrich and dignify what was excellent in the new; he would have the young democracy learn the decorum of a staid aristocracy. It is this fond lingering between worlds that sets Cooper apart from his fellows. He was an English squire of the old school turned republican, who did not quite like the company he found himself in. He was equally puzzled at the bumptious leveling of the coonskin democracy, and the

exploitative spirit of Wall Street Whiggery. But though he railed
at the newfangled ways with the testiness of a squire, he was too
confirmed a republican, too deeply concerned that the great
venture in republicanism should demonstrate its wisdom, to overlook its shortcomings. He would have it be so true to its ideal that
the world would acknowledge its excellence. He could not circumscribe his duties to election-day hurrahs; he must ferret out
treason in the market place; he must be faithful in counsel though
he utter unwelcome truths. It was the very faithfulness of Cooper
to his conception of an ideal republic that brought him into
collision with his fellows and filled his later days with bitterness.

It is easy to see where Cooper got those stubborn notions that
marked him as the last of our eighteenth-century squires and left
him obsolete after the adoption of the Constitution of 1821. From
his father, from the Tory rector of St. Peter's, Albany, who first
schooled him, from the Loyalist family of De Lancey into which
he married, from Governor Jay and the old gentry with whom he
was brought up, he imbibed certain stalwart conservatisms—
political, religious, social, economic—that mingled in his blood
and nourished the tissues of caste prejudice from which
his maturer social philosophy struggled in vain to escape. In
spite of his deliberate acceptance of the democratic principle, as
he understood that principle, he remained at heart as sturdily
eighteenth-century as any fox-hunting master of English acres.
He had early been bred in the old traditions at Otsego Hall where
he spent his boyhood. His father, Judge William Cooper, "a
testy and choleric gentleman easily wrought into passion,"—whom
he idealized as Judge Temple in *The Pioneers*—was an old-school
politician of high Federalist persuasion, a vigorous, not to say
truculent, embodiment of the stake-in-society principle of state-
craft. Smitten with the common itch for large land holdings,
he had got his hands on a huge virgin tract which he managed
in the old baronial fashion. He was a real lord of the manor and
late in life he recalled that "there were 40,000 souls holding land,
directly or indirectly, under me"; and in the year 1800 "he set
up a claim to having placed the plough upon more acres than any
other man in America" (quoted in D. R. Fox, *The Decline of
Aristocracy in the Politics of New York*, p. 136). Otsego Hall in
Cooperstown was a frontier citadel of Federalism defending the
western marches against Jeffersonian democracy, and Judge

Cooper used his economic power over tenants with telling effect. He "rode far and wide in the cause of Jay and later Aaron Burr, always preaching the musty doctrine that government had better be left to gentlemen, and that simple folk should vote as they were told" (*ibid.*, pp. 136–137). When persuasion failed he resorted to threats, and in 1792 he was before the legislature on impeachment charges. From the testimony it appears that the patriarchal Judge used direct methods with tenants in arrears; he "had been round to the people and told them that they owed him, and that unless they voted for Mr. Jay, he would ruin them" (*ibid.*, p. 140). By such arguments it was thought some seven hundred votes had been brought into the Federalist column by this exemplar of the old virtues.

But Cooper had drifted with his age far from such old-fashioned methods of class domination. In spite of his great love for his father he seems never to have espoused the latter's political creed. With the disintegration of Federalism the young man went with the country in its turning towards French romanticism. When and why he adopted the democratic faith is not apparent, but until middle life it would seem that he concerned himself little with political theory. He remained a provincial American with an intense pride of patriotism. But his long stay in Europe, lasting from June, 1826, to November, 1833, and the Jacksonian revolution that took place during his absence, put him upon an anxious examination of first principles, and thereafter to the end of his life the social and political problems of America were a burden on his conscience. He arrived late at a reasoned political faith, as he arrived late at his literary art, and it is impossible to trace the steps of his intellectual development; yet confused though his thinking was, and shot through with narrowing prejudices, he persistently sought for the light; and the germinal source of his dissatisfactions was the deepening conviction that, in Franklin's phrase, the affairs of this world are preposterously managed. From this conviction Cooper never swerved. The contrast everywhere between the real and the ideal took hold of his mind as an obsession, and put an end to his contentment. His romantic art suffered from the intrusion of realism; the romancer was constantly impelled to turn critic. It was his travels more than anything else that destroyed his provincial contentment. The perturbing influence of that experience abroad has never perhaps been adequately considered by his critics. No other American was so unsettled by contact with European civilization. It was a Europe in the throes of revolution and Cooper threw himself with enthusiasm into French politics, hoping for a wise republican issue from the overturn. But it was a Europe also of dignified and generous culture that was a challenge to his Americanism. It made a critic of him and turned his mind to political and social problems. Europe appealed to his native aristocratic prejudices, but repelled his democratic; Jacksonian America appealed to his democratic prejudices, but rode roughshod over his aristocratic. He found himself nowhere at home. Puzzled and perturbed, he leveled his shafts at both worlds and sought a haven of refuge in vicarious existence, at times in the wilderness beyond the soil and smutch of the Jacksonian frontier, at times in the Utopian world of *The Crater* where an honest man could find free play for his creative energy, until the trouble makers came upon him.

In temperament and outlook this later Cooper was another John Adams modified by changing times. A realist in his long brooding over social and political evils, he was at heart an idealist greatly concerned with justice amongst men, with a romantic fondness for dwelling on the virtues of earlier days. Like Adams he understood very well that equality is a Utopian dream; that social classes exist in every society that has accumulated property, and that sovereignty in the long run will fall into the hands that control the social economics.[1] The problem he set himself to consider was the problem of reconciling this universal fact with his own predilection in favor of democracy. That he regarded himself as a democrat his emphatic assertions suffice to prove; but no more than Emerson was he deceived by the spurious democracy of the times. "The writer believes himself to be as good a democrat as there is in America," he said in the Introduction to *The American Democrat*. "But his democracy is not of the impracticable school. He prefers a democracy to any other system, on account of its comparative advantages, but not on account of its perfection. He knows it has evils; great and increasing evils, and evils peculiar to itself; but he believes that monarchy and aristocracy have more. It will be very apparent to all who read this book, that he is not a believer in the scheme of raising men very far above their natural propensities." He would lift his voice in no hurrah for the ma-

[1] See the Preface to *The Redskins*.

jority, for he knew that the majority was very likely to be the tool
of the demagogue. He saw no peculiar virtue or special intelligence
in a coonskin cap, and he discovered no advantage in log cabins
and hard cider as a training school for statesmen. He had watched
the disgraceful campaign of 1840 with concern that gentlemen
should stoop to the demagoguery that marked that electoral
debauch; and it confirmed him in the conviction that "old-
fashioned, high principled gentlemen" of an earlier age would
never have been guilty of such traffic in votes—men like Chancellor
Livingston who devoted his later years to raising Merino sheep,
or John Jay who after filling with dignity many high offices retired
to his estate to concern himself with new varieties of melons.

Hating all humbug, Cooper made it his business to free his mind
from the several varieties of cant that were overrunning America
like pigweed. "Had a suitable compound offered," he said of
The American Democrat, "the title of this book would have been
something like 'Anti-cant.' " Roughly, the history of his essays in
criticism falls into two broad phases: the struggle to pull himself
out of the bog of eighteenth-century caste philosophy—from that
stake-in-society theory which his father upheld; and the struggle
to escape the fallacies of the nineteenth-century philosophy rising
about him—from the rude equalitarianism of Jacksonian democracy, and the materialism of capitalistic exploitation. His abandonment of the principle of gentleman-rule marks his definite break
with the philosophy of Federalism and the substitution of democracy. It cost him a prolonged struggle, for the social-stake theory
ran with many of his oldest predilections, and the evidence of that
struggle is scattered broadly through the pages written in the late
thirties; but having convinced himself of the social wrong involved
in the principle, he was tireless in refutation. In *The American
Democrat* he laid down the principle that "A government founded
on the representation of property, however direct or indirect, is
radically vicious. . . . It is the proper business of government to
resist the corruptions of money, and not to depend on them" (*On
Property,* p. 141). But it is *The Monikins,* a strange book much
laughed at by the critics, rarely read and little understood, that
concerns itself most largely with the theory. Sadly bungled though
the satire quite obviously is, it is nevertheless a spirited attack on the social-stake principle that reveals how far Cooper
had traveled from the doctrines of Hamilton and Webster, of

Federalist and Whig. Both England and America—Leaphigh and Leaplow—show meanly under his caustic analysis, the former perhaps more meanly than the latter; their institutions, societies, politics, manners, are an unlovely compound of cant and hypocrisy; and the root of the common meanness he discovers in human selfishness. He conceives of man as a queer mixture of good and evil from whom much is not to be expected; something nearer to Swift's conception than William Ellery Channing's; with too much of the Monikin in him to pass for a child of God; prone to error even under a republican system; insolent, tyrannical, loving fetishes, given to brag, too poor-spirited to be free, gilding his fetters and belying Locke's saying that chains are an ill wearing. There are depths of bitterness in *The Monikins* that startle the reader. It is a tale of doubt and disillusion, Gulliver-like in its fierceness of attack, that strikes through all the shoddy romanticisms of the times and reduces the current democracy to humbug. Subjected to such analysis the old Federalist shibboleth of men of principle and property is no more than the East wind in empty bellies. The possession of money does not change human nature; rich as well as poor are driven by selfish interest, and to give a loose to property power is to invite political disaster.

Your social-stake system supposes that he who has what is termed a distinct and prominent interest in society, will be the most likely to conduct its affairs wisely, justly, and disinterestedly. This would be true, if those great principles which lie at the root of all happiness were respected; but unluckily, the stake in question, instead of being a stake in justice and virtue, is usually reduced to be merely a stake in property. . . . Now, all experience shows that the great property-incentives are to increase property, to protect property, and to buy with property those advantages which ought to be independent of property, viz., honors, dignities, power and immunities. I cannot say how it is with men, but our [Monikin] histories are eloquent on this head. We have had the property-principle carried out thoroughly in our practice, and the result has shown that its chief operation is to render property as intact as possible, and the bones, and sinews, and marrow of all who do not possess it, its slaves." (*The Monikins*, Chapter XXVII.)

But though Cooper might deny the validity of the eighteenth-century social-stake theory, he saw no valid reason to abandon his eighteenth-century economics. In his preference for a social order founded on agriculture he was as confirmed a Physiocrat as Franklin or Jefferson; and this preference determined his judgment on the economic revolution under way in America. A people living close to the soil was living more wholesomely, he believed, than a city people immersed in trade and manufacture. For the capitalistic expansion that followed the new fiscal system of the seventeen-nineties, he felt an instinctive repugnance. Banking and the manipulation of credit seemed to him mean and sordid, and the spirit of speculation that was overrunning the land he believed was destructive of common morality. The activities of Wall Street he looked upon with the eyes of an English squire. To expect any sane progress from such worship of money, to assume that a high and excellent civilization could result from such worship, seemed to him plain madness. "God protect the country that has nothing but commercial towns for capitals," he wrote his wife in 1839 (Cooper, *Correspondence of James Fenimore Cooper*, Vol. II, p. 404), and the comment found amplification in many a caustic passage in his novels of criticism. A materialistic middle class with its gospel of progress interpreted in terms of wasteful exploitation seemed to him the hateful progeny of a period of "moral occultation"; and against this "Yankee" philosophy he waged an unrelenting warfare. In *The Monikins* he drew a gloomy picture of the America of the thirties when the land had come under a great moral eclipse; and in *Home as Found* and *The Redskins* he commented bitterly on the universal restlessness that was driving thousands to the new West to seek their fortunes. The settlement of the Inland Empire was no romance for him. The Great Migration seemed to imply the break-up of the older America he loved; and the impact of the frontier spirit upon the country seemed likely to destroy the last excellence of an earlier age. It marked for Cooper the final triumph of the acquisitive Yankee spirit, grasping and lawless in its crude leveling.

From these germinal sources—his love of the dignified ways of the old manorial families, his contempt for the middle class, his dislike of a bumptious leveling, his hatred of brag and cant and enterprise—came those sharp contrasts in his pictures that set the vulgar present over against the dignified past. His criticism was in no small part the reaction of a romantic to the unlovely works of an economic revolution. From his loyalty to the old came that subtle romanticizing of the eighteenth century that lends a charm to his tales, and from it came also that vindictive hatred of the frontier that spurred him to ill-balanced criticism. He could not like the new that was destroying the old. Like Emerson he was a man without a party, but unlike him he sought consolation in the past rather than the future. The excellence he yearned for he found in that older world whose stable ways were as yet unsettled by the romantic revolution, and from the meanness of the present he stole away to find consolation in the dignity and worth of honester times. The late eighteenth century became, therefore, his romantic haven and City of Refuge to which he returned gladly. He was always seeking to revitalize the old in an environment where, as he lamented, "the eighteenth century may be set down as a very dark antiquity."

That Cooper unconsciously romanticized the past is only too evident. Too often he accepted its self-proclaimed virtues as sober fact and created a race of squires that never existed outside his pages. Realist though he was in certain moods, he abandoned his realism in the presence of the tie-wig gentry. His father was as graspingly eighteenth century as Gouverneur Morris and saw to it that his own nest was well feathered; yet the son failed to perceive that the dignified professions of those old gentlemen were little more than splendid gestures. He made the mistake of taking them at their face value. Honest himself, he attributed an equal honesty to the older generation, and he watched with unfeigned regret the disintegration of an order that seemed to him the repository of much that was excellent. Fragments of its ideals he clung to; its dignity, its concern for breeding and manners, its fine distinction. Fragments also of its political convictions: its concern for law and order, its belief that all just law is founded in morality, its insistence that American government is one of principles and not of men. He put his finger shrewdly on certain fallacies of eighteenth-century theory, but he took too many of its values at par. The twilight is a mighty sorcerer and Cooper was bewitched by the half light that lingered softly on the familiar past.

This suffices to explain the grounds of the charge of aristocratic leanings that Cooper was persistently brought under. His bold defense of the landed gentry gave mortal enmity to the Jacksonians, and the tactlessness with which he pointed out the crude provincialisms of America—the bumptious plebeians he set over against the priggish gentlemen—was rubbing salt on open sores. *Home as Found* and *The Redskins* were onslaughts on the ways of the sacred majority that America could not forgive him for. Yet no counter criticism ever moved Cooper from his conviction that gentlemen of an earlier generation possessed dignity, principles, character, far beyond the speculators and politicians and "small-potato lawyers" of the present time of "moral occultation"; and the difference in favor of the old he traced to the economic basis of the tie-wig gentry. Believing with John Adams that an aristoc-racy is implicit in every established society, he frankly preferred a landed to a capitalistic aristocracy. Gentlemen of the old school were neighborhood patriarchs. Secure in position and possessions they disdained to keep an ear to the ground or court a silly pop-ularity. They were squires with a high sense of responsibility to themselves and society. Their stake in the land was a stabilizing influence in their lives; and their ample way of living, their well-bred leisure, their courteous bearing learned from a cosmopolitan experience, seemed to Cooper a desirable influence in a society lacking refinement and exact standards. To supplant them with the new gentry of Wall Street seemed to him plain folly, and he watched the decay of the old families with a pathetic concern. The Anti-Rent novels are a long defense of a thesis that comes to final expression in such a passage as this from *The Redskins:*

I say that, in a country like this, in which land is so abundant as to render the evils of a general monopoly impossible, a landed gentry is precisely what is most needed for the higher order of civilization, including manners, tastes, and the minor principles, and is the very class which, if reasonably maintained and properly regarded, would do the most good at the least risk of any social caste known. (Chapter XXVI.)

It is not hard, indeed, to understand Cooper's preference for Stephen Van Rensselaer the Patroon, to John Jacob Astor the fur trader, or Commodore Vanderbilt the ferryman; yet such preference was charged against him as un-American.

It was this revulsion from the meanness of the present that sent Cooper into the wilderness or out on the high seas, to seek adventure in the company of nature's noblemen, and forget the sordidness of the real. Here again the French school prompted his thinking, if only to supplement the romance of his boyish recollections. Natty Bumppo is quite evidently man as he came from the hand of nature, uncorrupted by the vices of the settlements; indeed one might question whether the back-to-nature literature can show another figure so enduringly vital as the Leatherstocking. From this same material is fashioned Uncas and the younger Chingach-

gook and still other lovable figures of his romances. They belong to
the free wilderness beyond the settlements, where the dramatic
flight and pursuit go on unchecked by impertinent fences. Here
their native virtues expand and their generous gifts find ample
play. They shunned the settlements as Cooper shunned them.
On the frontier, the middle ground between nature and civilization,
Cooper's spirits flagged. He had no love for the stumpy clearings,
the slovenly cabins, the shiftless squatters; the raw devastation of
the ax grieved him and he breathes contentedly only after he has
left the last scars behind and is in the deep woods beyond the smell
of rum. Such a man obviously was unfitted to write a just account
of the frontier as it straggled westward. He hated its ways too
fiercely to do justice to it, and when he comes upon it in his tales,
when he introduces a frontier figure such as Ishmael Bush in *The
Prairie* or old Aaron Thousandacres in *The Chainbearer*, it is to
depict the unhappy state of society where the virtues of nature are
gone and the refinements of civilization not yet come. No writer
has set down a more sweeping indictment of the frontier than
Cooper, and he set it down because the frontier seemed to him the
muddy source of the vulgar leveling he hated so heartily. A
gentleman, whether Indian or squire or scout, Cooper loved to be
with; but a vulgarian he could not endure, and a rascal stirred his
Puritan wrath. In consequence there runs through his work little
of the amusing picaresque strain that the heartier nature of Gilmore
Simms delighted in, and that made him a truer chronicler of frontier
ways.

Democrat though he professed to be, Cooper shrank from the
logical application of the democratic principle. The adoption of
manhood suffrage in New York brought in its train a sorry scramble
of demagogues to sway the popular will, a debasement of the
press, and a vulgarizing of political life that proved a sore trial
to Cooper's faith. He was too severely moralist to enjoy the little
weaknesses of human nature, but must set himself up as custodian
of public morals. Affronted by a bumptious vulgarity, he became
the assailant rather than the critic of Jacksonian ways. The land
to which he returned in 1833 was a broad target for his shafts and
he sent them into the white. The America of log cabins and hard
cider seemed to him to have repudiated the traditional standards,
moral as well as cultural, and he attributed the disintegration to
the corruption that came from the extension of the suffrage to

classes unprepared to use it wisely. It was this that embittered
his criticism in the caustic pages of *Homeward Bound* and *Home
as Found*. He was startled and resentful at the changes. "You
have been dreaming abroad," remarked one of the characters in
the former, "while your country has retrograded, in all that is
respectable and good, a century in a dozen years" (*Homeward
Bound*, Chapter XVII). The colossal brag, the meaningless unrest, the abysmal provincialism, he marked as the natural by-
products of the mob mind. In throwing off its old restraints
America was coming to deny all standards of decency and excellence. "What then do you deem our greatest error—our weakest
point?" asks one of his characters, and the reply is explicit:

> Provincialisms, with their train of narrow prejudices, and a disposition
> to set up mediocrity as perfection, under the double influence of an ig-
> norance that unavoidably arises from a want of models, and of the irre-
> sistible tendency to mediocrity in a nation where the common mind so
> imperiously rules. (*Home as Found*, Chapter XXV.)

It was during the bustling decade of the forties, when the agrarian unrest in York State was putting in jeopardy the old
manorial system, that Cooper's antagonism to the spirit of leveling became bitterest; and it was in defense of the old system that
he wrote the Anti-Rent trilogy that should always be set over
against the Leatherstocking tales. Taken together the two series
contain pretty much the whole of Cooper, his sea tales excepted;
either alone gives an inadequate and partial view. The one is a
social study, the other a romantic epic. The one gives a picture of
the changes the years have brought to a given region, the other
follows the retreating wilderness as the frontier moved westward.
The Anti-Rent novels present the reverse of the romantic picture
of the Leatherstocking tales. Their central figure is Aaron Thousandacres the squatter, who has come out of Connecticut to
possess what pleases him, regardless of legal rights. Offspring
of generations of covetous, psalm-singing Puritans, he has no
difficulty in justifying his lawlessness by Yankee logic. The
devil can quote Scripture, and in this respect old Thousandacres
is the devil's own son. When Scripture fails the easy gospel of
natural rights comes to his aid; the written law may be on the
side of the title-holder, but natural law is on the side of the
squatter.

"There's two rights to all the land on 'arth, and the whull world over," the squatter replied to Chainbearer's legal argument. "One of these rights is what I call a king's right, or that which depends on writin's, and laws, and sich like contrivances; and the other depends on possession. It stands to reason, that fact is better than any writin' about it can be." (*The Chainbearer,* Chapter XXV.)

Such lax doctrine, to Cooper, was the evil fruit of the spirit of lawlessness that was laying a blight upon America. A retributive bullet ends the fierce career of old Thousandacres, but his tigress wife, his rough sons and slattern daughters are driven from their home to plunge deeper into the wilderness, there to beget other generations of squatters whose vicious doctrines return to plague society. No romance blends with the tale of their lives; no sympathy softens the picture of the stern old Yankee. He has set himself against law and order and must yield or be destroyed. It is the old story of the struggle for land, a struggle that went on for generations between speculator and squatter, between rich and poor, with much wrong and much right on both sides; yet Cooper's sympathies are cold to the squatter's plea and he enlists God, morality, and the law, in defense of a title to forty thousand acres wheedled from the Indians for ninety-six pounds, York currency, spent in trinkets. Righteousness without a sense of humor is not easy to live with.

In much of his later work Cooper's romantic impulses are held in check by a growing tendency towards realism. It was there from the first but as he grew more critical it spread over more of his pages. He tried to hold the scales of his judgment even, but his realism was marred and distorted by his vehement nature. A mind exuding prejudice is ill equipped to deal objectively with material, and Cooper was too inveterate a moralist to accept the principle of impersonal detachment. He prided himself on facing fact, but he loved to preach; and having pointed out the wrongfulness of vicious morals he must follow it with a vigorous homily on right conduct. And yet despite his gross shortcomings there is a deal of realism scattered through his volumes. He consciously tried to be a chronicler of manners, to depict America truly, to recreate fairly present and past, red man and white, Dutch and Yankee. His prejudices certainly got the better of him in dealing with New England, and his romance certainly got the better of him in describing the Mohicans. Yet though he might romanticize Uncas he did not romanticize Saucy Nick in *Wyandotté*, but drew an excellent picture of the struggle between the drunkard and the warrior in the heart of the Tuscarora that reveals much of the Indian nature—an analysis that holds the scales more evenly than they are held in *The Last of the Mohicans* or in Bird's *Nick of the Woods*. The book as a whole, indeed, is an excellent example of Cooper's desire to substitute a critical for a romantic treatment of materials. In his discriminating analysis of the motives separating families in the Revolutionary war, there is no glorification of partisanship, no prejudiced espousal of a sacred cause, no division of sheep and goats. Cooper will have none of the cheap romance of patriotism, but probes skillfully into the motives and impulses that divided honest men amid the difficulties of civil war. More than that, he makes his villain one of the patriot party who uses the unsettlement of the times to cover his dirty tracks. It is a characteristic document that deserves to stand beside *Satanstoe* as an example of his later work.

Politics was all about Cooper while he was writing these tales, and his sporadic incursions into criticism led him into the field of political theory. So doughty a warrior must break a lance when all America was engaged in a great political tourney. While Whig and Democrat were loudly professing allegiance to the new doctrine of majority rule, Cooper was making his way back to the principles of the eighteenth century and discovering the essence of good government in self-restraint. The mistake of the new school, he was convinced, lay in confusing the present will of the majority with the rule of the people; the mistake of the old school lay in confusing the will of the minority with the rule of the people. Above and beyond both majority and minority is the eternal principle of justice, and any government that flouts that principle is bad government, no matter how sanctioned. In a republic which foolishly believes that the voice of the people is the sole criterion of right, the problem of justice is peculiarly difficult, for what remedies are available in cases "in which the people themselves happen to go astray, *en masse*"? It is the problem that attends every ethical interpretation of sovereignty, and it awakened acute concern in Cooper's mind. He could find no solution except in the good sense of the people, and with a vicious press and persuasive demagogues doing their best to befuddle the public mind, the outlook seemed dark. It was not the people he distrusted, but the self-seekers who set up to be leaders of the people. All the noise was made by demagogues who proclaimed their own mouthings to be authentic public opinion. How ineffectively Cooper struggled with the problem is written down in many a passage in his critical novels.

God help the nation [he said in *The Redskins*] where self-government, in its literal sense, exists. . . . When a people that has been properly educated by experience calmly selects its agents, and coolly sets to work to adopt a set of principles to form its fundamental law or constitution, the machine is on the right track, and will work well enough so long as it is kept there; but this running off and altering the fundamental principles every time a political faction has need of recruits, is introducing tyranny in its worst form—a tyranny that is just as dangerous to real liberty as hypocrisy is to religion. (Chapter XIII.)

Some observers pretend that . . . respect for law is gradually decreasing among us [he argued in *The Chainbearer*] and that in its place is sensibly growing up a disposition to substitute the opinions, wishes, and interests of local majorities, making the country subject to men instead of principles. The last are eternal and immutable; and coming of God, men, however unanimous in sentiment, have no more right to attempt to change them, than to blaspheme His holy name. All that the most exalted and largest political liberty can ever beneficially effect is to apply these principles to the good of the human race, in the management of their daily affairs; but when they attempt to substitute for these pure and just rules of right, laws conceived in selfishness and executed by the power of numbers, they merely exhibit tyranny in its popular form, instead of in its old aspect of kingly and aristocratic abuses. It is a fatal mistake to fancy that freedom is gained by the mere achievement of a right to govern, unless the manner in which that right is to be both understood and practised is closely incorporated with all popular notions of what has been obtained. The right to govern means no more than the right of the people to avail themselves of the power thus acquired to apply the great principles of justice to their own benefit, and from the possession of which they had hitherto been excluded. It confers no power to do that which is inherently wrong, under any pretense whatever. (Chapter XXVIII.)

Like Hugh Henry Brackenridge before him, Cooper was a democrat who criticized the ways of a reputed democracy because of his love for an ideal republic. Too few of his kind have arisen in America; too few who dare to speak their minds unterrified by public opinion. An individualist of the old English breed, he could not be intimidated or coerced in the matter of his rights by any clamor, whether of newspapers or mobs. He had his shortcomings in plenty, both as romancer and critic. Testy, opinionated, tactless, forever lugging in disagreeable truths by the ears, he said many wise things so blunderingly as to make truth doubly offensive, and he hewed at his art so awkwardly as well-nigh to destroy the beauty of his romance. Yet the more intimately one comes to know him, the more one comes to respect his honest, manly nature that loved justice and decency more than popularity. His daily life became a long warfare with his fellows, who exacted of him a great price for his idealism; but later generations should love him none the less for the battles he fought. That America has been so tardy in coming to know him as a man and a democrat, as well as a romancer, is a reflection upon its critical acumen.

CHAPTER V

SOME CONTRIBUTIONS OF NEW ENGLAND

It was the good fortune of New York to draw to the bustling city some of the best and most vigorous minds of New England. If the sons of Yankees flocked thither, the sons of Puritans came likewise, and the contributions of these latter to the idealism of a society rather too fond of material progress must not be overlooked. The literature of New York in particular was heavily indebted to New England. One need only run over a list of writers who came from New England to realize how great was its total contribution to the production of the New York group. Bryant and Halleck and Willis and Greeley and Beecher and Curtis and Tuckerman and Parke Benjamin and Stedman and Stoddard and even, in a sense, Melville, were products of that more serious-minded world that was to create transcendentalism and issue in strange projects of social reform; they were men who would easily share the ethical enthusiasm of their Puritan fellows, and create a literature concerned with other than aesthetic values. Not all of them were Puritan in ideals; Halleck and Willis quite evidently not; nevertheless the severe idealism of their work sets it apart from the productions of the Knickerbocker school. Perhaps not above, but certainly apart; and this unlikeness calls for some special consideration. Over against Irving and Paulding and Cooper may be set Bryant and Greeley and Melville, and the sharp contrast between them will serve to differentiate the native mind of New York from that of New England.

I

WILLIAM CULLEN BRYANT
Puritan Liberal

For upwards of half a century now too much of Bryant has been obscured by the brightness of his early fame. Since his death a serious injustice has been done him by the critics, who have dwelt too exclusively on his work in the field of verse to the neglect of other work in fields perhaps quite as significant. The journalist has been forgotten in the poet, the later democrat who spoke for American liberalism has been displaced by the youthful versifier who described American scenery. For this our bellettristic historians, who are impatient of any incursions into matter of fact, are to blame. Yet to ignore so much of Bryant results in underestimating him, and this serves to explain the thin and shadowy quality of his present reputation. He was a much larger man and more significant than the critics have made him out to be. His active and many-sided life is very inadequately expressed in the slender volume of his verse, excellent as much of that is. The journalist and critic who for fifty years sat in judgment on matters political and economic as well as cultural, who reflected in the *Evening Post* a refinement of taste and dignity of character before unequaled in American journalism, was of service to America quite apart from his contribution to our incipient poetry. He was the father of nineteenth-century American journalism as well as the father of nineteenth-century American poetry. In the columns of the *Evening Post* the best liberalism of the times found a place, inspired and guided by Bryant's clear intelligence. The lucidity of his comment and the keenness of his humanitarian criticism set the editor apart from shriller contemporaries, and made him a power for sanity in a scurrilous generation. But with his death the evanescent character of even the highest journalism asserted itself, and with the fading of his journalistic reputation the earlier Bryant of *Thanatopsis* shouldered aside the Bryant of the *Evening Post*, and an unconscious distortion of his career began, a distortion made easier by the fact that no outstanding work of the later period remained to restore the balance. In this he is like Jefferson. He is scattered piecemeal through his occasional writings as the latter through his letters, and the task of piecing him together and visualizing his work as a whole has not yet been done.

It will not prove an easy task. The narrow but real genius of Bryant is peculiarly elusive. His was essentially a self-pollenizing nature that needed few contacts with other minds. He lived within himself, little swayed by modes of thought, slowly maturing the native fruit of his speculation. The very tenacity and persistence of his intellectual life, the rigid integrity of his thinking, suggest the confidence of one who drew his nourishment from within, whose life was an organic growth. It is impossible to mistake his origins. The roots go down to deep substrata of Puritan seriousness and Puritan austerity, and the fruits which they nourish —somewhat scanty it may be but of firm texture and good keeping qualities—possess the slightly acrid flavor of old Puritan orchards where the care of the husbandman is pitted against harsh seasons and a meager soil. There is no pagan luxuriance, no riot of color or scent. The ethical idealism of New England is given stately form if not rendered altogether lovely; the passion for righteousness is held in restraint but it retains much of its tempered acidity. Happily there was little of the schools in Bryant, and nothing of the intellectual play-boy. His early life in the Berkshire hills, on his father's farm, as student at Williams College for a few months, and as a country lawyer, threw him upon his own intellectual resources and made possible a normal unfolding of his mind. He was fortunately spared a much-coveted life at Yale, where the narrow classicism and ungenerous dogmatisms could have done him little good. From Timothy Dwight the young Bryant could have got little to enrich his mind, and he might have got some disastrous checks. Left to himself he appropriated such nourishment as fell in his way and went forward on the path of a sober liberalism.

That he went forward at all is sufficient testimony to his native integrity of character. In 1825 when he removed to New York, the intellectual renaissance of Boston was just at the beginning, and in his new environment he never quite kept pace with the transcendental enthusiasms that so stimulated the New England radicals. At Great Barrington where he had been growing more discontented with his "shabby" profession of the law, he discovered little to encourage an independent liberalism. Bred up in an environment of intolerant Federalism and an equally intolerant Calvinism, he had much to outgrow and little to feed on. Few innovating ideas penetrated to the Berkshire hills where he was brooding on life and poetry, and the training of his youth was strong upon him. As a mere boy he had expostulated with President Jefferson in shrill heroic couplets, declaiming on the latter's reputed moral lapses and inviting him to resign his high office. He had summoned Napoleon to the bar of Cummington respectability and adjudged him guilty of high crimes against humanity; but such rhetorical outbursts were only echoes of a narrow world he was soon to outgrow. The blight of the tie-wig school of Fisher Ames did not fasten itself deeply on him, and by the time he had reached his twenties he was moving towards the twin goals towards which liberal New England was moving—the Unitarianism of Channing and the democracy of Jefferson. It was far more difficult for a Berkshire man to think his way through to such revolutionary goals than for a Concord; yet the unschooled Bryant who had never visited Boston till he went there in his twenty-seventh year to read a poem before the Phi Beta Kappa society at Harvard had already outstripped the Cambridge scholastics in the great work of setting his mind free. The stages through which he passed cannot easily be traced, but the fact of his decisive break with the dogmas of his youthful world is plain enough. During the last years at Great Barrington he put himself upon a course of reading and thinking, and from that provocative experience emerged the Bryant that we know. Calvinism and Federalism he put away, and he went up to New York completely new-outfitted in a fashion he never afterwards saw reason to change. In politics and religion, as in poetry, he was a man of few ideas, but those ideas were creative, and determined all his thinking.

For this change that was unconsciously preparing him for his later work on the *Evening Post*, Bryant owed something to his father, who had turned moderate Unitarian, but very much more to the Berkshire family of Sedgwicks, one of whom, Catherine M. Sedgwick, was just beginning her modest career as a "lady novelist;" another, Henry M. Sedgwick, was at the head of the New York bar, wealthy and liberal-minded; and a third, Theodore Sedgwick, Jr., was a trusted adviser on legal and economic matters, on whose pen Bryant came to rely in a difficult situation. Theodore Sedgwick seems to have been a liberal of the English school of Bright and Cobden, a confirmed free trader, and he induced Bryant to undertake a course of reading in political economy. During the years 1822 to 1824 the young man turned away from poetry and law to study Adam Smith, Thornton, and Ricardo, together with a number of pamphlets that issued from the Parliamentary debates over free trade in 1820. The adventure proved stimulating and definitely determined his attitude towards men and measures at a moment when American ideas were in a state of flux. It was therefore as an English liberal that he judged Jackson and

Clay and Webster, and as an English liberal that he weighed the
Utopian programs of Greeley and Brisbane and Ripley. There
is no evidence that he read the works of the French romantics,
although the major ideas of Rousseau came to him in the guise of
Unitarianism; and this aloofness from the social enthusiasm of
French thought, this failure to sympathize with the idealism of the
new sociology, may perhaps be accounted his greatest intellectual
shortcoming. Rousseau and Godwin and Mary Wollstonecraft
could have taught him much that he needed to know, could have
warmed his cool blood and awakened his Puritan sense of justice
to the wrongs of an exploitative order. A dash of Utopian enthusiasm would have made him a better poet and a better editor; but
lacking that he found himself sometimes out of sympathy with
men and women whom he should have understood better. A
liberal might smile at the measureless zeal of Fanny Wright and
Robert D. Owen; might dislike the militancy of the Abolitionists;
he might well counsel moderation; but he should not add his shaft
to the flight sent against them. But unfortunately Bryant too
often distrusted those who outran him, and would rather attack
than restrain them.[1]

As an English liberal it was inevitable that Bryant should turn
Democrat and support Jackson against Clay and Adams; and an
ardent Democrat he remained till the re-alignment over the
slavery question turned him into a free-soiler. He early supported
Lincoln for the Republican nomination—the more easily because
members of his family had removed to Illinois and there followed
the career of Lincoln sympathetically—and he accepted the Republican faith till the open alliance of the party with post-war capitalism aroused his opposition and weakened his allegiance.
Democrat though he was in conviction and sympathy, Bryant
was never a Jeffersonian, perhaps not even a Jacksonian, but
rather an anti-Whig, who measured the new America of the industrial revolution and capitalistic finance by the yardstick of
eighteenth-century liberalism. As a disciple of Adam Smith,
believing in the sufficiency of *laissez faire*, he looked askance at
an engrossing political state that enlisted its sovereign powers on
the side of the longest purses, and he viewed with scorn the mercenaries of the bench and Senate who defended the new citadels

---

[1] See his satire on Fanny Wright in *The Evening Post*, January 29, 1829, quoted by
Allan Nevins, *The Evening Post, etc.*, pp. 126-127.

of capitalism. In spite of his augmenting wealth he remained a simple countryman at heart, never a city man, never liking the ways of Wall Street, concerned with other things than money-making. If he had supplemented Adam Smith with Du Pont de Nemours he might easily have followed Jefferson into a Physiocratic agrarianism; if he had been bred in the frontier West he might have discovered more sympathy for a coonskin equalitarianism with its engrossing majority will. As it was, he occupied a middle ground between Jefferson and Jackson, an economic individualist who refused to conceive of the political state as a fat cow to be milked by whoever could lay hands on her. He wanted no share of the milk for himself and he saw no reason why others should have any. He turned his back on all middle-class temptations, refusing to speculate, not grasping at unearned increment, believing that America had a nobler destiny in store than could be measured by exploitation. An old-fashioned liberal, he set himself resolutely against the exploitative spirit that was clamoring for internal improvements, a protective tariff, speculative profits. The bitter struggle over the Bank and the American System, in which he was drawn to Jackson by principle as well as by admiration for his courage, laid the emphasis in his mind on financial and industrial problems and made him the outstanding journalistic opponent of Henry Clay. From first to last Bryant was anti-Whig.

There were times, to be sure, when he went further than that; times when his ingrained liberalism threw off its cool restraint and flamed up in dangerously disturbant fashion. In the depths of his Puritan nature was a quick sense of justice that might uncover strange potentialities; and associated as he was in the intimacies of daily work with two of the most radical spirits in New York, William Leggett and Parke Godwin, he could not remain untouched by their social enthusiasms. The former was a man of immense vitality and boundless sympathies, to whom social justice was a religion. A left-wing equalitarian democrat, Leggett hated all tariffs, subsidies, monopolies, credit manipulation, everything that the new capitalism represented. His sympathies were enlisted on the side of the new proletarian movement, and with the zeal of a knight-errant he greeted every opportunity to do battle for the cause. A home-made radical, created out of the native economics of the industrial revolution, he has been called by a late historical writer "one of the most sincere and brilliant apostles of democracy that America has ever known." His political leaders in the *Evening Post* aroused the admiration of such different men as Whittier and Walt Whitman, and were "perhaps the most potent force in shaping the ideas of democracy" held by the latter (Allan Nevins, *The Evening Post, etc.*, p. 141). His son-in-law, Godwin, on the other hand, was a radical of the imported school, an ardent disciple of Fourier, deeply concerned with communistic experiments at Brook Farm and elsewhere, and an assistant editor of *The Harbinger*, the mouthpiece of Brook Farm after it passed from transcendental to Fourierist control. His *Democracy, Pacific and Constructive*, was accounted by Horace Greeley the best of the contemporary studies of collectivism. Less militant than Leggett, his radicalism ebbed with the years and growing prosperity, but it sufficed to instruct Bryant in the elements of the current Utopian philosophies.

With such associates the older man was led somewhat unwillingly into the thick of social struggle and his mind shifted unconsciously to the left. The movement of Locofocoism in particular absorbed Leggett and drew Bryant after him. Set on foot by a combination of reforming economists opposed to banks, paper money, and monopolies, and the rising proletarian movement then beginning its long struggle to unionize the city workers, Locofocoism represented the extreme left wing of democratic equalitarianism, the avowed objective of which was to take government out of the hands of bankers and lodge it in the hands of the producers. It was one of the first native attempts at conscious class alignment between capital and labor. "What distinguishes the present from every other struggle in which the human race has been engaged," wrote Fanny Wright, "is that the present is evidently, openly and acknowledgedly a war of class. . . . It is the ridden people of the earth who are struggling to overthrow the 'booted and spurred riders' whose legitimate title to work and starve will no longer pass current" (quoted by Fox, *Aristocracy in the Politics of New York*, p. 396). How the democratic radicalism of Leggett was received by conservative New York is thus described by the historian of the *Evening Post:*

He was charged [says Nevins] with Utopianism, agrarianism, Fanny-Wrightism, Jacobinism, and Jack Cade-ism. His writings were said to set class against class, and to threaten the nation with anarchy. Gov. William M. Marcy called Leggett a "knave." The advance of the Locofoco movement was likened to the great fire and the great cholera plague. of these years. When Chief Justice Marshall died in the summer of 1835, Leggett unsparingly assailed him and Hamilton as men who had tried "to change the character of the government from popular to monarchical," and to destroy "the great principle of human liberty." . . . Ex-Mayor Philip Hone was handed that editorial on the Albany steamboat by Charles King, and dropped the journal with the vehement ejaculation, "Infamous!" "This is absolutely a species of impiety for which I want words to express my abhorrence," he entered in his diary. (Allan Nevins, *The Evening Post, etc.*, p. 152.)

The enthusiasm of Leggett sometimes carried further than the more tempered liberalism of Bryant could follow. He shared Leggett's distrust of Marshall and Hamilton, but he seems to have been only a moderate supporter of Locofoco principles. The paper had been brought close upon financial breakers by its attack on the money-interests. The working classes read it eagerly, but their indorsement could not make good the loss of advertising and patronage by the wealthy; yet even in such straits Bryant remained true to his liberalism and joined his associates in upholding the proletarian cause. The labor union movement had aroused the wrath of the employers and the courts were appealed to to suppress it. In May, 1836, "twenty-one journeymen tailors who had formed a union were indicted for a conspiracy injurious to trade and commerce," and after a trial the presiding judge charged the jury to bring in a verdict of guilty. Bryant at once attacked the judge in the *Evening Post:*

We do not admit, until we have further examined the question, that the law is as laid down by the Judge; but if it be, the sooner such a tyrannical and wicked law is abrogated the better. . . . The idea that arrangements and combinations for certain rates of wages are injurious to trade and commerce, is as absurd as the idea that the current prices of the markets, which are always the result of understandings and combinations, are injurious. (*Ibid.*, pp. 164–165.)

When the tailors were heavily fined by the court Bryant returned to the attack. He again pointed out the fatuousness of the legal logic by showing how the very price current was a similar evidence of conspiracy, and then appealed to a sense of common fairness:

Can anything be imagined more abhorrent to every sentiment of generosity and justice, than the law which arms the rich with the legal right to fix, by assize, the wages of the poor? If this is not slavery, we have forgotten its definition. Strike the right of associating for the sale of labor from the privileges of a freeman, and you may as well bind him to a master, or ascribe him to the soil. (*Ibid.*, p. 165.)

From defending the rights of free labor to defending the rights of free speech, was an easy step. When James G. Birney's Abolitionist press was suppressed by a Cincinnati mob, Bryant spoke out vigorously. "So far as we are concerned, we are resolved that this despotism shall neither be submitted to nor encouraged. . . . We are resolved that the subject of slavery shall be, as it ever has been, as free a subject for discussion, and argument, and declamation, as the difference between whiggism and democracy, or the difference between Arminians and Calvinists" (*ibid.*, p. 171). And when Elijah P. Lovejoy was murdered and his press thrown into the river, Bryant replied to those who believed that the Abolitionists had got their deserts: "Whether they erred or not in their opinions, they did not err in the conviction of their right, as citizens of a democratic State, to express them; nor did they err in defending their rights with an obstinacy that yielded only to death" (*ibid.*, pp. 171–172). From the defense of free speech Bryant went forward to the defense of free soil, and in 1848 he bolted Lewis Cass, the Democratic nominee, and joined the "Barnburner" movement that nominated Martin Van Buren. The terse pronouncement of the convention, indeed, might well be taken as an epitome and summary of Bryant's lifelong liberalism—"We inscribe on our banner Free Soil, Free Speech, Free Labor, and Free Men."

A trenchant critic of the rising capitalism, delighting in exposing the fallacies of the new economics and in pricking the bladders of political reputations—suggesting, for example, that it was scarcely god-like of the great Webster to accept a purse of $65,000 from his high tariff friends—Bryant was perhaps the most distinguished of the liberals created by the revolutions that were enthroning the middle class in power. The simplicity of his *laissez-faire* philosophy, like his admiration for "Old Bullion" Benton—whom he rated one of the greatest statesmen of the times—may seem somewhat old-fashioned today; but his ingrained democracy, his sturdy defense of the rights of free men, his championship of unpopular causes, his tolerance and fairness and keen sense of justice, ought not to seem old-fashioned. He may not have been a great poet, but he was a great American.

HORACE GREELEY
Yankee Radical

Horace Greeley has suffered far more disastrously than Bryant the common fate of journalists, yet his place in nineteenth-century America was too important and his influence on current democratic ideals too great, to be carelessly ignored. A Yankee radical transported to New York, he was the spokesman of the common sense and practical intelligence of the plain people of the North, seeking to understand the revolutionary upheaval then going forward, and bring it if possible to some issue in elementary justice. Far from being the visionary he was so often accounted, he was the most practical of men, accepting fact and seeking to square theory with reality; as ready to adopt new social machinery as the mill-owner to adopt a new invention. If there were social maladjustments, why should they not be set right? The patent confusions of the times seemed to him a challenge to the common intelligence. If civilization meant anything it ought to mean a generous life for the producing mass, and with the abundant resources of America the common well-being would never lie in jeopardy if simple justice prevailed. America had not yet fulfilled its promise; it had not yet become the haven for the poor and outcast its potential means allowed; nor with its growing cities where poverty found a congenial home, and its patrimony of raw lands flung to speculators, was it likely to become so unless greater ingenuity were applied to the problem. The industrial revolution was driving western civilization into uncharted seas; clearly, it was only common sense to take bearings and lay as fair a course as possible. To accomplish this Greeley was ready to entertain any promising suggestion. Intellectually curious, he had the wit to understand that the older agrarian America was being destroyed by forces that could not be stopped; they could only be guided. His eyes were wide open to what was taking place. He foresaw certain consequences implicit in the industrial revolution that his fellows were blind to. If it brought material advancement and the multiplication of conveniences—things excellent in themselves —it brought as well a sinister exploitation of the producers, as England with her Manchester slums had learned to her sorrow. If America were driving straight toward such dead-seas of wretchedness, surely only a conscienceless fool would refuse to help trim the sails.

No more admirable Yankee than Horace Greeley ever went West to make his fortune. With his Yankee capacity for hard work, his daring enterprise, his vigorous independence, he embodied an extremely sensitive social conscience, keen sympathy for those who do the work of the world, and a transparent honesty of mind and purpose. Bred up in the narrow poverty of the Vermont hills, remote from the culture of Boston and Cambridge, he retained the angularities that marked his frontier origin. His ungainly and shabby exterior was the outward, visible sign of a niggardly youth; yet underneath the uncouth exterior was as warm a heart as ever beat in Yankee bosom. His early life was a bitter struggle, aggravated by the succession of economic depressions that from 1819 to 1838 repeatedly brought hardship upon the country. Cradled thus in the anxieties attending the transition from an agrarian to a capitalistic order, nurtured in the harassing uncertainties that followed the break-up of the old static economy, he longed for a more rational social system, unsoiled by the heart-breaking wreckages that drifted into the new slums, unembittered by the lonely tragedies that laid a blight on the frontier. He believed that the honest worker, whether in the factory or on the farm, deserved a better fate than commonly fell to his lot. It was a scandal that poverty should dog his footsteps in a land potentially so rich as America; that those who did the necessary work of society should find themselves reduced to the status of the slave, whether black or white; and he early determined to explore the reasons why the workingman received so small an increment of the augmenting wealth of the industrial revolution. His struggles to gain a foothold in New York set him upon thinking, and before he was thirty he began those speculations on ways and means of returning to the producer a fair reward for his work, that were to occupy his mind to the last. The farmer and the wage-earner he took to his heart, and the furtherance of their well-being—despite the persistent and vindictive opposition he encountered—became a major objective of *The Tribune*.

Greeley's mind was as homespun as his clothes, and he never quite outgrew certain Vermont parochialisms that retarded his intellectual development. The environment in which he was bred was staunchly Federalist-Whig, marked by the exuberantly nationalistic spirit that sprang from the War of 1812; and the seeds of his national economy were sown in those years when to become nationally self-sufficient was the great ideal of America. It was natural for him to accept the leadership of Clay, whom he idolized, and to look to the Federal government for an adequate policy of internal improvements and national development. "We Vermonters were all Protectionists," he said in his *Recollections*. In 1828 the village of Poultney, where he was serving his apprenticeship, gave 334 votes for John Quincy Adams and only four for Jackson. Starting with this back-country faith in a benevolent paternalism, Greeley early began his speculations on an ideal national economy; and the conclusion to which he came, and which he never saw reason to question later, was that government must impose an intelligent wardship upon economic forces, that, left to themselves, tend always to the anarchy of individualism. He had suffered in his own person from the inadequacy and uncertainty of the financial and industrial machinery of the times; he was impatient of all purposeless floundering; the more he read the more rational it seemed that statesmanship must be judged by its intelligent concern to lessen the social waste and reduce the social friction. *Laissez faire* he pronounced a "suicidal" policy; it was an invitation to anarchy; it had impoverished India, and must impoverish America. From a critical study of the teachings of the Manchester school he came to two major conclusions: that agriculture and manufacturing are complementary industries, and the closer they are drawn together the better for the nation; and that a wide national economy can result only from investing the state with adequate regulatory powers. Hence his approval of Clay's American System. The judicious intervention of government by means of a protective tariff to foster the "infant industries," would secure them a domestic market that would—he allowed himself to hope—be regulated by domestic competition, would do away with the waste represented by transportation charges, and would return to the farmer an increase in price represented by those charges. In his opinion, however, protection was a temporary expedient, necessary only until American industries should get on their legs. "Protection is the shortest way to get free trade," he said in 1851 (*The Tribune*, January 23).

Greeley was never the tool of capitalistic interests that such an argument might seem to imply. All his mature life he persistently fought the aggressions of capitalism; yet in this crucial matter of protection his influence was thrown powerfully on its side, and the ingenious argument he expounded was at once taken over by the industrialists and used with telling effect. What particular turn he gave to the older Whig statement, adapting it to the prejudices of a more democratic electorate, a present-day economist has thus summarized:

The protective tariff, favored by the Whigs, was something different in his hands. The tariff arguments of his boyhood had been capitalistic arguments. Protect capital, their spokesman said, because wages are too high in this country. Eventually wages will come towards the European level and we shall not need protection. Greeley revised this plea; protect the wage earner, he said, in order that he may rise from this present condition of slavery. The only way to protect him against the foreign pauper is to protect the price of his product. But since capital owns and sells his product, we must needs protect capital. We know right well, he says, that a protective tariff cannot redress all wrongs. . . . The extent of its power to benefit the laborer is limited by the force and pressure of domestic competition, for which Political Economy has as yet devised no remedy. (John R. Commons, "Horace Greeley and the Working Class Origins of the Republican Party," *Political Science Quarterly*, Vol. XXIV, pp. 468–488.)

The argument for protection has been little improved since it came from Greeley's hands in the late forties and early fifties.[2] Nor, it must be added, has political economy devised the remedy for the evils of competition, that Greeley was concerned about, unless monopolistic control be regarded as such. Considering his extraordinary influence with the mass of farmers north and west, it must be accounted a calamity to agrarian prospects that *The Tribune*—a paper that Professor Commons characterized as "the first and only great vehicle this country has known for the ideas and experiments of constructive democracy"—should have thrown its influence on the side of artificial industrial expansion. That the mind of the northern farmer became so deeply inoculated with protectionist views, and has since persistently remained so, was due to Horace Greeley far more than to any other man.

The irony of it becomes apparent when the deeper spirit of Greeley's life is probed. Though he called himself a Whig, he was in all fundamental interests and conceptions a Jeffersonian, seeking in the spirit of the great Virginian to fashion a new philosophy to suit

[2] For his statement, see "Labor's Political Economy," in *Hints toward Reforms.*

the new times, more like him in free speculation than any other northern thinker of the day. It needed years for him to throw off the Federalist-Whig prepossessions of his youth, and work back to Jeffersonian fundamentals; but in the end he did work back, and in the end—always excepting this one matter of protection with its corollary of state paternalism—he came by his own path to the major conclusions Jefferson had reached a half century before. He was a spokesman of the older America seeking a way out of the confusions the middle class was bringing on the later America. In his social-mindedness that set justice above exploitation; in his readiness to change existing institutions in order to achieve justice; in his strong preference for an agrarian order as more wholesome than an industrial; in his trust in the good will of the plain people and faith in the local democracies; in his acceptance of the principle of states rights that during the struggle over slavery led him to advocate that the South be suffered to depart in peace:—in such conceptions he was a Neo-Jeffersonian, seeking to adapt the old principles to the needs of a different order. Greeley had never read the works of the French Physiocrats; he was unacquainted with their doctrine of the *produit net;* very likely he would not have accepted their teachings to the extent that Jefferson did. Nevertheless from his own experience he had come to agree with them in the exaltation of agriculture over other forms of labor, as he had come to agree with them in their social-mindedness. Greeley may be accounted a stepson, at least, of the old French school.

That for so long a time he should have turned aside from the path of Jeffersonianism to immerse himself in Utopian speculations and adventures may appear strange; and yet for so eager and hopeful a temperament it was the most natural thing in the world. It marked a step in the speculations through which he passed in pursuit of that remedy for domestic competition which the political economists had not provided. He was twenty-nine when Albert Brisbane's *The Social Destiny of Mankind* appeared in 1840, and on October 21, 1841, the first comment on Fourier socialism was printed in *The Tribune,* then only six months old. Thereafter for years *The Tribune* was the chief organ for the spread of collectivistic principles in the United States, Brisbane expounding Fourierism in the fifties, and Karl Marx contributing a weekly letter on European movements in the sixties, while lesser men contributed freely according to their special Utopian lights. With all this Greeley was in profound sympathy. Much of the theory he did not agree with; many of the plans and specifications seemed to him ill conceived; but convinced of the gross evils of civilization he welcomed free speculation as promising the only hope for their cure. Like Jefferson and William Ellery Channing, he put his trust in the unshackled mind, for like them he believed in the essential excellence of human nature when unperverted by vicious institutions.

It was this romantic faith that induced him to invest heavily in time, thought and money, in the Fourieristic foundations of the forties, the North American Phalanx in particular offering an opportunity for experiment on a considerable scale. In his deep concern over the selfishness of the competitive struggle, he was willing to turn from the bankrupt political economists to consider the plans of the "social architects." From Plato down those architects had been engaged on plans of ideal commonwealths, wherein the principle of brotherhood should supersede the principle of competition, and he believed the time had come when the great experiment might be tried with some reasonable hope of success. If the principle of collectivism could be successfully substituted for a chaotic individualism, the solution of the ancient problem of social injustice might be in a way to be achieved. This in itself, he believed, "would do for domestic competition what protection would do for foreign competition" (John R. Commons, *Horace Greeley, etc.*). When associationism failed, Greeley turned his thoughts eagerly to coöperation as a promising means of eliminating the waste of the middleman and destroying the wage system.[3] Somehow the middleman must be got rid of, he believed, if labor were to reap an adequate reward from its work. If one method did not achieve the result, another must be tried. To leave off seeking a solution was to acknowledge that society must remain a pigsty, with the strongest hogs appropriating the swill.

Such persistent venturing into Utopian experiment made Greeley the laughing-stock of more practical men who accepted the acquisitive instinct as the voice of God and were busily engaged in exploitation for their individual advantage; more important, it reveals how tenuous were the ties that held him to the Whiggery he still professed. Stalwart Whigs of the Webster

[3] See "The Organization of Labor," in *Hints toward Reforms*

school, middle-class bankers and industrialists, grew impatient with such pestilent heresies as exuded from *The Tribune*, and denied that Greeley was a Whig. In 1847 *The Courier and Enquirer* angrily protested:

> There can be no peace in the Whig ranks while the old New York Tribune is continued to be called Whig. . . . The *principles* of the Whig party are well defined; they are *conservative* and inculcate a regard for the laws and support of all established institutions of the country. They eschew *radicalism* in every form; they sustain the constitution and the laws; they foster a spirit of *patriotism*. . . . The better way for the Tribune would be at once to admit that it is only Whig on the subject of the Tariff . . . and then devote itself to the advocacy of Anti-Rent, Abolition, Fourierite, and Vote Yourself a Farm doctrines. (*The Weekly Tribune*, August 21, 1847; quoted in Commons, *Horace Greeley, etc.*, p. 473.)

The real animus of the middle-class dislike of Greeley is to be sought in his active championship of the great exploited classes, the farmer and wage-earner. He was always sowing the seeds of discontent amongst them. The betterment of their condition, he believed, was fundamental to any sound social progress. He was convinced that their well-being was interrelated; that whatever affected the one must affect the other. If the city proletariat were prosperous, the farmer's produce sold at better prices; and if the farmers were prosperous, the country would draw off the surplus labor from the towns and thereby sustain the wage scale. The key to the situation, he came to believe, lay in the land situation. The application of science to farm processes was a necessary preliminary to agrarian improvement, and he put the great influence of *The Tribune* behind the movement for scientific instruction in crop handling. But far more fundamental and immediate was the need of a drastic change in the Federal laws governing land sales. Believing that the wild lands of the West were a natural refuge for those who fled from the exploitation of the factory, he was concerned that those lands should be made available to the poorest settler. Greeley very well knew that the ruthless exploitation of the English proletariat was an inevitable consequence of the enclosure movement. Dispossessed of their land and lacking means to emigrate, the peasant had been thrown like sheep to the industrial wolves. Sunk in a hopeless wage-slavery, the Manchester factory-hand was an object-lesson in the fate that awaits the landless, too striking for a shrewd observer like Greeley to miss; and his agrarian program was proof that he had taken Goldsmith's warning to heart:

> Ill fares the land, to hastening ills a prey,
> Where wealth accumulates and men decay.

The freeholder, whatever the hardships of his lot, was still a free man and a free citizen, no fodder to fling to a huge-bellied industrialism.

To keep him thus free and independent, Greeley put himself vigorously into the great agrarian movement of the forties and fifties—the movement to democratize the national land policy that eventuated in the Homestead Act of 1862. The conception of the strategic usefulness of the western lands as a refuge for the city proletariat he derived from George Henry Evans, who in 1828 had established *The Working Man's Advocate*, was active in organization work with the mechanics of New York City, and contributed to the cause numerous pamphlets, one of which, issued in 1844, was entitled *Vote Yourself a Farm*. The pioneer work had been well done when, in 1845, Greeley joined the movement, accepted the arguments, and thenceforth was tireless in spreading the doctrine. The principle on which he should work he laid down in *The Tribune:*

> The freedom of the public lands to actual settlers and the limitation of future acquisitions of land to some reasonable amount, are . . . measures which seem to us vitally necessary to the ultimate emancipation from thraldom and misery. What is mainly wanted is that each man should have an assured chance to earn and then an assurance of the just fruits of his labors. (Quoted in Commons, *Horace Greeley, etc.*, p. 482.)

To accomplish this result Greeley introduced into Congress the first Homestead bill, according to the proposed terms of which any *bona fide* settler might file on one hundred and sixty acres of public land, to be paid for within seven years at the rate of $1.25 an acre; all public lands not thus filed on by actual settlers were to be listed at $5.00 an acre.[4] Greeley's bill was aimed directly at the old scandal of favoring wealthy speculators at the expense of the small man, a scandal that ran far back into the past. The traditional argument had been that the government could not go into the retail land business, but should sell in great blocks to responsible men who should in turn put settlers on the land. The

[4] See Charles Sotheran, *Horace Greeley*, p. 255.

policy had bred huge corruption, it had aroused bitter opposition, and had roiled the politics of more than one state holding western lands. In the early years of the century the province of Maine had repudiated Massachusetts Federalism and turned to the Republican party by reason of discontent with the old system [5] and the fierce Anti-Rent riots in New York State were of recent occurrence. It was against this policy of favoritism that Greeley protested, thereby bringing on his head sharp criticism from the respectable class, who declaimed bitterly against the demagoguery of a man who openly advocated a "vote yourself a farm" policy. To pay a middleman's price for public land, after that land had been wheedled from Congress in the dark of the moon, seemed to many gentlemen the only honest and patriotic way; but Greeley was unconvinced by such reasoning, and his concern over the problem became acute when the railroads began to appropriate huge tracts of the public domain. The policy of subsidizing them thus seemed to him wasteful and vicious; it ran directly counter to his fundamental principle of limitation of land holdings; it was repeating on a vast scale the ominous landlordism of the past.

Man has a *natural right* to produce and acquire property [he wrote], and therefore, I condemn a system of Land Monopoly, which robs the producer of one-half to seven-eighths of the fruits of his toil; and often dooms him to absolute starvation on the soil which he has faithfully and effectively tilled! The right of owning land is one thing: the right to own thousands and even millions of acres of land is another. The problem is learning to distinguish the one from the other. (*The Tribune*, April 24, 1849.)

"Settle the lands compactly and railroads will be constructed through them rapidly and abundantly," he said later. "The grants do essentially interfere with the true policy of granting lands in limited allotment to actual settlers" (*ibid.*, March 16, 1852). His proposed policy was far-sighted and socially just, but it was repudiated by a speculative middle class that would not have its unearned increment curtailed by visionaries.

Thoughtful as was Greeley's concern for the farmer, his concern for the city worker was even greater. The wretchedness of the New York slums was daily under his eye, and his honest heart was troubled at what he saw. That he should have sympathized with the emerging labor movement was inevitable; his conscience dic-

[5] See William A. Robinson, *Jeffersonian Democracy in New England.* pp. 43-45.

tated his stand, but his eager mind drove him to intelligent inquiry and vigorous support. He was the first American of wide reputation and influence to give serious consideration to the effects on the working class of the industrial revolution with its gospel of exploitation. The exploitation of natural resources was well enough; but the exploitation of human life was a different matter. A material prosperity based on social injustice, a civilization founded on slavery, he would have none of. That this great matter of slavery was inadequately understood and too narrowly interpreted by the Abolitionists, he was early convinced. He agreed with William Grayson and the southern apologists, that slavery existed in New York as well as in Charleston. "The worker of the Nineteenth Century," he said in *The Emancipation of Labor*, "stands a sad and care-worn man"; in America as well as in Europe he is falling into "that train of thought which is beginning to encircle the globe, and of which the burden may be freely rendered thus—'*Why should those by whose toil ALL comforts and luxuries are produced or made available enjoy so scanty a share of them?*'" If Theodore Parker could have lived a few years longer he must have shared Greeley's concern; but amongst the Abolitionists only Wendell Phillips joined with him in espousing the cause of the working class. Others held aloof. When appealed to in the middle-seventies to aid the labor movement, William Lloyd Garrison denied the existence of wage-slavery in America, and indignantly declined to take part in the proletarian agitation.[6]

Greeley's views would be reckoned advanced even today; before the Civil War they were regarded as incendiary, calculated to awaken class prejudice in a country where, as all patriotic Americans knew, classes did not exist. What, for example, could simple-minded Abolitionists make of a letter he wrote declining to attend an anti-slavery convention in Cincinnati in 1845?

You will readily understand that, if I regard your enterprise with less absorbing interest than you do, it is not that I deem Slavery a less but a greater evil. If I am less troubled concerning the Slavery prevalent in Charleston and New-Orleans, it is because I see so much Slavery in New-York, which appears to claim my first efforts. . . . [I would not] undertake to say that the Slavery of the South is not more hideous in kind and degree than that which prevails at the North. The fact that it is more flagrant and palpable renders opposition to it comparatively easy and its speedy downfall certain. But how can I devote myself to a crusade

[6] Garrison, *Life of Garrison*. Vol. IV, p. 248.

against distant servitude, when I discern its essence pervading my immediate community and neighborhood?

*I understand by Slavery, that condition in which one human being exists
mainly as a convenience for other human beings*—in which the time, the
exertions, the faculties of a part of the Human Family are made to sub-
serve, not their own development, physical, intellectual, and moral, but
the comfort, advantage, or caprices of others. . . .   In short, wherever
service is rendered from one human being to another . . . where the
relation . . . is one not of affection and reciprocal good offices, but of
authority, social ascendency and power over subsistence on the one hand,
and of necessity, servility, and degradation on the other—there, in my
view, is Slavery. ("Slavery at Home," in *Hints toward Reforms*.)

Here is a definition that may well be considered Utopian; but
however transcendental his general conception, Greeley was far
too practical to pursue abstractions. Having diagnosed the common disease that infects all modern civilization, he was willing
to use remedies that came to hand. Before 1845 he opposed
labor legislation, on the ground that the evil was social; but later
he supported the movement to limit the legal working day by statute. More and more, however, he came to believe that any lasting betterment must come from effective organization of the workers; that the salvation of labor lay in its own hands; and the great
end towards which he looked was coöperation. The stumbling-
block that stood in the way of coöperative effort was the common
distrust and suspicion that poisoned the minds of working men;
until they emptied their hearts of that evil, the path that labor must
follow would be flinty and its life meager and hard.

An incorrigible idealist, clearly, was this Yankee plebeian whom
Cooper believed a vulgarian, Godkin held in contempt, and
Bryant turned his back on and would not speak to—a strange,
child-like figure, with his round moon-face, eyes blinking through
spectacles and a fringe of whiskers that invited the pencil of the
cartoonist—yet carrying the sorrows of the world in his heart
and vexing his soul with all the problems of society; an idealist
who in the most sordid place in America, and after years of fruitless experiment, could still stand before his fellow Americans and
thus sum up his social philosophy—"the avocations of Life, and
the usages and structure of Society, the relations of Power to
Humility, of Wealth to Poverty, of served to servant, must all
be fused in the crucible of Human Brotherhood, and whatever
abides not the test, rejected" (*Hints toward Reforms*, p. 400).

In this faith—foolish it may be accounted by practical men, and futile, but certainly not mean, not ignoble—Horace Greeley lived and worked; to it he gave such strength and powers as were his, and he died at sixty-one of a broken heart. He foolishly wished to be President, but the American electorate that read his paper refused its votes, and his hopes were destroyed by the careless many who were untroubled about industrial pigstys.

III

HERMAN MELVILLE

Pessimist

Set down beside the austere Bryant and the plebeian Greeley, Herman Melville seems grotesquely out of company; and yet such proximities may suggest, better perhaps than words, an explanation of the futility of his dreams and the irony of the bitter penance of his days. Lifelong he was lacerated by the coldly moral in his environment, and harassed by the crudely practical; and without forcing the comparison, one may feel that Bryant and Greeley embodied in nobler form the twin forces that seized upon his bold and rich nature, and bound it to the rocks to be fed on by eagles. Like Jacob he wrestled all night with an angel, yet got no blessing from the touched thigh. Instead, his free spirit was tormented and his adventurous heart seared with fire. Far more truly than of De Quincey might one say of Melville: *Eccovi*, this little child has been in hell! All the powers of darkness fought over him, all the devils plagued him. They drove him down into the gloom of his tormented soul, and if they did not conquer, they left him maimed and stricken. The golden dreams of transcendental faith, that buoyed up Emerson and gave hope to Thoreau, turned to ashes in his mouth; the white gleams of mysticism that now and then lighted up his path died out and left him in darkness. Life could not meet the demands he made on it, certainly not life in America in the eighteen-fifties; the malady lay deeper than Greeley thought—it lay in the futility of life itself; and so after pursuing his vain dreams to the ends of the seas, the rebellious transcendentalist withdrew within himself while awaiting annihilation. There is no other tragedy in American letters comparable to the tragedy of Herman Melville. Bryant's melancholy is only the gentle pensiveness of twilight compared to the midnight of his pessimism. Hawthorne's gloom is no more than the skeptical questioning of life by a nature that knew no fierce storms; Poe's is only the atrabilious wretchedness of a dipsomaniac.

In the presence of a nature so tempestuous and fiercely honest, it is a rash critic who will dogmatize. There is no simple clue to his mystery, no common pass-key to unlock his mind. Raymond Weaver in his brilliantly creative study has perhaps done all that the critic can to light up the darkness, and later commentators can only follow in his footsteps. In so far as a simple explanation may suffice, the biographer finds it in certain frustrations that curdled the milk of his romance and turned it sour. Like Mark Twain in later years, he recoiled savagely from the smug conventions of society; but when he spoke out his views—instead of discreetly locking them up in his safe—and found himself fiercely assailed for unorthodoxy, he bade the world go to the devil and would have nothing more to do with its praise or blame. A proud sensitive nature, he took the world's contumely *au tragique*, and suffered it to mortify him. Or perhaps he was more like James Branch Cabell than Mark Twain. An arch romantic, he vainly sought to erect his romantic dreams as a defense against reality, and suffered disaster. In love with the ideal, and pursuing it in a wild adventure into the South Seas—his magic realm of Poictesme—yet "not so much bound to any haven ahead as rushing from all havens astern," he found there only disenchantment. Seeking his satisfactions in love of mother and wife, he came upon utter disillusion. The austerely prim and coldly correct Maria Gansevoort, to whom his boyish heart yielded itself passionately, was clearly no woman to satisfy his need of intelligent sympathy, and he fled moodily from the pale negations of a stifling environment. Even the finely loyal Elizabeth Shaw whom he married seems only to have completed his disillusion, and he withdrew into his study, and falling into "Plato's honied head," like Tashtego into the whale's head, "sweetly," or wretchedly, "perished there." It is the plague of the idealizing mind that is forever comparing a wife in her morning kimono with the Helen of his dreams. It is the curse of possession that plays havoc with romance; and because Melville's dreams were passionately beautiful, because he made heavy demands on life, his disillusion was bitter. And so like Felix Kennaston in Cabell's *Cream of the Jest*, and like Shelley in *Epipsychidion*, Melville fashioned his dream-figure to love. The elusive figure of Yillah in *Mardi*, whom he loves and loses and seeks, in a madly grotesque and satirical pursuit through all the civilizations of his land of Poictesme, is so suggestive of Cabell's *Domnei*, that it perhaps may be accounted the latter's prototype.

Remembering the mingled strains of Melville's ancestry, the critic is tempted to discover in his New England blood the source of his transcendental visions. Yet the influence is not easy to trace. Half Dutch and half Yankee, he certainly got his vigorous physique and hot temper from the former. His maternal grandfather, Major General Peter Gansevoort, was a huge bulk of a man who achieved high distinction in the Revolutionary War, and whose traditional prowess filled the boy's heart with pride. His mother, Maria Gansevoort, whom the son closely resembled in physique, was crossed in blood with that of the Van Rensselaers, the Ten Broecks, the Van Schaicks—the proudest families of the old Dutch *régime*—and was deeply imbued with the distinction of her patroon ancestry—"a cold, proud woman, arrogant in the sense of her name, her blood, and the affluence of her forebears" (Weaver, *Herman Melville*, p. 34). His debt to the New England strain is not so easily appraised. His paternal grandfather, Major Thomas Melville of Boston, a graduate of Princeton and wealthy in his own name and through his wife Priscilla Scollay, was not without his flashes of enthusiasm in early life, taking part with Joseph Story's father in the Boston Tea Party. But his incipient radicalism was soon washed out of him; he turned rigidly conservative, and to his death in 1832 he lingered in the twilight of the eighteenth century. As Federal naval officer of the port of Boston, he was a familiar figure in his cocked hat and knee breeches; and it was of him that Holmes wrote the verses, *The Last Leaf*.

He was of Scotch descent, and Melville's father traced the family line back to the thirteenth century, Herman Melville being twentieth in direct descent from Sir Richard Melvill, who in 1296 was forced to swear allegiance to Edward I of England. The blood seems to have run somewhat thin in Allan Melville, a conventional, pragmatic soul, who after making five trips to Europe, at the age of thirty-two, having carefully weighed the advantages, fixed his affections on Maria Gansevoort whom he met at Albany, and wooed with more propriety than passion. He entered business in New York city as an importer of French goods;

but hard times descended on "the greatest universal mart in the world," and in 1832, when Herman was thirteen, Allan Melville died leaving Maria Gansevoort and her eight children pretty nearly penniless. The struggle with poverty set its mark on the cold, proud woman whose ambitions centered about the success of affluence; and it left a mark of quite another sort on the son who was soon to measure her ideals with devastatingly critical eyes. The ways of mother and son were at the parting.

The volcanic passions pent up in Herman Melville's heart, the ardent imagination that sent him forth on long quests and brought him home empty-handed, can scarcely be traced to any source in Maria Gansevoort or Allan Melville. A strange, incomprehensible child he seemed to his mother, and strange and incomprehensible he remained in the eyes of the family—an ugly duckling of another breed than theirs. A bitter sense of aloofness and alienation from the intimacies of family sympathy seems early to have taken possession of him, and he felt himself quietly thrust out of the circle of respectable contacts. Melville's writings are filled with thinly veiled autobiography, and it is a careless reader who does not see in *Pierre* and *Moby Dick* confessions as frank as Rousseau's. "Call me Ishmael," is the opening injunction of the latter, and the book closes with a glimpse of "the devious cruising *Rachel*, that in retracing search after her missing children, only found another orphan" (Weaver, *Herman Melville*, p. 62). An Ishmael Melville unhappily conceived himself to be, an outcast and wanderer on the earth because man is an outcast and wanderer, to whom Nirvana is the only comfort and hope; and when he returned disillusioned from the South Seas, when he found no home by his own fireside, when he discovered his transcendental craftsmanship driving on the rocks of economic necessity, when the public rejected his mystical dreams and he was inexorably "damned by dollars," he perforce turned in upon his own broodings and sought solace in Plato. Driven by need from his hill farm in the Berkshires, he buried himself in the "Babylonish brick-kiln of New York," to pass long years pottering about the customhouse. It was the vast futility of life as he experienced it, that sent him to his study to find there such compensation as he might.

The stages in Melville's progress towards Nirvana are sufficiently marked by the four books, *Typee*, *Mardi*, *Moby Dick*, and *Pierre*. The first is his answer to the French romantic Utopia of man in a state of nature. That the rankling wounds in man's heart are poisoned, if not originally inflicted, by social institutions, he was partly convinced, and he felt a lively concern lest western civilization should bring its futile restlessness to the simple island people. The kindliness and simplicity of life in the valley of Typee, the compensating virtues of the unsophisticated primitive, he found lovable; but as the unhappy heir of centuries of Christian conscience, as a child of Hebraic ideals of righteousness, he could not eradicate the deep roots of ethical unrest. With Fayaway it was different. "Civilization had given her no veils; Christianity had given her no compunctions. She was neither a mystery nor a sin" (*ibid.*, p. 260). But he could not become a simple child of nature had he wanted to. He could never find his Nirvana in mere sensuousness; he could not sink into the mud of animal existence. Even while he bathed in the languorous calm of Typee, floating idly with Fayaway on the stream of being, his heart was beyond the narrow hills, and a cosmic nostalgia seized upon him. That chapter of his life ended in futility, and so he made his way back once more to the familiar places, with expectation still undaunted. Certain of his experiences on that return journey he has recorded in *White Jacket*, the story of his cruise on a man-of-war; and how near it brought him to oblivion is told in the episode of the threatened flogging before the mast, when fate intervened to save Melville from flinging himself overboard, carrying with him the brutal captain of the *Neversink*.

Amidst the constrictions of the old world to which he had come back, a fresh vision of happiness opened to him in his love for Elizabeth Shaw, and he made a desperate plunge into marriage. The post-thalamion of that thwarted romance was *Mardi*—a far-ranging "pilgrimage for a lost glamour," "a quest after some total and undivined possession of that holy and mysterious joy that touched Melville during the period of his courtship" (*ibid.*, p. 279). *Mardi* is a vast welter of satire and idealism, formless and wild, which in turn was no more than prologue to *Moby Dick*. This colossal book, fierce as *Gulliver*, broad as Rabelais, with its *saeva indignatio* that laughs as it rends life, is the great confession of his defeat. "It is good to laugh," he says in *Mardi*, "though the laugh be hollow. Women sob, and are rid of their grief; men laugh and retain it. Ha! ha! how demoniacs shout; how all skeletons grin; we all die with a rattle. Humor, thy laugh is divine."

And the conclusion to which the philosopher comes is this: "Beat-itude there is none. And your only Mardian happiness is but exemption from great woes—no more. Great Love is sad; and heaven is Love. Sadness makes the silence throughout the realms of space; sadness is universal and eternal" (*ibid.*, p. 279).

After *Moby Dick*, what remained but to put the external world of experience aside and turn in upon his own thwarted hopes to analyze them? *Pierre, or the Ambiguities* is his spiritual autobiog-raphy, the confession of a stricken soul. In the inconsequential matter of plot, a story of incest and murder and suicide, in its deeper purpose, it is a wild fierce tale of mortal passions, that traces the *élan* of mystical idealism to the buried depths of pro-creative instinct. It is the last bewildering attempt to understand the sources of the dream that had ridden him, and it is discovered in the passionate struggles of Enceladus, titanic offspring of the incestuous union between Heaven and Earth, to regain the king-dom from which he has been thrust. In *Mardi* the search for Yillah had been carried on under the watchful eye of Hautia, the temptress, whom "his whole heart abhorred," yet to whom at last he went in her bower of Flozella-a-Nina—"The Last-Verse-of-the-Song"; for in "some mysterious way seemed Hautia and Yillah connected." In *Pierre* Hautia reappears as Isabel, likewise a child of Heaven and Earth, who is set over against Lucy—the pure daughter of Heaven alone; and this dark Isabel robed in the mid-night of her hair, by appealing unconsciously to Pierre's noblest impulses, draws him from the safe orbit of the Gansevoort moral-ities, and makes of him "the fool of Truth, the fool of Virtue, the fool of Fate." Isabel is wild, unquestioning, mysterious passion, untouched by any Hebraisms; and this half-sister of his blood, this lovely embodiment of his star-crossed dreams, drives him unwittingly to destruction. Pierre learns at last that the vision brings poison in its kisses, for the divine in the heart of Enceladus is mingled with the clay of earth. The dream is man's final ironical curse; Yillah and Hautia and Lucy and Isabel—changing embodi-ments of the same mystical idealism—bring death to their lovers—this is the conclusion of *Pierre*, a conclusion that Mr. Cabell would not take kindly to. It was a black and bitter book, like *Moby Dick* "broiled in hell-fire," to fling at an easy-going public that cherished its Gansevoort conventions. With its fierce disillusions *Pierre* is the apogee and Nirvana of the spiritual romanticisms of the day.

That Melville was the spiritual child of Jean Jacques, that the consuming nostalgia he suffered from was mortal, the most casual acquaintance with his passionate rebellions should make clear; and that his pessimism was a natural end and outcome of his transcendental speculations, once those speculations had come to intimate contact with life, is perhaps equally clear. Transcendentalism in Concord village and at Walden pond, was one thing. Emerson's infrequent anger at the folly of men was soothed by the perfect art with which he phrased it, and never seriously ruffled his temperamental placidity. Thoreau's mystical communings were with the young god Pan; he was too wise to seek to domesticate a woodland nymph, and he was fortunate in escaping the dun twilight that gathers about the slow years of physical decay. But transcendentalism in the forecastle of the whaler *Acushnet*, transcendentalism that drove fiercely into the blood-red sunsets of dwarfing seas, transcendentalism in the hot and passionate heart of a man whose vast dreams outran his feet— this was something very different from the gentle mysticism of cooler natures and unembittered hearts where no Promethean fires were raging.

For Herman Melville, amidst the nameless obscenities of an alien environment, to keep his faith in the goodness of life strong and sweet, would have needed the boundless charity and simple paganism of Walt Whitman. But unfortunately for his peace of mind, though he might immerse himself in Plato, Melville was no Greek; he was Hebraic rather, out of Ecclesiastes, and Solomon and Jesus. "Away," he cries in *Pierre*, "ye chattering apes of a sophomorean Spinoza and Plato, who once did all but delude me that the night was day, and pain only a tickle. Explain this darkness, exorcise this devil, ye cannot. Tell me not, thou inconceivable coxcomb of a Goethe, that the universe cannot spare thee and thy immortality. . . . Already the universe gets on without thee. . . . Thou wert but the pretentious, heartless part of a man. Lo! I hold thee in this hand, and thou art crushed in it like an egg from which the meat hath been sucked" (Chapter XXII—3). From the lips of the ancient Preacher he had learned that all is vanity—even Pan. "The truest of men was the Man of Sorrows," he says, "and the truest of all books is Solomon's, and Ecclesiastes is the fine hammered steel of woe. All is vanity. ALL. . . . He who . . . calls Cowper, Young, Pascal, Rousseau, poor devils all of sick men; and throughout a care-free lifetime swears by Rabelais as passing wise, and therefore jolly;—not that man is fitted to sit down on tombstones, and break the green damp mould with unfathomably wondrous Solomon" (Weaver, *Herman Melville*, pp. 151–152). After *Pierre* came *Clarel*—years later— in which the theological doubts and religious unrest that mark the poetry of Arnold and Clough in England came to expression in a world that was untouched by them.[7] The abyss that lay between Melville and America had become deeper and wider.

Like all the transcendentalists Melville was a democrat, but his democracy sprang rather from his sympathies than from his philosophy. It was a democracy learned rather from Ecclesiastes than from Emerson; it sprang from his pessimism rather than from any transcendental faith in the divinity of man. He knew only too well how weak and foolish are the children of Adam; but in presence of the common fate to which the indifferent years hurry us, how stupid and callous are the social distinctions that society erects! Why should not life be a leveler, as well as death? His experience before the mast had taught him sympathy for the common man; he regarded quizzically the ways of the exploiting few and the sufferings of the exploited many; and he smiled ironically at the neat little classification that divides the human animal into sinners and saints. He was as comprehensive a democrat as Whitman, of the same all-embracing school that denied the common social and ethical categories of excellence; but alienated from his fellows, not drawn to them as Whitman was. It was not a sense of social aloofness that held him apart, but the isolation of loneliness. "When you see or hear of my ruthless democracy on all sides," he wrote to Hawthorne, "you may possibly feel a touch of a shrink, or something of that sort. It is but nature to be shy of a mortal who boldly declares that a thief in jail is as honorable a personage as Gen. George Washington. . . . It seems an inconsistency to assert unconditioned democracy in all things, and yet confess a dislike to all mankind—in the mass. But not so"(*ibid.*, pp. 320–321). He then goes on: "But truth is the silliest thing under the sun," and does not deign to explain. "Believe me," he says of *Pierre*, "you will pronounce Pierre a thoroughgoing Democrat in time; perhaps a little too Radical altogether to your fancy" (*ibid.*, p. 37).

[7] See Weaver, p. 365.

Such a man would not so much turn critic as embody criticism. His life—even more than Emerson's—laid upon America, was a yardstick to measure the shortcomings of a professed civilization. Cooper was a critic whom America could understand, and America hated him for his unpleasant frankness. Melville it could not understand, and it turned away and ignored him. Perhaps it was well enough that his generation could not comprehend his devastating speculations, and called him mad; or it would have cried out to crucify this maligner of all the tribal fetishes. He would level every barrier against the unpleasant that his age was erecting. He outran Thoreau in contempt for current material ideals. To turn scornfully away from the triumphs of his fellows—from the fruits of the industrial revolution and the romantic gospel of progress—this was incomprehensible blasphemy! Yet what had Herman Melville in common with middle-class America? Its hopes and fears were not his. He was troubled about life, and not about things. He was not concerned about politics or the political state. He was not concerned with trade, or money-getting, or romantic imperialisms. He was not even greatly concerned with political democracy, although in his time he had been as hot a republican as the best of them. The shoddy democracy of his time made his gorge rise; and to this shoddy democracy that shrilly proclaimed its excellence he paid his respects in words that suggest Lowell's *Cathedral*, but with a depth of significance that Lowell was incapable of. In the poem *Clarel*, into which Melville crowded so much of his later speculations, he comments thus:

This world clean fails me: still I yearn. . . .

This side the dark and hollow bound
Lies there no unexplored rich ground?
Some other world: well, there's the New—
Ah, joyless and ironic too!

Ay, Democracy
Lops, lops; and where's her planted bed?
The future, what is that to her
Who vaunts she's no inheritor?
'Tis in her mouth, not in her heart.
The past she spurns, though 'tis the past
From which she gets her saving part—
That Good which lets her evil last.

Behold her whom the panders crown,
Harlot on horseback, riding down

The very Ephesians who acclaim
This great Diana of ill fame!
Arch strumpet of an impious age,
Upstart from ranker villeinage:
Asia shall stop her at the least
That old inertness of the East. . . .

But in the New World things make haste:
Not only things, the *state* lives fast—
Fast breed the pregnant eggs and shells,
The slumberous combustibles,
Sure to explode.   'Twill come, 'twill come!
One demagogue can trouble much:
How of a hundred thousand such? . . .

Indeed, those germs one now may view:
Myriads playing pigmy parts—
Debased into equality:
Dead level of rank commonplace:
An Anglo-Saxon China, see,
May on your vast plains shame the race
In the Dark Ages of Democracy. . . .

Your arts advance in faith's decay:
You are but drilling the new Hun
Whose growl even now can some dismay;
Vindictive in his heart of hearts.
He schools him in your mines and marts
A skilled destroyer. . . .

Old ballads sing
Fair Christian children crucified
By impious Jews: you've heard the thing:
Yes, fable; but there's truth hard by:
How many Hughs of Lincoln, say,
Does Mammon, in his mills, to-day,
Crook, if he does not crucify?

The impieties of 'Progress' speak;
What say *these*, in effect to God?
'How profits it?   And who art Thou
That we should serve Thee?   Of Thy ways
No knowledge we desire; *new* ways
We have found out, and better.   Go—
Depart from us!'   And if He do?
Is aught betwixt us and the hells? . . .

For Herman Melville, at least, the barriers betwixt him and the
hells had long been gone, and only Nirvana awaited him.

BOOK THREE: THE MIND OF NEW ENGLAND

BOOK THREE
THE MIND OF NEW ENGLAND

THE New England renaissance was tardy in appearing and of brief duration, yet in the few years of its extraordinary vigor it imparted a stimulus to American life that its historians have not greatly exaggerated. We are now far enough from it to see that it was the last flowering of a tree that was dying at the roots, but in the tumultuous thirties it seemed to be a new birth of the native New England mind, opening on new worlds and great adventures. Though its prophecies might be little heeded at its own fireside, and unheard in the vast stretches of the West where men were clearing and building after quite different plans than the Concord architects were drawing, its significance in the development of American idealism—the ethical imprint it stamped on American culture—endured long after it had spent its force. It was the last and in certain aspects the most brilliant of the several attempts to domesticate in America the romantic thought of revolutionary Europe; and with its passing, civilization in this western world fell into the hands of another breed of men to fashion as they saw fit.

The revolutions in thought that lie between the eighteenth century with its aristocratic rationalism that conceived of human nature as evil, and the nineteenth century with its middle-class economics that conceived of human nature as acquisitive, are more clearly defined in New England and more sharply differentiated, than elsewhere in America. The flood of romantic speculation with its humanitarian emphasis on the potential excellence of man and the equality of human rights, that in Europe had diffused itself widely, in Massachusetts flowed into narrow channels prepared by Puritan discipline, and swept away habits of thought that had dominated New England for two hundred years. The intensity of the Puritan nature, once it embraced the new conceptions, imparted to them an intellectual and emotional unity that serves to explain the creativeness of the New England renaissance, as it serves to explain its failure to spread widely

271

beyond the confines of Massachusetts. Appearing a generation later than in Virginia, it drew its inspiration more largely from Germany than from France; it was intellectual and ethical rather than political and economic; and in consequence it held little in common with the Physiocratic agrarianism of Jefferson. The latter was sufficiently native to American economics to appeal to the common man from Maine to Georgia; the former was native only to New England Puritanism. Its idealism appealed only to rare souls, disciplined by speculation and trained in ethical values, men of strong character and fine distinction who counted for much more than numbers.

After all it is the ethical note that marks the Puritan. That New England has run so different a course from other parts of America has been due chiefly to its desire to serve God even though it might be serving self. Its material life has always been plentifully seasoned with the salt of religion. It sat under the teachings of an austere ethics, as it lived under the compulsions of a narrow economics; and the result was the development of a middle class distinct from that of the West where the desire to get on was less hampered by the desire to get to heaven. The outstanding social figures in early New England were the minister and the merchant; and these twin authorities—joined after the Revolution by the rising profession of the law—ruled in patriarchal fashion the inarticulate mass of the yeomanry. From these traditional leaders the policy of New England received a twofold bent: a bent to the ethical and a bent to the practical. The two have rarely fused in a harmonious and fruitful life, but for the most part have dwelt side by side under a covenant of noninterference, the character of current social ideals taking its impress from one or the other as it gained a temporary ascendency. In the three hundred years of New England history the minister has enjoyed two periods of intellectual ascendency: the first during the early days of the theocracy, when the commonwealth was ruled by the laws of God and John Calvin; and the second, between the years 1830 and 1850, when John Calvin was finally put aside and New England was in the way of being remodeled in accordance with the plans of God alone. Between these brief periods of ethical enthusiasm lies the main history of New England, a history that counts for little in our intellectual and aesthetic development, but that meant much and ill to the cramped minds of her sons.

This long stretch, arid and unlovely, was dominated wholly by the merchant. Its parsimonious thrift, relieved by few generous impulses, was hostile to all change and o the romance that is bred of change. There was no rapid inflow of settlers to bring fresh energy and expansion. The exuberant growth of other parts of America was never shared by rural New England, and in consequence the harvest of unearned increment was rarely reaped from her sterile acres. Except in the shipping towns there was little economic development. On its secluded little farms New England was living a narrow parochial life, cooping up its mind in a rigid theological system and disciplining its character by a self-denying ordinance. Public affairs were managed by the squire, for the minister was too busy defending John Calvin against the Arminians to have a care for much except morality and dogma. The renaissance became of necessity, therefore, a movement of liberalism—a vehement protest against the torpor of the dogmatist whose mind was shut up in a dead system. It was a sudden reawakening of the ethical passion of Puritanism that had slept for two centuries; a vision of a new heaven and a new earth that it proposed to take by storm. It proposed to rid the mind of New England of its decadent loyalties—the nightmare dreams of Calvinism that debased human nature, and the counting-house dreams of Federalism that conceived of man as an exploitative animal. It had discovered anew the beauty of righteousness, and in the name of righteousness it proposed to throw off the old tyrannies and create a society wherein the mind should be free and the soul enjoy its religion. The battle against Calvinism was only preliminary to greater battles which constituted the intellectual revolution that marked the renaissance.

It was the New England minister, and the spiritual heirs of the minister—a group of intellectuals and reformers more notable than New England had before bred—that gave to the movement its pronounced ethical quality. It was freedom for individual righteousness that they sought; not freedom for intellectual epicureanism, for romance, for aesthetic or pagan beauty. The transcendentalists and reformers had little time to amuse themselves with such things. They were too eager for the coming of the kingdom to dawdle over fiction or patronize the playhouse. They had been bred from their youth up on printer's ink; they came of a race that had long respected the printed page. Literary men by inheritance, they esteemed themselves stewards of a great cause. In rejecting their fathers' hell they became the more zealous to make a heaven of this world; and although the more practical Yankee was skeptical of their plans and would not suffer them to turn Boston into a transcendental Utopia, they succeeded in making such a stir as New England had never before known. For a brief time, at least, liberal ideas found a welcome in homes where they had hitherto been strangers; for a brief time the intellectual and not the merchant dominated New England.

PART ONE: THE TWILIGHT OF FEDERALISM

CHAPTER I

THE PASSING OF THE TIE-WIG SCHOOL

I

OLD BOSTON

THE year 1815, that brought to a close the unfortunate American venture into the maelstrom of the Napoleonic wars, may be conveniently taken to mark for New England the transition to the nineteenth century. With the rise of Unitarianism and the development of the new industrialism, a ruder and more vigorous age entered Boston. It met with a somewhat chilly reception. The patriarchal eighteenth century still clung to its warm chimney corner, not liking to be dispossessed by heirs of whom it testily disapproved. The old order stood on its dignity, tenacious of its habitual authority. It lived quietly in an aristocratic past, unregardful of the vigorous commonwealths rising beyond the Appalachian mountains, and contemptuous of the new political philosophy that preached the rights of man. A persistent continuity of temper marked the ruling class, a continuity little disturbed by the tumultuous revolutions of the past two generations. Although nearly half the voters of Massachusetts, in the year 1800, were Jeffersonian republicans, the knowledge of that fact only stiffened the backbones of the regnant caste. It colored their minds with a virtuous pessimism, but it edged their temper with the zeal of righteousness. The Boston mobsters, it would appear, were republican, and when the present custodians of the ark of decency were gathered to their fathers, very likely evil days would come upon the land; but while the righteous lived they would be faithful to their stewardship. Their own households, at least, they would keep clean of all democratic pollution; and so Boston and New Haven and Hartford—the capitals of New England culture—drew about them the garments of Federalist righteousness. Since the Revolution of '76 a new authority had risen on the ruins of the old Tory authority, but in spite of the change of personnel and outward political forms, the spirit of respectable New England remained pretty much what it had always been. John Quincy Adams and Fisher Ames and Josiah Quincy were little different in character and aims from Thomas Hutchinson and Joseph Sewall and Daniel Leonard—they were common chips from the tough old New England oak. High-minded yet narrow; devout yet not emotionally religious; thrifty yet generous in approved causes; engaged in overseas commerce yet oddly parochial—they were men fashioned by a rugged environment into vigorous stock, that would hold tenaciously to what they had got and would tolerate no insubordination on the part of their social inferiors.

With its twenty-five thousand inhabitants Boston ranked fourth in size among American cities. Philadelphia, the social capital of America, was nearly three times as large; New York nearly two and a half times; and even Baltimore had lately come to exceed her in population. The economic forces that make for liberalism had become largely impotent. Free land had long since been exhausted in Massachusetts and social lines were fixed. The northern frontier of Maine and New Hampshire was rugged and uninviting, and York State lay to the West. Except in the Connecticut valley the soil was thin and farming unproductive, and in consequence the more ambitious turned to commerce and manufacture which the physical conditions of the country invited. The dominant interest of Boston was commercial, and the ruling coterie of merchants and lawyers was narrowly Whiggish. They had modified their pre-Revolutionary political philosophy no further than to substitute the word republican for monarchical. The aristocratic temper dominated the town meetings, and the principle of property rule was commonly accepted as the essence of political wisdom. In substituting Federalism for Toryism there was no easing of the restrictions on rebellious plebeians. Quite repudiated were the rude leveling ways of the great Revolutionary adventure. Boston gentlemen had come to understand too well the danger of encouraging the mob, for as Fisher Ames pointed out in 1787, "The people have turned against their teachers the doctrines, which were inculcated to effect the late revolution" (*Works*, p. 11). Boston had had enough of revolutions since Daniel Shays had got up one of his own aimed at the Boston purse, and French Jacobins had let loose their devastating ideas upon a gullible world. Revolutions that were not made in Boston, by Boston gentlemen, were quite certain to be wicked and seditious; and Boston had definitely gone out of the revolution business. It wanted above all things to undo the mischief that had already been done, and take back into safe hands the political power which in the days of revolutionary enthusiasm had been seized by the agrarian democracy.

In the last decade of the eighteenth century the intellectual isolation of New England was sharply accentuated and the consequent intellectual stagnation became more disastrous. In other portions of America French revolutionary theories of man and society were spreading widely and shouldering aside the outworn past. A romantic equalitarianism, based on the doctrine of human perfectibility, was displacing the traditional economic realism, established on the dogma of total depravity. The leveling movement, in consequence, was provided with a persuasive idealism that awakened troublesome aspirations in the disfranchised majority and gave a strong impetus to the democratic movement. But New England leaders stood resolutely apart, accounting all equalitarianism sheer romantic folly. The old stubborn realism held its ground, interpreting political principles in terms of economics, and dogmatically maintaining the sacred rights of property. Boston Federalism refused to have anything to do with "atheistic France," the fruitful mother of Jacobin follies. Pollution, it was convinced, must result from any commerce with infidel and innovating ideas. Gunpowder that was played with might explode, and New England wanted no blowing up of her excellent society. Virginia had lent credulous ears to the voice of France, and the result was the atheist Jefferson and the rabble of his licentious followers. Massachusetts was not gullible and it would tolerate no Jeffersonian atheisms. And so instead of adapting French romantic philosophy to new world needs, seizing upon its social idealism to leaven the crude American lump— as Jefferson and Colonel Mason and John Taylor and many another Virginia gentleman had done—Boston Federalism rejected French ideas in the mass, dubbed French idealism Jacobinism, and turned back upon a stubborn reaction.

The disastrous consequences of that rejection upon the mind of New England cannot easily be measured. It is clear enough, nevertheless, that the renaissance was delayed a full generation.

and when it came it assumed certain provincialisms that greatly lessened its permanent influence upon the rest of America. The impress of its contribution upon our national thought has been far less permanent than that of Virginia, that came a generation earlier and was primarily economic and political. It is a suggestive fact that in the work of adapting the new Federal Constitution to democratic ends, New England contributed no creative leader, none in any way comparable to Jefferson; but on the contrary her most representative leaders—and in particular Webster— followed the eighteenth-century tradition in combating the equalitarian advance in the interest of economic groups. Some explanation of this fact may be found, perhaps, in the selfish isolation of New England Federalism, that closed the door on the liberal thought of France.

In consequence of such isolation Boston became the recognized home of the philosophy of a stake-in-society. If it clung tenaciously to an old-fashioned Federalism after it had been abandoned elsewhere, it was because Boston was more middle-class than Charleston, and had not learned from experience with Jacksonianism how easily the majority will may be shaped and controlled to particular ends. It inherited the old Tory contempt for democracy and relied on the old stock arguments to combat it. Its habitual tone was one of virtuous arrogance. The one great and ever-present fear that haunted the pillows of worthy Boston merchants and turned their dreams to nightmares, was fear of the mob getting out of hand; and democracy, for them, was only a euphemism for the mob—the ever-present menace to sober and decent government. In the judgment of Theodore Dwight, brother of Timothy, "there could be nothing more dreadful this side of hell." Nowhere else in America did the reaction against the democratic ideal carry so far as in Boston. The church and the merchant associations joined with polite society to cry it down, and upon the head of the democrat fell the most extravagant vituperation. For a generation few respectable New Englanders raised their voices in defense of democracy, but gentlemen of principle and property followed the lead of the little clique that was driving straight towards the Hartford Convention—blind sailors navigating the Dead Sea of Federalist pessimism.

All this was before the reputed time of plain living and high thinking. Intellectual Boston was as parochial as political Boston.

The lights whom Bostonians regarded as the torch-bearers of New England culture have long since been extinguished and their names forgotten even in Beacon Street. Amongst the literati of the little Boston of 1800 the historian need concern himself with no more than two or three: Fisher Ames (1758–1808), the Federalist lawyer-wit, and Robert Treat Paine (1773–1811), esteemed the ninth wonder of the Boston world. Other figures there were, of course, in addition to the literati: Harrison Gray Otis, the eloquent voice of Faneuil Hall, and Josiah Quincy, whom Lowell likened to an old Roman of the elder virtuous days, and who during a long life of ninety-two years was an example of stalwart and antiquated Federalism. Old Boston bred dignified figures in plenty, men admirably equipped to be college presidents, ambassadors, orators on formal occasions, purveyors of cultivated inutilities and polished commonplace—men like Edward Everett, whom all Boston praised while they lived and forgot when they were dead; but it bred no thinkers or men of letters who count in the larger history of America. Boston was still parochial, content with little things.

II

FISHER AMES
The Oracle of the Tie-Wig School

Of this testy little world that clung to its smallclothes and tie-wig, refusing to adopt the Jacobin innovation in dress and manners and politics, declining to temper its prejudices to the gusty whims of a leveling age, Fisher Ames was the universal counselor and oracle. A vivacious little gentleman to whom politics was the breath of life, he achieved so tremendous a reputation in his short lifetime that all New England looked to him for leadership and Harvard College wanted to make him its president. He came of vigorous stock, prone to consult its own will and speak its opinions with no squeamish concern for a neighbor's views. His brother, Dr. Nathaniel Ames, was as violent a Republican as Fisher was a Federalist, a hater of all lawyers whom he accounted the "pettifogging interest"; and when the two members of the family came together at dinner the talk must have been worth hearing. Diverse worlds and hostile philosophies faced each other over the roast, and the sauce no doubt was well spiced. Dr.

Nathaniel had a pretty gift himself in the way of pungent speech,
and Fisher's wit was the admiration of all New England. When
Gouverneur Morris—reputed the greatest wit in America—visited
Massachusetts, Fisher Ames was pitted against him, and Boston
believed that the honor of the Bay State was worthily upheld.
His pet hobby was the inherent tyranny of all democracies, and
when he once got astride his wooden horse and dug in the spurs,
the onset was tremendous. The letters that have come down to
us are a gold mine of picturesque vituperation, from which one may
dig a wallet of choice nuggets. The vivacity of his anathemas is
delightful, and one would give much to have heard Dr. Nathaniel's retort militant.

There are the solidest grounds for regarding Fisher Ames as
the representative citizen of Boston in the year 1800. He was the
cleverest and most intelligent spokesman of a social and political circle quite untouched by the new French liberalisms,
content with the habitual and familiar, and mightily concerned
that the future should be as like the past as one generation of
oysters is like another. A lawyer who shared the strong property consciousness of the Boston merchant, and a churchman
who accepted the moral leadership of the Calvinist clergy, he
offered stout and uncompromising resistance to innovation.
"A change, though for the better, is always to be deplored by
the generation in which it is effected," he said. "Much is lost
and more is hazarded" (*Works*, p. 15, edition of 1809). The new
gospel of progress that came in with French romanticisms, he
would have none of. In the face of a noisy Jacobinism that threatened to carry all before it, he fought a spirited fight, turning
pamphleteer when his broken health removed him from Congress,
counseling and scolding his fellow Federalists with his last breath.
Others might truckle and compromise, but not Fisher Ames. His
faith was founded on the solid granite of Yankee prejudice.

The very solidity of that prejudice made him the trenchant
spokesman of the older Boston conservatisms—that and the vivacity of his prose style which is approved Augustan, uncorrupted
by what he dubbed "pompous Johnsonian affectation." His contemporary reputation was enormous. Accounted a great orator,
he was accounted an even greater political philosopher, and his
pamphlets were appraised by President Kirkland of Harvard
as "the light of genius and wisdom darted athwart the gloom of

our political chaos." "In the character of Mr. Ames," said the Harvard president, "the circle of the virtues seemed to be complete, and each virtue in its proper place" (*Works*, Introduction, p. xxviii). Yet in spite of so authoritative a pronouncement, Fisher Ames does not seem today so great a man as he seemed to his own generation. From the data collected in a stout volume published soon after his death as "a voice of instruction and warning to his country," and from the letters published by his son in 1854, it is plain enough that this "powerful and original genius" was a retailer of somewhat shopworn goods, a complete Federalist Tory after the current Boston fashion. To Fisher Ames Federalism, as understood in New England, was a religion. He defended it with the ardor of the moralist, convinced that it included all the political virtues, and that whoever rejected it was a child of the devil. Whenever he considered the unpromising state of the country—which luxury he often indulged—whether in the midst of Shays's Rebellion or of the Jeffersonian revolution, he fell into black pessimism. He grew hot from fires of his own kindling, and the gloomier he became the more vigorously he blew the bellows.

To the sinful publican self-conscious virtue is peculiarly irritating, and since Fisher Ames accounted most of his generation political publicans, he was at odds with all but a scant remnant of Federalist saints. From this isolation, from the defeat that overwhelmed his party in the great election of 1800, and from aggravating ill health, which beginning when he was thirty-seven incapacitated him three years later for public life, he fell into a state of chronic political despondency that extracted a grim pleasure from the contemplation of democratic follies and the anarchy towards which the country was hastening. During his last years his wit became acid; his letters are filled with caustic comment to sharpen the temper of those on the fighting line. Of these racy comments, so characteristic of Federalist spleen, a few examples must serve to convey the spirit: "Our country is too big for union, too sordid for patriotism, too democratic for liberty." "We are in the hands of the philosophers of Lilliput." "I have as loyal and respectful an opinion as possible of the sincerity in folly of our rulers." "As to liberty, we are to have none—democracy will kindle its own hell, and consume in it." "Democracy is a troubled spirit, fated never to rest, and whose dreams, if it sleeps, present only visions of hell." In his last years Fisher Ames had become a shrill Jeremiah crying in the gates of an Israel that mocked the old prophets.

His political philosophy was simple, yet so native to Calvinist-Yankee New England, and historically so characteristic, that it provides a useful candle to throw light into the old New England garrets. In certain aspects it is close kin to the Whiggery of Locke and Pitt, particularly in its concern for the sacred right of property rule—a principle that he casually recognizes in his frequent assertion that "the mass of the federalists are the owners of the commercial and monied wealth of the nation" (*Works*, p. 426). But in post-Revolutionary Boston, suffering from the acute fright inflicted by Daniel Shays, this English Whiggery had come to assume a particular native form that differentiated it from its original. In the primitive Calvinist-Yankee world political theory had been shaped by the theocratic conception of stewardship, by which was meant an authoritative leadership reposing in the best and wisest, yet subject to the will of God as revealed in the Bible. Minister and magistrate, therefore, professed to justify their acts, not by expediency or interest, but by absolute ethical standards. From this early practice developed the pronounced ethical temper of New England political thought that set it apart from the Virginia school, a temper that persisted after the transfer of authority from Puritan minister and magistrate to Tory merchant and lawyer. With the growth of the aristocratic spirit in the middle eighteenth century, the squirearchy assumed unchallenged political leadership, and it was from the remnant of the old gentry remaining after the expulsion of the Loyalists, strengthened by a new generation of merchants and lawyers, that Boston Federalism drew its personnel. It professed republicanism, but it was instinctively aristocratic. It was true to its Puritan origins in expounding its political philosophy in terms of an absolute morality, and true to its aristocratic origins in assuming to be the special custodians of law and order. It no more questioned its special right to rulership in the state than it questioned its social position; and in both politics and society it professed the ancient doctrine of stewardship.

The kinship between the political philosophy of Fisher Ames and John Adams is quite evident. They are cut out of the same Puritan-Yankee cloth, but the former is a more careless tailor. Founded on less adequate analysis and lacking the wide historical appeal of Adams, assuming rather than proving the fact of a universal property aristocracy, and the economic origins of political power, the philosophy of Ames postulates the same ideal of justice as the end of government, discovers in faction the dragon to be slain, and concludes that only a static division of powers can insure political stability. Nevertheless the difference between the two men is enormous. John Adams was a philosopher, and Fisher Ames was only a lawyer-politician. The ideal of justice which the former postulated was fundamentally noble, whereas the ideal of justice which the latter assumed was narrowly legal. Both accepted the Puritan doctrine of human wickedness—a doctrine derived from medieval Toryism—and from it deduced the necessity of a coercive sovereignty; but Fisher Ames went further and assumed that the Puritan doctrine of the elect and the Yankee doctrine of the successful were one and the same, and that God's remnant in Israel was no other than the prosperous merchants and lawyers of Boston. All the great multitude of the unprosperous, by the same doctrine, were the mass of the unregenerate, condemned for the good of society to be ruled by a rod of iron.

The noble doctrine of justice, therefore, became for Fisher Ames little more than the divine right of the minority to coerce the majority, in the name and through the agency of laws and statutes. In his view justice was little more than a drab realist in a lawyer's wig, adjudicating title deeds, and delivering its findings out of law books. Its one concern was to safeguard what had been got, rather than to secure just and equal rights. It dreaded all rude and tumultuary innovation, and would tolerate no change that was not implicit in legal principles. Its golden rule was due process of law. Love of one's neighbors was, no doubt, an excellent private virtue, but it was impractical, if not immoral, in the state. Concern for the improvident sinners must not influence government to impair the rights of the thrifty saints; for government was instituted and exists to safeguard established things. "The chief duty and care of all governments," he argued, "is to protect the rights of property and the tranquillity of society" (*Works*, p. 125). Hence to Fisher Ames government was the common policeman and judge, whose function was to arrest the turbulent and bring them to the bar of the Common Law. Its beginning and end was the Tory principle of coercion. Its sovereignty was arrogant and domineering, taking no account of the democratic

principle of good will. "The motives to refuse obedience to government are many and strong," he explained; "impunity will multiply and enforce them. Many men would rebel, rather than be
ruined; but they would rather not rebel, than be hanged" (*Works*,
"Lucius Junius Brutus"). With government thus conceived of,
naturally he desired that it should be strong; that it should impose its will ruthlessly upon the rebellious. Naturally also he
regarded every idealist, the Rousseaus and Paines and Jeffersons—
all the mischievous hosts of "democratick babblers"—as a dangerous enemy of law and order, desperately bent on overturning
the rights of vested interests and the tranquillity of society. This
is sufficient to explain the vindictiveness of his assault upon Shays
and his followers, as "bankrupts and sots, who have gambled or
slept away their estates"—while in the Revolutionary army—and
were now engaged in the business of treason against the commonwealth, and the characteristic conclusion that he draws—"the
certainty of punishment is the truest security against crimes"
(*Works*, "Lucius Junius Brutus," p. 3). To Fisher Ames and
Daniel Shays, justice seems to have had very different aspects.

To the uncritical there is a certain persuasive dignity in the
philosophy of Boston Federalism. Gentlemen like Fisher Ames
were careful to appear well in public; they liked to be regarded
as faithful stewards of the common weal. Concern for the *res
publica* they professed so heartily that it seems ungracious to
question their motives. How excellently they could make out a
case for themselves will appear from the following exposition of
Fisher Ames' philosophy, as it was understood by a Harvard president:

Mr. Ames was emphatically a republican. He saw that many persons
confounded a republick with a democracy. He considered them as essentially distinct and really opposite. According to his creed, a republick is
that structure of an elective government, in which the administration
necessarily prescribe to themselves the general good as the object of all
their measures; a democracy is that, in which the present popular passions,
independent of the publick good, become a guide to the rulers. In the
first, the reason and interests of the society govern; in the second, their
prejudices and passions. The frame of the American constitution supposes
the dangers of democracy. . . . [The constitutional checks] are contrivances and devices voluntarily adopted by the people to restrain themselves from obstructing, by their own mistakes or perversity, the attain-
ment of the publick welfare. They are professed means of insuring to the
nation rulers, who will prefer the durable good of the whole to the transient

advantage of the whole or a part. When these provisions become in-
effectual, and the legislator, the executive magistrate, and the judge become the instruments of the passions of a people, or of the governing majority, the government, whatever may be its form, is a democracy, and
the public liberty is no longer safe. True republican rulers are bound to
act, not simply as those who appoint them *would*, but, as they *ought;*
democratick leaders will act in subordination to those very passions which
it is the object of government to control. . . . Then it is, that men, not
laws, govern. (*Works*, Introduction, pp. xxiv–xxv.)

"The durable good of the whole" is an excellent phrase; but
when the skeptical critic asks for more exact plans and specifications,
the only answer is a request for a vote of confidence. The representative is presumed to be wiser and more patriotic than his
constituents—quite above passion or interest—and may safely
be intrusted with "the publick good." "The love of country,"
Fisher Ames was fond of insisting, "is the morality of politics,"
and the Federal Constitution he believed to be so happily balanced
that partisan selfishness must transmute itself into patriotism.
But when we dismiss these amiable generalities—which reveal to
what straits gentlemen were reduced in their contest with democracy—and examine the political principles that lie behind them,
they do not appear so amiable. They imply as necessary corollaries a continuous aggrandizement of the political state, the principle of coercion, and the psychology of fear. It is no other than
the old Tory arrogance, new-modeled to suit republican taste.
Fisher Ames seems to have had no faith in the principle of good
will or the expediency of compromise; his contempt for the opposition was as frank as Hamilton's.

Government does not subsist by making proselytes to sound reasons
or by compromise and arbitration with its members; but by the power of
the community compelling the obedience of individuals. If that is not
done, who will seek its protection, or fear its vengeance. ("Lucius Junius
Brutus," *Works*, p. 5.)

For let it be remarked, that a feeble government produces more factions
than an oppressive one; the want of power first makes individuals legislators, and then rebels. Where parents want authority, children are wanting in duty. It is not possible to advance further in the same path; the
one will conduct us first to anarchy, and next to foreign or domestick
tyranny; the other, by the wise and vigorous exertion of lawful authority,
will lead to permanent power, and general prosperity. I am no advocate
for despotism; but I believe the probability to be much less of its being

introduced by the corruption of our rulers, than by the delusion of the people. (" Camillus,' *Works,* p. 17.)

A weak government, Ames argues insistently, is no other than a hotbed of faction, and faction is the fruitful mother of democratic anarchy. Again and again he returns to an exposition of the familiar eighteenth-century dogma that found its classic exposition in the tenth number of *The Federalist;* and his argument takes on darker colors from the Calvinist background of his mind. To those who have been reared on the sour doctrines of reprobation and election, the children of Adam become a major political concern. If God has cast off and denied the mass of the unregenerate, how shall the political philosopher hope to redeem them? If divine wisdom has granted them no part in the congregation of the righteous, what rights have they in the republic of the patriotic? To Fisher Ames town and village and farm showed plentiful examples of those whom the devil had marked for his own, and if they were gathered into a numerical democracy with the saints, how should the minority of the latter safeguard the Ark of the Sanctuary? How should the durable good of the whole be provided for? Thrift and godliness were not exactly synonymous terms to the Calvinist-Yankee, but it was clear that the godly will practice thrift, and those who have thriven, have *ipso facto* made out a case for their godliness. In this uncertain world two things seemed reasonably clear: that the poor are in a more doubtful state than the rich; and that in a moral world only the elect may be expected to serve the cause of morality. The wicked incline to democratic faction, but the prosperous serve the durable good of the whole.

To one cradled in such prejudices, the current phrase, "gentlemen of principle and property"—a phrase that provides the chorus to his thought—lacked the savor of cynicism that it suggests to modern ears. It was compounded of the ideals of Puritan and Yankee, and Fisher Ames seems never to have questioned its adequacy, or doubted its finality. To gentlemen of principle and property he looked to provide a bulwark against the immoral multitude; they were the stewards of society, on whom devolved the duty of protecting the whole from democratic faction. They had erected the Federal Constitution, which Jacobins were seeking to destroy; and in defense of that Constitution he brought forth his heaviest artillery. He contributed nothing new to the discussion;

but he repeated the familiar arguments with the gusto of a dogmatist. "Simple governments," he asserted, "are despotisms; and of all despotisms, a democracy, though the least durable, is the most violent" (*Works*, "American Liberty," p. 382). The mortal weakness of all democracies he discovered in their immorality. A democracy will make every people "thoroughly licentious and corrupt." "The known propensity of a democracy is to licentiousness, which the ambitious call, and the ignorant believe to be liberty."

> The great object, then, of political wisdom in framing our constitution, was to guard against licentiousness, that inbred malady of democracies, that deforms their infancy with grey hairs and decrepitude. (*Ibid.*, p. 384.)

> There is universally a presumption in democracy that promises everything; and at the same time an imbecility that can accomplish nothing, not even preserve itself. (*Works*, "Falkland," p. 151.)

"Politics should have no passions," this caustic old Federalist professed to believe, yet his bitterness against the Jeffersonians who threatened to overturn the funding law, the national bank, the midnight judicial appointments, and other measures of the best Federalist minds, was almost unseemly. It would appear that "the durable good of the whole" flew out at the window, when danger to commercial interests came in at the door. To erect a strong government and then lose control of it was a disaster indeed. With the political state in the hands of atheistic democrats, Fisher Ames was prepared to welcome the coming of anarchy, and his pessimism throve on the prospect. But that no warning might be lacking he laid down the whole theory of government in plain terms, that even Jefferson might understand:

> But the essence, and almost the quintessence, of good government is, to protect property and its rights. When these are protected, there is scarcely any booty left for oppression to seize; the objects and the motives to usurpation and tyranny are removed. By securing property, life and liberty can scarcely fail of being secured: where property is safe by rules and principles, there is liberty. (*Works*, "Phocion," p. 181.)

This is pure Federalism, stripped of all cant, speaking out frankly. It is the philosophy of John Locke brought in to serve the rising capitalism of New England, threatened by a Physiocratic agrarianism. The dogma of political morality has yielded to economic realism. The stake-in-society principle is the reply of the Puritan-Yankee to the democratic romanticism of Jefferson and Madison —a principle which, fortunately, "these apostles from the race-ground and the cock-pit" paid little heed to.

To a sophisticated generation, long familiar with the political ways of gentlemen of principle and property, Fisher Ames appears as a caustic little gentleman, vivacious and intolerant, who nodded his tie-wig dogmatically, and spoke his opinions oracularly. He quite evidently relished his ample store of old-fashioned prejudices, cherished them carefully, and prided himself on the wit with which he set them forth. If he was not the repository of all political wisdom that he believed himself to be, he was at least no demagogue, and in honoring him the Boston of the year 1800 was but painting its own portrait. It would be ungracious, perhaps, to add that Fisher Ames and Boston Federalism, defeated in their cherished projects, were both suffering from an extraordinarily aggravated case of the political spleen.

III

ROBERT TREAT PAINE, JR.
Wit

Young Tom Paine, who took his brother's and his father's name—partly because a certain other Tom Paine had achieved a fame that Boston did not regard as enviable—shared with Fisher Ames the literary renown of the New England capital, a renown so great that Boston paid him quite astonishing sums for such couplets as his indolence suffered him to turn off. The popularity of his wares was a notable instance of the working of the law of supply and demand. The patriotism of Boston preferred domestic to imported goods, and he offered his verses to a public not very critical of quality. Boston had never had a poet of her own, while Connecticut with her Hartford Wits was the envy of all New England. Certain poetesses to be sure, had tried with "hallowed hands" to "attune Columbia's lyre"—to quote Paine's eulogy of Mrs. Sarah Wentworth Morton, "blest Philenia, noblest of the choir" (*Works*, "Menander to Philenia," p. 129)—but their sentimentality was a bit cloying, and when genius appeared in the person of a Harvard graduate, graced with wit and adorned with all the learning of the schools, Boston was quick to acclaim him as her own.

The young man thus seized upon, and as it were raped by fame, was the last of the eighteenth-century wits, the most dashing product of a generation that patched its verse with tags of the classics and called it lisping in numbers.   In temper and manners he belonged wholly to the tie-wig school that swaggered till the War of 1812 and then became obsolete overnight.   As a young man about town he displayed the latest London clothes and set himself up as the very glass of fashion.   Although he wore his own hair, he clung to smallclothes and like an honest Federalist refused to adopt Jacobin trousers.   He was indisputably clever and he cultivated a pretty wit as assiduously as any Augustan.   He talked in epigrams, and a convivial evening—of which he was quite too fond for his own good—was a failure that did not produce a *bon mot* to run through the town.   His biographer has preserved a number of such for the amusement of posterity, and one at least deserves to be remembered by our younger critics.   When the prohibition against the theater was repealed in 1793, he remarked, "The Vandal spirit of puritanism is prostrate in New-England." In cleaving to wit and abandoning Puritanism, Paine broke with sober Boston convention, and soon all respectable folk began to shake their heads.   A thriftless fellow, he played with the devil openly in the eyes of all Boston.   He drank too much, he gambled, he haunted the theater and was a favorite of the greenroom, he became the first dramatic critic born and bred in New England, and when he married the daughter of an English actor, his father disowned him.   Quite naturally he came to poverty, dissipated his strength, suffered many a humiliation, and died at the age of thirty-seven, leaving his widow and young children to be provided for by a public benefit at his beloved Federal Street theater.

Little of his wit, unfortunately, found its way into his verse, which, modeled ostensibly on Dryden and Pope, lacks their vigorous common sense, and laboring to be sublime succeeds in being heavy. His couplets swell sonorously, but his thought does not keep pace with his rhetoric.   He follows his recipe carefully; adjectives duly support the nouns; the caesuras are justly spaced and the balance of the parts is as nice as if weighed in an apothecary's scales. He seasons the whole with the staples of personification and poetic diction; everything has been provided for, and yet the cake is fallen that he takes from the oven.   Something is lacking to lighten the sodden mass. A contemporary critic, viewing the finished product, expressed his judgment thus:

> Of Mr. Paine, as an author, we cannot speak in terms of unmingled praise. His verse, indeed, seldom loiters into prose; but it must be confessed, that his prose is here and there "tricked and frounced, till it outmantles all the pride of verse." His numbers are, perhaps, never feeble or faultering, but a wild and frolic imagination, occasionally, wantons through his periods, and sometimes displays itself in contemning the chaster elegancies, and sometimes in neglecting the severer decencies of thought and diction. (*Works*, Introduction, p. lxxviii.)

It is certainly a partial eye that discovers a wild and frolic imagination in these lumbering imitations of Pope, or in the occasional excursions into the languorous fields of Della Cruscan sentiment. When Paine ceases to be a wit he becomes an offense. To his admiring contemporaries his poetry seemed to be pure metal, but to later generations it is only plate, with the brass showing through the worn spots. *The Ruling Passion,* delivered before the Phi Beta Kappa Society in 1797, is perhaps the first poem of Paine's that is much more than vacuous and turgid rhetoric; and this is redeemed, in spite of liberal helpings from Pope, by a certain vivacity of satire, phrased with Augustan smartness. Such couplets as these still preserve a jaunty literary swagger for later ears; how they tickled the more susceptible ears of our grandfathers must be imagined:

> Where you send genius, send a fortune too;
> Dunces by instinct thrive, as oysters woo!
> For ne'er were veins of ore by chymist found,
> Except, like Hebrew roots, in barren ground!

Paine early grew old, and before he had reached his thirties his mind had taken a rigid conservative bent. His affections were fixed upon a past that was visibly falling into decay, and its ways were endeared to him in the measure that they decayed. It was a matter of personal pride with him to embody in his own manners the aristocratic bearing of pre-Revolutionary times.

> Mr. Paine [says his biographer] attached great consequence to *manners.* . . . He was modelled upon the *old school.* Without being familiar, he was easy among friends, and courtly to strangers. In colloquial discussions, he rigidly adhered to the law of politeness; and in mixed society, he neither courted the *high,* nor avoided the *low.* . . . He frequently deplored a supposed decay of *manners.* With concern, he used to inquire

" In manners, where is the successor of Gen. Knox to be found?" It was with him a constant topick of complaint, that *" The old, genteel, town families, had been elbowed out of house and home, by newcomers:"* that *" instead of the polished manners of a city, we should soon exhibit that growth of gentility, which is produced by ingrafting dollars upon village habits and low employments."* (*Works*, Introduction, p. lxix.)

Affecting an aristocratic bearing, Paine was as complete a Tory as the republican environment permitted. If he despised the new, pushing middle class that had risen since the Revolution, he held in contempt the numerous company of those he dubbed the yokel, the peasant, the hind, or the plow-tail. Under the circumstances the best that he could do politically was to turn Federalist, and he embraced the principles of Fisher Ames with genteel conviction. "In politics," says his biographer, "Mr. Paine was a disciple of the old federal school. He understood the constitution, as Washington administered, and as Hamilton had expounded it" (*ibid.*, p. lxxvii). During his undergraduate days he had dabbled in French revolutionary philosophy, and "the fanatic Atheism of France, decorated in all the meretricious charms of eloquence and philosophy, took a transient possession of his mind" (*ibid.*, p. lxxviii). At graduation in 1792, he read a poem entitled *The Nature and Progress of Liberty*, in which he eulogized "liberal thought," proposed to follow "Reason," declared that "the rights of man" are a gift from heaven, proffered the hand of fellowship to France—

> May struggling France her ancient freedom gain,
> May Europe's sword oppose her rights in vain—

and launched a devastating couplet at the great English opponent of the Revolution—

> The fame of Burke, in dark oblivion rust,
> His pen a meteor—and his page the dust.

Three years later, on proceeding Master of Arts, he presented a poem in very different vein. Three years were a generation in those stirring times, and by 1795 the penetrating vision of this genius of twenty-two had discovered the atheist poison in the cup of French democracy. *The Invention of Letters* rises to a climax in a satirical elaboration of a line from the poem of 1792—"Licentious morals breed disease of state." Having learned his lesson from Fisher Ames, the sapient young Federalist announces that democracy is the mother of faction, and faction leads on to anarchy. In this poem for the first time Paine's wit runs freely, and certain lines are as jaunty as he ever penned.

> For place or power, while demagogues contend,
> Whirled in their vortex, sinks each humbler friend.
> See Crispin quit his stall, in Faction's cause,
> To cobble government, and soal the laws!
> See Frisseur scent his dust, his razor set,
> To shave the treaty, or to puff Genet!
> In doubtful mood, see Mulciber debate,
> To mend a horse-shoe, or to weld the state!
> The whip's bold knight, in barn, his truck is laid,
> To spout in favour of the carrying trade!
> While Staytape runs, from hissing goose, too hot,
> To measure Congress for another coat;
> And still, by rule of shop, intent on pelf,
> Eyes the spare cloth, to cabbage for himself!
>
> Envy, that fiend, who haunts the great and good,
> Not Cato shunned, nor Hercules subdued.
> On Fame's wide field, where'er a covert lies,
> The rustling serpent to the thicket flies;
> The foe of Glory, Merit is her prey;
> The dunce she leaves, to plod his drowsy way.
> Of birth amphibious, and of Protean skill,
> This green-eyed monster changes shape at will;
> Like snakes of smaller breed, she sheds her skin;
> Strips off the serpent, and turns—Jacobin.

In view of the fact that Governor Samuel Adams, chief of the New England Jacobins, was to occupy the stage, President Willard had diplomatically struck from the manuscript the ten lines last quoted; but Paine had the audacity to re-insert them in speaking, and the tumultuous applause was sufficient proof that it was not from a Harvard audience that Sam Adams got the votes that annually returned him governor.

Verse imposed some slight restraint on Paine's rhetoric, but in prose when he was in full career—as in the grotesque eulogy of Washington which stirred the patriotism of Boston Federalists—the reins are on the neck of his eloquence, and he takes all barriers with fiery abandon. Fact troubles his wild and frolic imagination not at all, but like any plebeian demagogue—whose factional appeals he so furiously condemned—he blew the bellows of Federalist partisanship with extraordinary vigor, stoking his fire with rumor and misrepresentation and party spleen. No slander was too gross, no lie too palpable to serve his end. He baited the democrats quite shamelessly, and aroused the mob of Boston gentlemen like a true Tory. One of his political orations has been preserved by his editor in the collected edition of his works, for the enlightenment of posterity—an oration delivered in 1799, "at the request of the young men of Boston," on the theme of France and democracy. In this extraordinary composition Paine seems to have been quite ravished by his own rhetoric, that flashes in many a feint and parry before it impales its victim. It is a Federalist philippic, designed to destroy the good name of all who have quitted the sacred Federalist tribe. Words could hardly go further; disregard for truth could scarcely be more brazen. Paine's delight in clever antitheses overweighs any scruples in regard to just statement. "The French Republick," he asserted, "has exhibited all the vices of civilization, without one of the virtues of barbarism." One or two bits from this tremendous oration, that in "the glow of feeling, the swell of language, and the brilliancy of sentiments" has "very seldom been surpassed," and that was "received with rapturous and enthusiastic applause," must suffice to illustrate the justice of the Federalist claim to the custodianship of political good manners. "Politics should have no passions," Fisher Ames asserted—which excellent principle young Robert Treat Paine exemplified thus:

Political Empiricism has never attained, in any age or nation, so universal an ascendency, as at the present day in the "Illuminated Republick." Unfettered by the fear of innovation, and unshackled by the prejudice of ages, the modern Frenchman is educated in a system of moral and religious chimeras, which dazzle by their novelty those volatile intellects, which prescriptive wisdom could never impress with veneration. Every Frenchman, who has read a little is a pedant; and the whole race of these hornbook Philosophers is content with the atheism of Mirabeau . . . the absurd philanthropy of Condorcet, and the visionary politics of Rousseau. These are the boundaries of their literary ambition, of their political science. Hence it is, that they pretend to be too enlightened for belief, too virtuous for government.

The feculence of party is not yet drained of its rankest sediment. The worshippers of democracy, though their altars are thrown down, are not yet converted from their devotions. The frozen snake has still some sparks of animation; and, if placed by compassion near your hospitable fires, he will revive with exasperated venom, and sting the hardy fool that fostered him. Deal therefore with these ferocious demoralizers, as our crafty mariners trade with the savages of the Indian ocean—with your men at their posts, your guns loaded, and your slow matches burning. (*Works*, p. 319.)

For all democrats Paine had the hearty contempt of an honest man for a rogue, but for the intellectuals who expounded the new romantic philosophy his indignation was measureless. "The legitimate plebeian democrat," he asserted, is "an enemy to all government, under which he holds no office"; but fling him a bone from the public table and "he becomes the very scavenger of administration." The "Illuminated Jacobin," on the other hand, "never changes his principles."

His whole science is directed to unhinge society, his whole ambition to plunder it. He is too ravenous to be content with a system of order himself; and too selfish to permit its enjoyment by others. Like a hog in a flower-garden, he sets no value on the variegated foliage he destroys, and seems only desirous to root out every twig of vegetation, that can satiate his voracity. (*Ibid.*, p. 321.)

To such fustian was he reduced when his wit left him. That a gentleman could talk like that, and other gentlemen applaud, is a sad commentary on the intellectual honesty of partisanship, even amongst decent Federalists. Fustian was the order of the day, and Paine was merely baying with his pack. If only he had not professed such virtues his extravagance might be forgiven; but extravagance ill becomes a distinguished repository of political wisdom. Once, indeed, his vivacity got him into a nasty mess. While editor of *The Federal Orrery*, he accepted in 1795 a political poem entitled *The Jacobiniad*, the satire of which Paine "new-pointed and new-edged" before printing. The democrats, at whom it was directed, were vastly incensed, and a mob gathered before his lodging but was dispersed. Later the son of one of the victims challenged him to a duel. Paine declined but armed himself with an unloaded pistol. Accidentally meeting his challenger in the street, he drew his weapon, but the young fellow, standing in no awe of a favorite of the muses, struck the pistol down and proceeded to give Paine a sound drubbing. To such base treatment may genius come, when wit forgets that a sally of the tongue may invite a counter sally of the fists. And so we leave him in the dust of the street, ignobly laid low by the strength of that vulgar democracy which was to bring down so many things held dear by Boston Tories. His was, very largely, a wasted life—wasted by sheer indolence and feeble will. He was a fellow of some parts, and a sentence from one of his dramatic criticisms may not inaptly apply to him: "The character is not a sot, but his humor has a mellower tilth for having been husbanded and manured by 'the excellent endeavor of drinking.'"

CHAPTER II

WINDS OF POLITICAL DOCTRINE

I

INTO the complacent little Boston of Fisher Ames and Robert Treat Paine came the Embargo, the War of 1812, and the industrial revolution to upset its static order and destroy its snug provincialism. The old Federalism with its Hartford Convention and plans for New England secession went the way of mortality, carrying with it to the grave the old pessimism and the old spleen. The jealous isolationist policy was quietly forgotten in Boston; the gospel of secession was preached no more; George Cabot and Timothy Pickering gave way to other leaders; and provincial Boston joined with Kentucky and Tennessee in extolling a romantic nationalism. It sent to Washington a new spokesman, who joined with Henry Clay in a paternalistic program of national expansion, and took command of the forces combating the rising separatism of the South Carolina school. By the year 1830 Boston had traveled far from the times of the Hartford Convention.

The sufficient explanation of so striking a change is to be found, of course, in the changing economics of Massachusetts. The Embargo had proved a major disaster to New England shipping; and the Boston merchants, counting their losses from idle and dismasted ships, water-logging at the wharves, found just cause for hating the policy of the administration. But if the shipping business was brought face to face with tragedy, the manufacturing interests stumbled upon unexpected prosperity. With British imports cut off, the home market offered a tempting opportunity to Yankee enterprise. The familiar story of the swift rise of New England industrialism need not be recounted here. It is enough to remark that with the growth of domestic manufactures a new group of economic leaders appeared, and the policy of New England shifted from pro-mercantilism to pro-industrialism. It was a difficult choice at first between the antagonistic claims of the Boston merchant and the Lowell manufacturer; between the carriers of foreign goods who demanded free trade, and the makers of domestic goods who demanded a protective tariff. The traditional view of

New England was strongly for free trade. In 1807 a Federalist lawyer asserted it to be "an unalienable right," and in 1820 Judge Story asked, "Why should the laboring classes be taxed for the necessaries of life?"[1] The tariff bill of 1824 got only one vote from Massachusetts; but in the four years between the passage of that act and the "Tariff of Abominations" of 1828, Massachusetts went over definitely to industrialism. Thenceforth she was to be the leader in the movement looking to governmental paternalism, substituting the expansive Federalism of Hamilton for the restrictive Federalism of Fisher Ames, and becoming in consequence whole-heartedly nationalistic.

Equally significant, though less observed, was the changed attitude of Massachusetts towards the great republican experiment. Gone was the older generation, with its face turned to the past and its heart bound up with the patriarchal ideals of a decadent squire-archy. Gone also were the disturbant fears of democracy. The menace of Daniel Shays, that had put the old Federalists in a rage at democracy, was long since forgotten; and the nervous panic over French Jacobinism, that had upset New England for a decade, had subsided. In the light of longer experience with its ways democracy was seen to be far from terrifying. The hobgoblin of faction that had benightmared the dreams of Fisher Ames was discovered to be only a bogey to frighten naughty boys. Massachusetts had kept off the agrarian reef, despite war and economic unrest, and with her new constitution of 1820 property interests were as secure as any old Federalist could have wished. Gentlemen of principle and property were still in control of the state; and if less emphasis was laid on principle and more on property—if less regard seemed to be paid to gentlemen of breeding and manners, and more to assertive self-seeking—business was no less secure than in the good old days, and its profits were greater. And so, master of its looms and a growing home market, New England industrialism regarded genially the great western movement, fostered by a benevolent paternalism, confident of extending its markets with every mile of westward expansion. To encourage the development of the West and South by a Federal policy of internal improvement became, therefore, common business foresight, provided of course that the Constitution should follow pop-

---

[1] Quoted in Theodore Parker, *Daniel Webster: Additional Speeches*, Vol. I, p. 195. Considerable information will be found in this excellent study.

ulation and safeguard business interests against local agrarianism and the menace of particularism.

By the year 1830 both dangers lay black against the political horizon. The triumph of Jackson had enthroned the agrarian menace at Washington and produced such a scrambling of frightened interests—such a rattling among the old bones of Federalism and scurrying among the young limbs of industrialism—as the country had not seen for many a year. Henry Clay appealed to his followers in the West, and Webster marshaled his adherents of the East, and from the coalescing of these incongruous elements emerged the Whig party to do battle with Old Hickory. It was a patchwork army at best. In the hour of peril, principles go by the board. The Whig party was lineal heir of the old Federalism, but it denied its philosophical patrimony. It substituted expediency for the old economic realism, and began and ended intellectually bankrupt. Its bitter and unseemly squabbles over the Bank and tariff, its platitudes of patriotism and its pose of disinterestedness, the venom of its personal attack upon Jackson, were the earmarks of a policy of shallow opportunism that failed to make use of such victories as fell to its lot, for the simple reason that it could never agree on what to do. Such cohesive power as held it together—aside from petty antagonism to Jackson—was the vague assumption that the well-being of the American people was dependent on governmental patronage; the belief that each economic group and section must receive its special favor, and that through tariffs and bonuses and internal improvements the country as a whole must prosper. Of this principle of special favors—a return to the seventeenth century from which eighteenth-century liberalism was a reaction—the American System of Henry Clay was the chief expression, and it remains the most significant bequest of the Whig party to our political history.

The Whig party was the first attempt of our rising middle class to erect a political platform in accordance with middle-class ideals, and its failure was due to the fact that the time was not ripe for undisputed middle-class control. The merchant aristocracy of the North was overthrown, but the planter aristocracy of the South was still to be reckoned with; and its particularistic ambitions in the end wrecked the Whig coalition of the West and East. By 1820 a revolutionary change had taken place in the political philosophy of the plantation school. From an ardent nationalism

Calhoun was leading his followers back to the earlier doctrine of states rights; and New England industrialism found itself confronted with the doctrine which the Hartford junto had played with, but now with far more drive behind it. The slave economy was entertaining imperialistic dreams, and to effect its ends was building up a new constitutional philosophy. Southern writers had long been at work, and the weight of their authority was behind the new particularism. *Rawle on the Constitution*, a states-rights exposition, was the official textbook on civics at the United States Military Academy, and from it, while a student at West Point, Jefferson Davis declared that he first imbibed states-rights principles. Other authoritative southern works that were widely read were John Taylor's two studies: *Construction Construed and Constitutions Vindicated* (1820), and *New Views of the Constitution of the United States* (1823); some years later came Henry St. George Tucker's *Lectures on Constitutional Law* (1843); and these were only preliminary to Calhoun's searching exposition in his *Disquisition on Government* and *An Inquiry into the Nature of the Constitution of the United States*.

To meet this theory of particularism there was need of a resurgent Federalism, with a new nationalistic interpretation of the Constitution. The compact theory of the Federal state must be refuted by the organic theory; the conception of federated commonwealths must yield to the conception of a coalescing sovereignty. The old battle must be fought over again with fresh arguments. The sanctity of the Constitution must be asserted, but that sanctity must be thrown over a nationalistic rather than a particularistic interpretation. It must be shown that despite the vehement protestations of southern loyalty, a particularistic Constitution was a denial of loyalty and must end in the destruction of the national union. For this difficult business New England was as yet unprepared. The old Federalist arguments were obsolete, and many of those Federalists had been deep in the Hartford Convention. The new industrialism must provide its own theory, and it was fortunate in discovering two men whose combined learning and eloquence proved equal to the task.

II

The name of Webster has been so closely associated with the movement of constitutional nationalism as to overshadow the

just fame of one who has many claims to be regarded as the intellectual leader of the school. Joseph Story was a Salem lawyer
whose reputation, considerable as it is, is scarcely commensurate
with his influence on our later constitutional development. Of the
same Harvard class with William Ellery Channing, he dabbled in
polite letters as a young man, but went into the law, entered
politics, became Associate Justice of the Supreme Court, and for a
time was Dane professor of law at Harvard. He came of radical
stock. His father, a physician at Boston till he removed to Marblehead, was a militant Revolutionary Whig, one of the score or so of
Indians who made up the Boston Tea Party, and a leader amongst
the group of Sons of Liberty who seized and gagged the sentinels
and carried off two brass fieldpieces from the Common where the
British commander had posted them to overawe the town. The
son grew up an ardent republican. As a very young man he became
an outstanding leader of the unfashionable party, then in the
minority, and suffered certain humiliations on account of his
political opinions; on one occasion, according to Theodore Parker,
being "knocked down in the street, beaten, and forced to take
shelter in the house of a friend, whither he fled, bleeding, and covered with the mud of the street" (*Additional Speeches*, Vol. I,
p. 178). Of these youthful heresies few indications appeared in his
later life. Republican though he might be, he was utterly devoid
of any radical tendencies, and when he took his seat on the Supreme
Court bench he was speedily drawn into the powerful orbit of John
Marshall, shared the latter's views on all major constitutional
questions, and turned Whig. He became a close friend of Webster
and from 1816 to 1842 he was his chief adviser on knotty legal,
constitutional, and international questions. "From that deep and
copious well of legal knowledge," Parker asserts, Webster drew
freely "whenever his own bucket was dry" (*ibid.*, p. 170).

This shift from Republican to Whig came about quite naturally.
New England liberalism, it must be remembered, produced no
intellectual leaders till late, and no clear-cut political philosophy.
Though it nominally accepted the leadership of Jefferson it never
was won over to the Physiocratic economics or states-rights principles of the Virginia school. Story was at no time a Jeffersonian,
but rather an eager and avowed disciple of Washington, "little
infected with Virginia notions, as to men or measures." In his
Autobiography he wrote:

The republican party then and at all other times embraced men of very different views on many subjects. Nay, a Virginia republican of that day, was very different from a Massachusetts republican, and the anti-federal doctrines of the former state then had and still have very little support or influence in the latter state, notwithstanding a concurrence in political action upon general subjects. I was at all times a firm believer in the doctrines of General Washington, and an admirer of his conduct, measures and principles. . . . I read and examined his principles, and have made them in a great measure the rule and guide of my life. I was and always have been a lover, devoted lover, of the constitution of the United States, and a friend to the union of the states. I never wished to bring the government to a mere confederacy of states; but to preserve the power of the general government given by all the states, in full exercise and sovereignty for the protection and preservation of all the states. (Story, *Life and Letters of Joseph Story*, Vol. I, p. 128.)

That he had as little sympathy with the Physiocratic economics of Jefferson is apparent from his early activities in furthering the new paper system. While a member of the Massachusetts legislature, as a young man, he was active in pressing for bank franchises, and upon the establishment of the Merchants' Bank of Salem he became its president. Like Washington and Marshall he espoused the new gospel of capitalism, with none of the agrarian prejudices of the landed gentry to hold him back. He was the political twin of the great Chief Justice, and a Whig in spirit long before Webster. "I seem to myself," he remarked late in life, "simply to have stood still in my political belief, while parties revolved about me; so that, although of the same opinions now as ever, I find my name changed from Democrat to Whig, but I know not how or why" (*ibid.*, Vol. I, p. 546). Though somewhat naïve the comment is just. Anti-federalism in Massachusetts would seem to have been largely a capitalistic protest against the narrow tie-wig Federalism; and while Joseph Story sat upon the Supreme Court bench, adapting legal principles to the new needs of business, the country was moving forward to the middle-class philosophy that he had early come to hold.

In the year 1833 he published his *Commentaries on the Constitution*, the fruit of long labors, which was at once accepted throughout the North as a classical authority, and which has held its ground pretty well since. In method and temper, as well as objective, the exposition of Story stands in sharp contrast to that of the southern school. In its particularism the latter appealed to the history of the Constitution in the making, and to French romantic

philosophy; whereas the former followed English constitutional
theories to nationalistic ends. Story was steeped in the Common
Law and his thinking reveals the strong influence of Blackstone.
In passing through the mind of the great Tory commentator,
English constitutional theory had received a pronounced Tory
bias, and something of this remains after filtering through the
mind of Story. The ideal of a strong and efficient political state,
with its corollaries of a coercive sovereignty, of the duties of a
subject rather than the rights of a citizen, of loyalty to government rather than concern for political justice, derives immediately
from English theory and practice. Much likewise he took from the
older Federalists: their fear of an encroaching legislative power;
their concern at faction; their faith in checks and balances to
restrain the majority will. But his chief inspiration came from the
spirit of the Common Law—that subtle influence that Jefferson so
greatly feared. His legalism was inveterate; the final, authoritative
answer to all questions he discovered in the decision of the courts.
Against such a mind, deeply read in the law and with scanty knowledge of economics and political theory, the waves of liberal and
romantic thought broke impotently. His reasoning may be convincing to a lawyer, but to the historian his exposition is often
weak, his data inadequate, and his conclusions not infrequently
contrary to fact.

In building his argument Story drew his materials freely from
The Federalist, from the writings and decisions of Marshall, and
from Blackstone. The backbone of the work is Hamilton and
Marshall, from whom he quotes constantly, supplemented by a host
of decisions by Federalist judges. With its pronounced bias *The
Commentaries* must be regarded as a partisan document, which
like *The Federalist* has grown in authoritativeness with the triumph
of its party principles. Its surprising weakness on the historical
side has come to be overlooked since the downfall of southern
particularism, but during the debates that preceded the Civil War
the work was sharply handled by southern historians, and in his
Constitutional View of the War between the States Stephens quite
demolished Story's feeble attempt at an historical justification of
the anti-compact theory. The weight of historical evidence, to
present-day students, would seem to be on the side of the states-
rights argument, although in certain aspects both sides were innovators: Story in overleaping the period of French ascendency

when the Constitution took shape, and going back to the older
English tradition; and the compact school in reasserting the compact theory at a time when the spirit of nationalism was undermining it.   Story seems to have been conscious of his weakness,
for he expressly repudiates the method of interpreting the work in
the light of contemporary testimony at the time of its formulation.
In so doing he not only violates the principle that a document is to
be construed in the light of the common understanding when it
was drawn; but with naïve inconsistency, he constantly appeals to
The Federalist, pretty much ignoring the opposition pamphlets,
and interprets the Constitution in accord with its commentary.
But for the most part he clings to the strict letter of the document.
He lightly brushes aside the whole compact argument by asserting dogmatically that the phrase, "We the people of the United
States," must be understood in its simple literal sense, and that
thus interpreted, the Constitution is seen to derive immediately
from the individual citizens acting in their sovereign capacity without the intermediation of the state governments.   The dispute
long waged furiously about this point and Story's analysis touches
only the fringe of the argument.

Very likely it is presumptuous for one who is not a lawyer to
express an opinion, yet these celebrated *Commentaries* seem today
very little more than a new-modeled Federalism, adapted to changing conditions.   Underneath the somewhat crabbed and narrow
legalism is a common-sense realistic political philosophy, an embodiment of English constitutional tradition as it grew up under a
Tory régime, that reveals scant sympathy with French romantic
theories.   The work is an unconscious testimony to the tenacious
hold of the English Common Law on the legal mind of America,
as well as to the rising spirit of nationalism.   It did much to
strengthen both.   It was a triumph of the lawyer over the historian
and political philosopher, and it marks the beginning of the lawyer's
custodianship of the fundamental law.   In spite of its somewhat
petty legalism and prosaic common sense, a note of veneration for
the great document runs through the tedious pages, constituting
the work at once both a commentary and a eulogy.

III

DANIEL WEBSTER

Realist and Constitutionalist

A far solider mind, strongly realistic and broadly philosophical, acute in analysis and with great powers of imagination, was the mind of the distinguished leader of the New England Whigs. Not the equal of Story as a lawyer, he was far superior as a political thinker. No man more richly endowed in mind and person has played a part on the stage of our public life, and in spite of gross shortcomings in character and the betrayal of his own promise, Webster retains an aura of the heroic about him. He was a great man, built on a great pattern, who never quite achieved a great life.

In Emerson and Webster were completely embodied the diverse New England tendencies that derived from the Puritan and the Yankee: the idealistic and the practical; the ethical and the rationalistic; the intellectual revolutionary, ready to turn the world upside down in theory, planting at the base of the established order the dynamite of ideas, and the soberly conservative, understanding the economic springs of political action, inclined to pessimism, neither wishing for Utopian change nor expecting it. The physical contrast was as striking as the mental. The child of the Puritan was slender, nervous, with a lambent energy that played freely in a rarefied atmosphere; the child of the Yankee was massive, solid, somnolently heavy till an idea awakened his faculties, a lover of the fleshpots, careless of conventional morals, rankly physical, and yet with an assured stateliness of manner, a slow imagination that expanded majestically and a rich eloquence that moved forward by regular stages to a great objective. Emerson was the child of a long line of ministers, and ministerial in his unworldliness; Webster was a Yankee squire, the descendant of some fox-hunting master of broad English acres, who by a freak of fortune had got born into the family of a New Hampshire yeoman. No Englishman was ever more English than he. He loved the substantial things of life: his Marshfield farm; his cattle and horses and crops; his rides afield and the return to good dinners and rich wines. Nothing is more characteristic or more likable—more redolent of the natural Webster—than his concern for agricultural improvements. His homely talk on *The Agricul-*

ture of England, filled with facts that had come under his observant eye, reveals a side that is too little known. It is an English country squire talking to his neighbors about the homely things they all care for; and when after long years and disappointed ambition and utter weariness, he returned to his Marshfield farm to die, it was his cattle and his fields that offered a last solace to the broken man.

Webster's intellectual development falls into distinct and rather sharply defined periods. Before 1825 his mental processes were still under the dominion of the solid, rationalist eighteenth century, with its realistic politics and its *laissez faire* economics. With the emergence of the constitutional disputes at the end of the twenties, when the lawyers and historians were busy at their commentaries, he came increasingly to take a legalistic view of government. During the acrimonious forties, with slavery dividing the country into hostile camps, he was bitten deeply by presidential ambitions, and thenceforth to the end of his life he was little more than a politician—a rôle for which he was singularly ill-fitted, and which brought bitterness and disillusion to his last days. Since his death both earlier and later phases of his career have fallen into the background, and the middle period of constitutional interpretation has stamped itself indelibly upon his fame. Yet in many respects the solid reasoning of the political philosopher is more valuable than the stately but somewhat ill-grounded declamation of the defender of the Constitution; and his just fame is increased rather than lessened by recalling his earlier contribution to our institutional development.

Webster was a sound political scholar, if not an outstanding creative thinker. He was of the distinguished line of political realists, from Harrington through Locke and Burke, to Hamilton, Madison and John Adams. He derived equally from seventeenth-century liberalism and eighteenth-century Federalism. He was widely read in the political classics, and his vigorous mind laid hold upon major principles and examined them closely. His intellectual master was the acute thinker of the English Commonwealth period, James Harrington, whom he pronounces "one of the most ingenious of political writers," and to whose suggestive doctrine of economic determinism he returns persistently. That Harrington was not the originator of the doctrine he was well enough read to have discovered; but he pays him high tribute as the

thinker who gave the doctrine form and currency. It is the substantial realism of the *Oceana* that appealed to a mind thoroughly
indoctrinated with political realism, before the rise of manhood
suffrage and the spread of equalitarianism had brought a change
in American political theory. Both his major premises and his
mode of reasoning bear the impress of the classic English school.
In the year 1820, within a single week, he made two speeches,
which as expositions of his political philosophy are the most illuminating he ever uttered, and which should stand side by side:
the *Basis of the Senate*, delivered before the Massachusetts Constitutional Convention, and the Plymouth speech on *The First Settlement of New England*. They supplement each other and together
give an admirable elucidation of the stake-in-society principle
that embodied a conviction he never abandoned. They are compact
of Harrington, Montesquieu and John Adams—the last authentic
expression of the old Federalism, before the democratic storms had
driven it into new roadsteads and whipped its flag from the hal-
yards where it had long waved.

In his admirable argument Webster accepts as axiomatic the
theory of division of powers, with the attendant machinery of
checks and balances. He accepts equally the familiar view of
eighteenth-century liberalism, that the legislature as the self-conscious custodian of the popular will is certain to prove the engrossing member of government whose ambition is most to be feared.
To expect a stable balance between Senate and House when their
characters are undifferentiated by diverse modes of selection—
a result that must follow from choosing both on the numerical
majority principle—seems to him the judgment of political inexperience. The wiser method, he believed, was to seek counsel
of the philosophers and the clear teachings of history. The first,
Webster insisted, have rightly laid down the principle of a stake-
in-society as the true measure of political justice:

> I take the *principle* to be well established, by writers of the greatest
> authority. In the first place, those who have treated of natural law have
> maintained, as a principle of law, that, as far as the object of society
> is the protection of something in which the members possess unequal
> shares, it is just that the weight of each person in the common coun-
> cils should bear a relation and proportion to his interest. Such is the
> sentiment of Grotius, and he refers, in support of it, to several institutions
> among the lesser states. ("The Basis of the Senate," in *Works*, Vol. III,
> pp. 13–14.)

At the basis of the stake-in-society principle is the doctrine of economic power as the controlling factor in determining the form and scope of the political state. In support of this doctrine of determinism Webster appeals to Harrington:

It is his leading object, in his *Oceana*, to prove, that power *naturally* and *necessarily* follows property. He maintains that a government founded on property is legitimately founded; and that a government founded on the disregard of property is founded in injustice, and can only be maintained by military force. "If one man," says he, "be sole landlord, like the Grand Seignior, his empire is absolute. If a few possess the land, this makes the Gothic or feudal constitution. If the *whole people* be landlords, then it is a commonwealth." "It is strange," says an ingenious person in the last century, "that Harrington should be the first man to find out so evident and demonstrable a truth as that property being the true basis and *measure* of power." In truth, he was not the first. The idea is as old as political science itself. It may be found in Aristotle, Lord Bacon, Sir Walter Raleigh, and other writers. Harrington seems, however, to be the first writer who has illustrated and expanded the principle, and given to it the effect and prominence which justly belong to it. To this sentiment, Sir, I entirely agree. It seems to me to be plain, that, in the absence of military force, political power naturally and necessarily goes into the hands which hold the property. In my judgment, therefore, a republican form of government rests, not more on political constitutions, than on those laws which regulate the descent and transmission of property. . . .

The English Revolution of 1688 was a revolution in favor of property, as well as of other rights. It was brought about by men of property for their security; and our own immortal Revolution was undertaken, not to shake or plunder property, but to protect it. The acts which the country complained of were such as violated the rights of property. An immense majority of all those who had an interest in the soil were in favor of the Revolution; and they carried it through, looking to its results for the security of their possessions. ("The Basis of the Senate," in *Works*, Vol. III, pp. 14–16.)

Harrington's principle that "if the *whole people* be landlords, then it is a commonwealth," Webster justified by appeal to American history. The spontaneous birth of republican institutions out of colonial experience he attributed to the wide diffusion of property. The land tenure of primitive New England was the creative source of her popular government.

Their situation demanded a parcelling out and division of the lands, and it may be fairly said, that this necessary act *fixed the future frame and form of their government*. The character of their political institutions was determined by the fundamental laws respecting property. . . . The property was all freehold . . . alienation of the land was every way facilitated, even to the subjecting of it to every species of debt. The establishment of public registries, and the simplicity of our forms of conveyance, have greatly facilitated the change of real estate from one proprietor to another. The consequence of all these causes has been, a great subdivision of the soil, and a great equality of condition; the true basis, most certainly, of a popular government. "If the people," says Harrington, "hold three parts in four of the territory, it is plain there can neither be any single person nor nobility able to dispute the government with them; in this case, therefore, *except force be interposed*, they govern themselves." ("The First Settlement of New England," in *Works*, Vol. I, pp. 35–36.)

Wholly English then, after the soundest English liberal tradition, was Webster's political philosophy in the year 1820, compact of sober eighteenth-century realism, quite unaffected by French romantic equalitarianism. The great principle to which he adhered was the principle that government to be stable must be founded in men's interests; thus founded no cause is given for revolutionary upheavals. "The disastrous revolutions which the world has witnessed, those political thunder-storms and earthquakes which have shaken the pillars of society to their very deepest foundations, have been revolutions against property." Such were Webster's convictions on the eve of those two great upheavals, the rise of Jacksonian democracy and the rejuvenation of the slave economy, that unseated the authority of the old school of political realism, and turned him aside from the plain path to lose himself in a tangle of constitutional legalism.

English also was his economic theory, to which, like Franklin before him, he gave close thought. In the year 1820 he was a frank disciple of Adam Smith and the *laissez faire* school. Mercantilism he derided as exploded; [2] and Physiocratic agrarianism seemed to him unduly hostile to commerce. He never concerned himself, like Franklin, with humanitarian ends. His sympathies went strongly for free trade, individual initiative, and a competitive order—sympathies which to the end of his life he never wholly outgrew. In those early days the mercantile interests commanded his loyalty far more readily than the manufacturing interests. Next to his Marshfield farm he loved a full-rigged ship, and the thought of Yankee skippers plowing the seven seas in well-freighted bottoms fired his imagination and kindled his patriotism.

---

[2] See "The Tariff," in *Works*, Vol. III, pp. 118–122.

But if in the background of his thought he remained *laissez faire*, with the necessary implications of a diminished political state and reliance upon the law of supply and demand above tariffs, bounties, and political regulations, unfortunately in the foreground of expediency were the loud demands of his constituents for protective tariffs, internal improvements, and a policy of governmental paternalism. His economics came into collision with politics, and under the drive of necessity he went reluctantly along the path which Hamilton had marked out a generation before.

The change came between the years 1824 and 1825. In the earlier year he aroused himself to a strong defense of *laissez faire* economics in opposition to Clay's clever campaign cry, the American System; in the later year he endeavored half-heartedly to defend New England interests in the game of subsidies. He was honestly ashamed of the whole mess; to Webster any tariff was a "tariff of abominations"; but his mouth was stopped by the clamor of the Lowell textile masters.[3] But having chosen his side, thereafter he defended his course vigorously, and joined forces with Clay in extolling the principle of protection. The same dubious shift is revealed in his changing attitude towards public finance. In 1815 he was an old-fashioned Federalist in his preference for a metallic currency and his belief that the public credit must rest on the public income; bank paper, stocks, bonds, and other agencies of the new finance he distrusted as likely to encourage speculation.[4] Twenty years later he was the outstanding champion of the Bank in its mortal quarrel with Jackson. In defending his public career before his constituents in Faneuil Hall in 1842, he said: "The subject of currency has been the study of my life, in preference to all other public topics"; and the result of those studies had made him a confirmed bullionist. Nevertheless when "Old Bullion Benton" proposed to restore a metallic currency, Webster derided the plan on the ground that bank money was necessary; and when the subtreasury system was established he denounced it bitterly.[5] He was a partisan to the cause of the Bank, and as its attorney he defended its case before the American public, as he defended its cases before the Supreme Court. He was no longer a free man but was deep in the subsidies of financial interests; nevertheless his old

---

[3] See his "Apology and Defense," in *Works*, Vol. V, pp. 146, 240.
[4] See "The Bank of the United States," *Works*, Vol. III, p. 35.
[5] See "Speech in Wall Street," in *Works*, Vol. II, p. 55.

realism convinced him—as it had convinced Hamilton—of the necessity of shaping the public policy to the desires of the bankers. He justified it not only on the grounds of economic determinism, but by professing to discover in business the strong friend of national unity. The planters and farmers were local and sectional in outlook, but the "mercantile classes, the great commercial masses of the country, whose affairs connect them strongly with every State in the Union and with all the nations of the earth, whose business and profession give a sort of nationality to their character"—these men, he argued, gave solidity and stability to government—they were the cohesive force that bound the whole together.[6] In serving such clients he was but serving a greater cause.

After 1824 the earlier Webster with his solid understanding, his frank realism, his honest exposition of fundamental principles, slowly gave way to the lawyer, the politician, the opportunist of the unhappy later years. With the change the last authentic voice of the eighteenth century was silenced; the break with the old English tradition was complete. Immediate, domestic issues muddied his thought, and Webster and America plunged into a bitter partisanship produced by the new alignments of an equalitarian agrarianism, a capitalistic industrialism, and a feudal slavocracy. Federalism was dead and in its stead was the Whig party, patched together of odds and ends, devoid of principles, seeking only expediency; and of this party Webster became an outstanding spokesman. It was an ignoble time, and his great abilities were not substantial enough to save him from the common meanness. Whoever wishes to understand how great was his fall need only compare the speech of 1820 on "The Basis of the Senate" with the "Declaration of Whig Principles and Purposes" of 1840 (*Works*, Vol. II, p. 41).

To his contemporaries, however, his position was secure. His reputation was extraordinary, and he seemed as fixed and brilliant as the north star. After the reply to Hayne, his fame as the defender of the Constitution was in every mouth. That celebrated speech, perhaps the most celebrated in our congressional history, was delivered on the January 26, 1830, and awakened an amazing response. Men were moved to tears by its eloquence, and its circulation in pamphlet form exceeded that of any other pamphlet

[6] See "The Landing at Plymouth," in *Works*, Vol. II, pp. 204–205.

since the founding of the government. It is not a great constitutional argument, but it better served the purpose of inspiring in the public a grandiose conception of national unity under the organic law, than any reasoned statement could have done. For political purposes rhetoric was more effective than historical argument, and its sonorous sentences, and in particular the stately conclusion, vastly appealed to the taste of the generation. Three years later Webster applied himself more closely to the subtleties of the question. Calhoun's masterly argument with its exposition of the theory of concurrent majorities could not be answered by rhetoric, and on February 16, 1833, Webster spoke on "The Constitution not a Compact between Sovereign States" (*Works*, Vol. III, p. 449). His argument is strictly legal and rests on four theses: that sovereignty inheres in the people; that as individuals acting collectively in their sovereign capacity, they ordained and established the Constitution; that the Constitution thus established is the supreme law of the land, acting immediately upon the individual citizen and recognizing no intermediary sovereign state; and that as an "executed contract" it is irrevocable and final, with the necessary functions to construe its powers and execute its will.

Of these four theses, two may be regarded as Webster's chief contribution to the great debate: the doctrine of immediacy, and the doctrine of an executed contract. The latter, quite obviously, is no more than Burke's theory of the British constitution as founded on a compact entered into following the Revolution of 1688, and as such, by analogy from the Common Law, inviolable without the consent of both parties to the instrument. As developed by Burke the theory is somewhat tenuous, but as applied by Webster to the interpretation of a written document it is extraordinarily plausible to the legal mind. The doctrine of immediacy, on the other hand, would seem to have been derived from Judge Story. The argument of Webster in expounding the principle of immediate contact between the individual citizen and the Constitution follows the argument of Story's *Commentaries* too closely to escape comment. Theodore Parker explicitly states that Webster got his argument from Story, and circumstances bear out his assertion. The two men had long been close friends. Webster's speech was delivered a month after the *Commentaries* was finished. In his earlier speeches such principle found no place, and it is reasonable to suppose that, confronted by the Calhoun resolutions

Webster should have turned to the materials gathered by his learned friend and frequent adviser. Here was his reply ready to hand, a mass of legal fact and constitutional exposition, together with a clear and simple theory. Nearly a month elapsed before Webster rose to speak, and then he threw *Story on the Constitution* at Calhoun's theory of compact. Whether such an interpretation is reasonable or not, the speech added greatly to Webster's reputation as an expounder of the Constitution.

In 1833 he stood at the meridian of his renown; thereafter the westering sun of his fame went slowly down. He had come to evil times when opportunism and compromise—so imperative if the country were to hold together at all—seemed immoral to men who insisted that righteousness be legislated upon America, and weakness to men who demanded their pound of flesh. The black shadow of slavery fell across his path, and despite his wish to avoid all controversy on the subject, he could not evade the issue. It drove him into a corner, and the sword of the Constitution that he sought to defend himself with was turned in the end against him. Webster's antipathy to slavery was of long standing and he gave frank expression to it in his speeches. The position which he finally came to assume, in face of the growing abolition sentiment in Massachusetts, was taken deliberately and was worthy of a lawyer. He would oppose the extension of slave territory, but he would not interfere with slavery in the old slave states. The Constitution, he argued, recognized slavery as existing in certain commonwealths by virtue of state laws, but those laws did not run beyond the confines of the state. The territories were under Federal law, and no injunction was laid upon Congress to extend the laws or institutions of any state or group of states over the territorial domain. In his speech on "Exclusion of Slavery from the Territories," on August 12, 1848, he stated his position thus:

It will not be contended that this sort of slavery exists by general law. It exists only by local law. I do not mean to deny the validity of that local law where it is established; but I say it is, after all, local law. It is nothing more. And wherever that local law does not extend, property in persons does not exist. Well, Sir, what is now the demand on the part of our Southern friends? They say, "We will carry our local laws with us wherever we go. We insist that Congress does us injustice unless it establishes in the territory in which we wish to go our own local law." This demand I for one resist, and shall resist. It goes upon the idea that there is an inequality, unless persons under this local law, and holding property by authority of that law, can go into new territory and there establish that local law, to the exclusion of the general law. (*Works*, Vol. V, p. 309.)

It was the unfortunate Seventh of March Speech that proved Webster's undoing—this and the Fugitive Slave Bill in which he was deeply implicated. The situation was desperately critical, Webster was pessimistic, and this was a last gesture of reconciliation with the South. Presidential ambitions and runaway slaves were stewing in a common political pot with Abolition societies and northern mercantile interests. Webster was puzzled, hesitated, emptied another glass of the wine of the Constitution, and went for the Fugitive Slave Bill. It was a tragic political mistake. To be sure a tremendous address was presented to him, signed by the most respectable persons in Boston and Cambridge, but it was an empty honor. Webster's influence was gone, never to be regained. There is something pathetic in his futile attempt to stifle the New England conscience by ramming the Constitution down its throat:

Sir, the principle of the restitution of runaway slaves is not objectionable, unless the Constitution is objectionable. If the Constitution is right in that respect, the principle is right, and the law providing for carrying it into effect is right. If that be so, and if there is no abuse of the right under any law of Congress, or any other law, then what is there to complain of? ("Speech on the Compromise Measures," in *Works*, Vol. V, p. 433.)

And there is something pathetic also in the hurt vanity of the old man that his judgment should be questioned. His self-pride was offended when the Abolitionists rejected his legal dogmatisms, and set up their own dogmatisms. He regarded them as mischief-makers. "I am against agitators, north and south," he exclaimed petulantly. He recognized no higher law than the Constitution and Blackstone, and he would suffer no popular interference with Congress.

Then, Sir, there are the Abolition societies, of which I am unwilling to speak, but in regard to which I have very clear notions and opinions. I do not think them useful. I think their operations for the last twenty years have produced nothing good or valuable. . . . They have excited feelings. . . . I cannot but see what mischiefs their interference with the South has produced . . . everything that these agitating people have done has been, not to enlarge, but to restrain, not to set free, but to bind

faster, the slave population of the South. (" Seventh of March Speech,"
in *Works*, Vol. V, p. 357.)

I desire to call the attention of all sober-minded men at the North, of
all conscientious men, of all men who are not carried away by some fanatical idea or some false impression, to their constitutional obligations. I
put it to all the sober and sound minds at the North as a question of morals
and a question of conscience. What right have they, in their legislative
capacity or any other capacity, to endeavour to get around this Constitution, or to embarrass the free exercise of the rights secured by the
Constitution to the persons whose slaves escape from them? None at
all; none at all. Neither in the forum of conscience, nor before the face
of the Constitution, are they, in my opinion, justified in such attempt.
(*Ibid.*, p. 355.)

If the later Webster had no message for the conscience of New
England, neither had he any for the intelligence of New England.
The realistic Federalism that had listened to him in 1820 was gone,
submerged by the flood waters of the renaissance; and the current
transcendentalism seemed to him insubstantial and dangerous.
The rising liberalism of the forties left him wholly untouched; it
could not leaven the heavy materialism of his nature. He was
quite unacquainted with the new Massachusetts that was coming
to expression; he had lived too long with "the lawyers, the politicians, and rich merchants and manufacturers," to understand
the greater world of Concord. While he had been living on the
subsidies of State Street, and contracting his mind to the compass
of a banker's, the intellect of Massachusetts had become liberal.
And in becoming liberal it aroused him from indifference to hostility. Writing to a friend in explanation of his refusal to visit Concord in his later years, he said:

Many of those whom I so highly regarded in your beautiful and quiet
village have become a good deal estranged, to my great grief, by abolitionism, free-soilism, transcendentalism, and other notions which I cannot but
regard as so many vagaries of the imagination. (Quoted in Sanborn,
Life of Thoreau.)

But if he was scarcely acquainted with the little group of thinkers and liberals—Emerson, Thoreau, Channing, Parker, Garrison,
Phillips, Edmund Quincy, Whittier, Lowell, Higginson, Harriet
Beecher Stowe, Margaret Fuller—they were well acquainted with
him and took his measure exactly. The intellect of Massachusetts
—so long ignored by Webster—had its revenge. Its voice carried

farther than his, and it painted his portrait in no flattering strokes. The fierce storm that suddenly beat upon him broke the old man's spirit. He had fed too long on adulation to endure censure. No doubt that censure was severe, but it was far juster than the earlier adulation had been. Whittier's *Ichabod* is familiar to every American schoolboy. Lowell, then in his liberal mood, characterized him as "a statesman who had communicated no impulse to any of the great ideas of the century, as a statesman whose soul had been absorbed in tariff, banks, and the Constitution, instead of devoting himself to the freedom of the future." Emerson, who had long studied him critically, gave an extraordinarily just analysis of his character:

Mr. Webster is a man who lives by his memory, a man of the past, not a man of faith or of hope. He obeys his powerful animal nature;—and his finely developed understanding only works freely and with all its force, when it stands for animal good; that is, for property. He believes, in so many words, that government exists for the protection of property. He looks to the Union as an estate, a large farm, and is excellent in the completeness of his defence of it so far. He adheres to the letter. . . . What he finds already written, he will defend. Lucky that so much had got well written when he came. For he has no faith in the power of self-government. Not the smallest municipal provision, if it were new, would receive his sanction. In Massachusetts, in 1776, he would, beyond all question, have been a refugee. He praises Adams and Jefferson, but it is a past Adams and Jefferson, that his mind can entertain. A present Adams and Jefferson he would denounce. So with the eulogies of liberty in his writings,—they are sentimentalism and youthful rhetoric. He can celebrate it, but it means as much from him as from Metternich or Talleyrand. This is all inevitable from his constitution. All the drops of his blood have eyes that look downward. ("The Fugitive Slave Law.")

To the transcendental mind Webster's economic realism was peculiarly repugnant, and it was this which inspired Theodore Parker's critical analysis of Webster's career—the most scathing and explicit of all contemporary estimates. What Parker discovers most hateful in Webster's career was his adherence to the principles of Federalism, from the "Basis of the Senate" speech in 1820, to the New York speech on November 18, 1850. The persistence of his economic realism was an affront to the liberals of the humanitarian school that had moved far from the position of Fisher Ames. Webster might do lip service to humanitarian ideals, Parker asserted, but always he came back in the end to his polar conception—"The great object of government is the protec-

tion of property at home, and respect and renown abroad" (*Works:
Additional Speeches*, Vol. I, p. 220).

It was this same persistent realism that made Webster so useful
to the rising capitalism. His work in the Senate was supplemented
by his work in the court room. He was the greatest corporation
lawyer of the day, certain to be found defending vested interests,
never on the side of the leaner purse. Probably more than any
other man except John Marshall, he contributed to the work of
bringing the Constitution under the sovereignty of the judiciary.
His most significant contribution, certainly, was his argument in
the celebrated Dartmouth College case, delivered before the
Supreme Court in 1818, which resulted in one of the foundation
decisions on which later has been erected the solid structure of our
corporation law.[7] By engrafting upon the Constitution the
principle that a contract lies beyond the reach of legislative power
to annul, the decision assured greater security for private property
than exists under any other judicial system in the world. Alexander Hamilton could not have asked for more.

It was the singular ill fortune of Webster to have been born too
late to profit from the old mercantile Federalism to which his
affections were always attached, and too early to profit by the
industrial Federalism that came to greatness after the Civil War.
If fate had been kinder to him, and he had appeared on the political
horizon a generation earlier or a generation later, he would have
reaped in far greater abundance those high civic honors he so
foolishly coveted. The economic groups whom he served would
have been in position to reward a servant so conspicuously able
and useful. As a contemporary of John Adams he might have
become a notable political philosopher—provided always that he
had not turned Tory as Emerson suggested. But unhappily for his
fame he was launched between tides on a stormy sea and his
stately bark foundered in the squall of Abolitionism.

[7] Theodore Parker denied Webster credit for the argument, pointing out that
"the facts, the law, the precedents, the ideas, and the conclusions of that argument,
had almost all of them been presented by Messrs. Mason and Smith in the previous
trial of the case" (*Additional Speeches*, Vol. I, p. 171). The statement is confirmed
by Beveridge.

PART TWO: THE RISE OF LIBERALISM

CHAPTER I

THE RENAISSANCE

To write a history of Massachusetts, I confess, is not inviting to an expansive thinker. . . . From 1790 to 1820 there was not a book, a speech, a conversation, or a thought in the State. About 1820, the Channing, Webster, and Everett era begun, and we have been bookish and poetical and cogitative since. (Emerson, *Journals*, Vol. VIII, p. 339.)

IN such summary fashion in the year 1852, Emerson recorded his judgment on half a century of intellectual life in Massachusetts. It was the comment of an exacting critic. In its characterization of the extraordinary ferment of thought that marked the decades of the thirties and forties, it is quite inadequate; but in its contemptuous dismissal of the age of Fisher Ames and Robert Treat Paine it was scarcely unjust. The utter sterility of those old times Emerson understood only too well. It was the world of his own youth, whose pale negations he had come to hate. The creative impulse was stifled, the mind had grown stale from tedious iteration. But at last the old barriers gave way, and into this narrow illiberal world, that had long fed on the crusts of English rationalism and Edwardean dogmatism—dry as remainder biscuit after voyage—broke the floods that had been gathering in Europe for years, the waters of all the streams of revolution that were running there bank-full. Before this inundation the old provincialisms were swept away, and for the first time in its history, and the last, the mind of New England gave itself over to a great adventure in liberalism.

Quite evidently the renaissance resulted from the impact of the romantic revolution upon the Puritan mind, and it issued in a form native to New England experience. Animated by the common spirit of Utopianism, its dreams were unlike those of Virginia or the West, founded on a different economics and seeking different ends. Massachusetts had discovered a particular road leading to Utopia by way of the industrial revolution, and the textile mills on the Merrimac began weaving a new pattern of life for New

317

England.   The old static agricultural order was broken in upon, and with the social disruption came naturally an intellectual disruption.   The mind of that older New England had been held in the close keeping of the church, and the movement of intellectual emancipation became therefore at the outset a movement leveled at theological conservatism; it was concerned first to rid New England of the incubus of Calvinistic dogma.   The Calvinists were of tough fiber and tenacious of opinion, and to turn their flank was no summer campaign.   The result was a long battle of ideas, a fierce struggle between the old deterministic theology and the new romantic philosophy, with victory slowly inclining to the latter. This major struggle gave to the renaissance its profoundly ethical spirit that set it off sharply from the earlier renaissance of Virginia; and not the least important of the results of the movement was the liberation of the New England conscience from its long bondage to dogma, setting it free to engage in a larger work in the world.   What that conscience accomplished in the brief period of its freedom; what causes it espoused and what reforms it carried through—how it quickened a humanitarian zeal in New England and imparted a militant spirit to its culture—these are phases of the total movement not to be neglected by the historian.

In the realm of ideas the renaissance was largely dominated by old-world thought.   From the abundant stores of European revolutionary doctrine the New England liberals drew freely— more freely perhaps from German idealism than from French Utopianism.   Germany meant much to the awakening mind of New England, by reason of its spiritual and intellectual kinship. Plato was their common father, a transcendental mysticism their common experience.   Philosophical idealism with its indwelling Godhood that exalted man to the divine and transformed a mechanical universe into the dwelling place of divine love—this was a dynamic faith, appealing to men long nurtured in faith, more seductive to the children of Puritanism than any political or economic romanticisms.   It opened to them new heavens when the old were closed and encouraged them to go forth on great ventures.

But the renaissance was very much more than a transplanting of German idealism.   France had a shaping hand in it, and England. Jean Jacques came before Hegel, and Unitarianism before transcendentalism.   It was social and literary as well as philosophical. In so far as that which was essentially one may be divided, the movement involved three major strands: the social Utopianism that came from revolutionary France; the idealistic metaphysics that emerged from revolutionary Germany; and the new culture that spread with the development of literary romanticism. To distinguish these three strands is one thing; to endeavor to separate them is quite another. They interweave and blend in varying patterns; they are but different, new-world phases of a comprehensive European movement that runs far back into the preceding century—a movement that in transferring economic and political mastery from the aristocracy to the middle class, in destroying the worm-eaten feudal order and clearing the way for the new capitalistic order, laid open a broad path into the nineteenth century. The extraordinary appeal of this vast movement to the liberal mind of America resulted from the fact that an identical revolution was under way here. In New England, perhaps more dramatically than elsewhere in America, the day of the middle class was dawning, aristocratic ideals were disintegrating, and the hopes of men were running high. To humanize this emerging society, to awaken it to a nobler faith in human destiny, to further the cause of social justice, to create a democracy of the spirit—this was the deeper romantic purpose, however vaguely comprehended, that was fermenting in the New England renaissance, and it was this that gave to it a spirit so warmly ethical.

Now quite evidently a movement so extraordinarily complex would appeal diversely to different minds, and in its development it drew to itself a singularly various following. To the sons of respectable Federalism it was the new romantic culture that appealed; to the militant conscience of Puritanism it was the inspiration of social Utopianism; to the emancipated intellectuals it was the metaphysical idealism. Its many-sidedness was both confusing and stimulating. How shall we explain a movement that embraced such different men as Everett and Channing and Parker and Garrison and Whittier and Emerson and Longfellow and Holmes; men often mutually repellent, sometimes sharply critical of each other? No single mind sums up the whole—the theological, humanitarian, mystical, critical, and cultural aspirations of the awakening—as perhaps Goethe may be said to have done for Germany. Emerson, Thoreau and Parker possibly embodied it most adequately; they were transcendental individualists, intellectual revolutionaries, contemptuous of all meanly material standards.   But quite evidently Everett would not travel far along the transcendental path they pointed out, nor Holmes, nor Longfellow.   These latter expected no romantic Utopias, wanted no such Utopias.   Cambridge and Boston satisfied their hopes; they found the world not such a bad place for those who knew how to meet it on its own terms.   Yet they too were children of the awakening, and in following their individual paths they contributed in their own way to the disintegration of the old authoritarian order that had long held the mind of New England in subjection. Each in some measure and after his own fashion was a rebel, and their total rebellions made up the sum of New England's bequest to a more liberal America.   Yet in this eager and somewhat vague liberalism to which the renaissance was dedicated in spirit, the note that runs through the several programs is a note of reaction from the aspirations of the middle class.   It was an ethical protest against the harsh and unjust realities of the industrial revolution that was so ruthlessly transforming the old order of life in New England; and it took the form of a return to a simpler life.   To struggle free from the chains of the eighteenth century, only to be bound in new chains, was an ignoble ending to the emancipation that free men could not envisage with satisfaction.

CHAPTER II

LIBERALISM AND CALVINISM

THE first stirrings of new life were felt within the church, the repository of such learning as Harvard College disseminated through the Massachusetts villages. For two hundred years the dogmas of Calvin had lain as a heavy weight on the mind of New England. Revolutions had taken place in English and continental theology, but New England Calvinism had kept closely within the narrow confines of its creed, annually turning over the exhausted soil and reaping an ever scantier harvest. Since the days of Edwards there had been abundant speculation and much exercise in syllogisms, but no scrutiny of major premises. Such an examination was long overdue, with the romantic revolution under way in France, and new theories of human nature and the relation of man to society and the state, spreading widely. But unfortunately the odium which New England conservatism quickly fastened upon the French school frightened the orthodox. The stigma of atheism was put upon every harmless bantling of the numerous French brood, and in the terror of reaction the pulpit, following the lead of the reactionary pew, aroused itself to cleanse the church of every innovation. English Arianism, even worse things, it was discovered, had stolen into Congregational pulpits during the relaxed period of the Revolution; a dangerous spirit of liberalism had spread silently through the tidewater churches, capturing the strongholds of Boston orthodoxy.

By the year 1800 it was high time for the old Congregationalism of Jonathan Edwards to take counsel with itself. "Let us guard against the insidious encroachments of *innovation*—that evil and beguiling spirit which is now stalking to and fro in the earth, seeking whom it may devour," exclaimed Jedidiah Morse, the arch reactionary, in the days when French ideas were knocking at the doors of New England. And by innovation the doughty Jedidiah meant any idea that had been stumbled on, new since the days of the great Edwards. To go back to the pure Edwardean doctrine, to purge the church of incipient Arminianism and Arianism and Socinianism—together with such other innovations as might show their faces anywhere—became thenceforth the chief business of the devout New England of 1800. To timid souls the ideas of their grandfathers seemed far safer than the ideas of their fathers; and so theology followed politics in turning its back upon the freer, more generous world that beckoned.

Nevertheless French liberalism slowly won its victories. It needs high walls to keep out ideas. Excluded from the drawing-rooms and counting-houses, ostracized in society and politics, romantic philosophy slipped quietly into Boston by the door of theology, and took lodgings in the homes of the first families. To those who enjoy the little ironies of history, the easy subjugation of respectable Boston by that very Jacobinical heresy against which Boston was so bitter is too amusing to be overlooked. Changing its name and arraying itself in garments cut after the best Yankee fashion, the gospel of Jean Jacques presently walked the streets of Boston and spoke from its most respectable pulpits, under the guise of Unitarianism. The heretical doctrines of the excellence of human nature and the perfectibility of man were preached to Federalist congregations so persuasively that instead of repudiating them and asserting the total depravity of their neighbors, simple-minded merchants approved the doctrines and cheerfully paid their pew-rent. It was a respectable and bloodless revolution. Under its discreet disguise Unitarianism accomplished for New England what Jeffersonianism had accomplished for the South and West—the wide dissemination of eighteenth-century French liberalism. It opened the New England mind to fresh ideas. Out of Unitarianism was to come the intellectual renaissance, with its transcendental philosophies and social reforms, its enlarged conception of democracy and its Utopian dreams, which made New England count so effectively in the developments of the half century.

The twenty-five years between 1790 and 1815 were the nascent period of Unitarianism, when it was reëxamining the old Calvinist dogmas in the light of the new liberalism, weighing the doctrines of election and reprobation in the scale with the doctrines of God's beneficence and man's excellence, and coming definitely to reject them as blasphemy against God and defamation of human nature. And it was during these critical years that the upholders of the traditional orthodoxy were most actively concerned to provide

a defense for the sacred dogmas of their grandfathers. The liberal
advance produced a conservative reaction, and the lines of battle
were sharply drawn. The capture of Harvard College by the
Unitarians in 1805, and the founding of Andover Theological
Seminary by the Calvinists in 1808, were dramatic events in a
long intellectual and legal struggle that aroused much bitterness
and bequeathed to the churches a rich legacy of unchristian
animosities. Good men on both sides—to recall a contemporary
witticism—were quite too ready "to fight for the glory of God
as if the very devil were in them."

The traditional Calvinism defended itself with spirit, asserting
so vehemently that it was still a living faith, that the corpse was
not yet an authentic corpse, that it succeeded at least in postpon-
ing its own burial. It was deeply entrenched in the inertia of custom, but intellectually it was in really desperate straits. It was
slowly disintegrating from dry-rot with which both minister and
theology were stricken. With its major premises tacitly denied
by Yankee experience, it was unfortunate in being defended by as
humorless and ungainly a breed of theologians as ever quarreled over
the loving-kindness of God. Clinging to the defenses which Jonathan Edwards had erected against the incursion of old-world ideas,
it declaimed its dogmas and damned the human race with tedious
iteration. Over-threshed straw makes poor fodder, and after a
two-hour battle with potential infidelities, many a good minister
descended from his pulpit lamenting that his exhortations had
been wasted on "a sermon-proof, gospel-glutted generation."
Yet he went faithfully back to his study to consume the day in
argument with a suppositious Arminian, and in spinning cobweb
systems between the worm-eaten rafters, quite oblivious to the
common-sense world without his walls. The difficulties in which
those old Calvinists found themselves very likely seemed tragic
to them; but to later generations, endowed with some saving grace
of humor, the situation was not without its spice. The good men
were undeniably caught in a distressing dilemma. They were
laboring prodigiously both to sit tight in the old dogma of determinism and yet wriggle out; to maintain election and reprobation and yet insert somehow the thin edge of personal responsibility; to prove to the satisfaction of the pew that man is both
bound and free. It was a hard necessity to be under, to damn man
by predestination, and "yet worry out enough freedom for him

to be decently damned on," as a late critic has remarked;[1] to send him to hell by divine decree, yet prove that he went of his own accord. Yet they must do that impossible thing if they were to justify their theology to common-sense congregations that were drifting into indifference.

The whole thing was monstrously unreal and it resulted in hatching such a brood of tenuous subtleties as we have difficulty in comprehending today. Theological fame in Massachusetts came to be measured by the skill with which the logician made out to stand on both sides of the fence at the same time. Had it not been for Jonathan Edwards New England Congregationalism would have drifted comfortably with the tide of liberalism; but his uncompromising spirit held it anchored. This masterly spinner of theological systems bequeathed to his successors an unfinished work; but he had clearly envisaged the problem and suggested a line of attack. In his great inquiry into the nature of will he had hoped to provide an infallible means of reconciling the irreconcilable by arguing that the will is dependent on desire. The natural man, according to the Edwardean logic, is free to serve God as the highest good if he desires, but he lacks the desire unless God reveals himself as that highest good, and such revelation rests with God's pleasure. "Moral responsibility lies in the choice, not in the cause of the choice." [2] With this distinction suggested between natural and moral freedom, Calvinistic speculation went on hopefully till it attained its culminating triumph in Nathaniel Walker's ingenious doctrine of certainty with power to the contrary. Walker was a pupil of Timothy Dwight's, and one of the foundation professors of the new Yale Divinity School, established to combat Unitarian heresies. A tremendous rattling of the bones of the Connecticut churches followed his pronouncement that man's acts are not necessitated by a rigid law of cause and effect, but that his choices are so connected with antecedent conditions of soul and environment, that to God's perception it is certain what they will be, although he possesses full power of contrary choice.[3]

As we contemplate those old theological abstractions, dead now as Lot's wife, the universe of our fathers shrinks to a petty compass,

---

[1] See Fenn, *Religious History of New England: King's Chapel Lectures*, p. 130.
[2] See Williston Walker, *A History of the Congregational Churches in the United States*, p. 283.
[3] *Ibid.*, p. 356.

not much larger than the snug little state of Connecticut, curiously egocentric, curiously anthropomorphic. Obviously such grotesqueries could not endure indefinitely. Presently there must appear the common-sense housewife with her broom, and the dusty cobwebs would disappear. English Arianism, emerging out of English Presbyterianism, and long under suspicion of the New England fathers, first opened the windows and let a little fresh air into the New England churches. But back of Arianism was the total body of eighteenth-century rationalism, with its theology rooted in new political and social philosophies, and its doctrines derived from conceptions of God and man hostile to Calvinistic determinism. There could be no reconciling them. Calvinism must extirpate English rationalism or be disintegrated by it.

But rationalism refused to be extirpated. Here and there in Massachusetts pulpits appeared a new order of preachers, young men who had broken with the old dogmas and were plainly bitten with the English distemper. Of these the most notable was Jonathan Mayhew, from 1747 to 1766 pastor of the West Church, and the freest-spoken minister in Boston. Mayhew was a thoroughgoing liberal, not to say radical, an intimate friend of Otis and John Adams, and chief clerical leader of the opposition to the English ministry. He had broken through the narrow parochialism of Boston; he corresponded with the intellectual leaders of English dissent, and while still a young man was on the highroad to Arianism. He seems to have been a brilliant fellow, bold and frank in speech, with great and popular powers as a preacher, and his early death alone prevented him from anticipating some of the work of Channing.[4] A like fate abruptly terminated the work of another able young man, Lemuel Briant, pastor of the Braintree church from 1745 to his death in 1753. Briant was John Adams's pastor and, like Mayhew, an Arian, with a ready wit that his adversaries must have found disconcerting. "I have always tho't," he remarked apropos of the familiar dilemma, "that so far as any Man is pure (let it be in a greater or lesser Degree) he is not filthy."[5] But the coming on of the Revolutionary disputes and the disturbance of war put a stop to the normal development of the movement; and the general reaction following the treaty of peace gave encouragement to the Calvinistic reaction and temporarily strengthened the Edwardean

[4] *Ibid.*, pp. 276–277.   [5] *Ibid.*, p. 272.

school. Nevertheless the liberal doctrines of Mayhew and Briant, falling in with the French philosophy, prepared the way for the conscious Unitarian revolt at the end of the century.

That revolt was fundamentally ethical rather than theological, and the name Unitarian, which the liberal movement accepted somewhat reluctantly from its opponents, very inadequately describes its special genius. The term derives from the middle eighteenth century, before religious thought had come under the influence of the new social philosophy; and it suggests a primary theological bias in a movement that was far more significantly ethical and social. The early liberals, forerunners of Unitarianism, were theologians given to probing in rationalistic spirit, the mystery of the Godhood. Now, denial of the Trinity has been common to all Unitarians, although individually they might profess an Arian or a Socinian interpretation of the nature and rôle of Jesus; but what is more important, they have been from the first close Scripturists, disliking exact theological systems and setting biblical authority above human. By the time the name had come to be generally accepted—about the year 1815—it had already lost much of its earlier significance, for emphasis had shifted from the mystery of the Godhood to the problem of the relations existing between the children and the Father. On the one hand supernaturalism tended to disappear in morality, and on the other religion tended to seek an authoritative basis in idealistic philosophy and justify itself by intuitionism. "The soul," argued Channing, in his exposition of a later Unitarian theology, "is the spring of our knowledge of God." "Here is our primitive teacher and light." "The only God, whom our thoughts can rest on, and our hearts can cling to, is the God whose image dwells in our own Souls" (*Works*, Vol. VI, Introductory Remarks, p. 21). Unitarianism, in other words, reversed the thought process of Calvinism. Instead of debasing man to a mean creature, subject to a God of wrath, it professed to discover a loving Father in the human heart of love. Here was a revolution indeed, a revolution in which were the seeds of transcendentalism, of social Utopias, of pretty much the entire intellectual awakening of New England. The old Calvinism had no weapons to meet such an attack; the new creed lay outside its realm of thought. What that creed finally came to be, under Channing's influence, is thus stated by a recent historian:

Man is God's child, made in His image and object of His love; his reason and conscience are divine witnesses to truth and light, and when governed by them he walks in the ways of God, safe in his Father's love and care. The God in whom their opponents believed—a God of election and reprobation, capable of dooming an entire race because its ancestors disobeyed a God of arbitrary will and discriminating grace—seemed to them simply an immoral being and they frankly said so. (Fenn, *Religious History of New England, etc.*, p. 125.)

In its noblest expression Unitarianism became essentially a humanistic religion, rational, ethical, individual, yet with deep and warm social sympathies. In Channing's excellent phrase, it discovered the apotheosis of religion in "the adoration of goodness." It issued in conduct because it developed character. The highest testimony to the excellence of the faith is the noble company of men and women who subscribed to its creed. And yet after all, Unitarianism was rather an attitude of mind than a creed. It was the recovery of the original principle of New England Separatism, lost during the long years of orthodox conformity—the principle of the open mind and free inquiry. Let each devout soul, each group of fellow believers, Unitarianism announced, seek the truth where it may be found; let each give to it such outward form as best reveals its divine nature; not seeking to impose a particular interpretation upon others, but each taking upon himself full responsibility for his spiritual welfare. Authority it regarded as the prop of the weak; dogma, as the body of a faith that is dead. As free souls, mature and self-reliant, the Unitarians would be their own authority, would fashion their own creed. The Scriptures lie open and the heedful eye will discover God's revelation in their pages. The deeper spirit of Unitarianism is not inadequately embodied in the text, "Search the Scriptures, for they are they which testify of me." No abler or more devout Scripturists ever preached in America than the Unitarian ministers, and if bolder souls like Theodore Parker went further than others, if their free handling of old interpretations gave offense to the timid, that fact provided no sanction to coerce or stifle free inquiry. Toleration of differences, respect for devout free thought—this return to the position of Roger Williams two centuries before was the vital principle of Unitarianism. Like him, the Unitarian was a seeker, open-minded and free. Others might be intolerant, others might regard themselves as the sole custodians of truth, but not he.

But if the Unitarians who followed Channing were liberals

in religion, they were conservatives in well-nigh everything else.
Amongst the laity the adoration of goodness was sufficiently
tempered by Yankee thrift to keep it from interfering seriously
with the practical business of getting on in the world; and in
consequence the new faith gathered its supporters from amongst
the prosperous rather than the needy, from Federalists rather than
Democrats.   The commercial dominated the intellectual and
emotional in their prim and somewhat cold congregations.   "The
Unitarians," it was commonly said, "were the cult of the arrived."
As successful men, these Boston merchants and manufacturers did
not believe that they were the sons of Adam, children of iniquity.
They thought better of themselves and of God than Calvinism
permitted them to think; "one who was born in Boston," the current jest put it, "had no need to be born again."   Generous in all
approved philanthropies these Unitarian laymen might be, but
emotionally religious they were temperamentally incapable of
being.   Until the infusion of the rich sap of transcendentalism, that
gave it new life and brought it to bloom, Unitarianism was in
grave danger of dying at the root.   But with the spread of the
philosophy of intuitionalism, the negative individualism of Unitarianism became positive, broke with the respectable conservatism
of commercial congregations, and overflowed in a rich and generous
faith.   Authority, dogma, creed, were swept away by this new
faith in an indwelling divinity, with its intuitive sanctions, and
Unitarianism merged in the larger movement of the renaissance.

II

WILLIAM ELLERY CHANNING

To the austerely spiritual Channing the guiding principle of
Unitarianism was identical with the spirit of primitive New England separatism—the principle of freedom in religious matters,
the individual speaking his mind frankly, shepherd and flock feeding as they would, without fear and without coercion.   The soul is
responsible to itself and its own conscience; there are no orthodoxies
and no heterodoxies, but a duty is laid upon the individual to seek
truth with an open mind and be steadfast in its service.   It was this
spirit of open-minded liberalism that led him along the path of
unmilitant individualism, seeking freedom only to the end of
righteousness, and counting righteousness the fine flower of freedom; desiring peace and universal fellowship; loath to found a

sect; yet driven by those who denied freedom to themselves as well as others to become the champion and leader of a great schism that sundered the traditional unity of Congregationalism, and erected a new faith on the altars of the old.

Channing's heritage was drawn from the deepest wells of New England idealism; and filtered through his finely ethical mind it emerged pure and limpid, the living waters of the new faith. His noble preëminence was due to the simple spirituality of his nature. Intellectually, he was neither great nor original. In scholarship he was distinctly inferior to academic theologians like Andrews Norton and to omnivorous students like Theodore Parker. Almost wholly introspective he was influenced slowly by world-currents of thought, and such alien ideas as found lodgment in his mind took on a native form and color from his own convictions. Nevertheless though his meditations revolved about the pole-star of his own experience, his theology cautiously took shape under the pressure of two ideas that came to him from the latter years of the eighteenth century—the ideas of God's beneficence and of man's excellence. Once lodged in his mind, those ideas led to quite revolutionary consequences, not only in their disintegrating effect upon the Calvinistic dogmas in which he had been reared, but in the generous romanticism which they bequeathed to Unitarian theology. His intellectual development was late and halting, yet that he liberated himself at all was remarkable considering the world that bred him—Newport, frequented by wealthy planters and enriched by the slave trade, Cambridge and Boston then in the stagnancy of Federalist complacency. Of the same generation with Robert Treat Paine and Josiah Quincy, only a few years older than Rufus Choate and Edward Everett, as a boy sitting under the preaching of Samuel Hopkins—the rugged expounder of the Hopkinsian doctrine of willing to be damned for the glory of God, a doctrine so repugnant to the major tenets of Channing's theology—he belonged by temperament and training to the parochial world that accounted Fisher Ames a great orator, and looked with suspicion on the new century that was crowding in on its comfortable preserves.

From the deep New England ruts Channing pulled himself with incredible difficulty. His frequent reactions almost kept pace with his progress. For years he oscillated between freedom and dogma, now dominated by the Hopkinsian influence and thrown back

upon a morbid Calvinism by ill health; then resolutely casting off
the evil spell; until the year 1815, when the conservative wing
declaring war upon the liberals, he was drawn into the controversy
and took upon himself the burden of defending the liberal cause.
He was then thirty-five, but it was not till four years later, in the
celebrated Baltimore sermon at the ordination of Jared Sparks,
that he offered a definitive statement of the new theology. The
sermon brought him wide fame and fastened upon him the leadership of the Unitarian movement. Comment upon the new doctrines was widespread, and the circulation of the sermon in pamphlet form, according to a late biographer, "was not exceeded by
any American publication until in 1830 Webster made his memorable reply to Hayne" (John White Chadwick, *William Ellery
Channing*, p. 147). The creative influence of that sermon in clarifying certain doctrines of Unitarianism and integrating the society
should not blind us to the fact that it embodies only a portion of
Channing's theology—the idea of God's beneficence. It is a
reasoned attack upon Trinitarian Calvinism, upon those dogmas
which reveal—in Channing's expressive phrase—"how mournfully
the human mind may misrepresent the Deity"; but it takes no
account of the idea which later he came to place first—the idea of
man's excellence.

Finer than the Baltimore sermon in its restrained eloquence—
an eloquence that burns with an intensity rare in Channing—and
in its dramatic exposition of the doctrine of the atonement, is the
sermon entitled *Unitarian Christianity most Favourable to Piety*,
delivered in 1826 at the dedication of the second Unitarian church
in New York City. In this sermon Channing made use of a daring
comparison which startled his friends and gave mortal offense to
orthodox Calvinists. It is probably the most dramatic passage
to be found in his writings, and it so well exemplifies the temper of
the controversy that it deserves quotation. After discussing the
Edwardean philosophy of infinite punishment and the nature of
atonement, he proceeded:

Let me, then, set it before you, in new terms, and by a new illustration;
and if in so doing, I may wound the feelings of some who hear me, I beg
them to believe, that I do it with pain, and from no impulse but a desire
to serve the cause of truth.—Suppose, then, that a teacher should come
among you, and should tell you, that the Creator, in order to pardon his
own children, had erected a gallows in the centre of the universe, and had

publicly executed upon it, in room of the offenders, an Infinite Being, the partaker of his own Supreme Divinity; suppose him to declare, that this execution was appointed, as a most conspicuous and terrible manifestation of God's justice, and of the infinite woe denounced by his law; and suppose him to add, that all beings in heaven and earth are required to fix their eyes on this fearful sight, as the most powerful enforcement of obedience and virtue. Would you not tell him, that he calumniated his Maker? Would you not say to him, that this central gallows threw gloom over the universe; that the spirit of a government, whose very acts of pardon were written in such blood, was terror, not paternal love; and that the obedience which needed to be upheld by this horrid spectacle, was nothing worth? Would you not say to him, that even you, in this infancy and imperfection of your being, were capable of being wrought upon by nobler motives, and of hating sin through more generous views; and that much more the angels, those pure flames of love, need not the gallows and an executed God to confirm their loyalty? You would all so feel, at such teaching as I have supposed; and yet how does this differ from the popular doctrine of atonement? (*Works*, Vol. III, pp. 197–198.)

In seeking an explanation of Channing's break with New England orthodoxy—a breach that widened greatly with years, coming to embrace politics and economics as well as theology, alienating many of his own congregation and bringing acute grief to him— one can scarcely over-emphasize the influence of his Virginia experience. During the twenty-one months that he spent on the southern plantation, painfully isolated and lonely, he grappled seriously with a body of thought from which the environment of his youth had pretty much shut him away. Virginia in 1798 was ardently Jeffersonian, and French romantic philosophy was a commonplace in Virginia libraries. While Channing never went over wholly to Jeffersonianism, but retained certain Federalist prejudices after the old foundations had turned to quicksand under his feet, he there began a long process of speculative brooding that was to carry him far from the political principles of Boston. French revolutionary thought provided his chief intellectual stimulus during the critical Virginia period. Rousseau he read with profound interest, together with Godwin's *Political Justice* and Mary Wollstonecraft's *Rights of Woman*. The Physiocratic economics that sanctioned the agrarian bias of Jeffersonian democracy seems to have made no appeal to a mind primarily ethical in outlook, yet he went so far as to dabble in communistic theory, and for a time contemplated joining a communistic community. From France, moreover, he derived the idea of the excellence of human nature and the perfectibility of man, ideas which became the mainspring of his later thinking, creatively determining both his theology and his social philosophy, and transforming his whole intellectual world.

In July, 1800, eight months before it took formal possession of the White House, "French infidel philosophy" made its appearance in New England in the person of a slight, health-broken youth, who returned to his quiet theological studies, quite unmindful of the gunpowder he had brought back in his intellectual luggage. It was long before a spark was to strike home, but the powder was there and would do its work eventually. In passing through Channing's mind, the contributions of French romanticism merged with the native heritage of New England idealism, and supplemented by contributions from English Arian thought, slowly assumed definite form that came to issue in three dominating ideas, namely: God is love, man is potentially noble, religion is an excellent life. Enveloping these master ideas, in which they were carried as in a medium, was a pervasive ethical spirit that colored all his thinking and eventually took form in that striking phrase into which all of Channing is compressed, "the adoration of goodness—this is religion." This constituted his reply to the Edwardean theology that debased man to the sole end of exalting a monstrous God— the doctrine of "sweetness and light" was set over against the dogmas of reprobation and election.

With his profound sense of justice, Channing could not follow "the adoration of goodness" into an aloof and mystical pietism. The temptation was strong, for his finely aristocratic and hesitant nature prompted him to stand apart from all turmoil and partisan struggle. He disliked controversy and distrusted all dogmatists. The world of economics and politics was exceedingly distasteful to him; he would gladly stop his ears against the clamor of organized groups and strident parties. The Abolitionists, with whose purpose he deeply sympathized, seemed to him intolerant and their tactics vulgar. There is a measure of justice in Garrison's comment after Channing's death: "His nerves were delicately strung. The sound of a ram's horn was painfully distressing to him. He was firmly persuaded that nothing but a silver trumpet was needed to cause the walls of Jericho to fall; and he did his best upon his own." [6] And yet, however unwillingly, he was drawn in-

[6] Compare a fuller estimate in Garrison, *William Lloyd Garrison*, Vol. III, pp. 239-242.

evitably into an agitation that touched both his religion and his humanity; and between 1835 and 1837 he issued three notable contributions to the controversy: *Slavery*, a reply to the Southern apologists; *The Abolitionists*, an open letter to James Birney, whose Abolition press had been wrecked by an Ohio mob; and a noble appeal to Henry Clay against the annexation of Texas. In the latter year he spoke in Faneuil Hall at a turbulent meeting called to protest against the murder of Lovejoy, the meeting at which Wendell Phillips made his dramatic first appearance on the Abolition platform.

The point of view from which Channing approached the problem of slavery is clearly set forth in his *Introductory Remarks*, written in 1841 for a collected edition of his works, and which constitutes his *apologia pro vita sua*.[7] In this extraordinarily lucid and just statement he reduces the master passions of his life to two—respect for human nature, and reverence for human liberty—passions which were inseparable in all his thinking. Of the first he says, "The following writings will be found to be distinguished by nothing more than by the high estimate which they express of human nature. A respect for the human soul breathes through them." This attitude he elaborates at length:

An enlightened, disinterested human being, morally strong, and exerting a wide influence by the power of virtue, is the clearest reflection of the divine splendour on earth. . . . The glory of the Maker lies in his work. . . . Those men glorify God most, who look with keen eye and loving heart on his works, who catch in all some glimpses of beauty and power, who have a spiritual sense for good in its dimmest manifestations, and who can so interpret the world, that it becomes a bright witness to the Divinity.

I have also felt and continually insisted, that a new reverence for man was essential to the cause of social reform. . . . There can be no spirit of brotherhood, no true peace, any farther than men come to understand their affinity with and relation to God and the infinite purpose for which he gave them life. As yet these ideas are treated as a kind of spiritual romance. . . . The reception of this plainest truth of Christianity would revolutionize society, and create relations among men not dreamed of at the present day. . . . Men would know the import of the word Brother, as yet nothing but a word to multitudes. None of us can conceive the change of manners, the new courtesy and sweetness, the mutual kindness, deference and sympathy, the life and efforts for social melioration, which

[7] In the Glasgow edition of 1844 it prefaces the sixth volume.

are to spring up, in proportion as man shall penetrate beneath the body to the spirit, and shall learn what the lowest human being is.

Out of this reverence for human nature flowed his "reverence for Liberty, for human rights; a sentiment which has grown with my growth, which is striking deeper root in my age, which seems to me a chief element of true love for mankind, and which alone fits a man for intercourse with his fellow-creatures."

It is because I have learned the essential equality of men before the common Father, that I cannot endure to see one man establishing his arbitrary will over another by fraud, or force, or wealth, or rank, or super-stitious claims. It is because the human being has moral powers, be-cause he carries a law in his own breast and was made to govern himself, that I cannot endure to see him taken out of his own hands and fashioned into a tool by another's avarice or pride. It is because I see in him a great nature, the divine image, and vast capacities, that I demand for him means of self-development, spheres for free action—that I call society not to fetter, but to aid his growth.

In such humanitarian idealism did French romantic philosophy come to flower in the generous mind of this son of New England. He was no longer narrowly Unitarian; he had become a social revolutionary with Utopian dreams. The minister's wealthy parishioners might worship the common Father complacently under the shadow of slavery, black or white, but the minister could not; he had caught a glimpse of the Promised Land and would lead his flock towards it. Unhappily, the vast abyss of negro slavery lay between, and Channing considered it with grow-ing concern. In his examination of the problem he was broadly philosophical rather than narrowly partisan. He rested his case against slavery on an ethical adaptation of the natural-rights theory.[8] Since man is both rational and moral, he argued, he cannot be deprived by law or custom of the essential preroga-tives of personality. The inalienable rights of man are in es-sence no other than the rights of personality—the right to exercise his reason, to seek light of his conscience, to enjoy the fruits of his labor, to enter into domestic relations, in short to be free to live as a man in a state of civilization. To treat man as property is the grossest denial and violation of that which by its nature is inviolable and inalienable. Channing pushed his argument further and asserted that the institution of slavery was not only irrational

[8] For a brief discussion, see Merriam, *American Political Theories*, pp. 217-221.

and immoral, but a fundamental denial of democracy. It must end in perverting the political state to its own evil. The southern conception of a Greek democracy resting on black slavery he looked upon as the final prostitution of the democratic ideal. "Those who tell us that slavery is a necessary condition of a republic, do not justify the former, but pronounce a sentence of reprobation on the latter." For those text-mongerers who professed to justify slavery by Scripture, he had only scorn. By such methods polygamy might as readily be justified.

Inquiry into the nature and scope of individual rights brought Channing face to face with the problem of the political state and the duties of citizenship. Here his break with Boston Federalism was final and complete. He judged men and institutions by ethical standards; State Street judged them by economic standards. By his own path he went back to the eighteenth century, and interpreting the functions and province of government in the light of Godwin's *Political Justice*, he arrived at the conception of a constantly diminishing political state that should eventually disappear. The dogma of political sovereignty he denied: "The state is equally restrained with individuals by the Moral Law" ("Slavery," in *Works*, Vol. II, p. 37). The expediency of some restraint upon individual action he accepted, but with the proviso that it be exercised only to the end of the common well-being. "The authority of the state to impose laws on its members I cheerfully allow; but this has limits, which are found to be more and more narrow in proportion to the progress of moral science" (*ibid.*, p. 38). "That government is most perfect, in which Policy is most entirely subjected to Justice, or in which the supreme and constant aim is to secure the rights of every human being" (*ibid.*, p. 38). To such a government loyalty will be given gladly; but in the event that expediency should prevail over justice, and the state should prostitute its power by exploiting one class for the benefit of another, then must loyalty be transferred from the state to the higher law. "Justice is a greater good than property, not greater in degree, but in kind." "The good of the individual is more important than the outward prosperity of the State" (*ibid.*, pp. 40, 44). In such doctrines Channing paid his respects to the political philosophy of Webster.

The final outcome of his political thinking was a close approximation to the position of Jefferson. His distrust of power grew more apprehensive as he reflected on the common abuse of power, and the cheap and paltry appeals by which the unthinking are swayed. Before the organized power of the mass, the individual is helpless. In the *Introductory Remarks* he went further than he had done in earlier writings in analysis of the state, and such a passage as this might have been penned by John Taylor of Caroline County. It is pure Jeffersonianism.

So fearful is the principle of which I have spoken, that I have thought it right to recommend restrictions on power and a simplicity in government beyond what most approve. Power, I apprehend, should not be suffered to run into great masses. No more of it should be confided to rulers than is absolutely necessary to repress crime and preserve public order. A purer age may warrant larger trusts; but the less of government now the better, if society be kept in peace. There should exist, if possible, no office to madden ambition. . . . One of the tremendous evils of the world, is the monstrous accumulation of power in a few hands. . . . Is any man pure enough to be trusted with it? Ought such a prize as this to be held out to ambition? Can we wonder at the shameless profligacy, intrigue, and the base sacrifices of public interests by which it is sought, and, when gained, held fast? Undoubtedly, great social changes are required to heal this evil, to diminish this accumulation of power. National spirit, which is virtual hostility to all countries but our own, must yield to a growing humanity, to a new knowledge of the spirit of Christ. Another important step is, a better comprehension by communities that government is at best a rude machinery, which can accomplish but very limited good, and which, when strained to accomplish what individuals should do for themselves, is sure to be perverted by selfishness to narrow purposes, or to defeat through ignorance its own ends. Man is too ignorant to govern much, to form vast plans for states and empires. Human policy has almost always been in conflict with the great laws of social well-being, and the less we rely on it the better. The less of power given to man over man the better. (*Works*, Vol. VI, pp. 26–27.)

Channing had evidently read his *Political Justice* to good effect, for the spirit of eighteenth-century liberalism had passed into his thought and given shape to his political philosophy. In his hatred of war, his pacifism, his humanitarian concern, his social-mindedness, his repudiation of all coercive centralizing power, he proved himself a child of Godwin. He would have no tyranny, whether by the organized state or by the unorganized mass. He extended to all men the right of free thought and free speech. In no other cause did he speak more vehemently than in defense of this democratic right. When the Abolitionists were mobbed and their presses broken he rejoiced in their refusal to be silenced.

"From my heart I thank them," he wrote. "I am myself their debtor. I am not sure, that I should this moment write in safety, had they shrunk from the conflict, had they shut their lips, imposed silence on their presses, and hid themselves before their ferocious assailants. . . . I thank the Abolitionists, that in this evil day, they were true to the rights which the multitude were ready to betray." Then follows a passage that is perennially true, considering how hardly won and easily lost is the right of free speech:

Of all powers, the last to be entrusted to the multitude of men, is that of determining what questions shall be discussed. The greatest truths are often the most unpopular and exasperating; and were they to be denied discussion, till the many should be ready to accept them, they would never establish themselves in the general mind. The progress of society depends on nothing more, than on the exposure of time-honored abuses, which cannot be touched without offending multitudes, than on the promulgation of principles, which are in advance of public sentiment and practice, and which are constantly at war with the habits, prejudices, and immediate interests of large classes of the community. Of consequence, the multitude, if once allowed to dictate or proscribe subjects of discussion, would strike society with spiritual blindness, and death. The world is to be carried forward by truth, which at first offends, which wins its way by degrees, which the many hate and would rejoice to crush. The right of free discussion is therefore to be guarded by the friends of mankind, with peculiar jealousy. It is at once the most sacred, and the most endangered of all our rights. He who would rob his neighbor of it, should have a mark set on him as the worst enemy of freedom. ("The Abolitionists," in *Works*, Vol. II, p. 161.)

High-minded and generous was this child of Puritan idealism who had gone to school to French infidel philosophy—never untrue to the principle of free inquiry which in demanding for himself he willingly granted others. He calmly accepted the fact of disintegration which is implicit in all liberalism—the denial of traditional authority and ancient custom—partly because he believed the old ways were bad, but in part also because he held strongly to his faith in human nature. Despite failure and discouragement he clung to his cardinal belief—"My one sublime idea, which has given me unity of mind, the greatness, the divinity of the soul." He broke the more willingly with an ungenerous past because he envisaged a nobler future. An intuitive individualist, he was a forerunner of transcendental individualism, and he found himself in hearty accord with Emerson's doctrines in the Divinity School address. With the later rationalistic phase of

Unitarianism which began with Theodore Parker's memorable South Boston sermon *On the Transient and Permanent in Christianity*, in May, 1841, he found himself only partly in intellectual sympathy. He remained a supernaturalist after the younger generation had rejected supernaturalism; but his sturdy adherence to the principle of liberalism would not suffer him to join in the Unitarian hue and cry raised against the young radical. Unitarianism turned orthodox, and bent on erecting new dogmas, seemed to him treasonable to every liberal hope. "As to Mr. Parker," he wrote, "I wish him to preach what he thoroughly believes and feels. I trust the account you received of attempts to *put him down* was in the main a fiction. Let the full heart pour itself forth!" (John White Chadwick, *William Ellery Channing*, p. 357.) Sixteen months after he penned those words Channing was dead, but the spirit of his life was embodied in the great ferment that was rising about him when he died. "Let the full heart pour itself forth"—to many sober Bostonians it seemed that New England had taken that injunction quite too literally and was pouring forth disturbant and gusty heresies, but Channing would scarcely have disapproved.

CHAPTER III

LIBERALISM AND THE SOCIAL CONSCIENCE

I

THE SOCIAL MIND

UNITARIANISM was generous in its bequests to New England, and amongst its contributions to a nobler life not the least valuable was its warm social sympathy. Channing's tender social conscience sprang directly from his humanitarian religion. Not from the hard old Calvinism did he get this fine flower of a humane life, but from the new French philosophy. Not from bounding his ethics by the Decalogue, or hating sin more than he loved generosity, did he break the hard shell of Puritan righteousness; but by metamorphosing the sinner into a child of God and sharing with him the divine promise. Other-mindedness came naturally to a religion established in a God of love. The social conscience could not remain indifferent to injustice visited upon the children of a common Father. Yet other-mindedness was a virtue practiced too little in Calvinist New England. That old world had been more concerned with hopes of individual salvation, with propitiating an angry God, than with its present obligations to its neighbors. Hard doctrine—which the old Puritan loved—was likely to make hard characters, and an ascetic society was likely to breed close-fisted natures. The conscience was tender in New England, but it was tender chiefly as the guardian and monitor of the Ten Commandments; it gave itself too little concern about the new commandment which Jesus laid upon his disciples. It disciplined men and women in personal righteousness, it created self-reliant characters, it scrutinized narrowly the neighborhood conduct; but its social issues were likely to be mean and petty. The righteousness of which it professed to be guardian and monitor too often fell far short of generous manly stature.

From this hardness of the old religion came the hardness of the social conscience. When the Yankee was driven by brutal fact to admit that he was his brother's keeper, he usually took care to get a few honest pennies out of his brother's board and lodging.

The village poor were provided for by farming out, as the taxes were farmed out. The town meeting haggled narrowly over the terms, and substantial deacons underbid each other. Though the price might be low, some profit might still be got from the pauper's keep. It was a cold, hard, unsympathetic world for the social unfortunate, whether pauper, debtor, or idiot; and it was harsh as well to the children of all but the wealthy. The hours of toil were long, and the public schools about which the historians have bragged rather too loudly, were poor affairs, starved by the common niggardliness, ill taught and ill provided. The academies and colleges that professed to keep the torch of learning aflame were largely perquisites of the gentry. It is beside the point to assert that public schools existed in New England long before Virginia had any, and that poor boys stinted and starved their way through Harvard and Yale. Well known as such facts are, they do not testify to a high social sense in a people supposed to have been tender of conscience. The Calvinist was taught to fear God rather than to love him. It was a strong man's business to save one's soul and make a decent living; and in the social code of New England the weakling must take his chance.

There was helpful neighborliness of course in old New England, and much honest kindliness. Some of the hardest of dogmatic Calvinists were the most considerate and gentlest of men. Old Samuel Hopkins of slave-running Newport was a generous soul who preached the gospel of love to one's fellows, and practiced the virtues of apostleship to the poor and outcast. He denounced the slave trade to parishioners who knew all the inlets of the West African coast, and got himself well disliked. His congregation preferred his hard theology to his inconvenient humanitarianism, and kept him poor all his days. The dogmatic Timothy Dwight scathingly attacked slavery in his *Greenfield Hill*, denounced the injustice done the negro, and even protested against the extension of capital punishment. Yet for all such protests the common conscience was untouched. The Yankee was always standing in the way of the Puritan's righteousness. Respectability was founded on property, and respectability was mightier in New England than even John Calvin. It was the brutal debtor laws that brought on Shays's Rebellion, which Federalist church members put down and denied the grievances. It was no tender conscience that extinguished slavery in Massachusetts, for long after it became un-

profitable there the Yankee skipper was still in the slave trade.
Dignified Tory Row on what is now Brattle Street, Cambridge,
was built by gentlemen who drew their wealth from West Indian
slave plantations.[1] William Lloyd Garrison's offense in Baltimore, for which he was thrown into jail, lay in publishing the
name of a Massachusetts shipmaster from Newburyport—Garrison's native town—who was engaged in the coastwise slave
traffic.[2] In the year 1830 there were somewhat more than a
hundred Abolition Societies in the United States, not one of which
was in New England; and in the first number of the *Liberator*
Garrison wrote, probably without exaggeration, that he found
"contempt more bitter, opposition more active, detraction more
relentless, prejudice more stubborn, and apathy more frozen,"
in New England, "than among slave owners themselves." [3] The
old Puritan conscience might be tender, but it refused pretty
steadily to take on any larger job than Sabbath-keeping and dogma-
saving. It was inquisitorial rather than humanitarian, and the
sins which it hunted down were theological rather than social.

The bridge between this older world and the later was thrown
across by Unitarianism. With its shift of emphasis from a God of
wrath to a God of love came the entering wedge that was to split
away the egoism of the old theology—its thralldom to the conception of personal sin—and lay bare an inner core of altruism.
It was another sort of conscience that Unitarianism discovered, a
conscience that welcomed the new social thought of romantic
Europe, and applying it to the facts of life in America created the
new humanitarianism which bit so deeply into the New England of
the forties. From this movement the intractable nature of the
Yankee held him back, but the Puritan speedily transformed the
hard theological conscience into a tender social conscience, that
bewildered the conventional morality with its sweeping program
of reform.

The awakening of the new spirit may perhaps be held to date
from the growing opposition to war that was an aftermath of the
Napoleonic period with its huge debts and vast social suffering.
The inhumanity of war profoundly impressed thoughtful minds
that had come under the influence of the sociological movement,

[1] See T. W. Higginson, *Old Cambridge*, p. 149.
[2] See Garrison, *William Lloyd Garrison*, Vol. I, Chapter VI. The court held
that it was libelous to seek to bring into disrepute an action that was legal.
[3] Quoted by S. E. Morison in *Harrison Grey Otis*, Vol. II, p. 263.

and when Channing in 1812 preached his first anti-war sermon the new humanitarian spirit found expression. In his espousal of pacifism Channing was following in the footsteps of the social revolutionaries of the preceding century. He fell short of Tom Paine in analysis of the economic and dynastic sources of war, and in appreciation of its social consequences; nevertheless his denunciation was significant of a changing social attitude. From this early attack to the rise of the Garrisonian Non-Resistance Society of the late thirties and early forties, the spread of the pacifist movement was rapid. Transcendentalism was eloquently anti-militaristic, and Emerson, Alcott and Parker were outspoken in denunciation of the war spirit. To the war against war soon was added the war against drink, and with the establishment in Boston in 1826 of the *National Philanthropist*, under the patronage of the "Massachusetts Society for the Suppression of Intemperance"—a paper of which Garrison was editor for a few months— began the long agitation for the suppression of the liquor traffic. From such feeble beginnings the ardor of reform grew and spread swiftly, enlarging its program to embrace anti-slavery, woman's rights, [4] prison reform, repeal of the harsh debtor laws, vegetarianism, associationism, until it caught the contagion of the perfectionist and transcendental movements and issued in a comprehensive program of universal reform. The golden age of New England was quite as much the golden age of the New England conscience as of the New England mind.

II

The fame of transcendentalism has too much obscured the contemporary movement of perfectionism, a movement which marked the extreme expression of the new conscience, the most revolutionary of its aspirations, the apotheosis of ethical radicalism. Its want of literary skill narrowed its appeal and the archaic quality of its enthusiasm lessened its following; yet in spirit it was native to Puritan idealism, and it enlisted the active sympathy of many of the finer souls of New England. How greatly reform was furthered by the movement of perfectionism is not easily determined,

---

[4] This was an outgrowth of the anti-slavery movement and emerged from the conservative opposition to women's appearing on the abolition platform. The reply of the Quakeress, Angelina Grimké, to Elizabeth Beecher's *Essay on Slavery and Abolitionism, with reference to the Duty of American Females*, in 1837, marks the definite beginning of the movement. See Garrison, *William Lloyd Garrison*, Vol. II, pp. 133–134.

but it is clear that its influence permeated much of the revolutionary activity of the times.   Scratch an ardent Abolitionist and you were likely to find a potential perfectionist.

The doctrine was first elaborated by John Humphrey Noyes, a young Vermont mystic, who, under the influence of the revivalist excitement of the early thirties, elaborated a social creed that re-embodied much of the teaching of the extreme left wing of English Commonwealth thought.   Noyes was a primitive religious nature, with the tenderest of consciences, vastly troubled over current materialisms; and his speculations reveal a curious throw-back to early English Puritanism.   He was a Yankee Fifth Monarchy man. Two hundred years of Yankee experience slipped from his mind, and he walked and talked with the old millennial spirits, the Diggers and Levelers of Commonwealth times.   A devout Scripturist, he took literally the injunction of Matthew, "Be ye therefore perfect, even as your Father which is in Heaven is perfect."   A primitive Christian, he proposed to re-order society with the naïve simplicity of the apostle Eliot.   In his mystical speculations, social, political, and religious radicalisms were stirred in a common pot and simmered down to what may be called spiritual anarchism. Noyes was a Yankee "root and branch" man, a single-minded apostle of "thorough."   He would not strain at gnats and swallow camels, but he rejected the camels first and then proposed to get rid of the gnats.   In 1834 he established a small monthly paper called the *Perfectionist*, which was very probably as revolutionary a sheet as was ever printed in America.   He made converts, including Garrison, Edmund Quincy, son of Josiah Quincy, the Grimké sisters, Henry C. Wright and other Abolitionists, and made an increasing stir in the world, to the great concern of respectable folk who swallowed their camels without a grimace.

Some notion of the main doctrines of this seventeenth-century creed may be gained from a letter of Noyes to Garrison, written in 1837, from which the following is taken:

I have subscribed my name to an instrument similar to the Declaration of '76, renouncing all allegiance to the government of the United States, and asserting the title of Jesus Christ to the throne of the World. . . . When I wish to form a conception of the government of the United States . . . I picture to myself a bloated, swaggering libertine, trampling on the Bible—its own Constitution—its treaties with the Indians—the petitions of its citizens. . . . I have renounced active co-operation with the oppressor on whose territories I live; now I would find a way to put an end to his oppression. But he is manifestly a reprobate: reproof and instruction only aggravate his sins. I cannot attempt to reform him, because I am forbidden to "cast pearls before swine." I must therefore either consent to remain a slave till God removes the tyrant, or I must commence war upon him, by a declaration of independence and other weapons suitable to the character of a son of God.

He then lays down seven reasons for choosing to make war upon the state, amongst which are the following:

1. As a believer in the Bible I know that the territory of the United States belongs to God, and is promised . . . to Jesus Christ and his followers. . . .
6. The Son of God has manifestly, to me, chosen this country for the theatre of such an assault—a country which, by its boasting hypocrisy, has become the laughing-stock of the world, and by its lawlessness has fully proved the incapacity of man for self-government. *My hope of the millennium begins where Dr. Beecher's expires*—viz., AT THE OVERTHROW OF THIS NATION.

I have stated to you only . . . the principal things which God has urged upon me by his Spirit, and by which he has moved me to nominate Jesus Christ for the Presidency, not only of the United States, but of the world. Is it not high time for abolitionists to abandon a government whose President has declared war upon them? I cannot but think that many of them hear the same great voice out of heaven which has waked me, saying, "Come out of her, my people, that ye be not partakers of her sins and of her plagues." . . . Allow me to suggest that you will set Anti-slavery in the sunshine only by making it tributary to Holiness; and you will most assuredly throw it into the shade . . . if you suffer it to occupy the ground, in your mind or in others, which ought to be occupied by UNIVERSAL EMANCIPATION FROM SIN. All the abhorrence which now falls upon slavery, intemperance, lewdness, and every other specific vice, will in due time be gathered into one volume of victorious wrath against *unbelief*. I wait for that time as for the day of battle . . . I counsel you, and the people that are with you, if you love the post of honour—the forefront of the hottest battle of righteousness—to set your face towards *perfect* holiness. (Garrison, *William Lloyd Garrison*, Vol. II, pp. 145–148.)

This curious appeal brought forth its fruit in a Peace Convention, held in 1838, which published a Declaration of Sentiments [5] that was quite as extraordinary a pronouncement—one that serves to explain the utter bewilderment of prosaic souls at the strange progeny of the times. It was only one of many strange conventions, marked by an ebullient faith of which Emerson remarked, "The core of the comet did not seem to be much, but the whole air was full of splendors" (*Journals*, Vol. VII, p. 5), and on which Josiah Quincy

[5] Written by Garrison; see *ibid.*, Vol. II, pp. 230–234.

commented, "Such a mass of free mind as was brought together I have never seen before in any one assembly. . . . There was much talent and a great deal of *soul*." Men who take their Biblical teachings literally are likely to be curious fellows. Righteousness may prove a potent drink for them that love it, begetting its own particular intemperance; and a conscience that has slipped its leash of the practical will run many a mad chase. If it followed its logic this perfectionism must make short shrift of political parties, of loyalty to government, of the political state itself, and set up instead a social order in which familiar things would be topsy-turvy, with the just sitting in high places and the rich and great of earth brought low; and this is precisely what Noyes did in the Oneida Community— the most successful of the contemporary ventures in communism—of which he was the founder. In spite of his taste for the wine of new vintages Emerson was somewhat taken aback at certain of its ebullitions, and when the sabbatarian Charndon Street Convention in 1840 gathered together the choicest repositories of New England holiness, he shook his head dubiously. His humorous catalogue of the miscellaneous enthusiasts suggests more than a spice of criticism.

Madmen, madwomen, men with beards, Dunkers, Muggletonians, Come-outers, Groaners, Agrarians, Seventh-Day Baptists, Quakers, Abolitionists, Calvinists, Unitarians, and Philosophers,—all came successively to the top, and seized their moment, if not their hour, wherein to chide, or pray, or preach, or protest. ("The Charndon Street Convention," in *Works*, Vol. X, p. 374.)

And even the catholic-minded Edmund Quincy, who was one of the callers of the Convention, confessed that "It was the most singular collection of strange specimens of humanity that was ever assembled." The wine of perfectionism was in high ferment in New England in 1840.

It was a curious anachronism in the midst of the industrial revolution—this revival of the religious Utopianism of 1650, this April renaissance of the faith of a dead *saeculum theologicum*. It was in no sense a by-product of transcendentalism—no lunacy fringe of metaphysical speculation. It owed nothing to French romanticism or German idealism, not in origin at least. It was far more primitive and native, and its affinities run back to Roger Williams and the Fifth Monarchy millennialism, rather than to Rousseau and Kant and Jacobi. It was a breaking through of the submerged New England spirituality, a volcanic release from sterile conformity; and it summoned the awakening soul to go forth and conquer the world for righteousness. Millennialism is the prophetic hope of a primitive faith. To its disciples it is certain of fulfillment because God's promises are certain; but to practical minds, unconvinced that Biblical phrases are authentic divine contracts, any expectation of the speedy coming of the Kingdom of God seems grotesque. The millennial enthusiast is a fair butt of ridicule, and the perfectionists came in for a large share. It was Lowell who leveled at the militant godliness of the new sects the wittiest attack. Forgetting his English history he found himself puzzled, and being puzzled he allowed himself to become ill-natured. His clever sentences explode smartly about his subject, but there is no light in them.[6]

III

Upon another venture in Utopianism, and one far better known, the years have laid a pleasant, idyllic haze, softening the prosaic outlines and clothing them with romance. Brook Farm has been singularly fortunate in the posthumous fame that has dealt with it so tenderly as to transmute it into poetry. By virtue of the light reflected upon it by the transcendental illumination and the literary skill it commanded, the little communal settlement at West Roxbury has come to be regarded as a homely Yankee pastoral, a sort of May Day adventure in brown holland tunics, an inspiring quest of the ideal amongst furrows and manures. It is a social poem fashioned out of Yankee homespun. No hint of rude social leveling is associated with its aims; even its communism suggests no stigma. Of the dozens of communistic experiments which marked the first half of the nineteenth century in America, few were native in origin or ventured upon in New England. They were mostly undertaken by old-world groups, chiefly German, who sought cheap land and a free environment for primitive religious experiments. But Brook Farm was true Yankee, using the familiar dialect to clothe its unfamiliar thoughts, and escaping the prejudice that confronts the uncouth and alien; and in consequence the vagaries that all New England once laughed at have become enshrined as a cherished New England possession.

Perfectionism and Brook Farm embodied diverse phases of the

[6] See the essay on Thoreau.

renaissance and made appeal to different temperaments. Fellowship founded on common ownership and communal labor was
an ideal that left the religious mystic cold, whereas the anarchistic
holiness of perfectionism seemed to the Brook Farmers grotesque.
Present economic maladjustment appeared to the latter the
fundamental problem of the times. They were deeply concerned
for the future that must emerge from the chaotic individualism
of the present. Unless society were brought back to a wiser understanding of values, they foresaw only chaos; and so in a small way
they set about a great experiment. Brook Farm grew out of the
impact of the industrial revolution upon the social conscience of
New England. Industrialism and social speculation were contemporary developments. The first cotton mill in New England
was established at Lawrence in 1822, and the following year the
Merrimac Mills were established in the newly founded city of
Lowell. By absorbing the vast Irish immigration the factory
system brought increasing wealth to Beacon Street homes, but it
brought other consequences in its train which Beacon Street carelessly overlooked. How those consequences affected more sensitive
and intelligent minds—men like William Henry Channing, Theodore Parker and George Ripley—is suggested by their eager talk
of mutualism, association, coöperation, as potential cures for the
growing evils of competition, discussions never before heard in
New England. Describing the state of mind of the Boston group
of social thinkers, John Weiss offers the following explanation:

A mutualism to secure culture and material welfare was consistently
desired by those who believed in a community of the sources of moral and
spiritual welfare. The social evils which result from the struggles of
competitive labour seemed to outweigh all its benefits. Modern civilization was thought to be the culmination of isolated selfishness, madly
struggling from bread to luxury and refined delights, which the strongest
and least scrupulous only could acquire. Prisons and punishments were
the defences of this artificial system, to repress instincts that were moral
till they become illegal. Hospitals and benevolent institutions were also
mere defences to absorb as much misery as possible ere it became malicious,
to get the social gangrene reduced to limits. The providential impulses
of the human being were forced to act in subversive ways and directions,
when they might all be harmonized by their own inherent laws, and the
blessing of mutualism succeed to the bane of antagonism. Each man
ought to be the guarantee to all men against disorder; the carefully adjusted elements of a selfishness which threatens continually to blow the
social fabric to atoms, would become not only innoxious but salutary in
its proper combination; and a new civilization might arise in fair propor-

tion from the serial development and movement of all possible human tendencies. Then all men and women might labor and be happy; all might earn with a minimum of toil a competence of culture. Property would be the ally of the whole instead of the oppressor of the many; and crime would disappear, because the instincts would no longer have motives to be criminal. (*Life and Correspondence of Theodore Parker*, Vol. I, pp. 106–107.)

The transcendental basis of such social speculation is evident enough. The new social thought was transcendental thought. A common belief in the excellence of human instincts drew these idealists together; but when it came to the vexing problem of reconciling individualism and mutualism, creating an economic fellowship out of electric personalities, the more ardent transcendentalists took fright and prudently kept without the gates of Brook Farm. Organization seemed to them the fatal poison in the bottom of the cup. When a community was planned in Massachusetts in 1841, by liberal Christians of the Universalist sect, a writer in the *Dial* subjected the proposal to sharp criticism:

A true community can be founded on nothing short of faith in the universal man, as he comes from the hands of the Creator, with no law over his liberty but the eternal ideas that lie at the foundation of his being. . . . The final cause of human society is the unfolding of the individual man, into every form of perfection, without let or hindrance, according to the inward nature of each. (Quoted by Frothingham in *Transcendentalism, etc.*, p. 157.)

Such a view is anarchistic rather than collectivistic, and as embodied in Alcott's Fruitlands, it may be regarded as the transcendental type of Utopia. Towards all systems of socialism the transcendentalists were instinctively hostile, as implying an industrial regimentation; and in planning Brook Farm, Ripley rejected industrialism and reduced regimentation to a minimum. With the agrarian background of Brook Farm the transcendentalists were in hearty sympathy, quite oblivious of the fact that agrarianism could offer no solution for industrialism; but they balked at the principle of task allotment as a hindrance to the unfolding of individual differences. Upon the later introduction of the Fourier Phalanx their doubts grew into certainty, and they lost their faith in the experiment. Of all the transcendentalists William Henry Channing was clearly the most confirmed associationist, except

perhaps Ripley; to the end of his life he remained a socialist, active
in collectivistic movements and clinging fondly to his memory of
Brook Farm as a "great college of social students." But few of
his fellow transcendentalists shared his faith.

This growing skepticism of organization is clearly shown in the
comments of Emerson's *Journals*. In October, 1840, he set down
his first reaction to the plan as follows:

Yesterday George and Sophia Ripley, Margaret Fuller and Alcott
discussed here the Social Plans. I wish to be convinced, to be thawed, to
be made nobly mad by the kindlings before my eye of a new dawn of
human piety. But this scheme was arithmetic and comfort; this was
a hint borrowed from the Tremont House and United States Hotel; a
rage in our poverty and politics to live rich and gentlemanlike, an anchor
to leeward against a change of weather; a prudent forecast on the probable
issue of the great questions of Pauperism and Poverty. And not once
could I be inflamed, but sat aloof and thoughtless; my voice faltered and
fell. It was not the cave of persecution which is the palace of spiritual
power, but only a room in the Astor House hired for the Transcendentalists. I do not wish to remove from my present prison to a prison a little
larger. I wish to break all prisons. I have not yet conquered my own
house. It irks and repents me. Shall I raise the siege of this hencoop,
and march baffled away to a pretended siege of Babylon? It seems to
me that so to do were to dodge the problem I am set to solve, and to hide
my impotency in the thick of a crowd. (*Journals*, Vol. V, pp. 473-474.)

In January, 1844, noting the spontaneity of life at Brook Farm,
he drew the conclusion "that in the arrangements at Brook Farm,
as out of them, it is the person, not the communist, that avails"
(*ibid.*, Vol. VI, p. 492). With the introduction of Fourierist
organization he became sharply critical. Neither in Fourier nor
in Owen did he see any hope.

Fourier learned from him [Owen] all the truth he had, and the rest of
his system was imagination, and the imagination of a banker. The Owen
and Fourier plans bring no *a priori* convictions. They are come at merely
by counting and arithmetic. All the fine *aperçus* are for individualism.
The Spartan broth, the hermit's cell, the lonely farmer's life are poetic;
but the Phalanstery, the "Self-supporting Village," are culinary and mean.
(*Ibid.*, Vol. VIII, pp. 134, 135.)

And a few days later he gave his final judgment, "Dear heart, take
it sadly home to thee, that there will and can be no coöperation"—
a judgment that explains the clever phrase with which he demolished Brook Farm, "It is the Age of Reason in a patty-pan."

The transcendentalist with his Puritan conscience could understand and sympathize with the perfectionist zeal for universal

righteousness; but collectivistic systems of economy seemed alien and a community of goods uncongenial to his Yankee individualism.   Albert Brisbane, the American apostle of Fourierism, might bring George Ripley, the least individualistic and most prosaic of the transcendental group, to his views of organization; but he got on badly with the others who were quite too fluid to take a mechanical set.   In consequence it was not at Brook Farm but at the North American Phalanx that the French system found its fairest experiment and met with its solidest success.

IV

With the awakening interest in social problems the conscience of New England could not longer remain indifferent to slavery. The incoming of French humanitarianism, the spread of idealistic sociology under the teachings of Unitarianism, above all the stimulus of English Abolitionism that provided argument and example in the freeing of slaves in the British West Indies, wore away the indifferentism that had calloused the mind of New England; and with the decay of her provincial particularism the conscience of New England slowly roused itself. The arrogance of the slave party nowhere else stirred such deep resentment. Southern steel, striking the flinty Yankee character, threw off sparks that would fire whatever combustible stuff lay near; and such combustible stuff was provided in plenty by the Utopian enthusiasts who gathered in conventions, each with a plan of universal reform in his waistcoat pocket. Little conflagrations were started in many an obscure Yankee soul, and the noise of the crackling spread over New England, to the anger of the South and the vast concern of respectable Boston merchants. Sooner or later Abolition sentiment was bound to make a tremendous stir amongst the children of Puritanism; and when that time came it was bound to arouse tremendous antagonism amongst the sons of Yankees. The dominant commercial group would not tolerate a movement that was certain to alienate its southern customers. A mighty collision between the conscience and the self-interest of New England was inevitable; and in that collision of flinty characters, arguments were likely to be countered with blows.

The New England Abolitionists, men and women, were an extraordinarily interesting group. They were good fighters, outspoken and tenacious of opinion, unsparing in attack, refusing to be browbeaten, resilient and tough as seasoned hickory. In them the Yankee Tory met his match; against them coercion and intimidation, all the usual Tory weapons, failed as earlier they had failed with the primitive Quakers. They were daily charged with being social incendiaries. The commercial newspapers thundered against them as atheists, Sabbath-breakers, socialists, anarchists; the absurdest myths were given circulation; the public mind was skillfully poisoned against them. Yet as a matter of sober historical fact, they were the kindliest of men, with generous sympathies and disinterested motives. No blackguard was ever an Abolitionist—no ward-heeler, or mob-inciter, or purse-patriot; all such convenient tools of power were found amongst the baiters and mobsters in the commercial opposition. John Brown was the only direct-action Abolitionist and what befell him is well known among men. There was no money to be made, no place of honor or power to be got by espousing Abolitionism, but only self-sacrifice and social ostracism. Ambitious men, self-seekers, went with the dispensers of social favors. It was the remnant in Israel that gathered to the cause, few in numbers but the best New England had. And what an excellent company they were: Garrison, Samuel J. May, Edmund Quincy, Jonathan Sewall, Theodore Parker, Lydia Maria Child, Mrs. Chapman, Wendell Phillips, Thomas Wentworth Higginson, Whittier, Henry Ward Beecher, Sumner, Maria White and the young Lowell—such a fighting phalanx as the New England conscience had never before mustered, nor has since. To them were gathered heroic souls from other states: Arthur and Lewis Tappan and Gerrit Smith from New York, James Birney from Kentucky, Lucretia Mott from Philadelphia, the Grimké sisters from South Carolina. Harriet Martineau, who knew the group intimately, has left on record her judgment of them: "A just survey of the whole world can leave little doubt," she wrote in 1838, "that the abolitionists of the United States are the greatest people now living and moving in it" (Carpenter, *John Greenleaf Whittier*, p. 107). They gave New England and the country no peace. From their persistent agitation came the Emigrant Aid Society, Sharp's rifles, and the bloody struggle in Kansas; and from it came the temporary overwhelming of the Tory minority in Massachusetts. For a few brief years New England threw off the stifling grip of the commercial mind and was the home of American humanitarianism.

CHAPTER IV
CERTAIN MILITANTS
I
WILLIAM LLOYD GARRISON

THE flintiest character amongst the New England militants, curiously enough, was the son of an immigrant family, brought to Newburyport and abandoned by a shiftless father. William Lloyd Garrison was not an offspring of generations of New England Puritanism, but a waif thrown by chance on the bleak shores of Massachusetts, and left to shift pretty much for himself. Born in Newburyport, half English and half Irish, with a heritage that promised ill, he was disciplined in the sternest of schools. His capable Irish mother had a bitter time providing for her three fatherless children, and the son suffered the privation and found the help that were the mixed portion of the destitute of old New England. Like Horace Greeley he ate the bread of poverty and grew strong on it. There was iron in his nature, and the narrow means that drove his father to drink and desertion, that sent his brother adrift, that broke his mother and killed his sister, only strengthened his will and toughened his fiber. As a lad he was put to the cobbler's bench to learn the trade that Whittier was learning at Haverhill; later he was apprenticed to a carpenter and cabinet-maker. In both trades he was unhappy, and it was not till a freak of fate turned him over to a friendly printer that he found himself. For seven years he stuck to his case, and at the end of the apprenticeship he was not only a first-rate practical printer, but with some little knowledge of books and master of a vigorous and serviceable prose style. With the amazing capacity for self-training so characteristic of the Yankee, he had picked up a sort of education and was ready to do whatever work in the world should come to hand.

Chance threw in his way the job of village editor, and inclination plunged him into politics. His political opinions, which he embraced more ardently than intelligently, were faithful reflections of current Massachusetts partisanship. He was quite ignorant of political principles and the economics that determined political parties, and with unconscious naïveté he espoused the cause of Boston commercialism. He was a dogmatic, unquestioning Whig. Clay was his idol, General Jackson his abomination; and his first political speech was in support of Harrison Gray Otis, the discredited boss of the old Federalist machine. But this was only a vagary of youthful hero worship. Enthusiasm for reform was already setting up a ferment in his ardent soul and preparing him for quite other alliances. The unhappy fate of his father was a lesson that he took home, and he interested himself in the temperance movement then just getting under way, serving for a time as editor of a small temperance paper. Shortly thereafter he stumbled upon his life work. Benjamin Lundy, a homespun hero of the Society of Friends, had long been publishing intermittently his *Genius of Universal Emancipation,* and in the itinerant work of begging support he fell in with Garrison. The two discovered kindred interests and they entered into a compact to go forth together to fight the dragon of slavery. They sought out the den of the beast in Baltimore and delivered their blows lustily; with the result that Garrison was indicted by the grand jury for printing the name of a Newburyport merchant who was picking up some honest dollars in the coastwise slave traffic, and spent seven weeks in jail. On his release he returned to Boston to replenish a lean purse, and January 1, 1831, he issued the first number of *The Liberator,* a little paper that was to make a mighty stir in the world during a long period of hand-to-mouth existence.

Never was there a more foolhardy venture, judged by the wisdom of this world. With no following, no weapon but a borrowed font of type in a mean little print-shop, no money or credit, he flung his defiance at the entrenched enemy with the courage of uncalculating youth. A prospectus issued in the fall of 1830 thus set forth the purpose of the venture:

I shall assume, as self-evident truths, that the liberty of a people is a gift of God and nature:—That liberty consists in an independency upon the will of another:—That by the name of slave we understand a man who can neither dispose of his person or goods, but enjoys all at the will of his master:—That no man can have a right over others, unless it be by them granted to him. . . . That that which is not just is not law; and that which is not law, ought not to be in force:—That he who oppugns the public liberty, overthrows his own. . . . That there is no safety where there is no strength, no strength without union, no union without justice, no justice where faith and truth are wanting:—That the right to be free is a truth planted in the hearts of men, and acknowledged so to be by all that have hearkened to the voice of nature. . . . *Vide Algernon Sidney's Discourses on Government—the Declaration of American Independence—the Constitutions and Bills of Rights of the several States, etc., etc.* (*Life of William Lloyd Garrison, by his Children.* Vol. I, p. 200.)

This pronouncement was amplified in the salutatory address in the first number, as follows:

Assenting to the "self-evident truth" maintained in the American Declaration of Independence, "that all men are created equal, and endowed by their Creator with certain inalienable rights—among which are life, liberty, and the pu suit of happiness," I shall strenuously contend for the immediate enfranchisement of our slave population. . . . I am aware that many may object to the severity of my language; but is there not cause for severity? I *will* be as harsh as truth, and as uncompromising as justice. On this subject, I do not wish to think, or speak, or write, with moderation . . . urge me not to use moderation in a cause like the present. I am in earnest—I will not equivocate—I will not excuse—I will not retreat a single inch—AND I WILL BE HEARD. (*Ibid.,* Vol. I, pp. 224–225.)

The young man just turned twenty-six who thus marked out the path he was to follow for thirty-five years was an extraordinarily single-minded and rugged character. His like has too rarely appeared in America. Arrogant, dictatorial, intolerant, he might be, as his warmest friends admitted; but it is a foolish judgment that will dismiss him thus. Unyielding as granite, sheer Yankee will driven by a passionate energy, he was born for hazardous leadership. He was a man utterly unacquainted with fear. Lied about daily, threatened, bullied, charged with every sin in the Decalogue and every crime on the statute-book, he could not be coerced nor intimidated nor turned aside from his purpose. An ascetic who cared nothing for ease or preferment; a pacifist who fought only with the sword of the spirit; a stern moralist prophesying wrath upon a nation of mockers, and pronouncing doom upon a people that had forgotten God, he was an agitator fashioned after the ancient Hebraic pattern. The stature of such a man cannot be measured by conventional standards. Outwardly a somewhat prosaic Baptist, deeply religious and in his younger days bigotedly orthodox, he was in reality a spiritual child of the Old Testament, a modern Puritan on whom had fallen the mantle of the Prophets. New England Calvinism never bred so Puritan a soul. Hebraism was in his marrow—its noble austerity, its

consuming passion. He daily walked with righteousness and
communed with conscience. He carried God's scales into the
market place. He would not accept his law of men. Constitutions
and statutes were vain and foolish pronouncements to him if he
judged them to be contrary to the divine enactments. He counted
property in negroes and cotton as nothing when weighed in the
balance of justice. A human soul, whether in black skin or white,
was of far greater worth in his eyes than all the warring kingdoms
of this world. As fully as John Humphrey Noyes he reëmbodied
the root-and-branch righteousness of English Commonwealth
times. Others might lash the sins of his generation with whips;
he would scourge them with nettles and scorpions. He would
raise such a clamor about men's ears that the drowsiest must
awake. He would light such a fire in the slave market of America
that the evil thing should be consumed as stubble in the white
flame of righteousness.

Such primitive Hebraism, quite evidently, is calculated to make
troublesome citizens who are certain to get themselves heartily
disliked by those who approve of the world as it is. Any invasion
of the devil's realms will create an uproar, for the devil is prompt
to defend his own. Righteousness may prophesy in the gates, but
the buying and selling of the poor goes on as usual. Amongst
comfortable folk conscience is rarely at home when justice knocks
at the door; it is gone a-visiting, or is busy, or is waiting upon
Caesar, or is gone forth to pray. Comfortable folk do not like
clamor, even from the prophets, and are content to leave justice
to God with the hope that He will not disturb business. If the
tithes are duly paid, it is a mean and censorious God that will ask
how the money was got. Hence comfortable folk, north as well as
south, did not like Garrison; and not liking him they were zealous
to damn him. He was made out to be a bogy man, busily engaged in stirring up Nat Turner insurrections, inciting peaceful
and contented slaves to discontent, flouting the Constitution and
seeking to disrupt the Union. His righteousness was so great
a stumbling-block that he was held to be an atheist by eminent
formalists who knew of righteousness only by hearsay, and learned
of God only from report. It was reckoned to him a major sin that
he forgot his manners, for must not the Lord's work be carried on
in seemly fashion, and the money-changers be scourged from the
temple politely? "The first movement here at the North, was a

rank onset and explosion," said the eminent Dr. Bushnell. "The first sin of this organization was a sin of ill manners. They did not go to work like Christian gentlemen. . . . The great convention which met at Philadelphia drew up a declaration of their sentiments . . . by which they willfully and boorishly cast off the whole South from them" (Garrison, *William Lloyd Garrison*, Vol. II, p. 132, Note). What could be done with a fellow who insisted that the devil is rarely put in a quake by courteous treatment, and who had never learned that the Hebrew prophets bore themselves like Christian gentlemen? That he spoke with plebeian directness was unquestionably true.

These are your men of "caution," and "prudence," and "judiciousness" [he exclaimed in a speech at Philadelphia, May 14, 1838]. Sir, I have learned to hate those words. Whenever we attempt to imitate our great Exemplar, and press the truth of God, in all its plainness, upon the conscience, why, we are very imprudent; because, forsooth, a great excitement will ensue. Sir, slavery will not be overthrown without excitement, a most tremendous excitement. (*Ibid.*, Vol. II, p. 215. Note.)

If clerical gentlemen disliked Garrison, gentlemen of State Street disliked him much more heartily, and being the responsible custodians of law and order, they upheld existing institutions in their own way. Your Tory is always a Fascist at heart, and the Boston Tories naturally adopted the principle of direct action. Unpleasant things happened to Garrison in consequence. He was denounced at a most respectable meeting in Faneuil Hall, "at which Washington was cheered for being a slave-holder." He was mobbed in his print-shop by "gentlemen of property and standing from all parts of the city," and was thrown into jail by a timid mayor to save his life. Not since the days of Tom Paine had such unmeasured vituperation been poured out on the head of an American. It would seem that it was a perilous business to defend the downtrodden or to remind church-members of the injunction "to undo the heavy burdens and let the oppressed go free." When conscience throws down the gauntlet to economics it is certain to get some hard knocks. It is ill-trained for a rough and tumble contest; its scruples will not permit it to hit below the belt. But the Tory suffers no handicap of scruple and plants his blows where he can. On the occasion of an Abolition convention announced to be held within the shadows of Wall Street, Bennett's *New York*

Herald exemplified the sweetness and light of the commercial mind in such pronouncements as this:

What business have all the religious lunatics of the free states to gather in this commercial city for purposes which, if carried into effect, would ruin and destroy its prosperity? . . . Public opinion should be regulated. These abolitionists should not be allowed to misrepresent New York. . . . When free discussion does not promote the public good, it has no more right to exist than a bad government that is dangerous and oppressive to the common weal. It should be overthrown. On the question of the usefulness to the public of the packed, organized meetings of these aboli-tionists, socialists, Sabbath-breakers, and anarchists, there can be but one result arrived at by prudence and patriotism. They are dangerous assemblies—calculated for mischief, and reasonable in their character and purposes. . . . That half-a-dozen madmen should manufacture opinion for the whole community, is not to be tolerated. (*Ibid.*, Vol. III, pp. 283–284.)

In consequence of which appeals to "prudence and patriotism" the meeting was broken up, public opinion was judiciously regu-lated, and the Bible and Constitution vindicated by a Bowery mob under the leadership of a ward-heeler. It was from the impact of such ruthless opposition that Garrison's strategy took form; and it was direct and uncompromising and outspoken—as sternly logi-cal as Calhoun's. There were no shades in his thinking but only black and white, righteousness and sin. Expediency was not in his vocabulary. He was as narrow as he was intense. The catholic intellectual interests of the times touched him but little. Tran-scendentalism lay quite outside his world of thought. He was a religious soul rather than a speculative intellect, and he measured all things by the principles of primitive Christianity. As a young man he preferred the Calvinism of Lyman Beecher to the Uni-tarianism of Channing, but later he came to perceive the intimate relation between the major premises of Unitarianism and his so-cial ideals. It is idle to seek a political philosopher in a Hebrew moralist. His somewhat naïve political conceptions were an amalgam of French equalitarianism and Yankee perfectionism. The Declaration of Independence was his one political textbook, in the light of which he judged Congressional enactments and in-terpreted the Constitution. With Channing he assumed an ethi-cal sanction for natural rights, and this assumption conducted straight to the doctrine of the higher law. As early as 1830 his conscience was prepared to appeal from laws and statutes to ethics, on the principle that "that which is not just is not law." By 1837 he had accepted the philosophy of spiritual anarchism as set forth in the new gospel of perfectionism, and from this flowed naturally the doctrines of Nullification and disunion.

With amazing frankness Garrison published his views to friends and enemies, bringing all the hornets of conservatism about his ears. A furious discussion arose within the Abolition ranks on the question of loyalty to the political state, and the scandal of Garrison's Fifth Monarchy doctrine spread far. What that doctrine was he was at great pains to make clear. Writing to Henry C. Wright on the Quaker doctrine of non-resistance, he insisted on the sinfulness of all force whether in a private or public capacity, and then asserted:

> Human governments will remain in violent existence as long as men are resolved not to bear the cross of Christ, and to be crucified unto the world. But in the Kingdom of God's dear Son, holiness and love are the only magistracy. It has no swords, for they are beaten into ploughshares—no spears, for they are changed into pruning hooks—no military academy, for the saints cannot learn war any more—no gibbet, for life is regarded as inviolate—no chains, for all are free. And that kingdom is to be established upon the earth, for the time is predicted when the kingdoms of this world will become the kingdoms of our Lord and of his Christ. (Garrison, *William Lloyd Garrison*, Vol. II, p. 149.)

From such premises he deduced the conclusion that government is a cross that God permits men to endure as punishment for their sins. When they shall voluntarily quit their sins political government will cease.

> Human governments "are the results of human disobedience to the requirements of heaven; and they are better than anarchy just as a hailstorm is preferable to an earthquake, or the small-pox to the Asiatic cholera." From the silence of the Bible as to the *form* of such governments, he inferred not that each might claim a divine sanction, "but that the kingdom which Christ has established on earth is ultimately to swallow up or radically to subvert all other kingdoms." . . . "Shall we, *as Christians*, applaud and do homage to human government? or shall we not rather lay the axe at the root of the tree, and attempt to destroy both cause and effect together?" Foolish are the speculations about the best form of human government: "What is government but the express image of the moral character of a people?" (*Ibid.*, Vol. II, pp. 150–151.)

This is of course undiluted perfectionism, in which Garrison was the most ardent of believers. Prosaic political theory had lost all significance for him; he had got himself drunk on the new wine and was in no mood to listen to the counsels of expediency. Like John Humphrey Noyes he declared war upon the existing political state. He voluntarily disfranchised himself. He raised the banner of "disloyalty" in the *Liberator*, and summoned the Abolitionists to separate themselves from the unclean government that protected the sin of slavery. That the Constitution recognized the hateful system was sufficient proof to Garrison that the Constitution itself was unclean. Let it be consumed by its own iniquity. In 1843 he began an uncompromising attack upon it by nailing to the masthead of the *Liberator* his famous phrase, "A Covenant with Death and an Agreement with Hell," to which he soon added the words, "No Union with Slaveholders." He broke with many of his oldest friends, with Whittier and Gerrit Smith and James Birney, assailing them bitterly for meddling with third-party movements in the hope of curing the evil by political action. There followed, in consequence, a whirlwind and tempest of debate that brought a disastrous schism upon the Abolition movement. Cries of disloyalty and sedition filled all ears; but Garrison was indifferent to the storms that gathered about his head. He would go forward though he went alone. With every advance of the slave power his hatred of the Constitution, under cover of which its advances were made, grew more bitter. He outran southern fire eaters in advocacy of Nullification and secession. It became his daily work to undo the labors of Webster and bring the fundamental law into common contempt. The doctrine of no compromise with sin made no account of the complexities of social problems—the immediate, root-and-branch eradication of slavery or immediate dissolution of the Union, were his alternatives. "We dissolved the Union by a handsome vote, after a warm debate," wrote Edmund Quincy in 1843; "the question was . . . wrapped up by Garrison in some of his favorite Old Testament Hebraisms by way of vehicle, as the apothecaries say" (*ibid*., Vol. III, p. 88).

It was at a Fourth of July meeting, following the Anthony Burns affair of 1854, that Garrison made use of the striking appeal that attests his extraordinary boldness and skill as an agitator. After contrasting the principles of the Declaration of Independence and the present state of the Republic, he went on:

He should now proceed to perform an action which would be the testimony of his own soul, to all present, of the estimation in which he held the pro-slavery laws and deeds of the nation. Producing a copy of the *Fugitive Slave Law*, he set fire to it, and burnt it to ashes. Using an old and well-known phrase, he said, "And let all the people say, Amen"; and a unanimous cheer and shout of "Amen" burst from the vast audience. In like manner Mr. Garrison burned the decision of Edward G. Loring in the case of Anthony Burns . . . the multitude ratifying the fiery immolation with shouts of applause. Then, holding up the U. S. Constitution, he branded it as the source and parent of all the other atrocities,—"a covenant with death and agreement with hell"—and consumed it to ashes on the pot, exclaiming, "So perish all compromises with tyranny! and let all the people say, Amen!" A tremendous shout of "Amen" went up to heaven in ratification of the deed, mingled with a few hisses and wrathful exclamations from some who were evidently in a rowdyish state of mind, but who were at once cowed by the popular feeling. (*Ibid.*, Vol. III, p. 412.)

In such fashion did this disciple of the gospel of peace carry the war into Macedonia. The law of conscience had come into collision with the law of the land, and he followed conscience. For Garrison majority votes held no mandate. He had come to regard the political state as the mother of all mischiefs; for behind this thing of shreds and patches he saw unscrupulous politicians whose profession was the deceiving of simple minds, befogging moral issues with their myths and cults—their appeals to patriotism and the Constitution—and bringing the law of God into contempt. It was the spiritual bondage of the North that held the negro in slavery, Garrison had come to believe, and to free the conscience of the North was the great duty devolving upon the Abolitionists. With his intense single-mindedness he saw no other duty, and in doing that duty he would use no other weapon than the sword of the spirit. It is fortunate, perhaps, that the prophet knows so little of the resourcefulness of the market place on which he pronounces judgment, or his zeal might suffer abatement. Slavery was not destroyed by the conscience of Massachusetts, but by the economics of free labor. The free-soilers were more dangerous to it for they fought with material weapons; and old John Brown of Ossawatomie, more Hebraic even than Garrison, was a sterner realist, who took care to load his Sharp's rifle while girding on the sword of the spirit. From the prophet to the soldier is but a step, from the sword of the spirit to musket and ball, from conscience to the Emancipation Proclamation. Single-minded men—the Garrisons and John Browns—marshaling the discontent of their generation, sometimes do succeed in removing mountains; but unfortunately they leave a great scar, and the débris litters the whole country-side. Other mountains may even arise from the waste of the leveling. After the Emancipation Proclamation came the Four-teenth Amendment, and out of that came the triumphant gospel of "due process of law." The devil understands the ways of the world too well to become discouraged at a temporary set-back, for if righteousness succeed in breaking the bonds that bind a genera-tion, he knows that the market place carries an ample stock of new cords to replace those that are broken.

II

JOHN G. WHITTIER
Puritan Quaker

If Garrison was the flintiest character amongst the militant Abolitionists, Whittier was certainly the gentlest. Among many lovable men he was perhaps the most lovable. Bred in a faith that had never been dominant in New England, he escaped the indura-tion that was the price the New England conscience paid for its hard dogma. No thick shell of Calvinism incrusted for him the soul of humanitarian religion. In the Society of Friends righteous-ness was not daily twisted into unloveliness, nor the beauty of holiness forgotten; and in consequence, it was easier for him than for his Calvinist neighbors to fashion his life upon the principles of the New Testament, and set Christ above the Prophets.

Whittier's family escaped many temptations by following quiet paths to their own ends. Prosperity had never wooed the Massa-chusetts Quakers away from the simple life, as it had done with so many Philadelphia Friends, but a narrow domestic economy and social non-conformity had nourished their religion of peace and good will. Long before Channing discovered the religion of love in the teachings of French humanitarianism, the early Quakers had found that primitive gospel in the byways of Carolinian England, and had brought it to the new world. There they had borne testimony in their daily lives to the excellence of Christian fellow-ship, and there they had suffered the reproaches and the blows of bigoted conformists. Their faith had been tried in the fires of persecution, and the Society of Friends had justified its use of that most excellent of sectarian names. In the sincerity of their equali-tarian fellowship the Quakers were the friends of humanity, of

the poor and the outcast of this world. Their religion was of the
week-day as well as the Sabbath. With its mystical doctrine of
the inner light—of the Holy Spirit that speaks directly to the soul
without the intermediation of priest or church—it unconsciously
spread the doctrine of democracy in an autocratic world. It
interpreted literally the principle that members of the Christian
fellowship are equals in the sight of God and in each other's eyes—
that on earth there is neither high nor low but a common brotherhood in Christ. It quietly set aside the pretentions of priestly
hierarchies, and substituted the principle that religion is a matter
that lies with the individual and God. Naturally a "hireling
ministry" could not look with favor on such doctrine, and the sharp
hostility it aroused in theocratic New England, sprang from the
realization that the ideals of the Quaker fellowship were dangerous
to the ideals of a priestly theocracy. The autocratic rulers of
Massachusetts Bay could see little good in the democracy of the
Friends.

As became a Quietist, the master passion of Whittier's life was
ethical. He was neither a transcendental nor a Utopian visionary,
but a primitive Christian, an apostle of good will and a friend of
justice. Sprung from a long line of New England yeomen, wholly
of the soil, simple in wants, quietly independent, he was the last
lineal expression in our literature of the primitive faith, the last
authentic echo of the spiritual democracy of the seventeenth
century. A thorough Yankee in character, the Yankee never
dominated him. As a young man, to be sure, he temporized with
his Quakerism and dreamed fond dreams of worldly ambition.
The stirrings of youthful romance awakened the desire to be a
Byronic poet, and a Yankee knack with politics led him to meddle
with the hope of representing his district in Congress. He was
hand-in-glove with the time-serving Caleb Cushing, and the temptations of political intrigue almost led to his backsliding; but he
soon put the devil behind him and gave security for his better
behavior by coming out for the cause of Abolitionism. That was
the end of his hopes of political preferment, and the more surely to
burn his bridges he published in 1833, at his own cost, a little
Abolition tract entitled *Justice and Expediency*, which was reissued by Lewis Tappan in a great edition and scattered broadcast.
The same year he attended as delegate the National Anti-Slavery
Convention at Philadelphia, and subscribed his name to its pro-

nouncement. Thenceforth for over thirty years he gave his best strength to the cause, writing abundantly in prose and verse, serving as editor of Abolition publications, and suffering the unpleasant experiences common to the group, at one time being hunted by a mob and stoned.

This deliberate alignment with an unpopular cause, this calm response to the summons of conscience, was the fruit of his Quaker training. It was no new experience for the Quaker to dissent. The Whittier family had been Come-outers for generations, sacrificing material well-being for their faith, and he had grown up in dissent. The long struggle for democratic freedom in Massachusetts was a familiar story to him. The record had come down by word of mouth and stories of early persecutions were fireside tales in the Whittier household. His ancestors had lived in the hard old Puritan theocracy, and yet detached from it; and this detachment had rendered them shrewdly critical and sensitive to injustice. With their quiet dissent from what the Quaker conscience regarded as unrighteous, and their practical nullification of unjust authority, Whittier was in full sympathy. His intimate knowledge of early Massachusetts history had taught him certain things which official historians had overlooked, the chief of which was that dissent had been the ally and friend of freedom in New England. From his youth up he had been a loving student of the old annals, of those intimate narratives that preserve the voice and manner of the past; and as he discovered how often persecution had left its stain on the record, he was drawn to consider the superstitious aberrations of a people supposedly devout. In middle life he gathered up in *Leaves from Margaret Smith's Journal of Massachusetts Bay, 1678-79*, materials that he had long been collecting, and which, interpreted by a sympathetic imagination, provides a surprisingly vivid account of life in New England in the second generation.

All in all, it is Whittier's most notable achievement in prose. Pieced together out of old records, it is authentic as the yellow documents from which it was drawn. The soft light of romance lies upon its pages, sobered by historical fact and tempered by creative sympathy. Loving yet critical, quite devastating at times in its implications, it is an amazingly intimate narrative. The mind of Puritan New England is uncovered in these unpretentious pages, and it does not show to advantage. There was many a knot and seam in the old Puritan life, much that was mean and ugly woven into the honest web. The Puritan proneness to Quaker-baiting—aggravated to be sure by the ill manners of the Ranters; their vulgar credulity that encouraged witch-hunting; their callous treatment of the Indian and negro; their hardness of nature that made them grasping and censorious: such knots and seams in the Puritan character did not escape Whittier's eye, but they appear in the sketches of avaricious deacons, sour women, intolerant magistrates—the Deacon Doles and Goody Lakes and Roger Endicotts, whose bigotry tyrannized over the better natures of the community. Whittier sifted his materials carefully to gather up what good wheat there might be, yet the showing it must be confessed is but paltry. Honest Robert Pine who will have none unjustly treated, good Mr. Russ who counsels moderation in dealing with the unhappy victims of mob suspicion, Captain Samuel Sewall who speaks up bravely for the outcast—these are the remnant in Israel, the generous minority that cannot leaven the dour and credulous mass. Yet even they are not heroic figures to Whittier. His heroes are the Come-outers, and in particular Peggy Brewster—reminiscent evidently of his great-grandmother, the Quakeress Mary Peaslee, who married Robert Whittier in 1694—who is the good Samaritan of the Puritan neighborhood, and whose loving-kindness wins a reluctant good will that stops short of toleration of her non-conformity.

Such intimate studies in the psychology of persecution were a liberal education, and Whittier would have been no Quaker had he not learned his lesson. He was justified in not thinking well of the social conscience of respectable New England. Religious conformity, he had come to understand, had not kept alive the torch of freedom in Massachusetts, nor had Puritan righteousness befriended justice. Not the great of earth but the simple may be counted on to do God's work. So taking his lesson to heart he quietly put aside ambition, and like Peggy Brewster numbered himself among the remnant. Like her he would be a Come-outer and bear his testimony against the uncleanness of the American people in this matter of negro slavery. Not with musket and ball would he fight, like old John Brown; but with the sword of the spirit. The solution must lie with the conscience of the American people. As a Friend, a man of peace, he would not deal harshly with the supporters of slavery; he would not counsel violence.

But as a Yankee with a gift for politics, he would use political means to jog a slothful conscience and marshal its forces. And so Whittier became the politician amongst the Abolitionists. He proved himself a skillful lobbyist. He was active in getting up petitions to Congress. He supported John Quincy Adams and put pressure on the slippery Caleb Cushing. He advocated the policy of boring from within the old parties, but when such methods proved futile he became an active leader in the third party movement. He was an early supporter of the Liberal party—that in 1844 drew enough votes from Clay in New York to defeat him for the Presidency—of the Free-Soil party, and later of the Republican party.

It was this insistence upon the use of political methods that brought about the unhappy break with Garrison. Immediately it was no more than a difference over tactics, but it was embittered by a wide cleavage of political theory. With Garrison's conversion to spiritual anarchism the Abolition movement was sundered by a division between the perfectionists and the political actionists. The principle of non-voting and of refusing allegiance to the Constitution aroused strong opposition, and Whittier went with Birney and Gerrit Smith, with Jonathan Sewall, John Pierpont and the Tappans in rejecting the perfectionist policy. His political common sense turned naturally to political agencies to accomplish his ends. "Moral action apart from political" seemed to him an "absurdity." But when he applied the Quaker principle of Come-outism, and advocated separate party alignment, Garrison attacked him with his habitual intolerance. The latter feared a third party movement as certain to provide a rallying cry for the commercial interest to muster the mob to its support, and overwhelm the minority with the unthinking and selfish mass. "All political minorities," he argued, "are more or less liberal," and by throwing the Abolition strength to such organized minorities, the movement would be "feared and respected by all political parties" (Garrison, *William Lloyd Garrison*, Vol. II, pp. 310–311). The wisest strategy, he believed, was to seek to hold the balance of power between the old parties—rewarding friends and punishing enemies—while laboring to arouse the conscience of America, for ballots without conscience were the enemies of justice.

Whittier was no such root-and-branch spirit as Garrison, and in the political field he was a practical, somewhat prosaic Yankee, little given to abstract speculation, skillful in minor strategical skirmishes, inclined to opportunism. He belonged to no school of political thought. His equalitarianism came as a heritage from his Quaker religion rather than from political theory. To prepare himself for his work he read Milton and Burke. The pamphlets of the great Puritan appealed to him as the voice of the moral fervor of a heroic age, but Milton's aristocratic republicanism he seems to have examined no more critically than Burke's Whiggish legalism. Neither held anything in common with Quaker equalitarianism. Rousseau and Tom Paine and Jefferson, with whom he certainly would have sympathized, he seems not to have been acquainted with. In Whittier's New England they were in ill repute, and the young Whittier was as naïvely provincial in his political partisanship as was Garrison. Economics had no part in his thought, and the economic interests that divided Federalism and Anti-Federalism he seems never to have understood. Though sprung from six generations of farmers who tilled the same acres, he reveals no sympathy with agrarianism. He swallowed Clay and the American System without a qualm, and as a young editor he wrote with pride of the developing industrialism of Massachusetts. Neither in politics nor in economics was he a rebellious soul. He was conscience rather than intellect. He felt rather than thought. Only a moral issue could draw him into strife, and even in such contests he was ill equipped to lead the prosaic debates. His moral indignation found its natural expression in verse, and he early took his place as the poet of the Abolition movement, distilling into ready lyrics the emotion of the moment.

A great, even a noteworthy poet, Whittier certainly was not. Compared with Whitman he is only a minor figure. Among the better known American poets Bryant alone is so narrow in range and barren in suggestion. His austere and meager life bred too little sensuousness of nature and too few intellectual passions. An over-frugal watering of the wine of paganism had left the New England character thin. The sap of humor that ran so boisterously through the veins of the West, exuding a rough wit from Davy Crockett to Mark Twain, was quite gone out of the Yankee blood. His homely imagination was unquickened by a hearty village life as was the case with the English Bunyan and the Scotch Burns. He had become a bundle of Yankee nerves, responding only to

moral stimuli. The comment of Whitman sums up the Quaker
poet adequately:

Whittier's poetry stands for morality . . . as filtered through the
positive Puritanical and Quaker filters; is very valuable as a genuine
utterance. . . . Whittier is rather a grand figure—pretty lean and ascetic
—no Greek—also not composite and universal enough (doesn't wish to
be, doesn't try to be) for ideal Americanism. (Carpenter, *Life of Whitman*,
p. 293.)

Never a great artist, rarely a competent craftsman, he wrote for
the most part impassioned commonplace, with occasional flashes
that are not commonplace.

The high-water mark of lyric indignation was reached in the
lines to Webster. Written at white heat, they have the passionate directness of Thoreau's prose. Like other Abolitionists, Whittier had clung to his hopes of Webster in spite of frequent signs of
the latter's backsliding. He did not sufficiently appreciate the
economic alliances that tied Webster to State Street, and he under-
rated his presidential ambitions. But when the blow came with
the Seventh of March Speech, it staggered him—not alone the
defection of Webster, but the demonstrative approval of his
wealthy constituents. For having "convinced the understanding
and touched the conscience of a nation," Webster was formally
thanked by some seven hundred addressers from the most respectable circles of Massachusetts—great men like Rufus Choate,
George Ticknor, W. H. Prescott, President Jared Sparks and
Professor Felton of Harvard, Moses Stuart and Leonard Woods
of Andover Theological Seminary. It was an hour of profound discouragement that laid bare what colossal difficulties stood in the
way of Abolitionism. "The scandalous treachery of Webster and
the *backing* he has received from Andover and Harvard," wrote
Whittier to Garrison, "show that we have nothing to hope for
from the great political parties and religious sects" (William
Sloane Kennedy, *John G. Whittier*, p. 113).

The scathing lines of *Ichabod* were read throughout the North,
and they must have rankled in Webster's heart. Even Whittier
was troubled by their severity and thirty years later he wrote a
second Webster poem which he set beside *Ichabod* in his collected
works. *The Lost Occasion* is a testimony to the kindliness of Whittier's Quaker heart that did not love to offend; but no kindliness
of memory could change or soften the just verdict of the lines:

> Of all we loved and honored, naught
>   Save power remains;
> A fallen angel's pride of thought,
>   Still strong in chains.
>
> All else is gone; from those great eyes
>   The soul is fled:
> When faith is lost, when honor dies,
>   The man is dead!
>
> Then, pay the reverence of old days
>   To his dead fame;
> Walk backward, with averted gaze,
>   And hide the shame!

If Whittier was ill acquainted with the Boston of State Street and the Back Bay, and the Cambridge of Harvard culture, he knew intimately the Massachusetts of the village and the farm, and the overwhelming repudiation of Webster and the Whig party, following the Seventh of March Speech, would seem to have justified his lyric confidence expressed in the vigorous heptameters of *Massachusetts to Virginia*. For those who lived in the social world of Commissioner Loring—professor of law at Harvard—and Rufus Choate, it was hard not to think that Massachusetts had come to degenerate days. The fine old-school Federalist, Josiah Quincy, commenting on the Boston that watched Sims returned to slavery, wrote:

When the [Fugitive Slave] law passed, I did think the moral sense of the community would not enforce it; I said that it never would be. But now I find that my fellow-citizens are not only *submissive* to, but that they are earnestly active for, its enforcement. The Boston of 1851 is not the Boston of 1775. Boston has now become a mere shop—a place for buying and selling goods; and I suppose, also, of *buying and selling men*. (Garrison, *William Lloyd Garrison*, Vol. III, p. 328.)

And Lowell, living in the same mean atmosphere, wrote:

> Massachusetts, God forgive her,
>   She's akneelin' with the rest,
> She, thet ough' to ha' clung ferever
>   In her grand old eagle-nest.
>   (*Biglow Papers*, Part I, 1.)

But Whittier professed to think better of the conscience of New England. A strong pride of the commonwealth runs through the

lines that name over the towns of Massachusetts, from "free, broad
Middlesex," westward and northward to the hills of Hampshire:

And sandy Barnstable rose up, wet with the salt sea spray;
And Bristol sent her answering shout down Narragansett Bay!
Along the broad Connecticut old Hampden felt the thrill,
And the cheer of Hampshire's woodmen swept down from Holyoke Hill.

The voice of Massachusetts! Of her free sons and daughters,
Deep calling unto deep aloud, the sound of many waters!
Against the burden of that voice what tyrant power shall stand?
No fetters in the Bay State! No slave upon her land!

When at last the long controversy was over and release from the
struggle came to Whittier, his poetry grew richer and mellower.
He was not made to be a fighter, and it was with a sigh of relief
that he turned to the Elysian fields he had dreamed of, while he
was turning with his plow the rough stubble of a cause. Looking
back upon those arduous days, he sketched half whimsically his
own portrait in *The Tent on the Beach.*

And one there was, a dreamer born,
    Who, with a mission to fulfill,
    Had left the Muses' haunts to turn
    The crank of an opinion-mill,
Making his rustic reed of song
A weapon in the war with wrong,
Yoking his fancy to the breaking-plough
That beam-deep turned the soil for truth to spring and grow.

Too quiet seemed the man to ride
    The winged Hippogriff Reform;
Was his a voice from side to side
    To pierce the tumult of the storm?
A silent, shy, peace-loving man,
He seemed no fiery partisan
To hold his way against the public frown,
The ban of Church and State, the fierce Mob's hounding down.

For while he wrought with strenuous will
    The work his hands had found to do,
He heard the fitful music still
    Of winds that out of dream-land blew.
The din about him could not drown
What the strange voices whispered down;
Along his task-field weird processions swept,
The visionary pomp of stately phantoms stepped.

> The common air was thick with dreams,—
>   He told them to the toiling crowd;
> Such music as the woods and streams
>   Sang in his ear he sang aloud;
> In still, shut bays, on windy capes,
> He heard the call of beckoning shapes,
> And, as the gray old shadows prompted him,
> To homely moulds of rhyme he shaped their legends grim.

Many excellent things he did in those quiet later years; old time pictures like *Snowbound*, with its homely fireside economy long since buried under the snows of forgotten winters; vigorous tales like *Abraham Davenport;* ballads like *Skipper Ireson's Ride*, that have something of the spirit of the primitive.   He had given thirty years of his life to the cause of social justice, and surely none would grudge him in old age his rambles in pleasanter fields. It was well that he could turn to the past, for the America of the new exploitative age, the New England of Lowell and Lawrence, he never understood.   Black slavery he understood, but wage slavery he comprehended no more than did Garrison.   To the end he remained a primitive soul, ill equipped to understand a materialistic philosophy of society.   There is something pathetic in his *Songs of Labor*.   His economics, like his democracy, was of a bygone time, having no kinship with a scrambling free-soil-ism or a rapacious capitalism.   There is scant room in this world for the Friend with his unmilitant dream of the fellowship.   With his passion for freedom, established in the gospel of righteousness, the Quaker Whittier was fast becoming an anachronism in indus-trial New England that was concerned about very different things. How old-fashioned he had become is suggested by certain lines that phrase his greetings to later times.   Spare, somewhat halting in rhythm, yet transparently sincere, they constitute an apologia that New England need feel no shame for.

> Yet here at least an earnest sense
> Of human right and weal is shown;
>   A hate of tyranny intense,
>   And hearty in its vehemence,
> As if my brother's pain and sorrow were my own.
>
> O Freedom! if to me belong
> Nor mighty Milton's gift divine,
>   Nor Marvell's wit and graceful song,
>   Still with a love as deep and strong
> As theirs, I lay, like them, my best gifts on thy shrine!

III

HARRIET BEECHER STOWE

A Daughter of Puritanism

No more Puritan mind than Mrs. Stowe's ever contributed to the literature of New England. Her remarkable native gifts were unconsciously given specific shape by a rigid environment. For years the artist in her struggled to subdue the moralist, and never quite succeeded. Before she dipped her pen in ink her mind had taken its set. She could not hope to escape being a preacher. Daughter of a minister and wife of a minister, with brothers and sons ministers, she lived all her life in an atmosphere of religion. She was baptized in creeds and prattled the language of sermons as the vernacular of childhood. Born at a critical time for the old New England faith, her youth was passed amid the storm clouds of the Unitarian controversy, in an atmosphere charged with electricity. Connecticut was the very citadel of the Edwardean orthodoxy, and Litchfield was as rugged in its faith as the hills it nestled among; and when the old-school Calvinism of Boston was in danger of utter rout, it naturally turned to a Connecticut Daniel to save the venerable cause. Stout old Lyman Beecher was a host in himself. Son of a Connecticut blacksmith and himself brought up at the forge before he quitted it to seek learning at Yale College under Timothy Dwight, able, kindly, practical, with pronounced literary tastes and a capable pen, he was a stalwart Edwardean, militantly conservative, who damned our perverse human nature with incontrovertible logic. Harriet was eight years old when Channing preached his Baltimore sermon, and fourteen when her father was summoned to Hanover Street Church, Boston. Her childish heart had already been given to Baxter's *Saint's Rest*, and her imagination awakened by Cotton Mather's *Magnalia Christi Americana*. Theocratic New England lay enveloped for her in a haze of romance, more fascinating than any Sir Walter had woven about the Scottish Highlands; she had discovered there noble figures and heroic deeds to kindle an ardent hero worship. At fourteen she was converted—too easily it seems, for she could not demonstrate to the satisfaction of her spiritual counselors that she had been sufficiently under conviction of sin. Thereafter to the end of her life the greatest of all dramas for her was the drama of the soul concerned with the great business of salvation.

The surest clue to Mrs. Stowe's literary secret is to be found in her sympathetic understanding of the spiritual life of Puritan New England. She was a lifelong student of New England psychology, with its "profound, unutterable, and therefore unuttered melancholy" that resulted from open-eyed contemplation of grim fact. The past that lay bleak and stern behind the sober present she understood as few others did. Before her sympathetic eyes it fell into just proportions, and quite naturally she became the historian of her people. The autobiographical material that fills her later work—her husband's recollections in *Old-Town Folks*, and her own in *Poganuc People*—is much more than autobiography; it is intimate history of New England, written by one who in distilling her own experience was writing the chronicle of a race. In a brilliant chapter of the former work she gives a remarkable analysis of the intellectual development of Puritan New England, and provides the setting against which her own intellectual life should be placed. To overlook it is to miss the most suggestive commentary on her work that has ever been written.

This daughter of Puritanism traces her intellectual antecedents back to the long struggle of Puritan rationalism with feudal custom and medieval ideas. The old English Puritans, "by nature the most reverential and most loyal portion of the community," in destroying the divine-right sovereignty of King Charles, were impelled to transfer that sovereignty to a higher King. In pulling down the temporal, they erected a divine sovereignty; and their passionate attachment to the new Sovereign was the natural response to "the pleading and yearning within them of a faculty robbed of its appropriate object, and longing for support and expression." But the theologies to which they yielded intellectual allegiance were a "legacy from past monarchical and medieval ages." To free themselves from this unhappy legacy, and create a democratic theology, was an arduous work that needed two hundred years to accomplish; and not until the Revolution spread a new social philosophy through America, did the work go forward rapidly. Wanting such a democratic philosophy Puritan New England wandered in the old theological fogs. It was Jonathan Edwards who first turned the New England mind to rationalism, and began that long "controversy" that was to unsettle so much. But unhappily the rationalism of Edwards was turned aside to reactionary ends, and his *Treatise on True Virtue* was "one of the strongest attempts to back up by reasoning the old monarchical and aristocratic ideas of the supreme right of the king and upper classes." Nevertheless he set all New England to rationalizing, and it was this severe discipline that carried her people soberly through the Revolutionary War, and preserved them from the excesses which followed the Revolution in France. And it was this same discipline that prepared them for the eventual re-discovery of the humanity of Jesus and the democracy of his religion. New England had been struggling towards democracy through the bog of its feudal theology; it became consciously democratic with the appearance of the new theology (*Old-Town Folks*, Chapter XXIX).

This rationalistic bias of eighteenth-century New England suffices to explain for Mrs. Stowe the stern temper and angular individuality of the old Puritan Yankee. Her particular hero and saint was Jonathan Edwards, and her lesser hero and saint was Samuel Hopkins; and in both it was the courageous rationalism that appealed to her. In them, and more particularly in the former, she discovered the creative force that quickened a religion that was falling into dead formalism, that gave it fresh vitality and made it the central fact of everyday New England life. Across the world of her youth lay the shadow—or the light—of the great Edwards, and the great Hopkins was his intellectual heir. In another chapter of *Old-Town Folks* she sketches the Edwardean influence in bold outline.

The ministers of the early colonial days of New England, though well-read, scholarly men, were more statesmen than theologians. Their minds ran upon the actual arrangements of society, which were in great measure left in their hands, rather than on doctrinal and metaphysical subtleties. They took their confession of faith just as the great body of Protestant reformers left it, and acted upon it as a practical foundation, without much further discussion, until the time of President Edwards. He was the first man who began the disintegrating process of applying rationalistic methods to the accepted doctrines of religion, and he rationalized far more boldly and widely than any publishers of his biography have ever dared to let the world know. He sawed the great dam and let out the whole waters of discussion over all New England, and that free discussion led to all the shades of opinion of our modern days. Little as he thought it, Waldo Emerson and Theodore Parker were the last results of the current set in motion by Jonathan Edwards. (Chapter XIX.)

In this flood let loose by the metaphysical saw of Jonathan Edwards, Mrs. Stowe found the material for her New England tales. In no other pages does one realize so fully the tremendous, vital significance of religion to the children of Puritanism, nor appreciate how narrow a course their lives ran between the farm and the meeting-house. A domestic economy and a parochial theology absorbed their energies, and they took on sharp and angular imprints from a severe routine. It was a school of discipline that created individual character, and Mrs. Stowe possessed a loving eye for the odd and original. She delighted in emphasizing the theological differences that ran through Yankee families, giving little twists to character, and rising to the tongue in scraps of confirmatory Scripture. Large-hearted, motherly Grandmother Badger, in *Old-Town Folks*, was a stern Calvinist who daily threw predestination in the face of her easy-going Arminian husband, and exchanged syllogisms in a Sabbath-day "battle of the Infinities" with her son from Yale. Theology provided the staple of talk in the farmer's kitchen; it was the axis on which turned the simple country life. *Old-Town Folks* and *Poganuc People* are cross sections of old New England, with its lingering prejudices in favor of rank,[1] its Arminian Parson Lothrop in wig and gold cane, and its Calvinist Dr. Cushing hostile to all democratic Jacobinism, its country yokels, its stubborn yeomen who parade their independence by voting the democratic ticket openly in the face of gentlemanly Federalists, its sharp contrasts of a stately old order and a somewhat bumptious new, yet with the hard New England granite snugly laid up and bonded with the mortar of religion —a strange dead world that emerges distinctly through the haze of Victorian sentiment. For Mrs. Stowe was a child of her own romantic generation as well as a daughter of Puritanism, and it was easy for her to discover suggestions of Utopia in a world where minister and people mingled theology with their corn-huskings and apple-bees.

Between these sketches and the Abolition novels stands *The Minister's Wooing*, with its Puritan heroine bleached into pure holiness under the cold sunshine of Hopkinsian theology, and its unworldly minister who demonstrated the sincerity of his creed of disinterested benevolence—of willing to be damned for the glory of God—by voluntarily yielding his betrothed to an earlier lover.

---

[1] " It's a hard struggle for our human nature to give up titles and ranks, though," said Miss Mehitable. "For my part, I have a ridiculous kindness for them yet. I know it's all nonsense; but I can't help looking back to the court we used to have at the Government House in Boston." (*Old-Town Folks*, Chapter VI.)

It is a love story without sex, as befits the wooing of a Puritan nun by her spiritual father, set against a Yankee background of capable housekeeping and dignified tea-drinking, subdued to proper decorum by religion, and touched with tragedy by the shadow of damnation that falls on the unregenerate—a world in which the beauty of holiness is somewhat pale and austere, and where disinterested benevolence finds a thin and obdurate soil to strike root in. Mrs. Stowe was drawn to the theme, very evidently, by the impulse of her two Utopian enthusiasms, her interest in Abolition and her affection for the ways of old New England. Such romance as blossomed under those bleak skies she loved to gather into a Yankee nosegay, and in her sympathetic hands the old slave-running Newport becomes almost lovable and human. She might find the theology hard, but she forgave the sermon out of love for the preacher. As the historian of the human side of Calvinism she tempered dogma with affection. In unsympathetic print those old sermons were almost unbelievably harsh and ungainly; as theologians those bewigged preachers were dry as the chips of last year's woodpile; but as husbands and fathers and neighbors, they were usually kind and unselfish and helpful. Her father Lyman Beecher was an arid dogmatist on the Lord's Day, but on week-days he fished and hunted rabbits and went nutting with his sons, made garden or smoked hams, or helped a neighbor with plowing or haying, and was an unusually capable and cheery member of a busy little world. In the light of such domestic exegesis the bleakness of his theology was softened, and the dogmatic theologian became a very human person.

Thus instructed Mrs. Stowe found no difficulty in discovering the human side of Dr. Samuel Hopkins, or understanding how the hard doctrine might cover the gentlest of souls—that the very intensity of devotion to the logic of a stern creed betokened a depth of religious sincerity that would find issue in generous deeds. A thinker who can dig from the harsh soil of Calvinism the doctrine of disinterested benevolence will discover a tender conscience in his own bosom. One might hazard a guess, indeed, that the story of Samuel Hopkins was an unconscious defense of the New England ministers against the sharp charges of the Abolitionists that the clergy were half-hearted in the cause or openly hostile. With her conviction of the unselfish nobility of their lives, Mrs. Stowe must have taken a secret pleasure in revealing the good Doctor as a forerunner of the Abolitionists, and in pointing out that the crabbed logician of the Edwardean school, the theologian immersed in the abstractions of a grotesque system, was nevertheless a light set upon a hill, a primitive Christian with heart overflowing with loving-kindness, who understood the iniquity of slavery and turned shepherd to the outcast to his own hurt. The figure of the unworldly minister is drawn with loving hand and his angularities made less rugged. His noble spirituality shrivels and consumes the mean excuses of his slave-running parishoner; it spreads quietly over the countryside, and his daily life is a sermon that quickens hearts that his theology leaves cold. There is preaching aplenty in the book—quite too much for later stomachs; but it scarcely detracts from the significance of the story as a document of Puritan New England, revealing how a tender conscience was stirring beneath the crabbed exterior of the old Calvinism.

In the light of such antecedents and such training Mrs. Stowe's passionate concern over slavery becomes easily comprehensible. Her Puritan conscience was quickened by her warm human sympathies. She had come close to the hateful thing during the years spent at Cincinnati, where the Abolition sentiment of the Lane Seminary students aroused such bitter opposition that President Lyman Beecher was forced to approve the decision of the trustees to forbid any discussion of slavery, with the result that so great a hegira of students took place from Lane to Oberlin that the seminary was forced to close. Only the fact that two miles of Ohio mud provided defensive outworks saved the building and the houses of the teachers from the hands of the Cincinnati mob. She had visited in Kentucky; she had been to the slave markets; she had seen her father and brother aid runaway slaves by means of the underground railway. A profound sense of the iniquity of the system oppressed her, and when the Fugitive Slave Bill came to fill up the measure of her wrath, she poured out her heart in *Uncle Tom's Cabin*. Despite its obvious blemishes of structure and sentimentalism it is a great human document that stripped away the protective atmosphere from the sacred institution, and laid bare its elementary injustice. It brought the system home to the common feeling and conscience. The strong religious coloring emphasized the Abolition argument that slavery trafficked in Christian souls, and rendered it hateful to every humanitarian instinct. It was noble propaganda, and the humor and pathos, the passion for social righteousness, still linger in its pages to make a later generation wonder that our fathers should so long have tolerated this evil thing.

Five years later she published *Dred, A Tale of the Great Dismal Swamp*, a thoughtfully elaborated statement of the complex problem, with a suggested solution that only thrust into relief the fact that it had indeed become an irrepressible conflict—the same solution that had been hinted at thirty years before in Kennedy's *Swallow Barn*, namely, a system of paternalistic emancipation, based on the historical analogy of the extinction of English villeinage, the slaves to be treated as wards by the masters and educated for gradual emancipation. It was a feudal solution of a feudal problem, but it took higher humanitarian ground than human nature can, and Mrs. Stowe recognized the complex of passion and interests in which the problem was involved, by removing her southern emancipationist to Canada to try his experiment. More striking, perhaps, is the shift from the Christian pacifism of *Uncle Tom's Cabin* to the economics of *Dred*. The former had made appeal to the humanitarianism of the North; the latter proposed to appeal to the self-interest of the South. The slave states, Mrs. Stowe's heroine argued, were being ruined by slavery, and if they were to expect a sane economic future, they must destroy the wasteful system. The contrast between Yankee thrift under free labor and plantation shiftlessness under slave labor had been pointed out by Whittier in his *Justice and Expediency* as early as 1833 and by Caruthers in his *Kentuckian in New York* in 1834—statements that perhaps drew Mrs. Stowe's attention to the economic phases involved; nevertheless the recognition of the complexity of the problem, and the attempt to deal with it adequately, lessened the popular appeal of *Dred*. The book is more skillfully done than *Uncle Tom*, it is far richer in background material—in vivid sketches of poor whites, of revivalist preachers, of plantation life—it provides in Old Tiff a delightful study of the negro servant and it suggests the perennial fear of a negro uprising; but it lacks the singleness of appeal that makes for telling propaganda. It was not its melodrama that hindered its success. The public had swallowed that in *Uncle Tom* with a hearty appetite. It was rather the dissipation of dramatic interest, the want of a striking figure to capture the imagination and sympathy. It is a better sociological study but a weaker story.

It was hard for the New England conscience to quit the pulpit and turn artist; and it was particularly hard for Mrs. Stowe with her ardent nature and multiplying domestic cares. She could bring her soul under discipline but not her art. She never trained herself in craftsmanship, never learned restraint, but suffered her pen to range freely as her emotions directed. The creative instinct was strong in her but the critical was wholly lacking. Richly endowed though she was her work has suffered the fate that pursues those who forget that beauty alone survives after emotion subsides.

PART THREE: THE TRANSCENDENTAL MIND

CHAPTER I

THE GENESIS OF TRANSCENDENTALISM

FROM the doctrine of the open mind that was the core of Unitarianism, came the transcendental movement that marked the full flowering of the New England renaissance. It was the native response of the mind of New England to the summons of revolutionary romanticism, and its ardor was the greater for being so long delayed. Creatively influenced though it was by French Utopianism and German mysticism, its manners and mode of thought received a particular impress from an environment long preparing and that was natively congenial. "Practically," says its most penetrating historian, transcendentalism "was an assertion of the inalienable worth of man; theoretically it was an assertion of the immanence of divinity in instinct, the transference of supernatural attributes to the natural constitution of mankind."[1] It was the glowing expression of philosophic Utopianism, the flaring up of old fires of idealism, before the scientific and materialistic reactions destroyed its romantic dreams. It accepted kinship with the social idealism of the Declaration of Independence; it accepted the dynamic principle of equalitarianism; but it sought to go farther and provide a sure defense and justification of an idealism that it professed to find established in human nature, by establishing it in metaphysics.

The explanation of this curious throwback to earlier times in the mind of transcendental New England is clear enough to anyone acquainted with the history of Puritan thought struggling with the mystical element of Christian experience. Since the far-off days of Roger Williams—the seeker and mystic who was so great a puzzle to his realistic brethren—idealism had been starved in New England. Its mystical aspirations had been repressed by dogma, and its elusive dreams brought to nothing. Jonathan Edwards struggled life-long to hold his idealism in subjection to theology, and ended in abortive reaction; a potential Emerson,

[1] See Frothingham, *Transcendentalism in New England*. Chapter VI.

another Berkeley, he re-welded the bonds of dogma on the mind of New England, putting off for two generations the day of its release. Even in the freer minds idealism suffered from the repressions of the common rationalism; with Locke and Hume in the ascendancy the mystic found the times uncongenial to his needs. The dawn of a new day seemed to be breaking with the shift of interest from theology to politics, during the stirring days of the Revolution. The submerged idealism of New England came to expression in the dreams of homespun democrats like Sam Adams, and expanded in the sunshine of French Utopianism; but unfortunately Boston Federalism reasserted the old dogmatisms and put a speedy end to the movement. It shut the door upon all democratic aspiration and bade it go about its business. It was from such a narrow environment that the rising movement of Unitarianism received its impress. From a sterile rationalism, a respectable close-fisted conservatism, it could not escape; and in consequence the new movement of liberalism was taken over by Federalism and became a new orthodoxy. "The pale negations of Boston Unitarianism"—to use Emerson's well-known phrase—provided little nourishment for transcendental hopes.

Nevertheless Unitarianism carried within it the seeds of the new faith—in its intellectual attitude, if not in its philosophy. "The Unitarians as a class," remarks Frothingham, "belonged to the school of Locke, which discarded the doctrine of innate ideas, and its kindred beliefs. . . . Unitarianism . . . has rarely, if ever, been taught or held by any man of eminence in the church who was a Platonist" (*Transcendentalism in New England*, Chapter VI). But in spite of its eighteenth-century nurture—because of it, indeed—Unitarianism was a profoundly liberalizing movement. It was a narrow and local phase of a world-wide revolution; the special contribution of Boston to the great work of disintegrating the past to make ready for the future. It loosened the grip of dogma on the Puritan mind and widened the field of reading and thinking. But it did very much more—it recovered the original principle of Protestantism, the principle of individual responsibility, that had been tacitly denied by Calvinistic orthodoxy. It asserted the essential decency of human nature—men may not be the children of God but they are assuredly not children of the devil; and it summoned this decent human nature to live decently in accordance with its nature. It would not coop up the mind in dogma; it would not close all roads to heaven but one. The Unitarians might be instinctively conservative, as was natural to prosperous persons, but they at least acknowledged "themselves to be friends of free thought in religion." Their doctrine was not a creed but an attitude of mind. If they themselves were not Seekers, they professed a willingness for others to become Seekers. Very likely few of them measured up to the full stature of such liberalism; nevertheless they "honestly but incautiously professed a principle broader than they were able to stand by, and avowed the absolute freedom of the human mind as their characteristic faith" (*ibid.*, Chapter VI).

All this was excellent, but it was not enough. It remained to see what the free mind should discover in its venturesome quest into the unknown. Intellectually emancipated, with the bleak dogmas of election and reprobation put away, with the God of wrath dethroned and the God of love lifted up, and with the dynamic principle of freedom of inquiry in their possession, the younger generation of New England intellectuals naturally opened their eyes to discover what winds of new doctrine were blowing in the world. They were pretty much all Unitarians—the young transcendentalists—and largely clergymen; their primary interest was metaphysical and they had already abandoned Locke for Plato. The rationalistic eighteenth century was dead to them and they set forth to discover another age. Hints and suggestions of that better age had come to them from overseas—from Wordsworth and Shelley, from Cousin and Madame de Stael, from Coleridge and Carlyle; and the fresh beauty of that new poetry, the enormous stimulus of that new metaphysic, fired them with a desire to seek this inspiration at its source and drink from the living waters. And so they discovered romantic Germany where the new idealism had quite routed the philosophy of sensationalism, and a great school of transcendental thinkers was in triumphant possession of the field. It was a profoundly stimulating discovery, and from it dated the rise of New England transcendentalism.

The immediate creative influence of the new contact with Germany was to strengthen the incipient Platonism of the rebellious intellectuals, and provide it with an added sanction. Transcendentalism, it must always be remembered, was a faith rather than a philosophy; it was oracular rather than speculative, affirmative rather than questioning; and it went to Germany to find confirmation of its faith, not to reëxamine its foundations. Faith preceded metaphysics, and if the metaphysics had been lacking intuition would have supplied its place, poetic inspiration would have sufficed the needs of transcendental minds. They had found God for themselves before the philosophers justified them; they took to Germany what they sought there. Nevertheless it was a tremendous experience to come upon their own philosophy there, erected into a system, supported by a complete metaphysic; a philosophy that had put to rout the fashionable skepticism of Voltaire and Condillac, established on the sensationalism of Locke, and offering justification for faith in God and man—faith in a divinity indwelling in nature and the individual soul—by a masterly dialectics. That experience determined the development of New England transcendentalism. The metaphysic of Kant, the mysticism of Jacobi, the idealistic egoism of Fichte, the transcendentalism of Schleiermacher—the new gospel of the renascent German spirit—these were the living waters of truth to the thirsty minds of the New England intellectuals, from which they drank eagerly, never doubting their sufficiency. They were poets and prophets; they were young and strong in faith; others might concern themselves with the dialectics of idealism, they would apply it in their daily lives.

In essence this new transcendental faith was a glorification of consciousness and will. It rested on the rediscovery of the soul that had been dethroned by the old rationalism; and it eventuated in the creation of a mystical egocentric universe wherein the children of God might luxuriate in their divinity. The Unitarians had pronounced human nature to be excellent; the transcendentalists pronounced it divine. They endowed it with great potentialities; made of it a dwelling place of the Most High; discovered the secret voice of God in the buried life that men call instinct; refused to heed any other command save this inner voice of God. With ebbing faith men may deny their own divine nature, but the divinity is not destroyed; the music of the indwelling Godhood murmurs in the shell till the tide returns to flood it again. The one great miracle is the daily rebirth of God in the individual soul; every day is a new day; every act is a fresh wonder; faith, hope, trust, accompany man in his adventurous journeyings. Why, therefore, demanded the transcendentalist, should he not **trust** himself? Why should he not walk confident in his own high purpose? Why should he doubt and question the buried compulsions that urge him forward? If he is indeed a child of God, let him live as unto God; and if it should turn out that there has been some mistake in the premises and he proves to be a child of the devil, then let him live as unto the devil. Better so than not to trust himself.

Quite obviously they were arch-romantics—these young poets of the new faith; children of an age given over to new hopes and disintegrating revolutions; inexperienced prophets of a world in flux, before the scientific spirit had stripped them of their wings. The fascinating book of nature and of man had been newly opened to them, and like Miranda they were ready to exclaim,

> O wonder!
> How many goodly creatures are there here!
> How beauteous mankind is! O brave new world,
> That has such people in 't!

They could see only God because in their thinking God had filled their minds. No evil lurked in the secret places of their hearts to whisper doubts concerning the goodness of life; no ominous clouds veiled the divine light that wrapped their universe about. After two hundred years of discipline in righteousness the old dogmatic pessimism was dissipated, leaving not a rack behind. The evil was gone and God remained; and in this new world the sons of God were to be henceforth heirs of the kingdom, free to fulfill that good which is the final reality. Arch-romantics, they were dreaming a transcendental dream, as other arch-romantics were dreaming their Jacksonian dream, their imperialistic dream, their Utopian dream. Romanticism comes to different issues in different men and different times: Emerson and Jefferson were unlike enough, as their worlds were unlike; but they were both romantics and their idealism was only a different expression of a common spirit.

Years after the transcendental ferment had subsided, one of the lesser prophets of the movement offered a statement of the faith that deserves to be recalled:

Transcendentalism [he said] relies on those ideas in the mind which are laws in the life. Pantheism is said to sink man and nature in God; Materialism to sink God and man in nature; and Transcendentalism to sink God and nature in man. But the Transcendentalist at least is belied and put in jail by the definition which is so neat at the expense of truth. He made consciousness, not sense, the ground of truth. . . . Is the soul reared on the primitive rock? or is no rock primitive, but the deposit of spirit—therefore in its lowest form alive, and ever rising into organism to reach the top of the eternal circle again, as in the well one bucket goes down empty and the other rises full? The mistake is to make the everlasting things subjects of argument instead of sight. . . . Our soul is older than our organism. It precedes its clothing. It is the cause, not the consequence, of its material elements; else, as materialists understand, it does not exist. . . . What is it that accepts misery from the Most High, defends the Providence that inflicts its woes, espouses its chastiser's cause, purges itself in the pit of its misery of all contempt of His commands, and makes its agonies the beams and rafters of the triumph it builds? It is the immortal principle. It is an indestructible essence. It is part and parcel of the Divinity it adores. It can no more die than he can. It needs no more insurance of life than its author does. Prove its title? It is proof of all things else. It is substantive, and everything adjective beside. It is the kingdom all things will be added to. (C. A. Bartol, quoted by Frothingham in *Transcendentalism in New England*, Chapter XIV.)

This is sheer mysticism, and mystics in greater or less degree all the transcendentalists were—isolated and lonely in the midst of men, seeking always a larger fellowship, awaiting those fleeting moments of illumination that should light up the meaning of life. "Mine is a certain brief experience," says Emerson, "which surprised me in the highway or in the market, in some place, at some time,—whether in the body or out of the body, God knoweth, —and made me aware that I had played the fool with fools all this time, but that law existed for me and for all; that to me belong trust, a child's trust and obedience, and the worship of ideas, and I should never be fool more" (*The Transcendentalist*). Fleeting and incommunicable are such illuminations, yet like the clear sunlight to eyes that are open. "If you do not need to hear my thought, because you can read it in my face and behavior, then I will tell it you from sunrise to sunset. If you cannot divine it, you would not understand what I say" (*ibid.*). And because the realist found himself quite incapable of such understanding, the transcendentalist turned away from him to live by himself. "They feel that they are never so fit for friendship, as when they have quitted mankind, and taken themselves to friend."

Such an attitude of mind may easily become the father of criticism. Communing with the ideal rarely begets complacency; the actual seems poor and mean in comparison with the potential. Hence the transcendentalists, willingly or not, were searching critics of their generation. They were impatient of any falling short of the ideal, and their lives in consequence became an open indictment of a Yankee world given over to materialism. "By their unconcealed dissatisfaction," said Emerson, "they expose our poverty, and the insignificance of man to man." "Their quarrel with every man they meet, is not with his kind, but with his degree. There is not enough of him,—that is the only fault. . . . They make us feel the strange disappointment which overcasts every human youth. So many promising youths, and never a finished man!" (*The Transcendentalist*.)

As to the general course of living, and the daily employments of men, they cannot see much virtue in these, since they are parts of this vicious circle; and as no great ends are answered by the men, there is nothing noble in the arts by which they are maintained. Nay, they have made the experiment, and found that, from the liberal professions to the coarsest manual labor, and from the courtesies of the academy and the college to the conventions of the cotillion-room and the morning call, there is a spirit of cowardly compromise and se?ming, which indicates a frightful skepticism, a life without love, and an activity without aim. (*Ibid.*)

Idealists though they were, they could not escape meddling with the real which encompassed them on all sides—with institutions, laws, society, with the state itself. They were far more interested in God than in Cæsar, and they found it impossible to divide loyalties that too often clashed. When Cæsar essayed to impose his will upon theirs, when he put their ideals in jeopardy by demanding allegiance to laws they did not approve, they quietly denied him sovereignty and followed their own paths. With such men nothing could be done; their very lives were a criticism and a judgment on New England and America. Transcendentalism may have run into its follies, but foolish in its critical judgment—blind to the gap between profession and reality—it was not. It might be severe, but it was honest and intelligent, and honest intelligent criticism America stood greatly in need of.

CHAPTER II

RALPH WALDO EMERSON
Transcendental Critic

AT the age of thirty-six the man who was to become the most searching critic of contemporary America expressed his conception of his mission in the following passage:

> What shall be the substance of my shrift? Adam in the garden, I am to new-name all the beasts of the field and all the gods in the sky. I am to invite men drenched in Time to recover themselves and come out of time, and taste their native immortal air. I am to fire with what skill I can the artillery of sympathy and emotion. I am to indicate constantly, though all unworthy, the Ideal and Holy Life, the life within life, the Forgotten Good, the Unknown Cause in which we sprawl and sin. I am to try the magic of sincerity, that luxury permitted only to kings and poets. I am to celebrate the spiritual powers in their infinite contrast to the mechanical powers and the mechanical philosophy of this time. I am to console the brave sufferers under evils whose end they cannot see, by appeals to the great optimism, self-affirmed in all bosoms. (*Journals*, Vol. V, p. 288.)

Seven days before Emerson set down this transcendental pronouncement, he had written in his journal a different comment:

> A question which well deserves examination now is the Dangers of Commerce. This invasion of Nature by Trade with its Money, its Credit, its Steam, its Railroad, threatens to upset the balance of man, and establish a new, universal Monarchy more tyrannical than Babylon or Rome. Very faint and few are the poets or men of God. Those who remain are so antagonistic to this tyranny that they appear mad or morbid, and are treated as such. Sensible of this extreme unfitness they suspect themselves. And all of us apologize when we ought not, and congratulate ourselves when we ought not. (*Ibid.*, Vol. V, pp. 285–6.)

In such comments and others scattered plentifully through his Journals, Emerson essayed to make clear to himself the function of transcendental criticism as he felt himself called to practice it. It was to be no trivial or easy duty. In the midst of a boastful materialism, shot through with cant and hypocrisy and every insincerity, fat and slothful in all higher things, the critic proposed to try the magic of sincerity, to apply the test of spiritual values to the material forces and mechanical philosophies of the times. His very life must embody criticism; his every act and word must pronounce judgment on the barren and flatulent gods served by his countrymen. He must be a thinker and as such he must summon to the bar of a nobler philosophy the current standards of value and conduct. Men of the greatest reputation must not be spared; he must "issue a *quo warranto* and revoke the characters of fame," overruling the verdict of newspaper editors and the acclaim of the electorate. Here was a revolutionary business indeed, that the critic was proposing to himself; and the calm serenity with which he set about it was disconcerting. A thinker loose in the America of Daniel Webster, a thinker who proposed to test men and measures by the magic of sincerity, was likely to prove an unpleasantly disturbant factor in a world of pretense. Measured by such standards the current philosophies must bate and dwindle, and the common ideals shrink to the mean and paltry. The life of an honest thinker laid on the America of 1840 would reveal how far short it came from the stature of intellectual manhood.

Emerson the critic has been too much obscured to common view by Emerson the brilliant dispenser of transcendental aphorisms. The oracular *Essays* with their confident wisdom—the sententious expression of the middle period of a life that came to late maturity—interpose themselves between the young priest whose intellectual interests quietly detached themselves from Unitarian orthodoxy, and the mature critic whose loyalties quietly detached themselves from the gods of his generation. The very brilliancy of the *Essays* conceals the laborious processes by which their abundant wisdom was distilled. One must go to the *Journals* for that—to those intimate records that reveal how patiently he sought for truth and how honestly he followed it. Wisdom did not come to him of its own accord; it was painfully groped for. As an introspective Puritan youth he began early to keep a diary of his intellectual life, gathering into successive journals the savings from his discursive readings. For years as a quiet student he lived in a world of moral aphorisms, a cold, thin atmosphere where gnomic phrases bloomed and ancient oracles uttered judgment. This was the seedtime of his mind. He was making acquaintance with the noble dead, gathering their utterances to make for himself a new testament. "No man could be better occupied," he said later, "than in making his own bible by harkening to all those sentences which now here, now there, now in nursery rhymes, now in Hebrew, now in English bards, thrill him like the sound of a trumpet." As a young man he made this his chief concern. His early journals are an ample nursery where cuttings from all philosophies are set out, there to grow into such plants as circumstance should permit. The ancestral cult of the book was in his blood, and living as he did under the threat of ill health, none too confident that the years would lengthen out before him, he forced himself to a severe intellectual regimen. To invest his days wisely was his single purpose. He wanted only the best securities for his investments, and what he got he carefully deposited, together with the increments of his own thought, to draw upon at later need. There were no wastrel forays in his intellectual life, no unpruned riot of growth, but the very odds and ends of his meditation were carefully treasured to be used when other materials were lacking. Fortunately the stuff was of good quality that outlasted many makings-over, till finally he got the cut to his liking. From this discipline of years came his superlative mastery of the sententious sentence; his brilliant utterances are rich with the thought he has crammed into them.

The cheerful serenity that never deserted him was a triumph of will over circumstance. It was a singularly cheerless world that bred him, subsisting by sheer will power, eating its heart out with heroic ambitions, too grimly earnest to enjoy what it got so laboriously—the lean aftermath of two centuries of asceticism. The business of plain living and high thinking was a joyless manner of life, and the young Emerson got little pleasure from it. A nature less insulated must have broken under the strain. It was a world stricken with tuberculosis. Of the five brothers one was mentally defective, another burnt up his vitality and went to the West Indies to die, a third of brilliant powers succumbed to consumption, his first wife died of the same scourge, his second wife and Emerson himself were long affected with incipient tuberculosis. To ease such anxious lives there was need of a great solace, and that solace was sought in religion. The ascetic youth ran as naturally to religious meditation as a normal child to play. No call to conversion ever came to him; the natural man postulated in Calvinistic dogma was washed out of him before he was born. The earlier jottings in the journals, before philosophy came to soften the inherited asceticism, and a transcendental revulsion from the common pessimism had turned him into a serene optimist, often are as bleak and austerely introspective as those morbid human documents that fill the old libraries of Puritanism. Such meditations are thin gruel for the nourishment of a vigorous life, and Emerson must have suffered from innutrition if he had not come upon more substantial food.

Fortunately the old Puritan anchors were already dragging, and Emerson was pretty well adrift when the romantic surge caught him and sent him far along new courses. The Puritan moralizer became the transcendental seeker; the curious-minded loiterer in the gates of the temple, who had studied the moral winds by watching the tiny straws of circumstance—erecting unconsidered trifles into ethical signposts—calmly quitted the church and set forth on his intellectual quest. The ties had long been loosening, but it was his year abroad where he discovered ways of thinking unknown to Concord and Boston, that effectively liberalized his mind and released him from the narrow Yankee provincialisms. On that momentous trip Goethe, Landor, Coleridge, Wordsworth, Carlyle, set him speculating on new themes, stimulating afresh the love of Plato, in whom he had long found inspiration. Continental idealism with its transcendental metaphysics refashioned Emerson and put him upon his life-work.

Speaking of the intellectual revival of New England later in life, he remarked that "Goethe was the cow from whom their milk was drawn"; but it would seem that the influence of Wordsworth proved more immediately stimulating, for on his return home Emerson set about the systematic contemplation of nature which left so considerable a deposit in his mind. Before this he had been too intent on his soul to consider the sunshine on the fields, but thereafter he made his pilgrimages into the country with the seriousness of one conducting a novel experiment. In this new concern for nature there was a deliberate self-consciousness. In temperament he was a bookish recluse, in love with the printed page. He was not a Thoreau to love his Walden Pond for its own sake, and it needed an effort of the will to send him as far as Auburn wood, to lie on his back and translate nature into metaphysic. But he had come to the point where his developing philosophy must send him into the fields. He had looked within himself and discovered the divinity of the individual soul; but he had not probed the non-self, the great encompassing universe of matter

by which the individual is circumscribed and of which he is a part.
To discover there the diffused presence of God, to feel his kinship
with man, to understand that the soul is a microcosm, were necessary preliminaries to the unfolding of his transcendental philosophy, and he went about the work with painstaking thoroughness.
From this creative contact with nature emerged the Emerson we
know, radiant with idealism, glad of life; and this radiant gladness
he put into his maiden essay, *Nature*.

This was in 1836 when Emerson was thirty-three years of age.
In the next two years he published *The American Scholar*, quintessence of transcendental individualism, and the *Divinity School
Address*, the bible of transcendental religion. With the appearance
of the second series of *Essays*, six years later, the major ideas of his
philosophy were fully elaborated. Stripped of its idealistic phrase-
ology, of its beauty and fervor, the master idea of the Emersonian
philosophy is the divine sufficiency of the individual. In accepting
himself he accepted his fellows, and he accepted God. The universe he conceived of as a divine whole, whereof each man is his
own center from whom flows the life that has flowed in upon him,
perennially fresh, perennially a new creation. The law for things
is not the law for mind; man is unkinged in acknowledging any
lesser sovereignty than the sovereignty of self. Statutes, constitutions, governments, schools, churches, banks, trade—the
coercing sum of institutions and customs—these things do not
signify; they are only idols with clay feet that blind men worship.
The true divinity dwells elsewhere, in the soul of man; and that
divinity must rule the world and not be ruled by it. The apotheosis of individualism—such in briefest terms was the gospel of
Emerson; new only in its radiant dress and idealistic sanctions, the
final transcendental form of a doctrine spread widely by the
French romantic school. It was the same revolutionary conception
that Channing had come upon, that Jefferson had come upon, that
Rousseau had come upon—the idea which in the guise of political
romanticism had disintegrated the *ancien régime*, and in the form
of philosophical romanticism had disintegrated eighteenth-century
rationalism—the idea that was providing Utopian dreams for an
ebullient democratic faith.

Thus equipped with a philosophy Emerson was prepared to
begin his work as a critic. The ideal he had drunk of was a perennial condemnation of the material. The mean and ignoble ends

pursued by a mean and ignoble society were a challenge to the serenity of his faith, and he must set himself to analyze the causes of the low estate to which the potential sons of God had fallen. Lesser revolutions in thought were implicit in this greater one, revolutions which Emerson was bound to go through with. Despite the jaunty optimism of which he was often accused, his eyes were never blind to reality; to see, and measure, and judge, was to become his life business. He did not shrink from the ugliest fact, and the unhappy condition he discovered men to be in would have discouraged a less robust faith. At times even he doubted. At times he seems half persuaded, with Cotton Mather, that the potential children of light are "strangely and fiercely possessed of the devil." "Human nature is as bad as it dares to be," he commented in his journal; and at another time, "If it were possible to repair the rottenness of human nature . . . it were well" (*Journals*, Vol. VIII, p. 259).

In seeking an explanation of the tragic gap between the real and the ideal, he came to attribute a large measure of the cause, like the eighteenth-century romantics, to pernicious social institutions which stifle the nobler impulses and encourage the baser; and he became convinced likewise that the work to which the critic was called was the work of liberation, setting the mind free from false and ignoble loyalties that it might serve the true. He prepared therefore to lay his transcendental yardstick on the little world of Yankee reality and judge how far short it came of its potential divinity. New England had never been scrutinized so searchingly, measured so justly. Serene, imperturbable, he set the ideal in one pan of the scales, and all the New England realities in the other, and bade his neighbors see how the balance tipped. For a generation he was the conscience of America, a pricker of inflated balloons, a gauger of the national brag and cant and humbug. With keen insight he put his finger on the mean and selfish and the great and generous. He surveyed his world with the detachment of posterity and anticipated the slower judgment of time. His penetration was uncanny and few of his judgments on men and measures have suffered reversal in the court of final jurisdiction.

So shrewd a critic must concern himself greatly with the Jacksonian revolution that was hurrying America towards the acceptance of political equalitarianism. By every compulsion of his transcendental philosophy Emerson was driven to accept the abstract principle of democracy. He understood well what hopes for human betterment were awakened by the principle of majority rule, and as he followed the noise and tumult of the political campaigns he was driven to definition. In 1834 he commented in his journal:

The root and seed of democracy is the doctrine, Judge for yourself. Reverence thyself. It is the inevitable effect of the doctrine, where it has any effect (which is rare), to insulate the partisan, to make each man a state. At the same time it replaces the dead with a living check in a true, delicate reverence for superior, congenial minds. "How is the King greater than I, if he is not more just?" (*Journals*, Vol. III, p. 369.)

Somewhat later in the same year he suggested:

Democracy, Freedom, has its root in the sacred truth that every man hath in him the divine Reason, or that, though few men since the creation of the world live according to the dictates of Reason, yet all men are created capable of so doing. That is the equality and the only equality of all men. To this truth we look when we say, Reverence thyself; Be true to thyself. (*Ibid.*, Vol. III, p. 390.)

When I . . . speak of the democratic element, I do not mean that ill thing, vain and loud, which writes lying newspapers, spouts at caucuses, and sells its lies for gold; but that spirit of love for the general good whose name this assumes. There is nothing of the true democratic element in what is called Democracy; it must fall, being wholly commercial. I beg I may not be understood to praise anything which the soul in you does not honor, however grateful may be names to your ear and your pocket. (*Ibid.*, Vol. IV, p. 95.)

His deepening concern over the state of politics in America—the property-mindedness of the Whigs and the mob-mindedness of the Democrats—drew him into an analysis of political parties and the nature of the political state. He was little read in the political classics, and although he professed a mild approval of Montesquieu and was never tired of praising Burke, he was little influenced by either. The latter's political theory, indeed, was so fundamentally hostile to Emerson's major convictions—so legalistic in its reverence for government from the grave, so explicit in denial of new-born rights—that it is a fair assumption that Emerson never took the trouble to understand him but was content to enjoy his glowing rhetoric. Later commentators are too much given to glossing over Emerson's political theory, not approving its implications; or explaining it away by appeal to certain com-

ments jotted down when his nerves were tried by enthusiasts; [1]
but there is no explaining away a theory that was the logical expression of his transcendental philosophy, unless his whole philosophy be explained away. Emerson knew very well where his
political theory led, and he had no timid compunction about following it through.

In his speculations on the nature and functions of the ideal
republic—a theme that was much in his mind—he elaborated
what we may call the transcendental theory of politics, a theory
closely akin to philosophical anarchism. All the elaborate machinery devised by political thinkers like Montesquieu and John Adams,
with their schemes of checks and balances to preserve the *status
quo*, he calmly throws overboard; constitutions he is not interested
in, nor the complicated props of coercive sovereignty. The
single, vital, principle on which the true republic must found itself,
he insists, is the principle of good-will. Since "governments have
their origin in the moral identity of men," the recognition of a
common human nature with common interests must induce rational
men to enter a common political brotherhood; and until men become wise enough voluntarily to coöperate to the common well-
being, no good government is possible. The history of governments hitherto is a history of the tragic failure of men to achieve
a rational political state. "The idea, after which each community
is aiming to make and mend its law," he suggests in the *Essay on
Politics*, following Carlyle, "is the will of the wise man. The wise
man, it cannot find in nature, and it makes awkward but earnest
efforts to secure government by contrivance." But he does not
push his "wise man" theory to the patriarchal absolutism of
Carlyle; with Channing he postulates an ethical sovereignty above
the instrument. "Absolute right is the first governor; or, every
government is an impure theocracy."

The doctrine of good-will establishes government in "moral
identity"; it "separates the individual from all party, and unites
him at the same time to the race"; and in so doing it accepts the
sovereignty of the ethical absolute. This major conception of
Channing's Emerson took over and made his own. He is explicit
in his assertion of the need of a moral interpretation of the doctrine
of natural rights. The doctrine of an ethical sovereignty, he
asserts,

[1] See, for example, *Journals*, Vol. VII, p. 221.

. . . promises a recognition of higher rights than those of personal freedom, or the security of property. A man has a right to be employed, to
be trusted, to be loved, to be revered. The power of love, as the basis of
a State, has never been tried. . . . There will always be a government of
force where men are selfish; and when they are pure enough to abjure the
code of force they will be wise enough to see how these public ends of the
post-office, of the highway, of commerce and the exchange of property,
of museums and libraries, of institutions of art and science can be answered.

    Every man's nature is a sufficient advertisement to him of the character
of his fellows. My right and my wrong is their right and their wrong.
Whilst I do what is fit for men, and abstain from what is unfit, my neighbor
and I shall often agree in our means, and work together for a time to one
end. But whenever I find my dominion over myself not sufficient for me,
and undertake the direction of him also, I overstep the truth, and come
into false relations to him. I may have so much more skill or strength than
he that he cannot express adequately his sense of wrong, but it is a lie, and
hurts like a lie both him and me. Love and nature cannot maintain the
assumption; it must be executed by a practical lie, namely by force. This
undertaking for another is the blunder which stands in colossal ugliness
in the governments of the world. . . . For any laws but those which men
make for themselves are laughable. . . . This is the history of government,—one man does something which is to bind another. . . . Hence
the less government we have the better,—the fewer laws, and the less
confided power. The antidote to this abuse of formal government is the
influence of private character, the growth of the individual . . . the
appearance of the wise man; of whom the existing government, is, it must
be owned, but a shabby imitation. . . . To educate the wise man the
State exists, and with the appearance of the wise man the State expires.
The appearance of character makes the State unnecessary. The wise
man is the State. (*Essay on Politics.*)

    Thus in transcendental fashion does Emerson range himself on
the side of Jefferson, in opposition to a coercive sovereignty. A
strong and energetic government he feared as an efficient instrument of tyranny; and of the several contrivancies by which it
enforced its will, he considered the police power the stupidest.
As a sensible man he bore with the state; he would pay his taxes;
he would not strain at gnats; but as a free man he would not suffer
the state to coerce him; he would destroy it first. There is a passage
in his journal, written at the time of the declaration of war against
Mexico—when Alcott and Thoreau refused to pay their taxes—
that states his position with whimsical directness:

    The State is a poor, good beast who means the best: it means friendly.
A poor cow who does well by you,—do not grudge it its hay. It cannot

eat bread, as you can; let it have without grudge a little grass for its four stomachs. It will not stint to yield you milk from its teat. You, who are a man walking cleanly on two feet, will not pick a quarrel with a poor cow. Take this handful of clover and welcome. But if you go to hook me when I walk in the fields, then, poor cow, I will cut your throat. (*Journals*, Vol. VII, p. 220.)

With equal emphasis he rejected the economic interpretation of politics. As a child of the romantic revolution he understood quite clearly how the waves of humanitarian aspiration broke on the reefs of property rights, how economic forces were in league against the ideal republic. There could be no true democracy till this matter of economics was put in subordination to higher values. Both the political parties, the respectable Whigs and the voluble Democrats, he was convinced, were debauched by it; the one served property openly, the other secretly. "From neither party, when in power, has the world any benefit to expect in science, art, or humanity, at all commensurate with the resources of the nation." Emerson did not deny the fact of the universal appeal of economics. He could not, of course, accept the theory of economic determinism; but he was convinced that the whole matter must be probed deeply:

The philosophy of property, if explored in its foundations, would open new mines of practical wisdom, which would in the event change the face of the world; would destroy the whole magazine of dissimulation, for so many ages reckoned the Capital art of Government. It would purge that rottenness which has defamed the whole Science until *politic* has come to mean cunning. . . . It would go deep into ethics and touch all the relations of men. (*The Present Age.*)

Pending such exploration it was clear to Emerson that the Federalist-Whig theory of a stake-in-society, or rulership by persons of principle and property, was wholly vicious:

The theory of politics which has possessed the minds of men, and which they have expressed the best they could in their laws and in their revolutions, considers persons and property as the two objects for whose protection government exists. Of persons, all have equal rights, in virtue of being identical in nature. This interest of course with its whole power demands a democracy. Whilst the rights of all as persons are equal, in virtue of their access to reason, their rights in property are very unequal. . . . Personal rights, universally the same, demand a government framed on the ratio of the census; property demands a government framed on the ratio of owners and owning. . . . That principle no longer looks so self-evident as it appeared in former times, partly because doubts have arisen whether too much weight had not been allowed in laws to property, and such a structure given to our usages as allowed the rich to encroach upon the poor, and keep them poor; but mainly because there is an instinctive sense, however obscure and yet inarticulate, that the whole constitution of property, on its present tenures, is injurious, and its influence on persons deteriorating and degrading; that property will always follow persons; that the highest end of government is the culture of men. (*Essay on Politics.*)

In such suggestions as he offered touching the form of the ideal republic, where "every child that is born must have a just chance for his bread," Emerson reveals a pronounced bias in favor of the Physiocratic theory of society. He was at one with Jefferson in preferring an agrarian to an industrial order. Manchester economics—the doctrine of the economic man, of the iron law of wages, and other obscenities of the school—he quite frankly loathed. He did not, he said, "look with sour aspect at the industrious manufacturing village, or mart of commerce"; but he would not glorify the machine, nor reduce man to a factory hand. He questioned the sufficiency or finality of the division of labor. There is more than a suggestion of William Morris in the doctrine elaborated in *Man the Reformer;* that the industrial revolution with its factory system, must be judged in the light of its effect upon the workingman, that the true function of work must be explored and every man ply his tool to his own good. The suggestion that "a man should have a farm or mechanical craft for his culture," was an implicit denial of industrialism in the days of its first triumphs—a denial that Morris would have indorsed.

We must have a basis for our higher accomplishments, our delicate entertainments of poetry and philosophy, in the work of our hands. We must have an antagonism in the tough world for all the variety of our spiritual faculties, or they will not be born. Manual labor is the study of the external world. The advantages of riches remains with him who produces them, not with the heir.
I should not be pained at a change which threatened a loss of some of the luxuries or conveniences of society, if it proceeded from a preference of the agricultural life out of the belief, that our primary duties as men could be better discharged in that calling. . . . But the doctrine of the Farm is merely this, that every man ought to stand in primary relations with the work of the world, ought to do it himself, and not to suffer the accident of his having a purse in his pocket, or his having been bred to some dishonorable and injurious craft, to sever him from those duties; and for this reason, that labor is God's education; that he only is a sincere

learner, he only can become a master, who learns the secret of labor, and who by real cunning extorts from nature its sceptre. (*Man the Reformer.*)

In all this—in the doctrine of the minimized state, of the sacred rights of the individual, of the wholesomeness of an agricultural life; in his concern for social justice and his tenderness for the poor and exploited among men—Emerson proved himself a child of the romantic eighteenth century, who by his own transcendental path had come upon the Utopia that an earlier generation had dreamed of, and which he sketched in the lovely poem prefacing the *Essay on Politics*. Much of Emerson is compressed in these lines:

> Fear, Craft, and Avarice,
> Cannot rear a State.
> Out of dust to build
> What is more than dust. . . .
> When the Muses nine
> With the Virtues meet,
> Find to their design
> An Atlantic seat,
> By green orchard boughs
> Fended from the heat,
> Where the statesman ploughs
> Furrow for the wheat;
> When the Church is social worth,
> When the state-house is the hearth,
> Then the perfect State is come,
> The republican at home.

The contrast between such Utopian conceptions and the realities of America in the forties was calculated to edge the critical judgment with a certain asperity. The older agrarian simplicity of New England was being submerged by the industrial revolution, and in the midst of the change Emerson quietly pronounced judgment upon the new idols of his generation, upon State Street and Beacon Street, upon Webster and Clay and Douglas, upon Everett and Choate, upon black slavery and white, upon the Mexican War and the Fugitive Slave Bill, upon the stolid poor and the callous rich. His judgment was severe but it was never unjust. His later journals are a rich storehouse of critical comment, keen, illuminating, disastrous in its analysis of all cant and humbug. At times—in his comment on Webster, in his hatred of State Street, in his criticism of the common materialism—he is almost savage; at other times he is consumed with a vast sympathy for the long-suffering, exploited mass of the people. "Alas, for the majority," he exclaimed, "that old, inevitable dupe and victim. What a dreary Iliad of woes it goes wailing and mad withal. Some dog of a Cleon or Robespierre or Douglas is always riding it to ruin" (*Journals*, Vol. VIII, p. 449). When the Fugitive Slave Bill passed he wrote: "This filthy enactment was made in the nineteenth century, by people who could read and write. I will not obey it, by God" (*ibid.*, Vol. VIII, p. 236). In smug and prosperous Boston he found no comfort—the Boston that applauded when "Thank-God Choate thanked God five times" in denouncing "the trashy sentimentalism of our lutestring enthusiasts." Emerson would have none of Boston:

In Boston is no company for a fine wit. There is a certain *poor-smell* in all the streets, in Beacon Street and Mount Vernon, as well as in the lawyers' offices, and the wharves, and the same meanness and sterility, and leave-all-hope-behind, as one finds in a boot manufacturer's premises. (*Ibid.*, Vol. VIII, p. 363.)

With Theodore Parker he judged Boston to be the home of Hunkers, of that "cotton aristocracy" that Webster served. It groveled servilely before State Street; how should the homely moralities get a hearing in such a place? Even Harvard College he charged with being a tool of the Boston counting-houses.[2]

It was the crass materialism of America, of the Democrats equally with the Whigs, of the northern capitalists equally with the southern planters, that drove him to exasperation, and tempered his optimism. There is no jaunty optimism in a passage written during the panic days of '37:

. . . Society has played out its last stake; it is checkmated. Young men have no hope. Adults stand like day-laborers idle in the streets. None calleth us to labor. The old wear no crown of warm life on their gray hairs. The present generation is bankrupt of principles and hope, as of property. I see man is not what man should be. He is a treadle of a wheel. He is the tassel at the apron-string of society. He is a money-chest. He is the servant of his belly. This is the causal bankruptcy, this the cruel oppression, that the ideal should serve the actual, that the head

---

[2] "Harvard College has no voice in Harvard College, but State Street votes it down on every ballot. Everything will be permitted there which goes to adorn Boston whiggism; . . . but that which it exists for,—to be a fountain of novelties out of heaven, a Delphi uttering warning and ravishing oracles to elevate and lead mankind,—*that* it shall not be permitted to do or to think of. On the contrary, every generosity of thought is *suspected*, and gets a bad name." (*Ibid.*, Vol. IX, p. 215.)

should serve the feet. . . . Pride, and Thrift, and Expediency, who jeered and chirped and were so well pleased with themselves, and made merry with the dream, as they termed it, of Philosophy and Love,— behold they are all flat, and here is the Soul erect and unconquered still. What answer is it now to say, It has always been so? I acknowledge that, as far back as I can see the widening procession of humanity, the marchers are lame and blind and deaf; but to the soul that whole past is but one finite series in its infinite scope. Deteriorating ever and now desperate. Let me begin anew; let me teach the finite to know its master. (*Journals*, Vol. IV, p. 242.)

To be a critic rather than a fighter, and a critic because he was a poet and philosopher—this was the duty laid upon Emerson; and yet he was sorely troubled when men from the skirmish line of social conflict reported to him the need of leaders. Why should he be privileged to remain in his study when slaves were abducted on the streets of Boston and John Brown was fighting at Harper's Ferry? With the extremest reluctance he was drawn into the struggle—it was not his fight.

I waked at night [he recorded in his journal] and bemoaned myself, because I had not thrown myself into this deplorable question of Slavery, which seems to want nothing so much as a few assured voices. But then, in hours of sanity, I recover myself, and say, "God must govern his own world, and knows his own way out of this pit, without my desertion of my post, which has none to guard it but me. I have quite other slaves to free than those negroes, to wit, imprisoned spirits, imprisoned thoughts, far back in the brain of man,—far retired in the heaven of invention, and which, important to the republic of Man, have no other watchman, or lover, or defender, but I." (*Ibid.*, Vol. VIII, p. 316.)

But always in the end he was drawn in, and none spoke wiser or braver words to a careless generation. He never faltered, never compromised; the prophet of the ideal faced the real and told the truth about it, serenely and with clear insight. His heroes were not the heroes of State Street; Horace Greeley, Theodore Parker, Horace Mann, Henry Ward Beecher, he accounted the great Americans of his day, and not Everett and Webster and Clay and Calhoun. A friend of civilization, he was partisan only to the ideal; to justice, truth, righteousness. A Yankee of the Yankees, a Puritan of the Puritans, he had emancipated himself from all that was mean and ungenerous in the one and harsh and illiberal in the other. A free soul, he was the flowering of two centuries of spiritual aspiration—Roger Williams and Jonathan Edwards come to more perfect fruition.

CHAPTER III

HENRY THOREAU
Transcendental Economist

"Wisdom crieth in the streets and no man regardeth her"; yet "she teacheth temperance and forethought, justice and fortitude; than which men can have in their life nothing more profitable."

The single business of Henry Thoreau, during forty-odd years of eager activity, was to discover an economy calculated to provide a satisfying life. His one concern, that gave to his ramblings in Concord fields a value as of high adventure, was to explore the true meaning of wealth. Honest, fearless, curiously inquisitive—a masterless man who would give no hostages to fortune—he proved his right to be called a philosopher by seeking wisdom as a daily counselor and friend, and following such paths only as wisdom suggested. Out of his own experience, tested in the clear light of the Greeks, he wrote a transcendental declaration of independence that may be taken as the final word of the Concord school touching the great issues of practical living. *Walden* is the handbook of an economy that endeavors to refute Adam Smith and transform the round of daily life into something nobler than a mean gospel of plus and minus.

It was the common opinion of his neighbors that Henry Thoreau was a queer fellow who had somehow got all his values topsy-turvy. And yet the more thoughtfully one considers him, the more doubtful it appears whether the queerness lay with him or with his critics. Unfortunately a wholly honest and original man is so rare as to fall under common suspicion. To the inmates of Bedlam a sane man will appear queer. In a society of serfs a masterless man will be accounted an outlaw. To the Concord farmers Thoreau appeared strange only because he applied in his daily life a truth they assented to on the Sabbath. The principle that life is more than the meat and the body than raiment was familiar enough to the Sunday doctrines of Concord; but that a man should seriously apply it on week-days; that he should propose to regulate his mid-week activities by the economy of the Sermon on the

Mount, passed the comprehension of practical Yankees who followed quite another economy. It was Thoreau's conduct that perplexed them, rather than his philosophy.

From first to last that conduct was serenely logical. To this disciple of the ancient wisdom, Sabbath and week-day were one, and in seeking to square his daily life with the ancient precept, Thoreau became the arch-rebel of his group, the most individual amongst the "lunatic fringe" of the transcendental movement, the one who escapes elusively from the grip of an adjective. He slips out of all phrases devised to imprison him. "A bachelor of nature," Emerson, with his gift for cryptic phrase, called him; "poet-naturalist," Ellery Channing who knew him intimately, chose to call him. "I am a poet, a mystic, and a transcendentalist," Thoreau said of himself, disregarding his nature writings. Yet none of these phrases, true as they are, quite adequately sums him up. At the risk of committing a fresh futility, one may perhaps suggest that he was a Greek turned transcendental economist. His life seems to have been a persistent experiment in values. A philosopher of the open air who kept his mind clear and his nerves robust by daily contact with wind and weather; a mystic who pried curiously into the meaning of nature and was familiar with Hellenic and Oriental systems of thought; a Yankee, skilled in various homely crafts, yet rather interested in proving for himself what things were excellent and taking nothing on hearsay— Thoreau's chief business would seem to have been with life itself, and how it might best be lived by Henry Thoreau; how a rational being, in short, might enjoy the faculties God has given him, following the higher economy and not enslaving himself to the lower, so that when he came to die he might honestly say, I have lived.

Amongst the members of the transcendental school Thoreau was the one Concord man, born and bred there, literally of the soil and loving the things of the soil. His tireless rovings were commonly bounded by the familiar Concord horizons. His life had taken deep root in the Concord fields, and he refused to join the restless multitude of the *déracinés*, who seek novel experiences in a succession of transplantings. No English peasant ever clung to the home-acres with more loving tenacity. He was a countryman in instinct, distrusting the great city twenty miles away that disseminated its virus through the outlying villages and farms. The city was wedded to the economy of industrialism and exploitation. But as a child of Jean Jacques, Thoreau chose to believe that the road to heaven ran through the fields and not over the cobble-stones of Boston; he discovered an honest integrity of character oftener in the country than in Lowell mills, yet none too often there. It was easier to be free there, yet even in Concord village the herd mind was always laying springes to catch the unwary; and Thoreau would not be caught. He was poet and philosopher as well as countryman, and he weighed his own life and the life of his neighbors in the scales of Hellenic thought. He was surveyor of broader fields than his neighbor's wood-lot; was acquainted with other mysteries than the mystery of pencil-making. He desired other ends than those his shopkeeping, farm-tending neighbors served; he would not be encumbered as they were. He could not carry such gross impedimenta in his pack and be a free man; the pack was too heavy; and he proceeded to lighten it with a thoroughness that startled Concord. He "signed off" from Dr. Ripley's church; with Alcott, he refused to pay his poll tax: he severed his allegiance to the Commonwealth of Massachusetts and the Federal government; he rid himself of all concern at what Concord thought of his ways; he spoke out his honest convictions in the village Lyceum—convictions about John Brown and slavery and Massachusetts' part in sending negroes back to their masters—quite careless of the disapproval of Judge Hoar and other Concord dignitaries. Such a man had never before walked the village streets, and the spectacle filled his neighbors with amazement.

With so much useless luggage got rid of, Thoreau was ready to set about the high business of living. To outward appearance a somewhat angular Yankee, practical and capable, he was at heart a Greek, with the delight in the simple round of the seasons and a responsiveness to natural beauty that belonged to the older civi-lization. Brought up under the "pale negations" of Dr. Ripley's theology, he emerged a pagan. He was the most widely read in Greek literature of the Concord transcendentalists; had translated *Prometheus Bound*, and much of Pindar; and was completely at home in the clear Greek atmosphere. Who but a Hellenist could utter such words as these which serve as his apology for the Walden experiment?

I went to the woods because I wished to live deliberately, to front only the essential facts of life, and to see if I could learn what it had to teach, and not, when I came to die, discover that I had not lived. I did not wish to live what was not life, living is so dear; nor did I wish to practice resignation, unless it was quite necessary. I wanted to live deep and suck out all the marrow of life, to live so sturdily and Spartan-like as to put to rout all that was not life, to cut a broad swath and shave close, to drive life into a corner, and reduce it to its lowest terms, and, if it proved to be mean, why then to get the whole and genuine meanness of it, and publish its meanness to the world; or if it were sublime, to know it by experience, and be able to give a true account of it in my next excursion. (*Walden*, "What I Lived For.")

To seek Pan in a tired world and recover joys that have long been forgotten is a business that only a romantic will engage in; yet Thoreau set out on the quest with a clear-eyed purpose:

. . . My Good Genius seemed to say,—Go fish and hunt far and wide day by day,—farther and wider,—and rest thee by many brooks and hearth-sides without misgiving. Remember thy Creator in the days of thy youth. Rise free from care before the dawn, and seek adventures. Let the noon find thee by other lakes, and the night over-take thee everywhere at home. There are no larger fields than these, no worthier games than may here be played. Grow wild according to thy nature, like those sedges and brakes, which will never become English hay. Let the thunder rumble; what if it threaten ruin to farmer's crops? that is not its errand to thee. Take shelter under the cloud, while they flee to carts and sheds. Let not to get a living by thy trade, but thy sport. Enjoy the land, but own it not. Through want of enterprise and faith men are where they are, buying and selling, and spending their lives like serfs. (*Ibid.*, "Baker Farm.")

If the day and the night are such that you greet them with joy, and life emits a fragrance like flowers and sweet-scented herbs, is more elastic, more starry, more immortal,—that is your success. All nature is your congratulation, and you have cause momentarily to bless yourself. . . . The true harvest of my daily life is somewhat as intangible and indiscernible as the tints of morning or evening. It is a little star-dust caught, a segment of the rainbow which I have clutched. (*Ibid.*, "Higher Laws.")

To save one's soul has always been accounted in New England a matter worthy of a man's best effort, and Thoreau's days were given over to it with a single-heartedness without parallel even in New England. The Puritan, he believed, had suffered his high spiritual mission to be sacrificed to the economic; he would recover that mission by sacrificing the economic to the spiritual; but he would interpret the spiritual as a Hellenist rather than a Hebraist. The Christian other-worldliness seemed to him unduly regardless of the loveliness of this world. "Christianity," he says in the *Week*, "only hopes. It has hung its harp on the willows, and cannot sing a song in a strange land. It has dreamed a sad dream, and does not yet welcome the morning with joy."

I am not sure but I should betake myself in extremities to the liberal divinities of Greece, rather than to my country's God. . . . In my Pantheon, Pan still reigns in his pristine glory, with his ruddy face, his flowing beard, and his shaggy body, his pipe and his crook, his nymph Echo, and his chosen daughter Iambe; for the great God Pan is not dead, as was rumored. Perhaps of all the gods of New England and of ancient Greece, I am most constant at his shrine. (*The Week*, "Sunday.")

His extraordinarily frank evaluation of the New Testament, and of Calvinistic New England that had too long chewed the cud of conscience—"they did not know when to swallow their cud, and their lives of course yielded no milk"—is the work of a pagan from whom all creeds slip easily. Few more searching sermons have been preached in Massachusetts than the sermon that composed itself as Thoreau's boat floated down the Concord River, past the Billerica meeting-house where the honest villagers were worshiping the God of New England—a sermon that with fine irony summons minister and congregation to consider the deeper teachings of their sacred book.

I know of no book that has so few readers. There is none so truly strange, and heretical, and unpopular. To Christians, no less than Greeks and Jews, it is foolishness and a stumbling-block. There are, indeed, severe things in it which no man should read aloud but once. "Seek first the kingdom of heaven."—"Lay not up for yourself treasures on earth."—"If thou wilt be perfect, go and sell that thou hast, and give to the poor, and thou shalt have treasure in heaven."—"For what is a man profited, if he shall gain the whole world, and lose his own soul? or what shall a man give in exchange for his soul?"—Think of this, Yankees! . . . . Think of repeating these things to a New England audience! thirdly, fourthly, fifteenthly, till there are three barrels of sermons! Who, without cant, can read them aloud? Who, without cant, can hear them, and not go out of the meeting-house? They never *were* read, they never *were* heard. Let but one of these sentences be rightly read from any pulpit in the land, and there would not be left one stone of that meeting-house upon another.
 . . . When one enters a village, the church, not only really but from association, is the ugliest-looking building in it, because it is the one in which human nature stoops the lowest and is most disgraced. Certainly, such temples as these shall ere long cease to deform the landscape. . . . Really, there is no infidelity, now-a-days, so great as that which prays, and keeps the Sabbath, and rebuilds the churches. (*The Week*, "Sunday.")

As Thoreau understood the problem of economics there were three possible solutions open to him: to exploit himself, to exploit his fellows, or to reduce the problem to its lowest denominator. The first was quite impossible—to imprison oneself in a treadmill when the morning called to great adventure, to burden oneself with useless fardels when the pack must be kept light, was the folly of a slave mind. He had observed his neighbors closely and found little good in their way of self-exploitation.

I have travelled a good deal in Concord; and everywhere, in shops, and offices, and field, the inhabitants have appeared to me to be doing penance in a thousand remarkable ways. . . . How many a poor immortal soul have I met well-nigh crushed and smothered under its load, creeping down the road of life, pushing before it a barn seventy-five feet by forty, its Augean stables never cleansed, and one hundred acres of land, tillage, mowing, pasture and wood-lot. . . . The better part of the man is soon ploughed into the soil for compost. (*Walden*, "Economy.")

To exploit one's fellows seemed to Thoreau's sensitive social conscience an even grosser infidelity. The leisure of a slave driver, got by imprisoning his fellows in a treadmill, was an ignoble leisure from which came the empty vulgarity of modern life. "If I devote myself to other pursuits and contemplations," he said, "I must first see, at least, that I do not pursue them sitting upon another man's shoulders. I must get off him first, that he may pursue his contemplations, too." Freedom with abstinence seemed to him better than serfdom with material well-being, for he was only giving up the lesser to enjoy the greater, as was the privilege of the philosopher.

To be a philosopher is not merely to have subtle thoughts, nor even to found a school, but so to love wisdom as to live according to its dictates, a life of simplicity, independence, magnanimity, and trust. It is to solve some of the problems of life, not only theoretically, but practically. . . . When he has obtained those things which are necessary to life, there is another alternative than to obtain the superfluities; and that is, to adventure on life now, his vacation from humbler toil having commenced. (*Walden*, "Economy.")

It was the reply of the arch-individualist to the tyrannous complexities of society, and it set him apart even in the world of transcendentalism. Other members of the group professed to have found a better way out of the dilemma—the way of Brook Farm and

Fruitland; a richer life was to be achieved not by espousing poverty but by coöperation. But Thoreau could not adopt the
coöperative solution; he must either accept society as it was
or remove. Convinced that it was not worth accepting—that one
made a foolish bargain in selling oneself to it—he was content
to remove to Walden Pond. "I came into this world," he said,
"not chiefly to make this a good place to live in, but to live in it,
be it good or bad." "I desire to speak impartially on this point,
and as one not interested in the success or failure of the present
economical and social arrangement." He did not advocate that
other men should build cabins and live isolated. He had no wish
to dogmatize concerning the best mode of living—each must settle
that matter for himself. But that a satisfying life should be lived,
that the fox should somehow get free even though he left his tail
in the trap, he was vitally concerned about. "The youth may
build or plant or sail, only let him not be hindered from doing
that which he tells me he would like to do." Let him at least rid
himself of the false gospel of creature comforts, which men pay too
high a price for.

The story of Thoreau's emancipation from the lower economics
is the one romance of his life, and *Walden* is his great book. More
restrained than the *Week* and lacking the exuberant beauty of
the latter—its noble talk and scathing criticism—it is "informed
by a more explicit unifying philosophy." It is a book in praise
of life rather than of Nature, a record of calculating economies that
studied saving in order to spend more largely. But it is a book of
social criticism as well, in spite of its explicit denial of such a purpose, and in its speculations much of Carlyle and Ruskin and
William Morris crops out. In considering the true nature of economy he concluded, with Ruskin, that "the cost of a thing is
the amount of what I will call life which is required to be exchanged
for it, immediately or in the long run." Conceive of life as cheap,
a poor thing to be exploited, and the factory system becomes the
logical economic order; but conceive of it as dear, and the common
happiness the great objective of society, and quite another sort
of industrialism will emerge. Thoreau did not look with approval
on the rising city of Lowell, with its multiplying spindles and increasing proletariat, and he did not understand why Americans
should boast of a system that provided vulgar leisure for the
masters at the cost of serfdom for the workers.

Where is this division of labor to end? [he asks] and what object does it finally serve? I cannot believe that our factory system is the best mode by which men may get clothing. The condition of the operatives is becoming every day more like that of the English; and it cannot be wondered at, since, as far as I have heard or observed, the principal object is, not that mankind may be well and honestly clad, but, unquestionably, that the corporations may be enriched. (*Walden,* "Economy.")

The whole middle-class philosophy of exploitation was hateful to him, the middleman equally with the manufacturer. "Trade curses everything it touches; and though you trade in messages from heaven, the whole curse of trade attaches to the business." Men have been deceived by a false economy—lured by the bog lights away from the open fields to flounder in the miasmic marshes. While Ruskin was still pottering over Turner, Thoreau was elaborating in *Walden* the text: The only wealth is life.

In other bits *Walden* is curiously like *Hopes and Fears for Art,* and the drift of the whole is one with the revolutionary teachings of Morris, that the abiding satisfactions are those which spring from free creative work. This Yankee Greek had learned that it is a beautiful life back of the tool that creates beauty, and that if the work of our hands is ugly, it is because our lives are mean and sordid, affording no outlet for the free creative spirit. In New England, Puritan and Yankee alike had conspired against beauty, and the gods had taken revenge by clothing life in drab.

Before we can adorn our houses with beautiful objects the walls must be stripped, and beautiful housekeeping and beautiful living be laid for a foundation: now, a taste for the beautiful is most cultivated out of doors, where there is no house and no housekeeping.

What of architectural beauty I now see, I know has gradually grown from within outward, out of the necessities and character of the indweller, who is the only builder,—out of some unconscious truthfulness, and nobleness, without ever a thought for the appearance; and whatever additional beauty of this kind is destined to be produced will be preceded by a like unconscious beauty of life. The most interesting dwellings in this country, as the painter knows, are the most unpretending, humble log huts and cottages of the poor commonly; it is the life of the inhabitants whose shells they are, and not any peculiarity in their surfaces merely, which makes them *picturesque;* and equally interesting will be the citizen's suburban box, when his life shall be as simple and as agreeable to the imagination, and there is no straining after effect in the style of his dwelling. (*Walden,* "Economy.")

Thoreau needed only to have lived in a world that honored crafts-manship to have opened fully the vein of gold that Morris dug his philosophy from; he had the instinct of the craftsman but not his training. His turning from the workshop to the fields, hearing no call in the humdrum village economy to develop a beautiful craftsmanship, was an implied criticism of the common sterility of labor in every-day Concord; yet the honest sincerity of his nature led him to the conclusion that lies at the heart of the philosophy of the great English craftsman:

> None have so pleasant a time as they who in earnest seek to earn their bread. It is true actually as it is true really; it is true materially as it is true spiritually, that they who seek honestly and sincerely, with all their hearts and lives and strength, to earn their bread, do earn it, and it is sure to be very sweet to them.
>
> In short, I am convinced, both by faith and experience, that to maintain one's self on this earth is not a hardship but a pastime, if we will live simply and wisely; as the pursuits of the simpler nations are still the sports of the more artificial. It is not necessary that a man should earn his living by the sweat of his brow, unless he sweats easier than I do. (*Walden*, "Economy.")

At Walden Pond and on the Merrimac River Thoreau's mind was serene as the open spaces; but this Greek serenity was rudely disturbed when he returned to Concord village and found his neighbors drilling for the Mexican War, and when authority in the person of the constable came to him with the demand that he pay a due share to the public funds. The war to him was a hateful thing, stupid and unjust, waged for the extension of the obscene system of negro slavery; and Thoreau was brought sharply to consider his relations to the political state that presumed to demand his allegiance, willing or unwilling, to its acts. Under the stress of such an emergency the transcendentalist was driven to examine the whole theory of the relation of the individual to the state. He was not political-minded; he had concerned himself little with political theory; he would gladly let the government alone if government would let him alone; he was even prepared to make excuses for government. But he would not compromise with his conscience; and when the state applied the principle of coercion, he applied the counter principle of passive resistance. It was while he was domiciled in Walden cabin that the hand of the law seized him and thrust him into Concord jail. He went with the constable quietly, but there was a dangerous contempt

in his heart. It seemed absurd that a man could not go to the
cobbler's for a pair of mended boots, but he must be interfered
with by a neighbor playing the rôle of constable. Constable,
jailer, the magistrate on the bench, all the elaborate machinery of
the law, Thoreau contemplated quizzically and judged his neighbors fools to have exchanged their freedom for such masquerades.
Those who got anything from such instruments—lawyers and prop-
ertied men—might think well of them, but they were a mere
impertinence to Thoreau who wanted to go huckleberrying. When
they let him out he went quietly after his berries, and discovered
there was "no state in sight among the berry bushes." "I saw,"
he remarked casually, "that the state was half-witted, that it was
as timid as a lone woman with her silver spoons, and that it did
not know its friends from its foes, and I lost all my remaining
respect for it and pitied it."

But Thoreau was not done with the comedy. It set him upon
thinking, and the result was the essay, *Civil Disobedience*. Taken
by itself alone, it is a somewhat astonishing performance. This
Yankee transcendentalist quite evidently has turned philosophical anarchist. But read in the light of Emerson's *Journals*, or
in the light of Godwin's *Political Justice*, it is easily comprehensible.
It is no more than transcendental individualism translated into
politics, with all comfortable compromises swept away. Its
sources run straight back to eighteenth-century liberalism with its
doctrine of the minimized state—a state that must lose its coercive sovereignty in the measure that the laws of society function
freely. Very likely Thoreau had never read Godwin, yet his
political philosophy was implicit in *Political Justice*. In Godwin's
thinking the problem of man in society is the problem of a voluntary adjustment of the individual to the state; and it is only by
establishing economics and politics on morality, that political
justice is possible. The moral law is the fundamental law, superior
to statutes and constitutions; and to it the citizen is bound to render allegiance. "The object of the present state of society is to
multiply labor," asserted Godwin; "in another state it will be to
simplify it." "The only adequate apology of government is necessity." "Government however reformed" is "little capable of affording solid benefit to mankind." "Give us equality and justice
but no constitution. Suffer us to follow without restraint the
dictates of our own judgment, and to change our forms of social

order as fast as we improve the dictates of our own judgment."
"The pretense of collective wisdom is the most palpable of all
impostures." "The true reason why the mass of mankind has so
often been the dupe of knaves, has been the mysterious and complicated nature of the social system. Once annihilate the quackery
of government, and the most homespun understanding will be
prepared to scorn the artifices of the state juggler that would
mislead him."

By his own path Thoreau came to identical conclusions. There
is little in *Civil Disobedience* that is not in *Political Justice*. To
neither thinker is there an abstract state, society or nation—only
individuals; and to both, the fundamental law is the law of morality. Political expediency and the law of morality frequently clash,
and in such event it is the duty of the individual citizen to follow
the higher law. Thoreau went even further, and asserted the
doctrine of individual compact, which in turn implied the doctrine
of individual nullification; no government, he said, can have any
"pure right over my person or property but what I concede to it."

I heartily accept the motto,—"That government is best which governs
least"; and I should like to see it acted up to more rapidly and systematically. Carried out, it finally amounts to this, which also I believe,—
"That government is best which governs not at all"; and when men are
prepared for it, that will be the kind of government which they will have.
Government is at best but an expedient; but most governments are usually,
and all governments are sometimes, inexpedient.
A government in which the majority rule in all cases cannot be based
on justice. . . . We should be men first and subjects afterwards. It is
not desirable to cultivate a respect for the law, so much as for the right.
. . . How does it become a man to behave toward this American government today? I answer, that he cannot without disgrace be associated
with it. I cannot for an instant recognize that political organization as
my government which is the *slave's* government also. . . . There is but
little virtue in the action of masses of men. . . . It is not a man's duty,
as a matter of course, to devote himself to the eradication of any, even the
most enormous wrong; he may still properly have other concerns to engage
him; but it is his duty, at least, to wash his hands of it, and, if he gives
it no thought longer, not to give it practically his support. If I devote
myself to other pursuits and contemplations, I must first see, at least,
that I do not pursue them sitting upon another man's shoulders. I must
get off him first, that he may pursue his contemplations too. . . . If
the law is of such a nature that it requires you to be an agent of injustice
to another, then, I say, break the law. Let your life be a counter friction
to stop the machine. . . . As for adopting the ways which the state has
provided for remedying the evil, I know not of such ways. They take

too much time, and a man's life will be gone. . . . Some are petitioning
the State to dissolve the Union. . . . Why do they not dissolve it themselves,—the union between themselves and the state,—and refuse to pay
their quota into its treasury? [1] (*Works*, Vol. X, pp. 131-170.)

"Let your life be a counter friction to stop the machine"—in
this doctrine of individual syndicalism Thoreau's conception of
the relation of the citizen to the state is tersely summed up. In
so far as he was a democrat it was of the transcendental school,
rather than the Jacksonian. He would be governed by the majority
no more than by the minority. The scorn of a fine ethical mind
for practical government by politicians could scarcely be more
tellingly phrased than in the bit of verse he tucks into *Civil Disobedience:*

> A drab of state, a cloth-o'-silver slut,
> To have her train borne up, and her soul trail in the dirt.

Such a man quite evidently would go for Nullification as fiercely
as Garrison. Even though he might wash his hands of society, the
cries of those who suffered injustice followed him, and when the
Fugitive Slave Law passed, it robbed him of his peace, destroying
his pleasure in wonted things. The slave hunters were in Boston
streets, and justice in the person of Commissioner Loring was
sending Anthony Burns back to slavery. As he contemplated the
spectacle his wrath against a coercive government flamed up.
"My thoughts are murder to the state," he complained bitterly,
"and involuntarily go plotting against her."

I would remind my countrymen that they are to be men first, and
Americans only at a late and convenient hour. . . . I hear a good deal
said about trampling this law under foot. Why, one need not go out of
his way to do that. This law rises not to the level of the head or the reason;
its natural habitat is in the dirt. It was born and bred, and has its life,
only in the dust and mire, on a level with the feet; and he who walks with
freedom, and does not with Hindoo mercy avoid treading on every
venomous reptile, will inevitably tread on it, and so trample it under foot,

[1] Compare the following entry in his *Journal* under date of March 26, 1842:
"I must confess I have felt mean enough when asked how I was to act on society,
what errand I had to mankind. Undoubtedly I did not feel mean without a reason,
and yet my loitering is not without defense. I would fain communicate the wealth
of my life to men, would really give them what is most precious in my gift. . . . I
know no riches I would keep back. I have no private good unless it be my peculiar
ability to serve the public. . . . This is the only individual property. . . . It is
hard to be a good citizen of the world in any great sense, but if we do render no
interest or increase to mankind out of that talent God gave us, we can at least
preserve the principal unimpaired."

—and Webster, its maker, like the dirt-bug and its ball. ("Slavery in Massachusetts," in *Works*, Vol. X.)

The law will never make men free; it is men who have got to make the law free. They are the lovers of law and order who observe the law when the government breaks it.

Thoreau was a stern judge, and he held his age in low esteem. His Concord neighbors seemed to him poor fellows with too little spirit to be free men; they were the raw material of standing armies, militia, jailors, constables, and the *posse comitatus*. And then one day into the field of his vision came a plain Yankee, primitive and heroic, John Brown of Ossawatomie. In the contemplation of his life and death Thoreau felt a shock of new faith run like an electric current through his veins. The age was no longer dead to him, for it had bred a man. "I rejoice that I live in this age," he exclaimed, "that I am his contemporary." He had found his hero—not in past times as Carlyle and Emerson had done, but in the present and among his own Yankee kind. He had talked with John Brown in Concord and recognized him as a primitive idealist of rugged mold, a stern moralist who set justice above the law. That this man should be so grossly misunderstood by lesser men, so foully slandered, filled him with sorrow and with wrath also. "When a noble deed is done, who is likely to appreciate it? They who are noble themselves. I was not surprised that certain of my neighbors spoke of John Brown as an ordinary felon, for who are they? They have either much flesh, or much office, or much coarseness of some kind" ("The Last Days of John Brown," in *Works*, Vol. X, p. 241). His trial and conviction Thoreau regarded as a judgment, not on John Brown, but upon America; the lawyers and editors and politicians who judged him were only convicting themselves.

His company was small indeed, because few could be found worthy to pass muster. Each one who there laid down his life for the poor and oppressed was a picked man, culled out of many thousands, if not millions; apparently a man of principle, of rare courage, and devoted humanity; ready to sacrifice his life at any moment for the benefit of his fellow-man. It may be doubted if there were so many more their equals in these respects in all the country,—I speak of his followers only,—for their leader, no doubt, scoured the land far and wide, seeking to swell his troop. These alone were ready to step between the oppressor and the oppressed. Surely they were the very best men you could select to be hung. That was the best compliment this country could pay them. They were ripe for her gallows. She has tried a long time, she has hung a good many, but never found the right one before.

I do not believe in lawyers, in that mode of attacking or defending a man, because you descend to meet the judge on his own ground, and, in cases of the highest importance, it is of no consequence whether a man breaks a human law or not. Let lawyers decide trivial cases. Business men may arrange that among themselves. If they were the interpreters of the everlasting laws which rightfully bind man, that would be another thing. A counterfeiting law-factory, standing half in a slave land and half in a free! What kind of laws for free men can you expect from that? ("A Plea for Captain John Brown," in *Works*, Vol. X, p. 197.)

In Thoreau the eighteenth-century philosophy of individualism, the potent liberalisms let loose on the world by Jean Jacques, came to fullest expression in New England. He was the completest embodiment of the *laissez-faire* reaction against a regimented social order, the severest critic of the lower economics that frustrate the dreams of human freedom. He was fortunate in dying before the age of exploitation had choked his river with its weeds; fortunate in not foreseeing how remote is that future of free men on which his hopes were fixed:

The life in us is like the water in the river. It may rise this year higher than man has ever known it, and flood the parched uplands; even this may be the eventful year, which will drown out all the muskrats . . . such is the character of that morrow which mere lapse of time can never make to dawn. The light which puts out our eyes is darkness to us. There is more day to dawn. The sun is but a morning-star. (*Walden*.)

With the dawning of that day perhaps men will sit once more at the feet of the ancient wisdom and fashion their lives upon the principle that the soul is more than the meat and the body than raiment. Perhaps they may even shape for themselves new heroes—"above and after all, the Man of the Age, come to be called workingman." He and his deeds are looked down upon in our time—"It is obvious that none yet speaks to his condition, for the speaker is not yet in his condition." "Literature speaks how much still to the past, how little to the future; how much to the East, how little to the West" ("Thomas Carlyle and his Works," in *Works*, Vol. X, p. 118). One of the great names in American literature is the name of Henry Thoreau. Yet only after sixty years is he slowly coming into his own.

CHAPTER IV
THEODORE PARKER
Transcendental Minister

THEODORE PARKER was described by one of his biographers as "the best working-plan of an American yet produced," and by a fellow minister as "a conscience since Luther unsurpassed." The two comments suggest still another, that he was completely and adequately New England. Yankee and Puritan contributed equally to his making. His rich and plastic mind was two-sided: one-half was wholly English, practical, logical, concrete, lucid; loving fact and tireless in its acquisition; master of everyday affairs and competent in dealing with this world; the other was emotional, mystical, idealistic, deeply and spontaneously religious, living daily with God as a son with the Father, carrying the sorrows of men in his heart and the wrongs of the world on his conscience. One of the greatest of New England ministers, he was shepherd as well as counselor, pastor as well as teacher. "I wish to stand on the earth," he said with true critical insight, "though I would look beyond the stars. I would live *with men*, but think with philosophers" (Weiss, *Life and Correspondence of Theodore Parker*, Vol. I, p. 115). The generous amplitude of his nature was too large for the narrow walls of a church; he took all Boston for his parish, all New England for his congregation. Amazingly active and vital, he consumed whole libraries in his pursuit of knowledge. "His mind," says Weiss, "was like the republican idea itself; it could afford to be hospitable, but could not afford to be exclusive" (*ibid.*, Vol. I, p. 178). Conversant with many fields of knowledge, with a memory extraordinarily retentive, he was master of many languages—nineteen or twenty, according to Thomas Wentworth Higginson—and at home in the most abstruse subjects. He spent his vast energy with the prodigality of Cotton Mather, and he achieved what Cotton Mather with his inbred parochialism could not achieve, an intellectual cosmopolitanism that judged Boston by broader standards than it could gauge.

A first-class fighting-man was this child of yeoman New England

—none braver, not even Garrison, none more effective; and yet tender-hearted, sympathetic, with the shrewd common sense of his homespun forebears. The son of a Lexington farmer and mechanic, self-trained, endowed with indomitable will, he came of the soundest stock in Massachusetts. His grandfather was captain of the Minute Men who faced the British troops on Lexington Common in April, 1775; and a conscious pride of ancestry broke out frequently in his speech. The words uttered before the Ministerial Conference in May, 1851, in justification of his repudiation of the Fugitive Slave Law, were characteristic: "I am not afraid of men, I can offend them. I care nothing for their hate, or their esteem. I am not very careful of my reputation." He then goes on:

I have had to arm myself. I have written my sermons with a pistol in my desk,—loaded, a cap on the nipple, and ready for action. Yea, with a drawn sword within reach of my right hand. This I have done in Boston; in the midst of the nineteenth century; been obliged to do it to defend the (innocent) members of my church, women as well as men! You know that I do not like fighting. . . . But what could I do? I was born in the little town where the first bloodshed of the Revolution began. The bones of men who first fell in that war are covered by the monument at Lexington, it is "sacred to Liberty and the Rights of Mankind"; those men fell "in the sacred cause of God and their country." This is the first inscription that I ever read. These men were my kindred. My grandfather drew the first sword in the Revolution; my fathers fired the first shot; the blood which flowed there was kindred to this which courses in my veins today. Besides that, when I write in my library at home, on the one side of me is the Bible which my fathers prayed over, their morning and evening prayer, for nearly a hundred years. On the other side there hangs the firelock my grandfather fought with in the old French war, which he carried at the taking of Quebec, which he zealously used at the battle of Lexington, and beside it is another, a trophy of that war, the first gun taken in the Revolution, taken also by my grandfather. With these things before me, these symbols; with these memories in me, when a parishioner, a fugitive from slavery, a woman, pursued by the kidnappers, came to my house, what could I do less than take her in and defend her to the last? (*Additional Speeches*, Vol. I, pp. 13–15.)

With his sensitive conscience visited by such memories—a child of '76 living in the evil days of the Fugitive Slave Law, a devout freethinker borne on the crest of transcendental thought— Theodore Parker became the embodiment and epitome of the New England renaissance. More completely perhaps than any other representative, he gathered up and expressed the major revolu-

tionary impulses of his time and world: the idealistic theism implicit
in the Unitarian reaction from Calvinism; the transcendental
individualism latent in the doctrine of divine immanence; and
the passion for righteousness, to make the will of God prevail in
a world where the devil quite openly kept his ledgers. He was an
eager and thorough iconoclast, impatient to break the false
images—the God of John Calvin with its slanders of human nature,
and the god of State Street with its contempt for justice—which
New England, he believed, had worshiped too long, forgetting
the ideals of the Revolutionary fathers. The mind and conscience
of Boston seemed to him stifled by the strait-jacket of respectability. Righteousness like a fugitive slave, was driven into hiding,
or must walk the open streets with a Derringer in its pocket. As
a free soul loving freedom, and a righteous man loving righteousness, he believed a duty was laid on him to cut away the strait-
jacket, to shame the Boston that sold the poor in the gates for a
pair of shoes. He must labor to set free the mind and conscience
of Boston that they might go forth purified to work a beneficent
work in a world that is God's and not the devil's. His attack was
keen and unsparing; he laid on with gusto; he used homely words;
he was just rather than polite. Impatient of humbug and self-
seeking he dealt in searching criticism rather than conventional
eulogy. At his touch distinguished reputations shrank to the mean
and commonplace, and inflated dignitaries collapsed like a pricked
balloon. Intellectually honest, he spoke the truth he had been at
immense pains to gather, and in consequence those who suffered
the sting of his attack—ministers and lawyers and merchants and
politicians, men in high position, distinguished leaders of Boston
society—were not slack in crying out against him as a demagogue
and agitator. Next to Garrison he became the most hated man in
New England; and something of that contemporary hatred, fierce
and unforgiving, clings to his name still, coloring later estimates
of his worth, hinting that his manners were not on a level with his
morals.[1] An extraordinarily vital and interesting person, in short,
was this Yankee preacher with his Puritan conscience—this transcendental critic with his quiver full of facts; one not to be ignored
in casting up the accounts of the New England renaissance.

With his memorable sermon *On the Transient and Permanent
in Christianity*, preached in May, 1841—a sermon that ranks in

[1] See Wendell, *Literary History of America*, p. 348.

the history of Unitarianism with Channing's Baltimore sermon—
the Unitarian movement entered upon its second broad phase.
It abandoned supernaturalism established on the sufficient authority of the Scriptures, and adopted the conception of an evolutionary theism, of God progressively revealing himself to the developing faculties of men and speaking through the conscience. Under
Channing's guidance Unitarianism had abandoned the major
dogmas of Calvinism—total depravity, predestination, a God of
wrath; it had shifted the emphasis from stable will to boundless
love; and by such teachings it had captured the greater churches
of Boston. By 1830 it had become securely established as the
religion of Boston respectability, with implied bounds set to its
intellectual liberalism. As the first ardor abated it fell to defining
the new orthodoxy, resting content with what already had been
won. It was against this new orthodoxy that held fast to the old
supernaturalism that Theodore Parker protested. "The defect
of the Unitarians was a profound one," he pointed out; "ceasing to
fear 'the great and dreadful God' of the Old Testament, they had
not quite learned to love the all-beautiful and altogether lovely
[God] of the universe." [2] He would have no pausing of the movement of adventurous thought, no settling back into the ruts of
dogmatism; and so he threw himself with immense energy into
the work of liberating Unitarianism from a premature orthodoxy.

For this work he was admirably equipped. The greatest scholar
of his generation of New England ministers, deep in German theology and philosophy, with the latest results of higher criticism on
his study table, he was critically trained to separate historical
fact from ecclesiastical tradition, and establish his theology on a
basis of naturalism. He was at once scientific and transcendental.
He had translated De Wette's *Introduction to the Old Testament* and
was intimately acquainted with Strauss's *Leben Jesu*. He knew
the oriental backgrounds of Hebraic thought, had studied comparative religion with its suggestive record of taboos and fetishism,
and was gathering materials for a comprehensive history of
religion from primitive times. Intellectually acquisitive and
curious, he far outran the less informed and courageous of his
Unitarian brethren. But he was far more than a critic, he

[2] See "Letter to the Members of the Twenty-Eighth Congregational Society of
Boston," in Weiss, *Life and Correspondence of Theodore Parker*, Vol. II, Appendix
II, p. 482. This account of his "Experience as a Minister" constitutes a brief
intellectual autobiography, of first importance to the student of Parker.

may well be accounted a religious genius. A convinced intuitionist, he tested every authority by appeal to transcendental experience. He frankly abandoned faith in the supernatural, with its corollaries of miracles and its "fetishism of the Bible," and was far advanced in a theism that compensated for the supernatural by a passionate love of God. Thus established in personal experience his religion issued in conduct. Love of God was more to him than historical faith embodied in an historical church; love to his fellow men was more appealing than dogma. Hence the profoundly ethical quality of his religion, warm, palpitating, generous, that set it apart from the colder and austerer ethicism of the conventional Unitarians. The spirituality of Channing was enriched in Parker by the ardency of his loving nature.

The three major doctrines of his theism, as elaborated in his "Letter to the Members of the Twenty-Eighth Congregational Society," were the infinite perfection of God, the adequacy of man to all his functions, and the sufficiency of absolute, natural religion. In his elaboration of these doctrines the controlling influence of transcendental thought is everywhere apparent. A metaphysical optimism throws a golden light on all his thinking. The trinitarian Godhead, equally with the devil, vanishes in "the infinitely perfect God," "immanent in the world of matter, and in the world of spirit, the two hemispheres which to us make up the universe"—a universe created "from a perfect motive, for a perfect purpose, of perfect substance, and as a perfect means." Hence it follows in Parker's logic, that

there must be a complete solidarity between God and the two-fold universe which He creates. The perfect Creator is thus also a perfect providence; indeed, creation and providence are not objective accidents of Deity, nor subjective caprices, but the development of the perfect motive to its perfect purpose, love becoming a universe of perfect welfare. I have called God Father, but also Mother . . . to express more sensibility, the quality of tender and unselfish love, which mankind associates with Mother more than aught else beside. ("Letter," etc., in Weiss, Vol. II, pp. 470–471.)

The doctrine of the adequacy of man flows logically from the doctrine of the immanence of God, but Parker was not content to rest it on such basis alone. The conception of human perfectibility, as it filtered down to him through different strata of thought, romantic and idealistic, found a high sanction in his transcendentalism; but his practical nature demanded that it be established if possible on a scientific foundation. Anthropology must substantiate philosophy. Parker was not convinced that it could be thus adequately established; nevertheless he would travel the objective path as far as it might lead. Darwin's *Origin of Species* was published after Parker was seized with his fatal illness, yet in much of the latter's thinking he was groping his way toward some similar conception of "the unity of life of the human race," with its "progressive development" from "the state of ignorance, poverty, and utter nakedness of soul and sense, the necessary primitive conditions of the race, up to the present civilization." In the deep-buried scattered records of the past, slowly being gathered together and interpreted by science, he found "proof of time immense, wherein man, this spiritual Cosmos, has been assuming his present condition, individual, domestic, social, and national, and accumulating that wealth of things and thoughts which is the mark of civilization." The doctrine of human perfectibility might not be capable of scientific proof, but it was more than a reasonable hope; it was implicit in all the past.

But this progressive development does not end with us; we have seen only the beginning; the future triumphs of the race must be vastly greater than all accomplished yet. In the primal instincts and automatic desires of man, I have found a prophecy that what he wants is possible, and shall one day be actual. . . . What good is not with us is before, to be attained by toil and thought, and religious life. (*Ibid.*, Vol. II, pp. 471–472.)

Of this slowly and painfully evolving man with his expanding ideals, religion Parker believed to be the highest ultimate expression; and religion, as the eyes of men slowly open to larger truths, will be seen to be answerable to the needs of daily life, to embody the highest ideal of social excellence. The noblest religion he believed was not supernatural, but natural. "The absolute religion which belongs to man's nature, and is gradually unfolded thence," "is the idea of humanity, dimly seen but clearly felt, which has flitted before the pious eyes of men in all lands and many an age, and been prayed for as the 'Kingdom of Heaven.'" It is forever refashioning its ideal, re-embodying its vision, in every devout soul, in every creative age. "The religious history of the race is the record of man's continual but unconscious efforts to attain this 'desire of all nations'" (*ibid.*, Vol. II, p. 473). But unhappily every new advance soon crystallizes in dogmas and institutions; taboos and fetishisms are quick to re-imprison the mind that struggles to be free. Old forms, therefore, must be daily broken to make room for evolving experience. Religion must be free; it must rise spontaneously from the depths of life. Christianity has suffered grievously from a fetishism of the Bible, from its worship of the supernatural, from an ungenerous sectarianism beloved of "ecclesiastic skeptics," who believe "there is no place for the Christian Church or the Bible till they have nullified the faculties which created both, and rendered Bible-makers and Church-founders impossible." Every age must write a new Bible out of its God-given instincts, permeated with the divine love that is slowly shaping society to the divine purpose.

No more is the atheistic mocker or the ecclesiastic bigot commissioned to stop the human race with his cry, "Cease there, mankind, thy religious search! for, thousand-million-headed as thou art, thou canst know nought directly of thy God, thy duty, or thyself. Pause, and accept my authenticated word; stop, and despair!" (*Ibid.*, Vol. II, p. 475.)

It was this ethical quality of his religion that kept Theodore Parker so sensitive to wrongs and so generous in response to the call of social justice. His religion quickened his social conscience and summoned him to serve the plentiful reform movements of the day. With Garrison and Wendell Phillips he organized the militants of Boston radicalism. His political principles were simple and uncompromising, woven from the strands of English and French libertarianism of the seventeenth and eighteenth centuries—from Sidney, Locke, Rousseau, the great leaders of the natural-rights school. One who accepted as axiomatic the nobility of human nature and the perfectibility of man, might be a political romantic, but he was certain to be a liberal. Parker was a primitive democrat, whose democracy was bone of his bone and flesh of his flesh. But the democracy that answered the needs of his dream of the kingdom was, like Emerson's and Channing's, ethical rather than political or economic—it was "the enactment of God's justice into human laws" ("The Nebraska Question," in *Additional Speeches*, Vol. I, p. 327). "The democratic idea has had but a slow and gradual growth even in New England," he pointed out; nevertheless he was convinced that it was spreading, and "government becomes more and more of all, by all and for all" [3] (*ibid.*, p. 33). He hated Federalism with an intensity equal-

[3] This phrase of Parker's was probably the source of Lincoln's phrase.

ing Jefferson's, and ecclesiastical Federalism that twisted the authority of the church to the side of wealthy pewholders, using Scripture as a sanction for exploitation, he denounced as scathingly as Garrison. The power of the political state he feared, because he discovered the political state to be the friend of the rich rather than the poor, of selfish advantage rather than of God's justice. With other Abolitionists he distrusted the machinery of centralization that was being skillfully erected at Washington. "Opposition to centralization of authority is very old in America," he remarked; "I hope it will be always young" (*ibid.*, Vol. II, p. 29). But he was no partisan to the rule of the majority, if it determined contrary to his conscience. A transcendental individualist, he went for the nullification of an immoral statute in the name of the Higher Law.[4]

Parker was never blind to the economic basis of politics. He saw so clearly, indeed, the close alliance between group interests and governmental statutes, that his political activities were almost wholly determined by that recognition. As a political critic he was the shrewdest realist of his generation. He was one constituent whom politicians talking for Buncombe could not befuddle. He was too deeply read in American history, gifted with too keen historical insight, to be impressed by the glittering rhetoric of the Rufus Choates. He had his own views of the American government, and majestic appeals to the Constitution left him cold. The Constitution, he asserted, "is a provisional compromise between the ideal political principles of the Declaration, and the actual selfishness of the people North and South." America was not a democracy. It had thrown off theocracy, aristocracy, and monarchy, only to set in their places the "institution of money—the master of all the rest." The economic basis of society in America he considered to be open and patent. In church and state, money "is this day the strongest power of the nation." He declined to be deceived by party cries and platforms, either Whig or Democratic; both parties served economics rather than justice.

So there is a party organization about the dollar as its central nucleus and idea. The dollar is the germinal dot of the Whig party; its motive

---

[4] See "The Law of God and the Statutes of Men," in *Additional Speeches*, Vol. II, p. 181.

is pecuniary. . . . It sneers at the poor; at the many; has a contempt for the people. It legislates against the poor, and for the rich . . . the few who are born with the desire, the talent, and the conventional position to become rich. "Take care of the rich, and they will take care of the poor," is its secret maxim. Everything must yield to money. . . . With this party there is no Absolute Right, no Absolute Wrong. . . . There is Expediency and Inexpediency. . . . Accordingly a millionaire is reckoned by this party as the highest production of Society. He is the Whig ideal; he alone has attained "the measure of the stature of a perfect man."

The Democratic party appeals to the brute will of the majority, right or wrong; it knows no Higher Law. . . . There is . . . no vital difference between the Whig party and the Democratic party; no difference in moral principle. The Whig inaugurates the Money got; the Democrat inaugurates the Desire to get money. That is all the odds. . . . There is only a hand rail between the two, which breaks down if you lean on it, and the parties mix . . . a Democrat is but a Whig on time; a Whig is a Democrat arrived at maturity; his time has come. A Democrat is a young Whig who will legislate for money as soon as he has got it; the Whig is an old Democrat who once hurrahed for the majority—"Down with money! there is a despot! and up with the desire for it! Down with the rich, and up with the poor!" The young man, poor, obscure, and covetous, in 1812 was a Democrat, went a-privateering against England; rich, and accordingly "one of our eminent citizens," in 1851 he was a Whig, and went a-kidnapping against Ellen Crafts and Thomas Sims. ("The Nebraska Question," in *Additional Speeches*, Vol. I, pp. 331–335.)

The America of Parker's day was fast becoming middle class and Parker knew it, and like Lincoln he did not disapprove. Honest thrift he found wholly desirable, and wealth if it were honestly got. But speculation dissociated from creative work he regarded with old-fashioned distrust. "If a man fully pay in efficient, productive toil and thought, he is entitled to all he gets, one dollar or many million dollars . . . and if his estate be but what he has thus actually and honestly paid for with service given, equivalent to the service received, what he can virtuously keep or humanely apply and expend, then it will never be too large." [5] But he believed there were other gods, and greater, than the god of getting on; social justice was more desirable than unearned increment; and he set his face like flint against the common materialism of America. "I come to build up piety and morality; to pull down only what cumbers the ground," he said; but he had learned that the temples of State Street were not easily leveled:

[5] Quoted in Weiss, Vol. II, p. 488.

that they would not fall without a mighty crash. A less courageous man would have hesitated, but Parker was utterly fearless. Boston he knew "was a Tory town." "The Mother city of the Puritans is now the metropolis of the Hunkers" (*Additional Speeches*, Vol. I, p. 111). But the spirit of '76 was strong in him and he would "appeal from Boston drunk with gold, and briefly mad with hate, to sober Boston in her hour to come." He would appeal from Whiggish Boston to Revolutionary Boston; from State Street to Lexington common; from the Faneuil Hall of Rufus Choate to the Faneuil Hall of Sam Adams. He would awaken the ancestral idealism of Boston that slept uneasily under the spell of middle-class ambitions—that had sold its Puritan heritage for southern trade profits. Such an appeal Boston had never before listened to, ardent, unsparing, the Hebraic and the Yankee vernacular curiously mingled; and Boston writhed uncomfortably and pronounced the prophet ill-mannered.

When the Fugitive Slave Bill passed, the six New England states lay fast asleep: Massachusetts slept soundly, her head pillowed on her unsold bales of Cotton and of woolen goods, dreaming of "orders from the South." Justice came to waken her . . . and she started in her sleep, and being frightened, swore a prayer or two, then slept again. But Boston woke,— sleeping, in her shop, with ears open, and her eye on the market, her hand on her purse, dreaming of goods for sale,—Boston woke broadly up, and fired a hundred guns for joy. O Boston, Boston! if thou couldst have known, in that thine hour, the things which belong unto thy peace! But no: they were hidden from her eyes. She had prayed to her god, to Money; he granted her the request, but sent leanness into her soul. ("The Boston Kidnapping," in *Additional Speeches*, Vol. I, p. 89.)

But he offended the Boston code of good breeding even more seriously. He became personal. He named names. Before vast congregations, in printed books, he pronounced judgment on Bostonians respected in the Back Bay, mighty in State Street. Boston gentlemen had never before suffered such tongue-lashings. How mercilessly he excoriated Commissioner Loring, judge of probate and Harvard professor, for soiling his hands in the Anthony Burns case! How neatly he pricked the empty culture of Edward Everett for his pro-slavery ardor—"a Cambridge professor of Greek, he studied the original tongue of the Bible to learn that the Scripture says 'slaves,' where the English Bible says only 'servants'!" (*Additional Speeches*, Vol. II, p. 115.) What an utterly devastating attack he made on the great Webster for the latter's subserviency to local economic interests! Much honest realism underlies that criticism, and much honest American history. The "Nebraska Address" and the "Webster Address" are notable historical documents, incisive analyses—rare in those romantic days—done by one who has kept a shrewd eye on current politics, and understands the hidden springs of party policy. Into the Webster address he put his vast knowledge, his power of analysis, his frank idealism. It was "a sad and dreadful day" when duty bade Theodore Parker speak on the man whose uncommon powers he had long admired; but he did his work thoroughly, refusing to shut his eyes to ugly fact, refusing to indulge in commonplace eulogy. It was the eighteenth-century economic realism of Webster that stirred the wrath of the transcendentalist—that and the lapses from integrity. Parker's text was found in Webster's dictum that "the great object of government is the protection of property at home, and respect and renown abroad"; and how starkly it runs counter to his own ideal of government, "the enactment of God's justice into human laws," is laid bare in page after page of scathing commentary. To the exacting ethics of Parker, Webster was wanting in principles; he followed expediency rather than justice; and how surely expediency digs pitfalls for its own undoing he discovered tragic illustration of in the career of the great senator. It is a hard fate for a politician, accustomed to the cheap praise of the gullible public, to fall into the hands of a critic who is honest and searching; and Webster had too many weak points to emerge from such an analysis with credit. It is probably the most critical examination of Webster's career that has ever been made, and withal just.

Surprisingly modern, far more so than Channing, was this brilliant preacher—impulsive, colloquial, natural, whose every arrow was pointed with a fact and feathered to fly true; concerned more with righteousness than with policy; hating the dull commonplace and empty dignity of Tory ways; careless of convention, somewhat spectacular, with a keen relish for combat—a vital, vivid man, the apostle of conscience, the advocate of every unpopular cause. He possessed an amazing gift of words, yet he was too impatient, too practical, to become an artist; preferring immediate ends to more lasting reputation, and spending himself with a free prodigality. He was always the speaker rather than the writer and his printed pages bear the unmistakable marks of impetuous oral discourse. Emerson accounted him one of the four great men of the age. Whether or not that judgment holds, whether he was too eager a militant to become a great transcendental philosopher, the historian sees in Theodore Parker one of the greatest, if not the last, of the excellent line of Puritan preachers.

CHAPTER V

MARGARET FULLER

Rebel

THE fame of Margaret Fuller has waned greatly since her vivid personality was blotted out in the prime of her intellectual development. Misunderstood in her own time, caricatured by unfriendly critics, and with significant facts of her life suppressed by her friends out of a chivalrous sense of loyalty, the real woman has been lost in a Margaret Fuller myth and later generations have come to underestimate her powers and undervalue her work. Yet no other woman of her generation in America is so well worth recalling. She was the completest embodiment of the inchoate rebellions and grandiose aspirations of the age of transcendental ferment; for to the many grievances charged against the times by other New England liberals, she added the special grievance of the stupid inhibitions laid upon women. Transcendental radical and critic, like Emerson and Thoreau and Parker, she was feminist also; and to the difficult business of freeing her mind from the Cambridge orthodoxies, she added the greater difficulty of freeing her sex.

The written record that Margaret Fuller left is quite inadequate to explain her contemporary reputation. In no sense an artist, scarcely a competent craftsman, she wrote nothing that bears the mark of high distinction either in thought or style. Impatient of organization and inadequately disciplined, she threw off her work impulsively, not pausing to shape it to enduring form. Yet she was vastly talked about, and common report makes her out to have been an extraordinary woman who creatively influenced those with whom she came in contact. Like Alcott, her power lay in brilliant talk. Her quick mind seems to have been an electric current that stimulated other minds to activity, and created a vortex of speculation wherever she passed. Hungry for ideas, intellectually and emotionally vibrant, she caught her inspirations from obscure impulses of a nature thwarted and inhibited from normal unfolding; and in her sensitive oscillations she was often

426

drawn away from polar principles to which she would later swing back. There was quite evidently a fundamental unrest within her, a conflict of impulses, that issued in dissatisfaction; and this contradiction was aggravated by intense emotions, which both quickened her mind and distorted it.

A product of Cambridge bookishness, Margaret Fuller was both a wonder and a riddle to a generation that made little account of the psychology of sex. She was commonly looked upon as an intellectual monstrosity, the most fearful of Yankee bluestockings, and a later Bostonian has gone so far as to suggest that she was "an unsexed version of Plato's Socrates" (Wendell, *Literary History of America*, p. 300). But to present-day psychology her character is an extraordinarily suggestive document, and a recent critic has read her seeming contradictions like an open book.[1] Before Miss Anthony's penetrating analysis the Margaret Fuller myth vanishes, and a very real, natural, and unfortunate woman takes its place. She came of vigorous stock, independent, outspoken, opinionated. Her grandfather was a clergyman who was unfrocked by his church for being lukewarm in the Revolutionary War. Her father, Timothy Fuller, and her four uncles, worked their way through Harvard. In Timothy Fuller there was a large measure of Puritan grimness and severity that locked the door on the passions of his heart, that none might know of them; yet there seems to have been a volcano in the man who held off the world so brusquely. The rebel was strong in him. The Fullers were not of Brahmin stock and had no wish to please their social superiors. While a Harvard undergraduate, Timothy Fuller turned Jeffersonian republican and lost his place as first honor man by joining in an undergraduate protest against certain hated regulations. As a lawyer and politician he repudiated respectable Federalism, and although he was representative in Congress for four terms and enjoyed certain other offices, his non-conformity in the end cost him dear. No doubt he had counted on that, for he was stubborn oak that might break but would not bend. The tragedy of Margaret Fuller's life seems to have been sketched before in the life of Timothy Fuller.

To an extraordinary degree the daughter was the child of the father, in ideas and sympathies as well as blood. Like him she was a rebel, but for the daughter to turn rebel involved greater

[1] See Katharine Anthony, *Margaret Fuller. A Psychological Biography*.

hazards than for the father. Her sex was a heavy handicap, foɪ
the experience of Fanny Wright and Lucretia Mott had revealed
that American chivalry had definite bounds; it did not shield the
woman who ventured beyond the pale. Yet considering her blood
and training, how could she help thus venturing into freer fields
without? From her earliest years her father treated her as a comrade and gave her the training of a boy. In her studies he dealt
with her as James Mill dealt with his brilliant son. Perhaps it was
a mistake to force her into the rigid groove of classical learning
when she should have been playing with her dolls. From it she
got very unusual acquisitions, but overstimulation broke her
health, and isolation turned her mind in upon itself and made her
the victim of somnambulism and freaks of imagination. The
result was the development, on one side of her nature, of a female
counterpart of Cotton Mather—precocious, domineering, moody,
visionary, given to long hours of greedy reading, gorging herself
on books and well-nigh ruining her intellectual digestion as well as
her health. Against this unfortunate overstimulation her vigorous
nature struggled for years, and never quite successfully. Her
emotions were forever embroiling her intellect. To conceive of
her as sexless is curiously to miss the point of her emotionalism.
She was rather the victim of sex. Her ardent friendships with
other women, her flashes of mystical experience, her fondness for
children, her love of luxury and creature comforts, her eager love
affair with James Nathan who unchivalrously found safety in
flight, her friendship with Mazzini and her more intimate friendship
with Count Ossoli, that ended in an unconventional marriage after
her situation rendered it necessary—such reactions can be explained on no other hypothesis. Her ardent nature was the victim
of disastrous frustrations, rendered the more acute by premature
development. If she had married early, as Harriet Beecher did,
and her excessive energy had been turned into domestic channels,
her life must have been less tragic, whatever the effect might have
been on her intellectual development.

The acutest contemporary analysis of her contradictory character
is that given by her friend William Henry Channing, who found
his clue in the clash between endowment and environment:

Here was one fond as a child of joy, eager as a native of the tropics for
swift transition from luxurious rest to passionate excitement, prodigal to
pour her mingled force of will, thought, sentiment, into the life of the

moment, all radiant with imagination, longing for communion with artists of every age in their inspired hours, fitted by genius and culture to mingle as an equal in the most refined circles of Europe, and yet her youth and early womanhood had passed away amid the very decent, yet drudging, descendants of prim Puritans. Trained among those who could have discerned her peculiar power, and early fed with the fruits of beauty for which her spirits pined, she would have developed into one of the finest lyrists, romancers and critics, that the modern literary world has seen. This she knew; and this tantalization of her fate she keenly felt. (*Memoirs of Margaret Fuller Ossoli*, by R. W. Emerson, W. H. Channing, and J. F. Clarke, Vol. II, pp. 36–37.)

This disastrous clash between endowment and environment is strikingly exemplified in her delight in Europe when at thirty-four she found herself there—in her admiration for Georges Sand, and in particular the extravagance of her love for Rome, where her starved heart found satisfactions she had long dreamed of. "Italy receives me as a long-lost child, and I feel myself at home here," she wrote in 1847; and a few weeks later, "I find how true was the lure that always drew me towards Europe. It was no false instinct that said I might here find an atmosphere to develop me in ways I need. Had I only come ten years earlier! Now my life must be a failure, so much strength has been wasted on abstractions, which only came because I grew not in the right soil" (*ibid.*, Vol. II, p. 225). She was too eagerly pagan to be satisfied with either Puritan or Yankee Cambridge. The pale ethicism of New England was thin gruel for such an appetite for life. Even Emerson she found cold, and her stomach rebelled at the food he throve on. But this was only half the story; the other half was this:

But the tragedy of Margaret's history was deeper yet. Behind the poet was the woman,—fond and relying, the heroic and disinterested woman. The very glow of her poetic enthusiasm was but an outflush of trustful affection; the very restlessness of her intellect was the confession that her heart had found no home. A "book-worm," a "dilettante," a "pedant," I had heard her sneeringly called; but now it was evident that her seeming insensibility was virgin pride, and her absorption in studying the natural vent of emotions, which met no object of life-long attachment. At once, many of her peculiarities became intelligible. Fitfulness, unlooked-for changes of mood, misconceptions of words and actions, substitutions of fancy for fact . . . were now referred to the morbid influence of affections pent up to prey upon themselves. And, what was still more interesting, the clue was given to a singular credulousness, by which, in spite of her unusual penetration, Margaret might be led away blindfold. As this revelation of her ardent nature burst upon me, and . . . I saw how faithful she had kept to her life purposes,—how patient, gentle, and thought-ful of others, how active in self-improvement and usefulness, how wisely dignified she had been,—I could not but bow to her in reverence. (*Ibid.*, Vol. II, p. 37.)

The inchoate rebellions in her heart were stimulated and given form by her reading. From the English, French, and German ro-mantics she drew much of her intellectual food. The long hours spent with her father over Jefferson's letters were the best of preparation for Rousseau and Mary Wollstonecraft, and French romanticism provided an excellent introduction to the German. Her emotions were in high ferment when she came upon the German school, and she yielded her heart to it without reserve. Novalis, Richter, above all Goethe, became a passion and swept her along the path that Hedge and James Freeman Clarke were following. For years she gathered materials for a life of Goethe, but a feeling of self-distrust held back the project. Her love for him was the great literary enthusiasm of her life. "It seems to me," she wrote in 1832, "as if the mind of Goethe had embraced the universe. . . . I am enchanted while I read. He comprehends every feeling I have ever had so perfectly, expresses it so beautifully; but when I shut the book, it seems as if I had lost my personal identity; all my feelings linked with such an immense variety that belongs to things I had thought so different" (*ibid.*, Vol. I, p. 119). Later, with more critical analysis of Goethe, she found her enthusiasm modifying; she was repelled by his calm, aloof intellectuality; [2] but she never wavered in loyal recognition of his commanding powers.

Her romantic idealism was in full career when the transcendental movement caught her up and put its stamp upon her. It came as an emotional appeal to the vague aspirations of a life inadequately motivated, and she threw herself eagerly into the new philosophy and became the most hectic of its expounders. The intellectual foundations of her transcendentalism were so slight in comparison with the equipment of Hedge and Parker as scarcely to justify her pretentions to their fellowship. But what she lacked in knowledge of Kant and Fichte she made up in enthusiasm, and none ques-tioned her right to speak for the group. The editorship of the *Dial* provided a convenient safety valve for her energy, but it neither absorbed her nor sufficed to satisfy her limitless desires.

[2] See *Life Without and Life Within*, pp. 23–60.

She needed to espouse a cause more concrete and dramatic, personal in its demands, calling for high sacrifice. Abolitionism was at hand, but it repelled her by its narrow dogmatisms. Garrison was never a hero of hers. She regarded him with "high respect" for his "noble and generous" course; but "he has indulged in violent invective and denunciation till he has spoiled the temper of his mind" ("Frederick Douglass," in *Life Without and Life Within*, p. 122). Later, when she was in Europe, she looked back half regretfully at her indifference to the movement.

How it pleases me here to think of the Abolitionists! I could never endure to be with them at home; they were so tedious, often so narrow, always so rabid and exaggerated in their tone. But, after all, they had a high motive, something eternal in their desire and life. (*Memoirs*, Vol. II, p. 229.)

Even Brook Farm repelled her as much as it attracted her. Though she loved many of the members, bore her share in the discussions preliminary to its establishment, and often visited there, she would not join the venture. She had had enough of farm life at Groton. To open a road to Utopia with a common plow was, perhaps, too prosaic a business for her romantic nature, and when the Fourier Phalanx was introduced she grew skeptical. Fourierism seemed to her too mechanical a conception, in spite of her sympathy for the humanitarian spirit that lay behind it. As she looked back upon it from the vantage point of her French experience, she modified her judgment somewhat, although the old transcendental bias that Emerson had voiced still colored her views.

The more I see of the terrible ills which infest the body politic of Europe, the more indignation I feel at the selfishness or stupidity of those in my own country who oppose an examination of these subjects,—such as is animated by the hope of prevention. Educated in an age of gross materialism, Fourier is tainted by its faults; in attempts to reorganise society, he commits the error of making soul the result of health of body, instead of body the clothing of the soul; but his heart was that of a genuine lover of his kind, of a philanthropist in the sense of Jesus; his views are large and noble; his life was one of devout study on these subjects, and I should pity the person who, after the briefest sojourn in Manchester and Lyons, the most superficial acquaintance with the population of London or Paris, could seek to hinder a study of his thoughts, or be wanting in reverence for his purposes. (*Ibid.*, Vol. II, p. 206.)

It was in part from Fourier, certainly from the collectivistic theories discussed so generally by the transcendental group, that she received her equipment for the cause which, more than any other except the dramatic Roman revolution, appealed to the deeper rebellions of her soul. She had dealt much with the woman question in her "Conversations," and in 1844 she published *Woman in the Nineteenth Century*, a work that made a great stir in America. The "little book was the first considered statement of feminism in this country" (Katharine Anthony, *Margaret Fuller*, p. 80), and its novelty was emphasized by its boldness. The question of woman's place had emerged sharply from the Abolition movement, when the appearance of women on the platform had aroused opposition even from radical reformers, and Angelina Grimké had encountered insults when she spoke at Abolition meetings. But Margaret Fuller was the first since Mary Wollstonecraft, fifty years before, to undertake a reasoned defense of the claims of woman to emancipation from man-made custom. It was a somewhat shocking book to fling at respectable Boston bluestockings— male as well as female—for not only did she discuss equality of economic opportunity and equality of political rights for women, but she went further and spoke frankly about sex equality, marriage, prostitution, physical passions—pretty much everything that was taboo in Boston society. It was a bold thing to do, needing more courage even than to engage in a Fourieristic onslaught upon the conventions of private property. Only a first-class rebel would have had the temerity to offer such morsels to wagging tongues.

This was her parting shot at a world that had done its best to stifle her. Thenceforth her field was to broaden out immensely. In 1844 she went to New York to live in the family of Horace Greeley and write critical reviews for *The Tribune*—a shift that marked the beginning of her intellectual maturity, the end of her mystical sentimentalism. She was thirty-four years of age, and she plunged vigorously into the work of criticism, never perhaps very successfully, certainly never with high distinction. Her judgments were penetrating and individual, she awakened some Cambridge animosities by her comment on certain Cambridge poets, but she was not a notable critic. A fine craftsmanship she never attained. A light touch she could never command. Nevertheless the experience was sobering. Honest, practical Horace Greeley, with his pugnacious fondness for social reform, was an excellent antidote to Concord transcendentalism; and an awakening sociological interest discovered ample opportunities in New York for the expression of her mother-instinct. She took to her stormy bosom the inmates of Sing Sing prison, the poor and out-cast of the city. At last she went to Europe, fell in with Mazzini, and found a cause dramatic enough and real enough to satisfy her rebellious instincts. She was profoundly stirred by the Roman revolution, took charge of one of the hospitals, and spent her strength freely. On the tragic failure of the revolt she started home with her husband and child, only to perish on the sandy shores of Fire Island—a fate she did not turn her finger to escape. Perhaps it was well. She had only too good reason to be fearful of her reception and of the future. Tongues that had wagged before would certainly have risen to a virtuous gabble over her misadventure in Italy. On the whole one must be glad that her friends refused to permit her good name to be thrown to the gos-sips. Why shouldn't gentlemen lie stoutly if by so doing they can cheat the salacious?

A sensitive emotional nature offers the best of social barometers, and Margaret Fuller's tragic life, despite its lack of solid accom-plishment, was an epitome of the great revolt of the New England mind against Puritan asceticism and Yankee materialism. She was the emotional expression of a rebellious generation that had done with the past and was questioning the future. Not a scholar like Theodore Parker, not a thinker like Thoreau, not an artist like Emerson, she was a ferment of troubled aspiration, an enthu-siasm for a more generous culture than New England had known—the logical outcome of the romantic revolution which, beginning with Channing's discovery of humanitarian France, and leading thence to idealistic Germany, was to break the indurated shell of life in New England, and release its conscience and its mind. She was the spiritual child of Jean Jacques even more than of Goethe—a fact that she eventually came to realize. Writing from Paris in 1847, she said:

To the . . . Chamber of Deputies, I was indebted for a sight of the manuscripts of Rousseau, treasured in their library. I saw them and touched them,—those manuscripts just as he has celebrated them, written on fine white paper, tied with ribbon. Yellow and faded age has made them, yet at their touch I seemed to feel the fire of youth, immortally glowing, more and more expansive, with which his soul has pervaded this century. He was the precursor of all we most prize. True, his blood was mixed with madness, and the course of his actual life made some *detours* through villainous places; but his spirit was intimate with the fundamental truths of human nature, and fraught with prophecy. There is none who has given birth to more life for this age; his gifts are yet untold; they are too present with us; but he who thinks really must often think with Rousseau, and learn him ever more and more. Such is the method of genius,—to ripen fruit for the crowd by those rays of whose heat they complain. (*Memoirs*, Vol. II, pp. 206-207.)

The rebel pays a heavy price for his rebellions, as Margaret learned to her cost. She suffered much in her daily life, but it was her art that suffered most. She was evidently a far richer nature than her printed works reveal. Intense in her extravagant demands upon life, a radical humanitarian in all her sympathies and instincts, generous in response to whatever was fine and high, living unduly an inner life as became a daughter of Puritanism—Margaret Fuller was too vivid a personality, too complete an embodiment of the rich ferment of the forties, to be carelessly forgotten. The deeper failure of her career—its vague aspirations and inadequate accomplishment—was a failure that may be justly charged against the narrow world that bred her. Perhaps no sharper criticism could be leveled at New England than that it could do no better with such material, lent it by the gods.

PART IV: OTHER ASPECTS OF THE NEW ENGLAND MIND

CHAPTER I

THE REIGN OF THE GENTEEL

I

THE discussion of the New England mind hitherto has kept pretty much to the outskirts of Boston, to Concord and Roxbury and undistinguished precincts; it has not penetrated the Back Bay where dwelt the authentic representatives of Brahminism, nor has it concerned itself greatly with Cambridge that was a lesser Back Bay. Nevertheless there were other ideals than those of transcendentalism and social reform in the New England of the renaissance—ideals of culture, of scholarship, of *belles lettres*, to which the Brahmin mind contributed, and which after the subsidence of the ferment came to dominate genteel New England and for a generation largely influenced American letters. To the revolutionary aspirations of the forties the Back Bay contributed little. Brahmin Boston might turn Unitarian with Channing, but it was at heart neither French romantic nor German idealist; it desired rather culture for its own sake, and scholarship it regarded as the handmaid of culture. It hoped of course that righteousness and the will of God should ultimately prevail in human affairs, but it was not exigent in its demands. Occasion and means it willingly left to God, anticipating that the walls of Jericho must fall of their own weakness. It is surprising how little the greater issues of the time ruffled the serenity of the Brahmin mind, and how uncritical were its judgments on such issues as came under its review. Divided between State Street and the Back Bay, its life ran a smoothly agreeable course with no hint of potential antagonisms between exploitation and culture. It followed so strictly the injunction, let not thy left hand know what thy right hand doeth, that the two were almost total strangers to each other. Like Edith Wharton's contemporary Knickerbockers, the Brahmins conceived the great business of life to be the erection of barriers

435

against the intrusion of the unpleasant. They took it ill when those barriers were assaulted by rude militants, and when indisputable Brahmins—men like Edmund Quincy and Wendell Phillips—took part in the assault, the Back Bay regarded them as more than a little queer.

The immediate consequence of this concern for defensive breast-works was the reign of the genteel in life and letters, a reign that set up a court of critical jurisdiction over the domain of American letters. The essence of the genteel tradition was a refined ethicism, that professed to discover the highest virtue in shutting one's eyes to disagreeable fact, and the highest law in the law of convention. Gone were the franker days of Robert Treat Paine when a wit might find his choicest *bons mots* in the bottom of his cups. Coarse-ness had given way to refinement. It was the romanticism of Brahmin culture, with all Falstaffian vulgarity deleted, and every smutch of the natural man bleached out in the pure sunshine of manners. It was Victorianism of a more maidenly purity than the English strain, so carefully filtered by passing through the close Puritan mesh that the smallest impurities were removed. The first of literary commandments was the commandment of reti-cence. Literature was conceived of as belonging to the library and the drawing-room, and it must observe the drawing-room amen-ities. Only a vulgarian would lug a spade there. Any venture into realism was likely to prove libidinous, and sure to be common. Certainly Margaret Fuller had overstepped the bounds of decency with her remarks about women of the streets. The Adamite school was the vulgar expression of the natural man, and Con-tinental realism—the French and the Russian—was only bringing the gutter into the library. Literature must be fine and pure and noble, and as such it will serve decency and manners; what excuse is there for it otherwise? The case for the true church of lit-erature, as against the Adamite and other heresies, was admirably stated by Lowell:

I have not seen Swinburne's new volume—but a poem or two from it which I have seen shocked me, and I am not squeamish. . . . Why should a man by choice go down to live in his cellar, instead of mount-ing to those fair upper chambers which look towards the sunrise of that Easter which shall greet the resurrection of the soul from the body of this death? *Virginibus puerisque?* To be sure! let no man write a line that he would not have his daughter read. . . . But I have outlived many heresies, and shall outlive this new Adamite one of Swinburne.

The true Church of poetry is founded on a rock, and I have no fear that these smutchy back-doors of hell shall prevail against her. (*Letters*, Vol. I, p. 377.)

II

Though it willingly recognized the superior claims of poetry and the essay, the Brahmin mind found a more congenial field for its literary ambitions in history; and the quiet scholarship that it pursued with exemplary diligence was likely to flower in substantial historical studies.   Excellent work much of it is, brilliant in certain instances; yet it too is subtly marked by the psychology of the environment that produced it.   The renaissance of Boston scholarship began with Everett and Ticknor, whose German training was imposed on natures instinctively aristocratic, swayed by the older Federalist prejudices.   The latter applied himself to Spanish literature, but his colleague and fellow historian, Jared Sparks, proved that in the American field even painstaking scholarship could not subdue the temptation to improve upon reality. Sparks applied Boston ethics to biography and conceived that his mission in writing the life of a great American like Washington was to portray a national hero as a model to the youth of the land. In pursuance of this aim he studiously perfected nature by correcting all the little blemishes of manner and little weaknesses of character in order to produce an immaculate effect.   He edited Washington's letters with a free hand, not only correcting the grammar and spelling, but silently deleting such passages as did not become the hero he had in mind.   He did not of course go to the absurd lengths of Parson Weems in inventing episodes and effects, but he refused to deal with his materials realistically and the result was a falsifying of the total impression.

The greatest and in certain respects the most characteristic work of the period was George Bancroft's *History of the United States*, to which with single-minded purpose he devoted sixty laborious years.   Trained in Göttingen, he gathered his materials with German thoroughness, but the underlying spirit and purpose of his exposition were native to the ardent nationalism of Jacksonian America.   Bancroft was the only important member of the New England group of historians who was a militant Democrat, and he set out to justify to the world the ways of democratic America.   It was a great undertaking and in the opinion of Ranke, the

German historian, it justified itself. "Your history is the best book ever written from the democratic point of view," [1] he wrote Bancroft. The praise was perhaps not excessive. Conceived in the early days of the Jacksonian triumph, it reflects the grandiose conception of the future of America and the beneficent influence of republican institutions on western civilization, that were common in the golden days of equalitarianism and that even such a scholarly legalist as Hugh Legaré shared. But unfortunately, with his generation Bancroft had lost his economic bearings, and he drove forward somewhat too confidently into the new seas of political idealism trusting to the pole-star of emancipated human nature. As a democrat he was too easily persuaded that democratic America lay in the particular keeping of Providence, and he assumed too readily that the democratic development of American institutions was in response to the divine will. It reflects something of the partisanship of honest patriots who believe God is on their side; but it served to correct the teachings of Federalists like Richard Hildreth who insisted that God was on the side of Federalism. Till Bancroft took up his pen the bias of American chronicles had been anti-democratic. Every Federalist with leisure, a quill, and a smattering of historical knowledge, had added his mite to the Federalist myths that long constituted the body of our history. The democratic interpretation ran so counter to Boston tradition that Bancroft found little congeniality amongst his fellow historians, and he eventually quitted his native state and took up his home in Washington.

More representative of the Brahmin spirit was the work of William H. Prescott, John L. Motley, and Francis Parkman, who constitute what may be called the romantic school of Boston historians. They sought the romantic in theme and aspired to the romantic in treatment quite as consciously as did the contemporary novelists. Of excellent Brahmin strain, with leisure, wealth, opportunity, they were free to pick and choose as they would. Prescott and Motley turned away from the partisanships of America, and while Jacksonianism was in full swing the former wrote his *Ferdinand and Isabella*, and while the country was wrangling over slavery the latter wrote his *Rise of the Dutch Republic*. Broad in conception and dramatic in treatment, they are admirable works, yet they suggest that aloofness from the sordid realities

---

[1] Quoted in Stanton, *Manual of American Literature*, p. 103.

of America so characteristic of the Brahmin mind. Far more brilliant and significant was the work of Francis Parkman who turned his imagination to the far West over which the struggle for exploration and conquest had long persisted between the French and English. In his twenties he had made a venturesome trip to the great plains, and that experience gave life and vitality to his later historical writings, that were enriched by close research, a brilliant style, and a creative imagination. The theme he set himself was not alone a "history of the American forest," but a clash between civilizations—the "feudal, militant, and Catholic France in conflict with democratic, industrial, and Protestant England"; and with fine tenacity of purpose, in the teeth of ill health, he wrought at his project till the America of the old French War times was gathered into his pages. The Brahmin mind has contributed to American letters no more brilliant work than came from the pen of Francis Parkman.

III

If the highest aspirations of the Brahmin nature sought satisfaction in poetry, Longfellow may be reckoned its most characteristic product. In his work the romantic, the sentimental, and the moralistic, blended in such just proportions, and expressed themselves with such homely simplicity as to hit exactly the current taste and establish a reputation that later generations have difficulty in understanding. A gentle, lovable soul, widely read and in maturer years possessing a ripe literary scholarship, he was a skillful purveyor of gentle, lovable ideals. Although he drew his materials from Spain and Sweden and Italy, from primitive New England and aboriginal America, it was Germany that largely provided the staple of his romance. With Emerson and Margaret Fuller and Theodore Parker, he found Germany a singularly congenial land—not Königsberg with its transcendental metaphysics, nor Weimar with its pagan culture, nor Tübingen with its higher criticism. Such things, transcendental and critical, he was not concerned about; it was the minor romantics, Freiligrath rather than Heine, the gentle melancholy and pervasive *Sehnsucht* of the German folk-nature, that drew him irresistibly and quickened his sympathetic pen. There was little intellect in Longfellow, little creative originality. He was the poet of an uncritical and unsophisticated generation, as yet untroubled by science and industrialism, and his mind was detached from politics and his conscience rarely disturbed by social questions. He came of excellent Federalist stock, his father having been a delegate from Maine to the Hartford Convention; and with his courteous manners he fitted easily into the little world of Cambridge Brahmins. However one might question his poetry, none could question that he was a gentleman amongst gentlemen.

If he was never the omnivorous bookman that Lowell was, he was distinctly a poet of the library. His placid and singularly happy life was pretty much bounded by his library walls. One could scarcely have lived more detached from contemporary America, more effectively insulated against the electric currents of the times. Though Thoreau might flee to Walden he carried his questioning intellect with him; even the constable would not leave him alone there. But Longfellow's door shut securely against all intrusion. The winds of doctrine and policy might rage through the land, but they did not rattle the windows of his study to disturb his quiet poring over Dante. The translation of the *Divina Commedia* would go forward even while the country was being torn asunder. In a sense such work was his refuge against the storm and stress of malignant forces that troubled him. He did not like the tumult and the shouting, and much of Longfellow is compressed into the sonnets that preface the translation, much of the gentleness of his evasion, and much of the finer craftsmanship of his later years.

> Oft have I seen at some cathedral door
> A laborer, pausing in the dust and heat,
> Lay down his burden, and with reverent feet
> Enter, and cross himself, and on the floor
> Kneel to repeat his paternoster o'er;
> Far off the noises of the world retreat;
> The loud vociferations of the street
> Become an undistinguishable roar.
> So, as I enter here from day to day,
> And leave my burden at this minster gate,
> Kneeling in prayer, and not ashamed to pray,
> The tumult of the time disconsolate
> To inarticulate murmurs dies away,
> While the eternal ages watch and wait.
>
> How strange the sculptures that adorn these towers!
> This crowd of statues, in whose folded sleeves
> Birds build their nests; while canopied with leaves

Parvis and portal bloom like trellised bowers,
And the vast minster seems a cross of flowers!
  But fiends and dragons on the gargoyled eaves
  Watch the dead Christ between the living thieves,
  And underneath, the traitor Judas lowers!
Ah! from what agonies of heart and brain,
  What exultations trampling on despair,
  What tenderness, what tears, what hate of wrong,
What passionate outcry of a soul in pain,
  Uprose this poem of the earth and air,
  This mediaeval miracle of song!

A single incursion Longfellow made into the field of Abolition
controversy, prompted perhaps by Dickens, whose "grand chapter on slavery" in *American Notes* he had read in London. The
seven poems were written to beguile the tedium of a sea voyage.
They are unreal enough to seem quite harmless, yet they created
a decided stir on their appearance. For a Harvard professsor
to express publicly even a mild sympathy with the Abolition
movement, may well have been somewhat perilous, considering the
fate of Professor Follen; and the sacred institution may have
scented a real danger in such romanticisms. Grotesque as these
academic poems were, with their burnt-cork figures, they perhaps served to romanticize and sentimentalize the negro for northern minds, as *Uncle Tom's Cabin* did a decade later with tremendous effect. Slavery had no weapon against such an attack,
and no doubt Longfellow's contributions proved serviceable to
the cause of Abolitionism. But this one venture satisfied him, and
having got safely back to his library, he shut the door on the whole
vexatious question of slavery. He was not made for battle, and
causes commanded an unwilling allegiance. Little remained of
his Puritanism save conscience, a sense of struggle against somewhat vague and indolent powers of evil, a pleasant melancholy
that transmuted itself into pleasant verse. He lived vicariously
the lives of other poets, sharing their emotions, repeating their
thoughts, reproducing their pictures; yet adding some individual
color from his own sincere nature. Not richly endowed, he was
more than an echo. He marked the transition from the nebulous
ferment of the creative renaissance to the scholarly culture of Brahmin Cambridge. After Longfellow came Charles Eliot Norton
in whose blameless life that culture flowered, and after that came
sterility.

CHAPTER II

NATHANIEL HAWTHORNE

Skeptic

AFTER his immersion for some months in the Utopian dreams of Brook Farm, Miles Coverdale in *The Blithedale Romance* discovered that he had drifted far from reality. "No sagacious man," he remarked, "will long retain his sagacity, if he live exclusively among reformers and progressive people, without periodically returning into the settled system of things, to correct himself by a new observation from that old standpoint."

It was now time for me, therefore, to go and hold a little talk with the conservatives, the writers of the North American Review, the merchants, the politicians, the Cambridge men, and all those respectable blockheads who still, in this intangibility and mistiness of affairs, kept a death-grip on one or two ideas which had not come into vogue since yesterday morning.

In this suggestive pronouncement the intellectual position of Hawthorne is revealed. Cool, detached, rationalistic, curiously inquisitive, he looked out upon the ferment of the times, the clash of rival philosophies and rival interests, only to bring them into his study and turn upon them the light of his critical analysis. One after another he weighed the several faiths of New England, conservative and transcendental and radical, and ended skeptic. He was too much of a realist to change fashions in creeds. Time, experience—he is always remembering—have created men as we find them, and very likely only time and experience can make them over into something different. The conservatives would seem to have common sense on their side, for they are seeking to retain what has hitherto been won; but the reformers are not without justification as well, for impelled by an ardent faith they are seeking to win new conquests. But whether that which the conservatives defend so valiantly is worth defending, or whether the goal towards which the reformers drive so furiously is worth the trouble, are questions about which the rationalist may be permitted his doubts. The universe in which he found himself was a moral universe, Hawthorne on the whole believed; and if that were true then man's chief business and urgent problem was the matter of a sufficient morality.

Radical in his intellectual processes, he could never become greatly interested in specific radicalisms. He is often thought of as a transcendentalist, and his association with the Peabodys and his venture into Brook Farm might seem to lend color to such an interpretation. Yet nothing in his intellectual sympathies marks him as of the school. The polar conceptions of transcendentalism repelled rather than attracted him. Political and metaphysical speculation left him cold, and the twin revolutionary forces of the time, French romanticism and German idealism, never deeply affected his thinking. Amid all the flux he retained much of the older Calvinist view of life and human destiny. Though nominally a Unitarian he did not share Channing's faith in the perfectibility of man. The buried voice of God that the transcendentalists professed to have discovered in instinct, he greatly distrusted. Man seemed to him quite as likely to turn out to be a child of the devil as the first-born of God. Perhaps through a long and uncertain process he may grow into something nobler than he now is, but for the present the fact remains that the human heart, if not desperately wicked, is at least on familiar terms with evil; too often it is cold, selfish, malignant, and its secret promptings need watching. Doubting the indwelling presence of the divine Over-soul, he could find no justification for the transcendental faith in the excellence of the universe, out of which came the genial optimism of the Emersonians. Too pronounced a rationalist to comprehend the mysticism that lurked in the heart of the transcendental faith, he remained cold to the revolutionary criticism that was eager to pull down the old temples to make room for nobler. Eager souls, mystics and revolutionaries, may propose to refashion the world in accordance with their dreams; but evil remains, and so long as it lurks in the secret places of the heart, Utopia is only the shadow of a dream. And so while the Concord thinkers were proclaiming man to be the indubitable child of God, Hawthorne was critically examining the question of evil as it appeared in the light of his own experience. It was the central, fascinating problem of his intellectual life, and in pursuit of a solution he probed curiously into the hidden, furtive recesses of the soul.

The isolation in which he chose to brood over the problem,

seeking to take the solution by surprise in unguarded moments, was the natural consequence of his temperament and his habits. He lived singularly remote from common interests, singularly self-sufficient.   Both as thinker and artist he suffered from his self-imposed isolation.   The twelve years of his apprenticeship, closely immured and given over to spinning cobwebs about the old Puritan rafters, drawing the stuff of his romance out of his own bowels, may have facilitated the development of technic, but it laid narrow limitations on the matter of his art.   Intellectually unlocalized in his Yankee world, he was the romancer of a dead but unforgotten past, at home only where the New England conscience brooded over sin—subduing the old nightmares to less terrifying dreams, intruding his doubts into old dogmas yet never emerging from the old shadows.   Although he was a child of the liberation and had broken the web that Calvinism had woven about the mind of New England, he did not choose to quit the world from whose bondage he had freed himself.   He would examine the old problem in a new light.   In rejecting Calvinism as a religion, he retained it as a background for his inquisitive probing.   It appealed to his imagination after his reason had rejected its dogmas; it determined his art after it had ceased to command his loyalty.   In consequence, all his life Hawthorne dwelt between worlds.   Though at times he tried to establish contact with Yankee reality, though he essayed to establish an intellectual *rapport* with his generation, he never quite succeeded, but remained to the last isolated, a frequenter of the twilight.

Only in a narrow and very special sense was Hawthorne a romantic.   With the romance of love and adventure he was never concerned; what interested him was the romance of ethics—the distortions of the soul under the tyranny of a diseased imagination. How little he shares in common with other romantics is revealed in his detachment from his native Salem.   The place was not lacking in picturesque charm, present and past.   During the long years he spent in his Salem study, the city was rising to the zenith of its brisk sea life, with its ships in the China trade, its venturesome fisheries, its echoes of the whaling industry at Nantucket. Materials for romance were lying all about the Salem wharves— such a show of canvas and spars and rigging, such briny smells, such suggestions of far voyages to outlandish places, such strange figures slipping in from the ends of the earth—such romantic

promptings in short as would have intoxicated the imagination of
Herman Melville, and that Joseph Hergesheimer wove into the
rich tapestries of *Java Head*. A romantic could scarcely have
found in America a setting better calculated to awaken a sense of
brave adventure than in old Salem; yet for three years Hawthorne
sat in the Custom House, with such materials all about him, and
then turned away to the seventeenth century to write of Hester
Prynne. For a man gifted with imagination to fail to lift his eyes
to the horizon beyond which the hurrying ships were seeking
strange markets, and instead to turn them in upon a shadowy
world of half unreal characters; to overlook the motley picturesque
in the foreground of the actual, in order to brood over an old adultery and twist it into theological sin, can be explained only on
the ground that Hawthorne was concerned with ethical rather
than romantic values, that he was interested rather in the problem
of evil than in the trappings of romance. Aloofness of time and
place served to isolate the problem, stripping away the wrappings
of the physical, delocalizing it, transmuting the individual act
into the universal. Thus isolated, Hester's sin becomes a symbol of
that ancient evil which forever waylays human life and by strange
perversions brings havoc to our hopes—the greatest havoc to him
whose heart, like Chillingsworth's, is cold, selfish, malignant.

This temperamental aloofness from objective reality was both
the strength and the weakness of Hawthorne's art. In choosing
to follow the way of the inner life he was true to his Puritan breeding. The perpetual turning-in of the mind upon itself, the long
introspective brooding over human motives, came naturally to
one who lived in the shadow of a Puritan past. In their anxious
concern over sin the Puritans had become in some measure psychologists; how else could the secret impulses of the soul be probed
and its dark workings laid bare? Hawthorne was only doing what
Jonathan Edwards before him had done in his psychological
clinic of the Great Awakening—examining the reactions of sin
on conscience and character. From this comes the simplicity of
his theme and the compelling unity of his handling. To be sure it
is pathological phenomena that he deals with, as the phenomena
that Edwards dealt with in his *Narrative of the Surprizing Work
of God*, were pathological; and like Edwards, Hawthorne is led
into insubstantial and tenuous regions where he breathes with
difficulty. The substantial world of Puritan reality that Samuel

Sewall knew, Hawthorne seems scarcely to have been aware of; he created instead his own Puritanism, fantastic and unreal. He was forever dealing with shadows, and he knew that he was dealing with shadows, and this consciousness was a perennial source of doubt and uncertainty that bred self-distrust. In setting himself the task of dramatizing sin rather than sinners, of creating romance out of the problem of evil, he encountered difficulties that oppressed him. The well-springs of his imagination were constantly running dry and he must wait till they filled again slowly. Hence the "development of his art is towards ever greater elaboration of scantier and scantier materials, until the joy of the whole becomes lost at last in the milder pleasures of detail."[1]

From the grave difficulties inherent in his theme came the inveterate habit of sliding into symbolism and allegory—from this and from the narrowness of his emotional life and the restrictions of his sympathies. The cold thin atmosphere of his work, one comes increasingly to feel, was due not alone or chiefly to the severity of his artistic restraint that forbade all rioting of the sensuous imagination; it was due rather to a lack of nourishment, to a poverty of ideas and sensuous imagery. His inveterate skepticism robbed him of much, but his inhibitions robbed him of more. A romantic uninterested in adventure and afraid of sex is likely to become somewhat graveled for matter. Like the Pyncheon fowls, Hawthorne's imagination had suffered from too long inbreeding; it had grown anemic, and every grain of fancy is clucked over and picked at and made much of. Once an idea comes into his head he is loath to let it go, but he must turn it about curiously and examine it from every angle. The striking chapter in *The House of the Seven Gables*, where the death of Judge Pyncheon is played upon so persistently, is only an extreme example of his habitual method. The tongues that wagged over the minister's black veil were no more inquisitive and tireless than Hawthorne's when his imagination is fired by a vivid image. He will not let it go till it is sucked as dry as last year's cider cask. It is the way of one to whom ideas are few and precious. Knowing how little is in the bottle he will linger out the flavor of every drop. Hence his fondness for symbolism, and hence his frequent lapse into allegory when imagination grows dull. Because Hawthorne was an

---

[1] Amy Louise Reed, "Self-Portraiture in the Work of Nathaniel Hawthorne," *Studies in Philology*, Vol. XXIII, No. I.

artist he was saved from the shipwreck that such a method might seem to invite; yet perhaps it is not unreasonable to suggest that he was an artist for the reason that only through the mastery of a refined technic could his scanty stock of ideas make any show at all.

The intellectual poverty that resulted from his long immuring himself in a void is sufficiently revealed in his *American Note-Books*. In the somewhat tedious volume covering the eighteen years between 1835 and 1853—the most vigorous years of the renaissance—there is no suggestion of interest in the creative ideas of the time, in metaphysics or politics or economics or humanitarianism. It is the occasional record of one who lived an unintellectual life, and it makes but a paltry showing when set beside the journals of Emerson for the same years. Few books are referred to; systems of thought lie beyond his ken. Compared with the thinkers and scholars of the time he is only an idler lying in wait for such casual suggestions as he may turn into stories. Almost childish is his delight in marvels. There is something of the spirit of Cotton Mather in his persistent recording of the gruesome and fantastic, in the hope that they will open a quarry for his art. In the year that Emerson wrote *Nature*, Hawthorne set down the following amongst some dozens of similar suggestions: "A snake taken into a man's stomach and nourished there from fifteen to thirty-five years, tormenting him most horribly. A type of envy or some other evil passion." The *Note-Books*, of course, are very inadequate records of his life, and yet that a mind should lie in wait for such grotesqueries, and treasure them, offers food for speculation. After his marriage they are much less frequent and his jottings become more normal—a change which the Freudians, no doubt, would be ready enough to explain.

The one great adventure of Hawthorne's life was the plunge into Brook Farm Utopianism, a plunge that only proved the waters colder and less hospitable than he had hoped. It was a curious adventure for one of his temperament to engage in, and his eventual disillusion might have been foretold. Perhaps it may be explained as reaction from his long isolation. The glowing enthusiasms of the times must often have tempted him to leave his narrow walls, and share the intellectual and emotional stimulus that others professed to discover in the work of making society over. Whatever the explanation the venture turned out to be a failure. His skepticism followed him there and came to later expression in *The Blithedale Romance*, a work as thin and unreal as anything he ever did. It is worse. There is in its pages more than a hint of ill humor that colors his interpretation of the Fourieristic stage of the experiment, and slips out in his portraiture of the major characters. Hollingsworth both fascinates and repels him. A dramatization of the intransigent spirit of reform, his single-minded zeal for righteousness, is subtly fused with an intolerant egotism that destroys Zenobia, cows Priscilla, and wrecks the venture. Perhaps Albert Brisbane may have been in the background of Hawthorne's mind when he drew Hollingsworth, for it was Brisbane who influenced the change he seems to have resented; perhaps Garrison may have served to fill out the picture. Whoever it was, the figure of Hollingsworth is Hawthorne's reply to the summons of the social conscience of the times, done by a critic whose insistent skepticism will not shut its eyes, but discovers under a new masquerade the ancient evil of a cold imperious heart. Seventeen years before he wrote *The Blithedale Romance*, he had jotted down in his *Note-Book* the conception out of which came the later portrait:

A sketch to be given of a modern reformer,—a type of the extreme doctrines on the subject of slaves, cold water, and other such topics. He goes about the streets haranguing most eloquently, and is on the point of making many converts, when his labors are suddenly interrupted by the appearance of the keeper of a mad-house, whence he has escaped. Much may be made of the idea. (*American Note-Books*, pp. 20–21.)

Hawthorne's interpretation of Margaret Fuller is not so easily explained. Perhaps it came out of a subconscious personal spleen. Her rich paganism may well have disturbed a nature so reticent as his, so restrained by certain Puritan inhibitions. In an early sketch he commented on the unfitness of authorship for women, on the ground that "there is a delicacy . . . that perceives, or fancies, a sort of impropriety in the display of woman's natal mind to the gaze of the world, with indications by which its inmost secrets may be searched out" (quoted by Amy Louise Reed, "Self-Portraiture in the Work of Nathaniel Hawthorne"). Margaret's frankness in displaying her natal mind to the gaze of the world, her bold discussion of prohibited subjects like prostitution, could not fail to rub across Hawthorne's deepest prejudices.

She was too vigorous and outspoken, too consciously endowed with sex, too frankly feminist, not to have ruffled his instinctive squeamishness. It was not her radical feminism in the abstract that offended him, if he may be trusted; but certainly in the concrete. A sexless feminism would not greatly disturb a mind tolerantly familiar with the current radicalisms; but the frank avowal of sex touched a sensitive nerve. It offended certain latent Puritanisms in him. He was fascinated by Zenobia and yet afraid of her—or of himself; so his hero falls in love with the anemic and witless Priscilla. How characteristic of a mind long fed on symbols, to turn away from the wealth of reality and prefer a shadow!

After Brook Farm came no further experiments in the unsatisfactory business of a *rapprochement* with his generation. His marriage with Sophia Peabody brought with it the prosaic duties of providing for a family, and he had no leisure to play with social reform. Abolitionism he would have none of, nor perfectionism, nor Jacksonianism—the futility of such things became for him a fixed idea. That he once had the courage to make his plunge he seems to have rejoiced over: "Whatever else I may repent of," Miles Coverdale wrote, "let it be reckoned neither among my sins nor follies that I once had faith and force enough to form generous hopes of the world's destiny,—yes!—and to do what in me lay for their accomplishment." Yet the truer Hawthorne is to be found in the judgments set down in the *Note-Book:* "It is my opinion that a man's soul may be buried and perish under a dung-heap, or in a furrow of the field, just as well as under a pile of money." "Oh, labor is the curse of the world, and nobody can meddle with it without becoming proportionably brutified." The man who wrote that had much to learn about life and society, much that he might have learned from Thoreau. But Hawthorne never grappled with economics as Thoreau did, and he learned no more from him than from Melville, or from Emerson, or from any of the books he read by the wise of other days. Self-sufficient he remained to the last, hard-headed and practical, yet missing many a deeper truth that more receptive minds discover. He was traveling the path that leads to sterility, and the lifelong business of playing Paul Pry to the secrets of the conscience brought him at last to the comment, "Taking no root I soon weary of any soil in which I may be temporarily deposited. The same impatience I sometimes feel, or conceive of, as regards this earthly life." He was the extreme and finest expression of the refined alienation from reality that in the end palsied the creative mind of New England. Having consumed his fancies, what remained to feed on?

CHAPTER III

THE AUTHENTIC BRAHMIN

I

OLIVER WENDELL HOLMES

Beacon Street Wit

SINCE the death of Holmes in 1894, his reputation has shrunk and dwindled with that of his group. With the rise of other literary schools, New England standards have been submitted to a somewhat rude overhauling, and Brahmin ideals are no longer reckoned so authoritative as they were once believed to be, nor the supremacy of Boston genius so indisputable. Concord has risen as Cambridge and Beacon Street have declined, and in the shadow of Emerson and Thoreau, the wit of Back Bay is in danger of being obscured. Unsupported by his physical presence, his writings seem far less vital than they did when the echoes of his clever talk were still sounding through them. Certain intellectual shortcomings are more obvious when his works are brought together in a library edition: in the mass his prose seems far more discursive and his verse thinner and more jingly than when the several bits appeared singly, personally sponsored by the author in whose cleverness everybody delighted. Read with sprightly vivacity to a group of sympathetic listeners at the mellowest hour of the dinner, his occasional verse must have sparkled brightly and have gone off with such a crackle of laughter as to convince the Back Bay that the asthmatic little gentleman with bubbling spirits was a veritable poet, on the same friendly footing with the muse that he was with Beacon Street. So frequently on pleasant occasions did Holmes appear before his classmates and friends copy in hand, so often and so happily did he respond to the invitation to write something, that it would have been ungenerous of Boston—and Boston meant the Back Bay, the Saturday Club and Harvard College—not to have crowned him with a wreath of her own ivy.

For upwards of half a century, throughout the prime and on past the Indian Summer of the New England renaissance, Holmes was Boston's own wit, inexhaustible in clever sayings, bubbling

over with satire and sentiment, the autocrat of her social gatherings, the acknowledged head of her mutual admiration society.
Not since Robert Treat Paine had there been such a master of
Yankee small talk.   If he monopolized the conversation he dealt
generously with his listeners.   The stream was copious and the
waters were never bitter or astringent, but with just enough effervescence to suit the Boston palate.   As a young man the wit
sparkled more brightly; as an old man the humor exuded more
gently.   At twenty-five he described William IV of England with
republican irreverence: "The King blew his nose twice, and wiped
the royal perspiration repeatedly from a face which is probably
the largest uncivilized spot in England"; late in life he commented
on his obvious fondness of praise: "I was always patient with those
who thought well of me, and accepted all their tributes with something more than resignation."   Taste had changed with the times
in Boston.   Wit was yielding place to humor; eighteenth-century
frankness had given way to nineteenth-century refinement; Victorianism was in full and vigorous bloom in the Beacon Street of
1850, and so Holmes became a Yankee Victorian.   The morals
of an impeccable society required no castigation, and he was under
no obligation to satirize vice.   Audacious sallies would have been
reckoned in bad taste.   If the old-fashioned masculine wit of Robert Treat Paine, with its echoes of Charles Churchill, had presumed to intrude itself into the teacup society of Back Bay drawing-rooms, the indignant Doctor would have shown it the door,
and the small talk would have flowed again, decorous and clean
and amiable, far more refined than the wit that had delighted their
fathers.

And yet, though a full-blown Victorian in manners and tastes,
Holmes was something of a child of the eighteenth century at
heart.   The situation in which he found himself might have proved
disconcerting if he had chosen to speculate upon it.   By nature
a thoroughgoing rationalist, he lived in a romantic age.   A gentleman of "parts and learning," with a quick and lively fancy that
blossomed in the pat phrase and neat couplet, he loved wit and
hated dullness with true Augustan zeal.   The great days of Queen
Anne were a perennial inspiration to him.   He clung to the heroic
couplet through all the changes of romantic styles.   He moralized
in rime with the fluency if not the finish of Pope.[1]   He satirized

---

[1] See *A Rhymed Lesson.*

Calvinism with an honest wrath that he might have learned of Swift. He commented in his table-talk on the manners of the times with the chatty discursiveness of Addison. Like the earlier wits, he discovered a deep sympathy for the maturity and ripe wisdom of the classics. Writing to his friend John O. Sargent, he remarked:

I wish I had become as familiar with some classic author as you are with Horace. There is nothing like one of those perennial old fellows for good old gentlemenly reading; and for wit and wisdom, what is there to compare with the writings of Horace? You make me envious,—I vow I shall have to get up Juvenal or Catullus, naughty but nice, or somebody that nobody else knows. . . . I get so tired of the damp sheets of all sorts of *literati* (worse than the "screeching women of Marblehead") and clamorous essayists, that I want something always by me, calm, settled beyond cavilling criticism,—a cool, clear draught of Falernian that has been somewhere near two thousand years in the cellar. (Morse, *Life and Letters*, Vol. II, p. 311.)

But unhappily what could he do? He was the most sociable of persons, and he lived and moved in an atmosphere surcharged with various and sundry romanticisms. How could he preserve the spirit of quiet rationalism, or assure himself gentlemanly leisure, with a host of "isms" clamoring in his ears? He was amongst them even if he was not of them. He strove to keep himself aloof, unfuddled by heady idealisms and untroubled by strident reforms, but he could not shut his study door against the infection. He could not deny his generation, and inevitably he suffered his thought to be streaked and pied with the current romanticism. He gave Lyceum lectures on Wordsworth and Keats and Shelley, and their influence seeped into his verse. The Longfellow fame was all about him, and he fell to composing ballads and idyls and tales, quite as if he did not know better. Romantic garments fitted him ill, yet he persisted in trying them on. He even got to like them, and came finally to prefer *The Chambered Nautilus* above his other poems—a strange perversion of taste for a rationalist. *The One-Hoss Shay* is worth a volume of such pretty moralizing. *Parson Turell's Legacy* and *The Moral Bully* are in better vein—witty, lucid, critical—than any half-hearted ventures in romanticism. The eighteenth-century wit does not appear to advantage patched with Victorian sentiment, and he should have been rationalist enough to know it.

As a Beacon Street Victorian Holmes was as full of virtuous prejudices as an egg is full of meat; but as a rationalist, with a modest scientific equipment that came from his professional training, he kept the windows of his mind open to the winds of scientific inquiry that were blowing briskly to the concern of orthodox souls. Many a barnacled craft was foundering in those gales, and Holmes watched their going-down with visible satisfaction. He was perhaps the most militant Unitarian amongst Boston laymen. Hatred of Calvinistic dogma was an obsession with him; it dominated his thought and colored much of his work, *Elsie Venner* and his table-talk as frankly as *The One-Hoss Shay*. The criticism to which he subjected the old-school dogmas was always vehement, often vindictive. Long after the battle had been won he kept annoying the retreating enemy. His father, Abiel Holmes, was a rigorous follower of the Edwardean school, who after nearly forty years' service lost his pulpit for refusing to compromise with Unitarian liberalism that had gained the fortress of the near-by College Yard; and the stalwart among his congregation, having to yield the building, the endowment and the communion plate, were forced to establish themselves anew. In this unhappy schism that came about the time Oliver Wendell Holmes was graduating from Harvard in 1829, the latter went with the liberals. He had broken with the Calvinism of his father, and in the reaction he went further than most along the path of Unitarian rationalism—not the path of Channing that led to French romanticism and transcendentalism, but the path of Andrews Norton that led to a harder-headed rationalism. The reasons for this shift are sufficiently evident in his writings. At his father's table he had watched too many "whey-faced" brethren to like the breed—men with "a weedy flux of ill-conditioned hair," whose

> acrid words
> Turn the sweet milk of kindness into curds,
> Or with grim logic prove, beyond debate,
> That all we love is worthiest of hate,
> As the scarred ruffian of the pirate's deck,
> When his long swivel rakes the staggering wreck!
> (*The Moral Bully.*)

The words are bitter, but they reveal the length of his reaction from the Calvinism on which he had been over-fed at home and at Phillips Andover Academy; and they suggest also why, next to Theodore Parker, Holmes came to be the best hated of Boston Unitarians amongst the orthodox. On this one subject he was militantly radical, never shirking debate, but whetting the edge of his satire and impaling his victim neatly with his logic. He took sardonic delight in turning Calvinism against itself, in the clever *reductio ad absurdum* of the Edwardean argument. Perhaps this major intellectual interest appears most adequately in his picture of the Master, the autobiographical rationalist whom he introduces into *The Poet of the Breakfast Table*. A dabbler in the law, theology and medicine, a philosophic contemplator of the Order of Things, who refused to permit "the territory of a man's mind" to be "fenced in," who agreed with the Poet in thinking somewhat ill of the specialist who dedicated his life to the study of beetles, preferring to range widely through time and eternity, who followed Darwin and was deep in bacteriology, trying "curious experiments in spontaneous generation"—this was Holmes on the intellectual side, a genial disseminator of the latest scientific speculations, a tolerant amateur of the things of the mind, a friendly dabbler in absolute moralities, who hoped "to do some sound thinking in heaven" if he ever got there, but who was too pleasantly engaged with Beacon Street to settle things now.

In his own special way, then, as a Brahmin of the Brahmins, Holmes was a rebel, a puller-down of worm-eaten structures, a freethinker rejoicing when free thought tossed a cargo of obsolete dogma into Boston Bay, or drew out a linchpin of some respectable social coach. He loved Boston the more because he believed that Boston was the home of free thought and free speech, the capital of American brains, the intellectual rebel of the continent. He did not agree with Emerson's strictures, or Parker's. He would not concede that Boston was the "home of the Hunkers." It was provincial; it had crooked little streets; but

I tell you Boston has opened, and kept open, more turnpikes that lead straight to free thought and free speech and free deeds than any other city of live men or dead men—I don't care how broad their streets are, nor how high their steeples. (*The Professor at the Breakfast Table*, p. 4.)

When he contemplated the future of America, with Boston as its intellectual leader, he was carried on the crest of an exuberant optimism:

A new nursery, Sir, with Lake Superior and Huron and all the rest of 'em for washbasins! A new race, and a whole new world for the new-born human soul to work in! And Boston is the brain of it, and has been any time these hundred years! That's all I claim for Boston—that it is the thinking centre of the continent, and therefore of the planet. (*Ibid.,* p. 104.)

If the mind is free other things will take care of themselves—this pretty much sums up Holmes's social philosophy. Only, he would add, when the mind is used to its freedom, it will create a culture that is well-mannered, that does not run to extravagant agitation, that considers time, place, and outward circumstance in effecting needful changes—the quiet decency of Channing rather than the noisier way of Parker. The Brahmin way, after all, was the better way, Holmes believed; and Channing was a Brahmin:

Parson Channing put a little oil on one linchpin, and slipped it out so softly, the first thing they knew about it was the wheel of that side was down. T'other fellow's at work now; but he makes more noise about it. When the linchpin comes out on his side, there'll be a jerk, I tell you! Some think it will spoil the old cart, and they pretend to say that there are valuable things in it which may get hurt. Hope not—hope not. But this is the great macadamizing place—always cracking up something. (*Ibid.,* p. 19.)

Certainly not on the intellectual side could Holmes be set down as a conservative. He did not relish any such imputation and defended himself with vigor:

If to be a conservative is to let all the drains of thought choke up and keep the soul's windows down—to shut out the sun from the east and the wind from the west—to let the rats run free in the cellar, and the moths feed their fill in the chambers, and the spiders weave their lace before the mirrors, till the soul's typhus is bred out of our neglect, and we begin to snore in its coma or rave in its delirium—I, Sir, am a *bonnet-rouge,* a red-cap of the barricades, my friends, rather than a conservative. (*Ibid.,* p. 18.)

It was this spirit of rationalism that made him—at some risk of unpopularity—an unsparing critic of romantic equalitarianism. Here again is an echo of the older century. Neither the Jacksonian nor the transcendental version of the new gospel found favor in his eyes; both seemed to run counter to the open facts of history. As a realist he discovered justification for John Adams's doctrine of economic determinism: all society, he was convinced, tends to stratify in lines of wealth distribution, in America as well as in Europe, and no dogmas can prevent it. He went further and insisted that the possession of wealth makes possible comfort, ease, leisure, culture; that those lacking wealth are necessarily unfree and their lives in consequence are meaner and narrower. Much of his criticism of Yankee villagers and countrymen—and except Cooper, he was perhaps the most critical commentator on Yankee provincialisms of speech and manners—springs from the conviction that a niggardly economics had created a niggardly society. He desired more wealth to the end of more culture. He was too completely Brahmin to set material well-being as the ultimate goal of the competitive struggle; that seemed to him the object of State Street and of the plutocracy he frankly detested. In *The Poet at the Breakfast Table* he apologizes for calling one of his characters a capitalist, on the ground that "the word seems to be equivalent to highway robbery in the new gospel of Saint Petroleum." Wealth as a means to power he would have none of; but wealth as a means to leisure, and leisure as a means to cultivated living, he was fond of extolling. The machinery of Brahmin life must be well oiled, but the life is more than the machinery. Always he returned to the intellectual as the hallmark of every society that may be accounted excellent, and his instinctive dislike of the middle class was founded on its intellectual sterility. It lived opulently but meanly; its rich dinners wanted the spice of wit, its ostentatious display lacked the salt of manners. It was vulgar at heart, and Holmes hated vulgarity even more than he hated John Calvin's dogmas.

Unfortunately his Brahminism sealed pretty tightly certain windows of his mind that might better have been kept open. A radical in the field of theology where personal concern brought him to serious grappling with the problem, a tolerant rationalist in the realm of the intellect, he remained a cheerfully contented conservative in other fields. He was unconsciously insulated against the currents of social and political thought flowing all about him. Economic inequality he accepted rather too complacently. His daily life ran so easy and comfortable a course as never to prod him into questioning how other lives might be running. By instinct and training he was an aristocrat, and he was never at pains to conceal his preference for the well born and well mannered. He professed a philanthropic sympathy for the cause of the slave, but he shared the Beacon Street dislike of agitation—it was not well bred and it might bring down more things than he cared to have brought down. The most completely class-conscious of the

Boston writers, he deprecated all proletarian appeals. They were not, in his opinion, "wholesome moral entertainment for the dangerous classes. Boys must not touch off their squibs and crackers too near the powder-magazine." The less said about the wrongs of labor, the better—at least publicly. Social strata being determined by economics, the agitator is little better than a firebrand.

You can't keep a dead level long, if you burn everything down flat to make it. Why, bless your soul, if all the cities of the world were reduced to ashes, you'd have a new set of millionaires in a couple of years or so, out of the trade in potash. In the meantime, what is the use of setting the man with the silver watch against the man with the gold watch, and the man without any against them both? . . . Here we are travelling through the desert together like the children of Israel. Some pick up more manna and catch more quails than others, and ought to help their hungry neighbors more than they do; . . . but we don't want the incendiary's pillar of a cloud by day and a pillar of fire by night to lead us in the march to civilization, and we don't want a Moses who will smite the rock, not to bring out water for our thirst, but petroleum to burn us all up with. (*The Poet at the Breakfast Table*, pp. 5–6.)

In his attitude toward the present comfortable arrangement of society, Holmes was no rebel. He was not callous to the evils of society, but he was willing to take a longer time in the march towards civilization than more exigent souls wished; it was a pleasant march on the whole, and why quarrel over the difference in packs? If his attitude was not the indifferentism of the well-to-do, it was near kin to it. He reflected the negative qualities of Unitarianism, rather than the positive, the free mind rather than the tender conscience. His social bias is sufficiently revealed in the tributes of praise he bestowed so generously. Among those whom he delighted to honor, the names of Garrison, Phillips, Parker, Thoreau, Greeley, John Brown, do not appear; instead he offered his praises to Everett, Webster, Bryant, Whittier, Agassiz, Parkman, Wilkie Collins, the Grand Duke Alexis, and a host of lesser celebrities known to the Back Bay. His heroes were respectable souls rather than militant. As a critic his vision seems to have been blurred by certain astigmatisms, and he discovered heroic qualities more readily in the militant dead than in the militant living. He delighted in the Boston of '76, but it is reasonably certain that if he had lived then he would have walked the streets of that older Boston as a genial Tory, and would have suffered the fate of other gentlemen who found it desirable to with-

draw with Gage's Redcoats—unless, indeed, his love of the place
had held him despite his politics.

In his literary work Holmes was always the talker rather than
the writer. The charm of the vivid and racy colloquial marks
every page. A clever aphorism or telling pun is the objective of
every paragraph, and it explodes with a brilliant shower of sparks.
But like every talker his discursiveness is inveterate; he wanders
far in pursuit of his point and sometimes returns empty-handed.
He was always an amateur; life was too agreeable for him to take
the trouble to become an artist. The essay was his most congenial
form—his novels are to be taken no more seriously than his occasional verse. *Elsie Venner* wraps up the familiar problem of moral
determinism in pleasantly discursive chat of Yankee bumpkin-
ism in contrast with Yankee Brahminism, and he returns his impeccable hero to Beacon Street, after his sojourn in the provinces,
to reward him with the Brahmin rewards—a munificent practice,
a charming wife, and an exalted social position. What richer
reward could be desired by one who had tasted to the full the
mellow flavor of that society? Staid, delightful, self-satisfied,
righteous little Beacon Street! Last refuge and citadel of the old
Brahmin respectability; basking in the afternoon sunshine of its
culture, not realizing that its sun is already well past the meridian;
in love with its own virtues and unaware that the morrow will
see the invasion of the Huns and Vandals of plutocracy, to whose
plethoric bank books Brahmin culture must eventually bow—
who would not have liked it? It was something after all to have
been its favorite wit, its ready oracle, its clever poet, who in praising his fellow Brahmins was well aware that he discreetly praised
his own admirable qualities. Kindly, delightful, fortunate Dr.
Holmes! chief citizen of the Hub of the Universe! He was born
and lived with a silver spoon in his mouth, and if a grudging
posterity inclines to rate him and his little world somewhat lower
than he rated them, what difference can that make to him? Tolerant himself, we should perhaps emulate his example, and not insist too rudely that he is only a minor figure in American literature.

II

JAMES RUSSELL LOWELL

Cambridge Brahmin

Whatever the critics may eventually come to say about Lowell, he was certainly the ablest and most distinguished of the old Cambridge breed, in the days when the Brahmin caste was disintegrating and Brahmin ideals losing their hold on New England—a man of fine native abilities in whom Harvard culture did its best to strike fire and light and understanding to serve as a beacon to the rest of America. He was not of the Concord line of transcendental individualists, nor of the militant strain of reforming enthusiasts; but of the true Brahmin line of Josiah Quincy and Edward Everett and Oliver Wendell Holmes—men of sound culture who could serve God valiantly in the social station in which He had placed them, without wanting to pull down the old church to build a new. Like Charles Eliot Norton—*clarum et venerabile nomen*—he had no plans of a new building in his pocket, but was content to enlarge and embellish the old. He would serve culture rather than causes. His gifts were Brahmin gifts, his prejudices were Brahmin prejudices; and so in spite of a "certain sprightliness of brain" that tempted him to rebel at the aridity of the scholastic commons on which he fed, and in spite of certain youthful vagaries and incursions into indiscreet places, he remained at bottom a Harvard conservative, content with his birthright, hopeful that his ways were God's ways. This suffices to explain the extraordinary reputation of Lowell in Cambridge circles, and the difficulty with which it made headway elsewhere. Though he traveled much in his library—as Thoreau would say—his prejudices remained narrowly local. To the last he remained extraordinarily parochial.

Yet the culture he served so faithfully never fruited in wisdom. He was never quite certain of himself, of what he really believed. He was fond of standing off and studying himself quizzically, to learn what sort of person he was; yet he was swayed by so many impulses he was never quite sure what sort of legs were under him. He was hopelessly bewildered by his own vast disorder. His mind was as cluttered as a garret, filled with an endless miscellany of odds and ends. Life puzzled him, as it puzzles every serious mind; but he allowed himself to be too easily discouraged by his inveterate unwillingness to think. He never speculated widely or analyzed critically. Ideas, systems of thought, intellectual and social movements, he had no interest in; he was content to remain a bookish amateur in letters, loitering over old volumes for the pleasure of finding apt phrases and verbal curiosities. With all his reading, history remained a blank to him; and science he would have none of. "I hate it," he confessed late in life; "I hate it as a savage hates writing, because I fear it will hurt me somehow." A good many things hurt him in those later years, and it was characteristic of him to say, "I continue to shut my eyes resolutely in certain speculative directions." He defined culture as "intelligent purpose"; yet of such intelligent purpose his intellectual life revealed little. Naturally he did not relish the theological unsettlement that came with the advance of scientific inquiry. Leslie Stephen's rationalism troubled him, and after reading the former's *English Thought in the Eighteenth Century*, he wrote, "I am very much in the state of mind of the Bretons who revolted against the Revolutionary Government and wrote upon their banners, 'Give us back our God!'" (*Letters*, Vol. II, p. 168.) Neither did he relish the economic unsettlement the industrial revolution was bringing to Cambridge and America, but he looked back longingly to the quiet days "before our individuality had been trampled out of us by the Irish mob." Standing between the older America and the new, with the foundations disintegrating under his feet, he confused the disorder in his own mind with the disorder in the external world of society, and desperately sought to cling to his ancient hopes. A pathetic yearning for orderliness in an age that has grown heedless of it was natural enough in a mind that had come to expect little of life; but surely orderliness, like charity, should begin at home.

It was, perhaps, not altogether his fault. His impulses were liberal and his mind generous, but he was never strong enough to overcome the handicap of the Lowell ancestry and training. When he spoke of himself half whimsically as a natural Tory, he was putting his finger on the Brahmin strain. The sanctity of the Lowell blood is a commonplace in New England; but that it was Tory blood is less frequently remarked. His grandfather, John Lowell, to be sure, was visited by certain humanitarian compunctions, and in 1772 convinced himself that at Common Law slavery could not stand, and was eager to put it to the test in Massachusetts. But John Lowell was high in the councils of the Federalist party, and a judge, and it is a safe guess that his radicalism did not go deep. Certainly, the next generation was stalwartly conservative. The three brothers represented the three major professions of law, theology, and business, that constituted the New England hierarchy. His father, Charles Lowell, after traveling abroad, was settled as pastor of the West Church, Boston— Jonathan Mayhew's church—a post he held for fifty-six years. He was a stout Federalist, a good hater of Jefferson,[2] a pleasant, cautious gentleman who refused to be drawn into the bitter Unitarian-Trinitarian controversy of the day—as unlike the militant Mayhew as a conventional soul could well be.[3] His uncle, John Lowell, was a capable lawyer-politician, one of the directing minds of the Federalist machine, earnestly engaged in defending Massachusetts against the wicked Republicans. Another uncle, Francis Cabot Lowell, was an enterprising capitalist, founder of the city of Lowell, whose multiplying spindles, it was hoped, would turn the wives and daughters of Yankee farmers, and the poverty-stricken Irish immigrants, into efficient revenue-producers for State Street securities.

From this pleasant background of Brahmin conservatisms, Lowell went forth into a world given over to momentous changes, contemptuous of all Brahmin standards, to find his way as he might. An original mind would have marked out its own path, as Emerson did; a conventional mind would have gone with the better sort, as Josiah Quincy did; but Lowell was neither Emerson nor Quincy. Sensitive to change, he was rarely self-reliant; generous in sympathies, he was timid in convictions. He was no Come-outer to stand alone against the world, but unconsciously he took color from his environment and was always glad to find a staff to lean on. It was fortunate for his peace of mind that he never realized how frequently he was no more than an echo of other minds; yet the confusions and contradictions that mark off the several periods of his life can be explained in no other way. From Brahminism he drifted to radicalism, and from radicalism back to a modified Brahminism; and these changes resulted from no native intellectual unfolding, but from certain dominant personalities who drew him aside from his natural or-

---

[2] See *Letters*, Vol. I, p. 82.
[3] See Hale, *James Russell Lowell and His Friends*, p. 10.

bit. He quitted college as a pleasant young Tory, who paused in his Commencement Poem to address some pointed remarks at Abner Kneeland—the last man imprisoned in Massachusetts for religious opinion—upon the wickedness of an atheism that denied the faith of Charles Lowell. But the ferment of the times was already working in him, and when he was nineteen he wrote with youthful fervor, "I am fast becoming ultra-democratic. . . . Liberty is now no longer a cant word in the mouths of knaves and fools" (*Letters*, Vol. I, p. 33). Within a year he had met Maria White, whose influence till her death in 1853 was the determining factor in his intellectual life. She was an ardent Abolitionist and reformer, and under her pleasant tutelage Lowell was indoctrinated in the current philosophy of radicalism. He spoke at Abolition meetings, and contributed to the Abolition press. More important, he conceived that he had come upon his true mission in letters. In an ode beginning "In the old days of awe and keen-eyed wonder," he put into verse his new creed, a prose statement of which he elaborated in a letter explaining his *Prometheus* in 1843, a year before his marriage to Miss White:

Although such great names as Goethe, Byron, and Shelley have all handled the subject in modern times, you will find that I have looked at it from a somewhat new point of view. I have made it *radical*, and I believe that no poet in this age can write much that is good unless he give himself up to this tendency. For radicalism has now for the first time taken a distinctive and acknowledged shape of its own. So much of its spirit as poets in former ages have attained (and from their purer organization they could not fail of some) was by instinct rather than by reason. It has never till now been seen to be one of the two great wings that up-bear the universe. . . . The proof of poetry is, in my mind, that it reduces to the essence of a single line the vague philosophy which is floating in all men's minds, and so renders it portable and useful and ready to the hand. (*Letters*, Vol. I, p. 73.)

Six years later he asserted confidently, "I am the first poet who has endeavored to express the American Idea, and I shall be popular by and by." Yet within a few months he found the vein nearing exhaustion. In a survey of his course up to 1850, he remarked that he had served love and freedom hitherto, and he now proposed to serve beauty, adding the significant comment, "I find that Reform cannot take up the whole of me, and I am quite sure that eyes were given us to look about us sometimes, and not to be always looking forward. . . . I am tired of controversy" (*ibid.*,

Vol. I, p. 173). Between these several confessions lies the bulk of Lowell's contribution to the "causes" of the times, and how adequately he served them is revealed in the successive poems that came from his pen.[4] Their equal as a whole is not to be found in the work of other contemporary radicals. The better work is solidly vigorous, with competent iambs that often rise to the dignity of such lines as "Slowly the Bible of the race is writ." The eager rhetoric of *The Present Crisis* was the highwater mark of Abolition argument in verse; but its serviceableness for quotation cannot make it so good a poem as *Prometheus* with its muscular blank verse, or as *A Glance behind the Curtain* with its portrait of Cromwell, strong in his faith, ready for all needful iconoclasms:

> I have no dread of what
> Is called for by the instinct of mankind;
> Nor think I that God's world will fall apart
> Because we tear a parchment more or less."

This is frank transcendental radicalism, yet the truer Lowell of those days of youthful enthusiasm is found in the *Biglow Papers*, first written with spontaneous gusto out of his hatred of the imperialism of the Mexican war, and later carefully embedded in the heavy machinery of the prose setting. The native clutter of Lowell's mind is there laid bare—the grotesque mixture of homely satire, moral aphorisms, Yankee linguistics, literary criticism— an unwieldy mass that he could neither simplify nor reduce to order. The machinery spoils the propaganda and weighs down the satire; yet the verse has survived because for once Lowell let himself go and hit such heads as he had a mind to.

Lowell saw fit to retain most of his radical verse in the definitive edition of his works, but his radical prose he disowned, and it was left for pious hands to gather together long after his death. It was perhaps as well for his reputation that the ambassador at the Court of St. James's should not be plagued by his youthful indiscretions. In those prose writings were combustible materials. He went with the Abolitionists in their brisk assaults on law, order, and the Constitution. Whatever revolution was stirring anywhere found him sympathetic. He was strong for the work-

---

[4] The more significant titles are: *Prometheus* and *A Glance behind the Curtain,* 1843; *Columbus* and *The Present Crisis,* 1844; *On the Capture of Fugitive Slaves near Washington,* 1845; *Biglow Papers,* begun in 1846; *The Pioneer,* 1847; *Bibliolâtres,* 1849; *Anti-Apis,* 1851.

ingman's revolution of 1848 in France; it was social injustice that was to blame for mob violence, and the fetish of *laissez faire* was a sorry enough god to worship.

The great problem of the over-supply of labor is not to be settled by a decimation of the laboring class, whether by gunpower or starvation. . . . The giant Labor did not merely turn from one side to the other for an easier position. Rather he rose up, "Like blind Orion hungry for the morn." . . . They had learned by bitter experience that it was on the body of old King Log *Laissez-faire* that King Stork perched to devour them. *Let-alone* is good policy after you have once got your perfect system established to let alone. (Quoted in Scudder, *James Russell Lowell*, Vol. I, pp. 205–206.)

In common with the Abolitionists, Lowell appealed to the Declaration of Independence against the Constitution. He took delight in satirizing his Federalist forebears, who, he asserts, beginning to fear the light of freedom, ingeniously constructed a "Sacred Parasol" for the new Goddess of Liberty, "to prevent her from being tanned":

A stout machine of parchment was accordingly constructed, and, under the respectable name of a Constitution, was interposed wherever there seemed to be danger from the hostile incursions of light. Whenever this is spread, a dim twilight, more perplexing than absolute darkness, reigns everywhere beneath its shadow. . . . This contrivance of ours, though the work of our own hands, has acquired a superstitious potency in our eyes. (*Ibid.*, Vol. I, p. 210.)

No wonder Lowell later disowned such apostasies, for after Maria White's death in 1853 came the dun professorial period of his life, when Harvard laid hands on him and came near to reducing him to its own ways. It revived the old Brahmin instincts that had lain dormant during the years of his Abolitionism, without reviving the old sanctions. Left without a cause, half ashamed of his youthful indiscretions yet ill content to drift, he turned bookman and for twenty-one years wandered with Norton and Longfellow and Child in the Sahara of medieval scholarship. It was not a happy time with him. There is plenty of evidence of his restlessness and dissatisfaction that occasionally prompted the wish to turn wholly scholar and keep his note-books in order; that prodded him to salvage the mass of his accumulation by turning his lecture-notes into literary essays; and that in other moods induced him to turn half savagely upon his dead enthusiasms and find solace in clever satire. His vigorous salvagings were scarcely worth the trouble. He had nothing important to say about Dante or Pope or Wordsworth, and he said it with a good deal of needless verbal exertion. The essay on Thoreau, written in 1865, was a different matter. Here he was brought face to face with a past which it still hurt him to remember; and the ill nature that colors his comment is sufficient testimony to the painfulness of his memories. Certainly he did not understand Thoreau, was incapable of understanding him; yet might not his dislike have been prodded by the consciousness that Thoreau had refused to make terms with Harvard culture as he had done? An intelligent reading of Thoreau must have been an unpleasant experience in Lowell's mood, keenly aware of certain backslidings of his own; and the essay is suggestive for the light it throws on Lowell, not on Thoreau.

To this period belong most of the essays on which rests Lowell's reputation as a critic of letters and politics. Bright as that reputation long was, it is beginning to show tarnish. Subjected to the scrutiny of eyes unblinded by the congenialities of the Cambridge coterie, it appears that Lowell's brilliancy covered over certain grave shortcomings that unfitted him for serious critical judgment.[5] He had no standards other than ethical, only likes and dislikes; no interest in ideas, only a pottering concern for the text; no historical backgrounds, only isolated figures dwelling in a vacuum. He was puzzled over new schools and unfamiliar technic, and was at ease only in praising established reputations and confirming approved judgments. He scoffed at Taine instead of going to school to him, and made merry over Masson's *Life of Milton;* yet he was wholly incapable of dealing with men from whose fruitful minds came ideas that summoned throngs of followers. In almost the last year of his life he spent weeks rereading Rousseau, and was satisfied to dismiss him with the comment, "a monstrous liar, but always the first dupe of his own lie" (*Letters*, Vol. II, p. 424). *Leaves of Grass* he dismissed as affected, not original. He was shocked at Swinburne's "Adamite" heresy —"When a man begins to lust after the Muse instead of loving her, he may be sure that it is never the Muse that he embraces" (*ibid.*, Vol. I, p. 377). He admired Howell's prose style and loved

[5] See C. Hartley Grattan, "Lowell," in *The American Mercury*, Vol. II, pp. 63–69.

the man, but he could not bring himself to approve his literary and social theories.

During those sterile professorial years he was closing one door after another. Scarcely an important movement of contemporary thought awakened his interest. The hypothesis of evolution he rejected somewhat flabbily. "I think the evolutionists will have to make a fetish of their protoplasm before long," he said in 1879. "Such a mush seems to me a poor substitute for the Rock of Ages —by which I understand a certain set of higher instincts which mankind have found solid under their feet in all weathers" (*ibid.*, Vol. II, p. 245). And as late as 1886 he wrote, "I am a conservative (warranted to wash) and keep on the safe side—with God as against evolution." Naturally so provocative a doctrine as economic determinism never showed its face in his study; Karl Marx was not one of his intellectual companions. Even the home-bred knight-errant, Henry George, did not greatly interest him. "Why, who in the world buys such a book as that," he exclaimed of *Progress and Poverty;* and learning that a friend had subscribed for a thousand copies, he remarked, "He *must* be getting eccentric." [6]

The political principles that he discovered in the smoke of his professor's pipe were equally naïve. He took himself seriously as a guide and mentor in matters political. He was fond of talking about the "noble science of politics"; yet he never took the trouble to ground himself in the elements of the subject. He had scarcely read the primer of political theory. Burke was probably the only political writer who ever made any impression on his mind. Of American constitutional history he was as ignorant as a politician, and when in Civil War days he began to scratch the field of politics, he only uncovered certain old Federalist prejudices that lay hidden under his later accumulations. The extreme parochialism of the Brahmin mind is revealed in Lowell's incapacity to understand the South. The comment on Sibley's *Harvard Graduates*—"I do not know when the provincialism of New England has been thrust upon me with so ineradicable a barb"—should be turned upon Lowell's dogmatic essays in American politics. He had not the slightest comprehension of Calhoun's doctrine of majorities; yet he dismissed it contemptuously, after attribut-

[6] Five years later he was more sympathetic, but hopelessly confused. See *Democracy*, Vol. VI, p. 35.

ing it to one of Calhoun's followers.[7] He speaks of the "weak and wicked element" of states rights—which he supposes the South owed to "the unhappy ingenuity of Mr. Jefferson"—as an unhistorical repudiation of the principle of coercive sovereignty established by the fathers, quite overlooking the Hartford Convention. His treatment of Jefferson Davis and Andrew Johnson is marked by the dogmatisms of one who is defending God's will against the devil's sophistries. He will have no other interpretation of history than an ethical interpretation, in which good and evil are eternally at combat; and he closes his volume of political essays with a comment that embodies for him the sum of all political wisdom:

> We have only to be unswervingly faithful to what is the true America of our hope and belief, and whatever is American will rise from one end of the country to the other instinctively to our side, with more than ample means of present succour and of final triumph. It is only by being loyal and helpful to Truth that men learn at last how loyal and helpful she can be to them. (*Ibid.*, Vol. V, p. 326.)

Into the stagnant atmosphere of the Elmwood study came on a happy day in the middle sixties the vibrant personality of Edwin Lawrence Godkin, and under the stimulus of his crisp thinking there began for Lowell what may perhaps be reckoned an intellectual renaissance. Godkin was a moderate English liberal, a man of complete self-assurance, whose tart comment on politics and economics was pointed by a conviction of the finality of his own conclusions. Under such teaching Lowell made rapid progress in the new school of criticism fathered by *The Nation*. The delight with which he read Godkin's comment and the eager faith with which he greeted his ideas suggest that his own ethical interpretation of politics was giving way under the strain of post-war experience. From Godkin he got some casual instruction in *laissez faire*, and certain of its teachings snuggled down comfortably in his mind beside the principles of coercive sovereignty and a centralizing state, without awakening any suspicion of their incompatibility of temperament. He never went over wholly to *laissez faire;* he was too strongly Brahmin Federalist for that; but his leanings often carried him into the English camp. It was a tonic to his native conservatism that was troubled about the new theories of collectivism, and

[7] See "The Rebellion," in *Prose Works*, Vol. V, p. 134.

it awakened strong doubts about the experiment in democracy. The reaction against the radicalism of his Abolition days became sharp and final. "We have got to work back from a democracy to our original institution as a republic again," he wrote Leslie Stephen in 1879 (*Letters*, Vol. II, p. 161); and in 1888 he asserted that the republic would endure only "so long as the ideas of the men who founded it continue dominant" (*The Independent in Politics*, Vol. VI, p. 207). He warned Thomas Hughes against the extension of suffrage in England,[8] and he was more and more inclined to think that democracy meant a slough of mediocrity underlain with the mud of corruption—that it might prove to be "a Kakistocracy rather, for the benefit of knaves at the cost of fools" (*Letters*, Vol. II, p. 159).

From the vigorous movements of protest of the seventies and eighties, the agrarian uprising of the Middle Border and the proletarian organization in the industrial centers, he drew added confirmation of his fears. In his attitude towards both he was little more than an echo of Godkin, who was laying about him briskly, hitting both farmer and workingman with fine impartiality. He shared the latter's contempt for all agrarian programs, without quite understanding them. He knew little of America. The continent was scarcely more than a hinterland to Cambridge, a hinterland that he explored with some bewilderment on a trip that carried him as far as Cincinnati. Equally ignorant of economics and of the Middle Border, he had no basis for any opinion; a juster man would have put the agrarian question aside as beyond his competency; at least he would have been careful to clear his mind of prejudice. But Lowell was as much a victim of capitalistic prejudice as Thomas Bailey Aldrich and other Boston pseudo-intellectuals. The old Brahminism was close to the surface in those later years, and a scratch would reveal it. In the matter of the "Haymarket Riot" he wrote Howells that "he thought those Chicago ruffians well hanged"—a comment that recalls the Abner Kneeland episode of fifty years before. Physically Lowell was in close proximity to the labor problem, but intellectually he was worlds removed. He looked upon the labor unions with heavy misgivings. He frankly feared the power of the proletariat and was bitter in denunciation of social legislation. In 1869 he wrote Godkin, "Pray give Henry Wilson a broadside for dipping his

[8] See *Letters*, Vol. II, p. 175.

flag to that piratical craft of the eight-hour men. . . . I have a thorough contempt for a man who pretends to believe that eight is equal to ten" (*Letters*, Vol. II, p. 31). And somewhat later he wrote Norton:

I sometimes feel a little blue over the outlook here, with our penny-paper universal education and our workingmen's parties, with their tremendous lever of suffrage, decrying brains. . . . But the more I learn, the more am I impressed with the wonderful system of checks and balances which history reveals (our Constitution is a baby-house to it!) and the more my confidence in the general commonsense and honest intention of mankind increases. . . . I take great comfort in God. I think He is considerably amused with us sometimes, but that He likes us, on the whole, and would not let us get at the match-box so carelessly, as He does, unless He knew that the frame of His Universe was fire-proof. How many times have I not seen the fire-engines of Church and State clanging and lumbering along to put out—a false alarm! And when the heavens are cloudy what a glare can be cast by a burning shanty! (*Ibid.*, Vol. II, p. 51.)

The ways of the Gilded Age were a rude shock to Lowell's ill-grounded idealism. The crude post-war exploitation and the political corruption that marked the buccaneer stage of the rising plutocracy filled him with anxiety. As an honest man he was angered by the common scoundrelism of the politicians and the press and troubled at the apathy of the public, but his dislike for economics did him a grave disservice. In seeking out the guilty he went wide of the mark. To trace the source of the virus that was poisoning the public life to an exploiting economics, would have brought him close home. He chose to think it was spread rather by western agrarians and city ringsters, than by respectable New Englanders; yet after passing through the *Crédit Mobilier* scandal he was visited by unpleasant suspicions. "I suspect," he wrote after his return from the Cincinnati Convention in 1876, "that few of our Boston men who have had to do with Western railways have been more scrupulous [than the western Grangers.] I rather think they set the example of tempting legislators with the hope of questionable gains" (*Letters*, Vol. II, p. 170). With the open facts of a Congressional investigation before him, Lowell got no deeper than that. Yet his indignation must find outlet and he contributed two poems to *The Nation*—"The World's Fair, 1876," and "Tempora Mutantur"—in one of which he wrote:

> Show 'em your Civil Service, and explain
> How all men's loss is everybody's gain; . . .
> Show your short cut to cure financial ills
> By making paper-collars current bills;
> Show your new bleaching-process, cheap and brief,
> To wit: a jury chosen by the thief;
> Show your State legislatures; show your Rings;
> And challenge Europe to produce such things
> As high officials sitting half in sight
> To share the plunder and to fix things right;
> If that don't fetch her, why, you only need
> Your latest style in Martyrs—Tweed:
> She'll find it hard to hide her spiteful tears
> At such advance in one poor hundred years.
>
> (Letters, Vol. II, p. 155.)

This is Godkin translated into the Lowell vernacular, and what issued from his indignation was Godkin also—an apostolic ardor for civil service reform. He had learned at least, that democracy had not yet been achieved in America; that, indeed, such spontaneous liberalism as had been bred by free land was in danger of being destroyed by evils that issued from the loins of this same heedless frontier order.[9] In 1876 he wrote, "Let us all work together (and the task will need us all) to make Democracy possible. It certainly is no invention to go of itself any more than the perpetual motion" (*Letters*, Vol. II, p. 159). Yet in spite of his zeal, one may be permitted to doubt that Lowell really desired any other than a Brahmin democracy. In those later years his conception of an ideal society was unconsciously colored by memories of Cambridge fifty years before—a simple, patriarchal world, amenable to the rule of the better sort. In such a world democracy seemed possible; but in the rising proletarian-plutocratic order, what reasonable hope was there?

From his growing perplexities Lowell found a happy relief in his mission abroad. The experience was a godsend to a mind that was growing torpid. In 1869 he had written, "I fancy if I were suddenly snatched away to London, my brain would prickle all over, as a foot that has been asleep when the blood starts in it again. Books are good dry forage; we can keep alive on them; but, after all, men are the only fresh pasture" (*ibid.*, Vol. II, p. 24). London, in this mellow autumn of his life, ripened Lowell. He slipped into the congenial environment as easily as Irving had

[9] See *The Independent in Politics*, Vol. VI, pp. 204–209.

done a generation before, and found English society as delightful. He loved England with unaffected heartiness, and under the stimulating experience he expanded into a kindly English Liberal. The extreme Liberals—men like Mill and Arnold and John Morley—he found less sympathetic; and radical thinkers like William Morris he seems not to have known of. But English Liberalism of the Gladstone type was own cousin to Cambridge Brahminism; it united dignity and conscience; it seemed to him the ideal type of government—the rule of God-fearing gentlemen who strove to be faithful to their trusteeship, and who ruled because they were best fitted to rule. Into such a world no other American of the times could have entered more appreciatively than Lowell. If congeniality to the host be a prime requisite in an ambassador, President Hayes made no mistake in sending him to the Court of St. James's. He was a distinguished representative of Brahmin culture; but whether he was a representative of the solid realities of America is not so certain.

CONCLUSION

To the ebullient romanticisms with which the foregoing pages have dealt, the Civil War brought diverse fortunes; and from the titanic conflict emerged an America rid of one of the feculent sources of domestic schism. The romantic imperialisms of the slave economy were gone forever. So much at least was cleared from the path of its destiny, and the field of potential conflict was narrowed to the rival imperialisms of eastern capitalism and western agrarianism. Both had been vastly strengthened by the war. In the eastern centers was a greatly stimulated industrialism, fed from the reservoirs of liquid capital gathered in the process of financing the northern armies, ready to turn to transcontinental railway-building, large-scale manufacture, and a gigantic exploitation of the raw materials of mine and forest and field. Along the Middle Border the old romance of the settlement came to new life as the flood of homesteaders, augmented by disbanded soldiers, poured over the prairie spaces beyond the Mississippi, to repeat there the story of commonwealth building. East and West would eventually clash, for their diverse economic needs were driving towards a collision; but that would not come for a generation till the conflict of interests was thrust into sharper relief.

In the meantime many familiar things were becoming anachronisms over night, though they might linger on for years. As the romantic revolution began with the laying aside of the small-clothes and tie-wig of eighteenth-century aristocratic conservatism, so the new age began with the putting away of the outworn dress of eighteenth-century romantic liberalism. In the hurrying new days there was no time or place for abstract theories of natural rights, for equalitarian democracy, for local home rule—these relics of the past were thrust aside in the scramble for wealth and power. The old philosophies were swept out on the rubbish heap—Jefferson and Lincoln with Calhoun and Stephens—and Hamilton and Marshall came to their own again. The lost cause carried down to defeat much more than slavery, it carried down the old ideal of decentralized democracies, of individual liberty; and with the overthrow of the traditional principles in their last ref-

473

uge, the nation hurried forward along the path of an unquestioning and uncritical consolidation, that was to throw the coercive powers of a centralizing state into the hands of the new industrialism. Here was a revolution that was to engulf the older romantic America, its dignified literary ideals as well as its democratic political theory. In the world of Jay Cooke and Commodore Vanderbilt, the transcendental dream was as hopelessly a lost cause as the plantation dream; it was in even worse plight, for it left no tragic memories to weave a new romance about the fallen hopes. Emerson in Concord was as much out of date as Lowell in Cambridge, or Gilmore Simms in Charleston. A new age had come and other dreams—the age and the dreams of a middle-class sovereignty, that was busily surveying the fields of its future conquests. From the crude and vast romanticisms of that vigorous sovereignty emerged eventually a spirit of realistic criticism, seeking to evaluate the worth of this new America, and discover if possible other philosophies to take the place of those which had gone down in the fierce battles of the Civil War. What form this critical spirit assumed, and what replies it returned to the strident challenge of the time, are questions not to be answered here.

BIBLIOGRAPHY

Only the more important titles dealt with in the present study are listed hereunder, together with selected biographical and critical material. The invaluable bibliographies in the *Cambridge History of American Literature*, 4 vols., New York, 1917–22, cover most of the writers considered, and the reader is referred to them.

BOOK I: PART I

Information will be found in the *Library of Southern Literature* by E. A. Alderman and others (16 vols., New Orleans, 1908–13) and in Montrose J. Moses, *Literature of the South* (New York, 1910). See also Carl Van Doren, *The American Novel* (New York, 1921).

I. THE OLD DOMINION. See Thomas J. Wertenbaker, *Patrician and Plebeian in Virginia* (Charlottesville, Va., 1910).

II. For the economics of Jeffersonianism, see Charles A. Beard, *The Economic Origins of Jeffersonian Democracy* (New York, 1915; Chapter XII). Also Charles Gide and Charles Rist, *A History of Economic Doctrines* (translated by W. Smart and R. Richards, Boston).

JOHN TAYLOR: His works are out of print. Important titles are: *An Inquiry into the Principles and Policy of the United States* (Fredericksburg, Va., 1814). *New Views of the Constitution of the United States* (Washington, 1823). *Correspondence* (edited by W. E. Dodd, Richmond, 1908).

See "John Taylor, Prophet of Secession" (by William E. Dodd, in *Branch Historical Papers, II*, Richmond, 1908). See also Beard, *Economic Origins of Jeffersonian Democracy*.

III. JOHN MARSHALL: Sufficient materials will be found in Albert J. Beveridge, *Life of John Marshall* (4 vols., New York, 1916–19).

IV. For the plantation tradition, see Francis Pendleton Gaines, *The Southern Plantation* (New York, 1924).

WILLIAM WIRT: His works are out of print. *Letters of a British Spy* (Richmond, 1803). *The Old Bachelor* (2 vols., Richmond, 1810). *Life and Character of Patrick Henry* (Philadelphia, 1817; also several later editions).

See John P. Kennedy, *Memoirs . . . of William Wirt* (Philadelphia, 1849).

NATHANIEL BEVERLEY TUCKER: His works are out of print. *George Balcombe; a Novel* (2 vols., New York, 1836).—*The Partisan Leader; a Tale of the Future*, by Edward William Sidney (printed for the publishers, by J. Caxton, 1856 [*i. e.*, Washington, printed by Duff Green, 1836], 2 vols.); reissued as *A Key to the Disunion Conspiracy*: *The Partisan Leader* (2 vols. in one, New York, 1861); edition issued at Richmond, 1862.

Some information about Tucker will be found in W. P. Trent, *William Gilmore Simms* (Boston and New York, 1892).

V. WILLIAM ALEXANDER CARUTHERS: *The Kentuckian in New York. Or, the Adventures of Three Southerns. By a Virginian* (2 vols., New York,

1834).—*The Cavaliers of Virginia, or the Recluse of Jamestown. An Historical Romance of the Old Dominion* (2 vols., New York, 1834–1835).—*The Knights of the Horse-Shoe; a Traditionary Tale of the Cocked Hat Gentry in the Old Dominion* (Wetumpka, Ala., 1845; New York, 1882, 1909).

JOHN P. KENNEDY: *Works* (3 vols., New York, 1854; 9 vols., New York, 1871, with life by H. T. Tuckerman, Vol. X). *Swallow Barn, or a Sojourn in the Old Dominion* (2 vols., Philadelphia, 1832; several later editions). *Horse-Shoe Robinson; a Tale of the Tory Ascendency* (2 vols., Philadelphia, 1835; numerous later editions, the latest in 1906). *Rob of the Bowl; a Legend of St. Inigoe's* (2 vols., Philadelphia, 1838; later editions). *Quodlibet: Containing Some Annals Thereof . . .* (Philadelphia, 1840; 1860).

EDGAR ALLAN POE: The bibliography is extensive. See the *Cambridge History of American Literature*.

BOOK I: PART II

II. JOHN C. CALHOUN: *Works* (6 vols., Columbia, S. C., 1851; New York, 1853–55). *Correspondence*, edited by J. F. Jameson (American Historical Association, *Annual Report*, 1899, Vol. II).

Biographies: W. E. Dodd, in *Statesmen of the Old South* (New York, 1911). H. von Holst, *John C. Calhoun* (*American Statesmen Series*, Boston, 1882, 1899). W. M. Meigs, *Life of John Caldwell Calhoun* (2 vols., New York, 1917). G. M. Pinckney, *Life of John C. Calhoun* (Charleston, 1903). W. P. Trent, *Southern Statesmen of the Old Régime* (New York, 1897).

ALEXANDER H. STEPHENS: *Constitutional View of the War between the States* (2 vols., Philadelphia, 1868).

See L. B. Pendleton, *Alexander H. Stephens* (Philadelphia, 1908).

FRANCIS LIEBER: *The Stranger in America* (2 vols. in one, London, 1834). *Political Ethics* (Philadelphia, 1838; edited by Theodore D. Woolsey, Philadelphia, 1890; with introduction by Nicholas Murray Butler, Philadelphia, 1911). *Essays on Property and Labor* (New York, 1841). *Civil Liberty and Self-Government* (2 vols., Philadelphia, 1853; London, 1859; edited by Theodore D. Woolsey, Philadelphia, 1891). *Miscellaneous Writings* (2 vols., Philadelphia, 1881; edited by Daniel C. Gilman, Philadelphia, 1916).

See L. R. Harley, *Francis Lieber: His Life and Political Philosophy* (New York, 1899).

III. For the southern position, see Jeannette Reid Tandy, "Pro-Slavery Propaganda in American Fiction in the Fifties" (in *South Atlantic Quarterly*, January–March, 1922). Francis Pendleton Gaines, *The Southern Plantation* (New York, 1924; Chapter III).

WILLIAM J. GRAYSON: *The Hireling and the Slave* (Charleston, 1856).

IV. WILLIAM CRAFTS: *A Selection in Prose and Poetry, from the Miscellaneous Writings of the Late William Crafts. With Memoir by Samuel Gilman* (Charleston, 1828).

HUGH SWINTON LEGARÉ: *Writings* (2 vols., Charleston, 1846; with memoir).

WILLIAM GILMORE SIMMS: His works have never been collected and most of them are out of print. *Border Romances* (17 vols., New York, 1859, 1866, 1879; 10 vols., New York, 1882; 15 vols., Chicago, 1885; 17 vols., Chicago, 1888; 17 vols., Atlanta, 1901 [?]).

See W. P. Trent, *William Gilmore Simms* (New York, 1892)—an excellent study. Also see J. Erskine, *Leading American Novelists* (New York, 1910).

BOOK I: PART III

Excellent bibliographical material for western literature will be found in Ralph Leslie Rusk, *The Literature of the Middle Western Frontier* (2 vols., New York, 1925). See also W. H. Venable, *The Beginnings of Literary Culture in the Ohio Valley* (Cincinnati, 1891).

II. Interesting material will be found in Claude G. Bowers, *Party B ttles of the Jackson Period* (Boston, 1922).

III. TIMOTHY FLINT: His works are out of print and rare. *Recollections of the Last Ten Years* (Boston, 1826). *Francis Berrian, or the Mexican Patriot* (Boston, 1826; Philadelphia and London, 1834). *The Life and Adventures of Arthur Clenning* (Philadelphia, 1828). *George Mason, the Young Backwoodsman; or, "Don't Give up the Ship"* (Boston, 1829; with changed title, London, 1833). *The Shoshonee Valley; a Romance* (Cincinnati, 1830).

See John Ervin Kirkpatrick, *Timothy Flint, Pioneer, Missionary, Author, Editor* (Cleveland, 1911)—an excellent study with bibliography.

JAMES HALL: *Works* (4 vols., New York, 1853–56). *Legends of the West* (Philadelphia, 1832, 1833; five later editions).—*The Soldier's Bride; and Other Tales* (Philadelphia, 1833).—*The Harpe's Head; a Legend of Kentucky* (Philadelphia, 1833): as *Kentucky. A Tale* (London, 1834, 2 vols.).—*Tales of the Border* (Philadelphia, 1835). *The Wilderness and the War Path* (New York, 1846; New York and London, 1849).

See J. L. Davis, "Judge James Hall, a Literary Pioneer of the Middle West" (in *Ohio Archæological and Historical Society Publications*, October, 1909).

AUGUSTUS LONGSTREET: *Georgia Scenes* (Atlanta, Ga., 1835; New York, 1840; several later editions).

See John Donald Wade, *Augustus Longstreet, a Study of the Development of Culture in the South* (New York, 1924), an excellent study with bibliographical material.

DAVY CROCKETT: Five titles are grouped under the name of Crockett: *Sketches and Eccentricities of Col. David Crockett, of West Tennessee* (1833). *A Narrative of the Life of David Crockett, of the State of Tennessee* (Philadelphia, 1834; seven editions in one year). *Life of Martin Van Buren* (1835). *An Account of Col. Crockett's Tour to the North and Down East* (1835). *Col. Crockett's Exploits and Adventures in Texas* (1836). The *Narrative* is reprinted with an introduction by Hamlin Garland, in *The Modern Student's Library*, under the title, *The Autobiography of David Crockett* (New York, 1923).

There is no life of Crockett; such so-called works are uncritical jumbles of fact and fiction. Some information will be found in John Donald Wade, "The Authorship of David Crockett's Autobiography" (*Georgia Historical Quarterly*, September, 1922); S. H. Stout, "David Crockett" (*American Historical Magazine*, Vol. VII, No. I, Jan., 1902)—uncritical; Chester T. Crowell, "Davy Crockett" (*American Mercury*, Vol. IV, No. 13).

BOOK II

For Philadelphia, see Ellis Paxson Oberholtzer, *The Literary History of Phila-delphia* (Philadelphia, 1906). Also H. M. Ellis, "Joseph Dennie and His Circle" (*University of Texas Bulletin*). For the politics of New York, see Dixon Ryan Fox, *The Decline of Aristocracy in the Politics of New York* (New York, 1918).

I. CHARLES BROCKDEN BROWN: *The Novels of Charles Brockden Brown. . . with a Memoir* (Boston, 1827; Philadelphia, 1857, 1887). *Wieland; or the Transformation* (New York, 1798; best recent edition in *American Authors Series*, New York, 1926). *Arthur Mervyn; or, Memoirs of the Year 1793* (Philadelphia, 1799; Second Part, New York, 1800; numerous later editions).
    No adequate life has been written. The best is by William Dunlap, *The Life of Charles Brockden Brown* (2 vols., Philadelphia, 1815). See John Erskine, *Leading American Novelists* (New York, 1910), and Annie R. Marble, in *Heralds of American Literature* (Chicago and London, 1907).
    ROBERT MONTGOMERY BIRD: For a list of his plays, see A. H. Quinn, *A History of the American Theatre* (New York, 1923).
    Calavar; or, the Knight of the Conquest: a Romance of Mexico (2 vols., Philadelphia, 1834; about ten later editions).—*The Hawks of Hawks-Hollow. A Tradition of Pennsylvania* (2 vols., Philadelphia, 1835; two London editions).—*The Infidel; or, The Fall of Mexico* (2 vols., Philadelphia, 1835; London, 1835).—*Nick of the Woods, or, the Jib-benainosay. A Tale of Kentucky* (2 vols., Philadelphia, 1837; upward of twenty later editions).
    For his life, see Clement Foust, *Life and Dramatic Works of Robert Montgomery Bird* (1919).

II. JAMES KENT: *Commentaries on American Law* (4 vols., New York, 1826–1830; many later editions).
    For his life, see William Kent, *Memoirs and Letters of James Kent* (Boston, 1898).
    FITZ-GREENE HALLECK: *Poetical Works* (New York and Philadelphia; eight editions between 1847 and 1859). *Poetical Writings with Extracts from those of Joseph Rodman Drake* (edited by J. G. Wilson, New York, 1869, 1885).
    For a life, see J. G. Wilson, *The Life and Letters of Fitz-Greene Halleck* (New York, 1869). Also see W. C. Bryant, *Some Notices on the Life and Writings of Fitz-Greene Halleck* (New York, 1869).

III. WASHINGTON IRVING: The standard edition of his works is in forty volumes, New York, 1887.
    The standard life is by Pierre M. Irving, *The Life and Letters of Washington Irving* (4 vols., London, 1864; New York, 1879, 1883).
    See also *The Letters of Washington Irving to Henry Brevoort* (edited by George S. Hellman, 2 vols., New York, 1915). A recent study is George S. Hellman, *Washington Irving, Esq.* (New York, 1925).
    JAMES KIRKE PAULDING: *Works* (15 vols., New York, 1834–1839; 4 vols., 1867–1868).—*The Diverting History of John Bull and Brother Jonathan* (New York, 1812).—*Letters from the South* (2 vols., New York, 1817).—*The Backwoodsman. A Poem* (Philadelphia, 1818).—*Salmagundi, Second Series* (2 vols., New York, 1820).—*Koningsmarke, the Long Finne, A Story of the New World* (New York, 1823; 2 vols.,

New York, 1834; three London editions, and a German).—*Westward Ho! A Tale* (2 vols., New York, 1832, 1845; three London editions, a French and a German).—*The Dutchman's Fireside. A Tale* (2 vols., New York, 1831; latest edition, 1900).—*The Puritan and his Daughter* (New York, 1849, 1850; also London, 1849, two editions, and one German).

No adequate life has been written, but see W. I. Paulding, *Literary Life of James K. Paulding* (New York, 1867).

IV. JAMES FENIMORE COOPER: The editions of Cooper's novels are numerous; as good as any is the one in thirty-two volumes (New York, 1895, 1896–97). Much of his controversial work and critical articles have not been reprinted. See *Notions of the Americans; Picked up by a Travelling Bachelor* (2 vols., Philadelphia, 1829). *A Letter to His Countrymen* (New York, 1834). *The American Democrat; or Hints on the Social and Civic Relations of the United States* (Cooperstown, 1838). *The History of the Navy* (2 vols., Philadelphia, 1839). Also his eight volumes of European travels.

No satisfactory life has been written. The best is by T. R. Lounsbury, *James Fenimore Cooper* (New York, 1883). See also *Correspondence of James Fenimore-Cooper* (edited by his grandson, James Fenimore Cooper, 2 vols., New Haven, 1922). W. C. Brownell, in *American Prose Masters* (New York, 1909). Carl Van Doren, in *The American Novel* (New York, 1921).

V. WILLIAM CULLEN BRYANT: The standard edition is edited by Parke Godwin (6 vols., New York, 1883–1889: 1–2, *Biography*, 1883; 3–4, *Poetical Works*, 1883, 1901; 5–6, *Prose Writings*, 1884–1889). Much information on his work in journalism will be found in Allan Nevins, *A Century of Journalism* (New York, 1921).

HORACE GREELEY: His works have not been collected. See *Hints towards Reform* (New York, 1850). *Recollections of a Busy Life* (New York, 1868). *Essays Designed to Elucidate the Science of Political Economy* (Boston, 1870). *The American Conflict* (Hartford and Chicago, 1864–1866).

For his life, see James Parton, *The Life of Horace Greeley* (Boston, 1868). Charles Sotheran, *Horace Greeley* (New York, 1915). See also John R. Commons, "Horace Greeley and the Working-Class Origins of the Republican Party" (*Political Science Quarterly*, Vol. XXIV, pp. 468–488).

HERMAN MELVILLE: The best edition is The Standard (16 vols., London, 1922–23). Also see *Works* (4 vols., edited by A. Stedman, New York, 1892, 1896; Boston, 1900, 1910). Convenient editions of *Typee*, *Omoo*, and *Moby-Dick* are plentiful.

The indispensable life is Raymond Weaver's *Herman Melville: Mariner and Mystic* (New York, 1921), with bibliography. Also see John Freeman, *Herman Melville* (in *English Men of Letters Series*, New York, 1926).

BOOK III: PART I

I. For the political backgrounds, see A. E. Morse, *The Federalist Party in Massachusetts to the Year 1800* (Princeton, 1909). W. A. Robinson, *Jeffersonian Democracy in New England* (New Haven, 1916). Samuel Eliot Morison, *Life and Letters of Harrison Gray Otis* (2 vols., Boston, 1913).

FISHER AMES: *Works* (with memoir by J. T. Kirkland, Boston, 1809).
Works, with a Selection from his Speeches and Correspondence (edited by his son, Seth Ames, 2 vols., Boston, 1854).

ROBERT TREAT PAINE: *Works in Prose and Verse* (with memoir, Boston, 1812).

II. JOSEPH STORY: *Commentaries on the Constitution of the United States* (3 vols., Boston, 1833; numerous later editions).
See W. W. Story, *Life and Letters of Joseph Story* (2 vols., Boston, 1851).

DANIEL WEBSTER: The best edition of his works is The National— *The Writings and Speeches of Daniel Webster* (18 vols., Boston, 1903). *Private Correspondence of Daniel Webster* (2 vols., Boston, 1857). *Letters* (edited by C. H. Van Tyne, New York, 1902).
See George Ticknor Curtis, *Life of Daniel Webster* (2 vols., New York and London, 1870). For a critical contemporary estimate see Theodore Parker, *Discourse Occasioned by the Death of Daniel Webster* (Boston, 1853). See also Charles A. Beard, *The Economic Basis of Politics* (New York, 1922).

BOOK III: PART II

I. UNITARIANISM: See George Willis Cooke, *Unitarianism in America: A History of its Origin and Development* (Boston, 1902). Williston Walker, *A History of the Congregational Churches in the United States* (New York, 1894).

WILLIAM ELLERY CHANNING: *Works* (5 vols., Boston, 1841; sixth volume added in 1843; numerous later editions).
An excellent life is J. W. Chadwick, *William Ellery Channing, Minister of Religion* (Boston, 1903). See also William H. Channing, *Memoir of William Ellery Channing* (3 vols., Boston, 1848).

II. PERFECTIONISM: For materials see Garrison, *Life of William Lloyd Garrison* (4 vols., New York, 1885–1889).

BROOK FARM: See Lindsay Swift, *Brook Farm; Its Members, Scholars and Visitors* (New York, 1906; contains bibliography). J. T. Codman, *Brook Farm: Historic and Personal Memoirs* (Boston, 1894). Nathaniel Hawthorne, *Blithedale Romance*.

ABOLITIONISM: Sufficient materials will be found in Garrison, *Life of William Lloyd Garrison* (4 vols., New York, 1885–1889). See also Catherine N. Birney, *Sarah and Angelina Grimké* (Boston, 1885); and *James G. Birney and His Times, by His Son, William Birney* (New York, 1890).

III. WILLIAM LLOYD GARRISON: See Garrison, *Life of William Lloyd Garrison* (4 vols., New York, 1885–1889).

JOHN G. WHITTIER: *The Writings of John Greenleaf Whittier* (Riverside Edition, 7 vols., Boston, 1885–1889).
See G. R. Carpenter, *John Greenleaf Whittier* (in *American Men of Letters Series*).—T. S. Pickard, *Life and Letters of John Greenleaf Whittier* (2 vols., Boston, 1894).—F. H. Underwood, *John Greenleaf Whittier. A Biography* (Boston, 1884).

HARRIET BEECHER STOWE: *Works* (Riverside Edition, 16 vols., Boston, 1896; with life by Mrs. Field, 17 vols., 1898).
See Mrs. J. T. Fields, *The Life of Harriet Beecher Stowe* (Boston, 1897).

BOOK III: PART III

I. TRANSCENDENTALISM: The literature is abundant. See *The Dial* (4 vols., Boston, 1840–1844).—*The Harbinger* (4 vols., New York, 1844–1848).—Harold Clarke Goddard, *Studies in New England Transcendentalism* (New York, 1908).—O. B. Frothingham, *Transcendentalism in New England. A History* (New York, 1876).—See also Sylvester Judd, *Margaret. A Tale of the Real and Ideal* (2 vols., Boston, 1845; revised edition, 1851).

II. RALPH WALDO EMERSON: *Works* (Riverside Edition, edited by James Eliot Cabot, 12 vols., Boston, 1884–1893; London, 1884–1893; Centenary Edition, with biographical introduction and notes by E. W. Emerson, 12 vols., Boston, 1903–04; London, 1904).—*Journals of Ralph Waldo Emerson, with Annotations* (edited by Edward Waldo Emerson and Waldo Emerson Forbes, 10 vols., Boston, 1909–1914).—*Uncollected Writings. Essays, Addresses, Poems, Reviews and Letters by Ralph Waldo Emerson* (New York [1912]).

See George Willis Cooke, *Bibliography of Ralph Waldo Emerson* (Boston, 1908). James Eliot Cabot, *A Memoir of Ralph Waldo Emerson* (2 vols., Boston, 1887). George Willis Cooke, *Ralph Waldo Emerson; His Life, Writings, and Philosophy* (Boston, 1881). Oscar W. Firkins, *Ralph Waldo Emerson* (Boston, 1915). W. C. Brownell, *American Prose Masters* (New York, 1909).

III. HENRY DAVID THOREAU: *Works* (Riverside Edition, 11 vols., Boston, 1894; Manuscript Edition, 20 vols. [Vols. VII–XX contain the Journals], Boston, 1906).

See Francis H. Allen, *A Bibliography of Henry David Thoreau* (Boston and New York, 1908). William E. Channing, *Thoreau, the Poet-Naturalist* (Boston, 1873, 1902). F. B. Sanborn, *Henry D. Thoreau* (in *American Men of Letters Series*, Boston, 1882, 1910); *The Personality of Thoreau* (Boston, 1901); *The Life of Henry David Thoreau* (Boston and New York, 1917). Léon Bazalgette, *Henry Thoreau—Bachelor of Nature* (translated by Van Wyck Brooks, New York, 1924).

IV. THEODORE PARKER: *Collected Works* (edited by F. P. Cobbe, 14 vols., London, 1863–71). *The Critical and Miscellaneous Writings of Theodore Parker* (Boston, 1843). *Speeches, Addresses and Occasional Sermons* (2 vols., Boston, 1876). *The American Scholar* (with notes by George Willis Cooke, Boston, 1907).

An excellent study is J. W. Chadwick, *Theodore Parker, a Biography* (Boston, 1900), containing a bibliography. John Weiss, *Life and Correspondence of Theodore Parker* (2 vols., New York, 1864)—indispensable.

V. MARGARET FULLER: Her works have not been collected. Important titles are: *Woman in the Nineteenth Century* (New York and London, 1845; with additional papers and introduction by Horace Greeley, New York, 1855). *Life Without and Life Within* (Boston, 1860; New York, 1869). *Papers on Literature and Art* (2 vols., New York and London, 1846).

An excellent study is Katharine Anthony, *Margaret Fuller: A Psychological Biography* (New York, 1920). See also R. W. Emerson, W. H. Channing, and J. F. Clarke, *Memoirs of Margaret Fuller Ossoli* (2 vols., Boston, 1852). Thomas Wentworth Higginson, *Margaret Fuller Ossoli* (in *American Men of Letters Series*, Boston, 1884), containing bibliography.

BOOK III: PART IV

I. HENRY W. LONGFELLOW: *The Writings of . . . with Bibliographical and Critical Notes* (11 vols., Boston, 1886 [Vols. I–VI, *Poetical Works;* VII–VIII, *Prose Works;* IX–XI, *Dante*]).

See Samuel Longfellow, *Life of Henry Wadsworth Longfellow* (3 vols., Boston and New York, 1891). T. W. Higginson, *Henry Wadsworth Longfellow* (in *American Men of Letters Series,* Boston and New York, 1902).

II. NATHANIEL HAWTHORNE: *Works* (12 vols., Boston, 1871–76; Fireside Edition, 12 vols., Boston, 1879; Riverside Edition, 12 vols., Boston, 1883; Standard Library Edition, 15 vols., Boston, 1891 [contains *Nathaniel Hawthorne and his Wife,* by Julian Hawthorne]; New Wayside Edition, 13 vols., Boston, 1902).

The best-known life is Julian Hawthorne, *Nathaniel Hawthorne and His Wife* (2 vols., Boston, 1885). Henry James, *Nathaniel Hawthorne* (in *English Men of Letters Series,* London, 1879; New York, 1885, 1887). See also W. B. Brownell, *American Prose Masters* (New York, 1909). John Erskine, *Great American Novelists* (New York, 1910). Carl Van Doren, *The American Novel* (New York, 1921); Stuart P. Sherman, *Americans* (New York, 1923).

III. OLIVER WENDELL HOLMES: *Works* (Riverside Edition, 13 vols., Boston, 1891, additional volume, 1892; Autocrat Edition, 13 vols., Boston and New York, 1904).

See George B. Ives, *A Bibliography of Oliver Wendell Holmes* (Boston and New York, 1907).—John T. Morse, *Life and Letters of Oliver Wendell Holmes* (2 vols., Boston and New York, 1896).—Lewis W. Townsend, *Oliver Wendell Holmes. Centenary Biography* (London, 1909).

JAMES RUSSELL LOWELL: *Works* (Riverside Edition, 13 vols., Boston and New York, 1902 [contains Scudder's *Life*]; Elmwood Edition, 16 vols., Boston, 1904 [four volumes of letters]). *Anti-Slavery Papers* (2 vols., Boston and New York, 1902). *Letters of James Russell Lowell* (edited by Charles Eliot Norton, 2 vols., New York, 1893; 3 vols., Boston, 1904). *Early Prose Writings of . . .* (2 vols., New York, 1903).

G. W. Cooke, *A Bibliography of James Russell Lowell* (Boston and New York, 1906). H. E. Scudder, *James Russell Lowell: A Biography* (2 vols., Boston, 1901). Ferris Greenslet, *James Russell Lowell: A Biography* (2 vols., Boston, 1901). Ferris Greenslet, *James Russell Lowell: His Life and Work* (Boston, 1905). See also C. Hartley Grattan, "Lowell" (*The American Mercury,* Vol. II, p. 69); Harry Hayden Clark, *Lowell's Criticism of Romantic Literature* ("Publications of the Modern Language Association," March, 1926); W. D. Howells, *Literary Friends and Acquaintances* (New York, 1902); Henry James, *Essays in London and Elsewhere* (New York, 1893); J. J. Reilly, *James Russell Lowell as a Critic* (New York, 1915); and John M. Robertson, *Lowell as a Critic* (*North American Review,* February, 1919).

INDEX

THE
BEGINNINGS OF CRITICAL
REALISM IN AMERICA

VERNON LOUIS PARRINGTON

THE sudden death of Professor Vernon Louis Parrington in England, June 16, 1929, cut tragically short his labors on the last volume of *Main Currents in American Thought*. Of this third volume approximately the first half had been completed, which, together with the outline of the work and some scattered essays in sections otherwise undeveloped, constitutes all that the author left. Unfinished it is, yet no completion by another can be justified. That anyone could duplicate his felicity of style, so unobtrusively individual, so sensitively adjusted to the freighted thought, is hardly to be hoped for; and more important, that another scholar could accurately reproduce his interpretation is an assumption not to be warranted. The decision to publish the author's incomplete work is a tribute to his brilliance.

Nevertheless it is possible to know Professor Parrington's chief intentions, particularly when one understands, as his associates did, his principles for organizing materials and his standards of value. Students as well as associates first of all noticed beneath the richness and complexity of his thought a constancy of purpose as clear as the treatment of mass in a Gothic cathedral. Indeed it was through a delight in architecture pursued as a hobby for many years that Parrington expressed this desire for a unity, balanced, harmonious, and properly proportioned.

This architectonic feeling, abundantly illustrated in his writing habits, was carried over not only into his classroom procedure and conversation, but also into his varied interests. Painting as well as architecture had long intrigued him. Though few people knew it, he wrote poetry distinguished for restraint in expression and clarity of form; while in conversation he persistently sought the appropriate phrase, spiced it with wit, salted it with homely realism; for no gentleman of the eighteenth century was more conscious of the charms of good discourse.

Professor Parrington's classroom procedure had a reputation that attracted students not much interested in literature and which appealed to all ranges of intellect. The source of that popularity was the personality of the teacher, together with his gift for presenting ideas and evoking a response. By means of a Socratic cross-examination Parrington made the student discover his intellectual deficiencies; while the class, to its astonishment and delight, found the quest for truth both elusive and exciting. Surprise and satisfied expectation kept the easily bored from sinking into apathy, for there was no telling from day to day just what Professor Parrington was going to do. He paired every occasion with a fitting response; yet this flexibility did not degenerate into an aimless drifting, since he persistently simplified his main objectives and concentrated the material to be studied, while expressing its meaning through a significant symbol or a telling phrase. His classes in the eighteenth century, for example, were given the concept of harmony, balance, and proportion. They found it in architecture, they saw it in dress, they heard it in conversation, they watched it work out in the heroic couplet, they pursued it in Addison, Pope, and Swift; in short, they analyzed the whole social structure of the age and discovered it everywhere. A germinal idea, Parrington liked to call it, while he held it before the class like a many-faceted crystal, slowly turning it around and around so the student could see every face. As a result no student who had taken the course ever forgot the significance of this architectonic trilogy.

In writing habits there was a similar all-encompassing purpose. He habitually began with his thesis—a phrase, a sentence, or a revealing figure. This was examined and stripped of its implications as one would peel an onion layer by layer. So imperious was the habit of this procedure that his ability to write would be blocked until he had in mind a perfectly crystallized concept expressible at the maximum in one sentence. An example of this occurred shortly before he left on his trip to England. He had been working on the period that Mark Twain had labeled the "Gilded Age," but found the title inadequate to his idea, and, as a result, his writing did not get on. Another day some weeks later there was an obvious satisfaction expressed in his bearing and an exceptionally pronounced twinkle in his eye. "I have found the phrase," he said; "I will call it The Great Barbecue." Similarly, the three volumes of this work began in a single paragraph which by progressive unfoldings he expanded to its present scope.

After having made a provisional outline, with each section condensed into a single sentence, he began writing, completing a unit here or there as circumstance and mood directed. When it was completed the process of readjustment began. Each portion was inspected for its length, which had to be fitted to its relative importance; an emphasis here was shifted to balance an emphasis there; the mood of one part was altered to make it harmonize with the mood of its neighbor. As many as twelve times he rewrote a single section in this complex and delicate effort for harmonious adjustment. Finally, he made from this his finished outline.

Knowing Professor Parrington's methods one can now understand the problem he faced and the solution he found when bent on the task of writing a history of American literature. Although he was by nature partial to the claims of aesthetics, yet it was obvious to him that such an approach was foredoomed to failure. All too few of the American writers would deserve treatment on any aesthetic test, while many who were undeniably significant could not possibly be left out even though inferior artistically. Moreover, one only had to look at the numerous attempts already made to see the failure of the belletristic interpretation. What were these histories of American literature? Sprawling lists of names arranged in a fashion that gave little save conventionalized data and some dubious evaluations. Already there was a widespread demand for a new interpretation growing out of these past failures.

Professor Parrington found the first step to a solution when he remembered the day he opened Taine's *Histoire de la littérature anglaise*. It had come as a new and inspiring discovery to find a method that envisaged the literature of a people as the inevitable outgrowth of their racial peculiarities, environment, and epoch. It is true that the claim set up by Taine, that his method was scientific and could account for every phenomenon, proved to be unfounded; but nevertheless his work was epoch-making; it gave a unity and a significance never before attained, and this was what attracted Parrington. Nothing less unifying than Taine's method was thinkable.

A second source of inspiration came from a close friend and colleague, J. Allen Smith, another pioneer figure, who applied to the abstract theorizings of political science the economic realities that underlie and determine them. The method was so fruitful of results that it quickly spread to a group of American political scientists, from whose findings much of Parrington's significant work received its first flattering confirmation. Under such a stimulus Parrington was quick to realize the fruitfulness of economic determinism when applied even to literature.

A third idea completed the synthesis. When he envisaged American literature as American thought, the trammel of the belletristic was broken and he was free to reëvaluate American writers, to follow the trail of their work wherever it led; for at last he had found a method true to facts, yet one which would satisfy his insatiable demand for a significant unity, balanced, harmonious, and properly proportioned. The economic forces imprint their mark upon political, social, and religious institutions; literature expresses the result in its thought content.

But a technique, though vitally necessary, is not the end of the story. There still remains, even for the most impartial scholar, the final and, be it admitted, inescapable evaluation. Parrington was too honest with himself to dodge the issue; he made his choice and abided the result. In the foreword to the first volume he made his confession: "The point of view from which I have endeavored to evaluate the materials is liberal rather than conservative, Jeffersonian rather than Federalistic; and very likely in my search I have found what I went forth to find, as others have discovered what they were seeking. Unfortunately the *mens aequa et clara* is the rarest of attributes, and dead partisanships have a disconcerting way of coming to life again in the pages of their historians. That the vigorous passions and prejudices of the time I have dealt with may have found an echo in my judgments is, perhaps, to be expected; whether they have distorted my interpretation and vitiated my analysis is not for me to determine."

Professor Parrington's *Main Currents in American Thought* has, then, for its subject the adventures of American liberalism. To anyone alive to the issue an adventurous story it is, as becomes more apparent when the author's own liberalism is completely understood. Those sections where his sympathies are kindled, where he stamps his seal of enthusiastic admiration, provide the clue which his treatment of Roger Williams, Benjamin Franklin, Tom Paine, Jefferson, Emerson, Thoreau, Channing, and Theodore Parker assuredly verifies. All of his latent enthusiasms burst into bloom until, as in his essay on Roger Williams, nothing less than the cadence and passion of the Song of Solomon would express it. "Running through his writings is a recurrent echo of the Hebrew love-song that Puritan thought suffused with glowing mysticism:

'I am my beloved's and my beloved is mine: he feedeth among the lilies. . . . I will arise now, and go about the city in the streets, and in the broad ways I will seek him whom my soul loveth.' But when he went into the broad ways of Carolinian England, seeking the rose of Sharon and the lily of the valley, he discovered only abominations. The lover was tempted by false kisses; the Golden Image was set up in the high places, and the voice of authority commanded to bow down to it. And so as a Christian mystic Roger Williams became a Separatist, and set his mind upon the new world where the lover might dwell with his bride."[1]

The liberalism of Parrington had this great virtue, which all too many creeds lack: it was built on an obligation first to examine and understand all points of view before exercising the right to condemn them. Although he disliked the personalities and groaned at the dreary pages of men like Cotton Mather, yet he was not satisfied until he got at their marrow. And again there was an abiding sense of the humane in Parrington before which all abstractions, generalizations, and logical systems had to pass in review. He feared above all, as did the sensitive Jefferson, the cancer of power. "Man," he used to say, "has never proved himself worthy of an unrestrained control of his fellows, nor has any special group of men ever been dominant without injustice to others." Combined with this love of freedom was an urbanity and a sense of personal integrity not subject to the interference of outside forces in convention or mob—an integrity which so impressed everyone having contact with the man, that he has been often called an aristocrat. Parrington would not have objected to the label, nor have seen it as contradictory to the principles of liberalism, since in his opinion only liberalism expressing itself in a democratic society provides for the free exercise of personal rights. Elevating oneself by riding on the shoulders of others, a common device of the pseudo-aristocrat, was to him but a vulgar gymnastic performance.

When he described Jefferson "with his aristocratic head set on a plebeian frame"[2] he was unconsciously describing himself, for there was a deep love of the soil in Parrington. One saw it, surprisingly, in his hands. They were thick and sturdy, blunted at the ends as if from too much delving into the black loam of his flower garden, where roses, peonies, and crocuses were cherished companions, and the delight of his leisure hours. He secretly suspected

[1] Vol. I, p. 65. [2] Ibid., p. 343.

the apartment dweller as any true farmer would; and though there was a twinkle in his eye when he called New York a Babylon or spoke of its corrupting influence on scholar and artist, yet there was a meaning implied more serious than the jest.

It was Parrington's hope to vindicate this liberalism "stemming," as he said, "from the fruitful loins of the eighteenth century." As he diagnosed it, that era had two creative currents of thought: a hopeful, vigorous liberalism, together with a sturdy realism which did not balk at men's selfishness or deny the economic basis of social forces. Unfortunately the nineteenth-century liberal attended only to hopes and neglected the realism, while the swelling forces of industrialism accepted the economic realities but cynically brutalized them. Failure was the inevitable result; the liberals despair while Babbitt, regnant, infests the country with his blustering agents. In the unfinished section of this last volume it was Parrington's purpose to show this parlous state of twentieth-century America, to discern the hopeful gleam in the darkness, and to uncover the hidden forces working for a more stable and just society. Parrington's point of view then, was that of a staunch and kindly liberalism, the motif in the three volumes, the theme never absent from a page of the whole composition. It is a liberalism not to be found in any program yet formulated by political party or economic sect; it is rather a generous idealism that can envisage a future richer in values, more humane in distribution of favors than any known past. Wise to the ways of man, such a liberalism refuses confinement in the strait-jacket of any set formula, yet escapes the emasculation awaiting mere enthusiasm; for it can separate foes from friends and recognize the point where compromise means surrender.

If my analysis thus far is to any purpose it will suggest what these main objectives that Parrington never completed were to have been. The unfinished Book Two was to chronicle three parties of revolt against the plutocracy born of the Gilded Age. Of these rebellions the first was engendered on the Middle Border, where the farmers, beset by hard times, struck out against the source of their ills. As the agrarians diagnosed the situation, these economic maladjustments were brought on by a currency manipulated for the benefit of creditors, and further enhanced by capitalistic control of the political machine. One of the last of Parrington's completed units deals with the economic phase of the revolt; the next section was to record the farmer's effort to democratize the government. Through pressure of third-party movements the farmers tried to inject such reforms as the initiative and referendum, the recall, the direct primary, and the income tax; until, seduced by Bryan's oratory, they joined with the Democrats in an attack upon the intrenchments of capitalism. As Parrington saw it, these agrarian descendants of Jefferson, lacking the intellectual leadership which the South had contributed in earlier days, at a tactical disadvantage, and already a minority economic group, were fated to lose their last great uprising.

Also out of the valley of the Mississippi came a literature of the Middle Border. Such writers as Edward Eggleston and E. W. Howe had already initiated a realism that revealed the drabness of frontier life and suggested its smoldering discontent, although the pastoral note fathered by the genial and romantic James Whitcomb Riley did not lack its prose children. Notably did Meredith Nicholson, William Allen White, and Booth Tarkington[3] portray the village neighborliness, its wholesomeness, its spirit of democracy, until they cast such a fog of sentiment over the scene as to blur all the realities. But the true spirit of Populism is represented in the impassioned work of Hamlin Garland, whose "admirable realism and passionate democracy" Parrington depicts in a chapter that he completed.

The second chorus of dissent came from the very citadels of plutocracy, for the wage-earners, unable to escape slavery by flight to an unshackled frontier that no longer existed, were brought to bay. The doctrine of class war, which had been ignored since the eighteenth century, was revived by the German socialists and given an added plausibility by the employers' unscrupulous use of injunction, black list, and lockout. T. V. Powderly, who found a solution to the labor problem in syndicalism, organized the Knights of Labor. Although this union had a promising inception, it was soon wrecked, while the craft unionism recommended by Samuel Gompers forged to the front because of its middle-class ideology and spirit of compromise. On the other hand the left wing of the labor cause embraced various brands of socialism. The tragic flare-up of the Haymarket riot, which resulted in a "red" scare and persecution of the humane Governor Altgeld, served Parrington as a dramatic illustration of the obloquy that descended upon the

[3] See Addenda for notes on these men.

leaders of socialism, Daniel De Leon, Eugene V. Debs, and Victor Berger. Needless to say, Parrington had planned a vindication of them born of his desire to see more justice in the world.

There were echoes of this proletarian strife manifested in the world of letters. Certain writers following Edward Bellamy joined the quest for a socialistic Utopia. Parrington had completed his passage on Bellamy, but of the party formed to agitate for principles advanced in *Looking Backward* and of the other writers of Utopian novels, such as Tourgee, he left no treatment. A second set of writers were grouped together by reason of their common concern over the darkening future of American civilization. Edwin Markham, his humanitarian sympathies aroused, penned an indictment of wage exploitation in his "The Man with the Hoe" that caused no little concern in its day and spurred defenders of the existing economic system to offer liberal prizes for an equally convincing reply. The emergence of naturalism, seen in Stephen Crane[4] and Frank Norris,[4] was also a response to the darkening social outlook. Parrington defined naturalism as "a pessimistic realism that sets man in a mechanical world." He traced this pessimistic determinism to the machine industrialism so overwhelming in its power as to impress man with his own impotence, to the centralization of wealth, which causes a caste regimentation of society, and finally to the great city, which reduces the inhabitant to an infinitesimal unit of a vast beehive. Other writers, equally oppressed by this state of affairs, concentrated on the phenomena of the city. It was here that Parrington intended to discuss Henry B. Fuller, Harold Frederic, Robert Grant, and Edith Wharton.[5]

The third party of revolt was a hesitant one—the South, still convalescing from the Civil War and further weakened by divisions in its counsels. Though burdened by parochial creeds, weakened by lack of intellectual leadership, the agrarian South, largely plebeian, joined the Middle Border in its uprising. The middle-class South, represented by Henry W. Grady, proposed a surrender to the Yankee principle of industrial exploitation, while the remnant of the old aristocracy resisted the new and clung to the traditions of the past. Thomas Nelson Page, Joel Chandler Harris, Mary Murfree, and George Washington Cable attended to these romantic traditions of the plantation, the negro, the mountaineer, and

---

[4] See Addenda for lecture notes on these writers.
[5] See Addenda for brief notes on these writers.

the creole; while Sidney Lanier [5] became the poet of southern landscape and sunrise. Far more significant in Parrington's eye was the rebirth of a southern intelligentsia represented in letters by Ellen Glasgow, W. W. Woodward, the debunker, and James Branch Cabell,[6] the ironic romanticist. Professor Parrington, who had been among the first to appreciate Cabell, admired the competence of his style and the effectiveness of his ironic commentary on American civilization.

Book Three was to present the movement of liberalism from 1903 to 1917, and the reaction to it following the war. Parrington called this period of liberalism the "great stock-taking venture." These liberals announced that the democratic hopes of earlier days had not been fulfilled, that the Constitution is not a democratic instrument nor was it intended to be, and that while Americans were professing to create a democracy, they had been creating in fact a plutocracy. They then determined upon a new program based on their discovery of the relations between economics and politics. Such relations made necessary the control of property by the collective will, and to that end they endeavored to squeeze the Hamiltonian state into a Jeffersonian mold.[7]

The muckrakers of 1903 to 1910 attacked the plutocracy where its joints creaked. In effect this group of writers from Henry D. Lloyd to Charles Edward Russell, Gustavus Meyers, and A. M. Simons popularized economics and made the liberals conscious of what was going on behind the closed doors of the directors' meetings. On the other hand, the movement of Progressivism, engaged in the hopeless task of directing the political machinery to democratic ends, was typified by Robert LaFollette, Theodore Roosevelt, and Woodrow Wilson. Only one, LaFollette, remained true to the colors; the other two compromised, then surrendered, and the hopes of liberalism went down in a tragic *débâcle*.

In the realm of letters this liberalism found expression in three major groups of writers. A set of intellectuals turned critical began to scrutinize the economic, political, and social institutions of America. Of these critics Parrington considered Randolph Bourne and Charles A. Beard [8] the most important. Another set turned

---

[5] See Addenda for brief notes on these writers.

[6] See Addenda for magazine article on Cabell.

[7] "A Chapter in American Liberalism," which is included in the Addenda, deals with this subject, with the muckraking movement, and with post-war realism.

[8] See Addenda, "A Chapter in American Liberalism."

to fiction, shifting their point of view from liberalism to radicalism, from politics to economics. Winston Churchill [9] had discovered the emptiness of the profit motive with its resultant destruction of beauty, freedom, and creative craftsmanship. Similarly Robert Herrick [9] became a pathologist of the city, investigated its ethics, and then rebelled at the predatory egoism which ruled its life to the destruction of all ethical integrity. At his best Jack London [10] wrote of the revolution, though later selling out to bigger and better royalties; while Upton Sinclair became the revolutionary sleuth spying upon the indecencies of the capitalist system. Perhaps these novelists were too seriously engaged in social criticism and reform propaganda to become great craftsmen, yet they were to Parrington important writers, because they were in touch with deep currents of American thought.

Still a third set of writers turned to a realistic technique appropriate to the times, yet avoided the weakness inherent in direct propaganda. The poets Masters,[11] Sandburg, Frost, and Robinson, Parrington chose for consideration as realists with an art, an underlying criticism of conditions, and a philosophy that set them above the other poets of the time. For the same reasons he had planned a section on Huneker. Theodore Dreiser,[12] because of his massive documentation, his deterministic philosophy, and his sense of the inevitable tragedy inherent in life, Parrington labeled a modern, meaning by this that Dreiser most adequately and most thoroughly represented modern America.

The last section of the book was to be a consideration of the post-war reaction to the liberalism of the preceding period. The economic democracy which liberals had marked for their goal was now attacked by the younger intellectuals. H. L. Mencken turned to farce and burlesque for methods adequate to express his contempt of American democracy. Biologists pointed to the inescapable laws of heredity as a refutation of the liberals' hopes for social improvement; while some psychologists, discovering morons, ruled out all equalitarian Utopias. Parrington could find little sympathy in his heart for a return to the spirit of aristocracy. This narrow, doctrinaire biology, denied by the more careful biologists and

[9] See "The Problem Novel and the Diversion from Naturalism," in the Addenda.
[10] See Addenda for notes on London.
[11] See Addenda, "Ole Rölvaag's *Giants in the Earth* "
[12] See Addenda for lecture notes on Dreiser.

the behaviorists who assert that environment is determining, cannot rule out all environmental changes. As long as the *milieu* is an effective force in molding the organism, room is left for social betterment by social readjustments. A disputed psychology dealing in primitive sex drives, gland secretions, and intelligence scores is no more conclusive on the subject.

The attack on industrialism is nearer to the heart of Parrington's ideals, because it proved to him that liberalism is not by any means dead. Such a comprehensive movement enlisting first-class minds —intellectuals, poets, novelists, dramatists—revealed clearly to him the increasing criticism of a dehumanized economics, and such criticism proceeds from an implicit liberalism.

The attack on the middle class is seen best in Zona Gale,[13] Evelyn Scott, and particularly in Sinclair Lewis,[14] whom Parrington rated the chief of our younger satirists. This satire is a searching criticism of the *bourgeois* ideals and habitat, its tyrannical herd-mind, its povery-stricken materialism. By its nature this satire clearly suggests a set of new ideals which grow out of a free individualism rather than a political or economic socialism. The emphasis is shifted by implication from externalities to things of the spirit. This is more clearly seen in the new philosophies just now arising, which deny the finality of economic law, turn in politics to the ideal of a decentralized state, and in science to new syntheses emphasizing the pragmatic and relative aspects of scientific law.

The latest literary fashions that Parrington intended to consider embody a psychological emphasis seen in the impressionism of biography, in the brutal but frank pacifism of war novels,[13] and most significantly of all in the impressionism and expressionism of Sherwood Anderson.[14] Parrington felt that there were rich potentialities latent in these new methods although the writers of the new school were themselves painfully at sea. In technique as well as in direct statement there was to be seen, though obscurely, a renewed emphasis upon individual integrity, the necessity for creative expression, and the reaffirmation of what some may choose to call spiritual values.

In effect he believed that all is not lost. Through the influence of science we are recovering the neglected realism of the past; we

[13] See Addenda for brief notes.
[14] See Addenda, " Sherwood Anderson: a Psychological Naturalist."

are not only reaffirming it but making its acquaintance more intimately than ever before. Weld that science to enlightened and
humane aspirations (Parrington believed that there was nothing
in the findings of science that prevented the union) and a revivified
liberalism will make the world a fit place to live in. It is by no
means an easy program, for it requires knowledge of fact, and
ability to carry knowledge into the sphere of effective action. It is
made doubly difficult by the untimely death of one of its chief proponents, yet in the young men and women whom he liked to have
around him there must be, however obscurely, a feeling and a
groping for the way out. They will be guided and inspired by such
utterance as Parrington's diagnosis of Sinclair Lewis, where he
quarries out a vein of his own enduring liberalism.

"Some lingering faith in our poor human nature he still clings
to. In the great American mass that human nature is certainly
foolish and unlovely enough. It is too often blown up with flatulence, corroded with lust, on familiar terms with chicanery and
lying; it openly delights in hocus pocus and discovers its miracle-
workers in Comstocks and Aimee Semple McPhersons. But for all
its pitiful flabbiness human nature is not wholly bad, nor is man
so helpless a creature of circumstance as the cynics would have us
believe. There are other and greater gods than Mumbo Jumbo
worshiped in America, worthier things than hocus pocus; and in
rare moments even Babbitt dimly perceives that the feet of his
idol are clay. There are Martin Arrowsmiths as well as Elmer
Gantrys, and human nature, if it will, can pull itself out of the trap.
Bad social machinery makes bad men. Put the banker in the scullery instead of the drawing-room; exalt the test-tube and deflate
the cash register; rid society of the dictatorship of the middle class;
and the artist and the scientist will erect in America a civilization
that may become, what civilization was in earlier days, a thing to
be respected. For all his modernity and disillusion learned from
Pullman-car philosophers, Sinclair Lewis is still an echo of Jean
Jacques and the golden hopes of the Enlightenment—thin and
far-off, no doubt, but still an authentic echo."

"Thin and far-off, no doubt," is this contemporary liberalism,
yet Parrington found hints of it in the midst of the war fiasco that
culminated in reaction and despair. Death did not grant him the
opportunity to show what he found, but the young men who learned
from him the love of sound craftsmanship, who were inspired by

his enlightened dreams, will some day complete the monument. In the meantime Vernon Louis Parrington would like to be held in memory as he held his friend, J. Allen Smith—as a "scholar, teacher, democrat, gentleman."

E. H. EBY

University of Washington
Seattle, Washington
March, 1930

FOREWORD

WITH the present volume I bring to a close my studies in the main currents in American thought. The broad drifts of American opinion, as I interpret that opinion, should now be sufficiently clear. The volume immediately preceding the present one dealt with the romantic revolution in America—one of the most stimulating experiences the American mind has undergone—which was traced to twin forces: the influence upon an expansive generation of French romantic thought, and the spirit of robust individualism resulting from a fluid economics; and the creative result was the spontaneous emergence in America of a buoyant spirit of hopefulness that expressed itself in democratic programs and faith in a benevolent progress. The present volume deals with the slow decay of this romantic optimism in more thoughtful minds, and the cause of that decay is traced to three sources: the stratifying of economics under the pressure of centralization; the rise of a mechanistic science; and the emergence of a spirit of skepticism which, under the pressure of industrialism, the teachings of the physical sciences, and the lessons of European intellectuals, is resulting in the questioning of the ideal of democracy as it has been commonly held hitherto, and the spread of a spirit of pessimism. The custodianship of America by the middle class has brought unsuspected consequences in its train.

Thus after three hundred years' experience we have returned, intellectually, to the point from which we set out, and the old philosophy brought to the new world from the compact societies of Europe, with its doctrine of determinism and its mood of pessimism, has come back in changed form to color the thinking of our generation. Emersonian optimism, that was the fullest expression of the romantic faith, is giving way to Dreiserian pessimism, and the traditional doctrine of progress is being subjected to analysis by a growing skepticism. Our intellectual history thus conceived falls into three broad phases: Calvinistic pessimism, romantic optimism, and mechanistic pessimism. Between the first and the last lies the America of yesterday that shaped the American mind and American institutions; and with the submergence of that native world we are in the way of repeating here the familiar history of Europe, with its coercive regimentations reproduced on a larger scale and in more mechanical fashion. Once more a gloomy philosophy stands on the threshold of the American mind. Whether it will enter and take possession of the household, no one can predict as yet. This much nevertheless is clear: an industrialized society is reshaping the psychology fashioned by an agrarian world; the passion for liberty is lessening and the individual, in the presence of creature comforts, is being dwarfed; the drift of centralization is shaping its inevitable tyrannies to bind us with. Whether the quick concern for human rights, that was the noble bequest of our fathers who had drunk of the waters of French romantic faith, will be carried over into the future, to unhorse the machine that now rides men and to leaven the sodden mass that is industrial America, is a question to which the gods as yet have given no answer. Yet it is not without hope that intelligent America is in revolt. The artist is in revolt, the intellectual is in revolt, the conscience of America is in revolt.

It ought not to be necessary to add that in these volumes I have not essayed to write a history of American literature—that rather difficult task for which no scholar is as yet equipped. But I have suffered so many gentle reproofs for failing to do what I did not set out to do, that it may be well to repeat what I said in the Foreword to Volume I, that I have been concerned in the present study with the total pattern of American thought—the broad drift of major ideas—and not with vagrant currents or casual variations. In particular I have been repeatedly taken to task for a seeming slight put upon certain of our artists, and it has been inferred that I slighted them because I chose to ignore whatever did not fit into a rigid scheme of economic determinism. Let me say in rebuttal that I hold no brief for a rigid scheme of economic determinism. I recognize the rich culture potentialities that inhere in individual variation from type, and I realize that the arts are likely to receive their noblest gifts from men who should be classed biologically as cultural sports or variations from the cultural type. But in such a study as I have undertaken, individual variation is significant not for its own sake, but rather for the help it may offer in determining the type. After due consideration I see no cause to apologize for my treatment of Poe, for example, if indeed I have done so. I am content to have placed him historically and culturally in relation to the whole, leaving the fascinating problem of his variation from type to those who deal with such problems.

V. L. P.

INTRODUCTION *

IN the second volume of my studies I laid down the thesis that
at the beginning of our national existence two rival philosophies
contended for supremacy in America: the humanitarian philosophy
of the French Enlightenment, based on the conception of human
perfectibility and postulating as its objective an equalitarian democracy in which the political state should function as the servant
to the common well-being; and the English philosophy of *laissez
faire*, based on the assumed universality of the acquisitive instinct
and postulating a social order answering the needs of an abstract
"economic man," in which the state should function in the interests of trade. And I pointed out further, with adequate backing
up, I hope, that the first of these antagonistic philosophies was
accepted by the agrarian leaders of America and found issue in
the Jeffersonian program; that the second came to dominate the
thinking of the mercantile, capitalistic America and took form in
Hamiltonian Federalism. Unfortunately this logical alignment of
diverse economic groups was obscured by the needs of practical
politics, and in passing through the explosive Jacksonian revolution both philosophies underwent subtle changes. Jacksonianism
imposed upon America the ideal of democracy to which all must
thereafter do lip service, but it lost its realistic basis in a Physiocratic economics and wandered in a fog of political equalitarianism;
and the Whiggery that issued from Federalism turned to the work
of converting the democratic state into the servant of property
interests. Both political parties contented themselves with an
egoistic individualism that took no account of social ends, forgetful
of the humanitarian spirit that underlay the earlier democratic
program. The finer spirit of the Enlightenment was lost, and in
consequence the major parties chose to follow the economic interests of master groups, heedless of all humanitarian issues.

* The Introduction, as will be readily seen by the reader, is not complete, yet it
undoubtedly contains the gist of what Professor Parrington intended to include in
it. He wrote several forms of some parts, from which the Introduction as it stands
has been pieced together in logical order. It is probable that the last words he wrote
were the significant closing words here—"to summon forth the potential intelligence
of the younger generation."—*Publisher*.

But the spirit awakened by the earlier democratic enthusiasm could not be kept in political strait-jackets. The Jacksonian revolution overflowed all narrow party dikes, expressing itself in diverse humanitarian and reform movements and quickening the minds of ardent Americans with larger democratic aspirations. The noble idealism of successive third parties that have sprung up reasserted the democratic principles flouted by the major parties. The Locofoco movement, the Free-soil Party, the early Republican Party, the Greenback Party, the Populist Party, the Progressive Party, have had a common objective, namely to carry further the movement inaugurated by the Jeffersonians to make of America a land of democratic equality and opportunity—to make government in America serve man rather than property. The third-party movements have always been democratic movements, and though they have failed in their immediate objectives they have served the purpose of reminding the major parties—oftentimes rudely— that America presumes to be a democratic country. Thus interpreted the history of the political struggle in America since 1790 falls into three broad phases: the Jeffersonian movement that asserted the ideal of political democracy; the Jacksonian movement that established it crudely in practice; and the successive third-party movements that attempted to regain such ground as had been lost, to extend the field, and to perfect the machinery of democratic government.

As a result of the long struggle the abstract principle of democracy—during the period under consideration—was firmly established in the popular mind; but as it fell under the successive custodianship of different economic groups it came to receive strangely diverse interpretations. Interpreted by the coonskin Jacksonians it meant political equalitarianism; by the slave economy it meant a Greek democracy; by the industrial economy it meant the right of exploitation. It has changed service with each new master. Always the principles of Jeffersonianism—of democracy as a humane social order, serving the common well-being— have been lost out of the reckoning, and except in so far as the tendency has been checked by the third-party threat, democratic professions have been only a thin cover under which the old class warfare has gone forward vigorously. In the decades immediately following the Civil War democracy passed under the custodianship of the middle class, who were busily engaged in creating a plutocracy, and the major ideas of the earlier movement took on a characteristic middle-class coloring. The idea of a beneficent progress, which was the flower of the doctrine of human perfectibility, came to be interpreted as material expansion with constantly augmenting profits; and the idea of democracy came to be interpreted as the right to use the government of the whole for the benefit of the few.

.   .   .   .

Considered historically perhaps the chief contribution of the Progressive movement to the democratic cause is to be found in its discovery of the fundamentally undemocratic nature of the federal Constitution. That so obvious a fact so long escaped recognition was due to political causes easily understood. For a century the Constitution had been a symbol of national unity, a cohesive force amidst the drift of expansion, a counter influence to the disintegrations of states-rights particularisms; and as such it had appealed to the national loyalties of men in every commonwealth. To criticize it was reckoned disloyal. The long process of interpretation had remained in the hands of the lawyers and had been wholly legalistic and antiquarian. In all this earlier commentary— except for a small group of left-wing Abolitionists who repudiated the entire instrument—no question as to the democratic spirit of the Constitution was raised, no doubts as to its sufficiency as a fundamental democratic law were suggested. The class divisions that presided at its making were ignored, and the aristocratic spirit of its creators was forgotten. But with the rising revolt against the custodianship of government by financial and industrial interests came a new critical interest in the fundamental law. Discovering that its hands were tied the democracy began to question the reason for the bonds that constrained its movements. The latent distrust was quickened by what was regarded by many as judicial usurpations of power, such as the act of the Supreme Court in declaring unconstitutional the federal income-tax law, and the question of the desirability of an eighteenth-century document that by its complexity unduly impeded the functioning of the democratic will, was thrust into the foreground of political debate. It was the struggle of 1789 over again.

The new school of criticism was historical rather than legalistic. It was concerned primarily with origins—and it must take into account the political theories and class interests of the eighteenth-century gentlemen who framed the document. It refused to look upon the Fathers as supermen, devoted unselfishly to high patriotic duty, but chose to regard them as capable statesmen, saturated with aristocratic prejudices, who fearful of losing control of the new venture in republicanism, took care to shape an instrument that threw sharp restrictions about the majority will.

. . . .

The theme of the present volume is the industrialization of America under the leadership of the middle class, and the consequent rise of a critical attitude towards the ideals and handiwork of that class. It concerns itself primarily with the spirit of realism that under the constrictions of industrialism and with the spread of scientific modes of thought emerged to question the ardent romanticisms of an earlier age, and bring under doubt the excellence of a social order created by the Industrial Revolution.

The field to be traversed is thus predetermined. The interpretation of our literature since 1860 must be fitted into the broad lines of our national experience and will follow the main divisions of development.

I. The conquest of America by the middle class and its custodianship of democracy. The philosophy of the middle class.

II. The challenge of that overlordship by:

    1. The older democratic agrarianism as expressed chiefly in the third-party movements.

    2. The new proletarian philosophy that came likewise out of the ferment of the French Revolution, but that traveled a different course—through Europe and the earlier continental Industrial Revolution, and thence to America.

III. The intellectual revolution brought about by science with the results:

    1. The recovery of a spirit of realism.

    2. The appropriation of science by the middle class.

IV. The rise of a detached criticism by the younger intellectuals.

In dealing with this material it will be necessary to follow sectional lines in the earlier decades until the encompassing movement of centralization finally obliterated them and produced a common national spirit and purpose.

In the welter that is present-day America militant philosophies with their clear-cut programs and assured faiths are wanting, and many feel, as Matthew Arnold felt fourscore years ago, that they are dwelling between worlds, one dead, the other powerless to be born. The old buoyant psychology is gone and in the breakdown and disintegration of the traditional individualism no new philosophies are rising. Builders of Utopias are out of a job. Political and economic theory is in charge of paymasters and is content with the drab rim of the familiar landscape. Retainer-fees have blotted out for it the lovelier horizons that earlier thinkers contemplated. Academic political scientists and economists have largely joined the Swiss guards, and abdicated the high prerogative of speculative thought. It is the men of letters—poets and essayists and novelists and dramatists, the eager young intellectuals of a drab generation— who embody the mind of present-day America; not the professional custodians of official views. They at least decline to block the path to the Promised Land with retainer-fees; they at least are free souls, and in the measure of their abilities, free thinkers. It is to them therefore that one must turn to discover the intellectual currents of later America—to their aspirations as well as to their criticisms. Literature at last has become the authentic voice of this great shapeless America that means so much to western civilization. Not theologians any longer, nor political philosophers, nor industrial masters, nor bankers, are the spokesmen of this vibrant life of a continent, but the intellectuals, the dreamers, the critics, the historians, the men of letters, in short; and to them one may turn hopefully for a revelation of American life.

The period dealt with in the present study marks the complete triumph of the middle class and the final defeat of the traditional agrarianism. The disintegration of the earlier romanticisms, both native and imported, has run its course. The philosophy of Jefferson and John Taylor, with its physiocratic bias, its antipathy to a money economy, its love of local autonomy, has been buried in the potter's field.

·   ·   ·   ·   ·   ·   °

Amidst all the turmoil and vague subconscious tendencies, certain ideas slowly clarified: first, that the earlier democratic aspirations had somehow failed, that an equalitarian philosophy adapted to frontier conditions could not easily be carried over into a centralizing and stratifying America and was doomed to eventual defeat; second, that even in the supposed heyday of our democracy, we had never achieved a democracy, but rather a careless individualism that left society at the mercy of a rapacious middle class; third, that we must take our bearings afresh and set forth on a different path to the goal. As these convictions slowly rose into consciousness, a quick suspicion of our earlier philosophies arose to trouble us. With the growing realism of the times came a belief that our French romantic theories were mainly at fault and we must somehow go back to the rationalistic eighteenth century and start once more to recreate a democratic philosophy. The crux of the matter seemed to lie in the romantic conception of human nature. Rousseau and Godwin were the false prophets who led us astray, and we must return to the solid realism of John Locke. In the light of a realistic psychology, with its discovery of morons, and its study of mob tendencies, it was no longer possible to take seriously that attractive figment of the romantic imagination—man in the state of nature, perfectible by following the light of reason, seeking justice. Morons do not fit nicely into the older theory—they jar one's faith in human perfectibility. In the light of intelligence tests perhaps the whole romantic theory of democracy was only a will-o'-the-wisp. With the very foundations of our traditional philosophy turning to quicksand under our feet, no wonder we are bedeviled by doubts and uncertainties. Utopias no longer seem so near at hand as they did; plans and specifications of the ideal commonwealth no longer seem simple matters to be drawn by any competent social carpenter. Our jauntiness is gone, speculation is less important than investigation, and in the spirit of sober realism we are setting about the serious business of thinking.

In this thinking two major forces are at hand: economics and psychology. In our economic realism we are returning to the spirit of the eighteenth century, and adapting the determinism that marked political thought from Harrington and John Adams to Webster and Calhoun; but we are equipped with a psychological knowledge that those earlier thinkers lacked. Wedding the new psychology to the older economic determinism, we may hope in a spirit of sober realism to make some progress in our thinking.

Yet not too hastily should we abandon our earlier faith: the eighteenth-century conception of environment as a creative influence in determining character is a vital idea not yet adequately explored. Even morons may be traced back to adenoids or diets of salt pork and whisky or to later machine labor, and aristocracies are still seen to be economic. And aristocratic albinos may well breed mobs and morons. Jefferson was not as foolish as many of his disciples have been, and Jeffersonian democracy still offers hope. Education begins to fail—except education to individualize and to summon forth the potential intelligence of the younger generation.

CONTENTS *

* This is given in full, as Professor Parrington left it, with those parts not completed by him in brackets. Some revision has been made for the parts he completed,
but notes have been added to the text to show his original intention. For some of the
bracketed headings after Part II of Book II some material is given in the Addenda
from other work of Parrington's.—*Publisher.*

xxxi

BOOK TWO: THE OLD AND THE NEW: STORM CLOUDS

PART I

The Middle Border Rises

CONTENTS

PART II

Proletarian Hopes

PART III

The Hesitant South

[1] See "Naturalism in American Fiction," in the Addenda—lecture notes including
Crane and Norris.

BOOK THREE: THE NEW AMERICA

PART I

The Rise of Liberalism [4]

[2] See Addenda for lecture notes on Lanier.
[3] See Addenda for magazine article on Cabell.
[4] See "A Chapter in American Liberalism," the last of the Addenda.

[5] See *Ibid.*
[6] See Addenda, "The Problem Novel and the Diversion from Naturalism."
[7] See Addenda for brief notes.
[8] See Addenda for notes of lecture on Dreiser.

PART III

Reaction

[9] See Addenda for reprint of pamphlet on Lewis.
[10] See Addenda for brief notes.

BOOK ONE: CHANGING AMERICA

BOOK ONE

CHANGING AMERICA

WHEN America laid aside its arms after Appomattox and turned back to the pursuits of peace it was well advanced toward the goal set by Alexander Hamilton three-quarters of a century before. The great obstacle that had withheld its feet hitherto had been swept from its path. A slave economy could never again thwart the ambitions of the capitalistic economy. The jealous particularism that for a generation had obstructed the inevitable drift toward a coalescing national unity had gone down in defeat. The agrarian South was no longer master in the councils of government; the shaping of the future had fallen to other hands and the unfolding of the new order could go forward without southern let or hindrance.

Other obstacles were falling away of themselves. North as well as South, the traditional domestic economy was already a thing of the past. An easier way to wealth, and one enormously more profitable, had been discovered. The future lay in the hands of the machine that was already dispossessing the tool. In the hurry of the war years the potentialities of the factory system had been explored and the ready resources of liquid capital had been greatly augmented. From the smoke of the great conflict an America had emerged unlike any the earlier generations had known. An ambitious industrialism stood on the threshold of a continental expansion that was to transfer sovereignty in America from a landed and mercantile aristocracy to the capable hands of a new race of captains of industry. Only the western farmers, newly settled in the Middle Border and spreading the psychology of the frontier through the vast prairie spaces of a greater Inland Empire, remained as a last stumbling-block. Other battles with agrarianism must be fought before capitalism assumed undisputed mastery of America; but with the eventual overthrow of the agrarian hosts in their last stronghold the path would lie broad and straight to the goal of an encompassing industrialism, with politicians and political parties its willing servants. There would be no more dissensions in the household. With southern Jeffersonians and western agrarians no longer sitting as watch dogs to the Constitution, the political state would be refashioned to serve a new age, and the old dream of a coalescing national economy become a reality. The American System was in the way of complete establishment.

Other changes impended, and greater. The enthronement of the machine was only the outward and visible sign of the revolution in thought that came with the rise of science. As a new cosmos unfolded before the inquisitive eyes of scientists the old metaphysical speculations became as obsolete as the old household economy. A new spirit of realism was abroad, probing and questioning the material world, pushing the realm of exact knowledge into the earlier regions of faith. The conquest of nature was the great business of the day, and as that conquest went forward triumphantly the solid fruits of the new mastery were gathered by industrialism. Science and the machine were the twin instruments for creating a new civilization, of which the technologist and the industrialist were the high priests. The transcendental theologian was soon to be as extinct as the passenger pigeon.

With the substitution of the captain of industry for the plantation master as the custodian of society, the age of aristocracy was at an end and the age of the middle class was established. A new culture, created by the machine and answering the needs of capitalism, was to dispossess the old culture with its lingering concern for distinction and its love of standards—a culture that should eventually suffice the needs of a brisk city world of machine activities. But that would take time. In the meanwhile—in the confused interregnum between reigns—America would be little more than a welter of crude energy, a raw unlovely society where the strife of competition with its prodigal waste testified to the shortcomings of an age in process of transition. The spirit of the frontier was to flare up in a huge buccaneering orgy. Having swept across the continent to the Pacific coast like a visitation of locusts, the frontier spirit turned back upon its course to conquer the East, infecting the new industrialism with a crude individualism, fouling the halls of Congress, despoiling the public domain, and indulging in a huge national barbecue. It submerged the arts and created a new literature. For a time it carried all things before it, until running full tilt into science and the machine, its triumphant progress was stopped and America, rejecting individualism, began the work of standardization and mechanization. It is this world in transition from an aristocratic to a middle-class order, turmoiled by the last flare-up of the frontier spirit, shifting from a robust individualism to a colorless standardization, which the chapters that follow must deal with. A confused and turbulent scene, but not without its fascination to the American who would understand his special heritage—perhaps the most characteristically native, the most American, in our total history.

PART ONE: THE GILDED AGE

CHAPTER I
THE AMERICAN SCENE

I
FREE AMERICA

THE pot was boiling briskly in America in the tumultuous post-war years. The country had definitely entered upon its freedom and was settling its disordered household to suit its democratic taste. Everywhere new ways were feverishly at work transforming the countryside. In the South another order was rising uncertainly on the ruins of the plantation system; in the East an expanding factory economy was weaving a different pattern of industrial life; in the Middle Border a recrudescent agriculture was arising from the application of the machine to the rich prairie soil. All over the land a spider web of iron rails was being spun that was to draw the remotest outposts into the common whole and bind the nation together with steel bands. Nevertheless two diverse worlds lay on the map of continental America. Facing in opposite directions and holding different faiths, they would not travel together easily or take comfort from the yoke that joined them. Agricultural America, behind which lay two and a half centuries of experience, was a decentralized world, democratic, individualistic, suspicious; industrial America, behind which lay only half a dozen decades of bustling experiment, was a centralizing world, capitalistic, feudal, ambitious. The one was a decaying order, the other a rising, and between them would be friction till one or the other had become master.

Continental America was still half frontier and half settled country. A thin line of homesteads had been thrust westward till the outposts reached well into the Middle Border—an uncertain thread running through eastern Minnesota, Nebraska, Kansas, overleaping the Indian Territory and then running west into Texas—approximately halfway between the Atlantic and the Pacific. Behind these outposts was still much unoccupied land, and beyond stretched the unfenced prairies till they merged in the sagebrush plains, gray and waste, that stretched to the foothills of the Rocky Mountains. Beyond the mountains were other stretches of plains and deserts, vast and forbidding in their alkali blight, to the wooded coast ranges and the Pacific Ocean. In all this immense territory were only scattered settlements—at Denver, Salt Lake City, Sacramento, San Francisco, Portland, Seattle, and elsewhere— tiny outposts in the wilderness, with scattered hamlets, mining camps, and isolated homesteads lost in the great expanse. On the prairies from Mexico to Canada—across which rumbled great herds of buffalo—roved powerful tribes of hostile Indians who fretted against the forward thrust of settlement and disputed the right of possession. The urgent business of the times was the subduing of this wild region, wresting it from Indians and buffalo and wilderness; and the forty years that lay between the California Gold Rush of '49 and the Oklahoma Land Rush of '89 saw the greatest wave of pioneer expansion—the swiftest and most reckless—in all our pioneer experience. Expansion on so vast a scale necessitated building, and the seventies became the railway age, bonding the future to break down present barriers of isolation, and opening new territories for later exploitation. The reflux of the great movement swept back upon the Atlantic coast and gave to life there a fresh note of spontaneous vigor, of which the Gilded Age was the inevitable expression.

It was this energetic East, with its accumulations of liquid capital awaiting investment and its factories turning out the materials needed to push the settlements westward, that profited most from the conquest of the far West. The impulsion from the frontier did much to drive forward the industrial revolution. The war that brought devastation to the South had been more friendly to northern interests. In gathering the scattered rills of capital into central reservoirs at Philadelphia and New York, and in expanding the factory system to supply the needs of the armies, it had opened to capitalism its first clear view of the Promised Land. The bankers had come into control of the liquid wealth of the nation, and the industrialists had learned to use the machine for production; the time was ripe for exploitation on a scale undreamed-of a generation before. Up till then the potential resources of the continent had not even been surveyed. Earlier pioneers had only scratched the surface—felling trees, making crops, building pygmy watermills, smelting a little iron. Mineral wealth had been scarcely touched. Tools had been lacking to develop it, capital had been lacking, transportation lacking, technical methods lacking, markets lacking.

In the years following the war, exploitation for the first time was provided with adequate resources and a competent technique, and busy prospectors were daily uncovering new sources of wealth. The coal and oil of Pennsylvania and Ohio, the copper and iron ore of upper Michigan, the gold and silver, lumber and fisheries, of the Pacific Coast, provided limitless raw materials for the rising industrialism. The Bessemer process quickly turned an age of iron into an age of steel and created the great rolling mills of Pittsburgh from which issued the rails for expanding railways. The reaper and binder, the sulky plow and the threshing machine, created a large-scale agriculture on the fertile prairies. Wild grass-lands provided grazing for immense herds of cattle and sheep; the development of the corn-belt enormously increased the supply of hogs; and with railways at hand the Middle Border poured into Omaha and Kansas City and Chicago an endless stream of produce. As the line of the frontier pushed westward new towns were built, thousands of homesteads were filed on, and the speculator and promoter hovered over the prairies like buzzards seeking their carrion. With rising land-values money was to be made out of unearned increment, and the creation of booms was a profitable industry. The times were stirring and it was a shiftless fellow who did not make his pile. If he had been too late to file on desirable acres he had only to find a careless homesteader who had failed in some legal technicality and "jump his claim." Good bottom land could be had even by late-comers if they were sharp at the game.

This bustling America of 1870 accounted itself a democratic world. A free people had put away all aristocratic privileges and conscious of its power went forth to possess the last frontier. Its social philosophy, which it found adequate to its needs, was summed up in three words—preëmption, exploitation, progress. Its immediate and pressing business was to dispossess the government of its rich holdings. Lands in the possession of the government were so much idle waste, untaxed and profitless; in private hands they would be developed. They would provide work, pay taxes, support schools, enrich the community. Preëmption meant exploitation and exploitation meant progress. It was a simple philosophy and it suited the simple individualism of the times. The Gilded Age knew nothing of the Enlightenment; it recognized only the acquisitive instinct. That much at least the frontier had taught the great American democracy; and in applying to the resources of a continent the lesson it had been so well taught the Gilded Age wrote a profoundly characteristic chapter of American history.

II

FIGURES OF EARTH

In a moment of special irritation Edwin Lawrence Godkin called the civilization of the seventies a chromo civilization. Mark Twain, with his slack western standards, was equally severe. As he contemplated the slovenly reality beneath the gaudy exterior he dubbed it the Gilded Age. Other critics with a gift for pungent phrase have flung their gibes at the ways of a picturesque and uncouth generation. There is reason in plenty for such caustic comment. Heedless, irreverent, unlovely, cultivating huge beards, shod in polished top-boots—the last refinement of the farmer's cowhides —wearing linen dickeys over hickory shirts, moving through pools of tobacco juice, erupting in shoddy and grotesque architecture, cluttering its homes with ungainly walnut chairs and marble-topped tables and heavy lambrequins, the decade of the seventies was only too plainly mired and floundering in a bog of bad taste. A world of triumphant and unabashed vulgarity without its like in our history, it was not aware of its plight, but accounted its manners genteel and boasted of ways that were a parody on sober good sense.

Yet just as such comments are, they do not reach quite to the heart of the age. They emphasize rather the excrescences, the casual lapses, of a generation that underneath its crudities and vulgarities was boldly adventurous and creative—a generation in which the democratic freedoms of America, as those freedoms had taken shape during a drab frontier experience, came at last to spontaneous and vivid expression. If its cultural wealth was less than it thought, if in its exuberance it was engaged somewhat too boisterously in stamping its own plebeian image on the work of its hands, it was only natural to a society that for the first time found its opportunities equal to its desires, a youthful society that accounted the world its oyster and wanted no restrictions laid on its will. It was the ripe fruit of Jacksonian leveling, and if it ran to

a grotesque individualism—if in its self-confidence it was heedless
of the smiles of older societies—it was nevertheless by reason of its
uncouthness the most picturesque generation in our history; and
for those who love to watch human nature disporting itself with
naïve abandon, running amuck through all the conventions, no
other age provides so fascinating a spectacle.

When the cannon at last had ceased their destruction it was a
strange new America that looked out confidently on the scene.
Something had been released by the upheavals of half a century,
something strong and assertive that was prepared to take possession of the continent. It did not issue from the loins of war. Its
origins must be sought elsewhere, further back in time. It had been
cradled in the vast changes that since 1815 had been reshaping
America: in the break-up of the old domestic economy that kept
life mean and drab, in the noisy enthusiasms of the new coonskin
democracy, in the romanticisms of the California gold rush, in the
boisterous freedoms discovered by the forties and fifties. It had
come to manhood in the battles of a tremendous war, and as it
now surveyed the continent, discovering potential wealth before
unknown, it demanded only freedom and opportunity—a fair
race and no favors. Everywhere was a welling-up of primitive
pagan desires after long repressions—to grow rich, to grasp power,
to be strong and masterful and lay the world at its feet. It was a
violent reaction from the narrow poverty of frontier life and the
narrow inhibitions of backwoods religion. It had had enough of
skimpy, meager ways, of scrubbing along hoping for something to
turn up. It would go out and turn it up. It was consumed with a
great hunger for abundance, for the good things of life, for wealth.
It was frankly materialistic and if material goods could be wrested
from society it would lay its hands heartily to the work. Freedom
and opportunity, to acquire, to possess, to enjoy—for that it would
sell its soul.

Society of a sudden was become fluid. With the sweeping-away
of the last aristocratic restraints the potentialities of the common
man found release for self-assertion. Strange figures, sprung from
obscure origins, thrust themselves everywhere upon the scene. In
the reaction from the mean and skimpy, a passionate will to power
was issuing from unexpected sources, undisciplined, confused in
ethical values, but endowed with immense vitality. Individualism
was being simplified to the acquisitive instinct. These new Ameri-

cans were primitive souls, ruthless, predatory, capable; single-minded men; rogues and rascals often, but never feeble, never hindered by petty scruple, never given to puling or whining—the raw materials of a race of capitalistic buccaneers. Out of the drab mass of common plebeian life had come this vital energy that erupted in amazing abundance and in strange forms. The new freedoms meant diverse things to different men and each like Jurgen followed after his own wishes and his own desires. Pirate and priest issued from the common source and played their parts with the same picturesqueness. The romantic age of Captain Kidd was come again, and the black flag and the gospel banner were both in lockers to be flown as the needs of the cruise determined. With all coercive restrictions put away the democratic genius of America was setting out on the road of manifest destiny.

Analyze the most talked-of men of the age and one is likely to find a splendid audacity coupled with an immense wastefulness. A note of tough-mindedness marks them. They had stout nippers. They fought their way encased in rhinoceros hides. There was the Wall Street crowd—Daniel Drew, Commodore Vanderbilt, Jim Fisk, Jay Gould, Russell Sage—blackguards for the most part, railway wreckers, cheaters and swindlers, but picturesque in their rascality. There was the numerous tribe of politicians—Boss Tweed, Fernando Wood, G. Oakey Hall, Senator Pomeroy, Senator Cameron, Roscoe Conkling, James G. Blaine—blackguards also for the most part, looting city treasuries, buying and selling legislative votes like railway stock, but picturesque in their audacity. There were the professional keepers of the public morals—Anthony Comstock, John B. Gough, Dwight L. Moody, Henry Ward Beecher, T. De Witt Talmage—ardent proselytizers, unintellectual, men of one idea, but fiery in zeal and eloquent in description of the particular heaven each wanted to people with his fellow Americans. And springing up like mushrooms after a rain was the goodly company of cranks—Virginia Woodhull and Tennessee Claflin, "Citizen" George Francis Train, Henry Bergh, Ben Butler, Ignatius Donnelly, Bob Ingersoll, Henry George—picturesque figures with a flair for publicity who tilled their special fields with splendid gestures. And finally there was Barnum the Showman, growing rich on the profession of humbuggery, a vulgar greasy genius, pure brass without any gilding, yet in picturesque and capable effrontery the very embodiment of the age. A marvelous company, vital with the untamed energy of a new land. In the presence of such men one begins to understand what Walt Whitman meant by his talk of the elemental.

Created by a primitive world that knew not the machine, they were marked by the rough homeliness of their origins. Whether wizened or fat they were never insignificant or commonplace. On the whole one prefers them fat, and for solid bulk what generation has outdone them? There was Revivalist Moody, bearded and neckless, with his two hundred and eighty pounds of Adam's flesh, every ounce of which "belonged to God." There was the lyric Sankey, afflicted with two hundred and twenty-five pounds of human frailty, yet looking as smug as a banker and singing "There were ninety and nine" divinely through mutton-chop whiskers. There was Boss Tweed, phlegmatic and mighty, overawing rebellious gangsters at the City Hall with his two hundred and forty pounds of pugnacious rascality. There was John Fiske, a philosophic hippopotamus, warming the chill waters of Spencerian science with his prodigious bulk. There was Ben Butler, oily and puffy and wheezy, like Falstaff larding the lean earth as he walked along, who yearly added more flesh to the scant ninety-seven pounds he carried away from Waterville College. And there was Jim Fisk, dressed like a bartender, huge in nerve as in bulk, driving with the dashing Josie Mansfield down Broadway—prince of vulgarians, who jovially proclaimed, "I worship in the Synagogue of the Libertines," and who on the failure of the Erie coup announced cheerfully, "Nothing is lost save honor!"

Impressive as are the fat kine of Egypt, the lean kine scarcely suffer by contrast. There were giants of puny physique in those days. There was Uncle Dan'l Drew, thin as a dried herring, yet a builder of churches and founder of Drew Theological Seminary, who pilfered and cheated his way to wealth with tobacco juice drooling from his mouth. There was Jay Gould, a lone-hand gambler, a dynamo in a tubercular body, who openly invested in the devil's tenements as likely to pay better dividends, and went home to potter lovingly amongst his exotic flowers. And there was Oakey Hall, clubman and playwright, small, elegant, and unscrupulous; and Victoria Woodhull who stirred up the Beecher case, a wisp of a woman who enraged all the frumpy blue-stockings by the smartness of her toilet and the perfection of her manners; and little Libby Tilton with her tiny wistful face and great eyes that looked out wonderingly at the world—eyes that were to go blind with weeping before the candle of her life went out. It was such men and women, individual and colorful, that Whitman and Mark Twain mingled with, and that Herman Melville—colossal and dynamic beyond them all—looked out upon sardonically from his tomb in the Custom House where he was consuming his own heart.

They were thrown up as it were casually out of the huge caldron of energy that was America. All over the land were thousands like them, self-made men quick to lay hands on opportunity if it knocked at the door, ready to seek it out if it were slow in knocking, recognizing no limitations to their powers, discouraged by no shortcomings in their training. When Moody set out to bring the world to his Protestant God he was an illiterate shoe salesman who stumbled over the hard words of his King James Bible. Anthony Comstock, the roundsman of the Lord, was a salesman in a dry-goods shop, and as careless of his spelling as he was careful of his neighbors' morals. Commodore Vanderbilt, who built up the greatest fortune of the time, was a Brooklyn ferryman, hard-fisted and tough as a burr-oak, who in a lifetime of over eighty years read only one book, *Pilgrim's Progress*, and that after he was seventy. Daniel Drew was a shyster cattle-drover, whose arid emotions found outlet in periodic conversions and backslidings, and who got on in this vale of tears by salting his cattle and increasing his—and the Lord's—wealth with every pound of water in their bellies— from which cleverness is said to have come the Wall Street phrase, "stock-watering." Jim Fisk was the son of a Yankee peddler, who, disdaining the unambitious ways of his father, set up for himself in a cart gilded like a circus-wagon and drove about the country-side with jingling bells. After he had made his pile in Wall Street he set up his own opera house and proposed to rival the Medici as a patron of the arts—and especially of the artists if they were of the right sex. A surprising number of them—Moody, Beecher, Barnum, Fisk, Comstock, Ben Butler—came from New England; Jay Gould was of Connecticut ancestry; but Oakey Hall was a southern gentleman; Fernando Wood, with the face of an Apollo and the wit of an Irishman, was the son of a Philadelphia cigar-maker and much of his early income was drawn from sailors' groggeries along the waterfront; Tweed was a stolid New Yorker, and Drew was a York State country boy.

What was happening in New York was symptomatic of the

nation. If the temple of Plutus was building in Wall Street, his devotees were everywhere. In Chicago, rising higgledy-piggledy from the ashes of the great fire, Phil Armour and Nelson Morris were laying out stockyards and drawing the cattle and sheep and hogs from remote prairie farms to their slaughter-houses. In Cleveland, Mark Hanna was erecting his smelters and turning the iron ore of Michigan into dollars, while John D. Rockefeller was squeezing the small fry out of the petroleum business and creating the Standard Oil monopoly. In Pittsburgh, Andrew Carnegie was applying the Bessemer process to steel-making and laying the foundations of the later steel trust. In Minneapolis, C. C. Washburn and Charles A. Pillsbury were applying new methods to milling and turning the northern wheat into flour to ship to the ends of the earth. In San Francisco, Leland Stanford and Collis P. Huntington were amassing huge fortunes out of the Southern Pacific Railway and bringing the commonwealth of California to their feet. Everywhere were boom-town and real-estate promoters, the lust of speculation, the hankering after quick and easy wealth.

In the great spaces from Kansas City to Sacramento the frontier spirit was in the gaudiest bloom. The experiences of three centuries of expansion were being crowded into as many decades. In the fifties the highway of the frontier had run up and down the Mississippi River and the golden age of steamboating had brought a motley life to Saint Louis; in the seventies the frontier had passed far beyond and was pushing through the Rocky Mountains, repeating as it went the old frontier story of swagger and slovenliness, of boundless hope and heroic endurance—a story deeply marked with violence and crime and heart-breaking failure. Thousands of veterans from the disbanded armies, northern and southern alike, flocked to the West to seek their fortunes, and daily life there soon took on a drab note from the alkali of the plains; yet through the drabness ran a boisterous humor that exalted lying to a fine art—a humor that goes back to Davy Crockett and the Ohio flatboatmen. Mark Twain's *Roughing It* is the epic of this frontier of the Pony Express, as *Life on the Mississippi* is the epic of the preceding generation.

The huge wastefulness of the frontier was everywhere, East and West. The Gilded Age heeded somewhat too literally the Biblical injunction to take no thought for the morrow, but was busily intent on squandering the resources of the continent. All things

were held cheap, and human life cheapest of all. Wild Bill Hickok
with forty notches on his gun and a row of graves to his credit in
Boot Hill Cemetery, and Jesse James, most picturesque of des-
peradoes, levying toll with his six-shooter on the bankers who were
desecrating the free spirit of the plains with their two per cent. a
month, are familiar heroes in Wild West tales; but the real plains-
man of the Gilded Age, the picturesque embodiment of the last
frontier, was Captain Carver, the faultless horseman and faultless
shot, engaged in his celebrated buffalo hunt for the championship
of the prairies. Wagering that he could kill more buffalo in a day
than any rival hero of the chase, he rode forth with his Indian
marker and dropping the miles behind him he left an endless trail
of dead beasts properly tagged, winning handsomely when his
rival's horse fell dead from exhaustion. It was magnificent. Davy
Crockett's hundred and five bears in a season was but 'prentice
work compared with Captain Carver's professional skill. It is
small wonder that he became a hero of the day and his rifle, turned
now to the circus business of breaking glass balls thrown from his
running horse, achieved a fame far greater than Davy's Betsy.
With his bold mustaches, his long black hair flying in the wind, his
sombrero and chaps and top-boots, he was a figure matched only by
Buffalo Bill, the last of the great plainsmen.

Captain Carver was picturesque, but what shall be said of the
thousands of lesser Carvers engaged in the same slaughter, market-
hunters who discovered a new industry in buffalo-killing? At the
close of the Civil War the number on the western plains was estimated at fifteen millions. With the building of the Union Pacific
Railroad they were cut asunder into two vast herds, and upon these
herds fell the hunters with the new breech-loading rifles, shooting
for the hide market that paid sixty-five cents for a bull's hide and a
dollar and fifteen cents for a cow's. During the four years from 1871
to 1874 nearly a million head a year were slain from the southern
herd alone, their skins ripped off and the carcasses left for the
coyotes and buzzards. By the end of the hunting-season of 1875
the vast southern herd had been wiped out, and with the building
of the Northern Pacific in 1880 the smaller northern herd soon suffered the same fate. The buffalo were gone with the hostile Indians
—Sioux and Blackfeet and Cheyennes and a dozen other tribes.[1]

[1] See Allan Nevins, "The Taming of the West," in *The Emergence of Modern
America.*

It was the last dramatic episode of the American frontier, and it wrote a fitting climax to three centuries of wasteful conquest. But the prairies were tamed, and Wild Bill Hickok and Captain Carver and Buffalo Bill Cody had become romantic figures to enthrall the imagination of later generations.[2]

It was an abundant harvest of those freedoms that America had long been struggling to achieve, and it was making ready the ground for later harvests that would be less to its liking. Freedom had become individualism, and individualism had become the inalienable right to preëmpt, to exploit, to squander. Gone were the old ideals along with the old restraints. The idealism of the forties, the romanticism of the fifties—all the heritage of Jeffersonianism and the French Enlightenment—were put thoughtlessly away, and with no social conscience, no concern for civilization, no heed for the future of the democracy it talked so much about, the Gilded Age threw itself into the business of money-getting. From the sober restraints of aristocracy, the old inhibitions of Puritanism, the niggardliness of an exacting domestic economy, it swung far back in reaction, and with the discovery of limitless opportunities for exploitation it allowed itself to get drunk. Figures of earth, they followed after their own dreams. Some were builders with grandiose plans in their pockets; others were wreckers with no plans at all. It was an anarchistic world of strong, capable men, selfish, unenlightened, amoral—an excellent example of what human nature will do with undisciplined freedom. In the Gilded Age freedom was the freedom of buccaneers preying on the argosies of Spain.

III

POLITICS AND THE FAIRY GODMOTHER

Certainly the Gilded Age would have resented such an interpretation of its brisk activities. In the welter of change that resulted from the application of the machine to the raw materials of a continent, it chose rather to see the spirit of progress to which the temper of the American people was so responsive. Freedom, it was

[2] It is the same story in the matter of the passenger pigeon. In early days the flights of these birds ran to untold millions. The last great nesting was at Petoskey, Michigan, in 1878, covering a strip forty miles long and from three to ten miles wide. Upon the nests fell the market-hunters and a million and a half squabs were shipped to New York by rail, besides the thousands wasted. Within a generation the passenger pigeon had become extinct. See W. B. Mershon, *Outdoor Life and Recreation,* February, 1929, p. 26 ff.

convinced, was justifying itself by its works. The eighteenth century had been static, the nineteenth century was progressive. It was adaptable, quick to change its ways and its tools, ready to accept whatever proved advantageous—pragmatic, opportunist. It was not stifled by the dead hand of custom but was free to adapt means to ends. It accepted progress as it accepted democracy, without questioning the sufficiency of either. The conception accorded naturally with a frontier psychology. Complete opportunism is possible only amongst a people that is shallow-rooted, that lives in a fluid society, scantily institutionalized, with few vested interests. In a young society it is easy, in a maturing society it becomes increasingly difficult.

Dazzled by the results of the new technique of exploitation applied on a grand scale to unpreëmpted opportunities, it is no wonder the Gilded Age thought well of its labors and confused the pattern of life it was weaving with the pattern of a rational civilization. It had drunk in the idea of progress with its mother's milk. It was an inevitable frontier interpretation of the swift changes resulting from a fluid economics and a fluid society in process of settling into static ways. It served conveniently to describe the changes from the simplicities of social beginnings to the complexities of a later order. It was made use of following the War of 1812 to explain the stir resulting from the westward expansion and the great increase in immigration; but it was given vastly greater significance by the social unsettlements that came with the industrial revolution. With the realization of the dramatic changes in manner of living—the added conveniences of life, release from the laborious round of the domestic economy, ease of transportation—that resulted from the machine order, it was inevitable that the idea of progress should have been on every man's tongue. The increase of wealth visible to all was in itself a sufficient sign of progress, and as the novelty of the industrial change wore off and the economy of America was more completely industrialized, it was this augmenting wealth that symbolized it.

In such fashion the excellent ideal of progress that issued from the social enthusiasms of the Enlightenment was taken in charge by the Gilded Age and transformed into a handmaid of capitalism. Its duties were narrowed to the single end of serving profits and its accomplishments came to be exactly measured by bank clearings. It was unfortunate but inevitable. The idea was too seductive to the American mentality not to be seized upon and made to serve a rising order. Exploitation was the business of the times and how better could exploitation throw about its activities the sanction of idealism than by wedding them to progress? It is a misfortune that America has never subjected the abstract idea of progress to critical examination. Content with the frontier and capitalistic interpretations it has confused change with betterment, and when a great idealist of the Gilded Age demonstrated to America that it was misled and pointed out that the path of progress it was following was the highway to poverty, he was hooted from the market-place.

Having thus thrown the mantle of progress about the Gold Dust twins, the Gilded Age was ready to bring the political forces of America into harmony with the program of preëmption and exploitation. The situation could hardly have been more to its liking. Post-war America was wholly lacking in political philosophies, wholly opportunist. The old party cleavage between agriculture and industry had been obscured and the logic of party alignment destroyed by the struggle over slavery. Democrat and Whig no longer faced each other conscious of the different ends they sought. The great party of Jefferson and Jackson was prostrate, borne down by the odium of slavery and secession. In the North elements of both had been drawn into a motley war party, momentarily fused by the bitterness of conflict, but lacking any common program, certain indeed to split on fundamental economic issues. The Whig Republican was still Hamiltonian paternalistic, and the Democrat Republican was still Jeffersonian *laissez faire*, and until it was determined which wing should control the party councils there would be only confusion. The politicians were fertile in compromises, but in nominating Lincoln and Johnson the party ventured to get astride two horses that would not run together. To attempt to make yoke-fellows of democratic leveling and capitalistic paternalism was prophetic of rifts and schisms that only the passions of Reconstruction days could hold in check.

In 1865 the Republican party was no other than a war machine that had accomplished its purpose. It was a political mongrel, without logical cohesion, and it seemed doomed to break up as the Whig party had broken up and the Federalist party had broken up. But fate was now on the side of the Whigs as it had not been earlier. The democratic forces had lost strength from the war, and democratic principles were in ill repute. The drift to centralization, the enormous development of capitalism, the spirit of exploitation, were prophetic of a changing temper that was preparing to exalt the doctrine of manifest destiny which the Whig party stood sponsor for. The middle class was in the saddle and it was time to bring the political state under its control. The practical problem of the moment was to transform the mongrel Republican party into a strong cohesive instrument, and to accomplish that it was necessary to hold the loyalty of its Democratic voters amongst the farmers and working-classes whilst putting into effect its Whig program.

Under normal conditions the thing would have been impossible, but the times were wrought up and blindly passionate and the politicians skillful. The revolt of Andrew Johnson came near to bringing the party on the rocks; but the undisciplined Jacksonians were overthrown by the appeal to the Bloody Flag and put to flight by the nomination of General Grant for the presidency. The rebellion of the Independent Republicans under Horace Greeley in 1872 was brought to nothing by the skillful use of Grant's military prestige, and the party passed definitely under the control of capitalism, and became such an instrument for exploitation as Henry Clay dreamed of but could not perfect. Under the nominal leadership of the easy-going Grant a loose rein was given to Whiggish ambitions and the Republican party became a political instrument worthy of the Gilded Age.

The triumph of Whiggery was possible because the spirit of the Gilded Age was Whiggish. The picturesque embodiment of the multitude of voters who hurrahed for Grant and the Grand Old Party was a figure who had grown his first beard in the ebullient days before Secession. Colonel Beriah Sellers, with his genial optimism and easy political ethics, was an epitome of the political hopes of the Gilded Age. With a Micawber-like faith in his country and his government, eager to realize on his expansive dreams and looking to the national treasury to scatter its fructifying millions in the neighborhood of his speculative holdings, he was no other than Uncle Sam in the boisterous days following Appomattox. The hopes that floated up out of his dreams were the hopes of millions who cast their votes for Republican Congressmen who in return were expected to cast their votes for huge governmental appropriations that would insure prosperity's reaching certain post-office addresses. Citizens had saved the government in the trying days that were past; it was only fair in return that government should aid the patriotic citizen in the necessary work of developing national resources. It was paternalism as understood by speculators and subsidy-hunters, but was it not a part of the great American System that was to make the country rich and self-sufficient? The American System had been talked of for forty years; it had slowly got on its feet in pre-war days despite the stubborn planter opposition; now at last it had fairly come into its own. The time was ripe for the Republican party to become a fairy godmother to the millions of Beriah Sellerses throughout the North and West.

It is plain as a pikestaff why the spirit of Whiggery should have taken riotous possession of the Gilded Age. With its booming industrial cities America in 1870 was fast becoming capitalistic, and in every capitalistic society Whiggery springs up as naturally as pigweed in a garden. However attractive the disguises it may assume, it is in essence the logical creed of the profit philosophy. It is the expression in politics of the acquisitive instinct and it assumes as the greatest good the shaping of public policy to promote private interests. It asserts that it is a duty of the state to help its citizens to make money, and it conceives of the political state as a useful instrument for effective exploitation. How otherwise? The public good cannot be served apart from business interests, for business interests are the public good and in serving business the state is serving society. Everybody's eggs are in the basket and they must not be broken. For a capitalistic society Whiggery is the only rational politics, for it exalts the profit-motive as the sole object of parliamentary concern. Government has only to wave its wand and fairy gifts descend upon business like the golden sands of Pactolus. It graciously bestows its tariffs and subsidies, and streams of wealth flow into private wells.

But unhappily there is a fly in the Whiggish honey. In a competitive order, government is forced to make its choices. It cannot serve both Peter and Paul. If it gives with one hand it must take away with the other. And so the persuasive ideal of paternalism in the common interest degenerates in practice into legalized favoritism. Governmental gifts go to the largest investments. Lesser interests are sacrificed to greater interests and Whiggery comes finally to serve the lords of the earth without whose good will the wheels of business will not turn. To him that hath shall be given. If the few do not prosper the many will starve, and if the many have bread who would begrudge the few their abundance? In Whiggery is the fulfillment of the Scriptures.

Henry Clay had been a prophetic figure pointing the way America was to travel; but he came a generation too soon. A son of the Gilded Age, he was doomed to live in a world of Jacksonian democracy. But the spirit of Henry Clay survived his death and his followers were everywhere in the land. The plain citizen who wanted a slice of the rich prairie land of Iowa or Kansas, with a railway convenient to his homestead, had learned to look to the government for a gift, and if he got his quarter-section and his transportation he was careless about what the other fellow got. A little more or less could make no difference to a country inexhaustible in resources. America belonged to the American people and not to the government, and resources in private hands paid taxes and increased the national wealth. In his favorite newspaper, the *New York Tribune*, he read daily appeals for the adoption of a patriotic national economy, by means of which an infant industrialism, made prosperous by a protective tariff, would provide a home market for the produce of the farmer and render the country self-sufficient. Money would thus be put in everybody's pocket. Protection was not robbing Peter to pay Paul, but paying both Peter and Paul out of the augmented wealth of the whole.

The seductive arguments that Horace Greeley disseminated amongst the plain people, Henry Carey purveyed to more intelligent ears. The most distinguished American economist of the time, Carey had abandoned his earlier *laissez-faire* position, and having convinced himself that only through a close-knit national economy could the country develop a well-rounded economic program, he had become the most ardent of protectionists. During the fifties and later he was tireless in popularizing the doctrine of a natural harmony of interests between agriculture and manufacturing, and to a generation expanding rapidly in both fields his able presentation made great appeal. It was but a step from protectionism to governmental subsidies. Beriah Sellers and Henry Clay had come to be justified by the political economists. (Note that amongst Carey's converts were such different idealists as Wendell Phillips and Peter Cooper.)

IV

THE GREAT BARBECUE

Horace Greeley and Henry Carey were only straws in the wind that during the Gilded Age was blowing the doctrine of paternalism about the land. A Colonel Sellers was to be found at every fireside talking the same blowsy doctrine. Infectious in their optimism, naïve in their faith that something would be turned up for them by the government if they made known their wants, they were hoping for dollars to be put in their pockets by a generous administration at Washington. Congress had rich gifts to bestow—in lands, tariffs, subsidies, favors of all sorts; and when influential citizens made their wishes known to the reigning statesmen, the sympathetic politicians were quick to turn the government into the fairy godmother the voters wanted it to be. A huge barbecue was spread to which all presumably were invited. Not quite all, to be sure; inconspicuous persons, those who were at home on the farm or at work in the mills and offices, were overlooked; a good many indeed out of the total number of the American people. But all the important persons, leading bankers and promoters and business men, received invitations. There wasn't room for everybody and these were presumed to represent the whole. It was a splendid feast. If the waiters saw to it that the choicest portions were served to favored guests, they were not unmindful of their numerous home-spun constituency and they loudly proclaimed the fine democratic principle that what belongs to the people should be enjoyed by the people—not with petty bureaucratic restrictions, not as a social body, but as individuals, each free citizen using what came to hand for his own private ends, with no questions asked.

It was sound Gilded Age doctrine. To a frontier people what was more democratic than a barbecue, and to a paternalistic age what was more fitting than that the state should provide the beeves for roasting. Let all come and help themselves. As a result the feast was Gargantuan in its rough plenty. The abundance was what was to be expected of a generous people. More food, to be sure, was spoiled than was eaten, and the revelry was a bit unseemly; but it was a fine spree in the name of the people, and the invitations had been written years before by Henry Clay. But unfortunately what was intended to be jovially democratic was marred by displays of plebeian temper. Suspicious commoners with better eyes than manners discovered the favoritism of the waiters and drew attention to the difference between their own meager helpings and the heaped-up plates of more favored guests. It appeared indeed that there was gross discrimination in the service; that the farmers' pickings from the Homestead Act were scanty in comparison with the speculators' pickings from the railway land-grants. The *Crédit Mobilier* scandal and the Whisky Ring scandal and divers other scandals came near to breaking up the feast, and the genial host— who was no other than the hero of Appomattox—came in for some sharp criticism. But after the more careless ones who were caught with their fingers where they didn't belong, had been thrust from the table, the eating and drinking went on again till only the great carcasses were left. Then at last came the reckoning. When the bill was sent in to the American people the farmers discovered that they had been put off with the giblets while the capitalists were consuming the turkey. They learned that they were no match at a barbecue for more voracious guests, and as they went home unsatisfied, a sullen anger burned in their hearts that was to express itself later in fierce agrarian revolts.

What reason there was for such anger, how differently rich and poor fared at the democratic feast, is suggested by the contrast between the Homestead Act and the Union Pacific land-grant. Both were war-time measures and both had emerged from the agitations of earlier decades. By the terms of the former the homesteader got his hundred and sixty acres at the price of $1.25 an acre; by the terms of the latter the promoters got a vast empire for nothing. It was absurd, of course, but what would you have? The people wanted the railway built and Collis P. Huntington was willing to build it on his own terms. The government was too generous to haggle with public-spirited citizens, and too Whiggish to want to discourage individual enterprise. Ever since the cession of California there had been much talk of a continental railway to tie the country together. In the first years the talk in Congress had all been of a great national venture; the road must be built by the nation to serve the common interests of the American people. But unfortunately sectional jealousies prevented any agreement as to the route the survey lines were to run, and the rising capitalism was becoming powerful enough to bring into disfavor any engagement of the government in a work that promised great rewards. Under its guidance political opinion was skillfully turned into the channel of private enterprise. The public domain backed by the public credit, it was agreed, must pay for the road, but the government must not seek to control the enterprise or look to profit from it directly; the national reward would come indirectly from the opening-up of vast new territories.

The definite shift in policy came about the year 1855. In 1837 Stephen A. Douglas had been the driving force behind the state enterprise of building the Illinois Central Railway. In 1853 he proposed that the Pacific Railroad should be built by private enterprise. With the change promptly came a request for a patriotic land-grant. The government was expected to provide the road, it appeared, but private enterprise was to own it and manage it in the interest of speculators rather than the public. For old-fashioned souls like Thomas A. Benton, who still remembered the Jeffersonian concern for the common well-being, it was a bitter mess to swallow.

I would have preferred [he said] that Congress should have made the road, as a national work, on a scale commensurate with its grandeur and let out the use of it to companies, who would fetch and carry on the best terms for the people and the government. But that hope has vanished . . . a private company has become the resource and the preference. I embrace it as such, utterly scouting all plans for making private roads at national expense, of paying for the use of roads built with our land and money, of bargaining with corporations or individuals for the use of what we give them.[3]

With this speech the old Jeffersonianism pulled down its flag and the new Whiggery ran up its black banner. The Gilded Age had begun and Old Bullion Benton had outlived his time. In the tumultuous decades that followed there was to be no bargaining with corporations for the use of what the public gave; they took what they wanted and no impertinent questions were asked. The hungriest will get the most at the barbecue. A careless wastefulness when the supply is unlimited is perhaps natural enough. There were hard-headed men in the world of Beriah Sellers who knew how easy it was to overreach the simple, and it was they who got most from the common pot. We may call them buccaneers if we choose, and speak of the great barbecue as a democratic debauch. But why single out a few, when all were drunk? Whisky was plentiful at barbecues, and if too liberal potations brought the

[3] Quoted in J. P. Davis, *The Union Pacific Railway*, pp. 67–68.

Gilded Age to the grossest extravagancies, if when it cast up accounts it found its patrimony gone, it was only repeating the experience of a certain man who went down to Jericho. To create a social civilization requires sober heads, and in this carousal of economic romanticism sober heads were few—the good Samaritan was busy elsewhere.

The doctrine of preëmption and exploitation was reaping its harvest. The frontier spirit was having its splurge, and progress was already turning its face in another direction. Within the next half-century this picturesque America with its heritage of crude energy —greedy, lawless, capable—was to be transformed into a vast uniform middle-class land, dedicated to capitalism and creating the greatest machine-order known to history. A scattered agricultural people, steeped in particularistic jealousies and suspicious of centralization, was to be transformed into an urbanized factory people, rootless, migratory, drawn to the job as by a magnet. It was to come about the more easily because the American farmer had never been a land-loving peasant, rooted to the soil and thriving only in daily contact with familiar acres. He had long been half middle-class, accounting unearned increment the most profitable crop, and buying and selling land as if it were calico. And in consequence the vigorous individualism that had sprung from frontier conditions decayed with the passing of the frontier, and those who had lost in the gamble of preëmption and exploitation were added to the growing multitude of the proletariat. It was from such materials, supplemented by a vast influx of immigrants, that was fashioned the America we know today with its standardized life, its machine culture, its mass psychology—an America to which Jefferson and Jackson and Lincoln would be strangers.

v

FOLK HEROES

Perhaps one cannot penetrate more directly to the heart of the Gilded Age than in taking account of certain of its heroes, figures of earth whom it accounted great in its generation, and to whom its admiration flowed out in unstinted measure. It is our own secret desires we attribute to our gods, and if from the muck of the times a queer lot of heroes was singled out, if an undisciplined generation rioting in its new freedoms chose to honor men who had scrambled upward in uncouth ways, it only suggests that such figures were a composite picture of the secret desires of an age vastly concerned with getting on. From a host of striking personalities two must suffice to suggest the spirit of the times, authentic folk-heroes of the Gilded Age, fashioned out of the commonest stuff and realizing such greatness as multitudes of Americans were then dreaming of; and over against them a third figure, a mordant intellectual, who sardonically swam with the stream of tendency and in serving all the gods of the Gilded Age gained for himself a brilliant career.

I

GENERAL GRANT

Greatest of all the heroes of the age was the victor of Appomattox. His fame was in all men's mouths, and his reputation was substantial enough to withstand the attacks of enemies and the gross shortcomings of his own character. It was not for any singular or remarkable qualities of mind or personality that General Grant was taken to the heart of his generation, but rather because he was so completely a product of the times, so strikingly an embodiment of its virtues and weaknesses. In his spectacular career were the sharp contrasts that appealed to a plebeian people wanting in fine and discriminating standards of appraisal. He had come up from the people and the marks of his origins—the slovenly manners and uncritical force of frontier folk-ways—were stamped on him as indelibly as they were stamped on his fellow soldiers who proclaimed his greatness. To a later generation he seems an odd and unaccountable figure for the high rôle of national hero, yet he was as native and homespun as Lincoln, like him sprung from the common stock and learning his lessons from harsh experience, a figure blown to huge dimensions by the passions of civil war. A generation that discovered something praiseworthy in the "smartness" of Jim Fisk, in the burly acquisitiveness of Commodore Vanderbilt, or in the clever humbuggery of Barnum the Showman, certainly would judge with no very critical eyes the claims to greatness of a grim leader of armies who succeeded where so many before had failed.

General Grant was no conventional military hero. It was not the gold stars on his epaulets that dazzled his generation. The people of the North had seen too many gold stars rise and set on the military horizon, they had been stricken too sorely by the bitter struggle, to be caught by military popinjays. They had gone through the fire and any hero of theirs must himself have passed through the fire. It was something veracious in the man, something solid and unyielding in the soldier, something plain as an old shoe in the field marshal of bloody battles, that caught the imagination of the North and made Grant a hero—this together with a certain gift of pungent phrase, befitting the leader of democratic hosts, that served to spread his fame amongst the common people. Vicksburg did much for his reputation, but the demand for "unconditional surrender," sent to a Confederate leader, did far more. The words fixed his character in the popular mind. Here at last was a fighting man who instead of planning how to fall back, as other generals did, thought only of going ahead; so the popular judgment shut its eyes to his dull plebeian character and set a wreath on his brows. It rested there somewhat grotesquely. In spite of a deep unconscious integrity and a stubborn will that drove him forward along whatever path his feet were set on, he was the least imposing of military heroes. Short, stooped, lumpish in mind and body, unintellectual and unimaginative, devoid of ideas and with no tongue to express the incoherent emotions that surged dully in his heart, he was a commonplace fellow that no gold braid could set off. He hated war and disliked soldiering, yet accepting life with a stolid fatalism he fought his bloody way to ultimate victory.

Graduated from West Point after four sterile years of drill, quite uneducated and unread even in his profession, he served for a time at different army posts, went through the Mexican War—which he looked upon as a stupid imperialistic debauch—as quartermaster without gaining distinction, and eventually, oppressed by the eventless routine of garrison life, he fell into the habit of solitary drinking and was dismissed from the service. Misfortune that it seemed, it was his making. Only as a volunteer could he have risen so quickly to high command; as a captain or major in the regular army he would have been detailed as drill-master to the raw troops and have had no chance. Nevertheless hard times came with his dismissal. Indolent by nature and inclined to drift, he was as incompetent a man in practical affairs as one could find in a frontier township. But with a wife and children to support he must turn his hand to something, so he tried his luck at farming, selling real estate, and various odd jobs, yet all the time growing poorer and seedier, till the war came and picking him up flung him to mountain

heights of popularity and reputation. Thereafter till his death he
was accounted the greatest American of his generation. No accumulating evidence of his well-meaning but witless incapacity in
civic and political affairs could pluck from his brows the wreath
that had been thrust upon him.

In his spectacular career Grant was an embodiment of the dreams
of all the Beriah Sellerses of the Gilded Age. He was a materialistic
hero of a materialistic generation. He was dazzled by wealth and
power, and after years of bitter poverty he sat down in the lap of
luxury with huge content. He took what the gods sent, and if houses
and fast horses and wines and cigars were showered upon him he
accepted them as a child would accept gifts from a fairy godmother.
He had had enough of skimping meanness; with his generation he
wanted to slough off the drabness of the frontier; he wanted the
good things of life that had so long been denied him, and he was not
scrupulous about looking a gift horse in the mouth. He sought out
the company of rich men. He was never happier than when enjoying the luxury of Jay Cooke's mansion in Philadelphia or riding
with A. T. Stewart in Central Park. As he grew fat and stodgy the
vulgar side of his plebeian nature was thrown into sharper relief.
He accepted gifts with both hands, and he seems never to have
suspected the price that would be exacted of the President for the
presents to the General. He never realized how great a bill was sent
to the American people for the wine he drank or the cigars he
smoked with his wealthy hosts; yet if the wine had been molten
gold and the cigars platinum they would have been far cheaper.
In return for a few boxes of choice Havanas, Jay Cooke laid his
hands on millions of western lands for the Northern Pacific Railway. It was the way of the Gilded Age, and Grant was only doing
what all his friends and associates were doing. If he accepted a
fifty-thousand-dollar house in Philadelphia, his comrade General
Sherman accepted a hundred-thousand-dollar house at Washington. Such gifts were not bribes; they were open and aboveboard; it
was the free and easy way of the times. What the age was careless
about is the fact that it is hard to refuse a reasonable request from
one's fairy godmother, and what the General never understood is
that if one is President such a godmother is certain to be a very
dangerous member of the family.

There was far too much of that sort of thing all about him for
Grant to serve as President with credit to himself or profit to the

country. Honest himself, he was the source of more dishonesty in others than any other American President. His eight years in the White House marked the lowest depths—in domestic affairs at least—to which any American administration has fallen. They were little better than a national disgrace. All the festering evils of post-war times came to a head and pock-marked the body politic from head to foot. Scandal and corruption whispered all about him, the hands of his closest advisers were dirty; yet he stubbornly refused to hear the whispers or see the dirt. In judging men and policies he was no more than a child. He could never distinguish between an honest man and a rascal. He was loyal to his friends and open-handedness he regarded as a mark of friendship. In the end it turned out that like the thieves of Jericho his blatant followers despoiled him of pretty nearly everything.

In what must pass for his political views Grant was as naïvely uninformed as a Wyoming cowboy. Utterly wanting in knowledge of political principles, he was a fit leader for the organized mob that called itself the Republican party, whose chief objective was the raiding of the treasure-box of which it was the responsible guardian. He had been nominally a Democrat and the first vote he cast for President he cast for Buchanan. After Lincoln's death he turned naturally to President Johnson and was one of his supporters till the wily Radical group got his ear and carried him over to the rival camp. They wanted his reputation to hide under, and they took possession of it with no great credit to the General's reputation. Thereafter he was a Republican of the Whig wing. It was where he belonged. He was swayed politically by his emotional reactions and it was natural for him to drift into the opulent camp of money and power. His frontier democracy sloughed away and with his generation he went over easily to a buccaneer capitalism. No social conscience obtruded itself to give him trouble. His millionaire friends were Whig Republicans and with his respect for rich men, his admiration for material success, he found himself in congenial company amongst the Whig group. About the only political policy he ever interested himself in was the policy of a protective tariff, and his Whig associates took care that his interest did not wane. Yet so completely did the naïve General reflect the spirit of the Gilded Age that his noisy followers, conspiring to confuse in the public mind southern reconstruction and capitalistic expansion, and hiding a precious set of rascals in the folds of the bloody flag, came near to making him President for a third term. The General was bitterly disappointed at their failure, and the General's wife, who liked to live in the White House, was even more disappointed. To millions of Americans Grant was an authentic hero, to Mark Twain he was a very great man, and to Jay Cooke he was a pawn to be used in the noble strategy of fortune-seeking. What a comedy it all seems now—yet one that leaves an unpleasant taste in the mouth.

Yet to dismiss the stolid General thus is scarcely to do justice to the substantial core of the man. There remains the work written in pain during his last days, the two volumes of *Memoirs* that in their plain directness—as uninspired, says a late biographer, as "a bale of hay"— laid bare his honest simplicity and rugged meagerness. No blackguard and no charlatan could have written such pages. If General Grant was not the great man so many thought, he was a native growth from American soil, endowed like his age with a dogged will and a plodding energy, and he gave his country what he had. Though the branches of the tree were ungainly and offered too hospitable shelter to unseemly birds of the night, the gnarly trunk was sound at the heart.

2

JAY COOKE

Another hero of the times likewise was flung up as it were casually out of obscurity and reaped an amazing harvest from the gigantic struggle. In those difficult years the name of Jay Cooke— "the financier of the Civil War," as his biographer calls him— became as familiar to the people of the North as the names of Grant and Lincoln, and was often joined with theirs as that of one of the saviors of the Union. He was the first great American banker, and good fortune sent him into the world at a moment when his skill in brokerage found opportunity for free play. The war was as great a godsend to Jay Cooke as it was to Grant, for alone amongst our money-lenders he realized the problems and foresaw the profits in a popular system of war financing. He was a pioneer in exploring all the potentialities of the banker's trade, and in his dramatic exploitation of salesmanship and his skillful manipulation of money and credit he marked out the highway our later financiers have traveled. Jay Cooke occupies too significant a place in the history of American capitalism to be overlooked in casting up the accounts of the Gilded Age.

Of Yankee-Puritan stock, he was born in the frontier hamlet of Sandusky, Ohio, when the Western Reserve was at the beginning of its development. His father was a country lawyer of Federalist-Whig affinities, proficient in high-flown western oratory, who liked to be much in the neighborhood eye. He was a pushing, self-confident fellow, highly patriotic, soberly moral, fearing God and loving his country, who felt that the government he supported so heartily should serve him and his town with equal heartiness. His readiness in florid speech won him a single term in Congress, and he used his position as a heaven-sent opportunity to promote a government road from Sandusky—which it seems was not prospering as its inhabitants had expected it would—deep into the Indian country. It was a good Clay-Whig scheme of internal improvement; it would open up a rich timber country, and be highly profitable to the real-estate promoters of Sandusky. Cradled thus in speculation and faith in a benevolent government, his three sons grew up native Whigs, with vigorous Puritan-Yankee minds, who found no difficulty in reconciling the interests of God and Mammon. Eager to get on "the right side of fortune," they went into the three professions of banking, journalism, and the law. The eldest, Pitt, found the law little to his liking; the youngest, Henry, labored diligently at journalism, at Sandusky and later at Columbus, where he was part owner of the *Ohio State Journal* and "boss" of young William Dean Howells, who was likewise seeking to rise through the medium of journalism. It was the family itch for politics that took him to Columbus, and although the venture was financially unsuccessful it brought him influential connections. He was useful to Governor Salmon P. Chase, afterwards to be Lincoln's Secretary of the Treasury, and to John Sherman, who was later to become a great influence on financial policies at Washington. His reward came in the shape of an appointment to do the government binding, reputed to be worth $25,000—a commission that allowed him to unload his paper on some investors who speedily lost the $20,000 they put into it.

Henry Cooke's Whiggery was justifying itself, yet to both Pitt and Henry it soon became clear that Jay had hit upon the true road to wealth. At twelve years of age he had begun his career in his father's store at Sandusky, and with characteristic enterprise he put in some side lines and became "quite a capitalist." At fourteen he ventured so far as St. Louis to help in a general store, and at the age of seventeen he went to Philadelphia and took a place in a broker-banker's office. That was in 1839, a golden time for brokers, when every business man must keep a sharp eye on the table of banknote discounts and see to it that bad paper was worked off. Into this world of discounts and premiums the young clerk plunged with immense zest. "The business I am engaged in is of the most respectable kind and the house is the first in the city," [4] he wrote to Pitt Cooke. "He was ambitious, industrious, and faithful to each day's duties," his biographer reports of him. His quick mind ran to calculations and his slender sensitive fingers seemed made for telling money. He was soon the admiration of the office, an expert in detecting counterfeits, a walking table of "wild-cat" currency, with a genius for smelling out possible commissions. Every art of extracting profits from note-shaving, gold-juggling, delayed payments, and other devices known to the world of brokerage, he speedily made himself master of. When he reached his majority he was entered a member of the firm, and before he was thirty he aided his partners—"noble" fellows he called them, of honest Puritan extraction—in squeezing huge commissions out of the financing of the Mexican War. "It was a grand time for brokers and private banking," he remarked; and late in life he wrote glowingly of his cleverness in twice overreaching the Secretary of the Treasury. It was quite legal and the patriotic banker was vastly pleased to report, "So we victimized him again." [5] He was the brains of the company and under his guidance the business piled up profits at an astonishing rate. During the panic of 1854 he wrote: "We use our money at 1 1/2 to 3 per cent. per month from day to day and frequently it pays 1/8 to 1/4 a day. We have done a noble business since 1st of January; profits up to 1st July $135,000." [6] On the reorganization of the firm in 1858 he withdrew, and three years later, on January 1, 1861, he opened the doors of what was soon to become the greatest banking-house in America, Jay Cooke and Company of Philadelphia.

He was then in his fortieth year and his private fortune he reckoned at $150,000. But with the breaking-out of the war, oppor-

[4] E. P. Oberholtzer, *Jay Cooke, Financier of the Civil War*, Vol. I, p. 52.
[5] *Ibid.*, Vol. I, pp. 81 and 83.
[6] *Ibid.*, Vol. I, p. 85.

tunity knocked at the door of the new bank. Ardently patriotic, Jay Cooke was anxious to do his bit for the cause, but he seems never to have thought of going to the front. He came of fighting Revolutionary stock, but love of the battlefield had died out of the family. His father had been drafted for the War of 1812, but hired a substitute who was unfortunate enough to be killed, and none of the three sons got nearer the front than the Treasury Department at Washington. It was there that the battles of the Cooke brothers were fought. Henry Cooke went to Washington to attend the inauguration of the new administration, and twenty-one days later Jay Cooke modestly proposed a plan for mobilizing the resources of the firm in defense of the country. On March 25, he wrote to his brother:

> What we wish to do with the Treasury is to have the Department allow us to make the frequent transfers that are made from point to point instead of giving the business to Adams and Company [Express]. We can make those transfers and the Department when flush can give us 30, 60, 90 or 120 days time, as it is no loss to them, and the interest in the meantime would be clear profit and to be divided.[7]

When the magnitude of the task in which the country was engaged became clear to him he was no longer content with a single banking-house at Philadelphia. A branch at Washington under the shadow of the Treasury was highly desirable, and Henry Cooke was the man for the business. A born lobbyist, a close friend of John Sherman—who was looking out for a profitable opening in some war business for a brother—and of Secretary of the Treasury Chase, he let no grass grow under his feet. The war loans had not been taken freely and in July, Jay Cooke wrote to Chase suggesting a close alliance between the Treasury and two Philadelphia firms, Jay Cooke and Company and Drexel and Company.

> We would wish to make our business mostly out of the Treasury operations and we feel sure that we could by having a proper understanding with yourself greatly help you in the management of your vast negotiations. . . . We could not be expected to leave our comfortable homes and positions here without some great inducement and we state frankly that we would, if we succeeded, expect a fair commission from the Treasury in some shape for our labor and talent. If you feel disposed to say to us . . . that you will give us the management of the loans to be issued by the government during the war, allowing us a fair commission on them, . . . we are ready to throw ourselves into the matter heartily. . . .[8]

---

[7] *Ibid.*, Vol. I, pp. 132–133. [8] See *Ibid.*, Vol. I, pp. 143–144.

It was quite an amazing proposal and one that Secretary Chase dared not accept. Bankers and brokers in New York and Boston would scarcely approve a monopoly of loan-commissions granted to two Philadelphia houses. But Jay Cooke would not acknowledge defeat. He cultivated the acquaintance of the Secretary, lent him money, entertained his family, presented him with gifts, and gave him sound advice. He took the harassed servant of the people to his warm and generous heart and was vigilant in keeping him out of the clutches of Copperhead profiteers. His opportunity came in October, 1861, when in competition with other brokers he undertook the sale of a new bond-series. His success was so great that he won the complete confidence of Secretary Chase, and it was only a matter of time when he should secure his coveted monopoly. In February, 1862, he opened the branch house at Washington, immediately opposite the Treasury building, and Henry Cooke soon made its offices an indispensable club for Congressmen and government employees. He was charmingly cordial and during the next ten years he knew everybody and every political move at the Capital. With the same bland and deacon-like appearance as his brother, he was master of the art of ingratiating himself into the confidence of influential men, and successive Secretaries of the Treasury—Chase and Fessenden and McCulloch—were easily induced to look with partial eye upon the firm of Jay Cooke and Company. When Grant returned to Washington after the war he was soon like a brother to Henry Cooke, and when the General had tasted the quality of cigars kept for his use at Jay Cooke's Philadelphia home, his heart warmed to the kindly banker.

Meanwhile the firm was discovering innumerable ways to help win the war; amongst others Henry Cooke put through a congressional franchise for a street railway at Washington, and the new cars were soon carrying citizens and soldiers to and fro, to their great content and the company's great profit. He was hourly in and out of the Treasury and he knew as much about the government business as the Secretary. The interests of the firm extended with amazing rapidity; other banks came under their control and their agents were everywhere. Their later successes in selling bonds were a revelation to older-fashioned brokers. On the day that Richmond fell the "financier of the Civil War" marked out the lines of a pretentious country house that was to cost a million dollars and to become a show place of America, where Secretaries of the Treasury,

Presidents, and great men from every walk of life were to find a welcome release from their cares. "As rich as Jay Cooke" had become a common saying from the Atlantic to the Pacific. The gigantic war had been no ill wind to the money-teller of 1861.

In certain aspects Jay Cooke may be reckoned the first modern American. He was the first to understand the psychology of mass salesmanship. It was his fertile brain that created the syndicate and conceived and executed the modern American "drive." Under his bland deacon-like exterior was the mind of a realist. He assumed that every man has his price, but he knew that few men like to acknowledge the fact even to themselves; so he was at immense pains to cover our poor human nakedness with generous professions. If he were to lure dollars from old stockings in remote chimney-corners he must "sell" patriotism to his fellow Americans; and to do that successfully he must manufacture a militant public opinion. The soldier at the front, he announced in a flood of advertisements, must be supported at the rear. It was every loyal American's war, and patriotism demanded that idle dollars—in greenbacks—should be lent to the boys in blue, and a grateful government would return them, both principal and interest, in gold. To induce slacker dollars to become fighting dollars he placed his agents in every neighborhood, in newspaper offices, in banks, in pulpits—patriotic forerunners of the "one-minute men" of later drives. They also served their country, he pointed out, who sold government bonds on commission. He subsidized the press with a lavish hand, not only the metropolitan dailies but the obscurest country weeklies. He employed an army of hack-writers to prepare syndicated matter and he scattered paying copy broadcast. His "hired friends" were everywhere. In a hundred delicate ways he showed his appreciation of patriotic coöperation in the bond-sales—gifts of trout caught with his own hand, baskets of fruit from his own garden. He bought the pressings of whole vineyards and cases of wine flowed in an endless stream to strategic publicity-points. Rival brokers hinted that he was debauching the press, but the army of greenbacks marching to the front was his reply. It all cost a pretty penny, but the government was liberal with commissions and when all expenses were deducted perhaps two millions of profits remained in the vaults of the firm, to be added to the many other millions which the prestige of the government agency with its free advertising brought in its train.

With such prestige and with the greatest fluid resources as yet accumulated by any American, it was inevitable that the Rothschild of the North should play a bold part in the speculations of the Gilded Age. Jay Cooke vastly enjoyed the game and it was idle to expect him to sit back quietly when others were playing for high stakes. In those halcyon days promoters were as thick as flies about a dead carcass; wild-cat railroads had succeeded wild-cat banks as short-cuts to wealth; and in an unlucky moment Jay Cooke was tempted. He had expected to be made Secretary of the Treasury by President Grant, but failing of appointment in spite of countless boxes of twenty-five-cent cigars provided for the General's pleasure, he determined to back the Northern Pacific Railway enterprise. The company had been chartered in July, 1864, receiving a congressional grant of 12,800 acres of public land for every mile of track laid in the states, and double that amount in the territories. As the proposed line would run almost entirely through territories the grand total was reckoned at 47,360,000 acres.[9] Early land-sales were at the rate of $6 an acre. At such valuation the prospective value of the grant through the territories was $153,600 for every mile of track, yet in portions of an earlier line absorbed by the company the road had been built for $8,225 a mile, and a stretch of 112 miles at the rate of $9,500.[10] To be sure there were great stretches of unsalable land, but in compensation the company was free to run its surveys so as to embrace choice mineral deposits, virgin timber, water-power, and town sites.

As Jay Cooke contemplated the possibilities his buoyant temperament took fire, and he dreamed of empire-building. He quickly rationalized the project into a great patriotic undertaking that would carry the blessings of civilization to the farthest Northwest. He would lay open to the poor man the rich wheat lands of the Dakotas, the mineral wealth of the Rockies, the vast timber resources of the Puget Sound territory. He would annex western Canada by benevolent absorption. It was a dream worthy of the Gilded Age and Jay Cooke was chief amongst the Beriah Sellerses of the day. He threw himself into the project with boundless optimism, and proved again his right to be called a great financier. He proposed to sell the Northern Pacific as he had sold govern-

[9] See *Ibid.*, Vol. II, pp. 97–98.
[10] C. E. Russell, *Stories of Great Railroads*, p. 19.

ment bonds. He had learned that to catch the little fish he must first catch the big fish, for the shilling is timid till the pound shows the way. He must create confidence, cost what it would, and to that end he opened a huge pool and created a special syndicate. Stocks, jobs, cash, influence, were distributed judiciously where they would do good. In the language of stock-jobbing much "sweetening" was used.[11] And there was need of much "sweetening," for the times were inauspicious. Jay Cooke drove the publicity work with his old vigor, but sales were slow, and as the great patriotic venture showed signs of lagging he turned for help to a sympathetic government.

His engineer had made a careful estimate of the prospective cost of the road, which including rolling-stock, terminals, a branch line to Portland, and interest on bonds during the construction, came to $42,638 a mile for the entire line.[12] But the financier was not satisfied "with the magnificent property the government has given us," and made ready to buy from Congress a revision of the terms of the charter, which amongst other things would widen the land-grant belt through the territories to 120 miles, convey a second right-of-way zone from the Rocky Mountains to the Pacific, and permit the company to hypothecate the whole before the terms of the contract were fulfilled. It was an audacious proposal even to a generation used to audacious proposals. There was bitter opposition, for the rumblings of the *Crédit Mobilier* scandal were already disturbing the halls of Congress; but his lobbyists used "the company's money freely" to bring in the common breed of Congressmen, and the Cooke brothers employed their well-practiced skill to take care of such important persons as Speaker Blaine of the House, Vice-President Colfax of the Senate, and President Grant. The matter was handled with great delicacy in the case of the latter—"the glorious honest man," the banker called him. "He sent a fishing-rod and creel to the President's little son Jesse, for which he was duly thanked in a childish hand." He invited

[11] The list of his "beneficiaries," some of whom were drawn in delicately and some realistically, included, according to his biographer, Vice-President Colfax, Speaker Blaine and James A. Garfield of the House, Governor Rutherford B. Hayes of Ohio and Governor Geary of Pennsylvania, General Horace Porter, President Grant's private secretary, Senators John Sherman, William Windom, and Ben Wade, Delegate Garfielde of Washington Territory, Bayard Taylor. Amongst the papers were Henry Ward Beecher's *Christian Union*, Greeley's *Tribune*, the *Philadelphia Press*, the *Washington Chronicle*, the *London Times*.

[12] See Oberholtzer, Vol. II, p. 154.

the General to a day's fishing-trip, and together the heroes whipped the trout stream in the most charming comradeship. "It may be thought," remarks his biographer, "that such machinations were unbecoming in a man of Mr. Cooke's moral dimensions." [13] But surely delicate "machinations" were not unbecoming to such "moral dimensions." "We let the other side do most of the talking," wrote the deacon-like Henry Cooke, who kept the Sabbath as strictly as his brother, "and we do the voting." The President's cabinet was bitterly divided on the issue, but wheels turn on well-greased axles and delicate attentions have their reward. The bill was signed and the building of the Northwest empire could go forward.

Unfortunately, however, black days were pressing hard on the great success. The money of the company ran in fructifying streams through Europe and America but the expected crop was short. Thirty papers were subsidized in Germany; agents lived in ducal palaces; commissions, stocks, bonuses, were plowed in for manure; but the crop of bond-sales was still scanty. Ugly rumors were abroad. There was talk of a congressional investigation, and when General Banks offered a resolution of inquiry Jay Cooke was hurt to the quick. An investigation he regarded as no other than persecution of legitimate business, and he wrote to his brother: "He ought to be expelled from Congress for such outrageous attacks upon the great interests of the country. . . . If I get at him I will give him a piece of my mind, and no mistake, for his impertinence and foolishness." [14] Then the *Crédit Mobilier* scandal broke and in a panic he wrote to Henry Cooke denouncing the proposal to stop payment on the interest-coupons of the Union Pacific.

Now I want you to go to the Attorney General at once and tell him how wrong this whole procedure is. This whole persecution of the Union Pacific is nonsense, and is damaging our credit abroad. If the government sets the example of enjoining the payment of interest coupons, who will buy a bond abroad? The whole thing is wrong, ill advised and scandalous. . . . Williams ought to make a public apology for such an attack and instruct the lawyers to desist from anything of the kind. The bonds are long since in the hands of innocent holders, and, if they were not, they could never reach them in this way. Some wily speculators have put the idea into the heads of the government lawyers and they, without knowing anything of its effect upon business, have made this attack. It will damage us hundreds of millions unless withdrawn at once. No man of sense

[13] *Ibid.*, Vol. II, p. 176. [14] *Ibid.*, Vol. II, p. 322.

would buy a railroad bond or anything else in this country if such legal proceedings are to be permitted under the sanction of the highest officer of the government.[15]

Jay Cooke's ethics were simple. Whatever helped bond-sales was patriotic and right; whatever hurt them was wicked and immoral. Let government take care of business and business will take care of the country. That the newspapers could not see this great truth, but often indulged in wild demagoguery, was painful to one who had been generous to them. "It is too bad," he wrote of a certain attack, "that these newspapers are permitted by the law thus to interfere with great public works."[16] But the black days were at hand. The *Crédit Mobilier* scandal was a whirlwind reaped from the sowings of the Gilded Age. With the outbreak of the Franco-Prussian war bond-sales stopped short in Europe and the firm of Jay Cooke and Company was broken. September 18, 1873, the New York house suspended payment; the house of cards tumbled to pieces; and a panic swept the country. The crash was as spectacular as the rise; it had been built on credit and when credit was shaken it fell.

Because he had amassed a great fortune Jay Cooke was regarded by his fellow Americans as an intelligent man whose opinions were entitled to heedful consideration. A national figure in finance must become a national figure in the public councils; and this added function he assumed with the utmost seriousness. As the power behind the United States Treasury he regarded himself as responsible for the program of the Treasury; and he made use of his immense publicity-machine to shape public opinion in regard to taxation, funding, and the currency. His "views" of those questions were as simple as a child's primer. In brief they were: no taxes for the extinction of the debt; consolidate the debt and fund it in a form attractive to capital; retire the greenbacks and return at once to specie payments. Like others who had made money out of the war he did not take kindly to the idea of returning a part of it in taxes to pay off a debt that was highly profitable to him as a broker and banker. The men of '65 had fought and suffered to secure the blessings of liberty to their posterity, and it was only fair that posterity should help pay the bills. To popularize this pregnant thought he subsidized a pamphlet contributed by one of his hack-writers, entitled *Our National Debt a National Blessing;*

[15] *Ibid.*, Vol. II, p. 409.　　　　[16] *Ibid.*, Vol. II, p. 411.

but the Hamiltonian argument overshot the mark and aroused bitter opposition. In this as in his attitude towards currency-contraction and funding he was thinking exclusively in terms of the money-lender. Very likely he was probably not so much self-seeking as ignorant. Intellectually he was poverty-stricken and outside the narrow realm of brokerage and banking he was only a child. He read nothing, thought little and was unconcerned with social or economic principles. His business life was regulated by a set of ready-made formulas, in which ideas played no part. William Cullen Bryant rightly judged him in the following comment:

We counsel Mr. Jay Cooke in all good will, not to abandon his proper vocation of dealing in stocks and government securities, for the sake of giving lectures on political economy—a subject which he does not understand. We do not say that he might not understand it if he had given it his attention, but that he has evidently never done, and knows no more of the matter than Red Jacket knew of Greek. We advise all who have any money to invest to take Mr. Jay Cooke's seven-thirty bonds, and eschew his political economy. His seven-thirties are first rate, his political economy is a tissue of mistakes.[17]

Any program that lay outside the bounds of his formulas he regarded as dangerous radicalism, and any policy that threatened to reduce his commissions he regarded as unchristian. He bitterly disliked Secretary Boutwell of the Treasury, who rejected his guidance, and he wrote to his brother:

I observe . . . that Boutwell is to leave the Treasury. I think that if he does not propose to do any better than he has in the past it will be a grand move for Grant to put some more practical person in his place. A man who has no more breadth of thought . . . and no more spunk than to let the country drift along without even an attempt at funding the debt, and who insists upon keeping up an enormous taxation for the foolish object of paying off rapidly a debt that no one wants paid off, excepting gradually, it will be a great benefit to have replaced by some one who will take an opposite course.[18]

A month later one of the causes of the hostility was suggested by a member of the firm:

All of our transactions with Boutwell have shown conclusively that he will never permit one dollar to be made out of the business of the Treasury, if he can possibly prevent it. With all his friendly feelings I cannot remember a single dollar that we have made directly or indirectly out of his administration of the Treasury, . . .[19]

[17] *Ibid.*, Vol. I, pp. 643–644.   [18] *Ibid.*, Vol. II, pp. 267–268.
[19] *Ibid.*, Vol. II, p. 269.

Against the Greenback movement his hostility was bitter. He regarded it as an attempt to repudiate the "plighted faith" of the nation, and in 1867 he issued a pamphlet, written to order, aimed at combating the movement. In the opinion of a subsidized admirer it was "able, unanswerable and timely," calculated to do immense good in a country where universal suffrage encourages the "attempts of demagogues to excite the poor against the rich, labor against capital, and all who haven't money against the banks who have it." [20] How deeply the members of the firm felt in presence of any threat to the money interests is suggested in a letter from Henry Cooke of October 12, 1867.

You know how I have felt for a long time past in regard to the course of the ultra infidelic radicals like Wade, Sumner, Stevens, *et id omne genus*. They were dragging the Republican party into all sorts of isms and extremes. Their policy was one of bitterness, hate, and wild agrarianism without a single Christian principle to give it consistency, except the sole idea of universal suffrage. . . . These reckless demagogues have had their day and the time has come for wiser counsels. With Wade uttering agrarian doctrines in Kansas and fanning the flame of vulgar prejudices, trying to array labor against capital and pandering to the basest passions; with Butler urging wholesale conscription throughout the South and wholesale repudiation throughout the North so far as the national debt is concerned; with Stevens joining hands with the traitor Vallandigham and advocating the idea of a flood of irredeemable paper money sufficient in volume to drown the whole country; with Pomeroy and Wade and Sprague and a host of others clamoring for the unsexing of woman and putting the ballot in her hand . . . what wonder it is that the accumulated load was too heavy for any party to carry and that it broke down under it? [21]

There can be little doubt that the spectacular career of Jay Cooke quite dazzled his contemporary fellow citizens. Nothing like it had before appeared in America. The greatest salesman that the rising middle class had yet produced, a financier who understood the psychology of mass appeal, a propagandist of truly heroic proportions, he was reckoned no other than a magician by all the lesser money-grabbers of the Gilded Age. From nothing he built up a vast fortune. Scrupulous in all religious duties, a kind husband, a generous friend, benevolent in all worthy charities, simple and democratic in his tastes, ardently patriotic, uncreative and unintellectual, he exemplified all the substantial middle-class virtues of a people newly given to the worship of a sterile money economy.

[20] *Ibid.*, Vol. II, p. 56 note.   [21] *Ibid.*, Vol. II, p. 28.

To call him a vulgarian and the chronicle of his life nauseous would scarcely be charitable. The record of his days has been laid before us, naked and mean, by his biographer, who has done his best to construct a hero from the poor materials. No doubt he was a hero of his generation—and perhaps of ours also.

3
CHARLES A. DANA

If General Grant and Jay Cooke were naïve heroes, ignorant as the generation that delighted to honor them, Charles A. Dana, the journalist of the Gilded Age, was a disillusioned intellectual who after immersing himself in the golden dreams of the forties, put away all Utopian hopes and made use of his brains to serve himself. Disappointed with idealism, he turned materialist and dedicated to capitalistic exploitation the abilities that before had been given to a venture in coöperative living. A brilliant fellow, playing the new game in Gilded Age fashion and winning a brilliant success, he was a conspicuous victim of the bankruptcy of idealism that is the price of all wars, and his later triumph as editor of the *New York Sun* only served to measure the greatness of his fall. The career of Dana is a cynical commentary on the changing spirit of America from the days of Brook Farm to the days of Mark Hanna.

A child of the Puritan frontier, Dana early crossed over into New York State and became a shop-boy in the backwoods village of Buffalo at a time when the Indian trade was important enough to justify him in learning Algonquin. In these early manhood days he was living in the midst of the coonskin democracy, and falling in with the frontier spirit he became an ardent Jacksonian. He was eager for an education and quitting Buffalo he went to Harvard, but his eyes failing him after two years, he joined the Brook Farm community where he speedily became one of the chief counselors, and was deeply concerned for the success of the experiment. In those generous years he was a militant idealist, widely read in socialist literature and warmly espousing associationism as a cure for the evils of competition. Upon quitting Brook Farm after the burning of the Phalanstery he joined Greeley and for fifteen years was one of the directing minds on the *Tribune*. In 1848 he went abroad as foreign correspondent, saw much of the revolutions of that great year, studied the temper of the French and German people, analyzed the popular leaders and programs with singular acuteness, and found his sympathies warmly enlisted in the cause of the lower classes. He was then thirty-nine, and his active mind had gathered up all the diverse radicalisms—Jacksonian, Utopian, European proletarian—of his revolutionary generation. Shrewdly observant and with a sensitive social conscience, he was amply equipped to become such another critic of the Industrial Revolution as England had bred from its bitter experience.

But the war intervened, and after the war a dun twilight gathered about the hopes of the forties. Few generous enthusiasms survived those years of struggle and Dana in his editorial rooms underwent successive changes of heart. The realist slowly dispossessed the idealist and then the cynic swallowed up the realist. The last forty years of his life were spent undoing the work of his earlier years. His political philosophy went to pieces and the policy of the *Sun* became a mere hodge-podge of jingo programs, an irrational bundle of personal prejudices and private interests. His reaction from associationism carried him over to a stark and ruthless individualism. He saw all about him the strong and capable as the masters of the earth, with social justice an outcast and mendicant begging from house to house. The millennium to which belongs the ideal of social democracy which he had earlier served, he could no longer make out from any present bend in the road, and putting away his faith he went with the masters. The reaction began during the *Tribune* days with his espousal of the American System—the first outcropping of the middle-class qualities of his mind—and thereafter he drifted steadily to the right and the Dismal Swamp of exploitation. With augmenting wealth and the sense of power that came from the great success of the *Sun* he became the apologist and defender of capitalism, phrasing with clever vivacity all the sophistries of Gilded Age argument. Professing to be a Democrat, he made much of states rights and governmental *laissez faire*. He would countenance no interference with the principle of free competition, but would reduce the government to the rôle of policeman to keep the peace. He professed to believe that the dry bones of Manchesterism were a living democratic faith. He ridiculed the proposal for pure-food legislation, civil service reform, the control of monopolies, professing to see in every such move the insidious beginnings of an un-Ameri-

can bureaucracy. No social pretext justified in his eyes the regulation of business enterprise. Centralization of economic power he
accepted as in the nature of things, and the popular denunciation
of trusts he called "the greatest humbug of the hour." His argument was simple and to the Gilded Age wholly satisfactory.

The objects of trade being to buy as cheap as possible, to sell as dear as
possible, and to get control of the market as far as possible, the formation
for these purposes of these gigantic and widely extended partnerships is
just as natural and regular as the partnership of two shoemakers or of
two blacksmiths.[22]

Thus far Dana must be reckoned a belated disciple of the
Manchester school. The days of transcendental and Utopian
idealism were past and he knew it. The Gilded Age had traveled
far from such naïve enthusiasms and it was time to face reality.
But his realism was only a gesture to cover his surrender to capitalism. It was not honest. When his principle of individualism trod
on his own toes he threw it aside with no compunctions. He was
a *laissez-faire* Democrat only when a free field favored business,
but when business desired government assistance he made no
scruple to turn Whig. Accepting the principle of private exploitation under the drive of the acquisitive instinct, and content with
the social ethics of Captain Kidd, he would weaken government
or strengthen government as business profits dictated. In these
later years he became cynically class-conscious, while professing
to deny the existence of classes. He would disarm the government
as against the capitalist, but he would triple-arm it against the
farmer and workingman. He was shrill in his demands for a high
protective tariff for the manufacturers, huge grants of public lands
for speculative railway companies, and a monetary system in the
control of the bankers. But for the economic demands of the western farmers he had only contempt—the agrarians were flying in the
face of economic law as economic law was understood by the high
priests of capitalism. When he talked about "honest money" he
laid his brains on the shelf. He would have no other money than
the gold standard, and to achieve that object he never suffered
candor to weaken his plea. He bitterly opposed the income tax
and when the Democratic platform of 1896 suggested the reorganization of the Supreme Court to reverse the decision on its con-

[22] See James Harrison Wilson, *The Life of Charles A. Dana*, p. 479.

stitutionality, he turned demagogue and indulged in talk about "the destruction of the independence of the judiciary." When it was proposed that the railways be nationalized he protested that he could not "imagine anything more absurd, unpatriotic, and dangerous"—on the assumption no doubt that railways existed to pay dividends on their stock. "Still more alarming" to him was the "clearly implied approval of lawless violence contained in the denunciation of what is denominated in the [Democratic] platform 'government by injunction.' Veiled in the language of moderation, the wild light of anarchy shines through." [23] He urged upon government the necessity of holding the labor unions in strict control, he was eloquent in defense of the individual laborer's sacred right of "free contract," and he was loud in applause of President Cleveland's lawless suppression of the Pullman strike. When it came to Bryan and Populism he lost his head and became quite maudlin.

Dana was no fool to be deceived by his own insincerity. On the contrary he was highly intelligent and knew perfectly well what he was about. Having gone over to capitalism, he would fight its battles with whatever weapons came to hand, and like a son of New England he would cover his breast with a shield of morality. He became the chief journalistic exponent of the "lawless violence" he was fond of attributing to other social classes. He turned into a flaming jingo imperialist, talked patriotically about "adequate" coast defenses, demanded a great navy, and was the loudest spokesman of the blowsy doctrine of "Manifest Destiny." He was always peering through his glasses to discover some fresh territory to annex—Haiti, Cuba, Mexico—and so late as 1887 he was still calling for the annexation of Canada. Naturally he approved President Cleveland's Venezuelan proclamation and he probably would have enjoyed a tussle with the British lion. In his morality he was quite as truculent as in his patriotism and in his advocacy of capitalism. Perhaps it was a salve to a conscience that could not have been easy. He hated political corruption and he attacked the sordid looting that marked President Grant's administration with gusto. He took sardonic delight in giving the widest publicity to the classic corruptionist phrase of the day— "He understands addition, division, and silence." He erected into a fetish the cry "Turn the rascals out!" yet while helping to pry

[23] See *Ibid.*, p. 491.

loose one set of rascals from their spoils he was busily providing
another set with his demand for subsidies and tariffs.   It was a
situation that must have amused the cynical Dana.   He had long
since left off worrying about the damned human race.   It was more
sensible to pile up one's plate at the barbecue and send the bill to
the American people.   He had made a huge success and what mat-
tered it if his old Brook Farm associates, Ripley and Curtis, no
longer spoke to him when they met?

CHAPTER II

THE CULTURE OF THE SEVENTIES

It was in the seventies that good taste reached its lowest ebb. Not only in America, but in England as well, where rebels like William Morris were contemptuously rejecting a machine civilization. A veritable *débâcle* of the arts was in process, the lesser as well as the greater, in New York and Boston as well as in Chicago and San Francisco, from which literature could not wholly escape; and that *débâcle* was an expression of profound changes taking place at the bases of society. The dignified culture of the eighteenth century, that hitherto had been a conserving and creative influence throughout the Jeffersonian revolution, was at last breaking up. The disruptive forces that swept out of the great West, bringing the frontier spirit to every threshold, and the factory economy that displaced the wares of the craftsman with the products of the machine, were destroying that earlier culture and providing no adequate substitute. Distinction of manners and dress was gone, dignity and repose were gone, traditional standards were gone; and in their stead a bumptious restlessness, a straining for originality and individuality that exuded in a shoddy and meaningless grotesque. It was not without justification that Godkin contemptuously applied the phrase, "a chromo civilization," to the works of that singular generation dwelling between worlds, the one dead, the other seeming powerless to be born.

How much was lost in the break-up of the excellent culture of the eighteenth century the children of the seventies neither knew nor cared. Generations of growth had gone to its shaping. It had been formed by the needs of men and women conscious of the ties that linked them with the past. It was bound back upon the rich cultural life of medieval times, and in the aristocratic eighteenth century it had come to flower in forms of fine distinction and dignity. Touch that century on any side—dress, architecture, furniture, manners, letters—and the same note of refinement, of grace, of balanced harmonious form, is everywhere evident. The culture of the times of the Coffee House Wits was all of a piece, held to-

gether by an inner pervasive unity. The formality of the wig and
the heroic couplet was symbolic of a generation that loved dignity,
and the refinement of the Chippendale sideboard, wrought in
slender Honduras mahogany, was the expression of a society that
cultivated the graces of life. But when the tie-wig and smallclothes
disappeared before the social revolutions of the end of the century,
when the gentleman was pushed from his place by the banker and
manufacturer, and broadcloth gave way to tweeds, the culture of
the eighteenth century was doomed; and until another culture
should impose its standards upon society and reëstablish an inner
spiritual unity, there would be only the welter of an unlovely transition.

In no other field is the sprawling formlessness of the seventies
more grotesquely suggested than in its architecture and in interior
decoration, which is a lesser form of architecture. Upon the buildings of the times the hallmark of the Gilded Age is stamped in
gaudy colors. By the end of the thirties the fine traditions of
colonial craftsmanship were gone and the builders set forth on a
foolish quest for historical styles. Revivals followed on each other's
heels. The Greek revival and the Gothic revival marked the successive decline of the noble art of building, until at last, turning
away from the past, architecture erupted in what it conceived to be
a new American style, the expression of a free democratic people,
but which later generations reckon a sign and proof of cultural
bankruptcy. It was the golden age of the jig saw, of the brownstone
front, of the veranda that ran about the house like a spider web, of
the mansard roof, the cupola, the house of stilts. Flamboyant lines
and meaningless detail destroyed the structural unity of the whole;
tawdry decoration supplanted beauty of materials and a fine balance
of masses. A stuffy and fussy riot of fancy, restrained by no feeling
for structural lines, supplied the lack of creative imagination, and
architecture sank to the level of the jerry-builder. Bad taste could
go no further.

With this decay of aristocratic culture and the attendant disintegration of the earlier cultural unity, three diverse strands of
cultural impulse remained, each of an individual fabric that could
not easily be woven into a harmonious pattern: a decadent Federalistic culture that occupied the seats of authority in New England and wherever New England opinion was respected; the body
of social aspiration that had come from the French Enlighten-

ment, from which individual dreamers still drew nourishment; and the vigorous individualism of the frontier that bit so deeply into the psychology of the age. Behind these diverse impulses lay still another that would eventually shoulder them aside and provide the pattern for the America that was rising—the culture of an urbanized and mechanized society that in its vast warrens of business was creating the psychology and manners of a standardized, middle-class world of salesmanship.

I

NEW ENGLAND IN DECAY

In one spot in America, at least, the disruption of the fine old aristocratic culture would not be suffered without a protest. Brahmin New England would cling to its traditional standards though all the rest of America should go whoring after strange gods. The welter of the seventies it looked upon with undisguised contempt. It would not follow the way that other portions of the country were hastening. It would have nothing to do with a bumptious frontier spirit that recognized no obligations to the past—for the excellent reason that it had no past. It had had its fill of the visionary Enlightenment that had come to logical fruit in the vagaries of Thoreau and the grotesque vaporings of Alcott. It had had more than its fill of the strident causes that spawned like mushrooms in the rank soil of French romanticism. Emerson it could forgive, for Emerson was a Brahmin, but it quietly ignored his philosophic anarchism and chose to dwell on pleasanter aspects of his teaching. Wendell Phillips it regarded as a common nuisance, but Edmund Quincy it forgave, for after a season of vagrant wanderings he returned to the placid ways of his ancestral Brahminism. Of all these things, whether frontier or Utopian or what not, it had had enough, and so it turned back lovingly to the culture of earlier times and drew comfort from a dignified Federalism—enriched now by a mellow Harvard scholarship that was on intimate terms with Dante and Chaucer and Cervantes and Shakespeare—a Federalism that fitted the dignified Brahmin genius as comfortably as an old shoe.

It was an excellent heritage—that old culture. Never richly creative, never endowed with a fleshly paganism, it possessed nevertheless a solidity got from long wrestling with the eternities, a pleasantly acrid flavor got from crotchety old books, and a sober morality got from much contemplation of the sinfulness of the children of Adam. It was as native to New England as Boston brown bread, and it issued in self-respecting and dignified character. Underneath all transcendental and other eruptions it had lain unmoved like the granite foundations of the New England fields; and now after those eruptions had subsided it provided the solid footing on which the later culture might rear its chaste temples. But unhappily the building days of New England were over. Matters were going ill there. Emigration to the West was draining the vitality from farm and village, and in Boston disastrous changes were under way. The familiar places where Sam Adams and Josiah Quincy had dwelt with their fellows were being invaded by immigrants who brought with them another faith and discordant manners. The Roman Catholic church grew strong as the Old North declined; the Irish brogue displaced the Yankee on Boston Common; Faneuil Hall was given over to alien fishmongers. The Brahmin remnant was absorbed in banking and brokerage and railway investments. It still held the Boston purse but it was fast losing the Boston vote. The capital of the Puritan fathers was being destroyed by the Industrial Revolution that their descendants had set on foot. New England was visibly falling into decay and the years of its intellectual leadership in America were numbered.

The days of high thinking were over and the familiar home of humanitarian causes was inhabited by other tenants. All that remained of the golden forties was the quiet atmosphere of good breeding. Unitarianism, that Theodore Parker had kept openminded and militant, settled into a staid and respectable orthodoxy, its pale negations sufficing to soothe its placid congregations. Transcendentalism, that had thrown a lovely mist about the lean New England character, was evaporating in the rising sun of science; and the ardor of reform, that had burned fiercely in the Puritan heart, subsided into a well-bred interest in negro schools and foreign missions. The Abolition leaders laid aside their pens, convinced that the last injustice had been removed from American society. Their work was done and they turned unwilling ears to calls for new crusades. The New England conscience was tired. It had borne the burden and heat of a long day and was glad to be released from its cares to set up monuments to its sacred dead and to write the chronicles of its past. New England lost interest in

ideas and turned away from creative intellectual life to catalogue
its libraries and revere the men who had written those libraries.
The Enlightenment was over in Boston and the stir of reform
passed to New York and the West, where Amelia Bloomer and Elizabeth Cady Stanton carried forward the great crusades for temperance and women's rights, and Henry George was preaching the
gospel of a new social economics. Whatever militants existed in
New England were not likely to be Brahmins and their labors did
not roil the quiet waters. Clamorous distractions no longer disturbed the calm of Federalistic culture, and Cambridge and the
Back Bay quietly appropriated the literary earnings of Concord
and lived pleasantly on its revenues.

The inevitable fruit of such thin soil was the genteel tradition,
the excellence of which in the seventies New England maintained
in the face of all frontier leveling and romantic liberalisms—a
timid and uncreative culture that lays its inhibitions on every generation that is content to live upon the past. It was a penalty for
backsliding. The men of the preceding generation had got their
cheeses made—and excellent cheeses they were, with a fine native
flavor. But the transcendental cow had gone dry and with no
fresh cows coming in the Brahmins of the seventies were hard put
to it to live an adequate intellectual life. Translations and medieval
scholarship were no better than remainder biscuit after voyage.
Ever since Lowell put away his youthful radicalisms and turned
bookman, Brahmin culture had been undernourished. The story
of intellectual New England after 1870 is little more than a repetition of the story of New England after 1790—a resurgence of the
traditional Toryism that assumed an unquestioned custodianship
of all matters intellectual.

That was her own business, of course, and it would have been of
no great concern to the rest of the country if New England had
not set up a cultural dictatorship over American letters. It was
not content to follow its own path to sterility, but was bent on
dragging the country with it. Boston taste determined American
literary standards, and Boston taste rejected most of the new
movements then getting under way. Stoddard and Stedman in
New York, Boker in Philadelphia, and Aldrich in Boston, stoutly
upheld the genteel tradition, of which the *Atlantic Monthly* was
the authoritative spokesman. Great figures from the past—Emerson, Longfellow, Lowell, Whittier, Holmes, Motley, Parkman—

still walked the streets of Boston, and their extraordinary reputations were little less than tyrannous in the inhibitions they laid on younger men. It is incomprehensible today, the authority of these great reputations. Young William Winter walking twenty miles to stand in the moonlight at Craigie House gate and view reverently the silent walls within which the great Longfellow was sleeping; Mark Twain in the fullness of his powers abashed and put out of countenance at his temerity in speaking humorously of Emerson and Longfellow and Holmes at the *Atlantic* dinner—one understands such things with difficulty now that those reputations have so much bated and dwindled. Yet to the generation of the seventies the inhibitions of the genteel tradition were all-powerful, and the little Boston group set themselves up as a court of final jurisdiction over American letters. New England parochialism had become a nation-wide nuisance.

The genteel tradition, as Professor Santayana has pointed out, had long been a disease in New England. Some of the finest minds of the Renaissance—Emerson and Hawthorne in particular—had suffered from it; their mental processes "had all a certain starved and abstract quality," a lack of the rich paganism that endows life and art with sensuous beauty.

They could not retail the genteel tradition [he goes on]; they were too keen, too perceptive, and too independent for that. But life offered them little digestible material, nor were they naturally voracious. They were fastidious, and under the circumstances they were starved. . . . Therefore the genius of . . . Hawthorne, and even of Emerson, was employed in a sort of inner play, or digestion of vacancy. It was a refined labor, but was in danger of being morbid, or tinkling, or self-indulgent. It was a play of intra-mental rhymes. Their mind was like an old music-box, full of tender echoes and quaint fancies. These fancies expressed their personal genius sincerely, as dreams may; but they were arbitrary fancies in comparison with what a real observer would have said in the premises. Their manner, in a word, was subjective. In their own persons they escaped the mediocrity of the genteel tradition, but they supplied nothing to supplant it in other minds.[1]

If the thin pale atmosphere in which the genteel tradition throve starved the minds of greater men in a more vigorous age, it would play havoc with smaller men in an imitative age. After Emerson and Hawthorne came Stedman and Stoddard and Aldrich, upon

[1] *The Genteel Tradition in American Philosophy, University of California Chronicle,* Vol. XIII, Number 4.

whose studiously correct pages the genteel tradition laid a hand of death. In the seventies it had become the refuge of a stale mentality, emptied of all ideals save beauty, and that beauty become cold and anemic. Its taboos were no more than cushions for tired or lazy minds. The idea of morality—with its corollary of reticence—and the idea of excellence were well enough in the abstract, but become empty conventions, cut off from reality, they were little more than a refuge for respectability, a barricade against the intrusion of the unpleasant. In compressing literature within the rigid bounds of a genteel morality and a genteel excellence, New England was in a way of falsifying it. Highways are easy traveling, but the artist who will not venture from them misses much. In the seventies and eighties the incurious Boston mentality missed pretty much everything vital and significant in American life, and the more daring children of Boston—men like Henry Adams and, shall we add, Henry James—sought congenial atmosphere elsewhere.

I

THOMAS BAILEY ALDRICH AND THE GENTEEL

In the expansive days of Walt Whitman and Mark Twain the official custodian of the genteel in letters was Thomas Bailey Aldrich, who as editor of the *Atlantic* from 1881 to 1890 sturdily combated all literary leveling. Sitting in the high seat of Boston authority he would countenance none of the "Josh Billingsgate" corruptions of the English language that he professed to believe were sullying the purity of American literary taste. A Portsmouth, New Hampshire, boy, early transplanted to New York City, he lisped in numbers before he learned to think. At the age of nineteen he published a volume of poems entitled *The Bells*, *A Collection of Chimes*, the tintillations of which were little more than faint echoes of Keats, Chatterton, Tennyson, Poe, Bryant, Willis, and Longfellow; and to the end of his life his state of ideal felicity was to be "loaded to the muzzle with lyrics and sonnets" wherewith to do execution on all purveyors of realism with its "miasmatic breath blown from the slums." Transplanted to Boston from the Bohemian world of Pfaff's restaurant where Willis held court, he settled down into the staid atmosphere of the Back Bay with immense content. Though he was fond of calling himself only Boston-plated he was soon as completely Bostonian as the Autocrat himself. Intellectually and esthetically he had been Cambridge bred, and the influence of Longfellow, Lowell, and Holmes determined his every literary endeavor. Like the returned prodigal he wandered no more but was satisfied to feast on the dainties of Back Bay culture. He immersed himself in the genteel. His one ambition as editor of the *Atlantic* was to keep it as Lowell wished it kept. To the end of his life he remained completely insulated against the creative forces of the times, and in the year that Stephen Crane was writing *Maggie* he published *The Sisters' Tragedy*. He would have been shocked by *Maggie*, if he had read it, as a later generation wonders at *The Sisters' Tragedy*.

It is easy to see why Aldrich should have been taken to Boston's heart. His refined and delicate technique more than compensated for an intellectual sterility that seems never to have been apparent to his ardent admirers. Witty, charming in manners, in love with art and devoted to a painstaking craftsmanship, he was a hollow reed through which blew into flawless form the refinements of his world and group. Good taste found nothing to offend in his scanty pages. If he worshiped at the altar of beauty, beauty to him was always a chaste goddess, severe and pale and slight. A blowsy goddess like Whitman's, or a slattern like Mark Twain's, he would have none of. As a youthful poet, to be sure, he sometimes hinted that she had red cheeks and plump breasts and rounded limbs, but on his removal to Boston he discovered that she was quite Beacon Street with her slender form and modest reserve—no Greek but a lovely Puritan maiden; and the mature Aldrich came to prefer her chaste reticence to the freer ways the younger generation liked. They were destroying beauty—this younger generation—with their vulgar realism, besmirching the goddess with their vulgarities. In an interlude entitled "Realism" he gave voice to the following pastoral lament:

> Romance beside his unstrung lute
>   Lies stricken mute.
> The old-time fire, the antique grace,
> You will not find them anywhere.
> To-day we breathe a commonplace,
> Polemic, scientific air:
> We strip Illusion of her veil;
> We vivisect the nightingale
> To probe the secret of his note.
> The Muse in alien ways remote
>   Goes wandering.[2]

[2] *Poetical Works*, Vol. I, p. 45.

And in a dramatic monologue, quite evidently suggested by
The Grammarian's Funeral, he voiced the following protest against
an age enslaved to realism:

> A twilight poet, groping quite alone,
> Belated, in a sphere where every nest
> Is emptied of its music and its wings.
> Not great his gift; yet we can poorly spare
> Even his slight perfection in an age
> Of limping triolets and tame rondeaux.
> He had at least ideals, though unreached,
> And heard, far off, immortal harmonies,
> Such as fall coldly on our ear to-day.
> The mighty Zolaistic Movement now
> Engrosses us—a miasmatic breath
> Blown from the slums. We paint life as it is,
> The hideous side of it, with careful pains,
> Making a god of the dull Commonplace.
> For have we not the old gods overthrown
> And set up strangest idols? We would clip
> Imagination's wing and kill delight,
> Our sole art being to leave nothing out
> That renders art offensive. Not for us
> Madonnas leaning from their starry thrones
> Ineffable, nor any heaven-wrought dream
> Of sculptor or of poet; we prefer
> Such nightmare visions as in morbid brains
> Take form and substance, thoughts that taint the air
> And make all life unlovely. Will it last?
> Beauty alone endures from age to age,
> From age to age endures, handmaid of God.[3]

It was not the realists alone, he thought, who were fouling their
own nests, but all who turned aside from the narrow path of
Victorianism to explore new ways. Whitman he regarded as a
charlatan whose mannerisms were a "hollow affectation" representing "neither the man nor the time." Riley's formal verse
he preferred to his dialect poems—"The English language is
too rich and sacred a thing to be mutilated and vulgarized," he
wrote, overlooking the *Biglow Papers.* He held Kipling's cockney-
isms in contempt and said he would not have opened the pages of
the *Atlantic* even to the "Recessional." Lanier he thought a less
significant figure than Fitz-Greene Halleck, and of Poe he remarked that if he "had been an exemplary, conventional, tax-

[3] "At the Funeral of a Minor Poet," *Ibid.,* Vol. II, p. 94.

oppressed citizen, like Longfellow, his few poems, as striking as they are, would not have made so great a stir."[4] In such literary judgments the arch-conservative is engaged in defending the genteel tradition against every assault, convinced that the portals of creative literature open into the past and that in following in the footsteps of the dead we shall come upon a living world. The sterility of his own refined craftsmanship is perhaps sufficient commentary upon his faith.

When in later years he turned to prose his work revealed the same negative qualities. His prose style is finished, clean, and thin, wanting in homely idiom and a rich suggestiveness. The water trickled gently from the spring of his invention, cool and unroiled, but never abundant. The dignity that results from a strong nature held in restraint, he never achieved. There were no depths in him. He waited patiently for his vessel to fill and measured it out carefully. As a short-story writer he gained a surprising repute, and admirers like Sarah Orne Jewett were never tired of praising the sprightliness of his humor. Nevertheless his most celebrated story scarcely explains today the immense stir it made. *Marjorie Daw* is a clever *jeu d'esprit* but a bit thin and artificial, too consciously written backwards from its surprise ending. Other distillings of his wit and wisdom, done in the sententious manner and gathered up in *Ponkapog Papers*, are slight in content, and the effervescence is long since gone out of them. *The Story of a Bad Boy*, with its pleasant recollections of his Portsmouth youth, remains his most important work in prose and deserves much of the praise that has been lavished upon it; but set over against *Huckleberry Finn* its shortcomings are evident.

It is absurd, of course, to expect an aesthete to concern himself with ideas, or to care greatly about what goes on outside his ivory tower. The rumblings of the vulgar world beat ineffectually against the gate behind which he sits and dreams. For years the editor of the *Atlantic* was scarcely conscious of his complete aloofness from the world of reality, and he wrote in some surprise to Hamilton Wright Mabie, in 1897:

I like to have you say that I have always cared more for the integrity of my work than for any chance popularity. And what you say of my "aloofness" as being "due in part to a lack of quick sympathies with contemporary experience" (though I had never before thought of it) shows

---

[4] Ferris Greenslet, *Life of Thomas Bailey Aldrich*, p. 215.

true insight. To be sure, such verse as "Elmwood," "Wendell Phillips,"
"Unguarded Gates" and the "Shaw Memorial Ode" would seem somewhat to condition the statement; but the mood of these poems is not
habitual with me, not characteristic. They did, however, grow out of
strong conviction.[5]

Yet though he spoke rarely on social themes, during the long
years in Boston most of the Back Bay prejudices seemed to have
seeped into his mind and when the "strong convictions," to which
he refers, found utterance they proved to be Brahmin convictions.
In the vigorous poem "Unguarded Gates"—a poem tense, outspoken, almost unique in its deliberate declamation—he sallied
forth from his ivory tower to speak to the American people on the
dangers of uncontrolled immigration, a subject that Boston Brahmins had been talking about since the days of Harrison Gray Otis.

>Wide open and unguarded stand our gates,
>And through them presses a wild motley throng—
>Men from the Volga and the Tartar steppes,
>Featureless figures from the Hoang-Ho,
>Malayan, Scythian, Teuton, Kelt, and Slav,
>Flying the Old World's poverty and scorn;
>These bringing with them unknown gods and rites,
>Those, tiger passions, here to stretch their claws.
>In street and alley what strange tongues are loud,
>Accents of menace alien to our air,
>Voices that once the Tower of Babel knew!
>
>O Liberty, white Goddess! is it well
>To leave the gates unguarded? On thy breast
>Fold Sorrow's children, soothe the hurts of fate,
>Lift the down-trodden, but with hand of steel
>Stay those who to thy sacred portals come
>To waste the gifts of freedom. Have a care
>Lest from thy brow the clustered stars be torn
>And trampled in the dust. For so of old
>The thronging Goth and Vandal trampled Rome,
>And where the temples of the Caesars stood
>The lean wolf unmolested made her lair.[6]

What emotions lay back of the measured words of the poem, and
how deeply they were colored by the social passions of the times, he
tells in a letter to George E. Woodberry, written May 14, 1892:

I went home and wrote a misanthropic poem called "Unguarded Gates"
. . . in which I mildly protest against America becoming the cesspool of

---

[5] *Ibid.*, p. 200.   [6] *Poetical Works*, Vol. II, p. 72

Europe. I'm much too late, however. I looked in on an anarchist meeting the other night . . . and heard such things spoken by our "feller citizens" as made my cheek burn. These brutes are the spawn and natural result of the French Revolution; they don't want any government at all, they "want the earth" . . . and chaos. My Americanism goes clean beyond yours. I believe in America for the Americans; I believe in the widest freedom and the narrowest license, and I hold that jail-birds, professional murderers, amateur lepers . . . and human gorillas generally should be closely questioned at our Gates. Or the "sifting" that was done of old will have to be done over again. . . . A certain Arabian writer, called Rudyard Kipling, described exactly the government of every city and town in the . . . United States when he described that of New York as being "a despotism of the alien, by the alien, for the alien, tempered with occasional insurrections of decent folk!" [7]

Two years later he again gave private expression to one of his rare judgments on matters political and social:

When not otherwise engaged I sit and smoke, and smile at the present administration [President Cleveland's]. . . . The best kind of Democracy (as per sample) is no better than the worst kind of Republicanism. The Income Tax is the deformed child of Coxey and his brother scalawags. I vote for McKinley. We shall have bloody work in this country some of these days, when the lazy *canaille* get organized. They are the spawn of Santerre and Fouquier-Tinville. In about twenty years we shall bring out an American edition (illustrated with cuts) of the beautiful French Revolution.[8]

And again in 1899:

Personally I must confess that I have never been very deeply impressed by the administrative abilities of what we call the lower classes. The Reign of Terror in France is a fair illustration of the kind of government which the masses give us when they get the happy opportunity.[9]

The literary conservative, it appears, was no better than a social and political Tory. He has traveled back a hundred years and speaks again the very language of Robert Treat Paine. *Canaille* is not a nice word to apply to American workingmen, and the French Revolution has never been well thought of by the children of the *ancien régime*. Thomas Bailey Aldrich was a cultivated gentleman, on the pleasantest terms with the Muse of Beacon Street. Twice he traveled around the world; innumerable summers he spent in Europe; yet of many things that concern men greatly he was very, very ignorant. Of the American people beyond the

[7] Ferris Greenslet, *Life of Thomas Bailey Aldrich*, pp. 168–169.
[8] *Ibid.*, p. 176.   [9] *Ibid.*, p. 205.

Hudson River, he knew nothing. Of social economics he knew nothing. Fearful lest his art should get a smutch from the streets, he withdrew within his tower, where perhaps it is well to leave him. Yet it is odd to recall that he was once regarded as a significant literary figure and that intelligent people listened to him seriously.

2

THE NEW ENGLAND SCENE

In fields less distinguished than poetry and the essay the sway of the genteel was neither so magisterial nor so repressive. As fiction somewhat tardily encroached upon the older literary preserves of New England it brought with it a fresher and more realistic spirit that was eventually to deny the validity of the traditional standards. The group of fiction writers that arose in the seventies and eighties to chronicle the life of New England, was greatly concerned with the decay of the old New England world, and with the causes of that decay. As it set down with loving fidelity the characteristics of an earlier order it could not fail to consider the unloveliness of the new world that was rising on the decay of the old—the alien industrial towns with their polyglot workers that were flourishing as the native villages and quiet countryside declined. New England fiction, therefore, came to embody two main features, chronicle and criticism. It gathered up such picturesque bits of the past as time and change had left, and it questioned with some anxiety the ways of an industrialism that was destroying what it loved. It was not Boston fiction, but up-country fiction, given to exploring quiet villages and decaying towns; and in both its chronicles and its criticisms the spirit of realism became more searching as the years passed.

In its own fashion such fiction would finally be brought into service to the social conscience and issue as sociological studies. As the evils of sweated labor under the factory system were brought home to the common knowledge, one would suppose that New England would have been the first to conscript the novel to arouse the public conscience. There had been anxious discussion amongst the Concord intellectuals on the evils of industrialism, and in the early forties the talk had turned upon associationism as the likeliest cure; but though from such discussions came Brook Farm and other Utopian ventures, no fiction resulted. It was elsewhere, in the Pennsylvania iron district where exploitation was harsher and more brutal than in the textile mills, that fiction first turned to consider the ways of industrialism. In 1861 Rebecca Harding contributed to the *Atlantic* a story entitled "Life in the Iron Mills," that was stark and fierce in its drab realism.[10] Nevertheless ten years were to pass before Elizabeth Stuart Phelps published *The Silent Partner* (1871), a dithyrambic plea for justice for the mill-hands.

If this was not the first New England novel of industrialism it was certainly one of the earliest. In conception, temper, and technique it belongs to the emotional fifties, and is almost primitive in comparison with Rebecca Harding's work. Underlain with religion, it is sticky with sentiment. Although Miss Phelps professed to base her work on the Reports of the Massachusetts Bureau of Statistics of Labor, to which she says she was "deeply in debt for the ribs" of her story, the result is more a tract than a study. There is no realistic grasp of the materials. She was grieved that the mill-masters should reveal so little Christian understanding of the hard lot of the hands and so little sympathy with their poverty. "I believe," she said, "that a wide-spread ignorance exists among us regarding the abuses of our factory system, more especially, but not exclusively, as exhibited in many of the country mills." "Had Christian ingenuity been generally synonymous with the conduct of manufacturing corporations, I should have found no occasion for the writing of this book."[11] It was to lessen such ignorance and encourage Christian sympathy between the classes that she offered her study.

The book is a closet study done with more unction than skill. It is the work of an emotional woman who lived in a world of sentiment rather than reality. Miss Phelps was an Andover Brahmin, highly sensitive, whose deeply religious nature was ruffled by every vagrant wind. She was tremulous in her eager desire to lessen the injustice of men. *The Silent Partner* is a story of a young woman brought up in luxury, daughter of a manufacturer, who on her father's death wishes to join in the management of the factory, but on being politely rejected by her partners she engages in personnel work amongst her employees. There she comes upon

[10] Fred Lewis Pattee, *The Development of the American Short Story*, pp. 171–172. See the entire chapter for a discussion of early realism in the *Atlantic*.
[11] Preface, p. 5.

poverty as a sordid fact, and that discovery works a moral change
in her life. She is overwhelmed by it and cannot understand why
the conscience of the world is not overwhelmed. "Sometimes I do
not see," she exclaimed, "what else there can *be* to talk about in
such a world as this! I've stepped into it, as we have stepped out
into this storm. It has wrapped me in. . . ." [12] Of the complexity
of the problem she is wholly ignorant. Surely there must be some
road that leads to justice—justice based on understanding and
Christian kindliness; and the working girl whom she singles out for
heroine becomes in the end a street preacher to the textile workers,
after refusing to marry and bring children into a world of factory
toil. *The Silent Partner* is an emotional Puritan document that
was out of date when it came from the press.

While Miss Phelps was thus summoning the New England
conscience to cleanse the textile mills, her Brahmin sisters were
little inclined to engage in such thankless labors, but preferred to
gather up and preserve such fragments of the homely traditional
New England as had not been swept away in the engulfing stream
of industrialism. Female writers, from the days of Mrs. Sarah
Wentworth Morton, had long been busy in New England but never
had they written so well or so understandingly as in the days of
the New England decline. Harriet Beecher Stowe, Elizabeth
Stuart Phelps, Harriet Prescott Spofford, Rose Terry Cooke,
Mary Wilkins Freeman, and Alice Brown were not great writers,
but they essayed to be faithful recorders of what came under their
eyes. It was the earlier New England that quickened their imaginations, the rugged Yankee character that had taken form under a
homely domestic economy. They had no liking for the New England that was rising in the shadow of the mills; the cleavages of
race and religion that were sundering the old homogeneous society
were bitterly distasteful to them. The Irish, the French-Canadians,
the masses of raw immigrants that were swept into the hoppers of
the mills, were unwelcome gobbets to the Brahmin stomach. And
so these recorders of the New England decline turned away from
the sordid industrial scene, and it was not till thirty years later that
Mary Wilkins Freeman, in *The Portion of Labor* (1901), essayed
to do more adequately what Elizabeth Stuart Phelps had first
sketched.

From Catherine Sedgwick to Mrs. Freeman the note shifted

[12] Chapter VIII. p. 183.

from the moralistic to the sentimental, then to the idyllic, then to
the realistic; and the successive changes are sufficiently marked
by three writers, Harriet Beecher Stowe, Sarah Orne Jewett, and
Mary Wilkins Freeman. Seeking their materials remote from
Boston, amidst the old native stock pottering through the traditional round of life, they discovered a world of angular figures
that had grown knotty and gnarly from a harsh climate and a
meager soil. The stoic repressions that were a heritage from Puritan ancestors had bred a hard race that any twist of circumstance
was likely to turn into grotesques. Calvinists have always at hand
a providential justification of any freakish outcome to men's
struggles, and in piously denying freedom of the will they often
put the seal of God's approval on their own willfulness. Mrs.
Freeman's *Pembroke* is not unlike *Winesburg, Ohio*, as a record of
abortive lives; and Sarah Orne Jewett, in spite of a Brahmin temperament that chose to see the idyllic rather than the grotesque,
could not overlook what New England provided so abundantly.
In *A Country Doctor* a visitor in the village of Oldsfield thus analyzed the New England character:

. . . for intense, self-centred, smouldering volcanoes of humanity, New
England cannot be matched the world over. It's like the regions in Ice-
land that are full of geysers. I don't know whether it is the inheritance
from those people who broke away from the old countries, and who ought
to be matched to tremendous circumstances of life, but now and then
there comes an amazingly explosive and uncontrollable temperament
that goes all to pieces from its own conservation and accumulation of
force. By and by you will all be blown up,—you quiet descendants of the
Pilgrims and Puritans, and have let off your superfluous wickedness like
blizzards; and when the blizzards of each family have spent themselves
you will grow dull and sober, and all on a level, and be free from the
troubles of a transition state. Now, you're neither a new country nor an
old one. You ought to see something of the older civilizations to understand what peace of mind is. Unless some importation of explosive material from the westward stirs them up, one century is made the pattern
for the next.[13]

They deal wholly with the past—these chronicles of a decaying
New England—concerning themselves with a "primitive and
Biblical people" who dwelt in quiet inland towns or about the
lonely shores of the Maine coast; yet always under the shadow of
the meeting-house, with few defenses betwixt them and the eter-

[13] Chapter IX, p. 100.

nities. The age had traveled far beyond them and they were left pottering about in their narrow Hebraic world, unaware that science and industrialism were undermining the foundations on which village and meeting-house rested. "In that handful of houses," said old Captain Littlepage in *The Country of the Pointed Firs*, "they fancy that they comprehend the universe." But if they understood God's plan of redemption they knew nothing of the ways of capitalism. A certain romantic quaintness colors the realism of these country tales and imparts a note of the idyllic. Harriet Beecher Stowe first discovered the literary possibilities of decaying New England, and in *Old-Town Folks*, *Poganuc People*, and *The Minister's Wooing*, she turned back to the days of its prime and sketched the scene with a loving hand. But it was rather in *The Pearl of Orr's Island*, especially the first part before the heavy moralism that was always entrapping her art had closed upon the tale, that she revealed its possibilities to later writers. In a letter of July 5, 1889, Sarah Orne Jewett suggests the source of her own more finished work:

> I have been reading the beginning of *The Pearl of Orr's Island* and finding it just as clear and perfectly original and strong as it seemed to me in my thirteenth or fourteenth year, when I read it first. I never shall forget the exquisite flavor and reality that it gave me. . . . It is classical—historical—anything you like to say, if you can give it high praise enough.[14]

But Miss Jewett desired a more adequate realism and so she turned curiously to consider the technique of the great continental realists of the eighties. She read Zola and Flaubert, Tolstoi and Turgenev, and oddly enough was persuaded that she had long been trying to do what Tolstoi was doing. In a letter of 1888 she wrote:

> That story of Tolstoi's was such an excitement that I did not sleep until almost morning. What a wonderful thing it is! . . . It startled me because I was dimly feeling the same kind of motive (not the same plan) in writing the "Gray Man.". . . I have felt something of what Tolstoi has been doing all the way along. I can tell you half a dozen stories where I tried to say it, "Lady Terry," "Beyond the Toll-Gate," and this "Gray Man." Now and then it came clearer to me. I never felt the soul of Tolstoi's work until last night . . . but now I know what he means, and I know that I can dare to keep at the work I sometimes have despaired about. . . .[15]

[14] *Letters of Sarah Orne Jewett*, pp. 46–47.   [15] *Ibid.*, pp. 38–39.

Yet to later readers the tie that drew her to Tolstoi seems the thinnest of gossamers. The roots of her character—and of her art— went down too deep into Brahmin soil, she was too completely under the critical sway of Lowell and Fields and Aldrich, for her to turn naturalist. Her realism—if one may use the word—was as dainty and refined as her own manners—bleached out to a fine maidenly purity. In *The Country of the Pointed Firs*—a story that Willa Cather would destine for immortality in the select company of *Huckleberry Finn* and *The Scarlet Letter*—she discovers an innate gentility, or at least gentleness, in the simple fisherfolk of the Maine village, and she suggests as its source a primitive environment supplemented by an encompassing religion. Nowhere does she paint in the smutch of vulgarity, for in these eddies of New England life she discovers no vulgarity either of mind or manners. But in the cities it is different. There she found evidence in plenty of what she called the "cheap side of life," and she attributed it to the increasing material well-being of the country. Of the new middle class she held a low opinion—

Their grandparents or even their own parents went hungry and ill clothed, and it will take some time for these people to have their fling, to eat all they want and to wear fine raiment, and flaunt authority. They must get to a state, and by slow stages too, where there is going to be something fit for education. . . . The trouble is to us old-fashioned New Englanders that "the cheap streak" so often spoils what there is of good inheritance, and the wrong side of our great material prosperity is seen almost everywhere.[16]

There spoke the Brahmin. That this "cheap streak" should have spread so far through American life, that the vulgar middle class should have taken over the rule of the country, gave her concern. To one brought up on Carlyle and Lowell and Arnold the ways of the plutocracy were abhorrent, and she clung the more tenaciously to the land of her memories, where the gentry ruled, where the plain people respected themselves and their betters, and where vulgar display was unknown. "I think as Mr. Arnold does," she wrote in 1884, "and as Mr. Lowell did, that the mistake of our time is in being governed by the ignorant mass of opinion, instead of by thinkers and men who know something." [17] Though she disliked and distrusted the America that was submerging the old landmarks, she was as ignorant as her Maine fisherfolk of the

[16] *Ibid.*, pp. 186–187.   [17] *Ibid.*, p. 23.

social forces that were blotting out the world of her fathers, and she clung with pathetic futility to such fragments of the old order as remained. Like Lowell in his later years her heart was given to a Brahmin democracy where gentlemen ruled and where "the best traditions of culture and manners, from some divine inborn instinct toward what is simplest and purest," were held in universal respect.

What Miss Jewett with her love of the idyllic did not see—the grim and stark ugliness that resulted from the long Puritan repression—Mary Wilkins Freeman was to make the very warp of her work. She did not come of Brahmin stock. Bred up in the narrow village world of New England, she was a part of that world and she knew it as Miss Jewett could not. The decay of a social order was all about her in her youth. The more ambitious were drifting to the cities or to the new West, and those who remained were deeply marked by the constricting round of duties. Catastrophe seems always to be lying in wait for the characters that fill her meager pages. They are either timid and querulous, or fiercely "sot," yet in either case happiness has a way of slipping through their fingers. There was too little of the wine of paganism in their veins for them to enjoy what life offers. They held themselves in with too tight a rein. The New England conventions were always building higher the dams of their emotions until they broke and the roily waters rushed out in a wasting flood. Potential disaster peeps out of every page of her stories. *Pembroke* is an extraordinary collection of mean and petty and tragic lives, besotted with stubborn willfulness, without grace or comeliness, extracting no pleasant flavors from the crushed grapes of life. In that narrow world daily existence demands an unending struggle and the pinching meanness breeds miserly instincts and dour ways. *A Humble Romance* is a stark bit of sordid futility, and in many another of her short stories Mrs. Freeman etched in the familiar scene with a mordant pen. Drawn with realistic strokes the picture of New England in decay is not so lovely as Miss Jewett found it to be.

Realizing poignantly what was happening in the home of Puritanism, Mrs. Freeman turned eventually to deal with the problem of industrialism that was subduing New England to its will. *The Portion of Labor* picks up the theme where it had been dropped a generation before by Miss Phelps, and attempts in realistic manner to portray the life of the New England villager in the shoe factory. It is a tract rather than a story, and it finds no difficulty in reconciling industrialism with morality. It revives the old Puritan ethics of work—preached by Richard Baxter to his Kidderminster weavers two hundred and fifty years before; it discovers in discipline of character the great end of life; and it accepts the factory as a necessary instrument of civilization. It is the Cinderella story of a village girl who, refusing a chance to be sent to Vassar, enters a shoe factory, becomes a proletarian leader, engineers a strike, gains a wider vision of the function of labor, accepts the principle of exploitation, and is rewarded by marriage into the exploiting class. In her girlhood she was a radical in an untaught way, and from her valedictory essay at the High School Commencement to her organization of the factory workers she boldly attacked the factory owners. With the machine itself she had no quarrel. This is how she felt when she took her place for the first time in the mill:

Scared she was not; she was fairly exultant. All at once she entered a vast room in which eager men were already at the machines with frantic zeal, as if they were driving labor herself. When she felt the vibration of the floor under her feet, when she saw people spring to their stations of toil, as if springing to guns in a battle, she realized the might and grandeur of it all. Suddenly it seemed to her that the greatest thing in the whole world was work and that this was one of the greatest forms of work—to cover the feet of progress of the travellers of the earth from the cradle to the grave. She saw that these great factories, and the strength of this army of the sons and daughters of toil, made possible the advance of civilization itself, which cannot go barefoot. She realized all at once and forever the dignity of labor, this girl of the people, with a brain which enabled her to overlook the heads of the rank and file of which she herself formed a part. She never again, whatever her regret might have been for another life for which she was better fitted, which her taste preferred, had any sense of ignominy in this. She never again felt that she was too good for her labor, for labor had revealed itself to her like a goddess behind a sordid veil.[18]

Nevertheless she is ready to fight for control of the machine—for a return to the workers of a larger share of their earnings; but when the strike fails and she contemplates the misery that it has spread amongst the workers, she recants:

Her youthful enthusiasm carried her like a leaping-pole to conclusions beyond her years. "I wonder," she said to herself, "if, after all, this

[18] Chapter XXXV, p. 350.

inequality of possessions is not a part of the system of creation, if the righting of them is not beyond the flaming sword of the Garden of Eden? I wonder if the one who tries to right them forcibly is not meddling, and usurping the part of the Creator, and bringing down wrath and confusion not only upon his own head, but upon the heads of others? I wonder if it is wise, in order to establish a principle, to make those who have no voice in the matter suffer for it—the helpless women and children?" . . . She reflected, as she had so many times before, that the world was very old—thousands of years old—and inequality was as old as the world. Might it not even be a condition of its existence, the shifting of weights which kept it to its path in the scheme of the universe? [19]

Mrs. Freeman wisely chose a girl in her teens as the leader in a fierce labor battle, for Mrs. Freeman's own thinking on social questions was still in its teens. She had the warmest sympathy for the exploited poor; her conscience was as tender as Miss Phelps's; but her inadequate knowledge of economics served her ill. If economic inequality is necessary to keep the world from flying from its orbit, it serves the purpose likewise of character development. When an old factory-hand looks back upon a long life of futile labor he thus philosophizes:

Andrew quoted again from the old King of Wisdom—"I withheld not my heart from any joy, for my heart rejoices in all my labor, and that was my portion of labor." Then Andrew thought . . . of all the toilsome lives of those beside him, of all the work which they had done with their poor, knotted hands, of the tracks which they had worn on the earth towards their graves, with their weary feet, and suddenly he seemed to grasp a new and further meaning for that verse of Ecclesiastes.

He seemed to see that labor is not alone for itself, nor for what it accomplishes of the tasks of the world, not for its equivalent in silver and gold, not even for the end of human happiness and love, but for the growth in character of the laborer.

"That is the portion of labor," he said. [20]

So the book ends on a Hebraic note. In 1901 when Mrs. Freeman wrote *The Portion of Labor* the psychology of work had been pretty well explored. For years William Morris had been preaching a very different doctrine, pagan rather than Hebraic, yet Mrs. Freeman seems to have been acquainted with Morris no more than was Ellen Brewster, her girlish heroine. Even the starkest New England realism was not very critical of the industrialism that was destroying the traditional New England. A cynical reader

[19] Chapter LVII, pp. 519–520.   [20] *Ibid.*, p. 563.

might perhaps suggest that the explanation is to be found in the fact that the Yankee was profiting enormously from this fouling of the Puritan nest.

II

THE AFTERGLOW OF THE ENLIGHTENMENT— WALT WHITMAN

If the philosophy of the Enlightenment was fast disintegrating in the America of 1870, it still numbered its picturesque followers who sought to leaven the age with the social spirit of an earlier generation. It was a noble bequest—this gift of the French thinkers—with its passion for liberty, its faith in man, its democratic program. From that great reservoir had come pretty much all that was generously idealistic and humanitarian in the life of the two preceding generations. Its persuasive idealism had woven itself so closely into the fabric of national thought that our fathers had come to believe that America was dedicated in a very special sense to the principles of a free society. The democratic movement returned to it constantly to refresh its strength and take new bearings. At every great crisis the familiar pronouncement of the Declaration of Independence had been confidently appealed to in furtherance of social justice. And now in the days of an acquisitive individualism, when idealism was begging alms in the market-place, it still threw flashes of romantic splendor on the crude American scene. Old Peter Cooper still dreamed his dreams of social justice after eighty years had passed over his head; and Thaddeus Stevens, grown crabbed and surly from bitter struggles, mutely testified to his passionate equalitarianism on the day of his burial. But it was Walt Whitman in his den at Camden—culturally and in the things of the spirit countless leagues removed from Boston—who was the completest embodiment of the Enlightenment—the poet and prophet of a democracy that the America of the Gilded Age was daily betraying.

In his somewhat truculent pose of democratic undress Whitman was a singular figure for a poet, and especially an American poet. The amplitude and frankness and sincerity of his rich nature were an affront to every polite convention of the day. Endowed with abundant sensuousness and catholic sympathies, he took impressions as sharply as wax from the etcher's hand; and those impressions he transcribed with the careful impartiality of the modern

expressionist. His sensitive reactions to experience were emotional
rather than intellectual. A pagan, a romantic, a transcendentalist,
a mystic—a child of the Enlightenment yet heeding the lessons of
science and regarding himself as a realist who honored the physical
as the repository of the spiritual—to an amazing degree he was
an unconscious embodiment of American aspiration in the days
when the romantic revolution was at flood tide. His buoyant
nature floated easily on the turbulent stream of national being,
and his songs were defiant chants in praise of life—strong, abundant, procreative—flowing through the veins of America.

Oracular and discursive, Whitman lived and moved in a world
of sensuous imagery. His imagination was Gothic in its vast
reaches. Thronging troops of pictures passed before him, vivid,
vital, transcripts of reality, the sharp impress of some experience
or fleeting observation—his own and no one's else, and therefore
authentic. Delighting in the cosmos he saw reflecting its myriad
phases in the mirror of his own ego, he sank into experience joyously like a strong swimmer idling in the salt waves. Borne up by
the caressing waters, repressing nothing, rejecting nothing, he
found life good in all its manifestations. As an Emersonian he was
content to receive his sanctions from within, and as he yielded to
the stimulus of the environing present his imagination expanded,
his spirits rose to earth's jubilee, his speech fell into lyric cadences,
and from the exalted abandon of egoistic experience there issued
a strong rich note of the universal. His like had not before appeared in our literature for the reason that the childlike pagan
had not before appeared. Emerson with his serene intelligence
almost disencumbered of the flesh, and Hawthorne with his des-
sicating skepticisms that left him afraid of sex, were the fruits of a
Hebraized culture that Puritan America understood; but Walt
Whitman the caresser of life, the lover who found no sweeter fat
than stuck to his own bones, was incomprehensible, and not being
understood, it was inevitable that he should be inexorably damned.
The most deeply religious soul that American literature knows,
the friend and lover of all the world, the poet of the democratic
ideal to which, presumably, America was dedicated, Whitman was
flung into outer darkness by the moral custodians of an age that
knew morality only from the precepts of the fathers.

The early stages of Whitman's intellectual development are
obscure, but that in his twenties he caught most of the infections of

the times, literary, political, and social, is clear enough. The young printer-editor in frock coat and tall hat, with cane and boutonnière, who often joined the Bohemian society at Pfaff's restaurant, was a callow romantic, practicing the conventional literary arts of the time, writing formal verse, spinning romantic tales,[21] and seeking to approve himself a reputable littérateur. But the passion of reform was already stirring within him and a succession of causes— temperance, anti-capital-punishment, abolitionism—recruited his pen. As a child of Manhattan and of the Jacksonian revolution it was inevitable that his first great passion should have been political, and when in the late forties he found a suitable vehicle of expression in the *Brooklyn Eagle*, his native Jeffersonianism took stock of current political programs. His political master was the radical equalitarian William Leggett—whose praises in after life he never stinted—and from Leggett and the *Evening Post*, supplemented by Fanny Wright and Tom Paine and other disreputable influences, he seems to have got the first clear expression of the sweeping democratic postulates on which later he was to erect his philosophy. The times were stirring everywhere with revolution and on Manhattan Island Locofocoism, with the newfangled matches, ten years before had started its little local bonfire by way of preparation for a general conflagration that should consume the accumulated mass of wrong and injustice. The ardent young Whitman was deeply infected with Locofoco enthusiasm and his editorials for the *Eagle* were the pronouncements of an extreme left-wing Democrat, as became a disciple of Leggett.

In this early phase of his democracy he fixed his hopes on the great West where, he believed, a freer and more democratic America was taking shape. He was an expansionist, full of ardent hopes, an apostle of "manifest destiny." In such lesser matters as finance and governmental subsidies he was a good Jacksonian, following Old Bullion Benton in his preference for hard money and dislike of shin-plasters. He was opposed to the bankers and monopolists. He called himself a "free-trader by instinct," and so late as 1888 he said, "I object to the tariff primarily because it is not humanitarian—because it is a damnable imposition upon the masses."[22] But these lesser things were inconsequential in comparison with the

[21] See Mabbott, *Short Stories by Walt Whitman*, Columbia University Press, 1927.
[22] For his late views see Horace Traubel, *With Walt Whitman in Camden*, Vol. I, p. 99, and elsewhere.

great objective towards which America was moving—the ever-widening freedom of men in society. "There must be," he wrote in those early years, "continual additions to our great experiment of how much liberty society will bear."[23] On that grand theme he was never tired of speaking. With Tom Paine he believed that just government was a simple thing, fitted to the capacity of many heads; it is made complex to hide its dishonesty. After commenting on the "once derided, but now widely worshipped doctrines which Jefferson and the glorious Leggett promulgated," he went on:

. . . this one single rule, rationally construed and applied, is enough to form the starting point of all that is necessary in government: *to make no more laws than those useful for preventing a man or body of men from infringing on the rights of other men.*

And again:

There is not a greater fallacy on earth than the doctrine of *force*, as applied in government. . . . Sensible men have long seen that the best government is that which governs least.[24]

Such comments, of course, are only familiar echoes of the Enlightenment—echoes that run through all the thinking of the naturistic school, from Godwin and Paine to Channing and Emerson and Thoreau. In the minds of the children of the Enlightenment the creative ideal of individualism was always pointing toward the ultimate end of philosophic anarchism, and Whitman with his assured faith in the average man accepted the Godwinian political theory as naturally as did Thoreau. What other politics, indeed, was possible for those who built upon the postulates of the innate excellence of human nature and the measureless potentialities of men when vicious social codes have been swept away and the plastic clay is molded by a kindly environment? The perfectibility of man was no romantic dream to the disciples of the French school, but a sober statement of sociological fact, based on a rationalistic psychology; and Whitman was convinced that he was a competent realist in thus envisaging the social problem. If man's instincts are trustworthy, what justification is there for narrow repressions laid on his freedom? Hitherto those repressions have only maimed and distorted him, encouraging his baser rather than his better impulses; and before he can realize his potentialities he

[23] Cleveland Rogers and John Black, *The Gathering of the Forces*, Vol. I, p. 12.
[24] *Ibid.*, Vol. I, pp. 53, 54, 57.

must put away all external compulsions and learn to rely solely upon himself. Hence the immediate objective of the democratic revolution was individual freedom, the breaking of all chains, to the end that free men may create a society worthy of them.

So it was as a revolutionary that Whitman began his work; and a revolutionary he remained to the end, although in his last years he chose to call himself an evolutionist. A born rebel, he was always preaching the gospel of rebellion. "I am a radical of radicals," he said late in life, "but I don't belong to any school." [25] It was this revolutionary spirit that made him the friend of all rebellious souls past and present. "My heart is with all you rebels—all of you, today, always, wherever: your flag is my flag," [26] he said to a Russian anarchist; and it was this sympathy that enabled him to understand Fanny Wright and Tom Paine and Priestley, who "have never had justice done them." [27] "The future belongs to the radical," and so *Leaves of Grass*—he says in "Starting from Paumanok"—"beat the gong of revolt." Conventional law and order he frankly despised and those individuals who sought their own law and followed it awoke his admiration. Thoreau's "lawlessness" delighted him—"his going his own absolute road let hell blaze all it chooses." It is a coward and a poltroon who accepts his law from others—as true of communities as it is true of individuals. He was a good Jeffersonian in his fear of Federalistic consolidation that must put an end to local rights and freedoms.

> To the States or any one of them, or any city of the States,
> *Resist much, obey little,*
> Once unquestioning obedience, once fully enslaved,
> . . . no nation, state, city of this earth, ever afterward resumes
> its liberty.[28]
> I am for those that have never been master'd,
> For men and women whose tempers have never been master'd,
> For those whom laws, theories, conventions can never master.[29]

This is the spirit of the radical forties when men were prone to repudiate their allegiance to the political state; when left-wing Abolitionists were dissolving the Union by resolutions; and tran-

[25] Traubel, *op. cit.*, Vol. I, p. 215.
[26] *Ibid.*, Vol. I, p. 65.
[27] *Ibid.*, Vol. I, pp. 79–80.
[28] *Leaves of Grass*, inclusive edition ed. by Emory Halloway, Garden City, N. Y., 1927. Hereafter called *Leaves*. "To the States," p. 8.
[29] *Ibid.*, "By Blue Ontario's Shore," p. 297, ll. 21–23.

scendentalists were proclaiming the doctrine of nullification of
unrighteous law. It had come out of the Jacksonian upheaval, but
it was daily discovering fresh sanctions as the anarchistic premises
of the Enlightenment were more adequately explored and the
revolutionary spirit of Europe broke in upon America. During
these turbulent years Whitman's great plan was in gestation, but
before *Leaves of Grass* came to print in the first slender edition of
1855 other influences had been at work, confirming his earlier
views, endowing them with lyric passion and expanding them into
a grandiose whole. Those influences would seem to have been the
fervid emotionalism of the fifties, the monistic idealism of the
transcendental school, and the emerging scientific movement. On
the whole perhaps it was the first, with its vague and expansive
Utopianism, that bit most deeply, stimulating his rich pagan nature to unconventional frankness and encouraging him to throw off
the inhibitions of a Puritan ethicism that held American thought
in narrow bondage. The rude and ample liberalisms that so
shocked his early readers were in no sense peculiar to Whitman,
despite common opinion, but the expression of the surging emotionalism of the times, and *Leaves of Grass*, can best be understood
by setting its frank paganism against the background of the lush
fifties.

With its Calvinistic antecedents—Scotch-Irish and Huguenot
as well as New England Puritan—America had always been unfriendly to a pagan evaluation of man's duties and destiny, and
the revolutionary movement of the forties had been kept within
sober ethical bounds. John Humphrey Noyes was probably the
most radical American of the times, yet the Perfectionism of his
earlier years, with its ascetic religiosity, bore little resemblance
to the later communism of the Oneida Community. But the
liberalism of the fifties was casting off all Hebraic restraints and
running wild, proclaiming a new heaven about to appear on the
free continent of America, and bidding the youth of the land live
joyously as children of the earth. Paganism for the first time lifted
up its head and surveyed the American scene—a youthful paganism, lusty and vigorous, that suggested amazing applications of
the respectable doctrines of freedom and individuality, to the
scandal of older-fashioned folk. From the free spaces of the West,
carried on the tide of the Gold Rush, had come a spontaneous

reaction from the earlier repressions. Liberalism was passing from the political to the social—a free welling-up of repressed desires, a vast expansiveness. Too long had the natural human emotions been under the ban of asceticism; too long had a God of wrath dispossessed a God of love. Life is good in the measure that it is lived fully, and to live fully is to live in the flesh as well as the spirit. Emerson the prophet of the earlier decade had suffered from an extreme unfleshliness; Whitman the prophet of the fifties would recover the balance. As the current of emotionalism gathered force a frank *joie de vivre* submerged the old reticences; candor, frankness, a very lust of self-expression, was the new law for free men and women—a glorification of the physical that put to rout the traditional Hebraisms. A riotous sentimentalism ran about the land until it seemed to timid souls as if liberty were quite running away with decency. Freedom for black slaves was one thing, but freedom for women—the loosening of social convention—suggested terrifying eventualities like free love and the disruption of the family. They would countenance no such immoral freedom and under the leadership of young Anthony Comstock the forces of reticence and respectability made ready to do battle with the new liberalisms.

It was not alone Walt Whitman who threw down the gage to the Comstockian watchmen in the gates. The apostle of the new freedom, the high priest of emotional liberalism, was Henry Ward Beecher, lately come out of the West, who from the pulpit of Plymouth Church swept his thousands of idolizing followers along the path of Utopian emotionalism. With a rich amplitude and golden vagueness of metaphor he preached the new gospel. From his lips flowed a lyric chant, a vast paean, a very shout in praise of liberty and love, of godlike man and a manlike God. "Life—affirmative, immediate, in a highly ornamented Mayday world—he acknowledged and commemorated life!" [30] He bathed in a "perpetual tropical luxuriance of blessed love." "I never knew how to worship until I knew how to love," he cried; "and to love I must have something . . . that touching my heart, shall not leave the chill of ice but the warmth of summer." Like a good Emersonian he discarded reason—the discipline of the ancestral Calvinism—to follow the "secret chords of feeling," the "heart's instincts, whose channels you may appoint but whose flowing is

[30] Constance Mayfield Rourke, *Trumpets of Jubilee*, p. 171.

beyond control." A "magnificent pagan"—so Thoreau called
him—he reveled in sensuous beauty. His emotions mounted as
he contemplated this new land, this new people, the golden future
that beckoned—with all shackles broken, dedicated to freedom,
warm and palpitating from abundant life—a radiant world of
lovely women and manly men. He dwelt on Pisgah and from the
heights looked out on a divine democracy. "The life of the common people is the best part of the world's life," he exclaimed; "the
life of the common people is the life of God." And to his congregation intoxicated with his rhetoric he shouted, "Ye are gods! You
are crystalline, your faces are radiant!" [31] And the end and outcome envisaged by this prophet of the American Idea was a vaguely
grandiose fellowship, not of the Saints alone, but of all the thronging children of men, for of such is God's kingdom of this world.

As such lyric chants fell on Whitman's ears, they must have
quickened the ferment of thought that was eventually to clarify
for him the ideal of democracy, exalting it by making it warm and
human and social. The old Jacksonian leveling had been negative;
its freedoms had been individual, its anarchism selfish and unsocial. The great ideal of the fellowship had been lost in the
scramble for rights. Even transcendental democracy had narrowed its contacts. The hermit Thoreau in his cabin at Walden
Pond was no symbol of a generous democratic future. In the
struggle for liberty and equality the conception of fraternity had
been denied and the golden trinity of the Enlightenment dismem-
bered. It was this idea of fraternity, made human and hearty by
his warm love of men and women, that Whitman got from the
expansive fifties and built into his thinking. The conception of
solidarity, then entering the realm of proletarian thought through
the labors of Friedrich Engels and Karl Marx, was his response to
the new times—a response that infused his democratic faith with
a glowing humanism. Democracy spiritualized by Channing and
Emerson and Parker had suffered limitations from their lingering
Hebraisms—the Puritan passion for righteousness had imposed
strict ethical bounds on the democratic will. In Thoreau it
had been subjected to caustic skepticisms—the transcendental
individualist quizzically asked, "What *is* your people?" and refused to subject himself to the mass. But in Whitman all limitations and skepticisms were swept away by the feeling of comrade-

[31] *Ibid.*, p. 172.

ship. Flesh is kin to flesh, and out of the great reserves of life is
born the average man "with his excellent good manliness." Not
in distinction but in oneness with the whole is found the good life,
for in fellowship is love and in the whole is freedom; and love and
freedom are the law and the prophets. The disintegrations of the
earlier individualism must be succeeded by a new integration;
fear and hate and jealousy and pride have held men apart hitherto,
but love will draw them together. After all solidarity—the children
of America merging in the fellowship, sympathetic, responsive,
manlike yet divine, of which the poet should be the prophet and
literature provide the sermons.

It was a noble conception—washing away all the meanness that
befouled Jacksonian individualism—and it somewhat slowly found
its way to parity with his first master conception, the universal
ego, and settled into place in those later opening lines of *Leaves of
Grass*:

> One's-self I sing, a simple separate person,
> Yet utter the word Democratic, the word En-Masse.[32]

Then came the war to strengthen his faith in the common man.
As he watched the soldiers marching, fighting, suffering, he was
deeply impressed with their courage, patience, kindness, manliness, and came to reverence the deep wellspring of national being
from which issued such inexhaustible waters. It was not the few
but the many that gave him hope. "I never before so realized the
majesty and reality of the American people *en masse*," he wrote
of some regiments returning from the front. "It fell upon me like
a great awe." [33] And as he contemplated this fecund people, with
its sons and daughters issuing strong and wholesome from every
part of the land, there came to him a new conception of unity—
the Union that Lincoln loved—the drawing together into an indissoluble whole of the far-flung commonwealths—a realization of
the perfect State where reign liberty, equality, fraternity. Solidarity had taken on a political complexion but its life-blood was in
the veins of a free people.

But pagan though he was in his deeper nature, a child of the
emotional fifties, he was a transcendentalist also and his democratic
philosophy, as it took shape, bears unmistakable marks of the New
England school, supplemented perhaps by Quakerism. His well-

[32] *Leaves*, "One's-Self I Sing," p. 1, ll. 1–2.
[33] *Autobiographia*, p. 73. See also *Democratic Vistas*, p. 74.

known comment, "I was simmering and simmering; it was Emerson brought me to boil," suggests much, and in particular that the Enlightenment as it had come to him through the Jeffersonian heritage was supplemented and spiritualized by the Enlightenment as it had taken special form in passing through the transcendental mind. To this latter source must be traced the philosophic monism that served to draw his speculations together—a mystic sense of the divine oneness of life that took his major postulates in golden hands and fused them into a single spiritual whole. Thus instructed the "great Idea, the idea of perfect and free individuals," became curiously Emersonian in all its amplifications. There is the same glorification of consciousness and will, the same exaltation of the soul, the same trust in the buried life that men call instinct, the same imperious call to heed the voice of innate Godhood; and round and about this "perfect and free individual" is a mystical egocentric universe wherein the children of men may luxuriate in their divinity. The body is excellent as the soul is excellent; away, therefore, with all shamefacedness—the mean secretiveness, the putting of fingers to the lips in presence of the naked, the lies in presence of open palpable fact! For if this be indeed God's universe, and He is in and through it all, the children of Adam may stand in His presence unafraid—nay, rather with pride in their own excellence. "I exist as I am, that is enough," for "Divine am I inside and out, and I make holy whatever I touch or am touch'd from."

Whitman not only accepted Emerson with ungrudging loyalty but he dwelt much with Hegel and the German idealists, and with their help he penetrated curiously to the core of things, discovering there an inner spiritual reality that is the abiding substance behind the external manifestation. He had come upon food to sustain his faith in presence of the mean and base that compassed him about, and the puzzling contradictions of life no longer troubled him. If man be perfectible, if he be indeed a child of God though still in his infancy, how glorious must be the future toward which he is pressing! The evil will pass and the good remain.

Roaming in thought over the Universe, I saw the little that is Good
    steadily hastening towards immortality,
And the vast all that is call'd Evil I saw hastening to merge itself and
    become lost and dead.[34]

    [34] *Leaves*, "Roaming in Thought," p. 233.

When he turned from the oracular utterance of *Leaves of Grass* to sober exposition, he phrased it thus:

> There is, apart from mere intellect . . . a wondrous something that realises without argument . . . an intuition of the absolute balance, in time and space, of the whole of this multifarious, mad chaos of fraud, frivolity, hoggishness—this revel of fools, and incredible make-believe and general unsettledness, we call the *world;* a soul-sight of that divine clue and unseen thread which holds the whole congeries of things, all history and time, and all events however trivial, however momentous, like a leash'd dog in the hands of the hunter.[35]

To discover this divine clue and be drawn by the unseen thread into the orbit of things, to suffer the Me—the "human identity of understanding, emotions, spirit"—to fuse with the Not Me—"the whole of the material, objective universe and laws, with what is behind them in time and space"—became therefore for Whitman the grand objective of man's life and effort. This for him was the sum and substance of religion, which was no other than the binding of the individual back upon the whole. "A vast similitude interlocks all." And so from his conception of social solidarity he went forward to the conception of spiritual solidarity, and discovered religion to be the crown and glory of the "American Idea." Walt Whitman and America were to be the prophets of religion. "Easily at home in a natural world of prodigious brightness and scale, he . . . saw 'the most splendid race the sun ever shone upon,' and was urging the life of instinct and impulse. Love was the key— taking form and in 'Starting from Paumanok' he asserted his Love, Democracy, Religion—a new religion." [36] His message was purpose.

The soul,
Forever and forever—longer than soil is brown and solid—longer than water ebbs and flows.

I will make the poems of materials, for I think they are to be the most spiritual poems,
And I will make the poems of my body and of mortality,
For I think I shall then supply myself with the poems of my soul and of immortality.

I will make a song for these States that no one State may under any circumstances be subjected to another State,

. . . .

---

[35] "Carlyle from the American Point of View," in *Specimen Days, Prose Works*, pp. 174–175. [36] Rourke, *op. cit.*, p. 173.

I will sing the song of companionship,

         .   .   .

I will write the evangel-poem of comrades and of love,

         .   .   .

I am the credulous man of qualities, ages, races,
I advance from the people in their own spirit,

         .   .   .

I, too, following many and follow'd by many, inaugurate a religion, . . .

     .   .   .   .   .

Each is not for its own sake,
I say the whole earth and all the stars in the sky are for religion's sake.

I say no man has ever yet been half devout enough,
None has ever yet adored or worship'd half enough,
None has begun to think how divine he himself is, and how certain the future is.

I say that the real and permanent grandeur of these States must be their religion,
Otherwise there is no real and permanent grandeur;

         .   .   .

My comrade!
For you to share with me two greatnesses, and a third one rising inclusive and more resplendent,
The greatness of Love and Democracy, and the greatness of Religion.[37]

But this new religion of the mystical Whitman, in harmony with post-transcendental thought, was deeply impregnated with the spirit of science. He was in the very fullness of his powers when the conception of evolution came to him and he greeted it gladly, weaving it into all his thinking and discovering in it a confirmation of his idealistic philosophy. It was the evolution of Herbert Spencer, it must be remembered, that Whitman accepted—teleological, buoyantly optimistic, dominated by the conception of progress, shot through with the spirit of the Enlightenment; and such an evolution was a confirmation and not a denial of his transcendental premises. It supplemented rather than contradicted the tenets of his faith. Like Emerson as he saw the bounds of the material universe slowly pushed back by science he discovered amidst the constant change the presence of growth, development, the natural passage from the simple to the complex;

[37] *Leaves,* "Starting from Paumanok," p. 14, ll. 22–26; p. 15, ll. 1, 13, 19, 22–23; p. 16, ll. 2, 5–11; p. 17, ll. 7–10.

and like Theodore Parker he felt that this slow unfolding was no other than the unfolding of God, making Himself evident and unmistakable to man. Evolution was God's great plan. "The law over all, the law of laws, is the law of successions," he was persuaded; "for what is the present after all but a growth out of the past?" But noble as is the evidence of God's work discoverable by science, the soul is not content to rest with such evidence; it must seek out the reality behind the manifestation; and for this work the poet alone is fitted. The poet must complete the work of the scientist. The noble "Passage to India" is a lovely chant of human progress, the adventurous soul conquering the earth; but it must not pause there; it must seek God through the universe until it finds Him, and "Nature and Man shall be disjoin'd and diffused no more," and "All these hearts as of fretted children shall be sooth'd."

> Bathe me O God in thee, mounting to thee,
> I and my soul to range in range of thee.[38]

It was in this profoundly religious spirit that Whitman accepted science, built it into his poetry, rested confidently upon it; and it is this spirit that explains his formal statement in the "Song of Myself."

I accept Reality and dare not question it,
Materialism first and last imbuing.

Hurrah for positive science! long live exact demonstration!
Fetch stonecrop mixt with cedar and branches of lilac,
This is the lexicographer, this the chemist, this made a grammar of the
    old cartouches,
These mariners put the ship through dangerous unknown seas,
This the geologist, this works with the scalpel, and this is the mathematician.

Gentlemen, to you the first honors always!
Your facts are useful, and yet they are not my dwelling,
I but enter by them to an area of my dwelling.[39]

Equipped with such a philosophy and supported by such a faith Whitman accepted the twin duties laid upon him: to make clear to America her present failure in the great adventure—how far she had fallen short hitherto of any adequate democratic

[38] *Leaves*, p. 349, ll. 18-19. [39] *Leaves*, p. 43, ll. 9-17.

reality; and to mark out afresh the path to the Canaan of democratic hopes—reviving the early hopes of the Enlightenment and drawing in lovelier colors the democratic Utopia dreamed of for a hundred years. To be both critic and prophet—that he conceived to be his mission, a mission that he was faithful to for upwards of forty years. For the first duty he was admirably equipped. No other knew this America so intimately or so broadly—had penetrated so lovingly to the common heart and read so clearly its secret hopes and fears. That America was not yet a democracy— was very far indeed from a democracy—that it was a somewhat shoddy *bourgeois* capitalistic society shot through with cant and hypocrisy and every meanness, he saw with calm, searching eyes. No contemporary critic, not Godkin, not Emerson, saw more clearly the unlovely reality or dealt with it more scathingly, not only in *Leaves of Grass* but especially in his prose writings and in casual talk. Amongst scores of such passages a single one must serve for illustration.

I say that our New World democracy, however great a success in up-lifting the masses out of their sloughs, in materialistic development, products, and in a certain highly-deceptive superficial popular intellectuality, is, so far, an almost complete failure in its social aspects, and in really grand religious, moral, literary, and esthetic results. . . . Shift and turn the combinations of the statement as we may, the problem of the future of America is in certain respects as dark as it is vast. Pride, competition, segregation, vicious wilfulness, and license beyond example, brood already upon us. Unwieldy and immense, who shall hold in behemoth? who bridle leviathan? Flaunt it as we choose, athwart and over the roads of our progress loom huge uncertainty, and dreadful threatening gloom. It is useless to deny it: Democracy grows rankly up the thickest, noxious, deadliest plants and fruits of all—brings worse and worse invaders—needs newer, larger, stronger, keener compensations and compellers. Our lands embracing so much . . . hold in the breast that flame also, capable of consuming themselves, consuming us all. . . . Even today, amid these whirls, incredible flippancy, and blind fury of parties, infidelity, entire lack of first-rate captains and leaders, added to the plentiful meanness and vulgarity of the ostensible masses—that problem, the labor question, beginning to open like a yawning gulf, rapidly widening every year—what prospect have we? We sail a dangerous sea of seething currents, cross and under-currents, vortices,—all so dark and untried.[40]

As a realist Whitman granted the worst charges of the critics of democracy, but he probed deeper and brought other facts to light that modified the equation. It was the difficult question the old

[40] *Democratic Vistas, Prose Works,* pp. 254–255.

Federalists had posed and that Carlyle had lately revived—the question, is not this meanness inseparable from democracy? is not your people in fact a great beast, requiring the lash and the curb? It was the crux of the long debate over democracy and to it Whitman gave anxious and frequent consideration. In fighting the battle of 1790 over again, like Jefferson he rested his case on the native integrity and measureless potentiality of the "bulk-people"—they are the deep soil from which spring the abundant fruits and flowers of civilization. Gentle-nurtured folk do not understand this—they do not like the rank qualities of vital being. Matthew Arnold "always gives you the notion that he hates to touch the dirt—the dirt is so dirty! But everything comes out of the dirt—everything: everything comes out of the people . . . not university people, not F.F.V. people: people, people, just people!" In the rude, vital, natural man is the inexhaustible wellspring of good and evil; "He's got it all . . . not only the cruel, beastly, hoggish, cheating, bedbug qualities, but also the spiritual—the noble—the high-born"; [41] in "some ways" he is a "devil of a fellow," but he is not "all devil or even chiefly devil." [42] And because he is not chiefly devil such love and beauty and justice and comradeship as there is in the world, such progress in civilization as has been made hitherto, have been possible—how otherwise? If he has journeyed thus far out of the primeval slime, what bounds shall be set to his eventual journeyings? Why put out one's eyes with a mere handful of years?

So Whitman projected his democratic commonwealth far into the future; he would not have us believe that it had been realized here in America. Political democracy, the struggle for political rights that had engaged America hitherto, was only negative, a necessary preliminary to the ultimate reality. "I submit," he said, "that the fruition of democracy, on aught like a grand scale, resides altogether in the future," and its realization depends upon the use to which the people put their freedom. If from it emerges a proud and self-conscious individualism—"the quality of Being, in the object's self, according to its own central idea and purpose, and of growing therefrom and thereto—not criticism by other standards, and adjustments thereto"—then democracy on a grand scale will be possible and the self-reliant citizen will take his place in a free creative society. The ideal of the growing man, and the

[41] Traubel, *op. cit.*, Vol I, p. 174. [42] *Ibid.*, Vol. I, p. 285.

ideal of the perfect State—broadly social rather than narrowly political—these were his twin ideals; and the tie that is to bind men together in spontaneous solidarity is love. How characteristic is his sketch of the perfect city, and how deeply saturated with the Enlightenment! There is wanting only a physiocratic economics to make it perfect.

A great city is that which has the greatest men and women,

Where the city stands with the brawniest breed of orators and bards,
Where the city stands that is belov'd by these, and loves them in return and understands them,
Where no monuments exist to heroes but in the common words and deeds,
Where thrift is in its place, and prudence is in its place,
Where the men and women think lightly of the laws,
Where the slave ceases and the master of slaves ceases,
Where the populace rise at once against the never-ending audacity of elected persons,

Where outside authority enters always after the precedence of inside authority,
Where the citizen is always the head and ideal, and President, Mayor, Governor and what not, are agents for pay,
Where children are taught to be laws to themselves, and to depend on themselves,
Where equanimity is illustrated in affairs,

Where the city of faithfulest friends stands,
Where the city of the cleanliness of the sexes stands,

There the great city stands.[43]

Individualism, solidarity—on such strong bases he erected his ideal democracy, and the heaven-reaching temple will be overlaid with the rich arts and graces of a civilization worthy at last of the name. Such was the Enlightenment as it came to flower in the passionate idealism of Walt Whitman—a dream that was mocked and flouted and nullified by the Drews and Fisks and Goulds— the "hoggish, cheating, bedbug qualities" of a generation that scorned him for a beast. Even his stout faith was shaken at times

[43] *Leaves*, "Song of the Broad Axe," p. 160, ll. 7, 14–20, 21–22; p. 161, ll. 1–2, 6–7, 10.

by the infidelities of the Gilded Age. He was troubled by the gap
that opened between the free individual and the perfect State.
"I seem to be reaching for a new politics—for a new economy," he
confessed in 1888; "I don't quite know what, but for something." [44]
Although he protested, "The older I grow . . . the more I am
confirmed in my optimism, my democracy," he projected his hopes
farther into the future. He sympathized with the socialists but he
was not one of them. His revolutionary ardor abated and he
preferred in later years to call himself an evolutionist.[45] "Be
radical—be radical," he said to Traubel, "be not too damned
radical." [46] With his catholic sympathies that refused all bitterness he could not be a partisan—"after the best the partisan will
say something better will be said by the man." [47]

So in the twilight of the romantic revolution Whitman quietly
slipped away. The great hopes on which he fed have been belied
by after events—so his critics say;[48] as the great hopes of the
Enlightenment have been belied. Certainly in this welter of
today, with science become the drab and slut of war and industrialism, with sterile money-slaves instead of men, Whitman's
expansive hopes seem grotesque enough. Democracy may indeed
be only a euphemism for the rulership of fools. Yet in a time of
huge infidelities, in the dun breakdown and disintegration of all
faiths, it is not wholly useless to recall the large proportions of
Walt Whitman, his tenderness, his heartiness, his faith, his hope.
There was in him no weak evasion, no sniveling over the shards of
the goodly vessel broken at the well, but even when "old, alone,
sick, weak-down, melted-worn with sweat," a free and joyous
acceptance of life.

Thanks in old age—thanks ere I go,
For health, the midday sun, the impalpable air—for life, mere life,

   .   .   .   .

For all my days—not those of peace alone—the days of war the same,
For gentle words, caresses, gifts from foreign lands,
For shelter, wine and meat—for sweet appreciation,

   .   .   .   .

[44] Traubel, *op. cit.*, Vol. I, p. 101.
[45] *Ibid.*, Vol. I, pp. 193, 215.
[46] *Ibid.*, Vol. I, p. 223.
[47] *Ibid.*, Vol. I, p. 363.
[48] See Norman Foerster, *American Criticism*, pp. 211–222; Lucy Lockwood Hazard, *The Frontier in American Literature*, pp. 170–177.

For beings, groups, love, deeds, words, books—for colors, forms,
For all the brave strong men—devoted, hardy, men—who've forward
    sprung in freedom's help, all years, all lands,
For braver, stronger, more devoted men—(a special laurel ere I go, to
    life's war's chosen ones,
The cannoneers of song and thought—the great artillerists—the foremost
    leaders, captains of the soul:)
As soldier from an ended war return'd—As traveler out of myriads, to the
    long procession retrospective,
Thanks—joyful thanks!—a soldier's, traveler's thanks.[49]

A great figure, the greatest assuredly in our literature—yet perhaps only a great child—summing up and transmitting into poetry all the passionate aspirations of an America that had passed through the romantic revolution, the poet of selfhood and the prophet of brotherhood, the virile man and the catholic lover—how shall Walt Whitman become dumb or cease to speak to men unless the children of those who are now half-devil and half-God shall prove to be wholly devil—or wholly moron?

III

THE BACKWASH OF THE FRONTIER—MARK TWAIN

As Whitman contemplated the feeble literature purveyed by the worshipers of the genteel he asked with some irritation: "What is the reason in our time, our lands, that we see no fresh local courage, sanity, of our own—the Mississippi, stalwart Western men, real mental and physical facts, Southerners, etc., in the body of our literature?" That was in 1870 and the answer was at hand in the person of Mark Twain. Here at last was an authentic American— a native writer thinking his own thoughts, using his own eyes, speaking his own dialect—everything European fallen away, the last shred of feudal culture gone, local and western yet continental. A strange and uncouth figure in the eyes of Thomas Bailey Aldrich, yet the very embodiment of the turbulent frontier that had long been shaping a native psychology, and that now at last was turning eastward to Americanize the Atlantic seaboard. Yet in spite of a rare vein of humor, the outcropping of a rich and whimsical imagination, he made his way slowly to polite recognition. For years he was regarded by authoritative critics as little more than a buffoon, an extravagant fun-maker with a broad streak of western coarseness; and it was not till near the end, when he had long been an in-

[49] *Leaves,* "Thanks in Old Age," p. 435.

ternational figure, that the culture of the East accepted him. It was Howells then who pronounced him "the sole, the incomparable, the Lincoln of our literature . . . the very marrow of Americanism."

Just as that judgment was at the time, it needs qualification now. The marrow of Americanism is not the same substance from generation to generation. The outer environing life of a people works itself slowly into the bones and brings about subtle changes. Mark Twain was indubitably an embodiment of three centuries of American experience—frontier centuries, decentralized, leveling, individualistic; but the Americanism that issued from them came to its flower and was quickly succeeded by another kind as the fields of experience were re-plowed by industrialism and sowed to a different grain. Mark Twain was the child of a frontier past—as Lincoln was, as the Gilded Age was—and the America of today could no more breed him than it could breed Lincoln, or Greeley, or Whitman; his Americanism was the reflection of an environment that is no longer ours, in the slack folk-ways of the frontier that we have outgrown. Child of the Southwest in its early boom days, he was cradled in profitless schemes and nourished on dreams of vast potential wealth. The frontier spirit was an effervescence in his blood and golden expectations flung their mirage over the drab reality. As a boy he took impress from a kindly, ignorant, slave-holding, Calvinistic village world, and he quitted the slattern village life to plunge into the picturesque traffic of the Mississippi in the boom days when every river pilot drove his boat full steam ahead. Then the Far West of silver mines and the Golden Gate took him in hand—a gambling, romantic, optimistic frontier, feverish with flush times, "a beggar's revel of potential millionaires without the price of a square meal." [50] And finally this buoyant, irreverent adolescent was taken in hand by the Far East: by New England respectability in the persons of Olivia Langdon of Elmira, William Dean Howells of Cambridge, Twitchell and Warner of Hartford; and by New York in the persons of Carnegie and Gilder and Whitelaw Reid and Henry H. Rogers, to be made over into a man of the world.

Such were his origins and his schooling. All his life he remained a boy, with the imitativeness of youth, and yet with something deep within him that cherished its own integrity. Quick to take color from his environment and at home in crowds, he lived nevertheless in the solitude of his own heart. Acutely conscious of his

[50] Lucy Lockwood Hazard, *The Frontier in American Literature*, p. 223.

rough western ways, he admired the culture of the Langdons and
the refined art of Howells, and he wanted to be approved by them.
A kinsman of Beriah Sellers, he delighted in the great barbecue
and wanted to carve great portions for himself, to heap up his
plate as others were doing. His reactions to experience were always
emotional. He was not a Walt Whitman to penetrate curiously to
the core of his own being and grow thence outwardly, content to
wait till the world came round to him. He loved to make a splurge,
to be talked of, to be in the public eye, to live on an ample scale;
he accepted the world's standards and wished to be measured by
them. It was characteristic of the frontier. Wanting other standards, the frontier measured success by obvious material standards. Its aggressive individualism was never spiritual or intellectual or cultural. So with all his heritage of generations of
frontier individualism he never achieved an intellectual or spiritual
unity, an untroubled conscious integrity, as Emerson did and
Whitman did. He never was at home in the world of catholic
thought, but all his life he suffered from the petty inhibitions of
his origins. He could not throw off the frontier—its psychology
and its morality were too deeply intertwined with his primitive
self; and the result was a harassing inner conflict that left him
maimed.

Yet with all his shortcomings—because of them indeed—Mark
Twain is an immensely significant American document. He is a
mirror reflecting the muddy cross-currents of American life as the
frontier spirit washed in, submerging the old aristocratic landmarks. To know Mark Twain is to know the strange and puzzling
contradictions of the Gilded Age. With unconscious fidelity he
reveals its crudity, its want of knowledge, discipline, historical
perspective; its intellectual incapacity to deal with the complexities of a world passing through the twin revolutions of industrialism and science. And he reflects with equal fidelity certain
other qualities that go far to redeem the meanness: a great creative
power; an eager idealism, somewhat vague but still fine; a generous
sympathy; a manly independence that strove to think honestly;
a passionate hatred of wrong and injustice and an honest democratic respect for men as men. A significant if not an unsoiled or
heroic document!

That in his later years an impassable gulf opened between Mark
Twain and his generation, that the buoyant humorist of the sev-

enties ripened into the bitter satirist of the nineties, is a matter that has been much remarked upon. The fact is clear enough but the explanation is not so clear. In part no doubt—as Van Wyck Brooks has pointed out—the change resulted from a thwarting of the creative artist by a disastrous surrender to the ideals of the Gilded Age; in part, also, it was the inevitable toll exacted by the passing years. A humane and generous spirit cannot long watch with indifference the motley human caravan hastening to eternity—cannot find food for laughter alone in the incredible meanness and folly of men cheating and quarreling in a wilderness of graves. Tenderness, chivalry, love of justice, are poor bucklers to withstand the blows of fate, and Mark Twain had little skill in defense. The humorist like the poet is sensitively responsive to life and the scars multiply fast. Endowed with a nature not unlike Swift's in its fierce rage at inhumanity, not unlike Sir Philip Sidney's in its romantic chivalry, he was not a stoic to endure with equanimity. He was foredoomed to suffer vicariously. The comment he wrote Howells in 1899 throws a white light on the man. "I have been reading the morning paper," he said. "I do it every morning—well knowing that I shall find in it the usual depravities and basenesses and hypocrisies and cruelties that make up civilization, and cause me to put in the rest of the day pleading for the damnation of the human race."

Yet granting so much, and granting also a morbid conscience that harassed him with self-condemnation—"What a man sees in the human race is merely himself in the deep and honest privacy of his own heart"—it still remains true that the bleakness of his later years was due in part, at least, to the insubstantial dwelling he chose to live in. The architects of the Gilded Age were jerry-builders, and Mark Twain found his jerry-built house a poor protection against the winter winds. It was perhaps not greatly his fault that he built so flimsily. He was too willing to be caught in the web of material things. He could not reach out for companionship with the great earth. Hamlin Garland in a bleak Dakota shack found help and comfort in the philosophy of Taine, but Mark Twain could not get outside his own skin. He could not break a path through the provincialism of his environment. He was held prisoner to his own thoughts and his only release was through the window of imagination. When harassed beyond endurance he sought release in writing that hid the evidence of his rebellion.

What would Livy say, what would the American public say, if they knew he had come to deny all the tribal gods!

There is no more pathetic figure in American literature than Mark Twain, alone and solitary amid the blatant American crowd, living in a dreary wash of speeches and banquets, spinning the threads of a rebellious philosophy out of his own bowels, unaware of what others were spinning, regarding himself as a dangerous fellow and stowing away in his strong-box intellectual bombs that he thought too explosive for the Gilded Age to play with. In his intellectual isolation he could not take the measure of his speculations and he did not realize how common were such conclusions— that his own generation indeed, under the tutelage of the physical sciences, was fast drifting in the same direction, and that the clouds of pessimism were obscuring for many the brighter horizons of an earlier day. If he had known Henry Adams as intimately as he knew Henry H. Rogers, very likely his eyes would have been opened to many things that would have done him good. As it was he knew only that his speculations ran counter to the formal creed of his middle-class neighbors and friends. To deny the dogmas of the conventional orthodoxy and in the face of a smug optimism to assert a mechanistic pessimism, was an unpleasant business that he would have avoided if he could.

But he couldn't avoid it wholly, and in that fact is to be found the thread that runs through his later life, giving to it such unity and coherence as it possessed. It is this: here was a thoroughly honest mind, that hated all sham and quackery and humbug, and a singularly warm heart, that hated all wrong and cruelty and injustice; and this honest mind and chivalrous heart, deceived and led astray by the mass *mores*, espoused and defended such fragments of ideals, such bits of truth, as he came upon in his solitary brooding, until driven from one stronghold after another he came to doubt the adequacy of all strongholds and took refuge in a black pessimism—God is a malignant being, the universe is a machine, and man is a creature of determinism. It was a fierce and stark reaction from the emotionalism of the fifties—from Beecher's God of love and Whitman's religion of democracy. His earlier loyalty to half-gods had brought him at last to deny all the gods. And so a maimed giant, stumbling and uncertain, he made such way as he could; and his journeyings wrung from him many a fierce comment that his generation did not understand.

When the milk of western humor curdled in his veins, a Mark Twain emerged who was a puzzle to the Gilded Age. A humorist who was a good Republican and business man, the Gilded Age could understand; but a satirist who launched his shafts at sacred things —at evangelical religion, the Republican party, the government at Washington, the damned human race itself—it could not understand. The professional fun-maker had outgrown his audience. Expecting the familiar exaggeration, they accounted his bitterest sally a characteristic whimsy, and laughed when he commented bitterly on "this plodding sad pilgrimage, this pathetic drift between the eternities," or when he exclaimed, "Everything human is pathetic. The secret source of Humor is not joy but sorrow. There is no humor in heaven." But the significant thing is that in the end the tyrannizing *mores* did not conquer, they did not destroy him wholly; but such convictions as he had hewn from puzzling experience, however bleak or repellent they might be, he clung to firmly, desperately, and at last flung them in the face of the Gilded Age that had kept him prisoner.

The slow drift of Mark Twain's thought from humor to satire— it smacks of Philistinism to call it progress with its many false alarums and excursions and its huge frontier wastefulness—is plain enough to anyone who will take the trouble to chart his course. Roughly it falls into definite stages: the swaggering gayety of western youth in *Innocents Abroad* and *Roughing It*—the mood of flush times, down-grade with the brakes off; then a gay plunge into satire in *The Gilded Age;* then the West recalled in middle life—*Tom Sawyer, Life on the Mississippi, Huckleberry Finn*— living over again a youth that is gone; then an excursion into the Middle Ages—*The Prince and the Pauper* and *A Connecticut Yankee in King Arthur's Court*—a romantic flare-up of the democratic passions of the Enlightenment; then the search for the ideal in *Joan of Arc*—the dream of the perfect woman, the Domnei of James Branch Cabell; and finally *The Mysterious Stranger* and *What is Man?*—a fierce satire of disillusion, the cry of an idealist who realizes at last how greatly he has been cheated by his dreams.

That he should have begun by burlesquing life was itself a broad sign of his frontier origins. Since the first crossing of the Allegheny Mountains a swaggering extravagance of speech had been a hallmark of the Westerner. In part this swagger was an unconscious defense-mechanism against the drabness of frontier life; and in part it was the spontaneous expression of new experiences in an untrammeled world, the spirit of wilderness-leveling. Its procreative source would seem to have been the Ohio River where the rough flatboatmen bequeathed the Mike Fink legend to literature; and it expanded in the huge Davy Crockett hoax— a hoax that would have tickled the ribs of Mark Twain had he traced its genesis and progress, as a colossal example of how the damned human race loves to be humbugged. It developed further in Gus Longstreet's *Georgia Scenes* with its grotesque Ransy Sniffle —sorriest of backwoods heroes, too mean-spirited to ruffle like Canebrake Davy; and in Joseph Baldwin's *Flush Times of Alabama and Mississippi*, with its greasy frontier blackguard, Colonel Simon Suggs.

This earliest backwoods humor had been done in realistic colors and bears the impress of authenticity. But the school that succeeded—John Phoenix, Artemus Ward, Petroleum V. Nasby— quickly conventionalized its technique, relying on burlesque, tall lying, distorted spelling, genial philosophy. The picaresque strain was softened and perverted by deliberate human-interest touches— a better case must be made out for the untutored children of nature. It was this humor that Mark Twain inherited, and he enriched it with a wealth dug from his own large and generous nature. An incorrigible idealist, as all great humorists must be, he recreated some of the earlier types, translating Colonel Simon Suggs into Colonel Sellers, and Ransy Sniffle into Huck Finn. It was a glorious transformation, but the result lacked something of the soiled reality of the earlier blackguards. Yet underneath his idealism was a generous deposit of the common mud of life. The spirit of Mike Fink was never far from Mark Twain. It haunted him like an evil genius, refusing to be exorcised by Olivia Clemens, and it found vent in sly literary sprees that begot offspring to be handed about furtively and chuckled over by the sons of Adam; but for the most part it was kept in strict subjection to the proprieties of Elmira and Hartford.

Roughing It and *The Gilded Age* are brilliant complementary pictures of the gaudy frontier spirit that was washing in upon the staid realm of the genteel, to the vast concern of such genteelists as Thomas Bailey Aldrich. The former is a buoyant chronicle of the West of Captain Carver and Wild Bill Hickok, the West of the Pony Express, the Comstock lode, the bad man and the lynch law, a land of young men in red flannel shirts, heavy boots, and six-shooters, who feared neither God nor the devil. Bret Harte in San Francisco first realized the literary possibilities of this picturesque world, and his tales of life in the mining-camps were received with a shout of approval. But Bret Harte had never been a miner. He was not realist enough, nor honest enough, to portray the West in its stark, grotesque reality. He was only a literary middleman who skillfully purveyed such wares as his eastern readers wanted. In consequence he coated his tales with a sentimental picaresque—pandered to the common taste by discovering nuggets of pure gold in the dregs and outcasts of the mining-camps. But Mark Twain was too honest for that. He had been a part of the flush times and had seen the economic process work itself out. He had seen the grub-stake prospector succeeded by the wild-cat speculator, and him in turn followed by the eastern capitalist. He had seen the mining frontier become a thing of the past in a single decade, with the Comstock lode in the hands of competent exploiters and the pick-and-shovel miners plunging deeper into the mountains to pursue their feverish hopes. From that experience he had learned a lesson he was to carry East with him. "Because we judged that we had learned," he said, "the real secret of success in silver mining, which was, not to mine the silver ourselves by the sweat of our brows and the labor of our hands, but to *sell* the ledges to the dull slaves of toil and let them do the mining." [51]

It was the great lesson of his generation, and thus instructed he proposed to sell his brains in the best market. Exploitation was the royal road to wealth and he was eager to exploit both himself and his fellows. Yet not all of Mark Twain was thus eager. Deep in his heart was another Mark Twain, the artist, the chivalrous lover of justice, the simple child puzzled at life—and this Mark Twain was already plotting treason against the exploiting Mark Twain. For the first time this deeper self got out of hand in *The Gilded Age*. As he contemplated the common scoundrelism at Washington and elsewhere, his anger exuded in scathing satire. He hated the dirty thing, yet he seems never to have realized that such scoundrelism was only the backwash of the spirit of exploitation and that he himself was riding on its waves. With the soap-bubble dreams of Colonel Sellers he dealt lovingly, for he was sketching his own

[51] Vol. I, Chapter XXXIII, p. 237.

origins; the Colonel and the Hawkinses were his own flesh and blood and the Tennessee lands were an old investment about which the family dreams of wealth had been woven for years. He delighted in the Colonel's childlike faith that prosperity only awaited a vote of Congress—with adequate appropriations, of course. He asked no questions about unearned increment; to question that would have been treason to the frontier philosophy. So into Colonel Sellers he put all that was naïve and lovable in the Gilded Age. But Senator Dillworthy was another matter. Hypocrite and corruptionist, he was laying obscene hands on sacred things, betraying his high trust for sordid ends. Mark Twain hated graft—the word had not been coined but the ugly thing was there—and with the innocence of his generation he damned the agent and overlooked the principal. It was not his fault. The economics of history was a closed book to Americans of the seventies, and even Henry Adams in his analysis of the current corruption in his novel *Democracy* was no better than a mole nosing blindly underground.

He had opened another door to his genius and discovered the satirist. There lay the real Mark Twain. But the wares of the satirist were not in demand at the barbecue, so he closed the door and fell to purveying what the public wanted. *Tom Sawyer* was in part a malicious thrust at the Sunday School tale, and in part a whimsical pronouncement of the natural rights of the small boy. But it is in *Huckleberry Finn*—the one great picaresque tale of the frontier—that the western philosophy of Mark Twain, a philosophy that derives straight from the old naturistic school, crops out most sharply. It is a drama of the struggle between the individual and the village *mores*, set in a loose picturesque framework, and exemplifying the familiar thesis that the stuff of life springs strong and wholesome from the great common stock. Huck Finn is a child of nature who has lived close to the simple facts of life, unperverted by the tyrannies of the village that would make a good boy of him. He had got his schooling from the unfenced woods, from the great river that swept past him as he idly fished, from the folk-tales of negroes and poor whites, from queer adventures with Tom Sawyer; and from such experiences he had got a code of natural ethics. Then he found himself on the raft with Jim the runaway nigger, and his little pagan soul felt the stirrings of the problem of right and wrong. The village code and the natural code clashed and the conflict was terrifying. The village code warned him that hell yawned for one who helped a slave escape, and the human code warned him that betrayal was a blackguardly thing. With the fear of hell upon him he wrote to Miss Watson, and then his sense of the kindliness of Jim, the honest humanity under the black skin, rose up in fierce protest.

> It was a close place. I took [the letter] up, and held it in my hands. I was a-trembling, because I'd got to decide, forever, betwixt two things, and I knowed it. I studied for a minute, sort of holding my breath, and then says to myself:
> "All right, then, I'll *go* to hell"—and tore it up.
> It was awful thoughts and awful words, but they was said. And I let them stay said; and never thought no more about reforming.[52]

It was a triumph over the sacred tribal law of conformity—the assertion of the individual will in opposition to society—and it reveals the heart of Mark Twain's philosophy. The rebel Huck is no other than the rebel Mark Twain whose wrath was quick to flame up against the unrighteous customs and laws of caste. If men were only honest realists—that is, if they were men and not credulous fools—how quickly the stables might be cleansed and life become decent and humane. If only the good brains could be segregated and trained in a real "man-factory," the history of civilization might become something the angels need not weep over as they read it. It all comes back to an honest realism that in accepting fact will clear away the superstitious fogs in which men have floundered and suffered hitherto. The one sacred duty laid on every rational being is the duty of rebellion against sham—to deny the divinity of clothes, to thrust out quack kings and priests and lords, to refuse a witless loyalty to things. This creed of the rebel is written all through Mark Twain's later work, edging his satire and lending an Emersonian note to his individualism. In such a passage as this it emerges sharply:

> You see my kind of loyalty was loyalty to one's country, not to its institutions or its office-holders. The country is the real thing, the substantial thing, the eternal thing; it is the thing to watch over, and care for, and be loyal to; institutions are extraneous, they are its mere clothing, and clothing can wear out, become ragged, cease to be comfortable, cease to protect the body from winter, disease, death. To be loyal to rags, to shout for rags, to worship rags—that is a loyalty to unreason, it is pure animal; it belongs to monarchy, was invented by monarchy; let monarchy keep it. I was from Connecticut, whose Constitution declares "that all

[52] Chapter 31.

political power is inherent in the people, and all free governments are founded on their authority and instituted for their benefit; and that they have *at all times* an undeniable and indefeasible right to *alter their form of government* in such manner as they may think expedient."

Under that gospel, the citizen who thinks he sees that the commonwealth's political clothes are worn out, and yet holds his peace and does not agitate for a new suit, is disloyal; he is a traitor. That he may be the only one who thinks he sees this decay, does not excuse him; it is his duty to agitate anyway, and it is the duty of others to vote him down if they do not see the matter as he does.[53]

In the Middle Ages clothes-worship had been exalted to a religion, he believed, and he turned with gusto to reply to the aristocratic romanticism of Sir Walter, who, delighting in the picturesque company gathered in the great hall, forgot to penetrate to the *oubliettes*—is not the word commentary enough on the ways of the seigneur?—where nameless wretches were rotting under the walls of the castle. He had small patience with the cult of medievalism that was turning such men as Henry Adams and William Morris back to the Middle Ages as to their lost home. He had the frontier contempt for medieval ways, and for the *ancien régime* that was the last rags of the Middle Ages. The French Revolution had thrust the abomination away forever, and he thanked God for that "ever memorable and blessed Revolution, which swept a thousand years of . . . villainy away in one swift tidal wave of blood." He had no tears for Marie Antoinette. What was the Terror but "a settlement of that hoary debt in the proportion of half a drop of blood for each hogshead of it that had been pressed by slow tortures out of that people in the weary stretch of ten centuries of wrong and shame and misery the like of which was not to be mated but in hell . . . that unspeakably bitter and awful Terror which none of us has been taught to see in its vastness or pity as it deserves."[54] The past that had been consumed in that fierce conflagration had been a brutal, tyrannical, superstitious past, and not till king and priest had been flung out on the dung-heap did the people walk their native soil as free men. The whole king business was preposterous to him; with Freneau he cried, "Kings are the choicest curse that man e'er knew." The battle against medievalism had been fought and won and why go maundering back over past battlefields, when other battles await?[55]

[53] *The Connecticut Yankee*, N. Y., 1917, p. 107.
[54] *Ibid.*, Chapter XIII, pp. 105–106.
[55] Cf. Whitman's view, *The Gathering of the Forces*, Vol. II, pp. 284–286.

Mark Twain's passionate republicanism was a product of the Enlightenment as it had passed into the psychology of western Americans, and it retained the militant idealism of Jeffersonian times. It is shot through with the nature philosophy. In *The Prince and the Pauper*, the heir of Offal Court and the heir of the Tudors are both children of nature, endowed with warm hearts, generous sympathies, and clever wits. Put rags on the prince and robes on the pauper and their own kin cannot tell them apart. The latter, indeed, promises to make the better king, for he has suffered the lot of the subject, and not till the prince has put on rags does he come to know his people. It is caste that breeds cruelty and wrong; the brutalities of the English criminal code were deviltries devised by king and nobles to safeguard their stealings. Only when the laws spring from the people are they just. "The world is made wrong," cried the young king when he was brought out of prison to watch the burning at the stake of two women who had befriended him—women whose only crime was that of being Baptists—"the world is made wrong, kings should go to school to their own laws, at times, and so learn mercy." And this great lesson of mercy is exemplified in the acts of the pauper king, who during his brief reign tempers the harshness of the law with a sense of justice learned, like Huck Finn's, from sharp contact with reality.

It is in *A Connecticut Yankee in King Arthur's Court*—a curious medley, half philippic and half farce—that Mark Twain's passion for justice rises to white heat. The book has been grossly misunderstood. It is not an attack on chivalry—at least not primarily; it is rather an attack on thirteen centuries of reputed Christian civilization that under pretense of serving God has enslaved and despoiled the children of God. The keen satire is given point and edge by the long tragic perspective. Thirteen centuries heavy with sorrow and misery and frustrated hopes—a meaningless succession of foolish and futile generations, wandering in fogs of their own brewing, hagridden by superstitions, deceived and exploited by priest and noble, with no will to be free—here is a perspective to correct our callow enthusiasms, our revolutionary hopes! Why indeed should we expect men to possess the will to freedom, seeing that each generation is molded after the likeness of the past and none has been free? There is change, advance and recession, but the story of the generations is no more than a "sad drift between

the eternities," without purpose or meaning. In the brain of the
Connecticut Yankee are secrets hidden from the children of King
Arthur's time—a curious ability to use the forces of nature, some
glimmerings of social justice. But to what purpose have Hartford
and the nineteenth century used their knowledge? It is a world of
slaves still as it was in King Arthur's day. The human animal
cannot lift himself to heaven by his own bootstraps, and heaven
will not stoop to lift him. For a "clammy atmosphere of reverence,
respect, deference," it has substituted smartness, vulgarity, irreverence.

As one slips back and forth between the two worlds the satire
takes on vaster perspectives; it cuts deep into all civilizations, for
all alike are sham, all have issued from the conquest of man's native
intelligence by his superstitions that are too useful to his masters
to be dissipated. Clearly in Mark Twain's philosophy of history
the hopes of the Enlightenment are fading. Passionately dedicated
to the program of the Enlightenment—freedom, individuality,
humanitarianism, democracy—his faith in reason, free will,
progress, was burning low, in presence of the historical record.
The determinism that lurked at the bottom of John Locke's
psychology, unperceived by the French idealists, was revealing
itself to Mark Twain and he was already trimming his sails to the
chill winds blowing from the outer spaces of a mechanistic cosmos.

More immediately of course *A Connecticut Yankee* is an attack on the aristocratic romanticism of Sir Walter. There is little
loitering in the great hall—except to comment on the coarseness
of the knights and ladies—and much poking about in unlovely
secret places where one comes upon a rare collection of human
animals thrust away in the *oubliettes* or pigging together in mean
huts. Few chapters in American literature are so noble in their
saeva indignatio, so beautiful in their stern simplicity, as certain
sketches of the king's progress through his realm—not a royal
progress but a peasant's. There are no tears in them, they go far
beyond that. The scene in the smallpox hut where the wife is glad
her husband and daughters are dead—they are either in heaven or
hell, it makes little difference, for they are no longer in Britain
and so are happy; and the scene of the young mother hanged for
stealing a piece of cloth of an ell's length or so, hanged that property in Britain might be safe—such pictures reveal how far he had
traveled from the days of *Roughing It*. He was no longer a good

Federalist-Whig concerned about exploitation and the safeguards of property. Although he voted the Republican ticket he made merry over the tariff [56] and he frankly hated the dominant Republican property-consciousness. Like Lincoln he was for the man rather than the dollar when the rights of the two clashed. In these later years he was steadily drifting to the left, on the side of the social underling, sympathetic with those who do the work of the world. "He never went so far in socialism, as I have gone," said Howells, "if he went that way at all . . . but from the first he had a luminous vision of organized labor as the only present help for workingmen. . . . There was a time when I was afraid that his eyes were a little holden from the truth; but in the very last talk I heard from him I found that I was wrong, and that this great humorist was as great a humanist as ever." [57]

It is good for an American to read *A Connecticut Yankee*—and *Joan of Arc* as well; for in them is a flame that sears and shrivels the mean property-consciousness which lays a blight on every civilization. In the peasant girl of Domrémy, the rapt mystic led by her Voices, Mark Twain found his ideal, the lily that bloomed out of the muck of medieval times; and as he contemplated her life and work he was lifted to the plane of worship. She had waged heroic warfare against the embattled lies and shams and treacheries of a sordid age, and that she should have died at the stake was inevitable. What other reward was to be expected from bishops and kings and suchlike spawn of the devil? Not till the people grow to manhood can any savior help them, and in that day they will need no savior but themselves. The Sieur Louis de Conte struggles with the idea confusedly.

I believe that some day it will be found out that peasants are people. Yes, beings in a great many respects like ourselves. And I believe that some day *they* will find this out, too—and then! Well, then I think they will rise up and demand to be regarded as a part of the race, and that by consequence there will be trouble. Whenever one sees in a book or in a king's proclamation those words 'the nation,' they bring before us the upper classes; only those; we know no other 'nation;' for us and the kings no other 'nation' exists. But from the day I saw old D'Arc the peasant acting and feeling just as I should have acted and felt myself, I have carried the conviction in my heart that our peasants are not merely animals, beasts of burden put here by the good God to produce food and comfort for the 'nation,' but something more and better. You look incredulous.

[56] See Chapter 33.   [57] W. D. Howells, *My Mark Twain*, p. 43.

Well, that is your training; it is the training of everybody; but as for me, I thank that incident for giving me a better light, and I have never forgotten it.[58]

No Bayard ever did his devoir more knightly to his lady than Mark Twain to Joan, finding in the noble drama of her life the romance he had not found at Arthur's court. The knights of the Round Table were "but ghosts fighting in the fog," but Jeanne D'Arc was human and lovable and divine. And then the outlet through which his idealism had found release slowly closed in, and he was left alone with his comfortless speculations. What profits it to rail at the damned human race when man has about as much chance for happiness as a blind puppy in a sack? The bitter lot of humanity is due not to institutions alone or chiefly, it is a part of the mad plan of a bleak mechanical universe. For Mark Twain the solid earth was dissolving, leaving only a rack behind. It is futile to lament. A sympathetic heart, indeed, is the last and bitterest irony—for why weep over an evil exhalation! *"Life itself is only a vision, a dream . . . Nothing exists save empty space— and you."*

In a little while you will be alone in shoreless space, to wander its limitless solitudes without friend or comrade forever—for you will remain a *thought*, the only existent thought, and by your nature inextinguishable, indestructible. But I, your poor servant, have revealed you to yourself and set you free. Dream other dreams, and better. Strange, indeed, that you should not have suspected that your universe and its contents were only dreams, visions, fiction! Strange, because they are so frankly and hysterically insane—like all dreams . . . the silly creations of an imagination that is not conscious of its freaks—in a word that they are a dream, and you the maker of it. . . .[59]

So, like Cabell, Mark Twain asserts that man must build within and by letting his dreams flow out create for himself such shelter as he can against the chill of the eternal void. A flea on the epidermis of earth, nevertheless he is thought and thought is deathless. To such a conclusion did the buoyant youth of *Roughing It* arrive in the dun twilight years. *The Mysterious Stranger* is only *Tom Sawyer* retold in the midnight of his disillusion.

What an ending for a child of the Gilded Age! In his youth a complete frontiersman, with vast potential wealth within him, he hewed and hacked at his genius, working the easiest veins,

[58] *Joan of Arc*, Chapter 37, p. 290.
[59] *The Mysterious Stranger*, p. 151.

exploiting the most accessible resources, wasting much to cash in on a little.   And when in the end the fool's gold turned to ashes in his mouth, as a frontiersman still he pursued his way alone, a solitary pioneer exploring the universe, seeking a homestead in an ironical cosmos, until overwhelmed by the intolerable solitude he made mock at all the gods.   What a commentary on the Gilded Age!

CHAPTER III
CHANGING THEORY

UNLIKE as were Thomas Bailey Aldrich, Walt Whitman, and Mark Twain, they belonged equally to an America that was passing. In consequence of the silent drift towards consolidation new philosophies were preparing that were to rephrase the familiar American ideals and adapt current political and economic theory to the needs of the new order. For a decade or more the significance of that drift was obscured by the last great wave of decentralization that swept across the prairie commonwealths; but when the frontier had been pushed to the Pacific Northwest and the free lands had passed into private ownership, the movement of consolidation gathered momentum swiftly. Primarily economic in its origins, it went forward on even foot with the industrial revolution. The vast increase in population, the unprofitable expansion of agriculture, the augmenting resources of liquid capital, the new potentialities revealed by industrialism, were all engaged in the work of transforming a scattered agricultural people into an urbanized industrial people.

And then came the railways to hasten a movement that was implicit in the nature of things. Effective nationality in America issued more immediately from fluid communication than perhaps any other cause. A depressing spirit of isolation—of provincial aloofness—had lain like a heavy weight on the colonial mind. The barriers of distance were made formidable by a rugged untamed country, and to open up free communication was an arduous undertaking. Yet easy communication must be provided if economic development were to go forward. In the early years of the nineteenth century vast plans and great outlays of money went into the work of linking the sundered portions of the country by a system of waterways. The Erie canal, the great lakes, the Ohio and the Mississippi, were creating their own America, picturesque and individual, when the process of differentiation was rudely broken across by the iron rails that ran East and West, disregarding natural barriers and breaking down traditional frontiers. It was the railways that tied the continent effectively together, providing the needed transportation to make possible a national economic system. With the laying of the Union Pacific rails in the late sixties the destiny of America as a self-sufficient economic unity was fixed. Henceforth for an indeterminate period the drift of tendency would be from the outlying frontiers to industrial centers, and with that drift would come far-reaching changes in the daily routine of life. The machine would reach into the remotest villages to disrupt the traditional domestic economy, and the division of labor would substitute for the versatile frontiersman the specialized factory-hand. A new urban psychology would displace the older agrarian, and with the new psychology would come other philosophies in response to the changing realities.

I

WINDS OF ECONOMIC THEORY

So profound a revolution could not fail to dislocate the foundations of all traditional schools of thought. Economic and political theory were both thrown out of their earlier beds to flow in new channels. By force of gravitation the main stream of economic theory—like the main stream of political theory—poured into the broadening channels of capitalism, and only the lesser vagrant currents followed the old channels of agrarianism or the new channels of proletarianism. There was much speculation on the disturbing phenomena of the great change, and current economic theory was slow to settle into the conformities of a school. It divided sharply, not only between the advocates of capitalism and agrarianism, but between those who accepted the classical English theory and those who believed that economic conditions in America warranted an independent American school. The first group of professional economists—Henry C. Carey, Francis A. Walker, David A. Wells—made its appearance, and a very considerable group of amateurs—free-lance economists and fireside theorists—contributed to the speculation of the times in the measure of their intelligence. These latter have received scant attention, since the battle went against them; nevertheless they do not deserve to be forgotten, for most often they were an expression of the social conscience of the times—a homely protest against the exploitation of farmer and workingman by the rising capitalism.

But because they essayed to turn the course of "manifest destiny" they were ignored or roughly ridden down, and only one of them— Henry George—is still widely influential.

In the primitive early days of America economic theory had been a simple homespun product, woven on fireside looms, and following simple domestic patterns. With the rise of industrialism it passed into the keeping of stockbrokers and textile manufacturers and retail merchants who were looked upon as authoritative expounders of the new science of wealth. In his *Elements of Political Economy*, first published in 1837 and for forty years a standard textbook in American colleges, Francis Wayland accepted this view and offered an apology for treating of the subject at all. "It may possibly be urged," he said, "that the Author, having had no experience in mercantile business, should have left this subject to be treated of by practical men." In the days of Henry Clay this view established itself in the halls of Congress, where politicians who had never heard of Ricardo were on profitably intimate terms with Nick Biddle, and respected the interests of influential constituents far more than the principles of Manchesterism. With the appearance of professional economists the breach between economic theory and legislative votes widened to a chasm. Ignored by the politicians except in so far as their views fell in with the current paternalism, the economists retreated to the quiet of the schools and there spun their webs quite harmlessly. Youthful undergraduates were fed on a modified English classical theory in which the pessimism of Ricardo and Malthus, bred of the bitter dislocations of English industrial life, was diluted with an optimism more suited to the temper of the new world.

The academic economists, it must be confessed, were in an unhappy position, not unlike that of the earlier Calvinists. They lived as remote from the realities of life as did those old ministers. Trained in the orthodox English school they felt bound to defend *laissez faire;* yet as members of universities dependent on wealthy patrons they could not well offend powerful interests that wanted none of their free-trade theory. On the whole they stuck pretty manfully to their guns, and from Wayland to Sumner they upheld the abstract principle of free competition; but what they could do in other ways to appease the wrath of the protectionists they did heartily, and the steady rapprochement of academic economic theory and capitalism was foreordained in the nature of things academic. Agrarian and proletarian economics were granted no hearing in the colleges. Other schools than the English classical were not countenanced, Henry George was ridiculed and the left-wing European economists—great thinkers like Sismondi, Saint-Simon, Louis Blanc, Bastiat, Proudhon, Engels, and Karl Marx—were pretty much ignored by professors of economics in the America of the Gilded Age. Something of the intellectual sterility of the genteel tradition descended upon our academic economists; yet amongst them were vigorous and capable minds that must not be overlooked.

I

HENRY C. CAREY

Henry C. Carey, son of the vigorous Irish Republican, Matthew Carey, who made *The American Museum* one of the ablest of the eighteenth-century American magazines, may perhaps be justly called our first professional economist. The eighty-six years of his life were filled with enormous labors in the twin fields of economics and sociology. He did his own thinking from a basis of facts that he was at great pains to gather and tabulate, and his intellectual unfolding followed naturally the current material development of the mid-century. His statistics, of which he was excessively fond, no doubt were as unreliable as most statistics that economists love to dabble in, and like other purveyors of columned figures and impressive charts he certainly leaned too heavily on his knotty staff; but unlike academic economists such as Francis Wayland he tried to keep his thinking in contact with reality and in consequence his studies possess a solidity that is still impressive.

Although his father had early been interested in Hamilton's national system and for a time was president of a Philadelphia society concerned in furthering a protective tariff—for which the great German protectionist List published a number of letters in 1827—Carey began as a follower of the classical school, and in the thirties he published a treatise on political economy that expounded the Manchester doctrine of free-trade. But under the stirring leadership of Henry Clay the American System was making headway fast, and the facts of American expansion impressed him as earlier they had impressed the young List on his visit here. Turning statistician, he soon discovered, as he believed, certain fallacies in the English classical school, and he proceeded to examine afresh the Ricardian theory of rent. (The change came in 1848.) According to this most celebrated of all economic doctrines rent is measured by the difference in productivity between the best land, which is settled first, and the poorest, which social need later brings under cultivation; and hence in every growing community the increment of rent constantly increases at the expense of both labor and capital. But in the America which Carey was acquainted with, and where the story of social development was being swiftly recapitulated, the facts seemed to him to prove quite otherwise. Here the poorer lands were settled first, because their physical condition made them more easily available, and only later, when social pressure increased and larger means were available, were the rich bottom-lands cleared and the marshes drained.

As a result of his narrow interpretation of Ricardo's doctrine of social fertility, Carey lost faith in the Ricardian theory and turned frankly to the American scene to discover, if possible, a more adequate explanation. Soon the seeds of his intense nationalism were bearing their fruit. An inherited dislike of England led him to fear its industrial preëminence, and he abandoned the ideal of an international division of labor for the ideal of independent nationality, with America developing its individuality through the exploitation of its own resources. Free-trade, he came to believe, is international, it results in establishing a "single factory for the whole world, whither all the raw produce has to be sent whatever be the cost of transport"; whereas any society waxes individual and strong in the measure that it develops variety of employment with its demand for mutual help and service. Only through such associations can man develop his capacities and further his mastery of nature. His patriotism thus became involved in his economics and for years he waged a relentless warfare against Manchesterism. Not only were the English doctrines false to American fact, he pointed out, but they were vicious Tory doctrines which if followed here would keep America poor for the benefit of England. The great idea which came finally to dominate his thinking is suggested by the title of a pamphlet, written in 1852, *The Harmony of Interests: Agricultural, Manufacturing, and Commercial*—a work that suggests Frédéric Bastiat's *Les harmonies économiques*, published in 1850, and influenced by Carey's earlier speculations.[1] It was an age much given to discovering harmonies and Carey was

_____
[1] See Gide and Rist, *A History of Economic Doctrines*, pp. 282–284, 327–331.

not behindhand in the business. In the introduction he traced the
ills of contemporary economic life to the Manchester theories of
rent and population—theories which had thrown their black
shadows over English Parliamentary programs of relief and perverted the normal unfolding of western civilization. In consequence the "tendency of the whole British system of political economy is the production of discord among nations." [2]

In the background of Carey's mind was a Physiocratic dislike
of the sterile middleman which sharpened his antagonism to an
international division of labor, and a sensitive social conscience
that was concerned at the ruthless exploitation of English mill-
hands. An ardent believer in natural liberty and convinced of its
beneficence, he restricted economic freedom within national
boundaries. The harmony of interests is local and not international—the tying together of the several parts of the whole. Beyond the national boundaries it ceases. The pessimism of the
English school with its iron law of wages and its Malthusian law
of population was harshly repugnant to his buoyant optimism.
From these vicious roots, he was convinced, sprang the principle
of isolation and differentiation—that producer and consumer must
live apart, with the corollary that the poor must seek new lands in
far countries to supply the places of those from which they have
been thrust, there to produce agricultural staples to exchange for
the manufactured goods produced in thickly settled countries—a
principle that taxes both producer and consumer in the exact
measure of transportation tolls, and benefits exclusively the sterile
middleman. Applied to America the policy of free-trade must keep
this country dependent upon England—keep it agricultural for the
benefit of British merchants; and the program that Carey outlined, the complete sufficiency of which he never doubted, was a
return to the policy of Adam Smith, to that "general harmony of
interests" that must result from bringing the farmer and artisan
into neighborhood communities, fashioning the raw materials
where they are produced and consuming the farmer's produce
where it is grown. Adam Smith "saw well," says Carey, "that
when men came thus together, there arose a general harmony of
interests, each profiting his neighbor, and profiting by that neighbor's success, whereas the tendency of commercial centralization
was toward poverty and discord, abroad and at home." [3]

[2] *Miscellaneous Works*, Preface to *Harmony of Interests*.   [3] *Ibid.*

To his death in 1879 Carey was the most distinguished as he had been the most tireless advocate of a system of protection for American manufactures. He was one of the most pugnacious pamphleteers of a pugnacious generation.[4] He was a co-worker with Horace Greeley in the labor of convincing a suspicious people of the common benefits to be got from a subsidy to a class; and their joint influence gave respectability and popularity to the appeals of business men and politicians. Between 1849 and 1857 he "was the virtual editor of the *New York Tribune*" in all matters regarding protection. His chief antagonist in the long struggle was William Cullen Bryant and the *Evening Post;* and he made frequent appeal to Bryant to meet him in a pamphlet debate that should bring before the public both sides of the great question of protectionism. Bryant's refusal did not lessen his ardor, and in successive pamphlets he laid before the American people a well-rounded argument for tariff subsidies that ranks him in the history of economic thought with Friedrich List, the great German apostle of a nationalist economic system. American manufacturers owe a heavy debt to Henry Carey.

In these early years of industrialism the manufacturer was still dependent on the banker, and industrial development was held back, Carey came to believe, by a false financial policy imposed on the county by the bankers. From his boundless enthusiasm for the ideal of a national economy sprang likewise his unorthodox views on money that so greatly annoyed his fellow economists. Individual in his thinking on this as on other subjects, he espoused theories that to dogmatic bullionists like David A. Wells seemed incendiary at a time (during the post-war years) when so many Americans were bitten with "money heresies." On this theme his patriotism and his democratic sympathies ran together. He was opposed to the bullion system because it struck at nationalism. An English system, devised by Lombard Street, did not answer the needs of America. The price of gold is established in a world market and the flow of bullion is always toward the great centers already glutted with money. To throw the money of the world into a common pool was to subject the money of poorer and remoter countries to the control of the great financial capitals. Free-trade and the gold standard were the twin weapons forged by England for world-

---

[4] All told he published at his own print-shop some 3000 pages of pamphlet material of his own writing.

wide economic conquest, and for America to adopt a financial policy that held her subject to Lombard Street, seemed to Carey the height of folly. Gold follows the balance of trade, and until America had built up an adequate domestic economy her specie would continue to drain off, leaving too scanty a supply to do the necessary work of society.

The solution, he believed, lay in the creation of an independent national currency; and an efficient national currency, he held with Bishop Berkeley, was one that was non-exportable, that remained at home to do the day's work instead of gadding about. To provide such a medium of exchange he proposed a currency founded on the national credit—a "national system," he argued, "based entirely on the credit of the government with the people, and not liable to interference from abroad." [5] It was on such grounds that Carey supported the greenback issues and favored the remonetization of silver. The ideal of "societary circulation," he pointed out, was credit—"that great step towards civilization which consists in substituting *letters of credit* for material money"; and because "the steady and regular use of the *letter of credit* known to the world as the 'greenback,' or that other known as the 'national bank note,'" [6] tended to wean the minds of men from dependence on specie, he was warm in their favor.

With a sound national system, let foreigners take our gold for whatever balance of trade they can impose upon us, having no use among ourselves for any coin money except what we can retain under a wholesome foreign commerce.

What we most need today is the establishment of that monetary independence which results from maintaining absolute command over the machinery of exchange used within our borders, leaving to the gold dollar the performance of its duty of arranging for the settlement of balances throughout the world.[7]

Carey's insistence on a plentiful supply of money laid him under the charge of being an advocate of "cheap money," and therefore one of those wicked persons known as "inflationists." The charge in the main was true. He was pungent in his contrast between the prosperity of war times when an abundant currency released all the energies of the American people, and the stagnation that

[5] *Contraction or Expansion? Repudiation or Resumption? Letters to the Hon. Hugh M'Culloch, Secretary of the Treasury*, Philadelphia, 1866, p. 20.
[6] *Ibid.*, p. 22.
[7] Quoted in W. Elder, *Memoir of Henry C. Carey*, p. 13 (Philadelphia, 1880. With bibliography).

followed upon contraction. "Cheap money—low interest—enabled our working men to prosper," whereas dear money—high interest—was bringing distress and hardship. Every reduction in the amount of currency decreases the purchasing power of the people, and slows down the circulatory system. The attempt to retire the greenbacks he regarded as a class attack on the common welfare of the country. "To that end the greenback, everywhere claimed as the people's money, has by those in high places been denounced, small as is the quantity, when compared with the real need for it." [8] Paper money is "democratic in its tendencies," passing from hand to hand and never seeking a bank vault to hide in.

A war upon what is called "paper money" is . . . a war upon the poor in favor of the rich; and that the war being made upon it has precisely that effect is proved by the fact, that the western farmer is now being so impoverished by reason of such a reduction in the price of corn and oats that the former is being used as fuel, while the latter sold at 8 cents a bushel, [while] houses and lots in the neighborhood of Wall Street [are] commanding . . . prices such as had never before been heard of.[9]

Considering Carey's reputation as an economist and his wide influence, such doctrine, in the eyes of all "sound-money men," was distinctly pernicious. He was giving aid and comfort to the apostles of inflation and repudiation, and he suffered many a sharp attack. But that would not deter a warrior grown gray in battle, and in the very last year of his life he fell upon the bullion theory with the ardor of a young man. He would not suffer the bankers to go unrebuked in their mad attack on the prosperity of the country; he would not be silent while a policy of contraction, that so early as 1866 had reduced the per capita circulation to $12.50— according to his statistics—was still in full swing after the disastrous lesson of 1873. He had much in common with Peter Cooper, who in 1876 took up the battle against Wall Street for a "democratic" monetary system. The blood of the two old men, both born in the last decade of the eighteenth century, had not grown cold or sluggish with long years, but responded ardently to the great cause of democracy that had inspired their youth. That Carey's national system was a house divided against itself—that industry and finance were engaged in a mortal combat for supremacy—he

[8] *Shall We have Peace? Letters to President-elect Grant*, p. 39.
[9] *Contraction or Expansion? etc.*, p. 20.

probably never quite realized. He was concerned that America
should be free to create and enjoy the wealth that lay in the potentialities of the continent, and to that end he would have money
serve industry, and not industry money.

2

FRANCIS A. WALKER

The social conscience of Carey was colored with an optimism
that was the spontaneous expression of a generation that set no
limits to the beneficent development of American industrialism.
No storm-clouds had yet gathered on the horizon; no hostile systems challenged the sufficiency of capitalism. But a change was
at hand. By the end of the seventies the complacency of the
Gilded Age was disturbed by the rise of pestilent heresies in the
shape of new economic dogmas. The surplus-value theory of Marx
and the unearned-increment theory of Henry George were spreading widely through America, to the unsettlement of susceptible
minds; and the Knights of Labor were preparing to launch a general attack against the whole system of capitalistic exploitation.
Carey had sufficed the wants of his simpler day, but there was need
of a new champion to wield the sword of pure Ricardian doctrine
against these later heresies.

Francis A. Walker, son of the economist Amasa Walker, Brig-
adier General in the Civil War, Professor at Sheffield Scientific
School and later President of the Massachusetts Institute of
Technology, was to be the self-appointed champion of industrialism, the official economist of the Gilded Age, and forerunner of a
long line of academic purveyors of economic dogma. As the
author of a college textbook that superseded Francis Wayland's
naïve *Elements of Political Economy*—a work that had served
innumerable college generations as a quarry of economic doctrine—
he elaborated a complete system of economics with a geniality
that went far to popularize the "dismal science" with vast numbers
of undergraduates; and as an authoritative apologist for entrepreneur profits he rendered a service to capitalism that quite erased
his little Ricardian peccadillo of free-trade prejudice. There runs
through his solid pages the confident optimism of his generation—
an optimism that discovers in the heresies of socialism and single-
tax the only storm-clouds on the fair American horizons. He saw

no reason to question the ultimate good of industrialism, or to fear any deep-seated clash between labor and capital. He carried water easily on both shoulders, for he was so fortunate as to have worked out to his complete satisfaction, a magic economic formula that should return both to master and workman their just shares of the total production. In the light of his exegesis there could be no Marxian struggle of the classes. The captain of industry must no longer be regarded with sour aspect as a parasite upon labor, but as a fellow worker, the creator of those profits which are not subtracted for his benefit from the portion of labor. From Ricardo to Marx the economists had been barking up the wrong tree in their analysis of the rewards of the entrepreneur.

The classical school of the Gilded Age was in like position with the eighteenth-century Calvinists; they must either abandon their dogmas or reinterpret them to meet current needs. Walker was too good a Ricardian to abandon them, so he proposed to reinterpret them. The urgent problems to which he addressed himself were the sources of profits and of wages; and the examination of those problems led him to his theory of the function of the entrepreneur and to a rejection of the classical wage-fund theory. He refused to discard his suit of Ricardian clothes as Carey had done. They could never go out of style, he believed, so long as honest thinking was respected. He accepted most of the Ricardian dogmas without question. "Capital," he asserted soberly, "arises solely from saving. It stands always for self-denial and abstinence," and interest is the "reward of abstinence." But one important dogma, the classical wage-fund theory, he insisted on stripping away. He was too genial an optimist to rest content with the bleak conception that the margin of subsistence circumscribes the rewards of labor, and too enlightened an apologist of industrialism to assert that "profits are the leavings of wages." He could not hope to erect a theory suitable to the Gilded Age on such skimpy hypotheses, and he scourged them from the temple of economic law. Wages, to be sure, are the leavings after rent, interest, and profits have been deducted from the total production; but vast and dangerous misconceptions have arisen in regard to the portions that accrue to these several partners, and in particular mischievous perversions touching the share of profits. This was the crux of the problem of distribution and until the nature of profits should be determined the question of wages would remain to befuddle weak heads.

The heart of Walker's doctrine, therefore, is his theory of profits. He proposed to show that according to the true law of profits this flexible increment is never a moiety wrested from labor, but an additional earning of management that justly accrues to him who creates it. The doctrine from which he deduced his theory of the entrepreneur was the Ricardian theory of rent. On this point Walker was the most loyal of Ricardians, and he violently attacked Carey for repudiating the classical dogma. In a word "Ricardo's doctrine can no more be impugned than the sun in the heaven," he asserted, "and those who mouth at it simply show that they do not know what it was Ricardo taught." [10] What was needed was to understand its wide implications rather than to seek to destroy it— to trace in all its reaches the doctrine of fertility and discover how in other spheres than land the difference between fertile and unfertile measures the return upon economic endeavor. For the great doctrine of fertility, Walker pointed out, following Mill, is capable of expansion to cover wider fields than rent; it applies equally to management and labor; it broadens out into a comprehensive principle that exactly measures the most bitterly disputed of the several increments, the increment of profits.

This theory of fertility, introduced into the law of distribution, is Walker's most interesting contribution to economic speculation. By it he supplemented the trinity of land, capital, and labor—or in terms of distribution, of rent, interest, and wages—with a new entity—management and the earnings of management. The argument is highly ingenious. Assuming a no-profits employer at the lowest scale of the entrepreneur system, by analogy from the Ricardian no-rent grade of land, he asserted that similarly "profits are measured upwards from the level of the no-profits class of employers," and hence "it appears that the gains of the employer are not taken from the earnings of the laboring class, but measure the difference in production between the commonplace or bad, and the able, and shrewd, and strong management of business." [11] Profits, then, are an added increment of management, secured by foresight and business skill, the fruit of managerial fertility; and since they flow solely from the entrepreneur they belong to him alone and no portion may be justly claimed for rent, interest, or wages. The complete theory he states thus:

[10] *Land and its Rent*, p. 108.
[11] *Political Economy*, pp. 242, 348.

Under free and full competition, the successful employers of labour would earn a remuneration which would be exactly measured, in the case of each man, by the amount of wealth which he could produce, with a given application of labour and capital, over and above what would be produced by employers of the lowest industrial, or no-profits, grade, making use of the same amounts of labour and capital, just as rent measures the surplus of the produce of the better lands over and above what would be produced by the same application of labour and capital to the least productive lands which contribute to the supply of the market, lands which themselves bear no rent.[12]

It is a persuasive argument of which Walker was vastly proud. The germ of it later historians of economic thought have traced to Senior and John Stuart Mill, who had suggested the idea of "differential rent," or "rent of ability," which is the reward of "all peculiar advantages of extraordinary qualities of body and mind." [13] From whatever source it issued, the usefulness of such doctrine in the days of an expanding industrialism, and the ends it might serve in counteracting proletarian philosophies, are too evident to need comment. The Marxian dogma of surplus value—that profits are stealings from wages—was certainly calculated to breed dissatisfaction in weak proletarian heads. Marx was a good Ricardian in his major postulates and the Ricardians had failed to analyze adequately the true sources of profits; because of such failure the classical school had underestimated the social beneficence of the capitalistic system. Chained to the iron law of wages the school had been forced to envisage a bleak future with labor kept always at the margin of subsistence. From this pessimism Walker proposed to rid economic theory, by showing that entrepreneur profits augment the wage fund and hence that the entrepreneur is the benefactor rather than the exploiter of labor. With his business skill the captain of industry, like the inventor of a new machine, lays open new sources of wealth for all, and if he gains much for himself he gives more to society; for every improvement in business methods accrues in the end to society as a whole, for the new technique soon becomes a common possession.

The validity of Walker's theory of profits does not concern us here; it is a matter for economists to determine. To one who is under the spell of no doctrinaire system the theory seems some-

[12] *Quarterly Journal of Economics*, April, 1887. Quoted in Gide and Rist, *A History of Economic Doctrine*, p. 551.
[13] *Ibid.*, p. 549.

what too neat with its assumption of "free and full competition";[14] and in its conscious purpose to glorify the captain of industry it is freighted rather too heavily with the spirit of the Gilded Age. It not only throws the door wide to exploitation but it invites everybody to the feast. Yet the work of the apologist was only half done. Having established to his satisfaction the law of profits, Walker was prepared to take equally high ground in determining the increment that falls to labor. To glorify profits and at the same time defend the pessimism of the wage-fund theory, would have been foolish tactics in presence of the Marxian surplus-value theory; proletarian discontent must be dealt with and Walker was prepared to deal with it. Having ascertained exactly the several increments due to rent, interest, and profits—which in his system are rigidly determined by economic law—he confidently assigned all the residual increment to wages. Labor not only gets all it earns, he argued, but far more, since what does not fall to the just shares of the other partners falls to it—that is the "whole remaining body of wealth." If it be recalled that the total social fund of inventions, machinery, trade processes, systems of transportation, business methods, are alike in the service of all employers—the no-profit entrepreneur equally with the high-profit—it follows that the individual employer can derive from such social wealth no modicum of profit above and beyond what his individual fertility has produced. Where then can the income from such social fund flow except to wages? "Every invention in mechanics, every discovery in the chemical art, no matter by whom made, inures directly and immediately" to the benefit of labor.[15] This, to be sure, on the hypothesis of "full and free competition," which may be interfered with by various means but which in the long run prevails. How else shall one explain the constant rise in the wage-scale that has marked the Industrial Revolution and that has gone hand in hand with vast profits to the entrepreneur class?

It was a robust optimism that could lay down the theory that labor is "the residual claimant to the product of industry." Although Walker prided himself on his discovery, it seems to have made slight impression on later economic thought. Like too many members of the classical school the apologist of the Gilded Age

[14] For a critical examination see Gide and Rist, *A History of Economic Doctrine*, pp. 551–558.
[15] *Political Economy*, pp. 251–258.

failed to keep his feet on the plebeian earth; and his conclusions suggest how great mischief *a priori* reasoning may work in the speculations of academic gentlemen. A moderate dash of realism might have lessened his buoyant optimism; but Walker was too warm an admirer of capitalism, too eager to assert the beneficence of industrialism, to inquire curiously into the everyday facts of current exploitation. As a realistic statistician he was far inferior to Carey. But why demand a plodding realism of the economist when all America was romantic? If the economic theory of General Walker was a pleasant blend of Ricardo and Colonel Sellers, would it not hit the taste of the age to a nicety? Its sturdy optimism was a soothing antidote to the Jeremiads of the Marxians and the shrill demands of the single-taxers. The Gold Coast of America looked to its official economists for a confutation of all economic heresies, and who was so well equipped for that business as a doughty Colonel Sellers armed with a sharp Ricardian sword?

In this brisk work Walker engaged with gusto. In his onslaught upon Marx and Henry George he was untroubled by doubt. He first demolished the structure of their theory and then impugned their honesty. His condemnation of single-tax is bold and sweeping. There is a bitter asperity in his denunciation of the economic heresies of *Progress and Poverty*, and he dismisses the proposal to tax unearned increment with the comment, "Every honest man will resent such a proposition as an insult."[16] His discussion of the economics of the question is only casual and he hastens back to the safe haven of Ricardian doctrine.[17] In his commentary on the Knights of Labor he is somewhat vindictive for a well-bred gentleman. He charges the syndicalistic attack on the profits system to immigrant foreigners, asserts that the law of profit fertility is an insuperable obstacle to any proletarian control of industry, and finally damns it as un-American. The honest, native American "knows that for himself and his children the way is open clear to the top"; his "spirit is that of civility, reciprocity and fair play"; and he concludes:

Had it been left to our native population alone, not one of those violent and reckless attacks upon production and transportation, which have, within the past two or three years, shocked the whole industrial system and have come near to produce a general crisis of trade, would ever have taken place.[18]

[16] *Land and its Rent*, Preface, p. vi.   [17] *Ibid.*, pp. 181–182.
[18] *Political Economy*, p. 394.

Yet in spite of his genial optimism he discovered specks on the fair picture of society. To the Ricardian logic the stupidity of men is a constant irritant; if only men were rational the path of progress would be so much easier! After economic law has been demonstrated with the finality of a Euclidian theorem, it is disconcerting to see how the multitude will not be reasoned with, but persist in following after the last false prophet who cries in the market-place. The clamor raised by single-tax was especially annoying. "That such an argument," he remarked a bit testily, "should for a moment have imposed upon anybody, is enough to give one a new conception of the intellectual capabilities of mankind." [19] Fortunate it is for society, he concludes, that while man proposes, economic law disposes. False prophets will have their little day, but from their secure watch-tower the Ricardians calmly look out upon a world of which they alone hold the key.*

II

THE CONSCRIPTION OF POLITICAL THEORY

When the social fabric is being torn rudely across by a changing economics, political theory and practice will suffer from the attendant confusions. The America of the Gilded Age accounted itself a democracy and was outwardly content to make use of the familiar democratic machinery; but until it was determined whether majority or minority rule should prevail, whether the well-being of the many or the property of the few should be the chief object of government, there would be no serious effort to create a political state for adequate social control. In the meantime the old individualisms would range the land seeking what they might devour, and the common attitude toward the political state would remain one of good-natured contempt. A shambling government, corrupt and incompetent, awakened no man's hope or pride, and amidst the slovenly anarchisms of the times, with a crude exploitation in the saddle, the state would be pretty much ignored except when its services might prove useful to such exploitation. The plutocracy would oppose the erection of a vigorous state until such time as it felt strong enough to control its activities. The principle of the majority-will held grave potentialities that

[19] *Ibid.*, p. 433.
* In his original plan Professor Parrington included a third subsection on W. G. Sumner, but evidently decided against its inclusion.—*Publisher.*

might threaten the eventual mastership of wealth, and until the plutocracy had created its strongholds within the framework of the democracy it would bitterly oppose any extension of democratic control.

Broadly two great movements were going forward side by side in the unconscious drift of political tendency—the democratic and the plutocratic. The former, drawn chiefly from agrarian and labor elements with a considerable following of the middle and professional classes, was determined to carry forward and supplement the Jacksonian movement. It was honestly concerned for the development of the democratic principle. It would purify government by the application of civil service reform, it would steadily enlarge the bounds of social control of economic forces, and it would strengthen the political state to enable it to cope with corporate wealth and constrain the ambitions of the plutocracy into conformity with democratic ends. To such a democratic program the plutocracy was necessarily opposed. It professed the warmest loyalty to the abstract principle of democracy while bending every energy to emasculate effective democratic control. The problem confronting it was the familiar Federalistic problem— how to protect the minority from the majority and set property interests above human interests; but the problem had been immensely complicated by the strategic advances made by democracy. The democratic principle could not be easily thrust aside, it must be undermined. And so while awaiting the time when it should be strong enough to set up boldly its mastery of society, plutocracy took refuge in two principles, the superman theory and the *laissez-faire* theory, both of which it asserted to be democratic, the very essence of democracy. The former was "The public be damned" theory, which held that the economic leaders of society must be left free to manage their properties as they saw fit; and the latter was the familiar doctrine of individual initiative, that looked with suspicion on any interference by the political state with economic activity. If a bureaucracy may stick its nose into the citizen's private affairs what becomes of individual liberty?

But the plutocracy was building its real defenses elsewhere. Shrewdly aware of the potentialities of a Constitution that had been designed for the protection of property interests, it followed two main lines of development: it furthered the popular development of a cult of the Constitution by praising the excellence of a system of checks and balances, and spreading the view that to tamper with any provisions of the instrument was little short of sacrilege; and at the same time it bent every energy to extend the range of judicial prerogative and bring the legislative branch under control of the judiciary. It sought extra-constitutional indulgences that were dispensed by the courts in the name of the police power. The way had been prepared by Marbury vs. Madison and Dred Scott vs. Sanford, and during the Gilded Age a broad path to judicial control was opened by the elaboration of the "due process of law" principle discovered in the fourteenth amendment. With the development of the plutocracy the extension of the doctrine of judicial review went forward rapidly, providing an impregnable defense for property interests that promised ill for the principle of democratic control in the interests of the common well-being. The democracy was being driven from the inner keep of the castle.

While the real struggle was thus going on in the court-room, with the outcome in the hands of the judges, political speculation was playing havoc with certain of our oldest and most cherished doctrines. Pursuing the path suggested by Webster and Francis Lieber, it turned away from the particularism of Calhoun to explore the reaches of a consolidating nationalism. The inevitable drift towards unity—whether democratic or plutocratic—was daily gathering momentum. The destruction of the states-rights program and party had cleared the ground for a new conception of the dignity and powers of the political state. With the social shift from dispersion to centralization the federal government was destined to grow in authority; and political theory was destined to follow the same course, seeking to justify in principle what was being accomplished in fact. The end of the philosophy of dispersion was in sight. The tide was running toward an exaltation of the doctrine of sovereignty, with the consequent exaltation of the abstract political state. As the individual coalesced in the mass, the rights and dignity of the individual would lessen in the presence of an engulfing sovereignty. The traditional doctrine of natural rights was in for a slashing attack. Centralization must destroy the shambling Jacksonian structure and erect in its place a grandiose organic theory.

During the Gilded Age a number of systematic studies of political theory appeared, amongst which the most significant were, Woolsey's *Political Science, or the State* (1877), Bryce's *The American Commonwealth* (1888), Woodrow Wilson's *The State* (1889), and Burgess's *Political Science and Constitutional Law* (1891). Of these the formal studies of Woolsey and Burgess may serve to illustrate the changing thought of the times. Both are academic reflections of the current drift of tendency, and both reveal the academic sympathy with the master movement of centralization. The work of Woolsey was a revision of classroom notes used between 1846 and 1871 and strongly colored by pre-war views; the work of Burgess was the first-fruits of the influence of German speculation on the nature of the leviathan state.

I

THEODORE WOOLSEY

Theodore Dwight Woolsey, professor of Greek and president of Yale, was an heir in direct succession of Connecticut Federalism. Nephew of Timothy Dwight, a minister, and distinguished member of the social oligarchy that in its decadence still held Connecticut opinion in a strong grip, he could scarcely escape a predilection for the moralistic authoritative dogmatisms that marked the old Connecticut *régime*. The principle of coercive authority had lain at the heart of the political theory of Timothy Dwight, and Theodore Woolsey was true to his Puritan antecedents in asserting the supremacy of authority over liberty. The only important element in his thinking that sets him apart from his uncle was the influence of Francis Lieber, whose conception of organic growth in social custom he made his own, and whose disciple he professed to be. Naturally he retained the old Puritan dislike of leveling—the traditional Connecticut distrust of democracy. He would have no weakening of authority, no Jacobean license; and for anarchism, socialism, communism, which he reckoned the nastiest spawn of Jacobinism, his abhorrence was what one would expect of a Connecticut Federalist. The two ponderous volumes that he issued in 1877 are learned studies that bear on their dun pages many a telltale mark of earlier times. In them Theodore Woolsey was renewing the fight against an infidel philosophy that with its doctrine of natural rights denied the authority of the godly to police society.

In harmony with Lieber and Calhoun he rejected the romantic

doctrine of natural rights, and substituted a composite social-moralistic conception, that from John Winthrop and Roger Williams to Channing and Emerson had colored the Puritan thought of New England. Natural rights, he asserted, are those which belong to man by reason of the nature God has endowed him with; and the state is a moral agent, arising out of custom, to secure and guarantee such rights. It is "as truly natural as rights are, and as society is"; for established in the social nature of man it is the natural repository and guardian of his rights in a social order. It is an expression of the teleological purpose that underlies all things. The manner in which Woolsey elaborated his moralistic theory will be evident from the following passages:

The considerations that men exist together in society, that they have an irresistible impulse towards society, that their perfection of soul and of outward condition can be secured only in a social life, and, on the other hand, that recognition of rights and obligation alone make a social life a tolerable or even a possible thing, and that wherever men reflect on their own nature they admit the existence of certain classes of rights and shield them by public power, show a divine purpose which none who believe in a Creator of the world can deny. The Creator of man, having made him such that his temporal, moral, and spiritual perfection can be found only in society, prepared his moral feelings for the life for which he was destined. The destination for society; the means within human nature by which it is fulfilled; the means by which the individual and the community, when brought into society, are able to secure the good and avoid the evils possible in a state of coexistence—these form a complete, harmonious whole, which manifest comprehension of view and forethought. It is provided in our nature, when it is not perverted—that is, when it does not swerve from the true idea of human nature—that we shall form societies under law. A state of society is a state of nature, and the only true one.

When therefore *natural* rights are spoken of, we can accept the term, if it be used to denote such rights as grow out of our nature, and may be inferred from the destination to which it points us. Another and a heathenish kind of sense was attached to the words, when they were taken to mean the rights, or rather uncontrolled liberties, which men possessed in a state of human nature in which there was no organized society or government. . . . [Such a theory] contemplates men as enjoying certain powers of free action in this state of nature, and these powers must serve for a foundation of their state as members of society, or so many of them as it cannot be shown that they gave up, in order to make a state of law and order possible. In other words, the theory of the derivation of these rights from a state of nature may take a hypothetical shape, and deduce rights from what a man could do in a state of things which exists only in a jural fiction. . . .

We find no fault with the objects which the theories had in view, but with the want of conformity to truth. It must be pronounced, in *the first place*, contrary to fact, that such a state of nature ever existed. Man has always been under law; he is a ζῷον πολιτκον. . . .

Secondly, if it could be shown that he had such an origin, it would prove nothing.[20]

Having thus established both society and the state in the nature of man, and dismissed the romantic interpretation of natural rights as heathenish, Woolsey turned to examine the true sphere and function of the political state. He rejected in the main the *laissez-faire* view of Mill and Spencer, but he refused to go so far as Burgess. He will have no omnicompetent state. A just mean must be laid down between authority and liberty, and that mean he discovered in the dictum, "The sphere of the state . . . may reach as far as the nature of man and needs of man and of men reach";[21] that is to say, its control runs far beyond mere police powers, and concerns itself not only with material ends but with the "intellectual and aesthetic wants of the individual, and the religious and moral nature of its citizens." A state swollen to great powers he regarded as likely to swallow up liberty in paternalism, and a state immediately responsive to the popular will is certain to run into "extreme democracy." His ideal government he discovered in the rule of the Connecticut oligarchy, under which a homogeneous people, with simple agrarian habits, disciplined by religion and responsive to moral leadership, enjoyed a stable government administered by proved executives. Unfortunately with the nineteenth century began a decline in American government, resulting from economic changes, the growth of cities, lower-class immigration, and the "gradual reception of doctrines of political rights, which belong to extreme democracy." Such pernicious doctrines, in his judgment, were: the short term of office, popular election of judges to hold for a fixed period instead of for life, the debasement of the representative system by subjecting the representative to his constituents, and the spoils system.[22] In a later study he added two other evils: direct legislation through the initiative, and a popular referendum on war and peace.[23]

In spite of an imposing display of classical learning these two stout volumes reveal a childlike ignorance of *Realpolitik*, a naïve

[20] *Political Science*, Vol. I, pp. 23–25.
[21] *Ibid.*, p. 216.
[22] *Ibid.*, Vol. II, p. 141.
[23] *Communism and Socialism*, p. 232.

inability to grasp the significance of economic groupings that underlie all political alignments. Neither as minister nor as college president did Theodore Woolsey learn anything about the robust
materialisms which any realistic political theory must take into
great account. His knowledge of ancient Greek institutions no
doubt was adequate, but his knowledge of American constitutional
development was singularly inadequate. He accepted without
question the argument of Story and Webster that the phrase, "We
the people," proves the original, consolidating intention of the
document; he discussed the history of party government in the
United States without touching on the economic alignment of
agrarianism and capitalism; and he could discover only one thoroughly admirable political party—"the upright federal party."
He extols the Supreme Court as the triumph of the American
Constitution, without considering the desirability of a judicial veto
on legislative enactments, or suggesting a potential alignment of the
judiciary with the master forces of a generation. The moralistic
bias of his thought is perhaps sufficiently revealed in a comment on
the functions of the judges. "In a higher sense, they are not
representatives of the community nor of its chief magistrates, but
of justice and of God. . . . They are in fact more immediately
servants of God than any other men who manage the affairs of a
country, because expediency, departure from law or from the constitution, is for them in no circumstance a thing to be conceived
of."[24] Mark Twain, it would seem, was not the only humorist of
the Gilded Age.

In his later years Woolsey was much disturbed by the spread
of collectivist doctrine, and in the thick of the economic unrest
of the times he felt it to be his duty to assist in stemming the
advance of such doctrine. In his great work on political theory,
he demolished the communist-anarchist-socialist arguments in a
few pages, and then remarked with excellent candor, "There is
an extensive literature, relating to the subject . . . with much of
which I am not familiar." Fearful that he might not have delivered
a death-blow, after further reading he returned to the attack
three years later, and in 1880 published a volume entitled *Communism and Socialism*. For so difficult a business he was even
then inadequately equipped. He did not realize the magnitude of
his task. Marx's *Capital* could not be undermined in ten pages,

[24] *Political Science*, Vol. II, pp. 330–331.

even with the help of Cairnes, Mill, and Ricardo, and a political scientist with a theological background was scarcely competent to untie the close-knit threads of the Marxian economics. His exposition in consequence is incomplete and faulty; it largely overlooks the Marxian philosophy of history and ignores the doctrine of economic determinism. What troubles him most is the lack of religious faith amongst socialists. The validity of a theory he is satisfied to test by the morality of the theorist. One can easily guess that President Woolsey's opinions had turned into dogmatic conviction before a page of the literature to be examined had come under his eyes. Yet that so shallow a book should have issued from an academic pen will surprise no one who is aware of the incredible number of shallow books that actually have issued from academic pens. Provocative social thinking and the American university seem never to have got on well together.

In the fact that Woolsey's speculations on the nature of the state were accounted significant contributions to political science by his generation of Americans, the historian may find added confirmation of the shallowness of the Gilded Age. A stale Connecticut Calvinism, molding in the corner of the cupboard, is poor food to nourish thinking, and a man who knows nothing about the deeper springs of political struggle is singularly unqualified to elaborate a science of the state. Theodore Woolsey's weighty volumes were a dignified attempt to rehabilitate the old Connecticut Federalism and suit it to the taste of a new age. But what measure of political intelligence can one expect of a people fed on pious fictions by their most authoritative expounder of the noble art of government?

2

JOHN W. BURGESS

Woolsey has little to say about sovereignty. The speculations of Austin had not reached his quiet study, and the need for a coercive state in harmony with a centralizing industrialism was not likely to be realized by a man whose eyes were turned back fondly to a simple village life. It was left for a younger generation to examine the problem of sovereignty, and to that business John W. Burgess turned with zest. A thoroughgoing Austinian, a disciple of the German state-cult, a Hegelian, he would seem to have been ill fitted to interpret the functions of the state to America. And yet by virtue of his European detachment he saw clearly the direction in which America *

IV

BUTTRESSING THE DEMOCRATIC THEORY

I

A DEMOCRATIC ECONOMICS—HENRY GEORGE

While the academic economists were thus providing a new body of capitalistic theory, from the ranks of the people came a group that was bent on bringing economic principles into greater conformity to what they considered democratic needs. The economics of bankers and manufacturers they regarded as a selfish class economics and they proposed to democratize the body of economic thought as Tom Paine and Jefferson had democratized the body of political thought. Since the days of John Taylor such amateur economists had been plentiful in America, and in the post-war days when the country was in the throes of the Industrial Revolution, they sprang up at every cross-roads. George Henry Evans, Horace Greeley, Peter Cooper, Parke Godwin, Wendell Phillips, Albert Brisbane, Hinton R. Helper, "Coin" Harvey, were only a few out of the many who in their own way were seeking in economics a road to freedom. They were not formal economists; they were little read in the history of economic thought; in so far as they may be accounted a school they were mostly the unclaimed progeny of French Physiocratic theory who did not recognize their own father. Yet they were vastly concerned to bring economic theory into some sort of realistic contact with the facts of American experience and the ideals of democracy; and their immediate objective was the overthrow of current Manchester principles and the erection in their stead of a body of theory based on the needs of the producer and the consumer rather than the middleman.

Of this characteristic native group, largely ignored by our formal historians, by far the ablest and most influential was Henry George, a thinker created by the impact of frontier economics upon a mind singularly sensitive to the appeal of social justice, singularly self-

* The discussion of Burgess was not completed by Professor Parrington. At this point he planned a third section, "The New Ally: the courts: the police power and the fourteenth amendment; the injunction." None of this section was written, but he has dealt with these subjects *passim.—Publisher.*

sufficient in its logic. He remains still our most original economist. Beyond the Ricardian theory of rent, with its corollary of unearned increment, he owed little to Europe and nothing to academic American economists. From the first he was a free-lance, returning to the origins of things—as Tom Paine had advised long before— and thinking "as if he were the first man who ever thought." His major doctrines he arrived at largely independently, ignorant of the fact that his *impôt unique* had been earlier elaborated by the Physiocratic school, till long after he had come to identical conclusions. His matured philosophy was the outcome of the meditations of a Jeffersonian idealist contemplating the divergence between the crude facts of exploitation all about him and the eighteenth-century ideal of natural justice; and he became, in consequence, the voice of idealistic America seeking to adjust the economics of a rapidly changing society to the ends of democratic well-being. The passion of the reformer was in him, but wedded to the critical mind of the analyst; and this accounts for the wide appeal of *Progress and Poverty* that for thousands of Americans removed economic theory from the academic closet and set it in the thick of political conflict. Henry George humanized the dismal science and brought it home to the common interest. With his extreme simplification no doubt he fell into the same error the classical school had fallen into before him; he left too many elements out of his equation; but he succeeded in the same way they had succeeded—he made of economic theory a weapon to use in the struggle between the exploiters and the exploited. After *Progress and Poverty* the social economist could cross swords with the Ricardians.

Henry George is readily enough explained in the light of his environment. He was intellectually native to the West, but it was the West of the Gilded Age with its recollections of an earlier agrarian order. Upon the gigantic exploitation of post-war times, carried forward in the name of progress, he threw the experience of two hundred and fifty years of continental expansion. That experience had undergone a subtle change as the settlements moved through the Inland Empire, a change marked by the spirit of capitalistic expansion with its crop of unearned increment. On the frontier, land speculation was often the readiest means to wealth. To the west of the Allegheny Mountains land had long been the staple commodity, with the buying and selling of which every community was deeply concerned; and from the dramatic repetition of that experience in California, Henry George clarified the principle upon which he erected his social philosophy, namely, that a fluid economics begets an equalitarian democracy and homespun plenty, and that with the monopolization of natural resources a static econ-omy succeeds, with its attendant caste regimentation and aug-menting exploitation. In the days when he was meditating his social philosophy, California was still in the frontier stage of de-velopment, but amidst the hurrying changes a fluid economics was visibly hardening to the static, with a swiftness dramatic enough to impress upon him the significance of a story that had been ob-scured in earlier telling by the slowness of the dénouement. The vast cupidity of business in preëmpting the virgin resources of California, and in particular the technique of Leland Stanford and the Central Pacific Railway group, provided an eloquent object-lesson that set him to examining the long history of land-jobbing in America in its remoter social bearings. From such inquiry emerged the cardinal principles of an economic theory that must be reckoned the ultimate expression of a school of thought that begin-ning with Quesnay a hundred years before, and first interpreted for America by John Taylor and the Jeffersonians, was finally buried in a common grave with the kindred doctrine of natural rights.

It was no accident that his mind fastened upon land monopoly as the deeper source of social injustice. As a child of the frontier he thought in terms of land as naturally as the money-broker thinks in terms of discounts. His psychology was that of the producer rather than the middleman. Land, with all its potential wealth of field and orchard and forest and stream, with its unmeasured re-sources of coal and iron and oil and timber, was the fruitful gift of nature to man; and the true measure of social well-being, he be-lieved, is the measure in which labor is free to use such natural resources for productive purposes. Land monopoly was an ancient evil that had laid its blight on every civilization. The expropriation of natural resources was the origin of rent, and rent was a social tax parasitic in nature. Unearned increment was a moiety wrested from the producer, that waxed ever greater with the increase of production. Henry George was well aware how deeply rooted in American psychology was the love of unearned increment. Since the far-off days when the agent of the Transylvania Land Company wrote in 1775 that the Ohio Valley abounded in land-mongers, the rage for expropriative speculation had mounted steadily; and the railway land-grants of his day were a fitting climax to a policy that in every generation had brought forth such fruits as the Yazoo frauds. The land question was a perennial western problem. For years Horace Greeley in the *Tribune*, had spread amongst the farmers the "Vote Yourself a Farm" propaganda. The protest of the small western settler against the middleman policy of the government in alienating great blocks of the public domain to speculative companies, had added thousands of votes to the Republican party, and the result was the Homestead Act of 1862. But the fruits of the Act were partly destroyed by huge grants to railway promoters, and the time had come, George believed, when the problem must be envisaged in all its complexities and the American people brought to understand how great were the stakes being gambled for.

The disease had so long been endemic in America that the remedy must be drastic. No patent nostrums would serve. The vividness of his experience in the West had thrown into sharp relief his earlier experiences in the East, and made him distrustful of all social panaceas that hopeful idealists were seeking in Europe. With any form of collectivistic theory he would have nothing to do. Marxian socialism he looked upon as an alien philosophy, inadequate in its diagnosis and at fault in its prescription. The ills of America—perhaps of Europe as well—must be cured by another regimen. *Progress and Poverty* grew out of his experience as he watched the heedless alienation of the public domain. It was his reply to the policy of preëmption, exploitation, and progress of the Gilded Age. Philadelphia-born, he early suffered in his personal fortune from the periodic hard times that ran so disastrous a cycle in the days when America was in thoughtless transition from an agrarian order to an industrial. His scanty schooling came to an end before he had reached his fourteenth year, and at sixteen he saw no better opening in life than to ship before the mast to Australia. On his return he learned to set type, but times were bad and opportunity declining to knock at his door, he worked his way through the Straits of Magellan, landing in San Francisco in 1858, on his way to Salem, Oregon, where he worked for a time in a shop. With the exhaustion of the diggings he made his way back to San Francisco, and began a long series of restless ventures in the newspaper field, with only his hands for capital—none very successful, none quite a failure, but returning him useful dividends in the form of a serviceable prose style. At twenty-two he plunged into an improvident marriage with a girl of eighteen, and the next dozen years brought many privations to the little family.

Fate had not yet taken Henry George in hand to lead him into his life work. All the economics he then knew had been learned in the rough and tumble ways of a western print-shop. In 1869, at the age of thirty, while on a business trip to New York City, he was confronted by the contrast between wealth and poverty there nakedly exposed—so unlike what he had known at San Francisco. It was a prod to his social conscience, and as he contemplated the wretchedness of the East Side he registered a vow to explore the hidden causes of social disease. He had given no serious thought to economic questions, and now almost casually he went to the Philadelphia public library to look into John Stuart Mill's *Political Economy*. He accepted Mill's views on wages without critical examination, and wrote his first important article—on the Chinese question in California. In the meantime a group of California railway promoters had been buying and selling legislators in their work of building up private fortunes out of a public monopoly; and it was the contemplation of wealth acquired by such methods, together with the gamble of land speculation in Oakland in consequence of the proposal to establish there the western terminal of the continental railway, that clarified for Henry George the great principle he was to expound in *Progress and Poverty* ten years later.

The first drift in his intellectual development had been a drift back to the old Jeffersonianism from which the country was swiftly moving. As an editor he was an outspoken Democrat of the primitive school, opposed to protectionism, subsidies, a centralizing political state, and the corruption that follows in the train of paternalism as sickness follows infection. In a pamphlet written in 1870, he expounded his political faith thus:

Railroad subsidies, like protective duties, are condemned by the economic principle that the development of industry should be left free to take its natural direction. They are condemned by the political principle that government should be reduced to its minimum—that it becomes more corrupt and more tyrannical, and less under the control of the people, with every extension of its powers and duties. . . . They are condemned by the experience of the whole country, which shows that they have invariably led to waste, extravagance and rascality; that they inevitably become a source of corruption and a means of plundering the people.[25]

[25] George, *Life of Henry George*, pp. 216–217.

Having thus indoctrinated himself in the Jeffersonian liberalism with its foundations laid in natural rights and its conception of a decentralized society, the following year, at the age of thirty-two, he sat down to the serious elaboration of his views. *Our Land and Land Policy, National and State*, was an explorative pamphlet that went to the heart of the problem as he had come to understand it. The kernel of the work is the question of the relation of land to labor, of rent to wages; and the conclusion to which it led was the doctrine of the social ownership of socially created values, which justice requires shall return to society in the form of an equalized tax that shall absorb the unearned increment. Around this fundamental doctrine was grouped a considerable body of ideas that had been expounded by earlier liberals. How much he borrowed and how much he arrived at independently, cannot easily be determined; such diverse thinkers as James Harrington, Locke, the Physiocrats, Tom Paine, Karl Marx, John Stuart Mill, William Ellery Channing, might well have contributed to this provocative document, if George had been acquainted with them. Like Harrington was the assumption of economic determinism—that ownership of the land implies the rulership of society. From the school of Locke came the conception of natural rights, but interpreted rather in terms of Tom Paine and of William Ellery Channing. From Mill came the conception of unearned increment; from Marx the law of concentration; and from the Physiocrats the conception of a natural order and the doctrine of an *impôt unique*. And all this set in a framework of American economic history, which reveals with shrewd insight the disastrous tendency of the traditional policy of land alienation in great blocks to middle-men, with the attendant rise of rent.

How intimately he was related in his thinking to the French liberals of the eighteenth century, may perhaps be sufficiently suggested in his interpretation of the doctrine of natural rights—a doctrine the new realistic school from Calhoun to Woolsey and Burgess was subjecting to critical analysis. By uniting the individualism of Locke's doctrine of property with the Physiocratic doctrine of social well-being, he gave a sharp turn to the conception that, like Jefferson's, set it widely apart from the exploitative interpretation preferred by the Hamiltonian followers of Locke. The gist of his conception is thus set down:

Now the right of every human being to himself is the foundation of the right of property. That which a man produces is rightfully his own, to keep, to sell, to give or to bequeath, and upon this sure title alone can ownership of anything rightfully rest. But man has also another right, declared by the fact of his existence—the right to the use of so much of the free gifts of nature as may be necessary to supply all the wants of that existence, and which he may use without interfering with the equal rights of anyone else; and to this he has a title as against all the world.[26]

Much of Henry George is compressed within these few lines, that suggest as well the diverse liaisons of his thought. In his conception of the right of every man to himself he is in agreement with William Ellery Channing, who used the argument in his attack on slavery, and with Emerson, Parker, and the Transcendental radicals generally. It is an interpretation of natural rights that sprang easily from the Unitarian-Transcendental conception of the sacredness of the individual, and that was given wide currency by the anti-slavery propaganda. From his deduction that the right to property flows from the right to self, came his theory of tax-equity that was to play a major rôle in the formulation of his principle of taxation. If society may not justly take from the individual what the individual has created, it must seek its revenues elsewhere than in a personal-property tax; and where should it look if not to those values which society has created? The inalienable right of the individual to what he has produced does not extend to the appropriation of wealth he has not produced, and a sharp line is drawn between the rights of the individual and the rights of society, between production and exploitation. Herein lies the justification of the single-tax—a principle derived by crossing Locke with the New England school.

From the classical economists Henry George got little. He had a quiet contempt for them he was never at pains to conceal. He was convinced that they had distorted the whole science of economics. As the earlier Tories with their sacred *arcana imperii* had done with political government, they had involved economics in abstract theory, removing it from the comprehension of the common man. At the best they had dehumanized it to the status of a dismal science, with their postulate of an economic man and their pessimistic outlook. At the worst they had shaped it into a potent weapon for the exploiting class, who gravely invoked economic law—which none understood—to justify class policies of

[26] *Ibid.*, p. 223.

state. In an address delivered at the University of California, Henry George paid his respects to the classical school in these words:

> The name of political economy has been constantly invoked against every effort of the working classes to increase their wages or decrease their hours of labour. . . . Take the best and most extensively circulated text-books. While they insist upon freedom for capital, while they justify on the ground of utility the selfish greed that seeks to pile fortune on fortune, and the niggard spirit that steels the heart to the wail of distress, what sign of substantial promise do they hold out to the working man save that he should refrain from rearing children? . . .[27]

For political economy thus degraded from its high place and become the slut of private interest, Henry George proposed to do what Tom Paine had done for political theory a hundred years before—he would transfer it from the closet to the market-place by exposing the shabby *arcana imperii* and bringing it within the comprehension of common men. He would bring home to the popular intelligence a realization of the dynamics of economic law and its bearing upon social well-being, that men might plot a fairer course for society. This was the deeper purpose of *Progress and Poverty*—to humanize and democratize political economy, that it might serve social ends rather than class exploitation. *The Rights of Man* and *Progress and Poverty* may be reckoned complementary works, applying to related fields the spirit released to the modern world by the great thinkers of Revolutionary France. The foundations on which they both rest is the eighteenth-century conception of natural law, all-comprehensive, beneficent, free, enshrined in the common heart of humanity, and conducting to the ultimate of social justice.

As a necessary preliminary to his purpose, Henry George was forced to clear the ground of old growths. Before he could declare the truth he must uproot certain of the Malthusian and Ricardian heresies. He must substitute a sociological interpretation, based on historical reality in western civilization, for a set of economic abstractions, based on the political and economic accidents of England in post-Napoleonic days. The Manchester school, it must be remembered, was an embodiment of the aspirations of the rising middle class; it was a philosophical attack upon the vexatious restrictions laid upon capitalism by government in the hands of the landed aristocracy. It conceived of economic principles as cf con-

[27] *Ibid.*, p. 277.

cern only to the owning classes, and its theory took a special and narrow form from the current struggle between the landed and capitalistic interests. In a Parliamentary debate over the corn laws in 1814, Alexander Baring, the banker, assumed that the working classes had no interest at stake. To argue that they were affected, he said, was "altogether ridiculous; whether wheat was 130s. or 80s., the laborer could only expect dry bread in the one case and dry bread in the other." [28] In Francis Wayland's *Elements of Political Economy*, published in 1837, a similar narrow view of the field of economics was expressed. That an adequate political economy must be social, that it must be something very much more than a merchant's *vade mecum*, or handbook of profit rules, Henry George grasped as clearly as Ruskin; and he attacked certain of the Manchester principles with the ardor of a social prophet. Of these the classical wage-fund theory seemed to him the most vicious, and he was at vast pains to prove that wages are drawn from the produce of labor and not from a preëxistent capital-fund. Having established this to his satisfaction, he turned to consider the economic effects of monopolistic expropriation of natural resources, and discovered the explanation of the augmenting poverty of civilization in the shutting out of labor from the sources of subsistence, that is in land monopoly.

The argument is based on the Ricardian theory of rent. Though George rejected the classical wage-fund theory, he accepted without qualification the classical rent-theory, and discovered the kernel of his philosophy in the doctrine of social fertility. If rent is the difference between the income-value of a given piece of land and that of the least valuable in the neighborhood, it measures the difference between the yields per acre on the richest and the leanest soil with a like outlay of labor and capital. So in an urban community rent arises from what may be called social fertility— that is, from a monopoly-value in a given neighborhood. Such monopoly-value arises from strategic location; the desirability of a given tract for dwelling, factory, or shop. The number of persons daily passing will determine the rental value for shop purposes; the the accessibility to docks, railways, raw material, power, markets, labor-surplus, will determine its rental value for factory purposes. In every such case, however, it is society and not the individual

---

[28] Quoted by Wesley Clair Mitchell in *The Trend of Economics*, edited by R. G. Tugwell, p. 5

that augments rent, and this unearned increment increases with
the growth of the community. From every advance of civilization
it is the landlord who profits. He is a social parasite, the nether
millstone between which and material progress the landless laborer
is ground.

In every direction, the direct tendency of advancing civilization is to
increase the power of human labour to satisfy human desires—to extirpate
poverty and to banish want and the fear of want. . . . But Labour cannot reap the benefits which advancing civilization thus brings, because
they are intercepted. Land being necessary to labour, and being reduced
to private ownership, every increase in the productive power of labour but
increases rent—the price that labour must pay for the opportunity to
utilise its power; and thus all the advantages gained by the march of
progress go to the owners of land, and wages do not increase. . . [29]
Labour and capital are but different forms of the same thing—human
exertion. Capital is produced by labour; it is, in fact, but labour impressed
upon matter. . . . The use of capital in production is, therefore, but a
mode of labour. . . . Hence the principle that, under circumstances which
permit free competition, operates to bring wages to a common standard
and profits to a substantial equality—the principle that men will seek to
gratify their desires with the least exertion—operates to establish and
maintain this equilibrium between wages and interest. . . . And this
relation fixed, it is evident that interest and wages must rise and fall together, and that interest cannot be increased without increasing wages,
nor wages be lowered without depressing interest.[30]

There is no inherent antagonism between labor and capital,
Henry George was early convinced. The Marxians with their
theory of a class war were mistaken in their analysis. It is rent that
is the true source of social injustice, and the clash of interests in
society lies between the producer and the parasitic rent-collector.
In every society the appropriation of measured increment has
enslaved the ownerless. In all civilizations, from ancient Peru to
modern Russia, it has subjected the worker to exploitation. Helot,
villein, serf, are only different names for a common slavery, the
profits of which go to the landlord. In modern times the Industrial
Revolution has changed the form of serfdom, only to intensify and
embitter it. The Manchester factory-hand was in worse plight
than the medieval villein after the Black Plague. Dispossessed of
his acres by the enclosure movement, he had been thrown into the
hoppers of industrialism and ground to pieces. He was helpless in

[29] *Progress and Poverty*, Book IV, Chapter 4.
[30] *Ibid.*, Book III, Chapter 5.

the hands of the masters, who with their monopoly of land and the machine, in control of the common heritage of trade processes, raw materials, transportation, credit, and the law-making and law-enforcing machinery, were taking from labor an augmenting toll of its production. Hence the close correlation between material progress and proletarian poverty. Hence the logical outcome of the Industrial Revolution, when it should have run its course, was the reduction of the worker to the level of a slave, compared with whose material condition the status of the southern bond-slave was enviable. The southern apologists of slavery had been right; the negro on the plantation enjoyed advantages denied to wage-labor under industrialism.[31]

Having thus analyzed the forces at work in modern society, and wedded a flamboyant material progress to a slattern poverty, Henry George proposed his sovereign remedy—the return to society of social values, hitherto expropriated by means of the private ownership of land, and the removal of the burden of indirect taxation from the back of productive labor. The Ricardian theory of rent, interpreted in the light of eighteenth-century *laissez faire*—of free competition, of a beneficent natural law, of social justice—conducted to unforeseen social issues. If labor and capital are individual, the fruits of both should return to their producers. Society has no just claim on what society has not produced, and the individual has no just claim to that which his labor or capital has not produced. Render unto Cæsar the things that are Cæsar's, and to the individual citizen the things that are his—such to Henry George was the sum of the law of distribution. Land monopoly was a refined denial of natural rights. "The equal right of all men to the use of the land is as clear as their equal right to breathe the air—it is a right proclaimed by the fact of their existence."[32] Unearned increment was the shackles wherewith labor was bound. In the name of social justice strike those shackles from the limbs of men and progress would never again have its ears filled with the wailings of poverty. The workman would once again sing at his work, and the sunshine of well-being fall pleasantly on the land.

A brilliant thinker, with a passionate sympathy for the exploited of earth, this knight-errant from out the newest West ardently believed in the sufficiency of his social philosophy to all

[31] See *Ibid.*, Book VII, Chapter 2.   [32] *Ibid.*, Book VII, Chapter I.

needs. In him the French Revolutionary doctrine came to its most original expression in America. No doubt, like his progenitors, he oversimplified the problem. Society is more complex than he esteemed it; individual motives are more complex. It is perilous to subordinate psychology to abstract theory; the ideal of justice is always running afoul of immediate and narrow interest. Later academic economists have dealt sharply with Henry George, but what have they done to justify their magisterial tone? The science of economics is still cousin-german to philosophy in its fondness for spinning tenuous subtleties; it is still system-ridden, still too much the apologist for things as they are. From its servitude to a class Henry George essayed to deliver it. In fastening upon monopoly as the prime source of social injustice, he directed attention to the origins of exploitative capitalism. He did more than any other man to spread through America a knowledge of the law of economic determinism. He opened a rich vein and one that needs further exploring. The suggestive principle of unearned increment calls for further expansion to embrace other forms than rent, to fit it to the needs of a complex society. What he seems not to have seen was the wider range of economic determinism—that changes come only when the existing order has become intolerable to great classes, and the grip of use and wont is loosened by the rebellions born of exigent need. "For ever the fat of the whole foundation hangeth to the priest's beard," asserted a quaint Beggars' Petition in appeal to Henry VIII against the monasteries, and in that comment were the seeds of the Reformation. When the beards are few to which the fat hangs, the time is ripe for an upheaval. An arch-idealist, Henry George would hasten the change by appeal to reason. Like Godwin and Tom Paine he believed that reason will make its own way, forgetting that reason waits upon interest, and the day of its freedom is long delayed. Yet if he was oversanguine, why account that to his discredit? *

* The discussion of Henry D. Lloyd, planned as the second subsection, was not written.—*Publisher.*

CHAPTER IV

THE BEGINNINGS OF CRITICISM

FOR many thoughtful Americans the welter of frontier individualism was a severe trial to their faith in American institutions. An ambitious industrialism colliding with a shambling Jacksonian democracy was forecasting consequences to government and to society that intelligent men could not shut their eyes to. The America of Fisk and Gould, of Boss Tweed and the *Crédit Mobilier* scandal, was far from satisfying the requirements of any rational civilization. After a hundred years to have come to such heroes, to have bogged down in such filth, was an outcome to the great experiment that one could not contemplate with pride. It was no time to be silent. No people was ever saved by dumb preachers. The present generation was answerable for the new evils that were springing from the graves of the old, and intelligent Americans must not lose their heads in the thick of the common hurly-burly. So amidst the ruck and clamor of the times a tiny note of criticism was lifted up, timid and uncertain at first, but growing more confident and more strident as the decade grew older. It was not searching criticism. Sooner or later it was pretty certain to run into a blind alley of moral indignation, overlooking the major issues and leaving the vital factors of the problem unconsidered. Yet such as it was—shallow and feeble enough often to excite wonder in a later generation—it marks the rise of a spirit of skepticism towards the blowsy doctrine of manifest destiny that since the fifties had been blowing about the land.

The determining factors in the situation confronting criticism were political and economic, and the immediate problem that pressed for solution was the problem whether an undisciplined people, wedded to an old-fashioned agrarian democracy, could cope with an ambitious industrialism that was quite cynically buying and selling the political state. To deal with that problem most of the critics were singularly ill equipped. Two generations of constitutional debate, seasoned with a dash of equalitarian dogma, had left them intellectually lean and impoverished. They had forgotten the sober realism of the eighteenth century that never overlooked the intimate ties between economics and politics, and with no anchors down in the plebeian mud they were likely to drift helplessly in the moral squalls they were always blowing up. The more distinguished critics—those who commanded the most serious attention—were in a particularly unfortunate situation, for not only were they uninstructed idealists with no understanding of *Realpolitik*, but they had been reared in the classical tradition and their minds were saturated with a decadent aristocratic culture. To many of them the present evils of America served only to quicken an inherited skepticism of democracy. How can society expect to function adequately, they asked, without capable and honest leadership; and how can such leadership be hoped for in a rough and tumble democracy that loves the noisiest demagogue? Of this very considerable group of belated Federalists James Russell Lowell was the most distinguished representative. In the middle seventies he had come to believe that America was suffering from too much democracy, and that competent government could be had only by working back to the responsible Federalism of earlier times, with leadership reclaimed by the better elements of society. To the economics of the problem—the antagonistic interests of capitalist, proletarian, and farmer, with their struggles to control the political state—he gave no serious thought, but he viewed with instinctive suspicion the mounting ambitions of labor and he foresaw only evil from the bitter unrest of the farmers.

A second very considerable group, of which George William Curtis may be taken as spokesman, rejected all such antiquated Federalistic hopes as the foolish dreams of defeatists. They held fast to their faith in democracy, but they were convinced that more adequate democratic machinery must be provided. The root of the evil, they had come to believe, was political and must be sought in the vicious Jacksonian spoils system. With every change of administration to turn over the country to hungry partisans to devour, was not democracy but the negation of democracy? Government would not function satisfactorily until a trained civil service was provided, and the need of the hour, they pointed out, was an honest civil service reform. A third group, very much smaller than the others, of which Edwin Lawrence Godkin was the spokesman, was inclined to trace the plentiful evils of the times to an unwise paternalism, asserting that the real source of the common political scoundrelism was the lauded American System devised by Henry Clay, as a result of which government was seduced from its proper business of keeping the peace and was turned into a fairy godmother to shower gifts on favored interests. The only cure for the evil was to divorce business and politics and reëstablish in practice the police theory of government.

In the thinking of all three groups little consideration was given to the social consequences of the venture on which America had entered with the vigor of thoughtless youth. Concerning the ultimate consequences of the collision between a shambling democracy and an ambitious industrialism, few troubled themselves greatly. To find those who confronted the problem frankly and realistically, one must search out obscure men, labor leaders for the most part, or *déclassé* radicals like Wendell Phillips. The middle-class mind refused to see what its feet were stumbling over. In consequence the Gilded Age produced no critics of industrialism comparable to the great English critics—Carlyle, Kingsley, Ruskin, Morris, Tawney; no social philosophers like the great continental expounders of proletarian ideals—Marx, Engels, Bakunin, Sorel; no left-wing economists like the great French school—Louis Blanc, Bastiat, Proudhon. The genteel culture of America was no better than bankrupt in presence of brutal reality, quite unequipped to interpret the sprawling America that was transforming itself before its eyes into something it hated but did not understand. The time for searching criticism had not come, and would not come until the Industrial Revolution had created in America a proletariat such as swarmed in the English black country and amongst the hovels of continental cities. Nevertheless such criticism as there was must be taken into consideration, and for our present purpose it will suffice to single out three spokesmen—a grizzled warrior of the earlier renaissance who had the courage to face unpleasant fact, and two critics who brought to bear on political themes the best culture of the time. With these may be conveniently grouped certain novelists who more or less casually suffered their pens to deal with social problems.

I

THE NEW ENGLAND CONSCIENCE AND CAPITALISM— WENDELL PHILLIPS

Social criticism was by no means a new thing in America. For half a century it had filled all ears with its strident clamors, and from it had issued the motley group of reform movements that had been cheered or mocked at by thousands. From Channing and Cooper down to Parke Godwin and Horace Greeley it had been mustering its forces, vivid and picturesque figures for the most part—men and women like Fanny Wright, George Henry Evans, and Hinton R. Helper; ardent souls who beyond the dun horizon discovered a golden morrow that only awaited the rising of a new sun, and who lectured and wrote and argued till pretty much all America had caught something of their contagious enthusiasm. In this work New England came eventually to take the lead, and the golden forties were a time when in many an obscure Yankee head programs of reform were fermenting like a vat of malt. But unfortunately an excess of eagerness wore out the first enthusiasm, and when the shackles had been loosened from the negro bondmen the militancy of the New England leadership subsided and the tired New England conscience went on vacation.

But in these slothful times the conscience of one great New Englander was not tired, though he gave it no rest while life lasted. Wendell Phillips was a soldier of Puritan soul who did not lay down his arms in '65, but for nearly a score of years warred upon the injustices of the Gilded Age as he had warred before upon the obscenities of negro slavery. No sooner was the cause of abolitionism won—a cause to which he had sacrificed much in ease and the good opinion of Beacon Street, but from which he had gained more in self-respect and the decent opinion of mankind—than he turned to whatever new work offered. The lovers of justice, he knew very well, can indulge themselves in no vacations, for the devil is on the job day and night, and while the assailants sleep he is at work repairing any breaches in the walls of his citadel. When conscience is tired he counts on gaining his greatest victories.

The love of freedom has always been a dangerous possession in Massachusetts, given to exploding in unforeseen moments and unexpected places. No one could have foretold—certainly not he himself—that Wendell Phillips would put away all his Brahmin

loyalties and devote forty-seven years to an unresting attack on the
diverse Toryisms from which he and his class had hitherto prospered. Son of the first mayor of the city and a distinguished member of the Boston gentry, he was a patrician in the fullest Boston
sense. All the loyalties of his caste summoned him to uphold the
Brahmin authorities, but something deep within him, a loyalty to
other and higher ideals, held him back. When a frock-coated mob
laid its hands on Garrison to lynch him for abolition propaganda,
he drew back; he refused to follow the Mayor and the Colonel of
his regiment and other gentlemen if they betrayed the Boston for
which their grandfathers had fought. An instinctive love of justice
held him back. A fierce indignation flamed up within him at the
wrong done a citizen of Massachusetts for exercising his natural
right of free speech, and in that wild hour he discovered that he was
a child of '76 with the mentality of a revolutionist. His conscience
was aroused and he proceeded to put it in the safe keeping of Ann
Terry Greene, a brilliant young woman of radical mind, who quickened his sense of social justice as Maria White was to quicken
Lowell's. There was to be no backsliding in his case. From the
December day in 1837 when he replied to Attorney-General
Austin's slanders of the Revolutionary fathers in Faneuil Hall, to
the end of a life filled with enormous labors—a life daily stabbed by
Tory hornets, and that at the last is said to have inspired the re-
mark of Judge Hoar that he did not attend the funeral of Wendell
Phillips but he approved of it [1]—he followed his conscience into
many an unpopular cause and spoke for those for whom few were
willing to speak.

The story of his anti-slavery labors belongs to an earlier time and
need not be recounted here. His devotion to abolitionism equaled
Garrison's and his services were as great. It is rather the nineteen
years that remained to him after Appomattox that are of present
concern—what later battles he fought and how he bore himself in
those battles. It was a difficult time for Puritan liberalism, face to
face with a new age that had forgotten the old liberalisms. The
Grand Army of Abolitionism had disbanded and new armies of
other causes had not yet been recruited. Garrison and Edmund
Quincy and Whittier had laid aside their arms, and Lowell had long
since settled back into a comfortable Brahminism; the long struggle
had left them drained of their energy. But for Wendell Phillips the

[1] See Charles Edward Russell, *The Story of Wendell Phillips*, p. 53.

battle was not over; it was unending and he was enlisted for life. At a vast meeting that marked the formal close of the abolition movement he took leave of his old associates with these words: "We will not say 'Farewell,' but 'all hail.' Welcome, new duties! We sheathe no sword. We only turn the front of the army upon a new foe." [2] He had long spoken for prohibition, woman's rights, the abolition of capital punishment, and he now joined heartily with the courageous women engaged in such reform work. But more provocative business was at hand, and more dangerous—causes that touched the northern pocketbook as abolitionism had touched the southern. The banker's exploitation of the national currency, and the manufacturer's exploitation of factory labor—these were issues that a cautious man who was careful of his good name would not meddle with. But Wendell Phillips was never cautious and his good name had long since been flung to the wolves. And so in the evening of his days, with a courage that took little counsel of expediency, he embarked on a campaign that had for its ultimate objective the impregnable citadel of State Street. He would destroy capitalistic exploitation in all its works. It was as hopeless a battle as King Arthur's "last, dim, weird battle of the west," and entered upon as courageously.

How he came to hold the heretical views on money and labor that he expounded from the lecture platform cannot easily be traced. Perhaps they came from the radical fringe that envelops every great social movement; perhaps they were the inevitable expression of his left-wing temper. A man who had fought all Tory programs for thirty years must eventually come to hate the ways of capitalism, and so confirmed a democrat as Wendell Phillips would be certain to espouse the doctrine of thorough. One who had passed through the fires of abolition nullification, who had spoken of the Union as "built i' the eclipse and rigged with curses dark," who had repudiated his citizenship and equaled Garrison in contempt for a slave-protecting Constitution, would have pretty well cleared his mind of conventional respect for capitalistic law and order. He was not impressed by political cant. He had taken the measure of existing law and order and was casting about for a juster law and a more generous order.

In these later years, as a program of social reconstruction took shape in his mind, he was coming to essential agreement with the

[2] Quoted in Martyn, *Wendell Phillips: The Agitator*, p. 372.

program of socialism. With the Marxians he based his thinking upon economics, and his final objective came to be the substitution of coöperation for the profit-motive. As ardently as Horace Greeley he asserted the rights of labor. As early as 1860–1861 he had come to recognize a similarity in the economic status of the wage-slave and the bond-slave, and in 1865, in a speech on the eight-hour movement, he accepted as true the southern thesis that in western civilization all labor, whether bond or wage, was unfree, held in the grip of a master, bought and sold in the market; [3] and now that the shackles had been struck from the negro, it remained to strike them from the wage-earner. To turn the negro from a bond-slave to a wage-slave would be a sorry ending of abolitionism; but such must be the inevitable outcome, he believed, unless all labor should win freedom. The question of the hour for Wendell Phillips had become the question of the relation of labor and capital.

In his thinking on the currency question—a question that became acute in the seventies—he was soon caught up by the Greenback movement. It may have been that his contact with Thaddeus Stevens helped to mold his views on the money question; yet that he should have become a Greenbacker was foreordained. He had no amiable illusions in regard to State Street. As a tribune of the people he had long been intimately acquainted with its ambitions, and he would not turn over the country to its custodianship. He would have no bankers' control of the national currency, to augment or deflate as banking profits dictated. His democratic sympathies recoiled from a class control of the common medium of exchange, and in 1875 he offered a drastic solution of the vexing question that brought down on his head all the wrath of State Street. His plan provided for three things: the rejection of the national banknote system; the issue of honest greenbacks, secured by the wealth of the country, and receivable in payment for all debts public and private—not dishonest greenbacks like the old, which the government had repudiated at issue by refusing to accept them in payment of custom dues; and finally the retirement of interest-bearing bonds and the return to a cash basis for government business. How deeply he felt in the notorious matter of credit manipulation is suggested in the following passage with its echoes of an older America that looked with suspicion on a consolidating capitalism.

[3] See *Speeches*, Second Series, p. 139.

Three times within a dozen years, [he said] capitalists with their knives on the throat of the Government, have compelled it to cheat its largest creditor, the people; whose claim, Burke said, was the most sacred. First, the pledge that greenbacks should be exchangeable with bonds was broken. Secondly, debts originally payable in paper . . . were made payable in gold. Thirdly, silver was demonetized, and gold made the only tender. A thousand millions were thus stolen from the people.[4]

At other times he went further. Speaking on the labor question in 1872, he said:

I say, let the debts of the country be paid, abolish the banks, and let the government lend every Illinois farmer (if he wants it), who is now borrowing money at ten per cent., money on the half-value of his land at three per cent. The same policy that gave a million acres to the Pacific Railroad, because it was a great national effort, will allow of our lending Chicago twenty millions of money, at three per cent., to rebuild it.[5]

When we get into power, there is one thing we mean to do. If a man owns a single house, we will tax him one hundred dollars. If he owns ten houses of like value, we won't tax him one thousand dollars, but two thousand dollars. . . . We'll double and treble and quintuple and sextuple and increase tenfold the taxes. . . . We'll crumple up wealth by making it unprofitable to be rich. . . . You will say, "Is that just?" My friends, it is safe. Man is more valuable than money. You say, "Then capital will go to Europe." Good heavens, let it go! If other States wish to make themselves vassals of wealth, so will not we. We will save a country equal from end to end. Land, private property, all sorts of property, shall be so dearly taxed that it shall be impossible to be rich; for it is in wealth, in incorporated, combining, perpetuated wealth, that the danger of labor lies.[6]

The mad wicked ravings of a demagogue, such talk was accounted by sober financiers of Boston. But it was rather the talk of an honest equalitarian who understood how incompatible was property rule and the ideal of equality. The arch-enemy of a worthy civilization, Wendell Phillips had become convinced, was private capitalism with its dehumanizing profit-motive. There could be no adequate civilization, no Christianity, until coöperation had displaced competition, and men were become equal in economic rights as they were in franchise rights. At a Labor-Reform Convention held at Worcester on September 4, 1871, resolutions drafted by him were adopted—resolutions that reveal "just where Mr. Phillips stood for the last thirteen years of his life."

[4] Quoted in Martyn, *op. cit.*, pp. 412–413.
[5] *Speeches*, Second Series, p. 176.
[6] *Ibid.*, p. 167.

In this "full body of faith," and in two later speeches—*The Founda-tion of the Labor Movement*, and *The Labor Question*—the man who called himself "a Jeffersonian democrat in the darkest hour," wrote down as the great objective of the labor party the principle that has long been accepted as the cardinal plank of the Socialist platform.

We affirm, as a fundamental principle, that labor, the creator of wealth, is entitled to all it creates.

Affirming this, we avow ourselves willing to accept the final results of the operation of a principle so radical,—such as the overthrow of the whole profit-making system, the extinction of all monopolies, the abolition of privileged classes, universal education and fraternity, perfect freedom of exchange, and . . . the final obliteration of that foul stigma upon our so-called Christian civilization—the poverty of the masses. . . . *Resolved*, —That we declare war with the wages system, which demoralizes alike the hirer and the hired, cheats both, and enslaves the workingman; war with the present system of finance, which robs labor, and gorges capital, . . . war with these lavish grants of the public lands to speculating com-panies, and whenever in power, we pledge ourselves to use every just and legal means to resume all such grants heretofore made; war with the sys-tem of enriching capitalists by the creation and increase of public interest-bearing debts. We demand that every facility, and all encouragement, shall be given by law to co-operation in all branches of industry and trade, and that the same aid be given to co-operative efforts that has heretofore been given to railroads and other enterprises. . . .[7]

When he was about to take the platform on another occasion his wife is reported to have said to him, "Wendell, don't shilly-shally!" Certainly in this pronouncement, and in the speeches supporting it, there is no shilly-shallying. He will have no halfway measures, but goes straight to the economic core of the problem. Pretty much all of Marxianism is there, even to the class war. The capitalists had whetted their swords and he would have labor put its sword likewise to the grindstone. If the war were cruel, where did labor learn it—"learned it of capital, learned it of our enemies." In a world of economic concentration where caste follows property accumulation he had come to rest his hopes on the international solidarity of labor. The cause of democratic justice was committed to the keeping of the workingman, and if he were defeated in his hopes the future was black indeed. The American Revolution and the French Revolution had prepared the way gloriously for a greater event, the revolution of labor

[7] *Ibid.*, pp. 152–153.

He was not afraid of revolution. In America he hoped the battle would be fought with ballots, but if it must come to bullets, so be it. The Paris Commune met with his heartiest approval: "I have not a word to utter—far be it from me!—against the grandest declaration of popular indignation which Paris wrote on the pages of history in fire and blood. I honor Paris as the vanguard of the Internationals of the world." [8] And in the Phi Beta Kappa address, delivered in 1881 before all the assembled conservatisms of Boston, the old warrior with seventy years upon his head, went so far as to defend Russian Nihilism.

Nihilism is the righteous and honorable resistance of a people crushed under an iron rule. Nihilism is evidence of life . . . the last weapon of victims choked and manacled beyond all other resistance. . . . I honor Nihilism, since it redeems human nature from the suspicion of being utterly vile, made up only of heartless oppressors and contented slaves. . . . This is the only view an American, the child of 1620 and 1776, can take of Nihilism. Any other unsettles and perplexes the ethics of our civilization. Born within sight of Bunker Hill, in a commonwealth which adopts the motto of Algernon Sydney, *sub libertate quietem* ("accept no peace without liberty"); son of Harvard, whose first pledge was "Truth"; citizen of a republic based on the claim that no government is rightful unless resting on the consent of the people, and which assumes to lead in asserting the rights of humanity,—I at least can say nothing else and nothing less; no, not if every tile on Cambridge roofs were a devil hooting my words! [9]

"It was a delightful discourse," said one gentleman, "but preposterous from beginning to end." The doctrine was strange to Harvard ears—wicked and perverse. And strange and disconcerting also was his roll-call of great and noble deeds done in America in which Harvard scholarship had had no part. To an audience of Brahmin scholars it was not kind to say, "The greatest things have not been done for the world by its bookmen"; nor this, "It is not the masses who have most disgraced our political annals. I have seen many mobs . . . I never saw or heard of any but well-dressed mobs, assembled and countenanced, if not always led in person, by respectability and what called itself education." [10] It was a curious scene—that gathering in a Harvard hall listening to a son of Harvard who had gone to school to other teachers than those brought up on Brahmin culture. The liberalism of the forties was speaking to a generation that was concerned about other

[8] *Ibid.*, p. 154.   [9] See *Ibid.*, pp. 356–359.   [10] See *Ibid.*, p. 347.

things than a just and humane civilization. Wendell Phillips was hopelessly old-fashioned in America of the Gilded Age—a lone Puritan in a land of Yankees. He used to speak of himself grimly as "that Ishmael"; his home, he said, was the sleeping-car and his only friends the brakeman and the porter. He spent his strength and his earnings with generous prodigality, and when he died the only treasures he had laid up were in heaven. He was the last survivor of the great age of Puritan conscience, and the words he spoke of Theodore Parker may well stand for his epitaph: "The child of Puritanism is not mere Calvinism—it is the loyalty to justice which tramples under foot the wicked laws of its own epoch."

II

MORALITY AND POLITICS—GEORGE WILLIAM CURTIS

A child of Puritan conscience also was George William Curtis, like Wendell Phillips sprung from the Puritan gentry, but unlike him wanting in a passionate Hebraism that sought justice in all the byways and would not turn aside from pursuing it. A reformer but never a radical, he was a gentleman who was a lifelong friend of civilization. An idealist, he refused to serve the gross materialisms that swept so many of his fellows from the old moorings, but throughout a long and honorable career he preserved unshaken his early faith in republican ideals and the way of liberty. As an abolitionist he faced hostile audiences with admirable poise, and as a civil service reformer he fought off the attacks of greasy politicians with quiet contempt. A cultivated gentleman, high-bred if not heroic, was George William Curtis.

Born in Providence, Rhode Island, of excellent stock, living most of his life in New York City whither his father had removed to engage in the banking business, he was brought up in affluence and spent his days amidst dignified surroundings. Broad-minded and generous, with wide sympathies and urbane manners, he followed his conscience and weighed life in the scales of Puritan morality. He was no friend to compromise or expediency, yet he was content to serve God in the station whereunto he had been called, declining to turn rebel and become an outcast and pariah. Endowed with excellent parts, his training was unusually fortunate. At eighteen with his brother Burrill he went to Brook Farm, where he spent two profitable years in an atmosphere he found stimulating. After

quitting Brook Farm he passed the better part of two years at
Concord with his brother, living at farmhouses, helping with the
crops, and for a time indulging in an experiment not unlike Thoreau's at Walden Pond. Then followed four years overseas—from
1846 to 1850—rambling about the continent, sloughing off the
provincial asceticism of New England, and practicing his pen by
means of letters and diaries. On his return he drifted into journalism, wrote several volumes of travel essays and social satire,
caught the Lyceum infection, then at its malignant stage, lectured
voluminously to pay off an unfortunate debt, wrote for *Putnam's
Magazine*, became connected with *Harper's Weekly*, finally settling
into the Easy Chair of *Harper's Magazine*, from which comfortable
seat for years he sent forth gracefully pointed comments on manners, society, politics, life, yet more and more turning to politics as
his particular field and serving as volunteer political mentor and
critic to the Gilded Age.

Of his several early ventures into the field of polite letters little
need be said. The work of a high-spirited young man, they were
a cross between Nathaniel Parker Willis and Thackeray with a
suggestion of Disraeli. He took his place naturally as a member of
the New York group of littérateurs who were gaily exploiting the
conventional sentimentalism of the fifties. With its pose of clever
sophistication the New York school could do no good to a serious
young writer, and the pretensions of the new-rich society of the
town were a cordial invitation to go wrong. *Nile Notes of a Howadji*
(1851), written before the young traveler had caught the current
note of social satire, was a conscious correction of the ascetic
Puritanism imbibed at Concord, and with its frank delight in the
sensuousness of the East it gave offense to the professional blue-
stockings of the time. But in *The Potiphar Papers* (1853) he turned
to satirize New York society, then hastening to transform itself
from a staid Knickerbocker world into a Gold Coast of social
climbers. That his treatment of the theme should have been a
slighter edition of Thackeray's *Vanity Fair*—less searching and
more sentimental—might be guessed even if we did not know how
greatly Curtis loved and admired the English satirist. "He seems
to be the one of all authors who takes life precisely as he finds it,"
he wrote of him. "If he finds it sad, he makes it sad: if gay,
gay. You discover in him the flexible adaptability of Horace,
but with a deep and consuming sadness which the Roman never

knew, and which in the Englishman seems to be almost sentimentality.[11]

But in spite of their excellent model these sketches do not now
seem so sprightly as they seemed to his fellows on the staff of
Putnam's Magazine. Moralism scented with patchouli is no longer
the vogue, and they have long since been laid away with the hoops
and crinoline of the fifties. His most important venture in polite
literature—if indeed even that deserves the name important—was
Prue and I (1856), written in a golden summer when his pen was
dipped into the inkwell of love and he foresaw the years of his life
lengthening out in the most intimate of companionships. They are
charming essays in contentment that teach the familiar lesson that
the only abiding riches are the riches of mind and character. The
old bookkeeper in black coat and white tie who voyages to the
realms of romance while watching from the Battery outgoing ships,
has discovered the vicarious pleasure of the imagination, and the
Aurelia of his dreams is Prue as she was in her youth, and both are
Anna Shaw to whom soon after he was married. The first three
sketches—"Dinner Time," "My Chateaux," and "Sea from the
Shore"—are humorous and tender fancies in the graceful Victorian
manner; but "Titbottom's Spectacles" is Hawthorne-like in the
tenuous play of a grotesquely moralistic fancy, and the succeeding
sketches reveal the exhaustion of the vein. Later he tried his hand
at a novel—*Trumps*—but it refused to turn into anything but a
tract and in the early sixties he settled down in the Easy Chair
which he had first occupied as early as 1853.

Thereafter to his death in 1892 his work followed three diverse
lines. For thirty years he was essayist, orator, and political critic,
to a generation sorely in need of wise and urbane counsel. His
audience was wide and his influence great, and to his work he
brought the weight of his sane and just character. Not a great
scholar and not an acute critic, he was an enlightened and sensitive
conscience, and to the bar of his conscience he summoned the
parties and policies of a heedless and selfish generation. From the
Easy Chair he sent forth his genial comment on matters of current
interest, satisfying his love of creative writing by the grace of his
talk, and recognizing his kinship with the age of Queen Ann by
adopting the words of *The Tatler*, "I shall from time to time Report
and Consider all Matters of what Kind soever that shall occur to

[11] Edward Cary, *George William Curtis*, p. 78.

me." But such work at the best is ephemeral, and ephemeral likewise were the polished pronouncements of the occasional orator on
which far too much time and labor were expended. But New York
City must have its spokesman for formal occasions, and after
Bryant's death George William Curtis was summoned with increasing frequency. The rich context of his speeches, elaborated
with formal dignity and embellished with literary allusions, hit to
a nicety the taste of a generation that still delighted in oratory and
preferred dignity to informality. His addresses on Charles Sumner,
Wendell Phillips, Bryant, and Lowell, are excellent examples of a
style that is no longer the fashion. In their polished sentences
eulogy is tempered with criticism, but the criticism is sympathetic
and refuses to render judgments that may strike his hearers as
severe. It would be ungracious to intrude unpleasant facts on dignified occasions.

But his most significant work during these busy years lay in the
field of political criticism, and it was as editor of *Harper's Weekly*,
from 1863 to his death, and as a leader in the movement of civil
service reform, that he made the deepest impress on the age. The
Weekly, with Nast as cartoonist, was then at the height of its
popularity and influence, and by means of its editorial page Curtis
was able to marshal a very considerable following for whatever
cause or party he espoused. He had long taken part in practical
politics, was active in caucuses and conventions, was much on the
stump and kept his fingers on party wires. Yet influential as he
was—the scholar in politics, as his own generation loved to say—he
was never a serious student of politics in the broader meaning. He
was essentially an English gentleman politician, with a fine scorn
of mean and sordid policies, a warm love of country but an equally
warm love of civilization, devoted to the cause of liberty, a friend of
justice, yet with all his excellent traits an inadequate political philosopher. Like Lowell's his horizon was curiously limited. Abstract
political theory did not interest him and he never critically examined
diverse systems of government. Of economics he was as ignorant
as his generation. Again like Lowell the single standard by which he
judged politics was the moral standard, and in his anxious concern for
"good government" he failed to probe deeply the sources of "bad
government." In presence of the vast corruptions of the Gilded
Age he was as helpless in diagnosing the evil as Lowell or Norton.

Such helplessness is the more surprising considering what rare opportunities he had enjoyed for intelligent understanding. During the impressionable years of youth he daily associated with the most militant group of intellectual radicals in America and heard the ideas of Saint-Simon and Fourier and Owen eagerly canvassed. Associationism as a cure for the evils of competition was the cardinal doctrine of the Brook Farmists; yet his individualism passed unaffected through all such discussions. He seems to have sympathized with the skepticism of Hawthorne rather than the faith of Ripley and Dana. Writing to his father from Brook Farm he fell into the genial transcendental vein and gaily poked fun at those who would make the world over.

No wise man is long a reformer, [he wrote] for Wisdom sees plainly that growth is steady, sure, and neither condemns nor rejects what is, or has been. Reform is organized distrust. It says to the universe fresh from God's hand, "You are a miserable business; lo! I will make you fairer!" and so deputes some Fourier or Robert Owen to improve the bungling work of the Creator.[12]

It was as a transcendental optimist that he set out on his travels in 1846. The Europe he visited at the age of twenty was seething with discontent that was to flame up in the revolutionary year of '48, yet though he wandered leisurely through Italy, Hungary, Germany, France, and was at Paris during the great overturn, the evidence that his biographer has gathered indicates that he was not deeply affected by the experience. Unlike his friend Margaret Fuller, who was a passionate volunteer in the struggle of Mazzini at Rome, or like Dana, who followed the movement closely as foreign correspondent, he felt none of the promptings of a revolutionist. A romantic sympathy for Kossuth is clearly indicated, but his feelings carried him little further than that. Even in England, seething as it was with the proletarian unrest that culminated in the great Chartist movement, he came upon little to quicken his transcendental pulse. It was not till he got back home and found himself in presence of negro slavery that his reforming ardor took fire and he proposed to engage in the business of "organized distrust." He threw himself into the cause with enthusiasm and spoke from many an abolition platform. Then came the war and during those passionate years he was swept unconsciously along the path of consolidation, emerging from the fire a confirmed Hamiltonian with transcendental democratic leanings.

[12] See *Ibid.*, pp. 25–26.

Have you thought [he wrote Charles Eliot Norton in 1864] what a vindication this war is of Alexander Hamilton? I wish somebody would write his life as it ought to be written, for surely he was one of the greatest of our great men, as Jefferson was the least of the truly great; or am I wrong? Hamilton was generous and sincere. Was Jefferson either? [13]

Such Hamiltonian sympathies suffice to explain some of his votes in the New York Constitutional Convention of 1867, of which he was a member. He advocated the appointment of the attorney-general and certain other state officers, opposed the principle of municipal home rule, and approved the extension of the authority of the state over local police systems. With Tammany Hall and Boss Tweed before his eyes it was perhaps natural that he should have sought in the power of the up-state voter some external control over the city machine. But in spite of such obvious leanings towards the Whig branch of the Republican party Curtis was never a Whig. The transcendentalism he had imbibed at Brook Farm remained with him to color much of his thinking and restrain him from an uncritical advocacy of capitalism. He never went over body and soul to the new gospel of exploitation. He never lent a willing ear to the seductive appeals of the American System. He early became a free-trader and throughout his life was opposed to all tariffs and grants and subsidies. Discovering in the principle of liberty the cardinal principles of American democracy, he was disposed to accept a wide application of *laissez faire;* yet when it opened the door to extortion he was willing to curb an anti-social individualism. When in the seventies it was proposed by the western farmers that a national railroad should be built from Chicago to the Atlantic seaboard, Curtis looked upon the proposal with sympathy as likely to rescue the farmer from extortionate tolls.[14] Unlike Dana and Godkin, he declined to grow bitter and lose his head over the economic proposals of the western agrarians. In the sharp alignment between agrarianism and capitalism he stood in the main outside both parties, and although opposed to greenbackism he discussed the question with moderation and good sense—a rare thing in those blatant times.

But it was political decency rather than capitalistic or agrarian programs that he was chiefly concerned about. He looked to his conscience as guide and as editor of *Harper's Weekly* he used his influence to cleanse America of the corruption he abhorred. Week

13 See *Ibid.*, pp. 180–181.　　　　14 See *Harper's Weekly*, Sept. 20, 1873.

after week he appealed to the American voter to turn rascals out of office and put honest men in. The corrupt political machine was the source of the evil, and the machine had grown powerful through its control of patronage. There would be vicious government so long as politicians could create a machine by means of the spoils system. Two remedies, he believed, were necessary to cure the evil—independent voting and civil service reform; and to the spread of these two ideas he devoted the last twenty years of his life, thereby bringing on his head much abuse and incurring eventually a break with the Republican party.

His troubles began with his proposal of independent voting. To that party-ridden generation on whom the passions of war had fastened a tyrannical machine, the scratching of the party ticket seemed no better than treason. It was a Copperhead device to undo the results of the war and reëstablish the rebel leaders at Washington, and it needed courage to advocate it publicly. Curtis put the matter fairly in a speech to Independent Republicans at New York in 1880:

The first powerful and conclusive remedy for the tyranny of the machine . . . is scratching. The word has become a sneer, a taunt, a bitter reproach, but the test of the power and effectiveness of the remedy is the fury with which it is assailed. . . . The machine denounces scratchers as lustily as Laud denounced the Puritans, or George III the rebellious Yankees, or slave-driving Democrats Republican woolly heads. . . . The scratcher is the minute-man of politics. He is always in light marching order. He has only to consult his own knowledge and conscience, and with one stroke his work is done. Fortunately, also, his stroke may be as secret as his ballot. Those who do not choose to publish the fact need not be known, and may smile serenely at the blind fury of those whose plots are quietly foiled. This is the reason of the impotent anger with which scratching is assailed. It cannot be reached. . . . Scratching is denounced as dishonorable. Oh, no! the secret ballot is not dishonorable. The shot of the Middlesex farmer from behind a tree was no more dishonorable than the immortal volley from behind the breastworks of Bunker Hill. [15]

He then proceeded to lay open what seemed to him the core of the problem:

But useful as scratching is as a corrective, it does not strike at the heart of the machine, and it is therefore *only* a corrective and not a radical remedy. That remedy can be found only by finding the source of the power of the machine, and that source is official patronage. It is the command of millions of the public money spent in public administration; the control

[15] *Orations and Addresses*, "Machine Politics and the Remedy," Vol. II, pp. 157-159.

of the vast labyrinth of place, with its enormous emoluments; the system which makes the whole Civil Service, to the least detail and most significant position, the spoils of party victory; which perverts necessary party organization into intolerable party despotism. It is upon this that the hierarchy of the machine is erected. Strike at this system strongly, steadily, persistently, and you shiver the machine to pieces.[16]

Seeing his duty clearly, Curtis did not spare himself, but while most of his fellows were seeking fame or wealth for themselves he gave his time and strength without stint to the cause, and it was due to his efforts more than to those of any other man that a reform in the civil service was eventually brought about. He had to fight his way against bitter opposition. It was charged that he was seeking to create in America an undemocratic bureaucracy. His old friend Charles A. Dana—from whom he had become estranged—was quite frank. "Above all I do not believe," he said, "in the establishment in this country of the German bureaucratic system, with its permanent staff of office-holders who are not responsible to the people, and whose tenure of place knows no variation and no end except the end of life." [17] But it was the politicians who fought most bitterly, and when to civil service reform he added the sin of bolting the party, throwing over Blaine and supporting Cleveland, he was subjected to plentiful insults. Nevertheless as the leader of the Mugwumps, preaching to a party-ridden generation the gospel of independency, he did his country a real service. He could not foresee, of course, how easily the menace of the independent voter was to be met; how through the control of both party machines and both nominees by the political bosses the independent would have only the choice betwixt tweedledum and tweedledee, and in disgust would largely refrain from voting. But the open and crying political evils of the Gilded Age he saw clearly, and in seeking to lessen them he proved himself a useful citizen as well as a cultivated American.

III

ENGLISH LIBERALISM AND POLITICS—GODKIN AND "THE NATION"

The severest critic of the Gilded Age was Edwin Lawrence Godkin, founder of the *Nation*. More caustic than George William Curtis, equipped with a complete social philosophy, and armed with

[16] See *Ibid.*, p. 160.   [17] J. H. Wilson, *The Life of Charles A. Dana*, p. 466.

perfect self-assurance, he devoted thirty-five years to the task of instructing America in the principles of government as those principles were understood by John Stuart Mill. He was at once an idealist and a realist, and the intellectual history of the critic is revealed in the shift from the one to the other. To Godkin the English liberal—who had studied the American experiment from overseas—as to Karl Schurz the German liberal, America was the torchbearer of the democratic faith; and any defection from the cause, any betrayal of that faith, was a desecration of the temple of liberalism by its own priesthood. Liberalism, he was persuaded, was the handmaid of civilization; the hope of any rational progress, rested on the principle of free inquiry and free endeavor. To Godkin, therefore, and to Schurz and the hundreds of European liberals who sought refuge here following the *débâcle* of the revolutionary hopes of 1848, it was a matter of deep import that America should remain true to its liberal tradition, trusting freedom, refusing to repeat the unhappy experience of a Tory Europe. He would say to America what John Wise had said nearly two centuries before: "Ye have been called unto liberty, therefore hold your hold, brethren! Pull up well upon the oars, you have a rich cargo, and I hope . . . day-light and good piloting will secure all." But he would do more than that; he would pull an oar himself; and with high hopes, at the age of twenty-five, he cast in his lot with America to serve the cause in whatever ways might offer.

Godkin came of an English Protestant strain that for seven centuries had lived in County Wexford, at the extreme southeastern point of Ireland. He was neither Scotch like the men of Ulster, nor Irish like his neighbors of Kilkenny and Wicklow, but as English in blood and temperament as Jonathan Swift. Educated at Queen's College, Belfast, he studied law for a time at Lincoln's Inn, went through the revolutionary years of 1848–1851 with their great hopes, and entered the field of journalism as correspondent for the London *Daily News* during the Crimean War. In 1856 he came to America with the intention of entering the law, but returned to journalism. During the Civil War he was correspondent for the *Daily News* of London, laboring to counteract British Tory opinion that ran strongly pro-South, and marshal the forces of English liberalism on the side of the North. Three months after Appomattox he founded the *Nation* as an organ of criticism, through the columns of which he proposed to appeal to the intelligence and the conscience of America in support of the principles of Victorian liberalism.

For this excellent work of criticism Godkin was provided with a sound equipment. Endowed with a vigorous intellect, he kept his mind free from shifting fogs and rarely mistook immediate for ultimate ends. His training had been in a distinguished tradition. His father was a Presbyterian minister and journalist, and the strain of robust dissent that contributed so richly to Victorian liberalism came to him as a birthright. He was "brought up," he said, "in the Mill-Grote school of radicals." "When I was in college," he wrote in later years, "I and the young men of my acquaintance were Liberals, in the English sense. John Stuart Mill was our prophet, and Grote and Bentham were our daily food." [18] Already his heart was overseas; America as it had been described by de Tocqueville was his "promised land," the home of a free democracy on which his hopes for civilization were fixed. His first book, written at the early age of twenty-two, was a history of the land Kossuth was striving to set free, and he there defined the word democrat as he had come to interpret it—the democrats, he said, are "all those whose hopes and sympathies are not bound up in a party or class, but look for the welfare and progress of humanity as the goal of their striving." [19]

Thus he wrote in the aftermath of the revolutionary years of 1848–1851. But the glowing idealism of the young radical was to suffer discouragements and setbacks from the experience of later years. One suspects that his liberalism never possessed the whole of him, never grew from within out, but was overlaid on a nature fundamentally aristocratic that at heart preferred Tory to liberal ends. Though as a young man he spred his canvas to the winds of liberalism, he was always a little distrustful of the bellying sails and he never quite liked the crew. There is a curious suggestiveness in his changing attitude towards England and English society. He had quitted the old world out of dislike for it, and a dozen years later he declined to go back except as a "last extremity." "It would be going back," he said, "into an atmosphere that I detest and a social system that I have hated since I was fourteen years old." [20] At the bottom of this repugnance was an obstinate pride. He was ambitious, capable, and sensitive, and a caste society that refused

[18] Ogden, *Life and Letters of Edwin Lawrence Godkin*, Vol. I, p. 11.
[19] *Ibid.*, Vol. I, p. 17.   [20] *Ibid.*, Vol. II, p. 140.

to open its doors to him he looked upon as pernicious. To assert that his espousal of democracy was due to his brusque rejection by a more distinguished mistress, is a severe judgment, yet it is a judgment that his friend Henry Holt quite frankly implied.[21]

He had come to America in the hope of getting on in the world. He had a strong regard for social position. His standards were severe and his sympathies so narrow as to lay him open to the frequent charge of snobbery. He would mingle in none but good society, and it was easier in America than in England to gain entrance to good society. Until he had made his mark he would not go back; but when as a distinguished editor he ventured to return, and found himself accepted by the best people, his hatred for the English social system oozed away, and the eager delight he experienced in upper-class society was an unconscious testimony to the value he had set upon a system from which as a young man he had been excluded. Godkin was too English to make himself over into an American, too natively aristocratic to be a democrat. A disciple of John Stuart Mill, he lacked the complete intellectual integrity of Mill that brushed aside all caste prejudices and personal ambitions, as he lacked his vast intellectual accumulation. Godkin's liberalism was founded on Mill, but it was never quite Mill.

The philosophy to which, as a disciple of the Bentham-Mill-Grote school, the young Godkin gave his allegiance, was a Utilitarian adaptation of *laissez faire*—the doctrine that the greatest happiness of the greatest number is the ultimate social objective, and that such objective can be attained only through the completest liberty under the sway of reason and justice. As presented by John Stuart Mill it was a singularly persuasive philosophy that awakened a response in every generous mind. Liberty, he insisted, is the thing chiefly to be desired, for where men are free they will shape social organisms to their needs. Man is both an economic and a political animal, and the difficult problem of the political philosopher is to keep the one from trespassing upon the rights of the other. The economic man, under the drive of the acquisitive instinct, regards the political state as an ally in the present business of acquisition; and the political man looks upon business as subject to strict regulation and control in the interests of the state. To prevent this meddlesome interference of each with the other, Mill laid down the principle of liberty in terms as uncompromising as

[21] *Nation*, July 8, 1915, p. 47.

those of the Physiocrats. The "sole end," he asserted, "for which mankind are warranted, individually or collectively, in interfering with the liberty of action of any of their number, is self-protection," and "the only purpose for which power can be rightfully exercised over any member of a civilized community, against his will, is to prevent harm to others. His own good, either physical or moral, is not a sufficient warrant." [22]

From this excellent school the young Godkin emerged a political theorist of no mean ability; somewhat too dogmatic, perhaps, a bit overconfident of the finality of his logic, but with a shrewd dialectic, quick to separate reality from pretense, severe upon all flummery and buncombe. That his philosophy was sharply opposed to the current tendencies of American political life he saw clearly: to Whiggery with its ambitious paternalisms; to centralization with its glorification of a Bismarckian state. His thought was erected on a foundation of *laissez faire*, and he sharply differentiated economics and politics. As a realist he recognized differences in individual capacity, but he was keenly suspicious of any attempt on the part of government to compensate for such differences. Any interference with natural law, he was convinced, entailed greater evils than benefits. Economic competition is a struggle between individuals, and government must content itself with its proper rôle of policeman to keep the peace. With Mill he refused to recognize the state as a separate entity. He never confused the personnel of government with "what is called 'the state'"; and as he contemplated the honesty and capacity of the several members who administered government in a given commonwealth, he was disinclined to entrust them with regulative powers. Disinterested honesty and capacity, it seemed, too rarely got into office, governments were too little acquainted with common morality, to justify hopes of equalizing the inequality of nature by political means.

To the sound philosophical equipment brought from England Godkin added a very considerable understanding of American political history. The ten years spent here before the founding of the *Nation*, had been employed in getting at home upon the new scene. He had carefully checked the findings of de Tocqueville and was convinced that the French critic had gone far astray in his interpretation of the great American experiment. In his analysis of democratic tendencies he had fallen into the fallacy of *post hoc*

[22] *On Liberty*, Chapter I.

ergo propter hoc, with the result that he had got the cart before the horse; and in an article published in the *North American Review* of January, 1865, Godkin entered the lists in defense of America against the criticisms of English Tories founded on such fallacies. In its emphasis on historical realism "Aristocratic Opinions of Democracy" is a surprisingly modern study that might almost have been written by one of our younger historians. It is an interpretation of our political development in terms of environment, and it traces the rise of democracy to the leveling influence of decentralization. For a hundred and fifty years, he pointed out, old-world habits and customs, the spirit of aristocracy, prevailed in the closely grouped settlements along the Atlantic seaboard, where physical conditions restrained the tendency to social disruption; but with the breaking through of the Appalachian barrier, and the influx of new waves of immigration, the conditions were prepared for a vast movement of decentralization. It was the Inland Empire that made possible the democratic revolution in America. "How was it," he asks, "that that democratic tide, which within the last fifty years, has overwhelmed everything, during the previous hundred and fifty years gave so few signs of rising?" And his reply to the question antedates Professor Turner's theory of the frontier by thirty years:

If we inquire what are those phenomena of American society which it is generally agreed distinguish it from that of older countries, we shall find . . . that by far the larger number of them may be attributed in a great measure to what, for want of a better name, we shall call "the frontier life" led by a large proportion of the inhabitants, and to the influence of this portion on manners and legislation, rather than to political institutions, or even to the equality of conditions. In fact, we think that these phenomena, and particularly those of them which excite most odium in Europe, instead of being the effect of democracy, are partly its cause, and that it has been to their agency more than aught else, that the democratic tide in America has owed most of its force and violence.

The agency which, in our opinion, gave democracy its first great impulse in the United States, which has promoted its spread ever since, and has contributed most powerfully to the production of those phenomena in American society which hostile critics set down as peculiarly democratic, was neither the origin of the Colonists, nor the circumstances under which they came to the country, nor their religious belief; but the great change in the distribution of the population, which began soon after the Revolution, and which continues its operation up to the present time.[23]

[23] "Aristocratic Opinions of Democracy," in *Problems of Modern Democracy,* pp. 25–26, 30–31.

Godkin was thirty-four when he entered upon his life work of pouring a stream of fresh and free thought upon the ways of the Gilded Age. It was somewhat in the spirit of Matthew Arnold that he interpreted the function of criticism. "The highest allegiance of every man," he wrote Norton in 1865, "is due to liberty and civilization, or rather civilization and liberty"; [24] and the creed of the *Nation*, which Godkin unconsciously modified as culture dispossessed liberty in his affections, may be summed up in the words democracy, individualism, morality, culture, to the end of a free life in a humane and well-ordered society. Throughout the Gilded Age this transplanted English liberal was the high priest of criticism in America. His caustic intelligence played ironically about the current shibboleths and fetishes, reducing them to shreds and patches. He could discover little that was good in the Gilded Age, in its tariffs and land grants, its *Crédit Mobilier* and other scandals, its buccaneer plutocracy, its undisciplined proletarianism, its bitter agrarianism; and he was prompted to a severity of judgment that easier-going natures thought harsh. Enemies sprang up in his every footprint; but too much was at stake, he believed, to temper his criticism to flabby minds, and he laid about him with what he considered a fine impartiality.

It was a cold plunge into a dirty pool, and a nature less robust would have scrambled out quickly. His realism was a profound discouragement to his idealism, and his native aristocracy of temperament closed his mind to the virtues of certain homely American liberalisms. As an intellectual he distrusted all Jacksonian frontier freedoms. The doctrine of liberty did not appear to advantage in the garb of agrarians and proletarians; Thaddeus Stevens and Terence V. Powderly were an ungainlier breed of libertarians than Gladstone and Mill; with such leadership it seemed to Godkin that liberty was running away with civilization and a smash-up was likely. It was the duty of the *Nation*, therefore, to arouse the culture of America to its political obligations, to the end that the custodianship of liberty should be taken over by the intelligence of America. It proved a discouraging job, and slowly on the horizon of his mind rose the shadow of the doubt that had troubled de Tocqueville and Cooper and Fisher Ames— must a democracy prove a leveling influence that destroys a fine individuality and a generous social culture? Careless of his trus-

[24] Ogden, *op. cit.*, Vol. II, p. 48.

teeship, was not the American democrat throwing his heritage to the demagogue and the spoilsman?

As he watched the scrambling heedlessness of the times his liberalism oozed away, his democratic faith lost its sanctions, and he slowly drifted to the right and the dead-sea of pessimism. The mass was too powerful in America, and the mass was shot through with the spirit of selfish leveling. The democracy had been distorted by the frontier, and the sense of responsibility, of individual duty, was well-nigh atrophied. The vulgar West threw its crudity upon all America. "I do not like the western type of man," Godkin confessed to Norton; and to another friend who praised California, he wrote, "No scenery or climate I had to share with western people would charm me." He never spared his mordant adjectives in commenting privately on all America west of the Hudson River. In his gloomy later years he found consolation in Brahmin culture. For years he lived in Cambridge, and in the company of Lowell and Norton he felt at home. Here were democratic gentlemen worthy of his ideal. If all America were only like Cambridge his faith in a cultivated liberalism would be justified. In those years he called himself "an American of the *vieille roche*," which being interpreted, meant a liberal of the Brahmin school.

The immediate problems on which Godkin was called to pass judgment brought him into the thick of the struggles of the Gilded Age. As an editor he confronted the bitter antagonisms that sprang from the rivalries of the farmer, the wage-earner, and the industrial capitalist. Each group was seeking to enlist government on its side and use the political state for special and narrow ends. To a disciple of Mill all such attempts were no better than treason to democracy, and when such treason was justified by what he considered specious economic theory Godkin's hostility was edged with acerbity. All the trenchant dogmas of his philosophy—his police theory of the state, his Ricardian *laissez faire*, his individualism—rushed to the attack of such impudent impostors. With no organized forces at his back he made war on every major group in America. He essayed to rally the scattered minority of the intellectuals and overthrow the citadel of economic power by appeal to reason. It was magnificent but it was scarcely war. The culture of the Gilded Age was undisciplined, lacking faith and unnurtured in philosophy, fastidious rather than vigorous—the poorest of material for shock troops. It applauded every clever thrust of its captain, but preferred to keep its own hands unsoiled. In consequence, to the end of his life Godkin was a leader without a following, little more than a voice crying in the wilderness.

For the rising plutocracy Godkin felt the scorn of a gentleman for the vulgar new-rich. Its hands were dirty, and it was soiling all American life. Its gospel of Whiggery, that under pretense of furthering prosperity had turned Congress into an auction room, was an insult to his Manchester liberalism. Just as surely as government meddles with subsidies and tariffs and grants, he pointed out, will it be defiled. Men are but indifferent honest, and if statesmen are not to become mere political hucksters they must stand apart from the temptations of business. The plea for a national economy had brought Congress to the *Crédit Mobilier* scandals, and it would breed other scandals so long as it was heeded. The only cure for Whiggery was to destroy it. In a scathing leader he early paid his respects to the Whiggish system of governmental subsidies:

> The remedy is simple. The Government must get out of the "protective" business and the "subsidy" business and the "improvement" and the "development" business. It must let trade, and commerce, and manufactures, and steamboats, and railroads, and telegraphs alone. It cannot touch them without breeding corruption. We care nothing about the wonderful stories we hear about what can be achieved in the way of "promoting industry" by all these canal and steamboat and railroad schemes. Were the material prospect twice as tempting, the state could not profitably meddle with them, because neither it nor any other government in the world *can command the virtue necessary to carry them on.* This is not a matter of speculation; we know it as a matter of experience. It is almost as much as this Government can do to maintain order and administer justice. It may one day be able to do a great deal more, but not until a great change has occurred in the social condition of the country. We have gone far enough, heaven knows, on the road of "protection" and "promotion," and have found at every step that it leads straight to the bottomless pit; that for every hundred dollars voted by these poor men to whom we pay scanty wages for passing bills at Washington, we lessen, and perceptibly lessen, the stock of individual honor, of self-respect, and of public spirit, of a loyalty to ideals, to which far more than to any triumphs of material industry, we must look for continued national greatness. We are making money fast enough in all conscience; what needs fostering just now is honesty.[25]

Godkin found it exceedingly difficult to foster the austere honesty that he desired in the body politic, and in his fury at the

[25] *Nation*, January 30, 1873, p. 68.

common political scoundrelism he came to ascribe much of the virus that was poisoning America to the party of western agrarians. He was rapidly drifting to the right and the defense of capitalism, and as the agrarian platform was slowly built up of successive planks—greenbacks, free silver, subtreasuries, railway regulation, the income tax—he turned upon it all the batteries of his wrath. Godkin never understood the American farmer, but he professed to understand economics and political science, and the agrarian platform aroused his implacable hostility. In his frequent discussions of the currency question, a question that for thirty years was a subject of passionate debate, he was at some disadvantage. Intellectually he was ill equipped to deal with it. Although a Ricardian he failed to grasp Ricardo's quantitative principle of money or the function of paper currency. As a gold-standard advocate he accepted the English monetary system as it was given form by the Parliamentary Bank Act of 1844, and he would have no tampering with it. To Godkin money was a measure of value, and a fluctuating standard, implied in the quantitative theory, was as immoral as a fluctuating yardstick. The use of greenbacks—"rag money"—he reckoned a scheme by which dishonest debtors might cheat their creditors.[26] He was forced to regard gold and silver as commodities, fluctuating in price with supply and demand; but he looked upon them as possessing a stable natural value that placed them beyond political manipulation. Any attempt to disturb this natural value by artificial means he called dishonest.[27] He was almost indecent in the vehemence of his adjectives applied to the "dishonest money men." He called the Greenbackers "communists,"[28] and speaking of the Grangers, he said, "There is nothing unnatural or deplorable in a Granger turning from one form of swindle to another."[29]

By the middle nineties it was hard to distinguish Godkin's views on the agrarian program from those of a Wall Street banker. In discussing free silver he abandoned economic principles and fell to mouthing like any newspaper writer. The currency question he regarded as a simple question of public morality. There was only one issue, the issue between honest and dishonest money.

[26] See "Public Opinion and the Currency," *Ibid.*, February 27, 1873; "The Political Situation in 1896," in *Problems of Modern Democracy.*
[27] See "On Gold and Silver," *Ibid.*, July 6, 1876.
[28] *Ibid.*, May 25, 1876.
[29] *Ibid.*, June 1, 1876.

"The demand for free-silver coinage is a demand for a division of property," [30] he said in the early days of the campaign of 1896, and a fortnight later he took extreme ground:

. . . the bold and wicked scheme of repudiation . . . is presented without a blush in the platform. Upon this question the campaign must be fought. If the party of repudiators cannot be put down, the republic cannot be preserved and is not worth preserving.[31]

Such pronouncements bear none of the earmarks of dispassionate criticism. It may seem severe to suggest that they are the comments of a very ignorant or shallow critic, blinded by his prejudices; yet it is true. The equipment of Manchester economics with which he had outfitted himself in the late forties, was no longer adequate in the nineties; yet he seems not to have been aware of the fact. The mid-Victorian still regarded himself as an authority on all economic questions, although he seems to have done no serious reading in economic theory for half a century, and was scarcely conscious how far he had drifted towards the right. The old liberal was fighting the battles of capitalism with weapons as antiquated as the old cap-and-ball musket. "The great trouble with all silverites and currency lunatics, North and South," he said, "is that, when monetary crises arise, they cannot be got to go to the right quarter for information"—a comment that one might retort upon Godkin himself. The intellectual knew far less about money than "Coin" Harvey, whom he would have laughed at.

The same drift to the right is evident in the pronouncements on the Populist movement of the times. Writing on "The Kansas Situation," when the farmers' unrest was becoming militant, he remarked:

Such an unexpected outbreak as this of the last two or three years shows at least that it is not only in the cities, where the foreign-born swarm, that demagogues may thrive and the doctrine of revolution be preached.[32]

The "ravings of the Farmers' movement" he regarded as no more than a "vague and visionary discontent," that was seeking political cures for its economic ills. The hard times from which the West was suffering were the result of economic law. It was not the currency or excessive railway rates that were the cause. The vast

[30] "The Issue of the Campaign," *Ibid.*, July 2, 1896.
[31] "The Platform of Revolution," *Ibid.*, July 16, 1896.
[32] *Ibid.*, January 19, 1893.

extension of railway systems had brought under cultivation too many acres, and the reduction of transportation costs would serve only to bring additional acres under cultivation, thereby increasing competition and forcing prices still lower. High railway rates were the surest safeguard against further extension of an industry much overdeveloped; and for state legislatures to attempt to fix railway tariffs by law—to attempt to control economic forces by statutes—was sheer folly. In discussing the celebrated Illinois railway legislation Godkin spoke in defense of the roads:

> The locomotive is coming in contact with the framework of our institutions. In this country of simple government, the most powerful centralizing force which civilization has yet produced has within the next score years, yet to assume its relation to that political machinery which is to control and regulate it. . . . The corporations of course contested the validity of the law. If the legislature could establish one rate at which they should do the work of transportation, it could establish another. They were fighting for their lives and property; it was against taxation without representation. . . . An arbitrary power is claimed in the supreme legislative body to decide on the reasonable rates of the cost of private services. Just as three hundred years ago the price of bread and labor was regulated by act of Parliament, so now the cost of transportation is to be fixed by a jury of twelve men. . . . Thus far, therefore, the results of the Illinois railroad war must be regarded as rather portentous than satisfactory.[33]

The "watered-stock hallucination," that had taken possession of the agrarian mind and aroused such bitterness, he dismissed with a curious comment that did no great credit to his intelligence.

> There is . . . one difficulty in the way, which is the difficulty common to many of the proposed reforms in railroad management—the practice alleged has absolutely no existence except in the heated brain of the agitators who have imagined it. There are no roads in the United States on which any attempt has been made to increase the freight earnings in proportion to the watered stock or debt.[34]

The passions aroused by the campaign of '96 swept Godkin from his moorings and left him adrift. He quickly convinced himself that the real issue at stake was the moral integrity of the nation. As he studied the platforms and leaders he found little comfort in either. For McKinley he had the contempt of the intellectual for a purveyor of heavy platitudes, and he flayed him in a two-

[33] *Ibid.*, April 10, 1873.
[34] "The Watered Stock Hallucination," *Ibid.*, October 9, 1873.

column leader with his old skill.[35] But for Bryan, the "boy orator of the Platte," his dislike passed the bounds of decency; and for the Chicago convention that put him in nomination—"the roaring mob" with its "Populistic, anarchistic platform"—his contempt outran his command of invective.

No such collection of inflammatory and reckless men ever put themselves on exhibition in a national convention. Beside them the Populists are lamb-like, and the socialists sucking doves. The country has watched their mad proceedings with disgust and shuddering, only impatient for the coming of November to stamp out them and their incendiary doctrines.[37]

To what lengths his overheated brain carried him in those political dogdays, how starkly reactionary he had become, is suggested by his comment on the plank in the Democratic platform attacking the scandal of injunctions:

This blow at the courts shows how true are the instincts of the revolutionaries. They know their most formidable enemies. Judicial decisions have again and again drawn the fangs of confiscatory and revolutionary legislation, and the courts have come more and more to stand as the great bulwarks of property and personal rights.[37]

Godkin's last years were not happy. The wave of imperialism that swept over England and America, with its Boer War and Spanish War, brought him acute concern. The world that he knew was slipping from its moorings, and he was fearful of the seas into which it was plunging. The conquest of the Philippines seemed to him a badge of national degradation. Writing in November, 1899, he said:

We are dragging wearily in the old way, killing half a dozen Filipinos every week, and continually "near the end." The folly of ignorance and rascality we are displaying in the attempt to conquer and have "subjects" would disgrace a trades union.[38]

As he watched the tedious process of subjugation he inclined to attribute to Kipling a large share of the current imperialism. "I think most of the current jingoism on both sides of the water is due to him," he wrote a few weeks later. "He is the poet of the barrack-room cads," a "most pernicious, vulgar person"; and his

[35] "Prosperity's Advance Orator," *Ibid.*, June 18, 1896.
[36] "The Chicago Platform," *Ibid.*, July 16, 1896.
[37] "The Platform of Revolution," *Ibid.*, July 23, 1896.
[38] Ogden, *op. cit.*, Vol. II, pp. 238–239.

"White Man's Burden," cabled to America and printed on the
front pages of the newspapers as a message to imperialist America,
must have rubbed across Godkin's raw nerves. The pious cant
of Kipling's imperialism was a bitter cup for a disillusioned liberal.
The Jubilee with its fulsome laudation of "fat, useless royalty,"
was fittingly commemorated by this noisy poet of imperialism,
and Godkin turned away from it all in disgust.

But turn where he might he found no comfort. His old dreams
of a free and enlightened democracy rising in America, were dead.
Victorian liberalism had been laid away in the grave of John Stuart
Mill, and only its ghost was walking in these latter times. Godkin's
last days were bitter, and the gloom that was settling upon him
crept into his letters. It is a malady common amongst liberals, and
how deeply it had struck in is revealed in such passages as these:

I am not sanguine about the future of democracy. I think we shall have
a long period of decline . . . and then a recrudescence under some other
form of society.[39]

I do not know what the future of our modern civilization is to be. But
I stumble where I firmly trod.[40]

Things look very black. I think that while money-making will long
continue on a great scale, the government will shortly undergo great
changes which will be presided over not by men of light and learning, but
by capitalists and adroit politicians.[41]

I came here fifty years ago with high and fond ideals about America.
. . . They are now all shattered, and I have apparently to look elsewhere
to keep even moderate hopes about the human race alive.[42]

The idealist is prone to be exigent in his demands upon civilization. He marks out a straight path to the goal of his hopes, and
takes it greatly to heart when society chooses to follow other ways
to other ends. Godkin's mind was keenly critical, but his sympathies were narrow and his prejudices great. It is well to be a friend
to civilization, but it is foolish to set up as a custodian; for civilization, like Topsy, will shift for itself. A just and liberal government
is an excellent ideal, but it is one for which few amongst the mass
of men greatly care; and because America chose to follow its own
nose, because it would not become like the America of his dreams,
Godkin allowed his heart to fill with bitterness. It is true that his
recompense for long years of labor was scanty; the Gilded Age

[39] *Ibid.*, Vol. II, p. 199.
[40] *Ibid.*, Vol. II, p. 217.
[41] *Ibid.*, Vol. II, p. 243.
[42] *Ibid.*, Vol. II, p. 237.

was not to be frightened from its fleshpots by his warnings. But long ago it was said, "Wisdom crieth in the streets and no man regardeth her," and why should Godkin have become discouraged with civilization because certain blackguard years clove to their blackguardry, instead of mounting to the somewhat arid heights he pointed out? One must choose at the last between tolerance and pessimism, and Godkin chose pessimism.

It is difficult today to understand his great influence with cultivated readers of his generation. In part perhaps it was due to his crisp assurance. He put things so plumply, he wrote so brilliantly, that his readers were persuaded he must think as neatly. Yet his trenchant prose style cannot hide a certain slightness of matter. His later comments tended to become ever thinner and shriller—not criticism at all, but the sharp expression of aging prejudice. When he talked about the tariff he had Mill at his elbow; but when he talked about the agrarian or the proletarian movements he was little more than a blue-jay scolding at a world he disliked. Unlike his great master he did not go forward to meet new times; he did not reinterpret Victorian liberalism in the light of the lessons taught by the Industrial Revolution; but by standing still he did liberalism a real disservice.

IV

FICTION CONSIDERS THE STATE OF THE COUNTRY

It was only a question of time before the novel would throw off the inhibitions of the genteel and turn to consider the state of the country. A changing social order would not fail of reflection in the pages of fiction, and as the novelists fell to scrutinizing the familiar scene, comparing the reality with the patriotic professions, it was certain that the workings of democracy would come in for sharp criticism. In the last decades of the century the problem novel spread swiftly, expanding the field of its inquiry, and seeking to understand the new ways. Making its first essays in the familiar field of the political, it soon turned to consider the economic problems arising out of the new industrialism, espousing either capitalism or labor as the social sympathies of the author might determine. The class passions of the times found a reflection in its pages, and in consequence the sociological novel became increasingly a repository of the social ideas of a perplexed and troubled generation.

I

THE POLITICAL NOVEL

Of the early political novels three are of sufficient interest to reward attention: *The Gilded Age* (1873), *Democracy* (1881), and *An American Politician* (1884). The first, written by Mark Twain in collaboration with Charles Dudley Warner, is a satire of Gilded Age ways with particular attention to the political corruption of General Grant's administration. The fictional disguise is slight. The actual Washington is presented vividly and familiar figures —Ben Butler, Oakes Ames, President Grant, Secretary Boutwell —move through the scene. The central figure, Senator Dillworthy, was modeled upon Senator Pomeroy of Kansas, who had recently lost a reëlection through an unlucky exposure of an attempt to bribe the Kansas legislature. The heroine, Laura Hawkins, is a western lobbyist who in order to put through a congressional steal under pretense of providing an industrial school for the freedmen, twists Congressmen about her fingers, turns adventuress and ends in tragedy. Out of the West comes the spirit of corruption that the respectable East is unable to withstand, until the itch of speculation infects the whole country. It is Colonel Sellers who embodies the slackness of frontier political morals, that in turn vitiates his political principles. The genial Colonel is quite frankly a Greenbacker.

The country is getting along very well, [he said] but our public men are too timid. What we want is more money. I've told Boutwell so. Talk of basing the currency on gold; you might as well base it on pork. Gold is only one product. Base it on everything! You've got to do something for the West. How am I to move my crops? We must have improvements. Grant's got the idea. We want a canal from the James River to the Mississippi. Government ought to build it.[43]

The analysis is not penetrating. The real sources of political corruption—the rapacious railway lobbyists that camped in brigades about the capitol building—are passed over, and attention is fastened on small steals—the Knobs University bill and the Columbus River Navigation scheme—that do not touch the real rascals of the day. The implication is unmistakable that the source of corruption is the Jacksonian West with its heritage of the spoils spirit. The Federalistic East is victimized by the rapacities

[43] Vol. II, Chapter 13, p. 128.

of mid-western politicians with their religious cant, their talk of the rights of the people and the greatness of the plain democracy. Senator Dillworthy is fairly unctuous in his oily Christian spirit, and Brother Balaam is his fellow. The portraits, one suspects, need not be taken seriously as pictures of the chief apostles of preëmption and exploitation. To have sketched the real leaders of the great barbecue might have involved too many unpleasantries.

Democracy, written seven years later, is an inferior book in every way, less penetrating, less amusing, less creative. To essay to penetrate the dark places of political jobbery through the eyes of a society woman, too high-bred to turn lobbyist and inveigle secrets out of ambitious politicians, is sufficiently absurd, yet not uncharacteristic of the Henry Adams whose home was a distinguished salon and who in pottering about the political world of Washington deceived himself in thinking he had his finger on the web of intrigue. It is an amazing book for such a man to write. The attitude is that of the kid-gloved reformer who goes in for civil service reform, and who views the uncultivated West as the source of all political corruption. The hero, Senator Silas Ratcliffe of Peoria, Illinois, like Senator Dillworthy, is a past master in political organization who covers his dishonesty with religious cant. The economic sources of political corruption are ignored, and the evil is traced to the principle of democracy. Whatever political convictions are in the book are expressed by Representative Gore, a civil service reformer from Massachusetts, and quite evidently Henry Adams himself; and the conclusion is thus set forth:

"Do you yourself think democracy the best government, and universal suffrage a success?"

Mr. Gore saw himself pinned to the wall, and he turned at bay with almost the energy of despair:

"These are matters about which I rarely talk in society. . . . But since you ask for my political creed, you shall have it. I only condition that it shall be for you alone, never to be repeated or quoted as mine. I believe in democracy. I accept it. I will faithfully serve and defend it. I believe in it because it appears to me the inevitable consequence of what has gone before it. Democracy asserts the fact that the masses are now raised to a higher intelligence than formerly. All our civilization aims at this mark. We want to do what we can to help it. I myself want to see the result. I grant it is an experiment, but it is the only direction society can take that is worth its taking; the only conception of its duty large enough to satisfy its instincts; the only result that is worth an effort or a risk. Every other step is backward, and I do not want to repeat the past.

I am glad to see society grapple with issues in which no one can afford to be neutral."

"And supposing your experiment fails," said Mrs. Lee; "suppose society destroys itself with universal suffrage, corruption, and communism."

". . . I have faith; not perhaps in the old dogmas, but in the new ones. . . . faith in science; faith in the survival of the fittest. Let us be true to our time, Mrs. Lee! If our age is to be beaten, let us die in the ranks. If it is to be victorious, let us be first to lead the column. Anyway, let us not be skulkers or grumblers. There! have I repeated my catechism correctly? You would have it! Now oblige me by forgetting it. I should lose my character at home if it got out."[44]

And the conclusion of the matter is thus summed up:

"I want to go to Egypt," said Madelaine, still smiling faintly; "democracy has shaken my nerves to pieces. Oh, what rest it would be to live in the Great Pyramid and look out forever at the polar star!"

Not a hint of the Industrial Revolution; not a hint of the sordid Whiggery that was fouling American politics; not a suggestion of any creative social philosophy on which to establish an adequate theory of democracy. A dreary place at best, with no faith in human nature and no trust in democratic machinery, but only a gentlemanly belief that an antiquated Federalism may somehow pull this venture in republicanism out of the bog in which Jacksonianism had mired it. No wonder Henry Adams would not set his name on the title-page, but left it an orphan to make its own way in the world. In his life of John Hay, William Roscoe Thayer has explained the situation thus:

The Adamses, the Hays, and Clarence King formed an inner circle, which somebody named "The Five of Hearts," and out of this came, in 1882, a novel entitled *Democracy*, a strikingly clever satire on Washington society. Its authorship was at once attributed to them, but one after another denied it. If it was a joint product no individual could monopolize the credit; and as it seems to have been read chapter by chapter to the group, and discussed by them all, it might be said, technically, to be a composite. Clarence King is still commonly regarded as its author; and there are many supporters of Hay; but I believe that only Mr. Adams possessed the substance, and style, and the gift of Voltairean raillery which distinguish it.[45]

Mr. Thayer is generous in his praise.

An American Politician is even less consequential as a political study than *Democracy*. Marion Crawford was a professional ro-

[44] Chapter 4, p. 78.   [45] Vol. II, pp. 58–59.

mancer and in this naïve venture into a field little known to him he carried his complete romantic kit. The political theme is tied about with so many love strands as almost to strangle it. The hero, John Harrington, we are assured is a very remarkable man, a Bostonian with a Mayflower teapot in his family treasures, an idealist of primitive Puritan intensity. But we must take him upon hearsay. Nothing that he does or says suggests his greatness. Politically the book is reduced to a little glimpse of the methods of selecting a United States senator—an Irish ward boss with twenty votes in his belt, a gentlemanly railway attorney who handles offal skillfully with a handkerchief at his nose—set in between two set speeches by the hero. The rest is Newport and the Back Bay, not quite stupid yet with no distinction. The romancer does not move easily in an unfamiliar field, and he sends his hero forth to battle for righteousness with small intellectual equipment. His speeches are heavily oratorical and his political philosophy is naïve; it is pretty much George William Curtis, the sufficiency of civil service reform and the virtues of non-partisanship.

The unreality of the book is furthered by a conception worthy of Poe—a mysterious council of three that meets in London and directs political movements in America. We are dimly aware that the council is both ancient and honorable; that it goes back historically to post-Revolutionary days and is self-perpetuating; and its uncanny power has resulted from supreme intelligence supplemented by exact information gathered during many years. In its secret archives every public man in America is tagged and docketed; his political and financial affiliations are set down in detail; and on the basis of this knowledge the cryptic three send forth instructions that are faithfully carried out. The danger to America lies in sectionalism—North, South, and West struggling for supremacy in the national councils; and upon the three rests the self-imposed responsibility of saving America from itself. The idea is sufficiently absurd, as the book is absurd. Crawford was a cosmopolitan who knew little about American political conditions, and the crisis of the novel is the Hayes-Tilden *impasse* of 1876. The influence of the novel, one may safely assume, was negligible.*

* In his original scheme Professor Parrington included Tourgée's *A Fool's Errand*, but the text shows that he decided against its inclusion.—*Publisher.*

2

THE ECONOMIC NOVEL

The theme of these earlier novels was politics as revealed by the Gilded Age; on the other hand *The Bread-winners* was one of the early economic novels. Like *Democracy* it was an outcome of the discussions of the vivacious trio, John Hay, Clarence King, and Henry Adams. Written in 1882 by Hay, it was published anonymously in the *Century Magazine* from August, 1883, to January, 1884. Hay never publicly acknowledged the authorship, and it was not until the edition of 1915 appeared with an introductory note by his son, that his name appeared on the title-page. It achieved a notable success—far beyond that of *Democracy;* was warmly praised and sharply criticized; was replied to in other novels; all of which goes to show that it fanned the coals that were smoldering in the industrial life of the day, threatening a general conflagration. It was the first recognition on the part of literature that a class struggle impended in America—a first girding of the loins of polite letters to put down the menace that looked out from the under-world of the proletariat; and as such it assumes importance as an historical document quite beyond its significance as a work of art.

The motive of *The Bread-winners* is the defense of property against the "dangerous classes"; its immediate theme is a satire of labor unions. In an introductory note to the later edition, Clarence Leonard Hay explicitly denies this. "*The Bread-winners,*" he says, "is not directed against organized labor. It is rather a protest against the disorganization and demoralization of labor by unscrupulous leaders and politicians who, in the guise of helping the workingman, use his earnings to enrich themselves." He then states the theme thus:

It is a defense of the right of an individual to hold property, and a plea for the better protection of that property by law and order. Civilization rests upon law, order, and obedience. The agitator who preaches that obedience to lawful authority is a sin, and patriotism an illusion, is more dangerous to society than the thief who breaks in at night and robs the householder.

The editor thinks well of the American workingmen. At heart they are sound; their motives are honest; but their ignorance of fundamental economic principles too easily suffers them to fall victim to unscrupulous demagogues whose only object is their exploitation. To prevent such "disorganization and demoralization of labor," which can bring only suffering and failure upon men ill prepared to endure them, is therefore the patriotic duty of the educated classes. The proletariat is groping blindly for leadership; it is stirring uneasily; if the educated classes do not offer an enlightened leadership, the laborer will follow low cunning to immoral ends and blind leaders of the blind will bring irretrievable disaster upon civilization. Selfish appeal will kindle envy and hate; the rich and prosperous will go down before brute force; the rights of property will be destroyed; law, order, and obedience will give place to anarchy.

Such, briefly developed, is Clarence Hay's exposition of *The Bread-winners;* and the exposition seems to suggest the social views of John Hay. He probably had no antipathy to labor unions which are guided in their policy by "sound economic principles" and right "morality"—as the capitalist understands such things. But labor unions which follow their own leaders, which persist in thinking out a proletarian economy, which are bent on substituting a social morality for a property morality, which refuse to be led by the "educated classes," he was bitterly hostile to. It is the unrest furthered by rebellious labor unions that he fears, and it is this that gives point and animus to his satire. That *The Bread-winners* was conceived in a spirit of beneficent paternalism towards the proletariat, the present-day reader will have difficulty in discovering. It is too frank in defense of vested interests, it looks with too stern a disfavor upon all labor leaders who refuse to accept the finality of the present industrial order, it exudes too strong an odor of property-morality, to deceive an intelligent reader. Read today it is clearly a partisan defense of economic individualism, an attack upon the rising labor movement, a grotesque satire smeared with an unctuous morality—and because of this, a perfect expression of the spirit of upper-class America in those uneasy eighties with their strikes and lockouts and Haymarket riots.

The plot of the book is slight—it is the story of the oily machinations of Ananias Offitt, a professional agitator who lives off simple honest workmen whom he seduces, organizes a secret Brotherhood of the Breadwinners, urges on riot and robbery at the time of a great strike, is checkmated by the hero—a cultivated and elegant clubman by the name of Captain Arthur Farnham—betrays his tool, and in the end is murdered by him. Fortunately for the wel-

fare of property interests there are "honest" workmen, men like
Leopold Grosshammer, who rally to the support of law and order
and eventually break the strike. The love-story is provided with
two heroines, and the contrast between them emphasizes the class
line which property draws. The upper-class heroine is as correct
and colorless as Cooper's Eve Effingham: the lower-class heroine
is as vulgarly handsome and as brazen as "such people" are supposed to be. A high-school education has spoilt her for the factory
or domestic service, filling her empty head with foolish ambitions,
but it could not make a lady of her.

Hay was in Cleveland at the time of the great strike in 1877, and
he was profoundly disturbed by the experience. Writing to his
father-in-law, he said:

The prospects of labor and capital both seem gloomy enough. The very
devil seems to have entered into the lower classes of workingmen, and
there are plenty of scoundrels to encourage them to all lengths. . . . I
am thankful you did not *see* and *hear* what took place during the strikes.
You were saved a very painful experience of human folly and weakness,
as well as crime.[46]

The crying evils of a buccaneer industrialism which lay behind the
strikes, Hay ignored completely. To provide his idyllic background
of contented labor before it is seduced by demagogues, he goes back
to a decadent domestic economy. His "honest and contented
workman" is a carpenter who works for another carpenter—not a
factory-hand tending a machine; and when the demagogue comes
with his specious appeal he is triumphantly refuted.

"What are we, anyhow?" continued the greasy apostle of labor. "We
are slaves; we are Roossian scurfs. We work as many hours as our owners
like; we take what pay they choose to give us; we ask their permission
to live and breathe."
"Oh, that's a lie," Sleeny interrupted, with unbroken calmness. "Old
Saul Matchin and me come to an agreement about time and pay, and both
of us was suited. Ef he's got his heel onto me, I don't feel it."[47]

John Hay was convinced that an "educated leadership" alone
could save American democracy. But unfortunately—despite his
great reputation in diplomacy and statesmanship—his own education seems to have been faulty. He had lately risen into the exploiting class, and he accepted the ready-made opinions of that

[46] William Roscoe Thayer, *Life and Letters of John Hay*, Vol. II, pp. 5–6.
[47] Chapter V

class. His biographer has admirably stated his position during the days of the strike riots when he was clarifying his views:

> Those riots of 1877 burnt deep into Colonel Hay's heart. Like the rest of the world, he had theorized on the likelihood of war between Capital and Labor; but he had reassured himself by the comfortable assumption that under American conditions—equal opportunity for all, high wages, equal laws, and the ballot-box—no angry laboring class could grow up. The riots blew such vaporing away: for they proved that the angry class already existed, that the ballot-box instead of weakening strengthened it, and that not only the politicians of both parties but also the constituted authorities would avoid, as long as possible, grappling with it.
>
> The event was too large to be dismissed as an outburst of temper: it must be accepted as a symptom, a portent. Did it mean that a cancer had attacked the body politic and would spread to the vital organs? Was Democracy a failure,—Democracy—for more than a century the dream of the down-trodden, the ideal of those who loved mankind and believed in its perfectibility, the Utopia which good men predicted should somehow turn out to be a reality? Hay had sung his paean to liberty; Hay had throbbed at the efforts of patriots in Spain and in France to overthrow their despots; he had even exulted over the signs of democratization in England. Had he been the victim of mirage? Was Democracy not the final goal of human society, but only a half-way stage between the despotism of Autocracy and the despotism of Socialism?
>
> These questions he could not evade. . . . But he held, as did many of his contemporaries, that the assaults on Property were inspired by demagogues who used as their tools the loafers, the criminals, the vicious,—Society's dregs who have been ready at all times to rise against laws and government. That you have property is proof of industry and foresight on your part or your father's; that you have nothing, is a judgment on your laziness and vices, or on your improvidence. The world is a moral world; which it would not be if virtue and vice received the same rewards.[48]

John Hay, it must be recalled, had enjoyed a college education through the aid of relatives, he had been taken under the wing of Lincoln and become his private secretary, he had been thrust forward by influential politicians, and finally he had married wealth—were these things proofs of virtue in a moral world that rewards foresight and punishes improvidence? Or were they rather the marks of a skillful climber? John Hay was a charming and cultivated gentleman, but he was also a child of the Gilded Age, with the materialisms of his generation in his blood. The young man had been an Abolitionist and a political radical; the old man was a McKinley conservative whose chief claim to reputation lay in

[48] Thayer, *op. cit.*, Vol. I. pp. 6–7.

the "open-door" policy in China. The beginnings of this shift
to conservatism seem to have coincided with his marriage to Miss
Stone, daughter of a Cleveland capitalist whose interests were
threatened by the great strike. He was temperamentally one of
John Adams's "natural aristocrats," and having gained entrée into
aristocratic circles he took the coloring of his new environment.
A son of the frontier, he became a man of the world. Prosperity
was necessary to him.

Professing a deep attachment to democratic institutions and
hatred of all monarchical principles—in Spain and France—John
Hay ceased to be a Lincoln democrat, and took his place amongst
the ruling class, accepting the principles of the rising plutocracy.
The Bread-winners is a dramatization of the Federalistic principle
that government exists for the protection of property. "Remembering the date when *The Bread-winners* was written," says his
biographer, "we must regard it as the first important polemic in
American fiction in defense of Property." [49] John Hay had become
a thoroughgoing Hamiltonian. In his younger days his sympathies
had gone out to radical republicans everywhere, and he watched
the rising tide of liberalism with great satisfaction. In his first
visits to Europe he followed closely the liberal movements. He
was a warm admirer of Castelar, eulogizing him as one of the heroic
figures of modern times. In a lecture in 1869 on "The Progress of
Democracy in Europe" he spoke with the zeal of an advanced
liberal. But soon thereafter the ardor of his zeal lessened. On
later trips to Europe he did not display a like sympathy with the
program of the Social Democrats. As economic unrest crept into
politics, as strikes and boycotts began to disturb his father-in-law's
business, he discovered less sympathy for revolutionary movements. Political revolutions sponsored by respectable middle-class
leaders, were one thing; economic revolutions sponsored by the
proletariat were quite another thing. A democracy that breeds
more democracy is clearly dangerous. So much as has already
been accomplished is excellent, of course; but nothing further must
be attempted.

There is sound strategy in offensive epithets. And so, taking
counsel of fear, he applied to the current economic unrest the words
most offensive to polite American ears, and called it socialism,
anarchism. Without pausing to weigh the demands of the farmer

[49] *Ibid.*, Vol. II, p. 15.

and the workingman, with no understanding of the meaning of the great proletarian movement then going forward in Europe, he appealed in defense of property to the specter of economic leveling before which every good American of the eighties recoiled in horror. As early as 1869, speaking of Castelar, he said: "He has too much sense and integrity to follow the lead of the Socialist fanatics."[50] Commenting on the unsettled state of things in Paris in 1883, he wrote: "The laborers have had the mischief put into their heads by trade-unions."[51] As he contemplated the agrarian unrest of the seventies and later, he discovered in Greenbackism and Populism only another form of this hateful socialism. It was the work of agitators who were plain rascals.

He was greatly disturbed in 1875 at the state of politics, "with half the Republicans and all the Democrats inflationists at heart, and carrying on a campaign on the bald issue whether the nation shall be a liar and a thief or not."[52] And so late as 1900 he exclaimed petulantly: "This last month of Bryan, roaring out his desperate appeals to hate and envy, is having its effect on the dangerous classes. Nothing so monstrous has as yet been seen in our history."[53] Unhappily even in free America with its equal opportunity, and equal laws, there had come to be "dangerous classes"—rather a good many of them, taking the populistic farmers and discontented wage-earners into the account—so many, indeed, that John Hay grew gloomy over the outlook. And the outlook was all the gloomier because of our form of government; for is not the ultimate test of our democratic institutions the test of whether they are adequate to protect the property and "civilization" of the few against the "hate and envy" of the discontented many?

That *The Bread-winners* was a dishonest book Hay certainly could not have been brought to believe; nevertheless a Tory who covers his Tory purpose with a mantle of democracy can scarcely be reckoned intellectually sincere. The men of the seventies and eighties—cultivated and intelligent gentlemen like Godkin and Aldrich and Hay—were little more than demagogues in their fustian attacks on agrarian Greenbackers and militant labor unions; they feared and hated them too much to understand them, and they took advantage of their social position to cry them down. The "educated leadership" of the Gilded Age was a somewhat

---

[50] *Ibid.*, Vol. I, p. 321.
[51] *Ibid.*, p. 414.
[52] *Ibid.*, p. 426.
[53] *Ibid.*, Vol. II, p. 256.

sorry thing; it was ethically bankrupt while appealing to high moral standards. The best of such leaders were second-rate men—mediocre minds cramped by a selfish environment, imbued with no more than a property-consciousness. Of such a world John Hay in his *Bread-winners* was a distinguished spokesman and representative.*

3

THE BEGINNINGS OF THE SOCIOLOGICAL NOVEL

It was in the nineties that the sociological novel expanded into a great movement that in the next decade and a half was to engulf pretty much all American fiction and bring it into service to the social conscience. Such a development was in the nature of things. The artist would not sit forever in his ivory tower, content to carve his statuettes while the country without was turmoiled with revolution. Sooner or later he would venture forth and once he had been caught up in the swirl his art would take new forms and serve other purposes than the traditional genteel. Realism was in the air, the realism of Zola and the Russians, and from such a realism would come in America a more critical attitude towards the social revolution at work in the land.

It was the city that played havoc with our older fictional methods, as it played havoc with our traditional social philosophy. America was late in discovering the import of the huge Babbitt warrens it had been building with such fierce energy; but slowly the realities of the economic city rose to challenge the respectability of the romantic city. It was the discovery of this new lair of business that created the school of sociological fiction. The older city of literature had been a polite world wherein ladies and gentlemen drank tea and made love and talked proper scandal—a pleasant background of clubs and drawing-rooms, against which moved well-dressed figures. It was an echo of Thackeray—the world of the West End and Beacon Street and Fifth Avenue, too well-bred and prosperous to recognize slums or stockyards or stock-gambling. But with the nineties the old complacency was disturbed. A note of unrest crept into the current fiction. As the *protégés* of Mr. Howells looked out upon their world in search of reality, they discovered that polite society was being undermined. Too many

* In his plan Professor Parrington included here H. F. Keenan's *The Money-Makers*, but apparently he decided against its inclusion.—*Publisher.*

social climbers were thrusting themselves forward; too much vulgarity was displayed by the new-rich. The social primacy of the old families was being challenged by western pork-packers. Here was a rich field to harvest. *Le document humain* was the latest cry of realism, and so under the inspiration of M. Paul Bourget a new crop of realism came to fruit—clever studies in feminine psychology—the last word in contemporary reality. The social climber was analyzed mercilessly, her shallow and silly ambitions revealed to the least petty maneuver; her blighting influence upon an idealistic husband or her stimulus to a money-grabbing mate, is traced shrewdly. Such are Boyesen's *Mammon of Unrighteousness*, Robert Grant's *Unleavened Bread*, and Edith Wharton's *House of Mirth*—studies that were symptomatic of a generation disturbed by the consciousness of a vulgar plutocracy rising in its midst, and yet ignorant of the nature of the disease.

Nevertheless their vogue was brief. As economic unrest rose more menacingly upon the horizon of the new century, realism quickly tired of its Kate Van Schaaks and Selma Whites and Lily Barts, and turned away to prospect for a richer vein. Psychology was losing its fascination and social analysis was supplying a new inspiration; M. Bourget was yielding authority to Emile Zola. Even so whole-hearted a romantic as Mary Johnston was to turn from tales like *To Have and to Hold* to write *Hagar*, a novel of suffrage propaganda. There was to be not less realism but more. The change may be summarized in the word *background*. The old individualism had unconsciously insulated its hero from economic contacts; he moved in a polite environment detached from the larger play of social forces. An individualism so wanting in sociological verity could make scant appeal to the new spirit of sociology. That old world is dead. With the rise of the philosophy of determinism came another mood. To the realism of environment that conceived of the individual as a pawn on the chessboard of society, M. Zola had given the name *naturalism*. It was realism wedded to a deterministic sociology—the first reaction of a generation awakening to the subjugating power of the mass, and bent on studying the resultant phenomena in the clear light of science. The change was no less than revolutionary. The new school thought in terms of group and class and movement, rather than in terms of individuals each nursing his petty hopes and fears. The individual counts for so little in the enveloping stream of social tendency. Let us have no more shoddy heroes, foolish little egoisms in an unreal world; but figures of men and women, encompassed by the great stream, carried along on a resistless current. If they prove to be little better than puppets the novelist is not to blame, but society that reduces them to impotency. So the emerging school abandoned Howells and James and followed Frank Norris into the camp of the naturalists. Their work might be bad art—as the critics love to reiterate —but it was the honest voice of a generation bewildered and adrift.

The discovery of environment led imperceptibly to another discovery—the economic basis of society; and this in turn led to the rejection of the polite city of older literature. Once the eyes of the novelist opened to the significance of the economic, the world of the spenders became less significant than the world of the makers, the drones became less interesting than the workers. If a novel were to be true to American life, it must adjust its perspectives to the facts of the great American game of money-chasing; it must shift its habitat from Fifth Avenue to Wall Street, from the club to the factory. So the business man entered the portals of fiction, no longer the stock figure in broadcloth and top-hat who discarded business with his dirty collar in order to shift into respectability; but bringing with him his talk of deals and squeeze-outs, playing the great game of exploitation at his mahogany desk—the central, dominating figure in a capitalistic world. He was subjected to acute analysis—his philosophy, his ethics, the machine of industrialism he was creating, the intricate system of exploitation that he had elaborated, the jungle city that was his lair where he fought his battles. The more acutely he was analyzed the clearer it became that here was a figure greater than kings or presidents—a figure that had taken our traditional American life in his hands and was reshaping it to his ends; and that if realism were to be true to its ideal it must paint him as he was without detraction and without glorification. So of necessity the younger novelists turned from polite society to economics, and fell to dramatizing the life of the city jungle where business men fought their fierce battles.

The forerunner of the new school was a Norwegian-American, Hjalmar Hjorth Boyesen. An essayist and philologist, for a number of years professor of German at Columbia University, Boyesen began publishing as early as 1874, and thereafter contributed freely to the several fields of the essay, poetry, and fiction; but it was not until 1891 that he opened the new vein of realism which he worked industriously the remaining four years of his life, the life brought to a premature close in 1895. Three novels belong to this last phase of his work: *The Mammon of Unrighteousness* (1891), *The Golden Calf* (1892), and *The Social Strugglers* (1893). The books made considerable stir upon their publication, for they were the nearest approach to the Tolstoian type of realism which till then had appeared in America. They contain in germ many of the ideas which the later city realists were to amplify and develop; but these ideas were still entangled in the mesh of the current psychological realism and their sociological bearings obscured. In consequence they largely failed of their purpose, and within a decade they had fallen into oblivion. They are of interest today chiefly as historical documents of the early nineties.

In the preface to *The Mammon of Unrighteousness* Boyesen sets forth his purpose thus:

> My one endeavor in this book has been to depict persons and conditions which are profoundly and typically American. I have disregarded all romantic traditions, and simply asked myself in every instance, not whether it was amusing but whether it was true to the logic of reality—true in color and tone to the American sky, the American soil, the American character.

This, very evidently, is the realism of *milieu*—an endeavor to catch the reality of atmosphere; and as such it is of no great significance. In his choice of "types," moreover, he reflected the current taste. The crude self-made millionaire who dimly conscious of failure founds a university; the young idealist who fails because he is conscientious and the young realist who succeeds because he has no scruples against playing the game; and the aristocratic climber who marries to further her social ambitions—these are the stock figures of the realism that was to culminate in Robert Grant's *Unleavened Bread*, nine years later. But in the delineation of the character of Horace Larkin—the hero of a book that does not realize its promise—the note of the new realism is heard distinctly for the first time. The business man frankly breaks with the old ethics and erects a new ethics in conformity with his ambition; and it is the elaboration of the ethics of the Will to Power that justifies one in regarding *The Mammon of Unrighteousness* as a first study in the new city realism.

Horace Larkin, like Herrick's Van Harrington, is a Nietzschean who learned his ethics not from the German philosopher, but from the world of cut-throat business. It is the flower of the competitive system. The old pretense that business is an uplifting and civilizing agency—that trade breaks down barriers and carries in its shipments the gospel of fraternity and good will—is flung out on the scrap heap. Horace Larkin is no smug hypocrite. He faces the facts frankly; he will not deceive others any more than himself.

He was a beast of prey, asserting his right of survival; nothing more. If he succumbed to sentiment (and it is far easier to succumb to it than to resist it) he would merely be eliminating himself from the battle of existence as a potent and considerable force, and consigning himself to the rear ranks. And he felt in every fibre of his being that he was born for leadership.[54]

. . . nobody has a right to sacrifice himself to anybody else. If he does he simply eliminates himself from the struggle for existence, proves his unfitness to survive. It is natural for every strong man to try to make every other life tributary to his own; but the man who consents to make his life tributary to somebody else's is from Nature's point of view a weak man. . . . She may allow him to exist in a small way; but what is existence without predominance? . . . The man who is in advance of the morality of his age is, for practical purposes, a fool. It is no use quarreling with Fate; and in the United States the average man is the Fate that rules us and determines our place in the world.[55]

"The majority of our politicians are a low-lived lot, and many of them corrupt. But they have the courage to be American—crudely and uncompromisingly American—and that is, in my eyes, a virtue which is not to be lightly rated."

"And may I ask, Mr. Larkin, what do you mean by being American?"

"Being frankly, ably, enterprisingly plebeian. It is the plebeian after all, who shall inherit the earth—"

"I beg your pardon. According to the Bible it is the meek."

"I must differ with the Bible, then; for the meek, in my experience, if they inherit anything, never manage to keep it. It passes, sooner or later, into the hands of the strong, the self-assertive, the grasping. But these, as you will admit, are plebeian characteristics. A universally prosperous, comfortable, impudent, and enterprising mob—that is the goal toward which we are steering; and in my opinion it is a good and desirable one." [56]

This is a note that is to be heard more insistently as the new realism went further in its probing. Armed with this conviction Horace Larkin set forth as a conqueror, and it only adds to the dramatic fitness of things that in his rise he came across a will to power stronger, cleverer, than his own. Kate Van Schaak climbs upon his back to rise with him; she buys him with her money and social position, and having made the deal she realizes on the invest-

[54] Chapter XXXI.   [55] Chapter XXXVI.   [56] Chapter XXXIII.

ment. She is mistress henceforth, and the Nietzschean smiles at the irony of the situation.

In the third work Boyesen fails to maintain the level of *The Mammon of Unrighteousness. Social Strugglers* is simpler, more dramatic, better told. It carries the reader forward more easily. But it belongs with such novels of social analysis as Charles Dudley Warner's *The Golden House*—mildly critical of the vulgarizing influence of the new-rich, mildly sympathetic with the slum workers —rather than to the new realism. The heroine—daughter of a new-rich family that has come to New York to climb socially—awakens to the realization of parting ways: one the path of luxury which the four hundred travel, the other the path of service which leads to the slums and settlement work. It is a sentimental awakening, not an intellectual, induced by the hero, who on the fringe of the four hundred is mildly discontented with the ways of luxury. The vague idealism of the latter has been stirred by the Toynbee Hall experiment in London, and the persuasiveness of the lover rather than the conclusions of the thinker carries Maud Bulkley away from her conventional moorings.

The movement of the book is little clogged with sociological discussions; there is too little, indeed, to justify the conclusion. Only once does Philip Warburton lift the curtain upon the idealism which ostensibly is the determining factor in his life.

"I frankly confess that I am something of a red. I think the world is out of gear, and I can perfectly well conceive of a civilization far better than ours, without yet proposing any radical amendment to human nature. . . ."

There was to Maud something so wholly unexpected in this ebullition that she scarcely knew what to say. She had never philosophized concerning life and its problems; nay, she had never suspected that to a person who had money enough, and the access to good society, it could present any problems whatever. She knew that some terribly disreputable, shaggy, and wild-faced foreigners came here from Europe and proposed to turn our admirable civilization upside down; but that a gentleman of Warburton's culture and social standing could sympathize with such criminals had never occurred to her as a remote possibility. . . .

After this disturbing introduction Warburton proceeds to disclose what being "a red" means to him in the way of social revolutions:

"Have you ever heard of a London experiment known as Toynbee Hall?" he asked. . . .

"Yes: it's a place in the slums, where young men of good family go to live; isn't that it?"

"Yes; and, do you know, that is to me the most beautiful modern instance of a real desire to help the poor and helpless—to lift the world to a higher level. It is what I should like to do myself—and what I shall hope some day to do. . . ."

"Then you really think it a misfortune to be rich?" she ejaculated. . . .

"Yes, if wealth entails the loss of human sympathies, as in nine cases out of ten it seems to do, I regard it as a misfortune. If it means, as in this country it seems to mean, the loss of vital contact with humanity, the contraction of one's mental and spiritual horizon, a callous insensibility to social wrongs and individual sorrows, a brutal induration in creature comforts and mere animal well-being, the loss of that divine discontent and noble aspiration which alone makes us human—if it means this or any part of it, it is the greatest calamity which can befall a man. And it is because Christ foresaw that these were the natural effects of great wealth, and the security and ease which it engenders, that he declared that it was easier for a camel to pass through the eye of a needle than for a rich man to enter the kingdom of heaven." [57]

That is all. There is no dramatic justification of Warburton's views; they are without motive and foundation. *Social Strugglers* does not advance far along the path of the new realism.

As the years drew nearer the new century, the business man usurped an ever larger place in American fiction; the romance which had been sought in the deeds of 1776 was now discovered in the achievements of enterprise. It was the unconscious testimony of literature to the hold which business had got on the imagination of Americans. In the golden days of the "full dinner-pail," following the great victory of '96, the Captain of Industry reached the apogee of his fame. The voice of detraction had not yet been lifted against him; the muckraker had not yet set forth on his devastating career. To young reporters on city papers looking ambitiously towards fiction as the goal of success, what could offer greater appeal than the unwritten romance of Wall Street and the Stock Exchange? They had described it for the daily news columns, they had seen it extolled on the editorial page, why not dramatize it in fiction? Here was the real interest of America—the only reality that signified; yet the novelists had stupidly overlooked it, because they lacked the journalist's sense of news values, his *flair*.

Of the abundant crop of fiction which resulted from this discovery, no more characteristic examples need be sought than *The*

[57] Chapter VII.

Short Line War (1899) and *Calumet "K"* (1901), written in collaboration by Samuel Merwin and H. K. Webster. Their popular
success was immediate and maintained surprisingly. The former
ran to six editions, the last in 1909; the latter, to twelve editions,
the last so late as 1915. They are brisk stories, all action stripped
of descriptive superfluities, with plenty of newspaper punch:
dramatizations of hustle and bluff and the tricks of a cut-throat
game. Charlie Bannon, hero of *Calumet "K,"* is the boss who does
things, who is on the job, who takes long shots and "makes good"
—a "movie" hero of efficiency. He has no time nor inclination to
think, possesses no philosophy, asks no questions and is troubled by
no doubts or scruples; his fertile brain and cool nerve make him a
first-class fighting man, and he fights as the good soldier should on
orders from above. The hero of *The Short Line War*, Jim Weeks, is
another Bannon with the same fertile brain, cool nerve, calm
tenacity of purpose, quick decisiveness, and the same lack of
intellectual interests. In war it is sound strategy to strike quick
and hard; and the Captain of Industry, let it be clearly known, is a
war captain. To play the game hard, to beat the other fellow by
whatever means serve, that is the ideal of a competitive *bourgeoisie:*
not to be too nice about the law, for everybody knows that the law
is the chief weapon of the strong; not to cherish foolish idealisms,
for everybody knows that success alone pays. No more heartless,
brutal, anarchistic books could be conceived—a mad philosophy for
a mad world.

The broad movement towards a realistic portrayal of the economic city produced its eddies and minor currents, which at times
brought such a commotion of the waters as to appear like the main
current. Such was the flood of political novels which came with the
new century and lasted well upwards of a decade. These were a by-
product of the muckraking movement—a part of the propaganda
of the group of young insurgents within the Republican party who
were bent on rescuing the party from control of the old bosses, and
who prepared the way for the more significant movement of Progressivism which followed. Such studies as Francis Churchill
Williams's *J. Devlin—Boss* (1901), and Elliott Flower's *The Spoils-
men* (1903), were early examples; and Winston Churchill's *Coniston*
and *Mr. Crewe's Career* were probably the most notable. They were
journalistic for the most part, *exposés* of the "Boss" and the evils
of the political machine. The "Boss" is painted in various guises, as

brutal, cunning, thoroughly vicious, or as a man who plays the game with the same unsocial conscience that marks the capitalist. Most frequently Lincoln Steffens is followed and the human side of the "Boss" is "played up" equally with his political cunning. It is the characteristic journalistic touch—a bit cheap but immensely effective. As the movement of naturalism gained headway it became increasingly apparent that the "Boss" was only a part of the "System," and the political novel merged in the economic. These brisk studies constitute, however, a suggestive episode in our history—the literary echo of our political history between the years 1900 and 1910.

Little in the way of social analysis was to be expected from a group of clever journalists. They were reporters of fact, transcribers of externals. They note the social unrest, but it is little more than an undertone of the chorus of prosperity—a snarl of inconsequential criticism. It is the sting of a troublesome mosquito that is brushed off by the Captain of Industry who is too busy with big projects to bother about insects. Such is Will Payne's *Mr. Salt* (1903)—a sympathetic study of a coal-baron who is caught in the panic of '93 but pulls out and rises higher. To provide dramatic contrast there is the ineffective idealist who is growly and surly— "The whole thing is rotten—the whole business scheme. It's just a gold brick game operated by Salt and his kind. I'd like to stick a fuse to it and touch it off." [58] It is feeble enough—this protest. The rebel joins wildly in the great strike, is struck down by the hand of the law, rebels and strikes again and gets nowhere. Only a bitter, ineffective hate rankles in his heart, while Salt goes on triumphantly to greater power and a sort of moral regeneration through love—a regeneration that does not interfere with his keeping the title-deeds to his loot. An earlier study—*The Money Captain* (1898)—seemed to give promise of honester work than this. It is the story of a struggle between a corrupt gas-magnate and an enterprising editor whose *exposé* puts the magnate afoul of the law as interpreted by the magnate's judges, and who is saved from disaster by the timely death of the "duke." At the end is a touch of prophecy, quite startling in its forecast. These money-kings with their strong prehensile fingers are the spawn of a common plebeian America; the world of the makers is vulgarly democratic; but there follows the age of the spenders, and that shall be finely, altruistically

[58] Chapter IX.

aristocratic. The death of the hero "expunged from his fortune that color of greedy vulgarity and left its gold untarnished."

Dexter, for all his success, was a figure in the common democratic foreground of business; he was intimately and solely of the great everyday warp and woof of toil. He bore all his fruit at once—when he died. An heirship was required to give the fortune value. . . .

In a way it was fine and beautiful—all that huge accumulation of pillage coming to the white, firm hands of this pretty, amiable capable, good-hearted woman. The sudden substitution of her graceful and gracious figure for the swart and iron figure of the duke was like an apt transformation scene, prophetic of the future.[59]

These earlier books are mere preliminary sketches—first studies in economic backgrounds, hesitating between admiration and censure—satisfied to exploit the "human interest" in the dour figure of the money-grabber. The clever newspaper men did not know enough to do better, more realistic work; they saw the daily activities of business but they understood little of economics, less of sociology. And the new realism was soon to yield itself captive to sociology—to inscribe the name of Zola boldly on its pennant and go forth to conquer. It was Frank Norris who wrote the pronunciamiento of the new school, boldly, magnificently, with immense faith in the finality of his own conclusions. *The Responsibilities of the Novelist* was to become the textbook of the young naturalists.

[59] *The Money Captain*, Chapter 22.

CHAPTER I

DISINTEGRATION AND REINTEGRATION

THE figures of the Gilded Age, colossal yet grotesque, belonged to an America that was passing. Another world of thought and experience was rising above the horizon—a world in which the divinities were science and the machine—that was to disintegrate the traditional society of the dispersion and reshape the plastic materials in new forms. The long tide that for two centuries and a half had been running out had come at last to the turn. For six generations the pattern of life had been woven by the impulse of dispersion that in scattering men along a wide frontier had disintegrated the philosophies and rejected the social order brought from the old world, transforming America into such a society of free men as the Enlightenment had dreamed of—decentralized, individualistic, democratic. Dispersion, disintegration, individualism, anarchism—such was the inevitable drift under the compulsions of a fluid economics and frontier ways, of which the ultimate philosophical expression had been Thoreau at Walden Pond, discovering in his bean patch the same anarchistic principles that Godwin had learned of the French naturists—of which the prophet had been Walt Whitman, dreaming amidst the formless crowds of Manhattan his generous dreams of the democratic brotherhood—and of which Jay Gould the sordid wrecker in Wall Street was the prosaic reality.

Then had come the Industrial Revolution that in creating great cities and in drawing men from the plow to the machine was to undo in a few brief years the long work of the dispersion, repudiate the ideals of the Enlightenment, and provide a new pattern for a consolidating urban society. Thenceforward the drift was increasingly toward concentration, with its compulsions to reintegration and conformity—the imperious subjection of the individual to a standardizing order, the stripping away of the slack frontier freedoms in the routine of the factory, the substitution of the ideal of plutocracy for the ideal of Jacksonian democracy. And this revolutionary work of the machine was hastened by the new spirit of science that spread silently through the land, effecting a revolution in men's thinking as great as the machine was effecting in men's lives. Provincial America had been theological- and political-minded; but with the staying of the dispersion and the creation of an urban psychology, the ground was prepared for the reception of new philosophies that came from the contemplation of the laws of the material universe. The incoming of science had two immediate results: the application of technology to industry that was to further the Industrial Revolution; and the impact on speculative thought of the newly discovered laws of science that was to create a new philosophy. In the second of these twin influences lay an intellectual revolution that was to disintegrate the old theological cosmos, push far back the boundaries of space and time, reorient the mind towards all ultimate problems, and bring into question all the traditional faiths—political and social as well as theological and philosophical. Out of science was to come a new spirit of criticism and realism that was to set the pattern for later thought.

The story of disintegration and reintegration is a striking chapter in American life, a story that runs through two generations—the generation that came to maturity in the seventies, and the generation that came to maturity in the nineties. Between 1870 and 1900 the broad movement of thought passed through two sharply differentiating and contradictory phases: the extension of the philosophy of the Enlightenment, and the final rejection of the Enlightenment in consequence of a more rigid application of the law of causality in the light of a mechanistic universe. During the seventies biological evolution was interpreted in the light of earlier philosophies that had come out of the eighteenth century. It was reckoned a fulfillment and justification of the ideals of the Enlightenment, sanctioning the doctrine of progress that had risen from the conception of human perfectibility by a teleological conception of cosmic progress, glorifying the ideal of democratic individualism, and putting the seal of scientific approval on the philosophy of anarchism that had been the flower of two and a half centuries of the dispersion. And then in the nineties the clouds drew over the brilliant Victorian skies. With the substitution of physics for biology came a more somber mood that was to put away the genial romanticism of Victorian evolution, substitute a mechanistic conception for the earlier teleological progress, and reshape its philosophy in harmony with a deterministic pessimism that denied purpose or plan in the changing universe of matter. It was an unconscious return to the dark spirit long before brought hither by Puritanism from the complexities of English society—the spirit that dominated Calvinistic dogma before it disintegrated in the freedoms made possible by the great dispersion.

The great changes came swiftly because the machine had made ready the soil. Farmers and bankers do not think alike; country and town create different psychologies. A simple, decentralized America had been content with theology and metaphysics, and the intellectual history of New England for two hundred and forty years is not greatly skimped by being compressed into three words, Calvinism, Unitarianism, Transcendentalism. What was true of New England was true of America generally, except for the lesser influence of metaphysics. So long as society was mainly agricultural—and in those portions where the frontier spirit lingered on into later days—the church would retain its dominant influence and theology would still bound men's thought. But with the revolutions in economics and industry, with the rise of an urban society, the mind of America was making ready for the reception of science and the realism that was eventually to spring from science.

Venturesome pioneers had been at work long before, digging about under the thick crust of theology. Even in theocratic Massachusetts Increase and Cotton Mather had professed a zeal for scientific investigation, and the latter was vastly proud of his membership in the Royal Society. In the eighteenth century Franklin and Rittenhouse and William Bartram were evidences of a new spirit, and at Yale College President Ezra Stiles made a small beginning of scientific study that was swept away by his successor Timothy Dwight. In the early decades of the nineteenth century an interest in science was spreading widely, as *Silliman's Journal* witnesses. Asa Gray, Le Conte, and Agassiz encouraged the general interest in geology, and in the sixties and seventies Lewis H. Morgan turned to anthropology and R. L. Dugdale stimulated sociology by his significant study of the Jukes family.

Our present concern, however, is not with the contributions of America to abstract science, but rather with the changing mental attitude that resulted from familiarity with scientific methods—the shift from deductive reasoning to inductive investigation, with the consequent breakdown of theology and the slow drift from metaphysical idealism to scientific materialism; and such a changing attitude concerns us because of its enormous influence on the fabric of our later thinking, the total body of our intellectual and cultural life. Considered in this light the intellectual revolution that resulted when the mind of America, long shaped by theological dogmas, turned away from those dogmas to consider the new universe presented by science, cannot be made too much of. With the pushing out of the frontiers of space and time, the discovery of a vast impersonal cosmos that annihilated the petty egocentric world of good and evil postulated by the theologians, the substitution of universal energy for a beneficent providence, the conception of a ceaseless flux and flow that took no account of teleological ends, the assumption of universal law and universal causality, the mind of America quitted its quiet theological retreats and set forth on a great adventure that was to carry far and the results of which were to unsettle what before had been sure.

In this great work we have been engaged since European science first rose on our horizon a half-century and more ago. To speak exactly, it is not so much science that has taken possession of the mind, as certain postulates of science, certain philosophies presumably derived from science and justified by science, which we have felt bound to incorporate in our thinking as a hundred years before the conclusions of the Enlightenment had been incorporated. In that earlier philosophy of the Enlightenment the whole drift had been towards a dissolvent individualism, a disintegration of the earlier integration. In the new interpretation after 1870 the emphasis came to rest on the whole rather than the parts: in sociology, upon the historical growth of human societies; in biology, upon the evolution of the higher from lower forms. The individual, thus conceived of socially and politically, is no longer an isolated, self-determining entity, but a vehicle through which is carried the stream of life, with a past behind and a future before. He is a portion of the total scheme of things, tied by a thousand invisible threads to the encompassing whole. From the parts to the totality, from freedom to determinism—such has been the drift of thought that science has laid upon us and from which there is no easy escape.

With the advent of such a conception the long movement towards philosophical anarchism was brought to a stop. The integrating principle of unity must eventually shoulder aside the disintegrating principle of individualism; order must supersede willfulness. In the outcome a conception so coercive was to deny all the aspirations of our traditional social philosophy, surrendering society to a new regimentation and reducing the individual to an impotent victim of things as they are. Out of it was to spring the passionate protests of later rebels like Theodore Dreiser and Thorstein Veblen. Yet for the moment the rigid determinism of the premise was overlooked and man was accepted as the first-born and heir of God's benevolent universe. In the seventies the new postulates of science were looked upon as no other than fresh sanctions for the Comtean principle of continuity—of evolution from lower to higher in biology, of growth and progress in sociology. It was this middle ground that Herbert Spencer came to occupy in the minds of his American disciples—holding to the older individualism with its implications of anarchism, yet creating a cosmic philosophy that foreshadowed the eventual dwarfing of the individual.

I

THE VICTORIAN MOOD

The sturdy optimism that was a genial hallmark of the Victorian, was erected on more substantial foundations than a middle-class prosperity arising out of the Industrial Revolution; it was founded on a systematic philosophy, built of excellent materials and laid up with nice mortar-work, to which many hands contributed and in the finality of which many minds believed. Its master idea was the conception of growth, a conception that by contrast with the ideal of the static of earlier times, was profoundly revolutionary. Perhaps the most stimulating suggestion that came out of the Enlightenment, it was evolved by Turgot in France and by Price and Priestley in England, from the psychology of John Locke. If the human mind at birth is an empty vessel, wanting in innate ideas and waiting to be filled by sense perceptions, or if—to accept the familiar figure—it is a clean slate on which the finger of experience writes what it will, then it follows from the philosophy of Locke that the shaping of the individual is determined by the environment that cradles him. It is not an unfolding from within but a molding from without. Hence the idea of growth, and hence the vast preoccupation of the Enlightenment with sociology—or the science of environment—the hand of the sculptor that models the plastic clay. **From** such a conception the principle of progress was an inevitable deduction.

I

SOCIOLOGY AND THE ENLIGHTENMENT

It is convenient, if not quite exact, to trace the rise of the new gospel to Condorcet, who in the midst of the Terror and whilst in hiding from the Jacobins, wrote his stimulating *History of the Progress of the Human Mind* [1]—a work that was early reprinted in America and profoundly influenced Jefferson, who professed to find its principles exemplified in the history of his native Virginia. Condorcet was a humane and liberal spirit, a mathematician, a physicist, a sociologist, one of those eager Revolutionary minds passionately devoted to the creation of a more generous social order; and his celebrated work deserves a distinguished place in the history of social thought. He begins as a good Lockean with the psychology of sense perception, on which he erects his entire superstructure. Here is his opening paragraph:

Man is born with the faculty of receiving sensations; of perceiving and distinguishing the simple sensations of which they are composed; of retaining them, reproducing them, combining them; of comparing these combinations; of grasping what they have in common and what sets them apart; of fixing signs on all such objects in order to reproduce them more clearly and to facilitate new combinations. [2]

He then proceeds to trace the growth of the scientific attitude from the time of Bacon, till it culminated in the rise of social science, with the new politics of natural rights and the new conception of man as perfectible. It is commonly believed that the philosophers of the Enlightenment were speculative dreamers who created a fantastic natural man that flouted the sober realism of experience. Such a notion is grossly absurd. Condorcet was immersed in the scientific spirit of his age; it was to science that he looked for guidance and he had acquired a remarkable understanding of the data already gathered in western Europe. When he set down the following passages, therefore, he was writing not as a speculative dreamer, but as a sociologist who relied solely on

[1] The French title is, *Esquisse d'un tableau historique des progrès de l'esprit humain* See *Œuvres*, Vol. VI, Paris, 1847.
[2] *Œuvres*, Vol. VI, p. 11, Paris, 1847.

scientific inquiry to find a way out of the social mess into which western civilization was plunged by the selfish stupidity of rulers who were hostile to scientific truth.

> After long errors, after having lost their way in incomplete or vague theories, the publicists have finally come to recognize the true rights of man, to deduce them from this single truth, that he is a being endowed with sense perceptions (*un être sensible*), capable of shaping a train of reasoning (*capable de former des raisonnements*), and of acquiring moral ideas.[3]
>
> Finally, we have seen a new doctrine appear. . . . It is that of the indefinite perfectibility of the human species, a doctrine of which Turgot, Price and Priestly, were the first and most distinguished apostles; it belongs to the tenth epoch, in which we shall develop it broadly.[4]

In such passages is contained the kernel of Condorcet's philosophy, the grounds of that hope for human betterment which awakened his generous sympathies. The *Esquisse* is a noble contribution to the work which the heirs of the Enlightenment, from Turgot to Comte, so eagerly and hopefully engaged in—the work of tracing scientifically the changes of the past in order to forecast the path of the future. After dividing the history of social evolution into nine periods, Condorcet projects the outlines of the tenth which is still to come.

> If man can predict, with almost complete assurance, the phenomena of which he knows the laws; if, while they are still unknown in him, from the experience of the past he can forecast, with much probability, the events of the future; why should one regard as a chimerical undertaking the attempt to trace with some likeness the picture of the future destiny of the human species, in accordance with the facts of its history (*d'après les résultats de son histoire*)? The sole ground of faith in the natural sciences is this idea, that the general laws, known or unknown, that rule the phenomena of the universe, are necessary and constant; and on what grounds would this principle be less true for the development of the intellectual and moral faculties of man, than for the other operations of nature? Finally, since opinions formed from the experience of the past, in matters of the same kind, are the sole rule of conduct for the wisest men, why should one deny the philosopher the right to rest his conjectures on the same base, provided he does not attribute to them a certainty beyond that which springs from the number, the constancy and the exactness of his observations?
>
> Our hopes for the future state of the human species may be reduced to these three important points: the destruction of inequality between nations; the progress of equality amongst a common people; finally, the

[3] *Ibid.*, p. 176.   [4] *Ibid.*, Vol. VI, pp. 194–195.

growth of man towards perfection (*le perfectionnement réel de l'homme*). May not all nations one day approach the state of civilization to which have arrived the most enlightened peoples, the freest, the most emancipated from prejudice, such as the French and the Anglo-Americans? The vast distance that divides these peoples from the servitude of nations subject to kings, from the barbarism of African tribes, from the ignorance of savages, must it not gradually disappear? [5]

Condorcet was an idealist, and the grand object towards which he was working was an adequate social philosophy that should interpret justly the evolution of civilization. True to the genius of the Enlightenment he believed that in reason and in the moral sense man possessed the keys to his own progress—that the general reason under the guidance of humane feeling must assure a progressive amelioration of life that will eventuate in the common well-being of men in a rational society. The age of the Enlightenment, he believed, had "opened new paths to the political and moral sciences," and laid bare what to him were "the true principles of social happiness." The American Federalists, who were prodigal of vituperative rhetoric in assailing all French theorists, might have read the pages of Condorcet with profit.

The idea of progress with its corollary of a philosophy of history, thus elaborated by Condorcet, was taken over by Saint-Simon, but came to its most elaborate expression in the work of Auguste Comte. The grandiose philosophy of history to which Comte gave the name of Positivism, was an attempt to formulate the law of progress in civilization; and his dynamic sociology, which emerged naturally from his conception of history, was an attempt to apply that law to society. That the principle of progress is the law of nature Comte professed to discover in the unity of all natural processes and the historical unfolding of all systems; there are no breaks and no fresh beginnings, but everywhere and always, continuity. From this principle emerged the Comtean law of historical evolution with its three phases: the theological, the metaphysical, and the scientific-industrial. If continuity is the law of nature, such continuity presupposes an objective—presumably benevolent; and in view of such continuity towards a benevolent objective, it is only logical to endeavor to dispose the forces of society in harmony with the teleological purpose, and through the application of positive knowledge hasten the advent

[5] *Ibid., Dixième Époque,* pp. 236–237.

of the Golden Age. Hence the grand science, hitherto neglected, is sociology. Earlier generations had placed the Golden Age in a dim past; Comtean philosophy, in harmony with the Enlightenment, placed it in the future as the ultimate goal of an evolving society. To forecast the lines along which such progress will move, to read the future as a child of the past, became therefore a prime objective of the new school of history. The tracing of social laws was the great business at hand, and as the founder of a new social science Comte carried further and systematized the work begun by the Physiocrats. Before Comte history had been little more than chronicles, without pattern or meaning, unconcerned with the sources of change and providing no basis for forecast; after Comte history became an interpretation and a philosophy.

One would have supposed that Positivism would have appealed to American intellectuals, as it appealed to liberal English thinkers like Mill and Spencer. Not only has the American mind taken kindly to sociology, but the history of America, as Woodbridge Riley has pointed out, offers too pat an illustration of the Comtean law of progress to be overlooked.[6] The three centuries of American existence—the seventeenth with its theocracy, the eighteenth with its abstract theories of political rights and its faith in constitutions, and the nineteenth with its industrialism based on science—would seem to be pages out of the Positivist philosophy of history. That Comte made so slight an impression on the mind of New England was due, no doubt, to the current influence of transcendentalism with its metaphysical backgrounds. Although eager young intellectuals like John Fiske might accept it while awaiting a more adequate evolutionary philosophy, the country was not yet ripe for Positivism. When that time came it was Spencer rather than Comte who became the master of American intellectuals—Spencer and in a lesser degree John Stuart Mill. Both Spencer and Mill had come under the influence of the French sociological school, and it was through their writings that the new social philosophy penetrated America.[7]

2

BIOLOGY AND THE ENLIGHTENMENT

The appeal of Spencer to the generation born after the Civil War was extraordinary. Ardent young minds, for whom the candles

[6] *American Thought*, p. 172, New York, 1915.
[7] Woodbridge Riley, *American Thought*, Chapter XI.

of theology were burnt out and who were seeking new light to their feet, were drawn to him irresistibly. Young rebels who had thrown off the guidance of their elders and were bent on discovering fresh paths through the tangle of dead faiths—independent souls like Hamlin Garland and Jack London and Theodore Dreiser who were to become leaders of the realistic revolt against the genteel tradition in life and letters and faith—went to school to him to prepare themselves for the great work of freeing the American mind from the old theological inhibitions. Young men in colleges no longer read *Butler's Analogy*, as their fathers had done before the war, but turned with zest to Spencer's *Data of Ethics* to discover a more scientific theory of conduct. Everywhere the influence of the great Victorian penetrated, and wherever that influence spread the old theological prepossessions disintegrated. It is probably no exaggeration to say that Spencer laid out the broad highway over which American thought traveled in the later years of the century.

If the supreme excellence of Comte, as has been suggested by Lester F. Ward, was his insistence on the ultimate unity of all processes of nature,[8] if before him the continuity of forces had been inadequately understood, his intellectual kinship with Spencer cannot fail to be remarked. The latter's master conception, which he arrived at independently of Darwin and which life-long he applied systematically to the several fields of thought, was the master creative conception of the nineteenth century—the conception of pervasive unity and organic growth. In his well-known phrase it was the law of continuous development from the homogeneous to the heterogeneous, from the simple to the complex; and this principle he found exemplified in the total history of nature and man. Here then is the Comtean law of continuity, but vastly strengthened and given a cosmic significance by deductions from the new science. Lamarck and Darwin laid the foundations for Spencer's philosophy, as Condorcet and Saint-Simon had provided the backgrounds for Comte. Trained thus in the new school of biology, Spencer erected his synthetic philosophy upon the broadest foundations; the principle of organic evolution sufficed to explain for him not only the history of civilization, but the total history of life in a physical universe; and biology, psychology, sociology, politics, ethics—all the congeries of ideals and institutions and bodies of knowledge that shape civilization—were but

[8] *Ibid.*, p. 401.

variant expressions of the development from the homogeneous to the heterogeneous.

The final effect of the synthetic philosophy was not to overset but to confirm the major postulates of the Enlightenment. In his social theory are unforeseen confirmations of the glowing hopes of Turgot and Condorcet. From his studies in biology Spencer had come to think primarily in terms of the individual, and only secondarily in terms of the species and the genus. Now variation is the mark of the individual, for strictly considered, nature knows no duplication of life forms, but always and everywhere individual differentiation; yet since likenesses are far greater and more cohesive than unlikenesses, the instinct of gregariousness impels individuals to associate in ever larger groups, interacting through association and coöperation, whence arises a human society that tends continuously to pass from the simple to the complex. On these two major premises then—individual variation and the instinct of association—Spencer established his social and political theory; and when the elaborate data drawn from biology and ethnology and psychology are stripped away, the underlying conceptions reveal a curious likeness to the master principles of French romantic philosophy. This likeness becomes more striking as he explores the fields of sociology and politics; and his final deductions tally so closely with earlier theory as to warrant a disciple of Jefferson in becoming a disciple of Spencer.

There is no break between Condorcet and the synthetic philosophy. The great Victorian completed the work of the Enlightenment. In establishing his individualism on the principle of biological variation, Spencer was only restating in scientific terms the earlier metaphysical individualism; in establishing his psychology upon an unbroken sequence "from the simple reflex action by which an infant sucks, up to the elaborate reasoning of the adult man," with its corollary of continuously expanding powers, he was rebuilding on the foundation of Locke a fresh argument for the doctrine of indefinite development, or perfectibility; in establishing his sociology on the organic principle of "natural development," which shapes the individual to social ends, with an accruing wealth of individuation that is the final objective of true social life, he justified the French enthusiasm for liberty as the great desideratum, but liberty enriched and augmented by association in a free society; and finally, in establishing his ethics on the principle that "increas-

ing fullness of life is the 'end' of evolution," and the "highest conduct is that which conduces to the greatest length, breadth, and
completeness of life"—that the ultimate criterion of social ethics is
justice and that "every man is free to do that which he wills, provided he infringes not the equal freedom of any other man"—he
rephrased the earlier Godwinian principle that rational liberty
under the reign of justice is the ultimate end of society.[9]

That Spencer's social theory should have been shot through with
older ideals is not surprising when one considers his origins and
training. Sprung from radical nonconformist stock, a congenital
rebel, extraordinarily self-sufficient and coming to intellectual maturity in the tempestuous forties with their Benthamism, their
Chartism, their exigent democracy, he was molded by forces that in
large part were a reëmbodiment of the aspirations nullified by the
Napoleonic wars and the Tory reaction, and now come again to
birth. As a consequence his political theory, like Mill's, was deeply
affected by the revolutionary heritage. He accepted the social
contract as a "theoretical, though not a historical, basis of political
authority and institutions";[10] the doctrine of natural rights, which,
with Jefferson, he interpreted in terms of the rights to life, liberty,
and the pursuit of happiness; and the theory of a constantly
diminishing political state, on the hypothesis that the ultimate
form of society—as in Godwin's *Political Justice*—will, be anarchistic.

At least, such he conceives to be the forecast suggested by the
law of social evolution. As the coercive authority of the political
state diminishes, its place will be supplied by the cohesive force of
association, until voluntary coöperation extends to all the necessary
functions of society; and since the state tends to disappear with the
growth of a rational society, the great desideratum is an adequate
sociology rather than a political theory. The net result, therefore,
of Spencer's wide studies was a fresh justification, based on the
findings of Victorian science, of the master principles of eighteenth-
century speculation; its individualism, its liberalism, its passion for
justice, its love of liberty and distrust of every form of coercion.
The power of the majority must be curbed equally with that of the
minority and he concluded his *The Man versus the State* with the

[9] For a brief exposition of Spencer's major ideas see, William Henry Hudson,
"Herbert Spencer," in *Philosophies Ancient and Modern*, London, 1908.

[10] William Archibald Dunning, *A History of Political Theories from Rousseau to
Spencer*, New York, 1920, p. 400.

well-known words, "The function of Liberalism in the past was that of putting a limit to the powers of kings. The function of true Liberalism in the future will be that of putting a limit to the powers of Parliament." In the scientific speculations of the great Victorian the aspirations of romantic thought came to fresh vitality; embodied in a comprehensive evolutionary system they were given a fresh currency. Herbert Spencer completed the work begun by Locke a hundred and fifty years before, and his *Synthetic Philosophy* brought to conclusion the greatest intellectual movement of modern times.

As the young intellectuals, trained in the school of Spencer, looked out on the universe in the last quarter of the nineteenth century, they discovered, amid all its complexities an encompassing unity, a continuous growth, a creative purpose; and from such assumptions they justified the theory of progress, cosmic in scope and plan, that opened wide the doors to a vaster future. If in the backgrounds of their minds lurked the conception of determinism, it gave them no concern, for a benevolent determinism that shapes all things to a divine end, is no monster to be feared. In the evolutionary science were the grounds of a genial optimism that nothing could shake. If they had lost something of the jauntiness of the transcendental faith that beheld God plowing furrows at Brook Farm, they were armed with a scientific faith that by tapping stones and comparing fishes they should find His plan in an evolving series of life forms. Browning's Fra Lippo was a good Spencerian in his vigorous pronouncement:

> This world's no blot for us,
> Nor blank; it means intensely, and means good:
> To find its meaning is my meat and drink.

That progress was the law of the universe was held to be axiomatic by the new evolutionary school, and the American read in the new philosophy an added confirmation of a prepossession common to all Americans since Franklin and Jefferson, and become the common faith after the War of 1812. In sober minds it led to a complete reshaping of the outlook upon life, and in unbalanced minds it ran riot in all sorts of blowsy enthusiasms. Freedom, love, benevolence, progress towards a millennial perfection—these were the clarion notes in a huge symphony in praise of human perfectibility that assaulted American ears in the Gilded Age. Not Henry

Ward Beecher alone was the prophet of the new day. In the early seventies Mrs. Victoria Woodhull, one of the minor prophetesses, established a paper dedicated to the high end of "the Universal Religion of the Future . . . the Universal Home . . . the Universal Science, called Universology, based on the discovery and demonstration of Universal Laws . . . and an accompanying Philosophy of Integralism"—the "organ of the most advanced thought and Purpose in the World . . . the Organ of Cardinary News . . . News of the Aspiration and Progression of Mankind toward Millennial Perfection." [11] By contrast with such rhythmic enthusiasms the familiar lines of Tennyson are sober prose.

> Yet I doubt not thro' the ages one increasing purpose runs,
> And the thoughts of men are widen'd with the process of the suns.

How logically to young intellectuals of the seventies it all followed from the premises! If man is a rational being, potentially excellent and capable of indefinite development, the idea of a humane and rational progress in civilization is an inevitable deduction; and the evolutionist above all men was certain to build into his philosophy the cardinal idea of a unified progress, but given a cosmic sweep, accepted as the master principle in all fields of the material and the spiritual. It was the law of life, as the static was the law of death. No thinker who had grasped the idea of organic growth, could escape its larger implications; and no student in the seventies could think seriously without coming upon it.

3

THE END OF THE HOPES OF THE ENLIGHTENMENT

Then a film of haze slowly gathered upon the face of the brilliant sun and the light of men's hopes grew dimmer. As physics encroached upon the interest in biology, and leadership in speculation based on scientific findings passed from Spencer to Ernst Haeckel, young Americans of the next generation found the membership of the current philosophical trinity changed for them, and instead of unity, growth, purpose, they discovered unity, flux, chance. Purpose had disappeared from the grim face of the material universe, and they found themselves in the coils of a determinism that was more likely to prove malignant than benevolent. The idea of

[11] Quoted in Constance Mayfield Rourke, *Trumpets of Jubilee*, p. 201.

progress slipped quietly from their minds, and in its stead was only a meaningless and purposeless flux of things. But unity remained to bind the individual upon the whole and dwarf him to a pin-point in a vast macrocosm. The intellectual history of the last quarter of the nineteenth century—in America as well as elsewhere —in its teleological aspects is the history of the shift from the benevolent evolutionism of Spencer to the mechanistic materialism of Haeckel, with all the dislocations and readjustments involved in the cataclysmic change; and *The Education of Henry Adams*, that curiously suggestive study in disillusion, is saturated with the pessimism that followed upon the transition—a pessimism exuding from the contemplation of the bleak unity of a mechanistic universe. Of the earlier period before hope was gone, he wrote thus:

> For the young men whose lives were cast in the generation between 1867 and 1900, Law should be Evolution from lower to higher, aggregation of the atom in the mass, concentration of multiplicity in unity, compulsion of anarchy in order; and he would force himself to follow wherever it led, though he should sacrifice five thousand millions more in money, and a million more lives.[12]

Was there purpose in it all? To this Adams and the younger men more and more declined to make answer. Yet this much is clear, for them the end of the theological age had come, and the end also of the great hopes of the Enlightenment. The idea of progress was given over henceforth to the middle class to become the plaything of material expansion.

II

THE SCHOOL OF SPENCER—JOHN FISKE

Of the distinguished group that labored to naturalize in America the philosophy of evolution John Fiske was the most authoritative spokesman. As a brilliant popularizer of the Synthetic Philosophy, and an historian who applied the Comtean law of continuity to the American past, he brought to the Gilded Age the revolutionary influence of English and French thought. Deeply immersed in Victorian speculation, he threw over his acquisitions the genial mood of his generation and infused the doctrines of evolutionary science with the spirit of religion. He reveled in the cosmic philosophy of Herbert Spencer, but within the material cosmos the scientists were revealing, controlling its eternal flux, he perceived a

[12] *The Education of Henry Adams,* p. 232.

directing will that was shaping man's destiny to noble ends. New England scholarship had served God for too many generations to put aside its teleological prepossessions, and John Fiske was too completely New England to deny his spiritual obligations. The duty laid upon his conscience was plain. It was not enough to lay open to the New England mind the wealth of evolutionary science; he must justify its conclusions by binding them back upon the old faith and discover God revealed in biology as before he had been revealed in the Bible. And so in the heyday of Spencerian influence, before the bleak conception of a mechanistic universe had risen upon the horizon of men's thought to disperse the genial glow of optimism, this learned son of Connecticut was the prophet in America of the new order of thought.

John Fiske was a brilliant Yankee with a voracious appetite for ideas and a passion for cosmic syntheses. In certain respects he was the most richly endowed of the young students of his generation of Americans. Intellectually curious and acquisitive, he refused to be confined by orthodox fences but ranged far in pursuit of knowledge. The pale negations of the current New England theology, on which he had fed in his youth, soon lost their savor, and following his natural impulses he sought out the strongest food available. While still in his teens he had absorbed Emerson, Theodore Parker, and other New England radicals, and was reaching out for an ampler diet. That was in the late fifties, when a new cosmos was taking shape in men's minds and old faiths were disintegrating. The several rivulets of science—geology, zoölogy, chemistry, physics—that hitherto had followed diverse and vagrant courses, were slowly converging and making ready to mingle their waters in a vast common stream. Some further dredging needed to be done first, and on that great job Darwin had long been patiently engaged. It was a time of high hopes and young John Fiske, about to enter Harvard College, was not one to miss the significance of so great an awakening.

Amidst his quiet Connecticut lanes he had already been making his own discoveries. Although he had early gone through a form of conversion to dogmatic Calvinism he had not long been content with its arid provender, but turned to the English disciples of Positivism—George Henry Lewes, Buckle, Mill—and was absorbing Comte with the help of Voltaire and Goethe. In June, 1860, two months before taking his examinations for advanced standing at Harvard, he came upon a prospectus of Herbert Spencer's proposed system of philosophy, and this boy of eighteen was one of the first dozen Americans to subscribe to the undertaking. It was a golden day in his life, that was to determine his whole intellectual development. He became a devoted disciple of Spencer, dedicating his labors to the great cause of evolution. To that end he felt called to study prodigiously. As a Harvard undergraduate he found it difficult to treat his conventional instructors with due respect, for while his classmates were struggling with Greek roots he was exploring the whole field of philology and rioting in Comtean sociology. Instead of exhausting his energies with the usual undergraduate themes, he wrote in his junior year, at the age of nineteen, a critical examination of *Buckle's History of Civilization* for the *National Quarterly Review;* and while preparing for his final examinations he wrote a learned article on "The Evolution of Language" that was accepted by *The North American Review.*

Such intellectual precocity, suggesting to timid souls a lack of respect for orthodox opinions, was not without its dangers. From his first entrance to Harvard he was marked by certain tutors as a dangerous influence. Positivism and evolution were in ill repute in the college circles, and he was eventually summoned before the faculty and admonished for undermining the faith of Harvard undergradugtes. Outside the college he was becoming known as the "young atheist of Cambridge." The reasons for such a reputation were quite sufficient to Unitarian dogmatists who had forgotten the cardinal principle of Unitarianism—the principle of devout free thought—for young John Fiske had already gathered a huge pile of combustible materials that threatened the established orthodoxy. Before entering Harvard he had planned to write a history of early Christianity, but his interest in science drew him into other fields— the new sociological interpretation of history that he discovered in Grote's *History of Greece,* and the broad field of scientific speculation that opened to him in Humboldt's *Cosmos.* To this latter field he turned greedily, reading amongst other works Cuvier's *Règne Animal distribué d'après son Organisation,* Herschel's *Outlines of Astronomy,* Laplace's *Système du Monde,* Agassiz's *Zoölogy* and his *Essay on the Classification of the Animal Kingdom* (1857), and with the joy of a great discovery Darwin's *Origin of Species* (1859). From Agassiz's defense of special creation he dissented vigorously, and this dissent prepared him for an enthusiastic reception of Darwin's careful exposition. Certainly no other young student in America followed so closely or so intelligently the unfolding of the English school of evolutionary thought. In solid acquisition and in intellectual curiosity he was far in advance of Henry Adams, then a young diplomat in London.

Upon his graduation in 1863 he determined upon the law, read through the two-year course of the Harvard Law School in nine months, was admitted to the bar, waited two years for clients who never came, threw it over, and turned to his first love, the life of the scholar. He had his eye on a chair at Harvard, but so long as the old orthodox *régime* lasted no opening offered there. In the first year of President Eliot's administration (1869) an opportunity was provided and he was invited to give a course of lectures in Holden Chapel on the Positive Philosophy. The opposition was still too strong to permit the offer he sought—a chair in history—but he was eventually given a place as Assistant Librarian, where he spent five years amongst the books of Gore Hall. Driven to other means of support he turned to lecturing, was received with immense applause in London, and thereafter to the end of his life he suffered much of his vast energy to drain off into that most fruitless of jobs for a creative mind. A certain genial egoism was to blame for his playing willingly the rôle of lackey to women's clubs. He liked to talk to sympathetic audiences, and he was greatly effective on the platform. The inevitable result was that he fell short in accomplishment of the fine promise of his early years. His style became diffuse, his materials picturesque rather than solid, his thinking flabby. Pretty much all his significant work was done before he was forty.

The greater part of Fiske's intellectual life, despite his later incursions into certain waste places of history, was dedicated to the indoctrination of the American people in the principle of evolution as that principle was outlined in Spencer's *Synthetic Philosophy*. He was a man of one idea, but that idea was so vast and germinal, so comprehensive in its implications and so constructive in its suggestions, as to set afoot the greatest intellectual revolution in western civilization. He called himself a philosopher, but he meant by the term not a metaphysician, but a cosmic historian whose business was to interpret the universe in the light of the great laws that science was revealing. By 1860 science had revealed three such general laws: the law of gravitation, the law of biological variation and the survival of the fittest, and the law of the conservation of energy; and from them Spencer had deduced the principle of a unitary cosmos, with a common force sustaining both the organic and the inorganic, working to a single "far-off divine event, to which the whole creation moves." An intimate friend of Fiske's, and an ardent Spencerian, puts the intellectual situation in these terms:

The conceptions of the Universe generally held at the time when Fiske was in college were fragmentary and chaotic, each phenomenon or each group of phenomena being, like language, a special creation of an anthropomorphic God, turning out different jobs piecemeal like a man. The conception of one power behind all had been a dream of not a few philosophers and poets, but as a fact comprehensible by the average mind, it was not known until the discovery about 1860 of the Conservation of Force. About the same time was discovered the unity of all organic life, in its descent from protoplasm, and the identity of its forces with those of the inorganic universe. The nebular cosmogony, the persistence of force and the biologic genesis, united together, showed the power evolving, sustaining and carrying on the entire universe known to us, to be *one*, and constantly acting in one unified process; and that every detail—from the most minute known to the chemist, physicist and biologist, up to the greatest known to the geologist and astronomer, and including all known to the psychologist, economist, and historian—was caused by a previous detail. It having been established that the same causes always produced the same results, these uniformities were recognized as Laws, and it was also recognized that conduct in conformity with these laws produced good, and conduct counter to them produced evil. . . .

These great discoveries were at once grasped by Fiske's great intelligence, and welcomed with enthusiasm. To their dissemination he mainly devoted his next twenty years, and to their illustration in the origins and foundation of our national commonwealth, the rest of his career.[13]

While still at Harvard, as a result of the publication of his two undergraduate essays already referred to, he was sought out by Edward L. Youmans and urged to join with him in spreading the new evolutionary philosophy.[14] Youmans was an ardent proselytizer who had volunteered for the job of instructing the American people in the meaning of science. He attached himself to Spencer as spokesman and publicity agent, and was on the lookout for helpers. Encouraged thus by Youmans, Fiske threw himself impetuously into the work of furthering the new philosophy of

[13] Henry Holt, *Garrulities of an Octogenarian Editor, with Other Essays somewhat Biographical and Autobiographical*, Boston, 1923, pp. 327-328.
[14] See John Spencer Clark, *Life and Letters of John Fiske*, Vol. I, pp. 273-278.

evolution. As the task unfolded before his maturing mind it came to involve three major problems: to dissociate in the popular mind the potential theism of Spencer's *First Principles* from the materialism of Comte's Positivism, with which it was widely confused; to elaborate the teleological implications of evolution and demonstrate that the grand objective of all natural processes was "the production of happiness, and that, despite occasional lapses, all records of them prove that, on the whole, they tend not only to produce happiness, but to increase it";[15] and finally to apply the principles of the cosmic philosophy to historical writing and reveal how the law of evolution determines the forms of social institutions —to do more adequately in the field of American history what Buckle had tried to do in a larger field without the aid of evolution.

In all his intellectual interests and attitudes Fiske was a complete New England Victorian, but scarcely a British Victorian. In his erection of the doctrine of progress into a cosmic law, and in his resultant optimism, he was at one with Spencer and the English group. But he was a son of New England before he was an evolutionist, and although he had broken with the grotesque, anthropomorphic dogmas of Calvinism, he remained profoundly religious, and like Henry Drummond he sought to transfuse science with spiritual qualities. He was effectively a Unitarian, the leader of the Cambridge intellectuals who were carrying on the work that Theodore Parker would have done had he lived twenty years longer—the work of bridging the chasm between science and religion. To that end his vast concern with teleology—that God is the great wellspring out of which flows the unfolding cosmos, and that the unfolding is guided and controlled to beneficent ends. Natural law, working in a realm of causation, and shaping matter to forms more and more complex, to John Fiske was no other than the beneficent purpose known to theology as Divine Providence.

Pretty much all that he had to say on the question is contained in the four volumes of *Outlines of Cosmic Philosophy*, published when he was only thirty-two. Written with great enthusiasm and complete confidence, it was an attempt to summarize and restate the conception of cosmic evolution as Spencer had defined it in *First Principles*, and partly elaborated it in his *Biology* and *Psychology*. It was a timely presentation, and with its lucid exposition of the evidence drawn from the several fields of science it furthered

[15] Henry Holt, *op. cit.*, p. 328.

the spread of the evolutionary philosophy. But it sought to do more. Not content with arraying in due order the scientific proofs of a vast unitary cosmos—as Spencer had done—Fiske essayed the rôle of apologist and supplemented the facts of science with ontological and teleological speculations. Whereas Spencer had remained agnostic, refusing to speculate on the unknowable, and clearly implying a deterministic cosmos, Fiske took high theistic ground, asserting that evolution implies the existence of a creative mind, vaster than the anthropomorphic conceptions of theology and far nobler, whose cosmic plan unfolding in the material universe compels a belief in a benevolent God, and a belief also in the "eternal source of a moral law which is implicated with each action of our lives, and in obedience to which lies our only guarantee of the happiness which is incorruptible." And this "eternal Power, not ourselves, that makes for righteousness"—to use Arnold's phrase which Fiske was fond of quoting—is making also for altruism and the spirit of love that lies at the heart of Christianity; for is not the prolongation of infancy with its demands on altruism—a principle that was Fiske's contribution to evolution, of which he was justly proud—a master biological device for individual variation? In consequence the evolutionist becomes not only a theist, but a Christian in the truest meaning of the term. The fatherhood of God and the brotherhood of man—to which New England Unitarianism had come to restrict its dogmas—are in reality "two great interrelated cosmic truths—the existence of righteousness as an active principle in the Infinite Power or Reality back of the cosmos, and its correlative manifestation in the altruistic consciousness of man."[16]

Such speculation concerning the unknowable exercised an increasing fascination for Fiske as his deeply religious nature slowly colored the acquisitions of the scientist, and in a succession of tracts—*The Destiny of Man* (1884), *The Idea of God* (1885), *Through Nature to God* (1899), and *Life Everlasting* (1900)—he definitely rejected the negative attitude of agnosticism that was a common mark of the English evolutionary school, and turned to outline the religious faith of an evolutionist. George Eliot's dictum that God is unknowable and immortality is unthinkable, was too thin a diet for his robust nature; instead he elaborated the argument that faith in God and immortality is reasonable in the light of

[16] John Spencer Clark, *op. cit.*, Vol. II, p. 50.

the evolving cosmos that science was revealing. To John Fiske that cosmos was not bleak and impersonal, a vast congeries of physical forces that reduced man to the status of a flea on the epidermis of earth, but the expression rather of a benevolent will unfolding in accordance with a divine purpose. "The process of evolution is itself the working out of a mighty Teleology, of which our finite understandings can fathom but the scantiest rudiments." To Henry Holt this recovery of teleology was Fiske's great contribution to evolutionary thought.

He did more just there than any modern philosopher, perhaps than any philosopher, to show that this teleology is beneficent, and to restore in this way the attitude of mind which it may not yet be too late to call Faith in God and Immortality.[17]

No doubt it was due to such emphasis on the theistic implications of evolution that the doctrine was so quickly accepted in New England amongst the Unitarians and liberals; but for Fiske it marked the end of his intellectual leadership. After the battle had been won he turned away to engage in less fruitful activities, no longer followed keenly the new discoveries of science, and finally set himself to write the history of America. The venture on the whole was not fortunate. In his attempt to reinterpret the American past he suffered from grave handicaps, an inadequate knowledge and an inadequate philosophy. He was led into the field of history by his interest in the English school of Grote and Maine and Stubbs and Freeman, and his ultimate purpose was to present "the drama of American civilization, of which the political organization of the United States was the crowning feature, as an evolutionary development from antecedent causes and of great significance to the future civilization of the world." [18] But for this undertaking he was inadequately equipped and his conscious search for a Comtean continuity in social growth did him a real disservice. The economics of historical change he seems never to have considered, and his analyses of social forces are never acute or penetrating. Although he attempted to apply sociological evolution to history he was really little more than a political and military historian with a special fondness for wars and the details of battle strategy. In his first venture, *American Political Ideas*—written for his London lectures of 1880—he simplified American political develop-

17 Henry Holt, *op. cit.*, p. 339.
18 John Spencer Clark, *op. cit.*, Vol. II, p. 456.

ment to two germinal ideas—the town meeting and the principle of federation, and these two conceptions he traces back to the Teutonic folkmote and the Teutonic principle of shire representation. The theme with which he deals is thus stated in the preface:

> The government of the United States is not the result of special creation, but of evolution. As the town-meetings of New England are lineally descended from the village assemblies of the early Aryans; as our huge federal union was long ago foreshadowed in the little leagues of Greek cities and Swiss cantons; so the great political problem which we are (thus far successfully) solving is the very same problem upon which all civilized peoples have been working ever since civilization began. How to insure peaceful concerted action throughout the Whole, without infringing upon local and individual freedom in the Parts,—this has ever been the chief aim of civilization, viewed on its political side; and we rate the failure or success of nations politically according to their failure or success in attaining this supreme end. When thus considered in the light of the comparative method our American history acquires added dignity and interest, and a broad and rational basis is secured for the detailed treatment of political questions.[19]

Only a New England historian could write so naïvely as that, for only to a New Englander does the town meeting become a germinal source of American democracy. Not a great historian, Fiske ceased to be in his wandering later years a great intellectual influence. The rare promise of his young manhood he never fulfilled, but like his generation he suffered his energies to be dissipated and he ended in a somewhat blowsy optimism. To Henry Holt he was a very great and learned man, but to a later generation it is difficult to make out his vast stature. Nevertheless as a purveyor of Victorian science to the American people he did a useful and important work.

[19] John Fiske, *American Political Ideas*, Preface, pp. 4–5.

CHAPTER II

THE SKEPTICISM OF THE HOUSE OF ADAMS

In the welter of change that resulted from the revolutionary transitions of the Gilded Age, one man at least stood apart, skeptical about the worth of the current revolutions, unconvinced that all the hurly-burly meant a rational progress. To Henry Adams skepticism early became a habit. Doubt persistently dogged his footsteps and the more critically he examined the ways of his generation of Americans, the more certain it seemed to him that any were unworthy the name of civilization. He was not at home in the new world of the Gilded Age; and as he watched the disintegrations of the older New England in which he had been brought up, an incurable nostalgia seized upon him and he set about seeking another home where he might live the good life he had not lived heretofore. The America of the Gilded Age was alien to him; its gods were not his gods, nor its ends his ends. And so began for him a long pilgrimage of the spirit that was to carry him far and return him at last with no solider gains than a handful of curious relics in his pilgrim's scrip.

The sturdy New England character, with its self-sufficing individualism and granite integrity, never came to finer flower than in the Braintree-Quincy house of Adams. Intellectually curious, given to rationalism, retaining much of the eighteenth-century solidity of intellect and honest realism, refusing to barter principle for the good will of men, the Adams line produced no more characteristic offshoots than came in the fourth generation. In Charles Francis Adams, Jr., Henry Adams, and Brooks Adams, the family virtues of independence, intellectual integrity, and disinterested criticism, found abundant expression. All three were children of an earlier century, endowed with the solidest Yankee-Puritan qualities of mind and heart, unyielding as the rock ledges of their native fields; and they found the experience of living in the late nineteenth century, of adjusting their eighteenth-century minds to the demands of a sordid capitalistic order, a difficult business. Though they tried to bridge the chasm between the two worlds, though they

212

honestly sought some working compromise that would suffer them to share in the work of their generation, they met with failure. It was not possible for the House of Adams, with its old-fashioned rectitude, to accept the ways of the Gilded Age, and in the end they turned aside from the main-traveled road to follow their own paths.

I

CHARLES FRANCIS ADAMS—THE BUSINESS FAILURE

Of the three Charles Francis Adams most nearly succeeded in his experiment of a *rapprochement* with capitalism, with the result that his life came nearest to shipwreck. Perhaps there was less of the Adams granite in his character. He refused to turn rebel but consciously sought to win the prizes offered by his generation, training himself to serve financial interests, making overtures to business, and achieving a very considerable financial success. Yet nothing was more incongruous than an Adams serving as lackey to State Street, and when after abundant experience he came finally to realize it he turned away to pick up the scattered threads of a life largely wasted. For years he had suffered from a long mal-adjustment. When he quitted the army at the close of the war with the brevet rank of brigadier-general, he found himself adrift. The world of his youth was gone and the future seemed drab and un-promising. Intellectually he was caught between tides. The tradi-tional idealisms had burnt out in the bitter struggle, and in the sterile post-war years his Puritan nature found no adequate nour-ishment. The crusading ardor was gone, and the new world of science had not yet risen on the horizon of young men who had given their youth to the army. In 1865 he came upon John Stuart Mill's essay on Auguste Comte, which he said revolutionized his whole mental attitude—"I emerged from the theological stage, in which I had been nurtured, and passed into the scientific. . . . From reading that compact little volume of Mill's . . . I date a changed intellectual and moral life." Yet from this accidental foray into Victorian rationalism he got little more than a sense of release from a dead Puritanism. Creative intellectual enthusiasms were not to be his portion.

Disillusioned with the law, over which he had been pottering, and wanting to ally himself with the dominant forces of his genera-tion, he "fixed on the railroad system as the most developing force and largest field of the day." He delved into the history of certain railways and established a reputation as a student of transportation. For upwards of a quarter century—from 1866 to 1890—as a member of different public commissions and finally as president of the Union Pacific system—Jay Gould's road—he devoted his best energy to the work, only to be disillusioned in the end. In 1912 he wrote this confession:

> Indeed, as I approach the end, I am more than a little puzzled to account for the instances I have seen of business success—money-getting. It comes from a rather low instinct. Certainly, as far as my observation goes, it is rarely met with in combination with the finer or more interesting traits of character. I have known, and known tolerably well, a good many "successful" men—"big" financially—men famous during the last half-century; and a less interesting crowd I do not care to encounter. Not one that I have ever known would I care to meet again, either in this world or the next; nor is one of them associated in my mind with the idea of humor, thought, or refinement. A set of mere money-getters and traders, they were essentially unattractive and uninteresting. . . . In the course of my railroad experiences I made no friends, apart from those in the Boston direction; nor among those I met was there any man whose acquaintance I valued. They were a coarse, realistic, bargaining crowd.[1]

Yet not till he had reached his late fifties did he finally cut the ties that held him to the "bargaining crowd," and turn to the business of salvaging the remnant of his days. He gave himself over with zest to the writing of Massachusetts history, but it was then too late to do notable work. He had laid too many offerings on an altar he had come to loathe. Not a lifelong student like Henry, he had been unable to gather great stores of knowledge. Not a militant rebel like Brooks, he had never been given to searching inquiries into the laws of civilization. And so when he found himself free at last, he set himself to the business of local chronicles. That was better than nothing; it was the one thing in his life he took solid pride in; the work was honestly and capably done; but it was small savings from a lifetime of conscientious work. His venture into the realm of business had been a disaster.

II

HENRY ADAMS—INTELLECTUAL

From a similar disaster Henry Adams was saved by an early disillusionment. His efforts at *rapprochement* were little more than a gesture. While casting about after the war for a promising opening

[1] *Autobiography*, pp., 190-195.

for a career he hit upon finance as a likely field and published a number of essays that drew attention to him. But it was quite impossible for him to go forward along such lines. He was too completely the intellectual, too aloof from his generation in spirit and will, to ally himself with the economic masters of the Gilded Age. Sooner or later he would go his own way, and luckily good fortune took the matter in hand promptly. No suitable opportunity offering, he was dragooned by family and friends into an assistant-professorship at Harvard, where he spent seven years trying to explain to himself and his students the meaning of the Middle Ages. Those years were his introduction to history. The passion of the student was in his blood, and he turned with zest to brood over the scanty records of past generations, seeking a clue to the meaning of man's pilgrimage on earth, trying to arrange the meaningless fragments in some sort of rational pattern, in the hope of discovering an underlying unity in what seemed on the face only a meaningless welter of complexity and irrationality. A rationalist, he followed his intellect in an eager quest for the law of historical evolution, and he ended fifty years later in mysticism. It was a natural outcome for a lifetime of rationalizing—a compensation for the mordant dissatisfactions that issued from the restless play of mind.

Dissatisfied with his labors he quitted the Harvard post in 1879 and thereafter made his home at Washington in the atmosphere of politics. From the Middle Ages he turned to the American past and set out to explore the period during which the first Adams had played his part. He could not deal with narrow parochial themes; he would not fall into the "sink of history—antiquarianism," that satisfied Charles Francis Adams. From the beginnings of his intellectual life he had been concerned with the ideas and ideals that presumably lie behind periods and civilizations; so he went back to what he regarded as the great age of American political history, to inquire into the meaning of the struggle between Federalism and Jeffersonianism for control of the venture in republicanism. But finding little satisfaction there, as he had earlier found none in Victorian England, where he had studied closely contemporary English statesmen—Palmerston and Lord Russell and Gladstone— only to convince himself that they were bankrupt of ideas and morality, and had nothing to teach concerning the good life, he abandoned the field, threw over his familiar studies, and set about the great business of reëducating himself.

From his long studies in the American past one significant thing had emerged—he had come to understand the source of certain of his dissatisfactions with current American ideals that set him apart from his fellows. He had gone back to his own origins and had traced the rise of the defiant Adams prejudices that were as strong in the fourth generation as they had been in the first. The Adams family was eighteenth-century—Henry Adams had come to understand—and he himself in mind and education and prejudices, was of that earlier time. He was a child of Quincy rather than Boston—a simple world with simple virtues that capitalism and industrialism were destroying in the name of progress. From such village loyalties he could not rid himself. Perhaps in reason he should not have preferred that earlier homespun world; but affection does not heed logic, and as Henry Adams traced the decline of Quincy to Hamilton's financial policy that started the new capitalism on its triumphant career, he was filled with bitterness. It was a vulgar order that was rising and an evil day. Since 1865 the bankers had ruled America, and they were coming finally to cajole the American people into accepting their vulgar ideals and putting their trust in a bankers' paradise. As he watched the temples of the new society rising everywhere in the land, his gorge rose at the prospect. He had no wish to dwell in a bankers' paradise. Dislike of a capitalistic society was in his blood. From father to son all the Adamses had distrusted capitalism and hated State Street. The "only distinctive mark of all the Adamses," he said late in life, "since old Sam Adams's father a hundred and fifty years before, had been their inherited quarrel with State Street, which had again and again broken out into riot, bloodshed, personal feuds, foreign and civil war, wholesale banishments and confiscations, until the history of Florence was hardly more turbulent than that of Boston."[2]

And so when at the climax of the capitalistic revolution he watched the change going on noisily all about him, when the transition to the bankers' paradise was called progress and capitalistic feudalism was hailed as the advent of Utopia, he seemed to himself a somewhat pathetic anachronism. Shades of the prison house were falling about him. "He had hugged his antiquated dislike of bankers and capitalistic society," he said bitterly, "until he had become little better than a crank."

[2] *The Education of Henry Adams*, p. 21.

He had known for years that he must accept the régime, but he had known a great many other disagreeable certainties—like age, senility, and death—against which one made what little resistance one could. . . . For a hundred years, between 1793 and 1893, the American people had hesitated, vacillated, swayed forward and back, between two forces, one simply industrial, the other capitalistic, centralizing, and mechanical. In 1893, the issue came on the single gold standard, and the majority at last declared itself, once for all, in favor of the capitalistic system with all its necessary machinery. All one's friends, all one's best citizens, reformers, churches, colleges, educated classes, had joined the banks to force submission to capitalism; a submission long foreseen by the mere law of mass. Of all forms of society or government, this was the one he liked least, but his likes and dislikes were as antiquated as the rebel doctrine of State rights. A capitalistic system had been adopted, and if it were to be run at all, it must be run by capital and by capitalistic methods.[3]

But while he clung tenaciously to his obsolete prejudices in favor of an earlier century, the pugnacious realism of that century was oozing out of him. The middle years of his life, between the acceptance of the Harvard post in 1870 and the final break with Victorianism in 1892, were intellectually an unhappy period. He was losing his grasp on realities and becoming narrowly and exclusively political-minded. It was not good for him to live daily in the presence of politics. In so "far as he had a function in life," he said of the Henry Adams of 1877, "it was as stable-companion to statesmen, whether they liked it or not."[4] The term "statesmen" was of course only a polite euphemism for the breed of politicians who played their sordid game under his critical eyes. He was rarely under any illusions in regard to them except when blinded by friendship. Certainly his etchings of Grant and Blaine and Sherman and Conkling and other servants of democracy were done with acid.

Yet in all his penetrating comment on men and measures there is a curious failure to take into account the economic springs of action. He had let slip the clue old John Adams had followed so tenaciously. An acute historian, not thus wanting, would never have traced the triumph of the gold standard to the "mere law of mass," would never have substituted a physical determinism for an economic, would never have confused the principle of mass with a minority. How far an intelligent man and a competent historian could go astray in his criticism of current ways is suggested by the curious novel *Democracy*, that he wrote in 1880 while living in the

[3] *Ibid.*, pp. 343–344.   [4] *Ibid.*, p. 317.

daily companionship of John Hay and Clarence King. In dealing with the phenomena of political corruption he had none of the acuteness of old John Taylor of Carolina, who would have put his finger unerringly on the cause, or of the first Adams. If he had written *Democracy* after he had studied the funding operations of the Federalists under Hamilton's leadership, very likely he would have dealt with the problem more searchingly; but in 1880 Henry Adams revealed no more critical intelligence than did Godkin or Lowell or other critics of the Gilded Age.

The historical work done during those middle years at Washington was abundant and excellent, marked by rigorous use of sources, a dispassionate attitude towards partisan issues, and excellent form. It was easy for an Adams to take middle ground between Jefferson and Hamilton, however much his sympathies inclined to the former. In all this work, however, in the *Life of Albert Gallatin* (1879), in *John Randolph* (1882), as well as in the nine-volume *History of the United States during the Administrations of Jefferson and Madison* (1889–1891), the point of view remains too narrowly political, with the result that it fails to thrust into adequate relief the economics of the great struggle between agrarianism and capitalism; and without that clue the interpretation is wanting in substantial realism.

By 1891 he was convinced that he had got all he could from the curdled milk of politics, and he became dissatisfied with his work. There can be little doubt that it was a growing realization of the inadequacy of his analysis of social forces that determined him to abandon the field he had tilled so long and set about the business of reëducating himself. If *Mont-Saint-Michel and Chartres* and *The Education* tell anything about Henry Adams they reveal that his dissatisfactions welled up from deep springs within himself— from the consciousness of his failure to penetrate beneath the surface, to probe the hidden forces that move the puppets on the historical stage. He had long been seeking an adequate philosophy of history—for a unity behind the multiplicity—and in these early years of the nineties he was stimulated by Brooks Adams, who was then deep in his theory of the law of civilization and decay and had come to lean heavily on the principle of economic determinism.[5] "Brooks Adams had taught him," he said later, "that the relation between civilizations was that of trade," and stimulated by this

[5] *Ibid.*, pp. 338–339.

rediscovery of the philosophy of the first Adams he set about the business of orienting himself to the realm of science, of substituting for a meaningless political interpretation a broader philosophical interpretation.

Very likely it was his reading in the sociology of the Enlightenment that first turned his thought to the philosophy of history—chiefly Turgot and Comte. Speaking of the years 1867–1868 he said he "became a Comteist, within the limits of evolution."[6] He had long been interested in such clues as science offered—in the geological theories of Sir Charles Lyell and the biological deductions of Darwin. But the theory of biological evolution with its implications of a benevolent progress from the simple to the complex, failed to satisfy him; and he turned to the physical sciences for a guide, discovering as the ultimate reality behind all appearances—force. This physical principle he transferred to the field of sociology. Coal-power, electrical power, he concluded, were to civilization what the gaseous theory was to physics. It was a creative suggestion and it revolutionized his conception of history. It runs through all his later speculations and provided the basis of his thinking. "Adams never knew why," he said, "knowing nothing of Faraday, he began to mimic Faraday's trick of seeing lines of force all about him, where he had always seen lines of will."[7] "To evolutionists may be left the processes of evolution; to historians the single interest is the law of reaction between force and force—between mind and nature—the law of progress."[8] "The great division of history into phases by Turgot and Comte first affirmed this law in its outlines by asserting the unity of progress."[9]

Thus by the aid of the physical sciences Henry Adams came back to the philosophy of determinism—a conception that may lead either to pantheism or to mechanism as one's temperament determines. In such a choice there would be no doubt which way Henry Adams would go; he must somehow reconcile determinism and progress, he must discover unity in multiplicity—and that unity and progress he found in a mystical pantheism. "Continuous movement, universal cause, and interchangeable force. This was pantheism, but the Schools were pantheist . . . and their deity was the ultimate energy, whose thought and action were one."[10]

[6] Ibid., p. 225.
[7] Ibid., p. 426.
[8] Ibid., p. 493.
[9] Ibid., p. 493.
[10] Ibid., pp. 428–429.

How creatively this pantheistic mysticism was to determine his later thinking is sufficiently revealed in the pages of *Mont-Saint-Michel and Chartres*. With incredible labor Henry Adams had at last made his way out of the Sahara of politics in which he had long wandered.

Phrased in less transcendental terms his philosophy of history, as he came finally to understand it, was expressed thus:

The work of domestic progress is done by masses of mechanical power— steam, electric, furnace, or other—which have to be controlled by a score or two of individuals who have shown capacity to manage it. The work of internal government has become the task of controlling these men, who are socially as remote as heathen gods, alone worth knowing, but never known, and who could tell nothing of political value if one skinned them alive. Most of them have nothing to tell, but are forces as dumb as their dynamos, absorbed in the development or economy of power. They are trustees for the public, and whenever society assumes the property, it must confer on them that title; but the power will remain as before, who-ever manages it, and will then control society without appeal, as it con-trols its stokers and pit-men. Modern politics is, at bottom, a struggle not of men but of forces. The men become every year more and more creatures of force, massed about central power-houses. The conflict is no longer between the men, but between the motors that drive the men, and the men tend to succumb to their own motive forces. This is a moral that man strongly objects to admit, especially in mediaeval pursuits like poli-tics and poetry, nor is it worth while for a teacher to insist upon it.[11]

From a civilization thus tyrannized over by coal-power and elec-trical power, he turned away to discover if possible a civilization in which men had lived the good life that he longed for; and in his second incursion into medieval times he found what he had long been seeking. Two centuries, from 1050 to 1250, came to represent for him in the evening of his days the crown and glory of all human endeavor; the first century with its Norman Mont-Saint-Michel and its *Chanson de Roland*, with its forthright strength and sim-plicity, its uncritical acceptance of life and God, its hope encom-passed by a sufficing unity—a strong, naïve, credulous world, yet with men's minds buttressed like their cathedrals by a faith that held in equilibrium the soaring arches of their aspirations, with every cranny and nook flooded with radiant color: and the second century, that expressed itself in the cathedral of Chartres, with its adoration of the Virgin, its courtly love of Guillaume de Lorris and Marie de Champagne, its passionate mysticism of Saint Louis and

[11] *Ibid.*, pp. 421–422.

Saint Bernard and Saint Francis, and its soaring scholasticism of Thomas Aquinas—a tender, feminine age, that worshiped woman and erected its altars to Our Lady of Love rather than to Our Lady of Sorrows, that found in Isolde the ideal woman and expressed itself in Eleanor of Guienne and Blanche of Castile, in Héloïse and Marie de Champagne, more adequately than in Richard Cœur-de-Lion, till it finally went the way of mortality "with the death of Queen Blanche and of all good things about the year 1250":—to such idealization of medievalism did this child of Puritanism come in the wistful twilight of his days. He had never evaded life, nor professed himself satisfied with mean or cheap substitutes, but had sought persistently till he had come to believe that the good life had been lived once, though it might not ever be lived again. So much at least was clear gain, even though it should end in wistfulness.

Mont-Saint-Michel and Chartres is a beautiful book, the more beautiful because of its wistfulness; and the theme that runs through its pages is a denial of the values that embodied for his countrymen the sum of all excellence. It is an account of certain happy generations—so few amongst the countless many—who worshiped in love, before fear had come to the western world and crept into the message of the church; a love that elevated Mother Mary above the Christ of the Cross, and that in her shrine at Chartres would allow no hint of sorrow or suffering to appear, but represented her as looking out upon the world with a gracious and regal kindliness and mercy, quick to succor and to forgive—the spirit of love that suffices life in all its needs. *Mont-Saint-Michel and Chartres* is rich and tender and wise, perhaps beyond anything else that his generation of Americans wrote, with a mellow scholarship that walks modestly because it has learned how little it knows. Yet in its every implication it is a sharp and searching criticism of Boston and America of the nineteenth century. It repudiates every ideal of a generation that had gambled away the savor of life—that does not comprehend "and never shall," the greatness of that earlier time, "the appetite" for living, the "greed for novelty," "the fun of life." [12] It was precisely these things, unimportant though they might seem to the acquisitive mind, that Henry Adams had missed in his own life and passionately resented having missed. To come to know great men and great deeds and great ages is perhaps of doubtful expediency for one who must live amongst small men; and Henry

[12] *Ibid.*, p. 139.

Adams was forced to pay a heavy penalty for his catholic under=
standing and sympathy.

The profound suggestiveness of *Mont-Saint-Michel and Chartres*
lies in the skill with which the brilliant threads of medieval art and
thought and aspiration are woven into a single pattern, and the
splendor of its unity traced to a mystical *élan* that found its highest
expression in faith. It was the ideal of love that he discovered in the
golden twelfth century—love above law, above logic, above the
church and the schools: a love that explains for him the passionate
worship of Mother Mary, together with the new *"courtoisie"* that
sought to shape manners and morals to humane ends. The humanity of the Virgin set her above the Trinity, as the humanity of Saint
Francis set him above Thomas Aquinas, for all the latter's soaring
scholasticism. To one who entered those bygone times through the
portals of Chartres cathedral, it was natural to interpret the total
age in the light of the gentle smile of the Mother of God, and to feel
her presence as a transforming spirit amongst men. Has any other
Yankee interpreted so lovingly the mission of the Virgin, as Henry
Adams analyzed it in such a passage as this?

True it was, although one should not say it jestingly, that the Virgin
embarrassed the Trinity; and perhaps this was the reason, behind all the
other excellent reasons, why men loved and adored her with a passion
such as no other deity has ever inspired: and why we, although utter
strangers to her, are not far from getting down on our knees and praying
to her still. Mary concentrated in herself the whole rebellion of man against
fate; the whole protest against divine law; the whole contempt for human
law as its outcome; the whole unutterable fury of human nature beating
itself against the walls of its prison-house, and suddenly seized by a hope
that in the Virgin man had found a door of escape. She was above law;
she took feminine pleasure in turning hell into an ornament; she delighted
in trampling on every social distinction in this world and the next. She
knew that the universe was as unintelligible to her, on any theory of
morals, as it was to her worshippers, and she felt, like them, no sure conviction that it was any more intelligible to the Creator of it. To her, every
suppliant was a universe in himself, to be judged apart, on his own merits,
by his love for her,—by no means on his orthodoxy, or his conventional
standing in the Church, or according to his correctness in defining the
nature of the Trinity. The convulsive hold which Mary to this day maintains over human imagination—as you can see at Lourdes—was due much
less to her power of saving soul or body than to her sympathy with people
who suffered under law,—divine or human,—justly or unjustly, by accident or design, by decree of God or by guile of Devil. She cared not a
straw for conventional morality, and she had no notion of letting her

friends be punished, to the tenth or any other generation, for the sins of their ancestors or the peccadilloes of Eve.

So Mary filled heaven with a sort of persons little to the taste of any respectable middle-class society, which has trouble enough in making this world decent and pay its bills, without having to continue the effort in another. Mary stood in a Church of her own, so independent that the Trinity might have perished without much affecting her position; but, on the other hand, the Trinity could look on and see her dethroned with almost a breath of relief. . . . Mary's treatment of respectable and law-abiding people who had no favours to ask, and were reasonably confident of getting to heaven by the regular judgment, without expense, rankled so deeply that three hundred years later the Puritan reformers were not satisfied with abolishing her, but sought to abolish the woman altogether as the cause of all evil in heaven and on earth. The Puritans abandoned the New Testament and the Virgin in order to go back to the beginning, and renew the quarrel with Eve.[13]

Thus at last, in another land and a remote age, Henry Adams found the clue that explained for him his own failure and the source of the dissatisfactions that had tracked him doggedly through his far wanderings. He had come to understand the reasons for the sterility of his Massachusetts past, and the last shreds of his Puritan-Federalist heritage were cast off. In comparison with the vision that came to him in the choir of Chartres, how unspeakably poor and mean were the activities he had portrayed in *Democracy*, or even those he had dealt with in his history of the early days of the republic. He had discovered the highest existence in emotional response to noble appeal; the good life was the unified life, possible only on a grand scale in those rare and great periods of social *élan* when the individual is fused in an encompassing unity. Of that golden age of the Transition—so he finally cast up the account— "the sum is an emotion—clear and strong as love and much clearer than logic whose charm lies in its unstable balance."

The Transition is the equilibrium between the love of God—which is faith—and the logic of God—which is reason; between the round arch and the pointed. One may not be sure which pleases most, but one need not be harsh toward people who think that the moment of balance is exquisite. The last and highest moment is seen at Chartres, where, in 1200, the charm depends on the constant doubt whether emotion or science is uppermost. At Amiens, doubt ceases; emotion is trained in school, Thomas Aquinas reigns.[14]

Of all the elaborate symbolism which has been suggested for the Gothic cathedral, the most vital and most perfect may be that the slender

[13] *Mont-Saint-Michel*, pp. 276–277.   [14] *Ibid.*, pp. 321–322.

nervure, the springing motion of the broken arch, the leap downwards of the flying buttress,—the visible effort to throw off a visible strain,—never let us forget that Faith alone supports it, and that, if Faith fails, Heaven is lost. The equilibrium is visibly delicate beyond the line of safety; danger lurks in every stone. The peril of the heavy tower, of the restless vault, of the vagrant buttress; the uncertainty of logic, the inequalities of the syllogism, the irregularities of the mental mirror,—all these haunting nightmares of the Church are expressed as strongly by the Gothic cathedral as though it had been the cry of human suffering, and as no emotion had ever been expressed before or is likely to find expression again. The delight of its aspiration is flung up to the sky. The pathos of its self-distrust and anguish of doubt is buried in the earth as its last secret. You can read out of it whatever else pleases your youth and confidence; to me, this is all.[15]

One may enter the past, of course, through such portals as one chooses; but one is likely to choose the portals that promise to open upon the world of one's desires. It was a fortunate accident, no doubt, that led Henry Adams to Chartres to study the cathedral glass under the guidance of John La Farge; nevertheless it finally determined for him his total interpretation of the Middle Ages and of all history, and that interpretation followed naturally a subtle ancestral bias. Even in his rebellion against his past he could not get away from it, but like Ruskin and John Henry Newman he came to affirm—whether rightly or wrongly, who shall say?—that the singular glory of the Middle Ages was the mystical *élan* that came to expression in the adoration of the Virgin. As a child of generations of Puritans he came back finally, in the twilight of his studies, to the great ideal of faith. And yet it is not without suggestion that William Morris, who more nearly than any other modern expressed in his daily life the spirit of the Middle Ages, never concerned himself much with the medieval church—neither its cathedrals nor its scholasticism nor its miracles—never talked about an age of faith, would scarcely have understood, indeed, what was meant by the drive of a mystical *élan;* but discovered the secret of that earlier civilization in the gild rather than the church, and traced the source of the haunting beauty that clings to all its works to the psychology of craftsmanship that found delight in shaping the raw material to the craftsman's dreams.

The difference between Morris and Adams is great enough, and at bottom it is the difference between the artist and the intellectual; yet it is a pity that Henry Adams, with his wide acquaintance in

15 *Ibid.*, p. 383.

England, should never have known the one Victorian he should most have delighted in—the nineteenth-century craftsman who found in his workshop the good life the historian dreamed of, and was unhappy because it had been lost. Perhaps it would not have greatly changed the latter's interpretation. He was not a pagan in temperament to enter sympathetically into the medieval world that Morris had discovered and of which the Church was only a drapery—a drapery that never quite covered a frank *joie de vivre* that was an emotion far more realistic and human than any mystical *élan*, and that persisted long after the apogee of faith in the early twelfth century, filling all the later Middle Ages with its abundant beauty till it was finally destroyed by the economic revolution that came out of the Reformation. But at any rate he might have been led by such knowledge to set the craftsman beside the poet and the schoolman and the mystic—the nameless artist who wrought such marvels beside the patron who took care to have his name and his arms emblazoned on window and wall to remind posterity of his generosity; and certainly, his interpretation of the Middle Ages would not have suffered by such addition. Instead, an excessive intellectualism drove him back upon the naïve.

The disillusion of Henry Adams is abundantly instructive to the student of our flamboyant transition, so different from the golden Transition. Here was an honest man and an able—none honester and none abler in his generation—who devoted his life to finding a path out of the maze of middle-class America, that should lead to a rational and humane existence. He was never overconfident of his conclusions. All arrogant dogmatisms he had long since left behind; they had become for him pathetically futile and foolish. Creeds and faiths, whether in religion or politics or economics, he no longer subscribed to; but a certain residuum remained, from his long meditations—a sense of interfusing unity, mystical, pantheistic, that his lurking skepticism dealt tenderly with. *"Inter vania nihil vanius est homine,"* he asserted as a skeptic, and as a mystic he replied, "Man is an imperceptible atom always trying to become one with God. If ever modern science achieves a definition of energy, possibly it may borrow the figure: Energy is the inherent effort of every multiplicity to become unity." [16] In these later years he called himself half whimsically a "conservative Christian Anarchist" [17] and the explanation probably is to be found in his

---

[16] *Mont-Saint-Michel*, p. 332.   [17] *The Education*, p. 405.

shift from intellectualism to emotion as the crown of a satisfying life. "The two poles of social and political philosophy seem necessarily to be organization or anarchy; man's intellect or the forces of nature." [18] In rare and happy periods—as in the glorious Transition—freedom finds its fullest life in a spontaneous drawing together of the whole; but as the social *élan* dies away, institutions, organization, remain. Thomas Aquinas follows Saint Francis, form remains after emotion has subsided. Nevertheless the free man must cling to his freedom, in spite of society, in spite of the political state.

Absolute liberty is absence of restraint; responsibility is restraint; therefore, the ideally free individual is responsible only to himself. This principle is the philosophical foundation of anarchism, and, for anything that science has yet proved, may be the philosophical foundation of the universe; but it is fatal to all society and is especially hostile to the State. [19]

Though he lived in the midst of a centralizing politics and found his friends in such servants of centralization as John Hay and Henry Cabot Lodge, Henry Adams had no faith in the dominant ideals. He was never a friend to an acquisitive society with its engrossing political state. In the light of his favorite dictum that "Power is poison," he may perhaps be regarded as an old-fashioned Jeffersonian; it is another evidence of the persistence of his eighteenth-century mind. He was an arch-individualist who would go his own way and reach his own conclusions, quite unconcerned that his views were wholly at variance with those of his generation. How could it be otherwise? How should men who lived in the counting-house understand even the language of this pilgrim returned from other and greater worlds? It was foolish to talk of what he had seen. And so when he wrote *Mont-Saint-Michel and Chartres* he published it privately, and was incredulous when it was proposed to republish it and give it to the world. What had he, or the twelfth century, to say to the land of Theodore Roosevelt and Pierpont Morgan? Was not this America of theirs peopled by the descendants of the *bourgeoisie* who, six hundred years before, resentful at having been cheated—as they supposed—in their heavy investments in shrines and churches of Our Lady, had turned away from all such unprofitable business, and put their savings in lands and houses and ships and railways and banks—of which

[18] *Mont-Saint-Michel*, p. 344.   [19] *Ibid.*, p. 372.

things politics was the sluttish servant? How should one who had known Saint Francis and Eleanor of Guienne take such men or such a world seriously?

III

BROOKS ADAMS—REBEL

The difference between Henry Adams and Brooks Adams is, perhaps, sufficiently revealed in the distinction between the intellectual and the rebel. The youngest of the brothers was a militant nonconformist, a searching and outspoken critic of all the faiths of his generation. In Brooks Adams the family skepticisms were pointed and barbed, and the family distrust of capitalism issued in a broadside attack upon the hateful system. Few Americans of his day were so little pleased with the bankers' Utopia dreamed of by the middle class, or subjected the capitalistic mind to such critical analysis. Not content with rejecting that Utopia, he pursued his studies in the history of western civilization with a view to determining whether the economic mind, instead of being the friend and ally of a human society—as it professed to be—were not rather the foul wellspring of a disintegrating egoism that must destroy every civilization that yields to its siren appeal. In the theory he eventually elaborated, the capitalistic mind proves to be a greedy spider spinning his web to catch the simple imaginative minds—warrior and priest and artist and craftsman—and suck them dry. The sterile middleman becomes master of society and with the inevitable enslavement of the producer, and the drying-up of production at its source, civilization withers and decays, to be followed by another cycle in the long struggle between the creative and acquisitive instincts.

None but a congenital rebel could have arrived at such conclusions from the studies in which his youth was passed. As a son of the house of Adams the profession of the law was the predestined path to politics and diplomacy, and like Charles and Henry he devoted his younger years to the ancestral study, receiving such training as the Harvard Law School could give. He made greater progress than his brothers, eventually getting so far as to write legal treatises; but finding such work a bit arid he supplemented his legal studies with the writing of Massachusetts chronicles. His dissatisfactions seem to have culminated in the late eighties, during the lean years that preceded the crash of 1893; and he turned away from local chronicles to speculate on the deeper causes of social vigor and decline. The result was the publication in 1895 of *The Law of Civilization and Decay*, a study in social dynamics that took its point of departure from psychology, and based its conclusions on physics and economics. Before Henry Adams he elaborated the theory that civilization is the product of social energy, and social energy obeys the physical law of mass, accelerating or retarding in ratio to the density of population reduced to order. As society draws together in great centers its activity increases until exhaustion finally slows it down; whereupon follows a period of disintegration that breaks up the integrated mass and disperses its energy. The social ebb and flow, therefore, is always from decentralization to centralization and back again to decentralization, and as it flows it thrusts into the foreground different types of mind that express themselves in diverse ideals.

The master types that appear and disappear in this ceaseless flux are determined by two psychological drives that always and everywhere shape human activity—fear and greed: the one culminating in the social rule of the priest, the other in the social rule of the usurer. Decentralization with its isolation breeds the imaginative mind which, seeing more devils than vast hell can hold, turns to the priest for succor—to one who deals in miracles and professes to be able to fend off malignant powers, and who in consequence grows rich by his traffic in relics and rises to economic power. But imagination produces as well the creative mind that finds in isolation the promptings to revery, expresses its dreams in terms of beauty, and fashions a realm of art in which to dwell. Priest, artist, and warrior,—shrine, cathedral, and castle—were the creation of medieval times, the naïve products of the golden age of decentralization. Whereas centralization, with the rubbing away of singularity by daily contact and the greater rewards that lie open to activity, breeds automatically the economic mind—a mind that is necessarily unimaginative, practical, competitive, acquisitive, skeptical, preferring administration to creation, and setting exploitation as the single object of activity. And since centralization offers increasing rewards to greed, the economic mind subdues the imaginative, and the money-lender with his control of wealth rises to mastery. As he expropriates the resources of society he inevitably dominates the political state. His wealth enables him to maintain a hired police to safeguard his gains, until expropriation having run its course, the police fail to hold in check the mass of the exploited, and an unmartial class discovers that money can no longer buy security against the strength of numbers. The usurer is overthrown, his wealth is expropriated, and the social cycle must be run again.

This suggestive theory, which he works out with conspicuous skill in his interpretation of the Middle Ages and the rise of capitalism, implies a perennial conflict between fear and greed, that turns finally upon the relative development of the arts of attack and of defense. Centralization, it is clear, results from the superiority of the former; when attack is superior to defense the lesser strongholds of exploitation must fall and the defeated must become subject to the coalescing masters. After the disruption of the Roman Empire western Europe created its feudal system, by means of which the baron in his stout castle flouted the centralizing ambitions of the impotent monarchy; and it was not till the wealth of the church and of the *bourgeoisie* was thrown on the side of the king, and the development of the art of attack through the use of gunpowder, that the rise of the monarchical state was possible. But having aided the king to reduce the power of the barons, thereby rendering trade secure on a large scale, the *bourgeoisie* turned against the medieval church with its vast wealth that invited expropriation. In the primitive age of faith, under the dominion of fear, the burgesses had spent their money prodigally to build shrines and churches and cathedrals—in France alone between the years 1170 and 1270, eighty cathedrals and nearly five hundred large churches had been built, that by a calculation made in 1840, would cost a billion dollars to replace [20]—but with the development of the economic mind such amazing expenditures seemed wasteful, and the *bourgeoisie* looked about for a cheaper way of salvation. The money cost to the worshipers of saints and relics was a sharp prod to their skepticism as to the efficacy of such worship. This explains for Brooks Adams the origins of the Reformation; it was due to the economic dissatisfaction of the burgess class; the church had grown rich and grasping from its monopoly power. Speaking of the rise of English Lollardry, he argued:

The Lollards were of the modern economic type, and discarded the miracle because the miracle was costly and yielded an uncertain return . . . gifts as an atonement for sin were a drain on savings, and the econo-

[20] See Henry Adams, *Mont-Saint-Michel*, pp. 94-95.

mist instinctively sought cheaper methods of propitiation. The monied class, therefore, proceeded step by step, and its first experiment was to suppress all fees to middle-men, whether priests or saints, by becoming their own intercessors with the deity . . . [and] as the tradesman replaced the enthusiast, a dogma was evolved by which mental anguish, which cost nothing, was substituted for the offering which was effective in proportion to its money value. This dogma was "Justification by Faith," the corner-stone of Protestantism. . . .

But the substitution of a mental condition for a money payment led to consequences more far-reaching than the suppression of certain clerical revenues, for it involved the rejection of the sacred tradition which had not only sustained relic worship, but which had made the Church the channel of communication between Christians and the invisible world. That ancient channel once closed, Protestants had to open another, and this led to the deification of the Bible. . . . Thus for the innumerable costly fetishes of the imaginative age were substituted certain writings which could be consulted without a fee. The expedient was evidently the device of a mercantile community, . . . and made an organized priest-hood impossible. When each individual might pry into the sacred mysteries at his pleasure, the authority of the clergy was annihilated.[21]

With warrior and priest superseded by the tradesman as the dominant type—the imaginative mind by the economic—came the inevitable triumph of greed over fear. The ancient defenses of the church were razed and it stood naked to its enemies. In presence of the skepticism of the burgesses it could no longer sell its miracles in the open market, could no longer persuade men that it was God's vicegerent with powers of binding and loosing; and with its divine sanctions gone, its wealth-hoards lay unprotected before the cupid-ity of king, noble, and commoner. The spoliation of the monas-teries was the prelude to the long movement of the Reformation in England, and made possible its success. So long as the church re-tained its lands and treasure it could not easily be overturned; so a greedy King and greedy nobles took effective measures to disarm it, and having got their hands on the substantial plunder they left to Genevan ministers the lesser business of disputing over the form and doctrine of the new church. The revolution had already been accomplished; and this revolution—the transfer from priest to lay-man of a third of the wealth of England—was but prelude to still greater revolutions that were preparing, and which began with the pouring into England of the gold and silver from the Spanish treas-ure-ships. The spoiling of Rome and the spoiling of the Spaniard were both buccaneering adventures undertaken by zealous Protestants. Drake and Hawkins—pirate and slaver—were "hot gospellers," ready to fight, plunder, or rape for the glory of God and the profit of England; and it was such men who diverted to London the flood of Spanish-American silver that issued from the rich mines of Potosi.

Potosi was discovered in 1545, and from that event Adams dates the rise of the commercial activity that was to prepare the way for the Industrial Revolution, which came to flower two centuries later. This vast upheaval that destroyed the older feudal England, was the immediate outcome of the plundering of India that brought to London the vast treasure-hoards of the East. The eviction of the peasants from their lands had already provided a plentiful supply of cheap labor, the machinery of credit and exchange had been created, and with this immense influx of capital the Industrial Revolution was a matter of course. The manufacturers seized control of England and ruled till approximately 1810, when their authority was disputed by the financiers who gradually displaced them. The Bank Act of 1844, which yielded the control of the currency to the bankers, marked the definite transfer of sovereignty to Lombard Street; Samuel Lloyd, the banker, completed the work begun in 1523 by Thomas Cromwell, burgess-adventurer—the work of bringing England under the authoritative sway of the principle of greed. Since 1844 western civilization has lain helpless under the heel of the usurer, who levies his tax upon production by expanding and contracting the currency at will, and rules society through his control of the political state. The triumph of the economic mind is complete.

The aristocracy which wields this autocratic power is beyond attack, for it is defended by a wage-earning police, by the side of which the legions were a toy—a police so formidable that, for the first time in history, revolt is hopeless and is not attempted. The only question which preoccupies the ruling class is whether it is cheaper to coerce or bribe.[22]

The Law of Civilization and Decay is an extraordinarily provocative study, the main principles of which he elaborated and applied in later historical studies, the result of which was to emphasize for him the determining influence of economics and geography in the rise and fall of empires.[23] Equipped thus with a comprehensive

[22] *Ibid.*, p. 292.
[23] See *America's Economic Supremacy*, New York, 1900; *The New Empire*, New York, 1902.

philosophy of history, he turned in a later work to examine certain aspects of the play of social forces in America, in the light of universal social experience. The particular object of his inquiry in *The Theory of Social Revolutions* is the machinery of social control developed in America during the movement of capitalistic centralization, and its probable adequacy to meet the future stresses of acceleration. The problem of security for the capitalistic order resolves itself, he decides, into the problem of a sufficient protective police; and since every non-military master class must depend upon some form of mercenary Swiss guard, the solution in America has assumed a form not uncommon in earlier European experience, but which every European country has learned at bitter cost to reject. In the face of a strong anti-militaristic public sentiment that forbids a coercive army and navy, the financial masters have had recourse to the courts; and it is the eventual effect of such perversion of the courts to non-judicial ends that he considers in this frank inquiry.

Historically, he points out, the courts have at times exercised two diverse functions, the judicial and the political; and the problem of justice and equity before the law, it has been found by long and bitter experience, resolves itself into the total separation of the one from the other. The judicial function is that of impartial arbitrament in accordance with an established *corpus juris;* it is judgment and not will. The enactment of the law, on the other hand, is a political function, residing in the legislature. When therefore, the courts exercise the political function, they not only assert that the judicial will is sovereign, but they engage in a perilous struggle for mastership and involve themselves in all the passions of partisan objectives. Every "dominant class, as it has arisen, has done its best to use the machinery of justice for its own benefit." The temptation to such perversion is perennial; it is the particular and besetting temptation of an unmartial monied class; and in times of social stress it becomes acute. In revolutionary crises—as in England under Lord Chief-Justice Jeffreys and in France under the Revolutionary Tribunal—the political function overrides the judicial, the last protection of the individual is swept away, and society lies helpless before the ruling power. Thus to pervert the legitimate functions of the courts is a dangerous game to play—most dangerous for a non-military group for whom the courts are protectors; and yet it is precisely this game that capitalism in America, heedless of the teachings of experience, has long been playing. Using the courts as a police power it has brought contempt upon them and thereby weakened the arm upon which alone it can hope to rely in periods of acute stress. In short, capitalism has assumed the functions of sovereignty in America, but it has refused to assume the responsibilities of sovereignty. To gain immediate ends it has shut its eyes to future consequences; and what those future consequences are likely to be Brooks Adams is at pains to point out.

The kernel of his argument, obviously, lies in the thesis that the federal courts have assumed political functions; and into this question he delves with the equipment of the lawyer added to that of the philosophical historian. "Politics," he asserts realistically, "is the struggle for ascendancy of a class or a majority." Under the "American system, the Constitution . . . is expounded by judges, and this function, which, in essence, is political, has brought precisely that quality of pressure on the bench which it has been the labor of a hundred generations of our ancestors to remove."[24] Hence, "from the outset, the American bench, because it deals with the most fiercely contested of political issues, has been an instrument necessary to political success. Consequently, political parties have striven to control it, and, therefore, the bench has always had an avowed partisan bias."[25] From so anomalous a situation two curious developments have resulted: in the rôle of guardians of the Constitution the courts have assumed sovereign powers over the legislature, and at the same time, by a clever non-judicial hocus-pocus they have declared themselves superior to the Constitution, possessed of the prerogative of dispensation. How the first came into being Adams traces in detail from the time of Marbury vs. Madison in 1803, when Marshall asserted a supervisory jurisdiction over Congress, to Standard Oil Company vs. United States in 1911, when the Court amended an act of Congress that Congress had declined to amend. How the second came into being is a curious story. It arose, according to Adams, from the rigidity of a written constitution, that having been interpreted narrowly must somehow be stretched to meet public needs. In such an emergency the "Supreme Court of New York imagined the theory of the Police Power," saying in effect, "in our discretion, we suspend the operation of the Constitution, in this instance, by calling your act an exercise of a power unknown to the framers of the Constitution."[26]

[24] *The Theory of Social Revolution*, p. 45.   [25] *Ibid.*, pp. 47–48.   [26] *Ibid.*, p. 128.

In other words, having, by the assumption of sovereignty, nullified the legislative power from which relief would naturally come, and having awakened a hostile public opinion by its narrow interpretation of contractual rights, the court was embarrassed and looked about for a loophole of escape; and the most convenient loophole was the novel doctrine of judicial prerogative:

> No legislature could intervene, and a pressure was brought to bear which the judges could not withstand; therefore, the Court yielded, declaring that if impairing a contract were, on the whole, for the public welfare, the Constitution, as Marshall interpreted it, should be suspended in favor of the legislation which impaired it. They called this suspension the operation of the "Police Power." It followed, as the "Police Power" could only come into operation at the discretion of the Court, that, therefore, within the limits of judicial discretion, confiscation, however arbitrary and to whatever extent, might go on.[27]
>
> The effect of the adoption by the Supreme Court of the United States of the New York theory of the Police Power was to vest in the judiciary, by the use of this catch-word, an almost unparallelled prerogative. They assumed a supreme function which can only be compared to the Dispensing Power claimed by the Stuarts, or to the authority which, according to the Council of Constance, inheres in the Church, to "grant indulgences for reasonable causes." I suppose nothing in modern judicial history has ever resembled this assumption. . . .[28]

It is this amazing principle of the judicial prerogative which sets the Courts above the Constitution and grants them the privilege of dispensing Indulgences, that has perverted their functions from the judicial to the political. If Indulgences are for sale, naturally the wealthy will buy them. And since corporate wealth is regarded by the judiciary with a more than friendly eye, it rarely finds difficulty in securing such Indulgences as it seeks. The Courts have become, in consequence, not so much the Swiss Guards of capitalism, as a pliant sovereign lord who dispenses rewards to his favorites. The capitalist is "the most lawless" of citizens. In his attitude towards the state he is essentially anarchistic; he evades or nullifies a law that he does not like, while clamorous for the enforcement of a law that works in his favor.

If the capitalist has bought some sovereign function, and wishes to abuse it for his own behoof, he regards the law which restrains him as a despotic invasion of his constitutional rights, because, with his specialized mind, he cannot grasp the relation of a sovereign function to the nation

[27] *Ibid.*, p. 93.   [28] *Ibid.*, pp. 91–92.

as a whole. He, therefore, looks upon the evasion of a law devised for public protection, but inimical to him, as innocent or even meritorious.

This attitude of capital has had a profound effect upon shaping the American legal mind. The capitalist, as I infer, regards the constitutional form of government which exists in the United States, as a convenient method of obtaining his own way against a majority, but the lawyer has learned to worship it as a fetish. Nor is this astonishing, for, were written constitutions suppressed, he would lose most of his importance and much of his income. Quite honestly, therefore, the American lawyer has come to believe that a sheet of paper soiled with printers' ink and interpreted by half-a-dozen elderly gentlemen snugly dozing in armchairs, has some inherent and marvellous virtue by which it can arrest the march of omnipotent Nature. And capital gladly accepts this view of American civilization, since hitherto capitalists have usually been able to select the magistrates who decide their causes.[29]

The skepticisms of the House of Adams came to their frankest expression in the writings of Brooks Adams. The passion for social justice had brought him at last to a philosophy of history that made him a trenchant critic of the American of his generation. He rejected alike the humanitarian optimism that, from Condorcet to Herbert Spencer, had inspired generous souls with hope for future progress—and that even Henry Adams clung to—and the economic optimism that from the beginnings of the westward movement had inspired acquisitive souls with the hope of continuous gain. Nothing perhaps marked him more clearly as a rebel than his denial of the god worshiped by his fellows. The gospel of progress was for him no more than a fetish of the economic mind. In the ebb and flow of civilizations under the attraction of fear and greed, what justification was there for faith in a benevolent progress? His lot had been cast, unfortunately, in an age of capitalism, when the acquisitive mind was triumphing over the imaginative, the banker over the priest and craftsman and mystic; but he could see no reason in heaven or earth to brag of that fact, and he would have held himself a fool to apply the term progress to the spread of greed that was crowning the usurer as master of men. A thorough skeptic, with the comfortable illusions of his generation dissipated, he was in worse plight than Henry Adams, for he had created no golden twelfth century as a refuge against the present.

But if he was under no illusions, he was under no intellectual tyrannies; he had cleared his mind of all middle-class fetishes and could look out calmly upon a mad world. After a century and a

[29] *Ibid.*, pp. 213–215.

quarter this youngest of the House of Adams was still true to the sturdy intellectual honesty of his race. He refused to cry up a fool's paradise where his fellows were crowning the banker as king—professing to serve high ends while seeking vulgar profits: he would not shut his eyes to disagreeable truth or hold his tongue. In Brooks Adams one can almost hear the voice of the first Adams elaborating his doctrine of determinism, pointing out to a romantic generation the unpleasant realities that confuted its optimism, expatiating on the abundant follies of men that lay snares in their own path, yet clinging to a faith in justice that has become old-fashioned. Possibly Brooks Adams is not to be reckoned a great figure, but he was an honest man and worthy of his name—no mean accomplishment, for all in all the Adams family is the most distinguished in our history.

CHAPTER III

VICTORIAN REALISM

IT was not till the eighties that the movement of realism in fiction began to excite wide interest, and then began a brisk and often acrimonious discussion of the merits and shortcomings of the new technique that filled the pages of the literary magazines. The prejudices against it were many and robust. To most Victorians realism meant Zola, sex, and the exploitation of the animal, and all the pruderies of the Age of Innocence rose up in protest against defiling letters with such themes. The judgment of Aldrich's on realism—"A miasmatic breath blown from the slums"—was a characteristic Yankee echo of Tennyson's condemnation, "wallowing in the slough of Zolaism." All the high priests of the genteel rallied to combat such a desecration of literature, and when it knocked at the door of a respectable magazine in the person of Stephen Crane's *Maggie* the editor could do nothing else than turn it into the street. In the late nineties, when *Jude the Obscure* appeared in one of the family magazines, even the great reputation of Hardy was reckoned a poor excuse for such an offense to morality.

American taste was still romantic, and from his villa at Florence, F. Marion Crawford regularly sent forth heavy romances that were regarded as contributions to our literature. In defense of his wares he threw into the discussion of realism a compact little volume, *The Novel; What It Is*, in which he defined the novel as a pocket drama, the chief interest of which lies in the plot—a retort courteous to Howells's contention that plot is childish and a story ends well that ends faithfully; wedding bells at the end are of no interest to grown men and women, but rather what life brings after the wedding bells. To the aid of Crawford came the brilliant Scot, Robert Louis Stevenson, the literary idol of America in the nineties, whose brave tales were on every center-table. A confirmed romantic, Stevenson could not resist breaking a lance in the cause, and his *Humble Remonstrance* was a persuasive defense of the perennial appeal of romance.

But in spite of protests the spirit of realism spread quietly through the lesser works of fiction and the high-flown romantic was laid away in the grave of John Esten Cooke. The new realism was a native growth, sprung from the soil, unconcerned with European technique. In its earlier expression it inclined to a romantic or idyllic coloring, but as it developed it came to rely more and more on the beauty of truth. This primitive realism issued chiefly from the local color school of the short story, but it was supplemented by the sociological school. The influence of Lowell and the *Atlantic Monthly* on the development of the realistic short story had been encouraging, and in the next decade that development was to go forward swiftly. With the exploitation of local materials came a sharp division on sectional lines, and as Howells pointed out, America was soon parceled out geographically into local groups. Edward Eggleston in southern Indiana, George Washington Cable in New Orleans, Charles Egbert Craddock in eastern Tennessee, James Lane Allen in Kentucky, Octave Thanet in Arkansas, Sarah Orne Jewett and Mary Wilkins Freeman in New England, were representative of the new concern for local truth in fiction that was to tell against the romantic. In fixing attention on narrow and homely fields they were turning towards realism, for the charm of their work lay in fidelity to the *milieu*, the exact portrayal of character and setting. With the spread of an interest in the local the vogue of the strange and the remote declined and a quiet sobriety of tone displaced the romantic. The way was being prepared for a more adequate realism. "Nothing could testify with more force," said H. H. Boyesen in 1894, "to the fact that we have outgrown romanticism than this almost unanimous desire, on the part of our authors, to chronicle the widely divergent phases of our American civilization." [1]

But that waited upon profound changes in the American outlook on life. In the seventies and eighties conditions were not ripe for it and the naturalism that in France, Russia, Germany, and Scandinavia, was carrying everything before it, was still alien to the American temper. It was not so much that it offended our innate Puritanism as that it seemed to us belied by the open facts of American life. The psychology of the dispersion still marked us. Although we were feverishly building great cities we were still emotionally a country people, far from urban-minded. We still thought in terms of the slack earlier freedoms, uncritical of our

[1] *Literary and Social Silhouettes*, p. 73.

ways, untroubled about the future. For the American born before
the Civil War, naturalism was impossible; his mind had not been
shaped by the industrial city or come under the dominion of science.
The traditional outlook on life was unchanged; he still clung to the
old moralities, the old verities, the old faith in the goodness of life
in America. The intellectual revolution must be gone through with
before naturalism should be at home in America, a native expression of native conditions; and it would then be a vehicle only for
writers born and bred in the new city environment. In the meanwhile—in the genial years when the earlier optimisms still veiled
the harsher realities of science and industrialism—the movement of
realism got under way in the work of two distinguished craftsmen
who, bred up in Victorian culture, interpreted life in terms of the
middle and upper classes.*

II

HENRY JAMES AND THE NOSTALGIA OF CULTURE

There is a suggestion of irony in the fact that one of our earliest
realists, who was independent enough to break with the romantic
tradition, should have fled from the reality that his art presumably
would gird itself up to deal with. Like his fellow spirit Whistler,
Henry James was a lifelong pilgrim to other shrines than those of
his native land, who dedicated his gifts to ends that his fellow
Americans were indifferent to. Life, with him, was largely a matter
of nerves. In this world of sprawling energy it was impossible to
barricade himself securely against the intrusion of the unpleasant.
His organism was too sensitive, his discriminations too fine, to
subject them to the vulgarities of the Gilded Age, and he fled from
it all. He early convinced himself that the American atmosphere
was uncongenial to the artist.[2] The grotesqueries of the frontier
irruption, the crude turmoil released by the new freedoms, were no
materials to appeal to one in search of subtleties, to one who was a
lover of nocturnes in gray. And so, like Whistler, he sought other

---

* The first subsection of this chapter in the Contents is entitled "William James
and Pragmatism." None of this appears in the manuscript, and it seems likely that
Professor Parrington planned to transfer the subject to a later part of the book.
The numbering is, however, left as it is given in the Contents.—*Publisher*.

[2] "Civilization at its highest pitch was the master passion of his mind, and his
preoccupation with the international aspects of character and custom issued from
the conviction that the rawness and rudeness of a young country were not incapable
of cure by contact with more developed forms." Pelham Edgar, *Henry James, Man,
Author*, pp. 40–41.

lands, there to refine a meticulous technique, and draw out ever thinner the substance of his art.

The explanation of the curious career of Henry James, seeking a habitation between worlds and finding a spiritual home nowhere, is that he was never a realist. Rather he was a self-deceived romantic, the last subtle expression of the genteel, who fell in love with culture and never realized how poor a thing he worshiped. It was the first mistake of Henry James that he romanticized Europe, not for its fragments of the medieval picturesque, but for a fine and gracious culture that he professed to discover there. With the naïveté of the Age of Innocence he assumed that an aristocratic society—shall we say that of Mayfair or the Quartier Saint Germain?—is a complex of subtle imponderables that one comes to understand and embody only through heritage; and it was an assumption even more romantic that these imponderables were so subtly elusive as to escape any but the subtlest art. Like Edith Wharton he erected this suppositious culture into an abstract *tertium quid*, something apart from social convention or physical environment, something embodied in the choicer spirits of a class that for generations presumably had cherished them. Born of an unconscious inferiority complex in presence of a long-established social order to which he was alien, this romanticization of European culture worked to his undoing, for it constrained the artist to a lifelong pursuit of intangible realities that existed only in his imagination. The gracious culture that James persistently attributed to certain choice circles in Europe was only a figment of his romantic fancy—a fact that after long rambling on the Continent and nearly forty years' unbroken residence in England, he came finally to recognize. It was this failure to find the substance of his dream that imparted to his work a note of wistfulness. He had quitted the land of his birth to seek his spiritual home elsewhere, yet increasingly he came to question the wisdom of his act. He suffered the common fate of the *déraciné;* wandering between worlds, he found a home nowhere. It is not well for the artist to turn cosmopolitan, for the flavor of the fruit comes from the soil and sunshine of its native fields.

The spirit of Henry James marks the last refinement of the genteel tradition, the completest embodiment of its vague cultural aspirations. All his life he dwelt wistfully on the outside of the realm he wished to be a free citizen of. Did any other professed realist ever remain so persistently aloof from the homely realities of life? From the external world of action he withdrew to the inner world of questioning and probing; yet even in his subtle psychological inquiries he remained shut up within his own skull-pan. His characters are only projections of his brooding fancy, externalizations of hypothetical subtleties. He was concerned only with *nuances*. He lived in a world of fine gradations and imperceptible shades. Like modern scholarship he came to deal more and more with less and less. It is this absorption in the stream of psychical experience that justifies one in calling Henry James a forerunner of modern expressionism. Yet how unlike he is to Sherwood Anderson, an authentic product of the American consciousness!

III

WILLIAM DEAN HOWELLS AND THE REALISM OF THE COMMONPLACE

From such nostalgia, that left a note of wistfulness in his pages, William Dean Howells was saved by his frank and undivided loyalties. Intellectually and emotionally he was native to the American soil, and however widely he might range he remained always a conscious American. He had no wish to Europeanize his mind; he felt no secret hankerings for the ways of Mayfair or the culture of the Quartier Saint Germain. The homely American reality satisfied the needs of his art, and he accepted it with the finality of Walt Whitman. If he failed to depict it in all its sprawling veracity, if much of its crude robustness never got into his pages, the lack was due to no self-imposed alienation, but to the temperament of the artist and the refined discretions of his environment.

The current school of realism is inclined to deal harshly with Howells. His quiet reticences, his obtrusive morality, his genial optimism, his dislike of looking ugly facts in the face, are too old-fashioned today to please the professional purveyors of our current disgusts. They find his writings as tedious as the gossip of old ladies. To their coarser palates his respectable commonplace is as flavorless as biscuit and tea. Yet it must not be forgotten that for years he was reckoned new-fashioned. Whatever may be one's final judgment on his work it is certain that for twenty years he was a prophet of realism to his generation, the leader of a movement to turn American literature from the path of romanticism and bring it face to face with the real and actual. It was not his fault that the ways of one generation are not those of another, and it is well to remember that if his realism seems wanting to a generation bred up on Theodore Dreiser, it seemed a debasement of the fine art of literature to a generation bred up on Thomas Bailey Aldrich. Realism like dress changes its modes.

The Howells we know best was not a simple child of the frontier, like Mark Twain, whom all could laugh with and love because the sallies of his wit awakened a native response. He did not remain completely native to the older folk-ways. He was rather a composite of the ideals reckoned excellent by the post-war generation— an American Victorian, kindly, urbane, tolerant, democratic, accepting America as a land that God's smile rests on, and convinced that here, wedded to a generous democracy, culture must eventually produce offspring finer than the world has hitherto known. Bred up in the mystical Swedenborgian faith, he shrank from all fleshliness and loved purity with the devotion of a Galahad. A child of the Ohio frontier, he retained to the last the western feeling of democratic equality. An adopted son of Brahmin Cambridge, he immersed himself in culture—Italian, English, Yankee— and served the ideal of excellence with a lifelong devotion; a reverent pilgrim to the shrine of truth, he followed such paths as his generation knew to lay his art at the high altar. In all these things—in his ample culture, his kindly democracy, his high standards of workmanship—as well as in the instinctive reverences of a clean and sweet nature, he was an embodiment of the best in American life, a child of Jacksonian democracy who made use of his freedoms to serve the excellent cause of culture.

But he was much more than that, and if the critics who are wont to damn his Victorian squeamishness would penetrate to the inner core of Howells they would discover an intellectual, alert and sensitive to changing currents of thought, seeing with his own eyes, pursuing his own ends, who wrought out for himself a culture that was individual and native. If he was not, like Henry Adams, plagued with an itch of curiosity, he traveled widely in the realm of the mind. Culture meant to him open-mindedness, familiarity with diverse schools of thought, a willingness to venture upon the unorthodox and to defend the unpopular. He was never a child of the Gilded Age. He was unsoiled by its vulgarity, unconcerned with its sordid ambitions. Neither at heart was he a child of Brahmin culture. He loved Lowell and Norton and Godkin and Aldrich, and he wanted to be approved by them; but he ranged far more widely than they, into places they thought indiscreet. The mature Howells came to stand apart from Brahminism, dissatisfied with a literary Toryism, convinced that a sterile genteel tradition could not suffice the needs of American literature. His very drift toward realism was a negation of the Brahmin influence. On the whole it was unfortunate that he lived so long in the Cambridge atmosphere. The New England influence may not have been a factor in shaping his too leisurely technique, but certainly it postponed the day of his intellectual release. If he had removed to New York a decade earlier, before his literary method hardened into rigidity, his technique might have changed with his more radical intellectual outlook and become the vehicle of a more adequate realism than he ever achieved.

But the significant thing is that the mind of Howells refused to imprison itself in Brahmin orthodoxies, but set forth on perilous expeditions while Lowell and Norton were discreetly evading the intellectual heresies raging outside their libraries. While Henry James was moving towards aristocratic Mayfair, Howells was journeying towards the proletarian East Side. The scientific revolution seems early to have washed in upon him, undermining the theological cosmos of his youth and turning him into a liberal freethinker. His scientific views very likely came to him second-hand, through the medium of literature; but with his wide reading in Continental fields—Spanish, French, German, Scandinavian— he could not fail to become saturated with the evolutionary view then permeating all current letters. In this he was only following with John Fiske and Henry Holt and Henry Adams the path of a new orthodoxy; nevertheless in applying the scientific spirit to fiction and espousing an objective realism, he quite definitely broke with Brahmin tradition. And when, under the guise of fiction, he turned to social questions, and wove into the placid texture of his work the vexing problem of social justice, he ventured on perilous ground where his Brahmin friends would not follow. To espouse the teachings of Herbert Spencer was one thing, to espouse the teachings of Karl Marx was quite another.

Howells came late to an interest in sociology, held back by the strong literary and aesthetic cast of his mind. But in the eighties, when he had reached middle life, he was no longer able to ignore or evade the economic maladjustments of the Gilded Age. The social unrest that was coming to bloody issue in strikes and lockouts gave him acute concern, and slowly under pressure of a sensitive social conscience there began a quiet intellectual revolution that was to transform the detached observer of the American scene into a Marxian socialist. A democrat, a lover of his kind, a just soul endowed with a tender conscience, an idealist who dreamed of a brotherhood of free men who should create in America a civilization adequate to human needs, what else could he do? He loved peace but war was all about him. And so in the mid-afternoon of life he turned to the work of spreading the gospel of social democracy in the America of the Gilded Age. He had no private or personal causes to serve. He had not, like Godkin and Dana, given hostages to fortune in the shape of a newspaper or magazine; he had no call to be partisan to his own interests. He was free to plead the cause of justice in his own way and at his own time. It is easy for the later radical to sneer at him as a parlor socialist who talked well but carefully refrained from disturbing the capitalistic machine from which he drew his income; but that is to ignore the courage of the artist in confronting a hostile world. He stood stoutly for the rights of workingmen that the passions of the times swept rudely away. When the Haymarket Riot in Chicago brought its shameful hysteria, and all respectable America was crying for blood, Howells was one of the few intellectuals who spoke for justice, one of the few who held aloof from the mob spirit, thereby bringing on his head a wave of criticism. It was a brave thing in 1886 to speak for the "Chicago anarchists."

But it was not till his removal to New York, where he found himself at the center of the great revolution, that he set about seriously studying the ways of plutocracy. For the student of Cambridge society it involved a mental upheaval. The urbanity of his literary-manner conceals for most readers the intensity of emotion that underlies his quiet style; yet it is clear enough that having examined the ways of private capitalism and considered its works, he rejected it. Thenceforth to the end of his life he hated the thing and quietly preached against it. His affections went back fondly to the earlier agricultural order that had shaped his youth, and in the character of Dryfoos, in *A Hazard of New Fortunes*, he suggests the moral degeneration that he believed followed in the train of the substitution of a speculative capitalist economy for the wholesomer agrarian economy. But though, remembering his frontier youth, he might prefer the older ways, he was realist enough to understand that capitalism was the order of his generation, and he turned eagerly to explore the new proletarian philosophies that came out of Germany. Howells was the first distinguished American man of letters to espouse Marxian socialism. For a cultivated American in the Gilded Age to sympathize with proletarian theory and to proclaim himself a socialist, was enough to excite amazement in his fellows. In the eighties American social thought was still naïve and provincial. Old-world theories were as alien as old-world institutions, and in spite of the wide interest aroused by *Looking Backward* the intelligent American in 1890 knew as little about Marxianism as he knows today about Bolshevism.

The doubts and hesitations that troubled Howells during these years of changing outlook, are skillfully dramatized in *A Hazard of New Fortunes*. The story of the removal of the Marshes from New England to New York, told with more than usual leisureliness, is the story of the transition from the peacefulness of his earlier literary life to the anxieties of his later thought. Slowly into a story of the familiar Howells commonplace comes the note of social dissension. Antagonistic social philosophies meet and clash, and the movement draws inevitably to the great climax of the strike that brings tragedy into the scene. Of the mood that grew upon him as he wrote he afterwards said:

It became, to my thinking, the most vital of my fictions; through my quickened interest in the life about me, at a moment of great psychological import. We had passed through a period of strong emotioning in the direction of humaner economics, . . . the rich seemed not so much to despise the poor, and the poor did not so hopelessly repine. That shedding of blood which is for the remission of sins had been symbolized by the bombs and scaffolds of Chicago, and the hearts of those who felt this bound up with our rights, the slavery implicated in our liberty, were thrilling with griefs and hopes hitherto strange to the average American breast. Opportunely for me there was a great street-car strike in New York, and the story began to find its way to issues nobler and larger than those of the love-affairs common to fiction.[3]

The years of unrest marked by the great agrarian revolt were years of great intellectual activity for Howells, during which his

[3] Quoted in "The Social Consciousness of William Dean Howells," *New Republic* Vol. 26, p. 193.

thought ripened and mellowed. His own liberal spirit drew to him the liberal spirits of the younger generation, and he became the counselor and friend of many of the young rebels of the day. His sympathy went out to all who were concerned at the injustice of the world. He questioned the right of none to uphold his creed, nor sought to impose his own beliefs upon others. As he watched the great struggle of the times his heart was always on the side of the weak and exploited. Very likely he knew little about the economics of money and finance, over which rival partisans were quarreling savagely, but he understood the human side of the farmers' problem and it was always the balance in the human ledger that weighed with him.

He was a friend of Hamlin Garland and rejoiced when *Main-Travelled Roads* was given to the world, writing for it an introduction warmly and tenderly sympathetic. As an artist he grew concerned lest under the stimulus of B. O. Flower the zeal of the propagandist should submerge the art of the story-teller; but he had no quarrel with the "causes" that were fermenting in the mind of the young Populist, and would not lessen one whit the ardor of his social faith. Throughout the passionate campaign of 1896, that brought most of his friends to a blind and scurrilous partisanship of the gold standard, his heart kept his mind just and his sympathy for the unrequited producers served as counterbalance to the shrill vituperation of his friend Godkin. He had thought too long and too honestly to be moved by the *claque* of the press.

It was in the black days of the panic of '93 that he seems to have brooded most thoughtfully over the ways of capitalistic America, and in the following year he published *The Traveller from Altruria*, the first of his two Utopian romances in which he subjected the system of capitalism to critical analysis. It is a clever book that quite disarms the reader. Howells delivers no broadside attack on the capitalistic system, and he suggests its mean and selfish exploitation with such genial urbanity, such sly satire, as to arouse no sleeping lions. The concern in his heart is belied by the twinkle in his eye. He hints that the Altrurian critic is only the figment of a dream, and he smilingly suggests the sources of the Altrurian commonwealth in the long line of Utopian dreamers from Plato and Sir Thomas More to Bellamy and William Morris. But the urbanity is only a mask. Protected by it Howells delivers many a shrewd thrust at the ways of capitalism. American democracy does not show to advantage under his analysis. The Altrurian comes upon the canker of social injustice in every chink and cranny of life—a canker that is slowly destroying democratic America; and Howells takes a sly pleasure in contrasting our democratic professions with our plutocratic practice. There is a delightful irony in his attack on the professional classes—the professor, the minister, the writer—for their quick defense of the exploiting classes. What may we expect of the science of economics, he suggests, when our academic economists are only apologists for the existing order?

The Traveller from Altruria is a shrewd analysis of American life set against a Marxian background, and in forecasting the future Howells follows the Marxian law of concentration. The Age of Accumulation, with its gigantic monopolies gathered in ever fewer hands, prepared the way for a new order when industrialism, grown overbig, falls into the control of the state as naturally as the harvest is gathered into the granary. There was no need of a class war. When the times were ripe political means sufficed, for the democracy retained the effective weapon of the vote. Thirteen years later Howells completed his Utopian venture with *Through the Eye of the Needle*, in which he sketches in fuller detail the order of life in Altruria. It was not till men learned that coöperation is a better social cement than competition, altruism than egoism, that the new order was possible; and in this later work he depicts the kindly, rational society that emerged when men left off fighting each other and turned to working together instead. On every page the influence of William Morris is revealed—not only in the rejection of an urban society founded on the machine and a return to a decentralized anarchistic order, but in the emphasis on the psychology of work and the satisfactions that spring from free creative labor. *Through the Eye of the Needle* is curiously reminiscent of *News from Nowhere* and suggests how sympathetically Howells followed English social thought in its reaction against industrialism.

It was while he was thus engaged that he put into compact form his speculations on the theory of realism. For more than a decade he had been the most distinguished advocate of realism in America, and for longer still his successive novels had revealed to a critical world what substance and form he believed the realistic novel should possess. The immediate sources of his theory are obscure, though it is clear enough that the work of Jane Austen was a creative influence. From the school of French and Russian naturalism, then at the height of its vigor, he drew back in repulsion, and it was not till after his technique was matured that Tolstoi became an influence in his intellectual life. It is reasonable to assume that his realism was a native growth, the result of temperament unfolding through quiet years of reading in the English classics. A quizzical observer with the gift of humor is not likely to run into romanticism, and a youthful passion for Pope and Heine is not the best preparation for it. His intense dislike of the romantic, that led him to an inadequate and partial conception of it, seems to have sprung from certain instinctive feelings and convictions that strengthened with the years: a deep and sincere love of truth, a native sympathy with the simple homely phases of life, a quiet loyalty to American fact, and a sharp distrust of the aristocratic spirit. Endowed with such feelings he came to ascribe his own partisanships to literary methods; the romantic became for him the aristocratic, and the realistic became the democratic. As an American he was content to take the common stuff of life, as he found it in America, and depict it in unpretentious sincerity. Plain American life was not only worthy of literature, he was convinced, but the only material worthy of American literature. The path to the universal runs as directly through the commonplace American parlor as through the hall of the medieval baron or the drawing-room of Mayfair.

In *Criticism and Fiction* (1894), Howells ascribes the rise of modern realism to the twin sources of science and democracy. From science it derives its passion for truth, for "realism," he asserts, "is nothing more and nothing less than the truthful treatment of material." "We must ask ourselves before we ask anything else, Is it true?—true to the motives, the impulses, the principles, that shape the life of actual men and women." The question, what is essential truth, that has been the apple of discord amongst the realists, Howells answers in democratic fashion by appealing to the average. The "foolish man," he says, "wonders at the unusual, but the wise man at the usual." The realist, therefore, will deal objectively with the usual and common rather than with the unusual or strange, and in so doing he draws closer to the common heart of humanity, and learns the respect for simple human nature that is the source and wellspring of democracy. In delineating truthfully the prosaic lives of common people realism reveals the essential dignity and worth of all life. The romantic, on the other hand, is aristocratic. "It seeks to withdraw itself, to stand aloof; to be distinguished and not to be identified." "The pride of caste has become the pride of taste," and romance is the last refuge of the aristocratic spirit that, defeated elsewhere, has taken refuge in culture. Not aloofness, but comradeship, is the need of the world; not distinction, but identity. Realism is the child of democracy because the realist is one who "feels in every nerve the equality of things and the unity of men," and the great artist is one with a talent "robust enough to front the everyday world and catch the charm of its work-worn, care-worn, brave, kindly face."

To this characteristic conception that realism is democratic Howells adds certain other dicta that to his own generation seemed as true as to ours they seem doubtful: that art must serve morality, that it must teach rather than amuse, and that truthfulness to American life requires a note of cheerfulness. Art cannot flout the "eternal amenities," Howells asserted, for "morality penetrates all things, it is the soul of all things." Nor can it stand aloof, disdaining the office of teacher, for unless it "tends to make the world better and kinder" it is empty and futile; and it can do this only "from and through the truth." But the truth that will uplift society does not dwell in the kennel and pigsty; it will not be come upon by exploring the animal in man, or in wrapping the shroud of pessimism about life. In America at least, realism must concern itself with the "large cheerful average of health and success and happy life," for after all "the more smiling aspects of life" are "the more American." From such postulates Howells developed his familiar technique, which in minimizing plot, rejecting the unusual and strange and heroic, reduced his stories to the drab level that bores so many of his readers, and evokes the criticism that in elaboration of the commonplace he evades the deeper and more tragic realities that reach to the heart of life.

The criticism is just. More than any other thing this concern for the usual weakens Howells's work and renders it trivial. He does not probe the depths of emotional experience. Neither the life of the spirit nor the passions of the flesh is the stuff from which he weaves his stories. The lack—and allowing for all his solid excellence it remains grave—sprang in part from his own timid nature that recoiled from the gross and the unpleasant, and in part from the environment in which he perfected his technique. For years he lived in an atmosphere of complacent convention, a society dominated by women, culture, and conscience. Cambridge and Boston in the seventies and eighties were still in the Age of Innocence greatly concerned with erecting defenses against the intrusion of the unpleasant, reverencing the genteel in life and letters, soberly moral and making much of the eternal verities. In such a world of refined manners and narrow outlook what should the realist do but report faithfully of what he saw and heard? And so Howells, perforce, became a specialist in women's nerves, an analyst of the tenuous New England conscience, a master of Boston small-talk. It was such materials that shaped his leisurely technique until it falls about his theme with the amplitude of crinoline.

Through these chronicles of the Age of Innocence runs a persistent note of the neurotic. There are more scruples to a page of Howells than in any other writer except Henry James—for the most part filmy cobwebs invisible to the coarser vision of a later generation. The action percolates through the sand of small-talk, welling up from the tiniest springs and stopped by the smallest obstruction. Like Franklin's two-headed snake his characters are in danger of dying from thirst because of much argument over the right path to water. It is hard to weave a substantial fabric from such gossamer threads, and when in *The Rise of Silas Lapham* endless pages are devoted to the ethical subtleties of a woman's accepting the hand of a man who the family had believed was in love with her sister, or when in *April Hopes* the fantastic scruples of a neurotic girl are elaborated with a refinement of art worthy of a Fra Angelico Madonna, the stuff is too filmy to wear well. Commonplace men and neurotic women are poor materials from which to fashion an adequate realism, and with the passing of the Age of Innocence the scruples of Howells went out of fashion.

The fault, in part at least, must be traced to the artist's deep reverence for New England. From his youth he had cherished an exalted notion of the sufficiency of New England culture, and had accepted its parochialisms as ultimate standards. To a bookish lad, inclined to be too consciously literary, such loyalty to a declining school could only accentuate his native aloofness from life. His four years at Venice had been given over to an ardent pursuit of culture, as culture was understood by Lowell and Norton. It was the natural impulse of a sensitive mind, conscious of its limitations, reveling for the first time in the wealth that had been denied his

frontier boyhood. His poetic *Venetian Days* was an infallible pass-
port to Boston favor, and when after his return he was taken up
by the *Atlantic* group he carried with him to Boston an unconscious
inferiority complex that did his genius an evil turn. It was natural
for the self-taught western youth to be reverent in presence of the
great of earth; but it is not well for the artist to be humble in the
presence of his masters. Unless he is something of a rebel, given to
questioning the dogmas of the schools, he will never ripen into
creative originality.

An inferiority complex is a common mark of the frontier mind
that finds itself diffident in presence of the old and established, and
Howells suffered from it greatly. For years his keen eyes lacked
their usual shrewdness in judging Boston ways, and to the end of
his life he overestimated the greatness of the men to whom his
youthful loyalty had gone out. Not only did he accept Lowell and
Holmes and Longfellow at the Boston rating, but he regarded the
lesser group of cultivated Boston gentlemen with partial eyes. It
would have been far better for his art if like Hamlin Garland he
had never been received within the charmed circle; if he had had
to make his way alone. To justify his acceptance Howells felt that
he must prove himself as completely Bostonian as the best, and in
consequence he sloughed off his western heritage, perverted his
genius, and shaped his realism to the slender materials discovered in
Back Bay drawing-rooms. The genteel tradition was in the way of
strangling his realism.

Subjected to such refinements his realism in the end became little
more than technique—a meticulous transcription of New England
conventions, the casual action submerging itself in an endless
stream of talk. No doubt Howells was true to what he saw; certainly no one has ever fixed more exactly the thin substance of the
Age of Innocence. Nevertheless the fidelity of his observation, the
refinement of his prose style, and the subtlety of his humor that
plays lambently about the edges of his words, do not compensate
for the slightness of his materials. The record he has left is not
that of a great soul brooding over the meaning of life, puzzled,
uncertain, yet tender toward the victims that fate has seized and
crushed. He was restrained by too many inhibitions to deal frankly
with natural human passions. He felt deeply and tenderly, but he
was too diffident to let himself go. It is likely that Howells never
realized the inadequacy of his temperament and the futility of his

method to any serious realism. Even in his acutest study *A Hazard of New Fortunes*, which comes upon brutal economic reality, the story is entangled in a mass of minute detail and never quite breaks through. The indecisions, the repetitions, the whimsical descriptions, the drifting talk, are all true to life, but they are not essential or vital truth. The real issue toward which the story moves—the problem of social justice and the contrasting systems of wage-slavery, bond-slavery, and social democracy—is obscured in a welter of asides and never quite reaches the front of the stage. He is more effective in such works as *Indian Summer*, when he deals with characters on vacation who play whimsically with love, and in *April Hopes*, when he dwells fondly on the infinitely eloquent trivialities of young love-making. In such studies the minute fidelity to word and gesture, the humorous playing with invisible scruple, is a pleasant substitute for solider material.

Howells had real gifts, of which he made the most. Refinement, humor, sympathy—fidelity to external manner and rare skill in catching the changing expression of life—a passion for truth and a jealous regard for his art: he had all these qualities, yet they were not enough to make him a great realist. He belonged to the Age of Innocence and with its passing his works have been laid away. He has had no followers to keep his method alive. If one may hazard an explanation of the lot that has befallen him, it would be this. Howells the artist mistook his calling. He was not by temperament a novelist. He lacked the sense of drama, a grasp of the rough fabric of life, the power to deal imaginatively with the great and tragic realities. His genius was rather that of a whimsical essayist, a humorous observer of the illogical ways of men. He was an eighteenth-century spirit—a subtler Goldsmith—set down in another age and an uncongenial world. In his later years he must have come to realize this, for more and more he turned to the essay form. There his quiet humor and shrewd observation fitted his sinuous prose style to a nicety. In such sketchy autobiography as *My Literary Passions*, and more whimsically in such genial travel essays as *Certain Delightful English Towns*, his refined art arrived at its most perfect expression. Not an original genius like Mark Twain, far from a turbulent soul like Herman Melville, Howells was the reporter of his generation—the greatest literary figure of a drab negative age when the older literary impulse was slackening, and the new was slowly displacing it. He marks the transition between the earlier idealism and the later naturalism. A humane and lovable soul, he was the embodiment of all that was kindly and generous in an America that was not wholly given over to the ways of the Gilded Age—an America that loved beauty and served culture even amidst the turmoil of revolution.

BOOK TWO: THE OLD AND THE NEW: STORM CLOUDS

BOOK TWO

THE OLD AND THE NEW: STORM CLOUDS

THE quarter-century between the panic of 1873 that rudely disturbed the revelry of the Great Barbecue, and the campaign of 1896 that broke the agrarian opposition to capitalism, was marked by a fierce agrarian attempt to nullify in America the law of concentration. The silent drift toward plutocracy was too evident to escape comment even in the Gilded Age, and the ideal of plutocracy was too repugnant to a people drenched in Jeffersonian and Jacksonian prejudices to escape bitter hostility. The pursuit of wealth was an accepted democratic right, but it was assumed to be a fair race and no favors. The use of the political state by greater wealth to lay handicaps on lesser wealth had not been in the reckoning, and the law of progress that diminished the number of beneficiaries from the national policy of preëmption and exploitation had not been so interpreted. Something was wrong with a progress that augmented poverty as it increased wealth, and with the alarmist cry in their ears—the rich are growing richer and the poor poorer—the untutored democracy of the seventies and the eighties turned to question the drift of tendency that quite evidently was transforming a democratic people into a vast engulfing plutocracy. An older agrarian America was confronted by a younger capitalistic one, and the conflict of ideals and purposes was certain to bring on a bitter debate.

In the fierce struggle that turmoiled the politics of three decades the democracy went into battle as ill-equipped intellectually as it had been a hundred years before in the struggle over the Constitution. It was reaping the harvest of the long Jacksonian slackness that, content with the vote, had given no thought to the ultimate program of democracy but had suffered the lawyers to have their way. The Enlightenment had long since been submerged by Whiggish ambitions, and since the days of the Abolition Movement there had been no serious consideration of political theory. The success of the Jacksonian revolution had brought about its undoing. The abstract principle of democracy having won common

257

acceptance, it was assumed to be competent to shift for itself. But unfortunately a supposedly democratic state was functioning under a Constitution designed to thwart democracy, and, interpreted by lawyers, it buttressed the rights of property far more securely than the rights of man. Within this fundamental law capitalism had long been entrenching itself. Its stronghold could not be taken by frontal attack and its flanks were protected by the courts that had assumed the high prerogative of voiding statutory enactments by judicial decree. As a result in no other country was capitalism so safeguarded from hostile attack; it plowed its fields and gathered its harvests secure from disturbance.

Unfortunately the political state did not realize that it was not in reality the democracy it professed to be. The most intelligent liberalism of the times, failing to take into account the economic basis of politics, was satisfied to spend its energy in Civil Service Reform and similar tinkering with the political machinery, convinced that it was only necessary to recover the old aristocratic sense of responsibility in political agents to perfect a democratic government. Not till another generation did liberalism come to understand that the democratic program was still largely unfulfilled, and set about in all earnestness to complete it; but that did not happen till the philosophy of democracy had been far more adequately explored and the simple faith of Jacksonianism had been instructed by the experience of other lands. Popular discontent with the drift toward plutocracy was intensified by the successive economic crises that marked the transition from agrarianism to capitalism. The gospel of progress, it seems, had not taken due account of the price that must be paid in social disturbances, and the breakdowns of 1873–1879 and 1887–1896 with their harsh dislocations aroused a spirit of revolt that issued in broad popular movements. Those movements spun the thread of liberalism that runs through the years from the Gilded Age to the World War—a thread woven of the earlier liberalism that came from the frontier, and the new collectivistic theories that came from Europe. In the eighties and nineties it was still largely native agrarian, but in the early years of the new century it drew heavily on the proletarian philosophies of Europe—seeking to apply old-world experience to American problems. Through it all runs increasingly a note of sobering realism. After a hundred years political romanticism was slowly dying in America.

CHAPTER I

THE PLIGHT OF THE FARMER

I

DEMOCRATIC REACTIONS TO PLUTOCRACY

THE Middle Border was the first to recover from the heady romanticisms of Whiggery. The malady of preëmption and exploitation quickly ran its course there and after the first enthusiasm of settlement had subsided—the staking of claims, the scramble over townsites, the bidding for railway lines—the farmer settled down amidst his corn and wheat and cattle and hogs to learn what sort of living the prairies might provide. With his feet on the sobering earth he was no middle-class adventurer, no buccaneer lying in wait for the golden argosies of Spain, but a sober realist kept sane by wind and weather and kept honest by his daily occupation of tilling and reaping.

As the first wave of settlers spread over the prairies a mood of buoyant hopefulness colored their dreams. The earlier conquest of the Inland Empire had entailed exhausting labor in preliminary clearings, and the stumpage from great forests remained for years to obstruct clean tillage; but here in the Middle Border were treeless fields of black soil, level, uncluttered by stones, inviting the plow. For ages the prairie grass had been growing there, tall as a horseman in the bottoms and plentiful on the uplands; and as the unmarked seasons passed, the potash from the decaying vegetation added a richer fertility to the soil. In natural productiveness it was the fairest portion of America, and as the land-hungry settlers made their pitch there, filing on broad homesteads and building their cabins, a mood of buoyant expectation filled the land. It was not the flamboyant spirit of the Gilded Age, but the hopefulness of those who within a few short years were to transform a wilderness into the world's granary. In his wistful account of the glamour that lay upon the prairies in those first pioneer years—a glamour that soon passed like the morning dews—Hamlin Garland was no frontier romantic but a sober historian.

259

But as the seventies gave place to the eighties a subtle change came over the mood of the Middle Border. Disappointment and disillusion settled upon a land that before had smiled in the spring sunshine. The harvest was not fulfilling the expectations of the seedtime. The changed mood came in part from the harsh toil and meager living that were the necessary price the frontiersman must pay for his small winnings. It is no holiday job to subdue an untamed land and wrest abundance and comfort from a virgin soil. Only for the young who can project their hopes into the future is it endurable; for the middle-aged and the old it is a heart-breaking task. The history of the western frontier is a long drab story of hardship and privation and thwarted hopes, of men and women broken by the endless toil, the windows of their dreams shuttered by poverty and the doors to an abundant life closed and barred by narrow opportunity. It is true that the prairies took no such toll as the forests had taken; the mean and squalid poverty through which Lincoln passed was not so common in the Middle Border as it had been along the earlier frontier. Nevertheless a fierce climate and a depressing isolation added their discomforts to a bleak existence. The winds were restless on the flat plains, and the flimsy wooden houses, stark and mean, unprotected by trees and unrelieved by shrubbery, were an ill defense against their prying fingers. In winter the blizzards swept out of the North to overmaster the land, and in summer the hot winds came up from the Southwest to sear the countrysides that were rustling with great fields of corn. Other enemies appeared, as it were, out of a void. Endless flights of grasshoppers descended like a plague of locusts, and when they passed the earth was bare and brown where the young wheat had stood. Armies of chinch-bugs came from nobody knew where, and swarming up the tender corn-stalks left them sucked dry and yellow. It is nature's way, to destroy with one hand what it creates with the other; and for years the western farmers were fighting plagues that had possessed the prairies before the settlers came.

The disillusion of the Middle Border deepened into gloom as the widespread economic depression of the times added its discouragements. A period of falling prices was curtailing industry and forcing down the market values of all produce. From such depressions a debtor community always suffers most severely, for falling produce-prices mean rising money-values and a shifting standard of value for deferred payments. The farms of the Middle Border were heavily encumbered to provide tools and livestock and buildings, and the earnings were consumed by the interest that went East to the mortgage-holders. Debt was a luxury the farmer could ill afford, and when the debt was silently augmenting by the rising value of the dollar he was forced to consider his situation. The plight into which he had fallen was graphically summed up in the phrase "ten-cent corn and ten per cent interest"—a phrase that was to become a spark to all the tinder that was gathering from frontier hardships and disappointments. Falling market-values were at the bottom of his troubles. The prices of his staples were sinking below the cost of production. With four-cent eggs, five-cent butter, ten-cent corn, and fifty-cent wheat, with more hogs and cattle than the stockyards would take, and with debts contracted at interest-rates fixed by a higher scale of values, the economic position of the Middle Border was becoming desperate, and in the later eighties a sullen bitterness took possession of the land. As the farmer sat by the kitchen stove and stoked the fire with great ears of corn that were cheaper than coal, he had ample time to contemplate his lot. Ungathered crops for which there was no market would not pay interest. There was coming to be "too much hog in the dollar," as one commentator remarked quaintly. The Middle Border, all too clearly, was strangling from its own productiveness.

It was easy for newspaper critics, armed with the wisdom of the Board of Trade, to point out that overproduction was the trouble with the western farmer, and that so vast a development of staple crops resulting from sowing the prairie states to corn and wheat was certain to bring on disastrous market slumps. It was true. Production had outrun consumption; quantity output had brought on a glut. But it was also true—as the armchair critics were not so careful to point out—that other causes contributed equally to the deflation of the western farmer, the result of which was to despoil him of the last moiety of his earnings. He was in the grip of a complex middleman organization that gouged him at every turn. The gap between producer and consumer was widening to a chasm. The railways charged twenty cents a bushel cartage for wheat from the Mississippi to Chicago, and fifty-two and a half cents to the Atlantic seaboard. The elevator companies fixed monopoly tolls, swindled the farmer in their grain-gradings, and combined to force down the market price at harvest time and raise it after the crop came under their control. The "Livestock Ring," managed by the railways, controlled the Union Stock Yards at Chicago and squeezed the marginal profits from the farmer's cattle and hogs.[1] When on the other hand he bought implements or groceries or household goods he was at the mercy of a non-competitive market, protected by patent-rights and tariffs, to which were added extortionate transportation and middleman charges.

It was his own fault, of course. Due to his own political slackness the farmer had allowed himself to become the common drudge of society. All the exploiting classes had their hands in his pockets. His was the only considerable economic group that exerted no organized pressure to control the price he sold for or the price he paid. While capitalism had been perfecting its machinery of exploitation he had remained indifferent to the fact that he himself was the fattest goose that capitalism was to pluck. He had helped indeed to provide the rope for his own hanging. He had voted away the public domain to railways that were now fleecing him; he took pride in the county-seat towns that lived off his earnings; he sent city lawyers to represent him in legislatures and in Congress; he read middle-class newspapers and listened to bankers and politicians and cast his votes for the policy of Whiggery that could have no other outcome than his own despoiling. And now in the middle eighties he began to feel the rope about his neck, and realized the predicament he was in. It was not alone the local middlemen, or even the railways—he had come to believe—that were to blame. It was the money-power of the East, the grip of Wall Street, that was strangling him—a power that controlled the government at Washington, that manipulated the currency system, and that was engaged in a scheme to augment its holdings by forcing up the value of the dollar and automatically increasing the value of the indebtedness it had gathered in its vaults. Clearly it was high time for the deflated farmer to get into politics on his own account if he were to save himself from beggary, and so during the Gilded Age began a great agrarian revolt against capitalism that was to turmoil the next quarter of a century—a revolt that was to mark the last effective organization of the farmers to combat the new order, the last flare-up of an old-fashioned agrarian America before it was submerged by the middle class.

[1] See Nevins, *The Emergence of Modern America*, pp. 163–164.

II

THE FARMER CONSIDERS POLITICS

By the early seventies it was becoming clear to the Middle
Border that the policy of Whiggery took no account of the needs
of the farmer. Government was indifferent to him, whether at the
capital of his state or at Washington, and governmental programs
—whether in the matter of protective tariffs and land-grants, in its
unconcern at monopoly extortion, or in the contraction of the
currency with a view to the resumption of specie payments—ran
so counter to his interests that the dullest began to question the
fairness of the state. It had ceased to concern itself with the welfare of the whole. The combination of paternalism and *laissez faire*
that marked the Whiggery of the times could be interpreted by
the suspicious farmer, indeed, only as a surrender of government to
capitalism. It had lost all pretense of fairness in the distribution of
governmental favors, and withheld or granted aid with the single
objective of furthering the interests of powerful groups. It sanctioned the use of the state by business interests for purposes of
exploitation, and declined to exercise its power in the interests of
the consumer. It granted tariffs and subsidies, yet refused to regulate the monopoly power it had created. It was no longer a government of the people but a government of business, concerned for
the interests of exploitation, and if the farmer were to gain a
hearing he must first make himself feared.

Of necessity, therefore, the agrarian program entailed a political
struggle of great bitterness. There would be no adequate relief
granted until the farmers had wrested control of government from
the class that was exploiting them. The battle between agrarianism
and capitalism, in consequence, from the outset was a struggle for
control of the political state, that beginning in single commonwealths was eventually carried to the federal government. Hope of
effective aid from state governments quickly proved illusory, for
when the Illinois farmers passed a law to curb the railways the
federal courts set aside their enactment and bade the farmers—to
use a later phrase—go home and slop the hogs. They must not
meddle with matters beyond their comprehension. In consequence
of such slaps in the face the farmers fell to perfecting their organizations and arousing class consciousness until there issued from the
long debates of the Grange and the Farmers' Alliance the great

movement of Populism that proposed to reach as far as Washington, install there the representatives of the producing classes, and refashion the political state in accordance with the democratic needs of the plain people.

So ambitious a program needed time, not only for the farmers to organize but to clarify their policy. They were ill equipped for a serious struggle. With the rise of capitalism agriculture had been steadily falling in social prestige. As a result of the decline of the landed squirearchy in the North and the overthrow of the plantation economy in the South, agriculture had lost its traditional leaders who had furnished the brains and supplied the spokesmen in earlier political struggles. In the seventies agriculture was no longer reckoned a pursuit peculiarly suitable to gentlemen. The business man had risen in social prestige as the farmer declined, and instead of being recruited from the natural leaders of society agriculture suffered a draining-off of the more energetic and capable to the cities, leaving the farms in the hands of the less ambitious, who were supplemented in the seventies and eighties by European peasants who settled great portions of the Middle Border. With this loss of social prestige came a new urban contempt for farm life that expressed itself in "Hayseed" cartoons, and in the heedlessness of politicians who were quick to transfer allegiance from a decaying to a rising order.

The farmers of the Middle Border, drawn from many commonwealths and with a high percentage of aliens, were far from a homogeneous class-conscious group like the southern planters. Race, language, and cultural antecedents held them apart, intensifying the aloofness that was a common characteristic of the frontier. Week-days they stuck to their plows and Sundays, unlike the New England farmer, they were little given to churchgoing. The landholdings were commonly a homestead of a hundred and sixty acres, often running to an entire section of six hundred and forty acres. Much land was held idle by speculators, with the result that the isolation of the farmer—dwelling convenient to his fields rather than to neighbors—deepened the suspicious individualism that was an obsession of the agrarian mind, and unfitted him for effective coöperative effort. No political or social philosophy answerable to his needs was at hand, no intellectual leaders like Jefferson or John Taylor to adapt old-world theory to the conditions of the Middle Border, no commanding figure like Old Hickory to marshal the scattered hosts. The Physiocratic theory with its prestige of distinguished advocates and its elaborate social economics had never taken root in the Middle Border; although certain of its prejudices—that the farmer is the sole producer and the sterile middleman must somehow be got rid of—had taken possession of the western mind and largely influenced the ultimate program. But if the western farmer inherited no ready-made philosophy he was daily prodded by harsh reality. He got up and went to bed under the prick of economic necessity, and this made of him a realist and an opportunist, eager to apply homely remedies to homely ills. With the discipline got from hard times he was not easily gulled by bright young city lawyers with their handbooks of capitalistic economics. The new agrarianism of the prairies, in consequence, was a hard-headed, homespun theory, fashioned on the farms, intended to serve the producer rather than the middleman. It had behind it none of the high authority of the schools, and naturally it was mocked and scoffed at by all the spokesmen—editors, lawyers, bankers, scholars, intellectuals—of the prosperous middle class. The farmer had to make his way against the embattled prejudices and contempt of the rest of America.

But before he could become a power in political councils he must organize and use his voting strength as a unit; and as early as the late sixties the work of organization was got under way. It began as a social movement with the Grange that spread widely through the South and Middle West and even gained foothold in the East, bringing together in social groups the farmer families of the neighborhood. It professed to stand outside politics and strove to awaken an interest in coöperative buying and selling, but the community gatherings were certain to find politics waiting for them at the schoolhouse door, and after the program of coöperation had been discussed the talk ran easily into political debate. From the Grange issued in the eighties the Farmers' Alliance, more consciously political in its objective, active in arousing the farmers to political action; and with the hard times that came with the turn of the decade the different groups merged in the broad movement of Populism—a militant political uprising with a definite party program and organization. The flare-up came swiftly and in the first years of the nineties the prairies were aflame and even the cotton-fields of the South were fired. Populism swept from township to township, a militant agrarian movement, providing its own leaders—Tom Watson in Georgia, General Weaver in Iowa, Ignatius Donnelly in Minnesota, sockless Jerry Simpson in Kansas, with Hamlin Garland, and B. O. Flower, and other intellectuals rallying to the farmers' standard. It set up the banner of agrarian democracy, summoned its followers and drilled them for the battles that lay ahead. Huge meetings gathered of the farmers of a county and day-long they listened to speeches that came straight from the hay-fields and the corn-rows, speeches that were an echo of the daily experience of the farmer and the farmer's wife.

It was Mary Ellen Lease of Kansas who struck from the common bitterness a phrase that embodied the militant spirit of Populism. Week after week she traveled the prairie country urging the farmers to "raise less corn and more hell," and at her call the sunburned faces settled into grim purpose. The farmers had become class-conscious. They were enlisted in a class struggle. They used the vocabulary of realism, and the unctuous political platitudes and sophistries of county-seat politicians rolled off their minds like water from a duck's back. They were fighting a great battle—they believed—against Wall Street and the eastern money-power; they were bent on saving America from the plutocracy; and they swept over the county-seat towns, burying the old machine politicians under an avalanche of votes, capturing state legislatures, electing Congressmen and Senators, and looking forward to greater power. In 1896 Populism gained control of the Democratic party and entered on its great campaign to establish the principle of democracy at Washington. It was the last mortal struggle between agrarianism and capitalism, and to understand it one must turn back to the long agitation over the money question.

III

THE GREENBACK MOVEMENT

If in the early nineties the currency question had come to overshadow the questions of the tariff and railway regulation, it was because that problem lay at the heart of the struggle between the rival agrarian and capitalistic economies. The control of the national monetary system by the bankers was vital to the smooth functioning of a capitalistic order, and to assure such control it was desirable that monetary standards and emissions of currency be removed from the sphere of political action and lodged in the hands of business. The problem was difficult, for the right to "coin money and to regulate the value thereof" were functions of sovereignty specifically recognized in the Constitution; and it was a series of moves designed to transfer such functions to private groups that brought on a long political debate over systems of currency.

The intellectual background against which the struggle was set may be sketched briefly. Despite the long battle over the Bank in Jackson's time, little serious thinking on the principles of money and currency had been done in America. Financiers and economists alike followed the current English school, and since the appearance of the famous Bullion Report of 1811 that school had adhered to the intrinsic-value theory of money. While accepting banknotes as a useful medium of exchange, the English classical economists held that only coin is real money, and that the issue of notes must bear a definite ratio to the amount of coin and bullion in the vaults. Money is not a creature of the law. Government cannot create it. Rather it is a convenient token of labor done, and the stamp of the mint is only a certification of weight and fineness. There are but two ways, indeed, in which government can acquire money— through taxation and by borrowing. The "natural operation of the specie standard" was reckoned one of the fundamental "laws of trade," and for government to tamper with it—setting aside the intrinsic-value principle by the emission of irredeemable paper money—was to violate the sanctity of contracts, cheat creditors, increase prices, and disorder business. The law of supply and demand answered all the needs of money regulation.

This was no more than the application of the current theory of *laissez faire* to the problem of currency. But between the Bullion Report of 1811 and the Parliamentary Bank Act of 1844, English theory and practice had undergone two important modifications: the vast development of credit had suggested a free use of bank-notes based on securities other than coin or bullion, and the bimetallic standard had been superseded by the gold standard. By the terms of the Act of 1844 all banknotes were to be issued against securities and gold and silver coin and bullion in the bank vaults. The margin of issue was fixed at fourteen million pounds sterling. The total amount of banknotes thus "issued on the Credit of such Securities, Coin and Bullion," might not be increased, but within the limits set the Bank was free to increase or decrease issues at will. The Act further provided that "whereas it is necessary to limit the Amount of Silver Bullion on which it shall be lawful . . . to issue Bank of England notes," it should "not be lawful for the Bank of England to retain in . . . said Bank at any time an Amount of Silver Bullion exceeding One Fourth Part of the Gold Coin and Bullion." . . . [2] That gold should eventually have thrust silver aside was natural. In addition to its convenience as a commodity for international shipment, it was less in quantity, not widely dispersed or popularly held, and therefore more easily controlled by the money-brokers. With the function of government restricted to coining such gold as came to the mint, the whole business of currency emissions, with the attendant power of inflation and deflation of credit, would lie in the hands of the bankers who became the custodians of the national monetary system.

During the bitter discussions of currency policies that followed the dislocations of the Civil War, the two most authoritative spokesmen in America on the subject were Senator John Sherman of Ohio, for years Chairman of the Senate Committee on Finance, and David A. Wells, statistician, special Commissioner of the Revenue Bureau, and a scholar deservedly distinguished as an economist. In their views on the currency question both were followers of the classical English school. In two speeches in the Senate, of January 27, 1869, and January 24, 1870, the former stated his position definitely. "Let us," he said, "recognize as an axiom that nothing but coin is real money before we undertake to deal with the currency"; and in another place, narrowing his definition in terms of the English Bank Act, he asserted, "We must . . . recognize the immutable law of currency; and that is, there is but one true standard, and that standard is gold." [3] The weakness of paper money, he believed, was its instability; the ratio of exchange with gold fluctuates too greatly to make it a safe or convenient medium of business. "Last year the fluctuation in paper money amounted to forty-five per cent. Gold, however, remained as stable as the eternal hills, because it was not only the product of labor, but it was labor and value itself."[4] One may make of such an assertion what one will, but it is clear that John Sherman thought ill of the greenbacks, and wanted substituted for them a system of banknotes.

[2] *The Statutes at Large: 7 & 8 Victoriae*, Vol. 84, pp. 188–189.
[3] *Speeches and Reports on Finance and Taxation*, pp. 188, 190.
[4] *Ibid.*, p. 233.

It is impossible [he argued] to give a currency issued by a Government the flexibility to meet the movement of the exchanges. . . . It must have a flexibility which will enable it to be increased in certain periods of the year, and to flow back again into the vaults of the bank at others. I am convinced . . . that in time it will be wise to retire our United States notes and all forms of Government circulation, and depend upon notes issued by private corporations.[5]

Brief as these passages are, they suffice to make clear Sherman's position. He accepted without question the English theory and practice, and he wished to shape American legislation in conformity with them. The experience of the Civil War, and—shall we add—his intimate connections with Wall Street,[6] had confirmed him in his preference for a *laissez-faire* policy in currency matters. He would establish the gold standard, encourage the issue of banknotes, and turn over the custodianship of the national currency to private interests.

The position of David A. Wells was essentially similar. Wells wrote much and skillfully and he seems to have been the chief authority on whom such intellectuals as Godkin and Dana relied for materials for their editorials on the currency question. Indirectly, therefore, through the medium of editors and newspaper writers his opinions came to have wide influence. During the discussion of resumption of specie payments in the seventies his pen was particularly active. Amongst other things he then wrote *The Cremation Theory of Specie Resumption*, in which he advocated a policy of progressive contraction by the expedient of burning annually a fixed sum in greenbacks; *Robinson Crusoe's Money*, an exposition of the bullion theory of money for popular reading, illustrated by Nast and containing some witty thrusts at such well-known expansionists as Ben Butler, Wendell Phillips, Henry C. Carey, and Senator O. P. Morton; *Contraction*, in which he defended the thesis, "He who is not in favor of contracting the currency is not in favor of paying it, and he who is not in favor of paying it is a repudiator"; and certain other papers later gathered into his *Practical Economics* (1885).

Wells was an uncompromising bullionist and his theory of money is as simple as the doctrine of *laissez faire* on which it rests. Honest money represents labor and therefore possesses intrinsic value. The

[5] "Speech of January 24, 1870," *ibid.*, pp. 225–226.
[6] This laid him open to frequent and often bitter attack. See, among many, Mrs. Marion Todd, *Pizzaro and John Sherman* Chicago, 1891.

experience of the ages has demonstrated that of all commodities gold and silver are the most convenient for the purpose and in consequence they have come to be accepted universally as real money. Every dollar's worth of gold represents a dollar's worth of labor, always and everywhere, measured by the test of the world's needs. It is foolish for politicians and theorists to worry their poor heads over the supply of money, or attempt to predetermine the quantity best suited to the needs of business. The amount of money in circulation will always be regulated by the law of supply and demand. There is limitless gold locked up in the treasure-house of nature, and just so much is unlocked by human labor as the immediate needs of the world require. Gold can neither be inflated nor deflated, for, "There is one and the same law governing alike the supply of gold and of wheelbarrows. They are both tools or commodities, and the country will have and use all of either that it can use profitably." [7] Let government keep its hands off and money will regulate itself. "The value of the gold dollar is fixed and cannot be altered. The value of the paper dollar is constantly fluctuating." [8] That business conditions would be seriously affected by the withdrawal of the greenbacks, or that injustice would be done to debtors, Wells refused to believe. When the poison is withdrawn from the system a state of health reëstablishes itself. "I also count as an absurdity the idea that the business of the country is likely to be unfavorably affected by a deficiency of currency consequent upon contraction in the manner proposed." [9] The gold to take its place would be provided automatically by the infallible law of supply and demand. Thus triply armed with the logic of economic theory Wells pronounced for deflation, immediate and drastic:

I desire the federal government to get out of and abandon forever and as soon as possible this whole business of creating and issuing paper money, be it redeemable or irredeemable, for I believe as long as the federal government continues to recognize anything as money except hard matter-of-fact "labor representing" gold and silver, just so long the country will not have [a] stable and unfluctuating currency. . . .[10]

Such neat logic was out of date on the day that Wells penned it. The needs of business had outgrown the bullion theory of money

[7] *Practical Economics*, p. 54.
[8] *The Cremation Theory of Specie Resumption*, p. 10.
[9] *Ibid.*, p. 10.
[10] *Ibid.*, p. 13.

and credit was taking the place of a metallic currency. The fiction of a gold standard would be adhered to till another seismic dislocation proved its utter inadequacy to a world in confusion and it would be unofficially abandoned. Yet it was such logic that prevailed in America in post-war days, bringing acute distress upon the country as a whole and particular hardship to the Middle Border; and it prevailed because the banking interests followed a selfish and narrow policy marked out for them by the English theory and practice.

The financing of the war had been wasteful and slovenly beyond all precedent, and it had been fiercely criticized by the agrarians. It was a system, said the militant Greenbacker, Thaddeus Stevens, the like of which "no human folly had ever before witnessed." [11] When the war was over and the reorganization of the public finances was up for settlement, the bankers were shrewd enough to make the confusion serve their interests. Their great objective was to get back once more the control of the national credit that the war had taken from them. The National Bank Act of 1863—foolishly opposed by shortsighted state-bank advocates who were jealous of local rights—had been the first great step. By the provisions of the act the national banks were permitted to issue currency on the security of government bonds, in such quantities as they chose, on highly favorable terms, and the result was to drive out of circulation the wild-cat issues of state banks. But the crux of the problem was the question of the greenbacks that the necessities of the war had forced upon the government. The greenbacks were reckoned political money, the control of issues of which lay wholly with Congress. At any moment, responding to popular demand, Congress might deflate the bankers by the emission of new bills. At the time of first issue the financial interests had succeeded in vitiating the greenbacks by writing into the bill a repudiation of the issue by the government itself, and no sooner was the war over than they set about the business of retiring them. Their objective was the same end that English bankers had reached in 1844.

In the reorganization three broad policies were insisted upon by the banking interests: the speedy retirement of the greenbacks, in order to take government out of the credit market, the refunding of all debts on a gold basis, and an immediate return to specie payments. The result was a drastic policy of deflation that brought

[11] J. A. Woodburn, *The Life of Thaddeus Stevens*, p. 573.

further turmoil to the country. In ten years the money in circulation was reduced from somewhat over $2,100,000,000 to a little
over a billion, or from fifty-eight dollars per capita in 1865 to
seventeen dollars per capita in 1876.[12] The inevitable results
followed, a swift appreciation in the value of the dollar and the
automatic increase in the debt of the country, both public and
private, with the fall of commodity prices. Within a decade,
measured in commodity values, the liabilities of the American
people were nearly doubled by the simple device of changing the
standard of deferred payments. Gold might remain as stable as
the eternal hills, but somehow all other commodities were shrinking
daily. "Them steers," Solon Chase indeed said aptly, "while they
grew well, shrank in value as fast as they grew." This remarkable
result was brought about, it is well to remember, by the plea for
honest money and the plighted faith of the nation. Keeping the
public faith, it would seem, meant permitting the creditors to
change the terms of their payments after the contract was made.
"Who are these reasoners," cried Thaddeus Stevens, in disgust,
"who talk so learnedly of the laws of finance and the morality of
human dealings, whose consciences are so raw and stick out so
far from their excited coverings that no pharmaceutist can heal
their inward wound?"[13]

As a debtor community the Middle Border felt the pinch of deflation acutely, and in consequence the money question was thrust
sternly upon agrarian attention. On this issue it came finally to
fight its great battle, pitting its homespun experience against the
authority of the bankers and the teaching of the schools. To the
bankers' argument that note issues should be taken out of politics
and lodged in the hands of business men, it replied that the issue
of currency was a function of sovereignty, and to surrender it to
private corporations, as was done by the National Bank Act, was
undemocratic. The monetary system of the nation must not become the football of class interests. To the argument of the bullionists that gold was the only fixed and stable standard for deferred
payments, it replied that the gold standard was too narrow a base
on which to erect a monetary system for an expanding country,
that it was notoriously susceptible to manipulation, and that it
had been devised by Lombard Street in the interests of capitalism.
Since the days of the great struggle over the Bank a remarkable

[12] *Ibid.*, p. 573. [13] *Ibid.*, pp. 573–574.

change had come over the agrarian mind in its thinking on monetary affairs. In their distrust of all banks and bank-issues Jackson and Benton had swung sharply back to the bullion theory of money. They were militant hard-money men. But in the intervening years a new and revolutionary conception had been slowly making its way to recognition. In the minds of obscure economists the quantitative theory of money had risen to challenge the bullion theory. In unorthodox pamphlets and newspaper discussion it was being pointed out that the value of money is dependent on the amount in circulation, that gold and silver are commodities fluctuating in value like other commodities, and that it is the plain duty of the state to regulate the per capita circulation in accordance with business needs. To allow the bankers to erect a monetary system on gold is to subject the producer to the money-broker and measure deferred payments by a yardstick that lengthens or shortens from year to year. The only safe and rational currency is a national currency based on the national credit, sponsored by the state, flexible, and controlled in the interests of the people as a whole.[14]

By far the most suggestive of these obscure pamphleteers was Eleazar Lord, a New York banker, who for thirty-five years was a propagandist for a new currency system and who watched the bungling of the war finance with acute concern.[15] With the undemocratic nature of banknotes he was not concerned. As a banker he accepted them as desirable and wished to establish them on a sound national basis. He was in ardent sympathy with the patriotic nationalism of Henry C. Carey. The loose system of state-bank issues seemed to him chaotic and he was earnest in espousal of a common national system. Lord was an acute and stimulating thinker on monetary matters. He was one of the first Americans to understand the significance of credit, and he was realist enough to foresee that the system of the future would be a credit system. This was the clue to his dissatisfaction with the bullion theory of money, which he attacked with vigor, and to his acceptance of the

[14] See, amongst many, *Homo's Letters on a National Currency*, Washington, 1817; *Currency Explosions, their Cause and Cure*, New York, 1858; *Our Currency: Some of Its Evils, and the Remedies for them*, by a Citizen of North Corolina, Raleigh, 1861.

[15] His titles are: *Credit, Currency and Banking*, New York, 1828; *A Letter on the National Currency*, New York, 1861; *Six Letters on the Necessity and Practicability of a National Currency, etc.*, New York, 1862; and *National Currency: A Review of the National Banking Law*, New York, 1863.

quantitative theory.[16] He had the scantest respect for Sherman's dogma that gold is as stable as the eternal hills because it is "labor and value itself," or for Wells's belief that the law of supply and demand automatically produces gold enough to meet the needs of business. He would treat gold and silver as commodities varying in price with supply and demand, and make no attempt to relate the money scale to their fluctuations. For years, he said, America accepted the English "standard of currency, their aristocratic definition of wealth, and their distinction between capital and credit," to its disaster.

The so-called specie basis, whenever there is a foreign demand for coin, proves to be a mere fiction, a practical humbug; and whenever, by an excess of imports, this pretended basis is exported to pay foreign debts, the bank-notes are withdrawn from circulation or become worthless, the currency for the time is annihilated, prices fall, business is suspended, debts remain unpaid, panic and distress ensue, men in active business fail, bankruptcy, ruin, and disgrace reign.[17]

To provide a safe, flexible, and convenient currency, Lord proposed a system of national banknotes, based on the wealth of the country and responsive to the needs of a business world founded on credit.

Necessity must teach us whether we can and must have a currency of purely representative value, wholly disconnected from the precious metals, as a basis and standard, or prolong the conflict between coin and paper, commerce and exchange. The existing theory on the subject is too firmly fixed by education, prescription, prejudice and interest, to be overthrown. . . . Such words as *safe, secured, national, uniform, economical, inalienable*, when predicated of any thing but gold as currency, are to the specie-paying theorist mere sounds devoid of significance. . . . Credit must triumph. Can any one blame the well-meaning theorist if he manifests some degree of doubt and alarm in view of the extent to which the actual use of credit, and of the confidence in the use of credit, has already attained?[18]

In the writings of these obscure economists are to be found the seeds of the later agrarian program. Some of them were clearheaded and able men, but they underestimated the power of the banking group. They failed to realize that in a capitalistic society

[16] From what source Lord, and the other amateur economists, derived their theory is not clear. It is possible, of course, to assume that it was from Ricardo and the English economists. For an analysis and rejection of the quantity theory, see J. Lawrence Laughlin, *The Principles of Money*, Chapter VIII.

[17] *A Review of the National Banking Law*, p. 8.

[18] *Ibid.*, p. 34.

no monetary system would be tolerated that was not to the bankers' liking, and that if it were to their liking they would easily convince the public that it was the only honest and just system. It was this lesson that the Greenbackers and Free Silver men were to learn. No sooner was the issue joined between paper money and the gold standard than a scurrilous hue and cry was raised by the "sound-money" men. The bitter dispute that marked American politics for more than a score of years is a classic example of the distortion of fact for partisan ends that seems to be an inevitable consequence of referring a matter of policy to a democratic electorate. Denunciation took the place of exposition, and hysteria of argument; and in this revel of demagoguery the so-called educated classes—lawyers and editors and business men—were perhaps the most shameless purveyors of humbuggery. Stripped of all hypocrisy the main issue was this: Should the control of currency issues—with the delegated power of inflation and deflation—lie in the hands of private citizens or with the elected representatives of the people? It is a question on which wide disagreement may well exist, for it involves important differences of social and political theory. But the significant thing is that throughout the years when the subject was debated in every newspaper and on every stump the real issue was rarely presented for consideration. The bankers did not dare to present it, for too much was at stake and once it was clearly understood by a suspicious electorate their case was lost. Hence the strategy of the money group was to obscure the issue, an end they achieved by dwelling on the single point of inflation and charging the agrarians with a dishonest policy of repudiation.

Certainly in the minds of many conscientious men the fear of repudiation was very real and acute, and their fears made timid souls panicky. The newspapers took their cue from this bogey and beat the drums so loudly in the cause of "honest money" that all hope of calm discussion was lost. The issue became so distorted from class feeling that later historians find it difficult to view the question dispassionately. So late as 1916 Joseph Gilpin Pyle in his *Life of James J. Hill* could still speak of the Greenback movement as a vicious scheme of "inflation, the boon of the demagogue and the dream of the great debtor class in this new country," who "increased . . . by the opening up of the West on borrowed capital, welcomed any measure that might give them a specious justification for discharging their obligations with something worth less than what they had promised to pay." Describing the genesis of the free silver movement, he said:

Hence grew up a formidable coalition between mine owners, debtors unable or unwilling to pay, ambitious politicians, honest theorists led captive by barren and unpractical abstractions, and a host of men too ignorant to inform themselves, too impassioned by what they heard to wish to know the truth.[19]

Obviously it was not so simple—or so wicked—as that. To determine the justice of the charge of repudiation certain facts must be borne in mind. The gist of the money problem pressing so heavily on the Middle Border was the question of stabilizing the currency with a view to stabilizing prices. Under the prick of war-necessities a sharp inflation of prices had taken place. With the drastic contraction of the currency following the war, prices fell as sharply. From 1873 to 1896 a world-wide appreciation in the value of gold, aggravated by recurrent economic crises, further depressed the market values of commodities, rendering the question of the solvency of the Middle Border increasingly doubtful. Falling prices are only the obverse of rising money-values, and to stop the one it was proposed to cheapen the other, either through the issue of greenbacks as proposed by the Greenback party, or through the free coinage of silver as proposed in the plank of the Democratic platform of 1896. It was not a question of repudiation in favor of debtors, but a question of correcting an unjust deflation that favored the creditor class.

IV

GREENBACKISM AND PETER COOPER

The opposition to the program and methods of the rising plutocracy was not confined to the farmers of the Middle Border. It was nourished by a widespread distrust of banks and bank-currencies that was a heritage of the Jacksonian struggle. Amongst the leaders of the Greenback movement were many eastern men, some of wide industrial experience, whose economic views and prejudices were a hold-over from the days of John Taylor, and who discovered in the post-war finances the same class manipulations of public credit that marked the funding operations of Washington's administration. Men as dissimilar as Horace Greeley, Thaddeus Stevens, Wendell Phillips, Henry C. Carey, and Peter

[19] Vol. I, p. 485.

Cooper, made common cause with the western farmers in seeking to wrest control of government from the bankers, and establish what they conceived to be a just democratic economy. Picturesque militants grown old in warfare, they were of an earlier generation, inheritors of the ideals of simpler times before production for consumption had been superseded by consumption for profit, ardent equalitarians who would not see their hopes frustrated and America become a plutocracy without a struggle. Greeley, Carey, and Phillips have been considered elsewhere; Stevens was the last of the rugged equalitarians who followed their principles to the bitter end; and Peter Cooper was an unregenerate Jeffersonian who dedicated his last years to combating Wall Street, accepting in 1876, at the age of 85, nomination for the presidency by the National Independent Party, commonly called the Greenback Party.

Like Thaddeus Stevens an ironmaster, grown wealthy by a long life of useful and adventurous industry, builder of the first American locomotive that made possible the success of the Baltimore and Ohio railway, Peter Cooper was the most picturesque figure in New York City in the seventies. With Bryant he shared the distinction of being the patriarch of Broadway. Bred up amidst stern and harsh conditions, at a period when, he said, within his "own recollection unmarried white men could be sold for debt in the State of Connecticut," [20] he was not hardened by the struggle for subsistence. A tender social conscience mellowed an old-fashioned probity and gave character and dignity to a simple rugged nature. Transparently honest, with a certain innate austerity softened by a homely courtesy, he was not a reed to sway in every vagrant breeze, but a great oak with fibers toughened by the storms of years. Like Horace Greeley, whom he much resembled in honest kindliness, he carried the burdens of his country on his heart, and in the midst of abundant prosperity still reckoned himself his brother's keeper. By "nature and temperament a radical reformer," his strongest instinct was a quick sense of justice. He was oppressed by the poverty and misery he saw about him, and he gave so generously to all good causes that he was known to his generation as "the greatest philanthropist in the world." His chief accomplishment was the founding of Cooper Union for free instruction in 'practical art and science," on which he expended a fortune.[21] But

[20] *Ideas for a Science of Good Government*, p. iii.
[21] *Political and Financial Opinions of Peter Cooper*, p. 23.

he was not one to salve his conscience with a gift of superfluous wealth. His heart was as open as his pocketbook, and he must explore to its hidden sources the infection that was breeding social injustice in the new world. His private interests never blinded him to his larger duties, but he gave his time and strength as readily as his money to whatever cause he espoused.

Such a man was morally incapable of the buccaneering exploitation that marked the Gilded Age. Between Peter Cooper and Jim Fisk was an impassable gulf; they were products of different worlds and different economies. The speculative middleman who thrust himself between the producer and the consumer, with no sense of responsibility to either, but concerned only with immediate profit, was a figure to excite the wrath of an older-fashioned industrialist who had been taught that the only just reward is the reward that comes from productive labor; and in the days of the great barbecue Peter Cooper became deeply concerned for the future of America. It was the new breed of bankers with their control of the money system that were to blame, he came to believe, and he would have reckoned himself false to the obligations of citizenship if he failed to protest against their selfish manipulation of the public credit. He had watched the callous juggling of the national finances by the money-lenders during the Civil War, and had seen a debt of some three billions nearly doubled in the decade after Appomattox by the bond-holders. The new system of National Banks that issued from the emergencies of war had come to control the financial policy of the country, and to Peter Cooper it seemed that their purpose was to perpetuate a debt that enabled them to tax the productive labor of America and to squeeze wealth from a calculating expansion and contraction of the currency. To surrender to such mercenaries the sovereign power of issuing and regulating money seemed to him the abdication of sovereignty, and in so far as he could he felt called in honor to prevent it.

It needed rare courage and complete self-sacrifice to take up the gage of battle and in his old age to renew the war that Andrew Jackson had engaged in forty years before. His good name and his honorable career could not save him from the gibes of politicians or the caustic criticism of honest men. It was a losing fight at best. The struggle had been venomous in Jackson's day when the money-power was in its infancy; and now that the banking interests had grown mighty it was as hopeless as the charge of the Light Brigade

The cause had been lost on the day when Congress wrote into the bill establishing a legal tender for war purposes the single word "except," thereby invalidating the greenback for interest payments on bonds and duties on imports—an act that "drew tears from the eyes of Thaddeus Stevens"; and the bankers who could assert their control in war times had no intention a dozen years later of suffering that control to pass from hands that had grown enormously stronger.

Yet Peter Cooper refused to consider the outlook hopeless. With all the resources he could command he threw himself into the struggle. He scattered "more than a million of documents" broadcast—most of the matter of which he wrote; he appealed to Congress and the President, he challenged candidates, he cited the opinions of the Fathers, and when he was buried under an avalanche of votes—as Horace Greeley had been four years before—he preserved his faith in the "people's cause" and to the last day of his life kept up the great battle. "I always have been, am, and ever shall be with the poor toilers and producers; therefore I desire Congress to legislate for the poor as well as for the rich, who can take care of themselves," [22] he wrote in his ninety-second year, and the spirit that stirred in his old veins appears from such a comment as this:

I consider the persistent class legislation of Congress since the war, a worse despotism than that of Great Britain before the Revolution; because it reduces the laboring classes to periodic distress and starvation, that are worse than any despotism ever was; for monopolizing corporations, whether in the shape of banks or railroads, have no soul.[23]

Peter Cooper's political philosophy was simple and transparent. His teachers were Albert Gallatin, Henry C. Carey, and George William Curtis, and from them he drew three major ideas that had emerged from three generations of American experience: the need for a national monetary system based on legal tender; the necessity for a protective tariff; and the need for an effective civil service. The first was an adaptation of the old agrarian dislike of banknotes; the second came out of Clay's American System as it had been elaborated by Henry C. Carey in the fifties; and the third issued from the Civil Service Reform movement of the seventies. The exigencies of the political situation, however, thrust into the

[22] *Ideas for a Science of Good Government*, p. 272.   [23] *Ibid.*, p. 271.

foreground the money question, and nine-tenths of his writings deal with that pregnant issue. As an ardent Jacksonian he was deeply suspicious of the rising money-power, with its corporations and monopolies, its land-grants and railways and banks, for behind them he saw the specter of aristocracy. "In America," he said in 1882, "we have no aristocrats except those who have sprung up in a night—as toad-stools do in a dung-hill." [24] But class legislation must end in creating classes, and at another time he said, "There is fast forming in this country an aristocracy of wealth—the worst form of aristocracy that can curse the prosperity of any country. . . . Such an aristocracy is without soul and without patriotism. Let us save our country from this, its most potent, and, as I hope, its last enemy." [25]

His deep interest in political measures was quickened by an anxious concern at the hard times that resulted from the policy of drastic currency deflation. That matters were going ill in America during the middle seventies every fool knew, and Peter Cooper was only giving expression to the common knowledge in describing to President Hayes, in a letter dated August 6, 1876, the "appalling" economic situation. That it was equally bad in England he did not point out.

More than two hundred thousand men, within the last few weeks, have joined in "strikes" on the various railroad lines, the workshops and the mines of the country, on account of the further reduction in their wages, already reduced to the living point. That some of these strikes have been attended with lawless and unjustifiable violence, only shows the intensity of the evils complained of, and the despair of the sufferers. For four years past, since the "panic of 1873," millions of men and women, in this hitherto rich and prosperous country, have been thrown out of employment, or living on precarious and inadequate wages, have felt embittered with a lot, in which neither economy nor industry, nor a cheerful willingness to work hard, can bring any alleviation. Is it to be wondered at, that *enforced idleness* has made tramps of so many of our laboring population, or induced them to join the criminal and dangerous classes? [26]

After pointing out the disastrous effects of such hard times on mining, railways, real estate, and the western farmers, he asserted that the bankers, although they also were embarrassed, were "very patient with their troubles. . . for they know, that *money is appreciating in value all the time.*" He then uncovers the kernel of

[24] *Ibid.*, p. 261.   [25] *Ibid.*, p. 123.   [26] *Ibid.*, pp. 117–118.

his thought—that it is a sovereign duty of government to provide
an adequate national currency.

This bondage has its manifold centre and its secret force in more than
two thousand banks, that are scattered through the country. All these
banks, are organized expressly to loan out their own money and the money
of all those, who will entrust them with deposits. These loans are made to
men, whose business-lives will soon become dependent on money, borrowed from corporations, that have a special interest of their own. Such
a power of wealth, under the control of the selfish instincts of mankind,
will always be able to control the action of our Government, unless that
Government is directed by strict principles of justice and of the public
welfare. The banks will favor a course of special and partial legislation,
in order to increase their power . . . they will never cease to ask for more,
as long as there is more, that can be wrung from the toiling masses of the
American people.

Such a power should never be allowed to go out from the entire and
complete control of the people's Government. The struggle with this
money-power, intrenched in the special privileges of banks, has been going
on from the beginning of the history of this country. It has engaged the
attention of our wisest and most patriotic statesmen. Franklin, Jefferson,
Webster, Calhoun, Jackson, have all spoken of the danger of such a power
and the necessity of guarding against it.[27]

The solution he offered for the vexing monetary problem accorded with that of the Greenback Party,[28] namely, refusal to
recharter those banks *deceitfully styled national*" and the retirement of all bank currency; the abandonment of the policy of currency contraction; the issue of legal-tender notes to the amount last
found necessary for the functions of industry and business; the
rejection of a specie basis, the notes to be interconvertible with
government bonds bearing interest at 3.65 per cent; issued on
demand in any amount in exchange for legal-tender notes; and the
establishment of a Postal Savings Bank. No man ever believed
more ardently in the sufficiency of his program than Peter Cooper.
It was a suggestive proposal, that only a knave would call the
visionary scheme of a fool. He was tireless in explanation and
argument, the quality of which may be judged from the following
passage from a letter to Hayes and Tilden written during the campaign of 1877:

The worth or exchangeable value of gold is as uncertain as other products
of human labor, such as wheat or cotton. The exchangeable value of anything depends on its *convertibility into something else* that has value *at the*

[27] *Ibid.*, pp. 109–110.   [28] See *Ibid.*, pp. 59–60.

option of the individual. This rule applies to paper money as to anything else. But how shall Government give an exchangeable value to a paper currency? Can it be done by a standard which is beyond its control and which naturally fluctuates, while the sign of exchange indicated by the paper remains the same? . . .

. . . we must trust our Government with this *whole function* of providing the standards and measures of exchange, as we trust it with the weights and measures of trade. . . . We must require the Government to make this currency, at all times, and, at the option of the individual, *convertible.* But the currency must be convertible into something over which the Government has entire control, and to which it can give a definite as well as a permanent value. This is its own *interest-bearing bonds.* These are, in fact, a mortgage upon the embodied wealth of the whole country. The reality of their value is as sound and as permanent as the Government itself, and the degree of their value can be determined exactly by the rate of interest the Government may think proper to fix.[29]

The Jeffersonianism of Peter Cooper, like the Jeffersonianism of the Middle Border, had taken a bias from the confident nationalism that during the fifties so deeply colored American thought. To assure an adequate national economy, superior in its self-sufficiency to European—and especially English—policies, was a persuasive program that Henry C. Carey devoted his later life to formulating, and that men like Horace Greeley and Peter Cooper disseminated amongst their wide agrarian following. That such a program implied a paternalistic government did not trouble them. Peter Cooper accepted paternalism as a necessary governmental function. He would have the state build and own the great western railway systems; he would use the national domain for the benefit of the settler; he would not turn over the state to plunderers nor the resources of the nation to speculators. An honest man with a sensitive social conscience, he would have no hand in the great barbecue that wasted more than it consumed; but the times were heedless of the counsels of honest men, and he was loved and laughed at and ignored. Like Franklin in the Constitutional Convention, he had outlived his generation and was thrust aside by the new economy that was taking over the custodianship of America.*

[29] *The Political and Financial Opinions of Peter Cooper,* pp. 22–23.

* In his original plan Professor Parrington included here a discussion entitled "Bimetallism: A heritage of Jacksonian democracy; Ignatius Donnelly, 'Coin' Harvey," but from the references in the next chapter it seems evident that as he worked out his plan he decided to omit this.—*Publisher.*

CHAPTER II
THE DEMOCRACY OF THE AGE OF INNOCENCE

I

CAPITALISTIC ENCROACHMENTS

WITH its heritage of Jacksonianism it was natural for the agrarian movement to attempt to carry further the exploration of the democratic principle, seeking to complete the program that had been left unfulfilled by the Fathers. There were few as yet who questioned the finality of democracy as a political system or its adequacy to all social needs. The growing evils of American life were traced unhesitatingly to an imperfect democratic control of the forces of exploitation. If the plutocracy were making gains at the expense of the plain people it was due to defective governmental machinery, and the immediate problem was the readjustment of that machinery. There must be an extension of democratic control over the economics of society. The great principle of *laissez faire*, that had proved so useful in the earlier struggle against aristocratic paternalisms, was become a shield and buckler for the plutocracy that was rising from the freedoms of a let-alone policy. To curb the ambitions of that plutocracy and preserve the democratic bequest for the common benefit of all, was therefore the immediate problem of the times.

To this end two things remained to be achieved: to wrest possession of the government from the hands of the plutocracy that was befouling it, and to use it for democratic rather than plutocratic ends. The difficulties in the way were many. Entrenched behind the checks and balances of a complex constitution the plutocracy could not easily be dislodged from power; even if it were driven out of the legislative and executive branches of government it would find aid and succor in the judiciary, where a masterful corporation law was interpreted by a bench tender toward all property rights, and jealous of its sovereign prerogative of reviewing all legislative enactments. A surprising change had come over the attitude of the governing class towards democracy. Having gained control of the

283

machinery of government the plutocracy found no cause to quarrel with a situation wholly to its liking. It had mastered the gentle art of guiding the majority will, and secure —as it believed—in its control of the political state, it counted on an indefinite continuation of the policy of preëmption and exploitation. From such a group, whether in Wall Street or at Washington, no new theories of government were to be expected. Business men wanted to be let alone. They clung to the anarchism of the Enlightenment and were stout in defense of the principle of individual initiative. So late as 1916 a group of confirmed individualists reissued Spencer's *Man Versus the State*, with an introduction by Elihu Root, to combat the rising spirit of governmental control. They regarded the American system of government as adequate and final, and wanted no subversive changes. The Constitution had been completed by the post-war enactments that fixed the status of the negro, and for a generation thereafter—except for the silent changes wrought by the judiciary —it remained static. East of the Allegheny Mountains popular interest in political theory had come to an end. A group of academic thinkers like John W. Burgess and Woodrow Wilson, an occasional intellectual like Brooks Adams, isolated radicals like Johann Most and small Marxian groups in Chicago and New York, and leaders of the new proletarian movement like Terence V. Powderly, were still acutely concerned about political theory; but these men and their theories counted for little in the stodgy mass of capitalistic America. The political phase had passed over into the economic; politics was wholly divorced from reality.

But throughout the Middle Border and on to the Pacific Coast the spirit of political democracy was alive and vigorous. There the older frontier Jacksonianism still lingered. For upwards of a half a century creative political thinking in America was largely western agrarian, and from this source came those democratic ideas that were to provide the staple of a later liberalism. The conscious objective of this great movement was to complete the work begun by Jacksonianism, and create a political machinery that should enable the democracy to withstand the shock of the Industrial Revolution. Many thinkers contributed to the work—U'Ren of Oregon, Jerry Simpson of Kansas, Tom Watson of Georgia, "Coin" Harvey of Arkansas, General Weaver of Iowa, Ignatius Donnelly of Minnesota, Henry D. Lloyd of Chicago, to name a handful out of the mass—homespun realists who have been forgotten by a later generation, but whose labors were given to the necessary work of refashioning the political machinery of America, and whose program provided the materials for the later Progressive party. They were commoners, men of the people, unversed in the dogmas of the schools, idealists who drew their inspiration from the Declaration of Independence; they spoke for an older America that feared the rising plutocracy, and they were casting about for ways and means to cut its claws. From their labors came the Greenback Movement, the Farmers' Alliance, Populism; and from them came in turn the Progressive Movement that reaped what they had sown.

II

THIRD-PARTY MOVEMENTS

It is, perhaps, not extreme to interpret the political history of America since 1790 as largely a struggle between the spirit of the Declaration of Independence and the spirit of the Constitution, the one primarily concerned with the rights of man, the other more practically concerned with the rights of property. The humanitarian idealism of the Declaration has always echoed as a battle-cry in the hearts of those who dream of an America dedicated to democratic ends. It cannot be long ignored or repudiated, for sooner or later it returns to plague the councils of practical politics. It is constantly breaking out in fresh revolt. When the major parties have grown callous and indifferent to the wishes of the common people, it has reformulated its principles in third-party platforms. Without its freshening influence our political history would have been much more sordid and materialistic. With the exception of such sporadic outbursts as Antimasonry and Knownothingism, the third-party movements of the nineteenth century were democratic movements, inspired by a sense of social justice, founded on the Declaration of Independence, and promulgated to recall the American people to their heritage of idealism. The Locofoco party, the Freesoil party, the early Republican party, the Greenback party, the Populist party, the Progressive party, however they differed in immediate programs, have had a common objective, namely, to set man above property as the great object of governmental concern, and preserve in America the democratic principle of equal opportunity.

Despite the fact that they failed in their immediate objectives

they served the larger purpose of reminding the major parties that
America professes to be a democratic country, and that party
platforms must be brought to square with that fact. Thus interpreted the history of party struggle since 1790 falls into three broad
phases: the Jeffersonian movement that established the ideal of
political democracy; the Jacksonian movement that established
equalitarianism crudely in practice; and the successive third-
party movements that attempted, in successive reactions, to regain
such ground as had been lost, to extend the field, and to perfect
the machinery of democratic government. Since the rise of the
slavery controversy the major parties, allied with masterful
economic groups, have persistently ignored the Declaration of
Independence, and repudiated in practice the spirit of democracy.
To prevent if possible so grave a treason to our traditional ideals,
to assert the rights of the common man against the encroachments
of a class, has been therefore the common mission of the third-
party movements. The significance of their somewhat scanty
success is something the thoughtful American may interpret as he
will.

Since Civil War days, discontent has been endemic in the Middle
Border, and it has broken out in three great political upheavals:
the Greenback movement of the seventies; the Populist movement
of the eighties and nineties; and the Non-Partisan League movement of the second decade of the present century. Issuing from a
profound resentment at the exploitation from which the farmer suffered, they mark a persistent drift away from the old Jacksonian
individualism and an advance toward a socialized conception of the
political state. Disciplined by hard times the farmers were learning a lesson from capitalistic Whiggery; if the political state had
proved serviceable to business why should it not prove serviceable
to agriculture? Why should not a democratic state consider the
producers as well as the middleman? Why should it not provide a
national currency, a national system of transportation, a democratic banking system, a standard system of grain-grading, public
elevators, crop insurance, and the like? Why should the farmer be
squeezed at every turn by private companies who did badly what
the state could do well? By 1917, in short, the Middle Border had
got far from the simple individualism of earlier days and was well
advanced toward state socialism; and it was only the ruthless
opposition of the business interests, that had no wish to see their

private preserves thus rudely invaded, that put a stop to the movement.

Back of all these agrarian programs was the greater problem of the popular control of the political state. How could the undisciplined majority hold in check the disciplined minority? How could poverty meet wealth on an equal footing? The control of politics had fallen into the hands of the machine, and the machine served property interests. Legislatures were bought and sold like corner lots; senatorships went to the highest bidder; judges were more responsive to the wishes of bankers than to those of farmers. To break the power of the machine there must be an extension of democratic control, and to that end new machinery must be provided. Hence the vast agrarian concern with political machinery. From the agrarian agitation—supplemented by proletarian and middle-class recruits—has come the Australian ballot, the Initiative and the Referendum, the Recall, the Direct Primary, and popular election of Senators. The only important agrarian principle that has not been adopted is the principle of proportional representation. If agrarianism lost its great battle over the currency, it won the battle over the income tax. Nullified by a scandalous court decision after it had been long accepted, the income tax was finally established by the tedious method of constitutional amendment—an outcome that owed much to the Middle Border. In casting up the accounts of American democracy, the largest sums must be credited to the Middle Border, as in earlier years they were credited to the Jacksonian frontier. Whether the new machinery is useful or merely cumbersome, there is much disagreement, but it is agrarian in origin and it came from an honest attempt to democratize American politics.*

* The Contents here calls for a third section on the "Populistic Program" (see p. xxxiv for details) and a fourth on "William Jennings Bryan."—*Publisher.*

CHAPTER III

LITERATURE AND THE MIDDLE BORDER*

III

HAMLIN GARLAND AND THE MIDDLE BORDER

Iᴛ was not till the end of the eighties that the bitterness of the frontier began to creep into literature. Its slackness and drab poverty had got into the pages of *The Hoosier Schoolmaster*, as its neighborliness had got into Riley; but in these earlier studies there was no brooding sense of social injustice, of the wrongs done the Middle Border by unjust laws, of the hardships that are increased by the favoritism of government. In the year 1887, however, came a significant change of temper. Three very different writers— Harold Frederic, Joseph Kirkland, and Hamlin Garland—turned to the theme of farm life, and dealt with it in a mordantly realistic vein. It was the first conscious literary reaction to the subjection of agriculture to capitalistic exploitation and it was marked by the bitterness of a decaying order.

Seth's Brother's Wife, by Harold Frederic, is a drab tale of farm life in upper York State, as bitter as any tale of the western border. It is a story of defeat, of flight from country to town. The blight of failure is upon the farming community—a blight that embitters old and young; and the sketches of country louts, of soured lives, of broken men and women, do not make pleasant reading. No gentle idyllic light rests on the landscape such as Sarah Orne Jewett discovers on the fields and villages of New England. Sabrina Fairchild, an old maid embittered by the family failure, yet clinging to the family pride and hopeful that the family prestige will be restored, is a pathetic and desolate figure, gaunt and sharp-tongued; at mortal feud with another pathetic old woman, who with her husband had emigrated from Massachusetts years before, and held herself proudly above the mean and vulgar neighborhood in which

---

* In Professor Parrington's plan the section given here was to be preceded by a first section on "Edward Eggleston and Frontier Realism," and a second on "Whitcomb Riley and Folk Romance."—*Publisher.*

they had settled. The slack servants, gossipy and impudent, the petty lives, the grasping ways unrelieved by any grace or beauty, and set in a world of petty machine politics, make a drab and unattractive picture. Harold Frederic quite evidently hates this countryside that bred him. He will not, like Hamlin Garland, take up the battle for it against the town. He sees no hope in political programs; he is no Populistic agrarian fighting for justice; he wants only to escape from it to the city, where life may be lived more generously. The "trail of the serpent is over it all," he remarks, "rich and poor, big and little. The nineteenth century is a century of cities; they have given their own twist to the progress of the age —and the farmer is almost as far out of it as if he lived in Alaska. Perhaps there may have been a time when a man could live in what the poet calls daily communion with Nature and not starve his mind and dwarf his soul, but this isn't the century . . . get out of it as soon as you can."[1]

Much less bitter and hopeless is *Zury: The Meanest Man in Spring County* (1887), by Joseph Kirkland, son of Matilda Kirkland, who a generation before had written sketches of the Michigan frontier. In the preface the author points out that his study is "a palpable imitation of Thomas Hardy's 'Far from the Madding Crowd,'" an "attempt to reproduce, on American soil, the unflinching realism . . . of life down in actual contact with the soil itself." It is a tale of pioneer days in Illinois, in the second quarter of the nineteenth century, and it draws a full-length portrait of the son of a Pennsylvania immigrant who struggles up from mean beginnings to prosperity. The niggardliness of frontier life is drawn unsparingly—the harsh struggle for subsistence—but there is no outcry against governmental favoritisms or the law's injustice. It is nature that must be fought and conquered, and the battle needs strong men who must subdue their finer natures and more generous impulses to the work of acquisition. Zury Prouder is a masterful fellow who bends every energy to the business of accumulation. He makes one hand wash the other, and by dint of saving and squeezing and trading and foreclosing he slowly amasses wealth and power. He is a thrifty farmer as well as a shrewd trader, but his soul is seared by the frontier meanness—squeezed into land and stock and mortgages, consumed with the passion for grabbing. It was a reaction from the skimpiness of his youth. The bitterness of

[1] Chapter IV, pp. 26–27.

poverty had entered his heart as a boy, and his life took shape from the youthful resolve—

"Dad, I'm goin' t'own a mortgage 'fore I die; mind what I say."

"Hope ye will, Zury," his father replies. "Yew'll have a holt of the right eend of the poker then; 'n' t'other feller he'll have a holt o' the hot part, same's we've got naow."

"You bet! An' it'll sizzle his hands, tew, afore I'll ever let up on him."

But Kirkland will not let Zury remain a crabbed and hard-fisted son of the frontier. As the frontier hardships grow less the soul that has been seared by poverty is awakened to more generous impulses. Late in life Zury is taken in hand by a Boston woman who had come out as a schoolteacher years before, and whom Zury had given up for a bride with a rich farm, but to whom he eventually returns. Under her care the plates of mail are stripped from his heart, his better nature expands, and the meanest man in Spring County ripens into a kindly and lovable old age. What poverty and hardship had warped and twisted, love straightens out and ennobles; the meanness of the frontier is washed away as the rich soil yields a more abundant life. It is not a great book, but it is vigorous and honest, and its earlier chapters contain some admirable bits of realism. As one of the first stories of the western farmer it is secure of a place in the history of our American fiction.

It was this same year, 1887, that Hamlin Garland, alone and brooding over his studies at the Boston Public Library, wrote his first sketches of life in the Middle Border. The romance was fading from the prairies when he took up his pen. The Golden West of Mark Twain and the bucolic West of Whitcomb Riley had both slipped into the past and the day that was rising was to bring its discouragements that seared men's hopes as the hot winds seared the fields of rustling corn. The burdens of the western farmer were heavy on his shoulders and he could foresee no time when they would be lighter. Depression had settled on the Middle Border, and Hamlin Garland returning to the familiar fields from his Boston studies felt the depression in every fiber of his being. This was his land and his people. The blight laid upon men and women and children by the drab pioneer life was a familiar fact to him. The Garlands and the McClintocks had suffered from it as their neighbors suffered, and a rebellious wrath filled his heart as he contemplated the Middle Border—the barnyards where tired men did the evening chores, the ungainly houses where tired women stood over hot stoves, the fertile acres that produced more than the markets consumed. It was a life without grace or beauty or homely charm— a treadmill existence that got nowhere. If this were the Valley of Democracy then the democracy was a mean thing and hopeless, and having himself escaped from it he would do what he could to help others escape. In the completeness of his disillusion the glamour of romance was swept away and he proposed to set down in honest plain words the manner of life lived by these Middle Border folk, and the sort of earnings won by their toil. He would speak frankly out of the common bitter experience. The way to truth was the way of realism.

To a later generation that never knew the pioneer hardships of the Middle Border, Hamlin Garland seems strangely remote and old-fashioned; yet his intellectual antecedents are both ancient and honorable. At bottom he is an idealist of the old Jeffersonian breed, an earnest soul devoid of humor, who loves beauty and is mightily concerned about justice, and who, discovering little beauty and finding scant justice in the world where fate first set him, turned rebel and threw in his lot with the poor and the exploited. As a young man, consumed with a desire to speak for his people, he espoused a somber realism, for only by and through the truth could he hope to dislodge from men's minds the misconceptions that stood in the way of justice. The Middle Border had no spokesman at the court of letters and if he could gain a hearing there he must not betray his father's household by glossing ungainly reality; he must depict the life of the western farmer as it was lived under the summer sun and the winter cold, what harvests were brought to crib and what sort of wealth was finally gathered.

And yet in the light of his total work one hesitates to call Garland a realist. Perhaps more justly he might be called a thwarted romantic, and his early rebellious realism be traced to its source in a passionate refusal to be denied the beauty that should be a portion of any rational way of living; for when later he found himself in a land of nobler horizons, unsoiled as yet by crude frontier exploitation, when he looked out upon vast mountain ranges and felt the warm sun on the gray plains, he discovered there the romance of his dreams and fell to describing the strange splendors with the gusto of a naïve romantic. *Main-Travelled Roads* and *Prairie Folks* are the protest of one oppressed with the meanness of a world that takes such heavy toll of human happiness; *Her Mountain Lover* is the expression of a frank romantic who glories in the nobility of nature's noblemen; and *The Captain of the Gray-Horse Troop* is a tale in which romance is justified by ethics and the hero discovers in the protection of a weaker race the deepest satisfactions of life. Beauty is excellent, but beauty should walk hand in hand with service—not art for art's sake, but art subdued to the higher good of humanity.

Between these extremes of a stark realism and an ethical romanticism, stand two books, separated by many years and great changes, that embody in more finished form the theme which after all was the master passion of Garland's life—the Middle Border and the rebellions it bred. *Rose of Dutcher's Coolly* is a full-length portrait of an idealist in revolt against the narrowness of farm life, and *A Son of the Middle Border* is an idyll of the past, autobiography done in mellower years when the passions of youth have been subdued to less exigent demands. These books, together with the sketches of *Main-Travelled Roads* and the militant critical theory of *Crumbling Idols*, contain pretty much the whole of Hamlin Garland that after years have cared to remember—the saga of the Middle Border in the days of its great rebellion when the earlier hopes of boundless prosperity were turning to ashes in the mouth.

The striking originality of Garland's work, that sets it apart from other studies of the local-color school, sprang from the sincerity of his reaction to environment. His intellectual development followed the needs of his ardent, inquisitive nature. After quitting the little Academy at Osage, Iowa, he went forth in quest of an education that should explain to him the meaning of life as he had known it. In this search he was singularly fortunate. He was his own mentor and he took what he needed. Boston had long been the Mecca of his dreams and when he found himself there—having made a pious pilgrimage as Howells had done a generation earlier—he threw himself upon his studies with ascetic zeal. Fortunately he enrolled in the Boston Public Library instead of at Harvard, and his formless radicalisms there found food in plenty. Though he lived in Boston some ten years and made friends, he never penetrated the inner literary sanctuary. A somewhat forlorn outsider, unknown and unvouched for, he found no welcome as Howells and Twain had found, and he never entered the pleasant circles where Holmes and Lowell and Fields and Norton and Aldrich and Howells held sway.

Perhaps that fact unconsciously determined his scornful rejection of the Boston genteel in literature; at any rate his denial of the sovereignty of the New England literary rulers left him free to follow other masters who seemed to him more significant. In his bleak little room his ear had caught the greater voices then sounding in Europe and America. His masters were men of intellectual horizons unbounded by Beacon Street and Harvard Square: Taine and Ibsen and Björnson, Turgenev and Tolstoi, Zola and Millet, Darwin and Spencer and Fiske, Walt Whitman and Henry George, and the later Howells with his deeper sociological concern and graver realism. His three great masters came finally to be Whitman, Spencer, and Henry George. To these greater names should be added that of Edward Eggleston, who had been his boyhood idol, and that of Joseph Kirkland, who did much to stimulate and guide his earliest sketches. He did not absorb all these men had to give. He could not stretch his provincial mind suddenly to compass the intellectual realm of his masters. But something he got and that something, woven into the fabric of his thinking, was to make him free. It was the best school of the times, and from his studies Hamlin Garland emerged an uncompromising radical, one of a group of eager young men who gathered about B. O. Flower, and in the sympathetic pages of the *Arena* published their divers radicalisms to a hostile world. He was ready to proclaim new social and literary creeds, ready to go forth to do battle for democratic justice and a democratic art.

The gist of Garland's new literary creed is set forth in *Crumbling Idols*, written in the earliest years of the nineties, when Chicago was preparing the setting for the World's Fair, and gathered into book form in 1894. It is realism modified by the local-color school, by French impressionism, and by Whitman—intensely individualistic, ardently social, and militantly democratic. It would sweep away every fetish of great reputations and authoritative schools, and insist that the artist confront the life that he knows and tell of it truthfully. Following the French example he calls this iconoclastic realism, Veritism. "The *theory* of the veritist," he says, "is, after all, a statement of his passion for truth and for individual expression," and he then goes on:

Art, I must insist, is an individual thing,—the question of one man facing certain facts and telling his individual relations to them. His first care must be to present his own concept. This is, I believe, the essence of veritism. "Write of those things of which you know most, and for which you care most. By so doing you will be true to yourself, true to your locality, and true to your time." [2]

But Veritism in the hands of a disciple of Taine, Whitman, Henry George, and Herbert Spencer must take on ethical values and serve the common well-being. All art, he insists, is "sociologic," and realism is harsh because it is hopeful.

Because the fictionist of to-day sees a more beautiful and peaceful future social life, and, in consequence, a more beautiful and peaceful literary life, therefore he is encouraged to deal truthfully and at close grapple with the facts of his immediate present. His comment virtually amounts to satire or prophesy, or both. Because he is sustained by love and faith in the future, he can be mercilessly true. He strikes at thistles, because he knows the unrotted seed of loveliness and peace needs but sun and the air of freedom to rise to flower and fragrance.

The realist or veritist is really an optimist, a dreamer. He sees life in terms of what it might be, as well as in terms of what it is; but he writes of what is, and, at his best, suggests what is to be, by contrast. . . . He aims to hasten the age of beauty and peace by delineating the ugliness and warfare of the present; but ever the converse of his picture rises in the mind of the reader. He sighs for a lovelier life. He is tired of warfare and diseased sexualism, and Poverty the mother of Envy. He is haggard with sympathetic hunger, and weary with the struggle to maintain his standing place on this planet, which he conceives was given to all as the abode of peace. With his hate in his heart and this ideal in his brain the modern man writes his stories of life. They are not always pleasant, but they are generally true, and always they provoke thought. [3]

It is an excellent self-portrait of the young realist of that early time when all the rebellions of his blood cried out for expression— the troubled years between 1887 and 1893 when the Border was rising and the son of the Border found the flames of his discontent fanned by many winds. From such roots came the most acrid tales that had as yet fruited in American fiction. Few as were the stories of *Main-Travelled Roads* and *Prairie Folks*, they constitute a landmark in our literary history, for they were the first authentic expression and protest of an agrarian America then being submerged by the industrial revolution. No other man in our literature had known so intimately the Middle Border as Hamlin Garland— its restless swarmings from the old hive, never pausing long enough to gather the honey of the new fields, its heedless venturings for the reputed gold that lay beyond the farthest sunsets. He had re-

[2] Chapter III, p. 35.   [3] Chapter IV, pp. 51–53.

sponded to the spell that kept the pioneer moving West; the allure-
ment of the untamed prairie, the poetry of dawn and twilight. But
the poignant spell had been broken for him by the drab realities
that lay between the dawn and the twilight—the crushing round
of toil that took such heavy toll of men's development and wom-
en's happiness. He was familiar with the blight as well as the
bloom of the frontier. He had seen his uncle David McClintock
broken by the Border—the great wistful man with the soul of a
musician; he had seen his mother fail under the burden—the
cheerful, uncomplaining wife, joining with her rich voice in the
pioneer's song of "O'er the hills in legions, Boys!" And after the
disillusion of his final defeat on the bleak Dakota plains—by 1883
woodland and meadow were pretty much alienated from the public
domains and only plains and deserts and mountain valleys and
forests remained—his eyes were opened at last. "I clearly perceived," he said afterwards, "that our Song of Emigration had
been, in effect, the hymn of fugitives!" So he turned his face to the
East to seek the land of desire in Boston.

That chapter of his life was ended. He had learned that the old
romantic tales of the Border were lies to him, whatever they may
have been to earlier generations; but he had yet to naturalize himself in the realm of ideas, and analyze the experiences of his youth
in the light of current social liberalisms. He had begun that work in
1883 on his raw Dakota claim where his leisure hours were given to
Taine's theory of literary determinism, and Henry George's new
gospel of single-tax; and he carried it rapidly forward during three
years of eager reading. During those quiet months in Boston when
he was making himself at home in the world of contemporary
thought, he sketched the first of the stories of western life which
later he gathered together in *Main-Travelled Roads* and *Prairie
Folks*. "You're the first actual farmer in American fiction," said
his friend Kirkland, "now tell the truth about it." This handful of
short stories, fierce in the repressed passion of the writer's heart, was
Garland's reply to the old romantic myths of the West. In these
acrid pages life is not bucolic, it does not chew the cud of contentment "knee-deep in June," but it is stained with dust and
sweat, lacerated by raw nerves, depressed by a sense of economic
failure.

Of the lives of these labor-burdened men and women he intended
to tell the whole truth. But, as he confessed later, he could not.

"Even my youthful zeal faltered in the midst of a revelation of the lives led by the women on the farms of the middle border. Before the tragic futility of their suffering, my pen refused to shed its ink. Over the hidden chamber of their maternal agonies I drew the veil." It was hard for him to view it all with the calm detachment of the objective realist; the Border life was too deeply and intimately personal to him, it had marked him too harshly. And yet in the sense of conveying the spirit of reality he succeeded greatly, and these earliest tales remain notable work which later years have not forgotten. The subdued words of the Prologue offer the fittest of commentaries on the spirit in which they were done.

The Main-travelled road in the West (as everywhere) is hot and dusty in summer, and desolate and drear with mud in fall and spring, and in winter the winds sweep across it; but it does sometimes cross a rich meadow where the songs of the larks and bobolinks and blackbirds are tangled. Follow it far enough, it may lead past a bend in the river where the water laughs eternally over its shallows. Mainly it is long and weariful, and has a dull little town at one end and a home of toil at the other. Like the main-travelled road of life it is traversed by many classes of people, but the poor and the weary predominate.

Main-Travelled Roads, in its harsh objectivity, belonged to the earlier eighties, to the time when the spirit of unrest was still obscurely fermenting in the western mind, before it had clarified in definite agrarian movements and measures. It is clouded by doubt and harassed by uncertainty. No hope offers a way out of the weary tangle. Its psychology is that of the first mood of dejection that came with the failure of western agriculture with its virgin fields, its new machinery, and its specialized crops, to adjust itself to the new capitalistic order. The simple agrarian mind had not learned to play the new game. The sons of the Middle Border were children of the Gilded Age as truly as Colonel Sellers or Commodore Vanderbilt; they were plungers and speculators in land and crops; but they were no match for the Main Street plungers and speculators; and when bankruptcy instead of riches rewarded their hardships, they were embittered. Out of that very natural bitterness sprang the movement of Populism that proposed to take government out of the hands of Main Street and make it serve agriculture. It was the understanding of this fact that made Howells so sympathetic a critic of Garland. But he would encourage the artist rather than the reformer.

. . . these stories are full of the bitter and burning dust, the foul and trampled slush, of the common avenues of life, the life of the men who hopelessly and cheerlessly make the wealth that enriches the alien and the idler, and impoverishes the producer.

If any one is still at a loss to account for that uprising of the farmers of the West which is the translation of the Peasants' War into modern and republican terms, let him read *Main-Travelled Roads*, and he will begin to understand. . . . The stories are full of those gaunt, grim, sordid, pathetic, ferocious figures, whom our satirists find so easy to caricature as Hayseeds, and whose blind groping for fairer conditions is so grotesque to the newspapers and so menacing to the politicians. They feel that something is wrong, and they know that the wrong is not theirs. The type caught in Mr. Garland's book is not pretty; it is ugly and often ridiculous; but it is heart-breaking in its rude despair. [4]

Too soon, however, the will to remain objective weakened and his work took on a different note. "Obscurely forming in my mind," he says of the year 1889, "were two great literary concepts —that truth was a higher quality than beauty, and that to spread the reign of justice should everywhere be the design and intent of the artist. The merely beautiful in art seemed petty, and success at the cost of the happiness of others a monstrous egotism." [5] With this ethical conception of art he returned in 1889 to the old home, after a six years' absence, to experience a poignant reaction to the change that had come over the Border. "Another dry year was upon the land and the settlers were deeply disheartened," he wrote later. "The holiday spirit of eight years before had entirely vanished. In its place was a sullen rebellion against government and against God." [6]

Every house I visited had its individual message of sordid struggle and half-hidden despair. . . . All the gilding of farm life melted away. The hard and bitter realities came back upon me in a flood. Nature was as beautiful as ever. The soaring sky was filled with shining clouds, the tinkle of the bobolink's fairy bells rose from the meadow, a mystical sheen was on the odorous grass and waving grain, but no splendor of cloud, no grace of sunset, could conceal the poverty of these people; on the contrary, they brought out, with a more intolerable poignancy, the gracelessness of these homes, and the sordid quality of the mechanical routine of these lives. I perceived beautiful youth becoming bowed and bent. I saw lovely girlhood wasting away into thin and hopeless age. Some of the women I had known had withered into querulous and complaining spinsterhood,

---

[4] Introduction to *Main-Travelled Roads.*
[5] *A Son of the Middle Border*, Chapter XXVIII, p. 374.
[6] *Ibid.*, Chapter XXIX.

and I heard ambitious youth cursing the bondage of the farm. "Of such pain and futility are the lives of the average man and woman of both city and country composed," I acknowledged to myself with candor, "Why lie about it?" [7]

In such a mood the call of social justice was too insistent to be denied. "With William Morris and Henry George I exclaimed, 'Nature is not to blame. Man's laws are to blame'!" And so the young man of twenty-nine threw himself into the agrarian cause. He took the platform with Mary Ellen Lease and was glad of the farmers' approval of the new doctrine of less corn and more hell. Under the urging of his friend Flower he planned to put the Populist movement into fiction and wrote *A Spoil of Office*. The familiar Iowa backgrounds are in the story—the harsh lives and bent weary figures of men and women—but there is also an idealized heroine who suggests what life may become when injustice is done away with and the blighting toil is lessened—a figure who, as Grange lecturer and Farmers' Alliance speaker, may have been suggested by Mary Ellen Lease. Much inferior as it is to *Main-Travelled Roads*—a social tract rather than a work of art—we cannot well spare it from our Middle Border literature, for it has captured and preserves for later times the spirit of the passionate uprising of the farmers, and it recalls the vast hopes that fermented in that revolt —not well grounded, perhaps, but warm and human. "The heart and center of this movement," says Ida Wilbur, "is a demand for justice, not for ourselves alone, but for the toiling poor wherever found. . . . It is no longer a question of legislating for the farmer; it is a question of the abolition of industrial slavery." [8] There are echoes of an older and simpler America in these pages, of discontents that were put down but not removed—Jacksonianisms, Greenbackisms, anti-monopolistic crusades. Yet they look forward to a time when beauty and well-being shall be the common portion of those who do the work of the world. The way, alas, is "long and weary, and thousands and millions of us must die on the road, I am afraid," says the heroine; but go forward they must, along other paths than the path of capitalism.

Less significant is *Jason Edwards: An Average Man* (1891), that is an elaboration of the note, "The air is full of revolt against things as they are." It is a single-tax reply to the question of a young girl, "Are there any happy people in the world—any working people, I

[7] *Ibid.*, Chapter XXVIII, pp. 364-365.   [8] *Ibid.*, p. 245.

mean? Are they all cross and tired and worried and full of care, as we are here?" The story is two chapters in the life of a working-man—his struggle in Boston as a mechanic, and his struggle in Minnesota, whither he flees for a refuge on a homestead. Defeat awaits him in the end, and the conclusion is an illustration of Henry George's thesis that poverty is the entail of land rent. In this and in other studies done under the influence of B. O. Flower, whose appetite for reform literature was insatiable, Hamlin Garland had ceased to be an objective realist and turned propagandist, bringing down on his head the criticisms of conservative readers. One of his friends went so far as to expostulate over the folly of his course. "It is a mistake for you to be associated with cranks like Henry George and writers like Whitman," he said. "It is a mistake to be published in the *Arena*. Your book should have been brought out by one of the old established firms. If you will fling away your radical notions and consent to amuse the governing classes, you will succeed." [9]

It is the agrarian background of Garland's mind that makes him seem old-fashioned to a generation that has forgotten the agrarian roots of our past growth. He was so deeply colored by this earlier native America that he never outgrew it; and when the Populistic revolt had died down, when this last organized agrarian rebellion against the exploiting middle class had become only an episode in our history, he had outlived his day. He was too deeply stirred by Whitman's romantic faith in democracy, too narrowly a disciple of Henry George's Jeffersonian economics, to fit into an industrializing America. Despite his discipleship to European realism he refused to go with the group of young left-wing naturalists who were boldly venturing on new ways of fiction. He would not follow the path of naturalism. Of Norris's *McTeague* he said, "What avail is this study of sad lives? for it does not even lead to a notion of social betterment." [10] He could not bring himself to accept the major criteria of naturalism as they were exemplified in the work of Zola and Strindberg and Hauptmann. A native Jeffersonian, inspired by Whitman and instructed by Henry George and Herbert Spencer, would reject the somber, mechanistic background of naturalist thought. He had learned his science of the Victorian evolutionists, with their grandiose conception of a far-flung benefi-

[9] *A Son of the Middle Border*, Chapter XXXI, p. 417.
[10] *Critic*, Vol. 42, pp. 216–218.

cent progress from the homogeneous to the heterogeneous, and the backgrounds of his mind were radiant with promise. Neither a mechanistic science nor a regimented industrialism had risen in his outlook to bank the fires of his hope. No impersonal determinism had chilled his belief in man as a free-will agent in a moral universe. The vast bleak chemical cosmos that bewildered Theodore Dreiser did not rise before him to dwarf the individual nor overwhelm his aspirations. Like a French romantic of a hundred years before, he remained a confirmed optimist who believed that the future will correct the mistakes of the past, and the peace and beauty for which the human race longs lie immediately ahead. The art of the young man was becoming old-fashioned in the world of Stephen Crane; his ideals were Victorian in the days of Mark Hanna. And so after the agrarian revolt had failed and America lay fat and contented in the lap of McKinley prosperity, he found himself a man without a country, an alien in an industrializing order, and he turned away to the newer West and the romance he had always sought. While America was driving towards regimentation he traveled backward in time to recover a vanishing world of individualism, and the distance rapidly widened between them.

In those romantic wanderings through Colorado and California and into the far Northwest he found a new interest in the frontiersman's exploitation of the Indian, and in *The Captain of the Gray-Horse Troop* and *The Eagle Heart* he has wedded his social ethics to French romanticism, and endowed man in a state of nature with exalted social responsibilities. The old theme is dressed in new clothes and Captain Curtis of the Gray-Horse Troop becomes an Indian agent fighting the lawless and cruel encroachment of the frontiersmen upon the Indian rights; but the theme remains. Garland hated the frontier as fiercely as Cooper hated it, and like him he loved the clean free spaces; but when after his long and somewhat futile rambles he returned to the Middle Border, he found there a new light upon the familiar fields and in that light he wrote his saga of the Garlands and the McClintocks. This was to be his great bequest to American letters. To have sought the spirit of the Middle Border in its hopes and its defeat, to have written the history of the generation that swept across the western prairies, is to compress within covers a great movement and a great experience—one of the significant chapters in our total American history.

CHAPTER III
THE QUEST OF UTOPIA

FROM the welter of unrest of the later years of the century, with its labor struggles, its agrarian bitterness, its concern over the exhaustion of the public lands and a pinching monetary system, its acute distrust of monopolies and corporate power, sprang a very natural eagerness to forecast the future and blaze new roads that might lead to the democratic Canaan. Whither the main-traveled road would lead, discerning idealists knew only too well. To bog down in a mire of plutocracy would be a sorry ending to the great experiment; yet the mud was deepening with every mile of advance and unless another highway appeared the situation was unpromising. The crux of the problem seemed to reside in an extension of the powers of the political state, converting to social ends powers that hitherto had been serving private gain. The plutocracy was pointing the way. If the political state were fairly dedicated to democratic ends, why should not society go forward toward a true commonwealth, founded on a social economy and dedicated to common justice and the common well-being? There was need only to subordinate private interests to collective interests, and substitute coöperation for the present mad scramble of selfish individualism.

In elaboration of this pregnant thought a surprising number of social romances appeared during the last quarter of the century, that were native counterparts of the greater studies in collectivism by European thinkers. A recent study lists forty-eight titles of Utopian romances written between 1884 and 1900.[1] Of these several are communistic, and the rest are socialistic; yet in keeping with the American temper none openly makes use of the terms, and few apply the Marxian doctrine of the class war. Their appeal was directed primarily to the middle class of small business and profes-

* The first chapter of this section was to have been "Plutocracy and the Workingman," the second "The Rise of the Left." For the contents see p. xxxv.—*Publisher.*

[1] Allyn B. Forbes, *The Literary Quest for Utopia, 1880–1900.* "Social Forces," Vol. VI, No. 2, December, 1927.

sional men, and they were content to rely on political means to achieve economic ends. Troubled as was the American mind by the rise of a cutthroat exploitation, it was not yet ready to entertain ideas of direct action or trust the proletariat to enforce its will by mass strength. In one story, to be sure—Ignatius Donnelly's *Cæsar's Column* (1890)—there is a gloomy picture of the downfall of civilization caused by the class struggles; but the temper of Donnelly had lost its genial optimism through his long immersion in under-dog contests and had grown mordant and gloomy.

I

EDWARD BELLAMY AND "LOOKING BACKWARD"

When in 1888 Edward Bellamy published *Looking Backward* he gave a huge impetus to the Utopian romance. Third in the list of titles collected by Mr. Forbes, it was to have a wide influence on the thought of the times. It made instant appeal and successive editions were issued to meet the popular demand. Not since *Uncle Tom's Cabin* had an American novel reached so many readers, and Bellamy became at once a national figure, the prophet of a new industrial order. There is abundant evidence to the effect produced upon thoughtful readers. E. C. Stedman, the first critic of the times, spoke of it as a "remarkable and fascinating novel"; Frances E. Willard called it "a revelation and an evangel"; and Howells remarked on "the extraordinary effect which Mr. Bellamy's romance has had with the public." More significant still, *Looking Backward* speedily became the source and inspiration for a series of social organizations that beginning at Boston soon spread over the country. *The Nationalist* was established as the organ of the movement and thousands of eager men and women threw themselves into the work of reshaping American society to conform to the new social ideal. No doubt the enthusiasm was naïve, no doubt it sprang from a social inexperience that underestimated the complexity of the problem, yet the sources, clearly, were a sharp distrust of private capitalism and an idealistic faith in coöperation. In a pronouncement of the Boston "Nationalist Club," January 9, 1889, the cause was rested on two fundamental truths—"The principle of competition is . . . the application of the brutal law of the survival of the strongest and most cunning"; and, "The principle of the Brotherhood of Humanity is one of the eternal truths that govern the world's progress on lines which distinguish human nature from brute nature." [2]

It is not easy to trace the origins of Bellamy's interest in collectivism or the sources of his thought. A journalist and lawyer, he had studied in Germany, where presumably he had come in contact with Marxian socialism. Writing in the *Nationalist* for May, 1889, he commented thus on the origins of *Looking Backward*:

I never had, previous to the publication of the work, any affiliations with any class or sect of industrial or social reformers nor, to make my confession complete, any particular sympathy with undertakings of the sort. It is only just to myself to say, however, that this should not be taken to indicate any indifference to the miserable condition of the mass of humanity, seeing that it resulted rather from a perception all too clear of the depth and breadth of the social problem and a consequent skepticism as to the effectiveness of the proposed solutions which had come to my notice.

In undertaking to write *Looking Backward* I had, at the outset, no idea of attempting a serious contribution to the movement of social reform. The idea was of a mere literary fantasy, a fairy tale of social felicity. There was no thought of contriving a house which practical men might live in, but merely of hanging in mid-air, far out of the reach of the sordid and material world of the present, a cloud-palace for an ideal humanity. [3]

That the impulse did not come from the Marxians is sufficiently clear from his explanation of the idea of an industrial army. "The idea of committing the duty of maintaining the community to an industrial army, precisely as the duty of protecting it is entrusted to a military army," came to him, he said, from the object-lesson of European militarism. But however little he owed to the Marxians it is clear that Bellamy—the literary amateur who had dabbled in Hawthornesque fantasies—possessed a warm social conscience and a vigorous inquiring mind; and once his attention had been drawn to the evils of industrialism he would respond with the same direct competence that marked the thinking of Henry George. Nine years before *Looking Backward* he had dealt with a sociological theme. In 1879 he wrote *The Duke of Stockbridge, A Romance of Shay's Rebellion*, for the *Berkshire Courier*, which was reissued in book form in 1900. It was a hasty piece of work that falls off greatly in the latter part; yet in its sympathy for the agrarian rebels and its probing of the economic sources of the post-Revolutionary unrest, it was far removed from the temper of Federalist historians. It is an account of the tyranny of property rule—of the exploitation of the debtor farmer by the creditor gentleman made possible by the economic maladjustments resulting from the war. A bitter discontent is in the hearts of the common people. Hatred of lawyers and courts and process-servers, has taken the place of hatred of Tories. Soldiers who had conquered Cornwallis were returning home only to be conquered by writs and imprisoned by sheriffs. The exactions of a brutal law fell upon helpless victims; taxes outran incomes and there was no money to pay. Economic injustice was daily whetting the edge of class bitterness. The animus of Shays's Rebellion is compressed into a few paragraphs that suggest how clearly Bellamy had analyzed the social struggle.

"I use ter think ez there wuzn't no sech varmint ez a tory; but I didn't know nothin' 'bout lawyers and sheriffs them times. I calc'late ye could cut five tories aout o' one lawyer an' make a dozen skunks aout o' what wuz left over."

"I hearn as haow Squire Woodbridge says taxes is ten times what they wuz afore the war, an' its sartin that there ain't one shillin' inter folks' pockets ter pay 'em with where there wuz ten on 'em in them days. . . . It seems darn curis, bein' as we fit ag'in the red coats jest ter git rid o' taxes." [4]

So felt the agrarian. Now for the gentleman:

"That is the trouble nowadays, . . . these numskulls must needs have matters of government explained to them, and pass their own judgment on public affairs. And when they cannot understand them, then, forsooth, comes a rebellion. I think none can deny seeing in these late troubles the first fruits of those pestilent notions of equality, whereof we heard so much from certain quarters, during the late war of independence. I would that Mr. Jefferson and some of the other writers of disturbing democratic rhetoric might have been here in the State the past winter, to see the outcome of their preaching." [5]

Nine years after *Looking Backward* Bellamy published *Equality*, a critical examination of economic history with a view to creating an adequate social economics. The earlier work had drawn the outlines of the democratic society of the future, the later supplied a justification and a commentary. The great theme involved a twofold problem: an analysis of the failure of social justice under private capitalism, and a defense of the working of social capitalism. The two threads are closely interwoven, and the effect is heightened by the contrasts resulting from setting the two social

[4] *The Duke of Stockbridge*, Chapter II, pp. 22, 28.
[5] *Ibid.*, Chapter XXVI, p. 349.

orders over against each other. Innumerable questions, touching diverse phases, are propounded and answered. The apologist of private capitalism is pursued into every stronghold of his logic; he is assailed by a hundred vivid analogies which seek to lay bare the folly of a social system that breeds waste only to breed poverty, that puts a premium upon greed and yet takes away the security of possession, that bids the workers fight each other instead of uniting for the common welfare. But men must see a better before they will leave a worse, and so there is drawn the picture of another commonwealth that must arise when men shall put off the ass's head from their shoulders, and set intelligently to work. America is moving towards such a commonwealth, Bellamy is persuaded, and yet how slow it is to grasp the meaning of democracy! It holds back from its own good, loath to probe the depths of the revolutionary philosophy of liberty, equality, fraternity. Julian West awakes in this new world; his eyes are opened; the ass's head is gone; he knows for the first time the goodness of life in a rational society. And when in a hideous nightmare he returned to the old Boston he had lived in before he fell asleep, he tasted for the first time the full iniquity of the old pigsty arrangement. "I have been in Golgotha," he cried, "I have seen Humanity hanging on a cross!" It is knowledge of the good that must destroy the evil.

It was as a political economist that Bellamy attacked the problems of a democratic society, and his radicalism begins and ends with the interpretation he puts on the phrase. He was far from being a political economist of the schools. His contempt for the older classical dogmas was measureless. Manchesterism with its fetish of *laissez faire* he reckoned no better than a pseudo-science. " 'There were no political economists before the Revolution,' " remarks one of the scholars of the later age.[6] Such books as the *Wealth of Nations*, properly speaking, should be called "Examinations into the Economic and Social Consequences of trying to get along without any Political Economy." Before we shall get forward we must examine our terms.

Economy . . . means the wise husbanding of wealth in production and distribution. Individual economy is the science of this husbandry when conducted in the interest of the individual without regard to any others. Family economy is this husbandry carried on for the advantage of a family group without regard to other groups. Political economy, however, can

6 *Equality*, Chapter XXII, p. 189.

only mean the husbandry of wealth for the greatest advantage of the political or social body, the whole number of the citizens constituting the political organization. This sort of husbandry necessarily implies a public or political regulation of economic affairs for the general interest. But before the Revolution there was no conception of such an economy, nor any organization to carry it out. All systems and doctrines of economy previous to that time were distinctly and exclusively private and individual in their whole theory and practice. While in other respects our forefathers did in various ways and degrees recognize a social solidarity and a political unity with proportionate rights and duties, their theory and practice as to all matters touching the getting and sharing of wealth were aggressively and brutally individualistic, antisocial, and unpolitical.[7]

A social arrangement based on an individual economy must necessarily result in such monstrosities as the system of private capitalism with its cash nexus. It is no other than an organized system of social warfare, with all the appalling waste of war. Habit has blinded our eyes or we should see the utter bankruptcy of individual competition, that prides itself on its "famous process for beggaring a nation." "Were these serious men I saw about me," cried Julian West as he watched the folly of Washington Street, with its thousand shops madly bidding against each other, its vulgar advertising and cheating and swindling, "or children, who did their business on such a plan? Could they be reasoning beings, who did not see the folly which, when the product is made and ready for use, wastes so much of it in getting it to the user? If people eat with a spoon that leaks half its contents between bowl and lip, are they not likely to go hungry?"[8] What is it but such folly which prevents society from doing the thousand things which cry aloud to be done? So long as men must fight each other for individual subsistence how shall they be able to join forces to fight the common enemies, cold, hunger, disease? Our individualism keeps us poverty-stricken; we are too poor to destroy the social squalor, too poor to save our own lives.

If competition entails irretrievable waste, he points out, the system of competitive profit involves economic suicide. It is a pistol which private industrialism points at its own head. The struggle for profit is the hidden cancer that is eating out the heart of modern society, and Bellamy examines it searchingly in the chapter, "Economic Suicide of the Profit System."[9] Under private

[7] *Ibid*, p. 189.
[8] *Looking Backward*, Chapter XXVIII, p. 314.
[9] *Equality*, Chapter XXII.

industrialism profits are the oil to the wheels of industry, which turn in response to the market. By the market is meant those who have money to buy with; and demand is brisk or slack according to the diffusion of economic means. When the buyers are satisfied and abstain from further purchases, the market becomes glutted and the wheels of production cease to turn "though starving and naked mobs might riot in the streets." Profits, however, must come out of somebody's pocket; and the greater they are the more the pocket that pays is emptied; unless replenished by other profits, taken from still other pockets, it ceases to be able to buy in like proportion. In consequence the market slacks off and the wheels of industry run slower. The manufacturer takes his profits out of his workmen, the merchant takes his out of the public—which is another term for the workman; he who takes most grows rich fastest and is most successful. Obviously, however, such riches are acquired at the expense of the public capacity to buy; and such lessening capacity is ominous of gluts and crises to ensue, with losses which must be made good by greater profits when the wheels turn again. It is only too clear that society is suffering from a chronic dyspepsia of its industrial system; it cannot digest its food. The current maxim that a fair exchange is no robbery—so confidently urged—cannot apply to the profit system, for if the exchange is fair there is no profit, and if there is no profit there will be no exchange. The further maxim that demand governs supply and supply keeps pace with demand, refers only to the profit-market, and quite overlooks the important detail of social need.

The stupidity of such a system Bellamy never tires of pointing out. His striking analogy of the stage-coach has become a classic; the less known parable of the water-tank [10] is equally vivid; a hundred other shafts are directed at the profit-theory which underlies our individual economy. Until the sway of such anarchy is broken, until society learns to regulate its industrialism on the principles of a wise political economy, there can be no hope of betterment. To create and apply this wise political economy is the urgent business of democracy if it is not to perish. It must be such an economy as shall satisfy both our ethical ideals and our material needs. It must embody the spirit of democratic solidarity and it must look beyond the demands of the profit-market to the well-being of all. It must substitute coöperation for competitive war-

[10] *Equality*, Chapter XXIII, p. 195.

fare. The criminal waste which keeps the gray wolves forever snarling at the threshold of society, must cease; the specter of poverty which disorders the lives of men and distempers their hopes, must be banished by the united strength of all. If democracy cannot achieve such a democratic political economy it must flounder through deepening bogs until finally it sinks in the morass of plutocracy.

The fatal mistake of democracy heretofore has been the insufficiency of its program. It is incredible how limited has been its vision and how few and how minor have been its greatest revolutions. To overthrow monarchy was excellent, but it did not bring in democracy; rather, the unchecked sway of plutocracy. "'The people, indeed, nominally were sovereigns; but as these sovereigns were individually and as a class the economic serfs of the rich, and lived at their mercy, the so-called popular government became the mere stalking-horse of the capitalists.'"[11] Political revolutions have proved heretofore to be mere flashes in the pan; not until the economic revolution has been effected will the old tyranny be blown to pieces:

The second phase in the evolution of the democratic idea began with the awakening of the people to the perception that the deposing of kings, instead of being the main end and mission of democracy, was merely preliminary to its real programme, which was the use of the collective social machinery for the indefinite promotion of the welfare of the people at large. . . .

Which amounts to saying . . . that there never was a democratic government properly so called before the twentieth century. . . . The so-called republics of the first phase we class as pseudo-republics or negative democracies. . . .

Regarded as necessary steps in the evolution of society from pure monarchy to pure democracy, these republics of the negative phase mark a stage of progress; but if regarded as finalities they were a type far less admirable on the whole than decent monarchies. In respect especially to their susceptibility to corruption and plutocratic subversion they were the worst kind of government possible. . . . How could intelligent men delude themselves with the notion that the most portentous and revolutionary idea of all time had exhausted its influence and fulfilled its mission in changing the title of the executive of a nation from king to President, and the name of the national Legislature from Parliament to Congress? . . . The American people fancied that they had set up a popular government when they separated from England, but they were deluded. In conquering the political power formerly exercised by the king, the people had but

[11] *Equality*, Chapter II, p. 21.

taken the outworks of the fortress of tyranny. The economic system which was the citadel and commanded every part of the social structure remained in possession of private and irresponsible rulers, and so long as it was held, the possession of the outworks was of no use to the people, and only retained by the sufferance of the garrison of the citadel. The Revolution came when the people saw that they must either take the citadel or evacuate the outworks.[12]

The significance of the title of Bellamy's supplementary volume should now be clear. The problem of democracy always and everywhere is the problem of achieving economic equality. Without that all talk of liberty and fraternity, all equality before the law, is empty and sinister mockery. How can a man call himself citizen who must beg a fellow citizen to become his master? How shall the wage-taker treat his boss as a brother? Of what worth is equality before the law to one without a job? Democracy and servitude cannot lie down together. Wage-slavery debases the dignity of man; it puts upon him the greatest of indignities, servitude to things; it cheats him of his right to life, liberty, and happiness; it is the evil thing which degrades human society to the level of the pigsty, and puts a premium upon the hoggish instincts of men. It sows suspicion and hate between equals, changes the unsuccessful into cringing sycophants, sets its heel upon the weak and the helpless. The thing were too monstrous to be conceivable were it not the everyday fact of life—more than that, were it not the ideal of a supposedly democratic society, apologized for by our plutocratic culture, defended by all that accounts itself respectable, buttressed by the formidable turrets of the law, written down as a major premise in our treatises on political science: and all in the sacred name of individual enterprise. It is familiarity that blinds us to its evils, and makes its victims only callous or sullen. And it endures because men are deceived by its half-truths, seduced by its specious freedoms, led astray by its fatuous promises. Being taught to set the privilege of fighting above the privilege of helping, how should they not account their egoism more sacred than their altruism?

When men shall leave off bounding their democratic horizons by the old political economy and the old law, Bellamy was persuaded, they will see more clearly. The political science of private property conceived of government as a police power to safeguard the stake of

12 *Ibid.*, Chapter II, pp. 19, 20, 21, 22.

the individual in society. Very well, democracy needs only to re-
define the terms "stake-in-society" and "police power" to arrive at
a competent philosophy. The definition of the former is ready to
hand in the familiar words of the Declaration of Independence—the
stake of every man in society is no less than his life, his liberty, and
his happiness. To secure him in this stake is the primary function
of government. The property interpretation of the stake-in-society
principle was sound in its assumption of the economic as the
determining basis; we need only to democratize the interpretation
to arrive at our end.

"The primal principle of democracy is the worth and dignity of the individual. That dignity, consisting in the quality of human nature, is essentially the same in all individuals, and therefore equality is the vital principle of democracy. To this intrinsic and equal dignity of the individual
all material conditions must be made subservient, and personal accidents
and attributes subordinated. The raising up of the human being without
respect of persons is the constant and only rational motive of the democratic policy. Contrast with this conception that precious notion of your
contemporaries as to restricting suffrage. Recognizing the material dis-
parities in the circumstances of individuals, they proposed to conform the
rights and dignities of the individual to his material circumstances instead
of conforming the material circumstances to the essential and equal dignity of man."
"In short . . . while under our system we conformed men to things, you
think it more reasonable to conform things to men?"
"That is, indeed," replied the doctor, "the vital difference between the
old and the new orders." [13]

As a preliminary to this necessary end of conforming things to
men there must be a reinterpretation of the functions of the state.
Here again Bellamy's political economy gives a surprising twist to
the current police theory of government.

"In my day . . . it was considered that the proper functions of government, strictly speaking, were limited to keeping the peace and defending
the people against the public enemy, that is to the military and police
powers."
"And in heaven's name, who are the public enemies?" exclaimed Dr.
Leete. "Are they France, England, Germany, or hunger, cold, and nakedness?" [14]

The plutocratic interpretation of the police power signifies no
other than the protection of the individual in the enjoyment of the

---

[13] *Ibid.*, Chapter III, p. 26.
[14] *Looking Backward*, Chapter VI, p. 59.

fruits of his exploitation—that his right to keep and use what he
has got must be held more sacred than the welfare of society; that
the law, the military, the police, shall defend him in his right to do
with his winnings as he will. The democratic interpretation of the
police power, on the other hand, holds that the state must intervene
to the end that property shall serve a social and not a private interest; that the weak shall not be exploited by individual enterprise;
that all shall be protected in their right to life, liberty, and happiness. It demands an ethical basis for the social economy. The legal
maxim that a man may do as he will with his own, is open to question. The matter of ownership ceases to be a legal question of title,
and becomes a moral question of right and justice. Land, the
machinery of production, the profits of organized industry, coal,
ores, oil, lumber—are such things justly subject to private pre-
emption? Shall the complex structure of society be bottomed on the
law of contract, or on the ethics of social justice? Substitute one for
the other and a revolution is accomplished.

Our ethics of wealth is . . . extremely simple. It consists merely in the
law of self-preservation, asserted in the name of all against the encroachments of any. It rests upon a principle which a child can understand as
well as a philosopher, and which no philosopher ever attempted to refute—
namely, the supreme right of all to live, and consequently to insist that
society shall be so organized as to secure that right.[15]

Thus in the political science of democracy the old police theory
of government merges in an all-embracing trustee theory. To a
paternal state is entrusted the protection of the interests of society.
That the welfare of all shall be faithfully served, it is essential that
the common will control and direct the machinery for the production and distribution of wealth. The anarchy of individualism must
give place to an ordered regimentation, under a centralized authority. The social meaning of property must be probed to the
bottom and the exact line between public and private rights be
marked off. This brings Bellamy to his fundamental principle—the
collectivistic organization of industry as the *sine qua non* of a democratic society. How effectively such a centralized state must wage
war upon poverty, how adequately it must protect the citizen
against the common enemies of cold, hunger, and nakedness, it was
the purpose of *Looking Backward* and *Equality* to picture. "A hor-

[15] *Equality*, Chapter XI, p. 74.

rible cockney dream," William Morris called *Looking Backward,*
and by way of answer sketched his *News from Nowhere,* loveliest
of Utopias with its anarchistic freedom set in country fields.
Morris was an artist with an ample share of Ruskinian prejudice
against the machinery that Bellamy so greatly developed; nevertheless Bellamy was far more modern and realistic in his understanding of the part the machine will play in the society of the
future. To socialize the machine—to put upon it the slave-work
of society, surely means much to human freedom.

Looking Backward is a brief for no particular school of socialism,
although it inclines somewhat to Fabianism. Not through strikes,
boycotts and lockouts, was the great change brought about, but in
consequence of the spread of social intelligence and social ethics.
Unionism was not the father of the Revolution, nor agrarianism its
mother. Direct action and violence in any form rather hindered
than helped. Class propaganda was too narrow and too selfish.
The anarchists with their "red flag and talk about burning, sack-
ing, and blowing people up," retarded the Revolution by frighten-
ing the timid and making "a thousand enemies of their professed
cause to one friend." "The labor parties, as such, never could have
accomplished anything on a large or permanent scale."

It was not till a rearrangement of the industrial and social system on a
higher ethical basis, and for the more efficient production of wealth, was
recognized as the interest, not of one class, but equally of all classes, of
rich and poor, cultured and ignorant, old and young, weak and strong,
men and women, that there was any prospect that it would be achieved.
Then the national party arose to carry it out by political methods.[16]

To wait for the consent of all would seem to the impatient a long
postponement of the millennium; yet the postponement, Bellamy
argued, need not be long. The overreaching greed of private capitalism was daily hastening it. The new order must come about
speedily as a necessary consequence of two forces; the compulsion
of economic fact, and the stimulus of ideas. As the monopolistic
tendencies of private capitalism open the eyes of the dullest to the
growth of a plutocratic power beyond the control of the majority,
a quick fear of the impending tyranny must lead men to question
the larger scope and ultimate significance of the whole system.
Under the lash of this fear their minds will open to ideas which have

[16] *Looking Backward,* Chapter XXIV.

long been knocking in vain for admission. The sources of monopolistic power will be examined, and the successive steps by which the few have gained control of the machinery of production will become clear. Already the fertile idea of the unearned increment which the land-taxers have got hold of and are spreading widely, has prepared the way for the revolutionary doctrine of the social fund. Let the common man once understand how small a portion of wealth is produced by his private effort, and how large a portion by the agency of social organization with its heritage of experience and invention, and he will understand how unjustly private capitalism appropriates what it has not earned. The conclusion that wealth should belong to him who produces it, is a deduction of the most elementary ethics; and since the production of wealth in quantity is a consequence of the social organization and social heritage, the conviction becomes irresistible that such wealth belongs to society and cannot justly be appropriated by the individual.[17] Let such an idea spread widely and the way is prepared for the taking over by the state of the machinery of production, and the assumption by it of the obligation of universal trusteeship. Then will come the Revolution. Coöperation will take the place of competition; production and distribution for the common well-being will destroy the malevolent trinity of rent, interest, and profit, which have so long held the world in poverty; the intelligent strength of all will stand between the individual and cold, hunger, and nakedness. The noble words of the Declaration of Independence will no longer be a catch-vote and a mockery to the exploited multitude, but a reality. The democratic ideal, with its social philosophy summarized in the phrase, "the only wealth is life," will destroy the last vestiges of ancient tyranny and men will be free. Rooted in economic equality the fine flower of individualism will expand as it cannot now in unfertile soil; a generous and unstinted culture will spread the spirit of kindliness through society, and a new and nobler art and religion will go hand in hand with the new fellowship.

Only too clearly Edward Bellamy was an incorrigible idealist. He looked into the future with more confident eyes than most of us; he saw in the East the quickening of a new day where we see only darkness. A child of the Enlightenment, he put his trust in the natural goodness of men. They are not inherently base and ignoble, but the victims of an evil system that breeds what is base and ig-

[17] See *Equality*, Chapter XIII—"Private Capital Stolen from the Social Fund."

noble. "The folly of men, not their hard-heartedness, was the great cause of the world's poverty. It was not the crime of man, nor of any class of men, that made the race so miserable, but a hideous, ghastly mistake, a colossal world-darkening blunder." [18] In an arid land shall we waste the little store of water, or shall we regulate it strictly, that the desert may be brought to bloom as a garden?

The labor of men, I explained, was the fertilizing stream which alone rendered earth habitable. It was but a scanty stream at best, and its use required to be regulated by a system which expended every drop to the best advantage, if the world were to be supported in abundance. But how far from any system was the actual practice! Every man wasted the precious fluid as he wished, animated only by the equal motives of saving his own crop and spoiling his neighbor's, that his might sell the better. What with greed and what with spite, some fields were flooded while others were parched, and half the water ran wholly to waste. In such a land, though a few by strength or cunning might win the means of luxury, the lot of the great mass must be poverty, and of the weak and ignorant bitter want and perennial famine.

Let but the famine-stricken nation assume the function it had neglected, and regulate for the common good the course of the life-giving stream, and the earth would bloom like one garden, and none of its children lack any good thing. I described the physical felicity, mental enlightenment, and moral elevation which would then attend the lives of all men. With fervency I spoke of that new world, blessed with plenty, purified by justice and sweetened by brotherly kindness, the world of which I had indeed but dreamed, but which might so easily be made real. But when I had expected now surely the faces around me to light up with emotions akin to mine, they grew ever more dark, angry, and scornful. Instead of enthusiasm, the ladies showed only aversion and dread, while the men interrupted me with shouts of reprobation and contempt. "Madman!" "Pestilent fellow!" "Fanatic!" "Enemy of society!" were some of their cries, and the one who had before taken his eyeglass to me exclaimed, "He says we are to have no more poor. Ha! ha!"

"Put the fellow out!" exclaimed the father of my betrothed, and at the signal the men sprang from their chairs and advanced upon me." [19]

Like Henry George's noble study of social poverty, *Looking Backward* is a suggestive document of a generation that saw its finer spirits repelled by the vulgar individualism of the Gilded Age. In the long run, no doubt, its influence was slight and the hopes of the Bellamy Nationalists, like the hopes of the Single-taxers, were

[18] *Looking Backward*, Chapter XXVIII, p. 328.
[19] *Ibid*, pp. 328-9.

doomed to disappointment. Nevertheless it remains as a testimony to the fact that in a blatant world of preëmption, exploitation, and progress, were some who were concerned for a juster social order than the Gilded Age dreamed of—a true commonwealth that free men might build if they would.*

* At this point was to come a second section entitled "After Bellamy; 'Naturalism'; Tourgée's *Murvale Eastman.*"—*Publisher.*

CHAPTER IV

THE DARKENING SKIES OF LETTERS

So late as 1893, in spite of the stark ugliness of Hamlin Garland's pictures of the Middle Border, American realism was still unlike in temper those somber etchings, burnt into dark patterns by the caustic acids of European experience, that came from the hands of Russian and German and French naturalists—sketches that in their bitter gloom seemed tragically untrue to the homelier experience of America. In appraising such difference in temper Howells ascribed it to the gulf that separated American well-being from the poverty and injustice of European societies. American realism was hopeful because American life was hopeful. The novelist in this singularly favored land must reflect the temper of a people made kindly by an abundant prosperity and democratic justice, and in the sincerity of his realism he will necessarily concern himself with the "more smiling aspects of life, which are the more American." Whoever should strike a "note so profoundly tragic in American fiction" as was struck in Dostoevsky's *Crime and Punishment*, he asserted in 1891, "would do a false and mistaken thing." [1] And in a later work he spoke casually of our "gay American horizons"— surely the most romantic phrase ever applied to a sad and joyless people by a professed realist.

But while Howells was thus summing up the achievements of American realism and somewhat overconfidently forecasting its future temper, he was in fact writing the history of a past phase. Already the clouds were gathering upon our "gay" horizons, and the current optimisms were finding less food to feed on. The economics of this happy America were coming to be regarded by vast numbers as a class economics, forecasting a less democratic future. Young men born in the early seventies, when Mr. Howells was entering upon his new realistic studies, were coming to intellectual maturity in a very different age; a new science and a consolidating economics were creating a somber temper that was eventually to produce in *An American Tragedy*, a story not greatly unlike that

[1] *Criticism and Fiction*, p. 128.

Russian tale which Mr. Howells, a short generation before, had pronounced impossible to American experience. Stephen Crane and Frank Norris and Theodore Dreiser were the intellectual children of the nineties, and their art was a reflection of that sober period of American disillusion.

The artist, of course, in his creative work is only mediately influenced by the current science and philosophy; yet even in his aloofness from the specific problems of the laboratory and the study he can scarcely escape the pervasive influence of the *Zeitgeist*. And so, after Hamlin Garland, the realistic novel again took a new course from the shifting winds of scientific doctrine. The generation that succeeded the rebellious son of the Middle Border came too late to maturity to share his faith in the benevolent universe of Herbert Spencer, and got little comfort from a promised Utopia that only awaited the enactment of certain statutory laws—laws that would assure economic justice to all—to lay open its hospitable realm. Far-reaching changes were coming over the temper of scientific thought. The conclusions of the physical sciences were ravaging the orderly preserves of biological evolution, with its cardinal doctrine of organic growth and historical continuity; the hurrying march of scientific investigation was leaving far behind the benevolent universe conceived of by Victorian thinkers and was coming out upon higher and bleaker tablelands of speculation. The universe that unfolded itself to chemistry and physics was vaster and colder than biological evolution with its doctrine of the conservation of energy, had imagined—a vibrating mechanism shot through with energy, that revealed itself in action and reaction, impersonal, amoral, dwarfing all the gods dreamed of hitherto; a universe in which the generations of men have shrunk to a pin-point in limitless space and all teleological hopes and fears become the emptiest of futilities. It was the conception of determinism that after long denial was at last coming to wide acceptance—a conception that underlay the thinking of such diverse men as Comte and Spencer and Marx, a conception implicit in the doctrine of continuity, in the law of causality, in the Marxian law of concentration; and now disencumbered of its teleological wrappings, disillusioned with the doctrine of progress, it was to shape the new intellectual attitude towards life.

In presence of such an extraordinary intellectual revolution the old anthropomorphisms of metaphysics and ethics were doomed, and from the revelations of physics and chemistry and psychology must come an endeavor after a fresh evaluation of man's duty and destiny in a universe of immeasurable energy. An ethics that should square with the new data of science must take its departure from the bleak fact of a depersonalized universe, wherein man is but a single form of imprisoned energy, localized for a brief instant and rising to momentary consciousness in the eternal flux, about and through whom flows the energy of an unprobed universe. As this mechanistic conception found lodgment in minds prepared by a mechanical economics, the last remaining vestiges of the old French romanticism were swept away; a benevolent, egocentric universe was become unthinkable; progress was no longer the inherent law of matter and of life; but instead, everywhere change, disintegration and reintegration, a ceaseless and purposeless flux to what final end the human mind could not forecast. Thus at a stroke the benevolent cosmos of the fathers, wherein for generations men had been providing themselves with sure refuges, was swept away; and with its passing passed the old faiths—faith in freedom of the will, in a purposive providence, in a universe that had been long in travail to bring forth man, its last and dearest offspring for whom all things work together for good. And with the decay of the traditional faiths the younger generation was left to wander as best it might upon the bleak tablelands of impersonal energy. Spencer's "ultimate of ultimates," the Permanence of Force, that follows the law of evolution and dissolution, had given way to Faraday's electro-energy that is indifferent to purpose.

The intellectual backgrounds were thus preparing for a gloomier realism than Howells's or Garland's, a realism that took its departure from two postulates: that men are physical beings who can do no other than obey the laws of a physical universe; and that in the vast indifferentism of nature they are inconsequential pawns in a game that to human reason has no meaning or rules. To assume that fate which rules human destiny is malignant, is to assume a cosmic interest in man which finds no justification in science; Man at best is only an inconsequential atom in a mechanical flux, or at worst, as Jurgen puts it picturesquely, only a bubble in fermenting swill. Such a conception, of course, made slow headway against the traditional order of thought; and if it had not been aided by a changing economics it would have found few to follow a line of reasoning that led to such unpleasant conclusions. The mind of the artist is more susceptible to concrete social fact than to abstract physical principle, and the swift centralizing of economics in the eighties and the nineties provided the stimulus for the extraordinary reversal of thought marked by the contrast between Emerson and Theodore Dreiser. Emerson was the apotheosis of two centuries of decentralization that destroyed the pessimism brought to the new world by refugees from the old, and found its inevitable expression in the exaltation of the individual, free and excellent, the child of a beneficent order; whereas Dreiser was the first spokesman of a later America once more falling within the shadow of the pessimism that springs from every centralized society shut up within the portals of a static economics; that dwarfs the individual and nullifies his will, reducing him from a child of God to a serf.

Oddly enough it was in the West that the new spirit first expressed itself most adequately; amidst a society that was taking its first steps away from the traditional philosophy of the dispersion. Frank Norris in California, Dreiser in Indiana, Sherwood Anderson in Ohio, Masters and Sandburg and Vachel Lindsay in Illinois, were the spokesmen of the resentment welling up in the American heart at the loss of the older freedom and individual dignity.*

* The manuscript ends here. The first section of this chapter was to be "Edwin Markham and 'The Man with the Hoe.' " The second was to be on "The Rise of Naturalism: Stephen Crane; Frank Norris." The first item of the addenda gives material on this subject and on the two authors. The third would have been " Fiction Discovers the City."—*Publisher.*

ADDENDA

THE material given here comes from various sources, as indicated by the notes. The syllabus referred to is that for Professor Parrington's lectures at the University of Washington, *The American Novel Since 1890* (1925). The order here follows that of the contents of this book.

NATURALISM IN AMERICAN FICTION *

Naturalism originated in France. Term first used by Zola. Chief example—Flaubert's *Mme. Bovary.* Contrast between Zola and Flaubert reveals two diverse tendencies of the movement—a sociological study of background, with a multitude of characters dwarfed by the *milieu;* and psychological study of individual character.

Naturalism a child of nineteenth-century thought—offspring of Darwin, Marx, Comte, Taine. The scientific movement created a scientific attitude of mind and emphasized the law of causation. From this emerged two fruitful ideas: (1) biological determinism, (2) economic determinism. So Zola and Flaubert. Influence of Claude Bernard—"We take men from the hands of the physiologist solely . . . to solve scientifically the question of how men behave in society."

The criteria of naturalism are:

1. Objectivity. Seek the truth in the spirit of the scientist. "We naturalists, we men of science," Zola says, accepting Bernard's position, "we must admit of nothing occult; men are but phenomena and the conditions of phenomena."

2. Frankness. A rejection of Victorian reticence. The total man and woman must be studied —the deeper instincts, the endless impulses. The three strongest instincts are fear, hunger, sex. In the life of the ordinary person, the third is most critical, hence the naturalist makes much of it.

3. An amoral attitude toward material. The naturalist is not a judge, he holds no brief for any ethical standards. He records what happens. He "must possess a knowledge of the mechanisms inherent in man, show the machinery of his intellectual and sensory manifestations, under the influence of heredity and environment, such as physiology shall give them to us, and then finally, to exhibit man living in social conditions, produced by himself, which he modifies daily and in the heart of which he is undergoing constant transformation." (Zola.) This is difficult to accept. Puritanism.

* Notes for a lecture delivered at the University of California in 1922.—*Publisher.*

4. A philosophy of determinism. This is the vital principle of naturalism, setting it off from realism. The scientist has turned philosopher. It is the residuum of much pondering over life and its meaning, and may result from:

    a. Sociological emphasis—study of heredity and environment.

    b. A broader mechanistic philosophy—Flaubert, Dreiser.

    c. Fatalism: a world of malignant chance—Hardy.

5. A bias toward pessimism in selecting details. A reaction from the romantic conception of a purposive will.

Romance springs from the longings of a baffled and thwarted will, creating a world as we should like it wherein to find refuge. But the naturalist will tolerate no such refuge. He will envisage the truth, and the truth that he sees is that the individual is impotent in the face of things. Hence it is as the victim, the individual defeated by the world, and made a sardonic jest of, that the naturalist chooses to portray man. Always that conception creeps in. It is seen and felt throughout the texture of the story—a fate lurking in the background and visible to the reader—and at some dramatic moment the conviction comes home to the victim and is crystallized in bitter words wrenched from his baffled will. The business of the story is to lead him up to this crystallization.

There are two main forms—(1) Life is a trap. (2) Life is mean. So Strindberg's Countess Julie: "Everything is wreckage, that drifts over the water until it sinks, sinks." So Ray Pearson in Sherwood Anderson's *Winesburg, Ohio*: "Tricked, by Gad, tricked by life and made a fool of." So D. H. Lawrence: "We are prostituted, oh, prostituted by life." To Ma Westcott "Life is duty. It is a lie." This pressure may come from without—*milieu*—or from within—imperious desires—but the outcome is usually hopeless sorrow—sometimes stolid resignation, sometimes fierce protest, but with no other end than annihilation. An exception is Maugham's *Of Human Bondage*.

6. A bias in selection of characters. The naturalist commonly chooses one of three types:

    a. Characters of marked physique and small intellectual activity—persons of strong animal drives. They range all the way from morons like Norris's McTeague, Zola's Nana, and Dreiser's Jennie Gerhardt to natures like Hardy's Tess, and Sallie in *Of Human Bondage*.

    b. Characters of excited, neurotic temperament, at the mercy of moods, driven by forces that they do not stop to analyze. Such are Strindberg's Countess Julie, Sue, Emma Bovary, and the hero in *Of Human Bondage*. Sometimes this is aggravated by some physical defect, like a club-foot.

c. An occasional use of a strong character whose will is broken. Thus Hardy's Jude and the doctor in Strindberg's *By the Open Sea*. But such are comparatively infrequent.

Naturalism is pessimistic realism, with a philosophy that sets man in a mechanical world and conceives of him as victimized by that world. *Certain unconscious exaggerations of naturalism.* Since men are victimized either by outer forces—the *milieu*—or by inner drives—impulses and instincts—the naturalist from much brooding is subject to certain temptations:

1. From concern over a devastating *milieu* he may end in desiring to change that *milieu* to the end that men may achieve happiness. Hence he tends to lose his objectivity and scientific detachment, and becomes a partisan to a cause. Such was the fate of Zola. The philosopher of naturalism, in practice he abandoned his principles and became a reformer, attacking the church, the capitalistic order, etc. His *J'accuse* letter is characteristic of this. *Nana*, almost alone, preserves the naturalistic attitude. This was the failure of the first group of American naturalists—Frank Norris, Robert Herrick, Jack London.

2. From much study of inner drives of low-grade characters the naturalist is in danger of creating grotesques. Behavioristic psychology may prove to be a further temptation, in creating a "sex complex." So Masters's *Spoon River Anthology*, Sherwood Anderson, D. H. Lawrence, Frank Norris. Most common in the later American naturalists. So Brander Matthews.

3. From much emphasis on animal impulses the naturalist may turn man into an animal. Men are more than sex-driven creatures —the city is more than the slums. There are sewers, but why not accept the sewer without messing over its contents as they flow to disintegration? This is the commonest objection to naturalism. So Meredith: "The naturalist sees the hog in nature, and takes nature for the hog." It is certainly an overcorrection—a reaction against the complacent optimism of romanticism—against too much shutting of the eyes to slums and filth and sewers. To a mechanist like Dreiser, who traces life and conduct back to chemistry, or to the behaviorist, who traces it to ducts and glands, it is

rational. The charge may be true of Zola, of De Maupassant, of Anderson, of Lawrence, but it is not true of Hardy, of Maugham.

Naturalism and the Conception of Tragedy. Naturalistic books are almost inevitably tragedies, but the philosophy of naturalism that underlies them has played havoc with the Aristotelian conception of tragedy. As Ludwig Lewisohn says, it has "rendered the traditional principle of tragedy wholly archaic." According to the Aristotelian tradition, tragedy results when an essentially noble character of heroic proportions transgresses an immutable moral law by a self-originating will and suffers the punishment dealt by poetic justice. So Macbeth, Othello, Lear, Hamlet. But this assumes two thing: (1) an eternally changeless moral law; (2) the existence of a purposive will. Both of these the naturalist refuses to accept. Compare Hardy.

It became clear that the self-originating element in human action is small. The individual acts in harmony with his character, which is largely the result of complex and uncontrollable causes. It became even clearer that among the totality of moral values an absolute validity can be assigned to a few only. Hence the basic conception of tragic guilt was undermined from within and from without. The transgression of an immutable moral law by a self-originating will was seen to be an essentially meaningless conception, since neither eternally changeless moral law nor an uncaused volition is to be found in the universe that we perceive.[1]

The tragedy of naturalism lies in the disintegration and the pity or irony with which we contemplate man and his fate in the world.

Naturalism and the Traditional American Temper. The two most characteristic qualities of the American temper are Puritanism and optimism—the belief in the supremacy of the moral law, and the conviction that this is a good world that man shapes to his will. This is to be explained historically: the former is traditionally English, the latter a product of new-world economics—a decentralized society. Pessimistic determinism results inevitably from the sense of social pressure on the individual. Social complexity entails a feeling of coercive regimentation by forces too strong to contend against. These forces are both internal and external: environment or the social machine; heredity or the physical machine. The most complete dwarfing of the individual will and significance takes place in the most crowded societies, producing a corresponding philosophy and psychology. So the fatalism of the Orient and the dream of

[1] Ludwig Lewisohn, *Modern Drama*, New York, 1915, p. 3.

Nirvana. The first widespread philosophy of determinism among English people was spread by Calvinism. Predestination was an alien thought, the last expression of a world depressed by Roman regimentation and degeneration. Augustine preached that men are evil, and men are doomed. This old-world dogma was brought to America, where regimentation was impossible. A free economics created a free-will philosophy and psychology. The will to succeed. This flowered in Emerson. Philosophical optimism. The world is good, man is good: let him stand upon his instincts and there abide and the whole world will come round to him. "Trust thyself." Since Emerson's time a new world has been emerging. The old shadow is falling across the American mind. Determinism is in the air.

Complexity and American Determinism. Complexity springs from:

1. Machine industrialism. The bigness of the economic machine dwarfs the individual and creates a sense of impotency.

2. The great city reduces the individual to a unit. By machine methods of transportation and quantity output individual differences are worn away. We dress, live, think, work, play, alike. The *Saturday Evening Post* is fast regimenting the American mind. Standardization.

3. Centralization of wealth is creating a caste regimentation.

4. A mechanistic psychology. Behaviorism: stimulus and response; ducts and glands. The individual conceived as a mechanism driven by instincts and habits.

America today is the greatest, most complex machine the world has ever known. Individualism is giving way to regimentation, caste, standardization. Optimism is gone; pessimism is on the horizon. The psychology of naturalism is being prepared.

Three American writers began an experiment in naturalism in the middle nineties—Stephen Crane, Frank Norris, and Harold Frederic. The early death of all three stopped the movement, which was speedily overwhelmed by the romantic deluge and the muckraking zeal. Crane was tubercular and died at twenty-nine; Norris was cut down in the early thirties; Harold Frederic removed to England, where he died.

I

STEPHEN CRANE *

Stephen Crane was the genius of his generation. His work began
with *Maggie: A Girl of the Streets* (1893). "It was the first bit of
naturalism in American letters . . . an episodic bit of slum fiction
ending with the tragic quality of Greek drama." "The first ironical
novel ever written by an American." It was privately printed at
first, and not published until 1896. It is detached, objective,
amoral, dealing with a world without virtues but tyrannized by
taboos. It is a bit of life, beginning and ending casually. Here is
the end:

> In a room a woman sat at a table, eating like a fat monk in a picture.
> A soiled, unshaven man pushed open the door and entered.
> "Well," said he, "Mag's dead." [2]

It is a world without virtue and yet one that uses the social
taboo to condemn Mag—the only pure one of the lot. The story
was an attack on everything that was respectable in American literature—a notable achievement in a world of shoddy romanticism.
It was an affront to every instinct of the genteel tradition, and was
rejected by a public steeped in that same shoddy romanticism.

Crane's next novel was the first great American war story—
The Red Badge of Courage (1894). It was a *tour de force*, inspired
by Zola's *Le débâcle*, but more by Tolstoi—*War and Peace* and
perhaps *Sebastopol.* The individual is caught between the external
war machine and the inner instinct machine. There is a conflict of
impulses—fear, pride, the instinct of self-preservation, chiefly the
fear of fear. The hero is at the mercy of the crowd psychology and
blind chance. Crane follows Tolstoi in assuming that victories are
accidents, the outcome of a blind clash of unintelligent forces,
rather than due to strategy and generalship. The study is psychological—that of the fear of the recruit, his feeling that he alone is
marked as the target of the enemy. The impression of helplessness
is the same as in *Maggie*—both are atoms among a host of other
atoms.

Short Stories. The best are "The Blue Hotel," "The Experiment
in Misery," "The Open Boat." The first is a story of social responsibility and social guilt. The murder of the Swede is just part

* From lecture notes and the syllabus.—*Publisher.*
[2] Stephen Crane, *Works*, New York, 1926, Vol. 10, p. 216.

of the backwash of a topsy-turvy life: the victim of things. "Every
sin is the result of a collaboration." The second is a story of a
"hobo"—down-and-outer, who hears "the war of the city in his
ear." "The protest of the wretch who feels the touch of the imperturbable granite wheels, and who then cries with an impersonal
eloquence, with a strength not from him, giving voice to the wail
of a whole section, a class, a people." [3]

2

FRANK NORRIS *

The most stimulating and militant of our early naturalists—the
only one who wrote consciously with a definite creed. He had
thought out a naturalistic philosophy under the inspiration of Zola.
"He was never without a yellow paper-covered novel of Zola in his
hand," wrote his brother of him. His two chief novels reveal the
twin tendencies as revealed in *Nana* and *Le débâcle:* The study of
the individual in his reaction to environment, and the study of
social forces and their impact upon a group of related individuals.

His Work. Falls into three groups: (1) Romance—*Blix, Moran of
the Lady Letty*; (2) Naturalism—*McTeague, Vandover and the Brute;*
(3) *The Pit* and *A Deal in Wheat.* Between the two latter groups
stands *The Octopus.* The dates of the earlier works uncertain.
Commonly believed that Norris began as a romantic and worked
out of it slowly. Another view that he wrote romances as a means
of arriving, side by side with his serious work. Thus he seems to
have begun *McTeague* about 1894— although it was not published
till 1899.

Theory. His passion for truth more ardent—or more noisy—
than Crane's: his objectivity less. The strong conviction of a
deterministic universe was on him, but he never quite attained the
scientific detachment. His nature large and eager. Like Zola he
loved large canvases. This induced him rather to the sociological
than to the individualistic study. *The Octopus* more representative
of his genius than *McTeague.* Man in society, his theme: not mere
men and women as ends in themselves. This grew on him—the
second phase. The novelist must deal "with elemental forces,
motives that stir whole nations. These cannot be handled as
abstractions in fiction. . . . The social tendencies must be ex-

[3] *Ibid.*, Vol. II, p. 21.   * Lecture notes.—*Publisher.*

pressed by means of an analysis of the characters of the men and women who compose that society, and the two must be combined and manipulated to evolve the purpose—to find the value of x."[4] Above all, avoid propaganda.

Unskillfully treated, the story may dwindle down and degenerate into mere special pleading, and the novelist becomes a polemicist, a pamphleteer, forgetting that although his first consideration is to prove his case, his *means* must be living human beings, not statistics, and that his tools are not figures, but pictures of life as he sees it. . . .

Consider the reverse—*Fécondité*, for instance. The purpose for which Zola wrote the book ran away with him. He really did care more for the depopulation of France than he did for his work. Result—sermons on the fruitfulness of women, special pleading, a farrago of dry, dull incidents, overburdened and collapsing under the weight of a theme that should have intruded only indirectly.[5]

He never quite arrives at the amoral attitude. Ethical values persist in intruding themselves, sometimes quite incidentally, as in *McTeague*, but increasingly, as in *The Octopus* and *The Pit*.

"McTEAGUE"

Dedicated to Gates. The first considerable contribution to naturalism by an American writer. His carefully written work over which he labored five years.

Theme. A study in character disintegration that follows upon economic pressure. The unmaking of a man and woman by the caprice of events. The characters are simple. McTeague is heavy and stupid, slow in his movements but a blind bull when aroused. Trina neat and pretty but with unhappy potentialities in her thrift. In neither is there a will-to-power strong enough to give strength of character.

The Note of Determinism. A world of chance that victimizes them. The note struck by the lottery and the $5,000. By chance McTeague became a dentist, met Trina, proposed. But the chance that was making a man of him and a woman of Trina was preparing their downfall through Marcus Schouler. The wrestling-match was the turning-point. The two disintegrate together, each aggravating the weakness of the other. As Trina's neatness was pulling Mac up and making him self-respecting, so her thrift grew into miserli-

[4] *The Responsibilities of the Novelist*, "The Novel with a 'Purpose,'" Garden City, N. Y., 1928, Vol. 7, p. 22.
[5] *Ibid.*, p. 22.

ness under pressure of his failure to provide, and this embittered the essentially fair and generous nature of Mac.

Inner Drives. Little sex in the book after the first complication. Both Mac and Trina caught unexpectedly, yet handled differently. The latter pure naturalism. "The Woman is awakened, and, starting from her sleep, catches blindly at what first the newly awakened eyes light upon. It is a spell, a witchery, ruled by chance alone, inexplicable—a fairy queen enamored of a clown with ass's ears." [6] But in McTeague, oddly enough, the same instinct is judged and pronounced evil. Norris abandons the amoral attitude and argues that heritage from the lower life is evil. It is the weeds that spring up and stifle, as in Sherwood Anderson's "Seeds."

> Below the fine fabric of all that was good in him ran the foul stream of hereditary evil, like a sewer. The vices and sins of his father and his father's father, to the third and fourth and five hundredth generation, tainted him. The evil of an entire race flowed in his veins. Why should it be? He did not desire it. Was he to blame? [7]

The entire handling of sex in Trina, from the first frightened yielding to the later docile submission to Mac's brutality, his sadism, is admirably handled from the point of view of modern psychology. Norris was not a psychologist but in this he succeeded surprisingly.

Romantic Elements. Yet even in this severe study Norris has yielded to his romantic tendencies.

1. His patent effort to give dramatic unity to the whole through the symbol of gold. An exaggeration that is almost Dickens-like, with its warping singleness. The gold tooth, the $5,000, Trina's twenty-dollar gold pieces, the imaginary gold plate of Maria Macapa, the absurd canary in the gilt cage, the discovery of the gold mine. The wonder is that he didn't give Trina gold hair instead of black.

2. The use of a minor action: Maria Macapa and old Zerkow. The same pursuit of a phantom and the same outcome in murder. McTeague and Trina are real; Maria and Zerkow are grotesques.

3. The use of foils: Old Grannis and Miss Baker. Justified in romantic literature by contrast. The self-effacing, timid drawing together contrasted with the brute directness of McTeague. They do not marry, and preserve their dream world.

6 Frank Norris, *Complete Works*, New York, n. d., Vol. III, p. 58.
7 *Ibid.*, p. 22.

4. The use of the revenge motive: Marcus Schouler—the dramatic pursuit into Death Valley and the end.

"VANDOVER AND THE BRUTE"

An unfinished work—but a huge and terrible torso.

Theme. Revealed in the title. The two natures of man and the sloughing-off of the higher till the wolf is left. Done with a terrible directness, till the naked man is on all fours, padding up and down in his room. A grim and sordid theme but not quite achieved. The thing got away from him. If he had chiseled it as he chiseled *McTeague*, holding it off objective and amoral, it would have been a tremendous piece. But it is insufficiently motivated.

Determinism. A study in will. Vandover set over against Charlie Geary and Dolly Haight. The latter a victim of momentary weakness; the former a victim of constitutional pliability. A sensuous egotism that grows and consumes. Geary alone survives—the egoist who drives forward ruthlessly. A study of the slow, long descent—a chain of circumstances that finally binds him hand and foot. His props knocked away one by one—partly by fate, partly by himself: his father, the girl whom he loves, his concern for respectable opinion, his art, his money. The conclusion intensely dramatic—more so than the romance of *McTeague*.

The comment of Garland on *McTeague* applies equally to *Vandover:* "What avail is this study of sad lives? for it does not even lead to a notion of social betterment." His interest is "not that of the ethical teacher."

"THE OCTOPUS"

McTeague and *Vandover* are of the city and its sordid evil ways. They are studies in psychology. *The Octopus* is of the great California valleys and the evils that have come into the farm life with the railroad. It is a study in economics—the first of a long series of such studies. One can easily see how the theme caught the imagination of Norris, how his mind felt the relief from the narrow world and sordid wretchedness of *Vandover*. A certain magnificence in Norris responded to the epic breadth of the valleys—they fired his imagination—the vast sweep and power of nature: the rich soil, the brilliant sun that lays its palpitating heat upon the land, the quick response in flowers and fruit. The land is eager to produce; its fruitfulness is overpowering. There is an epic sweep of life and

reproduction here; and this epic of the soil is linked with the tragedy wrought by the Southern Pacific—the economic machinery
of man's making. The facts were well known and they took hold of
Norris's imagination. His sympathy is aroused and yet instead of
attacking the railroad he weaves it into his deterministic philosophy.

Theme. Ostensibly the wheat. Norris planned a huge trilogy of
its growing (*The Octopus*), marketing (*The Pit*), consumption (*The
Wolf*—never written). In reality, the impotence of unimportant
individuals in the struggle with things as they are. In *The Octopus*
the individual is dwarfed by the vast spaces, he is crumpled and
despoiled by the railroad. The flock of sheep destroyed by the
train is only a symbol of the men and women of the valley, under
the wheels of modern industrialism.

Action. A huge canvas with crowding figures and abundant
action. "The canvas swarms with actualities—plowing, planting,
harvesting, sheep-herding, merry-making, rabbit-killing, love,
labor, birth, death"—all keyed high and swept into a palpitating
background. A "strongly interwrought group of episodes," that
fall into certain series of developments too:

1. The atrophy of Magnus Derrick, which might well be a story
in itself.

2. The development of Annixter, "out of an absolute, yet not
gross, materiality," through the love of Hilma Tree; and then their
final annihilation.

3. A host of background characters—supernumeraries—that
give a sense of epic sweep.

The Note of Romance. The riot of color, of life, arouse the latent
romance of his nature. He cannot remain detached but projects
himself into the story in the person of Vanamee. He returns to the
use of the symbol as in *McTeague*—the wheat. He allows his villain
to perish melodramatically. How much more convincing is the
figure of Charlie Geary setting Vandover to work than S. Behrman
in the hold of the vessel.

In the end he abandons the amoral attitude. After proclaiming
the doctrine of determinism—that the railroads are the masters—
not the puppets of men—he takes refuge in a moral order. In the
large balance, the wheat remains, rectifying wrong—saving other
lives to make good what it here destroys. "The larger view always
and through all shams, all wickednesses, discovers the Truth that

will, in the end, prevail, and all things, surely, inevitably, resist-lessly, work together for good." [8] Nevertheless in contemplating the injustice done by the railroads, Norris neither demands nor expects relief.

The Octopus exemplifies Norris' theory of broad-scale work. It "draws conclusions from a whole congeries of forces, social develop-ment, race impulses." It "devotes itself not to the study of men but of man."

SIDNEY LANIER *

An original nature. Rejects both the genteel tradition and the ideals of the rising middle class. An artist to whom life means beauty.

He revivifies nature—is almost pagan in his adoration of the beauty of the sun and water. A half-personification of the sun-myth. He is essentially religious. To Longfellow and Tennyson nature is pretty embroidery; to Emerson it is a dwelling-place of the oversoul; to Lanier it is an object of adoration. See "The Marshes of Glynn."

He attacks industrialism—the first of the poets to cry out against it as a deadly blight on life and civilization. See "Corn," "The Symphony," "The Jacquerie."

He seeks a new religion, recognizing a quantitative element.

[8] Frank Norris, *The Octopus*, New York, 1906, p. 652.
* Lecture notes.—*Publisher.*

THE INCOMPARABLE MR. CABELL *

The successive volumes of James Branch Cabell have provided the tribe of critical Jeffries with a rich vein of diversion. They have recognized no closed season in their full-lunged pursuit of the strange heirs of Mr. Cabell's invention, and such Homeric absurdities of comment have been flung at him, that he is in a fair way to become our classic example of the fatuousness of contemporary estimates. As whimsical as Bernard Shaw, as provocative as Chesterton, he is more incomprehensible than either to all readers who do not choose to like what they have not always liked. Professing to be a romancer, and defending the glory of romance with inimitable witchery of phrase, he writes no romance that lovers of convention can understand. The lovely fabrics of his tales of Poictesme are all shimmer and sheen, woven of magic and veiling mysteries, instead of the correct taffeta and grosgrain; and the brilliant stuff of his tales of gallantry is fashioned of wit and poetry, instead of the customary wigs and sword play. Those to whom romance suggests *When Knighthood Was in Flower*, will find only obscurities and coarseness in *Figures of Earth* (1921) and *Jurgen* (1919, *enl.* ed. 1921); and those who delight in the stage rufflings of *Monsieur Beaucaire*, will discover only a libertine in *The Cords of Vanity* (1909, rev. ed. 1920). And if the reader boggles at such tales what can he hope to make of that strange, ironical whimsy, *The Cream of the Jest* (1917, rev. ed. 1922)? One needs to walk warily in dealing with Mr. Cabell, or the jest of which he is such a master will turn sardonically upon the critic. In all his thinking vague hinterlands lie behind the commonplace, cryptic meanings lurk behind the obvious; and the credulous, easy-going reader finds himself puzzled, and at last floundering quite hopelessly in a land of bogs and marsh-lights. And yet was ever another writer born to us Americans so insistent upon being understood? He has elaborated his views of life and art at length, and repeated them in successive volumes over nearly a score of years; and finally in what may have been a mood of sheer disgust at the stupidity of those who buy books, he reëlaborated his philosophy and wrote it out in good

* Reprinted by permission from *The Pacific Review*, December, 1921.—*Publisher*

set terms within the covers of a single volume. *Beyond Life* is an essay altogether remarkable for its haunting beauty of phrase, its honest agnosticism, its brooding irony. It is enough to turn one cynic to consider that so noble a book should have called forth from a reputable gentleman, presumably of good taste and sound judgment, the comment that it "contains cheap and shallow pessimistic observations on human limitations."

That *Beyond Life* (1919), with other of Mr. Cabell's books, contains "observations on the limitations of human nature," is quite obvious; for Mr. Cabell deals in comedy, and what is to become of comedy if it shall not observe those limitations and laugh at them? That it is even pessimistic may likewise be argued with some plausibility; but to assert that it is cheap and shallow is preposterous. An inquisitive mind, deeply concerned with ultimate values, cannot be cheap and shallow. And yet the fault of such widespread misinterpretation may lie in part at Mr. Cabell's own doorstep. An inveterate jester, his sallies often carry implications far beyond the obvious; his strange whimsies spring from depths of thought and emotion beyond the understanding of the careless. His attitude towards life is an odd mixture of the modern and the medieval: there is a medieval simplicity and frankness, a naïve wonder at the mystery that underlies the common, an incorrigible idealism; and this medieval attitude is drenched in modern agnosticism. He passes easily from a broad Chaucerian humor that laughs frankly at the relations of men and women, to a mystical idealization of those relations; and the problem of reconciling the humor and the ideal becomes a serious business with him. He hates the cant and dishonesty of our *bourgeois* existence, and he refuses to take seriously the host of petty concerns that most of us are very serious about. If he were less the artist he would join the disaffected and turn to rend this foolish world; but the spirit of comedy saves him and he contents himself with a jest. But the Cabellian jest uncovers depths of meditation that reveal the philosopher and the poet. In his own large meaning of the word Mr. Cabell is an economist. He is greatly dissatisfied with the "futile body-wasting," which under the "dynamic illusion known as common sense" passes for life, and is concerned to discover what abiding increment a man may get from his body during its brief existence as an entity. His mind is haunted with a sense of realities that lie beneath the surface appearances, and that insist on trickling from his pen in strange comments. It is a careless reader who is deceived or put off the scent by his whimsical vocabulary, who insists on conventional meanings for words which Mr. Cabell chooses to use otherwise than conventional persons use them. Romance and realism—words with which he plays constantly and upon which he hangs his philosophy—do not signify the spurious romance of childish minds, or the shoddy realism of practical minds. If one must insist upon translating his vocabulary into ordinary terms, let us understand that to Mr. Cabell romance and realism mean idealism and conventionalism; and to the profound distinction between these two attitudes towards life, he dedicates his work.

I have called Mr. Cabell a poet, and the justification lies in his persistent idealization of life in terms of beauty. At his birth he was endowed by an unkind fate with imagination. Now imagination may be a very pretty and amiable gift, highly useful for gilding one's egoism, putting honey in thistles, proving itself practical by arraying life in gay robes in order that it may seem an altogether lovely and desirable mistress; or it may prove a decidedly parlous faculty to play with. It can summon bogies, and terrors that are vaster and more real than bogies. A brooding imagination can work havoc with one's complacency. When Carlyle was in a mood to enjoy his nerves he would let his imagination range beyond the comfortable confines of convention, to consider the universe and the position of man therein—the black flow of time and the terrifying immensity of background against which man is set; and he would come back to dinner with Jane Welsh Carlyle with a sick stomach and an ill temper. It was not very gallant, but it was very natural to a man unnerved by what he had contemplated. Considered with open eyes reality is too overpowering for weak man, and because he could not relieve the tension with a jest, Carlyle's imagination inflicted chronic dyspepsia upon him. To conventional persons the dyspepsia and Jane Welsh Carlyle's sharp replies to her husband's ill humor, seem the important reality, and the overpowering visions of time and space that were at the root of the family discord, seem no other than romance. In this curious world of convention all things are topsy-turvy, and it needs a tremendous effort of will to set them only a little right.

To this effort Mr. Cabell's life work has been dedicated with unruffled urbanity. Like Carlyle he chooses to roam far in his philosophic quests, and like Thoreau he comes home at nightfall

with little more than a handful of stardust in his wallet. He loves
to sally forth on the greatest of adventures—the pursuit of reality
where it lies broadcast, hidden from practical eyes that refuse to
see. He is impelled by the old wonder that has haunted men from
the beginning of their long upward climb; the wonder and the fear
of life. Now to anyone but a fool or a poet, only too plainly life is
petty and gross and inconsequential, from the moment when with
superfluous blood and pain we are brought into the world, to the
time when we return by an unlovely process to chemical elements.
It is compounded of vanity, as the old poet long ago observed.
The practical, about which we make so much pother and over which
we chatter so foolishly, is only an illusion which men hug because
it keeps them in self-conceit. Mr. Cabell refuses to accept any such
illusions at their face value. He will not be humbugged by foolish
persons who pretend to talk wisely. What is man? he insists on
asking: A parasite on the thin rind of a planet that swings silently
through interstellar space—"an ape who chatters to himself of
kinship with the archangels while filthily he digs for groundnuts."
If this is the reality to which the philosopher must come finally—
and like Hamlet Mr. Cabell does not shirk the contemplation of
graveyard facts—then must the thoughtful man accept logically
a frank pessimism, and on this foundation build such a hut as may
best shelter him for the few days of his unintelligible life. Over this
sorry conclusion Mr. Cabell broods much, and because he is a
human being with a will to enjoy life and think well of himself, he
uses every faculty to scramble out of the pit and find a pleasanter
refuge for the brief time of his existence. The idealist in him
engages the pessimist, and like so many other moderns he goes out
in quest of that which may keep him sane. It is true that man is an
ape reft of his tail and grown rusty at climbing, but is that the
whole story? It is evident that men in all times have refused to
believe that they are not something other than apes—their very
dreams seem to belie a conclusion so mean and ignoble. Is there not
some deeper *élan vital*, some hidden impulse that drives man forward and upward even while his mind is on groundnuts? "Yet
more clearly do I perceive," argues the idealist, "that this same
man is a maimed god. . . . He is under penalty condemned to
compute eternity with false weights and to estimate infinity with a
yardstick; and he very often does it. . . . There lies the choice
which every man must make—or rationally to accept his own

limitations? or stupendously to play the fool and swear that he is at will omnipotent."

This would seem to be a hard choice, but Mr. Cabell does not hesitate. He patches up his agnosticism with the will to believe, on the pragmatic grounds that it seems to work. For man "rationally to accept his own limitations," is to defeat everything worth while in life; it is to yield the battle to a black pessimism. Whereas "stupendously to play the fool and swear that he is at will omnipotent," may end in creating the will to omnipotence, and the fool in some preposterous fashion may prove that he is indeed divine. Let man but accept his logical limitations and he returns to the ape reft of more than his tail, fallen to gibbering in the mud, refusing to take hold of that rope of sand by which miraculously he has drawn himself forward hitherto. For accepting his limitations means contenting himself with material fact, and "the trouble with facts seems to be, that if one treats them out of relation to the rest of life, they become lies." In the "stupefying mist of common sense" men walk blindly. The practical, the conventional, are alien to the deeper reality which is shadowed forth by emotions and dreams; which refuses to disclose itself nakedly, but hides behind symbols, haunting the mind even while one is pottering among inconsequentials. This deeper reality itself may be but a dream, but nevertheless it possesses the power of creating a will to believe, upon which hangs man's destiny. Hence the tales which we tell ourselves are significant because through some occult process they foreshadow the thing that may be; they prod the foolish will to omnipotence to believe that we shall outgrow the ape. For grown rusty at climbing, the ape-man "however dimly, feels himself to be a symbol, and the frail representative of Omnipotence in a place that is not home; and so strives blunderingly, from mystery to mystery, with pathetic makeshifts, not understanding anything, greedy in all desires, and honeycombed with poltroonery, and yet ready to give all, and to die fighting, for the sake of that undemonstrable idea."

It is because he is terrified at the meanness of what practical men call reality, that Mr. Cabell turns away from it to find the true life in dreams. Not only are they pleasanter, they are more useful; they are all that man has to aid him in the appalling task of getting himself out of the slime, that he may walk in green fields. We need to turn Prospero's words around—our dreams are such

stuff as we are made on. They alone are real and salutary, for
amid all their ramblings they seem dimly to suggest some end;
amidst their rank egoisms they seem to foreshadow a purpose: and
may not that end and purpose be the eventual creation of a life for
man that shall be worthy of his dreams? It is illogical to assume
that man can pull himself up by his own bootstraps, but how else
shall he pull himself up? Is not man the inveterate romancer somehow blindly creating a noble romance of man? "To what does the
whole business tend?" he asks at the conclusion of *Beyond Life*,
"—why, how in heaven's name should I know? We can but be
content to note that all goes forward, toward something. . . . It
may be that we are nocturnal creatures perturbed by rumors of a
dawn which comes inevitably, as prologue to a day wherein we and
our children have no part whatever. It may be that when our
arboreal propositus descended from his palm tree and began to walk
upright about the earth, his progeny were forthwith committed
to a journey in which today is only a way-station. Yet I prefer
to take it that we are components of an unfinished world, and
that we are but as seething atoms which ferment toward its making, if merely because man as he now exists can hardly be the
finished product of any Creator whom one could very heartily
revere. We are being made into something quite unpredictable, I
imagine: and through the purging and the smelting, we are sustained by an instinctive knowledge that we are being made into
something better. For this we know, quite incommunicably, and
yet as surely as we know that we will have it thus. And it is this
will that stirs in us to have the creatures of earth and the affairs of
earth, not as they are, but 'as they ought to be,' which we call
romance. But when we note how visibly it sways all life we perceive that we are talking about God."

From this persistent will to romance—the incorrigible propensity
to follow the dynamic illusion of dreams that is so deep an instinct
of human nature—Mr. Cabell deduces a conception of art that to
careless readers seems whimsically perverse; and from it likewise
emerges the lambent irony that plays like diffused lightning about
the horizons of his thought. The function of art in society, he
insists, is to comfort and inspire man with its divine beauty.
Without the artist this is but a grim and forbidding place where
men live; and unless every man is somewhat the artist, and seeks
his compensations in the lure of romance, it must remain grim and

forbidding. It is therefore the privilege and the duty of the artist "to prevaricate tenderly about the universe"; to create for life a meaning that is not apparent, by clothing it in beauty and adducing for it a noble significance. It is his mission to lure men away from the contemplation of facts which terrify or debase, from all ignoble and depressing realism, to pursue the ideal and entice the imagination to enter and dwell in a world as it ought to be. The artist, therefore, is a Moses in the wilderness, pointing men to the Promised Land, and even enabling them to go forward and taste its fruits while they still dwell in the wilderness.

Now of all the dreams which lure men, the one universal and potent dream, Mr. Cabell asserts with Freudian understanding, is the woman dream. Its roots are deep in the ape-animal; it drives men inexorably, for upon it depends the very existence of the race. And therefore, a shrewd mother-nature has somehow transmuted its base materials into the very stuff of romance, commingling with it all high and generous impulses, making of it the loveliest dream that visits man's weak head. In consequence of which ironic transmutation this lovely dream "hoodwinks humanity through the dynamic illusion known as love, in order that humanity may endure, and the groans of a lover be perpetuated in the wails of an infant." Considered in one light this is the very "cream of the jest" that nature perpetrates upon man; but considered in another light, does it not turn out to be the supreme jest which man has perpetrated upon nature? For once he has been taught the alphabet of romance, through the crude necessity of race preservation, he has gone far in his studies, and turned romancer on a great scale. From this raw material of biological sex-love he has woven the fabrics of his religion, of his art, of his idealism; he has dipped it in gleaming dyes, twisted it to quaint patterns, fashioned from it lovely robes to cover what is ugly. It is the wellspring and source of all romance.

Through this open door of woman-worship Mr. Cabell chooses to enter his world of deeper realities. "There is in every human being that which demands communion with something more fine and potent than itself," and this something more fine and potent he seeks in the woman of his dreams. It was so when the world was young, and it will be so as long as there is youth left in the world. In early times this object of adoration was the witch-woman, the Circes and Calypsos of ancient tales; later it became the lady-mistress of chivalric ideals; today it is the dream maiden whom the young man woos but never finds in marriage, and not finding her is impelled to turn to the ever-young and ever-lovely Helens and Ettarres of old romance. A good half of Mr. Cabell's work is given over to this curious celebration of woman-worship. It is elaborated in *Domnei* (1920), in *Jurgen*, in *Figures of Earth*. In the strange tales of the land of Poictesme the drama flows from the balking and thwarting of this woman quest by the Dame Niafers and Dame Lisas of the commonplace world, to man's undoing. Nevertheless "the long, high, fruitless questing does not ever end, but, rather, is temporarily remitted for the society of Dame Niafer and of Dame Lisa. For . . . one perceives that, even in remote Poictesme, those aging nympholepts, Dom Manuel and Jurgen—they also—were heartened to endure the privileges of happily married persons by a sure faith, discreetly left unvoiced, that these hard-won, fond, wearisome, and implacable wives were, after all, just temporary makeshifts. By and by would Freydis and Helen return, at their own season."—For the dream persists in the very face of present fact, and in this lies man's hope. "In youth all men that live have been converts if but in transitory allegiance, to that religion of the world's youth—to the creed of *domnei*, or woman-worship." Now it is "the very essence of *domnei*, that the woman one loves is providentially set between the lover's apprehension and God, as the mobile and vital image and corporeal reminder of Heaven, as a quick symbol of beauty and holiness, of purity and perfection. In her the lover views all qualities which can be comprehended by merely human faculties." "If but in honor, his heart stays bound to his first and only real love, that woman of whom he never tires. Her coming is not yet. He can but wait, sustained by his sure faith . . . that some day her glory will be apparent, and he will enter gladly into her secret kingdom, and will find her kisses all that in youth he foreknew to be not impossible. . . . And meanwhile this prescience, somehow, informs all art . . . and makes it to him a vital thing. . . . And there seems to be no beauty in the world save those stray hints of her, whose ultimate revealment is not yet. . . . And it is very often through desire to express his faith in this withheld perfection, of which he has been conscious in broken glimpses from afar, that he turns artist. . . . For every art is a confession of faith in that which is not yet."

But however adroitly man has turned the jest against nature, and erected a noble palace from base materials, the jest remains, mixed with the mortar, and the structure cannot endure for long. It is insubstantial, and at any moment the cloud-capped towers may disintegrate and the dream palace disappear, leaving not a rack behind. There remains only the jest. This unhappy ending Mr. Cabell foresees, and hence emerges the profound irony that underlies all his writing. To such disillusionment must all things come. Life is no more than a comedy, played by puppets; bitter, with more tears than laughter in it; yet because tears are futile and unnerving, what remains for the gallant gentleman but to confront life with a jest? Mr. Cabell does not wholly forego his chivalric ideal even while he is contemplating the vanity of all endings in the light of their beginnings. As Horvendile the clerk, he clings to it, even though he is doomed to walk the streets of Lichfield, Virginia, in the form of Felix Kennaston, who passes—to his own incredulous amusement—as a personage of some importance, with two automobiles and money in four banks. He possesses the magic sigil of Scoteia, by the potency of which he can send forth his soul to meet Ettarre, and recover the raptures that Felix Kennaston no longer knows. But the sigil of Scoteia turns out to be the half-top of a pomade glass from his wife's dressing-table; the potency is gone; and he remains at last no more than a respectable citizen with his automobiles and money in four banks. *The Cream of the Jest* reduces the chivalric ideal to pure irony.

By a transition more natural, perhaps, to a Virginian than to another American, Mr. Cabell turns from the contemplation of chivalry to the study of gallantry; and shifts the theme of his romances from the ecstatic adoration of the Woman, whom to possess is to lose, to the gay pursuit and enjoyment of women. In "The Rivet in Grandfather's Neck" he chooses to set a decidedly shabby and roué gallantry over against a somewhat futile and antiquated southern chivalry. He loves both the gallant and the gentleman, and he spares neither; they are equally the descendants of that Cavalier ideal which flourished so rankly in the soil of the old planter society; nevertheless the quaint and lovable Rudolph Musgrave with his gentle heroics comes off distinctly better than his brilliant half-brother, the novelist John Charteris. One might, indeed, wonder at Mr. Cabell's treatment of the artist Charteris, were it not so distinctly Shavian. It is odd how similar is his conception of the artist to the definition of Shaw—one who wriggles into the confidence of women to learn their secrets only to betray them. Nevertheless Jack Charteris, the brilliant thinker and talker of *Beyond Life*, mouthpiece of the Cabellian philosophy, deserves better treatment than he gets in the story of this sorry escapade; he comes quite too near the likeness of the mountebank Sheridan. In *The Cords of Vanity* gallantry reveals itself more attractively; it is gilded with youth and wit and poetry. It is Congreve at his best, scintillating, brilliant, with a delightful affectation of pose and gesture; and it is Marlowe also, with its galloping wit steeped in pure poetry. There is the true Elizabethan rapture of fine words and lovely images and quaint conceits. "Meantime," says young Robert Townsend, "being in love, I refined upon the notions of love with the ingenuity of an Elizabethan." There you have the spirit of the book. It is more than a pretty piece of paganism; it is the brightest tale of gallantry in our literature, masterly in the restrained irony of its inimitable conclusion.

It is obvious, however, that the mood which finally will receive dramatization from Mr. Cabell cannot be summed up in the ideal of gallantry. What that mood is one finds revealed at length by John Charteris in *Beyond Life*. It is the quintessence of irony distilled from long observation of human life, but it is not Congreve, much less is it Sheridan. Those shameless and selfish roués began as artists but they ended as mountebanks; life taught them cynicism and not tenderness; it sharpened their wit and dulled their sympathy. The higher irony lay quite beyond their natures. But with Mr. Cabell tenderness, sympathy, an ardent concern for the inevitable failure that lies in wait upon aspiration, are so strong and urgent that under the governance of a mind less intellectual, they must inevitably run into sentimentality. But there is in Mr. Cabell something of the intellectual austerity of Matthew Arnold, and it conducts him to the same ends. Consider such a passage as this: "Through a merciful dispensation, we are one and all of us created very vain and very dull. . . . Vanity it is that pricks us indefatigably to play the ape to every dream romance induces; yet vanity is but the stirrup-cup: and urgent need arises that human dullness retain us (as it does) securely blinded, lest we observe the wayside horrors of our journey and go mad. One moment of clear vision as to man's plight in the universe would be quite sufficient to set the most philosophic gibbering. Meanwhile with bandaged eyes we advance: and human sanity is guided by the brave and pitiable and tireless dullness of mankind. . . . Yet how varied are the amiable activities of human dullness, which tend alike to protect and to enliven human progress! Dullness it is, of course, that brews and quaffs Dutch courage; . . . that fosters salutary optimism as to the destiny of mankind, in flat defiance of everything mankind can do, and does unblushingly. . . . And finally dullness it is that lifts up heart and voice alike, to view a parasite infesting the epidermis of a midge among the planets, and cries, *Behold, this is the child of God, All-mighty and All-worshipful, made in the likeness of his Father!* . . . These and how many other wholesome miracles are daily brought about by our dullness, by our brave and pitiable and tireless dullness, by our really majestic dullness, in firm alliance with the demiurgic spirit of romance. . . . For that to which romance conducts, in all the affairs of life . . . is plain enough—distinction and clarity, and beauty and symmetry, and tenderness and truth and urbanity."

Here then is the note that still awaits adequate dramatization in a comedy greater than he has yet written—a cosmic irony suffused with tenderness and truth and urbanity. Above all, urbanity. Mr. Cabell has played too long with the ideal of gallantry; he has devoted too much precious time to creating Millamants to fall in love with; he has listened too credulously to the voice of Congreve. "I have read," says Charteris, out of Congreve, "that the secret of gallantry is to accept the pleasures of life leisurely, and its inconveniences with a shrug; as well as that, among other requisites, the gallant person will always consider the world with a smile of toleration, and his own doings with a smile of honest amusement, and Heaven with a smile which is not distrustful—being thoroughly persuaded that God is kindlier than the genteel would regard as rational." Surely the cosmic irony that loves men's dullness because it alone can preserve them from madness, and retorts upon the cosmic terrors with a jest, is higher than gallantry and more enduring. It arrives at tolerance for all human shortcomings; it embraces high and low in its sympathies; it achieves urbanity as a final goal. It is the stuff of which great literature is made. And Mr. Cabell is creating great literature. A self-reliant intellectual, rich in the spoils of all literatures, one of the great masters of English prose, the supreme comic spirit thus far granted us, he stands apart from the throng of lesser American novelists, as Mark Twain stood apart, individual and incomparable.

THE PROBLEM NOVEL AND THE DIVERSION FROM NATURALISM *

No sooner was naturalism fairly under way than it was well-nigh submerged under a wave of social speculation and inquiry. The years 1903–1917 were a distinctive period—a time of extraordinary ferment, when America was seeking to readjust her ideals and institutions to a revolutionary economic order that had come upon her. The popular phase was revealed in the muckracking movement, a movement which instructed the American middle class in certain elements of economics—particularly the close connection between economics and politics. But underneath, an intellectual revolution was in progress, setting steadily towards a new social philosophy. The old America had been intensely conservative, naïvely provincial and self-satisfied, compassed by a complacence founded on optimism—the gospel of the business man. The new America was eager and hopeful, impatient to square institutions to the new conditions. The total movement was profoundly democratic—a new Jacksonianism rising in protest against a menacing plutocracy.

1. *The Movement of Criticism.* The work of a vigorous social idealism. Passed through three broad phases:

a. Political. The movement of Progressivism, 1903–1912. An attempt to democratize the machinery of government to the end that the will of the majority shall prevail. Its impulse and much of its program came from Populism; and it resulted in a clarification of the issue between republicanism and democracy. An attack on the representative system and the checks and balances of the Fathers. It gave rise to a critical examination of the spirit and purpose of the Constitution.[1]

b. Economic. A growing conviction that talk of political democracy is futile except in so far as it leads to economic democracy. That power is economic in origin and that those who control the economics will control the government. The gospel of economic determinism. Certain conclusions emerged:

---

* Lecture notes.—*Publisher.*

[1] See J. Allen Smith, *The Spirit of American Government;* W. A. White, *The Old Order Changeth.*

1. That capitalism is no longer competitive but monopolistic.

2. That *laissez-faire*ism no longer suffices.

3. That centralization has submerged the individual citizen; that he is impotent before the leviathan corporation; and that henceforth the struggle is to be between organized groups for the control of the state.[2]

c. Literary. An examination and rejection of traditional literary and cultural ideas. An attack upon:

1. Puritan reticence and smug respectability.

2. Middle-class optimism and sentimentality. Led by H. L. Mencken, Ludwig Lewisohn, and the younger intellectuals. The bias aristocratic.

2. *The Incoming of Old-World Thought.* The breaking-down of the older provincialism and the reception of new ideas.

a. The philosophy of collectivism. Derived chiefly from Germany and England; largely Marxian and Fabian. The conviction that the state must absorb the trust. Later the appearance of syndicalism and guild socialism, based on a distrust of the bureaucratic, omnicompetent state. Anarchism has remained alien in spirit.[3]

b. The new aristocracy. A reversion from an easy-going Jacksonianism based on the doctrine of equalitarianism. A direct denial of that doctrine and the theory of leadership. In business the doctrine of the expert and the rule of efficiency. In philosophy the doctrine of the intellectual aristocrat—a suggestion of Nietzsche and the will to power. Thus Mencken joins hands with Judge Gary in upholding the ethics of the strong. The total result an effective denial of our traditional ideal of democracy.

c. The problem novel. All this ferment entered into literature, tyrannizing in its insistence. Old forms became old-fashioned overnight. The novel was so useful that it was drafted by the new crusading enthusiasm. Romance and naturalism alike were swept away; the political novel and the economic novel took their place to arouse public opinion to action. It was the glorification of propaganda. Except for James Branch Cabell and Edith Wharton not a writer escaped. There is something pathetic in the way the

[2] Representative books are: C. A. Beard, *An Economic Interpretation of the Constitution* (1913) and *The Economic Basis of Politics* (1922); Walter Lippman, *Public Opinion* (1922).

[3] See Bertrand Russell, *Proposed Roads to Freedom* (1919); Richard Roberts, *The Unfinished Programme of Democracy* (1920).

harmless bleating romantics were dragged at the chariot wheels of social problems. Booth Tarkington, Mary Johnston, Winston Churchill, William Allen White, were sacrificed equally with potential naturalists like Robert Herrick, Upton Sinclair, and Ernest Poole. Their careers may be seen from Churchill, Poole, and Herrick.

1. Winston Churchill. [The most representative of the spirit of Progressivism.] A conscientious middle-class romantic. Churchill was a faithful reflector of middle-class movements. His work falls into three phases:

[a. *Romantic historical tales*. *Richard Carvel* (1899) the type of Cavalier romance. A blend of Thackeray's *Henry Esmond* and *The Virginians*, John Paul Jones added for extra historical flavor. A double background: (1) the old South of the Revolution with a Loyalist villain and a patriot hero; (2) the London of Brooks Club and a gaming aristocracy, with Charles Fox. The heroine another edition of Beatrix Esmond the hero another Henry Esmond. *The Crisis* (1910) a romance of the borderland of the Civil War: a fire-eating Southern heroine and a sober Yankee-Puritan hero. *The Crossing* (1904) a romance of the settlement of the Inland Empire. A theme not yet adequately dealt with in American fiction. The story breaks in two: the first half Churchill's best work in romance; the last half his worst.*]

b. *Political novels*. Coincided with the rise of the Progressive movement. *Coniston* (1906) a study of the legislative boss in New Hampshire. A reflection of his experience in the state legislature. How the "interests," and in particular the railroads, manage to put their bills through. Jethro Bass sells political control to the highest bidder.

Mr. Crewe's Career (1908): the same theme a generation later. Consolidation of the railroads has brought about absentee dictatorship of state politics. The boss has removed to New York and manages the legislature through his local lawyer. The philosophy of big-business prosperity rests on property rights, held in trusteeship by the corporations that fill the empty dinner pails, make and unmake business confidence. The revolt of the younger generation —Austen Vane and Victoria Flint, in whom stirs a new social conscience.

* From the syllabus.—*Publisher.*

c. *Economic novels.* Began with *The Inside of the Cup* (1913), a venture in higher criticism and social interpretation. So compare *Robert Elsmere* (1888). An attack on old dogmas and an attempt to discover the democratic springs of Christianity. The clash between the reborn Son of God and an unregenerate society, and the need to establish the Kingdom of God in this world. The church today controlled by business subscriptions. The solution to be sought in a free pulpit, supported by the common people, preaching a new social Christianity.

A Far Country (1915), a study in the emptiness of the profit motive. A background of banking—J. P. Morgan and Company. The dissatisfaction of the prodigal son who has wasted his intellectual and moral patrimony—the lawyer who sells his brain to rise and loses the things that make life worth while. His conversion brings the call to self-education.

The Dwelling Place of Light (1917), a study of the blighting effect of industrialism on the native Yankee stock that has failed to rise into the exploiting class. The restlessness of modern life due to the failure of normal instincts to find satisfaction in daily existence— an emptiness due to loss of beauty, freedom, creative craftsmanship. The search for compensation brings death and not life. A background of the Lawrence strike and syndicalism.

2. Robert Herrick. The most promising of the potential naturalists. An intellectual fascinated by the crude materialism of Chicago in the late nineties. Suffered from the inhibitions of a Puritan idealism; the problems of this raw world cried aloud for solution— the woman question, the labor question, the problem of the professions—and warped him away from naturalism, making him an easy victim of the new social enthusiasm. The key to his thought— economic determinism.

The Memoirs of an American Citizen (1905). His best work and the nearest approach to naturalism. A detailed study of the American business man—the captain of industry who rises in a competitive society by his own will. The competitive order, he perceives, requires an ethics different from the Christian ideal. The survival of the fittest means the survival of the strongest, the most cunning and unscrupulous. The realist who deals with facts discovers that he lives in a world of pigs—little pigs of the village, larger hogs of the city. To get in the trough a man must have fingers and toes and use them. The world belongs to the strong

That which gives dignity is bigness: the larger the hog, the more imposing. Little business is dirty and petty, but big business may become poetic. To grind a mess of sausages is messy, but to provide sausages for every breakfast table in America is grandiose. To realize his ambition Van Harrington plays fast and loose with conventional ethics, but unlike Frank Cowperwood he seeks a new ethics. As a superman his work will be justified by its creativeness, by its service to humanity.

A Life for a Life (1910). In certain other of his work Herrick betrays naturalistic tendencies, notably in *The Web of Life* (1900), where he considers the problem of social complexity and how it binds the life of men and women and determines their fate. But in *A Life for a Life* he surrenders wholly to the problem. His theme is how the predatory egoism of the profit-struggle may be cured, and he presents alternative solutions: syndicalism and Christianity. The cure lies in individual self-conquest—breaking through the web of "things as they are" and choosing life instead of power.

Herrick was on the threshold of naturalism. He felt the complexity of life and the determining force of that complexity; but he failed to achieve the attitude of objectivity.

3. Ernest Poole. *The Harbor* (1915). The culmination of the novel of naturalistic propaganda and the most widely read. A dramatic record of a changing industrial order, traced through three stages: (1) The old world of small competitive business that is dead; (2) The present world of corporation control; (3) The world of syndicalistic control that struggles to be born.

Against this changing world stands the young idealist troubled in his loyalties, who sets up different gods to worship: (1) The idol of art—aloofness from the mass struggle; (2) The idol of efficiency by the supermen who rule in trusteeship; (3) The idol of mass solidarity and workers' control—the conclusion that is on the dawn of realization: "The world for all the workers." *Conclusion.* The ferment of social thought, shot through with Marxianism, familiarized the American novelists with one doctrine important for the naturalist—the doctrine of economic determinism. In none of them did it pass over into a larger conception of philosophical determinism, and this sets the limitation to their naturalism. The common zeal for reform or revolution, moreover, kept them from objectivity. In none is there the calm detachment and the amoral presentation of material without which naturalism sinks into propaganda. Their position presupposes a large confidence in individual initiative—a confidence in the power of men to alter the world they live in. It is admirable, but it is not the way of the naturalists, who do not seek to change what they regard as an essentially unresponsive world that changes only after its own way

JACK LONDON: THE NOVELIST OF THE PROLETARIAT*

Experienced the harsh contacts of a seasonal worker and tramp. Became a Marxian socialist and revolutionist, preaching the war of the classes in *The Iron Heel* (1908), *The Revolution* (1910), and other works. A man of strong vital energy with a philosophy shaped by Darwin, Spencer, and Nietzsche. Emphasizes a passionate will-to-power, a superman of swift and violent action.

The Call of the Wild (1903); a study in atavism, brilliant, poetic, set against a wild Alaska background. The resurgence of the primitive wolf-instincts in a domesticated dog.

The Sea Wolf (1904); the frankest statement in American literature of the unbridled will-to-power, egoistic, amoral. A malignant ferocity in a philosophical, herculean sea captain, whose body is destroyed by paresis, but whose malignancy is unconquered.

Martin Eden (1909); autobiographical. So compare *John Barleycorn* (1913). The former deals with his struggle to educate himself, to write, and to gain recognition. A background of his experience at the University of California. A profound contempt for *bourgeois* standards of life and thought. The note of revolution and the lapsing of the will-to-live.

London carries to the extreme the "elemental" of Norris, translating it into the primitive and abysmal. A potential naturalist in his amoral attitude and his underlying pessimism, but carried away by zeal of revolution. Lacks restraint and finish.

* From the syllabus.—*Publisher*.

UPTON SINCLAIR *

The most insistent and outspoken of the muckrakers. Began as a novelist, but his art submerged by propaganda—a profound suspicion of capitalism and all its ways.

The Jungle (1906); a story of the packing houses and the immigrant: the technique of "speeding up" and the labor scrap-heap. The social consequences of the profit principle—saving everything but the squeal of the hog and the health of the laborer.

King Coal (1917); a story of the Rockefeller coal fields in Colorado and the miners' union. Probably his most skillful story.

Numerous other titles, among them: *The Brass Check*, an examination of the American newspaper—the charge that these are the tools of plutocracy; *The Goose Step*, an examination of the American university—the charge that these serve wealth; *The Goslings*, an attack upon the public school as an agent of capitalism.

* From the syllabus.—*Publisher.*

353

THEODORE DREISER: CHIEF OF AMERICAN
NATURALISTS *

Against this background of eager ferment and various propaganda stands Theodore Dreiser, who is of this changing world and
yet apart from it: the most detached and keenly observant of all
our writers, a huge figure of ungainly proportions—a heavy-footed
peasant with unslaked curiosity and a boundless pity, who is
determined to examine critically "this animal called man" and
portray him truthfully. He tramps across fields straight to his
objective, messing sadly the neat little beds of American convention, peering into the secret places that are marked "Not Open To
The Public," keeping nothing hidden, ashamed of nothing, apologizing for nothing. Not since Walt Whitman has there been another
such frank and detached projection of reality, such insistence that
the world shall stop and consider those facts which convention has
politely agreed to ignore. Naturally a great hue and cry of the
Pharisees has been raised against him. The respectable middle
class will have none of this peasant directness and brutal truth. He
has entered our *bourgeois* society "murmurous of morality" with
an alien philosophy, which he must defend. At every moment he
feels under the necessity of assisting the truth as he sees it, and
instead of suffering his portrayal to stand on its own feet he props
it up with argument and interminable debate. The artist suffers
at the hands of the disputant.

The Man and his Philosophy. Marked by an immense and open-
eyed curiosity that ends in agnosticism. His anthropocentric
conceptions:

I have lived now to my fortieth year and have seen a good deal of life.
. . . But I am one of those curious persons who cannot make up their
minds about anything. I read and read. . . . But I find that one history
contradicts another, one philosopher drives out another. Essayists, in the
main, point out flaws and paradoxes in the current conception of things,
novelists, dramatists and biographers spread tales of endless disasters, or
silly illusions concerning life, duty, opportunity and the like. And I sit
here and read and read, when I have time, wondering.[1]

* Lecture notes.—*Publisher.*   [1] *Hey Rub-a-Dub-Dub*, New York, 1920, p. 1.

"Nothing is proved, all is permitted," he says in *The Titan*. Men will do what they think they can get away with. In briefest terms his philosophy may be phrased thus:

1. The world is without reason or meaning to us. Why we are here and to what end is unknowable.

2. Men are chemical compounds, existing in a world where they play about like water-flies, skipping restlessly and unintelligently as their legs drive them, whom the universe in its vast indifference suffers for a time.

3. Men divide into the strong and the weak; not the good and the bad. The will to power, the desire for pleasure, drive men on their courses. What restrains? Moral codes and social conventions, often useful, often harmful.

A metaphysical idealism will always tell him that it is better to preserve a cleanly balance, and the storms of circumstance will teach him a noble stoicism. Beyond this there is nothing which can reasonably be imposed upon the conscience of man.[2]

4. Hence the profound need of sympathy and mercy.

Let no one underestimate the need of pity. We live in a stony universe whose hard, brilliant forces rage fiercely. From the prowling hunger of the Hyrcan tiger to the concentric grip of Arcturus and Canopus there is the same ruthless, sightless disregard of the individual and the minor thing. Life moves in an ordered hierarchy of forces of which the lesser is as nothing to the greater . . . And in the midst of the rip of desperate things—in odd crannies and chance flaws between forces—there spring and blossom these small flowers of sentiment. Tenderness! Mercy! Affection! Sorrow! The Hindus worship an image of pain. And well they may. It is a classic amid the painless, the indifferent—Nirvana. Blessed are the merciful, for they shall receive mercy! No, no. Blessed are the merciful, for they create mercy. Of such is the kingdom of the ideal.[3]

His Attitude toward his Material. Dreiser possesses a vast and terrifying imagination. Like James Branch Cabell he broods over the plight of man in the universe. But he does not seek refuge in the ideal. He will confront things as they are. The very chemistry of decaying flesh fascinates him. It is a phenomenon of this impersonal and relentless universe. Compared with the realities of time and space and force—what is man and what are his puny efforts and ideals?

The damnable scheme of things which we call existence brings about conditions whereby whole masses suffer who have no cause to suffer, and

[2] *The Financier*, New York, c. 1912, p. 250.   [3] *Ibid.*, p. 409.

. . . whole masses joy who have no cause for joy. . . . We suffer for our temperaments, which we did not make, and for our weaknesses and lacks, which are no part of our willing or doing.[4]

His Objectivity. The larger view of life gives detachment. Only one who has emerged from the jungle can see the whole in broad perspective. In no other American writer, except Whitman, is such complete detachment achieved. His life is a long process of stripping away group illusions, of casting off group conventions. And for this the mass cannot forgive him, for the mass live in the strait-jacket of custom, thinking in no other terms than group or tribal terms, worshiping the communal idols, clinging to the tribal taboos. They cannot achieve individuality themselves and they hate Dreiser. It puts him outside the tribe, for the first law of the tribe is tribal-mindedness. Whoever is not of us is against us. Whoever questions the validity of the tribal sanctions is an enemy and must be destroyed. It is in vain that Dreiser asserts vehemently that he is telling the truth. Another version of the truth than the tribal version is not wanted.

The significance of Dreiser lies in the fact that he is an individual apart—one who has broken with the group and sits in judgment on the group sanctions. He is an anarchist who will be partisan to no taboos. This is a rare and perilous thing to do. He stands outside.

His Amoral Attitude. It is on this score that Dreiser stands condemned by our *bourgeois* censors. His amoral attitude is strangely metamorphosed into immorality. His indifference to the common preachments, his inability to accept Christian maxims, his refusal to do lip service to creeds—this is set down as evidence of viciousness, for *ipso facto* there can be no other moral standards than the tribal standards. What is Dreiser's justification? This, that in the physical universe he can discover no morality—no justice, mercy, pity, but everywhere great and indifferent force. And in society— in the instincts of men and in their hidden desires and secret acts —a disregard of conventional morality. Society is steeped in hypocrisy.

He saw no morals anywhere—nothing but moods, emotions, needs, greeds. People talked and talked, but they acted according to their necessities and desires.[5]

But in frankly revealing the hypocrisy of men Dreiser is no cynic. There is in him a profound morality—the morality of truth and pity

[4] *Ibid.,* p. 479.   [5] *The Financier,* p. 432.

and mercy. Let us not stone men for their sins but deal generously and kindly with them. What he protests against is superimposed codes. There is, for him, "in Nature, no such thing as the right to do, or the right not to do." [6]

But is there not social expediency? To which the individual for his own good should conform? Experience has taught men some excellent things.

His Work. Dreiser has given us full-length portraits of two women—Sister Carrie and Jennie Gerhardt—and of two men— Eugene Witla and Frank Cowperwood. These constitute his major contribution and on them his reputation rests.* In addition there is *Hey Rub-a-Dub-Dub,* a book of essays in which his philosophy is set forth, a naturalistic play, *The Hand of the Potter*—a study in pathology where the hand of the potter slipped—a book of travel, and some short stories. Of his four major characters the two women are passive and pliable, easily made victims of circumstance. Of the two men one—Eugene Witla—is weak, and the other—Frank Cowperwood—is the supreme example in American literature of the will to power.

The Financier and *The Titan.* A colossal study of the American business man, in two volumes of a total of 1332 pages. Compared with this all other studies are crude and unconvincing. Here the thing has been done once for all.

"These crude and greedy captains of finance had to be given some kind of literary embodiment, and Dreiser has hammered a raw epic out of their lives." [7]

Where did Dreiser get his intimate and detailed information concerning high finance? Where his knowledge of such a character? Out of his own powerful mind. Cowperwood a portrait of Charles Yerkes. Two periods: his Philadelphia life to 1873; his Chicago life to 1898. In both he molds circumstance to his advantage; in both he is caught by chance and fails.

The Man. Driven by three impulses: love of power, love of women, love of art. There is in him a unity of character and an inevitability of development that are overwhelming. Dreiser does not judge, apologize, praise, or condemn; he is content to permit the

---

[6] *Hey Rub-a-Dub-Dub,* p. 87.

* When this was written of course *The American Tragedy, A Book about Myself,* Dreiser's poems, *Moods Cadenced and Declaimed,* and his further books of travel had not been published.—*Publisher.*

[7] Randolph Bourne, *History of a Literary Radical,* p. 203.

character to develop. From first to last he is detached and objective. He presents Cowperwood as a magnificent physical and mental machine: a born fighter and leader, strong, alert, with a cool resourceful mind. A pronounced hardness that goes with strength —contempt for the weakling, impatience with the inefficient. In his sex passages there is no glamour of romance. They are direct and brutal—but more moral than glamorous. Nevertheless great personal charm—the magnetism of a virile mind and indomitable will. To men he is an inspiration, to women a fascination. And yet a frank egoist, self-centered, imperturbable.

The fate of the individualist: in pitting his will against life Cowperwood feared chance, which undid him in Philadelphia. But his very prevision, which carried him to triumph, brought his downfall. The many are stronger than the superman. And in the end, failure. Strength endures for so short a time and is so weak. Age, weakness, social forces—these undermine the strong. A vast irony. Cowperwood is punished not because he is evil but because he is a man.

Cowperwood's Philosophy. From his youth up life was a puzzle to him. Nothing was certain, for beyond and above all was a blind, irrational chance. Nevertheless within reasonable limits it was plain enough that strength and intelligence prevail. This lesson he first learned from the squib and the lobster, and it became his guiding principle. When chance had brought him within the shadow of the penitentiary, he summed it up:

It is a grim, bitter world we are all born into. . . . Who was to straighten out the matter of the unjust equipment with which most people began? Who was to give them strong minds in place of feeble ones, able bodies instead of wretched ones? Where were they to get pure-tendencies instead of impure ones, as the world looked on these things? . . . Some were sent into the world with a great lust and great ability for wealth like himself, a mind swift to see, a body strong to endure; and some were sent half equipped, almost shapeless and formless. . . . Strength and weakness—there lay the key, the answer.[8]

Stuart Sherman on Dreiser:

By eliminating distinctively human motives and making animal instincts the supreme factors in human life, Mr. Dreiser reduces the problem of the novelist to the lowest possible terms. . . . His philosophy quite excludes him from the field in which the great realist must work. He has deliberately rejected the novelist's supreme task—understanding and

[8] *The Financier*, p. 660.

presenting the development of character; he has chosen only to illustrate the unrestricted flow of temperament. He has evaded the enterprise of representing human conduct; he has confined himself to representation of animal behavior.[9]

And the two novels he says are "like a club sandwich composed of slices of business, alternating with erotic episodes." It is true, but the failure is one of art that does not merge them. What would Sherman have? Shall these impulses be eliminated from literature, or from human nature itself?

[9] Stuart P. Sherman, *On Contemporary Literature*, New York, 1923, p. 94. In the syllabus Professor Parrington says: "The most intelligent estimates of Dreiser are in Randolph Bourne, *History of a Literary Radical;* H. L. Mencken, *Prefaces;* and Carl Van Doren, *Contemporary American Novelists.* All other commentators are stupid."

SINCLAIR LEWIS: OUR OWN DIOGENES*

As the row of his pudgy orange-backed volumes lengthens on
the shelf, it becomes evident that Sinclair Lewis is the bad boy of
American letters whose thoughts are on bent-pins while the deacon
is laboring in prayer. His irrepressible satire belongs to a new and
irritatingly effective school. He has studied the technique of the
realists, and under the beguiling pretense of telling the truth
objectively and dispassionately, he insists on revealing to us un-
accommodated man as a poor, bare, forked animal, who like
Jurgen persists in thinking himself a monstrous clever fellow. He
is maliciously severe on all respectable dignities. In his hands the
noble *homo sapiens* of common repute is translated into an ignoble
homo libidinus et ventosissimus—an unattractive animal that runs
in herds, serves its belly, and has a taking way with the dams.
The free-born American citizen, master of the earth and its destiny,
is little flattered by the portrait he draws, and Mr. Lewis finds
himself, in consequence, *persona non grata* in any convention of
Elks or Rotarians.

The method he has chosen to adopt is a clever advance over the
technique of the eighteenth century, when pricking balloons was
the business of every wit. Those older satirists—nagging souls like
Pope and bold bad fellows like Churchill—were mainly concerned
to annoy their victims with pin-pricks. They were too completely
the gentleman to grow chummy with base fellows whom they
frankly despised; and in consequence they never discovered half
the possibilities of the gentle art of satire. Sinclair Lewis is wiser
than they were. He has learned that before one can effectively im-
pale one's victim, one must know all his weaknesses and take him
off his guard. So he ingratiatingly makes up to George F. Babbitt
of Zenith, drinks chummily with him, swaps greasy jokes, learns
all the hidden vanities and secret obscenities that slip out in the
confidences of the cups, beguiles him into painting his own portrait in the manly midnight hours; and when the last garment that
covers his nakedness is stripped off, the flashlight explodes and the

* Published as Number Five of *University of Washington Chapbooks*, 1927.—
Publisher.

camera has caught the victim in every feature of his mean and
vacuous reality.

No doubt it is an ungentlemanly thing to do—a calculating betrayal of trusting human nature done in the sacred name of art; and
it is certain that the unhappy victim will hate the artist when he
sees the developed print next morning. Yet the picture is extraordinarily lifelike. All the unlovely details of fat stomach and
flabby muscles are sharply revealed. It is too late to put on one's
clothes, and *homo sapiens* in the person of George F. Babbitt is
revealed as a shambling, two-legged animal, for the world to laugh
at. The method is immensely clever; it is the last word in the technique of despoiling one's victim of adventitious dignity, without
which life becomes a mean, bleak affair; but it is scarcely charitable.
To think well of oneself and to wish to impose that good opinion
upon others, are common human weaknesses that every tailor
blesses. Without clothes man is only a caricature of the godlike,
and the artist who betrays our nakedness to our enemies is very far
from a gentleman. The confidences of the cups must be held
sacred, for if we cannot drink without fear of our babbling being
reported, what becomes of goodfellowship?

But the charge of betraying goodfellowship leaves Sinclair Lewis
unconcerned. His satire knows no compunctions. An irreverent
soul, he dares the wrath not only of George F. Babbitt, but of the
innumerable clubs to which Babbitt belongs. A buoyant scoffer,
he does not permit even the organized wrath of the Chamber of
Commerce to disturb his equanimity. He provokes respectable
people on principle, and he has laid a devilish plan to work systematically through our sacred American decalogue, smashing one
commandment after another. Already behind him is strewn a sorry
wreckage of established creeds and authoritative slogans—a wreckage that delights the wicked and gives aid and comfort to all evil-
wishers in our comfortable and excellent society. Not even a
banker is sacred to him. Rotarians and Kiwanians, Billy Sundays
and Billy Bryans, voluble Congressmen and silent Presidents, even
our venerable Constitution itself, he scoffs at and makes merry
over. And to add insult to injury, he prospers in his sins. His calculating wickedness returns him a fattening bank account. His
impudent satires sell like bargain-counter silk stockings. We pay
handsomely to see ourselves most unhandsomely depicted. If we
would only take a lesson from the strategy of the heathen Chinese,

we might boycott Mr. Lewis's wares and reduce him to the beggary that is more becoming to wickedness than a wanton prosperity. But a Christian people will not go to school to the heathen, and so Mr. Lewis prospers in his wickedness and waxes vulgarly rich.

Now what is the tremendous discovery that Sinclair Lewis makes so much of, and that we pay so great a price to learn? It is no other than this: that the goodly United States of America are peopled by a mighty herd, which like those earlier herds that rumbled about the plains, drives foolishly in whatever direction their noses point— a herd endowed with tremendous blind power, with big bull leaders, but with minds rarely above their bellies and their dams. In the mass and at their own romantic rating they are distinctly imposing —big-necked, red-blooded, lusty, with glossy coats got from rich feeding-grounds, and with a herd power that sweeps majestically onward in a cloud of dust of its own raising, veritable lords and masters of a continent. But considered more critically and resolved into individual members, they appear to the realist somewhat stupid, feeble in brain and will, stuffed with conceit of their own excellence, esteeming themselves the great end for which creation has been in travail, the finest handiwork of the Most High who spread the plains for their feeding-grounds: with a vast respect for totems and fetishes; purveyors and victims of the mysterious thing called Bunk, who valiantly horn to death any audacious heretic who may suggest that rumbling about the plains, filling their bellies, bellowing sacred slogans, and cornering the lushest grass, are scarcely adequate objectives for such immense power: a vast middleman herd, that dominates the continent, but cannot reduce it to order or decency.

Consider, suggests Mr. Lewis, what this rumbling herd signifies in the light of rational and humane ideals. What sort of custodians of civilization are these lumbering mobsters with their back-slappings and bellowings? What becomes of the good life in a society that flowers in Rotarian conventions? The banker has reduced America to the level of a banker's Utopia, and now bids us admire his handiwork. Other societies, aristocratic and feudal, honored the priest and knight and artist above the usurer and tradesman; other generations professed to serve truth and beauty and godliness in their daily lives; but the great American herd cares nothing for such things. In the name of democracy priest and knight and artist are turned lackeys to merchants and realtors, to men who would not recognize faith or chivalry or imagination if they met them on the golf course, and who understand democracy as little as they understand Christianity. In this land of material abundance the good life is reduced to being measured in commissions and percentages; civilization comes to flower in the broker; the mahogany desk is the altar at which we sacrifice in a land of triumphant materialism. "God help the country," said Fenimore Cooper, years ago when the herd was small, "that has only commercial towns for its capitals." "Such a country is past helping," retorts Sinclair Lewis. "God cannot help it, or the Devil. In the name of George F. Babbitt and Dr. Almus Pickerbaugh and the Reverend Elmer Gantry, what can be expected of such a country? A people that worships the great god Bunk shall have its reward!"

To prove his amiable thesis Mr. Lewis has been at enormous pains to gather his materials at their sources. He has taken upon himself to become a specialist in depicting the *genus Americanus*. He has loafed along Main Street, played poker in back rooms with wicked young men, drunk in respectable clubs, and exchanged hearty back-slappings with the sons of Rotary. He has devoted days to the smoking-compartments of Pullmans, garnering the ripest wisdom and choicest stories of traveling salesmen. He has listened to philosophic brokers discourse on ethics, studied political and constitutional theory with realtors, learned all about Bolshevism from presidents of Chambers of Commerce, been instructed in the elements of economics by Republican Congressmen, discovered the fallacies in Darwinian evolution from clerical fundamentalists and the superiority of Fascism over democracy from the greatest captains of industry. No field of American experience has escaped his minute investigation, no authority has eluded his catechizing. In the course of his studies he has come to master the lusty American language in its subtlest shades and manliest *nuances*, from the comic supplement to Dunn and Bradstreet, and he talks easily with Main Street in its own vernacular. His rich and copious vocabulary fills a commonplace scholar with envy, and his ebullient slang, his easy slovenliness of enunciation, inflict on the simple-minded user of the King's English a hopeless inferiority complex.

Thus amply equipped with all the resources of scholarship, he has written four learned treatises in exemplification of the thesis that the *genus Americanus* is cousin-german to the scoffing Mr. Mencken's lately discovered *boobus Americanus*. The introductory study, *Main Street*, provided a comprehensive background and setting for the full-length portraits he was to draw later. Gopher Prairie, situated in the heart of agricultural America—in Meredith Nicholson's Valley of Democracy where the old-fashioned, kindly, neighborly, wholesome, democratic virtues are presumed to thrive in a congenial habitat—becomes in his unsympathetic analysis a place that William Allen White would not recognize as his home town. Here, he tells us, is respectability made sluggish and sterile. Here is "slavery self-sought and self-defended." Here is "dullness made God." Here, diluted and spread over a vast territory, the spirit of Babbitt has erupted in cheap and pretentious county-seats, parasites on the producing hinterland over whose politics and credit and morals Main Street tradesmen have set up a strict custodianship—futile and complacent and drab, mere echoes of the greater cities that lie on the horizon and to which the sons of Main Street turn for light and guidance.

It is these greater cities that constitute the true capitals of our red-blooded Americans who proclaim themselves "the greatest race in the world"—fruitful centers from which radiates the philosophy of pep, punch, and progress for the upbuilding and enlightenment of the world. Of these centers the hustling and mighty Zenith is the wonder and admiration of all right-minded citizens; it is the brightest and bloomiest sunflower of the great American garden. And in Zenith dwells George F. Babbitt, realtor, Sinclair Lewis's full-length portrait of a hero sprung from the loins of America, the completest embodiment of the triumphant American genius that is conquering the earth. Babbitt as an upstanding he-member of the great herd is a marvel, the apotheosis of the regnant middle class, the finished product of our snappy civilization. Other lands, no doubt, have produced men accounted great. Plato and Saul of Tarsus, St. Francis and Leonardo, Pascal and Galileo and Hegel, were no doubt esteemed in their own times and by their own cities; but Zenith does not go in for out-of-date merchandise; it is up-to-the-minute and it specialized in George F. Babbitts. And so when the Reverend Elmer Gantry rises to influence in Gopher Prairie, he is called to Zenith as its spiritual counselor, and becomes the custodian of the Zenith moralities, the apostle of Zenith Bunk, the devotee of the Zenith Mumbo Jumbo. And through Zenith passes also Martin Arrowsmith the rebel, the perverse outlandish scientist who refuses to worship Mumbo

Jumbo, on his solitary way to discover reality in a world of Zenith chicanery. Babbitt, Gantry, Arrowsmith—these are the figures that Sinclair Lewis comes upon in his exploration of the land of the free and the home of the brave. A somewhat curious showing at the best.

So slashing an attack upon our common creed and practice has naturally aroused vigorous protest. Human nature does not like to have its idols assailed; even the devotees of Mumbo Jumbo will defend their god against the heretics; and Sinclair Lewis has become the target for many a shaft. The critics have pressed home their counter attack with ardor. They insist that he is suffering from an aggravated case of astigmatism, and that in consequence he does not see eye to eye with those of normal vision. The world is out of focus to him—askew in all its structural lines; and this distorted vision prompts those jaundiced opinions and malicious judgments in regard to the ideals cherished by our best citizens. He has deliberately cultivated a spleen that makes him dislike his neighbors because they are comfortable and contented. Diogenes railing at mankind gained a vast reputation, but it is a nice question if Diogenes was a useful citizen. What did he do to further the well-being of his community? How much time and money did he give to charity and the upbuilding of his city? For all his talking Mr. Lewis does not seem to know what the good life is. He rails at Babbitt for not being Plato, but does he understand the A B C of service? To take a homely figure: the family cow, standing knee-deep in June and chewing the cud of contentment, would excite his Diogenic scorn. As a fault-finder and knocker, Brindle is not the equal of Diogenes; but to criticize her mentality and manners, forgetful of the fact that from the contented chewing of a plentiful cud will come a plentiful supply of milk and cream and butter to sweeten the bread of life, is a somewhat sorry business. In her modest, democratic sphere she is devoted to service, and if there is a nobler function, Rotary humbly confesses it had not discovered it. One must not, of course, press too far the analogy between Brindle and Babbitt; the figure is useful only to suggest that even in the lowliest spheres Mr. Lewis completely fails to understand the fine ethical values that underlie and animate the common American life at which he rails. How, then, shall he understand them in the higher? Comfort and service are excellent things in themselves, and if they can be merged in everyday experience, surely the good life is in the way of achievement.

The point is of vast importance, for it is here that Diogenes Lewis, his critics assert, has totally misread the meaning and faith of America. Here in this prosperous land the union between comfort and service—or to put it in more dignified phrase, the synthesis of Hellenism and Hebraism—has been achieved in practice. A rich and abundant life, motivated by a fine sense of ethical responsibility and disciplined by a democratic public school, is, in sober fact, the distinguishing characteristic of America that sets our country apart from all other lands in western civilization. Call it a Babbitt warren if you will, nevertheless where else has the industrial revolution been brought so completely and happily under dominion to the democratic ideal, or been so ennobled by ethical values? Here it has scattered its wealth amongst the plain people with a bountiful hand, until the poorest family enjoys its nickel-plated plumbing, its flivver, its telephone, its radio, its movies, its funnies, and all the thousand aids to comfort and intelligence which a few generations ago were denied kings—the result of all which is a standard of living that our forefathers would have envied. Our Hellenism is, happily, not Greek. That, as every schoolboy in America knows, was established in slavery; whereas our modern Hellenism is established in democracy and ennobled by a sensitive social conscience. Here the master serves. The richest and greatest amongst us—our Judge Garys and Andrew Mellons—are servants of the nameless public, and dedicate their creative genius to the common democratic prosperity. Our Hellenism, in short, is engrafted on a sturdy Hebraic root and flowers in righteousness—in charity, in education, in free clinics and hospitals, in scientific foundations, in great public libraries, in all the vast gifts that wealth freely offers to the cause of social amelioration. The Puritan strain is fortunately still the American strain, and we owe much to those excellent origins that Mr. Lewis scoffs at without understanding. Comfort and service—Hellenism and Hebraism: if this is not the good life, where shall one find it? In Bolshevik Russia? After all Diogenes Lewis is no more important—or useful —than the gad-fly that Brindle brushes from her glossy sides as she chews her cud. What gad-fly ever produced butter?

If Sinclair Lewis is unimpressed by such arguments it is because he is quite disillusioned with the current ideal of material progress. His dreams do not find their satisfaction in good roads and cheap gasoline. He would seem to be an incorrigible idealist who has been bred up on the vigorous Utopianisms of the late nineteenth century. In the golden days before the deluge he had gone blithely to school to all the current idealisms that flourished in the land—to Jeffersonian democracy and to Marxian socialism; and in the well-stocked pharmacopoeias of hopeful young liberals he professed to discover specifics for all our social ills. But the war destroyed his faith in nostrums and removed his Utopia to a dim and foggy future. He has not yet traveled so far in disillusion as Mr. Cabell, who has seen fit to dwarf man to the compass of a flea on the epidermis of earth; nor has he achieved the irony—or the technique—of Clarence Darrow, who suggests casually: "Of course I know that Confucius was as great a philosopher as Billy Sunday, and that as a thinker Buddha was the equal of Billy Bryan. But still all orthodox people know that Confucius and Buddha were spurious and the Billy brothers genuine." He has not even achieved the smug satisfaction of the psychologists who impose their preposterous intelligence tests on simple folk and triumphantly discover morons in respectable neighbors. Some lingering faith in our poor human nature he still clings to. In the great American mass that human nature is certainly foolish and unlovely enough. It is too often blown up with flatulence, corroded with lust, on familiar terms with chicanery and lying; it openly delights in hocus-pocus and discovers its miracle-workers in its Comstocks and Aimee Semple McPhersons. But for all its pitiful flabbiness human nature is not wholly bad, nor is man so helpless a creature of circumstance as the cynics would have us believe. There are other and greater gods than Mumbo Jumbo worshiped in America, worthier things than hocus-pocus; and in rare moments even Babbitt dimly perceives that the feet of his idol are clay. There are Martin Arrowsmiths as well as Elmer Gantrys, and human nature, if it will, can pull itself out of the trap. Bad social machinery makes bad men. Put the banker in the scullery instead of the drawing-room; exalt the test-tube and deflate the cash register; rid society of the dictatorship of the middle class; and the artist and the scientist will erect in America a civilization that may become what civilization was in earlier days, a thing to be respected. For all his modernity and the disillusion learned from Pullman-car philosophers, Sinclair Lewis is still an echo of Jean Jacques and the golden hopes of the Enlightenment—thin and far off, no doubt, but still an authentic echo.

Whether we like Mr. Lewis's technique or not, whether we agree

with his indictment of middle-class ideals or dissent from it, his
writings are suggestive documents symptomatic of a dissatisfied
generation given over to disillusion. The optimistic dreams of
middle-class capitalism are not so golden as they seemed to us
before the war; and these pudgy novels are slashing attacks on a
world that in mouthing empty shibboleths is only whistling to keep
up its courage. The faith of America is dead. These brisk pages
are filled with the doings of automata—not living men but the sim-
ulacra of men, done with astonishing verisimilitude, speaking an
amazingly realistic language, professing a surprising lifelikeness; yet
nevertheless only shells from which the life has departed, without
faith or hope or creative energy, not even aware that they are dead.

It is this consciousness of sketching in a morgue that differenti-
ates Mr. Lewis from the earlier satirists of middle-class America,
who in the hopeful years before the war were busily engaged in rebuilding the American temple. The preceding generation—earnest
souls like Robert Herrick and Jack London and Upton Sinclair—
were as well aware of the shortcomings of our industrial order as Sinclair Lewis, and hated them as vigorously. From the days of Emerson and George Ripley, of Carlyle and Ruskin, capitalistic society
had been persistently subjected to sharp and devastating analysis;
its drabness and regimentation, its sterility and emptiness and joy-
lessness, had been pointed out by many pens. The Victorians long
ago discovered that no generous or humane civilization was to be
expected from the hands of Plugson of Undershot—that the
banker conceiving of human felicity in terms of eight per cent. is a
mean and shabby fellow in comparison with St. Francis or Michel-
angelo. Long before Sherwood Anderson, William Morris had
observed that the workman no longer sings in the factory as in
other days he sang over his tool, and concluded that the creation
of beauty is more important for human happiness than figuring
profits from mass production.

But those earlier analysts were dealing with causes of which they
could only forecast the ultimate consequences, whereas Sinclair
Lewis is dealing with effects. Plugson of Undershot is now the
universal dictator. Before the war there was still life and hope in
western civilization; it was not yet reduced to being a common
Babbitt warren, with its Billy Sundays and Almus Pickerbaughs,
its artists and editors and scientists, on the Plugson pay-roll. What
emerges from the drab pages of Sinclair Lewis that is suggestive is

the authoritative pronouncement that the effects forecast by the earlier critics have become in our day the regnant order of things. Babbitt is the son of Plugson of Undershot, and Babbitt is a walking corpse who refuses to be put decently away to make room for living men. An empty soul, he is the symbol of our common emptiness. Historically he marks the final passing in America of the civilization that came from the fruitful loins of the eighteenth century. For a hundred and fifty years western civilization had sustained its hopes on the rich nourishment provided by the great age of the Enlightenment. Faith in the excellence of man, in the law of progress, in the ultimate reign of justice, in the conquest of nature, in the finality and sufficiency of democracy, faith in short in the excellence of life, was the great driving force in those earlier, simpler days. It was a noble dream—that dream of the Enlightenment —but it was slowly dissipated by an encompassing materialism that came likewise out of the eighteenth century. Faith in machinery came to supersede faith in man; the Industrial Revolution submerged the hopes of the French Revolution. And now we have fallen so low that our faith in justice, progress, the potentialities of human nature, the excellence of democracy, is stricken with pernicious anemia, and even faith in the machine is dying. Only science remains to take the place of the old romantic creed, and science with its psychology and physics is fast reducing man to a complex bundle of glands, at the mercy of a mechanistic universe. Babbitt, to be sure, has not yet discovered the predicament he is in, but Martin Arrowsmith knows; and while Babbitt is whistling somewhat futilely, Arrowsmith is hard at work in the laboratory seeking a new philosophy to take the place of the old. The outlook is not promising, but until a new faith emerges from the test-tube Sinclair Lewis will wander in the fogs of disillusion.

But enough of such crape-hanging at a time when our best minds are engaged in the great work of stabilizing prosperity. What are test-tubes in comparison with the infallible statistics patriotically disseminated by the National City Bank? To parade such heresies in the face of the progressive American public is enough to damn any man, genius or not. We want no carpers or cynics in our congenial membership. We must all get together to put across the drive for a bigger and richer and better America; and so, reluctantly, despite the fact that in many ways he is a good fellow, we blackball Sinclair Lewis.

SHERWOOD ANDERSON: A PSYCHOLOGICAL
NATURALIST *

Unlike our earlier naturalists in handling of material and dramatic interests. Concerned with inner life rather than outer, with hidden drives rather than environment. Accepts the main criteria of naturalism: determinism, distortion, pessimism. A lean and sparing writer whose symbolisms are obscure and puzzling. A single theme: the disastrous effect of frustrations and repressions that create grotesques. Due to (1) Crude, narrow environment that drives to strange aberrations; (2) Repressed instincts that break forth in abnormal action. The consequence a black loneliness—the hunger of fellowship and its denial. Limited in scope to episodic crises—hence his better stories short. Many failures· *Marching Men; Windy McPherson's Son; Poor White* (1920); *Many Marriages* (1923)—a clumsy account of a Babbitt gone on a psychological spree; *Horses and Men* (1923)—some more Grotesques; see in particular "A Chicago Hamlet."

Winesburg, Ohio (1918). A prose *Spoon River Anthology*, with an excellent collection of grotesques. Sharp vignettes; lonely, thwarted lives, "confused and disconcerted by the facts of life." A background of earlier America, crude and ugly, that drives to religious fanaticism in Steve Bentley; to passionate rebellion in Kate Swift; to bitter irony in Ray Pearson. Note the deterministic conclusion of "The Untold Lie"—"Tricked, by Gad, that's what I was; tricked by life and made a fool of"; and the pessimism: . . . "he shouted a protest against his life, against all life, against everything that makes life ugly."

The Triumph of the Egg (1921). A strange and difficult book with its subtle symbolisms. The theme is the common hunger for romance and fellowship that confuses itself with sex and is unsatisfied. Suggested in prefatory poem: "I have a wonderful story to tell but know no way to tell it."

1. *The Egg.* An epitome of his philosophy of grotesques. The egg breeds life that is futile, and life reproduces the egg. A morbid disgust that would bottle the egg, and the failure.

* The notes that follow are from the syllabus.—*Publisher.*

370

2. *Out of Nowhere Into Nothing*. Theme is the "white wonder of life"—what it is and the part it plays in shaping life; a sex illusion that in its mystic appeal to youth guarantees the perpetuation of the race. To age there is no "white wonder," but the life processes are dirty, and lead to final imprisonment in a common trap. Hence the "white wonder" is the supreme jest of nature, sardonic, beguiling, gathering its victims who eagerly run their predetermined course.

3. *Brothers*. A suggestion of the true "white wonder of life"— the brotherhood of man in a lonely world—"beyond words, beyond passion—the fellowship in living, the fellowship in life." But men cannot break through the walls of themselves to grasp it, and the dirt of the world destroys its beauty. "The whole story of man-kind's loneliness, of the effort to reach out to unattainable beauty, tried to get itself expressed from the lips of a mumbling old man, crazed with loneliness." "We have different names but we are brothers." "Already I have written three hundred, four hundred thousand words. Are there no words that lead into life?" See con-clusion of "The Man in the Brown Coat."

A Story Teller's Story (1924). An attempt to lay bare the emo-tional life of one seeking to be an artist in America; to plumb his own consciousness, to escape from a world he hates. Such escape comes from reaching down "through all the broken surface distrac-tions of modern life to that old craft out of which culture springs." He must pull himself free from a deadening and devastating routine of an industrial society with its empty ambitions. And having found his craft he finds a recompense in life. "I sang as I worked, as in my boyhood I had often seen old craftsmen sing and as I had never heard men sing in factories. And for what I had written at such times I had been called unclean by men and women who had never known me, could have no personal reasons for thinking me unclean. Was I unclean? Were the hands that, for such brief periods of my life, had really served me, had they been unclean at such moments of service?" A stimulating and suggestive document of modern life.

The note of determinism in Anderson expressed in two images, the wall and escape—running to get away from what holds us fast. But in running away from the old self to find a new, we carry the old self with us. Anderson one of the three or four most important men now writing fiction in America. Compare with D. H. Law-rence.

A NEW ROMANCE

The new romance and the new naturalism both spring from a common root—hatred of the meanness and ugliness of modern life; but romance seeks to evade and forget what naturalism examines curiously. It is a defense mechanism against things as they are and springs from:

1. Disgust at the verisimilitude of naturalism that parades the crude ugliness of life as if it were the reality. The dream more important than the fact, for our real existence is within the imagination, removed from material futilities, where we may satisfy our hunger for beauty, for far-ranging adventure, for ideal existence.

2. The impulse to free creation. Real life overshadowed and darkened by a sense of impotence; men are flies caught in the web of circumstance. But in romance the will is unshackled and the free imagination plays with time and space, shaping fate to its liking in terms of beauty, dwelling in a world as we should like it to be. Romance hence is the ideal cosmos of the ego.

3. The spirit of youth that has brooded over life and refuses to abandon its dreams. The inevitable outcome irony, an undertone of sadness, a recognition of the pessimism against which it desires to be a defense. This the final note. So compare the *Eros et mors* of old romance. . . .*

* Cabell omitted, as there is a fuller discussion of him given.—*Publisher.*

Introduction: With the entry of America into the war came a sharp change in literary development. Regimentation due to war psychology destroyed the movement of social criticism which dominated fiction between 1903 and 1917. The liberal movement in economics and politics came to an abrupt end, and the problem novel ceased to be written. Almost overnight it became old-fashioned. The year 1918 sterile.[1] With the year 1919 began a new literary period. Three major movements:

1. A resurgence of naturalism, inspired by psychology rather than by economics, with a tendency to impressionism in handling: represented by Sherwood Anderson.

2. A new romanticism, seeking ideal beauty as a defense against reality and emerging in irony: represented by James Branch Cabell.

3. A new criticism: A revolt of the young intellectuals against the dominant middle class—its Puritanism, its Victorianism, its acquisitive ideals: represented by Sinclair Lewis.

I

THE SMALL TOWN IN FICTION

The first expression of the new literature. Chiefly a middle-western development—and a late phase of the literature of the local. A reaction from the "economic city," with its centralizing economics, which dominated the problem novel. Two antagonistic interpretations: (1) The romantic small town, or the theory of a kindly, democratic world; (2) The realistic small town, or the theory of a petty, competitive world.

I. *The Romantic Interpretation of the Small Town.* A hold-over from an earlier period. Derives from Riley; elaborated and defended by Meredith Nicholson, *The Valley of Democracy* (1918). According to this theory the middle-western village is: (1) A land of economic well-being, uncursed by poverty and unspoiled by wealth; (2) A land of "folksiness"—the village a great family in its

---

* From the syllabus.—*Publisher.*

[1] For a statement of the reaction of a young intellectual to the war, see Randolph Bourne, *Untimely Papers*, 1919.

neighborliness, friendliness, sympathy; (3) Primarily middle-class, and therefore characteristically American, wholesome, and human in spite of its prosaic shortcomings; (4) The home of American democracy, dominated by the spirit of equality, where men are measured by their native qualities.[2]

WILLIAM ALLEN WHITE: A SON OF THE MIDDLE BORDER

Product of middle-class, Puritan Kansas. Dominated by sentiment, believes in the essential fairness of men. Two major ideas: (1) Belief in the excellence of western village life; (2) Fear lest this life be submerged by industrialism. A romantic and political Progressive. Formulated his political theory in *The Old Order Changeth* (1910)—thesis, that America is changing from representative republicanism to democracy. The problem is to make business honest. Not an intellectual. His plots resemble Thackeray's— leisurely, gossipy, confidential asides, a large canvas, many figures, a long period of time. His attitude admirably expressed in *Emporia and New York* (1906).

At the Court of Boyville (1899). The romance of youth set against the background of the small town. A world of dreams and loveliness: adventures that await beyond the horizon; the glory of pigtails and overalls. The democracy of the vacant lot: rivalry in marbles and hand-springs—the leadership of the capable. Sincerer work than Tarkington's *Penrod*. Contrast with Garland's *Son of the Middle Border*, and Mark Twain's *Tom Sawyer*.

A Certain Rich Man (1909). His plunge into the problem novel. Theme: fear of the economic city that draws the villager into its web. A contrast between the two worlds and two social ideals—the friendly democracy of the older America threatened by economic centralization.

In the Heart of a Fool (1918). One of the last of the problem novels. Theme—the invasion of the small town by industrialism and the disintegration of village virtues. The story of an idealist who opposes the ends of Main Street and his destruction by the herd. A suggestion of Sinclair Lewis. The conclusion—the excellence of love and the foolishness of selfishness. The background characters, studies in the reaction of the older ideal to the new egoism.

[2] For a criticism of Nicholson, see Randolph Bourne, *The History of a Literary Radical*, p. 128.

BOOTH TARKINGTON: THE DEAN OF AMERICAN MIDDLE-CLASS LETTERS

Possesses the virtues of cleverness, optimism, humor, respectability. Honors all the Victorian taboos. Life is an agreeable experience—to the successful, hence it is well to rise. His chief theme, middle-class romance as exemplified in the "valley of democracy": courtship of nice young people through the agencies of parties and picnics. A skillful writer, with a light touch, but his art destroyed by love of popularity—a novel ends well that ends happily. A perennial sophomore, purveyor of comfortable literature to middle-class America.[3]

The Gentleman from Indiana (1899). A dramatization of the "good, dear people" theme. The college man who goes back to his people to live and work with them. A satisfying life results from merging individual life in the common village life. A flabby and somewhat saccharine philosophy.

Alice Adams (1921). The story of an instinctive actress and her competitive struggle for social position and a man. A clever, attractive, lovable girl defeated by her background—led into foolish little deceits to keep up appearances—victim of middle-class conventionality. Shabby parlors versus conservatories as settings for proposals. The Adams family has fallen behind their acquaintances in the business of rising in the world, and Alice sinks to a lower social scale. An overrated book.

The Midlander (1923). A contribution to booster literature and an unconscious satire on the emptiness of the middle-class mind. A real-estate venture and what came of it. The conception that "man is a wealth-and-comfort-producing machine." Supposed to be tragedy, but the tragedy lies in preferring the imported to the domestic article—choosing a New York girl instead of a local one. The suburb thrives, the automobile business goes forward, and the gods of getting on smile in the end.[4]

The other numerous titles of Tarkington signify nothing except to lovers of comfortable literature. The clever Hoosier has ceased to be an artist—the great failure in contemporary American fiction.

DOROTHY CANFIELD (FISHER)

A clever dramatizer of the obvious: believes in the Woman Triumphant, and discovers in the right education of children—particularly girls—the solution of all problems. Two main themes

[3] See Mr. Cabell's criticism in *Beyond Life*, pp. 301–307.
[4] For a review see the *Nation*, March 19, 1924.

1. A protest against the demands of "social life." *The Squirrel Cage* (1912). A contribution to the problem novel. A William Morris suggestion of the sufficiency of handicraft as an escape from social demands. An arraignment of the American home where the father scarcely knows the children and the mother is shut away from the outside world.

The Bent Twig (1915). A study of university community life—the struggle between plain living and high thinking—of social pleasure and no thinking.

2. The defense of the village. The belief that community fellowship—a gathering to watch a century plant bloom—breeds an artistic spirit finer than old-world art and culture can offer. Especially a Vermont town is ideal for the proper bringing up of children. *The Brimming Cup* (1920). A story of the right bringing up of children. *Rough Hewn* (1922). The love of art and travel which leads inevitably to a Vermont town and marriage. *Raw Material* (1923). Sketches. The point of view given in "Paul Meyer"—the folly of thinking that a normal girl should prefer philology to matrimony.

II

THE REALISTIC SMALL TOWN AND THE NEW NATURALISM

The work of the younger intellectuals, more disciplined than the muckrakers, with wider culture and severer standards. Concerned for civilization, the things of the spirit, a free creative individualism, rather than political liberalism. A searching criticism of the triumphant middle class, its ideals and its habitat, the town and city; the repressive tyrannies of its herd mind; the futility of its materialism. Back of the novelists is a group of essayists, young critics of established ways: Van Wyck Brooks, Ludwig Lewisohn, Randolph Bourne, H. L. Mencken. They embody a reaction from: (1) The acquisitive ideal of a machine civilization. (2) "The great illusion of American civilization, the illusion of optimism"—the staple of middle-class business morale. (3) The sentimentalism of "comfortable literature," that evades reality and weakens the intellectual fiber. (4) The inhibitions of a Puritanism that has lost its sanctions. (5) The White-Tarkington doctrine of the "beautiful people" and "folksy village."

The movement began with Masters's *Spoon River Anthology*

(1915). An earlier work is E. W. Howe's *Story of a Country Town* (1883):—stark, grim, unrelieved, revealing the "smoldering discontent of an inarticulate frontier."

ZONA GALE—THE TRANSITION FROM ROMANCE TO REALISM

I. Friendship Village romance. *The Loves of Pelleas and Etarre* (1907). Everyone is helpful, everyone loves, or wants to, or is unhappy for lack of it. *Friendship Village* (1908). A world where there is no sorrow, or sickness, and where brotherly love rules. Of the "folksy" school.

II. The shift to realism. *Miss Lulu Bett* (1920). A homely village tragedy of the repressed soul that rebels under the irritation of domestic pin-pricks. Plebeian characters, thin, cheap, tiresome; set in a shoddy world and rubbing each other's nerves. Deacon Dwight a sadist; Miss Lulu a grotesque. Treated from the outside in contrast with Sherwood Anderson's method. *Faint Perfume* (1923). A glorification of martyrdom. The conviction that life is hard, and the excellence of the economy of pain. A partial return to the *Friendship Village* note, but like *Miss Lulu Bett* in the picture of a self-worshiping family.*

.   .   .   .

DONN BYRNE †

American born but Irish bred. His early work, *The Stranger's Banquet* (1919), half problem novel—industrialism—which offered little scope for the Celtic wistfulness in which he conceives romance to lie.

Messer Marco Polo (1921). The romance of distant times and places, of unfamiliar backgrounds and lovely worlds: medieval Venice and its pageantry; a far quest over burning sands; the loveliness of little Golden Bells at the court of Kubla Khan; the ardor of love that tangles itself in religion. A wistfulness and beauty of phrase that remind one of Synge's *Riders to the Sea.* The loveliest romance of recent years.[5]

The Wind That Bloweth (1922). A rich fabric—Gaelic folk; the woman of the boulevard; the white sun-baked road to Damascus;

* Sinclair Lewis omitted, as fuller material has been given.—*Publisher.*
† From the third section in the syllabus, which deals with "A New Romance."—*Publisher.*
[5] See Cabell's review of *Messer Marco Polo* in *Straws and Prayer-Books*, pp. 52–59 The writer's full name is Brian Oswald Donn-Byrne.

the fire of revolution; the crack of cordage as the ship rounds the Horn—a saga of the unquiet heart.

The Changeling (1923). Short stories of quaint places, forgotten people; the Bible and love of Ireland. Done with excellent craftsmanship.

Blind Raftery (1924). A tale of a blind harpist in Dean Swift's Ireland and of his wife, Hilaria, who sings the song of the women of the streets in Cadiz. Life teaches them a philosophy expressed by the harpist in these words: "We sit a little while by ourselves in an apart, dark place, and we learn truths, of how certain things one believes to be good are but vulgar selfish things, and how certain things the small think evil are but futile accidents. And we learn to be kind; such wisdom comes when we are dead. And those who have never died in life . . . are pleasant shallow people, soulless as seals."

ROBERT NATHAN

Began like Donn Byrne with a problem study—*Peter Kindred* (1919). A dual personality cut asunder and embodied in two characters: David the romantic fades out of the story, and Peter becomes a modern, absorbed in eugenics. A background of Phillips Exeter and Harvard.

Autumn (1921). An idyll of loneliness, with a commentary on materialism, done in simple, wistful language.

1. Mr. Jeminy, a village philosopher, disciple of Boëthius and St. Francis, half pagan and yet Christian. Troubled over the poverty of the world that does not amass "love, peace, the quiet of the heart, the work of one's hand."

2. A village background. Mr. Jeminy wished to teach the children the secret of happiness instead of the folly of plus and minus, and was turned out of his school. An echo of *Main Street* in its commentary on village narrowness, hardness, gossip. A frigid Puritanism that disapproves Mr. Jeminy for speaking disrespectfully of God and denies happiness to Mrs. Wicket who is under God's sentence of unhappiness.

3. A note of determinism. A world of grotesques—all are hemmed in and cramped, longing for fresh experience and strange adventures, all are unhappy. So Aaron Bade with his flute and his "awkward thoughts and clumsy feelings." Margaret Bade with her conviction, "Life is so much spilt milk"; Farmer Barly with his

commentary, "Folks are queer crotchets"; Anna Barly with her yearning for the "white wonder of life" and the trap. An indictment of New England for its destruction of natural happiness and the simple joy of life.

4. A profound irony. The end of Mr. Jeminy's hopefulness is disillusion. "Here within this circle of hills, is to be found faith, virtue, passion, and good sense. In this valley youth is not without courage, or age without wisdom." The outcome disproves this faith. Of his many pupils, "Not one is tidy of mind, or humble of heart. Not one has learned to be happy in poverty, or gentle in good fortune." Life as a whole is futile. The dead alone can ask God the meaning of life. "But for us, who remain, it has no meaning." The tale is Robert Frost done in prose—compare "Mending Wall."

The Puppet Master (1923). The most graceful fantasy in American literature. Papa Jonas, the puppet creator and master, watches the love of Annabelle Lee, a rag doll with shoe-button eyes, and Mr. Aristotle, a red-nosed, philosopher-clown puppet; and of Mary Holly and Christopher Lane, the poet. The theme is love— "Love is a man's soul: it does not grow like his hopes, it does not break like his heart. . . . But love goes by after a while." Papa Jonas is Mr. Jeminy, converted to the Stoic philosophy but lacking love. The note of determinism persists, but the Stoic attitude overcomes. "Yes," he said slowly, "one must make the best of what one has."

JOSEPH HERGESHEIMER: A SOPHISTICATED ROMANTIC

Began as a painter. After fourteen years' apprenticeship was accepted by the *Saturday Evening Post*, and began a career in popularity that rivals Tarkington's. Possesses the virtues and vices of the *Post* school. In earlier work a colorist, painting statuesques against artfully arranged backgrounds; a connoisseur of fabrics and poses and nature settings—nearly as "much concerned with the stuffs as with the stuff of life." In *Cytherea* the setting a sophisticated manipulation of the theme, as the hot Cuban night in *Cobra* with its naked primitive passions. A dabbler in psychology that develops into a crude Freudianism, particularly in *Cytherea*. Always a hint of artistic insincerity; something of a poseur yet a sensuous artist nature. His gorgeous prose style spotty and streaked by amazing crudeness.

The Three Black Pennys (1917). A study in the breaking out of willfulness in successive generations, set against a background of the history of iron-making in Pennsylvania. An elaboration of *Tubal Cain*. An anticlimax arranged for dramatic significance, suggesting the decay of romance in a hundred and fifty years of American industrial development. The first episode is Hergesheimer at his best. Howat Penny a study in moods that make him "angry at life"; but swept on by the will to possess. Ludowica Winscomb embodies a favorite theme—the suggestion of an older culture contrasted with the crude American reality. So compare Taou Yuen.

Linda Condon (1919). A study in the decay of surface beauty— an empty form caught in the web of a shallow mother and the demands of stronger natures, but preserved by lack of emotional concern. Handled skillfully, with a somewhat forced unity symbolized by Linda's straight black bang; but the story leaves one with a sense of unconcern for Linda and her fate. The ending melodramatic. Note Van Doren's curious comment—"nearly the most beautiful American novel since Hawthorne and Henry James."

Java Head (1919). The story of an exotic that languishes in an uncongenial habitat. A contrast in backgrounds: the romance of old Salem in the days of the clipper ship; the romance of a far older East that makes Salem seem raw and crude. Taou Yuen a decorative lay figure, with aristocratic suggestions beyond anything the West knows. The dramatic significance of opium, that hangs like a pall over the East and brings degeneration and death to Puritan Salem. The end with its cheap love adventure, a conscious satire on western life. Hergesheimer's best work. A romantic atmosphere got without archaic trappings of speech and manners; nevertheless makes much of costume.

Balisand (1924). A romance of a Virginia Federalist in the days of the Revolution and after. A rich background of plantation life, with a touch of somewhat cheap mysticism. Of the school of Washington rather than Jefferson. A better work than *The Bright Shawl* or *Cytherea*.

His other titles signify little. Yet see the *Saturday Evening Post* for a series of furniture stories. Characteristic of his concern for the "stuffs of life." See in particular, "Mahogany" (Vol. 195, no.

53, January, 1923); "Pewter" (Vol. 196, no. 23, January, 1924); "Oak" (Vol. 196, no. 3, July, 1923).[6]

IV
CERTAIN OTHER WRITERS

EDITH WHARTON—THE GENTEEL TRADITION AND THE NEW PLUTOCRACY

A temperamental aristocrat, endowed with keen intelligence and ripe culture. Observes the ways of a wealthy society without culture and unconcerned with standards. A protest against the domination of the middle class. Mrs. Wharton isolated in America by her native aristocratic tastes. The older New York society without real distinction, bound by convention and with middle-class concern for respectability; the new society a vulgar plutocracy; outside both a pushing *nouveau-riche* class eager to climb. Hence she turns to the authentic aristocracy of Europe for satisfaction of her genteel tastes. In spirit she belongs to the *ancien régime*. The highest law of society is convention, but it must be noble, not vulgar.

The House of Mirth (1905). A story of New York's gilded society, and how it served one of its daughters. Lily Bart, trained for social leadership in a plutocracy, a finished and costly parasite, seeking a market for her beauty, yet restrained by instinctive refinement from seeing the game through. Lacking money she is caught in a web of convention and destroyed. In her world convention is the social law, and the tragedy flows from her inability to rise above it or to keep it wholly. The contrast between Selden and Trenor—the aristocrat and the plutocrat—characteristic of Mrs. Wharton.

Ethan Frome (1911). A dramatization of the "narrow house" theme—life held relentlessly in the grip of poverty and duty. A bleak and joyless existence that seeks escape and suffers lingering tragedy. Thereafter a stern isolation and iron repression. Mrs. Wharton's finest work.

The Custom of the Country (1915). A study of the social climber. The best of a series of novels satirizing the encroachments on New York exclusiveness by the rising plutocracy and its daughters. The western plutocracy of pork presumably more vulgar than the

[6] For a striking characterization of Hergesheimer, see *The Bookman*, May, 1922 For an appreciation, see Cabell, *Straws and Prayer-Books*, pp. 195–221.

eastern plutocracy of Wall Street, yet between them the older
gentry crushed. So compare Boyesen, *Social Strugglers* (1893);
Robert Grant, *Unleavened Bread* (1900). Undine Spragg, like
Selma White, pushing, heartless, vulgar, showy, is set over against
Ralph Marvell, a refined "dabbler with life"; Peter Van Degen,
the "plunger"; and Elmer Moffatt, the self-made man. She embodies all that Mrs. Wharton most hates; all climbers are vulgar,
she believes, both men and women.

The Age of Innocence (1920). A study of the older world of the
eighteen-seventies. A loving yet satirical picture of a Pharisaic
society, "wholly absorbed in barricading self against the unpleasant"; that lives secluded, protected by its taboos, and fears
reality. A sterile world of clan conventions and negations; a
decadent Victorianism. The Van der Luydens of Skuytercliff are
of the same stuff as the Dagonets in *The Custom of the Country;*
and the dilettante Newland Archer is another Ralph Marvell. Into
this dead world enters Ellen Olenska with her vivid old-world
experiences, who threatens to rebel, yet finally yields to the clan
taboos. The book fades out like the lives of the Van der Luydens.
An admirable work.

Old New York (1924). Four carefully done tales that sketch
New York in the forties, fifties, sixties, and seventies. A return to
her best manner, with the finish of *The Age of Innocence.*

Her other later work not important. *Glimpses of the Moon* (1922)
inconsequential; and *A Son at the Front* (1923)—an attempt to
document the reactions of an artist with a son in the army—only
half successful.

Mrs. Wharton a finished artist who grasps her material firmly;
an intellectual attitude, delighting in irony. Unaffected by the
problem novel, and schools of naturalism or romanticism. Not a
thinker like Cabell, whose irony springs from an imagination that
contemplates man in his relation to cosmic forces, but an observer
whose irony springs from noting the clash between men and social
convention. The last of our literary aristocrats of the genteel
tradition. Her attitude expressed in the words, "*Je suis venue trop
tard dans un monde trop vulgaire.*"

WILLA CATHER: EPICS OF WOMEN

The Middle Border of Hamlin Garland seen through different
eyes. She looks back lovingly to a pioneer West, as the cradle of

heroic lives. An epic breadth of prairie spaces and industrious years, with a note of regret—*Optima dies prima fugit*. Against this background she sets her immigrant women, with their vigor and wealth of life, and considers how the West has dealt with them. Peasant heroines, with their strong natures hidden under queer speech and garb, set in a waste of wild red grass, bitter winters, burning summers, virgin soil and great loneliness. A long-ignored theme—the lot of the immigrant who has come on a desperate adventure—the struggle of their children with the soil. Compare *The Jungle*, for the industrial exploitation of the immigrant.

Has matured slowly. *The Troll Garden* (1905), and *Alexander's Bridge* (1910), are inconsequential. Her real work done late. Belongs to no school. Is neither naturalistic nor romantic. Is unconcerned with problems. Except for a single attack on the ugliness of the small western town—"The Sculptor's Funeral" in *The Troll Garden*—she ignores middle-class America and its Main Streets. An individual artist, sincere, capable; an excellent craftsman.

O Pioneers (1913). The story of Alexandra Bergson, a daughter of the Middle Border; calm, tenacious, capable; loving the soil and bringing it to abundant productiveness. The new world had brought out diverse qualities in the Swedish peasant family; the older brothers common, dull, vulgarized by Americanization; the younger brother suggestive of the better side of American opportunity. Alexandra the directing mind and controlling will. Over against her is set the Bohemian Marie Tovesky, childlike in her spontaneous enthusiasm. The tragic ending handled with great skill. Thrown about the whole, a harsh Nebraska countryside through changing periods. One who had not lived through similar experiences and loved the memory could not write so.

The Song of the Lark (1915). The story of Thea Kronberg, who by virtue of fierce energy and iron strength rises to triumph as an artist. There are no romantic stage-effects, only the passionate struggle of a tenacious will. Thea a peasant nature of vast solidity. The most convincing story of artist life written by an American. A changing background: the mean little Colorado town, the loneliness of Chicago, Europe, the great spaces of the Southwest.

My Ántonia (1918). The story of Ántonia Shimerda: an opulent peasant nature with strong mother instinct, thwarted by meager opportunities and vulgar environment. Her life runs a narrow round: the early pioneer experience with its loneliness and black tragedy; the town experience of the hired girl, who lives eagerly; the later life of a hard-working mother on a lonely farm. Ántonia "a rich mine of life like the founder of early races," loving, generous, eager, yet belonging to the soil. To vulgarize such natures by cramming them into a conventional mold, passes for Americanization—this the implied thesis.

One of Ours (1922). The story of Claude Wheeler, with strength imprisoned by a society that opens its opportunities to Main Street natures like Bayliss Wheeler. A suggestion of naturalism in the handling of the theme: Claude caught by the negative character Enid Royse because he fails to appreciate the complementary strength of Gladys Farmer—a true Cather woman, enmeshed in Gopher Prairie. A futile, ironical ending: better to die in battle than be destroyed by the pettiness of Gopher Prairie. The war atmosphere seems curiously old-fashioned.

The Lost Lady (1923). A change of theme. The story of Mrs. Forester, an embodiment of traditional feminine charm, quite superior to such incidents as age or loyalty—a type of woman outside Miss Cather's experience and understanding.*

V

SOME WAR BOOKS

The late war the first in our history that has produced an aftermath of searching criticism in fiction or drama. The romantic note dominant in all earlier accounts, particularly of the Revolution and the Rebellion. Such stories written by men who took no part in them. The Civil War produced only one book of realistic criticism, that was mutilated by the publisher to temper its cynicism, and that enjoyed no popularity—*The Recollections of a Private*, by Warren Goss. The late war is producing a considerable group, all realistic and critical; the romantic note has not yet appeared.

JOHN DOS PASSOS

Three Soldiers (1921). A naturalistic handling of war that serves as a commentary on *One of Ours*. The most notable American work on the theme since Stephen Crane's *The Red Badge of Courage.*

* See remarks on Miss Cather in the introduction to the text edition of Ole Rölvaag's *Giants in the Earth*, which follows these syllabus notes.—*Publisher.*

Similar in temper to Henri Barbusse, *Under Fire*, but dealing with
the barracks and the drill field. Compare with Andreas Latzko,
Men in War—impressionistic in handling. Dos Passos a young
artist from the university, an idealist who enlists and is disillusioned. A study of the war machine and the effect of regimentation
on different types of men—the contrast between army discipline
and a lax individualism, and the disasters that may ensue from
sudden change. Fuselli a low-grade character who wants to rise;
Chrisfield a solid animal who becomes sullen; Andrews a highly
nervous organism, to whom routine is killing. Coarse episodes set
in a brilliant background: the glamour of militarism gone.

E. E. CUMMINGS

The Enormous Room (1922). A brilliant revelation of the tortures
endured by an artist unjustly imprisoned in a French military
prison. Supplements *Three Soldiers* in destroying the appeal of
military glamour. An attack particularly on the common notion of
heroic, chivalrous France.

THOMAS BOYD

Through the Wheat (1923). An impressionistic handling of the
reactions of a normal American soldier, Private Hicks, to the war.
The keynote is numbness—a deadly numbness which offers the sole
defense of the normal mind against the horrors it confronts. Its
matter-of-factness, detached point of view, and the ordinariness of
the hero, set it apart from *Three Soldiers* and *The Enormous Room*.
An excellent bit of impressionism.

LAURENCE STALLINGS

Plumes (1924). A story of war by one who has suffered mutila-
tion from it. The theme—"If you are smashed badly . . . and if
you have any intelligence you must remake a world to live in."
A study of post-war disillusionment, naturalistically handled. So
compare the play in which he collaborated—*What Price Glory?*

VI

YOUTH IN REVOLT—CERTAIN PURVEYORS OF THE HECTIC

A group of youthful poseurs at the mercy of undigested reactions
to Nietzsche, Butler, Dadaism, Vorticism, Socialism; overbalanced
by changes in American critical and creative standards, and in love
with copious vocabularies and callow emotions. Given to satirizing

the educational methods of *alma mater;* quick to espouse new causes; enthusiastic for revolt as a profession. A prolific movement which as yet has accomplished nothing seriously creative.

F. SCOTT FITZGERALD

This Side of Paradise (1921); *The Beautiful and the Damned* (1922). A bad boy who loves to smash things to show how naughty he is; a bright boy who loves to say smart things to show how clever he is. Precocious, ignorant—a short candle already burnt out.

STEPHEN VINCENT BENÉT AND FLOYD DELL

Benét: *Heavens and Earth* (1920); *The Beginning of Wisdom* (1921); *Young People's Pride* (1923); *Jean Hugenot* (1923). Floyd Dell: *Moon Calf* (1921); *Briary Bush* (1922); *Janet March* (1923).

Luminaries of the school which holds that the sufficient tests of intellectual emancipation are rolled hose, midnight discussions, black coffee, and the discarding of wedding rings. Floyd Dell the most serious and ablest of the group.

BEN HECHT

Eric Dorn (1921); *Gargoyles* (1922). An almost naturalistic distrust of formal education, love, and government, and an unsubstantiated belief in the efficacy of revolt in general and the romance of city streets in particular. A burnt-out rocket. His last books— *1001 Afternoons in Chicago* (1923) and *Florentine Dagger* (1924) worse than inconsequential.

OLE RÖLVAAG'S "GIANTS IN THE EARTH" *

THE dramatic contrast between Per Hansa, type of the natural pioneer who sees the golden light of promise flooding the wind-swept plains, and Beret, child of an old folk civilization who hungers for the home ways and in whose heart the terror of lone-liness gathers, penetrates to the deeper reality of life as it was lived for three hundred years on the American frontier. It is not a late or rare phenomenon; it is only late and rare in literature. We have been used to viewing the frontier in broad and generous perspective and have responded most sympathetically to the epic note that runs through the tale of the conquest of the continent. It is the great American romance that gives life and drama to our history. It was this epic quality that de Tocqueville felt when he discovered the poetry of America in the silent march of a race toward the far-off Pacific, hewing its way triumphantly through forests and mountains to arrive at its objective. But the emo-tional side, the final ledger of human values, we have too little considered—the men and women broken by the frontier, the great army of derelicts who failed and were laid away, like the Norse immigrant lad, in forgotten graves. The cost of it all in human happiness—the loneliness, the disappointments, the renunciations, the severing of old ties and quitting of familiar places, the appalling lack of those intangible cushions for the nerves that could not be transported on horseback or in prairie schooners: these imponder-ables too often have been left out of the reckoning in our tradi-tional romantic interpretation. But with the growth of a maturer realism we are beginning to understand how great was the price exacted by the frontier; and it is because *Giants in the Earth*, for the first time in our fiction, evaluates adequately the settlement in terms of emotion, because it penetrates to the secret inner life of men and women who undertook the heavy work of subduing the wilderness, that it is—quite apart from all artistic values—a great historical document.

* Introduction to the text edition of Rölvaag's *Giants in the Earth*. Copyright 1929 by Harper and Brothers, by whose permission it is reprinted here.—*Publisher*

If in one sense the conquest of the continent is the great American epic, in another sense it is the great American tragedy. The vastness of the unexplored reaches, the inhospitality of the wilderness, the want of human aid and comfort when disaster came, these were terrifying things to gentle souls whom fate had not roughhewn for pioneering. Fear must have been a familiar visitor to the heart of the pioneer woman, and for a hundred and fifty years this fear of the dark wilderness was one reason why the settlements clung to the more hospitable seaboard. There, at least, was an outlook toward the old home. But with the crossing of the Allegheny Mountains, following the Revolutionary War, the frontier spirit came into its own. A spirit of restlessness took possession of men, and the thin line of settlements advanced swiftly, overrunning the Inland Empire with its interminable forests and malarial swamps, sprawling rudely from the Great Lakes to the Gulf of Mexico. To subdue the land was no easy task. Upon the old and the weak the wilderness laid a ruthless hand, and even of the strength of the young it took heavy toll. Tragedy was always lurking at the door of the backwoods cabin. In Beveridge's *Life of Lincoln* there is a grim story of the hardships suffered by the Lincoln family in Indiana that leaves no room for romance—husband, wife, two children, and later an old couple, were forced to pig together all winter in a brush camp open on one side to the weather, with only a fire in front for cooking and heating—a mode of life below that of the Indian in his skin teepee. And then a mysterious disease fell upon them, virulent and fateful, and the old couple were taken from their cots on the ground and put away beneath the soil to find what rest they might there. That men should break and women go mad under such strain is no more than may be expected of human nature. Beret, the wife of Per Hansa, brooding in her sod-hut in Dakota, afraid of life and of her own thoughts, and turning for comfort to a dark religion, is a type of thousands of frontier women who—as the historian Ridpath said of his parents—"toiled and suffered and died that their children might inherit the promise."

Very likely we should have felt the tragedy of the frontier long ago if we had been as much concerned with inner experience as with outward act, if we had been psychologists as well as chroniclers. But we have been too prone to romanticize the objective reality and disguise slatternly ways with the garb of backwoods independence. The realistic eighteenth century made no such mistake. Such infrequent glimpses of the first frontier as we catch in our early literature suggest a swift descent into grossness as the settlements were left behind. In the *Journal of Madam Sarah Knight*, which dates from the opening years of the eighteenth century, are brief notes of what fell under her sharp eyes on a horseback trip from Boston to New York. The sketches she has penciled are far from bucolic. Certain of the figures that emerge casually from her pages are no other than decivilized grotesques—animal-like creatures for whom returning to a state of nature meant living filthily in mean huts, traveling back centuries toward the primitive ways of the cavemen. Of the emotional reactions of these early children of the wilderness Madam Knight tells us nothing; so casual an observer would have no opportunity to penetrate beneath the unlovely surface.

A quarter century later Colonel William Byrd, the first gentleman of Virginia, wrote his graphic *History of the Dividing Line*, an account of a boundary survey run between the colonies of Virginia and South Carolina. As the survey leaves the seacoast behind and approaches the frontier, the same characteristics appear that Madam Knight noted—a rough and surly independence, a dislike of established law and order, and a shiftless way of life that is content to subsist off the country. "Lubberland," Colonel Byrd called the Carolina backwoods where a new race of poor whites was springing up—a rude decivilized existence that bore heavily on the women and was heedless of the common amenities of social life. In *Letters from an American Farmer* (1773) written by St. John de Crèvecœur, a cultivated Norman who established himself in the colonies after serving in the French army under Montcalm, the same sharp judgment is passed on the frontier. Crèvecœur was of the romantic school of Rousseau and eloquent in praise of life lived close to nature, yet even he discovers the frontier to be a blot on colonial civilization, the abode of rude and lawless figures who precede by a decade the sober army of occupation.

In the eighteenth century the testimony is clear that the frontiersmen—or "borderers," as they were commonly called—were rough bumptious fellows who fled the settlements partly because of a dislike of ordered and seemly ways. The colonial gentry, men like the Rev. Timothy Dwight, held them in deep contempt and rejoiced when they quitted the settlements and plunged deep into the wilderness beyond the jurisdiction of church and state. Lawlessness, shiftlessness, a passion like Jurgen's to follow after their own wishes and their own desires, seem to have been the characteristics of these rude men and slatternly women, as the aristocratic eighteenth century judged them. That is very far from the whole story, to be sure. Our later historians have made clear that from this same leveling frontier issued the spirit of American democracy, and that from these rough individualists came the great movement of Jacksonianism that swept away the class distinctions of an earlier century. Accepting so much, and recognizing the part played by the frontier in shaping the institutions and the psychology of America, it remains true, nevertheless, that the lot of the backwoodsman was hard and the price he paid in civilization for his freedom was great. The sod house of the Dakota plains was only a late adaptation of the primitive huts that were strung along the earlier frontier. What loneliness filled the hearts of the drab women who made hoecakes and dressed deer skins, what rebellions at their lot stirred dumbly within them, no record remains to tell and no literature has cared to concern itself about.

It was not till the nineteenth century that authentic accounts of the frontier, written by men who had come out of it, began to appear, yet even then in too scant volume. In Longstreet's *Georgia Scenes*, Joseph G. Baldwin's *Flush Times of Alabama and Mississippi*, and Davy Crockett's *Autobiography*, the frontier is painted in homely colors that time cannot fade. Their brisk pages seem to have been dipped in the butternut dye-pot of the backwoods cabin. By far the most significant of them is the braggart but naïvely truthful narrative of the life of Cane-brake Davy who in his several removals followed the advancing frontier the length of the State of Tennessee. Davy would seem to have been the authentic backwoodsman, and the life of the individual may be taken as a description of the genus. Restless, assertive, unsocial, buoyantly optimistic and obsessed with the faith that better land lay farther west, cultivating a bumptious wit that was a defense mechanism against the meanness of daily life, he was only an improvident child who fled instinctively from civilization. As a full-length portrait of the Jacksonian leveler, in the days when the great social revolution was establishing the principles of an equalitarian democracy, the picture is of vast significance. But it is incomplete. Concerning the wife and daughters who were dragged at his heels in the successive removals, the narrative is silent. It is a man's tale, unenriched by the emotional experiences of a woman, and as such it tells only half the story of the frontier.

The *Autobiography* was the last pungent note of realism before the romantic revolution swept over American literature; and it was not till two generations later, when the war was over and the glories of the Gilded Age were fading, that the frontier came to realistic expression again in the works of Hamlin Garland. *Main-Travelled Roads*, the first chapter in the tale of the Middle Border, is a prologue to *Giants in the Earth*, telling the story of the prairie settlement in the idiom of the generation that undertook the great adventure. In these brief tales is compressed the harsh temper of the eighties, when the spirit of revolt was running like wildfire across the prairies and the Middle Border was arming for battle. For a decade or more the farmers' affairs had been out of kilter, and a note of discontent had begun to appear in fiction. Before Garland, western life had been dealt with by Edward Eggleston in *The Hoosier Schoolmaster* and *The Circuit Rider*, and more searchingly by Ed Howe in *The Story of a Country Town*—a drab commentary on life in Atchison, Kansas, in the early eighties. But it is in Joseph Kirkland's *Zury, The Meanest Man in Spring County* (1887), that a deep sense of the meanness of frontier life is first adequately felt. The harsh constrictions of pioneer existence tightened about Zury as a boy when his father was struggling with debt, turning a naturally generous nature into a skinflint mortgage grabber. He early learned that he must fight to survive, and as a result his life was shut up in a narrow round of sordid accumulation. It was the poverty of the frontier, in Kirkland's eyes, that was the great hardship.

Hamlin Garland's more adequate story of the Middle Border, beginning militantly with *Main-Travelled Roads* (1887–92) and flowering in the idyllic saga of the Garlands and McClintocks (1914), is a chronicle that grows more significant as the times it deals with draw further into the past. Throughout his interpretation run two dominant notes: the promise of future fulfillment when the prairies have been brought under the plow—the Per Hansa note of pioneer optimism; and then later, rising slowly

into a ground swell, a note of discouragement suggesting the utter
futility of a laborious existence. Underlying *Main-Travelled Roads*
is a mood of bitterness that springs from a deep sense of failure—
a mood that grew harsher with the economic depression of the
Middle Border in the eighties. The harvest was not fulfilling
the expectations of seed time, and the bow of promise was gone
from the prairie fields. The figures of bitter men and despondent
women fill his pages and darken the colors of his realism. It is
the cost of it all that depresses him—the toll exacted of human
happiness. These early studies of Garland's strike the first note
of the tragedy of the frontier. Starkly objective, they are sociological sketches, the militant expression of a rebellious mood that
had been deepening since the panic of 1873 burst the romantic
bubble of frontier hopes. The history of two decades of economic
maladjustment, with their Granger Populism, their passionate
resentment at the favoritisms of government, their blind striking
out at the plutocracy that was visibly rising amid the American
democracy, is compressed within a few acrid tales that proposed
to tell the plain truth about life on the Middle Border farm.
Main-Travelled Roads is as complete an expression of the mood
of the last years of the century—the outlook upon life, the economic and political problems, the objective treatment of materials
—as *Giants in the Earth* is an expression of the vastly different
outlook and mood of our own day.

For a generation before 1917, when the movement was brought
to a sudden stop, the mind of America was deeply concerned with
problems of sociology. The growing spirit of realism was absorbed
in politics and economics and concerned itself little with subjective
analysis. The intellectuals were busily examining the Constitution
in the light of its economic origins and interpreting American
history in the light of frontier experience. The novelists, reflecting
the current interests, were fascinated by the phenomena of industrialism and were studying curiously the new race of captains
of industry who were weaving a strange pattern of life for America.
The city had already come to dwarf the country. Chicago bestrode
the Middle Border like a colossus, and the novelists found material
for their realism in the cut-throat ways of business men. Their
stories—harsh and strident as the grinding wheels on the over-
head "Loop"—were set against a background of sprawling cities

hastening to grow big, where the battles of giants were fought and where the *milieu*—a vast network of impersonal forces—was more significant than the individual men and women who were borne onward in the stream of tendency to submerge or rise as chance determined. A note of stark determinism runs through much of the work; but it was a determinism of environing forces— the objective world of the machine—rather than of character, and in consequence the deeper concern of fiction was sociological, the understanding of this impersonal machine order and the subduing of it to democratic ends. In such a world the farmer and the problems of the Middle Border were become as old-fashioned as ox-carts.

Ten years later, when *Giants in the Earth* was published, such objective treatment of materials was no longer the vogue. Since the war a revolutionary shift of interest has taken place, a shift from the sociological to the psychological. It is no longer the world of objective fact that obtrudes as the significant reality, but the subtler world of emotional experience, the furtive inner life of impulse and desire that Sherwood Anderson probes so curiously. The change of theme was first marked, perhaps, by *Spoon River Anthology*, with its mordant sketches of stunted and thwarted lives that Mr. Masters professes to regard as the natural harvest of a sterile village life. *Spoon River Anthology* is bitter in its sardonic rebellion against the genial optimisms of the "Valley of Democracy." From the epic thrust of expansion issued, as its natural progeny, a race of abortive grotesques, starved figures which suggest to Mr. Masters the cost in human values of severing the ties of kin and kind and throwing aside like an old shoe the creative wealth of social experience. The soil of the frontier village is too thin for men and women to strike deep root and grow to generous stature.

Since the publication of *Spoon River Anthology*, concern for psychological values has pretty much taken possession of our literature. In the lovely pages of Willa Cather's *O Pioneers!* and *My Ántonia* there is revealed a warm sympathy with the emotional life of pioneer women and a poignant understanding of their bleak lot. But the analysis—as in Hamlin Garland's work—draws back from the threshold of final tragedy, pausing before it has pene- trated to the hidden core of futility. The waste of all finer values exacted by the prairies is suggested by the queer figures of lonely immigrants who fade in the uncongenial environment, but it is not thrust into the foreground to dominate the scene. The vast stretches of the prairies are there—stern, inhospitable, breeding a dumb homesickness in alien hearts—where the red grass bends before the restless winds and the forces of nature are not easily tamed; but in the end the prairie is subdued and the scars it has laid on men's lives are forgotten. Since Willa Cather, others have dealt with the West—Ruth Suckow, Margaret Wilson, and Herbert Quick, to name a few—yet in none of their work is there the profound insight and imaginative grasp of the theme that gives to *Giants in the Earth* so great a sense of tragic reality.

In this creative return to the theme of the great American adventure the causes of human failure lie deeper than politics or economics. They are to be found in the impersonal forces of nature that are too powerful for the human will to cope with; and in the hidden weakness of fearful souls that cannot live when their roots have been pulled up from the congenial home soil. For all his titanic labors, Per Hansa, the viking, is struck down at last. There are few nobler passages in our fiction—the more telling for its restraint—than the final scene where, driven inexorably by circumstance, Per Hansa sets forth into the February blizzard to fetch a minister to the bedside of his stricken comrade. The note of determinism is there, subtle, pervasive. The Norns of his fathers had decreed that it should be so—in the urgings of the mystical Beret, in the dumb pleadings of the dying Hans Olsa and his broken-hearted wife. Per Hansa the strong, the capable one who never failed, who was cunning enough to outwit fate itself—Per Hansa would go out into the storm and return with the minister who would point the way to heaven to the troubled Hans Olsa. And so, driven by all the imperatives of fate, he sets out, skis on his feet and others at his back, to face the last great adventure. The blinding snow quickly wraps him about, the cold grips his heart, and Per Hansa is seen no more until on a soft May day, when the wheat is green in his fields and the corn is ready for planting, he is found seated by a haystack, his skis beside him and his face turned to the untrodden West. For all the heroic labors of Per Hansa, for all the tragic loneliness of Beret, the end is futility.

And Beret, the sick one, likewise is in the hands of the Norns. She had sinned through love of Per Hansa, and in the long brooding

hours on the Dakota plains her mind gives way. She cannot rise
to Per Hansa's delight in the newborn son. Peder Victorious—
symbol of Per Hansa's buoyant faith—for her is only another
evidence of sin. This dark land of Dakota is marked by God's
displeasure, and life for her becomes a silent struggle of renun-
ciation and atonement. A primitive Norse Calvinist, victimized
by a brooding imagination that sees more devils than vast hell
can hold, she dwells "on the border of utter darkness" where the
forces of good and evil struggle for the human soul. Across the
gloomy Puritanism of her nature fall the shadows of an older and
darker faith, and in her nostalgia the old Northland superstitions
merge with the somber Northland religion to her undoing. The
tragedy of Beret works itself out in the tender corridors of her
own heart and, as Professor Commager has suggested, it is as
universal as the tragedy of Goethe's Margarethe. In his portrayal
of the "sick soul" of Beret hungering for the far homeland the
Norse artist has achieved a triumph. The epic conquest of the
continent must be read in the light of women's sufferings as well
as in that of men's endurance. In whichever light it is read, it
becomes something far more suggestive than a drab tale of frontier
poverty or a sordid tale of frontier exploitation; it becomes vital
and significant as life itself.

Giants in the Earth is a great and beautiful book that suggests
the wealth of human potentialities brought to America year after
year by the peasant immigrants who pass through Ellis Island
and scatter the length and breadth of the land. Written in Norwegian, and stemming from a rich old-world literary tradition,
it is at the same time deeply and vitally American. The very
atmosphere of the Dakota plains is in its pages, and it could have
been written only by one to whom the background was a familiar
scene. The artist has lived with these peasant folk; he is one of
them, and he penetrates sympathetically to the simple kindly
hearts hidden to alien eyes by the unfamiliar folk ways. To gather
up and preserve in letters these diverse folk strains before they
are submerged and lost in the common American *mores*, would
seem to be a business that our fiction might undertake with profit.

Ole Edvart Rölvaag is himself a viking of the Per Hansa strain.
Born of fisher folk, 22 April, 1876, on the island of Donna at the
very edge of the Arctic circle, he took his name, following a com-

mon Norwegian custom, from the name of a cove on the shores of which he was brought up. It is a land barren except for the gorse and heather, and the long winter nights and the restless sea were certain to bring the imagination under their somber spell. At the age of fourteen, discouraged from further schooling by the family that contrasted him unfavorably with a brilliant brother, he turned fisherman, and for five years went off to the Lofoten Islands some two hundred miles away for the winter catches. Distrustful of the future, he made his great decision to come to America, landing in New York in 1896 with only a railway ticket to South Dakota. In the great West, still turmoiled by the agrarian upheaval of the nineties, he joined an uncle who had provided him transportation money, tried his hand at farming, worked at other jobs, and at the age of twenty-three, not having found himself, he turned once more to the formal business of schooling. In the fall of 1899 he entered Augustana College, a preparatory school in Canton, South Dakota. From there he went to St. Olaf College, Northfield, Minnesota, graduating in 1905 at the age of twenty-eight. After a year at the University of Oslo in Norway, he joined the staff of St. Olaf College, where he is now Professor of Norwegian Literature. In the larger sense, however, his education has been got from life, which he seems to have lived with a rich and daring intensity; and it is his own venturesome experience, certainly, that finds expression in the creative realism and brooding imagination of his work. Intellectually and artistically he is of the excellent old-world culture. How greatly his professional studies determined his literary technique only a competent Norwegian critic can judge; yet it is worth while comparing *Giants in the Earth* with Johan Bojer's *The Emigrants*—a work which, when announced as being in preparation, dramatically influenced his own novel.

THE SHORT STORY *

Introduction. With the ferment of the seventies and eighties a new school of literature, that was effectively a denial of the genteel tradition: it was effectively a popularization—a taking it out of the severe realm of the *Atlantic Monthly*. It was an appeal to the middle class. From Henry James to Hamlin Garland a steady shift from right to left. This implied:

1. A shift from genteel to homely material.

2. A shift to realism from the earlier sentimentality. This genteel tradition constantly cropping out anew—in Margaret Deland, in a changed form in Zona Gale. It has been strongest in New England—from Rose Terry Cooke through Sarah Orne Jewett to Mary Wilkins.

The short story commonly believed to be peculiarly representative of our genius—the stripping-away of the superfluous and the love of technical refinement. Derived from Poe and Hawthorne: both artists yet far removed from the tendencies which have controlled the development of the short story since.

Theme. The American short story has dealt largely with the two great themes of all romance, love and adventure. The form constitutes the great staple—is largely provided by women for women. The handling of this love theme reveals the inevitable shift from the genteel tradition to middle-class efficiency, and the spirit of the change is revealed in the changing dress of the heroine. In the seventies, crinoline, innumerable flounces of white muslin, lace parasols—no tan, no freckles, but a gentle pallor. Such dress and such heroines will exude sentiment. It will concern itself with atmosphere. Action brisk and efficient will appear unladylike, almost vulgar. What a change when the heroine clothes herself in a silk flour-sack—showing silk stockings, bare arms and neck—cultivating tan and freckles, bobbing her hair, going in for automobiles and golf and tennis! The older heroine dwelt in a world of sentiment without sex; the present-day heroine lives in a world of sex interest without sentiment. The more flounces in life and literature, the

---

* Lecture notes. This subject was not included in the contents, but contains some matter of interest.—*Publisher.*

less the animal is exposed. Hence action has superseded sentiment
—plot has superseded atmosphere. The hero becomes a Hart,
Schaffner and Marx young business man and the middle-class note
is struck loudly in the honk of the motor-car. The genteel tradition
is laid away with the flowers.

Major Influences during the Sixties. Through the fifties and
sixties literature uncertain and halting. The style largely set by
old-world fashions. Three in particular:

1. Influence of Charlotte and Emily Brontë. A sort of sentimental and mawkish passion. Stilted style, as in Harriet Beecher
Stowe. This fell in with the Irving note of the picturesque and was
exploited in *Godey's Lady's Book.*

2. Influence of Dickens. At its height in the fifties: an emphasis
upon the vulgar—plain and homely characters. Exploited in the
Atlantic by Lowell. So Rose Terry Cooke in *Miss Lucinda* (1861).

3. Influence of the French realistic movement: Balzac, Flaubert.
Only a faint beginning. Still a lot of romance stuff but given a local
color and garnished with humor.

Counter Tendencies. The inevitable development of the middle-
class city and the middle-class magazine, persistently affected by
certain throw-backs to an older American tradition. America is of
the city today, but day before yesterday it was still country, and in
the backgrounds of our minds is a country setting and love of simple people. Three main tendencies:

1. The discovery of the local. The picturesqueness of the strange
and remote in character, manners, speech. The charm of dialect
and interest in out-of-the-way places. This a reaction from too
much pavement and the rubbing-down of individual differences
from city contact. "Characters" are bred in isolated places. This
the dominant note in the short story from 1870 to 1900: to follow
it from Bret Harte on is almost to write a history of the short
story. It does not dominate the longer story. Constance Fenimore
Woolson.

2. The discovery of "human interest." The feeling that men in
the rough—with the bark on—may prove more interesting than
the products of an artificial civilization. This had been spread by
Dickens and by certain of the *Atlantic* writers.

3. The growing interest in realism. At first confused with the
commonplace—so Pattee in his comment on Rose Terry Cooke's
Miss Lucinda. A good deal of this earlier work is only another form

of romance—little affected by the rising French movement. Realism was to come slowly and late. All three of these made against the genteel tradition.

Henry James. His position peculiar. From his youth *déraciné*—his father hated American vulgarity, American journalism, and would not permit his son to take root. He grew up with an aristocratic conception of civilization—his sole interest lay in such civilization, and the manners of the polite society of that civilization. No other American has so hated and feared contamination from the vulgar. He was thus the last flower of the Genteel Tradition, transplanted to an environment more congenial. As the middle-class became more clamorous, he withdrew to the Continent, to England, where the older ideas still lingered. There in the spirit of the realist he wrote with refined art and persistent detachment—even to a punctilious and princely refinement. As Mr. Howells says, "To enjoy his work, to feel its rare excellence, both in conception and expression, is a brevet of intellectual good form."

His World. Always that of the spender, of assured position. His main interest lies in women; their refinement appeals to his refinement—no flappers or vulgarians but elegantly gowned women who never did the family washing. He is concerned with that which is dearest to the heart of aristocracy—standards of excellence. And in this he was true to his conception of civilization, for civilization begins after a competence has been assured. Those who are struggling to acquire have not the leisure, the inclination, for civilization. Hence *Daisy Miller* is a type of much of his work—the contrast between civilized Europe and uncivilized America, the one with standards of culture and manners and the other vulgarian. And his interest in American women results from the fact that they alone in America care for civilization and are painfully seeking to achieve it.

His Realism. The beginnings of the movement which has been called psychological realism, concerning itself with motives and processes of thought—the inner life. Developed by Bourget and far more fully by Dorothy Richardson in such a book as *Pilgrimage*, the inner life of Miriam Henderson in many volumes. Far removed from later psychological fiction founded on Freudian theory—as in D. H. Lawrence, Sherwood Anderson. Again the genteel tradition dealing with people who in the main have genteel impulses only. James held in horror this later naturalism—it was merely vulgarian.

The Spirit of the Local. Into this prim world with its incipient realism came the note of the Far West: Mark Twain and Bret Harte, who set a new style—the romantic, picturesque, human-interest story. This is a part of the Pike County idea of literature—a native rogue-tale but with touches of sentiment and shortened to effective form. This followed by Eggleston's *Hoosier Schoolmaster* (1871) and this in turn by the flood of local work of the eighties. The most notable the work of Charles Egbert Craddock, Joel Chandler Harris, Sarah Orne Jewett, and Mary Wilkins. The first discovered the hill people, the second discovered the Negro—his primitive folk-poetry. In the work of the last, a struggle between the genteel tradition and realism—and the final triumph of the latter.

A CHAPTER IN AMERICAN LIBERALISM *

Liberals whose hair is growing thin and the lines of whose figures are no longer what they were, are likely to find themselves today in the unhappy predicament of being treated as mourners at their own funerals. When they pluck up heart to assert that they are not yet authentic corpses, but living men with brains in their heads, they are pretty certain to be gently chided and led back to the comfortable armchair that befits senility. Their counsel is smiled at as the chatter of a belated post-Victorian generation that knew not Freud, and if they must go abroad they are bidden take the air in the garden where other old-fashioned plants—mostly of the family *Democratici*—are still preserved. It is not pleasant for them. It is hard to be dispossessed by one's own heirs, and especially hard when those heirs, in the cheerful ignorance of youth, forget to acknowledge any obligations to a hard-working generation that laid by a very substantial body of intellectual wealth, the income from which the heirs are spending without even a "Thank you." If therefore the middle-aged liberal occasionally grows irritable and indulges in caustic comment on the wisdom of talkative young men it may be set down as the prerogative of the armchair age and lightly forgiven.

Yet in sober fact there are the solidest reasons for such irritation. The younger liberals who love to tweak the nose of democracy are too much enamored of what they find in their own mirrors. They are indisputably clever, they are spouting geysers of smart and cynical talk, they have far outrun their fathers in the free handling of ancient tribal totems—but they are afflicted with the short perspective of youth that finds a vanishing-point at the end of its own nose. There is no past for them beyond yesterday. They are having so good a time playing with ideas that it does not occur to them to question the validity of their intellectual processes or to inquire into the origins of the ideas they have adopted so blithely. Gaily engaged in smashing *bourgeois* idols, the young intellectuals are too busy to realize that it was the older generation that pro-

---

* This was apparently not intended as the introduction to Part I of Book Three, but covers much of the ground indicated there.—*Publisher.*

401

vided them with a hammer and pointed out the idols to be smashed. It is the way of youth.

Middle-aged liberals—let it be said by way of defense—at least know their history. They were brought up in a great age of liberalism—an age worthy to stand beside the golden forties of last century—and they went to school to excellent teachers. Darwin, Spencer, Mill, Karl Marx, Haeckel, Taine, William James, Henry George, were masters of which no school in any age need feel ashamed; nor were such tutors and undermasters as Ruskin, William Morris, Matthew Arnold, Lester Ward, Walt Whitman, Henry Adams, to be dismissed as incompetent. To the solution of the vexing problems entailed by industrialism—in America as well as in Europe—was brought all the knowledge that had been accumulating for a century. It was a time of reëvaluations when much substantial thinking was done; when the flood of light that came with the doctrine of biological evolution lay brilliant on the intellectual landscape and the dullest mind caught some of the reflection. Few of the young scholars attended the lectures of Friedrich Nietzsche, and behavioristic psychology had not yet got into the curriculum; but Ladd and James were inquiring curiously into the mechanism of the brain, and animal psychology was preparing the way for the later Freudians. It was the end of an age perhaps, the rich afterglow of the Enlightenment, but the going down of the sun was marked by sunset skies that gave promise of other and greater dawns.

To have spent one's youth in such a school was a liberal education. The mind opened of its own will. Intellectual horizons were daily widening and the new perspectives ran out into cosmic spaces. The cold from those outer spaces had not yet chilled the enthusiasms that were a heritage from the Enlightenment, and the social idealism begotten by the democratic nature school still looked confidently to the future. They were ardent democrats—the young liberals of the nineties—and none doubted the finality or sufficiency of the democratic principle, any more than Mill or Spencer had doubted it. All their history and all their biology justified it, and the business of the times was to make it prevail in the sphere of economics as it prevailed in the realm of the political. The cure for the evils of democracy was held to be more democracy, and when industrialism had been brought under its sway—when America had become an economic democracy—a just and humane civilization would be on the threshold of possibility. To the achievement of that great purpose the young liberals devoted themselves and the accomplishments of the next score of years were the work of their hands. Certain intellectuals had been democrats—Paine and Jefferson and Emerson and Thoreau and Whitman and Melville—but they were few in comparison with the skeptical Whigs who professed democracy only to bind its hands. The Republican party had not been democratic since former days — and as Henry Adams said in 1880, it was accounted foolishness to believe in it in 1880. Autocracy was a toy to distract the voting man from the business of money-getting.

It was from such a school—richer in intellectual content, one might argue, than any the younger liberals have frequented—that the ferment of twenty years ago issued; a school dedicated to the ideals of the Enlightenment and bent on carrying through the unfulfilled program of democracy. Democratic aspirations had been thwarted hitherto by the uncontrolled play of the acquisitive instinct; the immediate problem of democracy was the control of that instinct in the common interest. Economics had controlled the political state to its narrow and selfish advantage; it was for the political state to resume its sovereignty and extend its control over economics. So in the spirit of the Enlightenment the current liberalism dedicated itself to history and sociology, accepting as its immediate and particular business a reëxamination of the American past in order to forcast an ampler democratic future. It must trace the rise of political power in America in order to understand how that power had fallen into the unsocial hands of economics. The problem was difficult. American political history had been grossly distorted by partisan interpretation and political theory had been dissipated by an arid constitutionalism. The speculative thinker had long been dispossessed by the eulogist and the lawyer, both of whom had subsisted on a thin gruel of patriotic myths. Even the social historians, though dealing in materials rich in suggestion, had been diffident in the matter of interpretation, without which history is no more than the dry bones of chronicle. Inheriting no adequate philosophy of historical evolution, the young school of historians must first provide themselves with one, in the light of which the American past should take on meaning, and the partisan struggles, hitherto meaningless, should fall into comprehensible patterns.

That necessary work was to engage them for years, but in the meanwhile, as critical realists, their immediate business was with facts and the interpretation of facts. John Fiske a few years before had essayed to interpret the rise of democracy in America by analogy from biological evolution, tracing the source of American democracy to the New England town meeting, which he explained as a resurgence of ancient Teutonic folk-ways. The theory was tenuous and it was not till Professor Turner drew attention to the creative influence of the frontier on American life that the historians were provided with a suggestive working hypothesis. Before that hypothesis could be adequately explored, however, and brought into just relations to a comprehensive philosophy of history, the rise of liberalism was well under way, marked by a rich ferment of thought that made the early years of the new century singularly stimulating. That ferment resulted from pouring into the vial of native experience the reagent of European theory—examining the ways of American industrialism in the light of continental socialism; and the result was an awakening of popular interest in social control of economics, a widespread desire to bring an expanding industrialism into subjection to a rational democratic program, that was to provide abundant fuel to the social unrest that had burst forth in sporadic flames for a generation. The great movement of liberalism that took possession of the American mind after the turn of the century—a movement not unworthy to be compared with the ferment of the eighteen forties—was the spontaneous reaction of an America still only half urbanized, still clinging to ideals and ways of an older simpler America, to an industrialism that was driving its plowshare through the length and breadth of the familiar scene, turning under the rude furrows what before had been growing familiarly there. It was the first reaction of America to the revolutionary change that followed upon the exhaustion of the frontier—an attempt to secure through the political state the freedoms that before had come from unpreempted opportunity.

For a quarter of a century following the great westward expansion of the late sixties America had been drifting heedlessly towards a different social order. The shambling frontier democracy that had sufficed an earlier time was visibly breaking down in presence of the imperious power of a centralizing capitalism. The railways were a dramatic embodiment of the new machine civilization that was running head on into a primitive social organism fashioned by the old domestic economy, and the disruptions and confusions were a warning that the country was in for vast changes. New masters, new ways. The rule of the captain of industry had come. The farmers had long been in ugly mood, but their great rebellion was put down in 1896, and never again could they hope to wrest sovereignty from capitalism. The formal adoption of the gold standard in 1900 served notice to the world that America had put away its democratic agrarianism, that a shambling Jacksonian individualism had had its day, and that henceforth the destiny of the country lay in the hands of its business men. Capitalism was master of the country and though for the present it was content to use the political machinery of democracy it was driving towards an objective that was the negation of democracy.

The immediate reaction to so broad a shift in the course of manifest destiny was a growing uneasiness amongst the middle class—small business and professional men—who looked with fear upon the program of the captains of industry. Industrialization brought its jars and upsets. The little fish did not enjoy being swallowed by the big, and as they watched the movement of economic centralization encroaching on the field of competition they saw the doors of opportunity closing to them. It was to this great body of *petite bourgeoisie* that members of the lesser intellectuals—journalists, sociologists, reformers—were to make appeal. The work was begun dramatically with the spectacularly advertised *Frenzied Finance*, written by Thomas W. Lawson, and appearing as a series in *McClure's Magazine* in 1903. The immense popular success of the venture proved that the fire was ready for the fat, and at once a host of volunteer writers fell to feeding the flames. The new ten-cent magazines provided the necessary vehicle of publicity, and enterprising editors were soon increasing their circulations with every issue. As it became evident how popular was the chord that had been struck, more competent workmen joined themselves to the group of journalists: novelists—a growing army of them—essayists, historians, political scientists, philosophers, a host of heavy-armed troops that moved forward in a frontal attack on the strongholds of the new plutocracy. Few writers in the years between 1903 and 1917 escaped being drawn into the movement—an incorrigible romantic perhaps, like the young James Branch Cabell, or a cool patrician like Edith Wharton; and with such popular novelists as Winston Churchill, Robert Herrick, Ernest Poole, David Graham Phillips, Upton Sinclair, and Jack London embellishing the rising liberalism with dramatic heroes and villains, and dressing their salads with the wickedness of Big Business; with such political leaders as Bob La Follette and Theodore Roosevelt and Woodrow Wilson beating up the remotest villages for recruits; with such scholars as Thorstein Veblen, Charles A. Beard, and John Dewey, and such lawyers as Louis Brandeis, Frank P. Walsh, and Samuel Untermyer, the movement gathered such momentum and quickened such a ferment as had not been known before in the lands since the days of the Abolition controversy. The mind and conscience of America were stirred to their lowest sluggish stratum, and a democratic renaissance was all aglow on the eastern horizon.

At the core it was a critical realistic movement that spread quietly amongst intellectuals, but the nebulous tail of the comet blazed across the sky for all to wonder at: and it was the tail rather than the core that aroused the greatest immediate interest. Lincoln Steffens, Charles Edward Russell, Ida Tarbell, Gustavus Myers, and Upton Sinclair were read eagerly because they dealt with themes that many were interested in—the political machine, watered stock, Standard Oil, the making of great fortunes, and the like—and they invested their exposures with the dramatic interest of a detective story. Up to 1910 it was largely a muckraking movement—to borrow President Roosevelt's picturesque phrase; a time of brisk housecleaning that searched out old cobwebs and disturbed the dust that lay thick on the antiquated furniture. The Gilded Age had been slovenly and such a housecleaning was long overdue. There was a vast amount of nosing about to discover bad smells, and to sensitive noses the bad smells seemed to be everywhere. Evidently some hidden cesspool was fouling American life, and as the inquisitive plumbers tested the household drains they came upon the source of infection—not one cesspool but many, under every city hall and beneath every state capitol—dug secretly by politicians in the pay of respectable business men. It was these cesspools that were poisoning the national household, and there would be no health in America till they were filled in and no others dug.

It was a dramatic discovery and when the corruption of American politics was laid on the threshold of business—like a bastard on the doorsteps of the father—a tremendous disturbance resulted. There was a great fluttering and clamor amongst the bats and owls, an ominous creaking of the machine as the wrenches were thrown into the well-oiled wheels, and a fierce sullen anger at the hue and cry set up. To many honest Americans the years between 1903 and 1910 were abusive and scurrilous beyond decency, years when no man and no business, however honorable, was safe from the pillory; when wholesale exposure had grown profitable to sensation-mongers, and great reputations were lynched by vigilantes and reputable corporations laid under indictment at the bar of public opinion. Respectable citizens did not like to have their goodly city held up to the world as "corrupt and contented"; they did not like to have their municipal housekeeping brought into public disrepute no matter how sluttish it might be. It was not pleasant for members of great families to read a cynical history of the origins of their fortunes, or for railway presidents seeking political favors to find on the newsstand a realistic account of the bad scandals that had smirched their roads. It was worse than unpleasant, it was hurtful to business. And so quietly, and as speedily as could be done decently, the movement was brought to a stop by pressure put on the magazines that lent themselves to such harmful disclosures. Then followed a campaign of education. Responding to judicious instruction, conducted in the columns of the most respectable newspapers, the American public was soon brought to understand that it was not the muck that was harmful, but the indiscretion of those who commented in print on the bad smells. It was reckoned a notable triumph for sober and patriotic good sense.

So after a few years of amazing activity the muckraking movement came to a stop. But not before it had done its work; not before the American middle class had been indoctrinated in the elementary principles of political realism and had rediscovered the social conscience lost since the days of the Civil War. Many a totem had been thrown down by the irreverent hands of the muckrakers, and many a fetish held up to ridicule, and plutocracy in America would not recover its peace of mind until at great cost the totems should be set up again and the fetishes reanointed with the oil of sanctity. The substantial result of the movement was the instruction it afforded in the close kinship between business and politics—a lesson greatly needed by a people long fed on romantic unrealities. It did not crystallize for the popular mind in the broad principle of economic determinism; that remained for certain of the intellectuals to apply to American experience. But with its sordid object—service—it punished the flabby optimism of the Gilded Age, with its object-lessons in business politics; it revealed the hidden hand that was pulling the strings of the political puppets; it tarnished the gilding that had been carefully laid on our callous exploitation, and it brought under common suspicion the captain of industry who had risen as a national hero from the muck of individualism. It was a sharp guerilla attack on the sacred American System, but behind the thin skirmish-line lay a volunteer army that was making ready to deploy for a general engagement with plutocracy.

With the flood of light thrown upon the fundamental law by the historians, the movement of liberalism passed quickly through successive phases of thought. After the first startled surprise it set about the necessary business of acquainting the American people with its findings in the confident belief that a democratic electorate would speedily democratize the instrument. Of this first stage the late Professor J. Allen Smith's *The Spirit of American Government* (1907) was the most adequate expression, a work that greatly influenced the program of the rising Progressive Party. But changes came swiftly and within half a dozen years the movement had passed from political programs to economic, concerned not so greatly with political democracy as with economic democracy. Of this second phase Professor Beard's notable study, *An Economic Interpretation of the Constitution* (1913), was the greatest intellectual achievement. Underlying this significant work was a philosophy of politics that set it sharply apart from preceding studies— a philosophy that unsympathetic readers were quick to attribute to Karl Marx, but that in reality derived from sources far earlier and for Americans at least far more respectable. The current conception of the political state as determined in its form and activities by economic groups is no modern Marxian perversion of political theory; it goes back to Aristotle, it underlay the thinking of Harrington and Locke and the seventeenth-century English school, it shaped the conclusions of Madison and Hamilton and John Adams, it ran through all the discussions of the Constitutional Convention, and it reappeared in the arguments of Webster and Calhoun. It was the main-traveled road of political thought until a new highway was laid out by French engineers, who, disliking the bog of eco

nomics, surveyed another route by way of romantic equalitarianism. The logic of the engineers was excellent, but the drift of
politics is little influenced by logic, and abstract equalitarianism
proved to be poor material for highway construction. In divorcing
political theory from contact with sobering reality it gave it over
to a treacherous romanticism. In seeking to avoid the bog of
economics it ran into an arid desert.

To get back once more on the main-traveled road, to put away
all profitless romanticisms and turn realist, taking up again the
method of economic interpretation unused in America since the
days of Webster and Calhoun, became therefore the business of the
second phase of liberalism to which Professor Beard applied himself. The earlier group of liberals were ill equipped to wage successful war against plutocracy. Immersed in the traditional equalitarian philosophy, they underestimated the strength of the enemies
of democracy. They did not realize what legions of Swiss Guards
property can summon to its defense. They were still romantic
idealists tilting at windmills, and it was to bring them to a sobering
sense of reality that *The Economic Interpretation of the Constitution*
was written. If property is the master force in every society one
cannot understand American institutional development until one
has come to understand the part property played in shaping the
fundamental law. Interpreted thus the myths that had gathered
about the Constitution fell away of themselves and the document
was revealed as English rather than French, the judicious expression of substantial eighteenth-century realism that accepted the
property basis of political action, was skeptical of romantic idealisms, and was more careful to protect title-deeds to legal holdings
than to claim unsurveyed principalities in Utopia. If therefore
liberalism were to accomplish any substantial results it must approach its problems in the same realistic spirit, recognizing the
masterful ambitions of property, recruiting democratic forces to
overmaster the Swiss Guards, leveling the strongholds that property had erected within the organic law, and taking care that no
new strongholds should rise. The problem confronting liberalism
was the problem of the subjection of property to social justice.

Yet interesting as was the muckraking tail of the comet, far more
significant was the core—the substantial body of knowledge
gathered by the scholars and flung into the scale of public opinion.
The realities of the American past had been covered deep with

layers of patriotic myths, provided in simpler days when the young Republic, suffering from a natural inferiority complex, was building up a defense against the acrid criticism of Tory Europe. Those myths had long since served their purpose and had become a convenient refuge for the bats and owls of the night; it was time to strip them away and apply to the past objective standards of scholarship, and to interpret it in the light of an adequate philosophy of history. To this work, so essential to any intelligent understanding of the American experiment, a group of historians and political scientists turned with competent skill, and the solid results of their labor remained after the popular ferment subsided, as a foundation for later liberals to build on.

The journalistic muckrakers had demonstrated that America was not in fact the equalitarian democracy it professed to be, and the scholars supplemented their work by tracing to its historical source the weakness of the democratic principle in governmental practice. America had never been a democracy for the sufficient reason that too many handicaps had been imposed upon the majority will. The democratic principle had been bound with withes like Samson and had become a plaything for the Philistines. From the beginning—the scholars discovered—democracy and property had been at bitter odds; the struggle invaded the Constitutional Convention, it gave form to the party alignment between Hamilton and Jefferson, Jackson and Clay, and then during the slavery struggle, sinking underground like a lost river, it nevertheless had determined party conflicts down to the present. In this ceaseless conflict between the man and the dollar, between democracy and property, the reasons for persistent triumph of property were sought in the provisions of the organic law, and from a critical study of the Constitution came a discovery that struck home like a submarine torpedo—the discovery that the drift toward plutocracy was not a drift away from the spirit of the Constitution, but an inevitable unfolding from its premises; that instead of having been conceived by the fathers as a democratic instrument, it had been conceived in a spirit designedly hostile to democracy; that it was, in fact, a carefully formulated expression of eighteenth-century property consciousness, erected as a defense against the democratic spirit that had got out of hand during the Revolution, and that the much-praised system of checks and balances was designed and intended for no other end than a check on the political power of the majority—a power acutely feared by the property consciousness of the times.

It was a startling discovery that profoundly stirred the liberal mind of the early years of the century; yet the really surprising thing is that it should have come as a surprise. It is not easy to understand today why since Civil War days intelligent Americans should so strangely have confused the Declaration of Independence and the Constitution, and have come to accept them as complementary statements of the democratic purpose of America. Their unlikeness is unmistakable: the one a classical statement of French humanitarian democracy, the other an organic law designed to safeguard the minority under republican rule. The confusion must be charged in part to the lawyers who had taken over the custodianship of the Constitution, and in part to the florid romantic temper of the middle nineteenth century. When the fierce slavery struggle fell into the past, whatever honest realism had risen from the passions of the times was buried with the dead issue. The militant attacks on the Constitution so common in Abolitionist circles after 1835, and the criticism of the Declaration that was a part of the southern argument, were both forgotten, and with the Union reestablished by force of arms, the idealistic cult of the fundamental law entered on a second youth. In the blowsy Gilded Age the old myths walked the land again, wrapped in battle-torn flags and appealing to the blood shed on southern battlefields. It was not till the advent of a generation unblinded by the passions of civil war that the Constitution again was examined critically, and the earlier charge of the Abolitionists that it was designed to serve property rather than men, was heard once more. But this time with far greater weight of evidence behind it. As the historians dug amongst the contemporary records they came upon a mass of fact the Abolitionists had been unaware of. The evidence was written so plainly, in such explicit and incontrovertible words— not only in *Elliott's Debates*, but in the minutes of the several State Conventions, in contemporary letters and memoirs, in newspapers and pamphlets and polite literature—that it seemed incredible that honest men could have erred so greatly in confusing the Constitution with the Declaration.

With the clarification of its philosophy the inflowing waters of liberalism reached flood-tide; the movement would either recede or pass over into radicalism. On the whole it followed the latter course, and the years immediately preceding 1917 were years when American intellectuals were immersing themselves in European collectivistic philosophies—in Marxianism, Fabianism, Syndicalism, Guild Socialism. New leaders were rising, philosophical analysts like Thorstein Veblen who were mordant critics of American economics. The influence of socialism was fast sweeping away the last shreds of political and social romanticism that so long had confused American thinking. The doctrine of economic determinism was spreading widely, and in the light of that doctrine the deep significance of the industrial revolution was revealing itself for the first time to thoughtful Americans. In its reaction to industrialism America had reached the point Chartist England had reached in the eighteen-forties and Marxian Germany in the eighteen-seventies. That was before a mechanistic science had laid its heavy discouragements on the drafters of democratic programs. Accepting the principle of economic determinism, liberalism still clung to its older democratic teleology, convinced that somehow economic determinism would turn out to be a fairy godmother to the proletariat and that from the imperious drift of industrial expansion must eventually issue social justice. Armed with this faith liberalism threw itself into the work of cleaning the Augean stables, and its reward came in the achievements of President Wilson's first administration.

Then the war intervened and the green fields shriveled in an afternoon. With the cynicism that came with post-war days the democratic liberalism of 1917 was thrown away like an empty whiskey-flask. Clever young men began to make merry over democracy. It was preposterous, they said, to concern oneself about social justice; nobody wants social justice. The first want of every man, as John Adams remarked a hundred years ago, is his dinner, and the second his girl. Out of the muck of the war had come a great discovery—so it was reported—the discovery that psychology as well as economics has its word to say on politics. From the army intelligence tests the moron emerged as a singular commentary on our American democracy, and with the discovery of the moron the democratic principle was in for a slashing attack. Almost overnight an army of enemies was marshaled against it. The eugenist with his isolated germ theory flouted the perfectional psychology of John Locke, with its emphasis on environment as the determining factor in social evolution—a psychology on which the whole idealistic interpretation was founded; the beardless philosopher discovered Nietzsche and in his pages found the fit master of the moron—the biological aristocrat who is the flower that every civilization struggles to produce; the satirist discovered the flatulent reality that is middle-class America and was eager to thrust his jibes at the complacent denizens of the Valley of Democracy. Only the behaviorist, with his insistence on the plasticity of the new-born child, offers some shreds of comfort to the democrat; but he quickly takes them away again with his simplification of conduct to imperious drives that stamp men as primitive animals. If the mass—the raw materials of democracy—never rises much above sex appeals and belly needs, surely it is poor stuff to try to work up into an excellent civilization, and the dreams of the social idealist who forecasts a glorious democratic future are about as substantial as moonshine. It is a discouraging essay. Yet it is perhaps conceivable that our current philosophy—the brilliant coruscations of our younger intelligentsia—may indeed not prove to be the last word in social philosophy. Perhaps—is this *lèse-majesté*—when our youngest liberals have themselves come to the armchair age they will be smiled at in turn by sons who are still cleverer and who will find their wisdom as foolish as the wisdom of 1917 seems to them today. But that lies on the knees of the gods.

BIBLIOGRAPHY

[Professor Parrington left no bibliography apart from the works mentioned in the text. It has been possible to formulate one with some certainty by reference to his personal library, theses written under his supervision, and the record of the books he borrowed from the University of Washington Library. In the two earlier volumes the bibliography is rigidly selective. Needless to say, I have not presumed such knowledge of his intentions. All the pertinent material which it is known that he used is included.—E. H. EBY.]

BOOK I: PART I

I. THE AMERICAN SCENE. For history of the period see Allan Nevins, *The Emergence of Modern America, 1865–1878* (in the series *A History of American Life*, Vol. VIII, New York, 1927); E. P. Oberholtzer, *History of the United States since the Civil War* (3 vols., New York, 1917–1926); Frederick L. Paxson, *Recent History of the United States* (Boston and New York, c. 1921).

For economic backgrounds see Harold Underwood Faulkner, *American Economic History* (New York and London, 1924); Gustavus Meyers, *History of Great American Fortunes* (3 vols., Chicago, 1910); Robert Irving Warshaw, *Jay Gould: The Story of a Fortune* (New York, 1928); and for the part played by railroads see John P. Davis, *The Union Pacific Railway* (New York, 1894); C. E. Russell, *Stories of Great Railroads* (Chicago, 1912); and Charles Francis Adams, Jr., and Henry Adams, *Chapters of Erie and Other Essays* (Boston, 1871).

For political corruption see Don Carlos Seitz, *The Dreadful Decade* (Indianapolis, 1926); and Denis Tilden Lynch, *"Boss" Tweed: The Story of a Grim Generation* (New York, 1927).

For journalism see Allan Nevins, *The Evening Post: A Century of Journalism* (New York, c. 1922); and Frank M. O'Brien, *The Story of the Sun* (New York, c. 1918).

General Ulysses S. Grant, *Personal Memoirs* (2 vols., New York, 1885–1886). For biography see W. E. Woodward, *Meet General Grant* (New York, 1928).

Jay Cooke. See E. P. Oberholtzer, *Jay Cooke, Financier of the Civil War* (2 vols. Philadelphia, c. 1907).

Charles A. Dana, *Recollections of the Civil War* (New York, 1902); J. H. Wilson, *Life of Charles A. Dana* (New York, 1907).

II. THE CULTURE OF THE SEVENTIES. For valuable sidelights on culture in the decade see Constance Mayfield Rourke, *Trumpets of Jubilee* (New York, c. 1927); Paxton Hibben, *Henry Ward Beecher: An American Portrait* (New York, c. 1927); Horace Greeley, *Recollections of a Busy Life* (New York, 1868); James Parton, *The Life of Horace Greeley* (Boston, c. 1896); Lewis Mumford, *The Golden Day: A Study in American Experience and Culture* (New York, 1926); and his *Sticks and Stones, A Study of American Architecture and Civilization* (New York, c. 1924).

For history of literature see Fred Lewis Pattee, *A History of American Literature since 1870* (New York, 1915); his *Sidelights on American Literature*

(New York, 1922); his *The Development of the American Short Story* (New York and London, 1923); and Carl Van Doren, *The American Novel* (New York, 1921).

Thomas Bailey Aldrich, *Prose Works* (7 vols., Boston, 1897); *The Poems of Thomas Bailey Aldrich* (2 vols., Boston, c. 1907). For his life see Ferris Greenslet, *The Life of Thomas Bailey Aldrich* (Boston and New York, 1908).

Mrs. Elizabeth Stuart Ward (Phelps), *The Silent Partner* (Boston, c. 1899); *A Singular Life* (Boston and New York, 1899); *Chapters from a Life* (Boston and New York, 1896).

Sarah Orne Jewett. *A Country Doctor* (Boston and New York, c. 1884); *A Native of Winby and Other Tales* (Boston and New York, c. 1893); *Deephaven* (Boston and New York, 1894). *Tales of New England* (Boston and New York, 1894); *The Life of Nancy* (Boston and New York, 1895); *The Queen's Twin and Other Stories* (Boston and New York, 1899); *The Country of Pointed Firs* (Boston and New York, c. 1910). For her life see *The Letters of Sarah Orne Jewett* (Boston and New York, 1911).

Mrs. Mary E. (Wilkins) Freeman, *A Humble Romance, and Other Stories* (New York, 1887); *The New England Nun, and Other Stories* (New York, 1891); *The Pot of Gold, and Other Stories* (Boston, c. 1892); *Pembroke; a Novel* (New York, c. 1894); *People of Our Neighborhood* (New York, 1901); *The Portion of Labor* (New York, c. 1901). *Young Lucretia, and Other Stories* (New York, 1903); *By the Light of the Soul* (New York and London, 1907).

Walt Whitman, *Leaves of Grass* (Inclusive edition edited by Emory Holloway, Garden City, New York, 1927); *The Complete Prose Works of Walt Whitman* (New York, 1898); *The Half-breed and Other Stories* (New York, 1927); *Autobiographia: or, the Story of a Life* (New York, 1892); *The Gathering of Forces* (New York and London, 1920); and *The Uncollected Poetry and Prose of Walt Whitman* (2 vols., Garden City, New York, 1921). For Whitman's life see Horace Traubel, *With Walt Whitman in Camden* (3 vols., New York, 1908–1914); Emory Holloway, *Whitman* (New York, 1926); John Addington Symonds, *Walt Whitman: a Study* (London, 1893); Léon Bazalgette, *Walt Whitman, the Man and his Work* (Garden City, New York, 1920); John Burroughs, *Whitman: a Study* (Boston and New York, c. 1924); Bliss Perry, *Walt Whitman: his Life and Work* (Boston and New York, 1906); and J. Johnston, M. D., and J. W. Wallace, *Visits to Walt Whitman* (New York, 1918).

For critical studies of his work see Norman Foerster, *American Criticism,* pp. 157–222 (New York, 1928); Basil De Selincourt, *Walt Whitman; a Critical Study* (London, 1914); Horace Traubel (ed.), *In re Walt Whitman* (Philadelphia, 1893).

Samuel Langhorne Clemens (Mark Twain), *The Writings of Mark Twain* (25 vols., New York and London, c. 1910–1911); *The Mysterious Stranger, and Other Stories* (New York and London, 1922); *What is Man?* (New York, 1917).

For his life see *Mark Twain's Autobiography* (New York and London, 1924); Albert Bigelow Paine, *Mark Twain, a Biography* (3 vols. New York, c. 1912); Van Wyck Brooks, *The Ordeal of Mark Twain* (New York, c. 1920); W. D. Howells, *My Mark Twain* (New York, c. 1910).

III. CHANGING THEORY. For a general history of economic theory see, Charles Gide and Charles Rist, *A History of Economic Doctrines from the Time of the Physiocrats to the Present Day* (Authorized translation from the second revised and augumented edition of 1913, Boston, New York, Chicago,

1913); *The Trend of Economics* (Edited by R. G. Tugwell, New York, 1924).

For material covered in this section see Francis Wayland, *Elements of Political Economy* (New York, 1837); Henry Charles Carey, *Principles of Social Science* (3 vols., Philadelphia, 1858–1860); his *The Harmony of Interests: Agricultural, Manufacturing, and Commercial* (2nd ed., New York, 1852); and his *Miscellaneous Works* (Philadelphia, 1875). Francis A. Walker, *The Wages Question, a Treatise on Wages and the Wages Class* (New York, 1891); his *Land and Its Rent* (Boston, 1891); and his *Political Economy* (New York, 1888).

For a general treatment of political theories see William A. Dunning, *A History of Political Theories from Rousseau to Spencer* (New York, 1920); Charles E. Merriam, *History of American Political Theories* (New York, 1920); and his *American Political Ideas: Studies in the Development of American Political Thought, 1865–1917* (New York, 1920).

Theodore Dwight Woolsey, *Political Science: or, the State Theoretically and Practically Considered* (New York, 1900); and his *Communism and Socialism in Their History and Theory* (New York, 1894).

John W. Burgess. *Political Science and Comparative Constitutional Law* (2 vols., Boston and London, 1896–1898); and his *The Sanctity of the Law; Wherein Does It Consist?* (Boston and New York, c. 1927).

J. Allen Smith, *The Growth and Decadence of Constitutional Government* (New York, 1930) is an invaluable aid to those wishing to get Parrington's viewpoint in political theory.

Henry George, *The Writings of Henry George* (Memorial edition, 10 vols., New York, 1898–1900). See particularly *Progress and Poverty* (Vols. I and II), and Henry George, Jr., *The Life of Henry George* (Vol. X).

Henry D. Lloyd, *Wealth Against Commonwealth* (New York, c. 1894); *Lords of Industry* (New York and London, 1910); *Man the Social Creator* (New York, 1906); *Strike of Millionaires Against Miners, or the Story of Spring Valley, with an Open Letter to Millionaires* (Chicago, 1890). For his life see Caroline Augusta Lloyd, *Henry Demarest Lloyd, 1847–1903* (2 vols., New York and London, 1912). (Parrington had intended to discuss Lloyd.)

IV. THE BEGINNINGS OF CRITICISM. Wendell Phillips, *Speeches, Lectures, and Letters* (2 vols., Boston, 1891–1892). For his life see Carlos Martyn, *Wendell Phillips, the Agitator* (Revised ed., New York, 1890); and Charles Edward Russell, *The Story of Wendell Phillips* (Chicago, c. 1914).

George William Curtis, *Nile Notes of a Howadji* (New York, 1851); *Trumps* (New York, 1861); *Potiphar Papers* (New York, 1854); *Prue and I* (New York, n. d.); *Orations and Addresses* (3 vols., New York, 1894); *From the Easy Chair* (3 vols., New York, 1894–1902); *Early Letters of George William Curtis to John S. Dwight; Brook Farm and Concord* (New York and London, 1898). For his life see Edward Cary, *George William Curtis* (Boston and New York, 1894).

Edwin Lawrence Godkin, *Reflections and Comments, 1865–1895* (New York, 1895); *Unforseen Tendencies of Democracy* (Boston, 1893); *Problems of Modern Democracy; Political and Economic Essays* (Third ed., New York, 1898). For his life see, *The Life and Letters of Edwin Lawrence Godkin* (Ed. by Rollo Ogden, 2 vols., New York and London, 1907). See also Gustav Pollak, *The Nation, Fifty Years of American Idealism: the New York Nation, 1865–1915* (New York, 1915).

The political novel: Mark Twain and Charles Dudley Warner, *The Gilded Age* (2 vols., New York, 1873); Henry Adams, *Democracy* (New York,

1880); F. Marion Crawford, *An American Politician* (New York, 1884). See also Albion W. Tourgee, *A Fool's Errand* (New York, 1880).

The economic novel: John Hay, *The Bread-Winners* (New York, 1883); H. F. Keenan, *The Moneymakers* (New York, 1885).

The sociological novel: Hjalmar Hjorth Boyessen, *The Mammon of Unrighteousness* (New York, 1891); his *The Golden Calf* (New York, 1892); and his *Social Strugglers* (New York, 1893); Robert Grant, *Unleavened Bread* (New York, 1900); Samuel Merwin and H. K. Webster, *Calumet K* (New York, 1901); and their *Short Line War* (New York, 1899). Francis Churchill Williams, *J. Develin-Boss* (New York, 1901); Elliot Flower, *The Spoilsman* (Boston, 1903); Winston Churchill, *Coniston* (New York, 1907); and his *Mr. Crewe's Career* (New York, 1908); Will Payne, *Mr. Salt* (Boston and New York, 1903); and his *The Money Captain* (New York, 1898).

For general accounts see Carl Van Doren, *The American Novel* (New York, 1921); Fred Lewis Pattee, *A History of American Literature since 1870* (New York, 1915); John Curtis Underwood, *Literature and Insurgency* (New York, 1914); and W. D. Howells, *Criticism and Fiction* (New York, 1891).

For material dealing with Henry Adams and John Hay see William Roscoe Thayer, *The Life and Letters of John Hay* (2 vols., Boston and New York, c. 1915). See also the bibliography on Henry Adams, Part II, section II.

BOOK I: PART II

I. DISINTEGRATION AND REINTEGRATION. For a general survey of philosophical thought during the period see W. H. Hudson, *Philosophies Ancient and Modern* (London, 1908); Woodbridge Riley, *American Thought from Puritanism to Pragmatism* (New York, 1915); William Archibald Dunning, *A History of Political Theories from Rousseau to Spencer* (New York, 1920).

Condorcet, Isidore, August Marie François Xavier, *Ouvres* (Paris, 1847). See also *A General View of Positivism* (Translated by H. J. Bridges, London, c. 1908).

Herbert Spencer, *Works* (18 vols., New York, 1915); see also his *Illustrations of Universal Progress; a Series of Discussions* (New York, 1890).

Ernst Heinrich Haeckel, *The Riddle of the Universe at the Close of the Nineteenth Century* (New York and London, 1900); and his *History of Creation* (2 vols., New York, 1914).

John Fiske, *American Political Ideas, Viewed from the Standpoint of Universal History* (New York, 1899); *Darwinism and Other Essays* (New ed. rev. and enl., Boston, 1892); *The Destiny of Man, Viewed in the Light of his Origin* (18 ed., Boston and New York, 1892); *Essays Historical and Literary* (2 vols., New York and London, 1902); *Excursions of an Evolutionist* (Boston and New York, 1892); *The Idea of God as Affected by Modern Knowledge* (Boston and New York, 1892); *Life Everlasting* (Boston and New York, 1902); *Outlines of Cosmic Philosophy, Based on the Doctrine of Evolution, with Criticisms of the Positive Philosophy* (4 vols., Boston and New York, c. 1903); *Through Nature to God* (Boston and New York, 1899); *Unseen World and Other Essays* (11th ed., Boston, 1876). For his life see J. S. Clark, *Life and Letters of John Fiske* (2 vols., Boston, 1917); and Henry Holt, *Garrulities of an Octogenarian Editor, with Other Essays Somewhat Biographical and Autobiographical* (Boston and New York, 1923).

II. THE SKEPTICISMS OF THE HOUSE OF ADAMS. Henry Adams, *The Degredation of the Democratic Dogma* (New York, 1920); *Democracy, a Novel* (New

York, 1880); *The Education of Henry Adams* (New York, 1918); *History of the United States during the Administration of Jefferson and Madison* (9 vols., New York, 1890–1898); *John Randolph* (Boston, 1895); *Letters to a Niece and Prayer to the Virgin of Chartres; with a Niece's Memoirs by Mabel La Farge* (Boston and New York, 1920); *Life of Albert Gallatin* (Philadelphia, 1880); *Mont-Saint-Michel and Chartres* (Boston and New York, 1913).

Brooks Adams, *America's Economic Supremacy* (New York, 1900); *Law of Civilization and Decay: an Essay on History* (New York, 1895); *The New Empire* (New York, London, 1902); *The Theory of Social Revolutions* (New York, 1913).

Charles Francis Adams, Jr., and Henry Adams, *Chapters of Erie and Other Essays* (Boston, 1871); Charles Francis Adams, Jr., *Charles Francis Adams 1835–1915; an Autobiography* (Boston and New York, 1916). See also W. C. Ford, *A Cycle of Adams Letters, 1861–1865* (2 vols., Boston and New York, 1920).

III. VICTORIAN REALISM. For material in Parrington's introduction to Chapter III see Francis Marion Crawford, *The Novel: What It Is* (New York, 1908); and H. H. Boyessen, *Literary and Social Silhouettes* (New York, 1894).

Henry James, *The Novels and Tales of Henry James* (24 vols., New York, 1907–1909); *Views and Reviews* (Boston, 1908); *The Letters of Henry James* (2 vols., New York, 1920). For criticism and biography see Pelham Edgar, *Henry James, Man and Author* (Boston and New York, 1927); Rebecca West, *Henry James* (New York, c. 1916); Van Wyck Brooks, *The Pilgrimage of Henry James* (New York, 1925).

William Dean Howells, *A Hazard of New Fortunes* (New York, 1891); *A Modern Instance* (Boston and New York, 1881); *Through the Eye of the Needle* (New York and London, 1907); *A Traveler from Altruria* (New York, 1908); *The Rise of Silas Lapham* (Boston, c. 1912); *April Hopes* (New York, 1888); *Certain Delightful English Towns; with Glimpses of the Pleasant Country Between* (New York and London, 1906); *Indian Summer* (Boston, c. 1914); *Venetian Life* (19th ed., new and enl., Boston, c. 1907); *Criticism and Fiction* (New York, 1891); *Literary Friends and Acquaintance* (New York and London, 1901); *Literature and Life* (New York and London, 1902); *My Literary Passions* (New York, c. 1895). For his life see *Life in Letters of William Dean Howells* (2 vols., Garden City, N. Y., 1928); *Years of My Youth* (New York, c. 1916). For critical estimates see Delmar Gross Cooke, *William Dean Howells; a Critical Study* (New York, c. 1922); Oscar W. Firkins, *William Dean Howells* (Cambridge, Mass., 1924); Alexander Harvey, *William Dean Howells; a Study of the Achievement of a Literary Artist* (New York, 1917).

BOOK II: PART I

I. THE PLIGHT OF THE FARMER. For general surveys of the Agrarian movement see Solon Justus Buck, *The Granger Movement* (In *Harvard Historical Studies*, Vol. XIX, Cambridge, 1913); and his *The Agrarian Crusade* (New Haven, c. 1920); F. E. Haynes, *Third Party Movements since the Civil War* (Iowa City, Iowa, c. 1916); F. J. Turner, *The Frontier in American History* (New York, 1920).

For discussions of the currency see *Homo's Letters on a National Currency* (Washington, 1817); *Currency Explosions, their Cause and Cure* (New York, 1858); *Our Currency: Some of Its Evils, and the Remedies for Them* (By a Citizen of North Carolina, Raleigh, N. C., 1861); D. H. Robertson, *Money*

(New York, c. 1922); J. Lawrence Laughlin, *The Principles of Money*, (New York, 1911).

David Ames Wells, *Practical Economics; a Collection of Essays Respecting Certain of the Recent Economic Experiences of the United States* (New York, 1885); *Robinson Crusoe's Money* (New ed. New York, 1896); *The Cremation Theory of Specie Resumption* (New York, 1875); *Contraction of Legal Tender Notes vs. Repudiation and Disloyalty* (New York, 1876).

Eleazar Lord, *Credit, Currency and Banking* (New York, 1828); *A Letter on the National Currency* (New York, 1861); *Six Letters on the Necessity and Practicability of the National Currency, etc.* (New York, 1862); *National Currency: A Review of the National Banking Law* (New York, 1863).

Peter Cooper, *Ideas for a Science of Good Government* (New York, 1883); *The Political and Financial Opinions of Peter Cooper* (New York, 1877).

William Hope Harvey, *Coin's Financial School* (Chicago, c. 1894); and J. A. Woodburn, *The Life of Thaddeus Stevens* (Indianapolis, c. 1913.)

III. HAMLIN GARLAND AND THE MIDDLE BORDER. For studies of the Middle Border see D. A. Dondore, *The Prairie and the Making of Middle America: Four Centuries of Description* (Cedar Rapids, Iowa, 1926); Lucy Lockwood Hazard, *The Frontier in American Literature* (New York, 1927).

For early realism of the Middle Border see Harold Frederick, *Seth's Brother's Wife* (London, 1898); and Joseph Kirkland, *Zury: The Meanest Man in Spring County* (Boston and New York, 1887).

Hamlin Garland, *Back-Trailers from the Middle Border* (New York, 1928); *Boy Life on the Prairie* (Revised ed., New York and London, c. 1899); *The Captain of the Gray Horse Troop: a Novel* (New York, c. 1902); *Crumbling Idols* (Chicago, 1894); *A Daughter of the Middle Border* (New York, 1921); *The Eagle's Heart* (New York, 1900); *Jason Edwards, An Average Man* (New York, 1897); *Main-Travelled Roads* (New York, c. 1891); *Her Mountain Lover* (New York, 1901); *Prairie Folk* (New and rev. ed., New York, 1899); *Rose of Dutcher's Cooly* (New York, c. 1899); *A Son of the Middle Border* (New York, 1917); *A Spoil of Office* (New York, 1897); *Trailmakers of the Middle Border* (New York, 1926).

BOOK II: PART II

II. THE QUEST OF UTOPIA. Edward Bellamy, *The Duke of Stockbridge; a Romance of Shay's Rebellion* (New York and Boston, 1901); *Equality* (3d ed., New York, 1897); *Looking Backward, 2000–1887* (Boston, c. 1889); see also *The Nationalist, a Monthly Magazine* (Vols. 1–3, May, 1889, to April, 1891. Edited by H. W. Austin).

For general material see Allyn B. Forbes, *The Literary Quest for Utopia, 1880–1900* (*Social Forces*, Vol. VII, 1927, pp. 179–189). Lewis Mumford, *The Story of Utopias* (New York, c. 1922); J. O. Hertzler, *The History of Utopian Thought* (New York, 1923).

INDEX

421